Reproductive Physiology of Vertebrates

ARI van TIENHOVEN, Ph.D.

Cornell University

W. B. SAUNDERS COMPANY
Philadelphia · London · Toronto · 1968

W. B. Saunders Company: West Washington Square
Philadelphia, Pa. 19105

12 Dyott Street
London, W.C.1

1835 Yonge Street
Toronto 7, Ontario

Reproductive Physiology of Vertebrates

To Ans

Preface

Je m'excuserais d'abord d'écrire cette préface, si déjà je n'écrivais cette préface pour m'excuser d'avoir écrit la pièce.

Préface du *Théâtre*
André Gide

This book is based upon lectures given in a course in the reproductive physiology of vertebrates. During the teaching of this course it became evident that no textbook was available in which the reproductive physiology of different classes was compared. It is the purpose of this book to try to fill this gap.

The arrangement consists of considerations of the control mechanisms which exist in different classes of animals. The coverage of the literature is meant not to be exhaustive but to be selective. An effort has been made to compare these control mechanisms and to evaluate similarities and differences. The reader should be familiar with basic concepts in endocrinology and reproductive physiology. I hope that the book will be useful to graduate students and researchers in reproductive physiology and it is for this reason that I have attempted to document many of the statements made. It was not judged desirable to overload the book with references and, wherever possible and justified, reference has been made to recent reviews and books.

I have on purpose not included considerations of a number of topics which might have been included in a book of wider scope but which seemed too specialized, e.g. lactation physiology, sperm physiology and metabolism, artificial insemination, the effects of x-irradiation and radioactivity, the pathology of the reproductive organs and processes, teratology and embryonic development. Excellent textbooks and reviews are available on these topics. Others might have made different choices in the topics to be covered and this book undoubtedly shows the bias of the author, but such bias seemed unavoidable and does not demand an apology.

Dr. James W. Atz has been helpful in making many reprints available to me. The personnel of the Mann Library deserve my thanks for their cheerful cooperation. Messrs. Bob Klein and Douglas Payne deserve my gratitude for making, developing, and printing some of the photographs. My secretary, Miss Theresa Rinkcas, has typed rough drafts and the final copy of much of the manuscript, and has been of considerable help in handling much of the correspondence. This is the place to let her know how much I appreciate her work. I thank Dick van Tienhoven for the help he gave in checking references. I am grateful to the staff of W. B. Saunders Company for their patience and encouragement.

To acknowledge the help, suggestions, and criticisms of all those who have aided me in preparing the final copy of the manuscript does not mean or imply shared responsibility for any controversies or errors which the book may contain. Many colleagues have offered valuable criticisms of portions of the manuscript. They are: James W. Atz, David T. Armstrong, David W. Bishop, Howard E. Evans, Franz Ellendorff, William Hansel, Oliver Hewitt, Jon Planck, and Hans R. Lindner. I would like to thank Dr. Malden C. Nesheim for the many valuable discussions we had, especially with respect to Chapter 12. I am grateful to my wife, who read the entire manuscript and typed and edited large sections of it, and who was patient throughout the labor of this book. Many authors have helped by allowing me to use either illustrations or tables; their generosity is acknowledged in the legends and footnotes.

Ithaca, New York   ARI VAN TIENHOVEN

Acknowledgment

I am indebted to the following publishers for permission to use the figures and tables indicted in parentheses: Academic Press Inc. (Figures 2.1, 6.2, 8.1, and 8.10; Tables 1.2 and 6.11); Akademia Kiado (Figures 8.2, 8.3, 8.6, and 8.11); the American Physiological Society (Figures 8.8 and 8.9); Annual Reviews (Figure 10.1); The Association for Research in Nervous and Mental Disease (Figure 13.1); Cambridge Philosophical Society (Figure 6.1); Dover Publications Inc. (Figures 3.10, 3.11, and 3.12); Elsevier Publishing Co. (Figures 3.6 and 3.7); Iowa State University Press (Figure 3.14); S. Karger AG. (Figure 8.5); Kuyushu University (Figure 3.16); J. B. Lippincott Co. (Figure 8.4); Longmans Green & Co. Ltd. (Figures 3.13 and 3.23; Table 3.2); Masson et Cie (Figures 5.2 and 5.3; Table 5.7); Pergamon Press Inc. (Figure 8.7); The Ronald Press Co. (Figure 3.21); The Royal Society of London (Figures 3.2, 3.3, 3.4, and 3.5); The Society for Endocrinology (Figure 3.8); The Society for the Study of Fertility (Figure 3.22); Springer-Verlag (Figure 3.15); John Wiley & Sons Inc. (Figures 3.18, 3.19, and 9.3; Table 3.1); The Williams & Wilkins Co. (Figures 2.2, 2.3, and 9.2; Table 6.7); The Wistar Institute (Figures 3.17 and 5.4); The University of Illinois Press (Figures 8.12 and 8.13).

Contents

INTRODUCTION 1

Chapter 1

SEX DETERMINATION 3

Chapter 2

EMBRYOLOGY 8
  Differentiation of the Gonads 8
  Differentiation of the Secondary Sex Organs 20

Chapter 3

THE ANATOMY OF THE REPRODUCTIVE SYSTEM 29

Chapter 4

INTERSEXES 68

Chapter 5

THE TESTIS 73
  Androgen Secretion 73
  Estrogen Secretion 89
  Spermatogenesis 89

Chapter 6

THE OVARY 104

    Estrogen Secretion 104
    Progestins or Progestogens 124
    Androgen Secretion 144
    Relaxin Secretion 145
    Oogenesis 146

Chapter 7

THE NONGONADAL ENDOCRINE GLANDS 160

    The Hypophysis 160
    The Thyroid 175
    The Parathyroids 181
    The Adrenal 181
    The Pancreas 188
    The Pineal Organ 190

Chapter 8

THE HYPOTHALAMUS 207

    Anatomy 207
    Damage to the Hypothalamo-Hypophyseal System 213
    Sex Steroids Administered into the Hypothalamo-Hypophyseal System 229
    Gonadotropins Implanted in the Hypothalamo-Hypophyseal System 233
    Electric Stimulation of the Hypothalamo-Hypophyseal System 233
    Correlations Between Histology, Histochemistry, and Biochemistry of the
        Hypothalamus and Reproduction 238
    Chemotransmitters (Releasing Factors) 243
    Effect of Pharmacological Agents 250
    Electric Activity of the Brain and Gonadotropin Release 252

Chapter 9

CYCLIC REPRODUCTIVE PHENOMENA 269

    Cyclostomes 269
    Elasmobranchs 269
    Teleosts 270
    Amphibia 271

Reptiles 272
Birds 272
Mammals 274
Description of the Estrous Cycle 280
The Menstrual Cycle 282
The Ovary During Pregnancy 288

Chapter 10

INSEMINATION AND FERTILIZATION 297

Copulation and Insemination 297
Sperm Transport 299
Spermatozoa Numbers at the Site of Fertilization 302
Capacitation 302
Penetration of the Egg Membranes 303
Polyspermy 305
Activation and Fertilization of the Egg 305
Fertilizable Life of the Egg and the Effect of Ageing of Eggs 307
Fate of Nonfertilized Ova and Unused Sperm 308
Parthenogenesis 308

Chapter 11

VIVIPARITY 311

Oviparity, Ovoviviparity, and Viviparity 311

Chapter 12

EFFECTS OF NUTRITION ON REPRODUCTION 355

Energy Intake 356
Protein Intake 365
Lipid Intake 368
Minerals 377
Summary 381

Chapter 13

ENVIRONMENT AND REPRODUCTION 388

Endogenous Rhythms 389
Synchronizing Stimuli 393

Chapter 14

HORMONALLY INDUCED REPRODUCTIVE BEHAVIOR 426

Migratory Behavior 426
Aggressive Behavior 429
Sexual Behavior 435
Parental Behavior 457

APPENDIX 467

LH Assays 468
Prolactin Assays 470
Assays for Human Chorionic Gonadotropin (HCG) 472
Pregnant Mare's Serum Gonadotropin (PMSG) 473

INDEX 477

INTRODUCTION

Reproduction of the species in vertebrates involves a series of complex phenomena even in the most primitive forms since, under virtually all normal conditions, it requires the bringing together of sperm and ova. Except in some unusual circumstances in which self-fertilization occurs, males and females need to be in proximity. The processes which cause the attraction of males and females or the migration of males and females, sometimes at separate times, to breeding grounds are not well understood, but interactions between hormones and migratory behavior have been established and information is accumulating on the interactions between the nervous system and the endocrine system.

In order to understand reproductive physiology one needs an understanding of embryology, anatomy, endocrinology, behavior, and biochemistry. This textbook is the result of an attempt to assemble available fundamental information about different classes of vertebrates. As will become obvious, even in well studied species such as rats much basic information is lacking and information about such animals outside the laboratory is often fragmentary. It is often difficult to discern a pattern, but it is hoped that bringing some diverse information together may encourage others to do some much needed research and provide a context which will aid in interpretation of the findings.

Chapter 1

Sex Determination

Sex is determined by a single pair of chromosomes in many species. In one sex (the *homogametic* sex) two homologous chromosomes are present; in the other (the *heterogametic*) sex only one of these chromosomes is present and the other chromosome is either absent or is different in size or form. The two chromosomes in the heterogametic sex may each have a part which is homologous with the other. These are the pairing segments.

It has become customary to use the notation XX-XY or XX-XO (depending on the presence of the second chromosome) for the cases in which the female is *homogametic* and ZZ-ZW or ZZ-ZO when the male is *homogametic*.

Table 1-1 shows which sex-determining mechanism is operative in different animals.

In some species the sex chromosomes can be recognized upon cytologic examination, usually in the metaphase of meiosis.

However, in many animals, especially fishes and amphibia (except South American salamanders [*Oedipina sp.*] and the aquatic African clawed toad [*Xenopus laevis*]), evidence of the presence of sex chromosomes and for the determination of the heterogametic sex is based on other evidence, such as sex-linkage and breeding from sex-reversed animals or from hermaphrodites. In other cases more indirect evidence has been used, such as data from hybridization and the application of Haldane's rule: "When in the F₁ offspring of two animal races one sex is absent, rare, or sterile, that sex is the heterozygous sex." See Beatty (1964) for a more extensive discussion.

The sex-determining mechanisms of cyclostomes and elasmobranchs are not known. The discussion of the mechanisms operative in the teleost fishes, for which there is evidence available, should start with the interesting case of the guppy *(Poecilia reticulata)*, in which the normal mechanism is apparently XX-XY. By selection it is possible to obtain a race of guppies in which the sex-determining mechanism is ZZ-ZW. In this race the XX-XY chromosomes become autosomes and a pair of the former autosomes become sex chromosomes. In the swordfish *(Xiphophorus maculatus)* races occur naturally in which the mechanism is XX-XY, whereas in other naturally occurring races the ZZ-ZW mechanism operates.

The question whether YY and WW individuals are viable and what phenotypic sex these animals have has been answered by an experiment using genetic males of the Japanese rice fish *(Oryzias latipes)* which had been treated with estrogens. The YY offspring were viable males. In *Xiphophorus* and *Xenopus laevis*, WW females have been obtained as well as viable W sperm (Blacker, 1965).

On the basis of a large number of cases of "abnormal" sets of sex chromosomes, (see Table 1-2) Beatty (1964) has formulated a general rule which may be applicable to all vertebrates. "There are factors determining the direction of the heterogametic sex-type on the 'odd' sex chromosome, while factors determining in the direction of homogametic sex-type lie on the 'even' chromosomes and/or autosomes."

This rule has not been proven to be

Table 1-1.   Sex Determining Mechanisms in Vertebrates

CLASS OR GENUS	GENETIC PATTERN	HORMONAL SEX REVERSAL	INDUCTIVE SEX REVERSAL	SELF-DIFFER-ENTIATION OF SECONDARY SEX CHARACTERS	REACTION OF OVIDUCT TO TESTOSTERONE	SEX CHROMOSOMES IDENTIFIED
Cyclostomes	?	?	?	?		
Elasmobranchs	?	m→f	?	?		No
Xiphophorus	XX–XY					No
	ZW–ZZ					
Oryzias	XX–XY	F→M;M→F				No
Hynobius	XX–XY					
Triturus†	XX–XY					
Oedipina	XX–XY					Yes
Pleurodeles	ZW–ZZ	M→F				No
Ambystoma	ZW–ZZ	M→F	F→M;m→f	Ambisexual	Positive	No
Xenopus	ZW–ZZ	M→F	F→M		Positive	Yes
Bufo	ZW–ZZ	m→f	M→F			
Rana‡	XX–XY	F→M;m→f	F→M		Negative	No
Reptilia	ZW–ZZ	m→f	F→M	Ambisexual	Positive	Yes
Aves	ZW–ZZ	m→f	F→M	Ambisexual and male*	Positive	Yes
Didelphis	XX–XY	m→f				
Macropus uabulatus	XY₁Y₂					
Potorous tridactylus	XX–XY₁Y₂					
Eutheria	XX–XY§	f→m	F→M	Female	Negative	Yes

M→F Complete sex reversal of a genetic male into a female.

F→M Complete sex reversal of a genetic female into a male.

m→f and f→m Incomplete sex reversal of male into female and vice versa.

* See Table 2-6.

† Possible exception, *Triturus cristatus*, which is ZZ–ZW (Gallien, 1965).

‡ Exception, *Rana arvalis*, in which female is heterogametic sex.

§ Exceptions are: *Sorex araneus* and *Gerbillus gerbillus*, which are all XY₁Y₂; *Microtus minutoides*, which is X_1X_2Y for the male and X_1X_2 for the female; and *Microtus oregoni*, in which the male is XO.

References: Altman and Dittmer, 1962; Beatty, 1960, 1964; Dodd, 1960; Gallien, 1965; and Witschi, 1959.

true for classes other than mammals, (in which, e.g., XXY + 2A have been found). Beatty points out that, for instance, in relation to amphibia an alternative hypothesis can explain the facts equally well. In this hypothesis, the "odd" chromosome is not considered and reads: "The number of 'even' sex chromosomes (e.g. Z or X) is less than the number of sets of autosomes in all specimens of the heterogametic sex-type (female and male, respectively) whereas the number of 'even' sex chromosomes is equal to the number of autosome sets in all members of the homogametic sex-type (male and female, respectively)."

Evidence from sex chromosome aneuploids is required in order to decide whether the first hypothesis is applicable to amphibia to the exclusion of the second hypothesis.

In the fruitfly (*Drosophila* sp.) the balance between the autosomes and sex chromosomes is important in determining the phenotypic sex (the Y chromosome is not important, contrary to the situation in mammals). Beatty (1964), by use of the method of least squares, has tried to evaluate the relative importance of the even and odd sex chromosomes and the number of sets of autosomes.

If X stands for the number of even sex chromosomes (X or Z), Y for the number of odd sex chromosomes, and a for the number of haploid sets of autosomes, and an F value < 0.5 predicts the homogametic sex type and > 0.5 predicts the heterogametic sex type, then the best "fit" is obtained by the formula:

$$F = 1.323 - 0.233X + 0.033X^2 + 0.00529X^3 + 1.957Y - 1.106Y^2 + 0.1882Y^3 - 1.288a + 0.459a^2 - 0.05087a^3.$$

One should not consider this formula as a law and the coefficients as absolute. However, it does indicate that the "odd" chromosome plays an important role in determining the heterogametic sex type and that the autosomes tend to determine the homogametic sex type, whereas the "even" sex chromosomes have little effect.

The mode of action of the sex chromosome has been investigated and the hypothesis of an inactive X chromosome has been postulated. In this hypothesis it is assumed that only one X chromosome in the somatic cell is active, so that in the female there may be cells in which one sex chromosome, carrying one set of alleles, is active, whereas in other cells, the alleles on the other sex chromosome are active. In effect, then, the female would be a mosaic with respect to the action of the genes on the sex chromosome. Gruneberg (1966) has, however, obtained evidence in mice with normal sex chromosomes that argues against acceptance of the "inactive sex chromosome" hypothesis. The characters investigated which gave these results were tabby, striated, and brindled. The autosomal and sex-linked heterozygotes, according to Gruneberg's results, do not differ in kind as presumed under the "inactive sex chromosome" hypothesis.

This hypothesis has been used to explain the occurrence of the XO pattern

Table 1-2. Chromosome Constitution and Gonadal Sex in Vertebrates, Excluding Chromosomal Mosaics

	MAMMALS			AMPHIBIA			AMPHIBIA			BIRDS*	FISH
SEX CHROMOSOMES	MAN	MOUSE	CAT	TRITURUS ALPESTRIS	TRITURUS PYRRHOGASTER	SEX CHROMOSOMES	AMBYSTOMA	PLEURODELES WALTLII	XENOPUS LAEVIS	CHICK	GASTEROSTEUS
						EUPLOIDS					
X +1A					♀	Z +1A	♂				
XX +2A	♀	♀	♀	♀	♀	ZZ +2A	♂	♂	♂	♂	♂?
XXX +3A				♀	♀	ZZZ +3A	♂	♂	♂		♂
XXXX +4A					♀	ZZZZ +4A	♂		♂		
XXXXX +5A						ZZZZZ +5A	♂				
XY +2A	♂	♂	♂	♂	♂	ZW +2A	♀	♀	♀	♀	♀
XYY +3A						ZWW +3A	♀	♀	♀		⚥
XXY +3A				♂†	♂	ZZW +3A	♀			⚥	
XXYY +4A					♂	ZZWW +4A	♀		♀		
XXXY +4A						ZZZW +4A	♀				
XXXYY +5A						ZZZWW +5A	♀				
XXXXY +5A					♂	ZZZZW +5A					
YY +2A						WW +2A	♀				
YYY +3A						WWW +3A	♀(?)				
						ANEUPLOIDS					
X +2A	♀	♀				Z +2A					
XXX +2A	♀					ZZZ +2A					
XXXX +2A	♀					ZZZZ +2A					
XXY +2A	♂	♂	♂			ZZW +2A					
XXXY +2A	♂					ZZW +2A					
XXYY +2A	♂					ZZWW +2A					
XXXXY +2A	♂					ZZZZW +2A					

♀ Female; ♂ Male; ⚥ Hermaphrodite.
* ZW:ZZ mechanism assumed.
† Sex reversed: initially female.
Reference: Beatty, 1964.

in the female somatic cells with an XX pattern in the ovarian tissue, and XO pattern in the male somatic cells but an XY pattern in testicular cells of the marsupials *Isoodon obesulus, I. macrouros,* and *Parameles nasuta* (Hayman and Martin, 1965). According to these authors, this phenomenon is an extreme case of chromosome inactivation with elimination having replaced inactivation.

The "inactive sex chromosome" hypothesis also would explain the presence of the sex chromatin or Barr body in the somatic cells and of the so-called "drumstick" in the polymorphonuclear leukocytes. In mammals the number of "Barr bodies" and "drumsticks" is one less than the number of X chromosomes, so that, e.g., in an XXXY individual there would be two Barr bodies in the somatic cells and two drumsticks in the polymorphonuclear leukocytes (Mittwoch, 1963). However, the presence of drumsticks in the leukocytes and the occurrence of sex chromatin in other somatic cells can occur independently (Beckert, 1962).

The sex chromatin of mammalian cells represents a heteropyknotic X chromosome (Melander, 1962) which frequently lies against the inner surface of the nuclear membrane, but may also be found, e.g. in the nervous tissue of the cat, against the nucleolus (Barr, 1966). The structure is about one micron in diameter and can be detected, e.g. in nervous tissue, by staining with cresyl violet or thionin; it also is stained by the Feulgen technique (Barr, 1966). The sex chromatin has been found to be present in a large number of mammalian species (see Barr, 1966, for extensive documentation).

Grinberg et al. (1966) used tritiated thymidine for in vivo and in vitro studies of the relationships between sex chromosomes, sex chromatin, and the "drumsticks" in cells of the nine-banded armadillo (*Dasypus novemcinctus*). In tissue cultures, one of the X chromosomes of the female synthesized DNA later than the other X chromosome; a peripheral focus of heavier labeling was found overlying the sex chromatin body, indicating that sex chromatin was formed by the late replicating X chromosome. In vivo localized labeling was found over several drumsticks, indicating a relationship between the drumstick and the late-replicating sex chromosome.

In birds, sex chromatin has not been found in the Charadriiformes, Passeriformes, Anseriformes, and Psittaciformes (Moore, 1962), but Kosin and Ishizaki (1959) reported its presence in female chickens. This poses a special problem since, as we saw before in birds, the female is the heterogametic sex. Barr (1966) suggests the possibility that the one Z chromosome of the female is heteropyknotic (dense and deeply chromatic), but that the two Z chromosomes of the male are isopyknotic. However, Barr (1966) cites other evidence which leaves the matter of sex chromosome heteropyknosis open to question.

The assumption that the heteropyknotic chromosome represents the "inactivated" sex chromosome leads to some difficulties with respect to the genetic evidence in chickens.

Cock (1964) has pointed out that an inactivated sex chromosome in the female would imply that none of the genes on this chromosome would be expressed, which is contrary to the genetic evidence available on sex-linked genes in the fowl.

An application of the detection of sex chromatin is the determination of the sex ratio of the embryos before sexual differentiation of the gonads has taken place (Picon, 1965). Such data would provide evidence about the differential mortality of male and female embryos at different stages of pregnancy. In man, cattle, and sheep it has been found that the sex ratio at birth favors the male, in spite of the higher number of male offspring aborted (Nalbandov, 1964). This implies that the sex ratio at conception is not unity. However, it is possible that the very early death of embryos (before sex differentiation) has been at the cost of females. Determining the sex of such embryos by sex chromatin detection would answer this question.

REFERENCES

Altman, P. L., and Dittmer, D. S. 1962. Growth, Including Reproduction and Morphological Development. Federation of American Societies for Experimental Biology, Washington, D. C.

Barr, M. L. 1966. The significance of the sex chromatin. Int. Rev. Cytol. *19*:35-95.

Beatty, R. A. 1960. Chromosomal determination of sex in mammals. Mem. Soc. Endocrinol. 7:45-48.

Beatty, R. A. 1964. Chromosome deviations and sex in vertebrates. *In* C. N. Armstrong and A. J. Marshall (eds.): Intersexuality in Vertebrates Including Man. Academic Press Inc., New York, pp. 17-143.

Beckert, W. H. 1962. Sex chromatin in nonmammalian vertebrates. Amer. Zool. *2*:505-506 (abstract).

Blackler, A. W. 1965. Germ-cell transfer and sex ratio in *Xenopus laevis.* J. Embryol. Exp. Morphol. *13*:51-61.

Cock, A. G. 1964. Dosage compensation and sex-chromatin in non-mammals. Genet. Res. (Camb.) *5*:354-365.

Dodd, J. M. 1960. Genetic and environmental aspects of sex determination in cold blooded vertebrates. Mem. Soc. Endocrinol. 7:17-44.

Gallien, L. G. 1965. Genetic control of sexual differentiation in vertebrates. *In* R. L. De Haan and H. Ursprung (eds.): Organogenesis. Holt, Rinehart, & Winston, Inc., New York, pp. 583-610.

Gowen, J. W. 1961. Genetic and cytological foundations for sex. *In* W. C. Young (ed.): Sex and Internal Secretions. Williams & Wilkins Co., Baltimore, Vol. 1, pp. 3-75.

Grinberg, M. A., Sullivan, M. M., and Benirschke, K. 1966. Investigation with tritiated thymidine of the relationship between sex chromosomes, sex chromatin, and the drumstick in the cells of the female nine-banded armadillo, *Dasypus novemcinctus.* Cytogenetics *5*:64-74.

Gruneberg, H. 1966. More about the tabby mouse and about the Lyon hypothesis. J. Embryol. Exp. Morphol. *16*:569-599.

Kosin, I. L., and Ishizaki, H. 1959. Incidence of sex chromatin in Gallus domesticus. Science *130*:43-44.

Hayman, D. L., and Martin, P. G. 1965. Sex chromosome mosaicism in the marsupial genera Isoodon and Parameles. Genetics 52:1201-1206.

Melander, Y. 1962. Chromosomal behaviour during the origin of sex chromatin in the rabbit. Hereditas *48*:645-661.

Mittwoch, U. 1963. Sex differences in cells. Sci. Amer. *(209:1)*:54-69.

Moore, K. L. 1962. The sex chromatin: its discovery and variations in the animal kingdom. Acta Cytol. *6*:1-12.

Nalbandov, A. V. 1964. Reproductive Physiology. Ed. 2. W. H. Freeman & Co., San Francisco.

Picon, R. 1965. Chromatine sexuelle du foetus de rat et détermination précoce du sexe. Arch. Anat. Microscop. Morphol. Exp. *54*:903-908.

Ryan, K. J., Benirschke, K., and Smith, O. W. 1961. Conversion of androstenedione-4-C[14] to estrone by the marmoset placenta. Endocrinology *69*:613-618.

Stolk, A. 1950. The ovarian occlusion apparatus in the viviparous Cyprinodont, Lebistes reticulatus Peters and Xiphophorus helleri Heckel. Proc. Kon. Ned. Akad. Wetensch. *53*:526-530.

Witschi, E. 1959. Age of sex-determining mechanisms in vertebrates. Science *130*:372-375.

Chapter 2

Embryology

DIFFERENTIATION OF THE GONADS

Description of Morphology

During embryonic development there is almost always a stage at which the gonadal tissue, formed from the intermediate mesoderm and lying on each side of the midline, is not differentiated into a male or female gonad. The genital ridge consists then of a cortex and medulla, which as we shall see will give rise to the ovaries and testes, respectively.

However, in order to become functional gonads, the genital ridge needs to acquire primordial germ cells. These cells originate in extraembryonic areas and in Lacertilia and birds (Dubois, 1965c), are transported by the blood to the genital ridge. In amphibia, chelonia, and mammals these cells are transported by ameboid movements (Franchi et al. 1962; Blandau et al., 1963; Dubois, 1965c).

In chicken and duck embryos the distribution of primordial germ cells is not equal in the left and right gonadal ridges; more cells are found on the left side. The ratio of the numbers found in the left and right gonads varies according to the stage of development. Until the third day of incubation the distribution is about equal, but at the end of four days the ratio of primordial germ cells in the left and right gonads is 2.5:1, and after five days about 5:1. The experimental evidence indicates that the primordial germ cells are required for the development of a normal gonad,

and thus the lack of development of the right female gonad may be the result of a lack of primordial germ cells. This supposition is strengthened by the observations of Stanley and Witschi (1940) that in the Cooper's hawk (*Accipiter cooperii*) and harrier (*Circus cyaneus hudsonius*), both of which have a well developed right ovary when adult, the ratio of primordial germ cells in the left and right gonads is close to 1:1; at the corresponding stage of development of the chicken the ratio is 5:1. On the other hand, in the red-tailed hawk (*Buteo jamaicensis borealis*), which does not have a developed right ovary, this ratio is closer to 3:1. This evidence indicates that the presence of the primordial germ cells is related to the subsequent development of the gonad.

The causes for the unequal distribution of the primordial germ cells have not been completely clarified. Van Limborgh (1957) has experimentally investigated this problem and found:

1. That sectioning of the developing embryo medially did not prevent an asymmetric distribution indicates that the asymmetry is not the result of a migration of these cells from left to right.

2. Turning the embryo around so that it lay on its left side (instead of on the right side as is normal) did not prevent asymmetry so that this is not the result of the orientation of the embryo during its early development.

3. The asymmetry is not the result of an asymmetric blood supply to the left and right gonadal ridges.

The mechanism which does cause the asymmetry is not known. It may be due to a differential between the two genital ridges with respect to some chemical agent which attracts the cells by chemotaxis.

There is evidence from a variety of sources that indicates that these primordial germ cells are important for the normal development of the gonad and affect the formation of the mature germ cells:

1. Removal of the primordial germ cells leads to formation of sterile gonads (Simon, 1960).

2. Blackler and Fischberg (1961) transplanted the germinal ridge of *Xenopus laevis* tadpoles with a genetic marker (two nucleoli per nucleus) to hosts (one nucleolus per nucleus) and found that the gonads of the host contained germ cells with two nucleoli per nucleus.

3. By parabiosis of chick and duck embryos and removal of the germinal crescent (the area of origin of the primordial germ cells) Simon (1960) was able to obtain chicks which had duck gonocytes.

How the genital ridge "traps" the primordial germ cells is not known. There is evidence in vivo (Simon, 1960) and in vitro (Dubois, 1965a) that the ridge attracts the primordial germ cells. In vivo transplantation of the genital ridge to another site still results in migration of the primordial germ cells to this ridge. In vitro, with the use of radioactively labeled primordial germ cells, it can be demonstrated that these cells migrate to a piece of germinal epithelium of a younger embryo (devoid of germ cells).

Dubois (1965b) has demonstrated, in subsequent experiments, that the undifferentiated germinal epithelium of young embryos can cause the migration of germ cells from the differentiated testes of a 12- to 13-day-old male embryo. The germ cells of female embryos lose their ability to migrate after the eighth day of incubation. The reason for the difference in ability to migrate of male and female germ cells is not known.

Sexual differentiation in cyclostomes and teleosts differs from that found in other vertebrates. The gonad in these two groups consists of only one type of tissue, which resembles that of the cortex of other vertebrates. It is worth noting that in cyclostomes and teleosts the tendency for hermaphroditism is more general than in the other vertebrates, suggesting that the expression of the phenotypic sex is more labile (Dodd, 1960b).

In the not yet sexually differentiated cyclostomes and teleosts each individual possesses germ cells or potential germ cells of both sexes. Differentiation into a male is the result of a reduction of the number of oocytes, and differentiation into a female is the result of a reduction in the number of male germ cells. In *Entosphenus,* male and female germ cells are more or less scattered throughout the gonadal tissue. In hagfishes *(Myxine* and *Bdellostoma)* and in the teleost families *Sparidae* and *Serranidae,* there are definite male or female germ cell areas in the same gonad. An excellent account of sex differentiation in cyclostomes can be found in the papers by Hardisty (1965a, b) and Lewis and McMillan (1965).

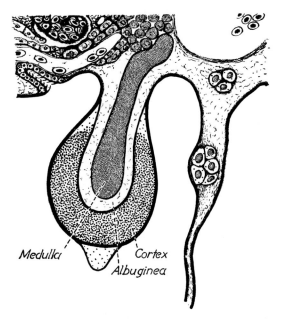

Figure 2-1. Cross section of the undifferentiated gonad of higher vertebrates showing the basic arrangement of medulla and cortex. (From Witschi, 1951.)

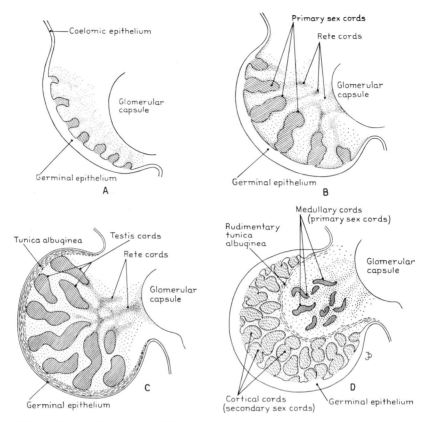

Figure 2-2. Differentiation of the gonad of higher vertebrates into testis and ovary. *A*. Origin of the primary sex cords from the germinal epithelium. *B*. The primary sex cords have developed but the gonad is still undifferentiated. *C*. Differentiation into a testis is taking place; the primary sex cords develop further; the germinal epithelium is reduced in size; and the tunica albuginea develops. *D*. Differentiation into an ovary consists of development of the secondary sex cords of the cortex and a reduction in the primary sex cords and of the tunica albuginea. (From Burns, 1961.)

The following account relates the different steps during sexual differentiation of the gonads of vertebrates other than cyclostomes and teleosts in accordance with the classical concept as described in recent reviews by Burns (1961) and Witschi (1951, 1965).

In these vertebrates the gonadal stroma consists of an outer cortex, which originates from the peritoneum, and an inner medulla, which, according to Witschi (1951), originates from the interrenal blastema (see Figure 2-1); according to others (see Franchi et al., 1962 for review) the medulla may be formed by proliferation of the germinal epithelium.

Differentiation into a testis is accompanied by a proportionally greater medullary development and differentiation into an ovary by a proportionally greater cortical development (Figure 2-3). The primordial germ cells become associated with the dominant component of the gonad.

In the male the primordial germ cells give rise to spermatogonia and so-called primary sex cords proliferate from the germinal epithelium (Figure 2-2). These sex cords form the seminiferous tubules. The Sertoli cells, according to Clermont and Perey (1957), originate from the supporting cells of the primary sex cords.

In the female the primordial germ cells give rise to oogonia, and a second proliferation of the germinal epithelium into the cortex occurs (Figure 2-2) to form the secondary sex cords. The primary sex cords and medulla decrease in relative size (see Figure 2-3). In some species, e.g. the

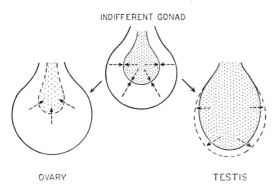

INDIFFERENT GONAD

OVARY   TESTIS

Figure 2-3. Diagram showing the comparative development of cortex and medulla of the undifferentiated gonad after differentiation into a testis or ovary in amphibia; arrows indicate the inhibitory effects of the two components according to Witschi's hypothesis. (From Burns, 1961.)

striped skunk *(Mephitis mephitis),* medullary development may precede cortical development. In this skunk, the primary sex cord follicles continue to enlarge for about 11 weeks after the female is born. There is very little accompanying cortical development (Leach and Conaway, 1963). Only after the medullary follicles have undergone atresia does the cortex start to develop. In other species the medulla may increase in size, but the cortex increases more, so there is a proportionally larger development of the cortex and, possibly, a subsequent decrease in the size of the medulla (Figure 2-3). The primordial germ cells give rise to oogonia, which become surrounded by follicle cells. As we mentioned, e.g. for the striped skunk, follicles can develop in the medulla and can be caused to ovulate by gonadotropin treatment.

An entirely different concept of gonadal differentiation in cattle, thought to be applicable to other mammals, has been formulated by Gropp and Ohno (1966). Use was made of the fact that the gonadal blastema of cattle gives a strong alkaline phosphatase reaction. This test was used to follow the development of the different elements involved in gonadal differentiation. Ages of embryos used were between one month after conception and near term. The genetic sex of the undifferentiated

embryos was determined from chromosome counts made from a piece of the donor's liver cultured in vitro.

Gropp and Ohno (1966) think that the gonadal differentiation takes place as follows: While primordial germ cells are still migrating the gonadal fold consists of a surface layer and underlying cell mass which are both alkaline phosphatase positive. The lining soon becomes alkaline phosphatase negative, whereas the alkaline phosphatase positive blastema occupies a large area along the medial wall of the mesonephric glomerular tuft and reaches down within the gonadal fold. The primordial germ cells, just after having completed their migration, can be found throughout the alkaline phosphatase negative layer. Primordial germ cells which might have migrated into the blastema would not be recognized because of the alkaline phosphatase positive reaction of both the blastema and the primordial germ cells.

In the female gonad the number of germ cells increases in the peripheral zone, whereas in the male this number decreases. These changes could be detected in the histochemical investigation but not in the histological (hematoxylin-eosin stain) investigation.

In the female the outer cell layers arrange themselves in cordlike columns at about 50 days after mating. The germ cells in the peripheral zone proliferate and the blastema forms alkaline phosphatase positive cords. Soon a layer of oogonia can be distinguished and eventually the cords from the gonadal blastema branch out and make contact with the layer of oogonia. These cords are the primordia of the follicles (follicular cords). In later stages, the oogonia are engulfed by the cords which Gropp and Ohno (1966) now label ovigerous cords. The follicle cells retain their alkaline phosphatase activity but the germ cells lose theirs gradually. Mitosis occurs at 75 days.

At about 80 to 85 days the onset of meiotic prophase can be seen, and most germ cells are incorporated in the oviger-ous cords.

At about 100 days primordial follicles are formed deep in the cortex. The pri-mordial follicles and the granulosa cells of the Graafian follicles are alkaline phos-phatase negative, but the theca interna cells are alkaline phosphatase positive.

A number of small areas, remnants of of the follicular cords which did not en-gulf germ cells, persist in the deeper cor-tical layers of the ovary. Such cords may be responsible for estrous cycles in mules, in which oocytes degenerate so that mules' ovaries lack oocytes.

In the male, spots which are alkaline phosphatase negative appear at 50 days. Shortly afterwards the tunica albuginea is formed and the mesenchymal cells below the coelomic lining are arranged in a densely packed layer, the primordial germ cells with alkaline phosphatase activity be-come rare in this zone. The alkaline phos-phatase negative spots enlarge and tubules are formed which contrast with the alka-line phosphatase positive interstitial cells. Mitosis of gonia within the newly formed tubules gives rise to precursors of the spermatogonia (60 days).

At about 100 days the germ cells can be recognized within tubules, which are now more sharply differentiated from the interstitial cells. The concept by Gropp and Ohno (1966) thus differs from the more classical formulation of Witschi and Burns in that it considers the function of the "germinal epithelium" minimal and that secondary sex cords are not observed.

Gropp and Ohno think that the ob-servation of secondary sex cords by others is the result of an illusion produced by the apparent lining up of the germ cells be-fore the follicular cords engulf them. In consequence, follicular cells of the ovary and the interstitial cells of the testis can be considered to be homologous; pos-sibly the tubular cells of the testis are also homologous to these two groups of cells.

The factors controlling or influencing sexual differentiation of the gonads have

been analyzed by a variety of techniques, which will be discussed before discussing the gonoduct systems.

Experimental Analysis of Gonadal Differentiation

Witschi (1965) has proposed that the medulla secretes a substance called medul-larin and the cortex a substance cortecin, which inhibit development of the cortex and medulla, respectively, and thus cause differentiation into either a testis or an ovary. These substances have not been iso-lated, and many experiments have been carried out to determine whether the gon-adal hormones secreted by the adult gon-ads, that is, the estrogens and androgens, simulate the effects of the proposed fetal gonadal hormones. A comparison between experiments in which fetal gonads of dif-ferent sexes develop in close proximity, and experiments in which estrogens or androgens are administered would sug-gest that the substances are not identical. The various experimental approaches used will be discussed.

GRAFTING

It seems a logical procedure to at-tempt sex reversals by transplanting a differentiating or differentiated gonad in the vicinity of an undifferentiated gonad in order to determine whether the dif-ferentiated gonad can influence the differ-entiation of the undifferentiated one. Table 2-1 summarizes some of these experiments for different genera.

To Table 2-1 we should add the case in which there is a natural chance for ex-change between the gonads of opposite genetic sexes. The classical example for this is the bovine freemartin, the genetic female twin to a bull calf. Such freemartins occur only when anastomoses of blood ves-sels of the two fetuses have occurred. The freemartin is characterized by a sterile testicular or ovotesticular gonad, the pres-

Table 2-1. Effect of Differentiated Gonad on Undifferentiated Gonad in Transplantation Experiments

GENUS	DIFFERENTIATED GONAD	UNDIFFERENTIATED GONAD (GENETIC SEX)	RESULT ON UNDIFFERENTIATED GONAD
Ambystoma	Testis	Ovary	Testis (sex reversal)
	Ovary	Testis	Ovary (sex reversal)
Xenopus	Testis	Ovary	Testis (sex reversal)
Triturus	Testis	Ovary	Sterile ovary
Gallus (domesticus)	Ovary	Testis	Right testis regresses
			Left gonad ovotestis
	Right rudimentary ovary	Testis	Left gonad ovotestis

References: Burns, 1961; Dodd, 1960a; Jost, 1960; and Wolff, 1959.

ence of a rather well-developed male duct system, but female external genitalia (sometimes with an enlarged clitoris), and female mammary glands. An ovine freemartin in which the anatomy of the sex organs resembled that of the bovine freemartin has been described by Alexander and Williams (1964). Biggers and McFeely (1966) mention that freemartins have also been found in pigs.

The explanation for the bovine freemartin originally proposed by F. R. Lillie (1917) was that a hormone secreted by the testes of the male twin caused the gonad of the female twin to develop in the male direction. It was subsequently shown that the male gonad is indeed endocrinologically active before the female gonad. However, as Bouters and Vandeplassche (1964) point out, not a trace of androgen (< 0.4 μg.) is found in the testes of fetal bull calves during the first two to four months of pregnancy, although lesions of the reproductive system of the freemartin can be found even before this time. Secondly, injections of androgens into cattle between the fortieth to forty-second day after insemination and continued until day 105, when the fetuses were examined, did not cause any changes in the ovaries of female fetuses although the external genitalia were masculinized (Jost et al., 1963). It is, of course, possible that androgen injections started earlier might have an effect.

This lack of experimentally induced freemartins has led Witschi (1965) to reiterate his theory of sex inductors and inhibitors. In this case the medullary antagonist from the male medulla would cause elimination of the female cortex. This medullary antagonist is different from the *arrhenogens* which control regression of the Müllerian ducts and stimulate the Wolffian duct system. The development of these systems is, according to Witschi (1965), dependent on the genetic female's own production of *arrhenogens* (term broader than androgens because the arrhenogens have not been proven to be steroids). Witschi bolsters his argument with the fact that androgen injections in female *Xenopus laevis* larvae are ineffective in inducing functional males but that implantation of differentiated testes will produce functional males. By breeding experiments with such sex-reversed genetic females, Mikamo and Witschi (1962) were able to produce colonies of 100 percent ZW females and 100 percent ZZ males and 100 percent WW females (not normally found).

An alternative hypothesis is that the anastomosis of the blood vessels leads to mosaics of the twins so that freemartins are the result of sex chromosome mosaicism. Evidence to support this has accumulated recently (Fechheimer et al., 1963; Goodfellow et al., 1965; Kanagawa et al., 1965; and Makino et al., 1965). Makino et al. (1965) and Goodfellow et al. (1965) reported that the normal male twin to the freemartin also was a mosaic, XX/XY. The earlier publication by Makino et al. (1962), which reported normal idiograms for free-martins, was probably based on sampling errors; fewer cells were counted in that report than in the later one. The occurrence of germ cell chimeras is confirmed by the presence of 2A-XX cells in bulls born as twins to freemartins (Ohno et al., 1962; Kanagawa et al., 1965). Gerneke (1965) has reported a case of XY chimerism in sheep also. That the freemartin is not the result of male primordial germ cells settling in the female gonad is suggested by the elegant experiments of Blackler (1965) conducted with *Xenopus laevis*. By the use of toads with different genetic nuclear markers (one or two nucleoli), transplantation of the primordial germ cell area from one larvae to another, and by mating the resulting offspring to normal toads, it was established that the gonad reversed the sex of the primordial germ cells. Thus ZZ males were obtained which were viable but produced W sperm with fertilizing ability. A similar situation seems to exist in the mouse: primordial germ cells of the fetal mouse ovary can be induced to differentiate into spermatozoa in the male mouse gonad (Turner and Asakawa, 1964). These experiments show, therefore, that the differentiation of primordial germ cells into either sperm or ova is apparently under the control of the genital ridge rather than under the control of the genetic information contained in the primordial germ cell itself.

The anastomosis of the fetal circulations of twins of unequal sex, the exchange of cells as evidenced by bone marrow chimeras, and the exchange of primordial germ cells do not cause freemartins in other species. In marmosets, young are always produced as twins. As the young are dizygotic, 50 percent of the twins differ in sex. Investigations of the common marmoset (*Hapale jacchus*) and of Geoffroy's tamarin (*Oepipomidas geoffroyi*) have revealed no abnormalities in either the males or females.

The occurrence of bone marrow chimeras was demonstrated in the lionheaded marmoset (*Leontocebus rosalia*), in *Tamarinus nigricollis*, and *Cebuella pygmea;* the exchange of primordial germ cells was found in *Callithrix jacchus, Cebuella pygmea,* and *Tamarinus mystax* (see Biggers and McFeely, 1966). These authors also point out that blood chimeras have been found in humans, but no authentic case of freemartinism in humans seems to exist.

According to Ryan et al. (1961), the lionheaded marmoset placenta can convert androstenedione-4-C^{14} to estrone, as is the case with the human placenta, but the bovine placenta cannot make this conversion; thus, bovine female fetuses would be exposed to androgen from their male twins, but marmosets and human female fetuses would not. This brings the "explanation" of freemartinism back to an effect of the male gonadal hormones on the female gonads. However, we have seen that experimentally it has not been possible to induce freemartins in cattle by injection of androgens. The special conditions which prevail in the development of the bovine freemartin are still not known and no definite explanation can yet be given for this phenomenon.

In addition to the classical bovine freemartin, there have been recent reports on duck freemartins, in which two embryos of opposite genetic sex developed in the same egg (Wolff and Lutz-Ostertag, 1961). In such freemartins the gonads of the females are never affected (analogous to the testes of the bull calf twin to the freemartin); however, the testicular hormone did cause a smaller than normal left oviduct in 10 out of 27 cases, caused a somewhat masculine kind of syrinx in 18 out of 27 cases, and caused a masculinized genital tubercle in 27 out of 27 cases.

In the genetic males, 24 out of 27 left gonads contained more or less extensive amounts of cortex (in controls this is about 30 to 40 percent). In 11 out of 27 embryos the Müllerian duct system had not regressed as far as in normal males. In the case of the avian freemartin, therefore, the testis is affected by the ovary. However, similar results can be obtained by

Table 2-2. Differentiation In Vitro of Duck and Chick Gonads

1. Male right testis 7d* duck embryo → normal testis
   Male left testis 7d duck embryo → normal testis
   Female right gonad 7d duck embryo → germ cells in cortex; gonad regressed
   Female left gonad 7d duck embryo → normal ovary
   Male right gonad 4–8d chick embryo → testis
   Male left gonad 4–8d chick embryo → testis
   Female left gonad 4–8d chick embryo → ovotestis
   Female right gonad 4–8d chick embryo → testis

For Duck and Chick:
2. Male left + female left, female gonad → ovary, male gonad → ovotestis
   Male left + female right, female gonad → regresses, male gonad → ovotestis

3. Male right + estrogen → ovotestis
   Male left + estrogen → ovotestis

4. Male gonad by parabiosis to ovary → ovotestis. This ovotestis incubated plus undifferentiated male gonad transforms the latter into ovotestis.

5. Male germinal epithelium (5d embryo) → no differentiation
   Male germinal epithelium (5d embryo) + female medulla (9–13d embryo): male germinal epithelium → cortex; medulla degenerated.

6. Female germinal epithelium (5d embryo) → ovary
   Female germinal epithelium (5d embryo) + medulla testis → germinal epithelium → ovary.

* d = -day-old.
Reference: Wolff and Haffen, 1965.

the injections of estrogens into the egg, a situation which differs from the one found in the bovine freemartin, in which exogenous androgens have no effect on the ovary.

The in vitro differentiation of undifferentiated gonads alone and in the presence of another differentiated gonad or of estrogen is summarized in Table 2-2. These results show that, as in in vivo experiments, the development of the right male gonad proceeds as a testis in the absence or presence of ovarian tissue. The left male gonad becomes a testis in the absence of ovarian tissue, but in the presence of the ovary becomes an ovotestis. It also shows that male gonadal tissue, transformed into an ovotestis under the influence of ovarian tissue, retains the induced properties of the ovarian development and can in turn cause the male gonadal tissue to differentiate in the female direction. Some of the substances which cause differentiation into ovarian tissue are present in the medulla, as is evident from the differentiation of male germinal epithelium into cortex in the presence of medullary tissue from a female. On the other hand, male medullary tissue does not seem to have an effect on either the undifferentiated female gonad or on the germinal epithelium.

In contrast to the lack of an effect of ovarian tissue on differentiation of the right male gonad is the effect of estrogen, which causes differentiation into an ovotestis. These data thus suggest differences between the female fetal gonadal hormone and estrogen, with estrogen being more potent. This is in contrast to the reaction of *Xenopus laevis* illustrated above, in which androgen was not capable of causing differentiation of an ovary into a testis but a testis transplant was capable of doing so.

STEROID HORMONE ADMINISTRATION

The effects of estrogen and androgen administration on sexual differentiation in different species have been summarized in Tables 2-3 and 2-4. The following con-

Table 2-3. Estrogen-Induced Sex Reversal in Genetic Males

SPECIES OR CLASS	RESULT	REFERENCE
Species in Which Estrogen Causes Sex Reversal		
Elasmobranchs	Prominent cortex	Chieffi, 1959; Dodd, 1960b
	Hypoplasia of medulla	Chieffi, 1959
Oryzias latipes	Functional female	Atz, 1964
Poecilia reticulata	Functional female	Atz, 1964
Salmo gairdneri	Ovotestis	Atz, 1964
Anguilla anguilla	Ovotestis	Atz, 1964
Gambusia affinis	Ovotestis	Atz, 1964
Xiphophorus maculatus	Ovotestis	Atz, 1964
Xiphophorus helleri	Ovotestis	Atz, 1964
Pleurodeles waltlii	Ovotestis; later became male	Gallien, 1961
Xenopus laevis	Ovotestis	Burns, 1961
Rana temporaria	Complete feminization but not permanent	Burns, 1961
Rana esculenta	Complete feminization at metamorphosis at low dosage; at high dosage masculinization	Foote, 1964
Rana sylvatica	As *Rana esculenta*	Burns, 1961; Foote, 1964
Rana catesbeiana	Complete transformation at metamorphosis	Burns, 1961
Bufo americanus	Complete transformation but not permanent	Burns, 1961
Bufo americanus	(Thyroidectomized) feminized	Dodd, 1960b
Bufo bufo	Partial but not permanent feminization	Dodd, 1960b; Foote, 1964
Pseudacris nigrita	Feminization	Dodd, 1960a
Ambystoma punctatum	Total feminization	Foote, 1964
Ambystoma trigrum	Total feminization	Foote, 1964
Ambystoma opacum	Total feminization	Foote, 1964
Hynobius retardatus	Total feminization	Foote, 1964
Hynobius nebulosis	Total feminization	Foote, 1964
Triturus alpestris	Total feminization	Foote, 1964
Triturus helveticus	Total feminization	Foote, 1964
Pelobatus cultipres	Total feminization	Foote, 1964
Discoglossus pictus	Partial but not permanent feminization	Foote, 1964
Alytes obstetricans	Partial but not permanent feminization	Foote, 1964
Emys leprosa	Ovotestis	Forbes, 1964
Lacerta sp.	Cortex induced	Dodd, 1960a
Coturnix coturnix	Left gonad with mature follicles eight weeks after hatching	Haffen, 1965
Gallus domesticus	Left gonad becomes ovotestis (not permanent)	van Tienhoven, 1957
Gallus domesticus in vitro	Ovotestis	Wolff and Haffen, 1965
Anas sp.	Ovotestis, not permanent?	Taber, 1964
Larus argentatus	Persistent cortex after two years	Boss and Witschi, 1947
Didelphis virginiana	Ovotestis, ovary	Burns, 1961
Species in Which Estrogen Does Not Cause Sex Reversal		
Tilapia aurea	Destruction of gonads	Eckstein and Spiza, 1965
Salmo trutta		Dodd, 1960b
Rana clamitans		Dodd, 1960b
Thamnophis sp.		Dodd, 1960b

Table 2-4. Sex Reversal Induced by Androgens

SPECIES OR CLASS	RESULT	REFERENCE
Species in Which Androgens Cause Sex Reversal of Females		
Oryzias latipes	Fertile functional male	Yamamoto, 1958
Salmo trutta	Ovotestis	Atz, 1964 (review)
Poecilia reticulata	Functional male	Atz, 1964
Gambusia affinis	Functional male	Atz, 1964
Xiphophorus helleri	Functional male	Atz, 1964
Rana temporaria	Permanent functional male	Burns, 1961 (review)
Rana sylvatica	Complete transformation at metamorphosis	Burns, 1961
Rana pipiens	Complete transformation at metamorphosis	Burns, 1961
Rana dalmatina	Feminization	Dodd, 1960b
Rana catesbeiana	Complete transformation	Dodd, 1960b
Rana clamitans	Complete transformation	Dodd, 1960b
Rana agilis	Complete transformation	Dodd, 1960b
Pseudacris nigrita	Complete transformation	Dodd, 1960b
Rhacophorus schlegelii	Almost complete transformation	Dodd, 1960b
Ambystoma punctatum	Ovotestis	Dodd, 1960b
Chrysemys marginata	Ovotestis	Dodd, 1960b
Species in Which Androgens Do Not Cause Sex Reversal of Females		
Tilapia aurea		Eckstein and Spira, 1965
Salmo trutta		Dodd, 1960b
Bufo americanus (ovary)		Dodd, 1960b
Bufo americanus (Bidder's organ)		Dodd, 1960b
Xenopus laevis		Witschi, 1965
Triturus sp.		Chieffi, 1965
Discoglossus sp.		Chieffi, 1965
Alytes obstetricans		Dodd, 1960b
Pelobates sp.		Chieffi, 1965
Pelodytes sp.		Chieffi, 1965
Bombina sp.		Chieffi, 1965
Ambystoma mexicanum		Dodd, 1960b
A. mexicanum x A. tigrum		Dodd, 1960b
Thamnophis radix		Forbes, 1964
Uromastix sp.		Forbes, 1964
Anolis sp.		Forbes, 1964
Lacerta sp.		Forbes, 1964
Effect of Androgens on Genetic Males		
Torpedo ocellata	Feminization	Dodd, 1960b
Xenopus laevis	Temporary feminization	Dodd, 1960b
Ambystoma opacum	Feminization	Atz, 1964
Pleurodeles waltlii	Feminization	Atz, 1964
Gallus domesticus	Ovotestis	Taber, 1964

clusions may be drawn from these data:

1. The higher the development on the phylogenetic scale the more difficult it is to obtain sex reversal. However, as the data of Table 2-3 show, permanent change is obtained in quail *(Coturnix coturnix)*, but in the fairly closely related chicken the change is not permanent.

2. Generally it is easier to obtain sex reversal in the homozygous sex. An exception is the Japanese rice fish *(Oryzias latipes)*, in which complete transformation in both directions can be obtained.

3. Androgens can cause feminization of male gonads; this, of course, would argue against the hypothesis that the androgen is identical with the hormones involved in normal differentiation of the testis.

It is of interest to know the approximate sequence of steroid hormone secretion during the development of the fetal gonads. For a number of species this has been determined.

The onset of steroidogenesis occurs in *Scyliorhinus caniculus* after sexual differentiation has started (Chieffi, 1965); in *R. pipiens* steroid hormones are secreted at the time of metamorphosis and sexual differentiation. The source of these steroids may be the adrenals (Chieffi, 1965). The time when sex hormone secretion starts in reptiles seems not to have been determined (Chieffi, 1965). In chickens sex steroid hormones can be demonstrated after sexual differentiation has started.

Price and Ortiz (1965) have compared mammalian sex differentiation in guinea pigs, rats, mice, hamsters, and rabbits, and found essentially the same sequence of events, i.e. testicular differentiation, androgen secretion, male Müllerian duct degeneration, female Wolffian duct degeneration, and prostate development. An exception is the rabbit, in which prostate development starts before female Wolffian duct degeneration starts. Androgen secretion occurred in guinea pigs before testicular differentiation was detectable. Ovarian cortical tissue develops at about the same time as the degeneration of female Wolffian ducts and male Müllerian ducts starts in guinea pigs. In the comparison of different species the initiation of ovarian cortical development is not indicated. According to Price and Ortiz (1965), evidence for inhibition of female Müllerian ducts by androgens is inadequate except in the case of the rabbit.

The effects of progesterone and desoxycorticosterone on gonadal differentiation have been investigated in relatively few species.

Progesterone (0.02 mg.) injected into embryos of *Torpedo ocellata* and *Scyliorhinus canicula* caused development of the cortex and reduction in the incidence of germ cells which migrate from the cortex into the medulla; autopsy at 3 to 4 months after the injections revealed that all animals had ovaries (Chieffi, 1959).

Rana esculenta, R. dalmatina, and *R. sylvatica* larvae injected with progesterone develop into males only.

Desoxycorticosterone causes feminization in *Torpedo ocellata, Scyliorhinus canicula, Rana esculenta, Rana dalmatina,* and *Hynobius nebulosus.* It seems to have no effect in *Rana temporaria, Hyla arborea japonica,* and *Triturus pyrrhogaster,* whereas it causes masculization in the wood frog *(Rana sylvatica),* and in *Rhacophorus schlegelii.*

EFFECTS OF THE HYPOPHYSIS AND ITS HORMONES

Hypophysectomy of the embryo, usually accomplished by decapitation, does not affect the sex differentiation of the gonads in sharks *(Scyliorhinus sp.),* frogs *(Rana temporaria, R. pipiens,* and *R. sylvatica)* (Chang and Witschi, 1955; Iwasawa, 1961), toads *(Bufo americanus)* (Chang, 1955), the chick (Fugo, 1940), the duck (van Deth et al., 1956), the rat and rabbit (Jost, 1953), and the mouse (Raynaud, 1959). The hypophysis is not required for exogenous sex hormones to have their effect on the differentiation of frogs *(Rana pipiens, R. temporaria,* and *R. sylvatica)* according to Chang and Witschi (1955).

The injection of gonadotropic hormones or the transplantation of pituitaries into embryos does not seem to affect sex differentiation. Burgos and Pisano (1958) have reported that injection of follicle stimulating hormone, FSH, in *Bufo arenarum,* after metamorphosis but before definitive sex differentiation, caused the development of males only, whereas luteinizing hormone, LH, caused appearance of females only. In each case one specimen had sperm and oocytes. Dufaure (1965) has reported that gonadotropin injection in *Lacerta vivipara* causes cortical development and female development of the medulla in genetic male embryos. Dufaure mentioned neither the gonadotropin nor the dosages used.

THYROID INHIBITORS

Iwasawa (1955a, 1955b, 1958, 1961) found that treatment of *Rhacophorus schlegelii* or of *Rana temporaria ornativentris* with thiourea caused sex reversal in females. Thyroidectomy of *Rana temporaria ornativentris* did not have this effect.

Thyroid inhibitors do not seem to affect the sex differentiation of birds and mammals; apparently, the effect of these chemicals has not been investigated in fishes and reptiles.

THE EFFECT OF THE ENVIRONMENT

In some vertebrates the environment or the condition of the ova at the time of fertilization affects sex differentiation. The temperature at which the eggs develop may cause a shift in the sex ratio. In the amphibians studied *(Rana sylvatica, Bufo vulgaris,* and *Hynobius retardatus)* larvae reared at 18 to 21°C. yield a normal sex ratio, whereas rearing the larvae at 10°C. yields only female offspring and at 15°C. only hermaphrodites are found. If the larvae are reared at 27°C. a normal sex

ratio is obtained at metamorphosis, but continued exposure to 27°C. results in destruction of the ovarian cortex and thus only males are obtained (Dodd, 1960a).

Lutz-Ostertag (1965) has reported that exposure of the eggs of *Coturnix c. japonica* to 39.5°C. between day 12 and 14 resulted in larger than normal right gonads in the females; these gonads did not have the lacunae found in controls.

An effect of environmental temperature on the development of the fetal gonad of the rat has been found by Torrey (1950). Transplantation of fetal gonads to the anterior eye chamber, where the temperature is somewhat lower, has no effect on differentiation of the testes but causes destruction of the cortex. When the eyelids were sewn closed (so that, presumably, the temperature did not differ from the deep body temperature) no effect of gonad transplantation was observed (Torrey, 1950).

Bellec and Stolkowski (1965) found that larvae of *Discoglossus pictus* differentiated predominantly into males (sex ratio 187) when reared in a Ringer's solution ($\triangle = -.48°C.$) with a K^+/Ca^{++} ratio of 0.11, whereas at a ratio of 0.14 the sex ratio was 42. At ratios of 0.48 and 0.03 the sex ratios were normal. The surprising observation was made that under these conditions no hermaphrodites were found. However, hermaphrodites were found if the larvae were raised in unbalanced Ringer's to 20 days and subsequently raised in normal Ringer's solution.

Atz (1964) points out that most eels *(Anguilla anguilla)* found in inland fresh water are females, whereas the majority of eels found in salt estuarine habitats are males. Whether the salt content of the water affects sexual differentiation or whether males prefer a higher salt content has not been established.

In *Rana esculenta* and *Rana temporaria* interruption of the "sexual embrace" causes failure of oviposition of the eggs. Such eggs can later be "stripped" from the oviduct. These "aged" eggs, when fertilized, give rise almost exclusively (299 out of 300) to male offspring. This result is not due to high mortality of female larvae. In the teleost fish studied, results of a delay in fertilization are not spectacular; e.g. in the rainbow trout *(Salmo gairdneri)* a delay of 21 days results in 55 percent males, 33 percent females, and 12 percent hermaphrodites (Atz, 1964); in the brown trout *(Salmo trutta)* a delay of 4 to 7 days results in a preponderance of females and an extended delay results in a preponderance of males (Dodd, 1960b). The significance of these shifts in sex ratio is not evident.

DIFFERENTIATION OF THE SECONDARY SEX ORGANS

Description of the Secondary Sex Organs

In many species a duct system is required to conduct the gametes, or, in the case of females, the gametes or the zygote, toward the outside.

The lampreys and hagfishes have no duct system to connect the testes to the outside, but sperm are shed into the coelomic cavity, which is emptied through abdominal pores (Gérard, 1954).

In male elasmobranchs and tetrapods the mesenchyme of the center of the gonad differentiates into a network, the *rete testis,* which connects with the seminiferous tubules and the anterior part of the mesonephric duct system, which gradually loses its kidney function. The anterior mesonephric ducts which do not degenerate and which form a pathway for the sperm are called the *ductuli efferentes.* These ducts plus the part of the primitive kidney duct form an elaborate network, the so-called epididymis. The primitive kidney duct serves for sperm transport and is called the ductus deferens. The development of the latter in different classes will be discussed later. In general, the ductus deferens opens into the cloaca and it may show a diverticulum, the seminal vesicle, or it may show an elaborate secretory membrane as is the case in some species of birds. In elasmobranchs "claspers" develop from the medial margin of the ventral fins. The clasper functions as an intromittent organ.

Table 2-1 (see also Figure 2-4) should be helpful in understanding the derivation of the various structures.

In teleosts there is no connection between the gonadal and the kidney tubules. The central cavity of the testes elongates posteriorly and a deferent duct is formed which originates from gonadal tissue. It may open into a separate opening between anus and the urinary papilla, into the anus, into a cloaca, or into a urinary duct or bladder. There are many anatomical variations in this class and no representative pattern applying to all teleosts can be given.

For cyclostomes the situation for the female is similar to that in the male. The ova of cyclostomes are shed into the body cavity, find their way to the cloaca, and are shed into the water at spawning.

In teleost fishes, the oviducts are either prolonged leaflike expansions of the ovary or they arise from mesenteries along the gonadal ridge; they are, however, not derived from the paramesonephric duct system. The guppy *(Poecilia reticulata)* and the swordtail *(Xiphophorus helleri)* possess a number of lobes which develop by invagination of the ovarian epithelium and pass over the wall of the oviduct. These lobes are covered by two layers resembling the occlusion tissue of the mammalian uterine cervix (Stolk, 1950), and may serve to retain the developing embryo in the ovary. At the posterior end of the oviduct the swordtail possesses two layers of tissue which close the posterior end of the oviduct. At copulation the gonopodium must penetrate these two layers (Peters and Mäder, 1964), and healing must be complete in about nine days. Presumably these layers serve to keep bacteria out of the oviduct.

In elasmobranchs and tetrapods the oviducts develop in close relation to the kidney duct system. In elasmobranch and

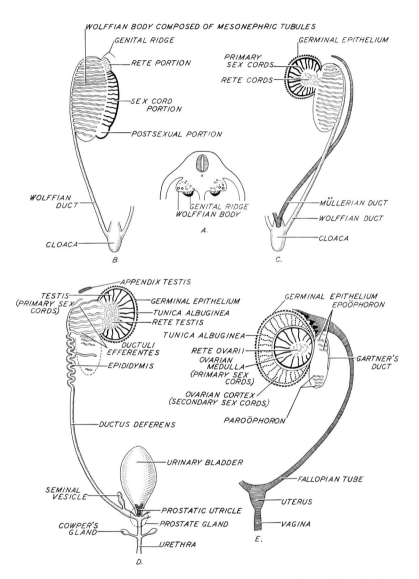

Figure 2-4. Embryogenesis of the genital system in amniotes. *A.* Section through the dorsal region of an early embryo. *B.* Sagittal section of the Wolffian body and genital ridge. *C.* The indifferent stage of development of the genital system. *D.* Differentiation of the male genital system. *E.* Differentiation of the female genital system. See text and also Table 2-5. (From Turner, 1966.)

Table 2-5. Homologies of Male and Female Reproductive Systems of Elasmobranchs and Tetrapods

MALE	INDIFFERENT	FEMALE
Testes	Gonadal medulla	
*Rete testis**		
		Rete ovarii
Bidder's organ (toads)†	Gonadal cortex	Ovary
Ductuli efferentes	Mesonephric tubules	*Epoophoron*
Paradidymis		*Paroophoron*
Ductuli aberrantes		
Epididymis	Mesonephric duct	
Ductus deferens		*Gartner's duct*
Ejaculatory duct		
Seminal vesicle		
Appendix of the epididymis		
Appendix testis	Paramesonephric duct (Müllerian duct)	*Hydatid*
		Fimbria of oviduct
		Oviduct
Prostatic utricle (uterus masculinus)		Uterus
		Upper vagina
Urethra	Urogenital sinus	Urethra vestibule
		Vagina
		Vestibular glands
Bulbo-urethral glands		*Para urethral glands*
Prostate		
Seminal colliculus	Müllerian tubercle	Site of hymen
Glans penis	Genital tubercle	Glans clitoris
Corpus penis		Corpus clitoridis
Raphe of scrotum and testis	Urethral folds	Labia minora
Scrotum	Labia scrotal swellings	Labia majora
Mesorchium	Genital ligaments	Mesovarium
Ligamentum testis		Ovarian ligament
Gubernaculum testis		Uterine ligament

* Italicized structures are rudimentary.
† After castration of male toads the organ of Bidder develops into a functional ovary.
References: Arey, 1946; Gorbman and Bern, 1962; and Nalbandov, 1964.

many amniotes the oviduct is a pinched off part of the primitive kidney duct (Ballard, 1964) (Table 2-5). In spite of asymmetrical ovarian development the elasmobranch oviducts develop symmetrically. Often the cranial ends fuse to form a single tube. In amphibia, reptiles, and mammals the oviducts are nearly symmetrical or symmetrical; in birds usually both oviducts develop in the embryo, but then a regression of the right oviduct takes place (in the chick at about the tenth day).

Experimental Analysis of Differentiation of the Secondary Sex Organs

GONADECTOMY

The absence of gonadal tissue during embryonic development has different effects upon different classes of vertebrates, as can be ascertained from Tables 1-1 and 2-6. In amphibia castration results in an intermediate sexual neutral type, whereas in birds the presence of the testes causes regression of the Müllerian ducts and the presence of the ovary causes differentiation of the genital tubercle and the syrinx. The right Müllerian duct regresses, apparently under the influence of the presence of either the testes or the ovary. Thus the gonadal influences on female gonaducts are mainly inhibitory. In mammals, the male gonad is required for normal sexual differentiation of the secondary sex characters. The testis is necessary, on the one hand to produce Müllerian duct regression, and on the other hand for Wolffian duct, prostate, urogenital sinus, and external genitalia development.

Table 2-6 Effects of Early* Gonadectomy on Embryonic Development of Secondary Sex Characters

AMPHIBIA

	MÜLLERIAN DUCTS	WOLFFIAN DUCTS	CLOACAL GLANDS
♂	Rudimentary	Persistent, sexually differentiated	Developed
♀	Developed	Persistent, functions as ureter	Absent
⚦	Present, undifferentiated	Present, undifferentiated posterior urogenital collecting duct M type	Absent
⚦	Present, undifferentiated	Present, undifferentiated posterior urogenital collecting duct M type	Absent

BIRDS

	MÜLLERIAN DUCTS	WOLFFIAN DUCTS	GENITAL TUBERCLE	SYRINX
♂	Absent	Present	M type	M type
♀	Left developed	Absent	F type	F type
⚦	Developed (both sides)	Present	M type	M type
⚦	Developed (both sides)	Present	M type	M type

MAMMALS

	MÜLLERIAN DUCTS	WOLFFIAN DUCTS	UROGENITAL SINUS	PROSTATE	EXTERIOR GENITALIA	MAMMARY GLANDS
♂	Absent	Developed	M type	Developed	M type	M type
♀	Developed	Absent	F type	Absent	F type	F type
⚦	Developed	Absent	F type	Absent	F type	F type
⚦	Developed	Absent†	F type	Absent	F type	F type

F = female; M = male; ♂ = normal male; ⚦ = gonadectomized male; ♀ = normal female; ⚦ = gonadectomized female.

* Before irreversible differentiation has occurred.

† In mice, partially persistent.

References: Burns, 1955, 1961; Gallien, 1965; and Jost, 1965.

Weniger (1965b) has obtained evidence that the hormones produced by chick and mouse testes in vitro may be different. Chick testes caused degeneration of the Wolffian ducts of the male mouse, whereas mouse testes caused development of these ducts. Chick testes also caused regression of female mouse Müllerian ducts of 12- to 13-day-old embryos and of 13½- to 18-day-old embryos; however, mouse testes caused regression of the female mouse Müllerian ducts of 12- to 13-day-old embryos but development of the Müllerian ducts of the· 13½- to 18-day-old mouse embryos.

HORMONE ADMINISTRATION IN VITRO AND IN VIVO

It seems logical to assume that the effects obtained through the presence of the gonads may be the result of hormone secretions. This assumption can be verified by different approaches which are listed here:

1. Incubation in vitro of the undifferentiated sex organs in the absence or presence of female or male sex hormones. Such experiments have shown that in the absence of sex hormones the sex organs react as in the castrated animals (Table 2-6), whereas androgen has the same effect as the presence of the testes, and estrogen the same effect as the presence of the ovary.

2. Administration of estrogens in physiologic doses causes development of Müllerian ducts in amphibia and of both Müllerian ducts in birds and the Müllerian ducts and vagina in mammals. These effects occur in males as well as in females. Estrogens have little or no effect on the de-

velopment of the Wolffian duct system. These effects are thus different from those obtained under the influence of the ovary in female embryos, e.g., in chick embryos only the left oviduct develops beyond 10 days of incubation.

3. Androgen administered early during embryonic life causes prevention of Müllerian duct development in amphibia. However, these ducts hypertrophy if the androgen is administered after the ducts are partly developed. In birds the oviduct development is prevented if androgen is given early enough. However, in mammals, androgens seem to have little effect on the female's oviducts, although in some species there may be regional effects such as, for instance, lack of development of the ostial portion of the oviduct in the hedgehog *(Erinaceus europaeus)* and of the vaginal portion of the oviduct of the opossum and the mouse, and failure to form the body of the uterus and vagina in the rabbit and mouse. It should be pointed out that in contrast to the lack of effect of androgens on Müllerian duct development in mammals, testis implants in castrates are effective in preventing this development. This suggests that the testes may secrete another hormone which causes involution of the Müllerian ducts. Androgens generally cause development and differentiation of the Wolffian duct system in amphibia, birds, and mammals.

4. Estrogens and androgens induce female and male development, respectively, of the urogenital sinus and cloacal derivatives provided the doses of these hormones are low. The external genitalia of birds include the genital tubercle, which does not develop after estrogen treatment, whereas androgen causes hypertrophy but is not required for its differentiation (see Table 2-6). In mammals estrogen causes development of female, androgen that of male genitalia.

Neumann et al. (1966) have reported that the injection of 10 mg./day of an anti-androgen (1,2-α-methylene-6-chloro-$\Delta^{4,6}$-pregnadiene-17-α-ol,-3,20-dione-17-α-ace-

tate = cyproterone acetate) during the second half of pregnancy in rats yielded male rats with vaginas capable of responding to estradiol administration. The penises of these animals showed a high incidence of hypospadias; no data on the histology of the testes were reported.

The conclusion that the embryonic gonads secrete androgens and estrogens which regulate the development of the male and female secondary sex organs seems justified from the evidence presented here so far. However, the objection has been made that the effects of androgen and estrogen administration are not specific, because so-called paradoxical effects have been observed. In these cases, androgen may cause development of female secondary sex structures, while male sex structures may be either stimulated or inhibited. An example of this is the opossum, *(Didelphis virginiana)*, in which *high doses* of androgen cause hypertrophy of the male genitalia and of the Müllerian ducts. The main argument against this objection is that these paradoxical effects usually occur after exceptionally high doses of the hormone in question have been given. With high doses, paradoxical effects are observed also in adult opossum; large doses of androgen can cause development of the chicken oviduct similar to that observed after estrogen injection (see van Tienhoven, 1961). The fact that most of the effects of castration can be prevented by steroid administration argues in favor of the hypothesis that secondary sex organ development in the embryo is controlled by steroid hormones secreted by the gonads.

A special case of gonaduct differentiation must be discussed. Despite attention from many embryologists, the mechanisms involved have not been completely elucidated. In most avian species the right oviduct regresses, even in those species in which the right ovary is not rudimentary and, apparently, becomes functional in the adult. Experimental analysis by the methods outlined has yielded the following facts (for review, see Hamilton, 1963, and Hamilton and Teng, 1965):

1. During normal development, both Müllerian ducts are present in the male at the fifth to sixth day of incubation; at days 9 to 10 involution starts, and at 14 days both oviducts have disappeared.

2. In the female embryo the left Müllerian duct develops and is retained, but the right one involutes in an anterior-posterior direction. This involution is slower than that of the Müllerian ducts of the male. At the same time, the right gonad is reduced in size, whereas the left shows development of the cortex.

3. Castration of either sex causes maintenance of both oviducts (see Table 2-6).

4. In vitro, the right oviduct, if taken before day 9, will develop like the left oviduct.

5. Androgen administration to embryos early in development results in involution of both oviducts.

6. Estrogen administration early in development leads to development of both oviducts, although in the adult the left oviduct is shorter than normal (resulting in ovulation into the body cavity because the oviduct does not extend far enough anteriorly) and the right oviduct often is not patent. It is possible that the adult ovary does not produce sufficient estrogen to maintain both oviducts. This would explain the selective advantage which birds with only one developed oviduct at hatching would have.

7. The rudimentary right gonad cultured in vitro secretes estrogen-like substances into the medium (Weniger, 1965a).

8. The presence of either ovary is sufficient to cause regression of the right oviduct.

Hamiltion has tried to explain these phenomena on the basis of different physiological competence of the left oviduct (as compared to the right oviduct) with respect to gonadal hormones. This hypothesis was tested by determining the ribonuclease level of the oviducts of male and female embryos at different stages of development. These results showed:

1. A sharp increase (to 4.5 times the initial value) in the activity of this enzyme in the right female and the left and right male Müllerian ducts between days seven and 11, and a subsequent steep decrease, which was slightly faster for the male ducts than for the right female duct. At the same time, the ribonuclease activity of the female's left Müllerian duct remained stable at the initial value, obtained for the four types of Müllerian ducts at seven days of age.

2. An increase in the deoxyribonucleic acid (DNA) and ribonucleic acid (RNA) levels of the developing female left Müllerian duct and a decrease in the male's left Müllerian duct between days 7 and 13 of incubation.

3. On the ninth day of development the anterior half of the right female Müllerian duct contains about 15 percent of the total ribonuclease extracted initially; for the posterior half this figure is about 5 percent. There is no such difference between left and right male Müllerian ducts.

The involutions of the right duct could thus be explained by a difference between the physiological competence of left and right duct under the influence of the same hormonal environment. When there is a high level of estrogen, both oviducts are "protected," whereas at low levels only the left one is.

Hamilton has pointed out that it is not established whether or not the hormones produced by the right and/or left gonad reach both ducts.

It might prove fruitful to test Hamilton's hypotheses by using embryos from strains of chickens in which there is a high incidence of two apparently normal oviducts (Morgan and Kohlmeyer, 1957). A comparison between these strains and "normal" strains might reveal what differences occur and whether such differences can explain the regression of the right oviduct in the "normal" strains.

Lutz-Ostertag (1965) has found that

exposure of Japanese quail *(Coturnix coturnix japonica)* eggs to 39.5°C. instead of 37.5°C. between days 12 and 14 of incubation gives rise to larger than normal right oviducts in 247 out of 252 females. The length of right oviducts varied from 33 to 75 percent of the length of the left oviduct. Among experimental males, 8 out of 199 had well developed left oviducts, but right oviducts were regressed except for the presence of a cloacal remnant; 39 out of 199 had left and right oviducts with a large diameter; 26 out of 199 had left and right oviducts with a small diameter; and in 91 out of 199 the anterior region of the left oviduct was present, but the right oviduct was regressed. It seems possible that exposure to higher temperatures at a critical period prevents synthesis of the enzymes required for the destruction of the Müllerian duct system.

REFERENCES

Alexander, G., and Williams, D. 1964. Ovine freemartins. Nature *201*:1296-1298.

Arey, L. B. 1965. Developmental Anatomy. Ed. 7. W. B. Saunders Company, Philadelphia.

Atz, J. W. 1964. Intersexuality in fishes. *In* C. N. Armstrong and A. J. Marshall (eds.): Intersexuality in Vertebrates Including Man. Academic Press, Inc., New York. pp. 145-232.

Ballard, W. W. 1964. Comparative Anatomy and Embryology. The Ronald Press Co., New York.

Bellec, A., and Stolkowski, J. 1965. Influence du rapport potassium calcium (K⁺/Ca⁺⁺) du milieu d'élevage sur la distribution des sexes chez Discoglossus pictus (OTTH)—nouvelles observations. Ann. Endocrinol. *26*:51-64.

Biggers, J. D., and McFeely, R. A. 1966. Intersexuality in domestic mammals. Adv. Reprod. Physiol. *1*:20-59.

Blackler, A. W. 1965. Germ-cell transfer and sex ratio in *Xenopus laevis.* J. Embryol. Exp. Morphol. *13*:51-62.

Blackler, A. W., and Fischberg, M. 1961. Transfer of primordial germ-cells in *Xenopus laevis.* J. Embryol. Exp. Morphol. *9*:634-641.

Blandau, R. J., White, B. J., and Rumery, R. E. 1963. Observations on the movements of the living primordial germ cells in the mouse. Fertil. Steril. *14*:482-489.

Boss, W. R., and Witschi, E. 1947. The permanent effects of early stilbestrol injections on the sex organs of the Herring gull *Larus argentatus.* J. Exp. Zool. *105*:61-77.

Bouters, R., and Vandeplassche, M. 1964. Het

mannelijke geslachtschromosoom als mogelijke oorzaak bij het ontstaan van het Freemartinisme by runderen. Vlaams Diergeneesk. Tijdsch. *33*: 229-241.

Burgos, M. H., and Pisano, A. 1958. Efecto de gonadotrofinas purificadas sobre la gonada de Bufo arenarum despues de la metamorfosis. Rev. Soc. Argent. Biol. *34*:162-174.

Burns, R. K. 1955. Urogenital system. *In* B. H. Willier, P. A. Weiss, and V. Hamburger (eds.): Analysis of Development. W. B. Saunders Co., Philadelphia, pp. 462-491.

Burns, R. K. 1961. Role of hormones in the differentiation of sex. *In* W. C. Young (ed.): Sex and Internal Secretions. Williams & Wilkins Co., Baltimore, Vol. 1, pp. 76-158.

Chang, C. Y. 1955. Hormonal influences on sex differentiation in the toad, *Bufo americanus.* Anat. Rec. *123*:467-485.

Chang, C. Y., and Witschi, E. 1955. Independence of adrenal hyperplasia and gonadal masculinization in the experimental adrenogenital syndrome of frogs. Endocrinology *56*:597-605.

Chieffi, G. 1959. Sex differentiation and experimental sex reversal in elasmobranch fishes. Arch. Anat. Micr. Morph. Exp. *42(Suppl.)*:21-36.

Chieffi, G. 1965. Onset of steroidogenesis in the vertebrate embryonic gonads. *In* R. L. DeHaan and H. Ursprung (eds.): Organogenesis. Holt, Rinehart, & Winston, Inc., New York, pp. 653-67.

Clermont, Y., and Perey, B. 1957. Quantitative study of the cell population of the seminiferous tubules in immature rats. Amer. J. Anat. *100*:241-267.

Dodd, J. M. 1960a. Genetic and environmental aspects of sex determination in cold-blooded vertebrates. Mem. Soc. Endocrinol. *7*:17-44.

Dodd, J. M. 1960b. Gonadal and gonadotrophic hormones in lower vertebrates. *In* A. S. Parkes (ed.): Marshall's Physiology of Reproduction. Longmans Green & Co. Ltd., London, pt. 2: pp. 417-582.

Dubois, R. 1965a. Sur l'attraction exerceé par le jeune épithélium germinatif sur les gonocytes primaires de l'embryon de poulet, en culture, *in vitro*: démonstration à l'aide de la thymidine tritiée. C. R. Acad. Sci. *260*:5885-5887.

Dubois, R. 1965b. Sur les propriétés migatrice des cellules germinales de gonades embryonnaires differenciées, chez l'embryon de poulet, en culture *in vitro.* C. R. Acad. Sci. *260*:5108-5111.

Dubois, R. 1965c. La lignée germinale chez les reptiles et les oiseaux. Ann. Biol. *4*:637–666.

Dufaure, J. P. 1965. Féminisation de l'embryon mâle de lézard vivipare *(Lacerta vivipara Jacquin)* par des gonadostimulines hypophysaires. C. R. Acad. Sci. *260*:2319-2322.

Eckstein, B., and Spira, M. 1965. Effect of sex hormones on gonadal differentiation in a cichlid, *Tilapia aurea.* Biol. Bull. *129*:482-489.

Fechheimer, N. S., Herschler, M. S., and Gilmore, L. O. 1963. Sex chromosome mosaicism in unlike sexed cattle twins. Proc. XI Int. Côngr. Genet. (The Hague) *1*:265 (abstract).

Foote, C. L. 1964. Intersexuality in amphibians. *In*

C. N. Armstrong and A. J. Marshall (eds.): Intersexuality in Vertebrates Including Man. Academic Press Inc., New York, pp. 233-272.

Forbes, T. R. 1964. Intersexuality in reptiles. *In* C. N. Armstrong and A. J. Marshall (eds.): Intersexuality in Vertebrates Including Man. Academic Press Inc., New York, pp. 273-283.

Franchi, L. L., Mandl, A. M. and Zuckerman, S. 1962. The development of the ovary and the process of oogenesis. *In* S. Zuckerman (ed.): The Ovary. Academic Press Inc., New York, Vol. 1, pp. 1-88.

Fugo, N. W. 1940. Effects of hypophysectomy in the chick embryo. J. Exp. Zool. *85*:271-297.

Gallien, L. 1961. Double conversion du sexe chez le triton *Pleurodeles waltlii*. C. R. Acad. Sci. *252*: 2768-2770.

Gallien, L. G. 1965. Genetic control of sexual differentiation in vertebrates. *In* R. L. DeHaan and H. Ursprung (eds.): Organogenesis. Holt, Rinehart, & Winston, Inc., New York, pp. 283-610.

Gérard, P. 1954. Organes uro-génitaux. *In* P. Grassé (ed.): Traité de Zoologie. Masson et Cie, Paris, Vol. 13, pp. 974-1043.

Gerneke, W. H. 1965. Chromosomal evidence of the freemartin condition in sheep, Ovis aries. J. S. Afr. Vet. Med. *36*:99-104. (Animal Breeding Abs. 34 ref. 382, 1966.)

Goodfellow, S. A., Strong, S. J., and Stewart, J. S. S., 1965. Bovine freemartins and true hermaphroditism. Lancet. 1040-1041.

Gorbman, A., and Bern, H. A., 1962. A Textbook of Comparative Endocrinology. John Wiley & Sons Inc., New York.

Gropp, A., and S. Ohno. 1966. The presence of a common embryonic blastema for ovarian and testicular parenchymal (follicular, interstitial and tubular) cells in cattle, *Bos taurus*. Z. Zellforsch. *74*:505-528.

Haffen, K. 1965. Intersexualité chez la caille *(Coturnix coturnix)*. Obtention d'un cas de ponte ovulaire par un mâle génétique. C. R. Acad. Sci. *261*:3876-3879.

Hamilton, T. H. 1963. Hormonal control of Müllerian duct differentiation in the chick embryo. Proc. XIII Int. Ornithol. Congr. *2*:1004-1040.

Hamilton, T. H., and Teng, C. S. 1965. Sexual stabilization of Müllerian ducts in the chick embryo. *In* R. L. DeHaan and H. Ursprung (eds.): Organogénesis. Holt, Rinehart, & Winston, Inc., New York, pp. 681-700.

Hardisty, M. W. 1965a. Sex differentiation and gonadogenesis in lampreys. I. The ammocoete gonads of the brook lamprey, *Lampetra planeri*. J. Zool. *146*:305-345.

Hardisty, M. W. 1965b. Sex differentiation and gonadogenesis in lampreys. II. The ammocoete gonads of the landlocked sea lamprey, *Petromyzon marinus*. J. Zool. *146*:346-387.

Iwasawa, H. 1955a. Transformation of ovaries to testes in thiourea treated frog larvae. Endocrinol. Jap. *2*:263-268

Iwasawa, H. 1955b. Relation between the concentration of thiourea solution and its masculinizing effect on frog larvae. Endocrinol. Jap. *2*:269-270.

Iwasawa, H. 1958. Sex reversal in female tadpoles induced by the treatment with methylmercaptoimidazole. Endocrinol. Jap. *5*:166-170.

Iwasawa, H. 1961. Effects of thyroidectomy, hypophysectomy and thiourea treatment on the development of gonads in frog larvae. Jap. J. Zool. *13*:69-77.

Jost. A. 1953. Problems of fetal endocrinology: The gonadal and hypophyseal hormones. Recent Progr. Hormone Res. *8*:379-413.

Jost, A. 1960. Hormonal influences in the sex development of bird and mammalian embryos. Mem. Soc. Endocrinol. 7:49-61.

Jost, A. 1965. Gonadal hormones in the sex differentiation of the mammalian fetus. *In* R. L. DeHaan and H. Ursprung (eds.): Organogensis. Holt, Rinehart, & Winston, Inc., New York, pp. 611-628.

Jost, A., Chodkiewicz, M., and Mauléon, P. 1963. Intersexualité du foetus de veau produite par des androgènes. Comparaison entre l'hormone foetale responsable du free-martinisme et l'hormone testiculaire adulte. C. R. Acad. Sci. *256*:274-276.

Kanagawa, H., Muramoto, J., Kawata, K., and Ishikawa, T. 1965. Chromosome studies on heterosexual twins in cattle. I. Sex-chromosome chimerism (XX/XY). Jap. J. Vet. Res. *(13:2)*:33-42.

Leach, B. J., and Conaway, C. H., 1963. The origin and fate of polyovular follicles in the striped skunk. J. Mammal. *44*:67-74.

Lewis, J. C., and McMillan, D. B. 1965. The development of the ovary of the sea lamprey (Petromyzon marinus L.) J. Morphol. *117*:425-466.

Lillie, F. R. 1917. The freemartin; a study of the action of sex hormones in the fetal life of cattle. J. Exp. Zool. *23*:371-452.

Lutz-Ostertag, Y. 1965. Action de la chaleur sur le développement de l'appareil génital de l'embryon de caille *(Coturnix coturnix japonica)*. C. R. Acad. Sci. 262 D:133-135.

Makino, S., Muramoto, J., and Ishikawa, T. 1965. Notes on XX/XY mosaicism in cells of various tissues of heterosexual twins of cattle. Proc. Jap. Acad. *41*:414-418.

Makino, S., Sasaki, M., and Sofuni, T. 1962. Notes on the chromosomes of freemartins. Proc. Jap. Acad. *38*:541-544.

Mikamo, K., and Witschi, E. 1962. Functional sex reversal in genetic females of Xenopus laevis induced by implanted testes. Genetics 48:1411-1421.

Morgan, W., and Kohlmeyer, W. 1957. Hens with bilateral oviducts. Nature *180*:98.

Nalbandov, A. V. 1964. Reproductive Physiology. Ed. 2. W. H. Freeman & Company, San Francisco.

Neumann, F., Elger, W., and Kramer, M. 1966. Development of a vagina in male rats by inhibiting androgen receptors with an anti-androgen during the critical phase of organogenesis. Endocrinology 78:628-632.

Ohno, S., Trujilo, J. M., Stenius, C., Christian, L. C., and Teplitz, R. L. 1962. Possible germ cell chimaeras among newborn dizygotic twin calves *(Bos taurus)*. Cytogenetics *1*:258-265.

Peters, G., and Mäder, B. 1964. Morphologische

Veränderungen der Gonadenausführgänge sich fortpflanzender Schwertträgerweibchen *(Xiphophorus helleri* Heckel*).* Zool. Anz. *173:*243-257.

Price, D., and Ortiz, E. 1965. The role of fetal androgen in sex differentiation in mammals. *In* R. L. DeHaan and H. Ursprung (eds.): Organogenesis. Holt, Rinehart, & Winston, Inc., New York, pp. 629-652.

Raynaud, A. 1959. Effects of destruction of the fetal hypophysis by x-rays upon sexual development of the mouse. *In* A. Gorbman (ed.): Comparative Endocrinology. John Wiley & Sons Inc., New York, pp. 452-478.

Simon, D. 1960. Contribution à l'étude de la circulation et du transport des gonocytes primaires dans les blastodermes d'oiseaux cultivés *in vitro.* Arch. Anat. Microscop. Morphol. Exp. *49:*93-176.

Stanley, A. J., and Witschi, E. 1940. Germ cell migration in relation to asymmetry in the sex glands of hawks. Anat. Rec. *76:*329-342.

Taber, E. 1964. Intersexuality in birds. *In* C. N. Armstrong and A. J. Marshall (eds.): Intersexuality in Vertebrates Including Man. Academic Press Inc., New York, pp. 285-310.

Torrey, T. 1950. Intraocular grafts of embryonic gonads of the rat. J. Exp. Zool. *115:*37-57.

Turner, C. D. 1966. General Endocrinology. Ed. 4. W. B. Saunders Company, Philadelphia.

Turner, C. D., and Asakawa, H. 1964. Experimental reversal of germ cells in ovaries of fetal mice. Science *143:*1344-1345.

van Deth, J. H. G. M., van Limborgh, J., and van Faassen, F. 1956. Le rôle de l'hypophyse dans la détermination du sexe chez l'oiseau. Acta Morphol. Neerl.—Scand. *1:*70-80.

van Limborgh, J. 1957. De Ontwikkeling van de Asymmetrie der Gonaden van de Eend. (The Development of Gonadal Asymmetry in the Duck Embryo). Ph.D. thesis, University of Utrecht.

van Tienhoven, A. 1957. A method of "controlling sex" by dipping of eggs in hormone solutions. Poultry Sci. *36:*628-632.

van Tienhoven, A. 1961. Endocrinology of reproduction in birds. *In* W. C. Young (ed.): Sex and Internal Secretions. Williams & Wilkins Co., Baltimore. Vol. *2:*1088-1169.

Weniger, J. P. 1965a. Extraction d'une substance oestrogène de milieux sur lesquels ont été cultivé des gonades droites femelles, atrophiques, d'embryon de poulet. C. R. Soc. Biol. *159:*464-466.

Weniger, J. P. 1965b. Étude comparée des actions hormonales des testicules embryonnaires de poulet et de souris en culture *in vitro.* Arch. Anat. Microscop. Morphol. Exp. *54:*909-919.

Witschi, E., 1951. Embryogenesis of the adrenal and the reproductive glands. Recent Progr. Hormones Res. *6:*1-23.

Witschi, E. 1965. Hormones and embryonic induction. Arch. Anat. Microscop. Morphol. Exp. *54:*601-611.

Wolff, E. 1959. Endocrine function of the gonad in developing vertebrates. *In* A. Gorbman (ed.): Comparative Endocrinology. John Wiley & Sons Inc., New York, pp. 568-581.

Wolff, E., and Haffen, K. 1965. Germ cells and gonads. *In* E. N. Willmer (ed.): Cells and Tissues in Culture. Academic Press Inc., New York, Vol. 2, pp. 697-743.

Wolff, E., and Lutz-Ostertag, Y. 1961. Free-martinisme spontané et expérimental chez l'embryon de canard. Arch. Anat. Mircroscop. Morphol. Exp. *50:*439-468.

Yamamoto, T. 1958. Artificial induction of functional sex-reversal in genotypic females of the medaka (Oryzias latipes). J. Exp. Zool. *137:*227-263.

Yamamoto, T. 1965. Estriol-induced XY females of the medaka *(Oryzias latipes)* and their progenies. Gen. Comp. Endocrinol. *5:*527-533.

Chapter 3

The Anatomy of the Reproductive System

The gonads of vertebrates perform two functions, which are reflected in their microscopic anatomy. They produce germ cells, so that zygotes can be formed, and they produce steroid hormones, which serve a number of functions to be discussed in detail later. In general the hormones stimulate the gonaducts, affect the secondary sex characteristics, and probably determine the organization of brain structures concerned with release of gonadotropic hormones and with sexual behavior.

In the discussion of the anatomy of the reproductive system we will present descriptions and illustrations of mature gonads during the reproductive season. Generally, animals reproduce at the time or during the season which gives the young an optimal opportunity to survive. This optimal opportunity may be created by the abundance of food, correct temperature, and conditions of humidity. The factors which regulate the breeding seasons and the physiologic pathways involved will be discussed more fully in another chapter.

Cyclostomes

In cyclostomes there is only one gonad in each sex. It is located near the midline and is attached to the body wall by a mesentery. The testis consists of lobules, each of which contains a number of ampullae lined by germinal epithelium. At the time of sexual maturity the ampullae break down and sperm cells are released into the body cavity. There are no gonaducts, and sperm cells leave the body cavity through two pores in the urinary sinus, which is connected with the urogenital papilla. According to Marshall (1960), interstitial cells secreting male sex hormones are found in *Petromyzon*.

Before spermatozoa are released, a number of other anatomical changes which indicate that the animal has reached adulthood take place. All fins enlarge, the dorsal and caudal fins are united by a thickening at the base, the postcloacal region curves upward, and the urogenital papilla becomes erect (Figure 3-1). A rather elaborate mating process occurs in the Petromyzontiformes. The male loops his tail over the body of the female so that the genital papilla is rather close to the female's vent. The animals spawn during mating. After spawning, a large number of dead males and females are found, but whether all the animals die after spawning has not been established (Breder and Rosen, 1966).

The ovary consists of follicles with a secretory theca interna (Busson-Mabillot, 1966); these follicles are all about the same size. In addition, there are "corpora lutea"* with unknown function and atretic

---

* "Corpora lutea" will be used when there is no convincing evidence available that progestins are secreted by this structure.

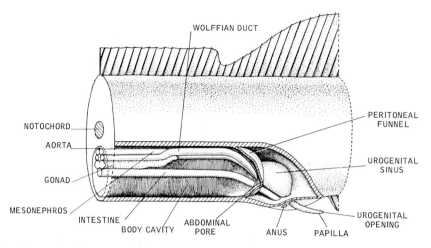

Figure 3-1. The urogenital system of the adult Lamprey *(Lampetra planeri)*. The mature germ cells reach the exterior via the body cavity, through the abdominal pores and the urogenital sinus. (From Turner, 1966.)

follicles, and, in the caudal position of the ovary, there may be testicular tissue remnants. The "corpora lutea" may be formed as the result of an invasion of the ruptured follicle by phagocytic cells (Gorbman and Bern, 1962).

Before spawning, a small ventral fin develops posterior to the cloaca, the postcloacal region curves upward, and the cloacal labia enlarge.

Elasmobranchs

An excellent description of the reproductive systems for the male and female of a representative of the elasmobranchs, the basking shark *(Cetorhinus maximus)*, has been given by Matthews (1950). We will largely use his description in the following account.

The testes are paired organs attached to the body wall by a mesorchium. In close proximity to the testis lies the epigonal organ consisting of lymphomyeloid tissue. In the basking shark it completely surrounds the testis so that the two organs form one body (Figure 3-2).

The testes of elasmobranch fishes can be divided into several zones: (1) the outer ampullogenic zone; (2) a zone with ampullae 120 to 150 μ in diameter that con-

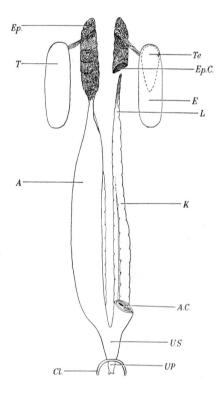

Figure 3-2. Reproductive organs of the male basking shark *(Cetorhinus maximus)*. Most of the ampulla on the right side of the drawing has been removed. *A* = ampulla ductus deferentis. *A.C.* = cut end of the ampulla. *Cl* = cut wall of the cloaca. *E* = epigonal organ. *Ep.* = epididymis. *Ep.C.* = cut end of the epididymis. *K* = kidney. *L* = Leydig's gland. *T* = testis and epigonal organ. *Te* = position of the testis (dotted line). *UP* = urogenital papilla. *US* = urogenital sinus. (From Matthews, 1950.)

tain spermatogonia that are slightly stainable with hematoxylin; (3) a zone of ampullae, with a diameter of about 300 μ, that contain spermatocytes either in premeiosis or in meiosis; the cytoplasm of these cell does not stain with hematoxylin or other stains; (4) a zone of ampullae that contain germ cells with small nuclei and the haploid number of chromosomes; (5) a zone with ampullae containing cells with elongated nuclei; and (6) a zone with empty ampullae in contact with the epigonal organ (Mellinger, 1965).

All the germ cells within an ampulla are in the same stage of development.* The ampulla grows from a single gonocyte; after proliferation into spermatogonia the germ cells become surrounded by follicle cells, which are homologous to the mammalian Sertoli cells. By a series of four mitotic and two meiotic divisions, each gonocyte gives rise to 64 sperm cells (Melinger, 1965).

Among the ampullae, Leydig cells can be found; these cells give a positive Schultz test for cholesterol (Chieffi, 1962). The fact that androgens can be extracted from the elasmobranch testes supports the concept that the Leydig cells of elasmobranchs and higher vertebrates are homologous (Chieffi, 1962).

The sperm traverse the testicular tubules to reach the ductuli efferentes and subsequently the epididymis. The epithelium of the latter in the basking shark consists of pseudostratified columnar epithelium and ciliated cells. The ductus deferens has a greatly expanded part, the ampulla, which, in the basking shark, may contain as much as 20 to 25 liters of spermatophores. The interior of the ampulla has many transverse folds; the epithelium is tall, cylindrical, and heavily ciliated. The spermatophores in the basking shark vary in size from a few millimeters to about 3.0 cm. They consist of hyaline material surrounding a central core of sperm.

The ampulla of the ductus deferens opens into the urogenital sinus (Figure 3-2). The spermatophores are introduced into the female reproductive tract via claspers, which contain a groove covered by glandular tissue that produces a secretion that may aid in the transport of the spermatophores (Figure 3-3). On the ventrolateral surface of the abdomen there are long wide siphon sacs lined by stratified epithelium with goblet cells which secrete a sticky fluid. These siphons are connected with the clasper grooves via siphon tubes. Gilbert and Heath (1955) have proposed that the secretion of the siphon sacs may make up a large part of the seminal fluid.

In adult viviparous sharks, as a rule, only the right ovary is functional although both oviducts are present; in adult rays, which give birth to living young, generally only the left ovary and left oviduct are developed, whereas in skates, which as a rule lay eggs, the left and right ovary and oviduct are present and functional (Gilbert, personal communication).

The general anatomy of the reproductive system of the female basking shark is illustrated in Figure 3-4. This shark, which may weigh 3 to 4 tons as an adult, has an ovary which may weigh as much as 12 kg. It is suspended from the body wall by a short mesovarium. The entire ovary is covered with a fibrous coat with an opening at the anterior pole through which ova are shed. The epigonal organ is present also in the females, and its anterior end may overlap the posterior end of the ovary. The ovary contains little stroma and consists mainly of follicles, "corpora lutea," and blood vessels.

From the center toward the periphery, the follicular wall consists of the zona radiata, the vitelline membrane, the granulosa, and the theca interna and externa. Upon examining the ovary of a sexually mature elasmobranch one may find ripe follicles, ruptured follicles, atretic follicles, and "corpora lutea."

Chieffi (1962) found that in *Torpedo*

---

*Mellinger uses the term ampulla, whereas Chieffi (1962) uses the term tubule.

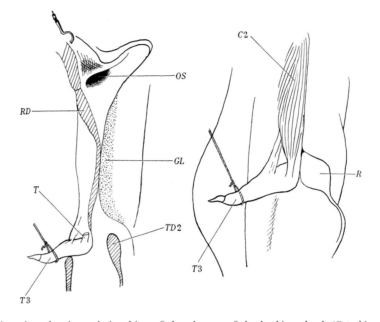

Figure 3-3. Dissection showing relationships of the clasper of the basking shark *(Cetorhinus maximus)*. *C2* = part of the compressor muscle inserted by a tendon onto the claw-cartilage. Its action is to extend the cartilage. *GL* = stippled area. It indicates the approximate extent of the clasper gland on the inside of the ventral marginal cartilage facing the lumen of the groove. *OS* = opening of the siphon tube. *RD* = cut edge of the marginal cartilage. *R* = base of the rhipidion. *T* = cut tendon of compressor muscle inserting on the base of the claw-cartilage. *T3* = claw-cartilage. *TD2* = cut surface of the base of the secondary dorsal terminal piece. (From Matthews, 1950.)

marmorata and *T. ocellata* the "corpora lutea" are formed from atretic follicles, with the granulosa cells contributing to the formation of the luteal tissue and the theca interna supplying the stroma. In these two species the ruptured follicle degenerates and never forms luteal tissue. In *Scyliorhinus stellaris* and *S. canicula,* on the other hand, the "corpora lutea" are formed by the granulosa layer, and the cuboidal cells of the theca interna by ruptured follicles; a supporting network is formed from the theca externa cells.

Viviparous Elasmobranchs. According to Gorbman and Bern (1962) there is evidence for progesterone secretion in the viviparous elasmobranchs. It may, therefore, eventually prove to be more correct to call the described structures corpora lutea in viviparous and the quoted form, "corpora lutea" in oviparous species.

The ova are collected in the ostium abdominale, which is formed by the fused anterior ends of the paired oviducts. The surface of the ostium abdominale has a number of furrows covered with stratified epithelium, and within the furrows the epithelium is composed of tall columnar cells. The oviducts also are covered by tall columnar epithelium.

In the basking shark each oviduct opens in a nidamentary gland, which is a swelling of the oviduct covered by ciliated epithelium. In this structure the albumen, mucus, and egg case are secreted. Posteriorly, the nidamentary gland opens into the isthmus covered by a tall columnar epithelium, which is ciliated in the anterior part but not ciliated in the posterior part.

The isthmus opens into a very large uterus, which is covered on the inside by villi-like projections, the so-called trophonemata. These structures are modifications of longitudinal ridges found in the uterus and are covered by single layers of polyhedral cells except in the distal part, which consists of a single layer of flattened cells.

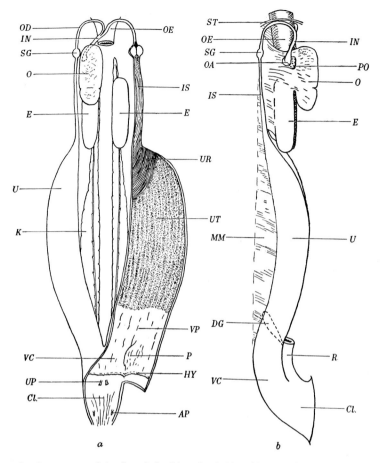

Figure 3-4. Reproductive system of the female basking shark *(Cetorhinus maximus)*. In (a) the oviduct is opened and the view is from the ventral surface; (b) is a lateral view from the right side. *AP* = abdominal pores. *Cl* = cloaca. *DG* = digitiform gland. *E* = epigonal organ. *HY* = hymen. *IN* = unpaired oviduct. *IS* = isthmus. *K* = kidney. *MM* = mesometrium. *O* = ovary. *OA* = ostium abdominale. *OD* = paired oviduct. *OE* = esophagus. *P* = pad in lateral wall of the common vagina. *PO* = pocket in right side of ovary. *R* = rectum. *SG* = nidamentary gland. *ST* = septum transversum. *U* = uterus. *UP* = urinary papilla. *UR* = uterus lined with folds. *UT* = uterus lined with trophonemata. *VC* = common vagina. *VP* = paired vagina of the left side. (From Matthews, 1950.)

Figure 3-5. Cloaca, common vagina and left-paired vagina of the basking shark *(Cetorhinus maximus)*. The asterisks show points which were in apposition before the incision was made and the arrow shows the direction in which the cut edge from which it springs has been displaced. *AP* = abdominal pore. *HY* = hymen. *P* = pad in the wall of the common vagina. *R* = rectum. *RO* = orifice of the rectum. *UP* = urinary papilla. *VL* = inner surface of left paired vagina. *VR* = right paired vagina. *VRL* = lumen of right paired vagina. The part between the stars and the hymen is the common vagina. (From Matthews, 1950.)

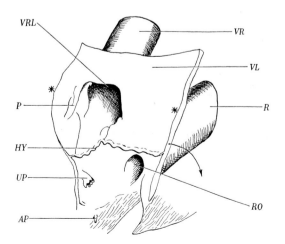

The posterior end of the uterus connects to the vagina, in which a hymen is present (see Figure 3-5).

The Bony Fishes

There is considerable variation among the anatomical details of the reproductive systems of bony fishes, which is not surprising in view of the large number of species (about 30,000) in this class.

Most teleosts, which comprise the vast majority of the bony fishes, have paired testes, which can be divided into two types, radial and acinus. In the latter, sperm cells are formed in small acini. All cells in a particular acinus are in the same stage of meiosis. The connective tissue membranes around each acinus break down when sperm are mature and they are thus released. In radial testis, tubules form the gonad with spermatogonia lining the outer ends of the tubules. Spermatocytes develop in clusters within each tubule (adjacent clusters may have spermatocytes in different stages of development), and sperm cells are randomly oriented in the lumen. The different tubules make connections with the ductus deferens (Smith, 1965). A tunica albuginea surrounds the testes. Each testis of the frillfin goby *(Bathygobius soporator)* has a broad, dark-red strip along the ventral surface; this is the testicular gland, which lies along the hilum of the testis and envelops the spermatic duct (Tavolga, 1955). Similar structures occur in some other species (Eggert, 1931).

The question whether Leydig cells are present in teleost fishes has been considered by Marshall (1960). According to him there are two quite different anatomical arrangements of these cells:

1. The interstitial gland cells or Leydig cells are found among the lobules, as is the case in most higher vertebrates; this condition is found, for example, in the three-spined stickleback *(Gasterosteus aculeatus),* the sprat *(Clupea sprattus),* and *Tilapia* sp.

2. The Leydig cells are found in the walls of the seminiferous lobules and are called lobule-boundary cells. These cells contain cholesterol during certain phases of the annual breeding cycle. During the period just before spawning the cholesterol disappears and after spawning it reappears, at about the same time that the lipoidal material, which filled the tubules after shedding of the sperm, starts to disappear. This anatomical arrangement is found, for example, in the pike *(Esox lucius)* and the char *(Salvelinus willughbii).*

Accessory reproductive glands have been reported in a number of species of teleosts; the term "seminal vesicle" has been used to designate these structures although they seem to vary in function. The "seminal vesicles" of the frillfin goby *(Bathygobius soporator)* are sperm reservoirs attached to the testes (Tavolga, 1955), whereas the "seminal vesicles" of the catfishes (Ictaluridae) consist of the posterior glandular portion of the lobate testes (Smith and Clemens, 1963). This posterior portion secretes material that is mixed with the sperm at spawning. On the other hand, the "seminal vesicles" of the male toadfish *(Opsanus tau)* (Hoffman, 1963), the marine mudsucker *(Gillichthys mirabilis)* (Weisel, 1949), and the South American catfish *(Trachycorystes striatulus)* (von Ihering, 1937) are separate glandular structures that secrete material, which, via the sperm duct, reaches the genital papilla. The function of the secreted material in most species is not well understood; in *Trachycorystes mirabilis,* however, the gelatinous material forms a "vaginal plug" after mating and thus may help to contain the sperm in the genital tract of the female.

Weisel (1949) points out that the "seminal vesicles" of the mudsucker should not be regarded as homologous with the seminal vesicles of reptiles and mammals since they are not part of the Wolffian duct system.

The intromittent organ of teleost fishes may be formed by a genital papilla, which is sometimes more or less elongated, for example, in the genus *Zenarchopterus* (family

Hemiramphidae) (Breder and Rosen, 1966), in a number of species of the family Cottidae (see Bolin, 1944; and Watanabe, 1960), and in the family Clinidae of the suborder Blennioidei. In the genus *Starksia* of this family, the anterior anal-fin spine may be attached to the genital papilla or may be completely free (Böhlke and Springer, 1961). The clasper-like penis found in some Ophidiidae (Brotulidae) is formed by a modification of the genital papilla (Hubbs, 1938; Turner, 1946). In some genera of one of the catfish families (Doradidae), the genital aperture is located at the apex of the anal fin and a fleshy intromittent organ is present (von Ihering, 1937). The organs with which this so-called pseudopenis is homologous cannot be determined from the description. In the viviparous sea perches (Embiotocidae) the front of the anal fin is enlarged and fleshy; this fleshy portion is modified posteriorly into a hard excrescence followed by an oval gland-like structure which opens anteriorly (Hubbs, 1918).

In other teleosts the anal fin is modified and forms the gonopodium, e.g. in the family Horaichthyidae (Breder and Rosen, 1966) and in the Poeciliidae, in which differences among the gonopodia and the gonopodial suspensoria are used for taxonomic purposes (Rosen and Bailey, 1963). Males of the genus *Tomeurus* (family Poeciliidae) and of the family Horaichthyidae do not deposit sperm in the female's genital system but rather deposit spermatophores at or near the female's genital opening. The male external sex organs are not intromittent organs in the strictest sense.

In the Jenynsiidae and Anablepidae, the intromittent organ is a true tube, which may be either dextral or sinistral. The genital openings in the females may also be either on the right or left in the Jenynsiidae; in the Anablepidae the females have a definite genital opening on either the left or the right (Breder and Rosen, 1966). The intromittent organ is formed by resorption of anal fin rays 1, 2, and 5 and by elongation of rays 3, 4, 6, 7,

8, and 9 with ankylosis of the elongated rays and thickening of rays 6 and 7 (Turner, 1948).

What seem to be the most bizarre intromittent organs are found in the families Phallostethidae and Neosthethidae; in which a large, fleshy priapus is located under the throat. This priapus contains the opening of the ductus deferens and of the anus on opposite sides. The skeleton of the priapus and its homologues have been studied by Regan (1916) and Bailey (1936). According to Bailey (1936), the priapal bones can be homologized with the missing pelvic girdle plus perhaps the postcleithrum and some of the pectoral pterygials. In the Neosthethidae, the ductus deferens opens into a glandular groove; in the Phallostethidae, the glandular groove is lacking. For details of anatomy, the reader should consult the papers of Regan and of Bailey.

Although it is not an intromittent organ, mention should be made of the internal muscular pseudopenis of *Skiffia lermae*, of the family Goodeidae. The ductus deferens, consisting of the fused left and right deferent ducts, opens into a pear-shaped pseudopenis which consists of an inner layer of longitudinal muscle, a thick layer of circular muscle, and a fibrous outer layer (Mohsen, 1961). The exact function of this organ is not known, but Mohsen has speculated that it may eject semen or that it may be everted to apply semen to the genital aperture of the female.

In many teleosts the ovaries are paired organs; there are, however, exceptions; e.g., the Japanese rice fish (*Oryzias latipes*), the guppy (*Poecilia reticulata*), the least killifish (*Heterandria formosa*), *Monopterus albus* (Liem, 1963), and some other species have one ovary only. As will be discussed later, hermaphroditism is encountered rather frequently among the teleosts; examples are found especially among the Sparidae and Serranidae.

The ovary of teleosts is a hollow organ, the cavity of which is continuous with the lumen of the oviduct. The follicles are embedded in connective tissue. The structure of the follicles varies among different species. In some species, e.g. the European bitterling *(Rhodeus amarus)*, there is, according to Bretschneider and Duyvené de Wit (1947), an inner epithelial layer of granulosa cells, a theca interna, and a theca externa (Figure 3-6).

The fate of the follicle varies. In some viviparous species, fertilization occurs within the follicle and the embryos develop within the ovarian or follicular cavity. In the Poeciliidae, the embryo does not leave the follicle until shortly before birth, but in the sea perches (Embiotocidae), clinids, and eelpouts (Zoarcidae) of the suborder Blennioidei, most development takes place within the lumen of the ovary. Under these conditions the ovarian epithelium becomes hypertrophied and glandular, and forms the *calyx nutricius.* Transfer of materials between mother and embryos often takes place by means of leaf-like extensions of the ovarian wall which penetrate into the gill cavities and the mouth of the embryo. The fate of the follicle is illustrated in Figures 3-7 and 3-8.

The system that conducts the eggs to the outside can have different anatomical origins. For the Salmonidae Gérard (1954) has stated that it consists of mesovaria, which form a funnel-shaped system. In a recent paper, Henderson (1967) illustrates the urinary and genital system of various species of the genus *Salvelinus*. She shows that the ova are discharged into the abdominal cavity and pass through a constriction of the posterior abdominal wall into a cavity that opens to the exterior through an opening on the urogenital papilla. In Anguillidae the posterior part of the coelom functions as a funnel—actually as two funnels because of the presence of the dorsal mesentery. Posteriorly, these funnels become one, forming a single channel that opens between the anus and urinary opening. In the Muraenidae, the two funnels remain separated; each opens into a separate opening behind the anus.

In the majority of teleosts, there are oviducts (not Müllerian ducts) formed by an extension of the ovarian cavity and open between the anus and the urinary pore.

In a number of species, the urogenital papilla is elongated, exterior to the body, and forms an ovipositor. An unusual illustration is the subfamily Rhodeinae (bitterlings), whose eggs are deposited in a mussel. Another unusual use for the ovipositor is characteristic of the family Syngnathidae (pipefishes and seahorses); the female deposits her eggs in the brood pouch of the male.

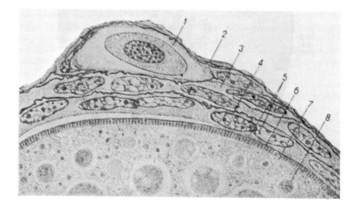

Figure 3-6.   Follicle of the European bitterling, *Rhodeus amarus.* 1. capillary. 2. theca externa. 3. theca interna. 4. basal membrane. 5. granulosa. 6. oolemma. 7. egg plasma. 8. yolk. (From Bretschneider and Duyvené de Wit, 1947.)

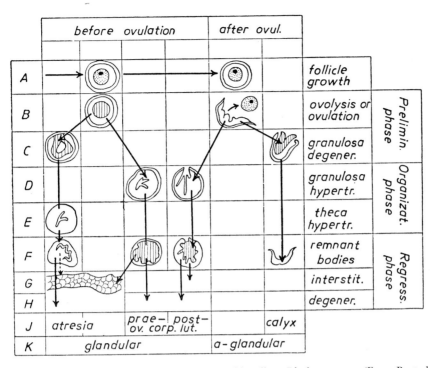

Figure 3-7. Fate of the ovarian follicle of the European bitterling, *Rhodeus amarus.* (From Bretschneider and Duyvené de Wit, 1947.)

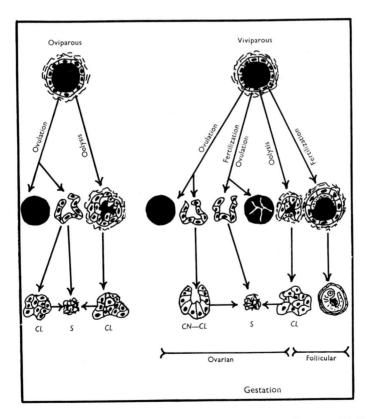

Figure 3-8. History of the ovarian follicle in different teleosts. *CL* = corpus luteum. *CN-CL* = calyx nutricius, which may be somewhat luteinized. *S* = scar. (From Hoar, 1955.)

Amphibia

The testes of Urodele and Anura are paired organs consisting of lobes, joined by thin segments in the case of the Urodele. In the Anura the testes consist of a mass of seminiferous ampullae, each with its own basement membrane and held together by an investing tunic. The histology of the testis of *Rana catesbeiana* is illustrated in Plate I-7; it shows the cell nests, or spermatocysts. The spermatocysts are formed from a primary spermatogonium which lays down the membrane around each spermatocyst. Each spermatogonium forms many secondary spermatogonia which undergo maturation divisions and form the spermatozoa. At this stage the cyst membrane disintegrates and the sperm heads become attached to the Sertoli cells. Since the spermatocysts may mature independently of one another, each ampulla may contain spermatocysts in different stages of maturation. Iwasawa and Asai (1964) have reported the occurrence of ova in testes of *Rana rugosa* (11 out of 32 males), *R. temporaria ornativentris* (12 out of 27 males), and *Rhacophorus schlegelii arborea* (one out of 118 males).

Interstitial cells are present in Urodele as well as Anura testes; whether they secrete the male sex hormone has not been determined. These cells may show considerable development at the time when the secondary sexual characters are undeveloped and may show no signs of development at the time that secondary sex characters are fully developed (Dodd, 1960; Forbes, 1961). The different sources of androgen in the amphibian testes will be discussed in a later chapter.

Bidder's organ, found in the Bufonidae, lies at the anterior tip of the testis. As we saw in Table 2-1, it is derived from the gonadal cortex and consists of small oocytes. After castration of the male it develops into a functional ovary.

The spermatozoa, upon shedding, take the following path: ampullae; efferent ducts of the ampullae; *ductuli*

efferentes; genital part of the kidney; *ductus deferens* (which is also the ureter). In some species the posterior end of the ductus deferens contains a vesicula seminalis which communicates with the ductus deferens by small ducts. The ductuli efferentes of *Ascaphus* of one side are connected to the longitudinal canal of the opposite kidney (Noble, 1954).

The cloacal gland and the pelvic gland (Figure 3-9) found in salamanders (Urodeles) together manufacture the spermatophore, which is picked up in the female by the cloacal lips. The follicular wall consists of a granulosa, theca interna, and theca externa.

Gymnophiona, primitive limbless amphibia resembling large earthworms, have a protrusible intromittent organ (see Figure 3-10). Fertilization in most frogs is external. One exception is *Ascaphus,* a primitive frog which has a cloaca extending into a tube that functions as a copulatory

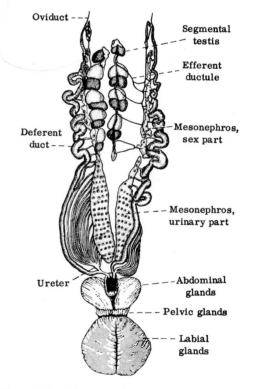

Figure 3-9. The reproductive system of the male salamander, *Tarichosa torosa.* (From Witschi, 1956.)

organ. This intromittent organ, unlike that of the gymnophiona, cannot be withdrawn into the vent. *Nectophrynoides vivipara,* as the name indicates, is viviparous and fertilization is therefore internal, but the males have no intromittent organ (Noble, 1954).

Vestigial Müllerian ducts are present in male Bufonidae. These ducts are stimulated by the secretions of Bidder's organs after castration so that eggs ovulated from Bidder's organ can be carried to the outside and the genetic male becomes a functional female.

The amphibian ovaries are paired, lobed organs consisting largely of a cortex covered by germinal epithelium. The medulla present during embryonic development has disappeared in the adult, and the ovary is a hollow organ, the cavity of which is lined by cells which are medullary in origin. As the follicles mature, they project into this cavity. On histological examination, the ovary is found to contain mature follicles, corpora atretica, "corpora lutea" formed, as in the European bitterling *(Rhodeus amarus),* from nonovulated follicles, and ruptured follicles which leave only a scar.

According to Gorbman and Bern (1962), "corpora lutea" occur in all viviparous species of Urodeles and they are absent in oviparous Anurana, whereas their

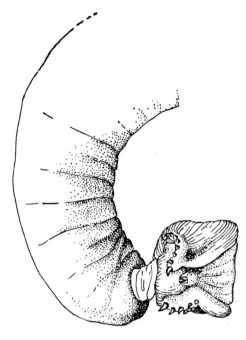

Figure 3-10.   Everted intromittent organ of the male *Scolecomorphus uluguruensis.* (From Noble, 1954.)

presence has not been established in oviparous Urodeles and viviparous Anurana. To the latter belong *Protopipa,* and *Pipa* in which the eggs are incubated in individual chambers on the back of the female (Figure 3-11), and *Gastrotheca marsupiata,* in which the eggs are carried in a pouch or marsupium on the back of the female (Figure 3-12).

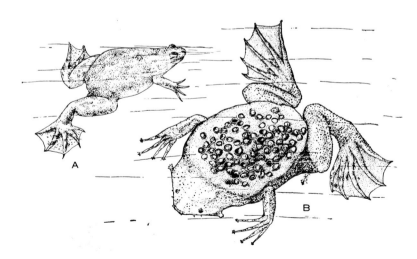

Figure 3-11.   Pipid toads: *A = Xenopus mulleri; B = Pipa pipa* female with eggs on the back. (From Noble, 1954.)

Bidder's organ shows maximal development during the spring preceding ovulation; afterward it regresses rapidly so that it may be difficult to find in older animals. During this period of development "corpora lutea" are formed, paralleled by the formation of "corpora lutea" in the ovary.

The oviducts derived from the Müllerian ducts are paired. In *Triturus viridescens*, six regions can be distinguished in the oviduct. From anterior to posterior,

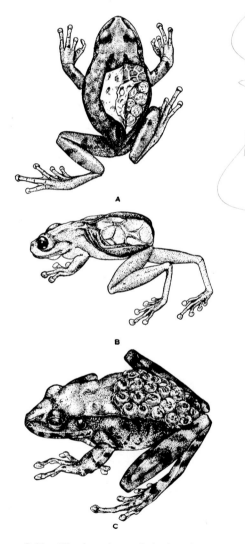

Figure 3-12. The brood pouch in females of different species of amphibians. *A. Gastrotheca marsupiata. B. Gastrotheca pygmaea*, eggs removed from the brood pouch. *C. Cryptobatrachus evansi.* (From Noble, 1954.)

they are the infundibular region (a transparent region which secretes a watery fluid), an opaque region with eosinophilic granules in the cells, a transparent wide region, an opaque white region, and a straight section leading into the cloaca (Dodd, 1960). The entire oviduct lumen is ciliated.

In *Rana* sp. the upper two-thirds of the oviduct are ciliated but the enlarged "uterus" is not. In *Xenopus* the entire duct is ciliated and no uterus is present.

In most Urodeles (exceptions: Hynobiidae and Cryptobranchidae) fertilization is internal. The males lack an intromittent organ; and internal fertilization is accomplished when the female picks up the spermatophores with the cloacal lips. In the female, pelvic glands may serve to store the spermatozoa after liberation from the spermatophore.

Reptilia

The reptilian testes are paired organs consisting of seminiferous tubules and interstitial cells which probably secrete male sex hormones. Interstitial cells have been found in lizards, snakes, and turtles (Forbes, 1961), but, according to Forbes, there is no information concerning their presence in adult Crocodilia. In 17 species of *Cnemidophorus* and in one species of *Ameiva* investigated, a circum-testicular subtunical band of Leydig cells is present (Lowe and Goldberg, 1966). The average thickness of this layer varies between 1.2 and 42.1 cells in different species. These cells show seasonal variation in storage of secretory granules (Lowe and Goldberg, 1966) and the morphology of these cells parallels that of the intertubular cells which are also present in these testes (De Wolfe and Telford, 1966). This arrangement of circum-testicular Leydig cells in Teiid lizards appears to be unique.

In sections of the testes one can recognize the Sertoli cells, and when spermatogenesis has proceeded to the stage of sperm formation one can distinguish spermatogonia, primary and secondary spermatocytes, spermatids, and spermatozoa forming different layers around the lumen of the tubule. The seminiferous tubules connect with the ducti deferentes via the ductuli efferentes. The ductus deferens opens into the genital papilla. In lizards and snakes the intromittent organ consists of paired posterior diverticula of the cloaca which lie within the tail (Figure 3-13); they are called hemipenes. During erection these pouches are everted through the cloacal opening and the semen can pass along a spiral groove in each hemipenis. The organ is withdrawn by contraction of a retractor penis muscle. In the same animal, each hemipenis may erect independently of the other. In turtles and crocodilians the penis is a single expandable structure on the floor of the cloaca. The semen flows over a groove on the surface.

Reptiles have paired ovaries in the body cavity suspended from the body wall by a mesovarium. The ovaries are hollow and consist mainly of follicles (which, when mature, project into the ovarian cavity from short stalks), corpora lutea, corpora atretica, and very little stroma. The central cavity is lined with a squamous epithelium. The follicular wall consists of a granulosa, a theca interna, and a theca externa. The corpora lutea are formed after rupture of the follicles as a result of luteinization and proliferation of the granulosa cells and the development of a supporting connective tissue derived from the thecal cells. The possible role of these corpora lutea and the mechanisms involved in their maintenance will be discussed further on.

The oviducts, which are derived from the Müllerian ducts, open into the cloaca. The anterior end of each oviduct secretes the albumen and shell around the egg. In some species of lizards and snakes there are special tubules in the vagina where sperm can be stored (Fox, 1956, 1963); these structures may help explain the long survival of sperm in the reproductive tract

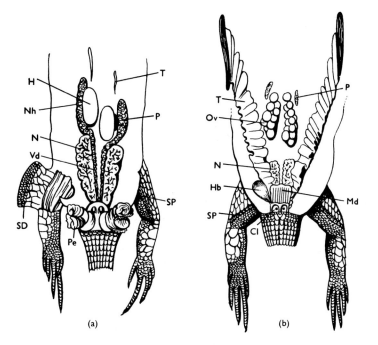

(a)   (b)

Figure 3-13.   Urogenital system of *Lacerta agilis*. (a) Male. (b) Female. *Cl* = cloaca. *H* = testis. *Hb* = urinary bladder. *Md* = rectum. *N* = kidney. *Nh* = epididymis. *Ov* = ovary. *P* = adrenal. *Pe* = penis. *SD* = femoral glands. *SP* = femoral pores. *T* = Müllerian ducts. *Vd* = ductus deferens. (From Dodd, 1960.)

of some reptiles (see Fox, 1956). Wilkinson (1966) found seminal receptacles in the infundibulum and also in the vagina of the snake *Diadophis punctatus.* Overwintering sperm cells were found in the vaginal receptacles only.

Aves

The avian testes are paired organs suspended into the body cavity from the body wall by a short mesorchium. As we shall discuss later, in most mammals the testes need to be maintained at lower than body temperature for the germinal epithelium to be maintained during the sexually active period. In these mammals the scrotum performs a cooling function.

Without presenting any evidence, Cowles and Nordstrom (1946) proposed that the air sacs might in birds cause cooling of the avian testes. Experimental evidence obtained with chickens (Williams, 1958a) indicates that the temperature of the testes (41.32°C.) is not different from the core body temperature (41.30°C.). However, Williams also showed that maintenance of the testes at lower than body temperature (by an "artificial scrotum") caused earlier spermatogenesis in such testes than occurred in controls. In subsequent experiments, Williams (1958b) also showed that transplanted testes exposed to saline of 44.4°C. prior to transplantation showed impaired spermatogenesis, whereas exposure to saline of 41.3°C. did not have this effect. Other workers have shown that destruction of the air sacs did not impair spermatogenesis in cocks (Herin et al. 1960).

Histologically it has been shown that the testes consist of seminiferous tubules, which in roosters may reach a total length of over 250 m. (Kumaran and Turner, 1949). Among the tubules are found the interstitial cells, the source of androgen secretion. More details will be discussed in another chapter.

Avian testes have small epididymides,

each one connected to a ductus deferens which, under the influence of androgen, becomes highly coiled (Figure 3-14). The distal end of the ductus deferens in some species, e.g. *Euplectes franciscanus* and *Junco hyemalis,* is enlarged; sperm can be stored in this *seminal glomulus* or *seminal vesicle* (not homologous with the mammalian seminal vesicle). The morphology of the copulatory organ varies considerably. In ducks and geese it consists of a grooved erectile "penis" (Figure 3-15), whereas in chickens it consists of a small erectile structure and lymph bodies (Figure 3-16).

In the majority of bird species investigated, only the left ovary is developed; the right is vestigial. Exceptions are found among the Falconiiformes, especially the Falconiidae. As we mentioned in Chapter 2, this may be the result of the more equal distribution of primordial germ cells between left and right gonads in these species. However, among sparrows (*Passer domesticus*) and pigeons (*Columba livia*) about 5 percent of the specimens have two developed ovaries (Romanoff and Romanoff, 1949).

It is difficult to explain the evolutionary significance of the frequent presence of two ovaries in one order when one takes into account that the right oviduct is not developed and thus eggs ovulated from the right ovary drop into the body cavity and probably are resorbed.

The ovary, when fully developed, resembles a bunch of grapes. Follicles are of various sizes; usually there are five to six large follicles 0.5 to 1.0 cm. in diameter filled with yellow yolk, a large group of follicles of about 2 to 3 mm. filled with yellowish yolk, and many smaller follicles. The follicle (see Figure 3-17) consists of the vitelline membrane, the granulosa, the theca interna, and the theca externa. During the early growth of the chicken follicles, the granulosa cells are in a single row which have abundant Golgi substance and granular endoplasmic reticulum. During growth the granulosa cells become

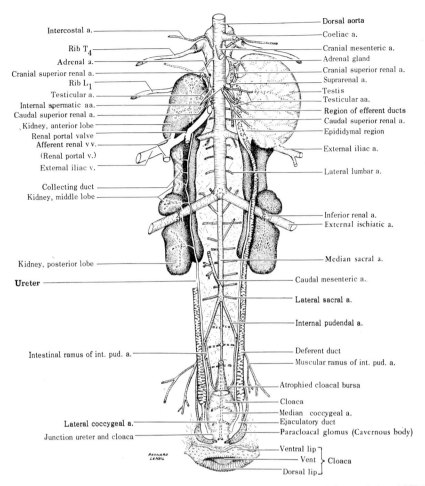

Intercostal a.
Rib T$_4$
Adrenal a.
Cranial superior renal a.
Rib L$_1$
Testicular a.
Internal spermatic aa.
Caudal superior renal a.
Kidney, anterior lobe
Renal portal valve
Afferent renal v v.
(Renal portal v.)
External iliac v.
Collecting duct
Kidney, middle lobe

Kidney, posterior lobe

Ureter

Intestinal ramus of int. pud. a.

Lateral coccygeal a.
Junction ureter and cloaca

Dorsal aorta
Coeliac a.
Cranial mesenteric a.
Adrenal gland
Cranial superior renal a.
Suprarenal a.
Testis
Testicular aa.
Region of efferent ducts
Caudal superior renal a.
Epididymal region
External iliac a.
Lateral lumbar a.
Inferior renal a.
External ischiatic a.
Median sacral a.
Caudal mesenteric a.
Lateral sacral a.
Internal pudendal a.
Deferent duct
Muscular ramus of int. pud. a.
Atrophied cloacal bursa
Cloaca
Median coccygeal a.
Ejaculatory duct
Paracloacal glomus (Cavernous body)
Ventral lip ⎤
Vent   ⎬ Cloaca
Dorsal lip ⎦

Figure 3-14. Reproductive system of a rooster. (From Lucas and Stettenheim, 1965.)

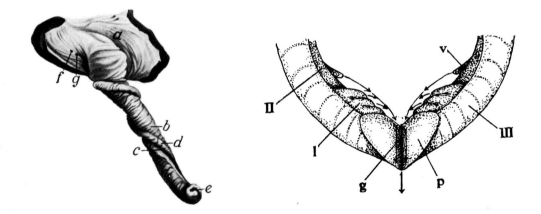

Figure 3-15. Penis of a drake. *a* = opened cloaca with the walls pulled back. *b* = penis. *c* = semen groove. *d* = border of semen groove. *e* = opening of glandular duct. *f* = opening of the ductus deferens. *g* = opening of the ureter. (From Ellenberger and Baum, 1932.)

Figure 3-16. *g* = longitudinal groove of erected copulatory organ. *l* = swelled lymph fold. *p* = erected copulatory organ. *v* = papillary process of the ductus deferens. *II* = second fold of cloaca. *III* = third fold of the cloaca. (From Nishiyama, 1955.)

43

separated by intercellular spaces filled with perivitelline substance. Just prior to ovulation the reticulum is agranular and the cell contains numerous lipid droplets (Wyburn et al., 1966). Electron microscopic examination also revealed that villus-like elevations arise on the oocyte cell membrane to form the zona radiata; these elevations may enhance the passage of yolk materials into the egg (Wyburn et al., 1965).

The large follicles are very vascular, with an enormously developed venous system and a small arterial system. A network of nerve fibers is present in follicular stalks; small bundles of fibers run to the wall of the follicle (Gilbert, 1965). An area on the follicle, which, on macroscopic examination, is free of blood vessels, is called the stigma. At the time of ovulation the follicle ruptures along the stigma. Granulosa cells remain identifiable for about 72 hours after ovulation. During the postovulatory period the cytoplasm of the granulosa cells becomes infiltrated by lipids (Wyburn et al., 1966). Histochemical investigations suggest that the granulosa cells and the theca interna cells can produce progesterone. It is not known whether progesterone or converted estrogen is released (Wyburn and Baillie, 1966).

After 3 to 7 days the chicken follicle disintegrates completely. No corpora lutea form from the ruptured follicle. Lutein cell tumors have been found; these structures resemble mammalian corpora lutea (see Plate I-28). In ring-necked pheasants *(Phasianus colchicus)* the ruptured follicles can still be recognized at the end of the breeding season (Kabat et al., 1948). There is little ovarian stroma; it contains interstitial cells which may be the source of androgen.

The ovulated yolk is either picked up by the fimbria of the oviduct or the egg falls into the ovarian pocket (formed by the body wall, the mesentery of the oviduct, and the air sac) and is then picked up by the oviduct.

In the oviduct there are different anatomical regions; their length is given in Table 3-1, their microscopic anatomy is illustrated in Figure 3-18, and the height of epithelium in different parts of the oviduct is given in Figure 3-19.

In the oviducts of chickens and turkeys there are two areas in which sperm can apparently be stored and maintain their fertilizing capacity. Van Drimmelen (1951) discovered so-called sperm nests, tubular glands, in the infundibulum of the chicken oviduct. Grigg (1957) could cause

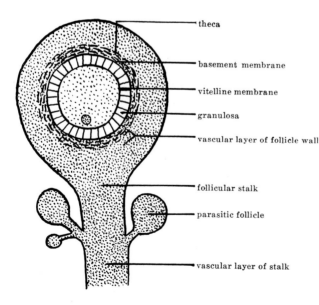

theca

basement membrane

vitelline membrane

granulosa

vascular layer of follicle wall

follicular stalk

parasitic follicle

vascular layer of stalk

Figure 3-17. Follicle of a chicken. **(From** Nalbandov and James, 1949.)

Table 3-1. Size of Various Sections of the Hen's Oviduct in Active and Inactive Periods

	SIZE OF OVIDUCT			
	ACTIVE STAGE		INACTIVE STAGE	
	LENGTH (CM.)	WIDTH (CM.)	LENGTH (CM.)	WIDTH (CM.)
Infundibulum (funnel)	7.0	8.6	2.4	—
Magnum	33.6	1.7	5.4	0.8
Isthmus	8.0	0.9	2.2	0.4
Shell gland	8.3	2.9	2.4	1.2
Vagina	7.9	0.9	3.0	0.4
Total	64.8	—	15.4	—

Reference: Romanoff and Romanoff, 1949.

the release of such sperm into the lumen of the oviduct by pulling a fluid-filled bag through the oviduct. Bobr, Lorenz, and Ogasawara (1964), however, found a glandular region in the uterovaginal junction in which spermatozoa are stored. According to these workers, the infundibular sperm nests are filled by spermatozoa only after unusual techniques of insemination are used, but the uterovaginal junction glands are those normally used for storage of sperm. At the time of oviposition presumably the sperm are released into the lumen and can fertilize the next ovum (Bobr, Ogasawara, and Lorenz, 1964). We will discuss this matter later. Verma and Cherms (1964) failed to find "sperm nests" in the infundibulum of the turkey but

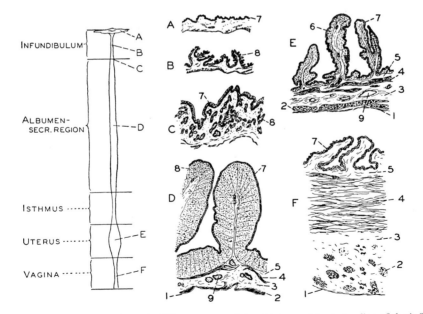

Figure 3-18. Transverse sections through different parts of the chicken oviduct. *A* = lips of the infundibulum. *B* = the neck of the infundibulum. *C* = transition region from infundibulum to magnum. *D* = magnum or albumen secreting region. *E* = Walls of the uterus. *F* = walls of the vagina. *1* = peritoneal membrane. *2* = longitudinal muscle fibers. *3* = connective tissue. *4* = circular muscle layer. *5* = inner layer of connective tissue. *6* = thick layer of convoluted tubular glands. *7* = epithelium of the duct. *8* = ducts of the convoluted glands. *9* = blood vessels. (From Romanoff and Romanoff, 1949.)

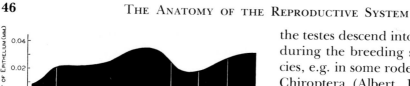

Figure 3-19. Height of the epithelial cells of different regions of the chicken's oviduct. (From Romanoff, 1949.)

found glands in the uterovaginal junction in which sperm cells were stored.

Mammalia

During embryonic development, the testes of all mammalian species are located in the abdomen. In the majority of species, the testes descend into the scrotum at least during the breeding season. In some species, e.g. in some rodents, Insectivora, and Chiroptera (Albert, 1961), the testes are intraabdominal during the nonbreeding period but are in the scrotum during the breeding season. In Table 3-2 the location of the testes in various orders is given.

The descent of the testis occurs through the inguinal canal, which, in some species, remains open postnatally (e.g. in rats) so that the testes can experimentally be placed in the abdomen and the effect of maintenance of the testes at body temperature can be studied. A number of facts are known about the testicular descent but the exact mechanisms which cause it are not known. It is

Table 3-2. Position of the Testes in Mammals

| | PERMANENTLY IN ABDOMEN | OUTSIDE ABDOMINAL CAVITY | | |
| | | SUBINTEGUMENTAL (INGUINAL OR PERINEAL) | SCROTAL | |
			PERIODICALLY	PERMANENTLY
Monotremata	Duckbill, spiny anteater	—	—	—
Marsupialia	—	Some (e.g. wombat	—	Most (e.g. opossum, numbat)
Xenarthra	Sloth, armadillo	—	—	—
Sirenia	Dugong	—	—	—
Proboscidea	Elephant	—	—	—
Hyracoidea	Hyrax	—	—	—
Cetacea	Whale, dolphin	—	—	—
Ungulata	—	Some (e.g. rhinoceros, hippopotamus)	—	Most (e.g. stallion, bull)
Carnivora	—	Some (e.g. hyena, seal)	—	Most (e.g. dog, lion)
Rodentia	—	Most* (e.g. rat, rabbit)	Some (e.g. ground squirrel)	—
Chiroptera	—	—	Most (all?) bats	—
Insectivora	Some (e.g. golden mole, tenrec)	Some* (e.g. mole, shrew)	—	—
Tupaiidae	—	—	—	*Tupaia*
Primates	—	—	Some (e.g. loris, potto)	Most* (e.g. monkey, man)

* Testes can be voluntarily or reflexly withdrawn into abdomen (in primates, only during infancy).
Reference: Eckstein and Zuckerman, 1956.

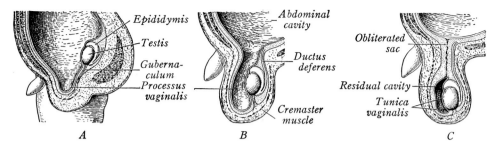

Figure 3-20. Relationships of the testes and processus vaginalis before, during, and after testicular descent in man. *A.* before descent. *B.* during descent. *C.* after descent. (From Arey, 1965.)

reasonably certain that androgen secretion promotes the descent into the scrotum. According to one hypothesis, the gubernaculum shortens and thus pulls the testes into the scrotum. The human gubernaculum at birth is indeed shorter than at the seventh month of fetal development. However, removal of the gubernaculum does not prevent the descent. According to another hypothesis the descent results from enlargement of the inguinal canal and the action of gravity on the testes. Prior to the descent of the testis through the inguinal canal the saclike pocket of peritoneum or *processus vaginalis* has entered the scrotal sac. The testis and gubernaculum are outside the peritoneum while in the abdomen and during descent into the scrotum, and thus lie outside of the vaginal process or sac (see Figure 3-20). Thus, the vaginal sac is invaginated by the testis to form a visceral layer close to the testis and a parietal or outer layer, the scrotal lining. As Figure 3-21 shows, the consequence of the testicular descent is that the ductus deferens loops over the ureter. The ductus deferens, as well as the spermatic nerves, arteries, veins, and lymphatics constitutes the spermatic cord which is wrapped, as is the testis, by the vaginal sac.

The anatomy of the scrotum and the temperature regulation of the testes is illustrated in Figure 3-22 and the discussion will be based on the structures shown.

1. The presence of the testes in the scrotum ensures that the testes will be at lower than body temperature under most conditions.

2. As the temperature measurements

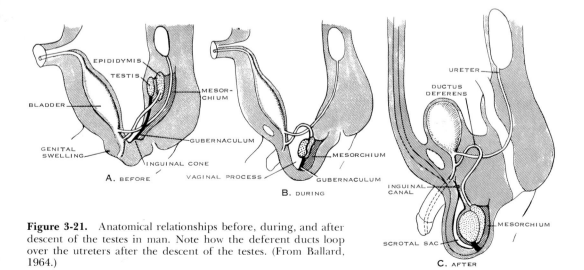

Figure 3-21. Anatomical relationships before, during, and after descent of the testes in man. Note how the deferent ducts loop over the utreters after the descent of the testes. (From Ballard, 1964.)

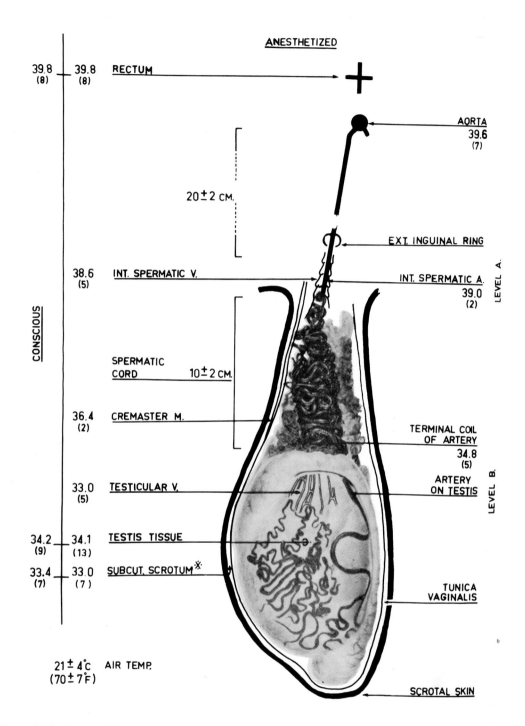

Figure 3-22. Anatomical relationships and experimental temperature readings at various sites in the scrotum of conscious and anesthetized rams. The internal spermatic artery had been filled with Neoprene and the cast had been exposed by removal of the pampiniform plexus and tunica albuginea over the artery on the testis. Figures in parentheses give the number of temperature readings from which the average was obtained.

Subcutaneous scrotum temperature readings were taken beneath the posterior skin and not the anterior (shown here for purposes of illustration only). The temperature in the artery of the testis was 34.4°C. based on seven observations. (From Waites, personal communication.)

show, the arterial blood is several degrees cooler at the terminal coil of the spermatic artery, which lies close to the epididymis.

3. The external cremaster muscle can, by contraction, pull the testes closer to the body if the temperature becomes too low.

4. The tunica dartos (not illustrated), which adheres to the skin of the scrotum, contracts on exposure to cold and thus brings the testes closer to the body and simultaneously reduces the surface area so that less cooling occurs.

In those species in which the testes are scrotal during the breeding season, prevention of cooling of the testes causes degeneration of the germinal epithelium.

In addition to the ductus deferens, which was discussed in Chapter 2, a number of secondary sex glands may be present in various species. These glands all possess secretory epithelium, a connective tissue layer, and smooth muscle fibers (Price and Williams-Ashman, 1961). These glands and their occurrence in the different mammalian orders are listed in Table 3-3. Of these, the ampullary glands and seminal vesicles are connected with the ductus deferens, whereas the prostate and bulbourethral glands are connected

with the urogenital sinus (Eckstein and Zuckerman, 1956). The seminal vesicles open generally into the pelvic urethra. In primates the distal part of the seminal vesicle and the ductus deferens join to form an ejaculatory duct.

In most mammals the urogenital and digestive systems have separate openings. Exceptions are the monotremes, marsupials, edentates, Aplodontia, and Castoridae. In the monotremes, the ductus deferens opens above the ureters, in all other mammals, below them because they end in the urinary bladder (Eckstein and Zuckerman, 1956).

In monotremes, the ventral part of the cloaca forms the penis. In all other mammals the cloaca is closed. The penis is attached to the outside of the body so that the urogenital sinus becomes a closed canal through which urine and semen pass. The penis of some marsupials, e.g. *Didelphis philander,* is split into two tips, each having one branch of the urethra.

In some species, e.g. cattle (see Figure 3-23), the penis is too long to fit into the preputial sac; a sigmoid flexure bends the organ so that in the nonerect condition it is contained within this sac. At copulation the flexure straightens out and the

Table 3-3. Occurrence of Secondary Sex Glands in Males of Different Mammalian Orders

ORDER	BULBOURETHRAL GLAND	PROSTATE	SEMINAL VESICLE	AMPULLARY GLANDS
Monotremata	+	?	−	−
Marsupialia	+	+	−	−
Insectivora	+	+	±	±
Chiroptera	+	+	±	±
Primates	+	+	±	±
Edentata	±	+	+	−
Pholidota	−	+	+	−
Lagomorpha	+	+	+	±
Rodentia	+	+	+	±
Cetacea	−	+	−	−
Carnivora	±	±	−	±
Proboscidea	+	+	+	+
Hyracoidea	+	+	+	−
Sirenia	−	+	+	−
Perissodactyla	+	+	+	+
Artiodactyla	+	+	+	±

References: Eckstein and Zuckerman, 1956; Price and Williams-Ashman, 1961; and Asdell, 1964.

semen can be deposited deep in the vagina. In Friesian cattle a condition occurs (due to a recessive autosomal gene [Hutt, 1964]) in which abnormalities of the retractor penis muscle (Figure 3-23) prevent the straightening of the flexure and the bulls are consequently impotent. Cutting the retractor penis muscle enables the bulls to mate but it is a questionable procedure since it spreads the undesirable gene through the population.

In most mammalian orders a bony or cartilaginous structure, the *os penis* or *baculum,* is present in the male and an *os clitoridis* in the female. Exceptions are man, ungulates, and whales.

For details on the anatomy of the genital system of different species, the reader should consult the well-illustrated chapter by Eckstein and Zuckerman (1956).

In most mammalian species the ovaries are paired organs suspended from the body wall by a short mesovarium. The right ovary of the duckbill *(Ornithorhynchus anatinus)* is atrophied. In some bats belonging to the family Vespertilonidae the left ovary is atrophied (Harrison, 1962). In a number of bat genera the left ovary

is present but no ovulations occur; this is the case in the free-tailed bat *(Tadarida brasiliensis),* the greater horseshoe bat *(Rhinolophus ferrumequinum),* the lesser horseshoe bat *(Rhinolophus hipposideros),* in *Miniopterus schreibersii,* and in *M. australis* (Pearson, 1949; Asdell, 1964). In *M. natalensis,* on the other hand, the ovulations occur only from the left ovary only (Pearson, 1949).

Among rodents, the mountain viscacha *(Lagidium peruanum)* has only one functional ovary, usually the right one, although up to two weeks prior to the first estrus the ovaries are indistinguishable morphologically. After removal of the right ovary ovulations from the remaining left ovary can take place (Pearson, 1949).

The mammalian ovaries are covered by an epithelium, usually one-layered cuboidal or low columnar, the so-called germinal epithelium (Harrison, 1962). Only in horses *(Equus caballus)* is the ovary not covered by epithelium except for a narrow groove, the ovulation *fossa,* into which follicles ovulate. In other mammals the germinal epithelium is interrupted

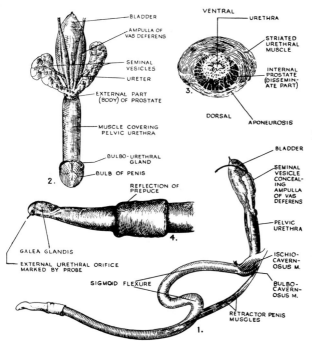

Figure 3-23. Penis and adjacent structures of the domestic bull. 1. General view from the left side. 2. Bladder and pelvic urethra in dorsal view. 3. Cross section through the upper part of the pelvic urethra. 4. Distal end of penis, partly withdrawn from the prepuce. (From Eckstein and Zuckerman, 1956.)

only at the time of ovulation of the follicles (Figure 3-24).

Under the germinal epithelium lies the tunica albuginea and under this lies a massive layer of follicles. In addition to the follicles one may find corpora lutea, corpora hemorrhagica, corpora albicantia, and large, polyhedral interstitial cells which are more prominent in some orders, e.g. Insectivora, Rodentia, and Carnivora, but less numerous or absent in others, e.g. Cetacea, Artiodactyla, and Primates (Harrison, 1962). According to Mossman (1966), these cells, in rodent ovaries, are derived mainly from relatively undifferentiated theca interna cells, atretic follicles, and, to

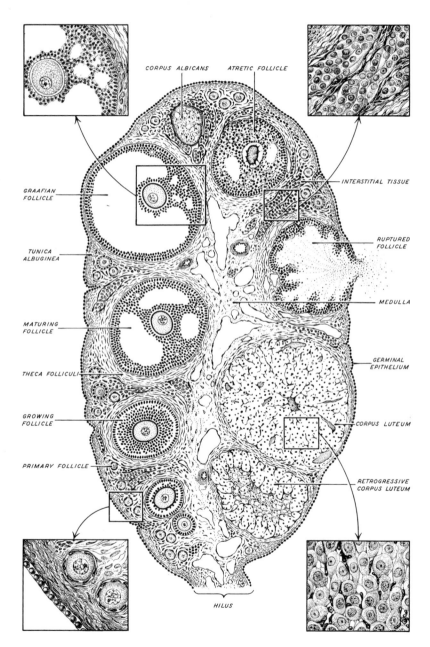

Figure 3-24. Mammalian ovary. (From Turner, 1966.)

a lesser extent, from cortical and medullary stromal cells.

In the infantile ovary there are, in addition to the cortical follicles, follicles in the medullary cords which are frequently in a further stage of development than the cortical follicles (Mossman, 1966). These medullary follicles are lost during further development.

A remnant of the epoophoron forms a blind duct system which becomes part of the ovary. A group of special cells is found along the ovarian hilus and in the mesovarium of armadillos *(Dasypus novemcinctus),* of the pika *(Ochotona princeps),* of the thirteen-lined ground squirrel *(Citellus tridecemlineatus)* (Seliger et al., 1966), and of women (Harrison, 1962). Harrison has stated that these cells are probably homologous to the Leydig cells. However, Seliger et al. (1966) found that after adrenalectomy this group of cells, in close relationship with the *rete ovarii* and medullary cords, resembles adrenal cortex cells. On in vitro incubation these cells secrete corticosterone and desoxycorticosterone in sufficient amounts to keep the animals alive; adrenalectomized animals die when the gonads and the adnexa are also removed. Identical cells are found in adrenalectomized males around the efferent ductules of the testes (Seliger et al., 1966).

The follicles can be divided into different groups according to their relative size and morphology:

1. *Primary follicles,* in which a single layer of epithelial cells surrounds the oocyte, and which have no theca layers. Polyovular follicles occur in a number of species. They are especially frequent in the opossum *(Didelphis virginiana)* and the striped skunk *(Mephitis mephitis).* Leach and Conaway (1963) found that polyovular follicles develop from the ovarian medulla in the skunk and that they are homologous with the seminiferous tubules of the testis. These follicles can be ovulated by gonadotropin treatment, but normally they degenerate during the summer after the animal is born. The degeneration of the ova within a medullary cord follicle leaves granulosa cells behind which may persist either as testis cords or as an anovular follicle. It is also possible that one ovum of a polyovular follicle degenerates and that the remaining ovum or ova plus the granulosa cells persist; they may degenerate later. The entire medullary cord follicle plus its ova may degenerate, while the theca proliferates to form a thecal interstitial gland, which eventually becomes a major part of the medullary interstitial tissue.

2. *Secondary follicles,* in which the epithelium is cuboidal or columnar and many layered to form the granulosa layer or membrane. On the outside the granulosa is surrounded by the vascular glandular theca interna and the outer theca externa which consists of connective tissue; the egg is at this stage surrounded by a membrane, the *zona pellucida.*

3. *Tertiary follicles,* which are filled with a (usually) clear fluid; the space filled by the fluid is called the antrum. The antrum is formed by cavities which develop in the granulosa (Harrison, 1962). In most rodents these follicles are surrounded by a thin thecal gland which is formed by the theca interna and secretes steroids. This gland degenerates shortly after ovulation (Mossman, 1966). In the pocket gopher *(Geomys bursarius)* this thecal gland is very prominent; it should not be confused with luteal tissue (see Mossman, 1966).

4. *Mature follicles,* which protrude like blisters on the surface of the ovary. The oocyte, surrounded by a layer of granulosa cells which form the *corona radiata,* is embedded in a mass of cells which form the *cumulus oophorus.* In hibernating vespertilionid bats the granulosa cells of the cumulus oophorus hypertrophy and are filled with glycogen, which may provide energy for the mature follicle during hibernation (see Harrison, 1962, for discussion).

5. *Degenerating follicles.*

6. *Atretic follicles,* in which, according to Nalbandov (1964), the beginning of

atresia can be recognized in the egg. Asdell (1946), however, found that changes could be discerned in the follicle before changes occurred in the ovum. According to Ingram (1962), the question whether the ovum or the follicle is affected first is not yet settled.

7. *Luteinized follicles,* in which luteinization occurs without rupturing the follicle.

8. *Anovular follicles,* which are apparently normal follicles but lack an ovum (Harrison, 1962). They do not usually form an antrum and do not become mature.

Corpora lutea are formed after ovulation and may have different life spans (to be discussed in Chapters 6 and 9). In many rodents a peripheral theca-like zone with cells in all transitional stages between stromal and luteal cells is found (Mossman, 1966). In many species accessory corpora lutea are formed, as mentioned on page 194. Mossman and Judas (1949) described the Canadian porcupine *(Erithizon dorsatum);* accessory corpora lutea from the ovary on the nonpregnant side usually disappear. For a further discussion of the accessory corpora lutea see Chapter 9.

The remainder of the female reproductive system consists essentially of the derivatives of the Müllerian duct system (fallopian tubes, or oviducts, uterus, and vagina) and the clitoris, urethra and vaginal vestibule.

Among the different mammalian orders the following main types of separation of the left and right·Müllerian ducts can be found:

1. Complete separation so that one finds two fallopian tubes, two uteri, two cervices, and two vaginas e.g. opossum *(Didelphis virginiana)* and kangaroo *(Macropus* sp.).

2. Two oviducts, no uterine body but two uterine horns completely separated (duplex uterus), and two cervices but one vagina; e.g. rabbit *(Oryctolagus cuniculus),* and rat *(Rattus norvegicus).*

3. Two oviducts, but two good sized horns (bicornuate uterus), a small uterine body, one cervix, and one vagina; e.g. pig *(Sus scrofa),* dog *(Canis familiaris),* and cat *(Felis catus).*

4. Two oviducts, one uterine body with two short horns, one cervix, and one vagina; e.g. cow *(Bos taurus)* and horse *(Equus caballus).*

5. Two oviducts, one uterine body without compartments, one cervix, and one vagina; e.g. primates.

The oviducts are generally highly convoluted tubes, of which the anterior end forms a funnel or infundibulum which lies close to the ovary in some species (rabbit, sheep, and man), or enclosed with the ovary (mouse and dog) by a fold of mesosalpinx which forms a capsule, called the ovarian *bursa.*

At the posterior end, where the oviduct enters the uterus, a number of different anatomical arrangements have been observed:

1. In marsupials only, the isthmus (just before the utero-tubal junction) is tortuous and has a wide lumen which is constricted at the posterior end.

2. The isthmus, which can be straight or tortuous, has a thick wall and a narrow lumen, is found in all eutheria with a bicornuate uterus. In most species it enters the side of the uterus where there are either villi or a sphincter (exceptions: cow, sheep) (Eckstein and Zuckerman, 1956). However, Edgar and Asdell (1960) found a marked flexure at the utero-tubal junction of sheep.

3. The tube enters the fundus and there are no villi or folds.

The oviduct is lined by a simple columnar, ciliated epithelium, with occasional goblet cells. There is an inner circular muscle and an outer longitudinal muscle layer. The uterus is surrounded by a serosa. The muscular myometrium consists of three indistinctly separated layers: an external longitudinal muscle, a vascular layer between the longitudinal ones, and the internal circular muscle layer. The endometrium, lining the inside of the ·uterus, consists of an epithelial inside layer and a glandular layer. The histology of the endometrium reflects the hormonal status of the animal, as we will discuss later. In certain bats (Vespertilionidae) sperm are stored in the uterus in a gelatinous matrix, whereas in others (Rhinolophidae) the sperm are stored in a ventral outpocketing of the vagina.

At the posterior end of the uterus, at the junction with the vagina, lies the cervix, which may be smooth or ridged, and is lined with columnar epithelium. The underlying mucosa contains large secretory goblet cells which secrete mucus.

The external genitalia consist of the clitoris, urethra, vaginal vestibule and the labia. Their respective size and development varies considerably among mammalian species. In the spotted hyena *(Crocuta crocuta)* the clitoris has the form of a penis and the urogenital canal runs through the clitoris so that the vagina passes through it (Asdell, 1964). In cats the clitoris contains cartilage and in sows it contains bone. The urethra may open either in the clitoris (e.g. in *Bassariscus astutus* and insectivore) or in the vagina or in the urogenital sinus; in primates it has a separate distal opening.

The outside of the vagina may have prominent skin folds or labia; only in women are there true labia majora and labia minora (Eckstein and Zuckerman, 1956). Marsupials have two lateral vaginas but parturition occurs through a temporary central vagina which develops at each parturition. In the rat kangaroo *(Potorous tridactylus)* birth takes place through the lateral vaginas (Asdell, 1964); the same is true for some more primitive marsupials (Sharman, 1959).

The epithelial lining of the vagina may reflect the stage of the reproductive cycle of the animal, e.g. in rats the epithelium is squamous during diestrus but is cornified during estrus (see Chapter 9).

The paired Bartholin's glands, which secrete mucus, open on the inner surface of the labia of nonprimates and labia minora of humans.

In a number of species, prostate glands are found in the females which are well developed, although they are not as big as in the corresponding males. Examples are the hedgehog *(Erinaceus europaeus),* rat, and eastern cottontail rabbit *(Sylvilagus floridanus).* For more complete listing see Price and Williams-Ashman (1961). In the rat, the incidence of females with prostate glands can be increased by selective breeding.

The reader interested in specific details of the anatomy of reproductive systems in different mammalian species should consult the paper by Eckstein and Zuckerman (1956).

Plate I, intended for reference, shows the reproductive systems of some of the experimental animals discussed.

PLATE I
Reproductive Systems in Different Classes of Vertebrates

1. Male lamprey *(Petromyzon marinus)*. *A* = testis.
2. Female lamprey *(Petromyzon marinus)*. Note the large ovary which almost completely fills the body cavity.
3. Male dogfish *(Squalus acanthias)*. *A* = testis. *B* = mesentery. *D* and *E* = ductus deferens. *F* and *G* = ampulla. *H* = urinary papilla. *I* = clasper.

PLATE I *(Continued)*

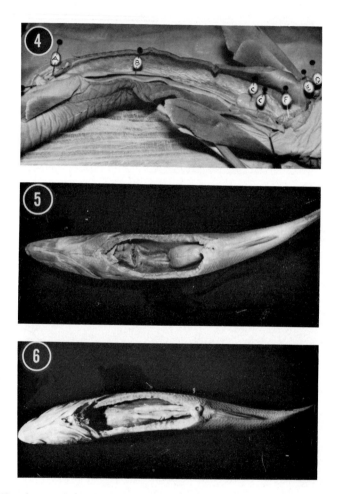

4. Female dogfish *(Squalus acanthias)*. *A* = uterus. *B* = oviduct. *C* = ovary. *F* = stomach.
5. Male yellow perch *(Perca flavescens)*. Note the large testis close to the cloacal opening.
6. Female yellow perch *(Perca flavescens)*. The two ovaries end posteriorly near the cloacal opening.

PLATE I *(Continued)*

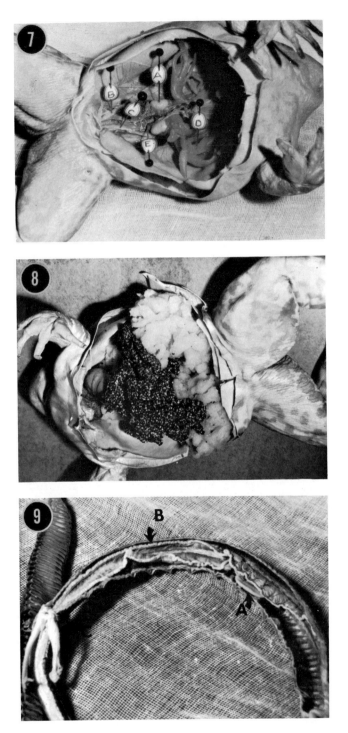

7. Male bullfrog *(Rana catesbeiana)*. *A* = testis. *B* and *C* = ductus deferens. *D* = fat body. *E* = kidney.
8. Female bullfrog *(Rana catesbeiana)*. Note the large ovary and the large oviduct. The walls of the oviduct of this specimen were extremely thick in comparison to other specimens.
9. Male garter snake *(Thamnophis* sp.)*. *A* = testis (the second testis had been removed). *B* = ductus deferens. *C* = hemipenis (dissected).

PLATE I *(Continued)*

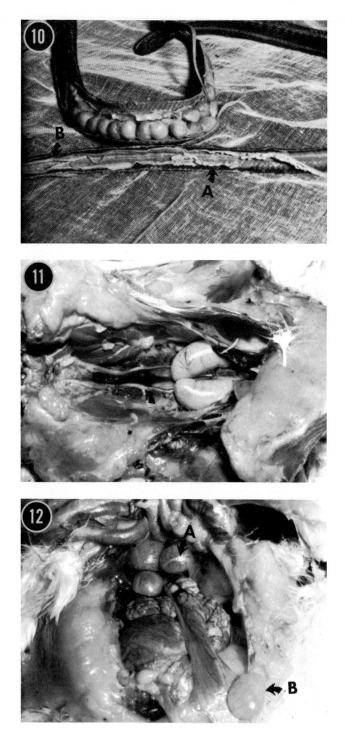

10. At the top is a pregnant garter snake *(Thamnophis sp.);* at bottom is a non-pregnant specimen. *A* = ovary. *B* = oviduct.

11. White Leghorn rooster. Arrow points to coiled ductus deferens.

12. White Leghorn laying hen. *A* = stigma on follicle. Oviduct is retracted posteriorly; *B* = cyst on wall of infundibulum (The cyst did not interfere with entry of the egg into the oviduct).

58

PLATE I *(Continued)*

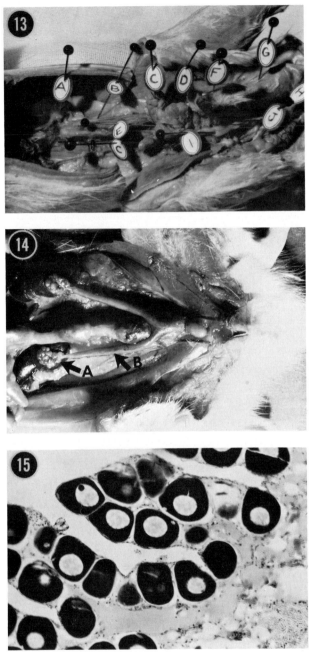

SCALE ⊢———⊣
            100 μ

13. Male rat. *A* = kidney. *B* = ureter. *C* = Seminal vesicle. *D* = urinary bladder. *E* = prostate. *G* = testis. *H* = epididymis. *I* = ductus deferens. *J* = bulbo-urethral gland.
14. Female rat. *A* = ovary with bursa. *B* = uterine horn.
15.* Cross section of the ovary of a lamprey (Hematoxylin-eosin stain).

───────────────

* Slides were bought from Turtox, Chicago, Illinois. The exact species is not known.

PLATE I *(Continued)*

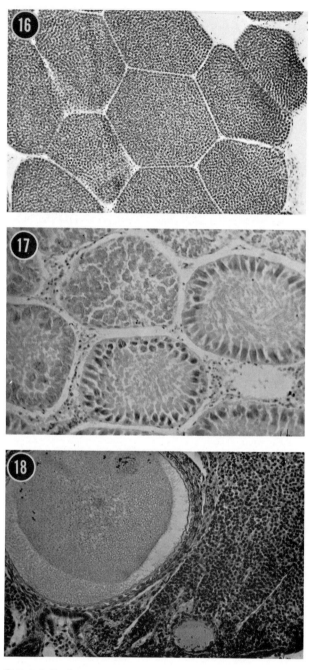

SCALE ⊢━━━┥
        100 μ

16.* Cross section of the testis of a lamprey. Note that germ cells in all lobules are in the same stage of spermatogenesis.

17. Section of the testis of a dogfish *(Squalus acanthias).* Note that in each tubule the germ cells are in the same stage of spermatogenesis but that there are differences among the tubules.

18. Section of the ovary of a dogfish *(Squalus acanthias).* Note the granulosa and thecal cell layers of the large follicle.

———————————

* Slides were bought from Turtox, Chicago, Illinois. The exact species is not known.

PLATE I *(Continued)*

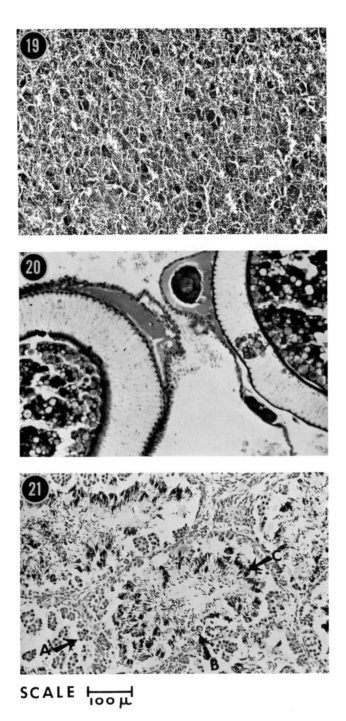

SCALE |——————| 100 μ

19. Section through the testis of a perch *(Perca flavescens)*. Note the small diameter of the tubules and the crowding of the germ cells.
20. Section of the ovary of a perch *(Perca flavescens)*. Note the large yolk droplets in the large follicle. The small, darkly stained follicle lacks these large droplets.
21. Section of the testis of a bullfrog *(Rana catesbeiana)*. *A* = cell nest with spermatogonia. *B* = cell nest with spermatids. *C* = sperm bundle.

61

PLATE I *(Continued)*

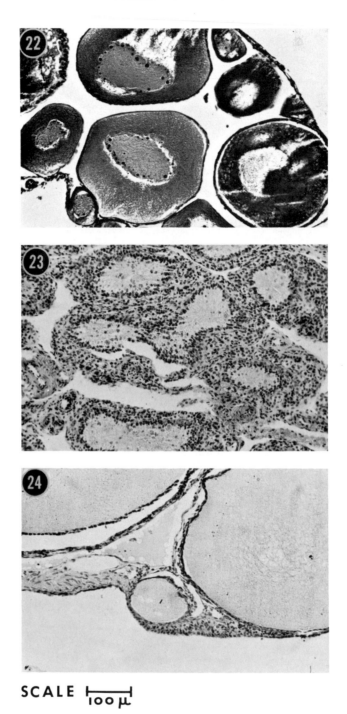

SCALE ⊢————⊣
100 μ

22. Section of the ovary of a bullfrog *(R. catesbeiana)*.
23.* Section of the testis of a turtle.
24.* Section of the ovary of a turtle. Note the layer of granulosa cells which has become detached from the follicular wall.

* Slides were bought from Turtox, Chicago, Illinois. The exact species is not known.

PLATE I   *(Continued)*

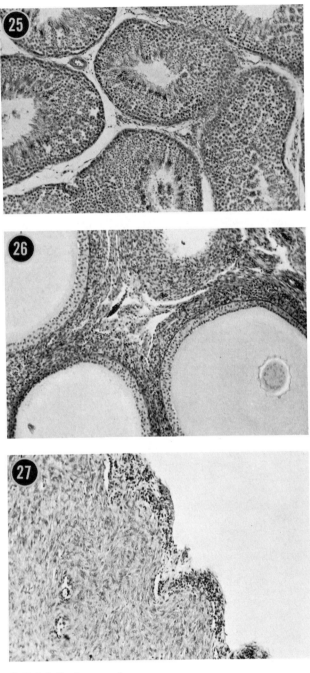

SCALE ⊢——⊣
      100 μ

25. Cross section of the testis of a mature White Leghorn rooster.
26. Cross section of the ovary of a laying White Leghorn hen. Compare with Figure 3-17 for identification of
     the follicular layers.
27. Section of a recently (less than 24 hours) ruptured follicle. Compare with numbers 28 and 30. Note the
     absence of large luteal cells.

63

PLATE I *(Continued)*

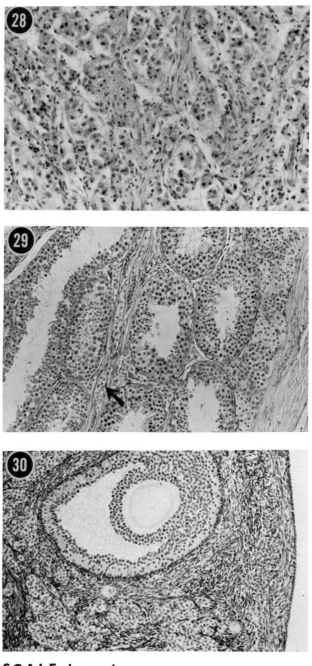

SCALE ⊢———⊣
100 μ

28. Section of a (luteal cell?) tumor from a chicken. (Slide from the collection of Dr. R. K. Cole, Department of Poultry Science, Cornell University.) Compare with numbers 27 and 30, and note the similarity to luteal cells of the rat.

29.* Cross section of the testis of a cat *(Felis catus)*. Arrow points to interstitial cells. Sperm bundles are in this section.

30.* Cross section of the ovary of a cat *(Felis catus)*. Mature follicle with antrum. See also Figure 3-24.

---

* Slides were bought from Turtox, Chicago, Illinois.

PLATE I *(Concluded)*

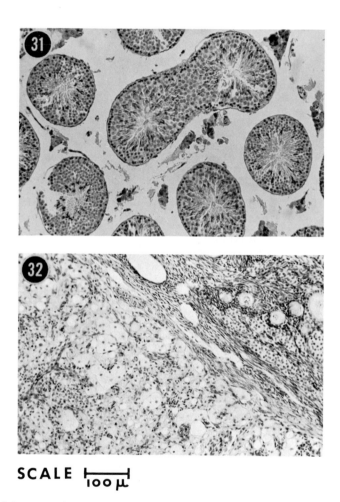

SCALE ⊢———⊣
100 µ

31. Cross section of the testis of a mouse *(Mus musculus)*. Sperm bundles are present. (Slide from collection of R. K. Coomes.)
32. Cross section of the ovary of the cat with corpus luteum on the left lower part of the picture. Compare with number 28.

REFERENCES

Albert, A. 1961. The mammalian testis. *In* W. C. Young (ed.): Sex and Internal Secretions. Williams and Wilkins, Baltimore, Vol. 1, pp. 305-365.

Arey, L. B. 1965. Developmental Anatomy. Ed. 7. W. B. Saunders Company, Philadelphia.

Asdell, S. A. 1946. *In* E. T. Engle (ed.): The Problem of Fertility. Princeton Univ. Press, p. 73.

Asdell, S. A. 1964. Patterns of Mammalian Reproduction. Ed. 2. Cornell University Press, Ithaca.

Bailey, R. J. 1936. The osteology and relationships of the phallostethid fishes. J. Morphol. *59*:453-478.

Ballard, W. W. 1964. Comparative Anatomy and Embryology. The Ronald Press Co., New York.

Bobr, L. W., Lorenz, F. W., and Ogasawara, F. X. 1964. Distribution of spermatozoa in the oviduct and fertility in domestic birds. I. Residence site of spermatozoa in fowl oviducts. J. Reprod. Fertil. *8*:39-47.

Bobr, L. W., Ogasawara, F. X. and Lorenz, F. W. 1964. Distribution of spermatozoa in the oviduct and fertility in domestic birds. II. Transport of spermatozoa in the fowl oviduct. J. Reprod. Fertil. *8*:49-58.

Böhlke, J. E., and Springer, V. G. 1961. A review of the Atlantic species of the clinid fish Starksia. Proc. Acad. Nat. Sci. Philadelphia *113*:29-60.

Bolin, R. L. 1944. A review of the marine cottid fishes of California. Stanford Icthyol. Bull. *3*:1-109.

Breder, C. M., Jr., and Rosen, D. E. 1966. Modes of Reproduction in Fishes. The National History Press, Garden City, N. Y.

Bretschneider, L. H., and Duyvené de Wit, J. J. 1947. Sexual Endocrinology of Non-mammalian Vertebrates. Elsevier Publishing Co., New York.

Busson-Mabillot, M. S. 1966. Présence d'une théque interne glandulaire, dans le follicule primaire de la lamproie de Planer (*L. planeri*, Block), vertébré cyclostome. C. R. Acad. Sci. *262*:117-118.

Chieffi, G. 1962. Endocrine aspects of reproduction in elasmobranch fishes. Gen. Comp. Endocrinol. Suppl. *1*:275-285.

Cowles, R. B., and Nordstrom, A. 1946. A possible avian analogue of the scrotum. Science *104*:586-587.

De Wolfe, B. B., and Telford, S. R. 1966. Lipid-positive cells in the testis of the lizard *Cnemidophorus tigris.* Copeia *3*:590-592.

Dodd, J. M. 1960. Gonadal and gonadotrophic hormones in lower vertebrates. *In* A. S. Parkes (ed.): Marshall's Physiology of Reproduction. Longmans Green & Co. Ltd., London. 1(pt. 2), pp. 415-582.

Eckstein, P., and Zuckerman, S. 1956. Morphology of the reproductive tract. *In* A. S. Parkes (ed.): Marshall's Physiology of Reproduction. Longmans Green & Co. Ltd., London. 1(pt.1), pp. 43-155.

Edgar, D. G., and Asdell, S. A. 1960. The valve-like action of the utero-tubal junction of the ewe. J. Endocrinol. *21*:315-320.

Eggert, B. 1931. Die Geschlechtsorgane der Gobiiformes und Blenniformes. Z. Wiss. Zool. *139*:249-558.

Ellenberger, W., and Baum, H. 1932. Handbuch der Vergleichenden. Anatomie der Haustiere. Ed. 17. Springer, Berlin.

Forbes, T. R. 1961. Endocrinology of reproduction in cold-blooded vertebrates. *In* W. C. Young (ed.): Sex and Internal Secretions. Williams & Wilkins Co., Baltimore, Vol. 2, pp. 1-87.

Fox, W. 1956. Seminal receptacles of snakes. Anat. Rec. *124*:519-539.

Fox, W. 1963. Special tubules for sperm storage in female lizards. Nature *198*:500-501.

Gérard, P. 1954. Organes uro-génitaux. *In* P. Grassé (ed.): Traité de Zoologie. Masson et Cie, Paris, Vol. 13, pp. 974-1043.

Gilbert, A. B. 1965. Innervation of the ovarian follicle of the domestic hen. Quart. J. Exp. Physiol. *50*:437-445.

Gilbert, P. W., and Heath, G. W. 1955. The functional anatomy of the claspers and siphon sacs in the spiny dogfish, (*Squalus acanthias*) and smooth dogfish (*Mustelus canis*). Anat. Rec. *121*:433 (abstract).

Gorbman, A., and Bern, H. A. 1962. A Textbook of Comparative Endocrinolgy. John Wiley & Sons Inc., New York.

Grigg, G. W. 1957. The structure of stored sperm in the hen and the nature of the release mechanism. Poultry Sci. *36*:450-451.

Harrison, R. J. 1962. The structure of the ovary. *In* S. Zuckerman (ed.): The Ovary. Academic Press Inc., New York, Vol. 1, pp. 143-187.

Henderson, N. E. 1967. The urinary and genital systems of trout. J. Fish. Res. Bd. Canada *24*:447-449.

Herin, R. A., Booth, N. H., and Johnson, R. M. 1960. Thermoregulatory effects of abdominal air sacs on spermatogenesis in domestic fowl. Amer. J. Physiol. *198*:1343-1345.

Hoar, W. S. 1955. Reproduction in teleost fish. Mem. Soc. Endocrinol. *4*:5-22.

Hoffman, R. A. 1963. Gonads, spermatic ducts, and spermatogenesis in the reproductive system of male toadfish, *Opsanus tau.* Chesapeake Sci. *4*:21-29.

Hubbs, C. L. 1918. A revision of the viviparous perches. Proc. Biol. Soc. Washington *31*:9-14.

Hubbs, C. L. 1938. Fishes from the caves of Yucatan. Publ. Carnegie Instit. Washington *491*:261-295.

Hutt, F. B. 1964. Animal Genetics. The Ronald Press Co., New York.

Ingram, D. L. 1962. Atresia. *In* S. Zuckerman (ed.): The ovary. Academic Press Inc., New York, Vol. 2, pp. 247-273.

Iwasawa, H., and Asai, O. 1964. Occurrence of testis-ova in adult frogs. Zool. Mag., Tokyo *73*:281-285.

Kabat, C., Buss, I. O., and Meyer, R. K. 1948. The use of ovulated follicles in determining eggs laid by the ring-necked pheasant. J. Wildlife Manage. *12*:399-416.

Kumaran, J. D. S., and Turner, C. W. 1949. Endocrine activity of the testis of the White Plymouth Rock. Poultry Sci. *28*:636-640.

Leach, B. J., and Conaway, C. H. 1963. The origin and fate of polyovular follicles in the striped skunk. J. Mammal. *44*:67-74.

Liem, K. F. 1963. Sex reversal as a natural process in Synbranchiform fish, *Monopterus albus.* Copeia 305-312.

Lowe, C. H., and Goldberg, S. 1966. Variation in the circumtesticular Leydig cell tunic of Teiid lizards *(Cnemidophorus* and *Ameiva).* J. Morphol. *119*:277-282.

Lucas, A. M., and Stettenheim, P. R. 1965. Avian anatomy. *In* H. E. Biester and L. H. Schwarte (eds.): Diseases of Poultry. Ed. 5. Iowa State Univ. Press, Ames, pp. 1-59.

Marshall, A. J. 1960. Reproduction in male bony fish. Zool. Soc. London Symp. *1*:137-150.

Marshall, A. J., and Coombs, C. J. F. 1957. The interaction of environmental, internal and behavioral factors in the rook, *Corvus f. frugilegus Linnaeus.* Proc. Zool. Soc. London *128*:545-589.

Matthews, L. H. 1950. Reproduction in the basking shark, *Cetorhinus maximus* (Gunner). Phil. Trans. Roy. Soc. London *234*:247-316.

Mellinger, J. 1965. Stades de la spermatogenèse chez *Scyliorhinus caniculus* (L): Description, donnés histochimiques, variations normales et expérimentales. Z. Zellforsch. *67*:653-673.

Mohsen, T. 1961. Sur la présence d'un organe copulateur interne, très évolué chez *Skiffia lermae,* Cyprinodonte Goodeidae. C. R. Aca. Sci. *252*: 3327-3329.

Mossman, H. W. 1966. The rodent ovary. Zool. Soc. London Symp. *15*:455-470.

Mossman, H. W., and Judas, I. 1949. Accessory corpora lutea, lutein cell origin, and the ovarian cycle in the Canadian porcupine. Amer. J. Anat. *85*:1-39.

Nalbandov, A. V. 1964. Reproductive Physiology. Ed. 2. W. H. Freeman & Co., San Francisco.

Nalbandov, A. V., and James, M. F. 1949. The blood-vascular system of the chicken ovary. Amer. J. Anat. *85*:347-377.

Nishiyama, H. 1955. Studies on the accessory reproductive organs in the cock. J. Agric. Fac. Kyushu Univ. *10*:277-305.

Noble, G. K. 1954. (Reprint of 1931 ed.) The Biology of the Amphibia. Dover Publications.

Pearson, O. P. 1949. Reproduction of a South American rodent, the mountain viscacha. Amer. J. Anat. *84*:143-173.

Price, D., and Williams-Ashman, H. G. 1961. The accessory reproductive glands of mammals. *In* W. C. Young (ed.): Sex and Internal Secretions. Williams & Wilkins Co., Baltimore, Vol. 1, pp. 366-448.

Regan, C. T. 1916. The morphology of the cyprinodont fishes of the subfamily Phallostethinae, with descriptions of a new genus and two new species. Proc. Zool. Soc. London, pp. 1-26.

Romanoff, A. L., and Romanoff, A. J. 1949. The Avian Egg. John Wiley & Sons Inc., New York.

Rosen, D. E., and Bailey, R. M. 1963. The poeciliid fishes (Cyprinodontiformes), their structure, zoogeography and systematics. Bull. Amer. Mus. Nat. Hist. *126*:1-176.

Seliger, W. G., Blair, A. J., and Mossman, H. W.

1966. Differentiation of adrenal cortex-like tissue at the hilum of the gonads in response to adrenalectomy. Amer. J. Anat. *118*:615-629.

Sharman, G. B. 1959. Marsupial reproduction. Monographiae Biologicae. *8*:332-368.

Smith, C. L. 1965. The patterns of sexuality and the classification of Serranid fishes. Novitates Amer. Mus. *2207*:1-20.

Smith, K. E., and H. P. Clemens. 1963. The morphology of the testes and accessory reproductive glands of the catfishes (Ictaluridae). Copeia pp. 606-611.

Tavolga, W. N. 1955. Effects of gonadectomy and hypophysectomy on prespawning behavior in males of the gobiid fish, Bathygobius soporator. Physiol. Zool. *28*:218-233.

Turner, C. D., 1966. General Endocrinology. Ed. 4. W. B. Saunders Company, Philadelphia.

Turner, C. L. 1946. Male secondary sexual characters of *Dinematichthys iluocoeteoides.* Copeia pp. 92-96.

Turner, C. L. 1948. The gonopodium of the viviparous fish *Jenynsia lineata.* Anat. Rec. *101*:675-676 (Abstr.).

van Drimmelen, G. C. 1951. Artificial insemination of birds by the intraperitoneal route. Onderstepoort J. Vet. Res. *Suppl. 1.*

Verma, O. P., and Cherms, F. L. 1964. Observations on the oviducts of turkeys. Avian Diseases *8*:19-26.

von Ihering, R. 1937. Oviducal fertilization in the South American catfish, *Trachycorystes.* Copeia pp. 202-205.

Waites, G. M. H., and Moule, C. R. 1961. Relation of vascular heat exchange to temperature regulation in the testis of the ram. J. Reprod. Fertil. *2*:213-224.

Watanabe, M. 1960. Cottidae. Tokyo News Service Ltd., Tokyo.

Weisel, G. F. 1949. The seminal vesicles and testes of Gillichthys, a marine teleost. Copeia pp. 101-110.

Wilkinson, R. F., Jr. 1966. Seasonal and hormonal changes in the oviducts of *Diadophis punctatus.* Diss. Abstr. *26*:5612.

Williams, D. D. 1958a. A histological study of the effects of subnormal temperature on the testis of the fowl. Anat. Rec. *130*:225-241.

Williams, D. D. 1958b. Effect of heat on transplanted testis material of the fowl. Transplant Bull. *5*:32-35.

Witschi, E. 1956. Development of Vertebrates. W. B. Saunders Co., Philadelphia.

Wyburn, G. M., and Baillie, A. H. 1966. Some observations on the fine structure and histochemistry of the ovarian follicle of the fowl. *In* C. Horton Smith and E. C. Amoroso (eds.): Physiology of the Domestic Fowl. Oliver and Boyd Ltd., London, pp. 30-38.

Wyburn, G. M., Aitken, R. N. C., and Johnston, H. S. 1965. The ultrastructure of the zona radiata of the ovarian follicle of the domestic fowl. J. Anat. *99*:469-484.

Wyburn, G. M., Johnston, H. S., and Aitken, R. N. C. 1966. Fate of the granulosa cells in the hen's follicle. Z. Zellforsch. *72*:53-65.

Chapter 4

Intersexes

In most classes of vertebrates intersexes occur with various frequencies. It is useful to give definitions before we continue. The terminology is from Atz (1964).

Hermaphroditism — the existence of male and female gonadal tissue in the same individual. The following types of functional hermaphroditism can be distinguished: in *synchronous hermaphroditism* the individual is capable of functioning as a male and female at the same time; in *protandrous hermaphroditism* the individual functions first as a male and later as a female, and in *protogynous hermaphroditism* the individual functions first as a female and later as a male.

Rudimentary hermaphroditism means that the animal functions either as a male or as a female, but still has testicular and ovarian tissue.

Sex reversal means that an animal that has one type of gonadal tissue, e.g. ovarian, in the absence of recognizable testicular tissue, changes so that it has recognizable tissue of the opposite sex, i.e. testicular tissue.

Sex inversion means that an animal belonging to one sex acquires characteristics belonging to the other sex, but without acquiring gonadal tissue of that sex. The term *pseudohermaphrodite* has been used for animals which have gonads of one sex but have retained secondary sex organs or secondary sex characters of the other sex.

We will discuss here, for the sake of brevity, only hermaphroditism which occurs in adults.

As was discussed in Chapter 2, in cyclostomes and teleost fishes the gonad is of cortical origin and no medulla exists. It may, therefore, be preferable to discuss the occurrence of hermaphroditism in these two groups first. In the hag fish (*Myxine glutinosa*) the tertiary sex ratio is very low. Atz (1964) states that only 19 males were found among 4000 specimens. This kind of observation was probably one of the bases for assuming that functional hermaphroditism is prevalent among cyclostomes. Recent investigations have shown that although rudimentary hermaphroditism occurred in about 13 percent of the *Myxine glutinosa* investigated, functional hermaphroditism did not occur.

In teleost fishes hermaphroditism has been reported more fequently than in any other group of vertebrates, but the frequency with which it occurs in each species is not well known. Atz (1964) gives an exhaustive listing of the occurrence of abnormal and normal hermaphroditism in different orders. The reader should refer to this important review for details about the distribution of hermaphroditism.

Only the groups in which synchronous, protandrous, or protogynous hermaphroditism occurs will be discussed.

They are as follows:

1. *Rivulus marmoratus,* of the family Cyprinodontidae, in which self-fertilization occurs (Harrington, 1961); the animal, incidentally, exhibits female secondary sex characters.

2. An abnormal case of self-fertilization in the guppy (*Poecilia reticulata*).

3. The normally occurring functional

hermaphroditism in the family Serranidae, in which synchronous and protogynous hermaphroditism occur. In *Serranus subligarius*, the belted sandfish, self-fertilization may occur but cross-fertilization can also take place.

4. The protandrous and protogynous hermaphroditism which occurs in the family Sparidae (rudimentary hermaphroditism also occurs in this family).

5. The protandrous hermaphroditism in *Cociella crocodila* of the family Platycephalidae.

6. The protogynous hermaphroditism of the family Maenidae.

7. The protogynous hermaphroditism which occurs in the Labridae (wrasses).

8. The protandrous hermaphroditism in *Monopterus albus,* of the order Synbranchiformes.

Atz (1964) stresses that too little is known about the utility of hermaphroditism for fishes living in different environments to provide an adequate explanation for its occurrence in different species.

The embryology of the gonads of elasmobranchs and tetrapods is, as we have discussed, similar in that the indifferent gonad consists of a medulla and cortex:

Hermaphroditism is rare among elasmobranchs; a few specimens have been found in *Scyliorhinus stellaris* and *Squalus acanthias,* whereas in *Notorhynchus* sp. and *Hexanchus* sp. it has been reported that a rudimentary testis is regularly present with the functional ovary.

In amphibia, hermaphrodites have been reported from time to time (Kolter, 1963), but there are no species in which functional hermaphroditism is a normal occurrence. In Chapter 2 we discussed the various experimental techniques which have produced intersexes of one type or another. For more details, the reader may want to consult Foote's review (1964).

Among reptilians, hermaphrodites have been reported in the European pond turtle *(Emys europea)* and the Greek tortoise *(Testudo graeca).* In both species an ovotestis was found in the presence of a testis. In both the painted turtle *(Chrysemys marginata)* and *Pseudemys troosti* a case has been reported of a specimen which had bilateral ovotestes with sperm and ova present (Forbes, 1964).

The most frequently cited cases of hermaphroditism in birds have been those of sex-reversal in chickens; the animals first laid eggs and then sired offspring. The only well-documented case of such a "sex reversal" was reported by Crew (1923). Autopsy revealed that the animal contained two testes and a diseased ovary. This case of true hermaphroditism is often confused with the sex-reversal which occurs after removal of the functional ovary (either by surgery or pathological agents). In such cases the animal, which first looks like a female, starts to take on secondary male sex characters, e.g. male type of feathers appear after molting (not as a result of the presence of male sex hormone, but rather of the absence of female sex hormone), and the male type of comb, spurs, crowing, and sexual behavior are noted. In these animals the normally undeveloped right gonad develops into an ovary or ovotestis. The earlier in life the left ovary is removed, the higher the incidence of ovaries (see van Tienhoven, 1961 for review). If an ovotestis develops, it may contain spermatozoa as well as ovulatory size follicles. However, the sperm cannot reach the cloaca because no ductuli efferentes and no ductus deferens are present.

The endocrinology of the development of the right gonad of the female has been studied in some detail. Kornfeld and Nalbandov (1954), Kornfeld (1958), Taber, and Salley (1954), Taber et al. (1958), and Taber et al. (1964) have presented evidence that estrogen in physiological doses (too small to stimulate the oviduct) inhibits development of the right gonad. It thus appears that estrogen secretion by the ovary can inhibit development of the rudimentary gonad in the intact female. Gardner et al. (1964) have, however, obtained inhibition of the rudimentary gonad by using a steroid-free extract of the ovary.

The inhibitory effect of estrogen on the development of the right gonad is apparently a direct effect. This conclusion is based on the observation that neither gonadotropins nor crude chicken pituitary extracts stimulate the development of the rudiment of intact, hypophysectomized, or estrogen-treated ovariectomized pullets (see van Tienhoven, 1961, for review). Hypophysectomy, to be sure, inhibits the development, but this need not be a specific effect of the lack of gonadotropins. It might be the result of a lack of thyroid hormone, adrenal cortical hormones, or a combination of these. Prolactin injections inhibit the development of the rudimentary gonad.

The age at which ovariectomy is performed affects the differentiation of the rudiment. If the operation is performed before the pullet is 30 days old, the right gonad develops into a testis or ovotestis, whereas ovariectomy at a later age results in a greater incidence of ovotestes and ovaries. This difference in differentiation may be the result of the longer time the estrogen has to act on the rudiment. Estrogen tends to inhibit the medullary tissue more than the cortical tissue; thus, after 30 days there might be more cortical tissue available, which would tend to make the gonad develp into an ovary.

The rudimentary gonad does not develop after ovariectomy in some species, e.g. turkeys, ring-necked pheasants, bobwhite quail (*Colinus virginianus*), and starlings; hypertrophy of the rudimentary gonad after ovariectomy occurs rarely in the duck (see Taber, 1964).

No cases of functional hermaphroditism have been reported in mammals, but a number of cases of intersexuality, including rudimentary hermaphroditism, have been found. Biggers and McFeely (1966) have reviewed these cases for domestic mammals and Armstrong (1964)

and Jacobs (1966) have done the same for man.

Among domestic mammals, the following cases of intersexuality have been studied most extensively:

1. Pseudohermaphroditic goats, all of which have testicular tissue, but the external genitalia vary from almost normal male to almost normal female (Biggers and McFeely, 1966). Male pseudohermaphrodites are always polled (the gene for polled is dominant) and the condition may be the result of a pleiotropic effect of the polled gene or of linkage between polled and a recessive gene for pseudohermaphroditism. This question has not been answered definitively. Genetically these male pseudohermaphrodites are females (sex chromatin present, karyotype XX), with one exception in which the XY has been reported (see Biggers and McFeely, 1966). In the majority of these male pseudohermaphrodites we would thus find testicular development in the absence of the Y chromosome (Biggers and McFeely, 1966).

2. Among pigs, hermaphrodites and pseudohermaphrodites have been reported, but in only a few cases has the genetic sex been determined. Biggers and McFeely (1966) mention three cases of male pseudohermaphroditism in which the genetic sex was $36 + XX$.

3. In cats the gene for yellow color is on the X chromosome; this gene is epistatic to the colors black and tabby, which are located on the autosomes. The allele ($^{y+}$) to yellow allows the expression of black and tabby. A tortoise-shell female cat is X^yX^{y+}; a male tortoise-shell cat would have to be $X^yX^{y+}Y$. In fact, a male tortoise-shell cat with the XXY constitution has been found (see Biggers and McFeely, 1966). In another case, a sterile male tortoise-shell cat was found to be an XY/XXY mosaic. Another mosaic was 38 XX/57 XXY. Exceptionally, fertile male tortoise-shell cats occur. In two cases the karyotype was 38 XY. The exact manner in which the tortoise-shell color is

Table 4-1. Chromosomal Intersexes in Man

NAME OF SYNDROME	KARYOTYPE	APPEARANCE
Turner's	45/XO	Streak gonad; hypoplastic ovarian tissue; uterus.
	46/XX	Streak gonad of hypoplastic ovarian tissue; uterus.
	46/XX	Gonadal agenesis; no uterus.
Triple XXX	47/XXX	Normal; primary or secondary amenorrhoea; fertile.
Klinefelter, Chromatin-positive	48/XXXY; 49/XXXXY; 46/47 XY/XXX	Apparent male; small testis; azoospermia; hyalinization of seminiferous tubular membrane.
	46/47XX/XXY; 46/ XX	Adenomatous clumping of Leydig cells; female type pubic hair.
Klinefelter, Chromatin-negative	46/XY	Small testes, female type pubic hair; majority of seminiferous tubules not hyalinized, some spermatogonia present; Leydig cells normal.
	XXY	Testes normal size, no spermatogenesis; external genitalia usually normal; average I.Q. below average of normal population.
	XXXY	Testes small; I.Q. lower than XXY.
	XXYY	Similar to XXY.
	47/XYY	Phenotype not clearly established (lack of sufficient number of cases).
	XXXX	Mentally defective; normal sex characteristics; normal menstruation.
	XO/XY	Female–features similar to Turner's syndrome; Male–normal.
Hermaphroditism	XX	Testicular and ovarian tissue present.
	XX/XY	Testicular and ovarian tissue present.

References: Armstrong, 1964; Jacobs, 1966.

caused in these cats is not established. They could be either $X^yY/X^{y+}Y$ or XY/XXY mosaics.

Cases of true hermaphroditism in domestic mammals have been reported for different species (see Hafez and Jainudeen, 1966), but not enough is known about the genetic constitution of these animals to explain their occurrence.

Intersexes among humans have been studied extensively. A number of the sex chromosome abnormalities and the effects on the phenotype have been listed in Table 4-1. It can be seen that hermaphrodites either have an XX constitution or are XX/XY mosaics.

REFERENCES

Armstrong, C. N. 1964. Intersexuality in man. *In* C. N. Armstrong and A. J. Marshall (eds.): Intersexuality in Vertebrates Including Man. Academic Press Inc., New York, pp. 349-393.

Atz, J. W. 1964. Intersexuality in fishes. *In* C. N. Armstrong and A. J. Marshall (eds.): Inter-sexuality in Vertebrates Including Man. Academic Press Inc., New York, pp. 145-232.

Biggers, J. D., and McFeely, R. A. 1966. Intersexuality in domestic mammals. Advances in Reprod. Physiol. *1*:29-59.

Crew, F. A. E. 1923. Studies in intersexuality. II. Sex reversal in the fowl. Proc. Roy. Soc. (B) *95*:256-278.

Foote, C. L. 1964. Intersexuality in amphibians. *In* C. N. Armstrong and A. J. Marshall (eds.): Intersexuality in Vertebrates Including Man. Academic Press Inc., New York, pp. 233-272.

Forbes, T. R. 1964. Intersexuality in reptiles. *In* C. N. Armstrong and A. J. Marshall (eds.): Intersexuality in Vertebrates Including Man. Academic Press Inc., New York, pp. 273-283.

Gardner, W. A., Wood, H. A., Jr., and Taber, E. 1964. Demonstration of a nonestrogenic gonadal inhibitor produced by the ovary of the Brown Leghorn. Gen. Comp. Endocrinol. *4*: 673-683.

Hafez, E. S. E., and Jainudeen, M. R. 1966. Inter-sexuality in farm mammals. Anim. Breed. Abstr. *34*:1-15.

Harrington, R. W., Jr. 1961. Oviparous hermaphro-ditic fish with internal self-fertilization. Science *134*:1749-1750.

Jacobs, P. A. 1966. Abnormalities of the sex chromosomes in man. Advances in Reprod. Physiol. *1*:61-91.

Kolter, P. C. 1963. A hermaphroditic bullfrog. Turtox News *41*:290-293.

Kornfeld, W. 1958. Endocrine influences upon the

growth of the rudimentary gonad of fowl. Anat. Rec. *130*:619-637.

Kornfeld, W., and Nalbandov, A. V. 1954. Endocrine influences on the development of the rudimentary gonad of fowl. Endocrinology *55*:751-761.

Taber, E. 1964. Intersexuality in birds. *In* C. N. Armstrong and A. J. Marshall (eds.): Intersexuality in Vertebrates Including Man. Academic Press Inc., New York, pp. 285-310.

Taber, E., and Salley, K. W. 1954. The effects of sex hormones on the development of the right gonad in female fowl. Endocrinology *54*:415-424.

Taber, E., Claytor, M., Knight, J., Flowers, J., Gambrell, D., and Ayers, C. 1958. Some effects of sex hormones and homologous gonadotrophins on the early development of the rudimentary gonad in fowl. Endocrinology *63*:435-448.

Taber, E., Knight, J. S., Ayers, C., and Fishburne, J. I., Jr. 1964. Some of the factors controlling growth and differentiation of the right gonad in female domestic fowl. Gen. Comp. Endocrinol. *4*:343-352.

van Tienhoven, A. 1961. Endocrinology of reproduction in birds. *In* W. C. Young (ed.): Sex and Internal Secretions. Williams & Wilkins Co., Baltimore, pp. 1088-1169.

Chapter 5

The Testis

ANDROGEN SECRETION

In Chapter 3 the anatomy and histology of the testis were reviewed, and mention was made of the presence or absence of Leydig cells, which presumably secrete androgens. A more detailed discussion of the methods used in order to show that the testes do indeed secrete androgens is, however, in order.

Evidence that the testis of a particular species secretes androgens can be direct or indirect. For instance, the effectiveness of replacement therapy in correcting the effects of castration indicates that the testes probably secrete androgens, but does not give any information about the chemical nature of the androgens secreted. Similarly, stimulation of the Leydig cells and the correlated increase in the size or activity of secondary sex organs or secondary sex characters are only indirect kinds of evidence. The presence of a hormone in the extract of the testes is more acceptable evidence, although it is not always possible to find a hormone in the spermatic vein even when it is present in the testicular extract. Such is the case, for instance, with estrogen in the dog testis (Eik-Nes and Hall, 1965). The presence of a hormone in the peripheral blood, or even better, a higher concentration of the hormone in the blood of the spermatic vein than in the spermatic artery, is the most convincing kind of evidence of androgen secretion.

There is no direct evidence that testes of cyclostomes secrete androgens; castration has not been performed successfully because the operation is difficult to per-

form. However, secondary sexual characters fail to develop after hypophysectomy, which, among other things, removes the gonadotropins which stimulate androgen secretion in higher vertebrates (Larsen, 1965). Administration of testosterone causes swelling of the labia, a phenomenon normally associated with sexual maturity.

In elasmobranchs, castration is also difficult to perform and animals survive only one month (Dodd et al., 1960). In successfully castrated animals secondary sex characters are not affected. Idler and Truscott (1966) have isolated testosterone from the blood of *Raja radiata* and *R. ocellata.* The free testosterone values were 2.8 to 10.2 μg./100 ml. and 2.2 to 20.8 μg./100 ml. for *R. radiata* and *R. ocellata,* respectively, whereas the testosterone glucuronide concentration for *R. radiata* was 4.3 to 6.7 μg./100 ml. Chieffi and Lupo (1961) isolated testosterone from testes of *Scyliorhinus stellaris.* The injection of testosterone propionate stimulated the growth of the claspers of the thorny skate *(R. radiata).* These experiments strongly support the hypothesis that the testes of elasmobranch fishes can secrete androgens.

The classic experiments of ablation and replacement therapy have been carried out on a number of species of teleosts (Table 5-1). The maximal development of the interstitial cells of the testes of the three-spined stickleback *(Gasterosteus aculeatus)* is correlated with full nuptial color. Extracts of salmon testes contain androgen, as revealed by bioassay techniques (Forbes, 1961). The peripheral blood of the sockeye salmon, *Oncorhynchus nerka,*

**Table 5-1. Effect of Castration and/or Androgen Administration
on Secondary Sex Characters of Teleosts**

SPECIES	TREATMENT	OBSERVATION
Salmonidae:		
Salmo salar	Castration	Sexual behavior is lost
Cyprinidae:		
Carassius sp.	Castration	Pearl organ regresses
Acheilognathus sp.	Castration	Nuptial color does not develop
Gasterosteidae:		
Gasterosteus aculeatus	Castration	Nuptial color does not develop
		No decrease in kidney tubule diameter
		No mucus secretion by kidney
		Lack of sexual behavior (nest building)
Cyprinodontidae:		
Oryzias sp.	Castration	Genital papilla regresses
		Nuptial color does not develop
		Sexual dimorphic color disappears
	Androgen administration to ♀	Reappearance of male sexual behavior
Poeciliidae:		
Gambusia sp.	Castration	Gonopodium regresses
	Androgen administration to ♂̶	Gonopodium develops
Xiphophorus helleri	Castration	Position in social hierarchy is lost
	Androgen administration to ♀	Gonopodium, sword and male color develop
	Androgen administration to ♂̶	Reappearance of male sexual behavior
Poecilia sp.	Androgen administration to ♀	Gonopodium develops
	Androgen administration to ♂̶	Reappearance of male sexual behavior
Platypoecilus sp.	Androgen administration to ♀	Gonopodium develops
Mollienesia sp.	Androgen administration to ♀	Gonopodium develops
Embiotocidae:		
Ditrema temmincki	Androgen administration to ♀	Elongation of seventh–tenth anal fin ray; thickening of anterior part of anal fin.
Cichlidae:		
Tilapia sp.	Castration	Genital papilla regresses
Gobiidae:		
Bathygobius soporator	Castration	Seminal vesicle regresses; no combat behavior; courted ♂, gravid and non-gravid ♀

♀ = intact female; ♂̶ = gonadectomized male; ♂ = intact male
References: Aronson, 1957; Atz, 1957; Dodd, Evennett and Goddard, 1960; Ishii, 1960; Forbes, 1961; Hoar, 1957a, 1957b; and van Oordt, 1963.

contains testosterone during the breeding season (Grajcer and Idler, 1963). There is thus rather good evidence that teleost testes are capable of secreting androgens.

In amphibia, ablation and replacement therapy techniques indicate that the testes secrete androgens. However, the source of androgen secretion within the testes is a matter of controversy. The Leydig cells show a definite seasonal cycle, e.g. in *Rana fusca* and *Rana esculenta*, but at the time of maximal Leydig cell activity, as judged by histological methods, the secondary sex characteristics are reduced (van Oordt, 1963). However, Lofts (1964) found

in *R. esculenta* and *R. temporaria* that the presence of *secretory droplets* in the Leydig cells was correlated with the development of secondary sex characters. In *Rana pipiens, R. esculenta*, and *Xenopus laevis*, histochemical evidence indicates production of ketosteroids (van Oordt, 1963). Della Corte and Cosenza (1965) were not able to detect androgens in extracts of *Triturus cristatus*, although 17-β-estradiol and progesterone were found. Chieffi (1962) reported the isolation of progesterone and of a trace of 17-β-estradiol from testes of *Bufo vulgaris*, but did not report on any androgens which might have been recovered.

For reptilia, the same problem as encountered for the amphibia exists. In some species there is a good correlation between development of the Leydig cells and secondary sex characters, e.g. *Lacerta*, whereas in others, e.g. the spiny-tailed night lizard *(Xantusia vigilis)*, no changes occur in the interstitial cells at the time the sex characters develop; this may mean that androgens in such species are secreted by the adrenals. Callard (1966) found, after incubation of the testis of the snake *(Natrix sipedon pictiventris)* with 16³H pregnenolone, that radioactive testosterone and progesterone could be extracted from the medium. However, the conversion to testosterone was only about 0.005 to 0.02 percent, whereas that to progesterone was 1.85 ± 0.16 percent.

Marshall (1955) states that there is a definite correlation between the interstitial cell activity and the sexual activity of birds. However, since the cycle of the Leydig cells is rather complicated, the view had been held that there was an inverse relationship between interstitial cell and sexual activity. In the young passerine bird the Leydig cells are heavily impregnated with lipids before the bird leaves the nest; after maturity and during the reproductive season the Leydig cells lose their lipids; at this time spermatogenesis and sexual behavior occur. The expanding tubules have dispersed the Leydig cells, which, after being exhausted, disintegrate. After the breeding season is over the tubules fill with lipids and a new interstitium forms.

Benoit (1950) has presented evidence that selective destruction of the germinal epithelium by x-rays (so that only the Leydig cells are maintained) does not affect comb size of chickens. The concentration of birefringent crystals in the Leydig cells of young cockerels is correlated with the increase in comb size (Kumaran and Turner, 1949).

Arrington et al. (1952) implanted pieces of frozen testes at the base of the comb of cockerels and into the seminal vesicles of castrated rats. The combs of the cockerels showed an androgenic response, indicating that the testis contains androgen. However, the seminal vesicles of the rat gave an ambiguous response. Connell et al. (1966), upon incubation of the testes of two-day-old chicks, found that acetate-C^{14} is incorporated into testosterone and androstenedione, and that either LH injection of the donor chicks or LH addition to the medium increases the incorporation of acetate. The ratio of testosterone to androstenedione produced by control testes was 2:3; after treatment of the chick with LH this ratio increased to 5:3, but after addition of LH to the medium the ratio dropped to 1:1. The testes also produce dehydro*epi*androsterone (DHEA), a weakly androgenic hormone that is a probable intermediate in testosterone biosynthesis (see Figure 5-1). Gorbman and Bern (1962) state that the testes of white-crowned sparrows *(Zonotrichia leucophrys gambellii)* can convert progesterone into testosterone. These observations indicate that in avian testes testosterone can be formed by either of the two pathways indicated in Figure 5-1.

Albert (1961) considers that the evidence in mammals favors the Leydig cells as the source of androgen secretion in the testis. In a recent paper, Christensen and Mason (1965) presented evidence that transformation of progesterone to testosterone occurred in tubules in vitro, although the activity of the Leydig cells was considerably higher.

Gorbman and Bern (1962) have pointed out that in some species, e.g. field mice *(Microtus arvalis)*, the maintenance of some secondary sex characters, during the nonbreeding season or in castrates, may be the result of maintenance of these structures, either by androgen secretion by the adrenal cortex or by extratesticular androgen sources, e.g. the "hibernating gland" (found in bats), which consists of a mass of brown fat, containing steroids, and is located between the scapulae of hibernating as well as of some nonhibernating animals (e.g. the rat). The maintenance of the sec-

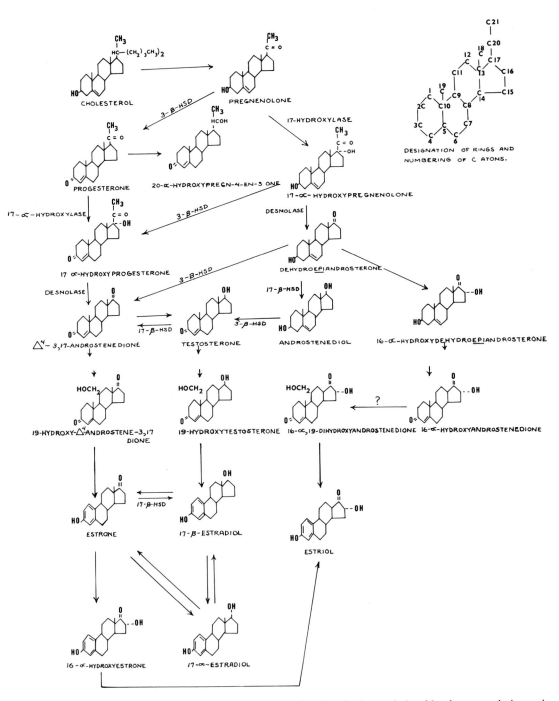

Figure 5-1. Biosynthetic pathway of steroid hormones showing the interrelationships between cholesterol, progesterone, estrogens, and androgens. 3β HSD = 3β-hydroxysteroid dehydrogenase; 17β HSD = 17β-hydroxysteroid dehydrogenase; 17α HSD = 17α-hydroxysteroid dehydrogenase. All three β-hydroxy = Δ^5 compounds can be in the three ester sulfate form. (From World Health Organization, 1965; Dorfman and Ungar, 1965; Baillie and Mack, 1966.)

ondary sex organs and, especially, the epididymides may be particularly important in those species in which live sperm are stored in the male genital system during the nonbreeding season (Gorbman and Bern, 1962).

The isolation of androgens from spermatic vein blood has revealed the secretion of testosterone, androstenedione, and DHEA by the testes. The ratio of testosterone to androstenedione in testicular venous blood is smaller than unity in immature rats. Near maturity and after maturity is reached this ratio is larger than unity. Injection of HCG does not increase the ratio in immature rats but increases it in adult rats (Hashimoto and Suzuki, 1966). In immature bulls, the ratio of testosterone to androstenedione is larger than unity and increases with approaching sexual maturity (see Eik-Nes and Hall, 1965). DHEA is a weakly androgenic hormone secreted by the testes that is a precursor for testosterone (see Figure 5-1).

The testosterone concentration in the peripheral blood of men is between 0.56 to 0.8 μg./100 ml.; for women it has been reported to be between 0.08 and 0.12 μg./100 ml. (Eik-Nes and Hall, 1965).

Control of Androgen Secretion

The evidence that androgen secretion in birds and mammals is under control of anterior pituitary secretions, specifically interstitial cell-stimulating hormone (ICSH) (luteinizing hormone, LH) has been well substantiated for a number of species, e.g. birds and mammals (see van Tienhoven, 1961, and Albert, 1961, for reviews).

Evidence of hormonal control is of a more limited nature in fishes, amphibia, and reptilia. The results of hormone injections obtained under a variety of conditions have been summarized in Table 5-2. Only positive results have been listed because it was judged that negative results might be caused by insufficient dosage or specificity of hormones. The interested student should consult the original references, which have been listed at the bottom of Table 5-2. It appears from these data that the pituitary gland controls androgen secretion by the testes in all species investigated. However, whether LH is the only controlling hormone in all species needs to be established. Whether the source of gonadotropin is specific also needs considerable more investigation, although tenta-

Table 5-2. Effect of Hypophysectomy and/or Gonadotropin Administration on Testicular Interstitium or on Secondary Sex Characters of Fishes, Amphibia and Reptiles

SPECIES	PROCEDURE	OBSERVATION
Lampetra planeri (ammocoete)	Ox AP administration	Cloaca swells; coelom connects to mesonephric duct
L. planeri (adult)	Ox AP administration	Cloaca swells
Lampetra fluviatilis	Hypophysectomy	Secondary sex characters do not develop; there is no release of sperm into body cavity
Salmonidae:		
Oncorhynchus nerka	*O. tshawytscha* AP	Spawning color heightened
	O. keta AP administration	Spawning color induced
Cyprinidae:		
Fundulus heteroclitus	Hypophysectomy	Nuptial color lost
	Hypophysectomy + androgen	Nuptial color returns
Phoxinus phoxinus	*Rana temporaria* AP administration	Nuptial color assumed
Acheilognatus tabira	Mammalian AP administration	Nuptial color assumed
Catostomidae:		
Misgurnus anguilli-caudatus	*Rana nigromaculata* AP administration	Slight development of secondary sex characters

**Table 5-2. Effect of Hypophysectomy and/or Gonadotropin
Administration on Testicular Interstitium or on Secondary
Sex Characters of Fishes, Amphibia and Reptiles (Continued)**

SPECIES	PROCEDURE	OBSERVATION
Gasterosteidae:		
Gasterosteus aculeatus	Mammalian AP administration	Interstitial tissue develops
Poeciliidae:		
Poecilia reticulata (I)*	Human pregnancy urine administration	Precocious secondary sex characters assumed
Poecilia reticulata (adult)	Pregnant mare's serum administration	Interstitial tissue increases
Poecilia reticulata	Sheep AP administration	Interstitial tissue increases
Centrarchidae:		
"Sunfish hybrid"	Hybrid or parental AP administration	Nuptial behavior appears (nest building, courting)
Cichlidae:		
Symphysodon aequifasciata	FSH administration	Blue color pattern of sexually mature fish induced
	LH administration	Intensifies blue color pattern of sexually mature fish and causes protrusion of genital papilla
Gobiidae:		
Bathygobius soporator	Hypophysectomy	Courtship and combat behavior abolished, territorial behavior lessens
Gobius paganellus	Hypophysectomy	Regression of auxiliary sex glands after 3 to 4 months
Amphibia:		
Rana pipiens	Hypophysectomy	Leydig cells atrophy
R. esculenta	Hypophysectomy	Leydig cell numbers increase; secretory and storage capacity decrease; thumb pad and Wolffian duct diameters decrease
R. temporaria	Hypophysectomy	Thumb pads decrease
R. pipiens	Hypophysectomy + LH administration	Interstitium stimulated
R. pipiens	LH administration	Interstitium stimulated
Reptiles:		
Thamnophis sirtalis	Hypophysectomy	Interstitial cells decrease
T. radix	Hypophysectomy	Interstitial cells decrease
Lacerta sp.	Mammalian AP administration	Secretion by sex segment of kidney
Alligator mississippiensis	Sheep AP administration	No effect on *ductuli efferentia* but gonads hypertrophy
Anolis carolinensis	Sheep AP administration	Secondary sex characters and sex behavior stimulated
Malaclemmys centrata	Sheep AP administration	Interstitium stimulated

* I = Immature.
References: Atz, 1957; Dodd, 1960; Dodd, Evennett and Goddard, 1960; Atz and Pickford, 1964; Blüm and Fiedler, 1965; Larsen, 1965; and Lofts, Pickford, and Atz, 1966.

tively it appears that mammalian gonadotropins can stimulate the interstitium of lower vertebrates.

Biochemistry of the Androgens

The suggested pathways for the formation of androgens and estrogens are given in Figure 5-1. Eik-Nes and Hall (1965) have pointed out that the occurrence of a certain pathway in vitro does not mean that such a pathway also exists in vivo. For instance, after incubation of dog ovarian slices in vitro, in the presence of tritiated dehydro*epi*androsterone (DHEA) and of C^{14}-labeled 17-hydroxyprogesterone, estradiol, and 19-hydroxyandrostenedione, each with the C^{14} and H^3 labels, were isolated. However, after perfusion of the dog ovary in situ via the ovarian artery with the same two substrates, only estradiol C^{14}, H^3 could be isolated; no evidence of the presence of 19-hydroxyandrostenedione was found.

A schematic presentation of the pathways utilized in synthesis of androgens and estrogens is given in Figure 5-1. The references cited give good introductions to further details.

Effects of Androgens

From early times, man has known that castration of animals and of his fellow man (slaves were sometimes made eunuchs) affected their sexual and aggressive behavior. The first proof that a substance present in the testes could restore some characteristics lost through castration was obtained by Berthold in 1849, when he stimulated the growth of combs and wattles of capons with testicular transplants. Since then, numerous effects of androgens upon a variety of species have been recorded. Only when these observations serve as an illustration of an effect will they be mentioned.

The principal effects can be divided into a number of main divisions and, in some cases, subdivisions.

EFFECTS ON THE GENITAL SYSTEM

Testis. In the rat, androgens can maintain spermatogenesis after hypophysectomy or after estrogen administration, or they can reinduce spermatogenesis if the testes have been allowed to degenerate by androgens.

Similar phenomena have been observed in hypophysectomized catfish *(Heteropneustes fossilis)* (Sundararaj and Nayar, 1966), killifish *(Fundulus heteroclitus)* (Atz, 1957; Lofts et al., 1966), and pigeons (see van Tienhoven, 1961). However, the conclusion that the restoration of spermatogenesis by androgens is a universal phenomenon among vertebrates should not be drawn. Basu and Nandi (1965) found that

testosterone not only failed to restore spermatogenesis in hypophysectomized frogs *(R. pipiens)*, but that it inhibited the FSH- and LH-induced restoration of spermatogenesis in these frogs, suggesting a direct inhibitory effect of testosterone on spermatogenesis. Subsequent studies in which the testis was cultured in vitro revealed that FSH + LH or FSH + LH + insulin + testosterone result in complete maintenance of the testis and occasionally stimulate spermatogenesis through the first meiotic division (Basu et al., 1966).

In vitro, testosterone had a slightly deleterious effect. For instance, the response to FSH + LH + testosterone was smaller than the response to FSH + LH, but in the presence of FSH + LH + insulin, testosterone had a stimulatory effect. A statistical analysis of the data presented is difficult, and the observations made about testosterone effects in vitro may have been the result of variability rather than of the treatment. In any event, there was no strong evidence for an inhibitory effect of testosterone on spermatogenesis. P. G. W. J. van Oordt (1960) states that in hypophysectomized *R. temporaria* testosterone injection did not affect the spermatogenetic response to pregnant mare's serum administration. Since no actual results were published it is difficult to compare the results with those of Basu and Nandi (1965). It should be noted that in rats a dose of testosterone, which reduces the testicular weight loss due to hypophysectomy from 57 percent to 10 percent, caused a weight increase of 77 percent if administered with gonadotropin (which by itself reduced the weight loss due to hypophysectomy from 57 percent to 10 percent [Gaarenstroom and de Jongh, 1946]). In other words, testosterone and gonadotropins act synergistically in the rat, but testosterone apparently inhibits the effect of gonadotropin in the frog *(R. pipiens)*.

The inhibitory effect of testosterone should be considered in connection with its effect in intact frogs, where it inhibits the formation of secondary spermatogonia (as it does in *R. esculenta*, see G. J. van Oordt, 1963). P. G. W. J. van Oordt concluded that in most amphibia the period of most intense spermatogenesis is *not* the period of most pronounced secretory activity of the interstitial cells. The hypothesis was formulated by P. G. W. J. van Oordt (1960) that in amphibia with a discontinuous spermatogenetic cycle, androgen may be one of the factors which prevent the onset of spermatogenesis during the resting or during the spermiation period. However, more information on the combined effect of androgens and gonadotropins in other amphibia is required before we should accept van Oordt's explanation.

In a variety of species it has been shown that androgen administration even in physiological doses reduces testicular weight and inhibits spermatogenesis (e.g. fishes [*Ditrema temmincki*], amphibia [*R. temporaria*], birds [pigeons, chickens], and mammals [rats, guinea pigs]). This effect is thought to be mediated mainly through an inhibitory effect of androgen on the pituitary's gonadotropin secretion. We mentioned that in *R. pipiens* there is evidence of a direct effect on the testes.

In intact immature rats and pigeons, testosterone has failed to induce spermatogenesis (Dorfman and Shipley, 1956; van Tienhoven, 1961). On the other hand, testosterone administration enhanced spermatogenesis in sparrows *(Passer domesticus)* provided spermatocytes were present in the tubules, and it has prevented testicular weight regression and degeneration of the germinal epithelium in slate-colored juncos *(Junco hyemalis)* and white-throated sparrows *(Zonotrichia albicollis)* when the amount of light was reduced from 16 to eight hours per day. Lofts (1962) found that androgen prevents the testicular collapse of the red-billed dioch *(Quelea quelea)* subjected to 17 hours of light per day, and restores spermatogenesis in birds in the regeneration phase.

Androgens also affect the gonads indirectly by inhibiting the gonadotropin secretion of the pituitary. Doses of androgen that induce spermatogenesis in the hypophysectomized pigeon cause regression of the testes of intact pigeons (Chu, 1940). Ludwig (1950) investigated in detail the effect of different doses of testosterone propionate to rats 30 and 60 days old. The results summarized in Table 5-3 show that:

1. A dose of 0.1 mg./day is sufficient to inhibit testicular weights and to depress the gonadotropin content of the pituitary.

2. At doses of 1.00 and 3.00 mg./day, testicular weights are less depressed than with doses of 0.1 mg./day, although the pituitary gonadotropin content is lower than after administration of 0.1 mg.

These results thus demonstrate that a high dose of androgen can overcome the inhibitory effect of a 0.1 mg. dose of tes-

Table 5-3.   Effects of Testosterone Propionate (TP) on Testicular Weight, Gonadotropin Potency of the Pituitary, and Spermatogenesis of Rats

AGE AT START	AGE AT AUTOPSY	DOSE TP	TESTES	AP POTENCY	SPERMATOGENESIS
			% of Body		
d.	d.	mg./day	Weight	% of Control	
60	90	—	1.036	100	Sperm present
60	90	0.05	.986	—	Sperm present
60	90	0.1	.780	31.15	Sperm present
60	90	1.0	.859	12.66	Sperm present
60	90	3.0	.954	14.27	Sperm present
30	60	—	1.183	—	Sperm present
30	60	0.1	.417	48.42	Spermatids, but no sperm
30	60	1.0	.878	2.69	Sperm present
30	60	2.0	1.006	5.38	Sperm present
30	60	3.0	1.050	—	Sperm present

Reference: Ludwig, 1950.

tosterone propionate on testicular weight and on spermatogenesis (in rats 30 to 60 days old). This stimulatory effect on spermatogenesis is further confirmed by the fact that pellets implanted into testes of rats receiving an inhibitory dose of 0.1 mg. testosterone propionate/day stimulate spermatogenesis in their immediate vicinity.

Davidson and Sawyer (1961) have determined by local implantation of small amounts of testosterone in dogs that the effect of testosterone probably occurs via the posterior median eminence. Implants in that region caused aspermia and testicular and prostatic atrophy, whereas implants into the pituitary had no effect on the size of the testes and prostate, although semen quality decreased.

Testosterone increases the FSH content of the pituitary without causing an immediate drop in FSH concentration of the blood, which does eventually decrease. The LH content of the pituitary and the LH concentration of the blood drop sharply shortly after testosterone treatment has started (Bogdanove 1964). It thus appears that testosterone inhibits LH synthesis and release and impairs the release of FSH, but to a much lesser extent.

Epididymis. Androgens prolong the life of sperm in the epididymides of mammals; as far as I know this function of androgens in inframammalian vertebrates has not been studied.

Secondary Sex Structures. The maintenance of the structural integrity and of secretory activity of the secondary sex structures, requires the presence of androgens. In chickens, androgen is not required for the maintenance of fertilizing capacity of sperm in the ductus deferens (see van Tienhoven, 1961), a situation which contrasts with the one which prevails in some mammals (see Bishop, 1961).

In the absence of secretory activity of the secondary sex glands, sperm cells are deprived of a large proportion of the seminal plasma which is a source of energy, a buffer preventing pH changes, and a suspending fluid (Mann, 1964). In the boar, for example, a large proportion of the total semen volume is contributed by the accessory glands. The average volume of the ejaculate is about 200 cc.; of this about 26 percent is contributed by the seminal vesicles, 19 percent by the Cowper's glands, and about 56 percent by the prostate and urethral glands. Removal of the seminal vesicles, Cowper's glands, or both does not affect fertility. The effect of removing the prostate and urethral glands was not reported (McKenzie et al., 1938). Greenstein and Hart (1964) found severe interference with fertility of rats only after they had removed the seminal vesicles and the coagulating gland. Removal of Cowper's glands, seminal vesicle, prostate coagulating gland, Cowper's glands plus seminal vesicles, Cowper's glands plus coagulating gland, seminal vesicles plus prostate, or prostate plus coagulating gland had no effect.

After castration the scrotum loses its ability to respond to changes in temperature, probably because of the lack of androgen, and, not because of the absence of the testes per se, since the scrotum did respond to temperature changes a few hours after castration but later (when the androgens had disappeared from the blood) failed to respond (Andrews, 1940).

Injection of testosterone propionate into neonatal female rats causes persistent estrus when they are adult (see p. 85). When such rats are ovariectomized and treated with estradiol the response of the uteri is less than that in the control ovariectomized rats treated with estradiol (van Rees and Gans, 1966).

SECONDARY SEX CHARACTERS

There are numerous cases of sexual dimorphism among the vertebrates. Most of these characters are influenced by androgen (in some cases they appear in the absence of estrogen, e.g. male feathering in most breeds of chickens), whereas in other cases they are under the influence of

Table 5-4. Morphological Seconday Sex Characters* under the Control of Male Sex Hormone

SPECIES	CHARACTER
Oryzias sp.	Dimorphic liver
Triturus cristatus	Nuptial dress (high tailcrest)
Bufo arenarum	Thumb pads
Leptodactylus ocellatus	Muscles and bone of foreleg
Terrapene carolina	Claws
Chelydra sp.	Claws
Pseudemys sp.	Claws
Anas platyrhynchos	Eclipse (hen feathering) plumage of drake prevented by early castration
Philomachus pugnax	Breeding plumage; skin tubercles around eyes
Passer domesticus	Black bill; result of androgen
Euplectes sp.	Blue-black bill; result of androgen
Passerina cyanea	Black bill tip; result of androgen
Hypochera chalybeata	White bill; result of androgen
Sturnus vulgaris	Orange bill; result of androgen
Larus ridibundus	Crimson bill; result of androgen
Larus argentatus	Red bill; result of androgen
Gallus domesticus	Comb size and color
Meleagris gallopova	Corunculated skin and topknot
Odocoileus virginianus	Antler calcification, loss of velvet, and delayed shedding; result of androgen
Homo sapiens	Voice; distribution of body hair

* Secondary sex organs not included.

References: Dorfman and Shipley, 1956; van Oordt, 1963; Witschi, 1961; Gorbman and Bern, 1962; Parkes and Marshall, 1960; and Forbes, 1961.

pituitary hormones, e.g. the male feather pattern of some African weaver finches (*Euplectes* sp., *Steganura* sp., and *Suelea* sp.).

No attempt has been made to furnish a complete list of the secondary sex characters under the control of androgen, but a few examples are cited in Table 5-4. Combined with data in Tables 5-1 and 5-2 they give an idea of the large number of characters that can be influenced by androgen. Androgen may affect a specific end organ in one species but not in another. One good illustration of this is Wilson's phalarope (*Steganopus tricolor*); the male incubates the eggs and the female does not. Androgen is required (together with prolactin) for the development of the incubation patch (Johns and Pfeiffer, 1963), whereas in the Passerines, estrogen (plus prolactin) is required and androgen (plus prolactin) is ineffective (Bailey, 1952).

BEHAVIOR

The effects of androgens on behavior are good examples of integration by inter-action between the nervous system and the endocrine system. For extensive discussions of the data collected on a variety of species the excellent reviews by Eisner (1960), Guhl (1961), and Lehrman (1961, 1964) should be consulted. A summary of effects on mating behavior is given in Table 5-5. For the sake of convenience I have divided the behavior patterns with which we are concerned into aggressive and sexual (mating) behavior, being fully aware that this separation is arbitrary, that there are all types of gradations, and that the two types of behavior are in many instances intertwined.

The aggressiveness of the frillfin goby (*Bathygobius soporator*) seems to be dependent on androgens, since castration causes disappearance of fighting. For three-spined sticklebacks, fighting behavior seems to depend on an interaction between the photoperiod under which the animals are kept and the hormonal status. Castration diminished aggressiveness under eight hours of light and 16 hours of darkness (8L-16D) but did not do so under 16L-8D.

Table 5-5.   Effect of Castration and/or Androgen Administration on Mating Behavior of Vertebrates

SPECIES	PROCEDURE	EFFECTS
Teleosts:		
Poeciliidae:		
Xiphophorus maculatus	Castration	Aspects of copulation behavior lost
Cichlidae:		
Hemichromis bimaculatus	Castration (not confirmed histologically)	No effect on courtship and fertilization
Gobiidae:		
Bathygobius soporator	Castration	Nondiscriminatory courting behavior
Anabantidae:		
Betta splendens	Incomplete ovariectomy (testicular regeneration)	Male behavior
Amphibia:		
Rana pipiens	Castration	Ejaculatory movements if tied to back of female
	Castration before breeding season	Clasp reflex disappears
	Castration after breeding season started	Clasp reflex persists
Rana pipiens	Androgen	Mating response persists
Birds:		
Pigeons		
Columba livia	Castration	Copulation attempts persist for several months
Fowl		
Gallus domesticus	Castration	Copulation behavior lost
Drake		
Anas platyrhynchos	Castration	Copulation behavior lost
Mammals:		
Rat	Castration	Decreases complete copulation
Rat, I*	Androgen	Induces copulation behavior
Rat, castrated	Androgen	Reinduces copulation behavior
Rat (Inbred colony, lack of copulations)	Androgen	Establishes complete copulation (including fertilizations)
Guinea pig	Castration	Reduces copulation behavior
Guinea pig, I*	Androgen	Induces copulation behavior
Guinea pig, castrated	Androgen	Reinduces copulation behavior
Rabbit	Castration	Reduces copulation behavior
Rabbit, castrated	Androgen	Reinduces copulation behavior
Dog	Castration	Reduces but does not abolish copulations
Cat, adult	Castration	Response varies. In some cats intromissions retained for months and mounting behavior retained for years, in other cats rapid decrease of mounting behavior.
Cat, I, castrated	Androgen	Mating behavior is induced; after androgen withdrawal same patterns occur as mentioned above after castration of adults.

* I = Immature
References: Aronson, 1957, 1959; Young, 1961, 1964.

Castration does not seem to affect the rank (based on aggressiveness) of the swordtail (*Xiphophorus helleri*); however, implants of testosterone propionate pellets causes an advance in rank.

The fighting behavior of American chameleons (*Anolis carolinensis*) does not seem to be affected by castration; however, treatment of castrated males with testosterone propionate causes an advance in rank. It is, of course, possible that either the castration was incomplete or that an extratesticular source of androgen provided the castrates with sufficient androgen to maintain their fighting behavior. In any event, it seems that in *Anolis carolinensis* androgen does play a role in aggressiveness.

Among birds, chickens have been used most extensively in studies of aggressiveness, but fortunately there are data on a number of other avian species. Castration reduces aggressive behavior of turkey toms and of roosters (Guhl, 1961). However, it does not diminish the fighting among pigeons and starlings (Carpenter, 1933a,b). Davis (1963) has claimed, on what seems insufficient evidence, that fighting behavior of the male starling is controlled by gonadotropic hormones. We will return to this is in a later chapter. The administration of androgens increases the aggressiveness of ringdoves *(Streptopelia risoria)*, capons, herring gulls *(Larus argentatus)*, and canaries *(Serinus canaria)*.

With respect to sexual behavior, specifically mating behavior, the evidence obtained seems to show the same trend: in the higher vertebrates aggressive behavior seems to depend on the presence of androgen, whereas in some of the lower vertebrates it is possible in the absence of androgens.

As Young (1961) has pointed out, one has to be careful in assessing the effects of castration. The mating behavior of the rat includes:

1. Mounting from the rear and clasping of his forelegs about the latero lumbar region of the female ("clasp without palpation").
2. Palpation of the sides with forelegs and simultaneous pelvic thrusts, and either:
3. a. Final forceful thrust, male lunges backward, indicative of intromission, usually failure to ejaculate, or
   b. Male continues to press against female prolonging intromission, releases clasp, slowly raises forelegs, emits ejaculate, withdraws penis.

The first two steps of this mating behavior are less affected by castration than steps 3a and 3b. In reading the literature one has to be careful to ascertain what is meant by "mating behavior." Table 5-5 lists the effects of castration and/or androgen administration on mating behavior.

The manner in which androgens, and for that matter estrogens, affects sexual behavior is not entirely clear, but there are data which warrant a discussion of this question. This problem is related to the differentiation of the neural tissue during prenatal or early postnatal development, depending on the species, and it may be better to discuss that question first and then return to the question of how sex hormones may affect the behavior pattern of the adult.

DIFFERENTIATION OF NEURAL TISSUE

The discussion will be limited to two related problems, the differentiation of gonadotropin regulating centers and of centers involved in behavior.

Gonadotropin Secretion Regulating Centers. It should be kept in mind that one of the essential differences between the gonadotropin secretion of male and female rats (the same probably applies to many other mammals) is the steady secretion of gonadotropin by the male anterior pituitary and the cyclic nature of gonadotropin secretion by the female anterior pituitary. This difference between male and female pituitaries was found not to be the result of any inherent differences between the pituitaries per se; e.g. male pituitaries were transplanted under the hypothalamus of a hypophysectomized female and normal estrous cycles, mating, pregnancy, and milk secretion ensued after the pituitary became vascularized (see Harris, 1964b).

A number of experiments have shown that the male and female hypothalamus differ with respect to the regulation of gonadotropin release, and that the differentiation into a male or female hypothalamus occurs during the first five days after birth in rats:

1. An ovary transplanted into an adult male rat which was castrated at birth will form corpora lutea.

2. Ovaries transplanted to an adult female, spayed at birth, caused normal estrous cycles in the recipient and formed corpora lutea (Harris, 1964b).

3. Ovarian transplants to male rats, with testes transplanted to the neck region at birth, show no evidence of corpus luteum formation.

4. Female rats which received a testicular transplant at birth do not show estrous cycles, form no corpora lutea, but have a permanently cornified vaginal epithelium (Harris, 1964b).

5. Injection of testosterone propionate into neonatal (first five days after birth) female rats causes lack of estrous cycles, failure of corpus luteum formation, and persistent vaginal cornification ("permanent estrus" or "persistent estrus") when the rats are adults.

Adams Smith, and Peng (1966) showed that the effect of the TP injection was not on the pituitary by transplanting pituitaries from androgen-treated rats under the median eminence of control rats and by transplanting pituitaries of control rats under the median eminence of androgen-treated rats. The rats treated with androgen but with "control pituitaries" still showed the persistent estrus syndrome, whereas control rats with the pituitaries from androgen-treated rats had normal cycles. These results are thus similar to those obtained by Harris (1964b) in rats with testicular transplants.

The dose of testosterone propionate injected determines the age at which persistent estrus will occur. In response to doses of 5, 10, and 50 to 100 μg. testosterone propionate, it occurred in ten-week-old rats in 0, 30, and 64 percent of cases, respectively. However, at 21 weeks of age,

90 percent to 100 percent of the rats were anovulatory whether the dose had been 5, 10, or 50 to 100 μg. testosterone propionate (Swanson and van der Werff ten Bosch, 1964). Barraclough (1966) injected 10 μg. testosterone propionate into neonatal rats and 55 to 70 percent became anovulatory rats at 60 days of age. Upon electric stimulation of the arcuate-ventromedial region, ovulation was obtained in five of 11 rats, whereas after stimulation of preoptic-suprachiasmatic area no ovulations were obtained unless the animals had been pretreated with progesterone (for discussion of this phenomenon see Chapter 8).

On the other hand, when 1.25 mg. TP was injected neonatally, 100 percent of the rats show sterility with persistent vaginal cornification. Electric stimulation of the arcuate-ventromedial region does not result in ovulation unless progesterone injections precede the stimulation. Preoptic electric stimulation fails to cause ovulation regardless of preceding progesterone treatment (Barraclough and Gorski, 1961; Barraclough, 1966).

An explanation offered by Barraclough (1966) is that low doses of androgen probably only affect the thresholds of activation of the preoptic region and that high doses affect the preoptic region and also the arcuate-ventromedial region of the hypothalamus. Progesterone treatment, according to Barraclough (1966), primarily affects the thresholds of excitability of the different hypothalamic regions to electric stimuli and the increase in pituitary LH content, which is observed after progesterone treatment of rats sterilized by the high doses of androgen, is secondary. Barraclough (1966) also proposed an alternate explanation, i.e. that high and low doses of androgen may affect the synthesis of LH releasing factor (LHRF) or the storage of LHRF differently. Which of these two explanations is correct cannot be decided on the basis of the available data.

Neonatal castration of male rats causes increased gonadotropin secretion, as is evident from prostate and seminal vesicle weights of intact males placed in parabiosis with these rats when 30 days old. Neonatal injection of castrated males with 2.5 mg. testosterone propionate does not affect their gonadotropin secretion at 30 days of age. However, a smaller dose of androgen is required to suppress the gonadotropin secretion of the androgen-treated castrated rats than of the castrated rats (Morrison and Johnson, 1966). These authors also found that neonatal androgen treatment increased the sensitivity of the ventral prostate and seminal vesicle to subsequent androgen treatment. Thus, there was an effect of the neonatal TP treatment on the sensitivity of the androgen feedback and on the sensitivity of the target organs of androgen. The question whether neonatal testosterone propionate treatment of females had an effect on the ovary was answered by the transplantation of ovaries of androgen-sterilized female rats to castrated controls. Such ovaries caused normal estrous cycles and showed normal corpus luteum formation, thus demonstrating that they were similar to control ovaries (see Harris, 1964b).

The differentiation of the brain of genetic male rats apparently occurs earlier than that of female rats, at least with respect to the effects of androgens. Harris (1964a) found that if male rats are castrated during the first 24 hours after birth, corpora lutea form in ovaries transplanted to such castrates and vaginal transplants show cyclic changes similar to those observed in intact female rats. Castration delayed beyond 24 hours results in lack of corpus luteum formation in transplanted ovaries. Apparently the testicular androgen causes differentiation of the male's brain as early as 24 hours after birth, whereas, in genetic females, androgen injections are effective in changing the hypothalamic mechanisms involved in gonadotropin release until the fifth day after birth.

In summary, androgen causes a differentiation of the hypothalamus in the neonatal rat such that LH is released steadily, not as an ovulatory surge (cyclic LH release). On the other hand, in the absence of androgen, regardless of the presence of the ovary (control females) or its absence, the hypothalamus differentiates so that cyclic release of LH can occur.

Kincl et al. (1965) report that an injection of thymocytes prior to androgen injection of neonatal rats prevents androgen from affecting ovarian activity. The mechanism involved in this protective action by thymocytes is not established.

Campbell (1966) has suggested that the effects of androgen can be obtained only during the first five days after birth because at about day 5 the primary plexus of the portal system starts to develop, and this event is correlated with hypothalamic differentiation.

Differentiation of the "Behavioral Substrate." The pertinent data have been summarized in Table 5-6. They show that:

1. Large doses of estrogen given neonatally to castrated males inhibit male mating behavior even when the male is given testosterone as an adult.

2. Estrogen given to intact neonatal rats results in some loss of male sexual behavior even after castration as an adult and testosterone therapy.

3. Estrogen administration to neonatal female rats results in a slight disturbance of normal female behavior.

4. Testosterone given to ovariectomized or to intact neonatal rats, or to intact guinea pigs during gestation, allows development of male behavior patterns of these young if testosterone is given when they are adult.

5. Neonatal administration of testosterone to female rats leads to loss of female sexual behavior. Ovariectomy of adult animals plus estrogen and progesterone therapy does not change this loss of female behavior patterns.

6. Adult male rats, castrated neonatally, show female mating behavior

Table 5-6. Effect of Gonadal Hormones on the Organization of the Hypothalamus as Measured by Behavior as Adult After Different Treatments

TREATMENT (NEONATAL)	SEX	SPECIES	TREATMENT AS ADULT	BEHAVIOR AS ADULT	REFERENCE
200 μg. Estradiol Benzoate (E.B.)	F	Rat	Ovariectomy; estrogen plus progesterone	29% showed lordosis	Whalen and Nadler, 1963
—	F	Rat	Ovariectomy; estrogen plus progesterone	100% showed lordosis	Whalen and Nadler, 1963
100 μg. E.B.	F	Rat	Ovariectomy; estrogen plus progesterone	1.23 frequency of lordosis	Levine and Mullins, 1964
—	F	Rat	Ovariectomy; estrogen plus progesterone	20.45 frequency of lordosis	Levine and Mullins, 1964
100 μg. E.B.	M	Rat	—	Fewer intromissions, fewer ejaculations, mounting bizarre	Levine and Mullins, 1964
100 μg. E.B.	M	Rat	Castration; testosterone propionate	Few intromissions and ejaculations, mounting normal	Levine and Mullins, 1964
50 μg. E.B.	F	Rat	♀ + estrogen plus progesterone	7/12 showed full receptivity. None showed agression or repulsive behavior	Harris and Levine, 1965
50 μg. E.B. day 4	M	Rat	—	17/31 showed no male behavior 13/31 showed partial male behavior 1/31 showed full male behavior	Harris and Levine, 1965
50 μg. E.B. day 4	M	Rat	♂ + TP 100 μg./day for 7 days	4/10 showed no male behavior 4/10 showed partial male behavior 2/10 showed full male behavior	Harris and Levine, 1965
Oil	M	Rat	—	17/25 showed full male behavior 6/25 showed partial male behavior 2/25 showed no male behavior	Harris and Levine, 1965
Oil	M	Rat	♂ + TP 100 μg./day for 7 days	5/5 showed full male behavior	Harris and Levine 1965
TP 500 μg. day 4	F	Rat	—	No lordosis (N = 18); all showed aggressive or repulsive behavior	Harris and Levine, 1965
TP 500 μg. day 4	F	Rat	♀ + estrogen plus progesterone	No lordosis (N = 10); all showed aggressive or repulsive behavior	Harris and Levine, 1965

Table 5-6. Effect of Gonadal Hormones on the Organization of the Hypothalamus as Measured by Behavior as Adult After Different Treatments *(Continued)*

TREATMENT (NEONATAL)	SEX	SPECIES	TREATMENT AS ADULT	BEHAVIOR AS ADULT	REFERENCE
Oil	F	Rat	♀ + estrogen plus progesterone	$^{15}/_{17}$ showed full sexual receptivity. No aggressive or repulsive behavior	Harris and Levine, 1965
TP 500 μg. day 4	F	Rat	♀ + TP 100 μg./day for 7 days	No lordosis (N = 10); all showed aggressive or repulsive behavior	Harris and Levine, 1965
Oil	F	Rat	♀ + TP 100 μg./day for 7 days	$^{5}/_{7}$ showed full receptivity; no aggressive or repulsive behavior	Harris and Levine, 1965
TP 500 μg. day 4	M	Rat	—	$^{10}/_{10}$ showed full male behavior pattern	Harris and Levine, 1965
1.25 mg. Testosterone prop. (TP)	F	Rat	—	No lordosis, aggressive behavior	Barraclough and Gorski, 1962
1.25 mg. TP	F	Rat	Castrated; estrogen plus progesterone	No lordosis, aggressive behavior	Barraclough and Gorski, 1962
—	F	Rat	Castrated; estrogen plus progesterone	Lordosis, normal mating	Barraclough and Gorski, 1962
10 μg. TP	F	Rat	—	Incidence of bizarre mating	Barraclough and Gorski, 1962

♀ = ovariectomized female; ♂ = castrated male.

when treated with estrogens and male behavior when treated with androgens. Grady et al. (1965) have summarized these findings as follows:

1. Feminization occurs in the intact female genotype and in either sex when gonads are absent.

2. Masculinization occurs when androgen is present regardless of genotype.

How androgens cause the "male" or "female" organization of the hypothalamus is not certain, but evidence is convincing that they affect both its endocrine and its neural (behavioral) function.

Location of the center of male and female behavioral control by androgens after neural tissue has been organized has been studied in mammals. Fisher (1956, 1964) injected testosterone into

various parts of the hypothalamus of male and female rats and found that the site of injection determined largely what type of behavior would ensue. In the medial preoptic region, testosterone induced maternal behavior in males as well as in females, whereas, in the lateral preoptic region, the same hormone induced male behavior in both sexes.

This indicates that a high enough concentration of testosterone *can* induce male behavior in a female, although its brain is presumably "organized for female behavior." On the other hand, it shows that male hormone in sufficient concentration can induce female behavior even in a male (although its brain "is organized for male behavior"). Fisher thinks that female behavior induced by testosterone could be the result of its progestational properties. Thus, the lateral preoptic center would be sensitive to progesterone and would react to the progesterone-like action of testosterone. This question needs further investigation, e.g. a comparison of the effect of testosterone and of progesterone at different concentrations in the same animal at the same site.

The mechanisms which operate after subcutaneous injection of hormones in castrated or intact animals are not known. Is it possible that the organizing effects of estrogen and androgen cause differences in their subsequent penetration so that after neonatal androgen treatment estrogens cannot reach the medial preoptic area? The center controlling female mating behavior has, as far as I know, not been located, but the situations may be similar.

METABOLIC EFFECTS

Androgens have a number of metabolic effects. In birds and mammals they generally cause nitrogen retention, increase the storage of creatine, and depress respiration of neural tissue. How androgen takes part in energy and nitrogen metabolism is not known.

ESTROGEN SECRETION

Estrogens have been isolated from the testes of a number of species (pig, horse, deer, man). In the horse the concentration of estrogen of spermatic vein blood is about 20 times higher than that in other venous blood (Leach et al., 1956). In vitro studies have shown that human testes slices can synthesize 17-β-estradiol and estrone from acetate (Albert, 1961).

The cellular source of estrogen production is probably the Leydig cell. Leach et al. (1956) arrived at this conclusion on the basis of the following evidence:

1. Leydig cell tumors are often associated with high estrogen excretion.

2. In cases in which the Leydig cells were the only elements present in the testes, estrogen excretion was higher than in castrates and only slightly lower than in normal men.

3. Chorionic gonadotropin injection in men stimulated the Leydig cells, increased estrogen excretion and necrosis of the seminiferous tubules, and caused no observable changes in the Sertoli cells.

It should be mentioned, however, that in cases of Sertoli cell tumors, estrogen excretion is also high, suggesting that these cells can secrete estrogens although they may not be the chief contributors to the estrogen secreted by the testes (Albert, 1961; Leach et al., 1956; Lacy et al., 1965).

SPERMATOGENESIS

Spermatogenesis is under the control of the pituitary hormones in all vertebrates if we consider the spermatogenetic cycle as a whole. Certain steps can proceed in the absence of the pituitary; others can proceed in its absence provided androgens are present in sufficiently high concentration; and others can continue in the absence of either of these hormones.

Hypophysectomy of cyclostomes has been performed on a limited number of animals, and the data collected indicate that pituitary hormones are required for the division of primary spermatogonia and possibly for the formation of primary spermatocytes. Once the latter are formed, spermatogenesis can proceed through the formation of spermatozoa. However, sperm are not released into the body cavity. In young brook lampreys (L. planeri) the injection of mammalian gonadotropin did not affect spermatogenesis. Whether this lack of effect is the result of specificity of the hormone or inability of the immature gonad to respond is open to investigation.

The number of experiments carried out with elasmobranchs is also fairly limited; in spite of this some clear cut results have been obtained. The removal of the ventral lobe of the pituitary of male *Scyliorhinus caniculus* causes breakdown of the transitional ampullae (between those which contain spermatogonia and those which contain primary spermatocytes). The tubulogenic zone and the proximal ampullae of the spermatogonial zone retain normal appearance. In distal ampullae which have more than three rows of cells, spermatogonia break down but the Sertoli cells apparently remain normal. According to Dodd et al. (1960) the ventral lobe of the pituitary is essential for the transformation of spermatogonia into primary spermatocytes. Removing the rostral and neurointermediate lobes does not affect spermatogenesis. The effect of gonadotropic hormones on spermatogenesis of elasmobranchs has been studied only in starved *S. caniculus*, in which the starvation inhibited the yield of sperm obtained by stimulating the urinogenital papilla. Mammalian gonadotropin injections (high in LH) caused the reappearance of sperm in such starved dogfish.

Information from a variety of sources on the effect of hypophysectomy, replacement therapy, and gonadotropin injections in fishes has been compiled by Atz (1957). Of all these data, only a few give information on the exact stages of spermatogenesis affected by hypophysectomy. In the common kille (*Fundulus heteroclitus*), stages beyond the spermatogonia are affected but the spermatogonia are not. Replacement therapy with *F. heteroclitus* pituitaries restores the testicular weight (which decreases after hypophysectomy).

It seems impossible to generalize about specificity of response to gonadotropins. The student who wants to obtain precocious spermatogenesis in a certain fish species should consult source materials reviewed by Atz (1957) and then select the hormones he wants to use from comparisons of potencies, of availability of hormone, of cost, and so on, and use the most suitable hormone.

The effects of hypophysectomy have been studied in a number of species of amphibia (see Dodd, 1960, and Hoar, 1966, for review). In virtually all species investigated, hypophysectomy resulted in testicular weight loss. However, if the operation occurred during the resting phase of the reproductive cycle, the weight loss could not be discovered. Basu and Nandi (1965) maintained frogs (*Rana pipiens*) at room temperature and found that at this temperature spermatogenesis became a continuous process rather than a discontinuous one, as under natural conditions. When frogs were kept at room temperature, hypophysectomy during the period when wild frogs were in the resting phase results in testicular weight loss. The operation has little effect on primary and early secondary spermatogonia of *Rana pipiens*, but mainly affects the later stages of spermatogenesis (Basu and Nandi, 1965). Burgos (1955), on the other hand, found that atrophic changes of spermatogonia occurred. Lofts (1961) observed that hypophysectomy of *R. temporaria* prevents formation of spermatocytes and causes lipid infiltration of the Sertoli cells if the operation occurs in March. FSH injection causes disappearance of these lipids and resumption of spermatogenesis. If hypophysectomy is performed during the postnuptial period, primary spermatogonia can still undergo division and form spermatocytes.

There is sufficient evidence to state that spermatogenesis is under hypophyseal control. However, the exact hormones required for either maintenance or reestablishment of complete spermatogenesis in hypophysectomized amphibia are not known. Either PMSG or HCG injections restore spermatogenesis and cause spermiation in hypophysectomized toads (*Bufo melanostictus*), although the response to HCG administration is more intensive. PMSG does not stimulate the Leydig cells, whereas HCG does (Basu, 1964). Basu and Nandi (1965) found that nearly complete spermatogenesis in hypophysectomized frogs kept at room temperature was obtained only in December and January by mammalian FSH and LH injections, and during other periods only incomplete spermatogenesis could be achieved. In view of the observed inhibition of gonadotropin-induced spermatogenesis in testosterone-treated hypophysectomized *R. pipiens*, one might expect LH to have an inhibitory effect. This possibility was not specifically tested since combinations of FSH and LH were injected. This relationship needs further evaluation. Burgos and Ladman (1957) noted that although LH caused spermiation in control and hypophysectomized frogs, FSH was required to increase the number of spermatogonia. The conclusion that FSH is indeed required needs, of course, ultimate confirmation from experiments in which amphibian gonadotropins have been used. There is, however, enough similarity in the response to amphibian and mammalian gonadotropins to tentatively accept that FSH is required for spermatogenesis, and that LH possibly has an inhibitory effect if enough is administered to cause androgen secretion by the Leydig cells.

The release of spermatozoa from the tubules is definitely under the control of LH (see Lofts, 1961, and Dodd, 1960). This release seems to be the result of water uptake, as shown by in vitro and in vivo experiments in which LH and adrenalin (van Dongen and de Kort, 1959; van Dongen et al., 1959; and van Dongen et al., 1960) caused spermiation.

The number of experiments in which hypophysectomized male reptiles have been used is limited. Hypophysectomy was found to cause degeneration of spermatocytes in *Thamnophis sirtalis, T. radix,* and *Agama agama)* which can be reversed by replacement therapy *(T. radix)* with either *T. radix* pituitaries or pregnant mare's serum gonadotropin (P.M.S.G.).

The injection of gonadotropins into intact reptiles results in increased testicular weights in *Alligator mississippiensis, Anolis carolinensis, Malaclemmys centrata,* and spermatogenesis in *Uromastix* sp., *Anolis carolinensis, Phrynosoma cornutum.*

Quantitative studies of the seminiferous epithelium have not, to my knowledge, been carried out for reptiles. The methods used to study birds and mammals should be applicable to reptilian testes, however. It seems, therefore, advisable to discuss these methods and the interpretations which have been made on the basis of the results obtained.

The spermatogenetic phenomena can, for the sake of classification, be divided into three main periods: (1) the period of multiplication of spermatogonia during which new spermatogonia and primary spermatocytes are formed; (2) the period of spermatocyte division that results in spermatid formation; (3) the period of spermiogenesis during which spermatids are transformed into spermatozoa.

Spermiogenesis can be divided into a number of stages. The total depends on the species being investigated. In ducks Clermont (1958) recognizes ten stages, illustrated in Figure 5-2. The proacrosomic granule (black in Figure 5-2) attaches itself to the nucleus (stages 1 to 4). This granule becomes the acrosome. The acrosome becomes a fine pointed structure at the tip of the nucleus (8 to 10). The chromatin material condenses (1 to 5), and the nucleus elongates (5 and 6). The chromatin material forms a spiral G and then becomes elongated (7 to 10). The tail is formed (8 and 9) and the cytoplasm is lost (10).

These stages of spermiogenesis can be correlated with changes in the seminiferous epithelium. Five generations of germ cells can be distinguished in the epithelium: the spermatogonia which lie close to the basement membrane, the primary and secondary spermatocytes lying closer to the lumen, and the spermatids and spermatozoa which are located more centrally.

Clermont (1958) divided the spermatogenic cycle into eight stages. His illustration (Figure 5-3) shows the composition of each stage with respect to the various cell types, as given in Table 5-7.

With the aid of such quantitative measures of the spermatogenetic cycle one can

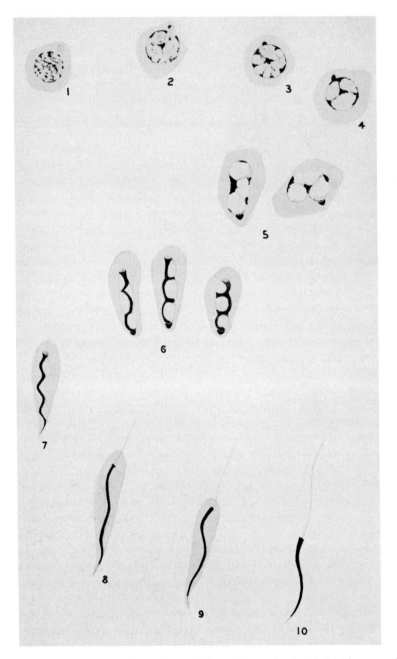

Figure 5-2. Spermiogenesis in the drake as observed in sections stained with PAS-hematoxylin. The series of changes which the spermatid undergoes are shown: 1, a young spermatid; 10, a mature sperm. The pro-acrosomic granule (in the cytoplasm in light gray) is shown as a black dot (2), which is attached to the nucleus (3) and becomes a triangular acrosome (4–6). The acrosome becomes more lightly stained (7) but persists as a fine point at the tip of the nucleus (8–10). (From Clermont, 1958.)

Table 5-7.   The Cell Types Found in Various Stages of the Spermatogenetic Cycle of the Drake.

STAGE	I	II	III	IV	V	VI	VII	VIII
Spermatogonia (G)	G	G	G	G	G	G	G	G
Spermatogonia in mitosis			M		M			M
Primary Spermatocytes								
Interphase (I)				I	L	L	L	L
Leptotene (L)	L,Z	L,Z	Z					
Zygotene (Z)								
Pachytene (P)								
Metaphase (S,Im)				P	P	P	P,D	D,S,Im
Secondary Spermatocytes (SII)								SII
Dividing Spermatocytes (SIIm)								SIIm
Spermatids, stages 1–10*	1 9	2 9	3 10	4 10	5	6	7	8

* See Figure 5-2.
Reference: Clermont, Y., 1958.

investigate the effects of hypophysectomy, changes in environment, hormone injections, and so on, on the cycle and ascertain the stage at which the experimental condition has its primary effect.

Unfortunately, quantitative measures of the spermatogenic cycle have not been used in studies of birds. We will, therefore, be able to describe only the more qualitative aspects of hypophysectomy and hormone administration.

Among birds, the pigeon and domestic chicken have been investigated most extensively. The results of these studies are in general agreement. Hypophysectomy causes regression of the testes, steatogenesis of the tubules, and degeneration of the germinal epithelium. No quantitative studies denoting the part of the spermatogenetic cycle primarily affected have been carried out. Replacement therapy with mammalian FSH restores spermatogenesis. Administration of LH causes an increase in the comb size of hypophysectomized roosters, but after 10 to 20 days of continuous administration the comb regresses. According to Nalbandov, Meyer, and McShan (1951) this is the result of either a qualitative difference between mammalian and avian LH or the result of a third (avian) gonadotropin. This interpretation was reached after it was established that administration of avian pituitary extracts could maintain comb growth and, later, maintain full comb size indefinitely. Histological examination of the testes reveals that there are two types of Leydig cells, one which requires avian pituitary extracts for transformation in the second type, which responds to mammalian gonadotropins by androgen secretion.

Lofts and Marshall (1959) made the interesting observation that hypophysectomy of pigeons causes progesterone to be present in the tubules and in the blood. This is quite remarkable because in females of other classes, progesterone secretion may be independent of the pituitary (e.g. some reptiles) or be dependent upon anterior pituitary gland secretions (e.g. mammals). In pigeons, ablation of the pituitary *causes* progesterone secretion by the testis. It remains to be seen whether the same phenomenon occurs in species other than pigeons. In pigeons, progesterone plays an important role in the regulation of paternal behavior and may thus be involved in a very specific response.

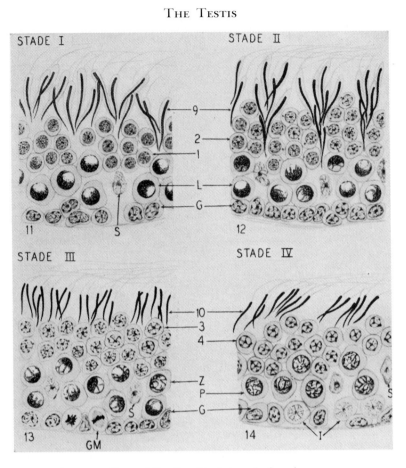

Figure 5-3. *See opposite page for legend.*

The spermatogenetic cycle of mammals has been studied in a number of species (rats [Clermont, 1962; Clermont and Perey, 1957], guinea pigs [Clermont, 1960], monkeys [Clermont and Leblond, 1959], and man [Clermont, 1966]). The essential methods used are the same as those described for ducks. The number of stages distinguished in spermiogenesis and spermatogenesis may vary. For instance, in rats, Clermont and Perey (1957) recognize 14 stages in spermiogenesis and 14 stages in the spermatogenetic cycle, whereas, in man, 16 stages are recognized in spermiogenesis and 14 in spermatogenesis (Albert, 1961). Various authors have used somewhat different classifications and have arrived at a different number of stages in the cycle of the same species (see Ortavant, 1959, for details).

An illustration of the morphological relationships to spermatogenesis is given in Figure 5-4.

The main advantages derived from the use of the quantitative methods in evaluating spermatogenesis are:

1. The manner in which the stem cells are renewed can be explained (see Figure 5-4).

2. The duration of the spermatogenetic cycle defined as "the interval between the appearance of the original spermatogonium and release of the spermatozoa which are produced from it" can be estimated (Ortavant, 1959), (see Table 5-8).

3. The efficiency of different stages of cycle can be measured.

Hypophysectomy of rats leads to some degeneration of type A spermato-

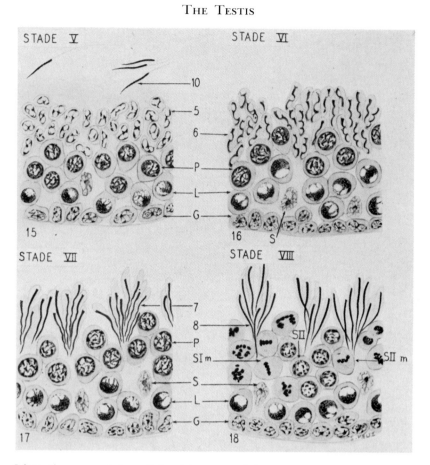

Figure 5-3. Schematic representation of the eight stages of the spermatogenetic cycle of the germinal epithelium of the drake. The numbers 1 through 10 indicate spermatids in different stages of spermiogenesis (see Figure 5-2). S = Sertoli cell. G = spermatogonium. GM = spermatogonium in mitosis. I = primary spermatocyte in interphase. L = spermatocyte in leptotene stage. Z = spermatocyte in zygotene stage. P = spermatocyte in pachytene stage. SIm = primary spermatocyte in metaphase. SII = secondary spermatocyte. $SIIm$ = secondary spermatocyte in metaphase. (From Clermont, 1958.)

gonia (Clermont and Morgentaler, 1955), but has no effect on type B spermatogonia or on mitosis as spermatocytes continue to be produced. However, the incidence of pachytene spermatocytes is severely reduced and there is degeneration of spermatids (stages 8 to 19 completely disappear); apparently, the spermatids are phagocytized by Sertoli cells. Results of hypophysectomy indicate that spermatogenesis through the premeiotic phase can occur in the absence of the pituitary gonadotropins; meiosis is apparently dependent on these hormones. Albert (1961) and Ortavant and Courot (1964) state that the postmeiotic phase is controlled by androgen. It is, however, not clear how androgen restores the germinal epithelium of hypophysectomized animals. Ortavant and Courot (1964) also conclude that the main effect of hypophysectomy is on the mitosis of the spermatogonia, reducing the number of spermatocytes formed by about 40 to 80 percent. There is also a marked degeneration during the zygotene phase of meiosis which can be prevented by FSH or LH administration.

The exact hormonal requirements for maintenance or reestablishment of spermatogenesis in hypophysectomized animals can be studied most conveniently in small laboratory mammals, because, pre-

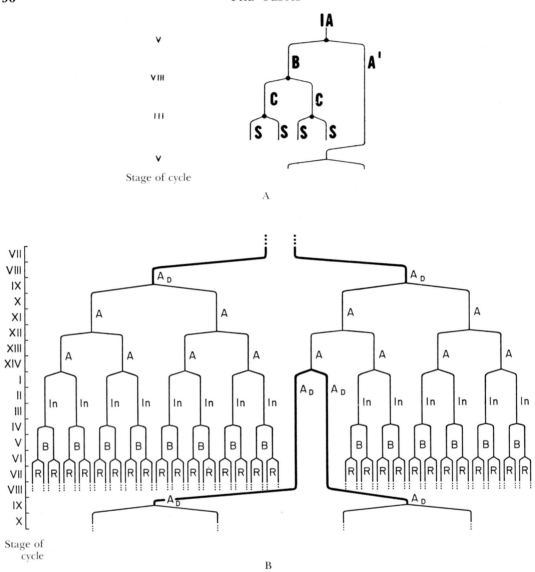

Figure 5-4. Probable patterns of development of spermatogonia in the drake and the rat. *IA* and *A'* = stem cell spermatogonia of the drake. A_D = dormant type A spermatogonia of the rat. *A* (for the rat) = type A spermatogonia (large cell, large nucleus, little chromatin). *In* = intermediate type spermatogonia (intermediate in appearance between types A and B). *B* and *C* (for the drake) = differentiated spermatogonia. *B* (for the rat) = type B spermatogonia (smaller cells than type A with smaller nucleus and peripheral chromatin). *R* = resting spermatocyte. *S* = spermatocytes. The junction of a vertical and two horizontal lines indicates a mitosis. In the rat, 10.6 percent of type A spermatogonia degenerate at stage XII; thus the yield of R is 10.6 percent less than indicated. (From Clermont, 1958, 1962.)

sumably, smaller amounts of hormones are required. Because most of the hormones available are of mammalian origin one would not expect great difficulties with specificity. Even in the case of growth hormone, for which specificity has been established, the rat will respond to prep-

arations of different origin. Consequently, we will mainly discuss the work done with rats. Some of the earlier literature is not included because the hormone preparations used were probably not pure; effects assigned to one hormone might well have been the result of either the contamina-

Table 5-8. Duration of the Seminiferous Epithelium Cycle* and of the Spermatogenic Cycle† in Various Mammalian Species

SPECIES	DURATION OF EPITHELIUM CYCLE (DAYS)	DURATION OF SPERMATOGENIC CYCLE (DAYS)
Rat (*Rattus norvegicus*)	12.3	49
Mouse (*Mus musculus*)	8.6	34
Bull (*Bos taurus*)	14.0	56
Sheep (*Ovis aries*)	10.0	40–49
Pig (*Sus scrofa*)	8.0	—
Rabbit (*Oryctolagus cuniculus*)	10.9	44
Man (*Homo sapiens*)	16	74

* Duration is time which elapses between two successive appearances of same cellular association.

† Interval between appearance of original spermatogonium and the release of the spermatozoa produced from it.

References: Ortavant, 1959; Ortavant and Courot, 1964; Swierstra and Foote, 1963, 1965; and Heller and Clermont, 1964.

tions present or a synergistic effect between the principal hormone and the contaminant.

In a very elaborate and thorough study, Woods and Simpson (1961) found that after hypophysectomy:

1. FSH injections (0.5 to 5 rat units [R.U.]/day) could not maintain testicular weight or the integrity of the germinal epithelium. At higher doses (10 to 40 R.U.) testicular weights could be maintained but at the dose of 10 R.U., .25 unit of LH was present as a contaminant and the seminal vesicles and prostate were heavier than those in the hypophysectomized controls. As will be discussed under point 2, this contamination may explain the effect.

2. At a dose of .25 R.U. of LH, testicular weight increased and few sperm cells were present whereas at lower doses this was not the case.

3. LH acted synergistically with FSH at a dose of 0.125 R.U. of LH (which by itself had no effect) together with 0.5 R.U. of FSH (which by itself had no effect), and testicular growth and spermatogenesis occurred.

4. Growth hormone and prolactin did not have an effect on the testes, but each acted synergistically with LH and with the combination of FSH plus LH.

5. ACTH and TSH had no effect on the testes or the response to gonadotropins.

After posthypophysectomy regression had occurred, no single hormone was capable of causing complete repair of the germinal epithelium although 15 R.U. of LH caused some. Combinations of FSH and LH acted synergistically to repair testicular epithelium and to restore the weight of the prostate and seminal vesicles. Growth and lactogenic hormone acted synergistically with the FSH-LH combination.

These data show rather clearly that, in the rat, LH is required for maintenance and for repair of the germinal epithelium. This effect of LH may be an indirect one in the sense that it acts via androgen secretion stimulated by the LH. As discussed in this chapter, androgens can prevent the testicular germinal epithelium degeneration and can restore spermatogenesis after the degeneration has occurred. Harvey (1965), in a preliminary note, confirms Woods and Simpson's data and states that the data obtained after LH injection and after androgen injection are remarkably similar.

Lacy and Lofts (1965) treated rats with estrogen (to inhibit gonadotropin secretion), which caused a gradual decline of germ cells other than spermatogonia. In many respects these changes are similar to those obtained after hypophysectomy. However, in this case, repair of the germinal epithelium was obtained by injecting FSH and not by injecting LH. One should not conclude that these data refute those of Woods and Simpson (1961). The data do indicate the possibility of an interaction between estrogen, the pituitary hormones, and the testes which is more complicated than the simple inhibition of FSH secretion.

The findings obtained in studies of rats may not be applicable to other species. Knobil and Josimovich (1961) found that LH injections in doses sufficient to stimulate the Leydig cells and to produce repair of the epithelium of the seminal vesicles of Rhesus monkeys did not repair the testicular germinal epithelium. FSH injections did, however, restore spermatogenesis without affecting the Leydig cells.

The effect of retaining the testes in the body cavity in species which normally have testes in the scrotum has been studied extensively by C. R. Moore and his co-workers (see review by Moore, 1939). These and subsequent investigations show that maintenance of the testes at body temperature or the exposure to higher temperature for short periods (20 minutes at 44°C. [Idäpään-Heikkilä, 1966]) led to disarrangement of the germinal epithelium, folding of the basement membrane, and infiltration of the Sertoli cells by lipids. This condition was reversible provided the exposure had not been too long. These effects have been observed in the lizard (Urosaurus ornatus) exposed for ten days to a temperature 1 to 2°C. above the preferred range (Licht, 1965), and in a number of mammals made artificially cryptorchid or in which the testes were exposed to high temperatures in other manners (e.g. rats, rabbits, sheep, and men).

Chowdhury and Steinberger (1964) exposed rat testes to 43°C. for 15 minutes and found that the damaging effect of heat was selective. Spermatids were damaged only in stages 1 and 2 of spermiogenesis; spermatids which had matured beyond these stages were not affected. Primary spermatocytes from stage 9 (see Table 5-6) to and including spermatocytes in stage 14 were damaged, but pachytene spermatocytes in stages 5 and 6 were not injured.

A number of recent investigations have been carried out to determine how applying heat causes damage to the germinal epithelium. Waites and Setchell (1964) applied heat to the testes of conscious rams so that they were above 39°C. for two to two and one half hours and established that this causes:

1. Damage to the germinal epithelium, determined by the incidence of dead and tailless sperm in the ejaculate.

2. An increased oxygen uptake so extensive that the low oxygen content of the venous blood probably causes tissue hypoxia.

3. An increase in glucose uptake by the testes. No change in blood flow was observed.

Waites and Setchell do not agree with the interpretation of data collected by Ewing and VanDemark (1963a,b), who used two different techniques. In the first, slices of rabbit testes exposed to abdominal temperatures for various lengths of time were incubated in vitro. The main criticism leveled at this experiment was that an unbuffered medium (Locke's) was used and that the data used in order to arrive at the conclusion that "spermatogenic arrest which results from exposure of the testis to elevated temperatures may be caused by reduced levels of substrate in the tissue" were based on incubation studies in air (where the center of the slice may be anaerobic). The studies carried out under an atmosphere of oxygen did not show a difference between control slices and slices from testes exposed to heat. As a second technique, Ewing and VanDemark (1963b) perfused testes in vitro with blood at 36.5 and 39.5°C. and measured glucose uptake. However, the rates of perfusion for the two temperature treatments were not the same, so one cannot be sure whether the effects observed were due to temperature differences or to perfusion rate differences.

The exact mechanism by which higher temperature causes degeneration of the testicular epithelium is still under investigation. However, it seems reasonable to assume that either lack of oxygen or lack of substrate causes the damage.

Nelson (1937) found that androgen secretion, as measured by seminal vesicle and ventral prostate weight, did not seem to be affected by cryptorchidism until 240 and 421 days, respectively, after the operation. Injections of a human pregnancy urine preparation restored these weights. Hall (1965) stated that biosynthesis of testosterone by rabbit testes in vitro was lower at 40°C. than at the scrotal temperature (38°C.) showing an impairment of steroid synthesis at abdominal temperatures. Eik-Nes (1966), measuring the testosterone concentration in spermatic venous blood, found that cryptorchid testes secreted less testosterone than scrotal testes; in both instances, gonadotropin administration increased testosterone production.

Nelson (1937) also noted that cryptorchidism causes the appearance of castration cells in the anterior pituitary of cryptorchid rats after about 65 days. Injections of a human pregnancy urine preparation caused the disappearance of these cells.

Johnson (1966), by using parabiosis (a hypophysectomized male joined with an intact male), found that after ten days of cryptorchidism of the intact partner, a significant weight increase in the testes and accessory sex organs of the hypophysectomized partner occurred. This indicates an increase in "total gonadotropin" and in LH secretion by the cryptorchid animals, although their own testes were smaller and the accessory sex organs not affected. This evidence suggests that some factor in addition to androgen affects pituitary gonadotropin and LH secretion.

Fachini and Ciaccolini (1966) deproteinized, defatted, and freed blood collected from spermatic veins of bulls of conjugated steriods, then deionized the remaining material and injected it into parabiotic female rats (ovariectomized adult with immature female). The ovary of the immature partner weighed 31.85 ± 2.67 mg. whereas that of controls was 72.65 ± 4.08 mg. and of corresponding females injected with jugular blood (processed as outlined) was 52.95 ± 1.62 mg. These results suggests that spermatic blood may contain a nonestrogenic, nonandrogenic substance which inhibits the anterior pituitary. The nature of this factor requires further elucidation and the question whether this factor is secreted by the tubules needs to be answered.

REFERENCES

AdamsSmith, W. N., and Peng, M. T. 1966. Influence of testosterone upon sexual maturation in the rat. J. Physiol. *185*:655-666.

Albert, A. 1961. The mammalian testis. *In* W. C. Young (ed.): Sex and Internal Secretions. Williams & Wilkins Co., Baltimore, Vol. 1, pp. 305-365.

Andrews, F. N. 1940. Thermo-regulatory function of rat scrotum. I. Normal development and effect of castration. Proc. Soc. Exp. Biol. Med. *45*:867-869.

Aronson, L. R. 1957. Reproductive and parental behavior. *In* M. E. Brown (ed.): Physiology of Fishes. Academic Press Inc., New York, Vol. 2, pp. 272-304.

Aronson, L. R. 1958. Hormones and reproductive behavior: Some phylogenetic considerations. *In* A. Gorbman (ed.): Comparative Endocrinology. John Wiley & Sons Inc., New York, pp. 98-120.

Arrington, L. R., Fox, M. H., and Bern, H. A. 1952. Androgen content of testis and adrenal of White Leghorn cockerels. Endocrinology *51*: 226-236.

Atz, J. W. 1957. The relation of the pituitary to reproduction in fishes. *In* G. E. Pickford and J. W. Atz (eds.): The Physiology of the Pituitary Gland of Fishes. New York Zool. Soc., New York, pp. 178-270.

Atz, J. W., and Pickford, G. E. 1964. The pituitary gland and its relation to the reproduction of fishes in nature and in captivity. FAO Fisheries Biology Techn. Paper No. 37.

Bailey, R. E. 1952. The incubation patch of passerine birds. Condor *54*:121-136.

Baillie, A. H., and Mack, W. S. 1966. Hydroxysteroid dehydrogenases in normal and abnormal human testes. J. Endocrinol. *35*:239-248.

Barraclough, C. A. 1966. Influence of age, prepubertal androgen treatment and hypothalamic stimulation on adenohypophysial LH content in female rats. Endocrinology *78*:1053-1060.

Barraclough, C. A., and Gorski, R. A. 1961. Evidence that the hypothalamus is responsible for androgen-induced sterility in the female rat. Endocrinology *68*:68-79.

Barraclough, C. A., and Gorski, R. A. 1962. Studies on mating behaviour in the androgen-sterilized female rat in relation to the hypothalamic regulation of sexual behaviour. J. Endocrinol. *25*: 175-182.

Basu, S. L. 1964. The effect of chorionic and serum gonadotrophin on the testes of normal and hypophysectomized toads, *Bufo melanostictus*. Folio Biol. *12*:203-210.

Basu, S. L., and Nandi, J. 1965. Effects of testosterone and gonadotropins on spermatogenesis in *Rana pipiens* Schreber. J. Exp. Zool. *159*:93-112.

Basu, S. L., Nandi, J., and Nandi, S. 1966. Effects of hormones on adult frog *(Rana pipiens)* testes in organ culture. J. Exp. Zool. *162*:245-255.

Benoit, J. 1950. Réproduction, charactères sexuels et hormones; Déterminisme du cycle saisonier. *In* P. P. Grassé (ed.): Traité de Zoologie. Masson et Cie, Paris, Vol. 15, pp. 384-478.

Bishop, D. W. 1961. Biology of spermatozoa. *In* W. C. Young (ed.): Sex and Internal Secretions. Williams & Wilkins Co., Baltimore, Vol. 2, pp. 707-796.

Blüm, V., and Fiedler, K. 1965. Hormonal control of reproductive behavior in some Cichlid fish. Gen. Comp. Endocrinol. *5*:186-196.

Bogdanove, E. M. 1964. The role of the brain in the regulation of pituitary gonadotropin secretion. Vitamins and Hormones *22*:206-260.

Bruce, H. M. 1965. Effect of castration on the reproductive pheromones of male mice. J. Reprod. Fertil. *10*:141-143

Burgos, M. H. 1955. Histochemistry of the testis in normal and experimentally treated frogs (Rana pipiens). J. Morphol. *96*:283-299.

Burgos, M. H., and Ladman, A. J. 1957. The effect of purified gonadotrophins on the morphology of the testes and thumb pads of the normal and hypophysectomized autumn frog *(Rana pipiens)*. Endocrinology *61*:20-34.

Callard, I. P. 1966. Testicular steroid synthesis in the snake, *Natrix sipedon pictiventris*. Amer. Zool. *6*:587.

Campbell, H. J. 1966. The development of the primary portal plexus in the median eminence of the rabbit. J. Anat. *100*:381-387.

Carpenter, C. R. 1933a. Psychobiological studies of social behavior in Aves. I. The effect of complete and incomplete gonadectomy on the primary sexual activity of the male pigeon. J. Comp. Psychol. *16*:25-57.

Carpenter, C. R. 1933b. Psychobiological studies of social behavior in Aves. II. The effect of complete and incomplete gonadectomy on second-

ary sexual activity histological studies. J. Comp. Psychol. *16*:59-97.

Chieffi, G. 1962. Endocrine aspects of reproduction in elasmobranch fishes. Gen. Comp. Endocrinol. Suppl. *1*:275-285.

Chieffi, G., and Lupo, C. 1961. Identification of oestradiol-17β, testosterone and its precursors from *Scylliorhinus stellaris* testes. Nature *190*: 169-170.

Chowdhury, A. K., and Steinberger, E. 1964. A quantitative study of the effect of heat on germinal epithelium of rat testes. Amer. J. Anat. *115*:509-524.

Christensen, A. K., and Mason, N. R. 1965. Comparative ability of seminiferous tubules and interstitial tissue of rat testes to synthesize androgens from progesterone-4-¹⁴C *in vitro*. Endocrinology *76*:646-656.

Chu, J. P. 1940. The effects of oestrone and testosterone and of pituitary extracts on the gonads of hypophysectomized pigeons. J. Endocrinol. *2*:21-37.

Clermont, Y. 1958. Structure de l'épithélium séminal et mode de renouvellement des spermatogonies chez le canard. Arch. Anat. Microscop. Morphol. Exp. *47*:47-66.

Clermont, Y. 1960. Cycle of the seminiferous epithelium of the guinea pig. Fertil. Steril. *11*:563-573.

Clermont, Y. 1962. Quantitative analysis of spermatogenesis of the rat: A revised model for the renewal of spermatogonia. Amer. J. Anat. *111*: 116-129.

Clermont, Y. 1966. Renewal of spermatogonia in man. Amer. J. Anat. *118*:509-524.

Clermont, Y., and Leblond, C. P. 1955. Spermiogenesis of man, monkey, ram and other mammals as shown by the "periodic acid–Schiff" technique. Amer. J. Anat. *96*:229-253.

Clermont, Y., and Leblond, C. P. 1959. Differentiation and renewal of spermatogonia in the monkey, Macacus rhesus. Amer. J. Anat. *104*: 237-273.

Clermont, Y., and Morgentaler, H. 1955. Quantitative study of spermatogenesis in the hypophysectomized rat. Endocrinology *57*:369-382.

Clermont, Y., and Perey, B. 1957. The stages of the cycle of the seminiferous epithelium of the rat: Practical definitions in PA-Schiff-hematoxylin and hematoxylin-eosin stained sections. Rev. Can. Biol. *16*:451-462.

Connell, G. M., Connell, C. J., and Eik-Nes, K. B. 1966. Testosterone synthesis by the two-day-old chick testis *in vitro*. Gen. Comp. Endocrinol. *7*:158-165.

Davidson, J. M., and Sawyer, C. H. 1961. Evidence for an hypothalamic focus of inhibition of gonadotropin by androgen in the male. Proc. Soc. Exp. Biol. Med. *107*:5-7.

Davis, D. E. 1963. The hormonal control of aggressive behavior. Proc. XIII Int. Ornithol. Congr. *2*:994-1003.

Della Corte, F., and Cosenza, L. 1965. Sur la présence d'hormones steroïdes dans les testicules de *Triturus cristatus carnifex* (Laur.). Gen. Comp. Endocrinol. *5*:679-680.

Dodd, J. M. 1960. Gonadal and gonadotrophic hormones in lower vertebrates. *In* A. S. Parkes (ed.): Marshall's Physiology of Reproduction. Longmans Green & Co. Ltd., London, 1 (Pt. 2), pp. 417-582.

Dodd, J. M., Evennett, P. J., and Goddard, C. K. 1960. Reproductive endocrinology in cyclostomes and elasmobranchs. Zool. Soc. of London Symp. *1*:77-104.

Dorfman, R. I., and Shipley, R. A. 1956. Androgens. John Wiley & Sons Inc., New York.

Dorfman, R. I., and Ungar, F. 1965. Metabolism of Steroid Hormones. Academic Press Inc., New York.

Eik-Nes, K. B. 1966. Secretion of testosterone by the eutopic and the cryptorchid testes in the same dog. Can. J. Physiol. Pharmacol. *(44:4)*:629-633.

Eik-Nes, K. B., and Hall, P. F. 1965. Secretion of steroid hormones *in vivo*. Vitamins and Hormones *23*:153-208.

Eisner, E. 1960. The relationship of hormones to reproductive behaviour of birds referring especially to parental behaviour: A review. Anim. Behav. *8*:155-179.

Ewing, L. L., and VanDemark, N. L. 1963a. Factors affecting testicular metabolism and function. II. Effect of temperature elevation *in vivo* on subsequent metabolic activity of rabbit testicular tissue *in vitro*. J. Reprod. Fertil. *6*:9-16.

Ewing, L. L., and VanDemark, N. L. 1963b. Factors affecting testicular metabolism and function. III. Effect of *in-vitro* temperature elevation on tissue slices and perfused testes in the rabbit. J. Reprod. Fertil. *6*:17-24.

Fachini, A., and Ciaccolini, C. 1966. Pituitary inhibition by effluent blood from the testis. Endokrinologie *50*:79-82.

Fisher, A. E. 1956. Maternal and sexual behavior induced by intracranial chemical stimulation. Science *124*:228-229.

Fisher, A. E. 1964. Chemical stimulation of the brain. Sci. Amer. *(210:6)*:60-68.

Forbes, T. R. 1961. Endocrinology of reproduction in cold-blooded vertebrates. *In* W. C. Young (ed.): Sex and Internal Secretions. Williams & Wilkins Co., Baltimore, Vol. 2, pp. 1035-1087.

Gaarenstroom, J. H., and de Jongh, S. E. 1946. A Contribution to the Knowledge of the Influences of Gonadotropic and Sex Hormones on the Gonads of Rats. Elsevier Publishing Co., Amsterdam.

Gorbman, A., and Bern, H. A. 1962. A Textbook of Comparative Endocrinology. John Wiley & Sons Inc., New York.

Grady, K. L., Phoenix, C. H., and Young, W. C. 1965. Role of the developing rat testis in differentiation of the neural tissues mediating mating behavior. J. Comp. Psychol. Physiol. *59*:176-182.

Grajcer, D., and Idler, D. R. 1963. Conjugated testosterone in the blood and testes of spawned Fraser River Sockeye Salmon, Oncorhynchus nerka. Comp. J. Biochem. Physiol. *41*:23-30.

Greenstein, J. S., and Hart, R. G. 1964. The effects of removal of the accessory glands separately or in paired combinations on the reproductive performance of the male rat. Fifth Int. Cong. Ann. Rep. (Trento) *3*:414-420.

Guhl, A. M. 1961. Gonadal hormones and social be-

havior in infrahuman vertebrates. *In* W. C. Young (ed.): Sex and Internal Secretions. Williams & Wilkins Co., Baltimore, Vol. 2, pp. 1240-1267.

Hall, P. F. 1965. Influence of temperature upon the biosynthesis of testosterone by rabbit testis *in vitro*. Endocrinology *76*:396-402.

Harris, G. W. 1964a. Female cycles of gonadotrophic secretion and female sexual behaviour in adult male rats castrated at birth. J. Physiol. *175*: 75P-76P.

Harris, G. W. 1964b. Sex hormones, brain development and brain function. Endocrinology *75*: 627-648.

Harris, G. W., and Levine, S. 1965. Sexual differentiation of the brain and its experimental control. J. Physiol. *181*:379-400.

Harvey, C. 1965. The effect of ICSH or FSH on the number of germ cells in the seminiferous tubules of the adult rats. Anat. Rec. *151*:359.

Hashimoto, I., and Suzuki, Y. 1966. Androgens in testicular venous blood in the rat, with special reference to puberal change in the secretory pattern. Endocrinol. Jap. *13*:326-337.

Heller, C. G., and Clermont, Y. 1964. Kinetics of the germinal epithelium in man. Recent Progr. Hormone Res. *20*:545-571.

Hoar, W. S. 1957a. The gonads and reproduction. *In* M. E. Brown (ed.): Physiology of Fishes. Academic Press Inc., New York, Vol. 1, pp. 287-321.

Hoar, W. S. 1957b. Endocrine organs. *In* M. E. Brown (ed.): Physiology of Fishes. Academic Press Inc., New York, Vol. 1, pp. 246-285.

Hoar, W. S. 1966. Hormonal activities of the pars distalis in cyclostomes, fish and amphibia. *In* G. W. Harris and B. T. Donovan (eds.): The Pituitary Gland. University of California Press, Berkeley, Vol. 1, pp. 242-294.

Idäpään-Heikkilä, P. 1966. Effect of local heat in vivo on the fine structure of the basement membrane and the Sertoli cells of the rat testis. Fertil. Steril. *17*:689-695.

Idler, D. R., and Truscott, B. 1966. Identification and quantification of testosterone in peripheral plasma of skate. Gen. Comp. Endocrinol. *7*: 375-383.

Ishii, S. 1960. Effects of testosterone on the ovary and anal fin of the viviparous teleost, *Ditrema temmincki* during gestation. Annot. Zool. Jap. *33*: 172-177.

Johns, J. E., and Pfeiffer, E. W. 1963. Testosterone-induced incubation patches of Phalarope birds. Science *140*:1225-1226.

Johnson, D. C. 1966. The use of non-castrate parabiotic rats for the evaluation of plasma gonadotrophins. Acta Endocrinol. *51*:269-280.

Kincl, F. A., Oriol, A., Pi, A. F., and Maqueo, M. 1965. Prevention of steroid-induced sterility in neonatal rats with thymic cell suspension. Proc. Soc. Exp. Biol. Med. *120*:252-255.

Knobil, E., and Josimovich, J. B. 1961. The interstitial cell stimulating activity of ovine, equine and human luteinizing hormone preparations in the hypophysectomized male Rhesus monkey. Endocrinology *69*:139-151.

Kumaran, J. D. S., and Turner, C. W. 1949. Endocrine activity of the testis of the White Plymouth Rock. Poultry Sci. *28*:636-640.

Lacy, D., and Lofts, B. 1965. Studies on the structure and function of the mammalian testis. I. Cytological and histochemical observations after continuous treatment with oestrogenic hormone and the effects of *F.S.H.* and *L.H.* Proc. Roy. Soc. London B. *162*:188-197.

Lacy, D., Lofts, B., Kinson, G., Hopkins, D., and Dott, H. 1965. Sertoli cells and steroid synthesis. Gen. Comp. Endocrinol. *5*:693.

Larsen, L. O. 1965. Effects of hypophysectomy in the cyclostome *Lampetra fluviatilis* (L.) Gray. Gen. Comp. Endocrinol. *5*:16-30.

Leach, R. B., Maddock, W. O., Tokuyama, I., Paulsen, C. A., and Nelson, W. O. 1956. Clinical studies of testicular hormone production. Recent Progr. Hormone Res. *12*:377-398.

Lehrman, D. S. 1961. Hormonal regulation of parental behavior in birds and infrahuman mammals. *In* W. C. Young (ed.): Sex and Internal Secretions. Williams & Wilkins Co., Baltimore, Vol. 2, pp. 1268-1382.

Lehrman, D. S. 1964. Control of behavior cycles in reproduction. *In* W. Etkin (ed.): Social Behavior and Organization among Vertebrates. University of Chicago Press, pp. 143-166.

Levine, S., and Mullins, R., Jr. 1964. Estrogen administered neonatally affects adult sexual behavior in male and female rats. Science *144*: 185-187.

Licht, P. 1965. The relation between preferred body temperatures and testicular heat sensitivity in lizards. Copeia *4*:428-436.

Lofts, B. 1961. The effects of follicle-stimulating hormone and luteinizing hormone on the testis of hypophysectomized frogs *(Rana temporaria)*. Gen. Comp. Endocrinol. *1*:179-189.

Lofts, B. 1962. The effects of exogenous androgen on the testicular cycle of the weaver-finch *Quelea quelea*. Gen Comp. Endocrinol. *2*:394-406.

Lofts, B. 1964. Seasonal changes in the functional activity of the interstitial and spermatogenetic tissues of the green frog, *Rana esculenta*. Gen. Comp. Endocrinol. *4*:550-562.

Lofts, B., and Marshall, A. J. 1959. The post-nuptial occurrence of progestins in the seminiferous tubules of birds. J. Endocrinol. *19*:16-21.

Lofts, B., Pickford, A. E., and Atz, J. W. 1966. Effects of methyl testosterone on the testes of a hypophysectomized Cyprinodont fish, Fundulus heteroclitus. Gen. Comp. Endocrinol. *6*:74-88.

Ludwig, D. J. 1950. The effect of androgen on spermatogenesis. Endocrinology *46*:453-481.

Mann, T. 1964. The Biochemistry of Semen and the Male Reproductive Tract. John Wiley & Sons Inc., New York.

Marshall, A. J. 1955. Reproduction in birds: The male. Mem. Soc. Endocrinol. *4*:75-89.

Marshall, A. J. 1961. Reproduction. *In* A. J. Marshall (ed.): Biology and Comparative Physiology of Birds. Academic Press Inc., New York, Vol. 2, pp. 169-213.

McKenzie, F. F., Miller, J. C., and Bauguess, L. C.

1938. The reproductive organs and semen of the boar. Research Bull., Mo. Agric. Exp. Sta. No. 279.

Moore, C. R. 1939. Biology of the testis, *In* Ed. 2. of E. Allen, C. H. Danforth, and E. A. Doisy (eds.): Sex and Internal Secretions, Williams & Wilkins Co., Baltimore, pp. 353-451.

Morrison, R. L., and Johnson, D. C. 1966. The effects of androgenization in males castrated at birth. J. Endocrinol. *34*:117-123.

Nalbandov, A. V., Meyer, R. K., and McShan, W. H. 1951. The role of a third gonadotrophic hormone in the mechanism of androgen secretion in chicken testes. Anat. Rec. *110*:475-493.

Nelson, W. O. 1937. Some factors involved in the control of the gametogenic and endocrine function of the testis. Cold Spring Harbor Symp. Quant. Biol. *5*:123-131.

Ortavant, R. 1959. Spermatogenesis and morphology of the spermatozoon. *In* H. H. Cole and P. T. Cupps (eds.): Reproduction in Domestic Animals. Academic Press Inc., New York, Vol. 2, pp. 1-50.

Ortavant, R., and Courot, M. 1964. Problèmes concernant l'action des hormones gamétocinétiques sur la spermotogènèse des mammifères. Arch. Biol. *75*:625-668.

Parkes, A. S., and Marshall, A. J. 1960. The reproductive hormones in birds. *In* A. S. Parkes (ed.): Marshall's Physiology of Reproduction. Longmans Green & Co. Ltd., London, 1 (Pt. 2) pp. 583-706.

Phoenix, C. H., Goy, R. W., Gerall, A. A., and Young, W. C. 1959. Organizing action of prenatally administered testosterone propionate on the tissues mediating mating behavior in the female guinea pig. Endocrinology *65*:369-382.

Sundararaj, B. I., and Nayar, S. K. 1966. Effect of testosterone and estrogen on the testes and seminal vesicles of hypophysectomized catfish, *Heteropneustes fossilis*. Anat. Rec. *154*:491 (abstract).

Swanson, H. E., and van der Werff ten Bosch, J. J. 1964. "Early-androgen" syndrome; its development and the response to hemi-spaying. Acta Endocrinol. *45*:1-12.

Swierstra, E. E., and Foote, R. H. 1963. Cytology and kinetics of spermatogenesis in the rabbit. J. Reprod. Fertil. *5*:309-322.

Swierstra, E. E., and Foote, R. H. 1965. Duration of spermatogenesis and spermatozoan transport in the rabbit based on cytological changes, DNA synthesis and labeling with tritiated thymidine. Amer. J. Anat. *116*:401-411.

van Dongen, W. J., and de Kort, E. M. J. 1959. Spermiation in the common frog *(Rana temporaria)*. I. Experiments on the isolated testis. Proc. Kon. Nederl. Akad. Wetensch. *62 C*:320-326.

van Dongen, W. J., Draisma, J. R., and de Kort, E. J. M. 1959. Spermiation in the common frog *(Rana temporaria)*. II. Experiments *in vitro*. Proc. Kon. Nederl. Akad. Wetensch. *62 C*:327-332.

van Dongen, W. J., Ballieux, R. E., Geursen, H. J., and Offermans, T. 1960. Spermiation in the common frog *(Rana temporaria)*. III. Histochemical and chemical investigations. Proc. Kon. Nederl. Akad. Wetensch. *63 C*:257-263.

van Oordt, G. J. 1963. Male gonadal hormones. *In* U. S. von Euler and H. Heller (eds.): Comparative Endocrinology. Academic Press Inc., New York, Vol. 1, pp. 155-207.

van Oordt, P. G. W. J. 1960. The influence of internal and external factors in the regulation of the spermatogenetic cycle in amphibia. Zool. Soc. London Symp. 2:29-52.

van Rees, G. P., and Gans, E. 1966. Effect of gonadectomy and oestrogen on pituitary LH-content and organ weight of androgen-sterilized female rats. Acta Endocrinol. 52:471-477.

van Tienhoven, A. 1961. Endocrinology of reproduction in birds. *In* W. C. Young (ed.): Sex and Internal Secretions. Williams & Wilkins Co., Baltimore, Vol. 2, pp. 1088-1169.

Waites, G. M. H., and Setchell, B. P. 1964. Effect of local heating on blood flow and metabolism in the testis of the conscious ram. J. Reprod. Fertil. *8*:339-349.

Whalen, R. E., and Nadler, R. D. 1963. Suppression of the development of female mating behavior by estrogen administered in infancy. Science *141*:273-274.

Witschi, E. 1961. Sex and secondary sexual characters. *In* A. J. Marshall (ed.): Biology and Comparative Physiology of Birds. Academic Press, New York, Vol. 2, pp. 115-168.

World Health Organization. 1965. Mechanism of action of sex hormones and analogous substances. W.H.O. Techn. Report Series 303.

Woods, M. C., and Simpson, M. E. 1961. Pituitary control of the testis of the hypophysectomized rat. Endocrinology *69*:91-125.

Young, W. C. 1961. The hormones and mating behavior. *In* W. C. Young (ed.): Sex and Internal Secretions. Williams & Wilkins Co., Baltimore, Vol. 2, pp. 1173-1239.

Young, W. C. 1964. The hormones and behavior. *In* M. Florkin and H. S. Mason (eds.): Comparative Biochemistry. Academic Press Inc., New York, Vol. 7, pp. 203-251.

Chapter 6

The Ovary

There are several differences and similarities between the testis and the ovary, which have been summarized in Table 6-1. It is evident that the ovary produces gonocytes and hormones, as is the case with the testis. These hormones, as we will discuss, serve in the female as the androgens do in the male; i.e. they are involved in the maintenance and stimulation of the gonoducts, in the differentiation of nervous structures, in the expression of secondary sex characters, and so forth.

ESTROGEN SECRETION

To a large extent, the knowledge concerning ovarian estrogen secretion by lower vertebrates is fragmentary and in many cases indirect. Some of this indirect evidence indicating estrogen secretion is tabulated in Table 6-2. Only in relatively few cases have estrogens been extracted from the ovary and in even fewer cases has the structure of the hormone been determined. Table 6-3 gives a list of the var-

Table 6-1. Comparison of the Ovary and the Testis

CHARACTER	OVARY	TESTIS
Location (Chapter 3)	Abdominal in all species	Abdominal in inframammalian animals, scrotal in many mammals (see Table 3-2)
Symmetry (Chapter 3)	In many reptiles, most birds, only left ovary developed; in Duck-bill platypus and some bats only 1 ovary developed	In most species, two testes function
Origin in elasmobranchs and tetrapods (Chapter 2)	Cortex of indifferent gonad	Medulla of indifferent gonad
Seasonal cycles	In many species	In many species
Cyclic phenomena during breeding season	In many mammals, pronounced cycles	No pronounced cycles
Hormones secreted (Chapters 5 and 6)	Estrogens Progestins Androgens	Androgens Progestins Estrogens
Control by gonadotropins (Chapters 5 and 6)	Follicular growth by FSH + LH Interstitial cells by LH Corpus luteum by LH (?)	Spermatogenesis by FSH or LH (?) Interstitial cells by LH
Mitosis (Chapters 5 and 6)	Mitosis continues in teleosts, amphibians, most reptiles after sexual maturity No mitosis after sexual maturity in cyclostomes, elasmobranchs, birds, and most or all mammals	Mitosis after sexual maturity

Table 6-2. Indirect Evidence Suggesting That Ovaries of Inframammalian Vertebrates Secrete Estrogens

SPECIES	TECHNIQUE USED	CHANGES OBSERVED
CYCLOSTOMES:		
River lamprey *(Lampetra fluviatilis)*	Estrone injection	Swollen labia in ³/₅ animals
ELASMOBRANCHS:		
Smooth dogfish *(Mustelus canis)*	Estrogen pellet implant	Stimulation of reproductive tract.
Spotted dogfish *(Squalus caniculus)*	Estrogen pellet implant	Stimulation of oviduct, horny secretions
HOLOSTEI:		
Bowfin *(Amia calva)*	Ovariectomy	Caudal ocellus appears (normally found only in males)
TELEOSTS:		
Tilapia sp.	Ovariectomy	Decrease in length of genital tube. Opercular coloration of immature female
Siamese fighting fish *(Betta splendens)*	Ovariectomy	No breeding behavior
Jewel fish *(Hemichromis bimaculatus)*	Ovariectomy	No breeding behavior
Guppy *(Poecilia reticulata)* ♂	Estradiol injection	Anal fin feminine
AMPHIBIA (Urodeles):		
Triturus cristatus	Ovariectomy	Regression if cloaca was swollen
American newt *(Triturus viridescence)*	Estrogen ⚲̷, ♀, ♂̷, ♂	Müllerian duct hypertrophy
AMPHIBIA (Anura):		
Meadow frog *(Rana pipiens)*	Ovariectomy	Oviduct regression
Meadow frog *(Rana pipiens)* I* & A†	Ovariectomy + estrogen	Oviduct hypertrophy.
REPTILES:		
Lizard *(Lacerta agilis)*	Ovariectomy	Lower oviducal epithelium
American chameleon *(Anolis carolinensis)*	Ovariectomy	Decrease in oviductal weight
American chameleon *(Anolis carolinensis)*	Estrogen ♂	Urge to fight increased. Ductus deferens, cloaca, Müllerian duct stimulated
Garter snake *(Thamnophis* sp.), pregnant	Estradiol dipropionate	Müllerian ducts stimulated
Testudo iberica I*	Estrogen	Stimulation of oviducts
American alligator *(Alligator mississippiensis*	Estrone injection	Stimulated oviducts
Lizard *(Sceloporus spinosus floridanus)*	Estrogen ♂	Hypertrophy of Müllerian ducts
Sceloporus occidentalis	Estrogen ♂	Hypertrophy of Müllerian ducts
Uromastix sp.	Estrogen ♂	Hypertrophy of Müllerian ducts

⚲̷ = gonadectomized female; ♀ = intact female; ♂̷ = gonadectomized male; ♂ = intact male.
*I = Immature
†A = Adult
References: Dodd, 1960; Forbes, 1961.

ious inframammalian vertebrate species from which estrogens have been isolated. The available evidence suggests that estrogen secretion by the ovary occurs in all classes of vertebrates and that these hormones play a role in stimulating female secondary sex characters and secondary sex organs in all classes of vertebrates.

Site of Estrogen Secretion

The site of estrogen secretion can be deduced from the histochemical demon-

stration of the key enzymes in the biosynthesis of the steroid hormones (see Figure 5-1). For a discussion of the interpretation and specificity of these histochemical methods see Deane and Rubin (1965).

The atretic follicle of *Torpedo marmorata* shows a positive reaction to the presence of Δ^5-3-β-hydroxysteroid dehydrogenase, but the postovulatory follicle shows a negative reaction, whereas in *Scyliorhinus stellaris* the situation is just the reverse (see Nandi, 1967). Bara (1965) has found that the enzyme is present in the thecal cells but not in the granulosa cells of maturing, ma-

Table 6-3. Species of Inframammalian Vertebrates in Which Estrogens Have Been Extracted from the Ovary or Blood

SPECIES	METHOD OF DETECTION	IDENTIFICATION	REFERENCE
CYCLOSTOMES:			
Sea lamprey (*Petromyzon marinus*)	Chemical	Estradiol-17-β, estrone	Botticelli et al., 1963
ELASMOBRANCHS:			
Pacific spiny dogfish (*Squalus suckleyi*)	Chemical	Estradiol-17-β, estrone	Wotiz et al., 1958
North Atlantic spiny dogfish (*Squalus acanthias*)	Chemical	Estradiol-17-β, estrone	Gottfried, 1964
Lesser spotted dogfish (*Scyliorhinus canicula*)	Chemical	Estradiol-17-β, estrone	Gottfried, 1964
Smooth dogfish (*Mustelus canis*)	Bioassay	Estrogen	Pickford and Atz, 1957
Torpedo (*Torpedo marmorata*)	Chemical	Estradiol-17-β, estriol	Chieffi and Lupo, 1963
DIPNOI:			
Lungfish (*Protopterus annectens*)	Chemical	Estradiol-17-β	Dean and Jones, 1959
TELEOSTS:			
Brown trout (*Salmo irideus*)*	Chemical	Estradiol-17-β	Gottfried, 1964
Carp (*Cyprinus carpio*)	Chemical	Estriol, 16-epi-estriol, estradiol-17-β	Gottfried, 1964
Swordfish (*Xiphias gladius*)	Bioassay	Estrogen	Forbes, 1961
Flounder (*Pseudopleuronectes americanus*)	Bioassay	Estrogen	Forbes, 1961
Angler fish (*Lophius piscatorius*)	Bioassay	Estrogen	Forbes, 1961
Cod (*Gadus callarias*)	Chemical	Estradiol-17-β, estrone	Gottfried, 1964
Conger eel (*Conger conger*)	Chemical	Estradiol-17-β, estrone, estriol	Lupo and Chieffi, 1963
Channel catfish (*Ictalurus punctatus*	Chemical	16-keto-estradiol, estriol, epiestriol, estradiol-17-α, estradiol-17-β, estrone	Eleftheriou et al., 1966
AMPHIBIA:			
Common European frog (*Rana temporaria*)	Chemical	Estrone, estradiol-17-β, estriol	Cédard and Ozon, 1962
Toad (*Bufo vulgaris*)	Chemical	Estradiol-17-β, estrone, estriol	Chieffi and Lupo, 1963
AVES:			
Chicken (*Gallus domesticus*)	Chemical	Estrogen	Marlow and Richert, 1940
	Chemical	Estradiol-17-β, estriol, estrone	Layne et al., 1958
	Chemical	Estradiol, estrone	O'Grady and Heald, 1965

* Gottfried (1964) refers to the brown trout as *Salmo irideus*. According to Hubbs and Lagler (1958) the brown trout is *Salmo trutta*, whereas the rainbow trout is *Salmo gairdneri* with *Salmo gairdneri irideus* considered a subspecies of *Salmo gairdneri*.

ture, and spent follicles of the mackerel (*Scomber scomber*). Atretic follicles, on the other hand, apparently lack this enzyme, suggesting that no steroidogenesis occurs in these follicles. Lambert (1966) found in the guppy (*Poecilia reticulata*) that the enzyme was present in the granulosa cells of the normal follicle. These observations, although indicating steroidogenesis in the follicle, do not prove that estrogens are formed; on the other hand, the presence of estrogen in the ovary and the presence of Δ^5-3-β-hydroxysteroid dehydrogenase would be evidence, albeit indirect, that estrogens are synthesized in follicular cells.

Among amphibia, this steroid dehydrogenase enzyme has been found in the granulosa cells, the thecal cells of the follicle, and the postovulatory follicle of *Triturus cristatus* and *Rana esculenta* (Nandi,

1967). Pesonen and Rapola (1962) could not detect 3-β-hydroxysteroid dehydrogenase in the ovaries of the South African clawed toad *(Xenopus laevis)* or in the toad *(Bufo bufo)*, suggesting a low level of steroidogenesis in the ovaries. However, Chieffi and Lupo (1963) identified estradiol-17-β, estrone, and estriol in ovarian extracts of *Bufo vulgaris,* indicating that steroidogenesis may occur in the ovary of this species. The possibility that estrogen is secreted by the adrenals and is found in the ovary cannot be excluded, particularly in view of the evidence that the adrenals of the South African clawed toad show a strong 3-β-hydroxysteroid dehydrogenase reaction.

The granulosa and theca of the water snake *(Natrix sipedon)* and the lizard *(Lacerta sicula)* show a positive reaction, as does the postovulatory follicle of the lizard (Nandi, 1967). The granulosa and theca of atretic and postovulatory follicles of the chicken also give a positive test for this enzyme. Marshall and Coombs (1957), mainly on the basis of histological and histochemical considerations, proposed that the estrogens are secreted by the thecal gland cells of the ovary, but the histochemical methods used were less specific than the Δ^5-3-β HSD test.

The estrogens found in different mammalian species are listed in Table 6-4.

Investigations to ascertain the site of estrogen production in the ovary are difficult, and much of the evidence that one cell type or another produces a particular hormone is indirect. For instance, the fact that a tumor of a certain cell type is associated with a high titer of a particular hormone has been used to identify the source of the hormone.

Destruction of certain cellular elements, for instance those of the follicles by x-rays, has been followed by measurement of hormone output by the animals with such ovaries. Rats in which all follicles have been destroyed by x-rays show irregular cycles for about six weeks. During the subsequent one to 14 weeks the animals may be in continuous estrus which is followed by permanent anestrus. Thus, there is evidence of estrogen secretion during a seven to 20 week period in the absence of follicles (Eckstein, 1962).

Many of the conclusions concerning the cellular origin of estrogen secretion must, therefore, be taken as tentative (Young, 1961). The cells of the theca interna, the thecal lutein cells of the corpus luteum, and the interstitial cells of the ovary have all been implicated as producers of estrogens (Young, 1961). Short (1964), on the basis of elegant experiments with follicles of the mare, has proposed a two-cell hypothesis explaining the synthe-

Table 6-4. Estrogens Found in Endocrine Organs of Female Mammals

SPECIES	ORGAN	ESTRONE	ESTRADIOL-17-β	ESTRADIOL-17-α	ESTRIOL	6-α-OH-ESTRADIOL-17-β
Pig	Ovary	+	+	−	−	−
Cow	Ovary, follicular fluid	7.3 μg./100 ml.	68.5 μg./100 ml.	−	−	−
Horse in estrus	Ovary, follicular fluid	16.9 μg./100 ml.	252 μg./100 ml.	−	−	−
	Ovary	+	+	−	−	+
Human	Ovary, luteal tissue of pregnancy	+ 24-89 μg./100 ml.	− 7-64 μg./100 ml.	−	+ 24 μg./100 ml.	−
Pig	Placenta	+	−	−	−	−
Cow	Placenta	+	+	+	−	−
Sheep	Placenta	−	−	+	−	−
Goat	Placenta	−	−	+	−	−
Human	Placenta	+	+	−	+	−
Cattle	Adrenal	+	−	−	−	−

References: Velle, 1963; Mellin and Erb, 1965.

sis of steroids. The hypothesis can be formulated as follows: the theca interna cells have all the enzymes required for synthesis of estradiol 17-β from cholesterol. The granulosa cells, on the other hand, have only a weak 17-hydroxylase ability and little or no 17-desmolase activity. In the intact follicle at estrus the theca interna probably secretes mainly estrogens, which can then reach the general circulation via the ovarian vein and lymphatic ducts. The granulosa cells, which are poorly vascularized, especially in comparison with the theca interna cells, probably synthesize little steroid hormone.

After rupture of the follicle, the theca cells regress, the granulosa cells become vascularized and form the corpus luteum. These cells can synthesize progesterone, some 17-α-hydroxyprogesterone and 20-α-hydroxypregn 4-en 3-one but little estrogenic hormone. In the mare, estrogen is, apparently, secreted by the theca interna cells. There may, however, be species differences with respect to the hormones that are produced by the various cell types as was pointed out by Savard in his discussion of Short's paper.

Control of Estrogen Secretion

Experiments performed to determine the control of estrogen secretion by the pituitary of lower vertebrates have not been numerous and some of the evidence available is difficult to interpret, because in some cases, e.g. *Rana pipiens,* the result may be due to a direct effect of pituitary hormones on the secondary sex organs (which were used to evaluate estrogen secretion by the ovary). In general, the indirect evidence suggests that in most species estrogen secretion is controlled by the secretions of the anterior pituitary as is the case in mammals. Lostroh and Johnson (1966), using hypophysectomized 28-day-old female rats, showed that FSH alone was not sufficient to induce enough estrogen secretion to stimulate uterine weights;

LH alone was also insufficient. A dose of 3 μg. FSH + 0.05 μg. LH per day for three days caused a small increase in uterine weight but 3 μg. FSH + 0.5 μg. LH per day for three days caused a substantial increase in uterine weight. These investigators used gonadotropin preparations of very high purity so that contaminations of FSH and LH and vice versa were negligible. A more detailed discussion about the control of estrogen secretions by pituitary hormones can be found in the papers by Dodd et al. (1960), and Jones and Ball (1962).

Effects of Estrogens

The effects of estrogens are most conveniently discussed with respect to the effects they have on various systems.

THE REPRODUCTIVE SYSTEM

One needs to distinguish between a direct effect of estrogen and an indirect one, which acts by virtue of its influence on the anterior pituitary or other endocrine gland involved in reproduction.

Effect on the Ovary. One direct effect of estrogen on the gonads has already been discussed under sex determination (Chapter 2). A direct effect of estrogens on the ovary of mature females has been noted in frogs *(Rana pipiens).* Ovaries of this frog can be made to ovulate in vitro by the addition of either pituitary preparation or progesterone to Ringer's fluid (Wright, 1961b). The addition of estrone and estradiol benzoate will reduce the number of eggs ovulated after adding pituitary extract, but will increase the number released after treatment with either progesterone or progesterone plus pituitary extract (Wright, 1961b). Edgren and Carter (1963), who used a better statistical design than Wright for their experiment, found no effect for estradiol-17-β or for estrone, but found that estriol inhibited the response to progesterone, thus indicating a direct effect of estriol on the ovary.

In birds, Chu and You (1946) did not find any ovarian stimulation by estrogen in hypophysectomized pigeons. Phillips and van Tienhoven (1960) found a synergism between estrogen and gonadotropin on follicle formation of mallard duck ovaries. In this case it was thought that the estrogen acted favorably by causing mobilization of the yolk precursors and that the gonadotropin enhanced or caused the transport of these precursors into the follicles.

There are several experiments which indicate that estrogens have a direct effect on the ovary in intact mammals. In some cases one cannot eliminate the possibility that the estrogens act via the hypophysis and, therefore, experiments with hypophysectomized animals are the most convincing. We will discuss both types of evidence.

Eckstein (1962) points out that it has been known since 1940 that estrogens stimulate the proliferation of the granulosa cells of hypophysectomized rodents. Recent investigations have shown that estrogens can cause an increase in ovarian weight of intact immature rats during the first eight days of administration and an increase in follicular size (Smith, 1961; Smith and Bradbury, 1961). After the eighth day, estrogen administration causes the ovarian weights to be smaller than those of controls. Aron et al. (1961) placed 20 to 50 μg. crystals of estradiol into the ovary of mature rats and observed in seven out of 18 cases luteinization of follicles. These "pseudo corpora lutea" had not ovulated. Aron et al., (1965) found subsequently that in pregnant rats, injection of estradiol on the tenth day of gestation caused formation of corpora lutea, with the incidence of corpus luteum formation higher in females that had mated than in females that had refused the male. Asch (1965) has reported that injections of 50 μg. estradiol in immature guinea pigs caused stimulation of follicles in 22 out of 26 and caused atresia in three animals, whereas in mature guinea pigs such injections caused luteinization in 11 out of 26 and atresia in ten out

of 26 animals. These experiments suggest gonadotropin release by estrogen, but do not exclude a direct effect on the ovary.

In hypophysectomized rats the granulosa proliferation is accompanied by heavier ovarian weights and larger follicles (Ingram, 1959; Croes-Buth et al., 1959; Smith, 1961; Smith and Bradbury, 1961). The doses of estradiol used to obtain these effects ranged from 0.5 to 1,000μg./day/rat. Aron and Marescaux (1961) observed that injecting 100 μg. of estradiol benzoate immediately after hypophysectomy prevented follicular degeneration in four out of six guinea pigs. When injected 24 hours after hypophysectomy follicular degeneration was prevented in four out of nine cases, and when it was injected 48 hours after the operation, follicular degeneration was prevented in one out of eight cases. These workers found that in the hypophysectomized guinea pig, 100 μg. estradiol benzoate acted synergistically with exogenous gonadotropins (of unstated origin) to cause the formation of corpora lutea, (CL) (1 out of 30 CL in gonadotropin treated, 30 out of 49 CL after gonadotropin plus estrogen treatment).

Intact immature rats injected with FSH and diethylstilbestrol (DES) showed formation of CL, but after injection of FSH alone, few CL were formed. DES injected in combination with human chorionic gonadotropin (HCG) yielded cystic luteinized follicles. Similar treatments of hypophysectomized rats yielded neither corpora lutea (in the case of FSH plus DES) nor luteinized follicles (in the case of HCG plus DES). DES treatment increased the ovarian weight in response to FSH and to pregnant mare's serum gonadotropin (PMSG) in immature and in hypophysectomized rats. DES increased ovarian weight in immature rats injected with HCG or with LH, but failed to do so in hypophysectomized rats (Smith and Bradbury, 1963). The difference in response between immature and hypophysectomized rats was, according to Smith and Bradbury, the result of estrogen-induced LH release from the pituitaries of the intact rats. Callantine et al. (1966) have presented evidence that estrogen can cause LH release, at least in adult rats. Smith and Bradbury (1963) also found that estrogen could stimulate the granulosa cells of the follicles directly.

There is evidence in the guinea pig for a synergistic effect between estrogen and gonadotropins, whereas in the rat the apparent synergistic effect on the induction of ovulation is the result of endogenous gonadotropin release induced by estrogen treatment. Takewaki (1964) found that HCG injected in estrogen-induced persistent diestrous rats, caused formation of nonfunctional CL; however, if estrogen was given before, during and after the HCG injections, functional CL (secreting progesterone) were formed.

Croes-Buth et al. (1960) noted that in intact immature rats small doses of estrogen reduce the size of the Leydig cells and the total amount of interstitium; large doses do not show such an effect. On the other hand, in hypophysectomized rats small or large doses reduce the total amount of interstitial tissue but do not affect cell size. It thus appears that estrogens act on the interstitium as well as on the granulosa cells; they inhibit the former but stimulate the latter.

The maintenance of the corpus luteum will be discussed later in more detail, but it should be mentioned here that estrogens can maintain the morphology and secretory function of the corpus luteum in hypophysectomized rabbits (see Eckstein, 1962) and rats (Bogdanove, 1964).

Effect on the Pituitary. The effect of estrogen on the pituitary, especially on gonadotropin secretion and release, has been the object of intensive studies. It is the classic concept that the gonadotropins stimulate ovarian follicular growth and ovarian steroidogenesis, and that these steroids in turn cause a decrease or an increase in gonadotropin secretion.

Much of the detailed experimental work with ovarian-pituitary relationships

has been done with mammals, mainly the rat, rabbit, and cat.

It is useful to define the terms to be used in the remainder of the discussions. "Gonadotropins" will refer to an unspecified mixture of FSH and LH or material assayed by a test that is not specific for either FSH or LH (see Appendix). "FSH," follicle stimulating hormone, will be used when either a "pure" hormone has been injected or when a bioassay presumably specific for FSH has been used. "LH" will mean luteinizing hormone and the term will be used when either a "pure" hormone is injected or a bioassay presumably specific for LH is used. "Interstitial cell stimulating hormone" (ICSH) and LH refer to the same substance. LH will also be considered the ovulation-inducing hormone. "Luteotropin" (LTH) or "prolactin" will be used for the hormone when a "pure" hormone is injected or when a bioassay specific for LTH has been used.

For an understanding of the relationship between the pituitary and the ovary, the effects of ovariectomy and estrogen administration on hypophyseal and blood serum concentrations of FSH and LH (van Rees, 1964) will be discussed.

In rats, ovariectomy causes an increase in the FSH and LH content of the anterior pituitary and in the concentration of these hormones in the blood (Table 6-5). One should keep in mind that ovariectomy not only removes estrogens from the circulation but that it may also remove progestins and androgens (Bogdanove, 1964). However, administration of 2 to 50 μg. of estradiol benzoate reduces the FSH and LH levels of the pituitary and serum in gonadectomized male and female rats. No decrease in the FSH content of the pituitary was found in intact female rats, although a reduction was observed in intact males. At very low doses, 0.1 to 0.2 μg. of estradiol per rat and 0.06 μg./100 gm. body weight, an increased pituitary LH content and a slight decrease in the serum concentration of LH were found (van Rees, 1964). This suggests that there may be different thresholds for the effect of estrogens on synthesis and release of LH. If this is indeed true, then the data would indicate a strong inhibiting effect on the release of LH (small doses inhibit the release) and a weaker inhibiting effect on synthesis (high doses inhibiting synthesis and thus causing a drop in pituitary LH content [van Rees, 1964]). Callantine et al. (1966) found an increase in plasma LH and a decrease in pituitary LH content after injection of 0.6 μg. of estradiol-17-β for seven days, thus showing that estrogen causes LH release.

Bogdanove (1964) has pointed out that if estrogens are given chronically and in sufficient doses, the LH and FSH release are both blocked, and that the dosage required to block FSH release is about eight times higher than the one for LH blockade.

Small doses of estrogen given for a short period can, under certain conditions (e.g. in prepubertal rats, pregnant rats, guinea pigs with ovaries transplanted to the spleen, anestrous ewes, rabbits after vaginal stimulation, anestrous cats after vaginal stimulation, and women with secondary amenorrhea [Everett, 1961; Greep, 1961]), cause ovulation by facilitating or causing the release of LH. Injecting estrogen into immature rats advances puberty (Ramirez and Sawyer, 1965).

Keeping in mind some reservations, one may generalize from present evidence that high doses of estrogens and chronic estrogen administration inhibit LH release, and in sufficiently high doses, FSH release, and that in short term experiments using low doses of estrogen LH release can be caused.

A number of studies, made to determine the site or sites at which estrogen has its effect, have thrown additional light on the question whether estrogens affect LH secretion and release. The data of some of these experiments, and a few experiments in which estrogen was given systemically and in which LH levels in the anterior pituitary and blood were determined, have been summarized in Table 6-5. (See also Table 8-3 and the discussion in Chapter 8.) In summary, these data show:

1. Implants of estrogen in the hypothalamus of rats and rabbits prevent the postcastration rise in plasma LH (Ramirez et al., 1964; and Kanematsu and Sawyer, 1964).

2. Estrogen implanted in the median eminence of intact rats causes a rise in plasma LH during the first four to five days after implantation (Palka et al., 1966), but after 18 days the LH concentration returns to normal. In ovariectomized rats such implants cause a depletion of LH from the pituitary 14 days after the implantation (Ramirez et al., 1964); in rabbits a similar LH depletion occurs (Kanematsu and Sawyer, 1964).

3. Intrapituitary implants of estrogen in rats prevent the postcastration plasma LH increase (Ramirez et al., 1964); the difference between the results obtained by these workers and Kanematsu and Sawyer (1963a) may be the result of bilateral implantations used by Ramirez et al. (1964) to ensure good distribution of the estrogen through the gland, and the unilateral implants by Kanematsu and Sawyer (1963a). In ovariectomized rabbits such implants cause an increase in the serum LH concentration (Kanematsu and Sawyer, 1964).

4. Castration cells do not appear in ovariectomized rats and rabbits if estrogen is implanted in the arcuate nucleus and the posterior median eminence, respectively (Lisk, 1963; Kanematsu and Sawyer, 1963b). According to Bogdanove (1963), who used pellets rather than estrogen in tubes, such implants fail to prevent the occurrence of castration cells. However, as Bogdanove (1963) pointed out, the area of contact of the pellet and median eminence may have been such that too little estrogen was available.

5. Intrapituitary estrogen implants fail to inhibit the occurrence of castration cells in rabbits (Kanematsu and Sawyer,

Table 6-5. Effect of Ovariectomy on Hypophyseal and Serum LH Levels

SPECIES	TREATMENT	SERUM LH	AP LH	AP WEIGHT	HISTOLOGY AP	REFERENCE
		% Ovarian ascorbic acid depletion	µg./AP	% Control value		
Rat (immature)	♀ Control	4*	19*	100*		Ramirez and McCann, 1963
	♀	16	18	95		
	♀ + Estradiol Benzoate 0.002 µg./100 g./day 14-23	16	—	100		
	0.02	13	—	100		
	0.04	0	12	85		
	0.06	3	10	87		
	0.18	3	2	100		
Rat (adult)	♀ Control	Not detected	16	100		
	♀	16	22	102		
	♀ + Estradiol Benzoate 0.002 µg./100 g./day 14-23	15	35	120		
	0.02	14	—	100		
	0.06	15	—	155		
	0.12	2	28	160		
	0.18	3	10			
				mg.		
Rat (adult)	♀ + Blank needle in mammary nucleus and arcuate nucleus			15.0 ± 0.38	Many castration cells	Lisk, 1963
	♀ + Estradiol in arcuate nucleus			15.8 ± 0.42	Few gonadotrops	
	in mamillary nucleus			15.8 ± 0.34	Many castration cells	
	in other points of the hypothalamus			16.0 ± 1.00	Many castration cells	
	in AP			—	Normal around the tip, at greater distance, castration cells	
	♀ Control			15.8 ± 1.01	Few gonadotrops	
		% Ovarian acid depletion				
Rat (adult)	♂ Control	15.3 ± 0.7				McCann and Taleisnik, 1961
	♂ + 0.1 µg. Estradiol benzoate 1X; 3 days later	9.6 ± 1.7				
	0.2 µg.	6.0 ± 1.7				
	1.0 µg.	4.7 ± 1.5				
	5.0 µg.	8.2 ± 1.9				
	3.7 µg.	3.7 ± 2.2				
		% Ovarian acid depletion	% Control value	mg.		
Rat (adult)	♂ Control	15.0 ± 0.8	100	9.8 ± 0.2		Ramirez et al., 1964
	♂ + Estradiol: Cholesterol 1:0 tube implant median eminence	− 1.6 ± 1.4		—		(Implants bilateral; rats killed after 12-14 days)
	1:5	6.2 ± 1.6	10	15.2 ± 0.8		
	1:10	3.4 ± 1.3	35	13.6 ± 1.2		
	1:12	5.4 ± 2.4		9.6		
	1:13	10.0 ± 0.9		10.3 ± 1.0		
	1:17	14.3 ± 1.7		12.0		
	1:26	11.1 ± 1.4		10.6 ± 0.5		
	♂ + Estradiol: Cholesterol 1:0 tube implant AP	6.3 ± 1.8	85	17.0 ± 1.0		
	1:10	7.8 ± 1.5		12.9 ± 1.1		
	1:12	9.6 ± 1.1		9.5 ± 0.8		
	1:13	8.7 ± 1.4		10.4 ± 1.1		
	1:17	14.2 ± 1.5		12.3 ± 0.6		

SPECIES	TREATMENT	SERUM LH	AP LH	AP WEIGHT		HISTOLOGY AP	REFERENCE
Rat (adult)	♀ Control					Castration cells	Bogdanove, 1963
	♀ + Estradiol: Cholesterol 1:8000 } Anterior Hypothalamus					Castration cells	
	1:2000 Anterior median eminence					Castration cells	
	1:500 Posterior median eminence					Castration cells	
	1:300 Mamillary body					Castration cells	
	1:100 }					Castration cells	
	0					Castration cells	
	♀ + Estradiol: Cholesterol 1:8000 in AP					Castration cells 5/5	
	1:2000 in AP					Castration cells 2/4	
	1:500 in AP					Castration cells 0/10	
	1:300 in AP					Castration cells 0/6	
	1:100 in AP					Castration cells 0/1	
	0					Castration cells 10/10	

SPECIES	TREATMENT	SERUM LH μg. LH/100 ml. plasma	AP WEIGHT IPSI-LATERAL mg./100 gm. body weight	AP WEIGHT CONTRA-LATERAL mg./100 gm. body weight	REFERENCE
Rat (adult)	♀ Control 5 days	0.2*	2.5*	2.5*	Palka et al., 1966
	♀ + Estradiol H³ median eminence 4 days	7.5	3.0	3.0	
	♀ + Estradiol 6,7H³ acetate median eminence 5 days	25.0	3.0	2.7	
	♀ + Estradiol H³ median eminence 18 days	0.2	3.5	2.2	
	♀ + Estradiol 6,7H³ acetate AP 4 days	0.2	3.2	2.8	
	♀ + Estradiol 6,7H³ acetate AP 5 days	0.2	3.1	2.5	
	♀ + Estradiol H³ AP 18 days	0.2	3.5	2.1	

SPECIES	TREATMENT	AP LH μg./gm. wet wt.	AP WEIGHT mg.	REFERENCE
Rabbit (adult)	♀ + Estrogen in tube in AP	0.50	13.9 ± 1.0	Kanematsu and Sawyer, 1963a (Animals killed 8 weeks after implant)
	♀ + Estrogen in tube in posterior median eminence	< 0.05†	13.2 ± 0.8	
	♀ + Estrogen in tube outside posterior median eminence	0.47	11.9 ± 0.9	
	♀ + Blank tube	—	11.4 ± 1.8	

SPECIES	TREATMENT	AP WEIGHT mg.	HISTOLOGY AP	REFERENCE
Rabbit (adult)	♀		5.26% GTH cells; GTH cells hypertrophied	Kanematsu and Sawyer, 1963b
	♀ + Estrogen in tube in AP	10.3 ± 0.8	3.67% GTH cells; GTH cells hypertrophied	
	♀ + Estrogen in tube in posterior median eminence	17.0 ± 2.5	0.66% GTH cells; GTH cells hypertrophied	
	♀ + Estrogen in tube in anterior median eminence	9.3	2.93% GTH cells; GTH cells hypertrophied	
	♀ + Estrogen in tube in mamillary body	12.1	4.76% GTH cells; GTH cells hypertrophied	

SPECIES	TREATMENT	SERUM LH % Ovarian ascorbic acid depletion	AP LH μg./gm. wet wt.	AP WEIGHT mg.	REFERENCE
Rabbit (adult)	♀ + Blank tubes	21.6 ± 3.3†	0.53 ± 0.05	10.5 ± 0.6	Kanematsu and Sawyer, 1964 (Animals killed 8 weeks after implant)
	♀ + Estradiol in tube in posterior median eminence	9.1 ± 3.4	< 0.1 in 5/7	19.6 ± 3.0	
	♀ + Estradiol in tube in other sites	24.1 ± 2.5	0.51 ± 0.06	11.7 ± 0.5	
	♀ + Estradiol in tube in AP	34.2 ± 1.8	0.34 ± 0.03	10.4 ± 0.8	

♀ = Gonadectomized female; ♀ = intact female.
* Values in this column were read from graph and are approximate.
† Associated with ovarian atrophy.

1963b). Bogdanove (1963) and also Lisk (1963) have reported the lack of such cells in the areas close to the implants in rats.

In addition to the difference obtained with respect to the pituitary cytology, there are differences of opinion about the interpretation of the data. Kanematsu and Sawyer (1963a) and Ramirez el al. (1964) state that estrogen, acting on the median eminence, inhibits the release of LH in rats and rabbits and causes pituitary hypertrophy. However, acting on the pituitary directly, estrogen causes release of LH in the rabbit (high blood LH concentration and a lowered pituitary LH content). Bogdanove (1963, 1964), on the other hand, is of the opinion that estrogen implanted in the hypothalamus is transported by the hypophyseal portal vessels to the anterior pituitary where it has its effect. Palka et al. (1966) have shown that such transport indeed occurs after the implanting of radioactive estrogens. More radioactivity was found in the contralateral pituitary half after a hypothalamic implant than after an intrapituitary implant.

The major objections to Bogdanove's interpretation have been stated clearly by Kanematsu and Sawyer (1964) and Palka et al. (1966). In brief, they are:

1. Cortisone implanted in the hypothalamus is not effective in the suppression of ACTH, but is effective when placed in the pituitary, thus demonstrating that a hormone that presumably would be transported in a way similar to estrogen is not effective in the hypothalamus but is effective in the pituitary.

2. Estrogen implanted in the rabbit AP causes an increase in plasma LH, but implants in the posterior median eminence (PME) cause a decrease in plasma LH. If the effects of estrogens were only on the AP cells then one would not expect the opposite from AP and PME implants.

The apparent discrepancy between the effects of intrapituitary estrogen implants on plasma LH concentration in ovariectomized rabbits and rats may be related to the different mechanisms involved in LH release for ovulation, although the time interval between implantation and measurement may also be the cause. The rat ovulates spontaneously every four days, whereas the rabbit ovulates only after coitus or after the injections of agents that cause LH release, or after LH injection. One might speculate that the neural stimulus, which causes ovulation, affects not only the release of an LH releasing factor but also causes an increased amount of blood to be diverted to the hypophysis so that estrogen acts in concert with the LH releasing factor and ensures ovulation. It is interesting to note that the rabbit is the only one of the mammalian species investigated in which the pituitary blood supply is not transported entirely via the portal system, but also via the anterior hypophyseal artery (Harris, 1947).

Worthington (1960), in a beautiful study, has shown that various agents (Nembutal, morphine) reduce the portal blood flow, whereas others (epinephrine, painful stimuli) increase it in the mouse. The speculation made above would thus be in line with known physiological phenomena, and the anatomical data may explain the difference that exists between the rat and rabbit after estrogen implants.

It should be mentioned that estrogen administration to males leads to atrophy of the testes, secondary sex organs, and secondary sex characters (dependent upon the presence of androgens). The evidence for and against a direct effect on the pituitary and an indirect one via the central nervous system is discussed at length by Bogdanove (1964), and will be reviewed in Chapter 8.

Mention was made that estrogens can maintain the corpus luteum of the hypophysectomized rabbit. This is due to a direct action. Estrogens also stimulate luteotropin (LTH) secretion by the anterior pituitary in the rabbit (Bogdanove, 1964) and the rat (Ratner et al., 1963). Kanematsu and Sawyer (1963a) found that estrogen implants in the median eminence of rabbits promote LTH synthesis and storage in the pituitary, whereas implants in the anterior pituitary cause LTH release. In the rat, estrogen injection causes an increase in LTH content of the AP (Ratner et al., 1963) and implants of estrogen either in the median eminence or in the anterior pituitary cause an increase in pituitary LTH content and an increase of LTH liberation, as indicated by mammary gland development (Ramirez and McCann, 1964).

The effect of estrogen addition to rat pituitaries cultured in vitro has not been consistent with respect to LTH secretion. Nicoll and Meites (1962) found that estrogen stimulated LTH secretion, whereas Gala (1965) found a depressed LTH secretion. Gala (1965) and Ratner et al. (1963) agree that injection of estrogen prior to removal of the pituitaries increases the LTH secretion of these pituitaries in vitro. Nicoll's and Meites' (1962) results suggest that estrogens can act directly upon the adenohypophyseal prolactin producing cells. This, of course, does not exclude other mechanisms.

Effect on the Oviducts. For the lower vertebrates (cyclostomes, elasmobranchs, teleosts, amphibia, and reptiles), effects of estrogens are listed in Table 6-3. For birds and mammals there is substantial evidence that ovariectomy prevents the normal development and growth of the Müllerian duct system and that estrogen administration causes development and growth.

However, the avian oviduct will not become functional, i.e. secrete proteins, unless either androgens or progestins are present with the estrogen. From the results of an extensive series of experiments, Dorfman and Dorfman (1963) concluded that progesterone decreases the response of the chicken oviduct to estrogen when this response is close to maximal, but that progesterone has a synergistic effect on the estrogen response if it is minimal. Estrogens also cause the breakdown of the occluding plate found at the junction of the oviduct and the vagina (Kar, 1947).

In mammals, as in birds, the Müllerian duct system's development is controlled by estrogens. This control can now be viewed from the point of view of gene-effector interactions (see Bonner, 1965). The events and mechanisms involved in protein synthesis are summarized briefly as follows: The information contained in the DNA of a gene is transcribed to cytoplasmic messenger RNA by base pairing so that the messenger RNA has a sequence of bases complementary to the DNA strand which formed the template. Amino acids are attached, through the interaction with enzymes, to transfer RNA (also called soluble RNA). The amino acid—transfer RNA combination ("activated amino acids") are transported to ribosomes. The ribosomes, moving along the messenger RNA, obtain information on the order in which amino acids attach to each other to form the polypeptide chain. When the polypeptide chain is completed it is released. Since each cell of an animal carries the same genetic information, the question of how cells and tissues differ remains.

The hypothesis for regulation of the genes is as follows: Regulator genes make repressors which then act on the operator gene, which, with the structural genes controlled by it, forms the operon. An effector substance, which may be a hormone, combines with the repressor to make it ineffective (derepresses it) so that the operon can now be expressed and the subsequent DNA transcription to messenger RNA and the formation of ribosomal RNA, which is required for protein synthesis, can occur. Estrogen injection causes water imbibition, hyperemia, an increase in RNA polymerase activity (Gorski, 1964), a ten-fold increase in RNA synthesis, and a subsequent increase in protein synthesis. Both RNA synthesis and protein synthesis are blocked by actinomycin D application; this antibiotic prevents the use of the DNA as a template and thus inhibits DNA-dependent RNA synthesis (Bonner, 1965). It has also been shown that a macromolecular cell fraction will inhibit the activity of RNA polymerase, but that this fraction combined with estrogen does not.

Segal et al. (1965), in an elegant series of experiments, demonstrated that the increased synthesis of RNA is the key to the action of estrogen on uterine cell growth. RNA, extracted from uteri of ovariectomized estradiol-treated rats and injected into the uteri of ovariectomized control rats stimulated cell growth. This stimulation was similar to that obtained with 6×10^{-4} μg. estradiol injected intraluminally in other ovariectomized rats.

Most studies of the events that occur after estrogen administration have dealt with the uterus, but similar changes occur in the Fallopian tube. The collagen content of the cervix decreases and the vaginal epithelium changes markedly. These changes in the epithelium are the basis for a number of estrogen bioassays. The presence of cornified cells in the vaginal smear is interpreted as a positive response (see Emmens, 1962, for details). The following measurements have been used to indicate a positive response to estrogen in the spayed mouse or rat:

1. The presence of cornified cells (with or without nucleated cells).

2. An increase in the rate of mitosis in the vaginal epithelium.

3. The thickness of the epithelium.

4. Increased vaginal respiration as determined by the reduction of 2, 3, and 5 triphenyltetrazolium to formazan. Emmens (1962) has given an exhaustive review of the methods used to estimate amounts of estrogens present in fluids and tissues by bioassay. In connection with estrogen bioassays, it should be mentioned that different estrogens can counteract each other's effects on the uterus. For instance, estriol and estrone both inhibit the effect of estradiol-17-β on the uterus of the ovariectomized rat and estriol depresses the response to estrone. Concentrations of estriol which inhibited the effect of estrone on the uterus did not show such an inhibition on the vaginal smear (Edgren, 1959).

SECONDARY SEX CHARACTERS

The effects of estrogen on secondary sex characters of the cyclostomes, elasmo-branchs, teleost fishes, and anuran amphibia have been relatively little studied and it is not possible to state whether or not the estrogens have an effect on such characters (in some cases they do not exist because the sexes are not dimorphic).

The male European newt *(Triturus cristatus)* has a dorsal crest and a silvery tail band; these characters are not the result of the presence of androgen but rather of the absence of estrogen. They develop when either sex is castrated. The development of the cloacal papilla also is depressed or inhibited by estrogens.

Reptiles generally show little sexual dimorphism, thus estrogens can be expected to have little effect. The femoral glands of the lizard *(Lacerta agilis)* are, however, less developed in the ovariectomized than in the intact female.

There are a number of secondary sex characters in birds which are controlled by estrogens.

Beak Color of Birds. The brown color at the base of the beak of female budgerigars *(Melopsittacus undulatus)* in the breeding condition is the result of estrogen secretion. In nonlaying females and intact and castrated males, the color is blue but it changes to brown after estrogen injection (Parkes and Marshall, 1960).

In the red-billed weaver *(Quelea quelea)*, the color of the bill of males, castrated males, and nonbreeding females is blood-red, whereas in the laying bird it is yellow, indicating that estrogen causes this change (Witschi, 1961).

Plumage Color and Structure. The male Brown Leghorn has black ventral feathers; the female has fawn ones. Estrogens cause the fawn color, as can be seen by administering estrogen to a capon from which the feathers have been removed. The barbs of the feather show a sensitivity gradient from tip to base. The estrogen effects on the growing feather vary with the intensity and duration of stimulation and the sensitivity of the feather (Parkes, 1952). The castrated female, the capon, and the rooster all have the male type of plumage, showing that this plumage results from a lack of estrogen rather than from the presence of androgen. Estrogen affects feather structure as well as color. The normal saddle feather of the capon is long and pointed and lacks barbules; after estrogen administration it is shorter and more rounded and has barbules.

In mallard ducks, pheasants (*Phasianus colchicus*), and quail (*Coturnix coturnix*), sexual dimorphism of the plumage colors is the result of the presence of estrogens in the female. Vevers (1962) discusses evidence that in Amherst pheasants (*Chrysolophus amherstiae*), pigmentation, barbule structure, and growth rate are estrogen-dependent, but that the angle of barring and the production of certain bars are not affected by estrogen.

Mammary Gland Development. Among mammals sexual dimorphism is quite common, but the number of secondary sexual characters proven to be controlled by estrogens is rather limited (Vevers, 1962).

1. The pouch of the brush tail possum (*Trichosuras vulpecula*) is formed only under the influence of estrogen; in the castrated male, estrogen administration causes formation of a pouch from the scrotum according to Bolliger and Tow (1947), suggesting homology of scrotum and pouch. These results have, however, not been confirmed by Sharman (1959) using the quokka (*Setonix brachyurus*). He also reviewed the evidence obtained by others and came to the conclusion that scrotum and pouch are not homologous. The evidence favors Sharman's conclusion that pouch and scrotum are not homologous.

2. The dewlap of the doe rabbit does not develop in the ovariectomized female or in the male. Injections of estrogen in the spayed doe will cause dewlap formation.

3. The sexual skin of the female baboon (*Papio* sp.), mandrill (*Mandrillus* sp.), mangabey (*Cercocebus* sp.), chimpanzee (*Pan satyrus*), and Rhesus monkey (*Macacus mulatta*) shows swelling during the follicular phase of ovarian development and after estrogen injection (in the Rhesus monkey).

On the other hand, in the small monkey (*Miopithecus talapoin*) there seems to be no correlation between the onset of menstruation and the swelling of the sexual skin (Eckstein and Zuckerman, 1960).

4. In most, if not all, mammals, estrogen causes initial development of the mammary glands, especially of the ducts.

EFFECTS OF ESTROGEN ON BLOOD COMPOSITION

Estrogen administration causes remarkable changes in the composition of the blood of teleosts, amphibia, reptiles, and birds, whereas no significant changes seem to occur in elasmobranchs, and except for lipemia, minor ones occur in mammals (see Table 6-6). The changes have been studied extensively in the chicken (Table 6-7) and the composition of the blood can be compared with that of the yolk of the chicken egg (Table 6-8). Urist and Schjeide (1961) have emphasized the relationship between hypercalcemia and hyperproteinemia to calcium protein complexes and yolk deposition. The phosphoprotein (X_1) and the phospholipid-lipoglycoprotein (X_2) present in avian blood serve apparently as precursors for the yolk. After passage through the follicular membrane the molecular weights of these protein complexes are reduced to half (Schjeide and Urist, 1959).

We have speculated that the following steps may occur, at least in birds, at the approach of sexual maturity.

1. Gonadotropins stimulate the secretion of estrogen and, possibly, of androgens by the ovary.

2. Estrogens cause mobilization of various precursors required for yolk, albumen, and shell formation, e.g. phospholipid, cholesterol, triglyceride, protein, calcium concentrations in the blood increase (Table 6-7). The changes in composition of the blood are largely the result of increased biosynthesis of these components in the liver (Ranney and Chaikoff, 1951; and Vanstone et al., 1957).

Table 6-6.　Effect of Estrogen on Blood Composition of Different Vertebrates

	CONTROL							ESTROGEN TREATED						
CLASS	CA mg. %	PROTEIN gm. %	LIPID (TOTAL) mg. %	STEROL ESTER + STEROLS %	TRIGLY-CERIDES %	PHOSPHO-LIPIDS mg. %	%	CA mg. %	PROTEIN gm. %	LIPID (TOTAL) mg. %	STEROL ESTER + STEROLS %	TRIGLY-CERIDES %	PHOSPHO-LIPIDS mg. %	%
Triukis semifasciatus (shark)	17.4	1.2	790	30	33	33	36	16.4	1.6	940	34	32	36	33.4
Paralabrax clathratus (Bass)	12.8	5.5	2210	29	17	54	54	108.2	14.4	4820	16	34.4	2430	49.4
Rana catesbeiana (Bull frog)	11.6	1.8	180	50	6.3	81	43.7	154.6	10.6	940	40	25.8	690	34.2
Pseudemys scripta troostii (Turtle)	8.5	2.9	680	47.7	9.4	290	42.9	36.8	3.7	1870	26.8	38.1	660	35.1
Gallus domesticus (Chicken)	10.2	3.4	1360	57.9	2.5	540	39.6	90.4	7.4	3290	44.4	20.2	1170	35.4
Mus musculus (Mouse)	9.9	6.3	565	—	—	200	—	11.0	6.2	1080	—	—	505	—

Reference: Urist and Schjeide, 1961.

3. Gonadotropins probably increase permeability of the follicular membranes and change the metabolic activity of these membranes so that yolk deposition occurs. This last effect of gonadotropins has not been studied and therefore remains speculative.

Indirect evidence in support of this sequence of events is the fact that in immature chickens yolk deposition cannot be induced, even by massive doses of chicken pituitary extracts or by mammalian gonadotropins. In chickens thus treated the oviducts are enlarged (van Tienhoven, 1961),

Table 6-7.　Changes in Blood Composition of Chickens After Estrogen Administration

COMPONENT	SEX	CONTROL	ESTROGEN
Total lipids, mg./100 ml. plasma	M	1100	14210
Phospholipids, mg./100 ml. plasma	M	162	934
Sphingomyelin, mg./100 ml. plasma	M	22	54
Cephalin, mg./100 ml. plasma	M	34	214
Cholesterol, mg./100 ml. plasma	M	235	1136
Total protein, gm./100 ml. serum	M	3.90	7.40
Albumen, gm./100 ml. serum	M	1.00	0.60
Globulin, gm./100 ml. serum	M	2.90	6.80
Vitellin (dilution detected)	F	0	40
Hemoglobin, gm./100 ml.	F	9	5.6
Total vitamin A, μg./100 ml.	F	5.1	46.8
Vitamin A ester, μg./100 ml.	F	0.9	42.8
Vitamin A alcohol, μg./100 ml.	F	4.2	4.0
Riboflavin, p.p.m.	F	Trace?	1.22
Biotin (water sol.), mμg./ml.	F	1.3 ± 0.22	8.3 ± 1.8
Ca, mg./100 ml.	M	10	97
Ultrafilterable Ca, mg./100 ml.	M	6.50	8.00
Mn, μg./100 ml.	F	None*	13.8
Inorganic phosphate, mg./100 ml.	M	6.20	20.00
Total sulfate, mg./100 ml.	M	5.80	1.70
Iron, μg./100 ml. plasma	F	100	700

* Controls were nonlaying hens, treated were 11-week-old pullets.
Reference: van Tienhoven, 1961.

Table 6-8. Composition of the Yolk of Chicken Eggs

COMPONENT	GRAMS	PERCENT
Total	18.7	100
Water	9.1	48.6
Solids	9.6	51.4
Organic matter	9.4	50.3
Proteins	3.1	16.6
Lipids	6.1	32.6
Triglycerides	4.0	21.4
Phospholipids	1.7	9.1
Cholesterol	0.4	9.1
Carbohydrates	0.2	1.1
Inorganic matter	0.2	1.1

References: Romanoff and Romanoff, 1949; O. S. Privet et al., 1962.

indicating that estrogen secretion occurs and precedes yolk formation. Other evidence, provided by the experiments of Phillips and van Tienhoven (1960), shows that pretreatment of adult wild mallard ducks with estrogen reduces the amount of gonadotropin required for yolk deposition.

The increase in blood calcium that occurs in chickens after estrogen administration consists mainly of an increase in the nondiffusible calcium (calcium protein complex). This increase is dependent, however, upon the level of diffusible calcium present at the time of estrogen administration. The concentration of diffusible calcium, in turn, is dependent on the parathyroids. The relationships between estrogen, parathyroid hormone, blood calcium levels, and bone calcium are not entirely clear. It has been established that:

1. Estrogen administration causes medullary bone deposition (Figure 6-1).

2. Laying hens show a greater increase in blood calcium after administration of parathyroid extract than do roosters or nonlaying hens (see Table 6-9).

3. Estrogen-induced elevation of blood calcium in the chicken is dependent on the level of diffusible calcium present at the time of estrogen injection (Polin and Sturkie, 1958). This agrees with the concept formulated by Urist and Schjeide (1961); estrogens affect the blood composi-

tion only in those classes in which there has been some evidence for regulation of blood calcium by the parathyroid hormone (in the case of teleosts it may be secreted by the ultimobranchial bodies [see Gorbman and Bern, 1962]).

4. Estrogen increases calcium retention; testosterone acts synergistically with estradiol benzoate in this respect (Table 6-10).

5. Estrogen administration causes an increase in parathyroid size (Landauer, 1954) and activity as measured histologically (Benoit, 1950; and von Faber, 1954).

6. Bone formed under the influence of estrogen administration in parathyroidectomized chickens is not calcified (Benoit and Clavert, 1947).

It appears from the available data that in the nonlaying hen estrogen increases calcium retention and bone deposition, and, at the same time, increases parathyroid activity. When egg laying starts and calcium is deposited in the shell, blood calcium levels decrease, which, in turn, causes parathyroid hormone release. The parathyroid hormone causes mobilization of the medullary bone deposited prior to the start of egg laying. Figure 6-1 illustrates that during egg shell formation, medullary bone is destroyed, whereas bone is formed when no egg shell formation is taking place. Inadequate calcium intake, which

Table 6-9. Parathyroid, Estrogen, and Blood Calcium: Relationships in Birds

ANIMAL	TREATMENT	N	TOTAL CA	DIFFUSIBLE CA	NON-DIFFUSIBLE CA	REFERENCE
			mg./100 ml.			
Laying hen	(Control)	73	24.7	7.0	17.1	
Laying hen	18–24 hour, starved	20	16.5	5.9	9.2	Polin and Sturkie, 1957
Laying hen	Sham-~~parathyroid~~‡	10	16.4	5.7	10.7	
Laying hen	~~Parathyroid~~	27	11.3	4.3	7.3	
Parathyroid rooster	100 mg. estrone	3	90	7.0	—	
Intact rooster	100 mg. estrone	1	101	7.9	—	Urist et al., 1960
Parathyroid hen	100 mg. estrone	2	66	4.8	—	
Intact hen	100 mg. estrone	1	114	9.0	—	
Estrogen treated rooster	Sham-~~parathyroid~~	28	24	6.0	—	
Estrogen treated rooster	~~Parathyroid~~	35	18	4	—	Polin and Sturkie, 1958
Laying hen	100 U PTE*	10	32	—	—	
Laying hen	(Control)	10	24	—	—	
Rooster	(Control)	6	11.8	—	—	Polin et al., 1957
Rooster	100 U PTE*	6	12.4	—	—	
Laying hen	(Control)	3	29.8	11.5	—	
Laying hen	500 U PTE*	3	47.7	12.0	—	
Laying hen	1000 U PTE*	3	33.2	12.6	—	
Nonlaying hen	(Control)	3	13.4	6.3	—	
Nonlaying hen	500 U PTE*	3	19.5	9.8	—	Urist et al., 1960
Nonlaying hen	1000 U PTE*	3	27.4	9.5	—	
Rooster	(Control)	3	10.0	6.0	—	
Rooster	500 U PTE*	3	19.5	10.5	—	
Rooster	1000 U PTE*	3	20.2	10.9	—	

* 4 Hours after parathyroid extract injection. ‡ ~~parathyroid~~ = parathyroidectomized.

Table 6-10. Effect of Gonadal Hormones on Average Daily Calcium Retention by Sexually Immature Pullets

TREATMENT	CONTROL	5 × 0.75 MG. TP	5 × 1.0 MG. ESTRADIOL BENZOATE	5 × 0.75 MG. TP + 5 × 1.0 MG. EB
Average daily Ca retention mg.	221	267*	286*	411*
Serum Ca mg./100 cc.	12.0	12.3	45.5*	48.3*

* $P < 0.01$.
Reference: Common et al., 1953.

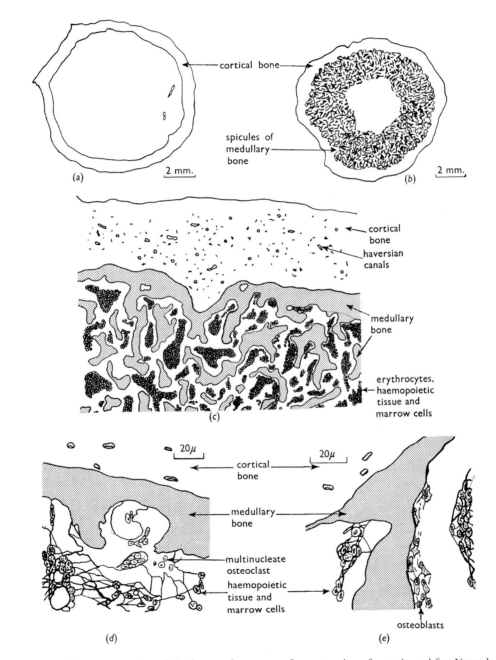

Figure 6-1. a. Transverse section of the femur of a rooster after extraction of protein and fat. Note absence of medullary bone. b. Similar section of the bone of a laying hen. Note the many trabeculae of medullary bone. c. Transverse section showing the invasion of the marrow by spicules of medullary bone in laying hen. d. High magnification view showing the destruction of medullary bone by an osteoclast during the time that an egg shell is being calcified in the oviduct of a laying fowl. e. A view similar to that in (d) showing bone being formed during osteoblastic activity in the absence of egg shell formation by the fowl. (From Simkiss, 1961.)

results in a negative calcium balance, will eventually lead to mobilization of all the medullary bone.

EFFECT ON APPETITE

In chickens and probably in other birds, treatment with synthetic estrogens is followed by an increase in appetite that is associated with the increased fat deposition (Hill et al., 1958). It has not been established whether naturally occurring estrogens have a similar effect. Meites (1949) has shown that diethylstilbestrol decreases appetite in rats and that estrone lacks this effect. It is thus possible that synthetic and naturally occurring estrogens may also have different effects on chickens. It may be that increased appetite as a result of estrogen secretion is an important adaptation that ensures the intake of the large

amounts of energy necessary for formation of eggs, but until it is proven that natural estrogens have such an effect this must remain a speculation. Whether estrogen affects the hypothalamic centers that regulate appetite directly and cause hyperphagia or whether changes in the blood composition induced by estrogen cause this phenomenon has not been determined.

EFFECT ON SEXUAL BEHAVIOR

With the exception of rabbits, ferrets, monkeys, and man (see Table 6-11), there is usually a rather limited period, called the estrous period, when the female will mate. This period may be as short as six to 12 hours, as in guinea pigs, or it may last several days, as in the mare. The estrus period coincides with the time of greatest ovarian follicular development and signs of estro-

Table 6-11. Cyclic Activity of Various Mammals

SPECIES*	CYCLE TYPE†	LENGTH (DAYS)	DURATION OF ESTRUS‡	OVULATION TYPE§	TIME	LUTEAL PHASE IN ABSENCE OF COITUS
Cat	S, P	14	4 days	I	24–30 hours after coitus	No
Cow	C, P	21	13–14 hours	Sp	12–16 hours after end of estrus	Yes
Dog	S, M	60	7–9 days	Sp	1–3 days after onset of estrus	Yes
Ewe	S, P	16	30–36 hours	Sp	12–24 hours prior to end of estrus	Yes
Ferret	S	—	Continuous	I	30 hours after coitus	No
Fox	S, M	90	1–5 days	Sp	1–2 days after onset of estrus	Yes
Goat	S, P	20–21	39 hours	Sp	30–36 hours after onset of estrus	Yes
Ground squirrel (Citellus tridecemlineatus)	S, P	14–28	3 days	I	8–12 hours after coitus	No
Guinea pig	C, P	16	6–11 hours	Sp	10 hours after onset of estrus	Yes
Hamster	C, P	4	20 hours	Sp	8–12 hours after onset of estrus	No
Man	C, Mn	28	None	Sp	14 days prior to onset of menses	Yes
Mare	S, P	19–23	4–7 days	Sp	6 days after onset of estrus	Yes
Mink	S, P	8–9	2 days	I	40–50 hours after coitus	No
Monkey (macaque)	C, Mn	28	None	Sp	11–14 days after onset of menses	Yes
Mouse	C, P	4	10 hours	Sp	2–3 hours after onset of estrus	No
Rabbit	C	—	Continuous	I	10 hours after coitus	No
Rat	C, P	4–5	13–15 hours	Sp	8–10 hours after onset of estrus	No
Sow	C, P	21	2–3 days	Sp	36 hours after onset of estrus	Yes

* Species either domesticated or in captivity.
† Cycle types: C, continuous, nonseasonal, will breed reasonably well during any part of the year; S, seasonal, cyclic activity occurs during specific time(s) of year; P, polyestrous, more than one period of heat during the season; M, monestrous, one period of heat during the season; Mn, menstrual cycle.
‡ Duration of estrus: Restricted time of the cycle during which the male may be accepted.
§ Type of ovulation: I, induced; Sp., spontaneous.
Reference: Zarrow, Yochim and McCarthy, 1964.

gen secretion (uterine stimulation, vaginal epithelium, vaginal smear) and thus presumably with a high titer of blood estrogens. Experimentally one can induce estrus by systemic administration of estrogen or by implanting estrogen into the hypothalamus (Harris, 1964b; and Sawyer, 1963). The site at which these implants are effective in inducing sexual behavior differs in different species; e.g. in the cat and rat it is the preoptic area, but in the rabbit it is the posterior and central medial basal hypothalamic area (Palka and Sawyer, 1964) and according to Lisk, (1964) it is in the mammilary body. On the other hand, ovariectomy abolishes estrus in many species but spayed rabbits continue to copulate, as do ovariectomized chimpanzees (Eayrs and Glass, 1962).

Estrogens alone, however, do not induce estrus in all species; there is evidence that in guinea pigs progesterone is also required (Nalbandov, 1964; and Eayrs and Glass, 1962) as is the case in sheep (Nalbandov, 1964). The constant heat (nymphomania) of cattle associated with cystic follicles presents a special problem. Chemical analysis reveals that the follicular cysts of such cows contain less estrogen than normal follicles (Mellin and Erb, 1965). Short (1962) found that follicular cysts contained larger than normal quantities of progesterone and androstenedione, and smaller than normal quantities of estrone and estradiol-17-β. He found no relationship, however, between the hormone content of the cysts and the behavior of the animals. Associated with the nymphomania condition, if it is allowed to persist, is a degree of masculinization and adrenal hyperfunction (Garm, 1949). The peculiar behavior of such cows may thus be the result of the interactions of several hormones. Asdell (1962) states that the ovariectomized cow remains in heat for less than a day after estrogen injection in spite of continued estrogen administration. He explains this reaction by assuming that the nervous system becomes refractory to the estrogens. This

hypothesis can be tested with more sophisticated techniques such as implanting estrogen in the hypothalamus. It is also possible that estrogen injection causes the release of other hormones initially and thus causes estrus, but that once these hormones have been metabolized there is no further release. The problem of the hormonal requirements for estrous behavior in the cow needs considerable further study.

In inframammalian vertebrates in which mating behavior occurs there is no estrous period, but the animal generally shows courtship behavior during the time the eggs develop and are ovulated. Ovariectomy abolishes such mating and courtship behavior (see Table 6-2). In chickens and turkeys the administration of diethylstilbestrol (DES) (which was used commercially) sometimes led to massive outbreaks of masculine behavior (Lorenz, 1954). These outbreaks were unpredictable, however, and seemed to depend on a number of other (undetermined) factors in addition to the estrogen administration.

Simpson et al. (1965) found that injections of 30 mg. DES in six- and eight-week-old turkeys consistently caused male behavior (strutting, gobbling) in males as well as in females. These doses of estrogen are, however, so high that the effects obtained cannot be interpreted in the light of normal physiological mechanisms involved in mating. Estrogen in more physiologic doses will induce crouching in castrated female chickens. During December and January, when the ovaries show no follicular development and when the testes show no evidence of spermatozoa in the tubules, copulations are frequently seen in mallard ducks. Presumably this behavior plays a role in pair-bond formation. The hormonal requirements for obtaining this behavior "out of season" are not known.

The effects of ovarian hormones on the mating and courtship behavior of reptiles, amphibians, and most species of fish are not well studied.

DIFFERENTIATION OF NEURAL TISSUE

As was the case with androgens, estrogens apparently affect the differentiation of gonadotropin regulating centers and centers involved in sexual behavior.

Gonadotropin Secretion Regulating Centers. The injection of 120 to 240 μg. estradiol benzoate in rats between days 1 and 5 after birth will cause infertility, characterized by azoospermia and reduced androgen secretion when the rats are adults. This effect is not obtained if the estrogen is administered after the rats are ten days old. It seems that such doses of estradiol benzoate have unphysiological effects, as such effects are not obtained if testes of 20-day-old donors are transplanted into 30- to 45-day-old females in which the hypothalamo-hypophyseal system has been exposed to physiological levels of estrogen. Such transplants show normal spermatogenesis.

The effect of these high doses given neonatally may prevent gonadotropin synthesis and/or release, as is also indicated by the persistent estrus and small ovaries without corpora lutea of female rats treated neonatally with estrogens (Arai, 1964).

The injection of the pups with thymus cell suspensions obtained from adult female rats prevents the effects of neonatal estrogen injections on the male's reproductive system (Kincl et al., 1965). The mechanism by which the thymus cells have their effect is not clear.

Injecting small doses of estrogen into immature rats advances the initiation of vaginal cyclic phenomena, probably via a neuro-hypophyseal mechanism that remains to be elucidated (Ramirez and Sawyer, 1965).

Behavioral Substrate. Male rats castrated at birth and injected with estrogen as adults will show female behavior, but if treated with testosterone as adults they will show aspects of male behavior, suggesting that the neural substrate can respond to either hormone if the animal was castrated at birth (Harris, 1964a).

Injecting large doses (100 to 200 μg.) of estradiol benzoate neonatally inhibits female behavior of females and aspects of male behavior of males when the animals become adult (Table 5-5). These inhibitions are not complete, as is evident from the male mounting behavior and ejaculation patterns of females treated with estrogen neonatally but given testosterone as adults.

Most of the questions that can be raised about the effect of estrogen on differentiation of the behavioral substrate have not been answered and experimentation in this field should be quite fruitful.

As far as we are aware, no experiments have been carried out to test whether gonadal hormones have effects on neonatal inframammalian vertebrates similar to those they have on neonatal rats. There are several natural phenomena that suggest that such is not the case. Examples are the protandrous and protogynous hermaphrodites among fishes, the castrated male toad in which Bidder's organ develops into a functional ovary (after which the animal functions as a normal female), and the domestic hen, which, upon removal of the ovary, may become phenotypically and behaviorally a male that will court females. In these examples, the animal's brain was exposed first to the hormones of the genotypic sex, but after sex reversal the animal behaves in accordance with its (new) phenotypic sex.

PROGESTINS OR PROGESTOGENS

Progesterone, first isolated from pig corpora lutea, was considered the principal or only progestin until other naturally occurring substances with progestin activity were discovered in the late fifties. The progestins isolated from different organs in females of various species are listed in Table 6-12. For reviews on the biochemistry of

Table 6-12. Progestins Found in Organs of Females of Different Species

SPECIES	PROGESTERONE	20-OH-Δ^4-PREGNENE-3-ONE		PROGESTIN ACTIVITY BIOASSAY
		α ISOMER	β ISOMER	
Cyclostomes:				
Petromyzon marinus	Ovary (bioassay)			
Elasmobranchs:				
Squalus suckleyi	Ovary			
Torpedo marmorata	Ovary			
Dipnoi:				
Protopterus annectens	Ovary			
Teleosts:				
Conger conger	Ovary			
Oncorhynchus nerka	Blood			
Serranus scriba	Ovotestis			
Amphibia:				
Bufo vulgaris	Ovary			
	Bidder's organ (trace)			
Reptiles:				
Thamnophis radix				Blood
Natrix s. sipedon				Blood
Bothrops jararaca	Ovary (bioassay)			
Crotalus t. terrificus	Ovary (bioassay)			
Birds:				
Gallus domesticus	Ovary			
Mammals:				
Equus caballus	Corpus luteum			
	Follicular fluid			
	Placenta		Placenta	
	Blood			
Sus scrofa	Corpus luteum			
	Follicular fluid			
Bos taurus	Corpus luteum		Corpus luteum	
	Follicular fluid			
	Adrenal	Adrenal		
	Blood			
	Placenta ?			
Ovis aries	Follicular fluid			
	Placenta	Placenta		
	Blood			
Rattus norvegicus	Corpus luteum	Corpus luteum		
	Placenta	Placenta		
	Ovary	Ovary		
	Ovarian vein	Ovarian vein		
	Blood	Blood		
Oryctolagus cuniculus	Ovary	Ovarian		
	Ovarian vein	Ovarian vein		
	Blood	Blood		
Elephant‡	Corpus luteum*			
Balaenoptera physalus	Corpus luteum†			
Seal‡	Corpus luteum			
Macaca mulatta	Placenta			
Homo sapiens	Corpus luteum	Corpus luteum	Corpus luteum	
	Follicular fluid	Follicular fluid	Follicular fluid	
	Placenta	Placenta	Placenta	
	Blood	Blood		

* No progesterone detected in CL of *Loxodonta africana* by Short and Buss, 1965.
† Given if no chemical determination is listed. ‡ Species not given.
References: Botticelli et al., 1963; Bragdon et al., 1954; Gomes and Erb, 1965; Hilliard et al., 1963; Kristoffersen et al., 1961; Lupo and Chieffi, 1963; Nandi, 1967; Porto, 1942 (as cited by Valle and Valle, 1943); Schmidt and Idler, 1962 and Velle, 1963.

progesterone, see Boscott (1962) and Fotherby (1964); see also Figure 5-1.

There seems to be a correlation between the production of progesterone and ovoviviparity or viviparity. However, the removal of the ovaries from pregnant ovoviviparous snakes did not lead to abortion in the garter snake *(Thamnophis radix)* (Bragdon et al., 1954), or the water snake *(Natrix s. sipedon),* (Bragdon, 1951). The function of progesterone in nonmammalian species has not been determined. It is possible that in a number of species its function is not related to maintenance of pregnancy, and that mammals "make use" of the progesterone (Hisaw and Hisaw, 1959) for regulation of the reproductive cycle, for control of behavior, for maintenance of pregnancy, and for development of the mammary glands. However, Callard and Leathem (1965) found that ovaries of ovoviviparous elasmobranchs (e.g. *Squalus acanthias*) and snakes *(Natrix sipedon pictiventris, N. taxispilota)* synthesize more progesterone than ovaries of oviparous elasmobranchs *(Raja erinacea)* and snakes *(Coluber c. constrictor).* They also found a greater progesterone synthesis by ovaries of pregnant than by ovaries of nonpregnant females, indicating a relationship between ovoviviparity and progesterone synthesis.

Site of Secretion of Progestins

The corpus luteum of mammals is usually considered to be the main source of progestin secretion (Nalbandov, 1964; Zarrow et al., 1964; and Gorbman and Bern, 1962). However, after coitus or LH injection, in rabbits it was found that progestins are secreted before ovulation occurs (Hilliard et al., 1963, 1964) and that the removal of the follicles prior to gonadotropin administration does not diminish the progestin output by the ovary significantly. Hilliard et al. (1963) proposed that the interstitial cells of the ovary secreted the progestins. These cells are well developed in

the rabbit and resemble luteal cells of the corpus luteum. This does not mean, however, that the corpora lutea are not normally important contributors to the progestin production by the ovary.

Mammalian corpora lutea, with the exception of those of *Elephantulus myurus* and those of Tenrecidae (Centetidae), are formed after ovulation. The follicular cavity is filled by proliferation of granulosa cells that become luteinized. The contribution made by the theca interna varies among different species (see Table 6-13).

The exceptional corpora lutea of *Elephantulus myurus* start to develop before ovulation. The corpora lutea enlarge, as a result of luteinization of the granulosa cells, and the ovum is pushed out of the corpus luteum (Eckstein, 1962). The theca interna cells that form the central core of the everted corpus luteum do not become luteinized.

The granulosa cells of the Tenrecidae swell before ovulation and fill the cavity of the follicle. Fertilization occurs in the follicle, the theca recedes, and the granulosa cells push the ovum out. The granulosa cells are pushed so that an everted corpus luteum is obtained as in *Elephantulus.* The theca interna cells form theca-lutein cells at the periphery of the corpus luteum (Harrison, 1962).

Progesterone can also be secreted by luteinized cystic follicles (Nalbandov, 1964). In the mammalian ovary, proven sites of progesterone production are the corpora lutea, luteinized follicles, and the interstitial cells.

Control of Progestin Secretion

The factors which control progestin secretion in inframammalian vertebrates are not well understood, largely as a result of the paucity of experimental data. It seems that corpus luteum formation and progesterone secretion by the ovary in elasmobranchs (Hisaw and Hisaw, 1959) and in ovoviviparous snakes (Bragdon, 1951)

Table 6-13. Contribution Which Theca Interna Cells Make to Mammalian Corpus Luteum of Pregnancy

SPECIES	THECA INTERNA CELLS
MONOTREMES:	
Ornithorhynchus anatinus, duckbill platypus	Invade CL, some in groups around periphery
MARSUPIALS:	
Dasyurus viverrinus, marsupial cat	Connective tissue ?
Didelphis virginiana, American opossum	No contribution
INSECTIVORA:	
Elephantulus myurus, elephant shrew	Form core of everted CL, also connective tissue ?
Neomys fodiens bicolor, water shrew	Enlarge in early pregnancy
Ericulus setosus (Setifer setosus)	Luteal cells at periphery
CHIROPTERA:	
Desmodus rotundus murinus, vampire bat	No contribution
Myotis lucifugus, little brown bat	No differentiation of theca cells
LAGOMORPHA:	
Oryctolagus cuniculus, rabbit	Invade CL, may form vascular and connective tissue
RODENTIA:	
Cavia porcellus, guinea pig	Hypertrophy, become indistinguishable from luteal cells
Mus musculus, mouse	Invade luteal tissue, may become connective tissue
Rattus rattus, black rat	Early proliferation, may form luteal cells
CETACEA:	
Sibbaldus musculus, blue whale	Invade CL in radial strands
Globicephala melaena, blackfish	Some cells at periphery
CARNIVORA:	
Callorhinus ursinus, northern fur seal	Paraluteal cells of early pregnancy
Felis catus, cat	Fibroblasts after day 3, some cells at periphery
Meles meles, European badger	No contribution
Mustela vison, mink	Migrate into gland
Phoca vitulina, harbor seal	Paraluteal cells of early pregnancy
PROBOSCIDEA:	
Loxodonta africana, African elephant	Investing layer, retained after parturition
PERISSODACTYLA:	
Equus caballus, horse	Incorporated into CL
HYRACOIDEA:	
Dendrohyrax arboreus, tree hyrax	CL consist of only theca interna cells
ARTIODACTYLA:	
Bos taurus, cow	Invade luteal tissue from sixth day, contribute to CL
Capra hircus, goat	Invade luteal tissue
Dama dama, fallow deer	Invade luteal tissue
Ovis aries, sheep	Invade luteal tissue, atrophy rapidly
Sus scrofa, pig	Some invade luteal tissue, some at gland periphery
PRIMATES:	
Homo sapiens, man	Form paraluteal cells, form eight percent of CL
Macaca mulatta, rhesus monkey	Paralutein cells
Papio porcarius, chacma baboon	Form vascular reticular system

References: Altman and Dittmer, 1962; Donaldson and Hansel, 1965b; and O'Donoghue, 1963.

can continue in the absence of the pituitary. As far as we know, no experiments have been carried out to investigate the effect of hypophysectomy on progesterone secretion by the avian ovary. However, as we mentioned before, the testes of pigeons will secrete progesterone after hypophysectomy, suggesting that at least in one species of birds there is a mechanism for progesterone synthesis independent of the pituitary.

The mechanisms controlling the maintenance of the corpus luteum and of its secretory activity have been studied in a number of domestic and laboratory animals. The initial stimulus for the luteinization may be the bursting of the follicle itself, whether this occurs as a result of a hormonal action (LH discharge or LH injection) or whether it occurs because the follicle is ruptured by hand (see Short, 1964, for review).

With the exception of the corpora lutea of rats, mice, and other mammals with short estrous cycles, the corpus luteum of nonpregnant animals formed after ovulation secretes progesterone for a number of days (Table 6-14) and subsequently regresses and stops producing progesterone. If the animal becomes pregnant, the corpus luteum is maintained and continues to secrete progesterone.

This regression can be the result of either a lack of a luteotropic hormone, the presence of a luteolytic factor, or a combination of both. Short (1964) has given a lucid and thought-provoking account of the probable mechanism involved in maintaining the corpus luteum of the ewe. The secretion of progesterone during the estrous cycle of the ewe is summarized in Figure 6-2.

The following salient facts are known about the control of the corpus luteum of the cycle:

1. Hypophysectomy on the day of ovulation in prepuberal ewes in which ovulation has been induced by gonadotropins does not affect the life span of the CL (which is 15 days in the controls).

2. Hypophysectomy of adult cyclic ewes, between days 2 and 5 of the cycle, results in a decrease of blood progesterone levels after day 9, whereas in control ewes (see Figure 6-2) such a decline does not take place until day 13. Hypophysectomy at day 9 to 10 causes a decrease of blood progesterone levels in four days. This indicates that in adult sheep a luteotropic factor from the pituitary is required for maintenance of the function of the corpus luteum (Denamur et al., 1966).

3. Stalk section either early or late in the cycle has no effect on the function of the corpus luteum (Denamur et al., 1966).

4. Hysterectomy prolongs the life of the corpus luteum (Short, 1964; Denamur et al., 1966).

5. If hypophysectomy and hysterectomy are performed on the same day early in the cycle, the progesterone secretion decreases about 12 to 15 days after the operation (Denamur et al., 1966).

6. Hysterectomy followed by hypophysectomy 20 to 30 days later leads to a rapid decline of the function of the corpus luteum (Denamur et al., 1966).

7. Stalk section either the same day

Table 6-14. Development and Regression of the Corpus Luteum of the Estrous Cycle and Duration of the Cycle in Different Mammals

SPECIES	DAY OF MAXIMAL DEVELOPMENT	DAY RETROGRESSIVE CHANGES NOTICEABLE	DURATION OF CYCLE
MARSUPIALS:			
Didelphis virginiana, opossum	3	7-8	28
RODENTIA:			
Cavia porcellus, guinea pig	9-10	11	16-19
Mesocricetus auratus, golden hamster	2	3	4
Mus musculus, mouse	2	3	4
Rattus rattus, black rat	2	3	4-5
PERISSODACTYLA:			
Equus caballus, horse	12-14	14	10-37
ARTIDACTYLA:			
Bos taurus, cow	9-10	14-16	20-24
Capra hircus, goat	9	12	21
Ovis aries, sheep	6-8	14	16
Sus scrofa, pig	6-9	13-16	18-24
PRIMATES:			
Homo sapiens, man	6	10	24-33
Macaca mulatta, Rhesus monkey	8	13	28
Papio porcarius, baboon	7-8	13	29-42

Reference: Altman and Dittmer, 1962.

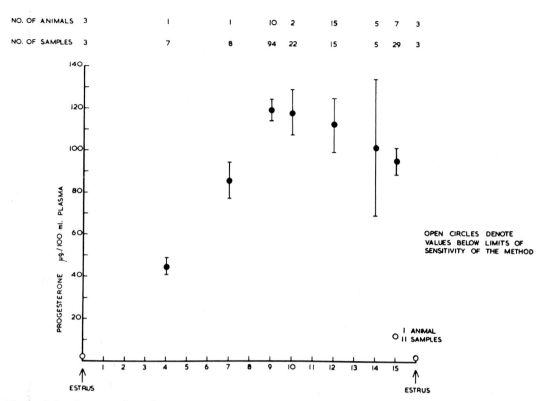

Figure 6-2. Concentration of progesterone in the ovarian vein blood of ewes at various stages of the estrous cycle. Mean, ± standard error of the mean. Recovery rate = 49.6 percent ± S.D. 10.5 (69 observations). (From Short, 1964.)

the hysterectomy is performed, or 20 to 30 days after hysterectomy apparently does not affect the function of the corpus luteum (Denamur et al., 1966).

8. Prolactin injections failed to prolong the life of the corpus luteum, as judged by histological criteria, and failed to restore progesterone secretion just after it has stopped (on day 15). In hypophysectomized ewes, prolactin also fails to extend the life span of the CL (Short, 1964).

9. Sheep LH administration fails to extend the life span of the CL in hypophysectomized sheep and fails to affect progesterone in intact ewes; the same results were achieved using human chorionic gonadotropin (Short, 1964).

10. Estradiol will increase the life span of the CL in intact but not in hypophysectomized ewes (see Short, 1964).

11. The presence of progesterone at

the time new CL are being formed tends to shorten the life span of the CL (Inskeep et al., 1964).

These data indicate that the function of the corpus luteum is under the control of the uterus and the pituitary (Short, 1964), and that the uterine control seems to dominate (points 4 and 5 above). The nature of the pituitary hormone involved has not been established, but apparently it can be secreted by the pituitary, isolated from the hypothalamus. However, an apparent conflict exists between these data and those presented by Nalbandov and St. Clair (1958). This is discussed in more detail in Chapter 8, in the section "Damage to the Hypothalamo-Hypophyseal System."

The data summarized in Table 6-15, for a number of species on which evidence obtained with rather pure hormones is available, show the variation which exists

Table 6-15.   Effect of Hypophysectomy and/or Hormone Administration on the Corpus Luteum of Different Species

SPECIES	TREATMENT	EFFECT	REFERENCE
Sheep	~~AP~~	No effect on PMS-HCG induced CL* of immature ewes	Denamur and Mauléon, 1963
	~~AP~~ day 2-5	Progesterone secretion normal until day 9, thereafter decreased	Denamur et al., 1966
	~~AP~~ day 9-10	After 4 days progesterone secretion decreased	Denamur et al., 1966
	Stalk section	CL not affected	Denamur et al., 1966
	Sheep LH injection	No effect on life span	Short, 1964
	Sheep prolactin injection	No effect on life span	Short, 1964
	Estradiol injection	Prolonged life span	Short, 1964
	~~AP~~ + estradiol	Normal life span	Short, 1964
Cow	Prolactin	No effect on life span	Smith et al., 1957
	Oxytocin	Decreased life span and progesterone content	Simmons and Hansel, 1964
	Oxytocin + sheep prolactin	Decreased life span and progesterone content	Simmons and Hansel, 1964
	Oxytocin + horse LH	Decreased life span and progesterone content	Simmons and Hansel, 1964
	Oxytocin + growth hormone	Decreased life span and progesterone content	Simmons and Hansel, 1964
	Oxytocin + HCG	Increased CL weight above controls; progesterone content same as controls	Simmons and Hansel, 1964
	Oxytocin + bovine AP	Increased CL weight and progesterone content above controls	Simmons and Hansel, 1964
	Bovine LH	Prolonged CL life	Donaldson and Hansel, 1965a
	Oxytocin days 2-6	Decreased progesterone content day 7	Donaldson et al., 1965
	Oxytocin + urea incubation HCG day 2-6	Smaller CL; normal progesterone content day 7	Donaldson et al., 1965
	Oxytocin + HCG	Increased progesterone content day 7	Donaldson et al., 1965
	Oxytocin + bovine LH	Increased progesterone content day 7	Donaldson et al., 1965
	Hysterectomy + bovine AP	Higher progesterone content than hysterectomy	Malven and Hansel, 1964
Pig	~~AP~~	CL maintained during luteal phase but regression later	du Mesnil du Buisson and Léglise, 1963
	Progesterone blockade	CL normal; progesterone content normal	Brinkley et al., 1964a
	Pregnant sow after repromix blockade	CL of pregnancy regressed	Brinkley et al., 1964b
	Pregnant sow + repromix blockade + HCG	CL of pregnancy regressed	Brinkley et al., 1964b
	CL induced in ovary with CL	CL regresses one cycle length after formation	Neill and Day, 1964
	Estrogen	CL decreases in size; progesterone content normal	Gardner et al., 1963
Hamster	Estrogen	Regression CL	Greenwald, 1965
	Estrogen + prolactin	Maintenance CL	Greenwald, 1965
	Estrogen + FSH	Maintenance CL	Greenwald, 1965
	Estrogen + LH	Regression CL	Greenwald, 1965
	LH	CL normal	Greenwald, 1965
	Ovine prolactin + ~~AP~~	CL maintained	Turnbull, 1966
	LH + FSH + ~~AP~~	CL regressed	Turnbull, 1966
	AP graft in ~~AP~~ animal	CL regressed	Turnbull, 1966
	AP graft in intact animal	CL hyperemic	Turnbull, 1966
Rat	AP auto transplant	CL life span extended	Everett, 1961
	AP auto transplant on day proestrus	CL life span extended 85%	Quilligan and Rothchild, 1960
	AP auto transplant on day estrus	CL life span extended 88%	Quilligan and Rothchild, 1960
	AP auto transplant on day metestrus 1	CL life span extended 78%	Quilligan and Rothchild, 1960
	AP auto transplant on day metestrus 2	CL life span extended 27%	Quilligan and Rothchild, 1960
	AP auto transplant + LH	CL regressed; progesterone content decreased	Rothchild, 1965a
	AP auto transplant + FSH	CL extended; progesterone content increased	Rothchild, 1965a
	AP auto transplant + LH + estrogen	CL larger than after transplant + LH	Rothchild, 1965a
	Pseudopregnancy	CL regressed by day 28	Rothchild and Schwarz, 1965
	Pseudopregnancy + estrogen	CL maintained beyond 28 days	Rothchild and Schwarz, 1965
	Pseudopregnancy + progesterone	CL regressed by day 28	Rothchild and Schwarz, 1965
	Pseudopregnancy + estrogen + progesterone	CL maintained beyond 28 days	Rothchild and Schwarz, 1965
	Pseudopregnancy + LH + estrogen + progesterone	CL regressed by day 28	Rothchild and Schwartz, 1965
	~~AP~~	CL pseudopregnancy regressed	Everett, 1961
	~~AP~~ + prolactin	CL maintained	Everett, 1961
Mouse	~~AP~~	CL regressed	Kovačič, 1965
	~~AP~~ + prolactin	CL maintained; decidual reaction	Kovačič, 1965
Rabbit	~~AP~~ + estrogen	CL maintained	Robson, 1947
	LH day 9	Regression old CL	Stormshak and Casida, 1965
	17-β estradiol + LH day 9	Old CL normal; new CL normal	Stormshak and Casida, 1965
	17-β estradiol + progesterone + LH	Old CL normal; new CL retarded	Stormshak and Casida, 1965
	Progesterone + LH	Old CL regressed; new CL retarded	Stormshak and Casida, 1965
	~~AP~~	CL regressed; no progesterone	Kilpatrick et al., 1964

**Table 6-15.   Effect of Hypophysectomy and/or Hormone Administration
on the Corpus Luteum of Different Species (Cont.)**

SPECIES	TREATMENT	EFFECT	REFERENCE
	H̸ + LH (day 7)	CL maintained; progesterone secreted	Kilpatrick et al., 1964
	H̸ + LH (day 7)	CL not maintained	Spies et al., 1966
	LH day 7	CL regressed	Spies et al., 1966
	HCG before day 4	Old CL and new CL maintained	Spies et al., 1966
	HCG after day 4	Regression old CL	Spies et al., 1966
	HCG on day 7	Regression old CL	Spies et al., 1966
	Estrone day 5-8	No effect on CL	Spies et al., 1966
	Estrone day 14-17	CL maintained week beyond controls	Spies et al., 1966
	Estrone day 5-8 + HCG Day 7	No regression of CL	Spies et al., 1966
	No LH + 2 conceptuses	Average wt. CL, 19.84 gm.	Stormshak and Casida, 1966
	No LH + 6 conceptuses	Average wt. CL, 17.75 gm.	Stormshak and Casida, 1966
	20 μg. LH day 9 + 2 conceptuses	Average wt. old CL, 8.36 gm.; new CL 5.4 gm.	Stormshak and Casida, 1966
	20 μg. LH day 9 + 6 conceptuses	Average wt. old CL, 13.37 gm.; new CL 6.8 gm.	Stormshak and Casida, 1966

H̸ = hypophysectom(y), (ized). * CL = Corpus luteum.

even among closely related species such as sheep and cattle. Some conclusions can, however, be drawn:

1. Prolactin is luteotropic, apparently, only in the rat and mouse. The maintenance of the corpus luteum by ovine prolactin, but not by a pituitary autograft, in hypophysectomized hamsters suggests that the ovine prolactin may be qualitatively different from hamster prolactin, or that ovine prolactin contains a contaminant that causes maintenance of the corpus luteum (Turnbull, 1966). In mice, LH may act synergistically with prolactin (Browning et al., 1965).

2. In cattle, HCG and LH are luteotropic. For hypophysectomized rabbits, LH has been reported to be luteotropic by Kilpatrick et al. (1964); however, Spies et al. (1966) could not confirm this effect. In intact rabbits, on the other hand, HCG and LH are both luteolytic if given after day 4 of pseudopregnancy.

3. In sheep and pigs, the corpus luteum of the cycle, once formed, is independent of the pituitary; however, the anterior pituitary is required for the formation of the corpus luteum.

4. FSH probably is luteotropic in the hamster as it can prevent estrogen-induced regression of the corpus luteum. We thus see that the life span of the corpus luteum of sheep and pigs seems to be independent of the pituitary, whereas in rats, mice, and rabbits the corpus luteum seems to be de-

pendent on pituitary hormone secretion. In rats and mice, the luteotropic hormone is LTH, whereas in rabbits it probably is LH. Opinion that LH is luteotropic in cattle is based on indirect evidence. On the other hand, after the corpus luteum has reached a certain age, LH becomes luteolytic.

The effects of various pituitary hormones and of HCG on the synthesis of progesterone by bovine corpora lutea in vitro have been studied in some detail (Savard et al., 1965, for review). Only substances having luteinizing activity, as measured by the ovarian ascorbic acid depletion test, are capable of stimulating in vitro progesterone synthesis that is a further confirmation of the luteotropic effect of LH in cattle. The injection of either oxytocin or prolactin to heifers does not affect the in vitro progesterone production, but HCG injections cause an increase in in vitro progesterone production; the HCG injections also cause a decrease in the progesterone content of the corpora lutea (Lynn et al., 1965).

The progesterone synthesis by human corpora lutea in vitro is stimulated by HCG and LH. On the other hand, the progesterone synthesis in vitro by pig luteal tissue is not stimulated by either pig anterior pituitary homogenate, PMSG, HCG, prolactin, or oxytocic principle (Duncan et al., 1961). However, endometrial extracts from uteri of day 12 and 13 of the estrous cycle increase, and filtrates from uteri of day 16 and 18 of the cycle inhibit the in vitro progesterone production by pig luteal tissue (Duncan et al., 1961).

There exists a considerable body of evidence that the uterus interacts with the ovary, either directly or indirectly, to regulate the maintenance of the corpus luteum.

Table 6-16 shows the effect of total hysterectomy on the life span of the corpus luteum for a number of species. The amount of tissue removed determines the extent of the reaction on the corpus luteum, as can be seen from the data summarized in Table 6-17. du Mesnil du Buisson (1961) obtained evidence that part of the effect of the uterus on the corpus luteum in pigs may be a local one (see Table 6-18). On one side the uterine horn and fallopian tube and part of the horn and tube on the opposite side were removed so that a segment of uterus less than 26 cm. was left intact. The gilts did not return to estrus and when they were killed 40 to 55 days after the operation it was found that the corpora lutea opposite the side of the remaining fragment looked like functional corpora lutea, whereas the CL on the ovary at the same side were completely regressed.

Anderson et al. (1966) confirmed the local effect of the uterus in pigs by finding a higher progesterone content in the corpora lutea of the ovary adjacent to the gravid horn in animals in which the posterior half of the right horn was removed. In guinea pigs, Fischer (1965) found the life span of the corpora lutea on the operated side of unilaterally hysterectomized animals increased (Table 6-18), whereas the corpora lutea at the unoperated side regressed.

Fischer (1965) found the same phenomenon in guinea pigs (see Table 6-18). These observations suggest that the effect of hysterectomy is not entirely an endocrine phenomenon since one would expect any possible hormone secreted by the uterus to have the same effect on both ovaries. However, the possibility of a local effect of a hormone cannot be excluded. There is another example of such a local endocrine effect in the case of the giant fruit bat *(Pteropus giganteus)*, in which only one ovum from one ovary is ovulated, and in which the uterine horn on the side

Table 6-16. Effect of Hysterectomy on the Corpus Luteum in Different Species

| SPECIES | TYPE OF OVULATION | LIFE SPAN OF CORPUS LUTEUM | | |
		NONFERTILE CYCLE	PSEUDO-PREGNANCY	PREGNANCY
Trichosurus vulpecula, brush possum*	Spontaneous	No change	—	—
Mus musculus, mouse	Spontaneous	No change	—	—
Rattus norvegicus, rat	Spontaneous	No change	Increase	No change
Mesocricetus auratus, golden hamster	Spontaneous		Increase	Immediate failure
Citellus tridecemlineatus, 13–lined squirrel	Induced	No change		No change
Oryctolagus cuniculus, rabbit	Induced	No change	Increase	Decrease
Mustela furo, ferret	Induced	No change	No change	
Didelphis virginiana, opossum	Spontaneous	No change		
Canis familiaris, dog	Spontaneous	No change		
Cavia porcellus, guinea pig	Spontaneous	Increase		Increase
Sus scrofa, pig	Spontaneous	Increase		
Ovis aries, sheep	Spontaneous	Increase		
Bos taurus, cow	Spontaneous	Increase		
Macaca mulatta, Rhesus monkey	Spontaneous	No change		
Homo sapiens, man	Spontaneous	No change		

*See Clark and Sharman, 1965.
Reference: Anderson et al., 1963.

Table 6-17. Effects of Subtotal Hysterectomy on Estrous Cycle of Gilts, Heifers, Ewes, and Rats

SPECIES	TISSUE REMAINING	INTERVAL OF FIRST CYCLE AFTER OPERATION; EFFECT ON CL*
Pig	Posterior half of cervix	No estrus after operation, ⁵/₅
Pig	Body and cervix	No estrus after operation, ⁴/₅; 26 day cycle ¹/₅
Cow	Body and cervix	No estrus after operation, ⁴/₄
Pig	Anterior ¼ of one horn and posterior ½ of cervix	No estrus after operation, ³/₅; 28 day cycles in ²/₅
Cow	Anterior ¼ portions of left and right horns	Cycles 25 days; preoperative cycles 20 days N = 4
Pig	Anterior ½ right horn, posterior ½ of cervix	Cycles of 32 ± 6 days N = 5
Pig	Posterior ½ of right horn, body and cervix	Cycles of 25 ± 2 days N = 5
Pig	Anterior ½ of both horns, posterior ½ of cervix	Cycles of 23 ± 1 day N = 5
Cow	Anterior ½ of both horns	Cycles of 55 days (20-113 days). N = 4; preoperative cycles 20 days
Pig	Sham operated	Cycles of 21 days N = 5
Sheep	Sham operated	No effect on corpus luteum (N = 3)
	Fallopian tube removed	No effect on corpus luteum (N = 3)
	Uterus removed	CL maintained ³/₃
	Unilateral, uterine horn removed on side of CL	CL maintained ¹/₃
	Unilateral anterior half uterine horn removed CL	CL maintained ¹/₃
	Unilateral posterior half uterine horn removed CL	CL maintained ¹/₃
	Veins and arteries ligated bilaterally	CL maintained ³/₄
	Veins and arteries ligated unilaterally	CL maintained ¹/₄
	Veins ligated bilaterally	CL maintained ²/₂
	Veins ligated unilaterally	No effect on CL (N = 2)
	Arteries ligated bilaterally	No effect on CL (N = 2)
	Arteries ligated unilaterally	No effect on CL (N = 2)
Rat	Control (Nembutal day 7 pseudopregnancy)	Cycles of 15 ± 0.6 days
Rat	Hysterectomy (Nembutal day 7 pseudopregnancy)	Cycles of 22.8 ± 0.8 days
	Hysterectomy (Nembutal day 7 pregnancy)	Cycles of 24.1 ± 0.6 days
Rat	Hysterectomy (Day 2 cycle)	Cycles of 5 or 6 days
	Unilateral hysterectomy (Day 7 pseudopregnancy)	Cycles of 17.7 ± 0.7 days
	Laparotomy (Day 7 pseudopregnancy)	Cycles of 13.6 ± 0.3 days
	Unilateral ♀ (Day 7 pseudopregnancy)	Cycles of 13.3 ± 0.3 days
	Unilateral hysterectomy (Day 7 pseudopregnancy)	Cycles of 15.8 ± 0.5 days
	Unilateral hysterectomy + ipsilateral, unilateral hysterectomy (Day 7 pseudopregnancy)	Cycles of 13.3 ± 0.2 days
Rat	Unilateral ♀ + control, unilateral hysterectomy (Day 7 pseudopregnancy)	Cycles of 17.4 ± 0.7 days
Rat	Unilateral ♀ + ipsilateral, unilateral hysterectomy remaining oviduct ligated and cut (Day 7 pseudopregnancy)	Cycles of 13.5 days
Rat	Unilateral ♀ + ipsilateral, unilateral hysterectomy + remaining oviduct and mesosalpinx cut	Cycles of 15.2 days
Rat	Unilateral ♀ + ipsilateral hysterectomy + oviduct and mesosalpinx cut and uterus retracted	Cycles of 16.6 days

♀ Gonadectomy of female. * CL = Corpus luteum
References: Anderson et al., 1963; McDonald, 1964; Barley et al., 1966.

Table 6-18. Interaction Between Hysterectomy and Different Hormones in Various Species

SPECIES	TREATMENT	EFFECT ON CL	REFERENCE
Guinea pig	Hysterectomy	Increase progesterone content day 62-64	Rowland and Short, 1959
	Hemihysterectomy + hemiovariectomy same side	CL normal	Fischer, 1965
	Hemihysterectomy + hemiovariectomy contralateral	CL life span twice normal	Fischer, 1965
	Hemihysterectomy	Increase life CL same side; CL unoperated side regressed	Fischer, 1965
Rabbit	Hysterectomy day 2	No effect	Mathis and Foote, 1965
	Hysterectomy day 2 + LH day 9	New CL formed; old CL regressed	Mathis and Foote, 1965
	Hysterectomy day 2 + LH day 9 + estrogen day 9 and 10	New CL formed; old CL increased luteal cell size	Mathis and Foote, 1965
	Hysterectomy pseudopregnant	CL 27.2 days (15 days for control)	Chu et al., 1946
	Hysterectomy pseudopregnant + uterine implant	CL regressed 10 days after implant	Chu et al., 1946
	Hysterectomy pregnant	CL regressed 9.5 days after operation	Chu et al., 1946
	Hysterectomy pregnant + placenta implant	CL as in normal pregnancy	Chu et al., 1946
	Placenta removed pregnant	CL regressed 10 days after operation	Chu et al., 1946
	Hysterectomy pseudopregnant + estrogen	CL regressed 10 days after last injection	Chu et al., 1946
	Hysterectomy 10 days before or 2-3 days after ovulation	CL persisted for 23-29 days	Spies et al., 1966
	Hysterectomy 10 days before + HCG day 3	CL persisted for 7-23 days	Spies et al., 1966
	Hysterectomy 10 days before + HCG day 7 or 13	CL regressed	Spies et al., 1966
Rat	Pseudopregnant	CL 12.7 days	Waynforth, 1965
	Pseudopregnant + hysterectomy	CL 22.7 days	Waynforth, 1965
	Pseudopregnant + hemihysterectomy	CL 19.2 days	Waynforth, 1965
	Pseudopregnant + endometrectomy	CL 18.7 days	Waynforth, 1965
	Pseudopregnant + hemiendometrectomy	CL 15.7 days	Waynforth, 1965
	Hysterectomy	CL 16.6 days	Malven and Hansel, 1965
	Hysterectomy + vasopressin	CL 12.6-13.4 days, ovulated earlier	Malven and Hansel, 1965
	Hysterectomy + oxytocin	CL 15.9 days	Malven and Hansel, 1965
	Hysterectomy + graft of uterus estrous rat	CL maintained 21 days	Hechter et al., 1940
	Hysterectomy + graft of uterus diestrous rat	CL normal; regressed 11-16 days	Hechter et al., 1940
	Hysterectomy + uterine implant of estrus after freezing	CL maintained 21 days	Hechter et al., 1940
		CL normal; regressed 11-16 days	Hechter et al., 1940
Pig	Hysterectomy	Maintenance of CL	DU Mesnil DU Buisson, and Léglise, 1963
	Hysterectomy + AP	CL of hysterectomy regresses	DU Mesnil DU Buisson, and Léglise, 1963
	Unilateral hysterectomy < 26 cm. remaining	CL ovary operated side maintained; CL contralateral ovary regressed	DU Mesnil DU Buisson, 1961
	Hysterectomy	Maintenance of CL for length of normal pregnancy	Spies et al., 1960
	Hysterectomy + transplant uterus	Maintenance of CL for length of normal pregnancy	Spies et al., 1960
	AP + sheep AP	CL regressed	Anderson et al., 1965
	AP + HCG	CL regressed	Anderson et al., 1965
	AP + hysterectomy + sheep AP	CL maintained for 20 days; regressed at 28 days	Anderson et al., 1965
	AP + hysterectomy + HCG	CL maintained for 20 days; regressed 25-28 days	Anderson et al., 1965
	Unilateral hysterectomy and later mated	Progesterone similar in left and right ovary of pregnant pigs	Anderson et al., 1966
	Posterior half right horn removed and later mated	Higher progesterone in ovary adjacent to gravid (left) horn	Anderson et al., 1966
Sheep	Hysterectomy	Prolonged life of CL.	Short, 1964; Kiracofe and Spies, 1966
	Hysterectomy + AP on day of ovulation	Life of CL 20 days (16 days in controls)	Short, 1964
	Hysterectomy day ovulation + AP on day 20	CL regressed in 6 days after AP	Short, 1964
	Estradiol	Maintains CL up to 50 days	Short, 1964
	Estradiol + AP	CL normal	Short, 1964
	Control	Normal cycle 16.6 days	Moor and Rowson, 1966a
	Unilateral ♀ + contralateral hysterectomy	Cycle 16.8 days	Moor and Rowson, 1966a
	Unilateral ♀ + ipsilateral hysterectomy	Cycle extended 22/31 cases	Moor and Rowson, 1966a
	Hysterectomy	Prolonged life of CL.	Denamur et al., 1966
	Hysterectomy + AP early in cycle	Progesterone decreased by day 12-15	Denamur et al., 1966
	Hysterectomy midcycle	Prolonged CL function	Denamur et al., 1966
	Hysterectomy midcycle + AP 20-30 days later	Progesterone declined within 48 hours	Denamur et al., 1966
	Hysterectomy + stalk section early in cycle	Some CL still secreting progesterone day 18	Denamur et al., 1966
	Stalk section early	No effect on CL	Denamur et al., 1966
	Stalk section late	No effect on CL	Denamur et al., 1966
	Hysterectomy midcycle stalk section 20-30 days later	Progesterone secretion high for at least 15 days	Denamur et al., 1966
	Hysterectomy during estrus	Maintenance CL of next estrus	Kiracofe and Spies, 1966

Table 6-18.   Interaction Between Hysterectomy and Different Hormones in Various Species (*Cont.*)

SPECIES	TREATMENT	EFFECT ON CL	REFERENCE
Cow	Hysterectomy	Increase life span CL	Malven and Hansel, 1964
	Hysterectomy + bovine AP extract	Increased progesterone content above hysterectomy	Malven and Hansel, 1964
	Oxytocin	Diestrus 8-12 days (21 days in controls)	{ Armstrong and Hansel, 1959;
	Hysterectomy + oxytocin	No return to estrus	{ Anderson et al., 1965
	Hysterectomy; removal cervix, body, horns posterior halves of oviducts between days 8-11	CL maintained for as long as 270 days. Progesterone 24.6 μg./gm. tissue	Anderson et al., 1963
	Removal uterine horns and posterior halves of oviducts day 8-11	First cycle 9 days longer than preoperative; second and third cycle 3 days shorter in ³/₄ heifers. One heifer no estrous behaviour for 250 days; 43 μg. progesterone/gm. CL	Anderson et al., 1963
	Removal cervix body and posterior ³/₄ of horns between days 8-11	Normal estrous cycles	Anderson et al., 1963
	Removal cervix body and posterior halves of uterine horns between days 8-11	²/₄ heifers near normal cycles (20 and 30 days); ²/₄ long first postoperative cycles (113-58 days); second cycle normal length; subsequent cycles short (7 and 8 days)	Anderson et al., 1963

AP = hypophysectomy; ♀ = gonadectomized female.

where ovulation takes place shows a progestational endometrium while the other horn retains an estrous appearance (Marshall, 1953).

The local effect of the uterus on the corpus luteum has been shown to exist by another experimental technique in which the uterus is distended on one side, i.e. a plastic coil inserted in the uterine horn of the ewe on day 4 of the cycle causes inhibition of the corpus luteum of the ipsilateral side (Ginther et al., 1966); similarly, in the guinea pig, a bead placed in one horn caused regression of the corpus luteum on the ipsilateral side.

There are, however, interactions between various hormones and the uterus, as can be seen from a comparison of similar hormonal treatments given to the same species in the absence and presence of the uterus (compare Tables 6-15 and 6-18). The data indicate that the anterior pituitary is required for the maintenance of corpora lutea of hysterectomy, for instance, in pigs, although the corpus luteum of the luteal phase does not seem to depend on the presence of the anterior pituitary.

Why uterine tissue affects the life of CL in one species but not in others is not entirely clear. One manner of investigating

would concern the presence of products of conception or of experimentally introduced stimulants, such as beads. In the species investigated, uterine distention affects the length of the cycle and, in these same species, hysterectomy causes extension of the life span of the corpus luteum. Unfortunately, there are no data that allow one to compare the effects of uterine distention between species in which hysterectomy affects the life of the corpus luteum and species in which there is no such effect.

How distention of the uterus acts to affect the ovary is not entirely clear. There is some evidence that the nervous system is involved. Denervation of the segments around the implanted bead causes a return to normal cycles in sheep (Nalbandov et al., 1955) and guinea pigs (Moore, as cited by Anderson et al., 1963). Sectioning the hypophyseal stalk also eliminates the effect of a bead in the uterus on cycle length (Nalbandov and St. Clair, 1958). Presumably, impulses mediated via the nervous system affect the activity of the hypothalamus with respect to the production or release of gonadotropin regulating factors, which in turn control the secretion and/or release of gonadotropic hormones by the pituitary.

On the other hand, the local effect of distention on the corpus luteum of the ipsilateral side suggests the production of a substance which is carried via blood vessels or lymph to the ovary. (Anatomically no vascular or lymph vessel system has been shown to drain from the uterus towards the ovary.) It is possible that both mechanisms play a role, depending on the extent of distention, the stage of the cycle, and other factors. In any event, this problem has not yet been resolved, but active investigation probably will soon yield sufficient data to propose a hypothesis to account for the observed phenomena.

That stimulation of the genital tract may play a role in ovulation and thus in corpus luteum formation, even in "spontaneous" ovulators, has been suggested by a number of experiments:

1. Mating to a vasectomized bull reduced the interval between the end of estrus and subsequent ovulation in heifers to 7.7 hours, whereas in unmated heifers the interval was 9.9 hours (Marion et al., 1950).

2. Mating induces oxytocin release in cattle (Hays and VanDemark, 1953).

3. Oxytocin injections given at the beginning of estrus cause earlier ovulation of cows (Hansel et al., 1958).

4. Oxytocin injection during the first week of the estrus cycle of heifers causes a reduction in the length of the estrous cycle to 8.12 days; an effect mediated by a shortening of the life span of the corpus luteum. In hysterectomized heifers, oxytocin did not have this effect (Armstrong and Hansel, 1959). Oxytocin does not affect the corpus luteum of golden hamsters (Ellett, 1964), guinea pigs (Donovan, 1961), or pigs (Duncan, et al., 1961; Rigor and Clemente, 1964). The significance of these species differences with respect to the ovarian response to oxytocin is not clear.

The variety of interactions between the uterus, the pituitary, and the ovary among different species makes it difficult to formulate a unifying concept for the regulation of the function of the corpus luteum. Rupture of the follicle, which usually occurs as the result of LH release, leads to corpus luteum formation. In animals with short cycles (rat and mouse) the corpus luteum is nonfunctional unless a release of prolactin occurs (in response to mating or other stimulation of the cervix). In pigs the corpus luteum, after it is formed, functions the normal length of an estrous cycle, independent of the anterior pituitary (Table 6-15). In sheep, the corpus luteum functions for about four days after the operation, but then progesterone secretion is reduced (Table 6-15). Short (1964) has proposed that progesterone secreted by the corpus luteum may stimulate the uterus to secrete a luteolytic hormone. Experiments with rats provide evidence that the uterus of the estrous rat and pseudopregnant rabbit may secrete a luteolytic substance (Table 6-18). However, in pigs, uterine transplants do not seem to affect the life span of corpora lutea in hysterectomized animals (Table 6-18). As we have seen, there may be a local effect of the presence of uterine tissue on the corpora lutea.

It has been proposed that the removal of the uterus of the rabbit has an estrogen sparing effect (Heckel, 1942; Chu et al., 1946) so that more estrogen circulates, which, in turn, causes maintenance of the corpus luteum. This hypothesis agrees with experimental evidence that estrogen maintains the corpus luteum of the hypophysectomized rabbit.

Further consideration of the maintenance of the corpus luteum will be given in Chapter 9.

Effects of Progestins

THE REPRODUCTIVE SYSTEM

The effects of progestins on the reproductive system will be divided, for the sake of convenience, into effects on the ovary and effects on the gonaduct system.

Effects on the Ovary. A number of investigations have shown that in toads *(Xenopus laevis)*, (Rothchild, 1965b) and frogs *(Rana pipiens)*, (Bergers and Li, 1960; Edgren and Carter, 1963; and Wright,

1961a, 1961b), progesterone can cause ovulation from ovaries kept in Ringer's solution in vitro, indicating a direct action of this hormone on the ovary.

In birds (chickens) and mammals (rats, rabbits, sheep, cattle, and monkeys [*Macaca mulatta*]) progesterone, if given at a critical interval and at the correct dose, will cause ovulation. In chickens and rats it has been shown that progesterone fails to elicit ovulation whenever the pituitary is removed within a specified interval after progesterone injection. This demonstrates that the ovulation-inducing effect of progesterone requires hormones from the anterior pituitary. Nallar et al. (1966) showed that progesterone caused an increase in serum LH concentration of cyclic rats only during the preovulatory phase of the cycle (day 2 of diestrus in rats with four day cycles, day 3 of diestrus in rats with five day cycles and during proestrus). Whether this effect of progesterone on the rat is dependent on the responsiveness of the hypothalamo-hypophyseal system to progesterone, or whether it depends on the responsiveness of the anterior pituitary to releasing factors from the hypothalamus has not been determined. In Chapter 8, evidence that progesterone acts via the hypothalamus will be discussed. Reviews by Bogdanove (1964) and Rothchild (1965b) should also be consulted.

The fact that the hypothalamo-hypophyseal system is required for progesterone-induced ovulation in chickens and in the mammals listed above does not exclude the possibility that progesterone also affects the follicle directly.

However, no proof that such an effect exists has been obtained. Progesterone pretreatment or the presence of a corpus luteum increases the incidence of ovulations obtained after gonadotropin injections in rabbits, sheep, goats, and cattle. This effect might be mediated through a direct effect on the ovary, but an effect on endogenous gonadotropin secretion has not been excluded.

There is evidence in a number of mammalian species that progesterone plays a role in estrogen secretion by the ovarian follicle. For instance, ovaries of hypophysectomized rats treated with HCG fail to secrete estrogen if no corpora lutea are present. Granulosa or luteal tissue that is not in contact with either the theca interna or interstitial tissue fails to secrete estrogen but will do so if contact is established (Rothchild, 1965b, for review). Lostroh (1966) has reported that progesterone, pregnenolone, 17-α-hydroxy-pregnenolone and 17-α-hydroxy-progesterone are capable of causing some repair of interstitial cells of hypophysectomized rats. (Complete repair is obtained in such rats after LH injections.)

Administration of progesterone in high doses, or given on a continuous basis or at certain intervals of the cycle, inhibits ovulation in pigeons, ring doves, chickens, rats, mice, rabbits, guinea pigs, cattle, sheep, goats, swine, dogs, monkeys, baboons, and women (Velle, 1963; Rothchild, 1965b). In chickens, continuous progesterone treatment or the injection of massive doses causes atresia of all follicles with yellow yolks. However, if the progesterone is given each day six to eight hours before the laying of the next egg, one can increase the number of eggs laid in sequence by 13 (Neher and Fraps, 1950). The timing of the injections is, however, critical.

In mammals, progesterone injections in high doses do not affect follicular growth except in the last preovulation phase. Estrogen secretion by these follicles apparently is also normal, and ovulation can be obtained with exogenous gonadotropins. However, rabbits, which normally ovulate in response to the injection of copper salts, will not do so if pretreated with progesterone for a number of days. This lack of response is not the result of a deficiency of gonadotropin content of the pituitary, but is probably the result of a blockade of the release of LH by progesterone.

Practical use is made of the inhibitory

effect on ovulation of progesterone and synthetic compounds with progesterone-like effects in the synchronization of the estrous cycles of cattle, sheep, and swine, and also for fertility control in women (Pincus, 1965). In sheep, cattle, and swine the fertility obtained after insemination at the first estrus is considerably below normal if progesterone is used; however, some of the synthetic progesterones have this undesirable effect to a lesser extent.*

Effects on the Gonaducts. Studies on the effect of progesterone, either alone or in combination with estrogens, on the oviducts of elasmobranchs, teleosts, amphibia, and reptiles have been few in number. The ovipositor of the European bitterling has been studied rather extensively; it enlarges upon addition of progesterone to the aquarium water (Bretschneider and Duyvené de Wit, 1947). The effect is not specific, for similar stimulations can be obtained with other hormones (Bretschneider and Duyvené de Wit, 1947).

Kambara (1962, 1963, 1964) found no effect of progesterone alone or in combination with estrogen and testosterone on oviduct weight of ovariectomized newts (*Triturus pyrrhogaster*). Progesterone did, however, increase the alkaline phosphatase activity of the epithelial cells of the oviducts; estriol, estrone, and diethylstilbestrol attenuated this response to progesterone, whereas testosterone and desoxycorticosterone acetate did not have this effect. Hypophysectomy also had no effect on the progesterone-induced increase in alkaline phosphatase.

Lee (1965) reported that estrogen plus progesterone can cause growth of the secretory glands in the oviduct of ovariectomized frogs (*Rana pipiens*) but not of the castrated males (in which the oviducts do not regress after castration).

The epithelium and the glandular portion of the oviduct of the snake (*Diadophis punctatus*) are stimulated in intact as well as in ovariectomized females. Progesterone alone causes edema of the submucosa and stimulates the oviduct of intact but not of ovariectomized females. Estrogen and progesterone do not act synergistically; the difference between the effect of estrogen and estrogen plus progesterone is the edema of the submucosa (Wilkinson, 1966).

The effect of progesterone on oviducts of pigeons (*Columba livia*), ring doves (*Streptopelia risoria*), and chickens has been investigated in some detail. Progesterone given alone has little or no effect on the weight of the oviduct in any of these species. However, in combination with estrogen it can either act synergistically or it can inhibit the effect of estrogen (Table 6-19 illustrates this point). Dorfman and Dorfman (1963) concluded from their data that progesterone acts synergistically with estrogen when the response of the oviduct to estrogen alone is small and that it acts antagonistically when the response to estrogen alone is near maximal.

In addition to its effect on oviduct weight, progesterone has an effect on the secretory activity of the oviduct (Table 6-20). Estrogen alone is not sufficient for the stimulation of albumen secretion; this process requires a combination of estrogen and progesterone, or of estrogen and androgen (Brant and Nalbandov, 1956). Progesterone also increases the amount of riboflavin secreted by the estrogen primed oviduct. Although avidin secretion can occur after treatment by progesterone, a higher secretion rate can be obtained by a combination of estrogen and progesterone.

Progesterone thus seems to play an important role in facilitating the normal function of the avian oviduct. In mammals, progesterone plays a very important role in preparing the uterus so that the egg can be implanted and in the maintenance of pregnancy.

After ovulation has occurred, the mammalian egg is transported through the fallopian tubes. At this stage, progesterone has an effect on the future of the ovum in

---

* For details on the application of the control of estrous cycles in livestock see the United States Department of Agriculture publication 1005 (1965).

Table 6-19. Effect of Hysterectomy and of Uterine Distention on the Estrous Cycle of Different Species

SPECIES	TREATMENT	NEXT CYCLE	REFERENCE
Sheep	Hysterectomy	Extended	Anderson et al., 1963
	Embryo introduced until day 12	No effect	Moor and Rowson, 1966b
	Embryo introduced on day 13-14	Extended	Moor and Rowson, 1966b
	Removal of embryo, day 13	Extended	Short, 1964
	Removal of embryo before day 12	CL regressed day 16	Short, 1964
	Bead 4 mm. day 3	Shortened; 12.8 ± 2.08 days	Nalbandov et al., 1955
	Bead 8 mm. day 3	Shortened; 13.0 ± 1.30 days	Nalbandov et al., 1955
	Bead 8 mm. day 8	Extended; 23.1 ± 1.80 days	Nalbandov et al., 1955
	Bead 8 mm. day 13	Normal; 16.3 ± 0.11 days	Nalbandov et al., 1955
	Bead 2 mm. day 3 or day 8	Normal; 16.3 ± 0.11 days	Nalbandov et al., 1955
	Stalk section	Failure of conception	Nalbandov and St. Clair, 1958
	Uterine denervation	Failure of conception	Nalbandov and St. Clair, 1958
	Plastic coil in uterine horn, day 4	Inhibition of CL on ipsilateral side	Ginther et al., 1966
Guinea pig	Hysterectomy	Extended (90 days)	Everett, 1961
	Bead 1.5 mm. day 3	Shortened; 11.7 ± 0.43 days	Moore cited by Anderson el al., 1963
	Bead 1.5 mm. day 8	Extended; 22.4 ± 0.42 days	Moore cited by Anderson et al., 1963
	Sham	Normal, 16.6 ± 0.16 days	Moore cited by Anderson et al., 1963
	Bead 7 × 3 mm. day 1-8	Normal, 16.6 ± 0.16 days	Donovan, 1961
	Bead 7 × 3 mm. day 9-16	Extended 17.45 days	Donovan, 1961
	3-4 beads 7 × 3 mm. day ?	Shortened 14.32 days, also for subsequent cycles	Donovan, 1961
	Bead in one side	CL on ipsilateral side regressed	Bland and Donovan, 1965
	Deciduomata	Extended 19-23 days	Loeb, 1927
Pig	Hysterectomy	Extended (no cycles observed after operation)	Anderson et al., 1963
	Cylinders 5/8", 5 gm. day 3-4	Normal	Anderson et al., 1963
	Cylinders 5/8", 32 gm. day 3-4	Normal	Anderson et al., 1963
	Cylinders 5/8", 74 gm. day 3-4	Normal	Anderson et al., 1963
	Cylinders 5/8", 5 gm. day 8-9	Normal	Anderson et al., 1963
	Cylinders 5/8", 32 gm. day 8-9	Normal	Anderson et al., 1963
	Cylinders 5/8", 74 gm. day 8-9	Normal	Anderson et al., 1963
	Removal of embryo during first 40 days	CL of pregnancy regresses	DU Mesnil DU Buisson and Rombauts, 1963
Cow	Hysterectomy	Extended	Anderson et al., 1963
	Dilation first 7 days	Shortened; 8-12 days	Hansel and Wagner, 1960
	Dilation day 2	Shortened; 12 days	Yamauchi et al., 1965
	Dilation day 6	Shortened; 15.5 days	Yamauchi et al., 1965
	Dilation day 1; midcycle; proestrus	No effect	Yamauchi et al., 1965
	Dilation day 14-18	Lengthened; 24-28 days	Yamauchi et al., 1965
	Cylinder in uterus day 8	Inconsistent shorter cycles	Anderson et al., 1965
Rat	Pseudopregnant	CL maintained 13.3 days	Peckham and Greene, 1948
	Pseudopregnant + 4 deciduomata	CL maintained 18.55 days	Peckham and Greene, 1948
	Pseudopregnant + 8 deciduomata	CL maintained 20.6 days	Peckham and Greene, 1948
	Pseudopregnant + 8 deciduomata formed and then removed	CL maintained 14.25 days	Peckham and Greene, 1948
	Pseudopregnant + deciduomata	Pseudopregnant 23 days	Carlson and De Feo, 1965
	Pseudopregnant + deciduomata + pelvic neurectomy	Pseudopregnant 15.1 days	Carlson and De Feo, 1965
Mouse	Deciduomata, pseudopregnant	CL as in pseudopregnant controls	Kamell and Atkinson, 1948

Table 6-20. Effect of Progesterone on Estrogen-Induced Increase in Oviduct Weight of Immature Fowl

BODY WEIGHT	ESTROGEN	DOSE PER DAY	PROGESTERONE DOSE PER DAY	OVIDUCT WEIGHT AS % OF OVIDUCT WITH ESTROGEN	PROGESTERONE	REFERENCE
gm. 580*	Estradiol benzoate	2.0 mg.	1.0 mg.	91.5		Bolton, 1953
150–200†	Stilbestrol	20 µg.	50 µg.	108.4		Mason, 1952
		20 µg.	500 µg.	176.1	508.9	
		200 µg.	50 µg.	143.2		
		200 µg.	500 µg.	61.4	2029	
	Estradiol benzoate	20 µg.	500 µg.	360.2	1246	
		200 µg.	500 µg.	82.1	3394	
100–150†	Diethyl stilbestrol	250 µg.	50 µg.	104.6		Hertz, Larsen and Tullner, 1947
		250 µg.	100 µg.	85.1		
		250 µg.	150 µg.	62.6		
		250 µg.	200 µg.	47.3		
		250 µg.	250 µg.	54.4		
		250 µg.	300 µg.	43.0		
1000†	Diethyl stilbestrol	13 mg. pellet	500 µg.	128.6	1516	Brant and Nalbandov, 1956
		13 mg. pellet	1000 µg.	281.8	2284	
		13 mg. pellet	2000 µg.	314.4	2835	
		13 mg. pellet	4000 µg.	240.7	2474	
180*	Diethyl stilbestrol	15 mg. pellet	0.57 mg.	169.0	1127	Adams and Herrick, 1955
550*	Diethyl stilbestrol	25 µg.	50 µg.	125.8		van Tienhoven, unpublished
		25 µg.	500 µg.	158.1		
		250 µg.	50 µg.	148.2		
		250 µg.	500 µg.	188.2		
500†	Estradiol dipropionate	25 µg.	5 µg.	59.9	373	Breneman, 1956
		25 µg.	25 µg.	70.0	444	
—‡	Stilbestrol	6 µg.	100 µg.	123.7		Dorfman and Dorfman, 1963
		6 µg.	400 µg.	138.0		
		6 µg.	1600 µg.	114.2		
		25 µg.	50 µg.	118.4		
		25 µg.	100 µg.	155.4		
		25 µg.	200 µg.	181.3		
		25 µg.	500 µg.	129.5		
		25 µg.	1000 µg.	144.3		
		25 µg.	2000 µg.	196.1		
		50 µg.	500 µg.	136.9		
		50 µg.	1000 µg.	151.6		
		50 µg.	2000 µg.	167.9		
		50 µg.	1000 µg.	131.0	450.0	
		50 µg.	4000 µg.	163.9	500.0	
		50 µg.	100 µg.	95.1		
		50 µg.	400 µg.	114.7		
		50 µg.	1600 µg.	165.9		
		50 µg.	500 µg.	6.56		
		50 µg.	1000 µg.	152.2		
		50 µg.	4000 µg.	168.9		
		60 µg.	1000 µg.	148.7		
		60 µg.	2000 µg.	153.2		
		60 µg.	4000 µg.	144.3	295.4	
		500 µg.	500 µg.	107.7		
		500 µg.	1000 µg.	101.0		
		500 µg.	2000 µg.	106.6		
		500 µg.	4000 µg.	74.9	482.1	
		1000 µg.	1000 µg.	94.1		
		1000 µg.	4000 µg.	70.7		

* Average body weight of groups.

† Weight estimated from age of birds from Table 9, Nutritional Requirements of Poultry, Nat. Res. Council, Publ. 301, 1954.

‡ These data were given as oviduct body weight ratios; the average estimated weight was 40-50 gm., using the Nat. Res. Council standards.

that it can speed up the transport of the egg (Blandau, 1961, for review). After its entry into the uterus, the ovum requires a suitable environment for maintenance of its metabolism and development and for implantation, although the latter can occur outside the uterus, as is evident from ectopic pregnancies. In the majority of cases implantation occurs in the uterus.

The importance of the correct hormonal and uterine conditions for implantation has been demonstrated beautifully by the transfer of ova from one rabbit to another in which the interval after ovulation between host and donors varied (Chang, 1950). A difference of one day was sufficient to prevent normal implantation and development. In the rat, ova that are transplanted to the uterus of a host that was mated one day earlier than the donor of the ovum degenerate. On the other hand, ova coming from a donor mated a day earlier than the host showed delayed development until ova and uterus were synchronized (Dickman and Noyes, 1960). That the condition of the uterus which allows implantation is dependent on steroid hormone has been shown repeatedly in rats ovariectomized at various intervals after mating. Progesterone in small doses (0.5 mg./day) can extend the life of ova in rats ovariectomized on day 2 after mating, and in higher doses, can cause implantation. If rats are ovariectomized on day 4, however, progesterone can cause maintenance of the life of the ova but it cannot cause implantation except in combination with estrogen.

After implantation has occurred, progesterone is required for the maintenance of pregnancy, which may be of ovarian or placental origin. Placentation and the maintenance of pregnancy will be discussed in another chapter. It should, however, be noted that progesterone can prevent embryonic mortality which normally occurs if rats are placed on a protein-free diet (Hays and Kendall, 1961).

Progesterone also plays an important role in determining the sensitivity of the uterus to posterior pituitary hormones, mainly oxytocin. Progesterone suppresses the electrical and mechanical activity of the rabbit uterus (Csapo, 1961; Csapo and Takeda, 1965). Progesterone administration can thus block parturition even when the uterus is under the influence of oxytocin, a hormone which normally provokes strong contraction by the myometrium. After progesterone administration is discontinued, parturition occurs (Nalbandov, 1964; Zarrow, 1961). Csapo (1961) showed that progesterone can have a local effect in preventing oxytocin-induced contractions. In ovariectomized, pregnant rabbits, each uterine horn can be caused to empty at different times if the placental function is suspended in one horn or if progesterone is injected intra-amniotically into one horn. The action of progesterone on uterine contractions is the result of the blocking of Na transport in the cell membranes (Jung, 1965).

In rabbits, calcium carbonate is secreted by the endometrium under the influence of the progesterone-dependent enzyme carbonic anhydrase. In mice, progesterone inhibits carbonic anhydrase activity whereas in rats the enzyme activity is not affected by progesterone (Pincus, 1965). It is difficult to formulate a unified hypothesis to explain the function of carbonic anhydrase in pregnant mammals.

Progesterone decreases the defense mechanisms of rabbit and cattle uteri against inoculated bacteria *(E. coli)*. Few bacteria can be recovered from rabbits inoculated during estrus or from spayed rabbits, but large numbers can be recovered from pseudopregnant rabbits or ovariectomized, progesterone-treated rabbits (Black et al., 1953; Black et al., 1954; and Hawk et al., 1957). This progesterone effect is not the result of a lack of leukocytic infiltration of the endometrium, for more leukocytes are found in the progesterone-influenced uteri than in uteri of estrous rabbits (Hawk et al., 1957). Nellor (1965) has ascertained that the leukocytes which invade the uterus under the influence of progesterone do not originate from the blood. He also proposes that these leukocytes release their products into the uterus at the start of the follicular phase and that this gives the uterus, under influence of estrogen, its bactericidal properties. Lamming and Haynes (1964) have found that during the time the uterus is susceptible to infection a polysaccharide material is secreted which inhibits phagocytosis by polymorphonuclear leukocytes, which may explain the increased susceptibility of the uterus to infection during this period.

The lack of resistance to bacteria during the luteal phase is probably the reason intrauterine insemination of pregnant cattle (a certain percentage of pregnant cattle show behavioral estrus) results in pyometria and resorption of the fetuses, whereas intrauterine insemination of estrous cattle does not result in pyometria. The incorporation of antibiotics in the semen diluent reduces the incidence of resorption of fetuses of pregnant cows after intrauterine insemination. (VanDemark et al., 1952).

It is important to know to what extent progesterone affects the anatomy of the Müllerian duct system.

After ovariectomy all parts of this system of monkeys regress. After regression has occurred, progesterone has little or no effect on uterine weight. Estrogen administration stimulates the uterus, cervix, and vagina; if this treatment is discontinued and progesterone is injected instead, the weight of the uterus is maintained but the weights of cervix and vagina regress. Administration of estrogen and progesterone to ovariectomized animals demonstrates that these hormones synergistically affect the uterus, but progesterone acts antagonistically to estrogen with respect to the cervix and vaginal weights (Hisaw and Hisaw, 1961).

Progesterone alone has little effect on the endometrium of castrated rabbits, but after estrogen priming it causes development of the endometrial glands. If estrogen and progesterone are given simultane-

ously, the endometrial development fails to occur, showing that sequential action is required (Gorbman and Bern, 1962).

Progesterone is required for the implantation reaction to occur. In primates, such a reaction consists of a proliferation of epithelial cells from the endometrial surface and from the glands. These proliferations grow into the surrounding stroma and may involve the inner endometrium bordering the lumen.

The growth of the cervix and the development of the uterine glands show a synergistic action of estrogen and progesterone.

The cytology of the vagina, however, shows different reactions to progesterone, estrogen, and a combination of these hormones. Estrogen alone causes cornification of the vagina in ovariectomized animals, but progesterone plus estrogen causes a thin epithelium, a diminution in the cornification and a reduction of the estrogen-induced increase in mitotic activity. Everett (1963) has demonstrated that progesterone prevents the estrogen-induced uterine epithelial mitoses in organ culture. Progesterone alone, on the other hand, induces slow growth of the vaginal epithelium; the growth consists mostly of an increase in the number of papillae and does not involve an increase in the thickness of the epithelium or cornification of cells.

SECONDARY SEX CHARACTERS

In human medicine, progesterone and some synthetic progestins have been used in cases of threatened abortions or in cases where a progesterone deficiency was indicated. A number of these compounds, e.g. progesterone, C_6 methyl 17-α-hydroxy-progesterone acetate, 6-α, 21-dimethyl-17-ethinyl testosterone, had a masculinizing effect on rat fetuses, and progesterone has been reported to cause pseudohermaphroditism in humans (Suchowsky and Junkmann, 1961).

Sexual Skin. The sexual skin of certain monkeys *(Macaca, Papio, Pan)* is under the influence of ovarian hormones. During the follicular phase it is edematous and red colored; this color and edema subside during the luteal phase. Estrogen administration causes changes in the sexual skin similar to those observed during the follicular phase. Injection of progesterone, after the sexual skin shows these changes, reduces the edema. After simultaneous injection of estrogen and progesterone to spayed monkeys, edema does not appear but the red color develops. Progesterone alone restores the red color (see Hisaw and Hisaw, 1961, for a more detailed review).

Progesterone affects the development of the mammary glands; it causes development of the alveoli and, after estrogen priming or when given in combination with estrogen, works synergistically to affect the development of the glands (Cowie and Folley, 1961).

EFFECT ON APPETITE

In mammals there are examples in which the luteal phase of the estrous cycle and pseudopregnancy in rodents are associated with increased gain in body weight and increased appetite. Rothchild (1965b) cites as examples baboons, women, and mice. However, a more systematic investigation is needed to establish whether these effects are indeed specific for progesterone and whether they are mediated via the hypothalamus. Dewar (1964) found that in pseudopregnant or in progesterone-implanted mice, weight gains still occur when the food intake is restricted to that of the control period. This increase in weight is the result of higher water, fat, and nitrogen retention. Dewar thinks that the increased food intake is partly a secondary response to the increased energy expenditure (about ten percent) and nitrogen retention induced by progesterone treatment, and that fat deposition takes place when the animals overadjust. However, he states that animals on restricted feed intake showed signs of increased appetite.

EFFECT ON SEXUAL BEHAVIOR

There is no evidence regarding the effect of progesterone on the sexual behavior of cyclostomes, elasmobranchs, teleosts, amphibia, and reptiles. In the birds studied so far, progesterone has no effect on sexual receptivity. In a number of mammals, estrus of castrated individuals can be obtained by administering estrogen and progesterone rather than by either hormone alone, e.g. guinea pig, rat, hamster, and mouse (see Young, 1961, and Rothchild, 1965b, for reviews). On the other hand, estrus can be induced in the cat by estrogen alone, as it can in cattle. However, pretreatment with progesterone lowers the dose of estrogen required to induce estrus in cattle. In sheep, progesterone must be present before estrogen can induce heat (Moore and Robinson, 1957). This sequence is thus in contrast to that found in rodents, where estrogen has to be followed by progesterone in order to give the highest incidence of estrus and the full development of estrous behavior. It is generally accepted (see Rothchild, 1965b) that the steroid hormones act on hypothalamic centers to induce estrous behavior. Goy and Phoenix (1963) obtained estrous behavior in two spayed guinea pigs after lesions were made in the anterior medial hypothalamus; however, lesions which prevented the estrogen-progesterone-induced estrus were more posterior.

Maternal behavior, and to be more specific, incubation behavior is induced in pigeons and ring doves by injecting progesterone (Lehrman, 1961). Progesterone implanted near the preoptic nuclei of the hypothalamus, and near the supraoptic decussation, elicits incubation behavior, whereas implants near the preoptic nuclei, anterior and lateral hypothalamus, paraventricular nucleus, and archistriatum result in depression of courtship behavior (Komisaruk, 1965). On the other hand, in domestic turkeys, the "spontaneous" sitting on eggs or remaining in the trap nest without eggs is interrupted by massive doses of progesterone (van Tienhoven, 1958).

Nest building by nonpregnant mice is induced by progesterone injections; this treatment is not effective in male mice, perhaps as a result of different "behavioral" substrate. It would be interesting to investigate whether this behavior could be induced in neonatally estrogen-injected mice. In pregnant rabbits, the drop in progesterone titer, caused either by approaching parturition or removal of the corpora lutea, leads to maternal nest building (see Lehrman, 1961).

Care of the young in a number of avian species (chickens, ring-necked pheasants, pigeons, ring doves, and turkeys) is apparently under the control of prolactin secreted by the pituitary (Lehrman, 1961). In rats, progesterone causes retrieving behavior (Riddle et al., 1942), while, as we mentioned earlier (Chapter 5), Fisher proposes that the retrieving behavior by male rats, induced by local testosterone injection into the hypothalamus, is the result of progestational properties of testosterone.

DIFFERENTIATION OF NEURAL TISSUE

As we noted earlier, the injection of either estrogens or androgens to neonatal rats causes abnormal reproduction at the time of sexual maturity (Chapter 5, under "Effects of Androgens," and this chapter, under "Differentiation of Neural Tissue"). Progesterone treatment, either before testosterone injection or simultaneous with estrogen injections of neonatal rats, prevents the effects of testosterone and estrogen on the reproductive system at sexual maturity (Kincl and Maqueo, 1965; Cagnoni et al., 1965). The manner in which progesterone affords this protection has not been established. Progesterone may perform an important role in protecting the male embryos against the effects of estrogen on the nervous system.

Progesterone by itself, given neonatally, does not affect the development or function of the genital system at sexual maturity. Whether progesterone affects the abnormal adult behavioral response obtained after neonatal estrogen or androgen injections has not, as far as I know, been established.

ANDROGEN SECRETION

There seems to be little or no evidence concerning ovarian androgen in cyclostomes, elasmobranchs, teleost fishes, amphibia, and reptiles. This is probably the result, in part, of the lack of sexual dimorphism in some species, and in part, the result of a general paucity of information concerning the hormones secreted by many species.

In many species of birds we find evidence that indicates androgen secretion by the female and, in some cases, specifically by the ovary. The comb and wattles of the sexually mature hen, the yellow bill color of the starling, the purple bill of the black-headed gull (*Larus ridibundus*), and the development of the ductus deferens of female starlings are examples. These changes occur at the time of full ovarian development, and they can be induced in either immature animals or animals with regressed ovaries only by administering androgens, and not progesterone or estrogens. However, the androgens might be secreted by the adrenal rather than by the ovary. Ovariectomy of starlings or bilateral gonadectomy of chickens results, however, in lack of development of the structures mentioned, showing that the androgen is secreted by the ovary at least in these two species (Witschi, 1961).

Evidence of various kinds indicates that the ovaries of at least some mammals can secrete androgens. Examples of this are:

1. Humans, in which the androgen concentration of blood of 13 women from 20 to 36 years of age was found to be 7.5 ± 3.5 μg./100 cc., whereas in seven ovariectomized women the concentration was 1.1 ± 0.5 μg./100 cc.; for 23 men between 20 and 29 years of age the concen-

tration was 4.69 ± 0.59, and for eight castrated men between 20 and 61 years of age 0.88 ± 0.18 (Tornblom, 1946). These data thus suggest a rather substantial androgen secretion by the ovaries of women. The source of androgen may be cells in the mesovarium and the hilus of the ovary. According to Eckstein (1962), these cells resemble interstitial cells morphologically, are sensitive to gonadotropins, and tumors of these cells are sometimes associated with virilizing syndromes.

2. Sow ovaries contain extractable androgens (Hill, 1962).

3. Guinea pig ovaries grafted in castrated male guinea pigs fully support the secretory elements of the seminal vesicles (Hill, 1962).

4. Mouse ovaries transplanted to the ears of castrated males will maintain a secretory epithelium and secretions in the seminal vesicles, provided the bearers of the grafts are maintained at a temperature of 27 to 28°C. (or lower, e.g. 22°C.). If such mice are kept at 33°C. no androgen is secreted. There is no correlation between the histological appearance of such ovaries and the secretion of androgen and it is thus not possible to identify the elements which secrete the androgens (Hill, 1962).

5. Rat ovaries transplanted to the tails of castrated males or spayed females will maintain the prostate in either sex (Hill, 1962).

6. The ovaries of rats made sterile by neonatal androgen injection (Chapter 5, under "Gonadotropin Secretion Regulating Centers") transformed about 7 percent of pregnenolone-4-C^{14} into androgens in vitro, and they transformed about 11 percent of progesterone-C^{14} into androgen, whereas for control ovaries no androgens were detected after incubation with pregnenolone-4-C^{14} and such ovaries converted only 0.9 percent of progesterone-C^{14} into androgens (Rosner et al., 1965).

7. Corpora lutea of rabbits can convert 34 percent of 4-C^{14}-(3-β-hydroxy-androstene-5-ene) into testosterone and 3.8

percent into androstenedione (Gospodarowica, 1965).

It is not clear to what extent the production of androgen by the ovaries affects the pituitary-ovary axis and what role androgens play in the normal reproductive physiology of different species.

RELAXIN SECRETION

Relaxin is a protein-like hormone, probably a combination of polypeptides (Frieden, 1959), which is secreted by the ovaries of sharks, rabbits, rats, mice, pigs, and whales (Boscott, 1962; Velle, 1963). The concentration is especially high in ovaries of pregnant sows; rabbit and guinea pig placenta are also fairly rich sources of relaxin; it is probably secreted by the corpus luteum (Zarrow and O'Connor, 1966).

This hormone has a number of effects which will be listed here:

1. Relaxation of the pelvic ligaments, especially of mice and guinea pigs. [Spayed guinea pigs or spayed mice are used for bioassays of relaxin (Hall, 1960a)]. The relaxation of the ligaments is probably the result of depolymerization of the connective tissue of the ligaments. In mice, pelvic ligament relaxation can be obtained by either estrogen or relaxin; however, progesterone inhibits this response but 17-α hydroxy progesterone caproate, which has progestational activity, does not. In guinea pigs, pelvic ligament relaxation can be obtained by either estrogen or progesterone, a combination of these two hormones, and by relaxin. Estrogen and relaxin are effective in the hysterectomized guinea pig but progesterone is not, suggesting that relaxin may be produced by the uterus in response to progesterone (Velle, 1963).

2. A transient water uptake by mature rat uteri is stimulated by relaxin (Kroc et al., 1959), but immature uteri do not give this response.

3. Relaxin softens the cervix of rats, mice, cattle, pigs, and women; this effect in pigs is accompanied by increased water

content. In cattle a pronounced fluid infiltration of the cervix occurs only if the animal has been primed with estrogen and progesterone and then treated with relaxin (Eggee and Dracy, 1966).

4. Relaxin has a number of effects on the uterus:

   a. In rats it has an uterotropic effect (Jablonski and Velardo, 1958), but not in mice (Hall, 1960b).

   b. It augments the action of estrogen on glycogen deposition in the myometrium of rats (Leonard, 1959) and mice (Hall, 1960b), and on the water uptake of the rat uterus (Zarrow and Brennan, 1959).

   c. It also augments the effect of estrogen on alkaline phosphatase of the myometrium of mice and on the edematous changes of the endometrium of mice (Hall, 1960b). The synergistic action of relaxin and estrogen on myometrial glycogenesis and on the endometrium are counteracted by progesterone, but those on alkaline phosphatase of the myometrium are not affected by progesterone.

   d. Relaxin augments the actions of progesterone in producing a progestational endometrium of rabbits (Zarrow and Brennan, 1959).

   e. The spontaneous activity of the uterine musculature of rats, mice, and guinea pigs is depressed after relaxin administration (Hall, 1960a; Velle, 1963), and there is evidence that the ratio between relaxin and progesterone determines the response to oxytocin (Boscott, 1962; Velle, 1963).

   f. The amount of progesterone required for maintenance of pregnancy in ovariectomized mice is reduced when relaxin is also administered (Hall, 1960b).

5. If progesterone (10 mg./day) is given to pregnant mice, delivery is delayed and there is a high mortality (92 percent); when relaxin is also administered delivery time is not affected but the mortality is reduced to about 50 percent (Kroc et al., 1959).

6. Relaxin can overcome the mucifying effect of progesterone on the vaginal epithelium of mice (Hall, 1960b).

7. Estrogen plus relaxin can cause lobular-alveolar growth of the mammary tissue of rats, rabbits and guinea pigs, but not of mice (Hall, 1960a).

These various effects of relaxin indicate a synergism with the steroidal hormones in stimulating the uterus for implantation and further indicate an interaction with the steroids to facilitate delivery (relaxation of the ligaments) and "on time" uterine response to oxytocin.

OOGENESIS

In Chapter 2 it was mentioned that: (a) the primordial germ cells migrate or are transported to the genital ridge; (b) the germinal and nongerminal elements of this ridge proliferate; (c) sexual differentiation, consisting of a differential development of cortex and medulla, occurs. In the genetic female, the cortex shows the greater development and the germ cells are retained in the cortex.

The number of germ cells increases rapidly through mitotic division in elasmobranchs and tetrapods. These germ cells are called oogonia; afterwards these oogonia enter the meiotic prophase and they are called primary oocytes. The beginning of the meiotic division does not occur simultaneously for all oogonia, but generally the oogonia located deeper in the cortex start to divide before those on the surface do (Franchi et al., 1962). The oocyte becomes surrounded by the ovarian zona granulosa which is probably derived from the surface epithelium of the genital ridge, as are the Sertoli cells of the testes, so that these two cell types are probably homologous (Witschi, 1951).

In essence, the remaining processes of oogenesis are the completion of the meiotic division, accompanied by the formation and extrusion of the first polar body, and the completion of the mitotic division

Table 6-21.   Stage of Development During Which Mitotic and Meiotic Divisions Occur During Oogenesis in Various Groups of Vertebrates

GROUP	MITOSIS	PROPHASE OF MEIOSIS
Cyclostomes	Ends before sexual maturity	Before sexual maturity
Elasmobranchs	Ends before sexual maturity	Before sexual maturity
Teleosts:		
Cottus bairdie	Throughout life	Throughout life
Gasterosteus aculeatus	Throughout life	Throughout life
Gobiiformes	Throughout life	Throughout life
Bleniformes	Throughout life	Throughout life
Cymatogaster aggregata	Throughout life	Throughout life
Plecoglossus altivelis	Throughout life	Throughout life
Poecilia reticulata	Before birth	Before birth
Merluccius merluccius	Six years before spawning	Six years before spawning
Amphibia	Throughout life	Throughout life
Reptiles*	Throughout life	Throughout life
Aves	Ends before hatching	At hatching
Monotremes	Before birth	Before birth
Marsupials	?	?
Eutheria†	Before birth	Before birth

* With possible exception of Sphenodon sp. and Sternotherus sp.
† With possible exception of Galago senegalensis moholi (G. mosambicus), G. crassicaudatus, G. demidovi, Perodicticus potto, and Loris lydekkerianus.
Reference: Franchi et al., 1962.

of meiosis and formation of the second polar body.

At this point it should be mentioned that there has been considerable controversy over the process of mammalian oogenesis and when it occurs in mammals (see Brambell, 1956, and Franchi et al., 1962, for reviews). The two main points of contention have been:

1. Whether oocytes are derived from oogonia or from the germinal epithelium.
2. Whether oogenesis occurs during reproductive life or whether mammals start reproductive life with a finite stock of oocytes.

With respect to point 1, evidence in all classes of vertebrates indicates that oocytes are derived from oogonia and evidence to the contrary is insufficient, since seldom, if ever, have intermediate stages between germinal epithelial cells and oogonia or oocytes been shown to be present. Experimental evidence supports the view that the germinal epithelium does not contribute germ cells to the population derived from the oogonia which was, in turn, derived from the primordial germ cells. For in-

stance, after x-ray treatment all oocytes are lost but no histologically recognizable changes occur in the germinal epithelium (Franchi et al., 1962), and oocytes persist in ovarian grafts although the germinal epithelium has disappeared (Franchi et al., 1962).

With respect to the second point, there is evidence in some teleosts, amphibia, and reptiles that mitosis can occur after sexual maturity (see Table 6-21). However, in elasmobranchs, birds, and the great majority of mammals, the histological evidence often shows no oogenesis after birth and no oogenesis after puberty. A number of experiments support the view that no oogenesis occurs after birth in mammals, e.g. (1) after partial ovariectomy, a compensatory hypertrophy of the remaining ovarian tissue occurs, resulting in about the same number of follicles with antra in the remaining ovary as occurred in the two ovaries together. In such cases the number of oocytes is exhausted faster than normal and the rate of loss is inversely proportional to the amount of ovarian tissue left (Franchi et al., 1962). (2) There is good correlation between the number of oocytes lost per unit of time in two strains of mice and the number of oocytes remaining at a certain age (Brambell, 1956; Franchi et al., 1962).

Kennelly and Foote (1966) injected thymidine-methyl H³ (which is incorporated in DNA) into rabbits at the day of birth. Rabbits were chosen as the experimental animals because the majority of the oocytes enter prophase I of meiosis during the first week after birth. Thus a possible relationship between oocytes in meiosis and definitive ova can be demonstrated from the labeling found in mature ova, which can easily be obtained by superovulation after hormonal treatment. Rabbit ovaries were sampled at 4, 12, 20, and 40 weeks of age after unilateral ovariectomy. Grain counts of the ova showed a significant decrease between four and 12 weeks and between four and 20 weeks; and even at 40 weeks 91 percent of the oocytes were still labeled. Eggs obtained by superovulation at 20 weeks of age were labeled in 82.5 percent of the cases; with increasing age the incidence of labeled ova remains constant. These very elegant experiments show that no significant de novo oocytogenesis occurs in the rabbit after puberty. The decrease in labeling between four and 20 weeks was due to nonrandom degeneration of older ova located deep in the cortical zone (Kennelly and Foote, 1966). Thus, one may conclude that all eggs originate before and during the neonatal period.

In all mammals except the dog and the fox (Blandau, 1961) the final phases of oogenesis occur before ovulation. These phases consist of loss of the nuclear membrane, disappearance of the nucleolus, condensation of the chromosomes, formation of the first maturation spindle, and extrusion of the first polar body. The changes can be induced in avian and mammalian eggs by the injection of luteinizing hormone before ovulation takes place (Brambell, 1956; Edwards, 1966; and Olsen and Fraps, 1950).

In the dog, the first polar spindle is not formed until after ovulation, and fertilization may occur before completion of the meiotic division. In the fox, the first polar spindle does not form until ovulation, and fertilization takes place when the second polar spindle is in metaphase (Brambell, 1956).

However, the maturation of mammalian oocytes can occur in vitro in the absence of LH, so that under these special conditions gonadotropins are not required (Edwards, 1966). The oocytes apparently do not mature if the basement membrane remains intact, and it may be that the rupture of this membrane initiates completion of the maturation process (Edwards, 1966).

Extrusion of the second polar body normally occurs after penetration of the vitelline membrane by one or more sperm, although there are a number of exceptions. In the dog, fox, and horse (Austin and Walton, 1960), the first polar body does not form until after ovulation and the sperm enters the oocyte when the second polar spindle is in metaphase. In *Ericulus setosus* the ripe follicles lack antra but have a spongy edematous granulosa. The sperm enters the egg when it has already formed the first polar body; fertilization occurs in the follicle and the egg is ovulated with two pronuclei formed (Strauss, 1950). Some eggs without the first polar body are also penetrated by the sperm; such eggs show cleavage but fail to ovulate.

By use of special procedures, it is possible to obtain fertilization of follicular eggs in chickens. Olsen (1952), by applying semen on the follicles of immature chickens, was able to obtain penetration of sperm into the follicle and cleavage of these immature ova. This situation, up to this point, resembles the one encountered in *Ericulus* for immature ova. However, in chickens these eggs are ovulated and in a few cases are fertile in spite of the fact that the interval between sperm application and ovulation was as long as 3 to 6 months. The sequence of events which occurs in these chicken eggs is not known. Olsen thought it improbable that the eggs would undergo maturation and extrude the two polar bodies, and that the two pronuclei subsequently unite.

Noyes (1952) obtained ova from ripe but not ovulated rat follicles and found that they can be fertilized in vivo in a host. The probability of fertilization increases as the eggs approach the stage of formation of the first polar body. The oocytes must be at least in the earliest phases of meiosis for fertilization to occur. Noyes (1952) found no polar bodies formed in vitro or in vivo in oocytes taken before the polar body had formed in the follicle.

With the extrusion of the second polar body, the nuclear changes involved in oogenesis are complete. However, a number of changes occur in the egg between meiotic prophase and extrusion of the second polar body. Among these changes are:

1. The deposition of yolk, which is considerable in elasmobranchs and birds, but small in mammals (except in the duckbill platypus and the spiny anteater).

2. The formation of the zona pellucida, which lies outside the vitelline membrane. The zona pellucida is a thin membrane in vertebrates other than marsupials and placental mammals (Brambell, 1956); it consists of a fairly homogenous inner zone and a radially striated outer zone. The origin of the zona pellucida is somewhat disputed. It may be formed by the cells of the corona radiata; however, the fact that in polyovular follicles some oocytes have a normal zona pellucida, although there are areas where the corona radiata does not touch part of the oocytes, suggests that the oocyte may form the zona pellucida (see Brambell, 1956, for review). In the baboon (*Papio anubis*) the zona pellucida is abnormal or lacking in a high percentage of follicles after stimulation of the ovary by human postmenopausal gonadotropin or human chorionic gonadotropin (Katzberg and Henrickx, 1966). The reasons for this abnormal development have not been elucidated.

The rupture of the follicle and the release of the egg are the final steps in the process of oogenesis. Several mechanisms have been proposed to explain the rupture of the follicular wall, and objections have been raised against many of them. It is entirely possible that more than one of these mechanisms operates in successful ovulation and there may be substantial variation between classes of animals with respect to these mechanisms. In many species of teleosts, amphibia, birds, and mammals, ovulation can be induced by administering mammalian luteinizing hormone. Lostroh and Johnson (1966) have, however, obtained evidence with hypophysectomized rats that shows that equal amounts of FSH and LH are equally effective in causing ovulation. How LH affects the mature follicle, and, in most cases, only mature follicles, is not clear. The following mechanisms have been proposed:

1. An increase in interfollicular pressure, as the result of continued deposition of yolk in the follicle, e.g. in birds, or continued secretion of the liquor folliculi in mammals. Phillips and Warren (1937) found that ovulation could not be induced in chickens by injecting fluid into the follicle. There is similar evidence contradicting the intrafollicular pressure theory dealing with mammals; in experiments with swine, the injection of fluid into the follicle did not cause ovulation (see Asdell, 1962).

2. External pressure on the follicle, as exerted by the oviduct at the time of ovulation. This theory not only fails to account for ovulation in cyclostomes and teleost fishes lacking an oviduct, but it also fails to account for the fact that the follicle of chickens can be removed several hours before ovulation and can be placed either in warm saline solution or in the body cavity without interfering with ovulation (Phillips and Warren, 1937; Neher et al., 1950). Also, ovulations from the right ovary of some hawks (*Accipiter cooperi*) will occur in the absence of the right oviduct, and in chickens ovulations occur normally in the absence of the left oviduct (Pearl and Curtis, 1914).

3. Smooth muscle fibers in the follicu-

lar wall, which cause rupture by localizing increased pressure within the follicle. The evidence against such a theory is somewhat indirect. Tetanic currents applied to the follicle to stimulate the contraction of such smooth muscle fibers are ineffective in causing ovulation; similarly, smooth muscle stimulants either injected or added to the medium with an excised follicle fail to cause ovulation in frogs and chickens (see Asdell, 1962).

4. Ischemia in the follicular wall with subsequent necrosis of this structure which causes weakening and subsequent rupture of the follicles. This theory is supported somewhat by the following evidence obtained with birds:

a. During the period shortly before ovulation one can observe an obliteration of the blood vessels which supply the area of the stigma (Plate 1-12) with blood. This shows at least the possibility that ischemia may occur.

b. Opel and Nalbandov (1961) noted that after hypophysectomy of laying chickens, the incidence of hens having multiple ovulations in response to an injection of LH increased between two and six hours after hypophysectomy and then returned to the zero hour level after about 18 hours. The authors think that hypophysectomy may cause regressive changes in the follicles, which makes them more sensitive to LH. However, there is no proof that these changes involve the vascular system specifically. In rats, LH injection causes an increase in the proportion of blood going to the ovary; this increase has a maximum of about 75 percent and it occurs 20 minutes after injection. This effect can be duplicated by histamine injection but not by FSH, prolactin, epinephrine or norepinephrine (Wurtman, 1964). These results seem to make it unlikely that lack of blood to the ovary is the cause of ovulation in mammals.

5. Recent evidence obtained with rabbits suggests that enzymes play a role in ovulation in mammals.

a. Injection of either puromycin or actinomycin D (antibiotics which block protein synthesis) into ovaries up to three hours after mating inhibits ovulation in rabbits (Lipner and Pool, 1965). This evidence suggests that ovulation involves protein synthesis, and, on the basis of morphological evidence, this synthesis seems to occur mainly in the granulosa.

b. Injection of PMSG followed by HCG results in the appearance of proteolytic enzyme activity in rat ovaries, which consist mostly of follicles (Lipner, 1965).

c. Injecting 30 Worthington units (in 1 to 3 μl.) of collagenase, Pronase (a protease) or Nagrase (a protease) into rabbit follicles caused most (62 to 100 percent) of these follicles to ovulate, whereas trypsin was less effective (21 percent) and papain, chymotrypsin, aminopeptidase, lysozyme, hyaluronidase, saline or polyvinyl pyrrolidone were ineffective. After the injection of collagenase, the intrafollicular pressure increased by 31 mm. Hg, but returned to normal values in about one minute and remained there until ovulation occurred. It is interesting to note that the preovulatory enlargement of follicles was induced after injection of the above named effective enzymes. Espey and Lipner (1965) propose that this may be the result of degradation of the ground substance in the follicular wall.

These three lines of evidence strongly suggest that, at least in mammals with follicles having antra, ovulation may be the result of an LH-induced proteolytic enzyme activity that causes breakdown of the follicular wall. To what extent the transient rise in intrafollicular pressure is required for ovulation remains to be determined.

On the basis of earlier experiments, Zachariae and Jensen (1958) had hypothesized that the follicular fluid was depoly-merized by an enzyme system. After incu-bation in vitro of the follicular fluid with hyaluronidase, there was a 3.5-fold in-crease in colloid osmotic pressure. Accord-ing to their hypothesis, this increase in col-loid osmotic pressure is abolished by an influx of fluid, which in turn plays a role in causing ovulation. The experiments by Es-pey and Lipner (1965) seem to rule out hy-aluronidase as the enzyme which causes ovulation, although it does not rule out the possibility that depolymerization of fol-licular fluid mucopolysaccharides occurs during normal ovulation. Espey and Lip-ner, however, (1965) question its signifi-cance in increasing intrafollicular pressure.

For the study of endocrine control of oogenesis (transformation of oogonia into primary oocytes by meiosis) one would need to use hypophysectomized fetuses in those species in which the animals hatch or are born with the germ cells present as oo-cytes (e.g. cyclostomes, elasmobranchs, birds, and most mammals). However, in tel-eosts, amphibia, and most reptiles, oogen-esis can be studied, in some cases, in adult animals. Hypophysectomy and/or the ad-ministration of gonadotropic hormones would reveal the extent to which oogenesis is under control of the pituitary.

It seems from the evidence available that oogenesis is independent of the pitui-tary in the teleosts and amphibia investi-gated (Jones and Ball, 1962). The same is probably the case in birds and mammals, although only a few species have been hy-pophysectomized before hatching or birth (e.g. chickens, rats, and rabbits) and no evi-dence that the ovary is dependent on the pituitary has been presented at this time.

Other phases of the maturation of the oocytes are, however, dependent upon the gonadotropic activity of the pituitary. In all vertebrate classes investigated, hypophys-ectomy prevents oocyte growth and yolk deposition and causes yolk resorption, regression and atresia of follicles, and restricts ovulation. Replacement therapy causes reversal to the normal condition

in hypophysectomized animals. Gonado-tropin injections can cause oocyte growth, yolk deposition, and ovulation in intact animals, which means completion of the first phase of meiosis and extrusion of the first polar body.

The available evidence thus indicates that oogenesis in the restricted sense (oo-gonia → primary oocyte) is independent of pituitary activity, whereas some of the sub-sequent phases, which culminate in ovula-tion, are dependent on the gonadotropic activity of the pituitary.

REFERENCES

Adams, J. L., and Herrick, R. B. 1955. Interaction of the gonadal hormones in the chicken. Poultry Sci. *34*:117-121.
Altman, P. L., and Dittmer, D. S. 1962. Growth. Fed. Amer. Soc. Exp. Biol., Washington, D. C.
Anderson, L. L., Bowerman, A. M., Melampy, R. M. 1963. Neuro-utero-ovarian relationships. *In* A. V. Nalbandov (ed.): Advances in Neuroen-docrinology. University of Illinois Press, Ur-bana, pp. 345-373.
Anderson, L. L., Léglise, P. C., DU Mesnil DU Buisson, F., and Rombauts, P. 1965. Interaction des hor-mones gonadotropes et de l'utérus dans le main-tien du tissu lutéal ovarien chez la truie. C. R. Acad. Sci. *261*:3675-3678.
Anderson, L. L., Rathmacher, R. P., Melampy, R. M. 1966. The uterus and unilateral regression of corpora lutea in the pig. Amer. J. Physiol. *210*: 611-614.
Arai, Y. 1964. Persistent-estrous and -diestrous condi-tions induced by early postnatal administration of estrogen in female rats. Endocrinol. Jap. *11*: 204-208.
Armstrong, D. T., and Hansel, W. 1959. Alteration of the bovine estrous cycle with oxytocin. J. Dairy Sci. *42*:533-542.
Aron, C., Asch, G., and Asch, L. 1961. Mise en évi-dence du rôle joué par la folliculine dans les variations de la sensibilité des ovisacs à la go-nadostimuline au cours du cycle oestral chez la ratte. C. R. Soc. Biol. *155*:1062-1066.
Aron, C., Asch, G., and Roos, J. 1965. Mise en évi-dence de l'action ovulatoire du rapprochement sexual chez la ratte gestante. C. R. Soc. Biol. *159*:2505-2508.
Aron, M., and Marescaux, J. 1961. Action de la fol-liculine sur l'ovaire chez le cobaye. C. R. Soc. Biol. *155*:1066-1069.
Asch, G. 1965. Modification de la réactivité de l'ovaire a la folliculine en fonction de l'age chez le co-baye. C. R. Soc. Biol. *159*:2495-2498.
Asdell, S. A. 1962. The mechanism of ovulation. *In* S. Zuckerman (ed.): The Ovary. Academic Press Inc., New York, Vol. 1, pp. 435-449.

Austin, C. R., and Walton, A. 1960. Fertilization. *In* A. S. Parkes (ed.): Marshall's Physiology of Reproduction. Longmans Green & Co. Ltd., London, 1 (Pt. 2) pp. 310-416.

Bara, G. 1965. Histochemical localization of Δ⁵-3β-hydroxysteroid dehydrogenase in the ovaries of a teleost fish, *Scomber scomber*, L. Gen. Comp. Endocrinol. *5*:284-296.

Barley, D. A., Butcher, R. L., and Inskeep, E. K. 1966. Local nature of utero-ovarian relationships in the pseudopregnant rat. Endocrinology *79*:119-124.

Benoit, J. 1950. Les glandes endocrines. *In* P. Grassé (ed.): Traité de Zoologie. Masson et Cie, Paris, Vol. 15, pp. 290-334.

Benoit, J., and Clavert, J. 1947. Analyse du processus d'ossification médullaire folliculinique chez les oiseaux. C. R. Ass. Anat. *34*:27-32.

Bergers, A. C. J., and Li, C. H. 1960. Amphibian ovulation *in vitro* induced by mammalian pituitary hormones and progesterone. Endocrinology *66*: 255-259.

Black, W. G., Simon, J., Kidder, H. E., and Wiltbank, J. N. 1954. Bactericidal activity of the uterus in the rabbit and the cow. Amer. J. Vet. Res. *15*: 247-251.

Black, W. G., Ulberg, L. C., Kidder, H. E., Simon, J., McNutt, S. H., and Casida, L. E. 1953. Inflammatory response of the bovine endometrium. Amer. J. Vet. Res. *14*:179-183.

Bland, K. P., and Donovan, B. T. 1965. Local control of luteal function by the uterus of the guinea-pig. Nature *207*:867-869.

Blandau, R. J. 1961. Biology of eggs and implantation. *In* W. C. Young (ed.): Sex and Internal Secretions. Williams & Wilkins Co., Baltimore, Vol. 2, pp. 797-882.

Bogdanove, E. M. 1963. Direct gonad-pituitary feedback: An analysis of effects of intracranial estrogenic depots on gonadotrophin secretion. Endocrinology *73*:696-712.

Bogdanove, E. M. 1964. The role of the brain in the regulation of pituitary gonadotropin secretion. Vitamins and Hormones *22*:205-260.

Bolliger, A., and Tow, A. J. 1947. Late effects of castration and administration of sex hormones on the male *Trichosurus vulpecula*. J. Endocrinol. *5*: 32-41.

Bolton, W. 1953. Observations on the vitamin metabolism of the common fowl. III. The effects of oestradiol dipropionate, testosterone propionate and progesterone injections on immature pullets on the riboflavin content of the magnum. J. Agric. Sci. *43*:116-119.

Bonner, J. 1965. The Molecular Biology of Development. The Oxford University Press, London.

Boscott, R. J. 1962. The chemistry and biochemistry of progesterone and relaxin. *In* S. Zuckerman (ed.): The Ovary. Academic Press Inc., New York, Vol. 2, pp. 47-79.

Botticelli, C. R., Hisaw, F. L. Jr., and Roth, W. D. 1963. Estradiol-17β, estrone and progesterone in the ovaries of the lamprey (*Petromyzon marinus*). Proc. Soc. Exp. Biol. Med. *114*:255-257.

Bragdon, D. E. 1951. The non-essentiality of the corpora lutea for the maintenance of gestation in certain live-bearing snakes. J. Exp. Zool. *118*: 419-435.

Bragdon, D. E., Lazo-Wasem, E. A., Zarrow, M. X., and Hisaw, F. L. 1954. Progesterone-like activity in the plasma of ovoviviparous snakes. Proc. Soc. Exp. Biol. Med. *86*:477-480.

Brambell, F. W. R. 1956. Ovarian changes. *In* A. S. Parkes (ed.): Marshall's Physiology of Reproduction. Longmans Green & Co. Ltd., London, 1 (Pt. 1) pp. 397-542.

Brant, J. W. A., and Nalbandov, A. V. 1956. Role of sex hormones in albumen secretion by the oviduct of chickens. Poultry Sci. *35*:692-700.

Breneman, W. R. 1956. Steroid hormones and the development of the reproductive system in the pullet. Endocrinology *58*:262-271.

Bretschneider, L. H., and Duyvené de Wit, J. J. 1947. Sexual Endocrinology of Non-Mammalian Vertebrates. Elsevier Publishing Co., Amsterdam.

Brinkley, H. J., Norton, H. W., and Nalbandov, A. V. 1964a. Role of a hypophyseal luteotrophic substance in the function of porcine corpora lutea. Endocrinology *74*:9-13.

Brinkley, H. J., Norton, H. W., and Nalbandov, A. V. 1964b. Is ovulation alone sufficient to cause formation of corpora lutea? Endocrinology *74*:14-20.

Browning, H. C., Brown, A. L., Crisp, T. E., and Gibbs, W. E. 1965. Response of ovarian isografts to purified FSH, LH, and LTH in partially and completely hypophysectomized mice. Texas Rep. Biol. Med. *23*:715-728.

Cagnoni, M., Fantini, F., Morace, G., and Ghetti, A. 1965. Failure of testosterone propionate to induce the early-androgen syndrome in rats previously injected with progesterone. J. Endocrinol. *33*:527-528.

Callard, I. P., and Leathem, J. H. 1965. *In vitro* steroid synthesis by the ovaries of elasmobranchs and snakes. Arch. Anat. Microscop. Morphol. Exp. *54*:35-48.

Callantine, M. R., Humphrey, R. R., and Nessel, B. L. 1966. LH release by 17β estradiol in the rat. Endocrinology *79*:455-456.

Carlson, R. R., and De Feo, V. J. 1965. Role of the pelvic nerve *vs.* the abdominal sympathetic nerves in the reproductive function of the female rat. Endocrinology *77*:1014-1022.

Cédard, L., and Ozon, R. 1962. Teneur en oestrogènes du sang de la grenouille rousse (*Rana temporaria* L.). C. R. Soc. Biol. *156*:1805-1806.

Chang, M. C. 1950. Development and fate of transferred rabbit ova or blastocyst in relation to the ovulation time of recipients. J. Exp. Zool. *114*: 197-225.

Chieffi, G., and Lupo, C. 1963. Identification of sex hormones in the ovarian extracts of *Torpedo marmorata* and *Bufo vulgaris*. Gen. Comp. Endocrinol. *3*:149-152.

Chu, J. P., and You, S. S. 1946. Gonad stimulation by androgens in hypophysectomized pigeons. J. Endocrinol. *4*:431-435.

Chu, J. P., Lee, G. C., and You, S. S. 1946. Functional relation between the uterus and the corpus luteum. J. Endocrinol. *4*:392-398.

Clark, M. J., and Sharman, G. B. 1965. Failure of hysterectomy to affect the ovarian cycle of the marsupial, *Trichosurus vulpecula*. J. Reprod. Fertil. *10*:459-461.

Common, R. H., Maw, W. A., and Jowsey, J. R. 1953.

Observations on the mineral metabolism of pullets. IX. The effects of estrogen and androgen administered separately on the retention of calcium by the sexually immature pullet. Can. J. Agric. Sci. *33*:172-177.

Cowie, A. T., and Folley, S. J. 1961. The mammary gland and lactation. *In* W. C. Young (ed.): Sex and Internal Secretions. Williams & Wilkins Co., Baltimore, Vol. 1, pp. 590-642.

Croes-Buth, S., de Jongh, S. E., and Paesi, F. J. A. 1960. The effect of small doses of oestradiol benzoate on the interstitial tissue of the ovary of the hypophysectomized immature rat. Acta Physiol. et Pharm. Neerl. *9*:303-314.

Croes-Buth, S., Paesi, F. J. A., and de Jongh, S. E. 1959. Stimulation of ovarian follicles in hypophysectomized rats by low dosages of oestradiol benzoate. Acta Endocrinol. *32*:399-410.

Csapo, A. 1961. Defence mechanism of pregnancy. *In* CIBA Foundation Study Group No. 9, Progesterone and the Defence Mechanism of Pregnancy. Little, Brown & Co. Inc., Boston, pp. 3-27.

Csapo, A. I., and Takeda, H. 1965. Effect of progesterone on electric activity and intrauterine pressure of pregnant and parturient rabbits. Amer. J. Obstet. Gynecol. *91*:221-231.

Dean, F. D., and Jones, I. C. 1959. Sex steroids in the lungfish (*Protopterus annectens* Owen). J. Endocrinol. *18*:366-371.

Deane, H. W., and Rubin, B. L. 1965. Identification and control of cells that synthesize steroid hormones in the adrenal glands, gonads and placentae of various mammalian species. Arch. Anat. Microscop. Morphol. Exp. *54*:49-66.

Denamur, R., and Mauléon, P. 1963. Effets de l'hypophysectomie sur la morphologie et l'histologie du corps jaune des ovins. C. R. Acad. Sci. *257*:264-267.

Denamur, R., Martinet, J., and Short, R. V. 1966. Sécrétion de la progestérone par les corps jaunes de la brébis après hypophysectomie, section de la tige pituitaire et hystérectomie. Acta Endocrinol. *52*:72-90.

Dewar, A. D. 1964. The nature of the weight gain induced by progesterone in mice. Quart. J. Exp. Physiol. *49*:151-161.

Dickman, Z., and Noyes, R. W. 1960. The fate of ova transferred into the uterus of the rat. J. Reprod. Fertil. *1*:197-212.

Dodd, J. M. 1960. Gonadal and gonadotrophic hormones in lower vertebrates. *In* A. S. Parkes (ed.): Marshall's Physiology of Reproduction. Longmans Green & Co. Ltd., London, 1 (Pt. 2) pp. 417-582.

Dodd, J. M., Evenett, P. J., and Goddard, C. K. 1960. Reproductive endocrinology in cyclostomes and elasmobranchs. Proc. Zool. Soc. London Symp. *1*:77-103.

Donaldson, L. E., and Hansel, W. 1965a. Prolongation of life span of the bovine corpus luteum by single injections of bovine luteinizing hormone. J. Dairy Sci. *48*:903-904.

Donaldson, L., and Hansel, W. 1965b. Histological study of bovine corpora lutea. J. Dairy Sci. *48*: 905-909.

Donaldson, L. E., Hansel, W., and Van Vleck, L. D.

1965. Luteotropic properties of luteinizing hormone and nature of oxytocin induced luteal inhibition in cattle. J. Dairy Sci. *48*:331-337.

Donovan, B. T. 1961. The role of the uterus in the regulation of the oestrous cycle. J. Reprod. Fertil. *2*:508-510.

Dorfman, R. I., and Dorfman, A. S. 1963. The response of chick oviduct to stilbestrol alone and in combination with various steroids. Steroids *1*:528-543.

DU Mesnil DU Buisson, F. 1961. Régression unilatérale des corps jaunes après hystérectomie partielle chez la truie. Ann. Biol. Anim. Biochim. Biophys. *1*:105-112.

DU Mesnil DU Buisson, F., and Léglise, P. C. 1963. Effet de l'hypophysectomie sur les corps jaunes de la truie. Résultats préliminaires. C. R. Acad. Sci. *257*:261-263.

DU Mesnil DU Buisson, F., and Rombauts, P. 1963. Réduction expérimentale du nombre des foetus au cours de la gestation de la truie et maintien des corps jaunes. Ann. Biol. Anim. Biochim. Biophys. *3*:445-449.

Duncan, G. W., Bowerman, A. M., Anderson, I. L., Hearn, W. B., and Melampy, R. M. 1961. Factors influencing *in vitro* synthesis of progesterone. Endocrinology *68*:199-207.

Eayrs, J. T., and Glass, A. 1962. The ovary and behavior. *In* S. Zuckerman (ed.): The Ovary. Academic Press Inc., New York, pp. 381-433.

Eckstein, P. 1962. Ovarian physiology in the non-pregnant female. *In* S. Zuckerman (ed.): The Ovary. Academic Press Inc., New York, Vol. 1, pp. 311-359.

Eckstein, P., and Zuckerman, S. 1960. The oestrous cycle in the mammalia. *In* A. S. Parkes (ed.): Marshall's Physiology of Reproduction. Longmans Green & Co. Ltd., London, 1 (Pt. 1) pp. 226-396.

Edgren, R. A. 1959. Modification of estrogen-induced changes in rat vaginas with steroids and related agents. Ann. N. Y. Acad. Sci. (*83:2*):160-184.

Edgren, R. A., and Carter, D. L. 1963. Studies on progesterone-induced *in vitro* ovulation of *Rana pipiens*. Gen. Comp. Endocrinol. *3*:526-528.

Edwards, R. G. 1966. Mammalian eggs in the laboratory. Sci. Amer. (*215:2*):72-81.

Eggee, C. J., and Dracy, A. E. 1966. Histological study of effects of relaxin on the bovine cervix. J. Dairy Sci. *49*:1053-1057.

Eleftheriou, B. E., Boehlke, K. W., and Tiemeier, D. W. 1966. Free plasma estrogens in the channel catfish. Proc. Soc. Exp. Biol. Med. *121*:85-88.

Ellett, M. H. 1964. Variations in the oxytocic content of the posterior pituitary lobe during the estrous cycle of the golden hamster (*Mesocricetus auratus*). Diss. Abst. *25*:3076.

Emmens, C. W. 1962. Estrogens. *In* R. I. Dorfman (ed.): Methods in Hormone Research. Academic Press Inc., New York, Vol. 2, pp. 59-111.

Espey, L., and Lipner, H. 1965. Enzyme-induced rupture of rabbit Graafian follicle. Amer. J. Physiol. *208*:208-213.

Everett, J. 1963. Action of oestrogens and progesterone on uterine epithelial mitoses in organ culture. Nature *198*:896-897.

Everett, J. W. 1961. The mammalian female reproductive cycle and its controlling mechanisms. *In* W. C. Young (ed.): Sex and Internal Secretions. Williams & Wilkins Co., Baltimore, Vol. 1, pp. 497-555.

Fischer, T. V. 1965. Local uterine inhibition of the corpus luteum in the guinea pig. Anat. Rec. *151*: 350 (abstract).

Forbes, T. R. 1961. Endocrinology of reproduction in cold-blooded vertebrates. *In* W. C. Young (ed.): Sex and Internal Secretions. Williams & Wilkins Co., Baltimore, Vol. 2, pp. 1035-1087.

Fotherby, K. 1964. The biochemistry of progesterone. Vitamins and Hormones 22:153-204.

Franchi, L. L., Mandl, A. M., and Zuckerman, S. 1962. The development of the ovary and the process of oogenesis. *In* S. Zuckerman (ed.): The Ovary. Academic Press Inc., New York, Vol. 1, pp. 1-88.

Frieden, E. H. 1959. Biochemistry of nonsteroidal ovarian hormones. Ann. N. Y. Acad. Sci. *75*: 931-941.

Gala, R. R. 1965. The synthesis and release of anterior pituitary lactogen *in vitro*. Dissertation Abstr. *25*:6031-6032.

Gardner, M. L., First, N. L., and Casida, L. E. 1963. Effect of exogenous estrogens on corpus luteum maintenance in gilts. J. Anim. Sci. *22*:132-134.

Garm, O. 1949. A study on bovine nymphomania with special reference to etiology and pathogenesis. Acta Endocrinol. Suppl. 3.

Ginther, O. J., Pope, A. L., and Casida, L. E. 1966. Local effect of an intrauterine plastic coil on the corpus luteum of the ewe. J. Anim. Sci. *25*:472-475.

Gomes, W. R., and Erb, R. E. 1965. Progesterone in bovine reproduction: a review. J. Dairy Sci. *48*: 314-330.

Gorbman, A., and Bern, H. A. 1962. A Textbook of Comparative Endocrinology. John Wiley & Sons Inc., New York.

Gorski, J. 1964. Early estrogen effects on the activity of uterine ribonucleic acid polymerase. J. Biol. Chem. *239*:889-892.

Gospodarowicz, D. 1965. La production *in vitro* d'androgènes par des corps jaunes de lapine. Biochim. Biophys. Acta *100*:618-620.

Gottfried, H. 1964. The occurrence and biological significance of steroids in lower vertebrates. A review. Steroids *3*:219-242.

Goy, R. W., and Phoenix, C. H. 1963. Hypothalamic regulation of female sexual behaviour; establishment of behavioural oestrus in spayed guinea pigs following hypothalamic lesions. J. Reprod. Fertil. 5:23-40.

Greenwald, G. S. 1965. Luteolytic effect of estrogen on the corpora lutea of pregnancy of the hamster. Endocrinology 76:1213-1219.

Greep, R. O. 1961. Physiology of the anterior hypophysis in relation to reproduction. *In* W. C. Young (ed.): Sex and Internal Secretions. Williams & Wilkins Co., Baltimore, Vol. 1, pp. 240-301.

Hall, K. 1960a. Relaxin. J. Reprod. Fertil. *1*:368-384 (review).

Hall, K. 1960b. Modification by relaxin of the response of the reproductive tract of mice to oes-

tradiol and progesterone. J. Endocrinol. *20*: 355-364.

Hansel, W., Armstrong, D. T., and McEntee, K. 1958. Recent studies on the mechanism of ovulation in the cow. *In* F. X. Gassner (ed.): Reproduction and Infertility. Pergamon Press, New York, pp. 63-74.

Hansel, W., and Wagner, W. C. 1960. Luteal inhibition in the bovine as a result of oxytocin injections, uterine dilation and intra-uterine infusions of seminal and preputial fluids. J. Dairy Sci. *43*:796-805.

Harris, G. W. 1947. The blood vessels of the rabbit's pituitary gland, and the significance of the pars and zona tuberalis. J. Anat. *81*:343-351.

Harris, G. W. 1964a. Female cycles of gonadotrophic secretion and female sexual behaviour in adult male rats castrated at birth. J. Physiol. *175*:75-76P.

Harris, G. W. 1964b. Sex hormones, brain development and brain function. Endocrinology *75*: 627-648.

Harrison, R. J. 1962. The structure of the ovary. *In* S. Zuckerman (ed.): The Ovary. Academic Press Inc., New York, Vol. 1, pp. 143-187.

Hawk, H. W., Simon, J., McNutt, S. H., and Casida, L. E. 1957. Investigations on the endocrine-controlled defense mechanism of estrous and pseudopregnant rabbit uteri. Amer. J. Vet. Res. *18*:171-173.

Hays, R. L., and Kendall, K. A. 1961. Maintenance of pregnancy with prolactin or progesterone in rats on a sucrose diet. Endocrinology *68*:177-178.

Hays, R. L., and VanDemark, N. L. 1953. Effect of stimulation of the reproductive organs of the cow on the release of an oxytocin-like substance. Endocrinology 52:634-637.

Hechter, O., Fraenkel, M., Lev, M., and Soskin, S. 1940. Influence of the uterus on the corpus luteum. Endocrinology 26:680-683.

Heckel, G. P. 1942. The estrogen sparing effect of hysterectomy. Surg. Gynecol. Obst. 75:379-390.

Hertz, R., Larsen, C. D., and Tullner, W. W. 1947. Inhibition of estrogen-induced tissue growth with progesterone. J. Nat. Cancer Inst. *8*:123-126.

Hill, F. W., Carew, L. B., Jr., and van Tienhoven, A. 1958. Effect of diethylstilbestrol on utilization of energy by the growing chick. Amer. J. Physiol. *195*:654-658.

Hill, R. T. 1962. Paradoxical effects of ovarian secretions. *In* S. Zuckerman (ed.): The Ovary. Academic Press Inc., New York, Vol. 2, pp. 231-261.

Hilliard, J., Archibald, D., and Sawyer, C. H. 1963. Gonadotropic activation of preovulatory synthesis and release of progestin in the rabbit. Endocrinology 72:59-66.

Hilliard, J., Hayward, J. N., and Sawyer, C. H. 1964. Postcoital patterns of secretion of pituitary gonadotropin and ovarian progestin in the rabbit. Endocrinology 75:957-963.

Hisaw, F. L., Jr., and Hisaw, F. L. 1959. The corpora lutea of elasmobranch fishes. Anat. Rec. *135*: 269-273.

Hisaw, F. L., and Hisaw, F. L., Jr. 1961. Action of estrogen and progesterone on the reproductive tract of lower primates. *In* W. C. Young (ed.): Sex and Internal Secretions. Williams & Wilkins Co., Baltimore, Vol. 1, pp. 556-589.

Hubbs, C. L., and Lagler, K. F. 1958. Fishes of the Great Lakes Region. Cranbrook Institute of Science, Bull. 26. Bloomfield Hills, Michigan.

Ingram, D. L. 1959. The effect of oestrogen on the atresia of ovarian follicles. J. Endocrinol. *19*: 123-125.

Inskeep, E. K., Howland, B. E., Pope, A. L., and Casida, L. E. 1964. Some effects of progesterone on experimentally induced corpora lutea in ewes. J. Anim. Sci. *23*:791-794.

Jablanski, W. J. A., and Velardo, J. T. 1958. Uterine growth promoting action of relaxin. Proc. Soc. Exp. Biol. Med. *98*:36-37.

Jones, I. C., and Ball, J. N. 1962. Ovarian-pituitary relationships. *In* S. Zuckerman (ed.): The Ovary. Academic Press Inc., New York, Vol. 1, pp. 361-434.

Jung, H. 1966. Zur Physiologie und Klinik der hormonalen Uterusregulation. Biol. Abst. *47* ref 6714.

Kambara, S. 1962. Effect of progesterone on activity of alkaline phosphatase in the oviduct of the newt, *Triturus pyrrhogaster.* Zool. Mag. (Tokyo) *71*:328-332. (Japanese with English summary.)

Kambara, S. 1963. Direct effect of progesterone on the activity of alkaline phosphatase in the oviduct of the newt, Triturus pyrrhogaster. Proc. Jap. Acad. *39*:600-604.

Kambara, S. 1964. Activity of alkaline phosphatase in the oviduct epithelium of the newt, *Triturus pyrrhogaster,* injected with estriol, diethylstilbestrol, estrone, testosterone or desoxycorticosterone acetate, singly or in combination with progesterone. Proc. Jap. Acad. *40*:536-540.

Kamell, S. A., and Atkinson, W. B. 1948. Absence of prolongation of pseudopregnancy by induction of deciduomata in the mouse. Proc. Soc. Exp. Biol. Med. *67*:415-416.

Kanematsu, S., and Sawyer, C. H. 1963a. Effects of hypothalamic estrogen implants on pituitary LH and prolactin in rabbits. Amer. J. Physiol. *205*:1073-1076.

Kanematsu, S., and Sawyer, C. H. 1963b. Effects of hypothalamic and hypophysial implants on pituitary gonadotrophic cells in ovariectomized rabbits. Endocrinology *73*:687-695.

Kanematsu, S., and Sawyer, C. H. 1964. Effects of hypothalamic and hypophysial estrogen implants on pituitary and plasma LH in ovariectomized rabbits. Endocrinology *75*:579-585.

Kar, A. B. 1947. Responses of the oviduct of immature female fowl to injection of diethylstilbestrol and the mechanism of perforation of the oviduct in the domestic fowl. Poultry Sci. *26*:352-363.

Katzberg, A., and Hendrickx, A. G. 1966. Gonadotropin-induced anomalies of the zona pellucida of the baboon ovum. Science *151*:1225-1226.

Kennelly, J. J., and Foote, R. H. 1966. Oocytogenesis in rabbits. The role of neogenesis in the formation of the definitive ova and the stability of oocyte DNA measured with tritiated thymidine. Amer. J. Anat. *118*:573-590.

Kilpatrick, R., Armstrong, D. T., and Greep, R. O.

1964. Maintenance of the corpus luteum by gonadotrophins in the hypophysectomized rabbit. Endocrinology *74*:453-461.

Kincl, F. A., and Maqueo, M. 1965. Prevention by progesterone of steroid-induced sterility in neonatal male and female rats. Endocrinology *77*: 859-862.

Kincl, F. A., Oriol, A., Pi, A. F., and Maqueo, M. 1965. Prevention of steroid-induced sterility in neonatal rats with thymic cell suspension. Proc. Soc. Exp. Biol. Med. *120*:252-255.

Kiracofe, G. H., and Spies, H. G. 1966. Length of maintenance of naturally formed and experimentally induced corpora lutea in hysterectomized ewes. J. Reprod. Fertil. *11*:275-279.

Komisaruk, B. R. 1965. Localization in brain of reproductive behavior responses to progesterone in Ring Doves. Amer. Zool. *5*:687 (abstract).

Kovačič, N. 1965. Prolactin assay by decidual reaction in the mouse. J. Endocrinol. *33*:295-299.

Kristoffersen, J., Lunaas, T., and Velle, W. 1961. Identification of 20β hydroxy-pregn-4-ene-3 one in luteal tissue from pregnant whales. Nature *190*:1009-1010.

Kroc, R. L., Steinetz, B. G., and Beach, V. L. 1959. The effects of estrogens, progestagens and relaxin in pregnant and nonpregnant laboratory rodents. Ann. N. Y. Acad. Sci. *75*:942-980.

Lambert, J. G. D. 1966. Location of hormone production in the ovary of the guppy, *Poecilia reticulata.* Experientia *22*:476.

Lamming, G. E., and Haynes, W. B. 1964. The influence of components of uterine flushings on phagocytosis. Fifth Int. Congr. Anim. Reprod. Art. Ins. *2*:355-360.

Landauer, W. 1954. The effect of estradiol benzoate and corn oil on bone structure of growing cockerels exposed to vitamin-D deficiency. Endocrinology *55*:686-695.

Layne, D. S., Common, R. H., Maw, W. A., and Fraps, R. M. 1958. Presence of oestrone, oestradiol and oestriol in extracts of ovaries of laying hens. Nature *181*:351-352.

Lee, P. A. 1965. Histological and biochemical analysis of the annual cycle of growth and secretion in the oviduct of *Rana pipiens.* Diss. Abstr. *26*:2932.

Lehrman, D. S. 1961. Hormonal regulation of parental behavior in birds and infrahuman mammals. *In* W. C. Young (ed.): Sex and Internal Secretions. Williams & Wilkins Co., Baltimore, Vol. 2, pp. 1268-1382.

Leonard, S. L. 1959. Physiology of relaxin in laboratory animals. (discussion) *In* C. W. Lloyd (ed.): Recent Progress in the Endocrinology of Reproduction. Academic Press Inc., New York, pp. 423-424.

Lipner, H. 1965. Induction of Graafian follicle proteolytic enzyme activity by human chorionic gonadotrophin (HCG) in rat Graafin follicles. Amer. Zool. *5*:727 (abstract).

Lipner, H., and Pool, W. R. 1965. Effects of antibiotics on the rabbit Graafian follicle. Fed. Proc. *24*:321 (abstract).

Lisk, R. D. 1963. Maintenance of normal pituitary weight and cytology in the spayed rat following estradiol implants in the arcuate nucleus. Anat. Rec. *146*:281-291.

Lisk, R. D. 1964. Hypothalamus and hormone feedback in the rat. Trans. N. Y. Acad. Sci. Ser. II 27:35-38.

Loeb, L. 1927. Effects of hysterectomy on the system of sex organs and on periodicity of the sexual cycle in the guinea pig. Amer. J. Physiol. 83: 202-224.

Lorenz, F. W. 1954. Effects of estrogens on domestic fowl and applications in the poultry industry. Vitamins and Hormones 12:235-275.

Lostroh, A. J. 1966. Steroids that mimic the effects of gonadotropins on the ovary and uterus. The Physiologist 9:234 (abstract).

Lostroh, A. J., and Johnson, R. E. 1966. Amounts of interstitial cell-stimulating hormone and follicle-stimulating hormone required for follicular development, uterine growth and ovulation in the hypophysectomized rat. Endocrinology 79:991-996.

Lupo, C., and Chieffi, G. 1963. Oestrogens and progesterone in the ovaries of the marine teleost, *Conger conger*. Nature 197:596.

Lynn, J. E., Collins, W. E., Inskeep, E. K., McShan, W. H., and Casida, L. E. 1965. Effects of gonadotropins, oxytocin and glucose on the bovine corpus luteum at the fourteenth day of the estrual cycle. J. Anim. Sci. 24:790-794.

McCann, S. M., and Taleisnik, S. 1961. The effect of estrogen on plasma luteinizing hormone (LH) activity in the rat. Endocrinology 69:909-914.

McDonald, M. F. 1964. Maintenance of the corpus luteum in the ewe. Proc. N. Z. Soc. Anim. Prod. 24:69-75.

Malven, P. V., and Hansel, W. 1964. Ovarian function in dairy heifers following hysterectomy. J. Dairy Sci. 47:1388-1393.

Malven, P. V., and Hansel, W. 1965. Effect of bovine endometrial extracts, vasopressin and oxytocin on the duration of pseudopregnancy in hysterectomized and intact rats. J. Reprod. Fertil. 9: 207-215.

Marion, G. B., Smith, V. R., Wiley, T. E., and Barrett, G. R. 1950. The effect of sterile copulation on time of ovulation in dairy heifers. J. Dairy Sci. 33:885-889.

Marlow, H. W., and Richert, D. 1940. Estrogens of the fowl. Endocrinology 26:531-534.

Marshall, A. J. 1953. The unilateral endometrial reaction in the giant fruit bat *(Pteropus giganteus* Brünnich). J. Endocrinol. 9:42-44.

Marshall, A. J., and Coombs, C. J. F. 1957. The interaction of environmental, internal and behavioural factors in the rook, *Corvus f. frugilegus,* Linnaeus. Proc. Zool. Soc. London 128:545-589.

Mason, R. C. 1952. Synergistic and antagonistic effects of progesterone in combination with estrogens on oviduct weight. Endocrinology 51:570-572.

Mathis, R. M., and Foote, W. C. 1965. Effects of estradiol, LH and hysterectomy on rabbit corpora lutea. J. Anim. Sci. 24:925 (abstract).

Meites, J. 1949. Relation of food intake to growth-depressing action of natural and artificial estrogens. Amer. J. Physiol. 159:281-286.

Mellin, T. N., and Erb, R. E. 1965. Estrogens in the bovine. A review. J. Dairy Sci. 48:687-700.

Moor, R. M., and Rowson, L. E. A. 1966a. Local uterine mechanisms affecting luteal function in the sheep. J. Reprod. Fertil. 11:307-310.

Moor, R. M., and Rowson, L. E. A. 1966b. The corpus luteum of the sheep: functional relationship between the embryo and the corpus luteum. J. Endocrinol. 34:233-239.

Moore, C. R. 1926. On the properties of the gonads as controllers of somatic and physical characteristics. IX. Testis graft reactions in different environments (rat). Amer. J. Anat. 37:351-416.

Moore, N. W., and Robinson, T. J. 1957. The behavioural and vaginal response of the spayed ewe to oestrogen injected at various times relative to the injection of progesterone. J. Endocrinol. 15: 360-365.

Nalbandov, A. V. 1961. Comparative physiology and endocrinology of domestic animals. Recent Progr. Hormone Res. 17:119-139.

Nalbandov, A. V. 1964. Reproductive Physiology. Ed. 2. W. H. Freeman & Co., San Francisco.

Nalbandov, A. V., and St. Clair, L. E. 1958. Relation of the nervous system to implantation. In F. X. Gassner (ed.): Reproduction and Infertility. Pergamon Press, New York, pp. 83-87.

Nalbandov, A. V., Moore, W. W., and Norton, H. W. 1955. Further studies on the neurogenic control of the estrous cycle by uterine distention. Endocrinology 56:225-231.

Nallar, R., Antunes-Rodrigues, J., and McCann, S. M. 1966. Effect of progesterone on the level of plasma luteinizing hormone (LH) in normal female rats. Endocrinology 79:907-911.

Nandi, J. 1967. Comparative endocrinology of steroid hormones in vertebrates. Amer. Zool. 7:115-133.

Neher, B. H., and Fraps, R. M. 1950. The addition of eggs to the hen's clutch by repeated injections of ovulation-inducing hormones. Endocrinology 46:482-488.

Neher, B. N., Olsen, M. W., and Fraps, R. M. 1950. Ovulation of the excised ovum in the hen. Poultry Sci. 29:554-557.

Neill, J. D., and Day, B. N. 1964. Relationship of developmental stage to regression of the corpus luteum in swine. Endocrinology 74:355-360.

Nellor, J. E. 1965. The leucocyte-like cells of the oviducts during the normal estrous cycle and their modification by progesterone and estrogen treatment. Anat. Rec. 151:171-182.

Nicoll, C. S., and Meites, J. 1962. Estrogen stimulation of prolactin production by rat adenohypophysis *in vitro.* Endocrinology 70:272-277.

Noyes, R. W. 1952. Fertilization of follicular ova. Fertil. Steril. 3:1-12.

O'Donoghue, P. N. G. 1963. Reproduction in the female hyrax *(Dendrohyrax arborea* Rawenzorii). Proc. Zool. Soc. London 141:207-237.

O'Grady, J. E. O., and Heald, P. J. 1965. Identification of oestradiol and oestrone in avian plasma. Nature 205:390.

Olsen, M. W. 1952. Intra-ovarian insemination in the domestic fowl. J. Exp. Zool. 119:461-481.

Olsen, M. W., and Fraps, R. M. 1950. Maturation changes in the hen's ovum. J. Exp. Zool. 114: 475-489.

Opel, H., and Nalbandov, A. V. 1961. Onset of follicular atresia following hypophysectomy of the laying hen. Proc. Soc. Exp. Biol. Med. *107*:233-235.

Palka, Y. S., and Sawyer, C. H. 1964. Induction of estrous behavior in the ovariectomized rabbit by estrogen implants in the hypothalamus. Amer. Zool. *4*:289 (abstract).

Palka, Y. S., Ramirez, V. D., and Sawyer, C. H. 1966. Distribution and biological effects of tritiated estradiol implanted in the hypothalamo-hypophysial region of female rats. Endocrinology *78*: 487-499.

Parkes, A. S. 1952. Relation between effect and method of administration of androgens and oestrogens to fowl. CIBA Foundation Colloquia on Endocrinology *3*:248-252.

Parkes, A. S., and Marshall, A. J. 1960. The reproductive hormones in birds. *In* A. S. Parkes (ed.): Marshall's Physiology of Reproduction. Longmans Green & Co. Ltd., London, 1 (Pt. 2) pp. 583-706.

Pearl, R., and Curtis, M. R. 1914. Studies on the physiology of reproduction in the domestic fowl. VIII. On some physiological effects of ligation, section or removal of the oviduct. J. Exp. Zool. *17*:395-424.

Peckham, B. M., and Greene, R. R. 1948. Prolongation of pseudopregnancy by deciduomata in the rat. Proc. Soc. Exp. Biol. Med. *69*:417-418.

Pesonen, S., and Rapola, J. 1962. Observations on the metabolism of adrenal and gonadal steroids in *Xenopus laevis* and *Bufo bufo*. Gen. Comp. Endocrinol. *2*:425-432.

Phillips, R. E., and Warren, D. C. 1937. Observations concerning the mechanics of ovulation in the fowl. J. Exp. Zool. *76*:117-136.

Phillips, R. E., and van Tienhoven, A. 1960. Endocrine factors involved in the failure of pintail ducks *Anas acuta* to reproduce in captivity. J. Endocrinol. *21*:253-261.

Pickford, G. E., and Atz, J. W. 1957. The Physiology of the Pituitary Gland of Fishes. Zool. Soc., New York.

Pincus, G. 1965. The Control of Fertility. Academic Press Inc., New York.

Polin, D., and Sturkie, P. D. 1957. The influence of parathyroids on blood calcium levels and shell deposition in laying hens. Endocrinology *60*: 778-784.

Polin, D., and Sturkie, P. D. 1958. Parathyroid and gonad relationship in regulating blood calcium fractions in chickens. Endocrinology *63*:177-182.

Polin, D., Sturkie, P. D., and Hunsaker, W. 1957. The blood calcium response of the chicken to parathyroid extracts. Endocrinology *60*:1-5.

Privett, O. S., Blank, M. L., and Schmit, J. A. 1962. Studies on the composition of egg lipid. J. Food Sci. *27*:463-468.

Quilligan, E. J., and Rothchild, I. 1960. The corpus luteum-pituitary relationship: The luteotrophic activity of homotransplanted pituitaries in intact rats. Endocrinology *67*:48-53.

Ramirez, D. V. (sic), and McCann, S. M. 1963. Comparison of the regulation of luteinizing hormone (LH) secretion in immature and adult rats. Endocrinology *72*:452-464.

Ramirez, V. D., and McCann, S. M. 1964. Induction of prolactin secretion by implants of estrogen into the hypothalamo-hypophysial region of female rats. Endocrinology *75*:206-214.

Ramirez, V. D., and Sawyer, C. H. 1965. Advancement of puberty in the female rat by estrogen. Endocrinology *76*:1158-1168.

Ramirez, V. D., Abrams, R. M., and McCann, S. M. 1964. Effect of estradiol implants in the hypothalamo-hypophysial region of the rat on secretion of luteinizing hormone. Endocrinology *75*: 243-248.

Ranney, R. E., and Chaikoff, I. L. 1951. Effect of functional hepatectomy upon estrogen-induced lipemia in the fowl. Amer. J. Physiol. *165*:600-603.

Ratner, A., Talwalker, P. K., and Meites, J. 1963. Effect of estrogen administration *in vivo* on prolactin release by rat pituitary *in vitro*. Proc. Soc. Exp. Biol. Med. *112*:12-15.

Riddle, O., Lahr, E. L., and Bates, R. M. 1942. The role of hormones in the initiation of maternal behavior in rats. Amer. J. Physiol. *137*:299-317.

Rigor, E. M., and Clemente, R. R. 1964. The effect of oxytocin injections on the oestrus cycle of gilts. Fifth Int. Congr. Anim. Reprod. Art. Ins. *3*:364-366.

Robson, J. M. 1947. Recent Advances in Sex and Reproductive Physiology. The Blakeston Co., Philadelphia.

Romanoff, A. L., and Romanoff, A. J. 1949. The Avian Egg. John Wiley & Sons Inc., New York.

Rosner, J., Delille, G. P., Tramezzani, J. H., and Cardinali, D. 1965. Production *in vitro* d'androgènes par l'ovaire de la ratte stérile. C. R. Acad. Sci. *261*:1113-1115.

Rothchild, I. 1965a. The corpus luteum-hypophysis relationship: The luteolytic effect of luteinizing hormone (LH) in the rat. Acta Endocrinol. *49*:107-119.

Rothchild, I. 1965b. Interrelations between progesterone and the ovary, pituitary and the central nervous system in the control of ovulation and the regulation of progesterone secretion. Vitamins and Hormones *23*:209-327.

Rothchild, I., and Schwartz, N. B. 1965. The corpus luteum-hypophysis relationship: The effects of progesterone and oestrogen on the secretion of luteotrophin and luteinizing hormone in the rat. Acta Endocrinol. *49*:120-137.

Rowland, I. W., and Short, R. V. 1959. The progesterone content of the guinea-pig corpus luteum during the reproductive cycle and after hysterectomy. J. Endocrinol. *19*:81-86.

Savard, K., Marsh, J. M., and Rice, B. F. 1965. Gonadotropins and ovarian steroidogenesis. Recent Progr. Hormone Res. *21*:285-356.

Sawyer, C. H. 1963. Induction of estrus in the ovariectomized cat by local hypothalamic treatment with estrogen. Anat. Rec. *145*:280 (abstract).

Schjeide, A. O., and Urist, H. R. 1959. Proteins and calcium in egg yolk. Exp. Cell Res. *17*:84-94.

Schmidt, P. J., and Idler, D. R. 1962. Sex hormones in the plasma of the salmon at various stages of maturation. Gen. Comp. Endocrinol. *2*:204-214.

Segal. S. J., Davidson, O. W., and Wada, K. 1965. Role of RNA in the regulatory action of estrogen. Proc. Nat. Acad. Sci. *54*:782-787.

Sharman, G. B. 1959. Marsupial reproduction. Monographiae Biologicae *8*:332-368.

Short, R. V. 1962. Steroid concentrations in normal follicular fluid and ovarian cyst fluid from cows. J. Reprod. Fertil. *4*:27-46.

Short, R. V. 1964. Ovarian steroid synthesis and secretion *in vivo*. Recent Progr. Hormone Res. *20*:303-333.

Short, R. V., and Buss, I. O. 1965. Biochemical and histological observations on the corpora lutea of the African elephant, *Loxodonta africana*. J. Reprod. Fertil. *9*:61-67.

Simkiss, K. 1961. Calcium metabolism and avian reproduction. Biol. Revs. *36*:321-367.

Simmons, K. R., and Hansel, W. 1964. Nature of the luteotropic hormone in the bovine. J. Anim. Sci. *23*:136-141.

Simpson, C. F., Harms, R. H., and Wilson, H. R. 1965. Alteration of sex characteristics of turkey poults with diethylstilbestrol. Proc. Soc. Exp. Biol. Med. *119*:435-438.

Smith, B. D. 1961. The effect of diethylstilbestrol on the immature rat ovary. Endocrinology *69*: 238-245.

Smith, B. D., and Bradbury, J. T. 1961. Ovarian weight response to varying doses of estrogens in intact and hypophysectomized rats. Proc. Soc. Exp. Biol. Med. *107*:946-949.

Smith, B. D., and Bradbury, J. T. 1963. Ovarian response to gonadotrophin after pretreatment with diethylstilbestrol. Amer. J. Physiol. *204*: 1023-1027.

Smith, V. R., McShan, W. H., and Casida, L. E. 1957. On maintenance of the corpora lutea of the bovine with lactogen. J. Dairy Sci. *40*:443.

Spies, H. G., Coon, L. L., and Gier, H. T. 1966. Luteolytic effect of LH and HCG on the corpora lutea of pseudopregnant rabbits. Endocrinology *78*:67-74.

Spies, H. G., Zimbelman, D. R., Self, H. L., and Casida, L. E. 1960. Effect of exogenous progesterone on the corpora lutea of hysterectomized gilts. J. Anim. Sci. *19*:101-108.

Stormshak, F., and Casida, L. E. 1965. Effects of LH and ovarian hormones on corpora lutea of pseudopregnant and pregnant rabbits. Endocrinology *77*:337-342.

Stormshak, F., and Casida, L. E. 1966. Fetal-placental inhibition of LH-induced luteal regression in rabbits. Endocrinology *78*:887-888.

Strauss, F. 1950. Ripe follicles without antra and fertilization within the follicle; a normal situation in a mammal. Anat. Rec. *106*:251-252 (abstract).

Suchowsky, G. K., and Junkmann, K. 1961. A study of the virilizing effect of progestogens on the female rat fetus. Endocrinology *68*:341-349.

Takewaki, K. 1964. Secretion of luteotropin by the anterior hypophysis following injections of estrogens in male rats and persistent-diestrous rats. Annot. Zool. *37*:195-200.

Tornblom, N. 1946. Androgens in human blood. Acta. Med. Scand. Suppl. *170*:10.

Turnbull, J. G. 1966. Luteotropic properties of pro-

lactin in the hamster. Dissertation Abstr. *26*: 4911.

Urist, M. R., and Schjeide, A. O. 1961. The partition of calcium and protein in the blood of oviparous vertebrates during estrus. J. Gen. Physiol. *44*:743-756.

Urist, M. R., Schjeide, A. O., and McLean, F. C. 1958. The partition and binding of calcium in the serum of the laying hen and of the estrogenized rooster. Endocrinology *63*:570-585.

Urist, M. R., Deutsch, N. M., Pomerantz, G., and McLean, F. C. 1960. Interrelations between actions of parathyroid hormone and estrogens on bone and blood in avian species. Amer. J. Physiol. *199*:851-855.

Valle, J. R., and Valle, L. A. R. 1943. Gonadal hormones in snakes. Science *97*:400.

VanDemark, N. L., Salisbury, G. W., and Boley, L. E. 1952. Pregnancy interruption and breeding techniques in the artificial insemination of cows. J. Dairy Sci. *35*:219-223.

van Rees, G. P. 1964. Interplay between steroid sex hormones and secretion of FSH and ICSH. *In* E. Bajusz and G. Jasmin (eds.): Major Problems in Neuroendocrinology. S. Karger, Basel, pp. 322-345.

Vanstone, W. E., Dale, D. G., Oliver, W. F., and Common, R. H. 1957. Sites of formation of plasma phosphoprotein and phospholipid in the estrogenized cockerel. Can. J. Biochem. Physiol. *35*:659-665.

van Tienhoven, A. 1958. Effect of progesterone on broodiness and egg production of turkeys. Poultry Sci. *37*:428-433.

van Tienhoven, A. 1961. Endocrinology of reproduction in birds. *In* W. C. Young (ed.): Sex and Internal Secretions. Williams & Wilkins Co., Baltimore, Vol. 2, pp. 1088-1169.

Velle, W. 1963. Female gonadal hormones. *In* U. S. von Euler and H. Heller (eds.): Comparative Endocrinology. Academic Press Inc., New York, Vol. 1, pp. 111-153.

Vevers, H. G. 1962. The influence of the ovaries on secondary sexual characters. *In* S. Zuckerman (ed.): The ovary. Academic Press Inc., New York, Vol. 2, pp. 263-289.

von Faber, H. 1954. Über die Beeinflussung der Nebenschilddrüse durch Verabreichung von Stilboestrol allein und kombiniert mit Thyroxin, bzw. Testosteronproprionat an Hähne. Endokrinologie *32*:295-302.

Waynforth, H. B. 1965. Uterine tissues in the regulation of corpus luteum life span in the rat. J. Endocrinol. *33*:XI-XII.

Wilkinson, R. F., Jr. 1966. Seasonal and hormonal changes in the oviducts of *Diadophis punctatus*. Dissertation Abstr. *26*:5612.

Witschi, E. 1951. Embryogenesis of the adrenal and the reproductive glands. Recent Progr. Hormone Res. *6*:1-23.

Witschi, E. 1961. Sex and secondary sexual characters. *In* A. J. Marshall (ed.): Biology and Comparative Physiology of Birds. Academic Press Inc., New York, Vol. 2, pp. 115-168.

Worthington, W. C. Jr. 1960. Vascular responses in the pituitary stalk. Endocrinology *66*:19-31.

Wotiz, H. H., Botticelli, C. R., Hisaw, F. L., Jr., and

Ringler, I. 1958. Identification of estradiol-17β from dogfish ova *(Squalus suckleyi).* J. Biol. Chem. *231*:589-592.

Wright, P. A. 1961a. Induction of ovulation *in vitro* in *Rana pipiens* with steroids. Gen. Comp. Endocrinol. *1*:20-23.

Wright, P. A. 1961b. Influence of estrogens on induction of ovulation *in vitro* in *Rana pipiens.* Gen. Comp. Endocrinol. *1*:381-385.

Wurtman, R. J. 1964. An effect of luteinizing hormone on the fractional perfusion of the rat ovary. Endocrinology *75*:927-933.

Yamauchi, M., Nakahara, T., and Kaneda, Y. 1966. Effects of intra-uterine administration of a viscous gel-like substance on the oestrous cycle in cattle. I. Oestrous cycle length and fertility following treatment. Animal Breeding Abstracts *34*, ref. 246.

Young, W. C. 1961. The mammalian ovary. *In* W. C. Young (ed.): Sex and Internal Secretions. Ed. 3. Williams & Wilkins Co., Baltimore, Vol. 1, pp. 449-496.

Zachariae, F., and Jensen, C. E. 1958. Studies on the mechanism of ovulation. Acta Endocrinol. *27*: 343-355.

Zarrow, M. X. 1961. Gestation. *In* W. C. Young (ed.): Sex and Internal Secretions. Williams & Wilkins Co., Baltimore, Vol. 2, pp. 958-1031.

Zarrow, M. X., and Brennan, D. M. 1959. The action of relaxin on the uterus of the rat, mouse, and rabbit. Ann. N. Y. Acad. Sci. *75*:981-990.

Zarrow, M. X., and O'Connor, W. B. 1966. Localization of relaxin in the corpus luteum of the rabbit. Proc. Soc. Exp. Biol. Med. *121*:612-614.

Zarrow, M. X., Yochim, J. M., and McCarthy, J. L. 1964. Experimental Endocrinology. Academic Press Inc., New York.

Chapter 7

The Nongonadal Endocrine Glands

The discussion of the nongonadal endocrine glands will be limited to the effects that these glands and their hormones have on reproduction and to some of the interrelationships between these glands and gonadal tissue. The reader who needs to acquaint himself with the comparative anatomy and physiology of these glands should read the books by Gorbman and Bern (1962) and Turner (1966).

THE HYPOPHYSIS

Comprehensive reviews of the comparative anatomy, physiology, and biochemistry of the pituitary gland have been published in the book edited by Harris and Donovan (1966). These reviews should be consulted by any serious student of reproductive physiology. A brief review of the aspects of hypophysectomy and replacement therapy as it pertains to reproduction and a summary of the most frequently used bioassay procedures for gonadotropins will be presented here.

Hypophysectomy

Hypophysectomy of the female river lamprey *(Lampetra fluviatilis)* results in a lack of ovarian development, although atresia of the developed follicles does not occur. Ovulation will take place in these hypophysectomized females in response to

injections with PMSG or HCG (Evennett and Dodd, 1963).

Removal of the pituitary of male river lampreys delays spermatogenesis and spermiogenesis, but both processes will continue to take place. After hypophysectomy there is a lack of development of secondary sex characters. In *L. planeri*, administration of ox pituitary powder results in cloacal swelling in immature males (see Table 5-2). Thus the evidence in the species investigated shows that the pituitary is required for ovarian development and it suggests that the pituitary is involved in the control of gonadal hormone secretion required for the development of secondary sex characters.

Ablation of the ventral lobe of the pituitary of *Scyliorhinus caniculus* causes abnormal transformation of the spermatogonia into primary spermatocytes (Dodd et al., 1960), and it causes atresia of yolk-filled follicles in the female. Follicular atresia has also been found in *Mustelus canis* and *Squalus acanthias* (Pickford and Atz, 1957). There is, apparently, no evidence published about the success of replacement therapy.

Table 7-1 illustrates that hypophysectomy results in malfunction of the ovary and the testes. After this operation a number of characteristics that also occur after gonadectomy become evident (see Table 5-2). Replacement therapy has been successful in a number of species. Hypophysectomized *Fundulus heroclitus* males

Table 7-1. Effects of Hypophysectomy of Teleosts on Reproductive Organs

SPECIES	EFFECT
MALES	
Gobius paganellus	Spermatogonia do not mature
Fundulus heteroclitus	Spermatogonia do not mature
Pleuronectes platessa	Spermatogenesis inhibited; spermatogenesis that had started not affected; no effect on spermiation
FEMALES	
Gobius paganellus	Ovaries do not grow; no vitellogenesis
Fundulus heteroclitus	Ovaries do not grow; no vitellogenesis
Pleuronectes platessa	Vitellogenesis suppressed; atresia; no oviposition
Carassius auratus	Vitellogenesis suppressed; atresia
Heteropneustes fossilis	No ovulation or spawning

Reference: Hoar, 1966; Sundararaj and Goswami, 1966.

treated with suspensions of *F. heteroclitus* pituitaries or with mammalian FSH or LH, and hypophysectomized female *F. heteroclitus* injected with *F. heteroclitus* pituitary suspensions, have shown a gonadal response demonstrating the dependence of the gonads on the pituitary and, more specifically, on gonadotropins.

Hypophysectomized gravid catfish (*Heteropneustes fossilis*) will ovulate and spawn after administration of either 5 mg. LH per fish, or 100 I.U. HCG per fish, or 250 I.U. PMS per fish, or 5 mg. desoxycorticosterone per fish. No response was obtained after the injection of any of the following hormones: FSH, TSH, LTH, STH, ACTH, oxytocin, estradiol, progesterone, and testosterone (Sundararaj and Goswami, 1966).

The literature concerning the control of gonadal function by the hypophysis has been reviewed in detail by Hoar (1966). The data show that the development of the gonads during larval stages is dependent upon the presence of the pituitary. After hypophysectomy, only spermatogonia develop in the testis; in the ovaries follicles fail to develop and gonadal hormones are not secreted, as is indicated by the absence of the oviducts.

The effects of hypophysectomy and replacement therapy have been discussed in Chapters 5 and 6. Very little is known about the identity of gonadotropic hormones in amphibia. FSH and LH activity have been found in pituitary bioassays, and mammalian gonadotropins affect the gonads of hypophysectomized amphibia.

The study of the effect of hypophysectomy and replacement therapy on reptiles has been limited to a few species. The evidence shows that gonadal weights and gametogenesis are dependent upon the presence of the anterior pituitary and that replacement therapy with mammalian gonadotropins is effective (Knobil and Sandler, 1963; Nalbandov, 1966). The available evidence, although contradictory, suggests that the pituitary is not required for maintenance of pregnancy, but is required for normal parturition in viviparous garter snakes and in the viviparous lizard (*Zootoca vivipara*).

Anterior Pituitary Hormones

Ablation of the pituitary leads to regression of the gonads, interruption of gametogenesis, and cessation of androgen and estrogen secretion, but surprisingly, in the case of the pigeon it causes accumulation of progesterone in the testicular tubules (see van Tienhoven, 1961a).

Replacement therapy with mammalian gonadotropins is effective with respect to spermatogenesis, but is only temporarily so with respect to androgen secretion, as measured by comb size. Avian pituitary extracts can, however, maintain comb size for an indefinite length of time. Nalbandov et al. (1951) have proposed that there is either a "third gonadotropin" in avian pituitaries or that avian LH is qualitatively different from mammalian LH. Further support for this hypothesis can be found in the fact that follicles in the ovaries of immature chicks fail to increase in size after mammalian gonadotropin injections, but do increase after the injection of chicken pituitary preparations; the same is true in hypophysectomized pullets (Das and Nalbandov, 1955). Follicular atresia, which normally occurs after all food is withdrawn from laying hens, is prevented by injection of either mammalian gonadotropins or by chicken pituitary extracts. Chicken pituitary extracts were more effective in inducing repeated ovulations (Morris and Nalbandov, 1961). In none of these experiments with hens can one exclude the possibility that the difference between the mammalian and avian pituitary preparation is not the result of the presence of tropic hormones other than gonadotropins in the avian material.

Nalbandov (1966) excludes this explanation because mammalian gonadotropins given in combination with ACTH, TSH, prolactin, and growth hormone are ineffective. However, there is good evidence that growth hormones differ between species (Knobil and Greep, 1959) and, therefore, mammalian growth hormone may have been ineffective for this reason.

During the nonbreeding season the ovaries of a number of birds, e.g. redbilled weavers (Quelea quelea), European goldfinches (Carduelis elegans), green finches (Carduelis chloris), canaries, and sparrows can be brought to full development with regular ovulations by injecting PMSG. In nonlaying chickens, FSH treatment can cause maturation of ova, and LH treatment results in ovulation (Nalbandov and Card, 1946). In all these cases the animal's own pituitary may have produced enough

avian LH to enable the mammalian preparations to be effective, but other hormones may have been present also. There remains, therefore, the difference between the effect of mammalian gonadotropins on immature and mature but regressed ovaries. The difference is probably the result of the inability of immature ovaries to respond. Das and Nalbandov's data show no ovarian weights indicating follicles of ovulatory size until the birds were 110 days old, at the beginning of the treatment. On the basis of the evidence obtained with females, one cannot state that the concept of an "avian" or "a third gonadotropin" has been proven. The evidence obtained with males is more convincing, although here also one cannot exclude the effect of other tropic hormones.

Ablation of the anterior pituitary of immature mammals prevents gonadal maturation; when the operation is performed in mature males and females, the gonads and the secondary sex organs regress, as do the mammary glands of the female. We have discussed the difference between species with respect to regression of corpora lutea after hypophysectomy in Chapter 6 (see Tables 6-15 and 6-17).

Replacement therapy is generally effective; in the male complete spermatogenesis can be obtained, whereas in the female follicular growth, ovulation, and implantation of embryos can be obtained by careful dosage of the appropriate hormones. Some of the hormonal requirements for obtaining spermatogenesis have been discussed in Chapters 5 and 6.

PROLACTIN

The presence of prolactin in the pituitaries of vertebrates has been investigated and the available data have been summarized by Nicoll et al. (1966), and Chadwick (1966). If prolactin activity is assayed by the "eft water drive" (causing the eft to migrate from a terrestrial to an aquatic habitat), its presence can be shown in pituitaries of elasmobranchs and all other higher vertebrates.

In a number of species of euryhaline teleosts (e.g. *Poecilia latipinna* and *Fundulus heteroclitus*) and of some fresh water teleosts (e.g. *Xiphophorus helleri, X. milleri,* and *X. maculatus*), hypophysectomy leads to death if the operated fish are kept in fresh water, although they will survive in brackish or in sea water. Such fish will survive in fresh water if given injections of either teleost pituitaries or mammalian prolactin (Schreibman and Kallman, 1966).

The ability to stimulate the pigeon crop gland is found in extracts from the pituitaries of dipnoans, amphibia, reptiles, birds, and mammals, whereas stimulation of mammary gland secretion is found after injections of amphibian, reptilian, avian, and mammalian pituitaries, and weak activity is found after injections of extracts from some teleosts and dipnoans. Proliferation of mammary tissue was found after injections of elasmobranch, teleost, and amphibian pituitaries.

The maintenance of rat corpora lutea has been established definitely only for mammalian prolactin. The definition of the presence of prolactin in the pituitary is thus dependent upon the assay used.

There is, apparently, no evidence that prolactin injections affect the gonads of cyclostomes, elasmobranchs, teleosts, amphibia, or reptiles. In birds the effects of exogenous prolactin may be related to the migratory activity of the species which is injected (Meier et al., 1966). In a sedentary or weakly migratory species prolactin injections cause regression of the testes, whereas in migratory species prolactin does not cause gonadal regression. The evolutionary significance of this difference may lie in the fact that prolactin causes migratory restlessness with concomitant hyperphagia in migratory species.

The decrease in gonadal size induced by prolactin injection of doves can be prevented by simultaneous FSH injections. According to Riddle (1963), prolactin prevents the release of gonadotropins from the pituitary.

Prolactin has a number of extra-gonadal effects which are involved indirectly with reproduction. Riddle (1963) has reviewed this evidence in detail and these effects are summarized.

Prolactin causes the formation of pigeon milk by the crop gland of birds in the order Columbiformes. Dumont (1965) has described the histology and the fine structure of the pigeon crop in nonbrooding pigeons and in birds which received prolactin injections. The pigeon crop gland lumen is lined by the stratum disjunctum, which consists of squamous epithelium; immediately under this lies the stratum spinosum, which is about three to four cell layers thick and consists of polyhedral cells. The stratum basale is a deeper layer and is followed by the lamina propria, which consists of connective tissue. After prolactin injection (1.75 I.U.) a number of histological changes occur, which become apparent about 12 hours after injection. These changes consist of a downward growth of the stratum basale into the lamina propria; after about two days the stratum basale becomes folded and the lamina propria tissue extends into the newly formed folds. After about four days the stratum basale becomes so thick that it obliterates the folds. The stratum disjunctum cells become polyhedral instead of flat, and intracellular fat droplets consisting of neutral unsaturated triglycerides appear in the stratum disjunctum and the stratum basale. These fat droplets appear subsequent to an increased mitotic activity. Dumont found, however, no striking changes in the organelle systems of any of the crop tissue except for the presence of ribosomes in single units in nonstimulated cells and the presence of polysomes in prolactin-stimulated cells. According to Riddle (1963) the mucosa (stratum disjunctum) cells slough off due to the proliferation of the stratum basale and the consequent poorer vascularization of the stratum disjunctum.

Prolactin is required for the formation of the so-called incubation or brood patch, which is formed on the breast of a number of avian species (but not all) that incubate their eggs by sitting on them. The formation of the incubation patch involves loss of down feathers from the ventral apterium of the breast and abdomen, and eventually results in fully developed patch feather papillae; follicles have disappeared (Selander and Yang, 1966), the epidermis increases in thickness (Selander and Yang observed a sixfold increase in breeding females), the vascularity (number and size of blood vessels) of the skin increases, and the water content of the skin may increase from the normal value (61.4 percent) to a maximum, during late incubation, of 84.9 percent (Selander and Yang, 1966). Bailey (1952) investigated the hormonal requirements for the formation of the incubation patch and found that in intact finches, estrogen implants will cause these changes, albeit not in the normal order, in birds that start nest building and incubation activities. Androgen pellets are ineffective, although estrogen is effective in males of species in which the male normally does not develop a brood patch. In the hypophysectomized birds, estrogen plus prolactin is required for normal brood patch formation, whereas estrogen alone causes only edema. Selander and Yang (1966) found that prolactin augments the effect of estradiol on the rate of defeathering, on dermal vascularity, and on edema in intact house sparrows. Progesterone increases the effect of estrogen on the thickness of the epidermis, but does not augment the estrogen-induced increased vascularity.

Selander and Yang (1966) also observed that in house sparrows, the normal incubation patch was more edematous than the hormone-induced patches, which may be due either to a requirement of a special sequence of hormone injections, or to a specific ratio of hormones or the requirement of tactile stimulation.

Johns and Pfeiffer (1963) have shown in the Northern phalarope (*Lobipes lobatus*) and Wilson's phalarope (*Steganopus tricolor*), in which the males incubate the eggs

and the females do not, that androgen plus prolactin is required for the formation of the brood patch in intact males. Selander (1964) has discussed the significance of the two mechanisms which operate in the male and female with respect to the timing of the brood patch formation. In the females, estrogen secretion reaches its peak at the time of egg laying, and estrogen can thus be used to time the formation of the brood patch; on the other hand, androgen secretion in the male reaches its peak before egg laying starts and thus, if testosterone is used to time the function of the incubation patch, events would start too early. In the male, the combination of testosterone with a stimulus to start prolactin secretion or release is required. This stimulus may be seeing the female sitting on the eggs, the sight of a nest with eggs, copulation, or other cue.

Lostroh and Johnson (1966), using 28-day-old hypophysectomized female rats and highly purified hormone preparations, showed that 3 μg. FSH + 1 μg. LH per day injected for three days tripled ovarian weight and caused development of follicles with large antra and evidence of luteinization; with only 2 μg. FSH, antra formation was found and an increase in ovarian weight of about 70 percent was obtained. Ovulation of these follicles was obtained in 100 percent of the cases by the injection of either 20 μg. FSH or 20 μg. LH eight hours after the third daily injection of 3 μg. FSH + 1 μg. LH. The experimenters also showed that LH and FSH are required for estrogen secretion (see Chapter 6).

Malven and Sawyer (1966a) produced ovulation and corpora lutea in hypophysectomized rats by the injection of 131 μg. FSH/day for three days and an injection of 21 μg. LH on day 4. These corpora lutea, in the absence of other treatments, remained normal morphologically, but upon traumatization of the uteri no deciduomata were found. Prolactin (10 I.U.), injected on the day after the last gonadotropin injection, caused progesterone secretion by the corpora lutea as determined by the formation of deciduomata. Prolactin was found to have a luteolytic rather than a luteotropic effect if the prolactin injections were delayed four or more days after the last gonadotropin injections. Rather small doses, e.g. 0.25 I.U./day, can induce this luteolysis (Malven and Sawyer, 1966b). The authors speculate that prolactin may be required for luteolysis because corpora lutea of cyclic rats persist for 13 to 17 days, but in hypophysectomized rats they persist for six to nine months, indicating that a pituitary factor is required for regression. They also refer to the fact that immediately after parturition, the corpora lutea of rats regress more rapidly if the dams are allowed to nurse their young (prolactin secretion is stimulated by suckling) than if the pups are taken away immediately after parturition. The amount of prolactin released during the cycle, therefore, has to be regulated well. In the absence of mating, enough prolactin needs to be released to cause corpus luteum regression, but the amount may not be high enough to cause functional maintenance of the corpus luteum, which normally occurs after mating.

Bartke (1966) has obtained evidence that the sterility of female dwarf mice (dw dw) or Ames dwarf mice (df df) can be prevented by ovine prolactin injections starting on the day insemination plugs are found. Similar results were obtained by grafting a hypophysis under the kidney of intact cyclic dwarf mice (Bartke, 1965). The low fertility of the males, also after artificial insemination, can be alleviated by such pituitary grafts, suggesting a prolactin effect on male fertility (Bartke, 1965). The mechanism by which prolactin has this effect has not been established. In general, the effects of prolactin on the male reproductive system have been limited. The following observations have been made:

1. Exogenous prolactin acts synergistically with androgen in stimulating the growth of the prostate of rats; seminal vesicles of guinea pigs are stimulated by prolactin as are the preputial glands of rats (see Meites and Nicoll, 1966).

2. Prolactin increases the glucuronidase activity of the rat and mouse testis (Meites and Nicoll, 1966).

3. Prolactin has an important influence on the development of the mammary glands and on the secretion of milk. These effects have been reviewed expertly by Lyons and Dixon (1966).

4. The effects of mammalian prolactin on the gonads seem to be limited to the luteotropic effect on the corpus luteum during pseudopregnancy and pregnancy, and to the luteolytic effect it may have during the estrous cycle in small rodents with short estrous cycles.

5. Prolactin does not affect progesterone synthesis by corpora lutea of a rat made pseudopregnant by gonadotropin injections, although LH increases the steroidogenesis by these corpora lutea.

6. The in vitro incorporation of acetate into cholesterol by normal rat corpora lutea can be caused by the injection of HCG plus prolactin, but not by either of these hormones alone (Meites and Nicoll, 1966).

In most species investigated, prolactin and growth hormone are separate entities (although it should be mentioned that Evans and Riddle disagreed, in the early years of endocrinology, on whether growth hormone and prolactin could be separated, Evans maintaining that they could, Riddle insisting that they could not). The human growth hormone and prolactin activity, apparently, cannot be separated (Lyons and Dixon, 1966) with respect to biological activities and antigenic properties, but human prolactin is antigenically different from sheep prolactin (Hayashida, 1966).

FOLLICLE STIMULATING HORMONE AND LUTEINIZING HORMONE

The effects of these hormones on the testis and ovary have been discussed in

Chapters 5 and 6 and need not be repeated here.

Up to this point a discussion of the question whether the pituitary secretes two chemical entities, namely FSH and LH, or whether one gonadotropic complex is secreted, has been avoided. This question has been differently answered, at various times, by the same investigator.*

Most of the evidence which can be cited in favor of one or the other hypothesis is indirect. The suggestion by Geschwind (Cole [ed.] 1964, p. 73) that two different fluorescent-labeled antisera (to FSH and LH) be used has, apparently, not been followed, probably because no pure FSH has been available. The use of rabbit antihuman FSH serum does not indicate fluorescence in any specific human pituitary cells (Hayashida, 1966).

In favor of the dualistic hypothesis, i.e. separate FSH and LH secretions, one can cite the following:

1. By using appropriate species, in which the presence of ripe follicles, ovulation, pregnancy, and lactation is distinctly separate (e.g. *Myotis myotis*), by using selected hormonal treatments (e.g. testosterone injections in adult female rats to obtain pituitaries high in FSH but free of LH, and by using special staining techniques, one can distinquish the separate cells in the pars distalis that produce FSH or LH. Results of these techniques can be combined with results of bioassay of one half of the pituitary gland, and histochemical and cytological investigation of the other half of the same gland. By using different solvents one can remove the FSH and LH activity and correlate this with the cytological and histochemical results. These techniques yielded results that support the dualistic hypothesis (Purves, 1966). On the other hand, Bogdanove and Gay (1966) have found that long term treatment with testosterone propionate of rats causes a high FSH and a low LH content;

however, this treatment causes regression of two types of gonadotropins that had been assumed to be FSH cells.

2. The bioassay of the anterior pituitary and of the plasma for LH and FSH reveals that after ovariectomy there is an increase in pituitary FSH potency, from 13 μg. in the normal mouse to 74 μg. in the ovariectomized mouse; while for blood FSH concentration the corresponding figures were: nondetectable amounts and 9.0 μg./100 ml. However, blood and pituitary levels of LH did not change (Parlow, 1964a). Similarly, estradiol injection in ovariectomized rats had a differential effect on FSH and LH contents of the anterior pituitary; testosterone injections in castrated rats also affected FSH and LH contents of the pituitary (Parlow, 1964b). Other experiments, showing similar principles of differential effects of hormones on pituitary FSH and LH concentrations, have been carried out with pigs (Parlow et al., 1964). These experiments are difficult to reconcile with an assumption of secretion of one gonadotropic complex.

3. Moszkowska (1959) found that after implantation of pituitaries in the absence of hypothalamic tissue, no corpora lutea were formed but follicular size increased, whereas with hypothalamic tissue present corpora lutea were formed, thus indicating FSH secretion in one case and LH secretion in the other.

As evidence in favor of a one gonadotropic complex hypothesis, one can cite as the main argument that no FSH free of LH activity has been obtained in spite of extensive purification procedures (Geschwind, 1966). On the other hand, single proteins which meet biochemical and physical characteristics of purity can have FSH and LH properties. The gonadotropin complex may thus be one hormone.

The reader interested in the physical and chemical properties of FSH, LH, and prolactin should consult the reviews by Geschwind (1964, 1966), Gemzell and Roos (1966), and Lyons and Dixon (1966).

Woods and Simpson (1961) have re-

---

*Cole, H. H. (Ed.) 1964. Gonadotropins. W. H. Freeman and Company, San Francisco, pp. 71-72.

ported the presence of a hypophyseal factor which antagonizes the effect of HCG on the ovarian and on uterine weight. The factor, during purification, is associated with LH, although the authors do not consider the antagonistic effect to be an inherent property of LH. Sairam et al. (1966) have isolated, from the urine of the Bonnet monkey *(Macaca radiata)*, a gonadotropin antagonist that inhibits the ovarian response to FSH in the Steelman-Pohley (1953) test for FSH and the effect of FSH after HCG administration on the uterus. Whether this antagonist is similar to the pituitary factor found by Woods and Simpson has not been established.

Gonadotropins of pituitary origin are sometimes excreted in the urine in significant amounts. Examples are human menopausal urine and the urine of castrates. Thus, under conditions in which the negative feedback from the gonads is removed, and when one might expect high levels in the blood (as is indeed the case), gonadotropins are excreted.

Gonadotropins that are not of pituitary origin are found in the urine of pregnant women and other primates, in the blood of pregnant mares, and in the placenta of mice, rats, hamsters, and humans. These hormones will be discussed here briefly.

The hormone found in the urine of pregnant women is called human chorionic gonadotropin; it originates in the chorion, as the name implies, and the secretion of this hormone may start as early as the third week of the cycle. Hormone excreted in the urine increases gradually until about 35 days after ovulation, when the maximum is reached. The hormone, when injected into hypophysectomized rats or mice, causes repair of the ovarian interstitial tissue, and in the hypophysectomized male it causes repair of the Leydig cells and androgen secretion; the latter may be responsible for the maintenance of the seminiferous tubules. The hormone has physiological effects similar to those caused by LH. An example of the luteinizing

effects of this hormone is the intense luteinization of ovarian follicles of rats that have been pretreated with PMSG, as is the case in the "Parlow" rat used in the assay of LH. Immunologically, LH and HCG are related, although not identical (Goss and Lewis, 1964).

The chorionic gonadotropins of other primates have not been investigated sufficiently to warrant further discussion here.

The gonadotropin found in pregnant mare's serum, often called pregnant mare's serum (PMS) instead of pregnant mare's serum gonadotropin (PMSG), is secreted by the endometrial cups of the mare. The hormone has FSH and LH-like properties which, unlike the pituitary gonadotropins, cannot be separated into two entities. In immature rats, PMSG causes follicular growth and ovulation, which, as we shall see, is dependent upon participation of the injected animal's own pituitary. These ovulations can be blocked by barbiturate injections (see Chapter 8). In hypophysectomized rats, PMSG injection causes follicular growth, interstitial cell repair, and estrogen secretion in the female, and causes spermatogenesis and androgen secretion in the male. Clegg et al. (1962) found that the gonadotropin secretion was affected by the genotype of the fetus. Gonadotropin secretion is ten times as high when the fetus is a horse as when it is a mule. PMSG secretion starts at about the thirty-seventh to forty-second day of pregnancy, and the concentration in the blood increases for three to four weeks, is maintained at this level for one to two weeks, and then declines. Small amounts are still present during the sixth and seventh months of pregnancy.

Other Perissodactylae also secrete gonadotropins during pregnancy; this secretion has been reported for the donkey, the giraffe, and the nilgar, and perhaps the African elephant also may secrete this hormone (Rowlands, 1964). Sufficient details for further consideration are not available.

The placenta of the rat contains a substance which can cause maintenance of the corpus luteum of the hypophysectomized rat; the same extract also gives a positive response in the pigeon crop gland assay for prolactin. The evidence thus favors the concept that the rat placenta secretes prolactin.

The human placenta secretes, in addition to the gonadotropin mentioned, a prolactin-growth hormone (Beck et al., 1965) that has both lactogenic and growth hormone properties, and in other ways resembles the pituitary prolactin-growth hormone (molecular weight and amino acid composition are similar) but, according to Friesen (1965) differs in other respects: mobilities differ, the pituitary hormone increases serum-free fatty acids, and the placental hormone does not.

Josimovich (1966) has determined that human placental lactogen (HPL) by itself has no growth hormone effect, in the hypophysectomized rat, on epiphysial cartilage growth (one of the standard growth hormone tests), but that HPL acts synergistically with human growth hormone (HGH) and bovine growth hormone. Neither HPL nor HGH afford protection against insulin-induced hypoglycemia, whereas a combination of HPL and HGH afford such protection.

These data suggest that the growth hormone effects observed by others with placental prolactin might be the result of contamination with growth hormone. The lack of a growth hormone effect of the placental hormone would also explain why pregnant women do not show evidence of acromegaly in spite of the high titers of placental hormone in the blood (Grumbach and Kaplan, 1965). The hormone may have a function in enhancing the positive nitrogen balance in pregnant women. The placental prolactin may also act in the development of the mammary glands, but the function which this hormone may have on the ovary does not seem to have been established.

Where and how gonadotropins have

their effects has been investigated intensively, using a variety of in vivo and in vitro techniques. In some of the in vitro investigations, perfusions of the ovaries were performed (Romanoff, 1966), whereas in other experiments tissue slices were incubated (Armstrong, 1966; Marsh and Savard, 1966; Savard et al., 1965).

In vitro incubation of either rat or bovine ovarian tissue reveals that addition of LH to the incubation medium increases the incorporation of acetate into progesterone (Marsh and Savard, 1966; Savard et al., 1965). Ying et al. (1965), similarly, observed that HCG increases the incorporation of acetate by testicular tissue suspensions. Armstrong (1966) has, however, presented evidence that the increased incorporation of acetate into progesterone is the result of an increased conversion of cholesterol into progesterone. Armstrong (1966), using rabbits in which ovarian cholesterol stores had been labeled with cholesterol-7^{3}H, found that intravenous LH injection causes increased secretion of 20-α-hydroxy-pregn-4-en-3-one (20-α-ol) and that a considerable part of this hormone originates from the labeled cholesterol. Channing and Villee (1966) found in in vitro experiments that LH stimulates conversion of cholesterol to pregnenolone in luteinized rat ovary homogenates.

In vitro experiments show that either injection of LH prior to removal of the ovary or addition of LH to the incubation medium causes increased synthesis of 20-α-ol, with a large proportion of the 20-α-ol being synthesized from cholesterol. The increased incorporation of acetate into progesterone could be partially dissociated from progesterone synthesis for both rat and bovine ovarian tissue. Romanoff (1966) also concluded, on the basis of perfusion experiments, that LH stimulated the conversion of cholesterol into progesterone by luteal bovine ovaries. Hall (1966) showed that LH promoted testosterone synthesis in rabbit testis slices by stimulating the conversion of cholesterol into pregnenolone. There is general agreement that LH acts between cholesterol and pregnenolone. Whether the stimulation of acetate incorporation into steroid hormones is the result of the stimulation of this conversion of cholesterol, as Armstrong (1966) has suggested, or whether the LH specifically stimulates acetate incorporation per se, is a matter of some controversy (Armstrong, 1966; Savard et al., 1965).

Marsh and Savard (1966) found that LH causes an increase in 3'-, 5'- adenosine monophosphate (cyclic AMP) in cattle corpora lutea; Hall and Koritz (1965) and Marsh and Savard (1966) obtained an increase in progesterone synthesis in bovine corpora lutea slices, similar to that obtained after either LH or cyclic AMP addition to the incubation medium. These data suggest that LH may stimulate cyclic AMP synthesis, which in turn increases progesterone synthesis. Sandler and Hall (1966) have obtained evidence that cyclic AMP stimulates steroidogenesis in rat testes in vitro.

In a discussion of steroidogenesis and of the effect of gonadotropic hormones on this metabolic process, it is important to point out that the rate of steroidogenesis may be dependent upon the generation of the reduced nicotinamide adenine dinucleotide phosphate (NADPH), which was formerly called reduced triphosphopyridine nucleotide (TPNH). However, Channing and Villee (1966) observed that the conversion of cholesterol in pregnenolone by luteinized rat ovary homogenates was independent of generation of NADPH.

Kidwell et al. (1966) measured glucose-6-phosphate dehydrogenase activity (this enzyme is one of the enzymes in the glucosephosphate-gluconate pathway which generates NADPH) and 20-α-hydroxysteroid dehydrogenase activities in the ovaries of immature rats that were injected with PMSG and HCG so that follicular maturation or ovulations were obtained as well as luteinization; other rats were treated with PMSG, HCG, and LH (started nine days after the PMSG injections). Glucose-6-phosphate dehydro-

genase was found in all corpora lutea, and 20-α-hydroxysteroid dehydrogenase was found first at the periphery and later in the centrally located corpus luteum cells. LH and HCG administration caused further increases in the activity of both enzymes in the luteinized granulosa cells. The increase in glucose-6-phosphate dehydrogenase activity was coincident with an increase in uterine weight, suggesting an association between the increased enzymatic activity and estrogen secretion. That estrogen secretion by corpora lutea can be increased by LH injection has been shown by McDonald et al. (1966).

Dorrington and Kilpatrick (1966) have shown that LH increases the in vitro production of progesterone and 20-α-ol in slices of rabbit ovaries, but has no stimulatory effect on progesterone synthesis in rabbit corpora lutea slices. NADPH, on the other hand, stimulates progesterone synthesis in ovarian slices and by corpora lutea, but has little effect on 20-α-ol production in ovarian slices. These data suggest that the effect of LH cannot be explained entirely by increasing the availability of NADPH. Armstrong (1966) has pointed out that although the effect of exogenous NADPH and LH may be different in in vitro experiments, the difference does not prove that LH does not make more endogenous NADPH available.

The increase in 20-α-hydroxysteroid dehydrogenase observed by Kidwell et al. (1966) might explain the ten-fold decrease in the progesterone to 20-α-ol ratio which was observed by Armstrong et al. (1964) after injection and subsequent incubation of rat luteal tissue, if it were not for the fact that the LH treatment also decreases the total amount of progesterone plus 20-α-ol.

It should be noted, although the interpretation of the data is not yet definitive, that puromycin, which blocks protein synthesis, also blocks LH- or 3'-,5'-AMP-induced progesterone synthesis by bovine corpora lutea; similar results are obtained with cycloheximide, another inhibitor of protein synthesis. Puromycin, similarly, blocks the effect of LH on testosterone synthesis (Hall and Eik-Nes, 1962). It is very probable that the protein synthesis inhibiting agents inhibit the synthesis of enzymes required for the completion of the pathway cholesterol → steroid hormone but this has not been proved.

Species specificity of the mammalian pituitary gonadotropic hormones has been investigated extensively by Geschwind (1966).

As pure FSH has not been available, no conclusions can be drawn with respect to this hormone. The specificity of LH seems to be limited; e.g. rabbit antiserum to ovine LH inhibits endogenous rat LH activity and can neutralize LH activity in humpback whale, pig, human, and rat pituitaries. The biological response (e.g. ovulation) has not been shown to be species specific. The half lives of LH activity from rat blood after injection of pituitary extracts of different species have yielded the following figures (Catchpole, 1964): rat pituitary, 15 minutes, pig pituitary, ten minutes, human pituitary, 65 minutes, and horse pituitary, 270 minutes; for PMSG the corresponding figure was 1560 minutes and for HCG 294 minutes. These figures suggest small differences among the pituitary extracts of the species investigated. Other investigations have shown that equine, bovine, ovine, and rat LH are immunochemically similar (Desjardins and Hafs, 1964).

The effects of the other anterior pituitary hormones (ACTH, TSH, growth hormone, and exophthalmos-producing substance) can be explained in terms of the effect on the hormone production by the target organ. According to Engel and Lebovitz (1966), there is no substantial evidence that any of these hormones, with the exception of ACTH, have extra-target organ effects. Of the extratarget organ effects of ACTH listed by these authors, none involve the reproductive system directly. In this chapter, discussion will be limited to the effects of the target organ hormones, e.g. thyroxine and corticosteroids, on reproduction.

Cehovic (1965) reported that α-melanophore-stimulating hormone (α-MSH) decreased the testicular weight and the diameter of the seminiferous tubules of guinea pigs, whereas β-MSH caused testicular edema, increased testicular weight, increased weight of the secondary sex organs, but did not affect the testicular tubules. How the α- and β-MSH exerted their effect, directly on the testis or via the pituitary or other endocrine gland, was not investigated.

Posterior pituitary hormones are, as will be discussed in Chapter 8, secreted in the hypothalamus, but may be stored in the posterior pituitary or pars nervosa. The removal of the posterior pituitary is, therefore, not always sufficient to create a posterior pituitary hormone deficiency. The hypothalamus can continue secretion of the hormones which may accumulate above the lesion (Sloper, 1966).

Posterior Pituitary Hormones

OXYTOCIN

The effect of oxytocin on gonadotropic secretion or release by the anterior pituitary, as assessed either by measurement of gonadotropin levels in the pituitary or plasma or by evaluation of gonadal function, has been studied mainly in mammals.

Chaudhury and Chaudhury (1962) found an effect of oxytocin injections on the pigeon crop gland, suggesting that prolactin might have been released but intradermal injection of oxytocin over the crop gland also gave a positive response. Others have not been able to confirm these results (Höhn, 1963; Mizuno and Meites, 1963). No other effects of oxytocin on gonadotropin secretion or release, or directly on the gonads of birds have apparently been noted.

Among mammals there are considerable species differences with respect to the pituitary and gonadal response to oxytocin. Intracarotid injection of oxytocin causes LH release in cyclic rats and rats in permanent estrus as a result of neonatal androgen treatment (Martini, 1966). In intact immature rats or in immature rats with hypothalamic lesions, infusion of oxytocin into the third ventricle causes premature vaginal canalization and increased weight of the reproductive organs, suggesting FSH and LH release (Corbin and Schottelius, 1961). In adult rats, on the other hand, infusion of as little as 5 mU. oxytocin into the third ventricle of cyclic rats at any day of the cycle except the day of proestrus causes pseudopregnancy, suggesting release of prolactin (Haun, 1966). Oxytocin injections, either prior to or after cervical stimulation, or injected for five days starting five days after cervical stimulation, do not affect the life span of the corpus luteum (Brinkley and Nalbandov, 1963), which may mean that once the corpus luteum is formed oxytocin cannot cause further prolactin release.

Studies concerning the effects of oxytocin on the rabbit gonad-pituitary system have given conflicting results. Martini et al. (1959) observed an increased urinary gonadotropin output after oxytocin injection of female rabbits. This observation is consistent with the increased testicular weight, increased tabular diameter, and increased sperm content of the epididymis after long term treatment with high (10 I.U./rabbit per day for five weeks, followed by 10 I.U./kg. per day for six weeks) doses of oxytocin (Armstrong and Hansel, 1958). Brinkley and Nalbandov (1963) found that subcutaneous injection of 50 U. of oxytocin four to 19 minutes prior to coitus prevented ovulation, whereas intracutaneous injections failed to do so. These data suggest, therefore, an inhibitory effect on coitus-induced LH release. Infusion of oxytocin into the pituitary of rabbits failed to induce ovulation (Campbell et al., 1964), but the effect of this infusion on coitus-induced ovulation was not studied.

Shibusawa et al. (1955) observed in dogs a slight and probably statistically not significant increase in testicular weight and an increase in urinary 17-ketosteroid (presumably indicating increased androgen production) following oxytocin injections.

Benson and Fitzpatrick (1966) cite evidence that oxytocin injections in ovariectomized guinea pigs bearing intrasplenic grafts caused luteinization of the follicles, thus indicating the release of the pituitary hormone responsible for luteinization in the guinea pig.

The effects of oxytocin and the possible pathways by which it acts have been investigated probably most extensively in cattle following the observation that mating causes oxytocin release and earlier than normal ovulation (see p. 136). Hansel et al. (1958) investigated the possibility of a causal relationship between oxytocin and ovulation by injection of 50 to 60 U. oxytocin. The cows thus treated ovulated about five hours earlier than the controls; this evidence thus supported the hypothesis that mating might cause earlier than normal ovulation via oxytocin release.

Armstrong and Hansel (1959) showed that oxytocin injections during the first week of the estrous cycle shortened the diestrual period; the next heat occurred eight to 12 days after the previous estrus. These effects were not observed in hysterectomized heifers (Armstrong and Hansel, 1959; Anderson et al., 1965; and see Table 6-15). The oxytocin-induced shortening of the life span of the corpus luteum can be prevented by atropine (Armstrong and Hansel, 1959; Black and Duby, 1965), reserpine (Armstrong and Hansel, 1959), and epinephrine (Black and Duby, 1965).

The effect of oxytocin on the corpus luteum depends, apparently, on the physiological status of this gland. For instance, oxytocin treatment during day 2 and 3 of the cycle does not decrease the weight nor the progesterone content, but treatments between day 2 and 6 decrease the weight and progesterone content, an effect which can be overcome by injections of either HCG or bovine LH, suggesting that oxytocin prevents release of endogenous LH. Donaldson et al. (1965), using the P^{32} uptake by chick testes for their bioassay of gonadotropins, found that the differences between the pituitary gonadotropin content of oxytocin-treated and control heifers were not significantly different at day 4 and 7 of the cycle, with treatments started at day 2. The correlation coefficients between gonadotropin content and total progesterone content for controls were $-.76$ on day 4 and $-.75$ on day 7; the corresponding figures for oxytocin-treated animals were 0.49 and 0.96. These correlations were interpreted to mean that in oxytocin-treated cows, the pituitary gonadotropin content reflects plasma gonadotropic hormone levels, but that in controls, pituitary gonadotropin concentration represents storage rather than plasma concentration. If this is true, the comparisons between the pituitary gonadotropin contents of control and oxytocin-treated animals should be reconsidered, since in the control animals the pituitary contents would lead to overestimation of the plasma levels; it thus would appear that oxytocin increases gonadotropin levels in the blood, a theory consistent with the follicular growth and ovulation observed by Armstrong and Hansel (1959), but it does not explain why the corpus luteum regresses and why the corpus luteum of such oxytocin-treated cows fails to regress when additional bovine LH is given. The fact that the bioassay method used was not specific for LH does not change the arguments proposed by Donaldson et al. (1965), although it may well be that oxytocin inhibits LH release or secretion and stimulates FSH release and secretion. In this case, one might propose that the maturation of the follicle as a result of the higher than normal FSH levels proceeds faster than normal, and enough LH is secreted to cause ovulation and to maintain the new corpus luteum. One would need to accept that oxytocin, during estrus,

causes LH release, but that during days 3, 4, 5, and 6 it inhibits LH release. Mares and Casida (1963) found that oxytocin injected on days 12 and 13 stimulated progesterone secretion, indicating that on days 4, 5, and 6 the response of the corpus luteum is different from days 12 and 13, an effect which should not be considered very surprising, since the gland undergoes rather rapid cyclic changes. These workers also established that injections of oxytocin on days 12 and 13 inhibited the progestogen production of corpora lutea in vitro, showing that the corpus luteum behaves differently in vivo than in vitro. Oxytocin, added to the incubation mixture, does not affect progestogen synthesis by the corpora lutea.

The entire question of the bovine corpus luteum maintenance and regression is under active study, and new data requiring new interpretations will undoubtedly be added rapidly. It seems, however, that satisfactory experiments will eventually require hypophysectomy of the animals and the use of bovine gonadotropins. The fact that equine LH is not capable of affecting the corpus luteum of the oxytocin-treated cow while bovine LH is (Simmons and Hansel, 1964) should be considered seriously in further investigations, for it is possible that similar specificities apply to FSH and prolactin.

The corpora lutea of pigs (Duncan et al., 1961; Rigor and Clemente, 1964) guinea pigs (Donovan, 1961), and golden hamsters (Ellett, 1964) are, apparently, not affected by oxytocin injections.

Telegdy and Fendler (1964) found that oxytocin injection (1.3 I.U./kg.) increased progesterone secretion by the adrenal but not by the ovary; this suggests that the increase in 17-ketosteroids in dogs noticed by Shibusawa et al. (1955) might also have been mediated via the adrenal rather than via the gonads.

Whether oxytocin releases prolactin (required for maintenance of the corpus luteum in rats and mice) has been a matter of controversy. Meites et al. (1963) have reviewed the evidence and concluded that in rats the experiments indicating pseudo-pregnancy after oxytocin administration are contradictory. In addition, lesions of the hypothalamus which inhibit oxytocin release do not interfere with milk secretion (dependent, among other things, upon adequate prolactin secretion).

Fitzpatrick (1966a) has critically reviewed the evidence concerning the effect of oxytocin on the genital duct system of female animals.

In a number of teleosts, injection of oxytocin causes premature expulsion of the young (e.g. the guppy, *Gambusia* sp.) or may cause expulsion of eggs under conditions which normally prevent oviposition (e.g. the Japanese rice fish). Fitzpatrick considers it possible that this effect is a pharmacological one.

In reptiles, gestation has been interrupted by injection of mammalian posterior pituitary extract, e.g. in *Natrix* sp., *Storeria* sp., and *Thamnophis* sp., and in the ovoviviparous lizard, *Zootoca vivipara* similar preparations cause expulsion of the eggs.

Riddle (1921), experimenting with doves, was the first to establish that posterior pituitary extracts can cause premature expulsion of eggs. Burrows and Byerly (1942) confirmed this effect in domestic chickens. Burrows and Fraps (1942) showed that vasopressin is more effective than oxytocin, and that effects of oxytocin can be explained in terms of vasopressin contamination. Later investigations have shown that vasopressin is not found in avian posterior pituitaries, but that these posterior pituitaries contain vasotocin (see Table 8-1). A number of studies have shown correlations between the vasotocin content of the posterior pituitaries of hens, the vasotocin concentrations in the blood plasma, and oviposition. Douglas and Sturkie (1964), and Sturkie and Lin (1966) found that the vasotocin concentration of a laying hen without an egg in the uterus is about 50 μU./ml., ten minutes before laying the

egg this value is about 150 μU./ml., and during oviposition the concentration was 30 to 150 times higher than during the resting stage (Douglas and Sturkie, 1964; Opel, 1966; and Sturkie and Lin, 1966); after oviposition the concentration dropped rapidly. Neither distension of the uterus nor injection of hypertonic saline injected into the carotid arteries caused a change in the blood vasotocin concentration. Ovipositions induced by acetylcholine or by pentobarbital injections are not accompanied by changes in vasotocin levels in the blood (Sturkie and Lin, 1966). Tanaka and Nakajo (1962) have found a sharp drop in vasotocin content of the posterior pituitary just prior to oviposition and a small decrease in oxytocin content at the same time. Shirley and Nalbandov (1956) have shown, however, that the posterior pituitary can be removed without affecting oviposition, a fact confirmed by Opel (1965). This investigator removed the posterior pituitary and, subsequently, made a piqûre of the preoptic region, an operation which caused premature oviposition in birds with and without posterior pituitaries. In further investigations, Opel (1966) established that both normal and piqûre-induced lay are associated with disappearance of vasotocin from the median eminence stalk region and with an increase in plasma vasotocin concentration. The release of posterior pituitary hormones after neural lobectomy has also been observed in mammals (to be discussed later in this chapter). These phenomena are in accord with the evidence that hypothalamic nuclei secrete these hormones, which can then be stored in the neural lobe of the hypophysis. There remains, however, the question why hens without posterior lobes can release vasotocin for oviposition but cannot release the posterior pituitary hormone that prevents polydipsia and polyuria (Shirley and Nalbandov, 1956). According to Table 8-2 this hormone should also be vasotocin.

Lesions of the preoptic hypothalamus delay but do not prevent oviposition

(Ralph, 1959); on the other hand, lesions of the supraoptic hypothalamus cause polydipsia but do not interfere with oviposition (Ralph, 1960). This indicates that an antidiuretic hormone is produced in the supraoptic nuclei, and that the oviposition-inducing hormone is produced in the preoptic area. These data suggest that a factor other than vasotocin is involved in water balance, although water balance regulation may involve vasotocin plus this other factor.

In mammals, a number of effects of oxytocin on the genital duct system have been noted, and these functions are thought to be important in sperm transport and in induction of labor.

Stimulation of the genitalia (vagina and cervix) leads to a milk ejection reflex in cattle, goats, and sheep. This ejection can be measured in either the animal stimulated, if it is lactating, or in a lactating partner connected by cross circulation (see Fitzpatrick, 1966a). Mating has been shown to cause milk ejection in cattle, horses, and women (see Fitzpatrick, 1966a) and antidiuresis has been observed in rats.

In sheep and cattle, semen is deposited in the vagina during natural mating and sperm have been reported in the fallopian tubes within 2.5 minutes in cattle and after six to 30 minutes in sheep. The presence of these sperm cannot be explained by they were going" and swam in a straight one assumes that the sperm "knew where they were going" and swam in a straight line from the vagina to the tube.

After a critical review of the available data about sheep and cattle, Fitzpatrick (1966a) concludes that uterine contractions may well be involved in the ascent of sperm, but that there is no proof that the release of neurohypophyseal hormones is an essential physiological component of mating. However, in vitro experiments with perfused cattle uteri have shown that sperm deposited in the cervix did not reach the upper part of the genital tract if hemostats were placed at different parts of this tract within five to ten minutes after semen deposition in control uteri, but sperm were found in the upper genital tract after oxytocin addition to the perfusion of fluid (VanDemark and Hays, 1954). It seems to this author that there is strong circumstantial evidence that oxytocin release may be involved in sperm ascent in some species such as cattle. Proof of such a concept would need to be obtained with animals with lesions which specifically destroy oxytocin-producing centers in the hypothalamus.

Evidence that oxytocin plays an important role in expulsion of the young is available for a number of species from a variety of experimental approaches. The evidence reviewed by Fitzpatrick (1966a) and Cross (1966) shows:

1. Injection of oxytocin can induce premature labor in rabbits and women.

2. In rabbits, cattle, pigs, horses and women, labor is accompanied by milk ejection from the mammary glands and increased intramammary pressure.

3. The concentration of an oxytocin-like substance in the jugular vein of sheep, goats, cattle, horses, and women in labor increases ten-fold within a 20 minute period, indicating a spurt of oxytocin release. Van Dongen and Hays (1966) found in calving cows that the concentration of an oxytocin-like substance in unextracted blood increased 10^6-fold a few minutes prior to expulsion of the calf.

4. Electrical stimulation of either the supraoptic (NSO) or the paraventricular nucleus (NPV) in the hypothalamus (see Chapter 8) causes uterine contractions, increases intramammary pressure, and can also induce premature labor.

5. Lesions of these hypothalamic nuclei, which produce oxytocin, cause abnormal parturition or lack of parturition in cats and guinea pigs, and cause prolonged gestation in rabbits.

The role of oxytocin in the initiation of labor will be discussed in the chapter on viviparity.

Hypophysectomized animals can give birth normally to their young, but they cannot nurse them as a result of lack of milk ejection. It is possible that any remaining oxytocin in the stalk median eminence area was released during labor and that the upper end of the stalk had not sufficiently reorganized to release oxytocin for milk ejection.

Cross (1966) and Fitzpatrick (1966b) have also reviewed the relationships between oxytocin and male secondary reproductive organs. A summary of the pertinent observations shows:

1. Rectal palpation of the seminal vesicles and ampullae of male sheep causes a release of neurohypophyseal hormones.

2. Injection of oxytocin in rabbits 30 seconds before access to males decreases the reaction time to the first ejaculate and increases the number of ejaculates which can be obtained.

These observations, considered with the increased rates of sperm discharge found after oxytocin injections of sheep and rabbits (see Cross, 1966), suggest the purely speculative hypothesis, in the absence of sufficient data for different species, that courtship may increase oxytocin release, as it does in females (see Fitzpatrick, 1966a), so that the number of possible ejaculations and successful matings within a given time increases. This may be important for species in which the male has a harem and the restricted mating season causes a relatively large number of females to be in heat simultaneously.

VASOPRESSIN

The effect of vasopressin on the ovary has been studied mainly in connection with a possible LH-releasing potency of this hormone. Injection of arginine vasopressin into the pituitary fails to cause ovulation in rats (Nikitovitch-Winer, 1962). In pseudopregnant rats, LH injections into the carotid artery cause LH release (Martini, 1966); LH release, as determined by LH concentration in the blood, is also ob-

served in castrated rats treated with estrogen and progesterone. This effect of vasopressin persists in hypophysectomized rats (McCann and Taleisnik, 1960); vasopressin injection into the ovarian vein also caused ascorbic acid depletion, suggesting a local effect of vasopressin not acting via LH release from the pituitary. Martini (1966) has argued that vasopressin may cause LH release in animals with high LH titers in the pituitary or that progesterone may sensitize the pituitary to the LH releasing effect of vasopressin.

Some support for Martini's suggestions is found in the experiments of Malven and Hansel (1965), which show that vasopressin hastens ovulation and shortens the diestrous period of hysterectomized rats. In such rats one may assume that progesterone concentrations in the blood and gonadotropin amounts stored in the pituitary are somewhat similar to those found in pseudopregnant rats.

In rats and women, coitus is associated with antidiuresis, indicating a release of vasopressin; in human males there are similar indications of vasopressin release during coitus (Fitzpatrick, 1966a,b). The functional significance of such vasopressin release is not established.

THE THYROID

The function of the thyroid in cyclostomes is not known (Dodd and Matty, 1964) and, consequently, no statement concerning the effects of hypo- or hyperthyroidism on reproduction can be made.

The evidence concerning the interrelationships between thyroid and reproduction in elasmobranchs seems to be limited to correlations existing between the activities of the thyroid and gonads during different periods of the reproductive cycle. It appears that thyroid activity is less in males than in females, and that in females, peaks of activity of the thyroid are associated with the period of initial growth of the ova and with gestation (see Dodd and Matty, 1964). For teleosts similar relationships have been noted (Dodd and Matty, 1964) and experimental hypothyroidism has caused delayed sexual maturation in swordtails (*Xiphophorus* sp.). In the guppy, thiouracil inhibits regeneration of the gonopodium of the male (Hopper, 1965).

We have mentioned in Chapter 2 that thiourea administration causes sex reversal of genetic females of *Rhacophorus schlegelii* and of *Rana temporaria ornativentris,* and that thyroidectomy failed to have such an effect in *R. temporaria ornativentris.* This suggests that the thiourea has its effect by a pathway other than the thyroid. It may be that the thyroid is required for the response, but this does not seem to have been investigated. The maturation of the gonads is normal in amphibia made hypothyroid to the extent that no metamorphosis occurs (see Dodd and Matty, 1964), but gonadotropin administration is necessary to obtain breeding behavior and spawning.

The influence, if any, of thyroid hormones in the reproduction of reptiles seems not to have been studied in any detail. Gorbman and Bern (1962) state that thyroidectomy arrests spermatogenesis and sex hormone secretion in *reptiles,* birds and mammals (emphasis mine).

Thyroidectomy or administration of goitrogens delays sexual maturity of ducks and chickens, prevents development of the penis of ducks and the comb of roosters, and reduces the response of the rooster's comb to exogenous androgen (van Tienhoven, 1961a). On the other hand, thyroid hormone administration causes earlier spermatogenesis in ducks and chickens and recrudescence of the testes and spermatogenesis in house sparrows during the sexual rest period (van Tienhoven, 1961a). In baby chicks, the response of the testis to exogenous gonadotropins is not affected by thyroxine administration, although the variability of

the response can be reduced by giving a daily dose of 2 μg. of D,L-thyroxine.

Thapliyal and Pandha (1965) observed larger testes and earlier spermatogenesis in juvenile spotted munias (*Uroloncha punctulata* = *Lonchura punctulata,* according to Ripley, 1960) thyroidectomized in December than in control birds. This size difference of the testes became apparent in February and persisted through December. In juvenile and adult birds, thyroidectomy prevented testicular regression, which normally occurred at the end of the breeding season. Woitkewitch (1940) had earlier reported the same effect of thyroidectomy in starlings (*Sturnus vulgaris*) with respect to testicular regression at the end of the breeding season. It would be of considerable interest to determine the extent to which the thyroid is involved in the regulation of the refractory period (a period after the end of the breeding season when no testicular activation can be obtained in response to increased light exposure). This period will be discussed in Chapter 13.

Ferrand (1963) injected large doses of thyroxine (50-150 μg./day.) into male greenfinches (*Ligurinus chloris* = *Carduelis chloris*) during October and November, which is probably the refractory period in this species, and found no effect on spermatogenesis, whereas from December to March such thyroxine injections stimulated spermatogenesis. Unfortunately, no experiments were carried out in which thyroxine injections were started toward the end of the breeding season and were continued until the testes of controls regressed.

The effects of thyroidectomy or goitrogen administration on reproduction of male mammals have been studied in the common laboratory species and domestic farm animals. In none of the species investigated did hypothyroidism stimulate spermatogenesis, increase fertility, or increase libido. On the other hand, thyroidectomy has been reported to decrease testicular size in rats, rabbits, and goats

(Nalbandov, 1964) and delay sexual maturity in rats thyroidectomized while immature (Maqsood, 1952). The operation seems to have no effect on fertility in any of the species investigated (Myant, 1964; Nalbandov, 1964). The administration of small doses of thyroid hormone has been reported to stimulate spermatogenesis in young rats (Talbert, 1962) and rabbits (Maqsood, 1951); in sheep, thyroxine treatment started before the breeding season may prevent the decrease in fertility associated with hot weather, but exposure of male rabbits to high temperature is more harmful when the animals have received thyroxine than in controls (Maqsood, 1952). Brooks and Ross (1962) did not find a beneficial effect of thyroxine treatment on semen quality of rams exposed to high temperatures; however, it should be kept in mind that "semen quality" is not a good predictor of fertility.

The relationships between the thyroid, the pituitary, and the gonads are complicated and may differ from species to species. Thyroidectomy of immature male rats causes a relatively small decrease in the size of the testis and seminal vesicles, and a decrease in anterior pituitary content of FSH and LH (Contopoulos et al., 1958); on the other hand, gonadectomy does not affect the TSH content of the pituitary. The administration of gonadotropin to control, hypo- and hyperthyroid rats and mice has different effects, according to the species used. The testicular response of mice to a standard dose of PMSG is increased by thyroxine and decreased by thiouracil administration, but in rats the response is decreased by thyroxine and increased by thiouracil administration (Meites and Chandrashaker, 1949). Similar results can be obtained with female rats and mice (Johnson and Meites, 1960). These data illustrate the danger of trying to generalize from data obtained with one species.

The effects of the thyroid on female reproduction will be discussed for birds and mammals only, because information on these relationships is rather inadequate for the lower vertebrates. Among birds most investigations have been carried out with domestic chickens. Thyroidectomy and goitrogen administration have generally yielded similar results, i.e. lack of sexual development in young birds.

Feeding thiouracil to immature pullets depresses estrogen-induced hypercalcemia, serum riboflavin increase, and serum vitamin A increase, but enhances the estrogen-induced increase in ovarian weight, liver weight, liver protein content, and liver fat content. The effect of thiouracil feeding on the response of the oviduct weight to estrogen depends on the timing of the estrogen injections. If the latter are given on alternate days thiouracil increases the response, but if estrogen is given daily thiouracil decreases the response (Common et al., 1950, 1958, and 1961).

Thyroxine administration depresses estrogen-induced hypercalcemia, increases serum riboflavin concentration, serum vitamin A concentration, serum vitellin concentration, liver weight, and liver protein content, but does not affect the estrogen-induced hypertrophy of the oviduct (see Common et al., 1955; Hosada et al., 1954). These effects of thyroxine on the composition of the blood may explain the decrease in follicular size in chickens (Lacassagne, 1957) and the decreased egg production, smaller egg size, and smaller yolk size (Thuillie et al., 1961), since one might expect smaller yolk deposition in case of a lower concentration of precursors in the blood.

Thyroidectomy of 35- to 40-day-old rats results in a decreased LH and FSH content of the pituitary; thyroxine injections partially restore the FSH content but have little effect on the LH content (Contopoulos and Koneff, 1963). Rabbits subjected to thyroidectomy show hypertrophied follicles that fail to ovulate after coitus but ovulate in response to pregnancy urine gonadotropin; pituitaries of thyroidectomized rabbits fail to induce ovulation in intact rabbits, showing that the anterior pituitary of these rabbits does not secrete sufficient LH (Chu, 1944). Krohn (1951) did not confirm these effects of thyroidectomy, but Thorsøe (1962) also found polycystic ovaries after thyroidectomy and a decrease in the incidence of coitus-induced ovulations. However, this decrease proves to be insignificant when tested by a Chi square test. Administration of thyroid hormone to rabbits increases the LH content but decreases the FSH content of the pituitaries (Chu and You, 1945).

Both thyroidectomy and administration of goitrogens have given conflicting results even within the same species. Sometimes the difference between results from different workers can be explained on the basis of the difference in time between the thyroidectomy and the time the animal was killed or between the duration of goitrogen administration. The literature is so voluminous that a summary of the data in a table or in a few paragraphs would, at best, be superficial. However, the interested student can refer to the original papers and obtain the critical information for evaluation of the data. We will list here the range of responses obtained by different workers for a number of species.

In rats, thyroidectomy has been reported to have no effect (Peterson et al., 1952; Myant, 1964), cause ovarian cysts eight to ten months after thyroidectomy (Janes and Bradbury, 1952) and retard follicular formation and prevent ovulation (Peterson et al., 1952). Longer than normal cycles with longer than normal diestrus and shorter than normal estrus (Kulcsár-Gergely and Kulcsár, 1961), and with greater variability than in control rats (Peterson et al., 1952; Reineke and Soliman, 1953; and Myant, 1964) have been reported rather consistently. A reduced incidence of pregnancies and a higher incidence of young born dead have been observed (Parrott el al., 1960;

Hohlweg et al., 1964, 1965). Schreiber et al. (1965) found that methyl-thiouracil inhibited the compensatory hypertrophy normally observed after unilateral thyroidectomy. The effects of thyroid hormone administration will not be discussed in detail because the dosage of these hormones is critical; an overdose will have toxic effects, and in experiments in which thyroprotein or desiccated thyroid has been fed, there was virtually no control over the individual dosage, and thus such experiments are open to severe criticism. One interesting experiment will be reported because of its unexpected results. Naller and Cedeno (1963) injected 5 μg. D,L-thyroxine/day into rats that had been spayed for a period of five months; the injections induced estrus after one to two weeks. This response could, in some cases, be prevented by bilateral adrenalectomy, suggesting that thyroxine may have increased estrogen secretion by the adrenals.

In mice, thyroidectomy by I^{131} injections caused prolonged estrous cycles, prolonged gestation periods, and decreased litter sizes, but it had no effect on fertility (Bruce and Sloviter, 1957). Thiouracil (a goitrogen) feeding causes constant estrus, and, in mice kept at 30° and 35° C., ovaries were packed with large follicles; in controls kept at the same temperatures such large follicles were lacking. In none of these groups were corpora lutea present (Reineke and Soliman, 1953). The uteri of the TU-fed mice showed an estrous histologic picture, those of controls an anestrous histologic picture, and those of thyroprotein-fed mice a progestational histologic picture. These observations agree with the ovarian condition, as ovaries of thyroprotein-fed mice have numerous corpora lutea.

Peterson et al. (1952) conducted a careful study with guinea pigs in which the effect of thyroidectomy, propylthiouracil given in the drinking water, and thyroxine injections was studied. The O₂ consumption was measured to monitor the effectiveness of the treatments. Thyroidectomy decreased the incidence of estrous responses, the percent fertility, and the percentage of young born alive. PTU had no effects on these parameters and thyroxine administration increased the percent young born alive.

The effect of thyroidectomy on the ovary of the rabbit has been discussed in connection with the effect of the operation on pituitary gonadotropin content. Chu (1945) thyroidectomized pregnant rabbits between days 2 and 29 and observed a high incidence of abortions, delivery of dead fetuses, and early death of young; thyroid feeding partly overcame these effects. These results were not confirmed by Krohn (1951) who found no effect on pregnancy after thyroidectomy on day 10, 16, or 20.

In dogs and cows, thyroidectomy does not affect the ovary or gestation; in the cow, symptoms of estrus are suppressed (Reineke and Soliman, 1953). Thiouracil (0.15 percent) feeding to gilts did not affect ovulation rate, fertilization rate, embryonic mortality during the first 25 days of gestation, or the number of pigs born alive, but gestation was lengthened significantly. Thyroprotein feeding had no effect on any of these parameters (Lucas et al., 1958). In a subsequent experiment, 0.15 TU in the diet fed to gilts pregnant for 38 days caused increased embryonic mortality (Brumstad and Fowler, 1959). In monkeys, hypothyroidism is usually associated with lengthened and irregular menstrual cycles (Myant, 1964).

Mild hyperthyroidism in a number of species has either no detrimental effect on reproduction or a possible beneficial effect as was discussed for the guinea pig. At doses of 120 μg. given on day 11, 240 μg. on day 12, and 480 μg. from day 13 till estrus, triiodothyronine caused somewhat smaller follicles in sheep, but so did drenching with glucose; when both treatments were given to the same ewe the ovaries were normal (Howland et al., 1966). In immature Rhesus monkeys, given 1.88 μg. triiodothyronine per kg. for 180 days, there was a decrease in pituitary gonadotropin content as measured by the mouse uterine assay; on the other hand, doses of 7.5 μg./kg. increased serum gonadotropins. Neither of these changes in gonadotropins were reflected by the condition of the genital system of the monkeys (Kar and Datta, 1965). That feeding thyroid hormone-containing materials can be economically harmful was shown by Travis et al. (1966). These workers found that gullet trimmings, used to make mink feed, contain large amounts of thyroid hormone; feed made with these trimmings reduced the number of females whelping, the number of young born, the birth weight of the young, and the viability of the young. These results can be partly simulated by adding triiodothyronine and sodium-L-thyroxine pentahydrate to a diet free of gullet trimmings.

From the data collected for the different species, it seems that mild hypothyroidism, as induced by low levels of goitrogens, and mild hyperthyroidism are compatible with normal or near normal reproduction, whereas severe hypothyroidism, at least in some species, reduces reproductive efficiency; severe hyperthyroidism can also have detrimental effects.

Several investigators have studied the effects of the gonadal hormones on thyroid activity, as assessed by thyroid histologic examination, I^{131} concentration by the thyroid, I^{131} release from the thyroid, and the peripheral metabolism of thyroid hormone.

Burger et al. (1962), on the basis of experiments in which dienestrol diacetate was fed to chickens in the presence and absence of thiouracil, with and without TSH injections, concluded that estrogen caused increased thyroid weights in otherwise untreated birds by destroying circulating thyroid hormone. Thyroid weights were measured, but no other parameters of thyroid function were made; therefore, these conclusions will require confirmation in experiments in which more sophisticated methods are used.

The most extensive studies of the

effects of gonadal hormones on thyroid activity have been carried out with rats and mice. Radioiodine (I^{131}) uptake and release are good measures of thyroid activity and allow the use of the same animals, thus reducing variability within the experiment.

Beckers and de Visscher (1957, 1961) observed that ovariectomy of rabbits increased I^{131} concentration by the thyroid, an effect which was reversed by estrogen injections. Estradiol benzoate inhibited the response of the thyroid to exogenous TSH, which suggests a direct effect of the estrogen on the thyroid.

In an interesting experiment, Soliman et al. (1964) determined blood thyroxine and TSH concentrations during estrus and diestrus of cyclic cattle, cows with inactive ovaries, and cows with cystic ovaries. Thyroxine levels were highest at estrus and in cows with cystic ovaries, while TSH concentration was highest at diestrus and was not detectable in cattle with cystic ovaries. The concentration of TSH was about equal in diestrous cows and cows with inactive ovaries. The high thyroxine concentrations were inversely related to TSH concentrations, which one might expect on the basis of the thyroid feedback of the pituitary. The data do not reveal how the estrogen has its effect, although estrogen does not seem to cause destruction of circulating thyroxine.

Radioiodine uptake by the thyroid is significantly higher during proestrus in mice and during estrus in rats (Soliman and Reineke, 1954a,b; Soliman et al., 1964). The variations during the other days of the cycle were not significant. Soliman and Badami (1956) found that TSH and thyroid hormone concentration were highest during estrus in rats, a situation different from that observed in cattle; the difference may mean that estrogen has its effect by different mechanisms in these two species. Several investigations have demonstrated that the I^{131} uptake can be affected by estradiol and progesterone in ovariectomized or in immature rats and

mice (Brown-Grant, 1966a; Elghamy and Soliman, 1965; Feldman, 1956; Grosvenor, 1962; Soliman et al., 1964; and Yamada et al., 1966). Estradiol increases I^{131} uptake and progesterone decreases the effect of estrogen (Elghamy and Soliman, 1965; Soliman and Reineke, 1955), but in rats decreases I^{131} uptake (Soliman and Reineke, 1955). A number of explanations of the mechanism by which estrogen has its effect have been offered. Grosvenor (1962) and Feldman and Danowski (1956) suggested that estrogen increases the degradation of circulating thyroid hormone, thus decreasing the feedback effect of thyroxine and increasing TSH secretion. Yamada et al. (1966), using thyroidectomized rats, found that estrogen lowered protein bound iodine (PBI) in thyroxine-injected rats, thus supporting the conclusion that estrogen lowers circulating thyroid hormone.

Brown-Grant (1966b) investigated the rise in I^{131} uptake prior to ovulation in rodents by blocking ovulation with pentobarbital. The blockade of ovulation also blocked the increased thyroid activity normally observed. Ovulation induced in these blocked rats by HCG or by LH injections did not increase thyroid activity. This suggests that the gonadotropin release does not cause increased thyroid activity via steroid secretions of the ovary, but that some neuroendocrine mechanism may be responsible. Hasselblatt and Ratabongs (1960) evaluated thyroid activity by histological procedures and found that PMSG and HCG increased thyroid activity in intact and hypophysectomized immature female rats, but not in gonadectomized female rats or intact male rats; the authors concluded that the effects of PMSG and HCG were mediated via steroid secretions acting directly on the thyroid. These conclusions and those of Brown-Grant (1966b) seem to be opposed to each other. However, it should be considered that Brown-Grant's experiments were short-term experiments in which the effect of one dose of gonadotropin or one release of endogenous gonadotropin was investigated, whereas Hasselblatt and Ratabongs studied the effect of ten days of injections. Brown-Grant (1966b) studied mature rats in which the pituitary thyroid axis had been exposed to fluctuating levels of estrogen and progesterone, whereas the immature rats had not been exposed to steroid hormones, or, if they were, the levels of these hormones must have been low.

The effect of castration or androgen administration on thyroid activity seems not to have been studied to the same extent as the effects of estrogens.

Aron et al. (1958) investigated the effects of castration on the TSH content of the pituitary and on thyroidal activity, as measured by histometric methods, in rats, during various months of the year. The correlation between TSH values and thyroid activity of the donors of the pituitaries was poor, indicating that at some times TSH content of the pituitary may reflect secretion and at other times may reflect storage. Castration caused a decrease in TSH content of the pituitary, but there was no consistent effect on thyroid activity. Inspection of the published graphs for thyroid activity gives the impression that castration causes a phase shift in the annual cycle of thyroid activity. The peak of activity in intact males occurs in January; for the castrates the peak occurred in November to December one year and in October the next year; the lowest activity in intact males and castrates occurred in May. Bogart et al. (1958) reported that testosterone injections in growing beef heifers and ewes increase thyroid weight and the TSH content of the pituitaries during the nonbreeding season, but during the breeding seasons of ewes, thyroid weights are lowered by testosterone treatment. Unfortunately, neither the statistical significance nor a measure of variability was given.

The effect on reproduction by thyrocalcitonin, a hormone secreted by the thyroid, and which lowers blood calcium, has apparently not been studied. Birds, with their very active calcium metabolism during egg laying, should be good experimental animals with which to study the effect of this hormone on shell formation.

THE PARATHYROIDS

Ablation of the parathyroids leads to hypocalcemia, which in some species, e.g. the dog, results in tetany and death. The survival rate of parathyroidectomized dogs is about five percent, but for rabbits about 75 percent; in bull frogs (*R. catesbeiana*) the operation leads to tetany, but in *R. pipiens,* in spite of a lowered blood calcium concentration, no overt symptoms develop (Gorbman and Bern, 1962).

Parathyroidectomy of laying hens causes eggs to be laid 3 to 5 hours earlier than normal; such eggs have little or no shell (Polin and Sturkie, 1957). Shell formation normally starts about 16 hours prior to oviposition, and the lack of shell can, therefore, reasonably be ascribed to the lack of the parathyroids rather than to the prematurity of the oviposition. After one to five weeks the parathyroidectomized hens lay normal eggs again, indicating that the parathyroids are not required for normal reproduction.

THE ADRENAL

The relationships between adrenal and reproduction are most conveniently discussed by subdividing the discussion into two parts. One part deals with the hormones of the adrenal medullary tissue, i.e. epinephrine and norepinephrine (adrenaline and noradrenaline); the other part deals with the hormones of the adrenal cortical tissue, the corticosteroid hormones.

Medullary Hormones

The effects of the adrenal medullary hormones on reproduction have not been studied in detail.

Injecting epinephrine causes release of spermatozoa in *Rana* sp. in intact and hypophysectomized frogs as well as in frogs with cut spinal cords, but no such response is obtained in toads, *Bufo* sp. (Forbes, 1961).

In English sparrows, epinephrine injected with gonadotropins prevents the testicular response to gonadotropins, but such is not the case in the Oregon junco (*Junco oregonus*) or the pigeon. Injections of epinephrine into sexually mature chickens interfered with spermatogenesis and caused damage to the nuclei of the sperm (see van Tienhoven, 1961).

The injection of epinephrine into rats caused testicular atrophy and regression of the secondary sex structures in a number of cases (Perry, 1941). Daily injections of epinephrine into dairy bulls for a ten week period caused a reduction in the semen volume and semen concentration, collected from these bulls with the aid of an artificial vagina (VanDemark and Baker, 1953).

The effects of epinephrine on female reproduction have been studied, apparently in even fewer species. Epinephrine, administered for 15 to 20 days to female sparrows caused regression of the ovaries and oviducts. In laying hens, injection of this hormone delayed the laying of the egg present in the shell gland at the time of injection (Sykes, 1955), and also caused a drop in egg production during the ten day period following the epinephrine injection; whether this treatment caused atresia was not established.

The role played by epinephrine and norepinephrine in ovulation of mammals will be discussed in Chapter 8. Spaying female rats increases the toxicity of epinephrine injections so that it becomes the same as in males (Astarabadi and Essex, 1952). Epinephrine injections into female rats causes the diestrous period to last from five to 29 days (Perry, 1941). In some strains of mice, epinephrine injections caused a blocking of pregnancy, probably because implantation does not occur (DeFries et al., 1965). The innervation of the Müllerian duct system by the sympathetic and parasympathetic nervous system suggests that epinephrine will have an effect on the motility of the uterus and its associate structures.

In chickens, epinephrine inhibits the circular and longitudinal muscles of the shell gland and causes contraction of the vaginal circular muscle, but it does not affect the vaginal muscle; epinephrine also prevents the response of the circular and longitudinal muscle to posterior pituitary extract (Sykes, 1955).

In mammals there are considerable differences among species in the response to epinephrine; within a single species the response is affected by the hormonal state of the animal.

Epinephrine has a motor effect on the myometria of pregnant and nonpregnant rabbits, squirrels, ferrets, hedgehogs, monkeys, and humans, and the pregnant cat and dog; on the other hand, epinephrine has an inhibitory effect on the myometria of the pregnant and on the nonpregnant guinea pig, rat, and mouse and the nonpregnant cat and dog (Reynolds, 1949). The dose of epinephrine and the route of administration play an important role; for instance, intravenous injection of large doses of epinephrine will cause a motor rather than an inhibitory effect on guinea pig uteri. The motor effect has been explained on the basis of vasoconstriction of the uterine arterioles, thus causing a local ischemia, which in turn causes contractions (Reynolds, 1949). The reason for the species differences is not clear and its significance, from an evolutionary point of view, is not readily obvious.

Corticosteroids

The metabolic pathways illustrated in Figure 7-1 show the key position of progesterone in the biosynthesis of corticosteroids and its structural similarity to the gonadal hormones. It is, therefore, not very sur-

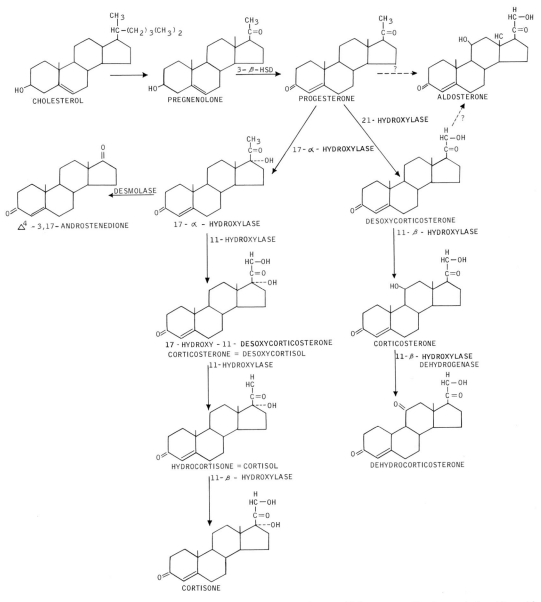

Figure 7-1. Biosynthetic pathway for some of the major corticosteroid hormones. For interrelationships with estrogens and androgens see Figure 5-1. (After Danowski, 1962; Gorbman and Bern, 1962.)

prising that some important interrelationships exist between the gonads and the adrenal cortex. In this discussion, the effect of corticosteroids and hypofunction or hyperfunction of the adrenal cortex on reproduction will be related first; subsequently, the effects of gonadal hormones on adrenal cortical function will be mentioned briefly.

The adrenal is essential for appropri-

ate mineral and carbohydrate metabolism. In elasmobranchs, birds, and mammals, ablation of the adrenals quickly leads to death unless the animals are given salt in the water or in the diet. But even when the animals are maintained in this manner, there are enough metabolic disturbances to make it difficult to evaluate the effect of adrenalectomy per se. Taber et al. (1956) prevented development of the rudimentary gonad in ovariectomized pullets, but the same result was obtained by restricting their food intake to the intake of the adrenalectomized animals. On the basis of such phenomena it seems that few reliable data can be obtained on the specific effects of adrenal cortical hormones on reproduction in adrenalectomized animals. In birds (van Tienhoven, 1961) and mammals (Parkes and Deanesly, 1966) there is little evidence of a specific effect of adrenal insufficiency on reproduction if the animals are kept in good health by regulation of the salt, caloric, and protein intake.

Administration of adrenocortical hormones can have effects on the gonads as well as on the secondary sex organs.

The injection of cortisone (5 mg.) into frogs (*R. pipiens*) implanted with two frog hypophyses in December or with one hypophysis in January and one in February, induced ovulation in 70 percent of the animals, whereas in controls (also bearing pituitary implants) this figure was 29 percent. Cortisone, under these conditions, also accelerated the rate of ovulation. Cortisone alone did not cause ovulations to occur. In vitro ovulation can be induced with pituitary hormones without the mediation of cortisone (Chang and Witschi, 1957).

Administration of cortisone, which is not secreted at all or is secreted in small amounts by the duck and chicken adrenal (Gorbman and Bern, 1962; Phillips and Bellamy, 1963), increased testicular weights, stimulated spermatogenesis, and increased comb size in drakes and six-week-old and four-month-old roosters (Leroy, 1952; Conner, 1959). However, in 20- to 40-day-old cockerels given essentially similar doses of cortisone, Dulin (1955) found no stimulation of the testis. Leroy (1959) injected 19-day-old cockerels with 10 mg. cortisone for 21 days and increased testicular weights, increased the diameter of the testicular tubules, and stimulated spermatogenesis; with 5 mg. cortisone per day no stimulation was

obtained. This same dose failed to increase the comb weight of capons. The differences between Dulin's results and those of Leroy (1952) may be comparable to those obtained with androgen, which was stimulatory after spermatocytes had been formed (Kumaran and Turner, 1949). Desoxycorticosterone acetate (not secreted by avian adrenals) injections into sexually mature roosters caused edema, atrophy of the germinal epithelium, and diminished comb size (van Tienhoven, 1961a).

Intravenous injection of 0.6, 1.0, or 5.0 mg. corticosterone (the adrenocorticosteroid secreted in largest amount by the chicken adrenal) had no effect on ovulation; however, 10 mg. either caused premature ovulation or blocked ovulation; apparently the reaction depends on the sensitivity of the particular animal. Injections of 20 mg. blocked spontaneous and progesterone-induced ovulations (van Tienhoven, 1961b).

The doses required to affect ovulation are unphysiological, and it seems, therefore, that corticosterone secretion is not a regulating factor in the timing of ovulation.

Spermatogenesis can be restored in hypophysectomized rats by cortisone, but in intact rats this hormone inhibits spermatogenesis, a situation analogous to that obtained with androgens, as Parkes and Deanesley (1966) have pointed out. In immature rats, cortisone injections stimulate testicular size when 1.0 mg. cortisone acetate/day is injected and increases the pituitary gonadotropin content (Hanson et al., 1957). On the other hand, Leroy (1953) found a decrease in testicular weight after injection of 2.5 mg. cortisone each day. In neither of the two sets of experiments did cortisone increase the weight of the secondary sex characters. Delost (1953) investigated the effect of castration, of castration plus adrenalectomy, and of replacement therapy in *Microtus arvalis* and found that cortisone stimulates the epithelium of the ductus deferens of the castrated adrenalectomized animal, but androgen is required for stimulation of the muscle layers of the ductus deferens.

Fendler and Endröczi (1965–1966) found that 17-β-estradiol implants into the hypothalamus of rats prevented compensatory hypertrophy of the ovary after unilateral ovariectomy, but if cortisone plus 17-β-estradiol were implanted, compensatory hypertrophy occurred, showing that cortisone can effect gonadotropin secretion under these conditions. Verheyden (1966) has reported that implants of hydrocortisone into pituitaries of adult female rats caused formation of persistent corpora lutea and caused mammary development, thus suggesting stimulation of prolactin secretion. Estradiol benzoate injections (50 μg./day) on days 1, 3, and 5 after the implant was made caused larger corpora lutea and more extensive mammary gland development. The effect of hydrocortisone on prolactin secretion is in accord with the observations by Nicoll and Meites (1964) that small doses of hydrocortisone (0.5 μg./ml.) added to the incubation medium stimulated prolactin synthesis in vitro by rat pituitaries, although large doses (10 μg./ml.) inhibited prolactin synthesis. On the other hand, adrenal hormones may have an inhibitory effect on prolactin secretion, as is suggested by the experiments of Swingle et al. (1951), in which adrenalectomy of cyclic rats resulted in pseudopregnancy, as verified by deciduomata formation after trauma to the uterus.

It is of interest that, according to a preliminary report by Campbell (1966), cortisone injections into neonatal rats are ineffective in inducing the persistent estrous sterility syndrome which can, however, be induced by estradiol, progesterone, testosterone, and some anabolic steroids, which are all effective steroids sharing the 11-β-H structure. According to a hypothesis proposed by Campbell, this free 11-β position may facilitate bonding to the hypothalamic polypeptides that are involved in gonadotropin regulation.

Blivaiss et al. (1954) found that cortisone injections increased ovarian weights, the number of follicles, the size of the antra, the weight of the uteri, and the amount of gonadotropin in the pituitary of immature rats. The vaginal epithelium of ovariectomized-adrenalectomized rats is stimulated by cortisone, but rarely could an estrous vaginal smear be obtained (Leroy and Moszkowska, 1952). Cortisone administration (1.6 to 25 mg./kg.) to intact or to adrenalectomized rats caused diestrus; guinea pigs gave a similar response. Monkeys injected with cortisone show a prolonged menstrual cycle (Donnet and Chevalier, 1961). Cortisone administration to pregnant mammals (rat, rabbit, and mouse) has an unfavorable effect on pregnancy (Parkes and Deanesley, 1966), and causes a high incidence of malformation in mice (Pinsky and George, 1964).

The physiological effects of desoxycorticosterone in rats are of more interest because desoxycorticosterone is the adrenal cortical hormone secreted in largest quantity by the rat. This hormone shows progestational activity if given in massive doses (Parkes and Deanesley, 1966). It is outside the scope of this book to discuss the reciprocal effects of the gonads on the adrenals. A review by Parkes and Deanesley (1966) treats this subject in detail.

Pacific salmon (genus *Oncorhynchus*) show increased activity of the anterior pituitary cells, as do migratory and nonmigratory rainbow trout (*Salmo gairdneri*). Before spawning, the pituitaries of the salmon show degenerative changes, the thyroid atrophies and degenerates, adrenal hyperplasia is severe, corticosteroids in the plasma are high (63.9 μg./100 ml.), and after spawning, males and females die. The migratory rainbow trout show some of these same phenomena, but to a lesser extent; plasma corticosteroids are 36.9 μg./100 ml.; the thyroid is normal; after spawning about 50 percent of the population survive; the testes of the survivors exhibit no signs of degeneration, but the ovaries contain damaged immature ova. The nonmigratory trout normally do not die as a result of spawning, and the incidence of the "pathological" changes which are found in salmon and to a lesser extent in migratory rainbow trout are not found or the changes are minor (Robertson et al., 1961). The nonmigratory males feed at the time of spawning and the females eat till shortly before shedding the eggs, but migratory males and females apparently stop feeding a considerable time before spawning. This lack of nutrition may contribute to the mortality, but the cause and effect relationships have not been established. Castration prevents the hyperadrenalism of salmon and also prevents the mortality at the time that control animals die. The exact interrelationships among the onset of sexual maturity, migration, hyperadrenalism, spawning, and death have not been determined.

The symptoms of hyperadrenocorticism of salmon resemble those of Cushing's syndrome in man, except that in salmon there is no evidence of hypertension (Robertson et al. 1966).

A congenital adrenogenital syndrome has been found in man. The condition can exist in the partial or in the severe form, but both conditions are carried by an autosomal recessive gene which causes a deficiency of 21-hydroxylase (Danowski, 1962). This leads to lower than normal secretion of hydrocortisone, which, in turn, means an insufficient negative feedback to the anterior pituitary to suppress ACTH secretion; consequently, ACTH secretion increases. As Figure 7-1 shows, an increase in Δ^4-3,17-androstenedione secretion is one of the consequences of this metabolic failure. Androstenedione has androgenic properties that cause virilization of the external genitalia and may cause pseudohermaphroditism. The discussion in Chapter 5 shows that in rats and guinea pigs the differentiation of the hypothalamus, with respect to both gonadotropin release and sexual behavior, is in the male direction in the presence of androgen. It is possible that such differentiation also occurs in women with the adrenogenital syndrome described above, especially if corrective measures are delayed. Injection of hydrocortisone will provide the necessary hormone for normal mineral and carbohydrate metabolism and will also suppress ACTH secretion. The reduced ACTH secretion diminishes the amounts of androstenedione and, apparently, normal sexual female development may follow. In men, this adrenogenital syndrome leads to enlarged external genitalia. Of course, the lack of hydrocortisone and aldosterone causes severe loss of sodium and dehydration; if not corrected, this may lead to circulatory collapse.

Symptoms similar to those found in the adrenogenital syndrome in man have been obtained in the offspring of rats injected with an inhibitor of 3-β-HSD during pregnancy. Female offspring show an enlarged clitoris, males show hypospadia, and in both sexes the adrenal is hyperplastic. Corticosterone injections after administration of the inhibitor prevent adrenal hyperplasia and clitoral enlargement, but do not affect the incidence of hypospadias (Goldman and Yakovac, 1966). Corticosterone apparently inhibits ACTH secretion, thus inhibiting the secretion of 3-β-hydroxysteroid androgens allowing normal clitoral development. The inhibitor also reduces testicular androgen secretion, thereby causing abnormal penile development. An experiment in which the inhibitor and testosterone are injected into pregnant females should be carried out to verify part of the hypothesis.

Christian and his co-workers, on the basis of a large series of investigations with different mammalian species, have proposed a hypothesis explaining the natural control of population densities and the occurrence of cycles of abundance in a species over the years. The activity of the adrenal is central in the formulation of this proposal. The evidence on which the theory is based has been obtained with "assembled populations" (in which the investigators put in the required number of animals to obtain the desired population density) with freely growing populations held in a confined space and with natural populations in the field. The subject has been reviewed in detail by Christian (1963) and Christian et al. (1965). For an amusing commentary, see also Deevey's account (1960) entitled: "The Hare and the Haruspex: a cautionary tale."

In brief, the hypothesis states that the density of a population with an ample food supply can become so high that the frequent encounters among animals (not necessarily fights with physical injuries) act as nonspecific stresses that cause adrenal hyperfunction. This adrenal hyperfunction interferes with a number of reproduction processes; it can delay sexual maturity, prolong estrous cycles, reduce the ovulation rate, decrease the incidence of implantation, increase embryonic mortality, lower milk secretion, and inhibit nursing, all of which lower the replacement of animals that die, so the population density decreases. Other factors (disease, lack of food, etc.) may contribute to this decline in population density, but lack of food is not required for the hyperadrenalism and reproduction failure to occur. The following experimental evidence supports Christian's hypothesis:

1. Hyperadrenalism in populations of high densities has been observed in a number of species. Different parameters have been used to measure adrenal activity, and in this summary the parameters used will be indicated in parentheses. Experimental evidence has been obtained in chickens (adrenal weight and cholesterol; Siegel, 1960), pheasants (adrenal weights; Flickinger, 1961), and in a number of mammalian species. Christian et al. (1965) have reviewed the evidence, and a summary is given here to indicate the rather general occurrence of this phenomenon: Mice (adrenal weight, adrenal ascorbic acid, circulating eosinophils, plasma corticosterone, and adrenocorticosteroid pro-

duction in vitro); white-footed deer mice, *Peromyscus leucopus* (adrenal weight); rats (adrenal weight, corticosterone secretion) microtus (adrenal weight, circulating eosinophils); woodchucks, *Marmota monax,* (adrenal weight, width of cortex, lipid depletion from fasciculate and reticular zones); rabbits (adrenal weight); Japanese deer, *Cervus nippon,* (adrenal weight).

2. In populations of chickens (three males and three females, four males and two females, and five males and one female) the males had heavier adrenals and thyroids than males housed with one female (at the same density as the other groups). The subordinate males among the roosters housed in groups with more than one male had slower testicular weight gains, showed delayed spermatogenesis, and showed degenerative changes in the testes, when compared to grouped, dominant males (Flickinger, 1961). A reciprocal relationship between adrenal weight and social rank was observed.

Christian (1959), Bronson and Eleftheriou (1964, 1965) have obtained evidence that social rank and psychological factors are more important than actual scaring or fighting in causing adrenal hypertrophy.

3. The density of the population is related to adrenal weight and egg production in chickens. At a density of one animal per 1.33 sq. ft. (0.12 m²) the incidence of birds laying, the number of eggs per laying hen, and the number of eggs per cycle were all below the corresponding values obtained for birds housed at one bird per 4.00 sq. ft. (0.36 m²) (Siegel, 1959).

In dense populations of mice, weights of testes, seminal vesicles and preputial glands decrease; delayed maturation, anestrus, and pseudopregnancy occur among females. Grouping 20 male and 20 female mice resulted in no births during the six weeks of grouping. The experience of grouping also had a carryover effect; after removal from the grouping, only 77 percent of the females had young and only 85 percent of this group reared their young. In white-footed deer mice, grouping increased resorption of fetuses.

Grouping increases in utero resorption of fetuses in *Peromyscus maniculatus.* Increased density in a freely growing population of voles *(Microtus)* inhibited maturation. In natural populations of voles and lemmings, the increased density is accompanied by decreased incidence of pregnancy, decreased litter size, and inhibition of sexual maturation. Rabbits, in a freely growing population, show diminished estrous behavior, decreased fecundity, and increased embryonic death.

4. The evidence cited above shows that increased density of populations causes adrenal hyperfunction and diminishes reproduction rates. Such a correlation might be statistically valid, but it does not prove a cause and effect relationship. In all probability the "stress" of the increased density causes increased ACTH release, leading to hyperadrenal function. Christian et al. (1965) have tested the effect of ACTH injections on reproductive events. Injections of large amounts of ACTH (1 to 8 units/day for ten days) caused follicular atresia, absence of mature follicles and corpora lutea, and decreased uterine weights in mature mice. ACTH also inhibited maturation of male and female *Peromyscus maniculatus bairdii* and *P. leucopus.* In adrenalectomized mice, maintained on either hydrocortisone acetate or corticosterone, ACTH interfered with reproduction of female mice, although to a lesser extent than in intact mice. Pituitaries injected with ACTH in intact or adrenalectomized mice (maintained on hydrocortisone acetate) stimulated the ovaries and uteri so that they were normal, suggesting that ACTH injections inhibited gonadotropin secretion or release.

The hypothesis of Christian is thus well supported by evidence from different types of experiments. It should be mentioned that the increased density of populations by no means affects only reproduction; it also decreases resistance to disease,

causes pathological changes in kidneys, and, in a number of other ways, reduces the size of the population (see Christian et al., 1965, for details).

Under sufficient stimulation of the adrenal by ACTH, adrenals can secrete estrogen as shown by Tullner (1966) in experiments with Rhesus monkeys *(Macaca mulatta).* Ovariectomized monkeys receiving 80 U.S.P. units of ACTH for 29 to 45 days had endometria that had the histological appearance of estrogen stimulation. In four of eight monkeys, cessation of ACTH injection resulted in withdrawal bleeding, as occurs when estrogen treatment is discontinued in ovariectomized monkeys. Another sign of estrogen secretion, the red sex-skin, was found.

THE PANCREAS

The comparative aspects of pancreatic hormone secretions have been discussed by Berthet (1963), Gorbman and Bern (1962), Turner (1966), and Young (1963); here only the effects of the two pancreatic hormones (insulin and glucagon) on reproduction will be discussed.

The effects of either pancreatectomy or of insulin or glucagon administration on reproduction of lampreys, elasmobranchs, teleosts, amphibia, and reptiles have not been investigated to any extent.

Insulin injections cause a decrease in serum vitellin of laying hens, a decrease which cannot be prevented by administration of FSH, although FSH prevents a starvation-induced drop in serum vitellin (Hosoda et al., 1955). The decrease in serum vitellin is accompanied by atresia of the follicles, as is the case in starvation.

The effects of pancreatectomy and insulin administration have been studied to the largest extent in rats. The experimental technique used most frequently for the induction of experimental diabetes in the rat consists of the administration of alloxan to destroy the beta cells of the pancreas. The induction of diabetes in male rats results in atrophy of the testes and degeneration of the tubules, but the Leydig cells and the secondary sex organs remain normal, indicating normal androgen secretion (Soulairac et al., 1948). However, Chatterjee (1966) found subnormal seminal vesicle weights in diabetic rats.

Diabetes in rabbits results in an increase in the amount of fructose in the semen, an increase which can be prevented by insulin injections. The increased amounts of glucose in the blood serve as a substrate for the formation of fructose by the seminal vesicles (Price and Williams-Ashman, 1961). Diabetes in 23-day-old rats caused cryptorchidism, failure of development of the germinal epithelium, and castrate type accessory sex organs. The injection of HCG caused hypertrophy of the interstitial cells and some development of the accessory sex organs, whereas testosterone administration resulted in development of these organs. This suggests that diabetes prevents the secretion of androgens, although the Leydig cells are stimulated. Insulin injection corrects the symptoms described (Hunt and Bailey, 1961). The authors suggest that the effect of insulin deficiency may be less the result of the high blood glucose than it is the result of protein malnutrition, which is also a consequence of the insulin deficiency.

Hypoglycemia, induced by either insulin or by tolbutamide (a sulfonylurea which causes insulin release from the pancreas), results in injury to the seminiferous tubules and edema of the interstitium in adult rats, but in prepuberal rats hypoglycemia has no apparent effect on the testes (Mancine et al., 1960).

Diabetes in female rats results in delayed sexual maturity, long and irregular cycles, sometimes, the cessation of cyclic events in the vaginal epithelium, and involution of ovaries, uteri and vagina; all of these symptoms can be prevented by insulin therapy (Lawrence and Contopoules, 1960). Houssay and Foglia (1946) also noted smaller than normal ovaries and

uteri in alloxan-diabetic rats; the gonadotropic potency of the pituitaries of these rats is lower than normal, suggesting that gonadotropin secretion is lowered by diabetes. Ovaries from diabetic donor mice, when transplanted into normal hosts, developed normally (Hummel et al., 1966). The mice used in this investigation were from a strain in which congenital diabetes was the result of a set of homozygous recessive genes. The testes of the males of this strain were normal, indicating that some gonadotropin was secreted, at least in the males. As will be discussed in Chapter 8, there is some evidence which indicates that the gonadotropin requirement for normal functioning of the testes may be lower than the gonadotropin requirement for normal ovarian function. The observation by Soulairac et al. (1948) that diabetic rats had ovaries with large corpora lutea but lacking large follicles might indicate that FSH secretion or release is specifically inhibited by diabetes.

In ovariectomized rats, the glycogen concentration of the uterus is higher in diabetic animals than in controls, and the estrogen-induced increase in glycogen concentration is also higher in diabetic animals (Swigert et al., 1960).

In alloxan-diabetic rats bred before the cycles cease, a lower incidence of pregnancies is found and a higher than normal incidence of stillbirth and early postnatal mortality occurs (Lunden and Morgans, 1950). Alloxan administration to pregnant rats on day 10 and 12 of pregnancy caused a higher than normal incidence of abortions, longer than normal gestation, and significantly ($P < 0.01$) but only slightly heavier than normal birth weight (5.36 ± 0.03 g. *versus* 5.13 ± 0.03 g.), according to Angerwall (1959). Diabetes induced by pancreatectomy results in larger than normal offspring with hyperplastic testes, adrenal cortices, parathyroids, and pineal bodies, and with pituitaries with a high incidence of chromophil cells but with normal ovaries (Hultquist, 1950).

Many of the phenomena described

for rats have also been found in diabetic women. Such women have a higher than normal abortion rate, even when the diabetes is well controlled by insulin injections. The most common complication of pregnancy in diabetic women is the large size of the baby. Pedersen (1955) found, for instance, that the average birth weight of 122 normal babies was 3045 g., whereas that of 122 babies from diabetic mothers was 3600 g. According to Jackson (1954), the genotype of the baby may be partly the cause for the "giant baby" syndrome, since children from diabetic or prediabetic fathers also were heavier than those of normal fathers.

The induction of a temporary hypoglycemia during crucial stages of pregnancy can affect the development of the offspring. Injections of insulin in rabbits during day 6, 7, 9, or 11 of pregnancy causes convulsions, which can be cured by glucose administration. If such insulin treatment is given on one day only, offspring are apparently normal; however, insulin given on two successive days results in *microphalia* and *ectopia cordis* (heart outside the body cavity). Injections of 20 to 22 units of insulin daily between day 6 and 13 of gestation result in fetal death and resorption, even when glucose is given to control the occurrence of convulsions (see Kalter and Warkany, 1959).

Smithberg and Runner (1963) found that the effects of hypoglycemia, induced by either insulin or tolbutamide, on the incidence of abnormalities in mice depends on the strain used. In addition, interactions were observed between niacin, insulin, and tolbutamide. In one strain (129), niacin increased the incidence of abnormalities induced by tolbutamide, but had no effect on those caused by insulin in strain BALB/C; on the other hand, niacin increased the incidence of insulin-induced abnormalities but did not affect that induced by tolbutamide. Fasting did not have effects as serious as those caused by either insulin or tolbutamide treatment.

Tuchmann-Duplessis and Mercier-Parot (1960), in comparing three hypoglycemic agents, found that tolbutamide and carbutamide caused a greater incidence of malfunctions in rat fetuses than did chlorpropamide, indicating that the teratogenic effect of tolbutamide is not entirely the result of its hypoglycemic effects. The suggestion may be made that these abnormal offspring caused by hypoglycemia (at least as induced by insulin) may not be the result of a malfunction of the maternal system. Abnormalities are induced in chicken embryos (Landauer and Rhodes, 1952) and duck embryos (Landauer, 1951) by insulin injections.

Injection of 300 μg. glucagon during day 7, 8, and 9 of development caused malformations of the eye, whereas 400-500 μg. caused microphtalmia and axial torsion of the skeleton and anuria (Tuchmann-Duplessis and Mercier-Parot, 1962).

The evidence thus indicates that either hypo- or hyperglycemia is harmful for embryonic development.

In summary, insulin deficiency causes lower than normal gonadotropin secretion, which is reflected in deficient steroid secretion and ovarian development. The deficient steroid secretion probably accounts for the lowered incidence of conceptions and the greater incidence of abortions. The repercussions of insulin deficiency in the male are less serious than those of insulin deficiency in the female.

THE PINEAL ORGAN

An excellent review of the literature and of recent experiments and morphological studies of the pineal organ and its associated organs can be found in the book edited by Kappers and Schadé (1965). This volume should be consulted for many details which cannot be mentioned here.

Kelley (1962) states that it is preferable to use the term "pineal systems" because the pineal organs appear to be double structures phylogenetically and embryologically. In the lower vertebrates, one structure, the pineal organ *(epiphysis cerebri)*, lies atop the roof of the diencephalon and its cavity is connected to the brain ventricle. The parapineal (parietal) part is an apparent outpouching from the pineal organ (e.g. in frogs), or it may be a separate diverticulum from the roof of the brain (e.g. in some lizards). In some lizards (e.g. Sphenodon) the parietal eye resembles the real eye by its possession of "a so-called cornea, a lens, a layer of sensory cells with a sort of fovea, ganglion cells and pigment cells" (van de Kamer, 1965). The parietal eye and the pineal organ may have the same embryological origin, but this needs further investigation (Kappers, 1965; Oksche, 1965).

Not all vertebrates seem to possess a pineal organ, although Oksche (1965) emphasizes that this problem needs to be reinvestigated with modern methods. The absence of this organ has been reported for *Myxine glutinosa, Torpedo ocellata, T. marmorata,* Crocodilia, the hairy armadillo *(Dasypus cillosus),* the nine-banded armadillo *(Dasypus novemcinctus),* the porpoise *(Phocaena communis),* the Javanese pangolin *(Manis javanica), Bradypus* sp., the collared anteater *(Tamandua tetradactyla),* the spotted dolphin *(Delphinus longirostris),* the striped dolphin *(Lagenorhynchus obliquidens),* and the sei-whale *(Balaenoptera borealis)* (Oksche, 1965).

One of the most interesting aspects of the development of the pineal organ is its change from a sense organ to a glandular organ. In some cyclostomes (e.g. *Petromyzon fluviatilis, P. marinus,* and *Geotria australis)* the pineal organ is a photoreceptor organ with neurosensory cells very similar to the sensory cells of the retina of the lateral eyes; the "lens" in the eyelike pineal organ is, however, of diencephalic origin, whereas in the lateral eye it is of epidermal origin (Kappers, 1965). A photosensory function of the pineal organ is also found in sharks (e.g. *Squalus acanthias* and *Galeus melastomus)* according to Altner (1965). Among tel-

eosts, the bluefin tuna *(Thunnus thynnus)* has a most elaborate pineal apparatus, consisting of a translucent dermal tissue and cartilagenous roof, which allows light to penetrate to the surface of the brain (see van de Kamer, 1965). Dodt (1963) has reported that light produces an inhibition of the spontaneous discharges recorded from the pineal organ of the rainbow trout *(Salmo gairdneri irideus).*

In anura, photosensory cells and the innervation of the pineal body are more developed than in urodeles (Kappers, 1965). The pineal organ, which is found in addition to the parietal eye in *Chalcides ocellatus,* also contains photoreceptorlike sensory cells. In other species of lizards, e.g. *Lacerta agilis,* the pineal organ shows a proliferation of cells, forming the possible basis for change into a glandular organ (Oksche, 1965). In snakes and turtles, development in the direction of a glandular organ is more pronounced.

The question whether sensory cells are present in avian pineal organs has not been answered definitely. Quay and Renzoni (1963) reported that cells resembling sensory cells (on the basis of their apical processes and synaptic modifications) are present in Passeriformes. A study of the ultrastructure of the pineal organ of the European magpie *(Pica pica)* by Collin (1966) showed that this organ contains rudimentary photoreceptors in the embryonic stage and early posthatching stage. In addition, photoreceptor cells with a very dense cytoplasm were found. At the end of the embryonic period, the Golgi apparatus of these cells hypertrophied and the cytoplasm became filled with granules. These changes indicate a possible change to secretory cells. Quay (1965a) suggests that the judgment concerning the presence or absence of nerve cell bodies in the avian pineal organ be delayed until data are available on a larger number of species. He says that the parenchymal pineal cells may be secretory, and that their proximity to blood vessels suggests a possible hormonal function.

Mammalian pineal organs do not contain photosensory receptor cells, but contain parenchymal cells that have structural and cytochemical characteristics that suggest a probable endocrine function.

PINEALECTOMY

The present discussion will be limited largely to the effects of pinealectomy and replacement therapy on reproduction, to correlations between the activity of the pineal body and gonadal activity, and to the relationships between illumination and pineal activity.

Removal of the pineal body from guppies (*Poecilia reticulata*) causes enlargement of the thyroid, an increase in the volume of the cell nuclei of the anterior lobe, and slightly earlier sexual maturity (Pflugfelder, 1953).

Pinealectomy of the water turtle (*Emys leprosa*) results in hyperactivity of the thyroid involution of the testicular tubules and a conspicuous secretion by the paraventricular nuclei (Combescot and Demaret, 1963). The effect of pinealectomy on the testes may be direct or indirect via the thyroid.

The evidence concerning the effects of pinealectomy on gonadal function in birds is contradictory. Even if one does not consider experiments in which controls are inadequate or absent, a number of contradictory observations remain. Shellabarger and Brenneman (1950) reported that pinealectomy of four-day-old cockerels depressed testicular weights until the animals were six weeks old, and increased testicular weights between their seventh and thirteenth weeks. The comparisons were made with sham-operated and nonoperated controls, with no difference noted between the latter two groups. In a subsequent series of experiments, Shellabarger (1952) confirmed that pinealectomy at two days of age depressed testicular weight at 20 days of age. He also ascertained that pineal extract injections in either sham-operated or pinealectomized

chicks stimulated testicular weight. Pinealectomy also reduced the gonadotropin content of the anterior pituitary. When chicks were killed at 40, 54, or 60 days, testes and comb were larger and gonadotropin content of the pituitary was higher than in nonoperated or sham-operated birds. Injection of pineal extracts prevented the effect of pinealectomy on testicular weights. Pineal extracts injected into intact cockerels depressed the gonadotropin content of the pituitary in only one of four experiments. Pineal extracts depressed the pituitary gonadotropin content of capons to that of intact males (Shellabarger, 1953). The results of these experiments would indicate that until about six weeks of age the pineal organ promotes testicular maturation, but after six weeks it inhibits it. Stalsberg (1965) removed the pineal gland of six-day-old chick embryos and found no effect on either testicular or comb weights at 18 or 63 days after hatching. The operation also failed to affect pituitary weight and pituitary histology. The main difference between the two experimental procedures is the age at which the pineal organ was removed, and it may be that this is a crucial factor. It is, for instance, possible that in the absence of the pineal organ the testis is stimulated to secrete sufficient androgen to inhibit the pituitary's gonadotropin secretion, and that this inhibition occurs at such low levels of androgen that the comb is not stimulated.

Moszkowska (1958) studied the gonadotropin secretion of pituitaries of chick embryos (16 days of incubation) in vitro by incubating the pituitaries with the testes of such embryos. The simultaneous incubation of pineal organs of these embryos tended to decrease the gonadotropin secretion, as evidenced by the lack of development of sexual cords of the testes.

Miller (1965), studying two strains of White Leghorn chicks that reached sexual maturity at very different ages, found that the change from a follicular structure to a lobular structure occurred

Table 7-2. Effect of Pinealectomy and/or of Pineal Extracts on the Pituitary and Reproductive System of Mammals in Comparison with Sham-operated or Intact Controls

TREATMENT	EFFECT	REFERENCE
A. IN THE GOLDEN HAMSTER (MESOCRICETUS AURATUS)		
Pinealectomy (16L-8D)*	No effect on ovarian or uterine weight	Reiter et al., 1966
Pinealectomy (1L-23D)	Increase of uterine weight	Reiter et al., 1966
Removal of eyes	Regression of reproductive organs, of AP and adrenal weights of males	Reiter and Hester, 1966
Removal of eyes	Regression of uteri of females	Reiter and Hester, 1966
Removal of eyes and Pinealectomy	No regression of reproductive organs, AP, or adrenal weights of males	Reiter and Hester, 1966
Removal of eyes and Pinealectomy	No regression of uteri of females	Reiter and Hester, 1966
Pinealectomy	Increased incidence of LH cells in AP	Girod et al., 1965
Pinealectomy in December	In January, 8 out of 9 animals had spermatozoa in the tubules. Controls had no spermatozoa in tubules	Czyba et al., 1964
B. IN THE RAT		
Pinealectomy	Larger ovaries	Wurtman et al., 1959
Bovine pineal extract injection	Smaller ovaries (?)	Wurtman et al., 1959
Pinealectomy and bovine pineal extract injection	Ovaries of similar weight as sham-operated controls	Wurtman et al., 1959
Pinealectomy	Hypertrophy and vacuolization of gonadotropin cells	Moreau, 1964
Pineal extract injection	Reduction of gonadotropin cells	Moreau, 1964
Pinealectomy	No effect on cell population of anterior pituitary	Holmes, 1956
Pinealectomy†	Increased incidence of eosinophils in AP	Thiéblot and Blaise, 1963
Pinealectomy and Pineal extract injection	Incidence of eosinophils close to normal	Thiéblot and Blaise, 1963
Pineal extract injection	Diminished storage of GTH; inhibited effect of endogenous and exogenous GTH	Thiéblot and Blaise, 1963
Pinealectomy†	Hypertrophy of testes and seminal vesicles	Thiéblot and Blaise, 1965
Pinealectomy	Hypertrophy of ovaries and uteri	Thiéblot and Blaise, 1965
Pinealectomy (under either continuous light, diurnal light, or predominant darkness)	Incidence of rats in estrus increased	Gittes and Chu, 1965
Pinealectomy and Pineal transplants	Incidence of rats in estrus similar to sham-operated rats	Gittes and Chu, 1965
Pinealectomy (24 hours light)	No effect on incidence of diestrus	Ifft, 1962
Pineal grafts (24 hours light)	No effect on incidence of diestrus	Ifft, 1962
Pineal extract injection (24 hours light)	Reduced incidence diestrus	Ifft, 1962
Pinealectomy	Maintenance of corpora lutea but no maintenance of deciduomata	Kehl et al., 1962
Pinealectomy	Persistent estrus for 3-4 days	Albertazzi et al., 1966
Pinealectomy and 5-Hydroxytryptamine (5HT)	Cycles tend to become normal	Albertazzi et al., 1966
Pineal extract injection to persistent estrus 18-month-old rats	Anestrus; ovarian weight decreased, larger but fewer corpora lutea, fewer follicles	Meyer et al., 1961
Pineal extract injection to cyclic rats	No effect on ovary or cycles	Meyer et al., 1961
Pineal extract injection (24 hours light)†	Delayed age of vaginal opening and first estrus; reduced incidence of follicular cysts	Moszkowska, 1963, 1965b
Pineal extract injection†	Earlier sexual maturity	Jöchle, 1956
Pineal extract injection	Prevented persistent estrus induced by continuous light	Jöchle, 1956
Melatonin injection†	Precocious spermatogenesis increased seminal vesicle weights	Thiéblot et al., 1966
Melatonin injection†	Increased ovarian weight, corpora lutea population, and uterine weight	Thiéblot et al., 1966
Melatonin injection†	Inhibition of ovarian growth, delay of vaginal opening and of first estrus. Inhibited "persistent" estrus of rats under continuous light, only after first injection	Wurtman and Axelrod, 1965; Wurtman et al., 1964
Melatonin injection†	No effect on reproductive system of females or males	Ebels and Prop, 1965
Melatonin injection†	No effect on cycle of adult females. No effect on persistent estrus induced by continuous light	Ebels and Prop, 1965

Table 7-2. Effect of Pinealectomy and/or of Pineal Extracts on the Pituitary and Reproductive System of Mammals in Comparison with Sham-operated or Intact Controls (*Cont.*)

TREATMENT	EFFECT	REFERENCE
Melatonin injection†	No effect on testis, seminal vesicles, or prostate weights	Moszkowska, 1965b
Melatonin injection†	Reduction of ovarian and AP weights	Moszkowska, 1965
Melatonin injection	No effect	Ebels and Prop, 1965
Serotonin injection (5HT)†	No effect on ovaries or estrous cycles	Wurtman et al., 1964
Serotonin injection†	Decreased testicular weight. Atrophy of ovaries in two of six cases. Pituitary weight decreased	Moszkowska, 1965b
5 Methoxytryptophol	Reduced ovarian weight; reduced incidence of estrus	McIsaac et al., 1964
	C. IN THE MOUSE	
Serotonin injection	Delayed vaginal opening, delayed onset of estrus, decreased ovarian, uterine and vaginal weights	Robson and Botros, 1961
Bovine pineal extract injection	Prevented effect HCG and human postmenopausal gonadotropin on uterus; no effect on estrogen-induced uterine weight increase	Soffer et al., 1965
Pinealectomy	Under continuous light, increase in incidence of estrous smear	Chu et al., 1964
Pinealectomy and Melatonin	Reduced incidence of estrous smears	Chu et al., 1964
Pinealectomy and Serotonin	No effect on incidence of estrous smears	Chu et al. 1964
	D. IN THE GUINEA PIG	
Sheep pineal extract injections	Prevent onset of puberty, follicular growth, corpus luteum formation, compensatory hypertrophy after unilateral ovariectomy	Moszkowska, 1963

* (16) hours of light–(8) hours of darkness.
† Immature animal treated.

at an earlier age in the strain showing the earlier sexual maturity. The initiation of spermatogenesis in both strains coincided with the change in pineal organ histology.

The effects of pinealectomy in mammals and of the injection of extracts of the pineal gland or of chemicals found in the pineal gland have been summarized in Table 7-2. The experiments listed show a considerable consistency with respect to the effect of pinealectomy on the pituitary-gonad axis, considering the variety of ages at the start and at the end of the experiment, the differences between measurements taken, and so forth. The general conclusion may be drawn that the pineal gland has an inhibitory effect, provided that its activity is not depressed by other conditions, such as long daylight. The effect of light on the pineal organ's activity will be discussed later.

The effects of pineal extract injections are somewhat difficult to evaluate because extracts are prepared differently by different workers. Generally, pineal extract injections reverse the effects of the operation in pinealectomized animals and have effects opposite to those of pinealectomy if given to intact animals.

The mammalian, or at least the bovine pineal organ has been found to contain a number of physiologically active substances, such as serotonin, (5-Hydroxytryptamine), histamine, catechol amine, melatonin (N-acetyl-5-methoxytryptamine) (Wurtman and Axelrod, 1965) and 5-methoxytryptophol, 5-hydroxytryptophol, 5-methoxyindole-3-acetic acid, and 5-hydroxyindole-3-acetic acid (McIsaac et al., 1965).

The synthesis of melatonin (see Figure 7-1) in mammals seems to be limited to the pineal organ, although in lower vertebrates such synthesis can also take place in the retinas of the lateral eyes (Quay, 1965b).

Injecting serotonin (in microgram amounts) and melatonin has not given consistent results in different laboratories. Sometimes differences may be due to difference in dose used, age of animal used, lighting conditions, or similar variables. However, this does not seem to be the case when one compares results obtained after melatonin injection by Wurtzman and Axelrod (1965) with those of Ebels and Prop (1965).

The differences between "no effect" and an inhibitory effect of melatonin on the reproductive system seem somewhat easier to reconcile than the stimulatory effect reported by Thiéblot et al. (1966), after administering large doses (100 to 500 μg.) of melatonin. Confirmation of these results should be awaited before making an attempt to interpret their biological significance.

Taking into account the evidence cited, it seems justified to designate the mammalian pineal organ an endocrine organ, which, under appropriate conditions, can have an inhibitory effect on the gonads.

Moszkowska (1965a) found that the secretion of gonadotropin into a medium during in vitro incubation was diminished by addition of ovine pineal pituitary powder. This effect was shown not to be the result of an effect of the pineal powder on the bioassay itself. In subsequent studies, Moszkowska found that serotonin did not affect the secretion of pituitary gonadotropins in vitro if the pituitaries were incubated in the absence of hypothalamic tissue. In the presence of hypothalamic tissue (which in itself increases gonadotropin secretion), serotonin had an inhibitory effect and reduced the gonadotropin content of the medium to that obtained after incubation of pituitaries alone. Under similar conditions, melatonin failed to affect gonadotropin secretion in vitro in either the absence or presence of hypothalamic tissue (Moszkowska, 1965b). The lack of an effect of melatonin on in vitro secretion of gonadotropin, although

melatonin in the hands of the same investigator showed an inhibitory effect in vivo, makes it difficult to interpret these data, especially with respect to the mechanism of action of melatonin. The question whether melatonin acts directly on the pituitary or via the hypothalamus cannot be answered with the data available.

Pinealectomy leads to hypertrophy and hyperplasia of the thyroid of rats (Scepovic, 1963), whereas injection of either pineal extract or melatonin inhibits the I^{131} uptake of rats (Reiter et al., 1965). In view of the interrelationship between the thyroid and the reproductive system, it might be interesting to determine to what extent the response of the genital system to melatonin is affected by the effect of melatonin on the thyroid. Experiments with thyroidectomized rats given a standard dose of thyroid hormone should provide an answer to this question.

Control of adrenal androsterone secretion has also been ascribed to the pineal. The evidence is controversial (van der Wal et al., 1965) and needs further investigation. However, for the interpretation of effect of the pineal on reproduction, it does not seem to be crucial whether the pineal secretes adrenoglomerulotropin.

The concentrations of serotonin, melatonin and noradrenaline in the pineal organ of rats show diurnal variations. Exposure of rats to continuous light decreases the concentration of melatonin, of the enzyme HIOMT (see Figure 7-2), abolishes the diurnal rhythm of melatonin, serotonin, and noradrenaline; exposure to continuous darkness abolishes the rhythm variations in the concentrations of melatonin and noradrenaline, but not of serotonin. However, exposure to one additional light period abolishes the diurnal rhythm of serotonin. Apparently, the serotonin concentration has an endogenous rhythm which can be affected by light (Axelrod et al., 1966; Snyder et al., 1965). The effect of light on pineal serotonin concentration is abolished by removing the

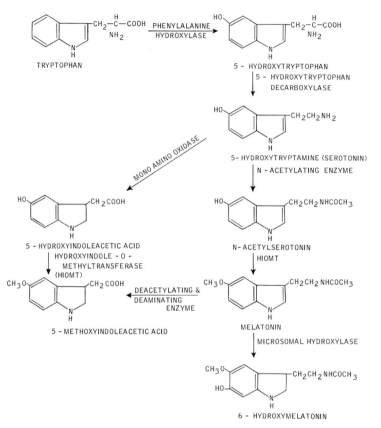

Figure 7-2. Synthetic pathway for biogenesis of melatonin. (After Erspanner, 1963; Wurtman and Axelrod, 1965.)

eyes. Superior cervical ganglionectomy abolished the pineal serotonin rhythm.

The pathway for transmitting the information from the environment to the pineal gland with respect to the regulation of HIOMT activity and probably of melatonin concentrations involves the retina, the inferior accessory optic tract, and the cervical ganglion (Moore et al., 1967).

Reiter and Hester (1966) found that blinding hamsters reduced testicular and secondary sex organs weights, but had no effect on ovarian weight, although uterine weight decreased. Exposure of hamsters to one hour of light and 23 hours of darkness led to decreased ovarian and uterine weights (Reiter et al., 1966). Pinealectomy under either of these two experimental conditions prevented these effects, suggesting that the pineal organ secretes a hormone (melatonin ?) inhibiting gonadal activity. Superior cervical ganglionectomy had the same effects as pinealectomy after either blinding or exposure to one hour of light per 24 hours. In hamsters under 16L-8D conditions, neither superior cervical ganglionectomy nor pinealectomy plus superior cervical ganglionectomy had an effect on the testis or the uterus.

The activity of HIOMT varies during the estrous cycle; lowest values are obtained during proestrus and estrus, and highest values during metestrus and diestrus (Wurtman, Axelrod, Snyder, and Chu 1965). Neither ovariectomy nor estradiol reproduced the effect of the estrous cycle, indicating that variations in HIOMT activity were not the result of inhibition by estrogen. Instead, variations in pineal activity may have been the primary effects, which in turn, regulated gonadotropin activity.

The role of the pineal organ in reproduction of mammals other than rats and hamsters has not been investigated experimentally in sufficient detail to evaluate its importance.

The administration of large amounts of serotonin (milligrams) will be considered separately because the effects observed may be pharmacological rather than physiological.

Injection of serotonin (10 mg./kg.) into male rats caused a decrease in testicular and secondary sex organ weights. The testis showed degenerative changes in the spermatids and primary spermatocytes (Boccabella et al., 1962).

Daily injections of serotonin (10 or 25 mg./kg.) into rats caused a delay in vaginal opening, and one injection of a dose of 1, 10, or 25 mg./kg. inhibited the number of ova recovered after PMSG treatment of immature rats (O'Steen, 1965). On the other hand, one serotonin injection did not interfere with the weight response of the ovary to PMSG plus HCG, although it decreased the response to PMSG. This suggests that serotonin may have prevented endogenous LH release (O'Steen, 1964). Injection of 1 to 1.25 mg./kg. serotonin inhibited the estrous cycle of mice (Botros and Robson, 1960), but 100 to 200 μg. given 16 to 17 hours prior to sacrifice, increased the incidence of mice ovulating in response to PMSG injection (Brown, 1966). Whether the difference between the response of rats and mice is the result of differences between doses used or whether it is the result of differences in response between the two species cannot be ascertained from the limited data available.

Serotonin administration interferes with the formation of deciduomata in mice, an effect which can be prevented by either prolactin or progesterone administration (Lindsay et al., 1961), indicating that serotonin interferes with prolactin secretion or release.

Pregnant mice injected with serotonin show a high incidence of abnormal embryos (Lindsay et al., 1963; Poulson et al., 1960, 1963) and high mortality of the fetuses. Pregnant rabbits given serotonin also show these symptoms (Poulson et al., 1960). Poulson et al., (1963) have suggested that serotonin administration may cause abnormal placental circulation resulting in mortality of the young. The effect on embryonic mortality cannot be reversed by progesterone administration.

REFERENCES

Albertazzi, E., Barbanti-Silva, C., Trentini, G. P., and Botticelli, A. 1966. Influence de l'épiphysectomie et du traitement avec la 5-hydroxytryptamine sur le cycle oestral de la ratte albinos. Ann. Endocrinol. 27:93-100.

Altner, H. 1965. Histologische and histochemische Untersuchungen an der Epiphyse von Haien. In J. A. Kappers and J. P. Schadé (ed.): Structure and function of the epiphysis cerebri. Progress in Brain Research. Elsevier Publishing Co., Amsterdam, Vol. 10, pp. 154-170.

Anderson, L. L., Bowerman, A. M., and Melampy, R. M. 1965. Oxytocin on ovarian function in cycling and hysterectomized heifers. J. Anim. Sci. 24:964-968.

Angervall, L. 1959. Alloxan diabetes and pregnancy in the rat. Acta Endocrinol. Suppl. 44.

Armstrong, D. T. 1966. Comparative studies of the action of the luteinizing hormone upon ovarian steroidogenesis. J. Reprod. Fertil. Suppl. 1:101-112.

Armstrong, D. T., and Hansel, W. 1958. Effects of hormone treatment on testes development and pituitary function. Int. J. Fertil. 3:296-306.

Armstrong, D. T., and Hansel, W. 1959. Alteration of the bovine estrous cycle with oxytocin. J. Dairy Sci. 42:533-542.

Armstrong, D. T., O'Brien, J., and Greep, R. O. 1964. Effects of luteinizing hormone on progestin biosynthesis in the luteinized rat ovary. Endocrinol. 75:488-500.

Aron, C., Asch, L., and Gandar, R. 1958. Fluctuations du contenu thyréotrope préhypophysaire et de l'activité thyroidienne chez le rat mâle entier ou castré. Contribution à l'étude des rapports entre la sécrétion et l'excrétion. Arch. Anat. Microscop. Morphol. Exp. 47:183-204.

Astarabadi, T. M., and Essex, H. E. 1952. Effect of epinephrine on male and female albino rats. Amer. J. Physiol. 171:75-77.

Axelrod, J., Snyder, S. H., Heller, A., and Moore, R. Y. 1966. Light-induced changes in pineal hydroxyindole-O-methyl transferase: Abolition by lateral hypothalamic lesions. Science 154:898-899.

Bailey, R. E. 1952. The incubation patch of passerine birds. Condor 54:121-136.

Bartke, A. 1965. Influence of luteotrophin on fertility of dwarf mice. J. Reprod. Fertil. 10:93-103.

Bartke, A. 1966. Reproduction of female dwarf mice treated with prolactin. J. Reprod. Fertil. 11:203-206.

Beck, P., Parker, M. L., and Daughaday, W. H. 1965. Radio immunologic measurement of human placental lactogen in plasma by a double antibody method during normal and diabetic pregnancies. J. Clin. Endocrinol. Metab. 25:1457-1462.

Beckers, C., and de Visscher, M. 1957. Mécanisme d'action de la folliculine sur la sécrétion thyroïdienne de la lapine, étudié au moyen du radioiode. Ann. Endocrinol. 18:1-9.

Beckers, C., and de Visscher, M. 1961. Ovary and thyroid secretion. Acta Endocrinol. 36:343-349.

Benson, G. K., and Fitzpatrick, R. J. 1966. The neurohypophysis and the mammary gland. In G. W. Harris and B. T. Donovan (eds.): The Pituitary Gland. University of California Press, Berkeley, Vol. 3, pp. 414-452.

Berthet, J. 1963. Pancreatic hormones: glucagon. In U. S. von Euler and H. Heller (eds.): Comparative Endocrinology. Academic Press Inc., New York, Vol. 1, pp. 410-427.

Black, D. L., and Duby, R. T. 1965. Effect of oxytocin, epinephrine and atropine on the oestrous cycle of the cow. J. Reprod. Fertil. 9:3-8.

Blivaiss, B. B., Hanson, R. O., Rosenzweig, R. E., and McNiel, K. 1954. Sexual development in female rats treated with cortisone. Proc. Soc. Exp. Biol. Med. 86:678-682.

Boccabella, A. V., Salgado, E., and Alger, E. A. 1962. Testicular function and histology following serotonin administration. Endocrinol. 71:827-837.

Bogart, R., Hudson, F., Nicholson, H., Mason, R. W., and Krueger, H. 1958. Effects of injected testosterone on fertility in female cattle and sheep. Int. J. Fertil. 3:105-119.

Bogdanove, E., and Gay, V. L. 1966. Effects of long-term testosterone propionate (TP) treatment on pituitary structure and gonadotrophin content. Fed. Proc. 25:315 (abstract).

Botros, M., and Robson, J. M. 1960. The effects of 5-hydroxytryptamine and iproniazid on sexual development. J. Endocrinol. 20:X.

Brinkley, H. J., and Nalbandov, A. V. 1963. Effect of oxytocin on ovulation in rabbits and rats. Endocrinol. 73:515-517.

Bronson, F. H., and Eleftheriou, B. E. 1964. Chronic physiological effects of fighting in mice. Gen. Comp. Endocrinol. 4:9-14.

Bronson, F. H., and Eleftheriou, B. E. 1965. Adrenal response to fighting in mice: separation of physical and psychological causes. Science 147:627-628.

Brooks, J. R., and Ross, C. V. 1962. Effects of ambient temperature and thyroxine therapy on semen quality of rams. J. Anim. Sci. 21:700-705.

Brown, P. S. 1966. The effect of reserpine, 5-hydroxytryptamine and other drugs on induced ovulation in immature mice. J. Endocrinol. 35:161-168.

Brown-Grant, K. 1966a. The effects of treatment with gonadotrophins or with oestrogen on the thyroid gland of the immature rat. J. Endocrinol. 35:263-270.

Brown-Grant, K. 1966b. The relationship between ovulation and the changes in thyroid gland activity that occur during the oestrous cycle in rats, mice and hamsters. J. Physiol. 184:402-417.

Bruce, H. M., and Sloviter, H. A. 1957. Effect of destruction of thyroid tissue by radioactive iodine in reproduction in mice. J. Endocrinol. 15:72-82.

Brumstad, G., and Fowler, S. H. 1959. Thyroid status and embryonic mortality in swine. Amer. J. Physiol. 196:287-290.

Burger, R. E., Lorenz, F. W., and Clegg, M. T. 1962. The effect of estrogen on the pituitary-thyroid axis in the immature domestic fowl. Poultry Sci. 41:1703-1707.

Burrows, W. H., and Byerly, T. C. 1942. Premature expulsion of eggs by hens following injection of whole posterior pituitary preparations. Poultry Sci. 21:416-421.

Burrows, W. H., and Fraps, R. M. 1942. Action of vasopressin and oxytocin in causing premature oviposition by domestic fowl. Endocrinol. 30:702-705.

Campbell, H. J., Feuer, G., and Harris, G. W. 1964. The effect of intrapituitary infusion of median eminence and other brain extracts on anterior pituitary gonadotrophic secretion. J. Physiol. 170:474-486.

Campbell, J. H. 1966. Effect of neonatal injections of adrenocortical hormones on reproductive phenomena in the female rat. J. Endocrinol. 34:XIV-XV.

Catchpole, H. R. 1964. Physiology of the gonadotropic hormones. In H. H. Cole (ed.): Gonadotropins. W. H. Freeman & Company, San Francisco, pp. 40-70.

Cehovic, G. 1965. Action des hormones mélanophoriques (α et β MSH) sur les gonades du cobaye mâle. C. R. Soc. Biol. 159:1491-1495.

Chadwick, A. 1966. Prolactin-like activity in the pituitary gland of fishes and amphibians? J. Endocrinol. 35:75-81.

Chang, C. Y., and Witschi, E. 1957. Cortisone effect on ovulation in the frog. Endocrinology 61:514-519.

Channing, C. P., and Villee, C. A. 1966. Stimulation of cholesterol metabolism in the luteinized rat ovary by LH. Biochem. Biophys. Acta 127:1-17.

Chatterjee, A. 1966. Prevention of gonadal degeneration in male diabetic rats by the use of insulin. Endokrinologie 50:11-14.

Chaudhury, R. R., and Chaudhury, M. R. 1962. Action of synthetic oxytocin on the crop gland of the pigeon. Nature 193:179-180.

Christian, J. J. 1959. Lack of correlation between adrenal weight and injury in grouped male albino mice. Proc. Soc. Exp. Biol. Med. 101:166-168.

Christian, J. J. 1963. Endocrine adaptive mechanisms and the physiologic regulation of population growth. *In* W. V. Mayer and R. G. Van Gelder (eds.): Physiological Mammalogy. Academic Press Inc., New York, Vol. 1, pp. 189-353.

Christian, J. J. Lloyd, J. A., and Davis, D. E. 1965. The role of endocrines in the self-regulation of mammalian populations. Recent Progr. Hormone Res. *21*:501-571.

Chu, E. W., Wurtman, R. J., and Axelrod, J. 1964. An inhibitory effect of melatonin on the estrous phase of the estrous cycle of the rodent. Endocrinology *75*:238-242.

Chu, J. P. 1944. Influence of the thyroid gland on pituitary gonadotrophic activity in the rabbit. Endocrinol. *34*:90-102.

Chu, J. P. 1945. The influence of the thyroid on pregnancy and parturition in the rabbit. J. Endocrinol. *4*:109-114.

Chu, J. P., and You, S. S. 1945. The role of the thyroid gland and oestrogen in the regulation of gonadotrophic activity of the anterior pituitary. J. Endocrinol. *4*:115-124.

Clegg, M. T., Cole, H. H., Howard, C. B., and Pigon, H. 1962. The influence of foetal genotype on equine gonadotrophin secretion. J. Endocrinol. *25*:245-248.

Cole, H. H. 1964. Gonadotropins. W. H. Freeman and Company, San Francisco.

Collin, J. P. 1966. Étude préliminaire des photo-récepteurs rudimentaires de l'épiphyse de *Pica pica* L. pendant la vie embryonnaire et post-embryonnaire. C. R. Acad. Sci. *263 D*:660-663.

Combescot, C., and Demaret, J. 1963. Histophysiologie de l'épiphyse chez la tortue d'eau, *Emys leprosa* (Schw.) Ann. Endocrinol. *24*:204-212.

Common, R. H., Keefe, T. J., and Maw, W. A. 1950. Some biochemical effects of thiouracil on the response of the immature pullet to estrogen. Can. J. Res. *28 D*:272-279.

Common, R. H., Maw, W. A., and Layne, D. S. 1955. The effects of thiouracil and of thyroxine on certain biochemical responses of the immature pullet to combined treatment with estrogen and androgen. Can. J. Biochem. Physiol. *33*:667-676.

Common, R. H., Maw, W. A., Layne, D. S., and McCully, K. A. 1958. The influence of thiouracil on the responses of the immature pullet to estrogen, with reference to oviduct hypertrophy, serum calcium, and liver composition. Can. J. Biochem. Physiol. *36*:1023-1035.

Common, R. H., Moo-Young, A. J., and McCully, K. A. 1961. Some effects of dietary thiouracil and dietary iodine supplementation on the responses of the immature pullet to estrogen. Can. J. Biochem. Physiol. *39*:1441-1450.

Conner, M. H. 1959. Effects of various hormone preparations and nutritional stresses in chicks. Poultry Sci. *38*:1340-1343.

Contopoulos, A. N., and Koneff, A. A. 1963. Pituitary hormone production and release in the thyroidectomized rat after thyroxine administration. Acta Endocrinol. *42*:275-292.

Contopoulos, A. N., Simpson, M. E., and Koneff, A. A. 1958. Pituitary function in the thyroidectomized rat. Endocrinol. *63*:642-653.

Corbin, A., and Schottelius, B. A. 1961. Hypothalamic neurohumoral agents and sexual maturation of immature female rats. Amer. J. Physiol. *201*:1176-1180.

Cross, B. A. 1966. Neural control of oxytocin secretion. *In* L. Martini and W. F. Ganong (eds.): Neurosecretion. Academic Press Inc., New York, Vol. 1, pp. 217-259.

Czyba, J. C., Girod, C., and Durand, N. 1964. Sur l'antagonisme épiphyso-hypophysaire et les variations saisonières de la spermatogénèse chez l'hamster doré *(Mesocricetus auratus).* C. R. Soc. Biol. *158*:742-745.

Danowski, T. S. 1962. Clinical Endocrinology. Williams & Wilkins Co., Baltimore, Vol. 4.

Das, B. C., and Nalbandov, A. V. 1955. Responses of ovaries of immature chickens to avian and mammalian gonadotrophins. Endocrinology *57*:705-710.

Deevey, E. S. 1960. The hare and the haruspex: a cautionary tale. Amer. Sci. *48*:415-430.

De Fries, J. C., Weir, M. W., and Hegmann, J. P. 1965. Blocking of pregnancy in mice as a function of stress: supplementary note. Psychol. Rep. *17*:96-98.

Delost, P. 1953. Action de la cortisone sur le canal déférent du campagnol des champs *(Microtus arvalis* P) castré et surrénalectomisé. C. R. Soc. Biol. *147*:1580-1584.

Desjardins, C., and Hafs, H. D. 1964. Immunochemical similarity of luteinizing hormones. J. Anim. Sci. *23*:903-904 (abstract).

Dodd, J. M., Evennett, P. J., and Goddard, C. K. 1960. Reproductive endocrinology in cyclostomes and elasmobranchs. Symp. Zool. Soc. London *1*:77-102.

Dodd, J. M., and Matty, A. J. 1964. Comparative aspects of thyroid function. *In* R. Pitt-Rivers and W. R. Trotter (eds.): The Thyroid Gland. Butterworth & Co. Ltd., London, Vol. 1, pp. 303-356.

Dodt, E. 1963. Photosensitivity of the pineal organ in the teleost, *Salmo irideus* (Gibbons). Experientia *19*:642-643.

Donaldson, L. E., Hansel, W., and Van Vleck, L. D. 1965. Luteotropic properties of luteinizing hormone and nature of oxytocin induced luteal inhibition in cattle. J. Dairy Sci. *48*:331-337.

Donnet, V., and Chevalier, J. M. 1961. Actions de la cortisone sur le cycle oestral des mammifères. La métamorphose des batraciens et la croissance des végétaux. Ann. Endocrinol. *22*:850-869.

Donovan, B. T. 1961. The role of the uterus in the regulation of the oestrous cycle. J. Reprod. Fertil. *2*:508-510.

Dorrington, J. H., and Kilpatrick, R. 1966. Effects of luteinizing hormone and nicotinamide adenine dinucleotide phosphate on synthesis of progestational steroids by rabbit ovarian tissue *in vitro.* J. Endocrinol. *35*:65-73.

Douglas, D. S., and Sturkie, P. D. 1964. Plasma levels of antidiuretic hormone during oviposition in the hen. Fed. Proc. *23*:150 (abstract).

Dulin, W. E. 1955. The effects of cortisone on the White Leghorn cockerel and capon. Poultry Sci. *34*:73-77.

Dumont, J. N. 1965. Prolactin-induced cytologic changes in the mucosa of the pigeon crop during crop-"milk" formation. Z. Zellforsch. *68*: 755-782.

Duncan, G. W., Bowerman, A. M., Anderson, L. L., Hearn, W. R., and Melampy, R. M. 1961. Factors influencing *in vitro* synthesis of progesterone. Endocrinol. *68*:199-207.

Ebels, I., and Prop, N. 1965. A study of the effect of melatonin on the gonads, the estrous cycle and the pineal organ of the rat. Acta Endocrinol. *49*:567-577.

Elghamry, M. I., and Soliman, F. A. 1965. I[131] uptake by the thyroids of ovariectomized mice after treatment with oestrogen and progesterone. Naturwissensch. *52*:210-211.

Ellett, M. H. 1964. Variations in the oxytocic content of the posterior pituitary lobe during the estrous cycle in the golden hamster *(Mesocricetus auratus)*. Diss. Abstr. *25*:3076.

Engel, F. L., and Lebovitz, H. E. 1966. Extra-target organ actions of anterior pituitary hormones. *In* G. W. Harris and B. T. Donovan (eds.): The Pituitary Gland. University of California Press, Berkeley, Vol. 2, pp. 563-588.

Erspamer, V. 1963. 5-Hydroxytryptamine. *In* U. S. von Euler and H. Heller (eds.): Comparative Endocrinology. Academic Press Inc., New York, Vol. 2, pp. 159-181.

Evennett, P. J., and Dodd, J. M. 1963. Endocrinology of reproduction in the river lamprey. Nature *197*:715-716.

Feldman, J. D. 1956. Effect of estrus and estrogen on thyroid uptake of I[131] in rats. Endocrinol. *58*:327-337.

Feldman, J. D., and Danowski, T. S. 1956. Effect of estrogen on the metabolism of protein-bound iodine. Endocrinol. *59*:463-471.

Fendler, K., and Endröczi, E. 1965/66. Effects of the hypothalamic steroid implants on compensatory ovarian hypertrophy of rats. Neuroendocrinol. *1*:129-137.

Ferrand, R. 1963. Spermatogenèse et mue du verdier soumis à des injections de thyroxine. Bull. Soc. Zool. Fr. *88*:221-229.

Fitzpatrick, R. J. 1966a. The posterior pituitary gland and the female reproductive tract. *In* G. W. Harris and B. T. Donovan (eds.): The Pituitary Gland. University of California Press, Berkeley, Vol. 3, pp. 453-504.

Fitzpatrick, R. J. 1966b. The neurohypophysis and the male reproductive tract. *In* G. W. Harris and B. T. Donovan (eds.): The Pituitary Gland. University of California Press, Berkeley, Vol. 3, pp. 505-516.

Flickinger, G. L. 1961. Effect of grouping on adrenals and gonads of chickens. Gen. Comp. Endocrinol. *1*:332-340.

Forbes, T. R. 1961. Endocrinology of reproduction in cold-blood vertebrates. *In* Ed. 3 of W. C. Young (ed.): Sex and Internal Secretions. Williams & Wilkins Co., Baltimore, Vol. 2, pp. 1035-1087.

Friesen, H. 1965. Purification of a placental factor with immunological and chemical similarity to human growth hormone. Endocrinol. *76*:369-381.

Gemzell, C., and Roos, P. 1966. The physiology and chemistry of follicle-stimulating hormone. *In* G. W. Harris and B. T. Donovan (eds.): The Pituitary Gland. University of California Press, Berkeley, Vol. 1, pp. 492-517.

Geschwind, I. I. 1964. The chemistry and immunology of gonadotropins. *In* H. H. Cole (ed.): Gonadotropins. W. H. Freeman and Company, San Francisco, pp. 1-34.

Geschwind, I. I. 1966. Species specificity of anterior pituitary hormones. *In* G. W. Harris and B. T. Donovan (eds.): The Pituitary Gland. University of California Press, Berkeley, Vol. 2, pp. 589-612.

Girod, C., Curé, M., Czyba, J. C., and Durand, N. 1965. Influence de l'épiphysectomie sur les cellules gonadotropes anthéhypophysaires du hamster doré *(Mesocricetus auratus* Waterh.) C. R. Soc. Biol. *158*:1636-1637.

Gittes, R. F., and Chu, E. W. 1965. Reversal of the effect of pinealectomy in female rats by isogeneic pineal transplants. Endocrinology *77*: 1061-1067.

Goldman, A. S., and Yakovac, W. C. 1966. Experimental congenital adrenal cortical hyperplasia: prevention of adrenal hyperplasia and clitoral hypertrophy by corticosterone. Proc. Soc. Exp. Biol. Med. *122*:1214-1216.

Gorbman, A., and Bern, H. A. 1962. A Textbook of Comparative Endocrinology. John Wiley and Sons Inc., New York.

Goss, D. A., and Lewis, J., Jr. 1964. Immunologic differentiation of luteinizing hormone and human chorionic gonadotropin in compounds of high purity. Endocrinology *74*:83-86.

Grosvenor, C. E. 1962. Effects of estrogen upon I[131] release and excretion of thyroxine in ovariectomized rats. Endocrinology *70*:673-678.

Grumbach, M. M., and Kaplan, S. L. 1965. In vivo and in vitro evidence of the synthesis and secretion of chorionic "growth hormone — prolactin" by the human placenta: its purification, immuno assay and destination from human pituitary growth hormone. Proc. II Int. Congr. Endocrinol. *1*:691-708.

Hall, P. F. 1966. On the stimulation of testicular steroidogenesis in the rabbit by interstitial cell-stimulating hormone. Endocrinology *78*:690-698.

Hall, P. F., and Eik-Nes, K. 1962. The action of gonadotropic hormones upon rabbit testis *in vitro*. Biochem. Biophys. Acta *63*:411-422.

Hall, P. F., and Koritz, S. B. 1965. Influence of interstitial cell-stimulating hormone on the conversion of cholesterol to progesterone by bovine corpus luteum. Biochem. *4*:1037-1043.

Hansel, W., Armstrong, D. T., and McEntee, K. 1958. Recent studies on the mechanism of ovulation in the cow. *In* F. X. Gassner (ed.): Proceedings of the Third Symposium on Reproduction and Infertility. Pergamon Press, New York, pp. 63-74.

Hanson, R. O., Blivaiss, B. B., and Rosenzweig, R. E. 1957. Sexual development in male rats treated with cortisone. Amer. J. Physiol. *188*: 281-286.

Harris, G. W., and Donovan, B. T. 1966. The Pituitary Gland. University of California Press, Berkeley, Vols. 1-3.

Hasselblatt, A., and Ratabongs, C. 1960. Die Bedeutung von Gonaden und Hypophyse für die Wirkung gonadotroper Hormone auf die Schilddrüsenfunktion. Acta Endocrinol. *34*: 176-188.

Haun, C. K. 1966. Involvement of neurohypophysial polypeptides in the secretion of luteotrophin. Anat. Rec. *154*:354-355 (abstract).

Hayashida, T. 1966. Immunological reactions of pituitary hormones. *In* G. W. Harris and B. T. Donovan (eds.): The Pituitary Gland. University of California Press, Berkeley, Vol. 2, pp. 613-662.

Hoar, W. S. 1966. Hormonal activities of the pars distalis in cyclostomes, fish and amphibia. *In* G. W. Harris and B. T. Donovan (eds.): The Pituitary Gland. University of California Press, Berkeley, Vol. 1, pp. 242-294.

Höhn, E. O. 1963. Failure of oxytocin to produce a prolactin-like response in pigeon's crop sac. J. Endocrinol. *26*:177-178.

Hohlweg, W., Dörner, G., Schumann, B., and Spode, E. 1964/65. Über die Fertilität radiothyreoidektomierter Rattenweibchen. Endokrinologie *47*:179-183.

Holmes, R. L. 1956. Effect of pinealectomy on the rat pituitary. Nature *177*:791.

Hopper, A. F. 1965. Inhibition of regeneration of the gonopodium of the guppy by treatment with thiouracil. J. Exp. Zool. *159*:231-240.

Hosoda, T., Kaneko, T., Mogi, K., and Abe, T. 1954. Serological studies on the egg production in fowls. III Effect of thryroxine on vitellin production. Bull. Nat. Inst. Agric. Sci. Ser. G. Anim. Husb. *8*:95-99.

Hosoda, T., Mogi, K., Kaneko, T., Abe, T., and Hiroe, K. 1955. Effect of insulin on the serum vitellin level in the fowl. Endocrinol. Jap. (2:2):137-142.

Houssay, B. A., and Foglia, V. G. 1946. Accion de la hipofisis de ratas con diabetes aloxanica. Rev. Soc. Biol. Argent. *22*:329-334.

Howland, B. E., Bellows, R. A., Pope, A. L., and Casida, L. E. 1966. Ovarian activity in ewes treated with glucose and triiodothyronine. J. Anim. Sci. *25*:836-838.

Hultquist, G. T. 1950. Diabetes and pregnancy. An animal study. Acta Path. Microbiol. Scand. *27*: 695-719.

Hummel, K. P., Dickie, M. M., and Coleman, D. L. 1966. Diabetes, a new mutation in the mouse. Science *153*:1127-1128.

Hunt, E. L., and Bailey, D. W. 1961. The effect of alloxan diabetes on the reproductive system of young male rats. Acta Endocrinol. *38*:432-440.

Ifft, J. D. 1962. Effects of pinealectomy, a pineal extract and pineal grafts on light-induced prolonged estrus in rats. Endocrinol. *71*:181-182.

Jackson, W. P. U. 1954. The prediabetic syndrome.

Large babies and the (pre) diabetic father. J. Clin. Endocrinol. *14*:177-183.

Janes, R. C., and Bradbury, J. T. B. 1952. Ovarian retention cysts in hypothyroid rats treated with diethylstilbestrol. Proc. Soc. Exp. Biol. Med. *79*:187-188.

Jöchle, W. 1956. Uber die Wirkung eines Epiphysenextraktes (Glanepin) auf Sexualentwicklung und Sexualcyklus junger weiblicher Ratten unter normalen Haltungsbedingungen und Dauerbeleuchtung. Endokronologie *33*:287-295.

Johns, J. E., and Pfeiffer, E. W. 1963. Testosterone-induced incubation patches of Phalarope birds. Science *140*:1225-1226.

Johnson, T. N., and Meites, J. 1960. Effects of hypo- and hyperthyroidism in rats and mice on ovarian response to equine gonadotrophin. Proc. Soc. Exp. Biol. Med. *75*:155-157.

Josimovich, J. B. 1966. Potentiation of somatotrophic and diabetogenic effects of growth hormone by human placental lactogen (HPL). Endocrinology *78*:707-714.

Kalter, H., and Warkany, J. 1959. Experimental production of congenital malformations in mammals by metabolic procedure. Physiol. Rev. *39*:69-115.

Kappers, J. A. 1965. Survey of the innervation of the epiphysis cerebri and the accessory pineal organs of vertebrates. *In* J. A. Kappers and J. P. Schadé (eds.): Structure and function of the epiphysis cerebri. Progress in Brain Research. Elsevier Publishing Co., Amsterdam, Vol. 10, pp. 87-151.

Kappers, J. A., and Schadé, J. P. 1965. Structure and function of the epiphysis cerebri. Progress in Brain Research. Elsevier Publishing Co., Amsterdam, Vol. 10.

Kar, A. B., and Datta, J. K. 1965. Induced hyperthyroidism and sexual development in prepuberal female Rhesus monkeys. Arch. Anat. Microscop. Morphol. Exp. *54*:119-128.

Kehl, R., Czyba, J. C., and Durand, M. 1962. Sur l'action lutéinique de l'épiphysectomie chez le rat. C. R. Soc. Biol. *156*:98-100.

Kelley, D. E. 1962. Pineal organs: Photo reception secretion, and development. Amer. Scientist *50*:597-625.

Kidwell, W. R., Balogh, K., Jr., and Wiest, W. G. 1966. Effects of luteinizing hormones on glucose-6 phosphate and 20α-hydroxysteroid dehydrogenase activities in superovulated rat ovaries. Endocrinology *79*:352-361.

Knobil, E., and Greep, R. O. 1959. The physiology of growth hormone with particular reference to its action in the Rhesus monkey and the "Species specificity" problem. Recent Progr. Hormone Res. *15*:1-58.

Knobil, E., and Sandler, R. 1963. The physiology of adenohypophyseal hormones. *In* U. S. von Euler and H. Heller (eds.): Comparative Endocrinology. Academic Press Inc., New York, Vol. 1, pp. 477-491.

Krohn, P. L. 1951. The effect of thyroidectomy on reproduction in the female rabbit. J. Endocrinol. *7*:307-309.

Kulcsár-Gergely, J., and Kulcsár, A. 1961. Über

die Gestaltung des Geschlechtszyklus in hypothyreotischen Ratten. Naturwissensch. 48:387.

Kumaran, J. D. S., and Turner, C. W. 1949. The endocrinology of spermatogenesis in birds. II Effect of androgens. Poultry Sci. 28:739-746.

Lacasssagne, L. 1957. Influence de l'ingestion de protéines iodées sur les réserves vitellines de l'ovocyte chez la poule domestique. Ann. Zootech. 3:283-290.

Landauer, W. 1951. The effect of insulin on the development of duck embryos. J. Exp. Zool. 117:559-572.

Landauer, W., and Rhodes, M. B. 1952. Further observations on the teratogenic nature of insulin and its modification by supplementary treatment. J. Exp. Zool. 119:221-261.

Lawrence, A. M., and Contopoulos, A. N. 1960. Reproductive performance in the alloxan diabetic female rats. Acta Endocrinol. 33:175-184.

Leroy, P. 1952. Réactions testiculaires de l'oiseau soumis à des injections de cortisone. Ann. Endocrinol. 13:991-997.

Leroy, P. 1953. Effets de la cortisone sur le tractus génital mâle. Symp. Europeo sul Cortisone, pp. 3-18.

Leroy, P. 1959. Réponse des gonades de poussins mâles Leghorn blanc traités à la cortisone ou à l'ACTH. Ann. Endocrinol. 20:1-23.

Leroy, P., and Moszkowska, A. 1952. Influence de la cortisone sur la réaction vaginale de la ratte castrée et de la ratte castrée et surrénalectomisée. C. R. Soc. Biol. 146:1861-1864.

Lindsay, D., Poulson, E., and Robson, J. M. 1961. The effects of 5-hydroxytryptamine and of an aminooxidase inhibitor on experimental deciduomata in mice. J. Endocrinol. 23:209-215.

Lindsay, D., Poulson, E., and Robson, J. M. 1963. The effect of 5-hydrotryptamine on pregnancy. J. Endocrinol. 26:85-96.

Lostroh, A. J., and Johnson, R. E. 1966. Amounts of interstitial cell-stimulating hormone and follicle-stimulating hormone required for follicular development, uterine growth and ovulation in the hypophysectomized rat. Endocrinology 79:991-996.

Lucas, J. J., Brunstad, C. E., and Fowler, S. H. 1958. The relationship of altered thyroid activity to various reproductive phenomena in gilts. J. Endocrinol. 17:54-62.

Lundan, O., and Morgans, M. E. 1950. Alloxan diabetes and pregnancy: A long-term observation. J. Endocrinol. 6:463-469.

Lyons, W. R., and Dixon, J. S. 1966. The physiology and chemistry of the mammo-trophic hormone. In G. W. Harris and B. T. Donovan (eds.): The Pituitary Gland. University of California Press, Berkeley, Vol. 1, pp. 527-581.

McCann, S. M., and Taleisnik. 1960. Effect of luteinizing hormone and vasopressin on ovarian ascorbic acid. Amer. J. Physiol. 199:847-850.

McDonald, G. J., Armstrong, D. T., and Greep, R. O. 1966. Stimulation of estrogen secretion from normal rat corpora lutea by luteinizing hormone. Endocrinology 79:289-293.

McIsaac, W. M., Taborsky, R. G., and Farrell, G.

1964. 5-Methoxytryptophol: effect on estrus and ovarian weight. Science 145:63-64.

McIsaac, W. M., Farrell, G., Taborsky, R. G., and Taylor, A. N. 1965. Indole compounds: Isolation from pineal tissue. Science 148:102-103.

Malven, P. V., and Hansel, W. 1965. Effect of bovine endometrial extracts, vasopressin and oxytocin on the duration of pseudopregnancy in hysterectomized and intact rats. J. Reprod. Fertil. 9:207-215.

Malven, P. V., and Sawyer, C. H. 1966a. Formation of new corpora lutea in mature hypophysectomized rats. Endocrinology 78:1259-1263.

Malven, P. V., and Sawyer, C. H. 1966b. A luteolytic action of prolactin in hypophysectomized rats. Endocrinology 79:268-274.

Mancine, R. E., Penhos, J. C., Izquierdo, I. A., and Heinrich, J. J. 1960. Effects of acute hypoglycemia on rat testis. Proc. Soc. Exp. Biol. Med. 104:699-702.

Maqsood, M. 1951. Influence of thyroid status on spermatogenesis. Science 114:693-694.

Maqsood, M. 1952. Thyroid function in relation to reproduction of mammals and birds. Biol. Revs. 27:281-319.

Mares, S. E., and Casida, L. E. 1963. Effect of exogenous oxytocin on the progestogen content of the bovine corpus luteum. Endocrinology 72:78-82.

Marsh, J. M., and Savard, K. 1966. Studies on the mode of action of luteinizing hormone on steroidogenesis in corpus luteum in vitro. J. Reprod. Fertil. Suppl. 1:113-124.

Martini, L. 1966. Neurohypophysis and anterior pituitary activity. In G. W. Harris and B. T. Donovan (eds.): The Pituitary Gland. University of California Press, Berkeley, Vol. 3, pp. 535-577.

Martini, L., Mira, L., Pecile, A., and Saito, S. 1959. Neurohypophysial hormones and release of gonadotrophins. J. Endocrinol. 18:245-250.

Meier, A. H., Davis, K. B., and Dusseau, J. 1966. Prolactin and the antigonadal response in the migratory white-throated sparrow. Amer. Zool. 6:312 (abstract).

Meites, J., and Chandrashaker, B. 1949. The effects of induced hyper- and hypothyroidism on the response to a constant dose of pregnant mare's serum in immature male rats and mice. Endocrinology 44:368-377.

Meites, J., and Nicoll, C. S. 1966. Adenohypophysis: Prolactin. Ann. Rev. Physiol. 28:57-88.

Meites, J., Nicoll, C. S., and Talwalker, P. K. 1963. The central nervous system and the secretion and release of prolactin. In A. V. Nalbandov (ed.): Advances in Neuroendocrinology. University of Illinois Press, Urbana, pp. 238-277.

Meyer, C. J., Wurtman, R. J., Altschule, M. D., and Lazo-Wasem, E. A. 1961. The arrest of prolonged estrus in "middle aged" rats by pineal gland extract. Endocrinology 68:795-800.

Miller, R. E. 1955. A Study of the Pineal Body in a Strain of Early Maturing White Leghorn Cockerels. M. S. thesis, Cornell University.

Mizuno, H., and Meites, J. 1963. Failure of oxytocin

to stimulate the pigeon crop gland. Nature *198*:1209-1210.

Moore, R. Y., Heller, A., Wurtman, R. J., and Axelrod, J. 1967. Visual pathway mediating pineal response to environmental light. Science *155*: 220-223.

Moreau, N. 1964. Contribution à l'étude de certaines corrélations endocrinnienes de l'épiphyse. Ann. Sci. Univ. Besançon Méd. *10*:5-189.

Morris, T. R., and Nalbandov, A. V. 1961. The induction of ovulation in starving pullets using mammalian and avian gonadotropins. Endocrinology *68*:687-697.

Moszkowska, A. 1958. L'antagonisme épiphyso-hypophysaire. Étude *in vivo* et *in vitro* chez l'embryon de poulet Sussex. Ann. Endocrinol. *19*:69-79.

Moszkowska, A. 1959. Contribution à la recherche des relations du complexe hypothalamo-hypophysaire dans la fonction gonadotrope. Méthode *in vivo* et *in vitro*. C. R. Soc. Biol. *153*:1945-1948.

Moszkowska, A. 1963. L'antagonisme épiphyso-hypophysaire. Ann. Endocrinol. *24*:215-225.

Moszkowska, A. 1965a. Contribution à l'étude du mécanisme de l'antagonisme épiphyso-hypophysaire. *In* J. A. Kappers and J. P. Schadé (eds.): Structure and function of the epiphysis cerebri. Progress in Brain Research. Elsevier Publishing Co., Amsterdam, Vol. 10, pp. 564-584.

Moszkowska, A. 1965b. Quelques données nouvelles sur le mécanisme de l'antagonisme épiphyso-hypophysaire—rôle possible de la sérotonine et de la mélatonine. Rev. Suisse Zool. *72*:145-160.

Myant, N. B. 1964. The thyroid and reproduction in mammals. *In* R. Pitt-Rivers and W. R. Trotter (eds.): The Thyroid Gland. Butterworth & Co. Ltd., London, Vol. 1, pp. 283-302.

Nalbandov, A. V. 1964. Reproductive Physiology. Ed. 2. W. H. Freeman and Company, San Francisco.

Nalbandov, A. V. 1966. Hormonal activity of the pars distalis in reptiles and birds. *In* G. W. Harris and B. T. Donovan (eds.): The Pituitary Gland. University of California Press, Berkeley, Vol. 1, pp. 295-316.

Nalbandov, A. V., and Card, L. E. 1946. Effect of FSH and LH upon the ovaries of immature chicks and low-producing hens. Endocrinology *38*:71-78.

Nalbandov, A. V., Meyer, R. K., and McShan, W. H. 1951. The role of a third gonadotrophic hormone in the mechanism of androgen secretion in chicken testes. Anat. Rec. *110*:475-494.

Naller, R., and Cedeno, G. A., 1963. Apparition d'oestrus par la thyroxine chez des rattes castrées. C. R. Soc. Biol. *157*:1805-1806.

Nicoll, C. S., and Meites, J. 1964. Prolactin secretion *in vitro*. Effects of gonadal and adrenal cortical steroids. Proc. Soc. Exp. Biol. Med. *117*:579-583.

Nicoll, C. S., Bern, H. A., and Brown, D. 1966. Occurrence of mammotrophic activity (prolactin) in the vertebrate adenohypophysis. J. Endocrinol. *34*:343-354.

Nikitovitch-Winer, M. 1962. Induction of ovulation in rats by direct intrapituitary infusion of median eminence extracts. Endocrinology *70*: 350-358.

Oksche, A. 1965. Survey of the development and comparative morphology of the pineal organ. *In* J. A. Kappers and J. P. Schadé (eds.): Structure and function of the epiphysis cerebri. Progress in Brain Research. Elsevier Publishing Co., Amsterdam, Vol. 10. pp. 3-28.

Opel, H. 1965. Oviposition in chickens after removal of the posterior lobe of the pituitary by an improved method. Endocrinol. *76*:673-677.

Opel, H. 1966. Release of oviposition-inducing factor from the median eminence-pituitary stalk region in neural lobectomized hens. Anat. Rec. *154*: 396 (abstract).

O'Steen, W. K. 1964. Serotonin suppression of luteinization in gonadotrophin-treated, immature rats. Endocrinol. *74*:885-888.

O'Steen, W. K. 1965. Suppression of ovarian activity in immature rats by serotonin. Endocrinol. *77*: 937-939.

Parkes, A. S., and Deanesly, R. 1966. Relation between the gonads and the adrenal glands. *In* A. S. Parkes (ed.): Marshall's Physiology of Reproduction. Longmans Green & Co. Ltd., London, Vol. 3, pp. 1064-1111.

Parlow, A. F. 1964a. Effect of ovariectomy on pituitary and serum gonadotrophins in the mouse. Endocrinology *74*:102-107.

Parlow, A. F. 1964b. Differential action of small doses of estradiol on gonadotrophins in the rat. Endocrinology *75*:1-8.

Parlow, A. F., Anderson, L. L., and Melampy, R. M. 1964. Pituitary follicle-stimulating hormone and luteinizing hormone concentrations in relation to reproductive stages of the pig. Endocrinology *75*:365-376.

Parrott, M. W., Johnston, M. E., and Durbin, P. W. 1960. The effects of thyroid and parathyroid deficiency on reproduction in the rat. Endocrinology *67*:467-483.

Pedersen, J. 1955. Weight and length at birth of infants of diabetic mothers. Acta Endocrinol. *18*:553-554.

Perry, J. C. 1941. Gonad response of male rats to experimental hyperadrenalism. Endocrinology *29*:592-595.

Peterson, R. R., Webster, R. C., Rayner, B., and Young, W. C. 1952. The thyroid and reproductive performance in the adult female guinea pig. Endocrinology *51*:504-518.

Pflugfelder, O. 1953. Wirkungen der Epiphysektomie auf die Postembryonalentwicklung von *Lebistes reticulatus* Peters. Wilh. Roux' Archiv. Entwicklungsmech. Organ *146*:115-136.

Phillips, J. G., and Bellamy, D. 1963. Adrenocortical hormones. *In* U. S. von Euler and H. Heller (eds.): Comparative endocrinology. Academic Press Inc., New York, Vol. 1, pp. 208-257.

Pickford, G. E., and Atz, J. W. 1957. The Physiology of the Pituitary Gland of Fishes. New York Zool. Soc., New York.

Pinsky, L., and DiGeorge, A. M. 1964. Cleft palate

in the mouse: A teratogenic index of gluco-corticoid potency. Science *147*:402-403.

Polin, D. and Sturkie, P. D. 1957. The influence of the parathyroids on blood calcium levels and shell deposition in laying hens. Endocrinology *60*:778-784.

Poulson, E., Botros, M., and Robson, J. M. 1960. Effect of 5-hydroxytryptamine and iproniazid on pregnancy. Science *131*:1101-1102.

Poulson, E., Robson, J. M., and Sullivan, F. M. 1963. Teratogenic effect of 5-hydroxytryptamine in mice. Science *141*:717-718.

Price, D., and Williams-Ashman, H. G. 1961. The accessory reproductive glands of mammals. *In* W. C. Young (ed.): Sex and Internal Secretions. Williams & Wilkins Co., Baltimore, Vol. 1, pp. 366-448.

Purves, H. D. 1966. Cytology of the adenohypophysis. *In* G. W. Harris and B. T. Donovan (eds.): The Pituitary Gland. University of California Press, Berkeley, Vol. 1, pp. 147-232.

Quay, W. B. 1965a. Histological structure and cytology of the pineal organ in birds and mammals. *In* J. A. Kappers and J. P. Schadé (eds.): Structure and function of the epiphysis cerebri. Progress in Brain Research. Elsevier Publishing Co. Amsterdam, Vol. 10, pp. 49-84.

Quay, W. B. 1965b. Retinal and pineal hydroxy-indole-O-methyl transferase activity in vertebrates. Life Sci. *4*:983-991.

Quay, W. B., and Renzoni, A. 1963. Comparative and experimental studies of pineal structure and cytology in Passeriform birds. Rev. Biologia *56 (new series 16)*: 363-407.

Ralph, C. L. 1959. Some effects of hypothalamic lesions on gonadotrophin release in the hen. Anat. Rec. *134*:411-431.

Ralph, C. L. 1960. Polydipsia in the hen following lesions in the supraoptic hypothalamus. Amer. J. Physiol. *198*:528-530.

Reineke, E. P., and Soliman, F. A. 1953. Role of thyroid hormone in reproductive physiology of the female. Iowa State Coll. J. Sci. *28*:67-82.

Reiter, R. J., and Hester, R. J. 1966. Interrelationships of the pineal gland, the superior cervical ganglia and the photoperiod in the regulation of the endocrine systems of hamsters. Endocrinology *79*:1168-1170.

Reiter, R. J., Hoffman, R. A., and Hester, R. J. 1965. Inhibition of I^{131} uptake by thyroid glands of male rats treated with melatonin and pineal extract. Amer. Zool. *5*:727-728 (abstract).

Reiter, R. J., Hoffman, R. A., and Hester, R. J. 1966. The effects of thiourea, photoperiod and the pineal gland on the thyroid, adrenal and reproductive organs of female hamsters. J. Exp. Zool. *162*:263-268.

Reynolds, S. M. R. 1949. The Physiology of the Uterus. Ed. 2. P. B. Hoeber, New York.

Riddle, O. 1921. A simple method of obtaining premature eggs from birds. Science *54*:664-666.

Riddle, O. 1963. Prolactin in vertebrate function and organization. J. Nat. Cancer Inst. *31*:1039-1110.

Rigor, E. M., and Clemente, R. R. 1964. The effect

of oxytocin injections on the oestrus cycle of gilts. Fifth Int. Congr. Anim. Rep. Art. Ins. *2*:364-366.

Ripley, S. D. 1960. Synopsis of the Birds of India and Pakistan. Bombay Nat. Hist. Soc.

Robertson, O. H., Krupp, M. A., Thomas, S. F., Favour, C. B., Hane, S., and Wexler, B. C. 1961. Hyperadrenocorticism in spawning migratory and nonmigratory rainbow trout *(Salmo gairdneri)*; comparison with Pacific salmon (Genus *Oncorhynchus*). Gen. Comp. Endocrinol. *1*:473-484.

Robertson, O. H., Krupp, M. A., Thompson, N., Thomas, S. F., and Hane, S. 1966. Blood pressure and heart weight in immature and spawning Pacific salmon. Amer. J. Physiol. *210*: 957-964.

Robson, J. M., and Botros, M. 1961. The effect of 5-hydroxytryptamine and of monoamine oxidase inhibitors on sexual maturity. J. Endocrinol. *22*:165-175.

Romanoff, E. B. 1966. Steroidogenesis in the perfused bovine ovary. J. Reprod. Fertil. Suppl. *1*:89-99.

Rowlands, I. W. 1964. Levels of gonadotropins in tissues and fluids, with emphasis on domestic animals. *In* H. H. Cole (ed.): The Gonadotropins. W. H. Freeman and Company, San Francisco, pp. 74-107.

Sairam, M. R., Raj, H. G., and Moudgal, N. R. 1966. Presence of gonadotrophin inhibitor in urine of the Bonnet monkey, *Macaca radiata*. Endocrinology *78*:923-928.

Sandler, R., and Hall, P. F. 1966. Stimulation *in vitro* by adenosine-3′, 5′-cyclic monophosphate of steroidogenesis in rat testis. Endocrinology *79*:647-654.

Savard, K., Marsh, J. M., and Rice, B. F. 1965. Gonadotropins and ovarian steroidogenesis. Recent Progr. Hormone Res. *21*:285-356.

Scepovic, M. 1963. Contribution à l'étude histo-physiologique de la glande thyroïde chez les rats épiphysectomisés. Ann. Endocrinol. *24*: 371-376.

Schreiber, F., Kmentová, V., and Zavadil, M. 1965. Relationships between gonadotrophin and thyrotrophin secretion; Inhibition of compensatory hypertrophy of rat ovaries by methylthiouracil. Biol. Abstr. 46, ref. 102493.

Schreibman, M. P., and Kallman, K. D. 1966. Endocrine control of freshwater tolerance in teleosts. Gen. Comp. Endocrinol. *6*:144-155.

Selander, R. K. 1964. Problem of timing of development of the incubation patch in male birds. Condor *66*:75-76.

Selander, R. K., and Yang, S. Y. 1966. The incubation patch of the house sparrow, *Passer domesticus* Linnaeus. Gen. Comp. Endocrinol. *6*:325-333.

Shellabarger, C. J. 1952. Pinealectomy vs pineal injection in the young cockerel. Endocrinology *51*:152-154.

Shellabarger, C. J. 1953. Observations of the pineal in the White Leghorn capon and cockerel. Poultry Sci. *32*:189-197.

Shellabarger, C. J., and Breneman, W. R. 1950. The

effects of pinealectomy on young White Leghorn cockerels. Indiana Acad. Sci. 59:299-302.

Shibusawa, K., Saito, S., Fukuda, S. M., Kawai, T., Yamada, J., and Tomizawa, K. 1955. Neurosecretion of oxytocin stimulates the release of pituitary gonadotrophin. Endocrinol. Jap. 2: 183-188.

Shirley, H. V., Jr., and Nalbandov, A. V. 1956. Effects of neurohypophysectomy in domestic chickens. Endocrinology 58:477-483.

Siegel, H. S. 1959. Egg production characteristics and adrenal function in White Leghorns confined at different floor space levels. Poultry Sci. 38:893-898.

Siegel, H. S. 1960. Effect of population density on the pituitary-adrenal cortical axis of cockerels. Poultry Sci. 39:500-510.

Simmons, K. R., and Hansel, W. 1964. Nature of the luteotropic hormone in the bovine. J. Anim. Sci. 23:136-141.

Sloper, J. C. 1966. The experimental and cytopathological investigation of neurosecretion in the hypothalamus and pituitary. In G. W. Harris and B. T. Donovan (eds.): The Pituitary Gland. University of California Press, Berkeley, Vol. 3, pp. 131-239.

Smithberg, M., and Runner, M. N. 1963. Teratogenic effects of hypoglycemic treatments in inbred strains of mice. Amer. J. Anat. 113:479-489.

Snyder, S. H., Zweig, M., Axelrod, J., and Fischer, J. E. 1965. Control of the circadian rhythm in serotonin content of the rat pineal gland. Proc. Nat. Acad. Sci. 53:301-305.

Soffer, L. J., Fogel, M., and Rudavsky, A. Z. 1965. The presence of a "gonadotrophin inhibiting substance" in pineal gland extracts. Acta Endocrinol. 48:561-564.

Soliman, F. A., and Badawi, H. M. 1956. Levels of thyroid and thyrotrophic hormones in the blood of rats at various stages of the oestrous cycle. Nature 177:235.

Soliman, F. A., and Reineke, E. P. 1954a. Cyclic variation in thyroid function of female mice as assessed by radioactive iodine. J. Endocrinol. 10:305-307.

Soliman, F. A., and Reineke, E. P. 1954b. Changes in uptake of radioactive iodine by the thyroid of the rat during the estrous cycle. Amer. J. Physiol. 178:89-90.

Soliman, F. A., and Reineke, E. P. 1955. Influence of estrogen and progesterone on radioactive iodine uptake by rat thyroid. Amer. J. Physiol. 183:63-66.

Soliman, F. A., Abdo, M. S., Soliman, M. K., and Abdel Wahab, M. F. 1964. Uptake of Iodine-131 by the thyroids of female mice during the oestrous cycle. Nature 201:506-507.

Soliman, F. A., Zaki, M., Soliman, M. K., and Abdo, M. S. 1964. Thyroid function of Friesian cows during the oestrous cycle and in conditions of ovarian abnormality. Nature 204:693.

Soulairac, A., Desclaux, P., and Katz, R. F. 1948. Action du diabète alloxanique sur le tractus génital du rat mâle et femelle. C. R. Soc. Biol. 142:311-312.

Stalsberg, H. 1965. Effects of Extirpation of the Epiphysis Cerebri in 6-Day Chick Embryos. Olaf Norlis Forlag, Oslo.

Steelman, S. L., and Pohley, F. M. 1953. Assay of the follicle stimulating hormone based on the augmentation with human chorionic gonadotropin. Endocrinology 53:604-616.

Sturkie, P. D., and Lin, Y. C. 1966. Release of vasotocin and ovipostion in the hen. J. Endocrinol. 35:325-326.

Sundararaj, B. I., and Goswami, S. V. 1966. Effects of mammalian hypophysial hormones, placental gonadotrophins, gonadal hormones, and adrenal corticosteroids on ovulation and spawning in hypophysectomized catfish Heteropneustes fossilis (Bloch). J. Exp. Zool. 161:287-296.

Swigert, R. H., Atkinson, W. B., and Goldberg, L. G. 1960. Deposition of glycogen in the uterus of the alloxan-diabetic rat. Anat. Rec. 136:287 (abstract).

Swingle, W. W., Fedor, E. J., Barlow, G., Jr., Collins, E. J., and Perlmutt, J. 1951. Induction of pseudopregnancy in rat following adrenal removal. Amer. J. Physiol. 167:593-598.

Sykes, A. H. 1955. The effect of adrenaline on oviduct motility and egg production in the fowl. Poultry Sci. 34:622-628.

Taber, E., Salley, K. W., and Knight, J. S. 1956. The effects of hypoadrenalism and chronic inanition on the development of the rudimentary gonad in sinistrally ovariectomized fowl. Anat. Rec. 126:177-193.

Talbert, G. B. 1962. Effect of thyroxine on maturation of the testes and prostate gland of the rat. Proc. Soc. Exp. Biol. Med. 111:290-292.

Tanaka, K., and Nakajo, S. 1962. Participation of neurohypophysial hormone in oviposition in the hen. Endocrinology 70:453-458.

Telegdy, Gy., and Fendler, K. 1964. The effect of posterior pituitary hormones on adrenocortical and ovarian progesterone secretion in dogs. Acta Physiol. Acad. Sci. Hung. 25:359-364.

Thapliyal, J. P., and Pandha, S. K. 1965. Thyroid-gonad relationship in spotted munia, Uroloncha punctulata. J. Exp. Zool. 158:253-262.

Thiéblot, L., and Blaise, S. 1963. Influence de la glande pinéale sur les gonades. Ann. Endocrinol. 24:270-285.

Thiéblot, L., and Blaise, S. 1965. Influence de la glande pinéale sur la sphère génitale. In J. A. Kappers and J. P. Schadé (eds.): Structure and function of the epiphysis cerebri. Progress in Brain Research. Elsevier Publishing Co., Amsterdam, Vol. 10, pp. 577-584.

Thiéblot, L., Berthelay, J., and Blaise, S. 1966. Effet de la mélatonine chez le rat mâle et femelle. I. Action au niveau des gonades et des annexes. Ann. Endocrinol. 27:65-68.

Thorsøe, H. 1962. Inhibition of ovulation and changes in ovarian mucopolysaccharides induced by thyroidectomy in rabbits. Acta Endocrinol. 41:441-447.

Thuillie, M. J., Lacassagne, L., and Calet, C. 1961. Étude de l'influence de la d-l-thyroxine sur le poids de l'oeuf, sur le poids du jaune et sa composition. Ann. Biol. Anim. Bioch. Biophys. *1*:134-140.

Travis, H. F., Bassett, C. F., Warner, R. G., and Reineke, E. P. 1966. Some effects of feeding products high in naturally occurring thyroactive compounds upon reproduction of mink *(Mustela vison)*. Amer. J. Vet. Res. *27*:815-817.

Tuchmann-Duplessis, H., and Mercier-Parot, L. 1960. Influence of three hypoglycemic sulfamides, carbutamide BZ$_{55}$, tolbutamide D$_{860}$ and chlorpropamide on pregnancy and prenatal development of the rat. Anat. Rec. *136*:294 (abstract).

Tuchmann-Duplessis, H., and Mercier-Parot, L. 1962. Production de malformations congénitales chez le rat traité par le glucagon. C. R. Acad. Sci. *254*:2655-2657.

Tullner, W. W. 1966. Adrenal-mediated endometrial stimulation and withdrawal bleeding in ovariectomized monkey. Endocrinol. *79*:745-748.

Turner, C. D. 1966. General Endocrinology. Ed. 4. W. B. Saunders Company, Philadelphia.

VanDemark, N. L., and Baker, F. N. 1953. The effect of daily injections of epinephrine on semen production of bulls. J. Anim. Sci. *12*:956 (abstract).

VanDemark, N. L., and Hays, R. L. 1954. Rapid sperm transport in the cow. Fertil. Steril. *5*:131-137.

van de Kamer, J. C. 1965. Histological structure and cytology of the pineal complex in fishes, amphibians and reptiles. *In* J. A. Kappers and J. P. Schadé (eds.): Structure and Function of the Epiphysis Cerebri. Progress in Brain Research. Elsevier Publishing Co., Amsterdam, Vol. 10, pp. 30-48.

van der Wal, B., Moll, J., and de Wied, D. 1965. The effect of pinealectomy and of lesions in the subcommissural body on the rate of aldosterone secretion by rat adrenal glands *in vitro*. *In* J. A. Kappers and J. P. Schadé (eds.): Structure and Function of the Epiphysis Cerebri. Progress in Brain Research. Elsevier Publishing Co., Amsterdam, Vol. 10, pp. 635-643.

van Dongen, C. G., and Hays, R. L. 1966. Oxytocic activity in unextracted blood plasma during calving. J. Reprod. Fertil. *11*:317-323.

van Tienhoven, A. 1961a. Endocrinology of repro-

duction in birds. *In* W. C. Young (ed.): Sex and Internal Secretions. Williams & Wilkins Co., Baltimore, Vol. 2, pp. 1088-1169.

van Tienhoven, A. 1961b. The effect of massive doses of corticotrophin and of corticosterone on ovulation of the chicken (Gallus domesticus). Acta Endocrinol. *38*:407-412.

Verheyden, C. 1966. Effet de l'implantation intrahypophysaire de cortisol sous forme anhydre chez la ratte. Ann. Endocrinol. *27*:509-512.

Woitkewitch, A. A. 1940. Dependence of seasonal periodicity in gonadal changes on the thyroid gland in *Sturnus vulgaris*. C. R. Acad. Sci. URSS *27*:741-745.

Woods, M. C., and Simpson, M. E. 1961. Characterization of the anterior pituitary factor which antagonizes gonadotrophins. Endocrinology *68*:647-661.

Wurtman, R. J., and Axelrod, J. 1965. The formation, metabolism, and physiologic effects of melatonin in mammals. *In* J. A. Kappers and J. P. Schadé (ed.): Structure and Function of the Epiphysis Cerebri. Prog. Brain Research. Elsevier Publishing Co., Amsterdam, Vol. 10, pp. 520-528.

Wurtman, R. J., Altschule, M. D., and Holmgren, U. 1959. Effects of pinealectomy and of a bovine pineal extract in rats. Amer. J. Physiol. *197*:108-110.

Wurtman, R. J., Axelrod, J., and Chu, E. W. 1964. The relation between melatonin, a pineal substance and the effects of light on the rat gonad. Ann. N. Y. Acad. Sci. *117*:228-230.

Wurtman, R. J., Axelrod, J., Snyder, J., and Chu, E. W. 1965. Changes in the enzymatic synthesis of melatonin in the pineal during the estrous cycle. Endocrinology *76*:798-800.

Yamada, T., Takemura, Y., Kobayashi, I., and Shichijo, K. 1966. Re-evaluation of the effect of estrogen on the thyroid activity in the rat and its mechanism. Endocrinology *79*:849-857.

Ying, B. P., Chang, Y. J., and Gaylor, J. L. 1965. Testicular sterols. III The effect of gonadotrophins on the biosynthesis of testicular sterols. Biochim. Biophys. Acta *100*:256-262.

Young, F. G. 1963. Pancreatic hormones: insulin. *In* U. S. von Euler and H. Heller (eds.): Comparative endocrinology. Academic Press Inc., New York, Vol. 1, pp. 371-409.

Chapter 8

The Hypothalamus

ANATOMY

To understand the pathways and possible pathways by which the environment affects reproduction, it is important to describe the anatomy and function of the hypothalamus as it pertains to the control of the function of the pituitary.

The hypothalamus is the part of the brain mainly concerned with autonomic functions (such as heat regulation, appetite regulation, sleep, and rage); these functions are regulated by neural mechanisms. However, the regulation of water balance and the regulation of the release of hormones from the anterior pituitary involve a hormonal control. The hypothalamus thus performs the task of being an intermediary between the nervous system, of which it is part, and the endocrine system, to which it can send "hormonal" information.

The schematic presentation in Figure 8-1 illustrates the major features of the hypothalamo-hypophyseal system with which this chapter will be mainly concerned.

In elasmobranchs, anurans, reptiles, birds, and mammals, the main blood supply of the anterior lobe of the pituitary is via a hypophyseal portal system (Daniel, 1966; Green, 1951, 1966a; and Gorbman and Bern, 1962). Adams et al. (1965/1966) have pointed out that the portal vessels have a rather localized distribution and that different types of cells in the anterior pituitary tend to be grouped in specific regions in a given animal species. Such

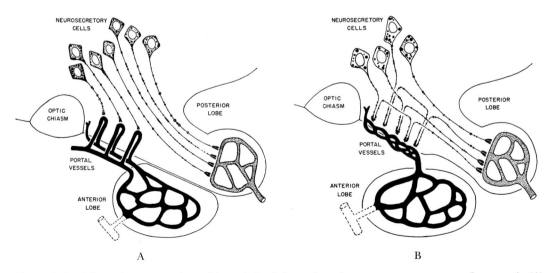

Figure 8-1. Schematic presentation of hypothalamic-hypophyseal neurosecretory system of mammals (A) and birds (B). Note that in birds the axons send loops to the portal vessels, whereas in mammals the portal vessels send loops to the axons. (From Scharrer and Scharrer, 1954a.)

207

a system would permit a blood supply of specific hypophyseal cells by blood from specific regions of the hypothalamus, so that different control centers are connected to different cell types.

In the two principal groups of cyclostomes, the lampreys and the hagfishes, there appears to be no vascular or neural connection between the brain and the pars distalis, although there is evidence that the amount of neurosecretory material (see later in this chapter) in the hypothalamus can be affected experimentally in lamprey larvae (Gorbman, 1965). In the lampreys a portal system is lacking, whereas in hagfishes a portal system carries blood from the hypothalamus to the roof of the neurohypophysis (Gorbman, 1965). Light and electron microscope investigations have revealed that this brain area, from which the blood is carried to the neurohypophysis, contains axon terminals containing small vesicles. The area is stainable with paraldehyde-fuchsin; in this manner it resembles the median eminence of the tetrapods. In addition, the area in the brain where it is located is comparable to the median eminence (Nishioka and Bern, 1966). Gorbman (1965) has cited evidence against the possible transport of neurosecretory material to the pars distalis as follows: (a) the neurohypophysis adjacent to the pars distalis is avascular; (b) the neurohypophysis is separated from the pars distalis by a layer of connective tissue; (c) the number of neurosecretory endings in the neurohypophysis is small; (d) it is unlikely that neurosecretory products would diffuse through capillaries which are 100 to 200μ from the nearest capillaries of the pars distalis. In cyclostomes there is thus a neurosecretory area in the brain from which neurosecretory material can reach the neurohypophysis via axons, but there is no connection, vascular or neural, between the brain and the pars distalis.

In elasmobranch fishes, the pars distalis receives blood from two "median eminences" so that, as in the tetrapods, there is a vascular pathway for transport of neurosecretory material to the pars distalis (Gorbman, 1965; Follenius, 1965). According to Follenius (1965) the ventral lobe of the adenohypophysis, where the gonadotropic and thyrotropic hormones are presumably secreted, is not under neurovascular or neural control. This part of the pituitary resembles that found for the adenohypophysis of cyclostomes. The intermediate lobe of the pituitary of elasmobranchs receives a rich nerve supply, in contrast to the situation found in tetrapods.

Among teleost fishes, considerable variation exists with respect to the connections between the brain and the pars distalis. In none of the species investigated has a communication between hypophyseal and hypothalamic vascularization been found. In several species, e.g. the perch (*Perca fluviatilis*) and the rainbow trout (*Salmo gairdneri irideus*), there are neurovascular junctions on the capillaries of the neurohypophyseal, primary longitudinal arteries which supply blood to the secondary capillary bed, which in turn vascularizes the adenohypophysis. Follenius (1965) considers this part of the neurohypophysis as a possible equivalent of the median eminence. Another anatomical arrangement is exemplified in the sea horse (*Hippocampus guttulatus*), in which axons from the hypothalamic area are in close contact with the cells of the pars distalis (Gabe, 1966). Neurovascular contacts between the neurohypophysis and adenohypophysis, without imposition of a basement membrane, have been observed in *Gadus morhua*, *Phoxinus* sp., and *Peocilia* sp. (Follenius, 1965). Knowles and Vollrath (1965) have reported that the pars distalis of the eel (*Anguilla anguilla*) receives aldehyde-fuchsin positive fibers as well as aldehyde-fuchsin negative neurosecretory fibers, which, after examination under the electron microscope, were found to contain vesicles with a central electron dense granule.

In anurans, reptiles, birds, and mammals, the main blood supply of the anterior lobe of the pituitary is via a hypophyseal portal system (Green, 1951, 1966a).

The anterior lobe of the pituitary, except in some lower vertebrates, does not receive nerve fibers from the hypothalamus. There is, however, a peripheral vegetative nerve supply, which has mostly a vasomotor function.

Substances are secreted by neurosecretory cells in the hypothalamus. The definition of a neurosecretory cell is "a neuron that also possesses glandular activity" (Yagi et al., 1963). That neurosecretory cells have full neuronal function (generation and conduction of action potentials) has been shown for the leech (*Theromyzon rude*) by Yagi et al. (1963) as well as for the rat (Yagi et al., 1966). Bern and Knowles (1966) have further emphasized that neurosecretion is distinguished from neurotransmitter liberation by ordinary neurons by the fact that the neurosecretory material is liberated into the blood, or regulates synthesis or release of blood-borne hormones from the endocrine system.

Originally, the determination of neurosecretory cells was based on the demonstration of glandular activity by cytological criteria; this was followed by the demonstration that some of the neurosecretory cells stain with stains, such as paraldehydefuchsin, or with chromalum hematoxylin-phloxin. However, these stains are not specific (e.g. pancreatic cells also give a positive reaction). The use of electron microscopy revealed the presence of granules with a diameter of 1000 to 3000 Å which seemed to be associated with neurosecretion, but the presence of such granules is not by itself an indication of neurosecretion. Bern and Knowles (1966) have stressed that neurons can be considered neurosecretory if they meet some of the above criteria *and* are an integral part of the endocrine system.

After the use of the paraldehyde-fuchsin stain and others, as well as after electron microscope studies, it has been suggested that the neurosecretory material (NSM) is produced in the cell perikaryon and transported in the axons; however, this material may also be formed throughout the axon (for discussions see Bargmann, 1966; Bern and Knowles, 1966; Green, 1966a; and Sloper, 1966). Some of the NSM produced by the paraventricular nucleus (PVN) and the supraoptic nucleus (NSO) is transported via the axons to the posterior pituitary or neurohypophysis. The posterior pituitary thus functions as a storage organ, and therefore is not an endocrine gland. Other neurosecretory cells may have axons ending on the portal blood vessels and the hormone secreted by the neuron is not stored in the posterior pituitary (Bern and Knowles, 1966). Jasinski et al. (1966) found that stimulation of the olfactory tract of goldfish depleted the stainable NSM from the axons of the preoptic nucleus. The calculated rate of movement of these granules showed that the granules appeared to move out of the perikaryon until the granulation in the axons was normal; after this the granules accumulated in the perikaryon.

This evidence indicates that NSM is synthesized in the perikaryon and transported to the terminal end of the axon. The structure of the hormones stored in the posterior pituitary has been established and their synthesis has been an accomplishment of great importance, since these were the first proteinlike hormones synthesized in the laboratory. This accomplishment was cited when duVigneaud was awarded the Nobel prize. The structure of these hormones and the occurrence in several classes of vertebrates are given in Table 8-1, and the potency of four of these hormones is given in Table 8-2. The methods of bioassay that were used also indicate some of the effects of these proteinlike hormones.

The blood vessels of the hypophyseal portal system make connections with some of the axons and the neurosecretory material may be transported to the anterior lobe of the pituitary. In a later section of

Table 8-1. Amino Acid Sequence of Neurohypophyseal Hormones Found in Different Species

```
        S_____S
        |                     |
H • Cys • Tyr • X • Y • Asp.NH₂ • Cys • Pro • Z • Gly.NH₂
```

AMINO ACIDS	NAME OF HORMONE	CLASSES OR SPECIES IN WHICH FOUND
X = Ileu Y = GluNH₂ Z = Leu	Oxytocin	Birds, mammals
X = Phe Y = GluNH₂ Z = Arg	Arginine vasopressin	Most mammals
X = Phe Y = GluNH₂ Z = Lys	Lysine vasopressin	Pig, hippopotamus
X = Ileu Y = GluNH₂ Z = Arg	Vasotocin	Fishes, amphibia, birds
X = Ileu Y = Ser Z = Ileu	Isotocin or Ichthyotocin	Fishes
X = Ileu Y = GluNH₂ Z = Ileu	8-Isoleucine oxytocin	Polypterus and some amphibia

Reference: Heller, 1962.

this chapter, evidence of the presence of substances in the median eminence that affect hormone release from the anterior pituitary (the so-called releasing factors) will be presented, and the effects of the posterior pituitary hormones on gonadotropin release from the pituitary will be discussed. The presence of neurosecretory material in neurosecretory nerve fibers, which are part of the hypothalamo-hypophyseal tract, and the presence of neurosecretory material in the portal vessels is strong evidence in favor of the hypothesis that the portal vessels are a neurovascu-

Table 8-2. Potency (Units/mg.) of Different Neurohypophyseal Hormones in Various Bioassays

ASSAY METHOD	ARGININE VASOPRESSIN	LYSINE VASOPRESSIN	OXYTOCIN	VASOTOCIN	ISOTOCIN
Rat uterus	20–25	15–20	360, 415	40	28
Blood pressure (rat) (increase)	400–450	270–340	10, 3.8	71	—
Blood pressure (hen) (decrease)	56	42	430	—	16
Antidiuresis (rat)	400–450	110–140	Diuretic	71	—
Milk ejection (rabbit)	70–80	50–60	371	119	—
Hen uterus	320	29	29	1030	—
Water balance (frog)	—	—	(360)	2600	< 1
Urinary balance (frog)	21	5	360	7800	—

References: Li, 1961; Heller, 1962.

lar link between the hypothalamus and the pars distalis (Arko and Kivalo, 1958).

In addition to these main features, which are illustrated, there are some additional anatomical findings that are important for the understanding of the regulation of anterior pituitary function:

a. A small venous system exists (see Figure 8-2) which passes from the posterior surface of the anterior lobe of the pituitary to the capillary network of the median eminence (Szentágothai et al., 1962).

b. In some species, a vascular link connects the neural lobe and the adenohypophysis so that some blood of the general circulation can reach the anterior pituitary without passing

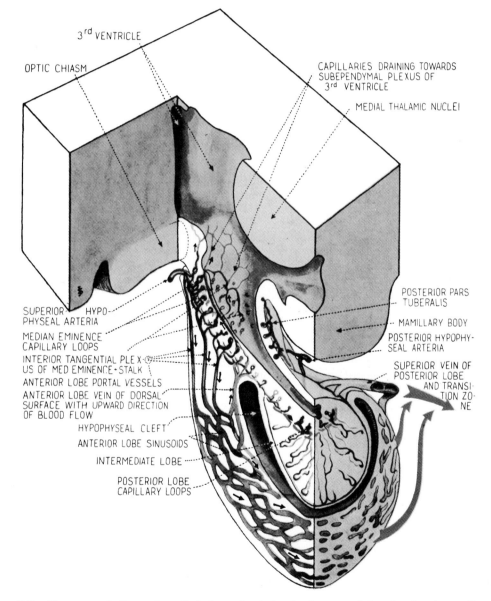

Figure 8-2. Diagrammatic illustration of pituitary circulation in the cat and dog showing the small venous system which passes from the posterior surface of the anterior lobe to the capillary network of the median eminence. (From J. Szentágothai et al., 1962.)

through the primary plexus of the median eminence.

Electron microscopy of the rat's median eminence by Kobayashi et al. (1966) and Matsui (1966b) has revealed that there are three kinds of vesicles or granules present, i.e.:

1. Large (90 to 160 mμ. diameter) electron dense granules; axons containing these granules may also contain synapse-like vesicles.

2. Small (70 to 150 mμ. diameter) electron-dense granules with or without haloes; axons containing these granules may also contain synapse-like vesicles.

3. Synaptic vesicle-like structures, which may be present in axons containing large granules, small granules, or no granules.

Kobayashi et al. (1966) and Matsui (1966b) have speculated that the large granules may be carriers of the neuro-hypophyseal hormones, that the small granules are carriers of catecholamines and that the synaptic vesicle-like structures are carriers of acetylcholine. The regions of contact between the axons with the synaptic vesicle-like structures and the capillaries may show aggregations of vesicles against the axon membrane in contact with the capillary wall similar to the so-called "active points" at the synapse in the central nervous system (Kobayashi et al., 1966). The presence of catecholamines in the median eminence of mammals has been demonstrated by Fuxe (1964) and the presence of a monamine oxidase in the median eminence was shown by Matsui and Kobayashi (1965).

Acetylcholine or an acetylcholine-like substance and neurohypophyseal hormones were shown to be present by bioassays (Kobayashi et al., 1966). Acetylcholine esterase has been found in the median eminence of the Japanese silver eye (Zosterops palpebrosa japonica) (Uemura, 1964a) and the white-crowned sparrow (Zonotrichia leucophrys gambelii) (Kobayashi and Farner, 1964).

Matsui (1966a), in an investigation of the median eminence of the pigeon (Columba livia), found that the posterior median eminence contained large granules (neurohypophyseal hormone carriers?) and small granules (monoamine carriers?), but that the large granules were more abundant in the anterior median eminence. Aldehyde-fuchsin stainable granules are more abundant in the anterior than in the posterior median eminence.

These observations show that neurosecretory cells may be present, although such cells cannot be demonstrated by the aldehyde-fuchsin stain or other stains mentioned in the unit on gonadotropins in this chapter. The observations also indicate that adrenergic and cholinergic neurons may be present in the median eminence.

With these anatomical characteristics in mind, consideration should be given to the physiologic consequences of this arrangement and to the physiologic evidence which has been gathered to support the concept of hypothalamic control of the anterior pituitary by a humoral pathway.

These considerations will be limited to the control of gonadotropic hormone secretion and release. A number of techniques has been used, and, where pertinent, the principal results and their interpretation will be given.

We owe the formulation of the current concept of the control of the anterior pituitary function to Green and Harris (1947). This concept involves:

1. The production of substances in the median eminence which can cause the liberation of hormones from the anterior pituitary gland.

2. The transport of these substances to the pituitary gland.

3. The release of such substances in the median eminence under the influence of neural impulses.

The different lines of evidence in favor of this concept and the various details which have been worked out will be discussed in more or less detail. Excellent recent reviews can be found in the books edited by Bajusz and Jasmin (1964), Cole (1964), Harris and Donovan (1966), Martini and Ganong (1966), Nalbandov (1963), Schreiber (1963), Szentágothai et al. (1962), and Yamamoto and Brobeck (1965), and in reviews by Bogdanove (1964), Everett (1964a), Guillemin (1964), and McCann and Ramirez (1964), and in the books by Scharrer and Scharrer (1963), and Turner (1966).

The present discussion will be limited to a presentation of the evidence that supports the above mentioned concept with respect to the neural control of gonadotropin secretion and release. The author is fully aware that this limitation is arbitrary and will only give a partial presentation of the overall concept of the control of pituitary function.

DAMAGE TO THE HYPOTHALAMO-HYPOPHYSEAL SYSTEM

Transplantation of the Pituitary In Vivo

When anterior pituitary glands are transplanted to sites other than the hypothalamus, one may be sure that any connections, either neural or vascular, are interrupted and that they cannot regenerate. Of course, one should ensure good vascularization of the gland. In many cases the kidney or the anterior eye chamber have been selected as ectopic sites. Piacsek and Meites (1966a) have presented evidence that after transplantation of the rat's pituitary (site not given), exposure of the animal to continuous light affects the cytology of the pituitary and stimulates the weight of ovaries and uteri. If we assume that light can affect the pituitary only via the nervous system, one needs to assume that sufficient hormone is produced by the hypothalamus

and released into the general circulation to affect the function of the transplanted pituitary. So far this has only been reported for mammals.

We will discuss the effects of pituitary transplantation in the different classes of vertebrates.

Teleosts. The transplantation of the anterior pituitary of the teleost *Poecilia formosa* reduces its rate of secretion of ACTH and growth hormone (GH), but it increases its capacity to secrete thyroid stimulating hormone (TSH) and prolactin (tested by measuring its adaptation to fresh water). This indicates an inhibitory effect of the hypothalamus on TSH and prolactin secretion (Ball et al., 1965). Mention should be made that according to Nicoll and Bern (1964) the pituitaries of teleost fishes do not contain prolactin, as tested by the pigeon crop assay. However, Ball and Oliverau (1964) have shown that hypophysectomized *Poecilia formosa* cannot survive in fresh water but will do so after prolactin administration (20 μg./day), thus making the survival in fresh water a suitable test. Similar observations with respect to the maintenance in fresh water by pituitary grafts have been made for the platyfish, *Xiphophorus maculatus* (Schreibman and Kallman, 1964). The same authors reported in 1966 that prolactin injections of 10 μg. or more prevented mortality of hypophysectomized *Xiphophorus maculatus*, whereas vasopressin, oxytocin, TSH, ACTH, and growth hormone were ineffective. This provides reasonably good evidence that the maintenance of life in platyfish with ectopic pituitaries was the result of prolactin secretion.

Amphibia. Assenmacher and Tixier-Vidal (1965) and Fontaine and Leloup (1964) have reviewed the literature on the effect of pituitary transplants in amphibia and higher vertebrates. Ectopic pituitary transplants of *Pleurodeles waltlii* larvae (Pasteels, 1957) fail to show differentiation of the gonadotropic cells, whereas in adults the FSH and LH cells degenerate after transplantation and the testes and ovaries become atrophied. The acidophils are maintained and continue to secrete growth hormone and ACTH (Pasteels, 1960). Autotransplantation of the pituitary of the red eft *(Diemyctylus viridescens)* caused the water drive to develop; this phenomenon (see Chapter 7) occurs in intact animals after injection of prolactin but not after injection of other pituitary hormones, thus suggesting that transplantation of the pituitary resulted in prolactin secretion (Masur, 1962). In *Rana temporaria* (Vivien and Schott, 1958) and in *Bufo bufo* (van Dongen et al., 1966) spermatogenesis continues at a somewhat lower level than in intact controls but at a considerably higher level than in hypophysectomized animals. Similarly, testicular weights are maintained at a higher level than in hypophysectomized males in *Bufo bufo.* In these toads the Leydig cells were generally nonsecretory after ectopic pituitary transplantation, although they were secretory when the pituitary was placed near the median eminence. The thumb pads of the toads with ectopic transplants regressed, but not as much as those of hypophysectomized males.

In general, the evidence suggests that in ectopic transplants of male frogs *(R. temporaria)* and male toads *(Bufo bufo)* FSH secretion continues at a somewhat lower rate than in intact males but that LH secretion is severely curtailed in toads. (No evidence was presented for this aspect for *R. temporaria).* The cytological evidence obtained with *Bufo bufo* pituitaries supports these conclusions.

In *Rana temporaria,* ectopic transplantation of the pituitary of females in the spring resulted in atresia of the ovarian follicles (Vivien and Schott, 1958), whereas in *Bufo bufo* females, ovarian weights were maintained while they increased somewhat in the controls (3.15 percent of body weight to 5.37 percent of body weight) and severely regressed in the hypophysectomized females (van Dongen et al.,

1966). In the fall, hypophysectomy of female *R. temporaria* led to ovulation (Vivien and Schott, 1958) (similar to the ovulations observed by Houssay et al., 1935, after extirpation of the hypothalamus) but the long term effect was regression of the ovary, which also occurred in *Bufo bufo* in which the pituitary was transplanted to the eye muscle in the fall (van Dongen et al., 1966). Ovulations were rare in *Bufo bufo* when the pituitary was transplanted to the median eminence. Female *Bufo bufo* with pituitaries transplanted to the median eminence showed atresia of the ovary in five out of eight cases; in the other females regression occurred immediately after the operation, but growth of the ovary occurred afterward. Doerr Schott (1965) has reported little effect of ectopic pituitary transplantation on the cytology of the hypophysis of *R. temporaria.* Assenmacher and Tixier-Vidal (1965) suggest that the low level of FSH secretion may still be dependent upon small quantities of hypothalamic mediator because destruction of the median eminence of metamorphosed *Ambystoma mexicanum* with ectopic pituitaries reduces testicular activity to that of hypophysectomized animals.

There seem to be no reports on the effect of pituitary transplants on the prolactin secretion in amphibia. In vitro studies of prolactin secretion gave inconclusive results for *Necturus maculosus* (Nicoll, 1965). Pasteels (1957) observed that after transplantation of the anterior pituitary in *Pleurodeles waltlii* larvae, gonadal, adrenal, and thyroidal development were similar to those found in hypophysectomized animals. In the grafts, no differentiation of chromophobes occurred, but if the transplantation took place after thyrotropes had appeared, degeneration of these cells was found. However, acidophils continued their normal development. Acidophils have been associated with prolactin secretion. Pasteels (1957) speculates, on the basis of one animal, that these cells may secrete ACTH.

Ectopic transplantation (under the oral mucosa) of the pars distalis of *Ambystoma mexicanum* has the same effect on male and female gonads as hypophysectomy. The pars distalis, grafted so that it was in contact with the cut edges of the wall of the third ventricle, also lacked gonadotropic activity, as indicated by the small testis weight in eight out of nine animals and the small ovarian weight of females subjected to this operation (Jørgensen and Larsen, 1963).

Birds. After transplanting pituitaries of drakes *(Anas platyrhynchos)* and roosters *(Gallus domesticus),* the testes, thyroids, and adrenals regress (Assenmacher, 1958; Nalbandov, 1964), although the changes in the thyroidal and adrenal weights are not as drastic as those in the testicular weights. Cytological examination and electron microscopy show that the erythrosinophilic (prolactin) cells are secretory in the transplants of drakes. The transplants of chicken pituitaries have not been examined for this, but in view of the selection against "broodiness" in most commercial breeds of chickens,' it is possible that the ability to produce prolactin has been lost. Experiments to determine the effect of pituitary transplants on prolactin producing cells should be carried out with breeds in which "broodiness" still occurs or with the red jungle fowl.

Pigeons *(Columba livia)* are well suited for investigations on the effect of pituitary transplants on prolactin production because the animal's crop glands can serve as indicators. After transplantation of the pigeon's pituitary to the kidney, erythrosinophilic cells become rare (Tixier-Vidal et al., 1966), and no proliferation of the pigeon crop gland occurs (Baylé and Assenmacher, 1965). These experiments thus indicate a difference between pigeons and ducks with respect to the control of prolactin secretion. However, this difference is not confirmed by the results of in vitro experiments, to be discussed later.

Differences between ducks and pigeons may well be related with the fact that the duck is migratory whereas the pigeon is not. Evidence is accumulating that indicates that in migratory species prolactin may play a role in the induction of hyperphagia and subsequent fat deposition without affecting gonadal integrity, whereas in nonmigratory species prolactin causes gonadal atrophy (Meier et al., 1966). If the data obtained from ducks and pigeons hold generally true for migratory and nonmigratory birds, then one might find in migratory species that a release from hypothalamic inhibition causes prolactin secretion, and that in nonmigratory species the hypothalamus is required for prolactin secretion. Recent experiments (Gourdji and Tixier-Vidal, 1966) have shown that hypothalamic extracts from drakes stimulate prolactin secretion by pituitaries in vitro, results very similar to those obtained with pigeon pituitaries cultured in vitro (Kragt and Meites, 1965). Thus in vivo transplanted pigeon and drake pituitaries show different prolactin secretion patterns, but in vitro there seems to be little or no difference.

Mammals. In rats and guinea pigs, transplantation of the anterior pituitary often does not result in complete testicular atrophy, and if atrophy occurs after the operation, there is usually subsequent recovery of spermatogenesis (Martinovitch et al., 1963; Everett, 1964a). One explanation is that the amount of chemotransmittor secreted by the hypothalamus is high enough to maintain essentially normal function of the pituitary. This is, thus, similar to the explanation given for the higher gonadotropin secretion found in female rats with pituitary transplants after exposure to continuous light.

The difference between male and female rats with respect to gonadal development after pituitary homotransplants may be the result of differences between the sensitivity of male and female pituitaries to hypothalamic hormones in the general circulation, differences between the hypothalamic hormone production of males and females, differences between the sensitivity of ovaries and testes to the same concentration of gonadotropins, or a combination of all three factors mentioned. Asakawa and Turner (1965) favor the explanation that testes are more sensitive to gonadotropin than ovaries.

That some gonadotropin secretion by the transplanted pituitary can occur is shown by the experiments by Martinovitch et al. (1966) in which hypophysectomized adult female rats received multiple anterior pituitary transplants under the kidney or in the anterior eye chambers, from 18 to 21-day-old donors. These pituitaries were transplanted either fresh or after 7, 14, or 21 days of in vitro incubation. The ovaries of the recipients were several times heavier than those of controls; follicles with antra were found in the animals with transplants and uterine growth was also observed. The grafts were healthy looking and gained weight in comparison with the weight at the time of transplantation. It seems thus that 7.5 to 17 pituitaries can secrete enough gonadotropin to stimulate the ovaries. That this stimulation is not the result of "leakage" of any gonadotropins present at the time of transplantation is evident from the fact that similar results were obtained with fresh and cultured pituitaries and from the interval of more than eight months between implantation and killing of the animals. Gittes and Kastin (1966) obtained results which agree with those of Martinovitch et al. (1966). Ten to thirty pituitaries were transplanted and evidence of luteinization was obtained, although no corpora lutea were formed. Hoshino (1964) reported that single subcutaneous pituitary grafts in three-week-old mice induced earlier vaginal opening and earlier estrus than in controls, suggesting that in mice, single, transplanted pituitaries may secrete enough gonadotropin to stimulate the ovaries. The difference between mice

and rats with respect to the number of pituitaries required for ovarian stimulation may be a reflection of a greater sensitivity of the ovarian tissue of the mouse or to a greater "autonomy" of the mouse pituitary or to a combination of these factors.

The ovarian follicles of rats regress after pituitary transplantation to the kidney or anterior eye chamber; however, corpora lutea present at the time of transplantation are maintained for several months and secrete progesterone, as is evident from the formation of deciduomata in response to uterine trauma (Everett, 1964a). The transplanted pituitary secretes more prolactin than the one in situ, but the secretion of FSH, LH, GH, and ACTH is sharply decreased. Petrovic and Aron (1958) found that anterior pituitaries transplanted to guinea pig testes activated the Leydig cells of the testis into which the implant was made, and sometimes also activated those in the other testis. These results are in agreement with the phenomena discussed above, that in males pituitary transplantation does not have as drastic an effect as hypophysectomy, although one might have expected an effect of the intratesticular transplants on spermatogenesis also.

Some of the consequences of transplantation of the anterior lobe of the pituitary are an extensive central infarct, a loss of large gonadotropic cells (Nikitovitch-Winer and Everett, 1959) and a loss of thyrotropes. One might thus argue that the gonadal atrophy and decreased thyroidal activity were the result of an insufficient vascularization. By an elegant series of experiments, Nikitovitch-Winer and Everett (1958, 1959) showed that the vascularization by the hypophyseal portal vessels causes a resumption of the gonadotropic function of such pituitary glands. The gland was transplanted under the median eminence after it had been established under the kidney capsule (with continued lack of follicular development in spite of a marked improvement in histological organization of the transplanted pituitary). The retransplantation caused severe necrosis, but the gland recovered and showed the reappearance of gonadotropic cells (Nikitovitch-Winer and Everett, 1959) and of gonadotropin release (rats with pituitaries retransplanted under the median eminence eventually showed estrous cycles and conceived) (Nikitovitch-Winer and Everett, 1958). Pituitaries retransplanted under the temporal lobe of the brain did not show a recovery of gonadotropic function. These experiments thus demonstrated that there was indeed some special function served by vascularization by the hypophyseal portal vessels, and that the infarct per se was not the cause of the loss of gonadotropin secretion. The technique of transplanting the pituitary can be used to determine to what extent the steroidal feedback requires the integrity of hypothalamic connections to the pituitary. Van Rees and Wolthuis (1962) found that testosterone injections prevented the depletion of FSH from immature rat pituitaries transplanted to the kidneys, indicating a direct effect of testosterone on the pituitary. Estrogen had a less dramatic, but still measurable, effect. Progesterone, on the other hand, was ineffective. The assay method was not specific for FSH, nor was the assay technique in accordance with acceptable standard procedures. Nevertheless, the data show a direct effect of the steroid on pituitary gonadotropin content.

The special case of transplantation of the anterior pituitary to different parts of the hypothalamus requires special attention.

Basophilic cells, which stain after periodic acid Schiff staining (PAS+), disappear from the pituitary after it is transplanted to the kidney or the anterior eye chamber. However, after transplantation to an area of the ventral hypothalamus (involving the arcuate nucleus, the ventral part of the anterior periventricular nucleus, and possibly the parvicellular region of the retrochiasmatic area) such PAS+ basophilic cells

reappear (see Figure 8-3) (Szentágothai et al., 1962; Flament-Durand, 1964) and often are hypertrophied (Szentágothai et al., 1962). According to Knigge (1962), rat pituitary grafts are functional only if they are in contact with the supraopticohypophyseal tract; however, Flament-Durand (1964) found functional grafts that were not in contact with this tract. It is important to state that these grafts did not establish connections with the capillary loops of the portal system of the median eminence, and thus were apparently maintained by humoral transmittors from the hypothalamic area. If the transplants were located in areas other than the median eminence or ventral hypothalamic area, no reappearance of basophils occurs.

The pituitaries transplanted to the so-called hypophysiotropic area secreted larger amounts of gonadotropins than those transplanted to other areas of the hypothalamus, as was evident from the testicular weights, which were about six times higher in the former group of rats than in the latter. Ovarian and uterine weights of females with such hypothalamic transplants were 22 and 151 mg./100 gm. body weight, respectively, whereas the corresponding figures for hypophysectomized rats and cats with transplants in nonhypothalamic areas were 10.6 and 34.2, and 8.7 and 40.2 mg./100 gm. body weight, respectively. In intact controls, these figures were 37.5 and 208 mg./100 gm. body weight (Halász et al., 1962). In other experiments, fresh follicles and corpora lutea were found (Halász et al., 1965).

In subsequent investigations, Halász and Pupp (1965) interrupted all the nervous connections to the hypophysiotropic area and then transplanted the pituitaries there. In the case of males, the testes were maintained to the same extent as in rats in which the area was not deafferentiated. Deafferentiation in females resulted in smaller ovaries and in either polyfollicular ovaries in rats with constant vaginal estrus, or ovaries with

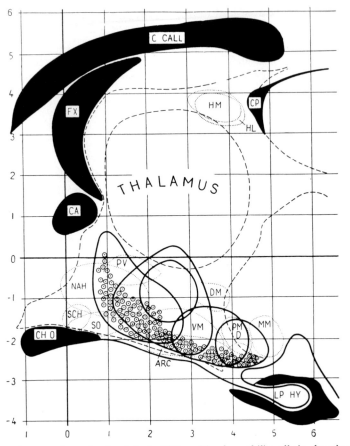

Figure 8-3. Pituitary homografts maintained their PAS positive basophilic cells in the places indicated by the small circle with a center dot. These locations have been projected on a midsagittal plane. (From Szentágothai et al., 1962.)

persistent corpora lutea, but not in new ovulations in rats that were in vaginal diestrus. These results were interpreted as a direct control of the function of the pituitary by humoral agents from the hypophysiotropic area and a control of this area by neural structures outside of it. As we shall discuss later, specific factors have been isolated from the hypothalamus and median eminence which control the release of different pituitary hormones.

May (1964) has presented evidence that the atrophied testes of hypophysectomized mice regenerate and contain sperm after two anterior pituitaries of neonatal mice are implanted into the cerebellum. Unfortunately, no controls in which pituitaries were placed in other parts of the brain were included in the experiment.

It is thus impossible to judge whether there is something special about cerebellar transplants. The experiment by Hoshino (1964) with female mice suggests that the mouse pituitary, transplanted subcutaneously, can also secrete enough gonadotropin to stimulate the ovaries. More critical evidence is required before a hypophysiotropic function is assigned to the cerebellar area.

Anterior Pituitaries Cultured In Vitro

The incubation in vitro of anterior pituitaries, in the absence or presence of hypothalamic tissue or extracts, allows for a rather precise control of conditions. The pituitary and medium can be assayed for activity of the different pituitary hormones, and one can thus evaluate the effects of different preparations on the synthesis and on the release of specific pituitary hormones.

With the use of tissue and organ culture techniques, evidence has been obtained that hypothalamic extracts can cause FSH release from rat pituitaries (Mittler and Meites, 1964) and LH release (Schally and Bowers, 1964). On the other hand, hypothalamic tissue or tissue extracts prevent prolactin synthesis and release by rat pituitaries (Talwalker et al., 1963; Gala and Reece, 1964). In pigeons, however, pigeon hypothalamic extracts are required for the release of prolactin (Kragt and Meites, 1965). Rat hypothalamus extracts do not affect pigeon pituitary prolactin release and pigeon hypothalamic extract does not affect rat pituitary prolactin release (Kragt and Meites, 1965).

It is of interest to compare the in vitro prolactin production by the anterior pituitaries of pigeons and ducks because of the cytological difference between the results obtained when pituitaries of these species are transplanted. Tixier-Vidal and Gourdji (1965) found, after incubation of duck pituitaries (in the absence of hypothalamic tissue), that a selective preservation of erythrosinophils occurred and prolactin was found in the medium. However, no determinations of the prolactin content of the pituitaties before and after incubation were made, so that it is impossible to decide whether prolactin production occurred or whether prolactin was released into the medium. The cytological evidence suggests that prolactin synthesis probably occurred. More recent experiments by Gourdji and Tixier-Vidal (1966) have shown that extracts from drake hypothalami increase the prolactin release into the medium by duck pituitaries cultured in vitro. Thus pigeon and duck pituitaries respond similarly to hypothalamic extracts in vitro with respect to prolactin production, but they behave differently after transplantation to the kidney.

Transection of the Hypophyseal Portal System

Portal vessels can regenerate after the pituitary stalk is cut; therefore, the only critically valid experiments are those in which a barrier is placed between the cut ends.

The anterior hypophysis' blood supply is mainly via the portal vessels, and one of the consequences of sectioning the stalk is necrosis of the anterior pituitary (Adams et al., 1963, 1964; Benoit and Assenmacher, 1959; Dávid, et al., 1965) and one might, therefore, expect a diminished secretion of hormones as the result of infarct per se and doubt that the portal vessels carry special messenger materials to the anterior pituitary. (This argument has been partially discussed in the section on pituitary transplants.) Benoit and Assenmacher (1959) have provided evidence of another nature to show that the infarct per se is not the cause of gonadal atrophy observed in ducks after stalk transection. After sectioning of the portal vessels, at least 20 percent of the anterior pituitary remains histologically normal. If incomplete hypophysectomies leave 20 percent of the gland intact, no testicular atrophy occurs in drakes. This implies that the amount left intact after section of the portal vessels should be sufficient to maintain normal testicular size, but, nevertheless, testicular regression occurs. Dávid et al. (1965) studied hypophyseal blood flow with the aid of ^{86}Rb after stalk sectioning, and found four weeks after the operation that the blood flow to the surviving hypophyseal tissue was normal.

The effect of stalk sectioning in different classes of animals has given different results because of different anatomical arrangements.

Amphibia: Interruption of the portal vessels of *Triturus cristatus* leads to a decrease in the number of gonadotropic cells and impairment of spermatogenesis (van Oordt, 1960). Destruction of the median eminence prevents the testicular response to an increase in temperature in this species.

Birds: In ducks, one can transect the stalk without destroying the portal vessels and one can destroy the portal vessels without damage to the stalk. After stalk section, but with the portal vessels left intact, no effect on testicular or adrenal size is shown in the drake, but often the thyroid function is decreased. On the other hand, destruction of the portal vessels causes atrophy of the testes, a lack of testicular response to increased amounts of light, and a lack of hypertrophy of the remaining testes after hemicastration; the thyroids and adrenals sometimes are smaller than normal and the response of the thyroid to propylthiouracil is abolished (Assenmacher, 1958). In laying hens *(Gallus domesticus)* Shirley and Nalbandov (1956) observed atrophy of the ovaries, oviducts and combs after stalk section, which also destroyed the portal vessels, but little effect was noticed on the size of the thyroids and adrenals.

Mammals: In mammals, the effects of stalk section, which includes disruption of the portal vessels, generally have been a decrease of testicular size, a lack of ovarian follicular development, and an interruption of the estrous cycle very similar to that observed after pituitary transplants. The effects have been studied in dogs, cats, sheep, rabbits, rats, and guinea pigs (see Assenmacher, 1958; Everett, 1964a; Everett and Nikitovitch-Winer, 1963; Greep, 1961; and Jacobsohn, 1966). Rats with cut stalks show an increased prolactin secretion (Nikitovitch-Winer, 1965), as do ferrets (Donovan, 1963). In women, when the stalk is sectioned for clinical reasons, lactation is induced (Eckles et al., 1958), suggesting a high prolactin secretion, whereas the disappearance of menstrual cycles, lack of ovarian follicles and corpora

lutea, and atrophic reproductive tract show that gonadotropin secretion has diminished; evidence of low ACTH, TSH, and GH secretion was also obtained.

Denamur et al. (1966) have presented evidence that stalk section in sheep does not affect the life of the corpus luteum of cyclic sheep. In hysterectomized sheep the corpus luteum was still secreting progesterone 18 days after stalk section, although after this time there was a decrease in the progesterone secretion. These results imply that the sheep pituitary secretes a luteotropic hormone after transection of the stalk, although the corpus luteum was not maintained in hypophysectomized or hypophysectomized and hysterectomized ewes in the hands of the same experimenters. These data seem to conflict with those found by Nalbandov and St. Clair (1958), in which implantation failed in mated, stalk-sectioned ewes. The fact that stalk transection in pregnant ewes between day 42 and 90 of pregnancy does not cause abortion does not help to answer the question raised, since hypophysectomy after day 50 of pregnancy does not cause abortion in sheep. On the basis of the available data, the apparent conflict between the data of Denamur et al., 1966, and Nalbandov and St. Clair cannot be resolved. It should be pointed out that in a species closely related to sheep, i.e. domestic goats, stalk section between day 44 and 129 of pregnancy causes abortion, as does hypophysectomy between day 38 and 120 (Cowie et al., 1963).

Donovan (1963) has found that in ferrets corpora lutea remain fully developed and that there is no interference with uterine growth during four weeks of pseudopregnancy after stalk section. However, after hypophysectomy the corpora lutea regressed and ovarian and uterine weights decreased. In the stalk-sectioned ferrets, ovarian and uterine weight fell below those of controls after the four week period. These data thus indicate that, as in sheep, the isolated ferret pituitary is capable of secreting a luteotropic hormone.

Lesions of the Hypothalamus

Hypothalamic lesions, depending upon their location, may destroy the nuclei in which the hypothalamic hormones are synthesized, the axons in which the neurosecretory material is transported, or the blood vessels which transport the material to the anterior pituitary. We have discussed the consequences of destruction of the portal vessels, and the present discussion will, therefore, be limited to the consequences of destruction of the hypothalamic nuclei.

The method employed in making the lesions affects the interpretation of the results obtained (Rowland, 1966). The three methods used are:

1. Surgical damage of the nuclei was employed by Assenmacher (1958), but this method has the disadvantage that it usually involves large areas; thus the lesions are not well delimited.

2. Electrolytic lesions, made by running a small direct current (DC) through an electrode which is placed stereotaxically in the desired area. If stainless steel electrodes are used, a deposit of iron will occur at the tip of the electrode and the observed effect may be the result of the destruction of the neural tissue *or* it may be the result of the deposition of the iron, which, as was shown by Everett and Radford (1961), can stimulate the hypothalamus. This problem of interpretation can be avoided by the use of platinum electrodes (Everett and Radford, 1961).

3. Electrocoagulation, in which stereotaxically placed stainless steel electrodes are heated by a radio frequency current and the neural tissue is destroyed by the heat, reduces the problem of irritative deposits.

An illustration of the different results that may be obtained by electrolytic lesions and electrocoagulations has been given by Reynolds (1963). After electrocoagulation of the ventromedial hypothalamus of rats, no hyperphagia was observed, whereas after electrolytic lesions in the same area, rats became hyperphagic. Hoebel (1965) found hyperphagia in rats after electrocoagulation of the ventromedial hypothalamus and Hoebel and Teitelbaum (1962) found hyperphagia after electrolytic lesions using platinum electrodes. Reynolds (1965) maintains that it is possible to destroy the ventromedial hypothalamus without obtaining hyperphagia. The difference between the results of different investigators may involve the extent of the lesions and the way the measurements are made. In any event, the results of Reynolds' (1963) experiments show that in the hands of the same investigator, the technique used to make lesions can affect the results.

4. Injections of goldthioglucose (GTC) into mice causes damage to the ventromedial nucleus and leads to obesity and hyperphagia. Liebelt et al. (1966) reported that in GTC-treated mice, persistent vaginal cornification occurs and that ovarian stromal cells are replaced by interstitial cells. Browning (1964) found that after GTC treatment, prolactin is released and that in ovariectomized GTC-treated mice with intraocular ovarian autografts (Browning and Kwan, 1964) the cycles were irregular, often with long metestrous periods. They found the mean cycle length to be 11.3 days, whereas in non-GTC-treated mice, the mean cycle length was 8.4 days. Uterine cystic hyperplasia accompanied mammary development. Obesity and abnormal cycles sometimes occurred independently of each other.

5. Radiation-induced lesions have been used by Gale and Larsson (1963) to study the effects of hypothalamic lesions on lactation in goats.

However, the majority of lesions reported in the literature have been made by electrolysis.

The literature on the effects of lesions on reproductive physiology is voluminous, but most of the information has been obtained with the rat and, apparently, little has been done from a comparative point of view.

In *Triturus cristatus* destruction of the preoptic nucleus leads to a decrease in the number of gonadotropic cells in the pituitary and to impaired spermatogenesis (van Oordt, 1960), whereas in *Rana temporaria* lesion of the preoptic magnocellular nucleus in the male has no apparent effect on the gonads and secondary sex characters; in the female such lesions do not affect ovarian weight or development of secondary sex characters, but they do prevent ovulation (Dierickx, 1963).

Lesions made in the infundibulum of the toad *(Bufo arenarum?)* cause an infarct of the central part of the pituitary and a release of gonadotropic hormone, so that between 20 and 57 percent of the operated females ovulate (Houssay et al., 1935).

We have discussed that in *Rana temporaria* transplantation of the pituitary may cause ovulations; a similar factor may be the cause of the ovulations observed by Houssay et al. (1935).

In male frogs, destruction of the diencephalon does not affect testicular growth but in the midwife toad *(Alytes obstetricans)* the gonads atrophy after such lesions.

Lesions of the anterior hypothalamus of drakes *(Anas platyrhynchos)* cause testicular atrophy and prevent compensatory hypertrophy of the remaining testicle after unilateral castration (Assenmacher, 1958).

In laying chickens *(Gallus domesticus)* lesions of the ventral part of the paraventricular nucleus block "spontaneous" and progesterone-induced ovulations (Ralph, 1959; Ralph and Fraps, 1959b; and Egge and Chiasson, 1963).

Studies carried out in a number of mammalian species, especially the dog and rat, have shown that lesions in the hypothalamus have rather specific effects on the secretion of the different adenohypophyseal hormones. Lesions which affect ACTH secretion, for instance in the dog, do not seem to affect GTH secretion, and vice versa (Fortier, 1963). There is a certain amount of overlap among the TSH, ACTH, and GTH "centers" in the rat, but it is possible to make selective lesions.

We will list the effects observed on reproduction after lesioning different parts of the hypothalamus.

Destruction of the magnicellular part of the paraventricular nucleus of adult rats does not interfere with the estrous cycles (Olivecrona, 1957).

Lesions placed in the anterior hypothalamus of immature female rats cause precocious follicular growth, increase estrogen secretion, cause precocious opening of the vagina, and increase uterine weights (Bogdanove and Schoen, 1959; Elwers and Critchlow, 1960; Donovan and van der Werff ten Bosch, 1959). The exact site of the lesion is important. Everett (1964a) has pointed out that if the lesions include the basal suprachiasmatic area and more dorsal regions, precocious sexual development is followed by regular cycles and ovulations, but that damage to the suprachiasmatic area alone causes constant estrus after the animal reaches precocious sexual maturity.

In adult rats, electrolytic anterior hypothalamic lesions cause hypertrophy of the anterior pituitary and of the uterus (Hillarp, 1949; D'Angelo, 1960; van Rees et al., 1962), while lesions made by electrocoagulation have the same effect (Schiavi, 1964). The ovaries of rats with anterior hypothalamic lesions have no corpora lutea and show persistent vaginal cornification ("constant estrus" or "persistent estrus"). Corpora lutea formation can be induced by the injection of progesterone (Greer, 1953) or by ovariectomy and transplantation of one of the ovaries to the spleen (Flerkó and Bárdos, 1961b; Desclin et al., 1962). This indicates that in spite of the lesions there is a response to either the progesterone or to a lowering of the estrogen level that allows for the release of sufficient LH for ovulation. On the other hand, if estrogen is lowered by hemiovariectomy there is no compensatory hypertrophy of the other ovary (D'Angelo and Kravatz, 1960; Flerkó and Bárdos, 1961a). However, Desclin et al. (1961) found compensatory ovarian hypertrophy after hemiovariectomy.

Exposure to cold (4° C.) of rats in persistent estrus, as a result of lesions, causes ovarian atrophy and a cessation of the vaginal cornification. This demonstrates the sensitivity of the pituitary gonadotropin activity to temperature changes as a result of the lesions (D'Angelo, 1960).

Assays for FSH activity have shown that the lesions cause a lower than normal blood FSH level but that they do not affect the amounts of FSH present in the anterior pituitary (D'Angelo and Kravatz, 1960).

On the basis of these data, Flerkó (1962) has proposed that the lesions destroy an estrogen-sensitive center that inhibits FSH secretion, causing a continuous release of FSH, which stimulates estrogen production, and sufficient LH to allow for estrogen secretion but not ovulation. An abrupt lowering of the estrogen level allows for LH secretion at levels high enough for ovulations to occur; similarly, progesterone can cause LH secretion, indicating that the centers which control LH secretion and release have been left intact. The contention that an estrogen-sensitive center controlling FSH secretion has been destroyed is further supported by a number of other observations, i.e.:

1. Lesions in the anterior hypothalamus between the optic chiasma and the paraventricular nuclei prevent the effects of estrogen administration on the ovary (decrease in weight and in number of corpora lutea) (Flerkó, 1962).

2. Such lesions prevent the effects of lowering the estrogen level by hemiovariectomy. (See point 1.)

3. Implants of pieces of ovary in this part of the hypothalamus cause a decrease in the uterine weight, indicating diminished FSH secretion (Flerkó, 1962). Everett (1964a) has pointed out that estrogen implanted in the suprachiasmatic region (where lesions will cause persistent estrus and uterine hypertrophy) do not affect the ovary of female rats or the weights of prostates and seminal vesicles of males.

4. In parabiotically joined immature rats in which one member of the pair is castrated, the ovaries and uteri of the intact member enlarge. Injection of estrogen to the spayed partner prevents this stimulation of the genital system. After lesions are made in the spayed member, estrogen does not prevent the stimulation of the genital apparatus of the intact member, although uterine weight is intermediate between weights of the estrogen and nonestrogen-treated pairs (Flerkó, 1962).

5. Testosterone causes an involution of the ovaries in spayed rats with ovaries transplanted to the spleen, but fails to do so in similar rats with anterior hypothalamic lesions (Flerkó and Ilei, 1960).

Bogdanove (1964) has proposed that the lesions per se may cause an increased FSH secretion without involvement of a steroid-sensitive feedback mechanism. Bogdanove's major points in challenging Flerkó's proposal are:

1. Physiological amounts of estrogen given to intact rats cause morphological changes in the anterior pituitary which are not prevented by hypothalamic lesions (Bogdanove 1963a).

2. Lesions do not prevent the castration-induced changes in the morphology of the anterior pituitary, nor do they prevent the effects of estrogen on the pituitary of ovariectomized rats (Bogdanove, 1963b).

3. Bogdanove (1964) found that the placing of a lesion in the anterior hypothal-

224 THE HYPOTHALAMUS

amus of immature rats can result in an increase in uterine weight. Thus, in the parabiotic rats, the lesions might have accounted for the difference between lesioned and nonlesioned estrogen-treated parabionts, so differences would not be the result of an impaired feedback mechanism.

The phenomenon of increased estrogen secretion by the ovary and lack of corpora lutea, after anterior hypothalamic lesions, has been observed in other species, e.g. the guinea pig (Dey, 1941). In the rabbit (which normally is continuously in heat and which ovulates only after coitus) lesions of the anterior hypothalamus result in cystic endometrial hyperplasia (Flerkó, 1962). In ferrets, lesions of the anterior hypothalamus during the period of anestrus cause earlier estrus (Donovan, 1960; van der Werff ten Bosch, 1963). These lesions thus are effective at a time when the amount of estrogen secreted by the ovaries is extremely small.

In cats, lesions of the suprachiasmatic nucleus do not affect the female reproductive system (Laqueur et al., 1955),

whereas similarly placed lesions in rats cause persistent vaginal cornification with a lack of corpora lutea (McCann and Taleisnik, 1960; Taleisnik and McCann, 1961; Barraclough et al., 1964), but after progesterone injection, ovulation occurs (Barraclough et al., 1964). If the lesion involves the suprachiasmatic nucleus and the periventricular portion of the medial preoptic area, persistent vaginal cornification and absence of ovulation are produced. However, no ovulations occur after progesterone administration (Barraclough et al., 1964), although ovulations occur after electric stimulation of the ventromedial-arcuate nuclear complex (Barraclough et al., 1964) (see Figure 8-4). This indicates that the suprachiasmatic-periventricular medial optic area controls the release of LH and that this area is sensitive to circulating steroid levels.

Tejasen and Everett (1966) found that the "electrochemical" stimulation of the right medial preoptic area, which normally causes ovulation in rats, did not do so in 19 out of 23 rats if a complete ipsilateral

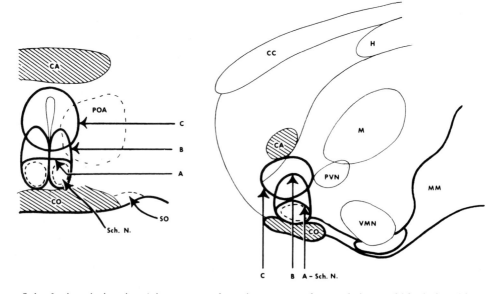

Figure 8-4. Lesions in location A in rats caused persistent estrus, but ovulation could be induced by progesterone. Lesions in location B produced persistent estrus but no ovulation was obtained after progesterone administration. Lesions in C did not cause persistent estrus and progesterone administration advanced ovulation by 24 hours. Abbreviations: *CA* = anterior commissure. *CO* = optic chiasma. *POA* = preoptic area. *CC* = corpus callosum. *Sch. N.* = suprachiasmatic nuclei. *PVN* = paraventricular nuclei. *VMN* = ventromedial nuclei. *A* = arcuate nuclei. *MM* = mamillary bodies. *H* = hippocampus. *M* = massa intermedia. (From Barraclough et al., 1964.)

transection rostral to the suprachiasmatic nucleus was made. Incomplete transections, either laterally, basally, or medially, did not interfere with ovulation. The authors concluded that a diffuse neuronal pathway exists from the preoptic area (see Figure 8-5).

Quinn and Zarrow (1965) have used a different experimental approach to localize the areas involved in LH release. Immature rats will respond to PMSG by ovulation; however, this requires the presence of the hypophysis for the release of endogenous gonadotropins. This release of endogenous gonadotropins can be prevented by lesions (made with platinum electrodes) in the medial preoptic and basal anterior hypothalamic regions. Lesions elsewhere in the hypothalamus fail to interfere with PMSG-induced ovulations of immature rats.

Lesions of the supraoptic nucleus do not affect reproduction of laying hens (Ralph, 1960), of roosters (Egge and Chiasson, 1963), or of male rats (Soulairac and Soulairac, 1956). Interruption of the supraoptic hypophyseal tract causes persistent estrus in adult rats (Kobayashi et al., 1959), but in cats causes failure to come into heat or to breed (Fisher et al., 1938).

In laying hens such lesions interrupt

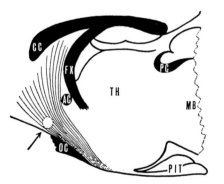

Figure 8-5. Diagram shows a postulated diffuse septal-preoptic-tuberal array of nerve fibers concerned with LH release, excitable under pentobarbital anesthesia. Opposite the end of the arrow a small lesion is indicated. *AC* = anterior commissure. *CC* = corpus callosum. *FX* = fornix. *MB* = midbrain. *OC* = optic chiasma. *PIT* = hypophysis. *PC* = posterior commissure. *TH* = thalamus. (From Everett, 1964b.)

laying (Ralph and Fraps, 1959a) and in drakes they cause testicular atrophy (Assenmacher, 1958), but in white-crowned sparrows they cause incomplete testicular regression (Wilson and Farner, 1965).

The implications of this difference in the importance of an intact supraoptic-hypophyseal connection have been discussed by Farner and Follett (1966). No definite reasons for the difference can be given because the techniques used were not identical and species differences may be important.

Electrolytic lesions in the nucleus infundibularis or in the posterior median eminence (interrupting the pathway from this nucleus to the anterior pituitary) caused testicular atrophy in white-crowned sparrows.

Farner and Follett (1966) have speculated on the possibility of two neurohemal control systems for the regulation of anterior pituitary function. There is evidence which supports this:

1. The experiments with electrolytic lesions in different parts of the hypothalamus of white-crowned sparrows.

2. The anatomical evidence, which shows that in this species the portal system contains separate anterior and posterior capillary plexuses, associated with the anterior and posterior parts of the median eminence, and which drain separately into the cephalic and caudal lobe of the adenohypophysis (Vitums et al., 1964).

It is important to recall that in pituitaries of drakes, at least the FSH cells are limited to the cephalic and the LH cells to the caudal lobe of the anterior pituitary.

Interruption of the hypothalamo-hypophyseal tract in drakes (Gogan et al., 1963) and roosters (McFarland, 1959) causes testicular regression.

Lesions of the paraventricular nucleus in laying hens interrupt egg laying (Egge and Chiasson, 1963), whereas similar lesions in immature rats cause precocious sexual development (Elwers and Critchlow, 1960; Horowitz and van der Werff ten

Bosch, 1962) and in mature rats persistent estrus (Flerkó, 1957; Bogdanove and Schoen, 1959). A temporary effect of the lesions has been reported by Flament-Durand and Desclin (1964). When a thread was placed in the uteri of rats with lesions (made by a lumbar puncture needle) in the laterodorsal part of the paraventricular nucleus four days after the operation, a strong decidual reaction was obtained; however, when the thread was introduced 11 days after the lesion, no decidual reaction was detected.

Lesions in a number of locations in the hypothalamus have interfered with reproduction in different species. Destruction of the interstitial laterodorsal hypothalamus in guinea pigs results in ovarian atrophy (Barry and Mazzucca, 1962); ventromedial nucleus lesions in cats have the same effect (Robinson and Sawyer, 1957), but in rats such lesions do not disturb the estrous cycle although they prevent mating behavior (Kennedy and Mitra, 1963). In sheep, lesions in the ventral hypothalamus just above the stalk lead to ovarian atrophy (Clegg and Ganong, 1960), as do lesions between the ventromedial nucleus and the mamillary bodies in adult rats (Soulairac and Soulairac, 1959; Corbin, 1963; and Montemurro, 1964). In immature rats, similar lesions delay puberty (Corbin and Schottelius, 1960, 1961). In rabbits (Sawyer, 1959b), cats (Robinson and Sawyer, 1957), and laying hens (Egge and Chiasson,

1963) such lesions cause ovarian regression. Destruction of the mamillary bodies of male rats leads to atrophy of the genital tract; this condition cannot be reversed by HCG injection (Soulairac and Soulairac, 1959), which is surprising, because such a restoration can be obtained in hypophysectomized but otherwise intact rats (Evans and Simpson, 1950).

Electrolytic lesions of the nucleus tuberalis of white-crowned sparrows result in testicular atrophy (Wilson and Farner, 1965). In sheep, lesions of the tuberal region lead to testicular atrophy (McFarland and Clegg, 1960).

In a series of experiments in which various connections to the medial basal hypothalamus were cut and in which different criteria for gonadotropic function were measured, Gorski and Halász (1966) obtained the results listed in Table 8-3. These data show that afferent pathways via the anterior hypothalamus are required for ovulation and that the medial basal hypothalamus may be able to respond to decreased steroid levels. However, for a complete response an afferent input is required. The anterior hypothalamic connections are not required in order for compensatory hypertrophy to occur.

Lesions of the arcuate nucleus in the posterior hypothalamus in adult rats cause persistent estrus without formation of corpora lutea. After HCG or LH injections corpora lutea form (van Dyke et al., 1957), whereas in immature rats such lesions lead

Table 8-3. The Effects of Interruption of Connections to the Medial Basal Hypothalamus on Gonadotropic Function of the Anterior Pituitary

PATHWAYS CUT	SPONTANEOUS OVULATION	COMPENSATORY OVARIAN HYPERTROPHY	AP LH AFTER ♀	PLASMA LH AFTER ♀
Dorsal and Lateral Posterior	Normal	Occurred	Increased	Increased
Anterior	None	Occurred	Increased	Increased
Dorsal and Lateral Posterior and Anterior	None	Failed to occur	Increased slightly	Increased slightly

♀ = gonadectomy (female).
Reference: Gorski and Halász (1966).

to precocious sexual maturity with normal subsequent cycles (Bogdanove and Schoen, 1959; Krejci and Critchlow, 1959; Gellert and Ganong, 1960). In mature male rats such lesions have had varied effects: Soulairac and Soulairac (1956) and D'Angelo (1960) have reported testicular atrophy, whereas Halász (1962) found no effect. The lesions made by D'Angelo include, however, the arcuate nucleus and the median eminence. Lesions of the arcuate nucleus and the base of the ventromedial nucleus in estrogen primed rabbits initiated lactation, suggesting prolactin secretion was induced by the lesions (Haun and Sawyer, 1961).

Lesions of the median eminence generally disturb reproductive performance, e.g. in ducks the testes regress (Gogan et al., 1963), and in ducks and in white-crowned sparrows the photoperiodic response of the testes is abolished (Gogan et al., 1963; Farner and Follett, 1966). In rats, ova fail to implant (Gale and McCann, 1961), permanent diestrus is induced (McCann and Friedman, 1960; McCann and Taleisnik, 1960), follicles fail to develop but corpora lutea persist, and no rise in plasma LH or pituitary LH levels is found after ovariectomy (Taleisnik and McCann, 1961). In cats, follicles regress (Laqueur et al., 1955), in guinea pigs, ovaries and uteri regress (Dey, 1941), and in rabbits, ovulation fails to occur despite normal mating (Sawyer, 1959a,b). Ovarian regression has been reported by Flerkó (1962). In sheep, no heat occurs and no corpora lutea form, although uterine histology is cyclic (Clegg et al., 1958); in dogs, testes regress and the pituitary FSH and LH are depressed (Davidson et al, 1960; Daily and Ganong, 1958); in goats, milk secretion is diminished (Gale, 1963, 1964). In rats, milk secretion occurs after median eminence lesions (de Voe et al, 1966), as it does in estrogen treated rabbits with such lesions (Haun and Sawyer, 1960; and Kanematsu et al., 1963).

Median eminence lesions often interrupt the vascular link between the hypothalamus and the anterior pituitary gland, and effects can then be expected to be quite similar to those observed after stalk transection or pituitary transplantation, for example, lactation and maintenance of corpora lutea. Prolactin secretion, as we have seen, is increased after severance of the hypothalamo-hypophyseal connections, thus indicating an inhibitory effect of the hypothalamus on prolactin secretion. Averill (1965) has, however, reported that lesions lateral to the paraventricular nucleus inhibit lactation but that this can be partially overcome by prolactin injections. Once lactation is established, no further prolactin injections are required for its continuance. These results are puzzling and require further studies on the effect of these lesions on the secretions of other pituitary hormones.

In males, precocious sexual maturity is difficult to induce by hypothalamic lesions. Donovan and van der Werff ten Bosch (1965) present data which show that anterior hypothalamic lesions in immature male rats do not cause sexual precocity, whereas similar lesions in female littermates cause precocious puberty. Bogdanove (1964) had tried to account for this on the basis of a low sensitivity of the whole reproductive system to gonadotropins. However, in a preliminary report, Bar Sela (1964) has stated that hypertrophy of the prostate and seminal vesicles occurred after anterior hypothalamic lesions. This may indicate that an androgen-sensitive center that regulates LH secretion was destroyed. In adult male rats, lesions in the periventricular area, which is part of the anterior hypothalamus, caused hypertrophy of seminal vesicles and the prostate without changing the FSH and LH content of the anterior pituitary in one experiment, but decreased LH content in two other ones. The lesion had no effect on the castration-induced rise in plasma and pituitary LH content (Bogdanove et al., 1964). The increase in prostate weight suggests that LH secretion and release are increased (The weight of

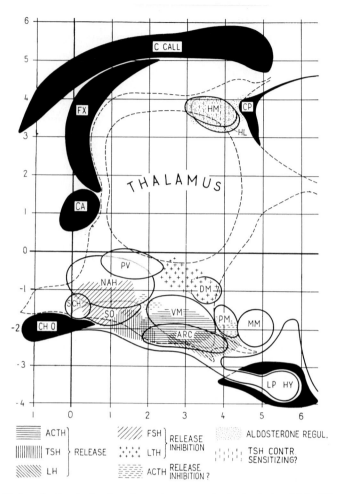

Figure 8-6. Midsagittal projection indicating the various areas in the brain in which different functions of the pituitary are controlled. (From Szentágothai et al., 1962.)

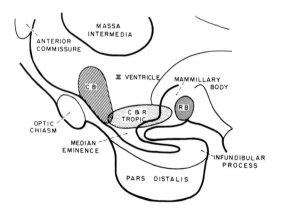

Figure 8-7. Localization of gonadotropic and sex behavioral areas in the hypothalamus of the female cat and rabbit. *C & R tropic* is the common area controlling release of pituitary ovulation-inducing hormone in the cat and rabbit. *CR* and *RB* are areas in which lesions induce permanent anestrus in the cat and rabbit, respectively. (From Sawyer and Kawakami, 1961.)

this organ is dependent upon androgen secretion, which, in turn, is dependent upon LH levels. Ventral prostate weights have been used as assays for LH).

Figure 8-6 illustrates the location of the hypothalamic centers involved in the release of gonadotropins and other hormones from the pituitary. The localizations are based on lesion experiments and also on electrical stimulations (which will be discussed later). This illustration is based on experiments carried out in one laboratory using the rat. The difference between two induced ovulators, i.e. the cat and the rabbit, with respect to the centers involved in sexual behavior is illustrated in Figure 8-7.

SEX STEROIDS ADMINISTERED INTO THE HYPOTHALAMO-HYPOPHYSEAL SYSTEM

The effects of estrogen administration to the hypothalamo-hypophyseal system on the secretion and release of gonadotropic hormones were given in Table 6-5. The influence of sex steroids injected or implanted into the hypothalamo-hypophyseal system on reproduction in birds and mammals has been summarized in Table 8-4. For an

illustration of the sites at which estradiol causes lordosis and ovarian atrophy, see Figure 8-8.

In each of these experiments, adequate controls were used to rule out the effects of implants or injections per se. The data are obtained from too few species to allow for comparative generalizations. Even general conclusions are controversial, e.g. Flerkó (1962) and Bogdanove (1964). With the reservation made that more extensive data may prove them wrong, it seems permissible to draw these conclusions:

1. Testosterone and estrogen implants can cause the same behavioral effect in rabbits after implantation of the steroids in the same areas.

2. The effects exerted by the sex steroids are quite localized if small amounts are administered.

3. There are considerable species differences with respect to the effect observed from implants in different loci, e.g. comparisons between rabbits and rats show that estradiol implants in the mamillary body of the rabbit result in failure to mate, but ovulation can take place after Cu salt injections, whereas in rats an apparently complete blockade of gonadotropin secretion occurs, as is evident from the ovarian atrophy and the lack of com-

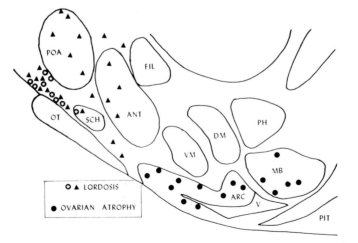

Figure 8-8. Midsagittal diagram of rat hypothalamus, showing sites at which estradiol implants promoted ovarian atrophy or behavioral estrus, as evidenced by lordosis. Lordosis response to 27-gauge implants is shown by black triangles and to 30-gauge implants by open stars. (From Lisk, 1962a.)

Table 8-4. Effects of Sex Steroid Administration into the Hypothalamo-hypophyseal System on Reproductive Organs of Vertebrates

SITE OF ADMINISTRATION	INJECTION OR IMPLANT	STEROID	SEX	SPECIES	EFFECTS	REFERENCE
Median eminence	Implant	Testosterone propionate	♂	Dog	Aspermia, atrophy of testes and seminal vesicles	Davidson and Sawyer, 1961a
	Implant	Estradiol benzoate	♀	Rabbit	Ovarian atrophy; failure to ovulate	Davidson and Sawyer, 1961b
	Implant	Estradiol benzoate	♀	Rabbit	Ovarian and uterine atrophy; LH content of AP lowered. Increase in prolactin content of AP. No mammary gland development	Kanematsu and Sawyer, 1963a,b
	Implant	Estradiol benzoate	⚥	Rabbit	Prevented hypertrophy of AF negative basophils; decreased number of AF negative basophils	Kanematsu and Sawyer, 1963c
	Implant	Estradiol benzoate	⚥	Rabbit	Decrease in AP weight; decrease in plasma LH and AP content of LH	Kanematsu and Sawyer, 1964
	Implant	Estradiol benzoate	⚥	Rabbit	Behavioral estrus, not reversible by progesterone treatment	Palka and Sawyer, 1964
	Implant	Norethindrone	♀	Rabbit	Blocked ovulation; no effect on LH content of AP; failed to mate unless estrogen treated; ovaries and uteri normal	Kanematsu and Sawyer, 1965
	Implant	17-OH-progesterone-caproate	♀	Rabbit	Anestrus, not reversed by estrogen; ovulated in response to Cu salt injections	Sawyer, 1966
	Implant	Testosterone	♂	Rat	Reduced ventral prostate weight, decreased LH content, decreased LHRF in median eminence	Chowers and McCann, 1965
	Implant	Testosterone	♂	Rat	Testes, seminal vesicle, and prostate atrophy	Lisk, 1962b
	Implant	Testosterone	♀	Rat	Ovarian atrophy	Lisk, 1962b
	Implant	Estradiol	♀	Rat	Diestrus, mammary glands develop	Ramirez et al., 1964a
	Implant	Estradiol	♀	Rat	Increased plasma LH 4–5 days after implant; after 18 days no plasma LH detectable; mammary glands develop, large CL, diestrous smears	Palka et al., 1966
	Implant	Estradiol	♀	Rat	Diestrus, no change in uterine weight, increase in AP weight, effect on LH in AP variable; decrease in LHRF	Chowers and McCann, 1965
"Above the anterior pituitary"	Injection	Dienestrol diacetate	♂	Chicken	Regression of testis and comb	Hohlweg and Daume, 1959a
Anterior hypothalamus	Injection	Dienestrol diacetate	♂	Rat	Regression of testis; decrease of gonadotropin content of AP	Hohlweg and Daume, 1959b
Arcuate nucleus	Implant	Estradiol	♀	Rat	Atrophy of reproductive tract	Lisk, 1960, 1964
	Implant	Estradiol	♀	Rat	Increase in size of AP	Lisk, 1965
	Implant	Estradiol	♂	Rat	Atrophy of reproductive tract	Lisk, 1960, 1964
	Implant	Estradiol	♂	Rat	Increase in size of AP	Lisk, 1965
	Implant	Estradiol	⚥	Rat	Decrease of gonadotropin cells in AP	Lisk, 1965
	Implant	Testosterone	♀	Rat	Labor prolonged, death of fetuses, no effect on cycle or conception	Lisk, 1965
	Implant	Progesterone	♀	Rat	Same effect as testosterone	Lisk, 1965
Mamillary region	Implant	Estradiol benzoate	⚥	Rabbit	Estrous behavior, not reversed by progesterone	Palka and Sawyer, 1965

* Versene injection had the same effect as Na testosterone sulfate.

♂ = intact male; ♀ = intact female; ⚥ = gonadectomized female; ♂ = gonadectomized male; CL = corpus luteum; AP = anterior pituitary; LH = Luteinizing hormone; LHRF = Luteinizing hormone releasing factor; AF = aldehyde-fuchsin.

Table 8-4.   Effects of Sex Steroid Administration into the Hypothalamo-hypophyseal System on Reproductive Organs of Vertebrates (Cont.)

SITE OF ADMINISTRATION	INJECTION OR IMPLANT	STEROID	SEX	SPECIES	EFFECTS	REFERENCE
	Implant	Testosterone propionate	♀	Rabbit	Estrous behavior	Palka and Sawyer, 1966
	Implant	Norethindrone	♀	Rabbit	Failed to mate in spite of estrogen injections; ovulated after Cu salt injections	Kanematsu and Sawyer, 1965
	Implant	Estradiol	♀	Rat	No effect on castration cells	Lisk, 1963
	Implant	Estradiol	♀	Rat	Atrophy of reproductive system; AP enlarged	Lisk, 1965
	Implant	Stilbestrol butyrate	♂	Cat	Normal mating behavior; genital tract atrophied	Harris and Michael, 1964; Michael, 1965
	Implant	Testosterone	♀	Rat	No effect on cycles or conception	Lisk, 1965
	Implant	b Estradiol	♀	Rat	No compensatory hypertrophy after unilateral ovariectomy	Littlejohn and de Groot, 1963
Midlateral preoptic region	Injection	Na Testosterone sulfate	♂	Rat	Male behavior	Fisher, 1966
	Injection	Na Testosterone sulfate	♀	Rat	Male behavior	Fisher, 1966
Medial preoptic	Implant	Estradiol	♀	Rat	Lordosis reflex obtained	Lisk, 1962a
	Implant	Estradiol + progesterone	♀	Rat	Mating behavior with shorter latency than after estradiol alone	Lisk, 1966b
	Implant	Estradiol + progesterone	♀	Rat	No effect on cycles or conception	Lisk, 1964
	Injection	Na Testosterone SO₄*	♂	Rat	Maternal behavior	Fisher, 1966
	Injection	Na Testosterone SO₄*	♀	Rat	Maternal behavior	Fisher, 1966
	Implant	Testosterone propionate	♂	Rat	Complete male sexual behavior	Davidson, 1966
Preoptic area	Implant	Testosterone	(?)	Chicken	Male sexual behavior	Fisher, 1966
	Implant	Estradiol	♀	Rat	Lordosis reflex obtained	Lisk, 1965
	Implant	b Estradiol	♀	Rat	No effect on compensatory hypertrophy after hemiovariectomy	Littlejohn and de Groot, 1963
	Injection	Progesterone	♀	Chicken	Premature ovulation	Ralph and Fraps, 1960
Anterior pituitary	Implant	Testosterone propionate	♂	Dog	Semen quality decreased	Davidson and Sawyer, 1961a
	Implant	Estradiol benzoate	♀	Rabbit	Mammary gland developed, no effect on AP, uterine or ovarian weight; small decrease in prolactin content of AP	Kanematsu and Sawyer, 1963a,b
	Implant	Estradiol benzoate	♀	Rabbit	No effect on ovary or ovulation	Davidson and Sawyer, 1961b
	Implant	Estradiol benzoate	♀	Rabbit	Small decrease in AF negative basophils	Kanematsu and Sawyer, 1963c
	Implant	Estradiol	♀	Rabbit	Decrease in LH content of AP; increase in AP weight	Ramirez et al., 1964
	Implant	Estradiol	♀	Rabbit	Small decrease in LH content of AP; increase in plasma LH	Kanematsu and Sawyer, 1964
	Implant	Norethindrone	♀	Rabbit	No effect on behavior or ovulation	Kanematsu and Sawyer, 1965
	Implant	Testosterone	♂	Rat	No effect on testes, seminal vesicles or prostate	Lisk, 1962b

Table 8-4. Effects of Sex Steroid Administration into the Hypothalamo-hypophyseal System on Reproductive Organs of Vertebrates (Cont.)

SITE OF ADMINISTRATION	INJECTION OR IMPLANT	STEROID	SEX	SPECIES	EFFECTS	REFERENCE
	Implant	Testosterone	♂	Rat	No effect on ventral prostate or pituitary weight or LH content of AP	Chowers and McCann, 1965
	Implant	Testosterone	♀	Rat	No effect on ovary	Lisk, 1962b
	Implant	Estradiol	♀	Rat	No effect on plasma LH; ipsilateral hypertrophy of AP; mammary glands developed; large CL; diestrus	Palka et al., 1966
	Implant	Estradiol	♀	Rat	No effect on uterus; AP enlarged; effect on LH in AP variable low. Rise in LHRF content of median eminence; rats in diestrus	Chowers and McCann, 1965
	Implant	Estradiol	♀	Rat	Around tip of cannula decrease of growth cells	Lisk, 1963
	Implant	Estradiol	♀	Rat	No effect on castration cells	Bogdanove, 1963a

pensatory ovarian hypertrophy after removal of one ovary.

Estrogen implants in the median eminence of rabbits (see Figure 8-9) inhibit the synthesis and release of LH and stimulate the synthesis of prolactin but not its release (no mammary gland development); in rats, however, these implants cause the synthesis and release of LH and prolactin (Ramirez and McCann, 1964). On the other hand, estrogen implanted into the pituitary of rabbits causes the synthesis of LH and release of LH and prolactin (Kanematsu and Sawyer, 1963b), but in rats it does not cause LH release but only prolactin secretion (mammary

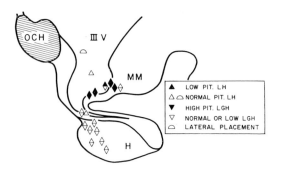

Figure 8-9. Location of effects of estrogen implant upon luteinizing hormone (LH) and prolactin (LGH) content of the pituitary in the brain of a rabbit. Low pituitary LH content is associated with an elevated prolactin content in these experiments. (From Kanematsu and Sawyer, 1963a.)

glands develop) (Ramirez and McCann, 1964). The reader is referred to Table 6-5 for quantitative data on the effects of estrogen on LH in the anterior pituitary and the blood.

One can suggest some tentative "explanations" for the species differences if one assumes that the effects of estrogen in the case of gonadotropin secretion are exerted via the hypothalamus. Accepting such an assumption, one can see that it is an advantage for rabbits to have estrogen inhibit the synthesis and release of LH and prolactin release because the animal is continuously in estrus. Estrogen would thus prevent the synthesis of a protein which would not be needed continuously and, at the same time, prevent it from trickling away. Similarly, the release of prolactin in the rabbit is inhibited to prevent mammary development while the animal is not lactating. At the proper stimulus (coitus) LH is released and, as we saw in a previous chapter, a positive feedback between the pituitary gland and the ovary is established (20-α-hydroxy-pregn-4-en-3-one is secreted after coitus and stimulates LH secretion). Whether this induction of progestin or other ovarian secretions also stimulates the secretion and release of prolactin remains to be investigated.

In the rat, on the other hand, ovulation occurs during each estrous cycle. The stimulation of LH synthesis and its release by estrogen would build the LH level high enough to induce ovulation while estrogens synchronize ovulation so that it occurs when the follicle is ovulable. The release of prolactin during the cycle may prepare the corpora lutea, which normally have a very short functional life, for the subsequent stimulation by the prolactin secreted in response to mating.

4. In the rat, the structures of the anterior hypothalamus, at which estrogen will cause estrous behavior, are separate from those (arcuate nucleus and mamillary body) at which estrogen will inhibit gonadotropin secretion. Reichlin, in a discussion of Lisk's paper (1966a), pointed out that there is an apparent difference between the hormone requirement of the spayed rat when the hormones are given intracerebrally and when they are administered by other routes. Estrogen implanted into the hypothalamus can cause estrous behavior, whereas this behavior can be obtained after subcutaneous injection only if estrogen *and* progesterone are given.

In subsequent experiments, Lisk (1966b) has shown that the latency between implantation and female estrous behavior is considerably shorter after estrogen plus progesterone implants than after estrogen implants alone. Nevertheless, the fact remains that estrogen, injected subcutaneously, cannot induce estrous behavior, but placed in the hypothalamus, it can.

The ovariectomized cat will show estrous behavior after subcutaneous estrogen injection and apparently does not require progesterone for sexual behavior. It is of interest that the cat (Michael, 1965) and the rat (Attramadal, 1964) both show selective accumulation of estrogen in the hypothalamus; use was made of labeled estrogens to establish this fact. On the other hand, ovariectomized sheep, which require administration of estrogen and progesterone for the induction of estrous be-

havior, apparently do not selectively accumulate estrogen in the brain (Robinson, 1965), although they do accumulate it in the anterior pituitary, as do rats and cats. It might be of interest to determine to what extent progesterone enhances the accumulation of estrogens in the critical areas of the hypothalamus.

GONADOTROPINS IMPLANTED IN THE HYPOTHALAMO-HYPOPHYSEAL SYSTEM

The implantation of small amounts of LH in the median eminence results in a decrease in the LH content of the anterior pituitary (Corbin and Cohen, 1966; Dávid et al., 1966). Implants of ACTH or FSH in the median eminence, LH implants in the amygdala (Corbin and Cohen, 1966) or in the anterior pituitary (Dávid *et al.*, 1966) lack this effect. There was no effect on the concentration of plasma LH after LH implants were made in the median eminence (Corbin, 1966). These results suggest a direct feedback of LH on the hypothalamus-regulating pituitary secretion. An anatomical basis for such a feedback is found in the small venous system that passes from the posterior surface of the anterior lobe of the pituitary to the capillary network of the median eminence (see Figure 8.2).

ELECTRIC STIMULATION OF THE HYPOTHALAMO-HYPOPHYSEAL SYSTEM

A convenient measure of the release of LH is to measure whether ovulation has occurred. In induced ovulators, it is easy to detect whether the stimulus caused ovulation, because in control animals there is a very low incidence of spontaneous ovulations. In spontaneous ovulators, one can use different preparations to evaluate whether a particular stimulus causes ovulation. In chickens, a very regular sequence of ovulation and oviposition occurs which makes it possible to predict when the next ovulation will occur with a fair degree of accuracy. It has been established that six to eight hours elapse between the intravenous injection of either LH or progesterone (to cause release of endogenous LH from the hen's own anterior pituitary) and ovulation (Fraps, 1955). One can thus estimate when the hen releases LH for a "spontaneous" ovulation. One can attempt to induce premature ovulation by stimulation a number of hours before this "spontaneous" LH release occurs. An experienced person can verify the occurrence of the premature or of the normal ovulation by digital palpation via the cloaca. In crucial experiments, the animal can either be laparotomized or killed to verify the correctness of the judgment based on palpation. The evaluation of the palpation is based on the known time intervals between ovulation and the presence of the egg in different parts of the oviduct. The advantage of the use of the chicken for this type of experimentation, or for any other type in which electrodes or cannulas have to be placed in the brain, is that the animal does not have to be killed, and one can do several experiments with the same animal, each time with the knowledge that the electrode is in the same place. This has certain statistical advantages because each animal can serve as its own control and thus one eliminates, to a large extent, variation among animals. Care should, of course, be taken that the sequence of treatments to which the animal is to be exposed is a random one.

In spontaneous ovulators, one can attempt to provoke premature ovulation by treating the animal far enough in advance of the expected time of ovulation, but one has to be sure that the follicles present can indeed respond to ovulation-inducing hormone at that time. It is, therefore, prudent to include a "positive" control group which is injected with physiological doses of LH at a time corresponding to the time the experimental animals are stimulated electrically. For such experiments it is highly desirable to use animals with a sufficiently long estrous cycle or animals in which ovulation occurs during a very limited part of the day, otherwise time differences may become so small that one needs a very large number of animals in each treatment to show that differences between controls and stimulated animals are statistically significant. It is worth mentioning that in horses and cattle one can verify the occurrence of ovulation by palpation, so the animals need not be killed.

For the study of the effects of electrical stimulation on the ovulation of rats or other mammals with short estrous cycles, special preparations need to be used. Stimulation can take place during diestrus so that any induced ovulation is well in advance of any spontaneous ovulation that might occur, or one can use rats which do not ovulate spontaneously, such as pregnant or pseudopregnant rats, persistent estrous rats (the persistent estrous can be induced by exposure to continuous illumination by treatment with androgen or estrogen during the first five days after birth, or by hypothalamic lesions). Of course, the lesions may interfere with any ovulation-inducing effect that the electrical stimulation might have in intact rats. Rats in which ovulation has been blocked by pharmacological agents such as atropine, Nembutal, or others (Everett 1964a) which will be discussed later in this chapter can also be used.

Under laboratory conditions in which artificial lights are on from 5 a.m. to 7 p.m., the blocking drug has to be effective between 2 and 4 p.m. the day of proestrus, for this is the time period during which the stimulus for LH release and LH release for ovulation occur (Everett, 1964a).

In evaluating the effects of electrical stimulation, a distinction should be made between stimulations made with the aid of iron-containing electrodes which may cause the deposition of iron deposits (Everett and Radford, 1961) and those made with platinum electrodes in which the stimulation is due to the electrical current per se.

Amphibia: In *Rana esculenta,* electric stimulation of the nucleus preopticus (NPO) resulted in spermiation in 15 out of 32 cases when the inferior part was stimulated, and spermiation in 32 out of 45 cases when the superior part was stimulated (Stutinsky and Befort, 1964). Spermiation was induced after stimulation of the superior part of the NPO even after hypophysectomy, demonstrating that the effect was not dependent on the release of LH. Subsequent investigations showed that this stimulation caused release of epinephrine, which causes spermiation. On the other hand, stimulation of the infundibulum resulted in spermiation only if the anterior pituitary was left intact, suggesting that in this case LH was released.

Birds: Electrical stimulation of the median eminence of laying chickens with the aid of stainless steel electrodes or stimulation of the preoptic hypothalamus with such or platinum electrodes resulted in delayed ovulation (Opel and Fraps, 1961; Opel, 1963). However, insertion of the electrodes into the preoptic hypothalamus without passing a current also delays ovulation, so apparently it is damage to this area that causes the delay in ovulation. One could study the effect of electrical stimulation dissociated from the introduction of the electrode by using permanent electrodes.

As we have seen, destruction of part of the hypothalamus in toads causes a release of ovulation-inducing hormone, whereas in hens a much smaller area of damage can cause a delay in ovulation. In subsequent experiments, Opel (1964) has found that the insertion of an electrode into almost any part of the brain (hyperstriatum, neostriatum, median thalamus, hypothalamus) causes premature oviposition if the insertion occurs during the period between 10 a.m. and noon. He speculates that these premature

ovipositions may be the result of LH release in quantities sufficient to cause oviposition but insufficient to cause ovulation.

Mammals: A large number of studies on the effect of electric stimulation of the brain of "induced ovulators" has been carried out with rabbits and cats. Reviews by Everett (1964a), Harris and Campbell (1966), and Sawyer (1964) provide extensive documentation so that here we will summarize only the major results.

In rabbits, stimulation of the medial preoptic area, the tuberal hypothalamus, the arcuate nucleus, or the mamillary region of the hypothalamus has resulted in ovulation. In cats, stimulation of the area from the ventromedial nuclei to the mamillary bodies leads to ovulation. An inhibitory effect is obtained by stimulation of the lateral hypothalamus, for stimulation of this region inhibits the ovulation normally induced after stimulation of the ventromedial nuclei.

In rats in which spontaneous ovulation has been blocked with pentobarbital, ovulation can be induced by stimulation via stainless steel bilaterally placed concentric electrodes in the median eminence. Everett and Radford (1961) showed that deposition of iron in the suprachiasmatic area, the medial preoptic area, the anterior hypothalamic area, and the septal area causes ovulation in rats with pharmacologically blocked spontaneous ovulations. Electric stimulation via platinum electrodes does not cause ovulations. However, when such electrodes are placed bilaterally, 2 mm. apart, across the medial preoptic areas of the brain and with stimuli of 1 m. amp. in biphasic pulse pairs of 1 m./second duration at frequencies of 30 c./s. in 30 second trains, at 30 second intervals for 60 minutes, nine to 12 ovulations occurred. When the stimulations lasted a shorter time, the number of ova ovulated decreased. The stimulation had to last more than ten minutes in order to obtain ovulations (Everett, 1965).

In a beautiful study, Everett (1964b), using a 10 μA D.C. and varying only the duration of the stimulation, established that the amount of electricity required by the diestrous, barbiturate-treated rat for ovulation is about twice as high as the amount required by a similarly treated proestrous rat. In a subsequent study, rats were stimulated with a train of 150 μA monophasic, positive, rectangular pulses of 1 msec. duration, administered at a frequency of 100 c./s. during diestrus and before the critical period of the day of proestrus (during this critical period the stimulus for the release of LH occurs). Hypophysectomies were carried out at different intervals after stimulation and the number of ovulations was ascertained. The diestrous rats required over 60 minutes to release sufficient LH for ovulation, whereas proestrous rats required 40 minutes. Further experimentation (Everett, 1964c) showed that the requirement for exogenous LH of diestrous barbiturate-treated rats during the critical period was about 30 percent higher than that of proestrous rats. It thus appears that as the stimulation becomes stronger, more LH-Releasing Factor (LH-RF) can be brought into action and a greater amount of LH can be released.

The lack of cyclic release of LH from male pituitaries has been discussed in Chapter 5. Electrical ("electrolytic") stimulation of the medial preoptic area at 10 μA D.C. for 20 seconds via bipolar concentric stainless steel electrodes will induce luteinization (some corpora lutea had entrapped ova) in 50 percent of ovaries transplanted to the kidney capsule of male rats, castrated when 30 days old. When the stimulation is longer, a higher proportion of ovaries will show corpora lutea (Quinn, 1966). Moll and Zeilmaker (1966), using monopolar, bilateral electrodes and using a current of 1.5 μA for ten seconds, found that corpora lutea were formed in the transplanted ovary when the electrodes were in the median eminence or in the preoptic area of castrated male rats. Progesterone given until

the day preceding stimulation prevented the ovulation-inducing effect of the stimulation.

Rats brought into persistent estrus by neonatal androgen treatment will ovulate in response to electrical stimulation (80-100 μA, 100 c./s., 0.5 msec., 15 seconds off, 15 seconds on for 15 minutes) of the hypothalamic regions, rostral or caudal to the arcuate and ventromedial nuclei, provided the animals have been pretreated with progesterone (to increase the LH content of the anterior pituitary gland). Stimulation of the medial or lateral preoptic region of such rats failed to induce ovulation (Barraclough and Gorski, 1961; and Barraclough, 1966b). These experiments have allowed an interpretation for the manner in which androgen causes the sterility syndrome which was discussed in Chapter 5. Figure 8-10 illustrates the interpretation suggested by Barraclough (1966b). Kordon (1964), using similar androgen-treated, persistent estrous female rats, treated with progesterone when adult, stimulated the area from the posterior end of the ventromedial nucleus to the anterior border of the mamillary bodies with rectangular 50-100 μA pulses, 100 c./s., 0.3 msec. for 15 minutes and found no ovulations, but the ovaries showed a weight increase of 32 to 46 percent, mostly as a result of follicular growth. Kordon found no evidence of ovulations but stated that in his preparation LH release may have been blocked as a result of techniques differing from those used by Barraclough and Gorski (1961).

Noumura (1957) joined intact female rats with castrated males or spayed females by parabiosis, causing persistent estrus in the intact rats; the follicles were large but no corpora lutea were present. After electric stimulation to the head of the gonadectomized partner, luteinization took place, and when the stimulation was repeated daily over a long time period the corpora lutea resembled those of pregnancy. A similar stimulus to the intact female parabiont was markedly less effective. This investigation, of course, does not

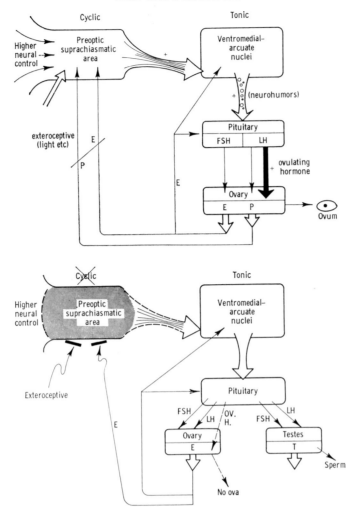

Figure 8-10. *Upper diagram:* Diagrammatic representation of events, which may occur at the hypothalamic, pituitary, and gonadal levels to result in steroid secretion and ovulation. When proper estrogen *(E)* and progesterone *(P)* ratios are reached, the preoptic area becomes responsive to exteroceptive and interoceptive influences, is activated, and in turn activates the ventromedial-arcuate area. Sufficient LH-releasing factor is released to cause discharge of ovulating hormone and ovulation occurs.

Lower diagram: Hypothalamic events, which occur after neonatal androgen treatment of female rats or which occur in rats in which the anterior preoptic area is destroyed. There is no cyclic control for ovulatory discharge of gonadotropins and only tonic hypothalamic influences on the pituitary function can be manifested. Sufficient FSH and LH are released to cause follicular development and estrogen secretion but ovulation fails to occur and the persistent estrus syndrome ensues. In the male the release of FSH and LH is adequate for spermatogenesis and androgen production. *OV. H.* = ovulating hormone. *T* = testosterone. (From Barraclough, 1966b.)

allow for any localization of effect within the brain. The experiment suggests, however, that stimulation of the head can cause LH release (CL formed) and prolactin secretion (CL of pregnancy).

Everett and Quinn (1966) have investigated the effect of "electrolytic" and of "electric" stimulation of various parts of the rat's hypothalamus on LH release (ovulation) and on prolactin secretion (maintenance of corpora lutea). Electrolytic stimulation of the medial preoptic area of pentobarbital-blocked rats during proestrus consistently caused ovulations, but only eight out of 38 rats became pseudopregnant. On the other hand, pseudopregnancy was invoked after "electrical" stimulation of an area that ranged from the anterior hypothalamic area and the paraventricular nuclei to the premamillary complex and which included the dorso-medial nuclei dorsally. These data strongly suggest that two separate regions of the hypothalamus are concerned with the release and/or secretion of LH and prolactin. The stimuli which cause prolactin secretion release an inhibitory factor which normally holds prolactin secretion in check.

The several lines of experimental evidence discussed so far support the concept of the hypothalamic control of pituitary function as discussed in the beginning of this chapter. One of the phenomena which gave considerable support to this concept was the observation that in certain species (particularly drakes and white-crowned sparrows) there existed a correlation between the reproductive state (mostly males were investigated) and the histology and histochemistry of the hypothalamus.

CORRELATIONS BETWEEN HISTOLOGY, HISTOCHEMISTRY, AND BIOCHEMISTRY OF THE HYPOTHALAMUS AND REPRODUCTION

The discussion of these relationships is restricted because it does not take into account the secretion of neurosecretory material and its transport to the pars nervosa, nor does it do justice to the relationship between hypothalamus and pars nervosa in response to dehydration or to "stress". For critical discussions on these aspects, the reader should consult the recent books by Gabe (1966), Harris and Donovan (1966), Scharrer and Scharrer (1963) and Symposia of Zoological Society of London (1963). Scharrer and Scharrer have published a beautifully illustrated paper with an excellent discussion (1954b).

The neurosecretory cells can be recognized by staining the neurosecretory granules with stains such as chromalum hematoxylin, paraldehyde fuchsin, or pseudoisocyanin (Bargman, 1966; Gabe, 1966) and alcian blue at a pH of 2. After oxidation with performic acid, according to some, this stain reaction is indicative of SH or SS groups (Green, 1966b), but according to Gabe (1966) this conclusion should be treated with reservation. The stain is, however, excellent for identifying NSM. Green (1966b) and Sloper (1966) give excellent discussions on the question whether the NSM is produced in the perikaryon of the cell and transported to the pars nervosa by "axoplasmic flow" or whether the NSM is synthesized along the entire nerve cell. A definite answer to these questions cannot be given. For the concept of neurohumoral control of the anterior pituitary the answer is, however, not a crucial one.

The hypothesis that material produced in the hypothalamus could affect the function of the anterior pituitary gland, specifically, the secretion and release of gonadotropins, has found considerable support from the evidence obtained with photoperiodic birds. In this review it is difficult to do justice, individually, to the admirable reports by Benoit and his colleagues and Farner and his associates. Limitations of space necessitate a condensation of their evidence.

Neurosecretory material can be demonstrated in the layer of contact of the median eminence and the portal capillaries (Farner and Oksche, 1962).

In *Z. leucophrys gambellii*, neurosecretory fiber bundles from the supraoptico hypophyseal tract penetrate into the anterior median eminence in greater numbers than into the posterior portion. These fiber bundles enter a plexus beneath the supraoptico hypophyseal tract. This plexus also contains fibers from the tubero-hypophyseal tract. In the anterior part of the median eminence, delicate radial fibers, stainable with aldehyde fuchsin, end in the outermost layer of the median eminence, the *stratum glandulare,* and can be traced to the walls of the capillaries; the neurosecretory material lies adjacent to the walls of these vessels (Farner and

Oksche, 1962). The looping fibers illustrated in Figure 8-1 are not found in the anterior part of the median eminence, but there are looping aldehyde fuchsin negative fibers of the tubero-hypophyseal tract in the posterior portion of the median eminence, where neurosecretory material is not as dominant as in the anterior portion.

Drakes and white-crowned sparrows show a spectacular increase in testicular weight if the animals are exposed to 14 to 20 hours of illumination per day, provided the animals are not in the so-called refractory period, which may last for several months after the testes have regressed. During this refractory period (to be discussed in more detail in Chapter 13) no response is obtained (Laws, 1961). Benoit and Assenmacher (1955, 1959) and Farner and Oksche (1962) noted that the activity of the neurosecretory cells (as assessed by size of the nuclei and nucleoli) was increased after exposure of their experimental animals to long photoperiods, whereas in birds kept on eight hours of illumination this increase did not occur. The neurosecretory material that was present in large amounts in the median eminence of birds exposed to eight hours of light per day disappeared after exposure to 20 hours of light per day. These changes could be correlated with the increase in testicular size. Subsequent investigations showed that photostimulation led to increased acid phosphatase activity in the NSO and median eminence, and to an increase in catheptic proteinase activity of the median eminence. The acid phosphatase activity may be an indicator of cellular activity; the catheptic proteinase activity probably reflects an increased rate of protein breakdown, which seems correlated with the disappearance of the neurosecretory material (Farner et al., 1964). Such changes do not occur in white-crowned sparrows exposed to long photoperiods during the refractory period (Farner et al., 1964). In other words, there is a correlation between

the observed lack of changes in the hypothalamus and the lack of a testicular response.

It has to be emphasized that photostimulation does not cause any definite changes in the neural lobe of the hypophysis, whereas dehydration or osmotic stress cause a depletion of neurosecretory material and an increase in acid phosphatase activity. No detectable changes occur in the median eminence. Dehydration or osmotic stress cause an increase in the activity of the neurosecretory cells of the NSO and in the acid phosphatase activity of these cells (Farner et al., 1964). These correlations have generally been confirmed for two other photosensitive species, the white-throated sparrow, *Zonotrichia albicollis* (Wolfson and Kobayashi, 1962) and the Japanese silver-eye, *Zosterops palpebrosa japonica*, (Uemura and Kobayashi, 1963). Rossbach (1966) found a correlation between the activity of the NPV cells and gonadal size in the European blackbird *(Turdus merula)* but found no correlation between NSM in the median eminence and gonadal size or between NSM in the median eminence and season. Subsequent investigations, already mentioned, show that destruction of the supraoptico hypophyseal tract only causes partial depression of the photoperiodic testicular response, whereas destruction of the posterior median eminence, where there are few neurosecretory fibers, abolishes this response (Farner and Follett, 1966). This evidence thus suggests that the correlations observed are not necessarily causal ones.

Graber and Nalbandov (1965) studied the effect of age, photoperiod, castration, and hypophysectomy on the presence of neurosecretory material in the median eminence of White Leghorn roosters, which are generally not very photosensitive. Between 44 and 64 days of age there was a rapid increase in the amount of aldehyde fuchsin positive material, and after this age it remained high. One week of exposure to different durations of illumination of roosters between 64 and 233 days of age had no effect on the median eminence. Unfortunately, there were no measurements of testicular and comb size, so the extent of a correlation between the presence of neurosecretory material and testicular activity is not known. The fact that neither castration nor hypophysectomy affected the concentration of NSM in the median eminence does not provide an answer, it shows the lack of an effect of testosterone on the median eminence histology and it indicates the lack of a feedback mechanism. Oksche et al. (1959) found that castration of white-crowned sparrows and subsequent exposure to long photoperiods did not deplete the NSM from the median eminence, but it did cause this depletion in intact controls. This suggests a feedback mechanism of gonadal hormones on the hypothalamus. Uemura (1964b) has demonstrated that administration of either testosterone or estrogen prevents the light-induced increase in phosphatase activity of the median eminence of photosensitive *Emberiza rustica latisfacia*. There seems to be an apparent difference between photosensitive passerines and White Leghorn chickens with respect to a gonadal-hypothalamic neurosecretory system feedback mechanism.

The sharp increase in NSM in the median eminence obtained by Graber and Nalbandov (1965) occurs at a time when normally there is an increase in testicular size. Unfortunately, no data were given, so one can only speculate on a possible relationship between accumulation of NSM in the median eminence and testicular activity.

Legait (1959) has studied the changes in the neurosecretory hypothalamo-hypophyseal system during the annual cycle of chickens. The average diameter of the cell nuclei of the NPV was about the same during sexual rest, molting, and the laying period. It fluctuated during the incubation period but was generally higher. In most cases the comparisons are based on observations made on one animal, so it is impossible to evaluate the effect of individual variability. During the incubation of eggs, the water metabolism of the hen may be disturbed because she eats little and may drink infrequently. The fact that neurosecretory materials are generally less abundant during the period of egg incubation than during the sexual rest (when the ovarian weight is about the same as in the incubating hen) suggests that the disturbed water metabolism may have affected the size of the cell nuclei of the NPV.

Exposure to darkness of female budgerigars (*Melopsittacus undulatus*) leads to depletion of neurosecretory material from the median eminence and increased ovarian weights in one experiment, whereas, in another, a similar treatment affected neither the hypothalamo-hypophyseal system nor the gonads (van Tienhoven et al., 1966). These data thus suggest that it is not the exposure to light per se which causes changes in the median eminence. It is, of course, possible that in opportunistic breeders, such as the budgerigar, other factors play a role similar to the one light plays in photosensitive species. Oksche et al. (1963) observed in zebra finches (*Taeniopygia castanotis*) that photoperiod does not affect the hypothalamo-hypophyseal neurosecretory system, but that a general correlation exists between depletion of neurosecretory material from the palisade layer of the median eminence and gonadal development.

It should be worthwhile to investigate the effect of photoperiod and the effect of stimuli that cause gonadal stimulation in nonphotoperiodic birds (e.g. ring doves) on the hypothalamo-hypophyseal neurosecretory system. Changes in the neurosecretory hypothalamo-hypophyseal system with respect to gonadal activity or changes in photoperiod are not limited to avian species, although they are more spectacular in birds.

In teleost fishes, results obtained vary

with the species investigated. Stahl and Leray (1961) found, among nine species investigated, that only in *Hippocampus guttulatus* was there a direct relationship between the preoptic neurosecretory material and the basophils of the hypophysis. Among species with a well developed tuberal nucleus, *Mugil cephalus, M. capito, M. auratus,* and *Gadus capelanus* showed a seasonal change in the neurosecretory material (which does not stain with aldehyde fuchsin or chromalum hematoxylin, but does stain with aniline blue, light green, eosin and phloxin). The appearance of these neurosecretory cells and the increase in their activity coincided with gonadal development and the multiplication of gonadotropic cells and their vacuolation. However, in *Morone labrax,* which has also a well developed tuberal nucleus, no such relationship appeared.

In many species of teleosts, no portal system is present and the question how the NSM is transported to the mesoadenohypophysis (equivalent of the distal lobe?) arises. In some species, fibers containing NSM have been found close to the cells of the mesoadenohypophysis (e.g. in *Hippocampus guttulatus, H. brevirostris, Typhle hexagonus*) (Gabe, 1966). In some other species (e.g. *Rhodeus amarus*) a vascular plexus in the neurohypophysis that has digitations and capillaries, going from this plexus to the mesoadenohypophysis, may be the equivalent of the portal system of higher vertebrates (Gabe, 1966).

In eels *(Anguilla anguilla),* the appearance of neurosecretory fibers giving a positive stain for NSM is correlated with increased gonadotropic and thyrotropic activity (Knowles and Vollrath, 1965).

Among amphibia, several important observations have been made on *Rana temporaria.* Dierickx (1965) isolated the pars ventralis of the tuber cinereum from the remainder of the brain, but maintained the connection of this structure with the pars distalis and left the vascular supply of this region intact. The ovaries and oviduct of such operated

female frogs were well developed, but in hypophysectomized females they were atrophied two and a half months after the operation. In such operated animals aldehyde fuchsin (AF) positive fibers were absent, but the hypothalamo-hypophyseal tract contained very fine AF negative fibers. No differences were found between the testes of males with the isolated pars centralis of the tuber cinereum and the testes of hypophysectomized males; in both groups mature sperm were present. However, the thumb pads of the hypophysectomized males were thinner. These results thus underscore the importance of the AF negative fibers originating from the tuber cinereum. The area periventricularis of the pars ventralis of the tuber cinereum corresponds with the nucleus infundibularis and the nucleus ventromedialis of mammals. We have already discussed the importance of lesions in these areas in the reproduction of mammals. The data also agree with the findings of Wilson and Farner (1965) for white-crowned sparrows.

In the turtle *(Testudo mauritanica)* Grignon (1960) observed that injections of 1 mg. diethylstilbestrol (DES) per day caused a small increase in neurosecretory material in the neurosecretory cells, but large doses of DES caused depletion of the material, mainly from the cells of the NSM.

In rats, one might not expect an observable effect on neurosecretion during the short estrous cycle because the changes would be relatively slow.

A comparison between rats exposed to constant illumination and rats exposed to constant darkness shows that NSM is more abundant along the hypothalamo-hypophyseal tract and cells of the NSM are larger and more active in the rats exposed to light, but the cells of the NPV seem unaffected by light treatment. Exposure to either constant light or constant darkness causes the depletion of the NSM from the neurohypophysis, compared to controls receiving 12 hours light and 12 hours darkness per day (Fiske and Greep, 1959).

De Groot (1957) observed in one out of three females and in two out of three males that gonadectomy caused a conspicuous accumulation of NSM around the blood vessels of the hypophyseal stalk, but in the other three animals no definite variations from normal were found. Lisk (1965/1966), using a considerably larger number of female rats, observed an immediate decline in the NSM present in the median eminence. This decline could be prevented by implants of 17β-estradiol, in stainless steel tubes, into the arcuate nucleus (implants elsewhere in the hypothalamus were not effective and neither were empty tubes implanted into the arcuate nucleus). These experiments by Lisk (1965-1966) not only show an effect of estrogens on neurosecretory material present in the median eminence, but they also pinpoint the estrogen feedback mechanism. Arko et al. (1963) reported that in rats, but not in rabbits, gonadectomy increased NSM in the median eminence. It is not known why there is a discrepancy between de Groot's and Arko et al.'s experiments, on the one hand, and Lisk's results, on the other.

A number of papers have been published on the histologic aspects of the laterodorsal-interstitial hypothalamic nucleus (LIHN) of the guinea pig under different conditions. This nucleus is characterized by the presence of neurosecretory cells which do not stain with aldehyde fuchsin or chromalum hematoxylin. Castration of male guinea pigs is followed by an immediate (24 to 72 hour) increase in the number of neurosecretory cells in the LIHN, which suggests an increase in synthetic activity (Barry and Torre, 1962). The long term effect of castration (five months after operation) is, however, a sharp reduction of such cells with neurosecretory activity (Barry and Léonardelli, 1965). A similar effect was noted for spayed guinea pigs (Barry et al., 1962) and a further decrease in the number of these cells occurs after progesterone administration. The number of these cells varies during the estrous cycle, with the lowest number occurring at proestrus and the highest immediately postestrus (Barry and Léonardelli, 1962).

In the European mole (*Talpa europaea*) the increased gonadal activity occurs at the time when the secretory activity of the cells of the LIHN appears highest (Barry, 1960).

Hagedoorn (1965) studied the relationship between the neurosecretory activity of the hypothalamo-hypophyseal system of the striped skunk (*Mephitis mephitis nigra*) in which the female has a long anestrus (middle of March till late February) and an estrous period which lasts for about a week. During estrus there is a lack of NSM in the NSO, NPV, and anterior hypothalamus. Hagedoorn also observed that during the anestrous period the ependymal lining of the third ventricle has fingerlike projections protruding into the lumen of the ventricle; these projections contain neurosecretory droplets. During estrus the ependymal lining is smooth. Similar differences were noted in the males between the quiescent and reproductively active periods. Artificial illumination activated the neurons of the preoptic part of the NSO. NSM is released from the preoptic NSO cells as the female enters preseasonal estrus in January.

Szentágothai et al. (1962) have investigated the effects of removing the gonads, thyroid, and adrenals on the size of the cell nuclei of different hypothalamic areas. The results of these investigations are summarized in Figure 8-11.

The hypothalamus and other parts of the central nervous system, areas especially high in nuclei, contain enzymes capable of inactivating oxytocin (Hooper, 1963). The material is found in the mitochondrial and supernatant fraction of homogenized tissue centrifuged at 600 g. In pregnant dogs, the enzymatic activity in the mitochondrial fraction of the hypothalamus is

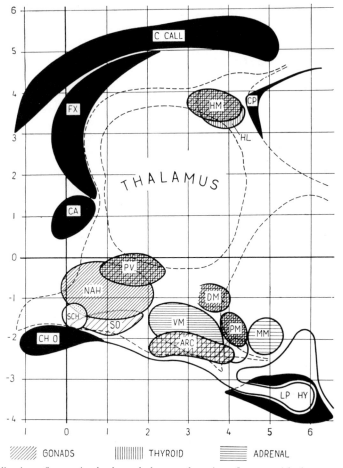

Figure 8-11. Localization of areas in the hypothalamus where interference with the target organs of pituitary hormones caused changes in the size of the cell nuclei. (From Szentágothai, et al., 1962.)

higher than that in nonpregnant dogs (Hooper, 1964), with highest activity present during the late stages of pregnancy. In rabbits the oxytocin inactivating activity in the particulate and in the supernatant fraction goes up sharply four days after mating, a time which is crucial in the transportation of the blastocyst in the uterine horns (Hooper, 1966a).

Ovariectomy caused a decrease in the activity of the supernatant, whereas estradiolbenzoate administration to intact nonpregnant rabbits resulted in an increase in this activity. The enzymatic activity of the particulate fraction was not affected by either of these experimental treatments (Hooper, 1966c).

After parturition, the enzyme activity

in the supernatant falls to the level found during pregnancy in about six hours, and then stays at this level for about 28 days. The activity in the particulate fraction falls to an indetectable level in ten days. Removal of the young causes a more rapid than normal decrease of activity in both fractions (Hooper, 1966b).

These experiments suggest that these enzymes may play a role in determining oxytocin concentrations in the blood and thus regulate uterine activity.

CHEMOTRANSMITTERS (RELEASING FACTORS)

The hypothesis of the neurohumoral control of hypophyseal function has been considerably strengthened by the isolation from the hypothalamus of factors that, upon injection or infusion into the anterior pituitary, cause the release of adenohypophyseal hormones. For an excellent general review about the various releasing factors, one should read the papers by Guillemin (1964) and McCann and Dhariwa (1966). The present discussion will be limited to a consideration of the hypothalamic factors which control the secretion and release of gonadotropins.

Most of the work on the presence of the gonadotropin releasing factors has been carried out with mammals, specifically rats and rabbits. We have cited the effect of hypothalamic extracts on in vitro prolactin production by pigeon pituitaries.

Observations in a number of laboratories indicated the presence of factors in the hypothalamus which cause the secretion of the release of gonadotropic hormones by isolated pituitaries. Moszkowska (1959) found that pituitaries from 50- to 60-day-old male rats caused the growth of follicles after the pituitaries were transplanted to the ovaries of immature female rats. The implantation of two hypothalami per pituitary together with the pituitaries caused earlier opening of the vagina and the appearance of corpora lutea.

In subsequent investigations Moszkowska and Kordon (1961, 1965) measured LH-RF by the percent luteinization and FSH-RF by the uterine weight of the recipients of the pituitary ovarian transplant. With this technique they found that: (1) Female hypothalamus contained more LH-RF than the male hypothalamus with respect to FSH-RF; (2) Castration increased the LH-RF content of male hypothalami, but decreased that of females. No effect of castration or spaying was found on the FSH-RF content. As we shall see, Chowers and McCann (1965) found no effect on the LH-RF content of hypothalami from either castration or spaying. These investigators used a rather

specific assay for LH-RF (ovarian ascorbic acid depletion in the "Parlow" rat). (3) Small lesions of the anterior hypothalamus decreased the LH-RF content without affecting the FSH-RF of female rats. (4) Continuous illumination increased the LH-RF content of male hypothalami but decreased that of females; no significant effect on FSH-RF content of either males or females was evident. (5) Neonatal testosterone injection did not affect the LH-RF of males but decreased that of females; this treatment also failed to affect the FSH-RF of males and females. (6) Hypophysectomy increased the LH-RF of female hypothalami but not of males; no effect on FSH-RF was found in either males or females.

In vitro experiments also showed that hypothalamus incubated with pituitary increased the secretion of FSH and LH by cultured pituitaries.

Donnet et al. (1960) found that administration of hypothalamic tissue to intact immature rats or mice caused precocious puberty, with the hypothalamus of prepubertal rats being ineffective and the hypothalamus of rats which just reached puberty most effective. Hypothalami of sexually mature rats and rats in constant diestrus had similar potencies and both were intermediate, between the prepubertal and the recently matured rats. Subsequent investigations showed that single hypothalamic implants, given every day for five days, caused precocious vaginal opening, and the appearance of typical estrous vaginal cells. In a minority of the cases, diestrus for 10 to 12 hours was observed, and in 17 percent, abnormal smears occurred while in six percent a transient diestrus lasting five to six days was found. Multiple implants caused vaginal opening in 24 to 36 hours and diestrous smears (Donnet et al., 1961a).

Single hypothalamic implants caused a transient diestrus, whereas repeated or multiple implants caused diestrus in 20 out of 22 sexually mature rats. Single hypothalamic implants from castrated or from adrenalectomized rats had the same effects as the multiple implants from intact mature rats. (Donnet et al., 1961b).

These experiments all suggest the presence in the hypothalamus of factors regulating the secretion or the release of gonadotropins. The development of sensitive assays for LH and FSH and the "creation" of animals sensitive for the assay of LH and FSH releasing factors (LH-RF and FSH-RF) have made it possible to obtain more concrete evidence.

In vivo, sheep median eminence extracts have been found to induce LH release in weaver finches (species not given) Johnson and Witschi, 1962). Frankel et al. (1965) have obtained evidence which suggests that hypophysectomy of roosters causes an appearance in the blood of a factor, which probably is LHRF.[*]

A number of "end points" have been used for the demonstration of LH-RF in median eminence extracts:

1. The incidence of ovulations in rabbits after intrapituitary infusion or intravenous injection of the extract, (Campbell et al., 1964; Campbell and Gallardo, 1965).

2. The increase in progestin secretion by the ovaries of pseudopregnant or pregnant rabbits after intrapituitary infusion of the extract.

3. The incidence of ovulations in:

    a. Immature rats pretreated with PMSG (Hopkins and Pincus, 1965)

    b. Mature rats treated neonatally with androgen. Johnson (1963) and Lloyd and Weisz (1966) have pointed out the apparent difference between the results obtained after electrical stimulation of the hypothalamus of such rats, which does not result in ovulation unless the LH stores have been built up by progesterone treatment (Barraclough and Gorski, 1961) and the apparent presence of sufficient

LH in the pituitary of "androgen sterilized" rats to induce ovulation after LH-RF administration. Barraclough (1966a), in a recent publication, has shown that the storage of LH as a result of progesterone treatment is probably secondary and that the primary effect of progesterone is the alteration of the thresholds of excitability (see p. 252-253 for further discussion).

    c. Mature rats with lesions of the median eminence (McCann and Ramirez, 1964).

    d. Pentobarbital blocked adult rats after intrapituitary infusion of the extract (Nikitovitch-Winer, 1962).

    e. Diestrous or pseudopregnant rats after the intrapituitary infusion of the extract (Nedde and Nikitovitch-Winer, 1964).

4. The increase in LH concentration of the blood of ovariectomized or ovariectomized-estrogen-progesterone-treated rats or of intact rats; the ovariectomized-estrogen-progesterone-treated rats being the most sensitive assay animal (McCann and Ramirez, 1964).

5. The decrease in ovarian ascorbic acid content of rats prepared according to the method of Parlow (see Appendix).

6. The release of LH by pituitaries incubated in vitro (Kobayashi et al., 1963; Cohen et al., 1966; Schally and Bowers, 1964; and Moszkowska and Kordon, 1965).

7. The release of LH from the pituitaries of immature male rats treated either with estradiol (10 µg./day) plus progesterone (1 mg./day) or with testosterone propionate (100 µg./day) (Johnson, 1964). No release was obtained, however, from the pituitaries of control rats injected with the median eminence extract. The possibility always exists that the median eminence extract may be contaminated by LH so that one has to be careful to differentiate LH-RF from LH activity. Boiling the extract just before use destroys the LH activity without affecting LH-RF activity.

Purification of the extract by filter-

---

[*] Nalbandov. 1966. J. Anim. Sci. 25(Suppl.): 82.

ing through a Sephadex G-25 column removes the LH activity. Verification that the LH is indeed removed can be obtained by testing the extract in hypophysectomized animals.

The LH-RF is probably a small polypeptide which is destroyed by trypsin and also by pepsin digestion (Jutisz et al., 1963). The molecular weight is less than 3000 (McCann and Ramirez, 1964). The LH-RF differs from oxytocin and vasopressin by the fact that the LH-RF is not destroyed by thioglycolate treatments, whereas oxytocin and vasopressin are destroyed (McCann and Ramirez, 1964).

The presence of LH-RF in the median eminence gives strong support to the Green and Harris (1947) hypothesis. The hypothesis is further strengthened by the fact that a number of experimental treatments affect the amount of LH-RF in the median eminence or in the blood.

The determination of the concentration of LH-RF in tissue is facilitated by the fact that for rat median eminence, there is a linear log dose relationship with the ovarian ascorbic acid depletion (McCann and Ramirez, 1964).

Ramirez and Sawyer (1966) observed that shortly before vaginal opening of immature rats, an abrupt rise in LH-RF concentration in the stalk-median eminence occurs, followed by an equally sharp drop in LH-RF on the day of vaginal opening. The onset of puberty (as indicated by vaginal opening) is accompanied by a sharp drop in pituitary LH and a rise in blood LH levels. The estrogen-induced advanced puberty is accompanied by similar changes.

During the estrous cycle the LH-RF concentration of the median eminence of rats fluctuates, with a very low concentration at late proestrus (4:30 p.m.) and estrus and a high concentration just prior to the sharp decrease (5:30 p.m. day of proestrus) according to Ramirez and Sawyer (1965), whereas Chowers and McCann (1965) found the highest concentration during late diestrus and the lowest concentration during early proestrus and estrus, with a slight increase observed between early and late proestrus.

Piacsek and Meites (1966b) found that ovariectomy resulted in a reduction of the LH-RF content of the hypothalamus to about 30 percent of the normal content. Injections of 0.8 μg. of estradiol benzoate daily decreased the LH-RF content of the hypothalamus of such rats and decreased the LH concentration of the pituitary (the LH concentration of the pituitary had increased about four times as a result of ovariectomy). Injections of 4 mg. progesterone daily had no significant effect on the LH-RF concentration, but the combined injections of estrogen and progesterone did not alter the LH-RF concentration either, showing that progesterone prevents estrogen from having its LH-RF-lowering effect. Piacsek and Meites drew the conclusion that ovariectomy stimulated release of LH-RF more than its synthesis, that estrogen inhibited release and synthesis of LH-RF, and that estrogen caused LH release by a direct effect on the pituitary. Chowers and McCann (1965) failed to find an effect of ovariectomy, two to three months after the operation, on LH-RF concentration. In intact males and females, estrogen injections did not affect LH-RF content but lowered hypophyseal LH content. Estradiol implants in the hypothalamus, on the other hand, decreased LH-RF concentration without consistently affecting pituitary LH content. The implantation of estrogen in the pituitary resulted in an increase in LH-RF content and had a variable effect on pituitary LH content.

Castration of male rats did not affect the LH-RF content two to three months after the operation, according to Chowers and McCann (1965), but Piacsek and Meites (1966b) found a 2.5-fold increase in rats killed three weeks after the operation. Testosterone propionate (1 mg./day) injections into castrated rats prevented the increase in LH-RF content (Piacsek and Meites, 1966b), but caused an increase in intact rats, according to Chowers and McCann (1965). Testosterone propionate implants into the hypothalamus altered neither the LH content of the pituitary nor the LH-RF content of the hypothalamus. The different results obtained after ovariectomy and castration by the two groups of workers makes it difficult to evaluate the control mechanisms involved in the synthesis and release of LH-RF. The mechanisms proposed to explain the results obtained with female rats by Piacsek and Meites (1966b) have been mentioned. An interpretation of the results offered by Chowers and McCann (1965) is that the steroid hormones exert a negative feedback on LH-RF secretion and that LH does the same. Thus, in the case of castration, there is a rise in LH secretion that negates any effect that withdrawal of testosterone or estrogen might have had on LH-RF secretion; similarly, steroid hormone administration lowers the LH secretion, which negates the effect that steroid hormones may have had on LH-RF secretion. The possibility of a negative LH feedback on LH-RF secretion is supported by the experiments of Nallar and McCann (1965), which show that hypophysectomy of rats results two to three months later in an increased LH-RF concentration of the peripheral blood, an effect which is prevented by lesions of the median eminence.

Ramirez and Sawyer (1965), on the basis of the decrease in LH-RF at a time during the estrous cycle when LH release probably had taken place (after the "critical period"—see p. 151-152), also assumed a negative feedback of LH on the median eminence. The dual control of hypothalamic activity by LH and steroid hormones agrees with the evidence presented in previous sections of this chapter, which demonstrates such negative feedback effects on pituitary LH contents and blood LH concentrations. In newborn rabbits, the median eminence contains a factor that, after extraction and upon infusion in the pituitary, causes ovulation, as does extract from adult rabbits (Campbell and Gallardo, 1965). No concentration was reported, however.

Median eminence extracts have been found to contain an FSH releasing factor (FSH-RF), which has been demonstrated by the following experiments:

1. Depletion of the amount of FSH from the rat anterior pituitary (assayed by the Steelman-Pohley test) was found after intracarotid injections of hypothalamic extracts. Control animals injected with cerebral cortex extracts showed no decrease in pituitary FSH content (Dávid et al., 1965b). Kuroshima, Arimura, Saito, Ishida, Bowers and Schally (1966) showed in an elegant experiment that intracarotid injections of pig or beef hypothalamic extract caused a decrease in pituitary FSH content and an increase in plasma FSH concentration of rats.

2. Injections of the median eminence extract cause an increase in plasma FSH (assayed by determining the uterine weights of intact mice injected with HCG plus the FSH-RF containing material [Igarashi and McCann, 1964a]) in (a) ovariectomized rats, treated with 50 μg. estradiol benzoate and 25 mg. progesterone, and (b) ovariectomized rats with median eminence lesions (to block FSH release). Adequate controls were used to ensure that the effect of the extract was not the result of contamination with FSH and to show that the FSH-RF was not present in cerebral cortex extracts (Igarashi and McCann, 1964b).

3. There was a release of FSH into the medium by mature female pituitaries cultured in vitro; extracts from the cerebral cortex did not cause such a release (Dávid et al., 1965a). Neither the median eminence extract nor the cerebral cortex extract as such affected the FSH assay when injected together with FSH (Mittler and Meites, 1964).

4. Release of FSH into the medium by

pituitaries of ovariectomized-estrogen-progesterone-treated rats (Kuroshima et al., 1965).

The FSH-RF content of the median eminence increases after ovariectomy and is reduced by estrogen treatment of spayed cats (Dávid et al., 1965b).

A similar situation prevails in the male rat: castration leads to an increase of FSH-RF, and androgen treatment of intact rats reduces the FSH-RF content of the median eminence (Mittler and Meites, 1966).

Investigations by Igarashi et al. (1964) revealed that FSH-RF and LH-RF behave similarly upon Sephadex-G25 column filtration. Both activities are located closely to the vasopressin, showing that LH-RF and vasopressin are not identical, as was already clear from the effect of thioglycolate on LH-RF and on vasopressin. The FSH-RF was contaminated with vasopressin but as much as 500 mμ. vasopressin could not cause FSH release, indicating that FSH-RF activity cannot be accounted for by this contaminant.

There is no proof that LH-RF and FSH-RF are separate chemical entities nor is there proof that they are not.

Gellert et al. (1964) found that injection of extracts of either the pars tuberalis or of the pars tuberalis plus median eminence of steers caused precocious vaginal opening in immature rats. Median eminence extract injected alone had no effect, but it acted synergistically with pars tuberalis extract in causing earlier vaginal opening and earlier first estrus. The extract did not have this effect in hypophysectomized rats. Both extracts did, however, contain LH, and the pars tuberalis extract did contain FSH. Injections of the amounts of LH found in the extracts and of an even larger amount of FSH failed to duplicate the results obtained with the extracts, so the data indirectly support the idea that the extracts cause FSH release from the pituitaries of the immature rats.

In a number of laboratories in France,

evidence has been obtained that the hypothalamic tissue, placed close to a transplanted pituitary or added to a pituitary cultured in vitro causes an increase in the secretion of gonadotropins. Moszkowska (1959) found that implantation of pituitaries of male rats to the ovary of immature rats caused an increase in follicular size. Only in the presence of hypothalamic tissue (two hypothalami per pituitary) were corpora lutea formed and was the vagina opened precociously. The effect of the hypothalamic tissue was stronger when it was obtained from castrated male or female rats than when it was obtained from intact ones (Moszkowska and Kordon, 1961). In vitro incubation of male rat pituitaries also showed that the presence of hypothalamic tissue caused secretion of LH (Moszkowska and Kordon, 1961).

The hypothalamus, which causes stimulation of LH and FSH release, inhibits prolactin secretion by the pituitary. The evidence for the presence of a prolactin inhibiting factor (PIF) is:

1. Fragments of hypothalamus inhibit the production of prolactin by pituitaries cultured in vitro (Gala and Reece, 1964); hypothalamic extracts have the same effect (Talwalker et al., 1963; Kragt and Meites, 1965). Meites (1966) mentions that there is a dose-response relationship between the dose of extract added in vitro and the amount of prolactin produced.

2. Extracts of pig hypothalamus prevent the depletion of prolactin from rat anterior pituitaries, which normally occurs after cervical stimulation (Kuroshima, Arimura, Bowers and Schally, 1966).

3. Injection of bovine median eminence extracts prevents the nursing-induced and the stress (bleeding and laparotomy)-induced depletion of prolactin from the anterior pituitary of lactating rats (Grosvenor et al., 1965).

4. Injection of rat hypothalamus extracts impairs milk secretion in rats (Grosvenor, 1966), but Meites et al. (1960)

found initiation of lactation with hypothalamus suspensions. The initiation of lactation is not specifically the result of prolactin, but involves other hormones. This evidence is, therefore, not specific enough to be used by itself as evidence for the presence of a PIF in the hypothalamus.

A number of experimental treatments affect the concentration of PIF in the median eminence; nursing, reserpine injections, or estradiol administration can cause a release of prolactin and also a diminished PIF concentration, as measured from the amount of prolactin released in vitro after addition of hypothalamic extract from these different groups (Ratner and Meites, 1964). Grosvenor (1965) used an in vivo assay; he measured the decrease in prolactin content of lactating rats after nursing their pups, and measured the hypophyseal prolactin content after stress (which normally induces a decrease in prolactin content of the pituitary). The extent to which the extract prevented these reductions in prolactin content was used as a measure of the potency of the extract. No significant effect of stress or nursing was found with respect to the effectiveness of hypothalamic extract inhibiting the decrease in prolactin content. These in vivo data are thus in contrast with the in vitro data obtained by Ratner and Meites (1964). Gala and Reece (1964) found no difference between the effects of hypothalamic extracts of lactating and cyclic rats on prolactin secretion of rat pituitaries in vitro. The data obtained by Ratner and Meites (1964) suggest a mechanism whereby different stimuli cause prolactin release by decreasing the PIF secretion. How this is accomplished remains to be discovered. Ben David et al. (1964), on the basis of pituitary-hypothalamus cultures in vitro, came to the conclusion that estrogen acted directly on the pituitary in stimulating prolactin secretion. As was discussed previously, the effect of estrogen on pituitary prolactin secretion in vitro has yielded different results in different laboratories (see Chapter 6), and it is difficult to determine the reason for these differences from the data presented.

LH-RF of either bovine or ovine origin fails to inhibit prolactin secretion in vitro, indicating that LH-RF and PIF are separate entities (Schally et al., 1964).

In general, the different investigators have used cerebral extracts as controls when they were investigating the effect of hypothalamic extracts. In most cases, the cerebral extracts were devoid of activity or the activity was extremely low. A few exceptions should be noted. De la Lastra and Croxatto (1964) found that human cortex, habenula, and pineal extracts caused an OAAD response in intact "Parlow rats" but failed to do so in hypophysectomized rats. The extracts also increased the LH activity in the plasma of ovariectomized-estradiol or estradiol-plus progesterone-treated rats.

Hopkins and Pincus (1965) found that median eminence homogenates and also cerebral homogenates from rats contain factors which can inhibit and which can facilitate ovulation in PMSG-treated rats. These factors can be separated by centrifugation at 10,000 xg for 20 minutes. The hypothalamic tissue homogenate inhibits PMSG-induced and also PMSG-HCG-induced ovulation, suggesting that it acts on the ovary. Further evidence with purified fractions is required before one can draw any conclusions about similarities with the LH-RF found by others in acid extracts of the median eminence but not found in similar extracts of cerebral tissue.

Some of the hypothalamic hormones, e.g. oxytocin and vasopressin, are stored in the neurohypophysis, and, therefore, it is of interest to evaluate the effect of these hormones on anterior pituitary function. The pertinent experiments have been reviewed in Chapter 7. This evidence suggests that oxytocin and vasopressin can affect pituitary gonadotropin release; however, there are several arguments against the hypothesis that these hormones are identical with the LH-RF. For instance:

1. Vasopressin and oxytocin activity are destroyed by thioglycolate treatment, and there is no destruction of activity in the LH-RF preparation.

2. The LH-RF activity of extracts cannot be accounted for by the amount of oxytocin and vasopressin present in the median eminence extracts.

EFFECT OF PHARMACOLOGICAL AGENTS

The administration of anticholinergic agents (e.g. atropine sulfate, Banthine), antiadrenergic drugs (e.g. Dibenamine, Dibenzyline, and SKF 501), anesthetics (e.g. ether), barbiturates, analgesics (e.g. morphine), or tranquilizers (e.g. reserpine and chlorpromazine) can prevent either induced ovulation or spontaneous ovulation provided that the administration takes place at the appropriate time. The effects of these agents on ovulation in a number of species have been reviewed and summarized by Sawyer (1964) and Everett (1964a). This type of evidence indicates that the autonomic and the central nervous system are involved in the release of ovulation-inducing hormone from the pituitary. However, the effect of some drugs on ovulation varies among species. For example, pentobarbital blocks ovulation in the rat (see Sawyer, 1964; and Everett, 1964a) but has no effect on the Syrian golden hamster (Mesocricetus auratus) (Alleva and Umberger, 1966), or in the chicken (see Fraps, 1955; Sawyer, 1964). Diallyl barbituric acid, on the other hand, induces ovulation in chickens (see Fraps, 1955; Sawyer, 1964). The question of the mechanism by which the drugs cause their effects on ovulation has not been definitely answered.

Evidence in favor of a specific effect of, e.g., antiadrenergic drugs is provided by experiments in which, in the rabbit, ovulation was induced by intracarotid injection of large doses of epinephrine; the rabbits were protected against the lethal effect of epinephrine by prior atropine treatment. Similarly, epinephrine, infused into the ventricle, will cause ovulation in rabbits (Everett, 1964a). Earlier experiments showed that epinephrine injection into the pituitary caused ovulation (Everett, 1964a). However, it was shown by Donovan and Harris (1965) that this alleged effect of epinephrine is a function of pH rather than of epinephrine or norepinephrine.

Moore (1961) has argued that the effects of drugs such as Dibenamine, Dibenzyline, and Pathilon block ovulation, not because they act as antiadrenergic or anticholinergic drugs, but because they act as nonspecific stress agents which cause ACTH release, which in turn prevents LH release. Evidence in support of this hypothesis is that after daily administration of these drugs, at 5 p.m., the cycle was interrupted but returned to normal. If the drug was then given during the critical period, 1 to 5 p.m. on the day of proestrus, ovulations were not blocked in 80 percent of the cases. However, an important argument against the hypothesis that "stress" is the stimulus for causing an ACTH release which in turn prevents LH release is the fact that different agents which cause stress (e.g. cold, heat, and ganglionic blocking agents) do not block ovulation (Sawyer, 1964).

Ramirez et al. (1964b) subjected Moore's hypothesis to further study and found that adrenalectomy (which should cause an increase in ACTH secretion) produced a border line rise in plasma LH; large doses of cortisol, given to rats to block ACTH secretion, failed to alter plasma LH concentration, whereas chronic cortisol treatment lowered pituitary ACTH and elevated pituitary LH slightly. Ovariectomized rats given large doses of estradiol benzoate showed a lowered plasma LH and pituitary LH when compared with ovariectomized controls, while the adrenal weight remained unchanged and pituitary ACTH was slightly elevated. These results show that ACTH and LH secretion can be increased simultaneously and that increases in ACTH secretion are accompanied by only slight changes in LH secretion. However, the effect of stress (formalin injection) was not tested in connection with LH and ACTH release. Moore (1966) found that formalin (0.2 ml.) injection every 12 hours for 48 hours caused a sharp decrease in plasma LH concentration of ovariectomized rats; this decrease could be prevented by pretreatment for two days with 60 mg./kg. cortisol (to inhibit ACTH release). The cortisol had no effect on plasma LH concentration in nonstressed rats; very similar results were obtained in ovariectomized-adrenalectomized rats, although Moore confirmed that neither adrenalectomy nor pretreatment with cortisol affects plasma LH concentrations.

The experiments show, at least in case of formalin injection, that ACTH release is not compatible with LH release.

The relationship between neurotransmitters and ovulation has been investigated by indirect approaches. Lippmann et al. (1966) and Coppola et al. (1965, 1966) studied the effect of catecholamine depleters (e.g. reserpine) alone and in combination with drugs that antagonize the catecholamine depletion effect of reserpine (e.g. Iproniazid) on hormone release. They concluded from their results that depletion of brain norepinephrine, or rather the rate of synthesis uptake and/or release of norepinephrine, is related to the suppression of LH release (failure of ovulation) and the stimulation of prolactin secretion (pseudopregnancy was induced) observed after administration of these drugs.

Zolovick et al. (1966) found an increase in monoamino oxidase activity in the frontal cortex, the amygdala, and the hypothalamus between diestrus and proestrus. They discuss this increase in connection with the fact that 5-hydroxytryptamine (5HT) administration inhibits ovulation (O'Steen, 1965) and suggest that the increase in enzyme activity overrides the effect of 5HT to allow LH release to occur. On the other hand, they point out that their data may "represent only the sum total of all neural activity in the brain leading to ovulation and does not represent the neurophysiological events controlling gonadotropin secretion." In the experiments by Coppola et al. (1966), monoamino oxidase inhibitors (e.g. Iproniazid and Pheniprazine) administered alone did not affect PMSG-induced ovulation in immature rats, although these two drugs were effective in overcoming the ovulation-inhibiting effect of reserpine. Further experiments are required to establish the relationship between neurotransmitters and ovulation. The attempts to relate ovulation to biochemical changes in the crucial areas of the brain involved in regulation of gonadotropin synthesis and release should lead to a better understanding of the manner in which other hormones can affect gonadotropin secretion.

A number of important findings have been made by the use of ovulation-blocking agents alone and in combination with electrical stimulation. These data have been discussed by Sawyer (1959a, 1963, 1964) and Everett (1964a); a brief summary is given here:

1. Atropine, morphine, pentobarbital, and alcohol prevent ovulation from occurring in estrogen-primed rabbits after stimulation of the posterior hypothalamus, but ovulation occurs after stimulation of the median eminence. These results indicate that the limiting site of blockade for these drugs lies just proximal to the median eminence (Sawyer, 1964); see Figure 8-12.

2. When lights in the animal rooms are on from 5 a.m. to 7 p.m., rats with a four day cycle will ovulate about midnight following the day of proestrus. By the administration of a blocking agent, such as Dibenamine, atropine and pentobarbital, at various times before ovulation, it was established that administration between 2 p.m. and 4 p.m. prevents ovulation from occurring. Hypophysectomy instead of drug administration had similar effects, indicating that LH release starts at the same time that the period "critical for

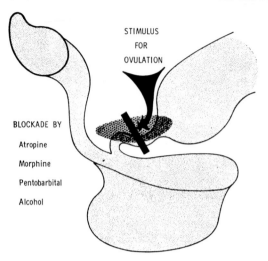

Figure 8-12. Critical sites of blockade of electrically stimulated release of pituitary ovulation-inducing hormone by certain drugs. (From Sawyer, 1963.)

drug administration" starts. This period from 2 to 4 p.m. on the day of proestrus will further be referred to as the "critical period." The discovery of this "critical period" is a very important one. However, of even more importance is the fact that LH release occurs 24 hours later after it has been blocked on the day of proestrus, and that this delayed release in turn can be blocked again between 2 and 4 p.m. This blockade can be carried out for three days, after which follicular atresia occurs (Everett, 1964a).

The time at which the critical period occurs is dependent upon the light schedule; a 12-hour shift will occur gradually if day and night are reversed. It appears that the animal's own internal rhythm becomes entrained to the lighting schedule; this phenomenon will be discussed in detail in Chapter 13).

PMSG injection into immature 30-day-old female rats will induce ovulation on day 33 of life. This ovulation is dependent upon the presence of the pituitary. Hypophysectomy before 2 p.m. the afternoon before ovulation takes place prevents ovulation, but hypophysectomy after 5 p.m. has no effect. Injections of sodium barbital between 2 and 4 p.m. in intact rats also prevent ovulation in such immature PMSG-treated rats (Strauss and Meyer,

1962; and McCormack and Meyer, 1962). Injections of 10 I.U. HCG cause ovulation in such "blocked" rats (McCormack and Meyer, 1962). In younger rats (24 days old) of a different strain, Quinn and Zarrow (1964) found that the time of day at which PMSG was injected had no effect on the incidence of ovulation, and that the effect of Nembutal was dependent upon the interval after PMSG injection and not upon the time of day. These workers also observed that atropine sulfate did not block ovulation if given later than 52 hours after PMSG, but SKF 501 (N-[9-fluorenyl]-N-ethyl-β-chloroethylamine hydrochloride) and Nembutal were still effective 56 hours after PMSG administration. Hypophysectomy 60 hours after PMSG injection permitted a full ovulatory response. The difference between the results of Strauss and Meyer (1962) and McCormack and Meyer (1962) on one hand and those of Quinn and Zarrow (1964) on the other are not explainable because there are several differences between the experimental conditions.

The copulation-induced ovulations in estrogen-treated rats mated on the first day of diestrus (see Chapter 6) can also be blocked by the injection of atropine (Aron and Asch, 1962).

ELECTRIC ACTIVITY OF THE BRAIN AND GONADOTROPIN RELEASE

Recordings of electric activity from the different parts of the brain during the stimulation for LH release and during and after LH release have been useful in providing data on the interaction between the endocrine and the nervous systems. Most of the studies concerning gonadotropin release have been carried out with the rabbit and cat (reflex ovulators), and the rat (spontaneous ovulators). Excellent summaries can be found in papers by Cross (1964, 1965), Sawyer (1959a, 1963) and Everett (1964a).

Sawyer and his co-workers evaluated

the effect of different hormones on the nervous system by measuring: (1) the minimum voltage necessary to obtain an arousal electroencephalogram (characterized by a desynchronized record obtained from the frontal lobe and a four to seven c./s. rhythm from the hippocampus) after electric stimulation of the reticular system, and (2) the occurrence of the EEG "after-reaction" (characterized by high amplitude slow waves and "sleep spindles" followed by high amplitude waves of eight to nine c./s. in the hippocampus, limbic cortex, and other related areas) after electric stimulation of the rhinencephalic and hypothalamic areas. The EEG "after-reaction" was given this name because it occurs in the female rabbit after coitus. Using these criteria it was found that:

1. Ovulation-inducing doses of HCG, PMSG, LH, prolactin, oxytocin, and vasopressin induce the EEG after-reaction without electrical stimulation, but FSH, TSH, ACTH, and growth hormone fail to do so.

2. During the first few hours after the injection of progesterone in the estrous rabbit, a reduction of the threshold (expressed as voltage) for the induction of the EEG arousal and for the EEG after-reaction is obtained. It is during these few hours that progesterone facilitates ovulation in the estrous rabbit in response to stimulation of the vagina with a glass rod. However, 24 hours after progesterone injection, the thresholds to obtain the EEG changes were raised considerably. It is at this time that progesterone has an inhibitory effect on the induction of ovulation in response to coitus or in response to injection of copper salts. At this time, progesterone has also caused a refusal to mate on the part of the doe.

In further experiments, rabbits were given testosterone or estrogen for a week. Such rabbits remained in estrus and had a lowered EEG arousal threshold but an elevated EEG after-reaction threshold, which was correlated with a failure to ovulate after mating. From this separation of the threshold changes for obtaining EEG arousal, EEG after reaction, and separation of behavioral estrus but lack of ovulation, it seems that the EEG arousal is related to the sexual behavior and the after-reaction to the release of pituitary hormones.

Several drugs which block ovulation in the rabbit, e.g. atropine, morphine, chlorpromazine, and pentobarbital, cause a greater increase in the threshold for the EEG after-reaction than in the threshold of the EEG arousal. Dibenzyline, which blocks ovulation, does not affect the EEG arousal threshold, but increases that of the EEG after-reaction.

A number of contraceptives, e.g. Norethindrone, Norlutin, and Nilvar, raise the EEG after-reaction threshold and block ovulation, but do not affect the estrous behavior.

In rats, doses of morphine, atropine, and chlorpromazine, sufficient to block ovulation, cause the appearance of slow waves with high amplitudes in several areas of the brain, suggesting an inhibition of the reticular activating system; this is accompanied by an increased threshold for EEG arousal after stimulation of the reticular system. However, reserpine and SKF-501, which block ovulation, do not have these effects.

Stimulation of the vagina of rats causes changes in the electrical activity recorded from the ventromedial hypothalamus and the amygdala. However, these changes can also be induced by non-specific stimuli. The changes do not seem to be related to the release of gonadotropic hormones. Ovariectomy, the stage of the estrous cycle, and sex do not seem to have an effect on the EEG response elicited after different stimulation techniques (pinching the tail, inserting a needle, etc.) (Margherita et al., 1965).

The recording of the electric activity by rather large electrodes gives an estimate of this activity on larger areas. By the use of microelectrodes one can obtain estimates of the electric activity of single cells. A number of stimuli were found to increase the firing rate of lateral hypothalamic neurones of rats. These stimuli, in descending order of effectiveness, are pain, cold, probing of the cervix (such probing causes prolactin release), smell, light, and noise. The stage of the estrous cycle affected the number of neurones affected by olfactory stimuli. In proestrus, more than twice as many neurones as during estrus or diestrus responded, and during estrus, fewer neurones responded to cold, pain, and probing of the cervix. Cross and Silver (1965) found that the percentage of hypothalamic neurones responding to stimuli from the genital tract was lower in pseudopregnant than in cyclic or ovariectomized rats, indicating that progesterone depresses excitation of hypothalamic neurones.

Slow, intravenous progesterone injection causes a depression of the unit responses to cervical probing, but does not affect the response to light or to pain stimuli (Barraclough and Cross, 1963).

The investigators suggested that the lowered activity during estrus, as a result of enhanced inhibitory connections to the lateral hypothalamus, might explain the luteotropic effect of estrogen. This argument was based on the known inhibitory effect of hypothalamic connections on prolactin secretion.

Abrahams et al. (1964) used the technique of recording evoked potentials (with macroelectrodes) and found that electric uterine stimulation of chloralose-anesthetized cats caused a response which was limited to the preoptic and tuberal regions of the hypothalamus. The latency and amplitude of the potential evoked after uterine stimulation were smaller than those obtained after cutaneous stimulation. These experiments show that a uterine-hypothalamic pathway exists, but the relationship with hormone release is not established and remains speculative at this time.

So far, we have considered the hypothalamus as if it operated in a vacuum, and it is, therefore, pertinent to determine which other parts of the central nervous system affect the function of the hypothalamus as it relates to gonadotropic function of the anterior pituitary. We will discuss the effect of lesions and electrical stimulation on reproductive phenomena. Figure 8-13 shows the anatomic relationship of the hypothalamus to other brain areas. For reviews of the connections of the hypothalamus see de Groot (1966) and Nauta (1963).

Karapetyan et al. (1963) reported that removal of the cerebral hemispheres of chickens interrupted reproduction, but that after a ten to 30 day recovery period, reproduction returns to normal. The hemispheres of chickens consist essentially of the basal ganglia; the presence of the cortex is a matter of controversy—if it is present it does not contribute more than one or two percent to the total volume of the hemispheres. Stimulation of the archistriatum of laying hens leads to delayed ovulation, but small lesions in the same areas had no effect (Juhász and van Tienhoven, 1964).

Captivity inhibits the development of ovaries and oviducts of wild Mallard ducks (*Anas platyrhynchos*). Lesions which interrupt the archistriatal-hypothalamic connections cause a lessening of the "escape behavior" of such ducks and also causes a significant increase in the size of ovaries and oviducts, suggesting an inhibitory effect of captivity mediated via the archistriatum on gonadotropin secretion by the pituitary (Phillips, 1964).

The effect of lesions and electrical stimulation in different parts of the brain have been studied mostly in laboratory and domestic animals.

Extirpation of the telencephalon of intact or ovariectomized rabbits (and feeding the animals by gastric intubation) induces mammary growth and milk secretion, suggesting release of prolactin. Lesions of the neocortex or removal of the olfactory bulbs are not effective in this respect (Beyer and Mena, 1965).

Removal of the cortex has no effect on coitus-induced ovulation in rabbits or on

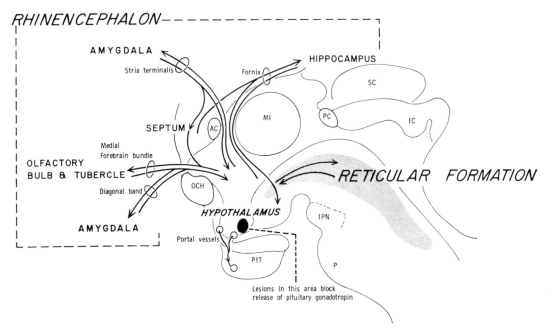

Figure 8-13. Some of the rhinencephalic and reticular formation nerve pathways projecting to and from the hypothalamus. The control of the pituitary is considered to be humoral via the hypophyseal portal vessels. (From Sawyer, 1963.)

gonadotropic output of male rabbits or female rats (Lundberg, 1962; see Sawyer, 1964). On the other hand, stimulation of the cortex of rats causes depletion ·of ovarian ascorbic acid, indicating LH release (see Sawyer, 1964). Bilateral temporal lobectomy of female *Macaca mulatta* caused significant lengthening of the menstrual cycle in two out of two animals (Wada and Erikson, 1962).

Extirpation of the frontal parts of the brain of ferrets and rats does not affect fertility (see Sawyer, 1964).

Ablation of the olfactory bulbs has different effects according to the species investigated. It should also be remembered that these lesions may not affect the estrous cycle of an animal under certain conditions; under other conditions there may be a very marked effect. Neither removal nor stimulation of these structures affect coitus-induced ovulation in rabbits (Sawyer, 1959b) or the estrous cycle of guinea pigs (Donovan and Kopriva, 1965). Ablation of the olfactory bulb of six-week-old female rabbits prevented the formation

of ripe follicles and corpora lutea and caused the interstitial gland cells to be small and the uteri to remain undeveloped (Franck, 1966). It also caused abnormal sexual behavior in these rabbits.

Ablation of the olfactory bulbs of female mice prevents the "van der Lee-Boot effect" (increased incidence of pseudopregnancies in female mice housed in small cages) and the "Bruce effect" (failure of implantation after a strange male is introduced in the female's cage) from expressing themselves (Bruce, 1966). However, in the rat the "Bruce effect" does not seem to occur (Davis and de Groot, 1964), which may mean that olfactory stimuli in rats may not be as important in the release of prolactin as they are in the mouse.

The removal of the olfactory bulb of female swine results in an absence of estrous cycles with, in some cases, involuted uteri and ovaries, but in other cases with normal uteri and active corpora lutea (Signoret, 1965). The effect of olfactory stimuli on reproduction will be discussed further in Chapter 13. Kling (1964) found that bilateral or unilateral lesions of either the olfactory stalk or the medial olfactory area caused delayed vaginal opening in rats. Bilateral transection of the olfactory stalk caused a decrease in testicular weights in six-week-old male rats. However, body weights of male rats with such lesions were also reduced. Part of the effect on the testicular weight may therefore have been the consequence of a general reduction in body weight.

Lesions in the amygdala of immature rats caused greater ovarian and uterine weights, whereas electrical stimulation of this area in similar rats caused delayed puberty (Bar Sela and Critchlow, 1962). In mature female rats, bilateral amygdala lesions cause pseudopregnancy-like vaginal smears, persistent corpora lutea, and a positive decidual response 35 days after the operation, indicating increased prolactin secretion (Moore et al., 1965). This suggests that the amygdala has an inhibitory effect on prolactin secretion, probably via the hypothalamus. However, Zouhar and de Groot (1963) observed that after bilateral amygdala lesions or after stria terminalis lesions there was evidence of decreased prolactin secretion. The reason for the differences between these experiments is not clear from the published data. Bilateral lesions of the amygdala depress spermatogenesis in rats (see Lundberg, 1962). Amygdala lesions in rabbits do not affect coitus-induced ovulation, but stimulation causes ovulation (Sawyer, 1959a, 1964).

Transection of the stria terminalis of immature cats causes precocious sexual development (Sawyer, 1964). Lesions in the thalamus, caudate nucleus or fornix of rats have no effect on the onset of puberty of immature rats (Sawyer, 1964). However, Herbert and Zuckerman (1958) found that lesions in these areas caused the onset of estrus in ferrets. These results have not been confirmed (Donovan and van der Werff ten Bosch, 1965). Bilateral lesions of the hippocampus made in one-

week-old rats delayed the onset of puberty, whereas pyriform cortex lesions caused precocious sexual maturity (Sawyer, 1964).

Lesions of the septum of rabbits do not interfere with coitus-induced ovulation. Electric stimulation of this area in one persistent estrous rat caused ovulation (Sawyer, 1964).

Damage to the medial habenula causes a lowered prolactin content of the pituitary (Zouhar and de Groot, 1963).

Critchlow (1958), investigating the involvement of the midbrain on ovulation in cyclic rats, found that lesions in the area of the mamillary peduncle blocked ovulation. Only lesions rostral to the interpeduncular nucleus were effective; lesions caudal to this level did not affect ovulation. Pekary and Davidson (1966) performed complete mamillary peduncle transections in adult male and female rats and found normal vaginal cycles after an interval of 0 to 27 days of diestrus. These rats had normal body, ovarian, adrenal, and thyroidal weights but smaller than normal uteri. Lesions made on the day of proestrus did not interfere with ovulation. Lesions in the males did not affect the reproductive organs.

Electrical stimulation of the mamillary peduncle in Nembutal-blocked rats failed to cause ovulation. These results thus indicate that the integrity of the mamillary peduncle is not required for gonadotropin secretion.

Removal of the cerebellum arrested the sexual development of sheep (Markaryan and Grigoryan, 1964).

Lesions in the area postrema of the medulla oblongata did not affect the testes of rats (Lundberg, 1962). The implantation of cupric sulfate in the ventromedial nucleus or in the median eminence plus the anterior pituitary causes ovulation in rabbits, but similar implants in the amygdala, hippocampus, septum, NSO, lateral hypothalamus, or close to the anterior pituitary do not cause ovulation (Hiroi et al., 1965).

It seems valid to state that, at least

in birds and mammals (reptiles not having been investigated in sufficient number of cases), there is substantial support for the hypothesis that the gonadotropic activity of the pituitary is regulated via a neurohumoral mechanism. The anatomical evidence supports the conclusion that the chemotransmitters are transported by the portal system. The chemotransmitters investigated, LH-RF and FSH-RF, have met all but one of the 13 criteria listed by Guillemin (1964) for assessing the validity of the concept of the releasing factors. This one criterion, presence of the substance in the portal system, has probably not been reported on because of technical difficulties in obtaining sufficient material.

The transplantation of the pituitary to the so-called hypophysiotropic area has shown that the material required for the maintenance of gonadotropic function does not require transport via the portal vessels but can act directly on the cells of the pituitary.

It is interesting to compare the areas designated as affecting gonadotropin secretion by different techniques in the same laboratory and to compare these areas with the area at which the hormones of the target glands cause morphological changes in the hypothalamic cells. A comparison of Figures 8-3, 8-6, and 8-11 shows very good agreement among the three methods used to localize the gonadotropin-regulating areas of the hypothalamus.

Intracerebral administration of steroid hormones has provided evidence that certain specific hypothalamic areas are involved in the negative feedback of estrogen and testosterone and that possibly there is also a direct feedback to the pituitary. The implants of LH into the hypothalamus have supplied evidence of pituitary-hypothalamus negative feedback.

The lesion and electrolytic stimulation studies have shown that specific areas of the hypothalamus and extrahypothalamic structures are, or are not, required for normal gonadotropic function.

In mammals, there is considerable evidence that certain hypothalamic and other brain areas have an inhibitory influence on prolactin secretion and that FSH secretion can be maintained, at least partially, in the absence of hypothalamic connections, although in the presence of such connections FSH activity of the pituitary is increased (Moszkowska, 1959). LH secretion seems to be more dependent upon the hypothalamic connections than FSH.

The pharmacological agents which aided considerably in formulating the hypothesis of neurohumoral control of the pituitary have been found to be extremely useful in determining the "critical period", when the stimulus for "spontaneous" LH release occurs, and in determining the approximate duration of this stimulus.

The recording of electrical activity per se has not provided evidence to support the hypothesis of neurohumoral-hypothalamic control of the pituitary activity. However, such recordings have provided evidence that steroid hormones can alter the thresholds of the neural tissue to certain stimuli.

The overall understanding of reciprocal hypothalamic-pituitary relationships has advanced the knowledge of how environmental factors affect reproduction.

REFERENCES

Abrahams, V. C., Langworth, E. P., and Theobald, G. W. 1964. Potentials evoked in the hypothalamus and cerebral cortex by electrical stimulation of the uterus. Nature 203:654-656.

Adams, J. H., Daniel, P. M., and Prichard, M. M. L. 1963. The volumes of pars distalis, pars intermedia and infundibular process of the pituitary gland of the rat, with special reference to the effect of stalk section. Quart. J. Exp. Physiol. 48: 217-234.

Adams, J. H., Daniel, P. M., and Prichard, M. M. L. 1964. Some effects of transection of the pituitary stalk. Brit. Med. J. 2:1619-1625.

Adams, J. H., Daniel, P. M., and Prichard, M. M. L. 1965/1966. Observations on the portal circulation of the pituitary gland. Neuroendocrinol. 1:193-213.

Alleva, J. J., and Umberger, E. J. 1966. Evidence for neural control of the release of pituitary ovulating hormone in the Golden Syrian hamster. Endocrinol. 78:1125-1129.

Anderson, L. L., Bowerman, A. M., and Melampy, R. M. 1965. Oxytocin on ovarian function in cycling and hysterectomized heifers. J. Anim. Sci. 24:964-968.

Arko, H., and Kivalo, E. 1958. Neurosecretory material and the pituitary portal vessels. Morphological evidence of a possible functional interrelation between the hypothalamo-hypophysial neurosecretory pathway and the pituitary portal system in the median eminence and the pars tuberalis of the rat. Acta Endocrinol. 29:9-14.

Arko, H., Kivalo, E., and Rinne, U. K. 1963. Hypothalamo-neurohypophysial neurosecretion after the extirpation of various endocrine glands. Acta Endocrinol. 42:293-299.

Aron, C., and Asch, G. 1962. Influence inhibitrice de l'atropine sur le déclenchement, par le rapprochement sexuel, de la ponte ovulaire chez la ratte mûre. C. R. Acad. Sci. 255:3056-3058.

Asakawa, H., and Turner, C. D. 1965. The capacity of ectopic pituitary grafts to induce growth and genital development in hypophysectomized male rats. Amer. Zool. 5:724 (abstract).

Assenmacher, I. 1958. Recherches sur le contrôle hypothalamique de la fonction gonadotrope préhypophysaire chez le canard. Arch. Anat. Microscop. Morphol. 47:447-572.

Assenmacher, I., and Tixier-Vidal, A. 1965. Hypothalamic-pituitary relations. Proc. Sec. Int. Congr. Endocrinol. 1:131-145.

Attramadal, A. 1964. The uptake and intracellular localization of oestradiol-17β.6.7-H³ in the anterior pituitary and hypothalamus of the rat. Acta Pathol. Microbiol. Scand. 61:151-152.

Averill, R. L. W. 1965. Restoration of lactation in rats with hypothalamic lesions which inhibit lactation. J. Endocrinol. 31:191-196.

Bajusz, E., and Jasmin, G. 1964. Major Problems in Neuroendocrinology. S. Karger, Basel.

Ball, J. N., and Olivereau, M. 1964. Rôle de la prolactine dans la survie en eau douce de Poecilia latipinna hypophysectomisé et arguments en faveur de sa synthèse par les cellules érythrosinophiles de l'hypophyse des Téléostéens. C. R. Acad. Sci. 259:1443-1446.

Ball, J. N., Olivereau, M., Slicher, A. M., and Kallman, K. D. 1965. Functional capacity of ectopic pituitary transplants in the teleost Poecilia formosa, with a comparative discussion on the transplanted pituitary. Phil. Trans. Roy. Soc. London B. 249:69-99.

Bargmann, W. 1966. Neurosecretion. Int. Rev. Cytol. 19:183-201.

Barraclough, C. A. 1966a. Influence of age, prepubertal androgen treatment and hypothalamic stimulation on adenohypophysial LH content in female rats. Endocrinology 78:1053-1066.

Barraclough, C. A. 1966b. Modifications in the CNS regulation of reproduction after exposure of prepubertal rats to steroid hormone. Recent Progr. Hormone Res. 22:503-528.

Barraclough, C. A., and Cross, B. A. 1963. Unit activity in the hypothalamus of the cyclic female rat: Effect of genital stimuli and progesterone. J. Endocrinol. 26:339-359.

Barraclough, C. A., and Gorski, R. A. 1961. Evidence that the hypothalamus is responsible for androgen-induced sterility in the female rat. Endocrinology 68:68-79.

Barraclough, C. A., Yrarrazaval, S., and Hatton, R. 1964. A possible hypothalamic site of action of progesterone in the facilitation of ovulation in the rat. Endocrinology 75:838-845.

Barry, J. 1960. Recherches sur la glande diencéphalique. C. R. Soc. Biol. 154:1250-1253.

Barry, J., and Léonardelli, J. 1962. Recherches sur les modifications des cellules neurosécrétoires acidophiles de l'hypothalamus latéral du cobaye au cours du cycle oestral. C. R. Acad. Sci. 254: 747-749.

Barry, J., and Léonardelli, J. 1965. Effets à long terme de la castration bilatérale chez le cobaye mâle sur la réaction de mise en charge printanière des cellules du noyau hypothalamique latérodorsal interstitiel. C. R. Soc. Biol. 159: 2371-2373.

Barry, J., and Mazzuca, M. 1962. Modifications du cycle oestral provoquées chez le cobaye par la destruction électrolytique bilatérale du noyau hypothalamique latérodorsal interstitiel (N H L D I). C. R. Acad. Sci. 255:2835-2837.

Barry, J., Slimane-Taleb, S., and Torre, J. F. 1962. Étude des variations morphologiques des cellules neuroglandulaires du noyau hypothalamique latérodorsal interstitiel du cobaye après implantations d'hormones sexuelles, isolées ou associés à la castration. C. R. Acad. Sci. 254: 1674-1676.

Barry, J., and Torre, J. F. 1962. Effets précoces de la castration sur la morphologie des cellules neurosécrétoires du noyau hypothalamique latérodorsal interstitiel (N H L D I) du cobaye mâle. C. R. Soc. Biol. 156:847-848.

Bar-Sela, M. E. 1964. Sexual development in male rats bearing amydaloid and hypothalamic lesions. Anat. Rec. 148:359 (abstract).

Bar-Sela, M. E., and Critchlow, V. 1962. Delayed puberty following electrical stimulation of amygdala in female rats. Program 44th Meeting Endocrinol. Soc. Abstract no. 38.

Baylé, J. D., and Assenmacher, I. 1965. Absence de stimulation du jabot du pigeon après autogreffe hypophysaire. C. R. Acad. Sci. 261:5667-5670.

Ben-David, M., Dikstein, S., and Sulman, F. G. 1964. Effect of different steroids on prolactin secretion in pituitary-hypothalamus organ co-culture. Proc. Soc. Exp. Biol. Med. 117:511-513.

Benoit, J., and Assenmacher, I. 1955. Le contrôle hypothalamique de l'activité préhypophysaire gonadotrope. J. de Physiol. (Paris) 47:427-567.

Benoit, J., and Assenmacher, I. 1959. The control by visible radiations of the gonadotropic activity of the duck hypophysis. Recent Progr. Hormone Res. 15:143-164.

Bern, H. A., and Knowles, F. G. W. 1966. Neurosecretion. In L. Martini and W. F. Ganong (eds.): Neuroendocrinology. Academic Press Inc., New York, Vol. 1, pp. 139-186.

Beyer, C., and Mena, F. 1965. Induction of milk secretion in the rabbit by removal of the telencephalon. Amer. J. Physiol. 208:289-292.

Bogdanove, E. M. 1963a. Failure of anterior hypothalamic lesions to prevent either pituitary reactions to castration or inhibition of such reactions by estrogen treatment. Endocrinology 72: 638-642.

Bogdanove, E. M. 1963b. Direct gonad-pituitary feedback: an analysis of effects of intracranial estrogenic depots on gonadotrophin secretion. Endocrinology 73:696-712.

Bogdanove, E. M. 1964. The role of the brain in the regulation of pituitary gonadotropin secretion. Vitamins and Hormones 22:205-260.

Bogdanove, E. M., and Schoen, H. C. 1959. Precocious sexual development in female rats with hypothalamic lesions. Proc. Soc. Exp. Biol. Med. 100:664-669.

Bogdanove, E. M., Parlow, A. F., Bogdanove, J. N., Bhargava, I., and Crabill, E. V. 1964. Specific LH and FSH bio-assays in rats with hypothalamic lesions and accessory sex gland hypertrophy. Endocrinology 74:114-122.

Browning, H. C. 1964. Luteotropin (prolactin) release in mice following administration of gold thioglucose. Amer. Zool. 4:289 (abstract).

Browning, H. C., and Kwan, L. P. 1964. Abnormal pituitary-ovarian relationship, with mammary gland stimulation, in gold thioglucose-treated mice. Texas Rep. Biol. Med. 22:679-691.

Bruce, H. M. 1966. Smell as an exteroceptive factor. J. Anim. Sci. Suppl. 25:83-87.

Campbell, H. J. 1966. The development of the primary portal plexus in the median eminence of the rabbit. J. Anat. 100:381-387.

Campbell, H. J., and Gallardo, E. 1965. Gonadotrophin-releasing activity of median eminence extracts from cattle of different ages. J. Physiol. 181:65P-66P.

Campbell, H. J., Feuer, G., and Harris, G. W. 1964. The effect of intrapituitary infusion of median eminence and other brain extracts on anterior pituitary gonadotrophic secretion. J. Physiol. 170:474-486.

Chowers, I., and McCann, S. M. 1965. Content of luteinizing hormone-releasing factor and luteinizing hormone during the estrous cycle and after changes in gonadal steroid titers. Endocrinology 76:700-708.

Clegg, M. T., and Ganong, W. F. 1960. The effect of hypothalamic lesions on ovarian function in the ewe. Endocrinology 67:179-186.

Clegg, M. T., Santolucito, J. A., Smith, J. D., and Ganong, W. F. 1958. The effect of hypothalamic lesions on sexual behavior and estrous cycles in the ewe. Endocrinology 62:790-797.

Cohen, A. I., Nicol, E., and White, W. F. 1966. Effect of luteinizing hormone releasing factor (LRF) on rat and pig pituitary monolayer cultures. Fed. Proc. 25:315 (abstract).

Cole, H. H. 1964. Gonadotropins. W. H. Freeman and Company, San Francisco.

Coppola, J. A., Leonardi, R. G., and Lippmann, W. 1966. Ovulatory failure in rats after treatment with brain norepinephrine depletors. Endocrinol. 78:225-228.

Coppola, J. A., Leonardi, R. G., Lippmann, W., Perrine, J. W., and Ringler, I. 1965. Induction of pseudopregnancy in rats by depletors of endog-

enous catecholamines. Endocrinology 77:485-490.

Corbin, A. 1963. Testicular and accessory organ depression in immature rats with posterior hypothalamic lesions. Amer. J. Physiol. 204:129-132.

Corbin, A. 1966. Pituitary and plasma LH of ovariectomized rats with median eminence implants of LH. Endocrinology 78:893-896.

Corbin, A., and Cohen, A. I. 1966. Effect of median eminence implants of LH on pituitary LH of female rats. Endocrinology 78:41-46.

Corbin, A., and Schottelius, B. A., 1960. Effects of posterior hypothalamic lesions on sexual maturation of immature female albino rats. Proc. Soc. Exp. Biol. Med. 103:208-210.

Corbin, A., and Schottelius, B. A. 1961. Estrogen therapy in immature female rats with posterior hypothalamic lesions. Proc. Soc. Exp. Biol. Med. 106:841-844.

Cowie, A. T., Daniel, P. M., Prichard, M. M. L., and Tindal, J. S. 1963. Hypophysectomy in pregnant goats, and section of the pituitary stalk in pregnant goats and sheep. J. Endocrinol. 28:93-102.

Critchlow, V. 1958. Blockade of ovulation in the rat by mesencephalic lesions. Endocrinology 63:596-610.

Cross, B. A. 1964. The hypothalamus in mammalian homeostasis. Symp. Soc. Exp. Biol. 18:157-193.

Cross, B. A. 1965. Electrical recording techniques in the study of hypothalamic control of gonadotrophin secretion. Second Int. Congr. Endocrinol. 1:513-516.

Cross, B. A., and Silver, I. A. 1965. Effect of luteal hormone on the behavior of hypothalamic neurones in pseudopregnant rats. J. Endocrinol. 31:251-263.

Daily, W. J. R., and Ganong, W. F. 1958. The effect of ventral hypothalamic lesions on sodium and potassium metabolism in the dog. Endocrinology 62:442-454.

D'Angelo, S. A. 1960. Hypothalamus and endocrine function in persistent estrous rats at low environmental temperature. Amer. J. Physiol. 199:701-706.

D'Angelo, S. A., and Kravatz, A. S. 1960. Gonadotrophic hormone function in persistent estrous rats with hypothalamic lesions. Proc. Soc. Exp. Biol. Med. 104:130-133.

Daniel, P. M. 1966. The anatomy of the hypothalamus and pituitary gland. In L. Martini and W. F. Ganong (eds.): Neuroendocrinology. Academic Press Inc., New York, Vol. 1, pp. 15-80.

Dávid, M. A., Fraschini, F., and Martini, L. 1965a. An in vivo method for evaluating the hypothalamic follicle stimulating hormone releasing factor. Experientia 21:483-484.

Dávid, M. A., Fraschini, F., and Martini, L. 1965b. Parallélisme entre le contenu hypophysaire en FSH et le contenu en FSH-RF (FSH-Releasing Factor). C. R. Acad. Sci. 261:2249-2251.

Dávid, M. A., Fraschini, F., and Martini, L. 1966. Control of LH secretion: Role of a "short" feedback mechanism. Endocrinology 78:55-60.

Dávid, M. A., Csernay, L., László, F. A., and Kovács, K. 1965. Hypophysial blood flow in rats after destruction of the pituitary stalk. Endocrinology 77:183-187.

Davidson, J. M. 1966. Activation of the male rat's sexual behavior by intracerebral implantation of androgen. Endocrinology 79:783-794.

Davidson, J. M., and Sawyer, C. H. 1961a. Evidence for an hypothalamic focus of inhibition of gonadotropin by androgen in the male. Proc. Soc. Exp. Biol. Med. 107:5-7.

Davidson, J. M., and Sawyer, C. H. 1961b. Effects of localized intracerebral implantation of oestrogen on reproductive function in the female rabbit. Acta Endocrinol. 37:385-393.

Davidson, J. M., Contopoulos, A. N., and Ganong, W. F. 1960. Decreased gonadotrophic hormone content of the anterior pituitary gland in dogs with hypothalamic lesions. Endocrinology 66: 735-740.

Davis, D. L., and de Groot, J. 1964. Failure to demonstrate olfactory inhibition of pregnancy ("Bruce effect") in the rat. Anat. Rec. 148:366 (abstract).

de Groot, J. 1957. Neurosecretion in experimental conditions. Anat. Rec. 127:201-217.

de Groot, J. 1966. Limbic and other neural pathways that regulate endocrine function. In L. Martini and W. F. Ganong (eds.): Neuroendocrinology. Academic Press, New York, Vol. 1, pp. 81-106.

de la Lastra, M., and Croxatto, H. 1964. Ovarian ascorbic acid depleting activity in human brain extracts. Nature 204:583-584.

Denamur, R., Martinet, J., and Short, R. V. 1966. Sécrétion de la progestérone par les corps jaunes de la brébis après hypophysectomie, section de la tige pituitaire et hysterectomie. Acta Endocrinol. 52:72-90.

Desclin, L., Flament-Durant, J., and Gepts, W. 1961. À-propos de l'activité gonadotrope de l'hypophyse chez des rats en oestrus permanent résultant de lésions hypothalamiques. Arch. Anat. Microscop. Morphol. Exp. 50:329-339.

Desclin, L., Flament-Durand, J., and Gepts, W. 1962. Transplantation of the ovary to the spleen in rats with persistent estrus resulting from hypothalamic lesions. Endocrinology 70:429-436.

de Voe, W. F., Ramirez, V. D., and McCann, S. M. 1966. Induction of mammary secretion by hypothalamic lesions in male rats. Endocrinology 78:158-164.

Dey, F. L. 1941. Changes in ovaries and uteri in guinea pigs with hypothalamic lesions. Amer. J. Anat. 69:61-87.

Dierickx, K. 1963. The extirpation of the neurosecretory preoptic nucleus and the reproduction of Rana temporaria. Arch. Int. Pharmacodyn. Therap. 145:580-589.

Dierickx, K. 1965. The origin of the aldehyde-fuchsin-negative nerve fibres of the median eminence of the hypophysis: a gonadotropic centre. Z. Zellforsch. 66:504-518.

Doerr-Schott, J. 1965. Cytologie fine de l'hypophyse antérieure d'un amphibien, Rana temporaria L. après greffe homéotypique et culture in vitro prolongée. Analyse de la fonction gonadotrope. Gen. Comp. Endocrinol. 5:672 (abstract).

Donnet, V., Chevalier, J. M., Duflot, J. C., and Pruneyre. 1961a. Actions des implants uniques ou multiples d'hypothalamus total sur le déclenchement de la maturité ovarienne chez la ratte normale. C. R. Acad. Sci. 252:3490-3491.

Donnet, V., Chevalier, J. M., Duflot, J. C., and Pruneyre, A. 1961b. Étude comparative des effets des implants d'hypothalamus et d'hypophyse sur le cycle oestral de la ratte pubère. C. R. Soc. Biol. 155:545-547.

Donnet, V., Chevalier, J. M., Jaquin, M., and Pruneyre, A. 1960. Étude comparative des implantations hypothalamiques et hypophysaires dans le déclenchement de la puberté chez la ratte et la souris. C. R. Soc. Biol. 154:1842-1844.

Donovan, B. T. 1960. The inhibitory action of the hypothalamus upon gonadotrophin secretion. Mem. Soc. Endocrinol. 9:1-15.

Donovan, B. T. 1963. The effect of pituitary stalk section on luteal function in the ferret. J. Endocrinol. 27:201-211.

Donovan, B. T., and Harris, G. W. 1956. Adrenergic agents and the release of gonadotrophic hormone in the rabbit. J. Physiol. 132:577-585.

Donovan, B. T., and Kopriva, B. C. 1965. Effect of removal or stimulation of the olfactory bulbs on the estrous cycle of the guinea pig. Endocrinology 77:213-217.

Donovan, B. T., and van der Werff ten Bosch, J. J. 1959. The relationship of the hypothalamus to oestrus in the ferret. J. Physiol. 147:93-108.

Donovan, B. T., and van der Werff ten Bosch, J. J. 1965. Physiology of Puberty. Edward Arnold Publishers Ltd., London.

Eckles, N. E., Ehni, G., and Kirschbaum, A. 1958. Induction of lactation in the human female by pituitary-stalk section. Anat. Rec. 130:295 (abstract).

Egge, A. S., and Chiasson, R. B. 1963. Endocrine effects of diencephalic lesions in the White Leghorn hen. Gen. Comp. Endocrinol. 3:346-361.

Elwers, M., and Critchlow, V. 1960. Precocious ovarian stimulation following hypothalamic and amygdaloid lesions in rats. Amer. J. Physiol. 198:381-385.

Evans, H. M., and Simpson, M. E. 1950. Physiology of the gonadotrophins. In G. Pincus and K. V. Thimann (eds.): The Hormones. Academic Press Inc., New York, Vol. 2, pp. 351-404.

Everett, J. W. 1964a. Central neural control of reproductive functions of the adenohypophysis. Physiol. Rev. 44:373-431.

Everett, J. W. 1964b. Preoptic stimulative lesions and ovulation in the rat: 'Thresholds' and LH-release time in late diestrus and proestrus. In E. Bajusz and G. Jasmin (eds.): Major Problems in Neuroendocrinology. S. Karger, Basel.

Everett, J. W. 1964c. LH quotas, apparent preoptic thresholds and LH-release times for ovulation in proestrous vs. late-diestrous rats. Fed. Proc. 23:151.

Everett, J. W. 1965. Ovulation in rats from preoptic stimulation through platinum electrodes. Importance of duration and spread of stimulus. Endocrinology 76:1195-1201.

Everett, J. W., and Nikitovitch-Winer, M. 1963. Physiology of the pituitary gland as affected by transplantation on stalk section. *In* A. V. Nalbandov (ed.): Advances in Neuroendocrinology. University of Illinois Press, Urbana, pp. 289-304.

Everett, J. W., and Quinn, D. L. 1966. Differential hypothalamic mechanisms inciting ovulation and pseudopregnancy in the rat. Endocrinology 78:141-150.

Everett, J. W., and Radford, H. M. 1961. Irritative deposits from stainless steel electrodes in the preoptic rat brain causing release of pituitary gonadotropin. Proc. Soc. Exp. Biol. Med. *108*: 604-609.

Farner, D. S., and Follett, B. K. 1966. Light and other environmental factors affecting avian reproduction. J. Anim. Sci. 25 suppl.: 90-115.

Farner, D. S., and Oksche, A. 1962. Neurosecretion in birds. Gen. Comp. Endocrinol. 2:113-147.

Farner, D. S., Kobayashi, H., Oksche, A., and Kawashima, S. 1964. Proteinase and acid-phosphatase activities in relation to the function of the hypothalamo-hypophysial neurosecretory systems of photo stimulated and dehydrated white-crowned sparrows. *In* W. Bargmann and J. P. Schadé (eds.): Lectures on the diencephalon. Progress in Brain Research. Elsevier Publishing Co., Amsterdam, Vol. 5, pp. 147-155.

Fisher, A. E. 1966. Chemical and electrical stimulation of the brain in the male rat. *In* R. A. Gorski and R. E. Whalen (eds.): Brain and Behavior. University of California Press, Berkeley, Vol. 3, pp. 117-130.

Fisher, C., Magoun, H. W., and Ranson, S. W. 1938. Dystocia in diabetes insipidus. Amer. J. Obstet. Gynecol. *36*:1-9.

Fiske, V. M., and Greep, R. O. 1959. Neurosecretory activity in rats under conditions of continuous light or darkness. Endocrinology *64*:175-185.

Flament-Durand, J. 1964. Morphologie et fonction de transplants hypophysaires dans l'hypothalamus chez le rat. C. R. Acad. Sci. *259*:4376-4378.

Flament-Durand, J., and Desclin, L. 1964. Observations concerning the hypothalamic control of pituitary luteotrophin secretion in the rat. Endocrinology 75:22-26.

Flerkó, B. 1957. Le rôle des structures hypothalamiques dans l'action inhibitrice de la folliculine sur la secrétion de l'hormone folliculo-stimulante. Arch. Anat. Microscop. Morphol. Exp. *46*:159-172.

Flerkó, B. 1962. Hypothalamic control of hypophyseal gonadotrophic function. *In* J. Szentágothai (ed.): Hypothalamic Control of the Anterior Pituitary. Akadémiai Kiado, Budapest, pp. 192-264.

Flerkó, B., and Bárdos, V. 1961a. Luteinisation induced in "constant oestrus rats" by lowering oestrogen production. Acta Endocrinol. *37*: 418-422.

Flerkó, B., and Bárdos, V. 1961b. Absence of compensatory ovarian hypertrophy in rats with anterior hypothalamic lesions. Acta Endocrinol. *36*:180-184.

Flerkó, V. B., and Illei, G. 1960. Zur Frage der Spezifität des Einflusses von Sexualsteroiden auf hypothalamische Nervenstrukturen. Endokrinologie. *35*:123-217.

Follenius, F. 1965. Bases structurales et ultra structurales des corrélations diencéphalo-hypophysaires chez les séleciens et les téléostéens. Arch. Anat. Microscop. Morphol. Exp. *54*:195-216.

Fontaine, M., and Leloup, J. 1964. Central nervous system and thyroid and gonadotropic function in poikilotherms. Proc. Second Int. Congr. Endocrinol. *1*:487-494.

Fortier, C. 1963. Hypothalamic control of anterior pituitary. *In* U. S. von Euler and H. Heller (eds.): Comparative Endocrinology. Academic Press Inc., New York, Vol. 1, pp. 1-24.

Franck, H. 1966. Ablation des bulbes olfactifs chez la lapine impubère. Repercussions sur le tractus génital et le comportement sexuel. C. R. Soc. Biol. *160*:389-391.

Frankel, A. I., Gibson, W. R., Graber, J. W., Nelson, D. M., Reichert, L. E., Jr., and Nalbandov, A. V. 1965. An ovarian ascorbic acid depleting factor in the plasma of adenohypophysectomized cockerels. Endocrinology 77:651-657.

Fraps, R. M. 1955. Egg production and fertility in poultry. *In* J. Hammond (ed.): Progress in the Physiology of Farm Animals. Butterworth & Co., Ltd. London, Vol. 2, pp. 661-740.

Fuxe, K. 1964. Cellular localization of monoamines in the median eminence and the infundibular stem of some mammals. Z. Zellforsch. *61*:710-724.

Gabe, M. 1966. Neurosecretion. Pergamon Press, Oxford.

Gala, R. R., and Reece, R. P. 1964. Influence of hypothalamic fragments and extracts on lactogen production *in vitro*. Proc. Soc. Exp. Biol. Med. *117*:833-836.

Gale, C. C. 1963. Non-essential role of prolactin in the hormonal restoration of lactation in goats with radio frequency hypothalamic lesions. Acta Physiol. Scand. *59*:269-283.

Gale, C. C. 1964. Further studies on the effect of radio frequency hypothalamic lesions on lactation and water metabolism. Acta Physiol. Scand. *61*:228-237.

Gale, C. C., and Larsson, B. 1963. Radiation induced "hypophysectomy" and hypothalamic lesions in lactating goats. Acta Physiol. Scand. *59*:299-318.

Gale, C. C., and McCann, S. M. 1961. Hypothalamic control of pituitary gonadotrophins. J. Endocrinol. *22*:107-117.

Gellert, R. J., and Ganong, W. F. 1960. Precocious puberty in rats with hypothalamic lesions. Acta Endocrinol. *33*:569-576.

Gellert, R. J., Bass, E., Jacobs, C., Smith, R., and Ganong, W. F. 1964. Precocious vaginal opening and cornification in rats following injections of extracts of steer median eminence and pars tuberalis. Endocrinology 75:861-866.

Gittes, R. F., and Kastin, A. J. 1966. Effects of increasing numbers of pituitary transplants in hypophysectomized rats. Endocrinology 78: 1023-1031.

Gogan, F., Kordon, C., and Benoit, J. 1963. Reten-

THE HYPOTHALAMUS

---

tissement de lésions de l'éminence médiane sur la gonado stimulation du canard. C. R. Soc. Biol. *157*:2133-2136.

Gorbman, A. 1965. Vascular relations between the neurohypophysis and adenohypophysis of cyclostomes and the problem of evolution of hypothalamic neuroendocrine control. Arch. Anat. Microscop. Exp. *54*:163-193.

Gorbman, A., and Bern, H. A. 1962. A Textbook of Comparative Endocrinology. John Wiley & Sons Inc., New York.

Gorski, R., and Halász, B. 1966. Neural pathways and gonadotrophin release in rats. Fed. Proc. *25*: 315 (abstract).

Gourdji, D., and Tixier-Vidal, A. 1966. Mise en evidence d'un contrôle hypothalamique stimulant de la prolactine hypophysaire chez le canard. C. R. Acad. Sci. *263*:162-165.

Graber, J. W., and Nalbandov, A. V. 1965. Neurosecretion in White Leghorn cockerel. Gen. Comp. Endocrinol. *5*:485-492.

Green, J. D. 1951. The comparative anatomy of the hypophysis, with special reference to its blood supply and innervation. Amer. J. Anat. *88*:225-312.

Green, J. D. 1966a. The comparative anatomy of the portal vascular system and of the innervation of the hypophysis. *In* G. W. Harris and B. T. Donovan (eds.): The Pituitary Gland. University of California Press, Berkeley, Vol. 1, pp. 127-146.

Green, J. D. 1966b. Microanatomical aspects of the formation of neurohypophysial hormones and neurosecretion. *In* G. W. Harris and B. T. Donovan (eds.): The Pituitary Gland. University of California Press, Berkeley, Vol. 3, pp. 240-268.

Green, J. D., and Harris, G. W. 1947. The neurovascular link between the neurohypophysis and adenohypophysis. J. Endocrinol. *5*:136-146.

Greep, R. O. 1961. Physiology of the anterior hypophysis in relation to reproduction. *In* W. C. Young (ed.): Sex and Internal Secretions. Williams & Wilkins Co., Baltimore, Vol. 1, pp. 240-301.

Greer, M. A. 1953. The effect of progesterone on persistent vaginal estrus produced by hypothalamic lesions in the rat. Endocrinology *53*: 380-390.

Grignon, G. 1960. Étude du complexe hypothalamo-hypophysaire chez la tortue terrestre (*T. mauritanica*) traitée par le diéthylstilboestrol. C. R. Soc. Biol. *154*:1256-1259.

Grosvenor, C. E. 1965. Effect of nursing and stress upon prolactin-inhibiting activity of the rat hypothalamus. Endocrinology *77*:1037-1042.

Grosvenor, C. E. 1966. Impairment of milk secretion in rats following injection of extract of hypothalamus. Fed. Proc. *25*:191 (abstract).

Grosvenor, C. E., McCann, S. M., and Nallar, R. 1965. Inhibition of nursing-induced and stress-induced fall in pituitary prolactin concentration in lactating rats by injection of acid extracts of bovine hypothalamus. Endocrinology *76*:883-889.

Guillemin, R. 1964. Control of pituitary hormone secretion. Recent Progr. Hormone Res. *20*:89-121.

Hagedoorn, J. P. 1965. Interrelationships Between the Central Nervous System, the Hypophysis, and the Gonadal System in the Common Striped Skunk (*Mephitis mephitis nigra*). Dissertation Abstracts, *26*:2970.

Halász, B. 1962. Influence of partial or total interruption of the hypophyseal stalk and of focal hypothalamic lesion on the weight and histological structure of endocrine organs. *In* J. Szentágothai (ed.): Hypothalamic control of the anterior pituitary. Kiado Akadémiai, Budapest, pp. 106-127.

Halász, B., and Pupp, L. 1965. Hormone secretion of the anterior pituitary gland after physical interruption of all nervous pathways to the hypophysiotropic area. Endocrinology *77*:553-562.

Halász, B., Pupp, L., and Uhlarik, S. 1962. Hypophysiotrophic area in the hypothalamus. J. Endocrinol. *25*:147-154.

Halász, B., Pupp, L., Uhlarik, S., and Tima, L. 1965. Further studies on the hormone secretion of the anterior pituitary transplanted into the hypophysiotrophic area of the rat hypothalamus. Endocrinology *77*:343-355.

Harris, G. W., and Campbell, H. J. 1966. The regulation of the secretion of luteinizing hormone and ovulation. *In* G. W. Harris and B. T. Donovan (eds.): The Pituitary Gland. University of California Press, Berkeley, Vol. 2, pp. 99-165.

Harris, G. W., and Donovan, B. T. 1966. The Pituitary Gland. University of California Press, Berkeley, Vols. 1-3.

Harris, G. W., and Michael, R. P. 1964. The activation of sexual behaviour by hypothalamic implants of oestrogen. J. Physiol. *171*:275-301.

Haun, C. K., and Sawyer, C. H. 1960. Initiation of lactation in rabbits following placement of hypothalamic lesions. Endocrinology *67*:270-272.

Haun, C. K., and Sawyer, C. H. 1961. The role of the hypothalamus in initiation of milk secretion. Acta Endocrinol. *38*:99-106.

Heller, H. 1962. Neurohypophyseal hormones. *In* U. S. von Euler and H. Heller (eds): Comparative Endocrinology. Academic Press Inc., New York, Vol. 1, pp. 25-80.

Herbert, J., and Zuckerman, S. 1958. Ovarian stimulation following cerebral lesions in ferrets. J. Endocrinol. *17*:433-443.

Hillarp, N. Å. 1949. Studies on the localization of hypothalamic centres controlling the gonadotrophic function of the hypophysis. Acta Endocrinol. *2*:11-23.

Hiroi, M., Sugita, S., and Suzuki, M. 1965. Ovulation induced by implantation of cupric sulfate into the brain of the rabbit. Endocrinology *77*:963-967.

Hoebel, B. G. 1965. Hypothalamic lesions by electrocauterization: Disinhibition of feeding and self-stimulation. Science *149*:452-453.

Hoebel, B. G., and Teitelbaum, P. 1962. Hypothalamic control of feeding and self-stimulation. Science *135*:375-376.

Hohlweg, W., and Daume, E. 1959a. Lokale hor-monelle Beeinflussung des Hypophysen-Zwischenhirnsystems bei Hähnen. Endokrinologie 37:95-104.

Hohlweg, W., and Daume, E. 1959b. Über die Wirkung intra-zerebral verabreichten Dienoestroldiacetats bei Ratten. Endokrinologie 38:46-51.

Hooper, K. C. 1963. The enzymic inactivation of physiologically active polypeptides by different parts of the nervous system. Biochem. J. 88: 398-403.

Hooper, K. C. 1964. Distribution of hypothalamic peptidases in pregnant and non-pregnant dogs. Biochem. J. 90:584-587.

Hooper, K. C. 1966a. Some observations on the behaviour of hypothalamic enzymes during the time of blastocyst implantation in the rabbit. Biochem. J. 99:128-132.

Hooper, K. C. 1966b. The metabolism of oxytocin during lactation in the rabbit. Biochem. J. 100:823-826.

Hooper, K. C. 1966c. The effect of injected oestradiol-benzoate on the concentration of some peptidases in the rabbit. Biochem. J. 100:37P.

Hopkins, T. F., and Pincus, G. 1965. Effects of rat hypothalamic and cerebral tissue on PMS-induced ovulation. Endocrinology 76:1177-1183.

Horowitz, S., and van der Werff ten Bosch, J. J. 1962. Hypothalamic sexual precocity in female rats operated shortly after birth. Acta Endocrinol. 41:301-313.

Hoshino, K. 1964. Gonadotrophic effects of iso-grafted pituitary glands in mice. Anat. Rec. 148:377 (abstract).

Houssay, B. A., Biassotti, A., and Sammartino, R. 1935. Modifications fonctionelles de l'hypophyse après les lésions infindibulo-tubériennes chez le crapaud. C. R. Soc. Biol. 120:725-727.

Igarashi, M., and McCann, S. M. 1964a. A new sensitive bio-assay for follicle-stimulating hormone (FSH). Endocrinology 74:440-445.

Igarashi, M., and McCann, S. M. 1964b. A hypothalamic follicle stimulating hormone-releasing factor. Endocrinology 74:446-452.

Igarashi, M., Nallar, R., and McCann, S. M. 1964. Further studies on the follicle-stimulating hormone-releasing action of hypothalamic extracts. Endocrinology 75:901-907.

Jacobsohn, D. 1966. The techniques and effects of hypophysectomy, pituitary stalk section and pituitary transplantation in experimental animals. In G. W. Harris and B. T. Donovan (eds.): The Pituitary Gland. University of California Press, Berkeley, Vol. 2, pp. 1-21.

Jasinski, A., Gorbman, A., and Hara, T. J. 1966. Rate of movement and redistribution of stainable neurosecretory granules in hypothalamic neurons. Science 154:776-778.

Johnson, D. C. 1963. Hypophysial LH release in androgenized female rats after administration of sheep brain extracts. Endocrinology 72: 832-836.

Johnson, D. C. 1964. Effects of hypothalamic extraction on hypophyseal LH in immature male rats. Proc. Soc. Exp. Biol. Med. 117:160-163.

Johnson, D. C., and Witschi, E. 1962. Gonadotropin-releasing activity of sheep median eminence extracts. Amer. Zool. 2:531-532 (abstract).

Jørgensen, C. B., and Larsen, L. O. 1963. Neuro-adenohypophysial relationships. Zool. Soc. London Symp. 9:59-82.

Juhász, L. P., and van Tienhoven, A. 1964. Effect of electrical stimulation of telencephalon on ovulation and oviposition in the hen. Amer. J. Physiol. 207:286-290.

Jutisz, M., de la Llosa, P., Sakiz, E., Yamazaki, E. V., and Guillemin, R. 1963. L'action des enzymes protéolytiques sur les facteurs hypothalamiques LRF et TRF stimulant la secrétion des hormones hypophysaires de lutéinization (LH) et de thyréotrope (TSH). C. R. Soc. Biol. 157:235-237.

Kanematsu, S., and Sawyer, C. H. 1963a. Effects of hypothalamic estrogen implants on pituitary LH and prolactin in rabbits. Amer. J. Physiol. 205:1073-1076.

Kanematsu, S., and Sawyer, C. H. 1963b. Effects of intrahypothalamic and intrahypophysial estrogen implants on pituitary prolactin and lactation in the rabbit. Endocrinology 72:243-252.

Kanematsu, S., and Sawyer, C. H. 1963c. Effects of hypothalamic and hypophysial estrogen implants on pituitary gonadotrophic cells in ovariectomized rabbits. Endocrinology 73:687-695.

Kanematsu, S., and Sawyer, C. H. 1964. Effects of hypothalamic and hypophysial estrogen implants on pituitary and plasma LH in ovariectomized rabbits. Endocrinology 75:579-585.

Kanematsu, S., and Sawyer, C. H. 1965. Blockade of ovulation in rabbits by hypothalamic implants of norethindrone. Endocrinology 76:691-699.

Kanematsu, S., Hilliard, J. and Sawyer, C. H. 1963. Effect of hypothalamic lesions on pituitary prolactin content in the rabbit. Endocrinology 73: 345-348.

Karapetyan, S. K., Mikaelyan, N. G., and Nazaryan, M. B. 1963. Experimental data on the role of various parts of the central nervous system in regulating reproduction in birds. Izvest. Akad. Nauk. Armiansk. S. S. R. Biol. Nauki 16:35-41.

Kennedy, G. C., and Mitra, J. 1963. Hypothalamic control of energy balance and the reproductive cycle in the rat. J. Physiol. 166:395-407.

Kling, A. 1964. Effects of rhinencephalic lesions on endocrine and somatic development in the rat. Amer. J. Physiol. 206:1395-1400.

Knigge, K. M. 1962. Gonadotropic activity of neonatal pituitary glands implanted in the rat brain. Amer. J. Physiol. 202:387-391.

Knowles, F., and Vollrath, L. 1965. A dural neurosecretory innervation of the pars distalis of the pituitary of the eel. Nature 208:1343-1344.

Kobayashi, H., and Farner, D. S. 1964. Cholinesterases in the hypothalamo-hypophyseal neurosecretory system of the white-crowned sparrow, Zonotrichia leucophrys gambelii. Z. Zellforsch. 63:965-973.

Kobayashi, H., Oota, Y., Uemura, H., and Hirano, T. 1966. Electron-microscopic and pharmacological studies on the rat median eminence. Z. Zellforsch. 71:387-404.

Kobayashi, T., Kobayashi, T., Kagawa, T., Mizuno, M., and Amenomori, Y. 1963. Influence of rat hypothalamic extract on gonadotropic activity of cultivated anterior pituitary cells. Endocrinol. Jap. *10*:16-24.

Kobayashi, T., Sato, H., Maruyama, M., Arai, K., and Takezawa, T. 1959. Persistent estrus produced in rats by hypothalamic lesions. Endocrinol. Jap. *6*:107-112.

Kordon, C. 1964. Retentissement de stimulation électrique de l'hypothalamus sur la fonction gonadotrope du rat. J. de Physiol. *56*:386 (abstract).

Kragt, C. L., and Meites, J. 1965. Stimulation of pigeon pituitary prolactin release by pigeon hypothalamic extract *in vitro.* Endocrinology *76*:1169-1176.

Krejci, M. E., and Critchlow, V. 1959. Precocious uterine stimulation following hypothalamic and amygdaloid lesions in female rats. Anat. Rec. *133*:300 (abstract).

Kuroshima, A., Arimura, A., Bowers, C. Y., and Schally, A. V. 1966. Inhibition by pig hypothalamic extracts of depletion of pituitary prolactin in rats following cervical stimulation. Endocrinology *78*:216-217.

Kuroshima, A., Ishida, Y., Bowers, C. Y., and Schally, A. V. 1965. Stimulation of release of follicle-stimulating hormone by hypothalamic extracts *in vitro* and *in vivo.* Endocrinology *76*:614-619.

Kuroshima, A., Arimura, A., Saito, T., Ishida, Y., Bowers, C. Y., and Schally, A. V. 1966. Depletion of pituitary follicle-stimulating hormone by beef and pig hypothalamic extracts. Endocrinology *78*:1105-1108.

Laqueur, G. L., McCann, S. M., Schreiner, C. H., Rosemberg, E., Rioch, D. McK., and Anderson, E. 1955. Alteration of adrenal cortical and ovarian activity following hypothalamic lesions. Endocrinology *57*:44-54.

Laws, D. F. 1961. Hypothalamic neurosecretion in the refractory and post-refractory periods and its relationship to the rate of photoperiodically induced testicular growth in *Zonotrichia leucophrys gambelii.* Z. Zellforsch. *54*:275-306.

Legait, H. 1959. Contribution a l'Étude Morphologique et Expérimentale du Système Hypothalamo-Neurohypophysaire de la Poule Rhode-Island. Thèse d'aggrégation de l'Enseignement Superieur. Université Catholique de Louvain.

Li, C. H. 1961. Some aspects of the relationship of peptide structures to activity in pituitary hormones. Vitamins and Hormones *19*:313-329.

Liebelt, R. A., Sekiba, K., Icchinoe, S., and Liebelt, A. G. 1966. Persistent vaginal cornification in gold-thioglucose-treated BALB/c/Ki mice. Endocrinology *78*:845-854.

Lippmann, W., Leonardi, R., Ball, J., and Coppola, J. 1966. Relationship between hypothalamic catecholamines and gonadotropin secretion in rats. Fed. Proc. *25*:353 (abstract).

Lisk, R. D. 1960. Estrogen-sensitive centers in the hypothalamus of the rat. J. Exp. Zool. *145*: 197-207.

Lisk, R. D. 1962a. Diencephalic placement of estradiol and sexual receptivity in the female rat. Amer. J. Physiol. *203*:493-496.

Lisk, R. D. 1962b. Testosterone-sensitive centers in the hypothalamus of the rat. Acta Endocrinol. *41*:195-204.

Lisk, R. D. 1963. Maintenance of normal pituitary weight and cytology in the spayed rat following estradiol implants in the arcuate nucleus. Anat. Rec. *146*:281-291.

Lisk, R. D. 1964. Hypothalamus and hormone feedback in the rat. Trans. N. Y. Acad. Sci. Ser. II *27*:35-38.

Lisk, R. D. 1965. Reproductive capacity and behavioural oestrus in the rat bearing hypothalamic implants of sex steroids. Acta Endocrinol. *48*:209-219.

Lisk, R. D. 1965/1966. Neurosecretion in the rat: Changes occurring following neural implant of estrogen. Neuroendocrinology *1*:83-92.

Lisk, R. D. 1966a. Hormonal implants in the central nervous system and behavioral receptivity in the female rat. *In* R. A. Gorski and R. E. Whalen (eds.): The brain and gonadal function. Brain and Behavior. University of California Press, Berkeley, Vol. 3, pp. 98-117.

Lisk, R. D. 1966b. Estrogen plus progesterone are neural trigger for behavioral estrus in the rat. Anat. Rec. *154*:472 (abstract).

Littlejohn, B. M., and de Groot, J. 1963. Estrogen-sensitive areas in the rat brain. Fed. Proc. *22*: 571 (abstract).

Lloyd, C. W., and Weisz, J. 1966. Some aspects of reproductive physiology. Ann. Rev. Physiol. *28*:267-310.

Lundberg, P. O. 1962. Extrahypothalamic regions of the central nervous system and gonadotrophin secretion. Proc. 22nd Int. Cong. Physiol. Sci. *1*:615-619.

McCann, S. M., and Dhariwal, A. P. S. 1966. Hypothalamic releasing factors and the neurovascular link between the brain and the anterior pituitary. *In* L. Martini and W. F. Ganong (eds.): Neuroendocrinology. Academic Press Inc., New York. Vol. 1, pp. 261-296.

McCann, S. M., and Friedman, H. M. 1960. The effect of hypothalamic lesions on the secretion of luteotrophin. Endocrinology *67*:597-608.

McCann, S. M., and Ramirez, V. D. 1964. The neuroendocrine regulation of hypophyseal luteinizing hormone secretion. Recent Progr. Hormone Res. *20*:131-170.

McCann, S. M., and Taleisnik, S. 1960. Hypothalamic regulation of luteinizing hormone secretion. Science *132*:1496 (abstract).

McCormack, C. E., and Meyer, R. K. 1962. Ovulating hormone release in gonadotrophin treated immature rats. Proc. Soc. Exp. Biol. Med. *110*: 343-346.

McFarland, L. Z. 1959. Effects of an electrolytic lesion in the avian hypothalamo-hypophysial tract. Anat. Rec. *133*:411 (abstract).

McFarland, L. Z., and Clegg, M. T. 1960. Sexual behavior in rams and the effect of hypothalamic lesions. Anat. Rec. *138*:366-367 (abstract).

Margherita, G., Albritton, D., MacInnes, R., Hayward, R., and Gorski, R. A. 1965. Electroencephalographic changes in ventromedial hypothalamus and amygdala induced by vaginal and other peripheral stimuli. Exp. Neurol. *13*: 96-108.

Markaryan, L. P., and Grigoryan. G. S. 1964. The role of the cerebellum in the sexual function of sheep. Biol. Abst. 45, ref. 19885.

Martini, L., and Ganong, W. F. 1966. Neuroendocrinology. Academic Press Inc., New York.

Martinovitch, P. N., Pavić, D., and Živković, N. 1963. The functional activity of infant rats' anterior pituitaries grafted into hypophysectomized males (heterotopic grafts). J. Exp. Zool. *153*: 89-97.

Martinovitch, P. N., Živković, N., and Pavić, D. 1966. The response of the ovary of the rat to heterotopically placed anterior pituitary transplants. Gen. Comp. Endocrinol. 7:215-223.

Masur, S. K. 1962. Autotransplantation of the pituitary in the red eft. Amer. Zool. 2:538 (abstract).

Matsui, T. 1966a. Fine structure of the posterior median eminence of the pigeon, *Columba livia domestica*. J. Fac. Sci. Univ. Tokyo (Sec. 4) *11*: 49-70.

Matsui, T. 1966b. Fine structure of the median eminence of the rat. J. Fac. Sci. Univ. Tokyo (Sec. 4) *11*:71-96.

Matsui, T., and Kobayashi, H. 1965. Histochemical demonstration of monoamine oxidase in the hypothalamo-hypophysial system of the tree sparrow and the rat. Z. Zellforsch. *68*:172-182.

May, R. M. 1964. Induction de la spermatogénèse par la greffe bréphoplastique intracérébelleuse de l'hypophyse chez le souriceau hypophysectomisé. C. R. Acad. Sci. 259:3083-3085.

Meier, A. H., Davis, K. B., and Dusseau, J. 1966. Prolactin and the antigonadal response in the migratory white-throated sparrow. Amer. Zool. 6:312 (abstract).

Meites, J. 1966. Control of mammary growth and lactation. *In* L. Martini and W. F. Ganong (eds.): Neuroendocrinology. Academic Press Inc., New York. Vol. 1:669-707.

Meites, J., Talwalker, P. K., and Nicoll, C. S. 1960. Initiation of lactation in rats with hypothalamic or cerebral tissue. Proc. Soc. Exp. Biol. Med. *103*:298-300.

Michael, R. P. 1965. The selective accumulation of estrogens in the neural and genital tissues of the cat. *In* L. Martini and A. Pecile (eds.): Hormonal Steroids. Academic Press Inc., New York, Vol. 2, pp. 469-481.

Mittler, J. C., and Meites, J. 1964. *In vitro* stimulation of pituitary Follicle-Stimulating-Hormone release by hypothalamic extract. Proc. Soc. Exp. Biol. Med. *117*:309-313.

Mittler, J. C., and Meites, J. 1966. Effects of hypothalamic extract and androgen on pituitary FSH release *in vitro*. Endocrinology 78:500-504.

Moll, J., and Zeilmaker, G. H. 1966. Ovulatory discharge of gonadotrophins induced by hypothalamic stimulation in castrated male rats bearing a transplanted ovary. Acta Endocrinol. *51*:281-289.

Montemurro, D. G. 1964. Weight and histology of the pituitary gland in castrated male rats with hypothalamic lesions. J. Endocrinol. *30*:57-67.

Moore, W. W. 1961. Failure of adrenergic and cholinergic blocking agents to block ovulation in the rat. Amer. J. Physiol. *200*:1293-1295.

Moore, W. W. 1966. Effect of stress on plasma LH activity in ovariectomized rats. The Physiologist 9:248 (abstract).

Moore, W. W., Woehler, T. R., and Tarry, K. 1965. Effects of lesions of the amygdala on adrenal, thyroid and ovarian function. Anat. Rec. *151*: 390 (abstract).

Moszkowska, A. 1959. Contribution à la recherche des relations du complexe hypothalamo-hypophysaire dans la fonction gonadotrope. Méthode *in vivo* et *in vitro*. C. R. Soc. Biol. *153*:1945-1948.

Moszkowska, A., and Kordon, C. 1961. Mise en evidence de facteurs agissant sur la décharge gonadotrope préhypophysaire (G.R.F.) dans les implants hypothalamiques de rat prélevés dans differentes conditions expérimentales. J. de Physiol. 53:431-432 (abstract).

Moszkowska, A., and Kordon, C. 1965. Contrôle hypothalamique de la fonction gonadotrope et variation du taux des G.R.F. chez le rat. Gen. Comp. Endocrinol. 5:596-613.

Nalbandov, A. V. 1963. Advances in Neuroendocrinology. University of Illinois Press, Urbana.

Nalbandov, A. V. 1964. Effects of pituitary transplantation in birds. *In* L. Martini and A. Pecile (eds.): Hormonal Steroids. Academic Press Inc., New York, Vol. 1, pp. 283-287.

Nalbandov, A. V., and St. Clair, L. E. 1958. Relation of the nervous system to implantation. *In* F. X. Gassner (ed.): Reproduction and Infertility. Pergamon Press, New York, pp. 83-87.

Nallar, R., and McCann, S. M. 1965. Luteinizing hormone-releasing activity in plasma of hypophysectomized rats. Endocrinology 76:272-275.

Nauta, W. J. H. 1963. Central nervous organization and the endocrine motor system. *In* A. V. Nalbandov (ed.): Advances in Neuroendocrinology. Univeristy of Illinois Press, Urbana, pp. 5-21.

Nedde, N. R., and Nikitovitch-Winer, M. B. 1964. Induction of ovulation in diestrous and pseudopregnant rats with median eminence extract treatment. Anat. Rec. *148*:317 (abstract).

Nicoll, C. S. 1965. Neural regulation of adenohypophysial prolactin secretion in tetrapods. Indications from *in vitro* studies. J. Exp. Zool. *158*: 203-210.

Nicoll, C. S., and Bern, H. A. 1964. "Prolactin" and the pituitary glands of fishes. Gen. Comp. Endocrinol. *4*:457-471.

Nikitovitch-Winer, M. 1962. Induction of ovulation in rats by direct intrapituitary infusion of median eminence extracts. Endocrinology *70*:350-358.

Nikitovitch-Winer, M. 1965. Effect of hypophysial stalk transection on luteotropic hormone secretion in the rat. Endocrinology 77:658-666.

Nikitovitch-Winer, M., and Everett, J. W. 1958. Functional restitution of pituitary grafts retransplanted from kidney to median eminence. Endocrinology 63:916-930.

Nikitovitch-Winer, M., and Everett, J. W. 1959. Histocytologic changes in grafts of rat pituitary on the kidney and upon re-transplantation under the diencephalon. Endocrinology 65: 357-368.

Nishioka, R. S., and Bern, H. A. 1966. Fine structure of the neurohemal areas associated with the hypophysis in the hagfish, *Poliostrema stoutii*. Gen. Comp. Endocrinol. 7:457-462.

Noumura, T. 1957. Changes in ovaries of female rat in parabiosis with gonadectomized co-twin following electrical stimulation applied to head of either parabiont. Ann. Zool. Jap. 30:18-25.

Oksche, A., Laws, D. F., Kamemoto, F. I., and Farner, D. S. 1959. The hypothalamo-hypophysial neurosecretory system of the white-crowned sparrow, *Zonotrichia leucophrys gambelii*. Z. Zellforsch. 51:1-42.

Oksche, A., Farner, D. S., Serventy, D. C., Wolff, F., and Nicholls, C. A. 1963. The hypothalamo-hypophysial neurosecretory system of the zebra finch, *Taeniopygia castanotis*. Z. Zellforsch. 58: 846-914.

Olivecrona, H. 1957. Paraventricular nucleus and pituitary gland. Acta Physiol. Scand. Suppl. 136.

Opel, H. 1963. Delay in ovulation in the hen following stimulation of the preoptic brain. Proc. Soc. Exp. Biol. Med. 113:488-492.

Opel, H. 1964. Premature oviposition following operative interference with the brain of the chicken. Endocrinology 74:193-200.

Opel, H., and Fraps, R. M. 1961. Blockade of gonadotrophin release for ovulation in the hen following stimulation with stainless steel electrodes. Proc. Soc. Exp. Biol. Med. 108:291-296.

O'Steen, W. K. 1965. Suppression of ovarian activity in immature rats by serotinin. Endocrinology 77:937-939.

Palka, Y. S., and Sawyer, C. H. 1964. Induction of estrous behavior in the ovariectomized rabbit by estrogen implants in the hypothalamus. Amer. Zool. 4:289 (abstract).

Palka, Y. S., and Sawyer, C. H. 1966. Induction of estrous behavior in rabbits by hypothalamic implants of testosterone. Amer. J. Physiol. 211: 225-228.

Palka, Y. S., Ramirez, V. D., and Sawyer, C. H. 1966. Distribution and biological effects of tritiated estradiol implanted in the hypothalamo-hypophysial region of female rats. Endocrinology 78:487-499.

Pasteels, J. L., Jr. 1957. Recherches expérimentales sur le rôle de l'hypothalamus dans la différenciation cytologique de l'hypophyse chez Pleurodeles waltlii. Arch. Biol. 68:65-114.

Pasteels, J. L., Jr. 1960. Étude expérimentale des différentes catégories d'éléments chromophiles de l'hypophyse adulte de Pleurodeles walthlii, de leur fonction et de leur contrôle par l'hypothalamus. Arch. Biol. 71:409-471.

Pekary, A. E., and Davidson, J. M. 1966. Role of the mammilary peduncle (MP) in reproductive processes in the rat. Anat. Rec. 154:400 (abstract).

Petrovic, A., and Aron, M. 1958. Maintien de la fonction gonadostimulante de greffons préhypophysaires intratesticulaires chez le cobaye hypophysectomisé. C. R. Soc. Biol. 152:144-146.

Phillips, R. E. 1964. "Wildness" in the Mallard duck: Effects of brain lesions and stimulation on "escape behavior" and reproduction. J. Comp. Neurol. 122:139-155.

Piacsek, B. E., and Meites, J. 1966a. Stimulation by continuous light of gonadotropic function in transplanted pituitaries of hypophysectomized rats. Fed. Proc. 25:191 (abstract).

Piacsek, B. E., and Meites, J. 1966b. Effects of castration and gonadal hormones on hypothalamic content of luteinizing hormone releasing factor (LRF). Endocrinology 79:432-439.

Quinn, D. L. 1966. Luteinizing hormone release following preoptic stimulation in the male rat. Nature 209:891-892.

Quinn, D. L., and Zarrow, M. X. 1964. Inhibition of pregnant mare's serum-induced ovulation in the immature rat. Endocrinology 74:309-313.

Quinn, D. L., and Zarrow, M. X. 1965. Inhibition of the release of the ovulating hormone in immature rats with hypothalamic lesions. Endocrinology 77:255-263.

Ralph, C. L. 1959. Some effects of hypothalamic lesions on gonadotrophin release in the hen. Anat. Rec. 134:411-431.

Ralph, C. L. 1960. Polydipsia in the hen following lesions in the supraoptic hypothalamus. Amer. J. Physiol. 198:528-530.

Ralph, C. L., and Fraps, R. M. 1959a. Long-term effects of diencephalic lesions on the ovary of the hen. Amer. J. Physiol. 197:1279-1283.

Ralph, C. L., and Fraps, R. M. 1959b. Effect of hypothalamic lesions on progesterone-induced ovulation in the hen. Endocrinology 65:819-824.

Ralph, C. L., and Fraps, R. M. 1960. Induction of ovulation in the hen by injection of progesterone into the brain. Endocrinology 66:269-272.

Ramirez, V. D., and McCann, S. M. 1964. Induction of prolactin secretion by implants of estrogen into the hypothalamo-hypophysial region of female rats. Endocrinology 75:206-214.

Ramirez, V. D., and Sawyer, C. H. 1965. Fluctuations in hypothalamic LH-RF (luteinizing hormone-releasing factor) during the rat estrous cycle. Endocrinology 76:282-289.

Ramirez, V. D., and Sawyer, C. H. 1966. Changes in the hypothalamic luteinizing hormone releasing factor (LHRF) in the female rat during puberty. Endocrinology 78:958-964.

Ramirez, V. D., Abrams, R. M., and McCann, S. M. 1964a. Effect of estradiol implantation in the hypothalamo-hypophysial region of the rat on the secretion of luteinizing hormone. Endocrinology 75:243-248.

Ramirez, V. D., Moore, D., and McCann, S. M. 1964b. Independence of luteinizing hormone and adrenocorticotrophin secretion in the rat. Proc. Soc. Exp. Biol. Med. 118:169-173.

Ratner, A., and Meites, J. 1964. Depletion of prolactin-inhibiting activity of rat hypothalamus by estradiol or suckling stimulus. Endocrinology 75:377-382.

Reynolds, R. W. 1963. Ventromedial hypothalamic lesions without hyperphagia. Amer. J. Physiol. *204*:60-62.

Reynolds, R. W. 1965. Hypothalamic lesions and disinhibition of feeding. Science *150*:1322.

Robinson, B. L., and Sawyer, C. H. 1957. Loci of sex behavioral and gonadotrophic centers in the female cat hypothalamus. The Physiologist *1*:72 (abstract).

Robinson, T. J. 1965. Accumulation d'oestradiol et hexoestrol tritiés dans le cerveau et quelques autres tissus chez la brebis. Ann. Biol. Anim. Biochim. Biophys. *5*:341-351.

Rossbach, R. 1966. Das Neurosekretorische Zwischenhirnsystem der Amsel *(Turdus merula)* in Jahresablauf und nach Wasserentzug. Z. Zellforsch. *71*:118-145.

Rowland, V. 1966. Stereotaxic techniques and the production of lesions. *In* L. Martini and W. F. Ganong (eds.): Neuroendocrinology. Academic Press Inc., New York, Vol. 1, pp. 107-132.

Sawyer, C. H. 1959a. Nervous control of ovulation. *In* C. W. Lloyd (ed.): Recent Progress in Endocrinology of Reproduction. Academic Press Inc., New York, pp. 1-18.

Sawyer, C. H. 1959b. Effects of brain lesions on estrous behavior and reflexogenous ovulation in the rabbit. J. Exp. Zool. *142*:227-246.

Sawyer, C. H. 1963. Discussion of paper by P. L. Munson. *In* A. V. Nalbandov (ed.): Advances in Neuroendocrinology. University of Illinois Press, Urbana, pp. 444-457.

Sawyer, C. H. 1964. Control of secretion of gonadotropins. *In* H. H. Cole (ed.): Gonadotropins. W. H. Freeman and Company, San Francisco, pp. 113-159.

Sawyer, C. H. 1966. Neural mechanisms in the steroid feedback regulation of sexual behavior and pituitary-gonad function. The brain and gonadal function. *In* R. A. Gorski and R. E. Whalen (eds.): Brain and Behavior. University of California Press, Berkeley, Vol. 3, pp. 221-255.

Sawyer, C. H., and Kawakami, M. 1961. Interactions between the central nervous system and hormones influencing ovulation. *In* C. A. Villee (ed.): Control of Ovulation. Pergamon Press, New York, pp. 79-97.

Schally, A. V., and Bowers, C. Y. 1964. *In vitro* and *in vivo* stimulation of the release of luteinizing hormone. Endocrinology *75*:312-320.

Schally, A. V., Meites, J., Bowers, C. Y., and Ratner, A. 1964. Identity of prolactin inhibiting factor (PIF) and luteinizing hormone releasing factor (LRF). Proc. Soc. Exp. Biol. Med. *117*:252-254.

Scharrer, E., and Scharrer, B. 1954a. Hormones produced by neurosecretory cells. Recent Progr. Hormone Res. *10*:183-232.

Scharrer, E., and Scharrer, B. 1954b. Neurosekretion. *In* W. Bargmann (ed.): Handbuch der Mikroskopischen Anatomie des Menschen. Springer Verlag, Berlin, 6 (pt. 5), pp. 953-1066.

Scharrer, E., and Scharrer, B. 1963. Neuroendocrinology. Columbia University Press, New York.

Schiavi, R. C. 1964. Effect of anterior and posterior hypothalamic lesions on precocious sexual maturation. Amer. J. Physiol. *206*:805-810.

Schreiber, V. 1963. The Hypothalamo-Hypophysial System. Publishing House Czechoslovak Acad. Sci., Prague.

Schreibman, M. P., and Kallman, K. D. 1964. Functional pituitary grafts in fresh water teleosts. Amer. Zool. *4*:417 (abstract).

Schreibman, M. P., and Kallman, K. D. 1966. Endocrine control of freshwater tolerance in teleosts. Gen. Comp. Endocrinol. *6*:144-155.

Shirley, H. V., Jr., and Nalbandov, A. V. 1956. Effects of transecting hypophyseal stalks in laying hens. Endocrinology *58*:694-700.

Signoret, J. P. 1965. Action d'ablation des bulbes olfactifs sur les mécanismes de la reproduction. Proc. Sec. Int. Cong. Endocrinol. *1*:198-202.

Sloper, J. C. 1966. The experimental and cytopathological investigation of neurosecretion in the hypothalamus and pituitary. *In* G. W. Harris and B. T. Donovan (eds.): The Pituitary Gland. University of California Press, Berkeley, Vol. 3, pp. 131-239.

Soulairac, A., and Soulairac, M. L. 1956. Effets de lésions hypothalamiques sur le comportement sexuel et le tractus génital du rat mâle. Ann. d'Endocrinol. *17*:731-745.

Soulairac, A., and Soulairac, M. L. 1959. Action de la gonadotrophine chorionique et de la testostérone sur le comportement sexuel et le tractus génital du rat mâle, porteur de lésions hypothalamiques postérieures. Ann. d'Endocrinol. *20*:137-146.

Stahl, A. and Leray, C. 1961. The relationship between diencephalic neurosecretion and the adenohypophysis in teleost fishes. Mem. Soc. Endocrinol. *12*:149-161.

Strauss, W., and Meyer, R. K. 1962. Neural timing of ovulation in immature rats treated with gonadotrophin. Science *137*:860-861.

Stutinsky, F., and Befort, J. J. 1964. Effets des stimulations électriques du diéncephale de *Rana esculenta* mâle. Gen. Comp. Endocrinol. *4*:370-379.

Szentágothai, J., Flerkó, B., Mess, B., and Halász, B. 1962. Hypothalamic Control of the Anterior Pituitary. Akadémiai Kiado, Budapest.

Taleisnik, S., and McCann, S. M. 1961. Effects of hypothalamic lesions on the secretion and storage of hypophysial luteinizing hormone. Endocrinology *68*:263-272.

Talwalker, P. K., Ratner, A., and Meites, J. 1963. In vitro inhibition of pituitary prolactin synthesis and release by hypothalamic extract. Amer. J. Physiol. *205*:213-218.

Tejasen, T., and Everett, J. W. 1966. Release of ovulating hormone after a unilateral preoptic stimulus. Blockade by ipsilateral transection at preoptic-anterior hypothalamic junction. Anat. Rec. *154*:431-432 (abstract).

Tixier-Vidal, A., and Gourdji, D. 1965. Évolution cytologique ultra-structurale de l'hypophyse du canard en culture organotypique. Élaboration autonome de prolactine par les explants. C. R. Acad. Sci. *261*:805-808.

Tixier-Vidal, A., Baylé, J. D., and Assenmacher, I. 1966. Étude cytologique ultrastructurale de l'hypophyse du pigeon après autogreffe ectopique. Absence de stimulation des cellules à prolactine. C. R. Acad. Sci. *262 D*:675-678.

Turner, C. D. 1966. General Endocrinology. Ed. 4. W. B. Saunders Company, Philadelphia.

Uemura, H. 1964a. Cholinesterase in the hypothalamo-hypophysial neurosecretory system of the bird, *Zosterops palpebrosa japonica*. Zool. Mag. *15*: 118-126.

Uemura, H. 1964b. Effects of gonadectomy and sex steroids on the acid phosphatase activity of the hypothalamo-hypophysial system in the bird *Emberiza rustica latifascia*. Endocrinol. Jap. *11*: 185-203.

Uemura, H., and Kobayashi, H. 1963. Effects of prolonged daily photoperiods and estrogen on the hypothalamic neurosecretory system of the passerine bird *Zosterops palpebrosa japonica*. Gen. Comp. Endocrinol. *3*:253-264.

van der Werff ten Bosch, J. J. 1963. Effects of cerebral lesions, blinding, and domestication on gonadal functions of the female ferret. J. Endocrinol. *26*:113-123.

van Dongen, W. J., Jørgensen, C. B., Larsen, L. O., Rosenkilde, P., Lofts, B., and van Oordt, P. G. W. J. 1966. Function and cytology of the normal and auto transplanted pars distalis of the hypophysis in the toad *Bufo bufo* (L). Gen. Comp. Endocrinol. *6*:491-518.

van Dyke, D. C., Simpson, M. E., Lepkovsky, S., Koneff, A. A., and Brobeck, J. R. 1957. Hypothalamic control of pituitary function and corpus luteum formation in the rat. Proc. Soc. Exp. Biol. Med. *95*:1-5.

van Oordt, P. G. W. J. 1960. The influence of internal and external factors in the regulation of the spermatogenetic cycle in amphibia. Symp. Zool. Soc. London *2*:29-52.

van Rees, G. P., and Wolthuis, O. L. 1962. Influence of testosterone, progesterone and oestradiol on the F.S.H.-release of hypophyses grafted under the kidney capsule. Acta Endocrinol. *39*:103-109.

van Rees, G. P., van der Werff ten Bosch, J. J., and Wolthuis, O. L. 1962. Prolonged vaginal oestrous and the normal oestrous cycle in the rat. I. Morphological observations. Acta Endocrinol.

40:95-102.

van Tienhoven, A., Sutherland, C., and Saatman, R. R. 1966. The effects of exposure to darkness on the reproductive and hypothalamo-hypophysial systems of budgerigars, *Melopsittacus undulatus*. Gen. Comp. Endocrinol. *6*:420-427.

Vitums, A., Mikami, S. I., Oksche, A., and Farner, D. S. 1964. Vascularization of the hypothalamo-hypophysial-complex in the white-crowned sparrow, *Zonotrichia leucophrys gambelii*. Z. Zellforsch. *64*:541-569.

Vivien, J. H., and Schott, J. 1958. Contribution à l'étude des corrélations hypothalamo-pituitaires chez les Batraciens. Le contrôle de l'activité gonadotrope. J. de Physiol. *50*:561-563 (abstract).

Wada, J. A., and Erikson, L. B. 1962. Menstrual irregularities in temporal lobectomized Rhesus monkeys (Macaca mulatta). Science *135*:46-47.

Wilson, F. E., and Farner, D. S. 1965. Effect of hypothalamic lesions on testicular growth. Fed. Proc. *24*:129 (abstract).

Wolfson, A., and Kobayashi, H. 1962. Phosphatase activity and neurosecretion in the hypothalamo-hypophyseal system in relation to the photoperiodic gonadal response in *Zonotrichia albicollis*. Gen. Comp. Endocrinol. Supp. *1*:168-179.

Yagi, K., Azuma, T., and Matsuda, K. 1966. Neurosecretory cell: capable of conducting impulse in rats. Science *154*:778-779.

Yagi, K., Bern, H. A., and Hagadorn, I. R. 1963. Action potentials of neurosecretory neurons in the leech, *Theromyzon rude*. Gen. Comp. Endocrinol. *3*:490-495.

Yamamoto, W. S., and Brobeck, J. R. (Eds.) 1965. Physiological Controls and Regulations. W. B. Saunders Company, Philadelphia.

Zolovick, A. L., Pearse, R., Boehlke, K. W., and Eleftheriou, B. E. 1966. Monoamine oxidase activity in various parts of the rat brain during estrous cycle. Science *154*:649.

Zouhar, R. L., and de Groot, J. 1963. Effects of limbic brain lesions on aspects of reproduction in female rats. Anat. Rec. *145*:358 (abstract).

Chapter 9

Cyclic Reproductive Phenomena

A number of cyclic phenomena may occur in the reproductive system and the reproductive behavior of vertebrates. For the sake of convenience we shall divide these cyclic phenomena into two types, seasonal breeding cycles and cycles which occur during the breeding season.

In the case of seasonal reproduction, one may generalize that the reproductive processes are so timed that the young will be born when there are optimal conditions for their development. Thus, time of ovulation, time of mating, length of incubation, etc., have to be synchronized rather accurately but still allow sufficient leeway for special conditions. Extensive documentation of the timing of the breeding season for a large number of groups of vertebrates can be found in the chapter by Matthews and Marshall (1956) in *Marshall's Physiology of Reproduction* and for mammals in Asdell's book, *Patterns of Mammalian Reproduction* (1964). We will discuss, in a later chapter, the environmental and other factors that regulate the breeding seasons. In this chapter the discussion is limited to cyclic phenomena during the reproductive season.

The breeding cycle consists of a series of events: spermatogenesis in the male, maturing of follicles and ovulation in the female, the coming in contact of sperm and oocytes, fertilization, embryonic development, and birth. These events have to be well synchronized, but can involve a large number of adaptations in the highly developed mammals and it can be relatively simple as in cyclostomes and in a

number of teleosts. The more maternal care necessary, the less one would expect more than one brood to be born. However, this is a somewhat oversimplified notion, as we shall see later in this chapter.

In any event, we will need to take account of such events as pregnancy and a concomitant lack of ovulations and mating. Here the reproductive events in the different classes will be described and the major patterns will be discussed.

CYCLOSTOMES

The lampreys, after they reach sexual maturity, have no cycle, as the males and females die after spawning. Insufficient evidence is available on the breeding of hagfishes to make any statement about cyclic events. However, corpora lutea resembling those of mammals have been found (Perry and Rowlands, 1962).

ELASMOBRANCHS

All fishes belonging to this group have internal fertilization. Among the sharks are ovoviviparous, viviparous, and oviparous species; the skates or Rajiformes are usually oviparous and the rays generally are ovoviviparous.

Among the sharks the lesser spotted dogfish *(Scyliorhinus canicula)* is sexually active through the year. However, the interval between ovulations is shorter than the gestation period, so that embryos of different stages of development can be found in the reproductive tract. In *Mustelus canis,* the smooth dogfish, which is also ovoviviparous, ovulation and fertilization occur in June and July and after a gestation of ten months the young are born.

Libby and Gilbert (1960) noted that the clear-nosed skate *(Raja eglanteria)* lays her eggs in pairs, with the interval between successive pairs diminishing as follows: 18, 12, 8, 6, 4 and from then on the interval stays at four days until about 60 eggs are laid. What factors control these intervals are not known.

TELEOSTS

There is a great variety of breeding patterns among the 30,000 species of this order. Only a small fraction of these species have been investigated. We will attempt to describe the main patterns.

Oviparous

Among the oviparous forms the following patterns have been described:

1. The male and female die after spawning, so there are no cyclic changes. An example of this is the Pacific salmon *(Oncorhynchus nerka).*

2. Sperm and eggs mature seasonally and are shed when the conditions are "right." For instance, in the three-spined stickleback *(Gasterosteus aculeatus),* temperature seems to be the important factor in determining the timing of breeding. The actual spawning by the female is induced by a complicated series of behavioral interactions between male and female. The male builds the nest and chases the female towards its entrance pushing her into the nest where she spawns. The maturation of eggs may take place throughout the year and may culminate during the breeding season (e.g. the three-spined stickleback). In other species, e.g. the Australian gar-

fish *(Reporphamus melanochir),* which has a spawning season from September to March, there is a succession of follicular cycles during the breeding season.

Some species, e.g. the Japanese rice fish *(Oryzias latipes),* will ovulate and shed the eggs only during a certain period of the light-dark cycle. In nature the fishes ovulate at dawn, but by experimental manipulations of the light-dark cycle the time of spawning can be shifted (Matthews and Marshall, 1956).

Preovulation "corpora lutea" are found, e.g. in the European bitterling, and postovulation "corpora lutea" are found, e.g. in the killifish *(Fundulus heteroclitus).* The possible significance of such corpora lutea for regulation of the breeding period has not been determined.

Viviparous

Among viviparous species, a number of different conditions have been found.

1. A short but definite cycle, during which the female will mate or will take the mating position, e.g. the guppy *(Poecilia reticulata),* which has a four to six day cycle. The preovulatory corpora lutea may regulate this breeding behavior (see Perry and Rowlands, 1962). Fertilization development of the young occurs in the follicle and a large number of young are born simultaneously. The oocytes which are in the ovary as the previous brood is born are well developed and can be fertilized within a few days. In *Gambusia* sp. and *Mollienesia* sp., on the other hand, the oocytes are small at the time the previous brood is born and the oocytes have to mature before fertilization can occur; thus the interval between brood expulsion and fertilization is longer than in the guppy.

2. In *Quintana atrizona* the eggs can be fertilized immediately after the previous brood is expelled.

3. Superfetation, the fertilization of

oocytes, occurs while the female is pregnant so that embryos at different stages of development are present simultaneously, e.g. in *Poeciliopsis pleurospilus* and *Poeciliopsis infans*, where two broods may be present and in *Heterandria formosa*, where there may be six to nine broods in different stages of development (Matthews and Marshall, 1956). In these examples there is a pseudoplacenta which allows for an exchange between embryonic and maternal blood. In *Heterandria formosa*, the placenta develops from the somatopleure of the pericardial sac; this placenta expands to cover the anterior part of the embryo.

4. Development of the embryos may take place within the ovarian cavity rather than within the follicular cavity. In these cases there is no superfetation. This pattern occurs in the Goodeidae and Jenynsiidae. The exchange between embryonic and maternal blood in Jenynsiidae occurs via flaps of ovarian tissue and the mouth and pharyngeal cavities of the embryo (Matthews and Marshall, 1956), whereas in Goodeidae many species have embryos which have large rectal processes (trophotaeniae) able to absorb nutritional material from the ovarian fluid.

5. In *Cymatogaster aggregata*, which has very small eggs with little yolk, young are born in June and July and the males, which are sexually mature at birth, inseminate the females immediately. A similar situation is found in *Micrometrus aurora* and *M. minimus*. The females are not sexually mature at birth and breed at about one year of age. The sperm stored in the ovarian cavities do not fertilize the eggs until December in *Cymatogaster aggregata*. The embryos are retained in the ovarian cavity and are born in June and July. During the period of early gestation, epithelial cells that line the ovarian cavity form internal fluid reservoirs and some ova degenerate.

These cyclic changes in teleost ovaries are thus associated with pregnancy and they are not similar to the more familiar estrous cycles of laboratory mammals.

AMPHIBIA

With few exceptions amphibia are oviparous. The exceptions are *Pipa* sp., *Protopipa* sp., *Gastrotheca marsupiata* in which the fertilized eggs develop on the back of the females either in small chambers or in a pouch, and a pseudoplacental connection is formed between mother and young. However, little is known about the cycles of these animals.

Fertilization is usually external, with the exception of the tailed-frog *Ascaphus truei* and in the Salamandroidea.

In oviparous amphibia with external fertilization, the breeding is seasonal and occurs usually only once a year, at least in the species of the temperate zone.

A number of patterns of gonadal and other changes have been recorded among amphibians, some of which we will mention:

Urodela

1. Spermatogenesis occurs at the end of the breeding season and sperm are retained in the testes to be released during the breeding season, e.g. the newt *(Triturus cristatus)* which breeds in April to June, but in which spermatogenesis is finished in the fall. Secondary sex characters, e.g. thumb pads, are well developed during the time of spermatogenesis in *Triturus viridescens*.

2. Spermatogenesis occurs shortly before the breeding season, e.g. in *Cryptobranchus alleganiensis*, in which spermatogenesis occurs in July and breeding in August and September.

3. Mating may take place before the breeding season, e.g. in the American salamander *(Eurycea bislineata)*, in which spermatogenesis begins in June. By September the *ductus deferens* develops and becomes distended with sperm. The males may mate and sperm can be found in the spermatheca of the females, although the breeding season is from late March to

early April (Matthews and Marshall, 1956). In all three groups ovulations occur during the breeding season.

Anura

One pattern is found in most anura: spermatogenesis and ovarian follicular development may be complete in the fall, but the animals hibernate and breeding occurs in the spring. However, by gonadotropin injections, spermiation and ovulation can be induced and the eggs can be fertilized (Matthews and Marshall, 1956).

No function has been assigned to the preovulatory and postovulatory "corpora lutea" of the oviparous amphibia. In the ovoviviparous species mentioned the corpora lutea may have a function according to Gorbman and Bern (1962).

REPTILES

In most species investigated, reproduction is seasonal and, generally, only one ovarian cycle is observed each year. Sperm may survive for as much as six years in the oviduct of the females so that spermatogenesis and mating do not need to be synchronous with the time of ovulation in the female.

There are, however, exceptions to the pattern of only one ovarian cycle per year, as has been pointed out by Perry and Rowlands (1962). For instance, the Saharan lizard, *Acanthodactylus* sp., and the oviparous *Amphibolurus* sp. of Australia ovulate twice per year, and *Dryoplylax* sp. and *Tomodon* sp. have eggs in the oviduct throughout the year. The time it takes follicles to mature varies; in some species maturation is very rapid, e.g. in the horned toad *(Phrynosoma solare)*, it takes two to three weeks for the follicle to increase in size from about 100 cubic mm. to 3600 cubic mm., whereas in the Yucca night lizard *(Xantusia vigilis)* it takes three years for the follicle to mature.

The function of corpora lutea found in oviparous species of reptiles is not established. According to Perry and Rowlands (1962) the persistence of these corpora lutea is not necessarily related with the interval between ovulations. The corpora lutea in viviparous species may inhibit the growth of follicles since, e.g. in the garter snake *(Thamnophis radix)* follicles do not mature during gestation, and corpora lutea are present at this time. However, experimental verification that this correlation is indeed a causal one is not available.

BIRDS

In most birds of the temperate zone, spermatogenesis is completed shortly before the breeding season and often the female reaches breeding condition after the males. During the last week prior to ovulation, yolk deposition is usually rapid and the ovary undergoes a considerable weight increase.

Birds can be divided into determinate and indeterminate layers. In the former, the clutch consists of a definite number of eggs regardless of the number of eggs removed from the nest. Indeterminate layers lay a clutch of a certain number of eggs, but if eggs are removed the number of eggs laid may be far in excess of the normal number. Phillips (1887) obtained 50 eggs from a yellow-shafted flicker *(Colaptes auratus)* by removing eggs from the nest.

In determinate layers, the number of eggs in a clutch is limited by the number of mature ova, e.g. in the brant *(Branta canadensis)*, or because massive atresia and yolk resorption occur when the clutch is finished, e.g. in the budgerigar *(Melopsitaccus undulatus)*.

Smith (1966) found in Thayer's gull *(Larus thayeri)* and in Iceland gulls *(L. glaucoides)* that the ovaries contained from five to seven ovulable follicles at the onset of the breeding season. After oviposition, more eggs were lost from Thayer's gull nests than from those of Iceland gulls. This was correlated with the fact that lost eggs were not replaced by Thayer's gull females but Iceland gull females laid additional eggs. The pattern of atresia was also different for these two species. In the ovaries of Thayer's gulls atresia started after the first egg was laid, but in Iceland gulls atresia started after the third egg was laid.

In indeterminate layers, egg laying may be interrupted by the incubation of eggs, which is accompanied by regression of the ovary. After the young are raised, another set of follicles may mature and a new clutch may be laid.

The laying cycle of chickens has been investigated in some detail (Fraps, 1955; van Tienhoven, 1961). In a somewhat oversimplified way, Figure 9-1 illustrates the laying and the ovulation pattern of a hen receiving light from 5 a.m. to 7 p.m. Experimental evidence indicates that a time interval of 6 to 8 hours elapses between the injection of LH or progesterone (which causes release of endogenous LH via a neural mechanism, as discussed in

Chapter 8) and ovulation. For instance, injection of LH or progesterone at 3 p.m. of the day the last egg of a sequence is laid (Thursday in the example of Figure 9-1) causes ovulation at about 10 p.m. It has been assumed that the release of LH would take place 6 to 8 hours before spontaneous ovulation and that it was taking place over a one to two hour period (Fraps, 1955; van Tienhoven, 1961). Injection of Dibenamine, which blocks the neural stimulation, at various times before expected ovulation, indicated that the injection was 87.5 percent effective at 14 hours, only 18.7 percent effective at 12 hours, but 57 percent and 50 percent effective at ten and eight hours before expected ovulation. At the time of its discovery this low percentage of blocked ovulations at 12 hours was difficult to explain (van Tienhoven et al., 1954).

In 1965 Nelson et al. found that three peaks of LH concentrations in the peripheral blood were present 21, 13, and 8 hours prior to ovulation of the third follicle. The changes in LH concentration prior to ovulation of the C_1 follicle have not been reported, but if one assumes that

SEQUENCE OF LH RELEASES, OVULATIONS, AND OVIPOSITIONS IN LAYING HENS ON A 14 HOUR LIGHT SCHEDULE: 4 EGG SEQUENCE.

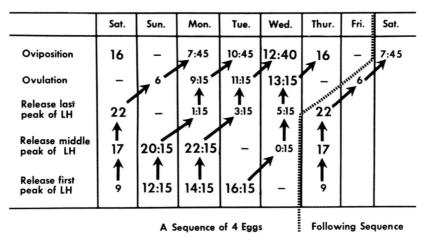

	Sat.	Sun.	Mon.	Tue.	Wed.	Thur.	Fri.	Sat.
Oviposition	16	—	7:45	10:45	12:40	16	—	7:45
Ovulation	—	6	9:15	11:15	13:15	—	6	
Release last peak of LH	22	—	1:15	3:15	5:15	22		
Release middle peak of LH	17	20:15	22:15	—	0:15	17		
Release first peak of LH	9	12:15	14:15	16:15	—	9		

A Sequence of 4 Eggs   Following Sequence

Figure 9-1. Sequence of LH release, ovulation, and oviposition in laying chickens kept under a 14-hour light schedule (hours 5 to 19). Illustrated is a schematized and somewhat oversimplified four-egg sequence. The numbers indicate the time of the day (see text). (Data for timing of ovulation and oviposition from Fraps, 1955; data for the timing of LH release from Nelson et al., 1965.)

the changes are similar to those reported from the C_1 ovulation, then the blockade observed by Dibenamine injection 12 hours before ovulation may mean blockade of the middle peak of LH. It is interesting to note that electric stimulation of the archistriatum or of the paleostrium primitivum of hens was most effective in causing a delay in ovulation between 14 and 16 hours before expected ovulation of the C_1 follicle. The same stimulus was ineffective at 11, 12, and 17 hours before ovulation and caused a delay in ovulation in two out of 13 hens stimulated in the archistriatum 13 hours before expected ovulation. It thus seems that electric stimulation of these areas 14 to 16 hours before ovulation may have depressed the 13-hour LH release but still allowed a sufficient release for ovulation to occur, albeit several hours later than normally expected. The significance of the peak in LH concentration 21 hours prior to ovulation has not been established.

Figure 9-1 shows that apparently the release of the last peak of LH has to occur in the dark or shortly after the lights are on. Presumably the light acts as a cue on which the internal rhythm of the regulatory processes for LH release can lock in. Under conditions of 24 hours of light, the ovipositions and presumably the ovulations become distributed over the entire 24 hour period. This shows that the last peak of LH release can occur when the light is on, but under continuous light the cue of the light going on is missing. The subject of rhythms and their regulation by external factors will be discussed in another chapter.

The hypotheses proposed to explain the shift in the time of day when ovulation occurs during a sequence have been reviewed by Fraps (1961) and van Tienhoven (1961). This shift does not seem to be a general phenomenon among birds, and a discussion of these theories here would require too much detail. The reader is therefore referred to these reviews and the original papers by Bastian and Zarrow (1955), Fraps (1955), Nalbandov (1959), and Nelson et al. (1965).

The time sequence of ovulations and ovipositions in the cycle of the Japanese quail (*Coturnix c. japonica*) has been investigated by Opel (1966). It was established that (1) the interval between oviposition and ovulation of the next egg in a sequence is about 30 minutes (from 15 minutes to two hours); (2) the interval between consecutive ovipositions is more than 24 hours but less than 25 hours regardless of sequence length; (3) the first egg of a sequence is ovulated eight to nine hours after the onset of light; (4) ovulation takes place between five to nine hours after LH injection (50 percent ovulating between seven and eight hours); (5) the difference in time of day between first and final ovulations in a sequence is 1.6 to 2.9 hours (4.5 to eight hours in chickens).

MAMMALS

It is among mammals that one finds the most pronounced cyclic phenomena in the female during the breeding season. For details concerning the seasonal cyclic activity of the testes and ovaries in individual species the student should consult the chapters by Eckstein (1962) and Eckstein and Zuckerman (1956) and the book by Asdell (1964).

Monotremes

The duck-billed platypus (*Ornithorhynchus anatinus*) and the spiny anteater (*Tachylglossus aculeatus*) breed in the spring. Both lay their eggs (two in the case of the duck-billed platypus) or their egg (in the case of the anteater) and the eggs are incubated in a nest by the duck-billed platypus, and in a brood pouch by the anteater. There are no breeding cycles within the breeding season. The ova of these monotremes are covered by albumen and a leathery shell as they pass down the genital tract. The egg of the duck-billed platypus has a diameter of about 3 mm. when it is ovulated and measures 16 to 18 by 14 to 15 mm. when it is laid (Asdell, 1964).

Marsupials and Eutheria

We have seen in Chapter 6 that oogenesis, in the strict sense of the word, is completed at birth in the majority of mammalian species. The maturation of the oocytes occurs after birth. Between birth and puberty there may be rhythmic waves of primordial follicle development, but these follicles and oocytes become atretic. Some follicles of the last wave before puberty survive, and these are involved in the follicular maturation and ovulations which occur after puberty. In the Nubian giraffe *(Giraffa camelopardalis)* the follicles do not undergo atresia but form corpus luteum-like structures.

The onset of puberty, which is probably partly the result of a change in the physiology of the hypothalamus, is marked by the appearance of behavorial estrus, maturation of the ovarian follicles, ovulation, greater development of the secondary sex organs, and opening of the vagina. Not all these changes take place at the same time. There is, for instance, evidence that ovulation may have occurred one or more estrous periods before the animal shows heat for the first time. This is an example of a so-called silent heat (Perry and Rowlands, 1962; Nalbandov, 1964). The maturation of follicles does not occur in hypophysectomized animals, and follicular development can be restored by injections of GTH, or FSH plus small amount of LH.

These experiments thus establish that follicular maturation is under control of gonadotropic hormones. Similarly, the other changes described above for the onset of puberty fail to develop in hypophysectomized animals and can be made to appear by GTH administration.

The onset of behavorial heat, which occurs in all mammals except some primates, is synchronized with ovulation and

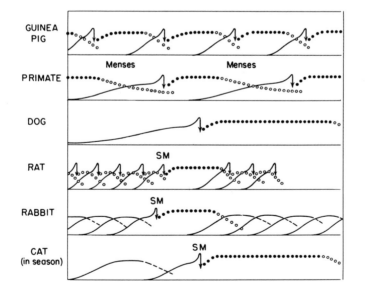

Figure 9-2. Diagrammatic presentation of reproductive cycles of some laboratory animals. ——— = follicular phase, schematized and inaccurate in detail; - - - - = atresia; ↓ = ovulation; • = fully active corpus luteum; ∘ = regressing or otherwise not fully active corpus luteum. *SM* = sterile mating. After *SM* or equivalent stimulation the cycles of rat, rabbit, and cat become directly comparable with those of the other species shown. (From Everett, 1961.)

can be brought about in most mammals by either estrogen or a combination of estrogen and progesterone (see Chapter 6).

Ovulation of the mature follicle can be brought about by injections of LH. After ovulation a corpus luteum is formed. The endocrine and other factors which control corpus luteum function have been discussed in Chapter 6. In small rodents (e.g. rat, mouse, and hamster) the corpus luteum has a very short life span and it probably does not secrete much progesterone. Different patterns of ovarian cyclic activity are illustrated schematically in Figure 9-2.

With respect to ovulation, we can distinguish two major groups among mammals: the "induced" ovulators, in which ovulation occurs after coitus, and the "spontaneous" ovulators, in which ovulation occurs without coitus.

INDUCED OVULATORS

The following Carnivora definitely belong to this group (Altman and Dittmer, 1962; Asdell, 1964, 1966; Everett, 1961): the northern fur seal (*Callorhinus ursinus*); the large brown weasel (*Mustela frenata*); the ferret (*M. furo*); the mink (*M. vison*); the raccoon (*Procyon lotor*); the domestic cat (*Felis catus*). The following rodents: the tree mouse (*Phenacomys longicaudus*); the California meadow mouse (*Microtus californicus*); an Asian vole (*M. guentheri*); the thirteen-lined ground squirrel (*Citellus tridecimlineatus*). The following lagomorpha: the common hare (*Lepus europaeus*); the jack rabbit (*Lepus californicus*); the eastern cottontail rabbit (*Sylvilagus floridanus*); the domestic rabbit (*Oryctolagus cuniculus*). The chiroptera are represented by the lump-nosed bat (*Corynorhinus rafinesquii*). The following Insectivora: the hedgehog (*Erinaceus europaeus*); the mole shrew (*Blarina brevicauda*) the common shrew (*Sorex araneus*); and the Madagascar hedgehog (*Setifer setosus*). Evidence suggests that a number of other species are induced ovulators, but this has not been proved. To these species belong the

following Carnivora: Canada otter (*Lutra canadensis*); *Martes* sp.; the mongoose (*Herpestes auropunctatus*). The Pinnepedia are represented by the elephant seal (*Mirounga leonina*); Insectivora by: the American mole (*Scalopus aquaticus*) (Conaway, 1959); the water shrew (*Sorex palustris*); the water shrew (*Neomys fodiens*); the Indian fruit bat (*Pteropus giganteus*). The rodents are represented by: nutria (*Myocaster coypus*); the marsupials by the long-nosed kangaroo rat (*Potorous tridactylus*).

Among these species, only a few have been investigated with respect to the maturation of follicles. In the domestic rabbit, which is in constant estrus, successive groups of follicles mature and degenerate in the absence of mating (Perry and Rowlands, 1962). The mink, which has a heat period that may last for a month or more (Asdell, 1964), shows waves of maturing follicles. The cat shows estrus seasonally, twice a year, spring and fall, in North America and Northern Europe (Asdell, 1964). During each estrous season it comes into heat and if the animal is not mated the heat period ends, the follicles regress, and a new wave of follicles matures (Perry and Rowlands, 1962) and there is a second heat period two to three weeks after the end of the first one. The ferret, on the other hand, may be in heat from April to August (Asdell, 1964) but the follicles remain ovulable during this period (Perry and Rowlands, 1962).

When mating occurs, there is a reflex release of LH from the pituitary, as can be determined from pituitary bioassays in the rabbit (Everett, 1961). Corpora lutea are formed from the ovulated follicles (see Chapter 6). If the mating is sterile there will be a pseudopregnancy of about 16 to 17 days; if the mating is a fertile one, pregnancy lasts 30 to 32 days. During this time the corpus luteum is well developed but mature follicles are present, since the doe can ovulate immediately after the end of pseudopregnancy or pregnancy (Asdell, 1964).

A reproductive pattern quite different from that of other laboratory and domestic mammals is found in the mink. Mating, early in the breeding season, is followed by induced ovulation, but subsequently new follicles develop. These follicles can be induced to ovulate if a new mating occurs more than six days after the first one. The new ova are fertilized and remain in the uterus together with the blastocysts from the previous mating. In the mink, implantation is delayed (to be discussed in Chapter 11). Enders and Enders (1963) reported that as the interval between matings increases to seven days there is a decline of offspring sired by the first male to about 14 percent. This decline is not the result of the new ovulations per se, since litter size is not affected if the second coitus is sterile.

Hansson (1947) found that separation of the two matings 1, 2, and 3 to 4 days yielded the following percentages of infertile females 9.1, 18.0 and 20.8, respectively, as compared to 32.6 percent infertility when females were mated only once. This relatively high infertility may have been the result of ovulations induced by infertile matings and by riding of the female by a male; the riding can induce ovulations. The mean litter size for one mating was 4.11 whereas for matings separated by 1, 2 and 3 to 4 days it was 4.21, 4.54, and 3.90 respectively.

Mating at intervals of five to six days increased infertility to above the control level (37.1 versus 32.6 percent) and decreased litter size (3.77 versus 4.11). At intervals over six days the percentage of infertile females fluctuated between 11.2 and 18.5 and litter size between 4.24 and 4.86 whelps per litter.

Enders and Enders (1963) state that in matings separated by one day, superfecundation occurs. Under these conditions the first male sires about one-third of the litter.

Hansson (1947) also established that the date of mating affected the length of gestation via an effect on the time implantation occurs. Quantitatively he found the following relationships:

$$Y = 62.0 - 1.0846 \ X + 0.01804 \ X^2$$

in which Y is the length of the gestation period and X the mating date in March.

SPONTANEOUS OVULATORS

In this group ovulation normally occurs "spontaneously." There are, however, a few examples in which, under certain conditions, coitus can affect the time of ovulation in animals of this group (see Chapter 6).

Under a number of special conditions ovulation can be induced by copulation in rats. Rats kept under continuous light will, after a certain period, go into permanent estrus without ovulations occurring. Mating of such females causes ovulation (Dempsey and Searles, 1943). Rats in which ovulation is prevented by pentobarbital injections between 2 p.m. and 4 p.m. on the day of proestrus will ovulate if mated during the estrous period (Everett, 1952). Aron et al. (1965) found that injection of 10 μg. estradiol on the first day of proestrus in rats with a four day cycle and injection on day 2 in rats with a five day cycle induced acceptance of the male, and ovulation occurred as a consequence of copulation; estrogen-treated rats which did not copulate failed to ovulate. The higher the number of copulations, the higher the incidence of ovulations. Taleisnik et al. (1966) found that mating caused an increase in plasma LH concentration and a decrease in LH content in normal female rats and in ovariectomized rats treated with estrogen and progesterone. On the other hand, stimulation of the vagina with a glass rod failed to cause LH release. Allen (1922) mentions that several virgin or unmated laboratory mice, which had shown more than one estrous cycle, failed to ovulate unless brought into sexual contact with a male.

Among the "spontaneous" ovulators one can distinguish two major groups, i.e.:

1. Those animals with nonfunctional

corpora lutea and short (four to five day) estrous cycles, e.g. rats, mice, and hamsters.

2. Those animals with functional corpora lutea and long estrous cycles, e.g. horse, cow, pig, sheep, guinea pig.

Nonfunctional Corpora Lutea and Short Cycles. In the animals of the first group, there are medium-sized follicles (300 to 500 μ) present during any phase of the estrous cycle. According to Perry and Rowlands (1962) a group of these follicles starts the final growth phase, but part of this group undergoes atresia and the other part will ovulate. The corpora lutea formed from these ruptured follicles grow for about two to three days in rats and hamsters, but they regress rapidly in the hamster (so that at the next ovulation the corpora lutea are difficult to find),

or more slowly in the rat (so that three to five generations of corpora lutea can be found at any time during the cycle).

These ovarian changes are accompanied by marked changes in the uterus (hyperemia, increased water content, hyperplasia and hypertrophy of the endometrium, and increased spontaneous contractions of the myometrium) and the vagina (see Table 9-1 and Figure 9-3). During estrus the animal also shows behavioral changes. If a finger or hand is laid on the animal's back she will exhibit lordosis, characterized by immobility and a concave back. If the pudendal region is touched the back is held concave, the hind legs are extended, and the posterior end is presented to facilitate mating (Nalbandov, 1964).

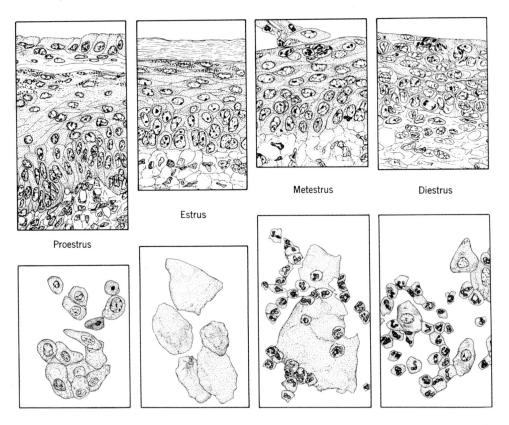

Metestrus

Diestrus

Estrus

Proestrus

Figure 9-3. Vaginal cycle in the rat. The upper row of figures shows the alteration in the lining epithelium of vagina as seen in histological sections. The lower row of figures shows the cell types obtained in a vaginal smear. In proestrus, nucleated epithelial cells are found in the smear; in estrus, cornified squamous cells only are present in the smear; during metestrus squamous cells and leukocytes are found, whereas in diestrus nucleated cells, leukocytes, and mucus are present. (From Gorbman and Bern, 1962, as redrawn from Long and Evans, 1922.)

Table 9-1. Summary of Events During Estrous Cycle of the Rat

STAGE	OVARY	UTERUS	VAGINA	VAGINAL SMEAR	BEHAVIOR
Proestrus 12 hours	Follicles grow rapidly. CL of previous cycle regress	Starts to distend with fluid	Epithelium thick. Cornified layer below epithelium	Epithelial cells only	Signs of acceptance of the male at end of this period
Estrus 12 hours	Follicles maximal size; germ vesicles start to break down	Maximal distention; hyperemic	Epithelium thick. Cornified layer on surface	Few cornified cells	Accepts male; lordosis
Early Metestrus 15 hours	Ovulation	Regression of uterine distention; epithelium shows vacuolar degeneration	Cornified layer becomes detached. If mated vaginal plug present	Many cornified cells	No acceptance of the male
Late Metestrus 6 hours	New CL	Degeneration and regeneration of epithelium	Epithelium thin. No cornified layer present	Cornified cells plus many leukocytes	No acceptance of the male
Diestrus 57 hours	CL larger than at late metestrus. Follicles larger than at late metestrus	Regeneration of epithelium	Epithelium thin	Leukocytes plus epithelial cells	No acceptance of the male
Proestrus	As before	As before	As before	As before	As before

Reference: Gorbman and Bern, 1962.

Young (1961) has pointed out that in the ovariectomized animal treated with estrogen, it takes 48 to 72 hours for the vaginal epithelium to proliferate, and that if ovaries of immature rats are removed 27 hours after injection of human chorionic gonadotropin (HCG), vaginal cornification can be obtained in 84 to 96 hours. This indicates that the estrogen causing these events was secreted two or three days before maximal size of the follicles was reached.

Hypophysectomized rats require administration of FSH and LH for follicular growth and ovulation (Velardo, 1960) and for estrogen secretion and estrous behavior (Nalbandov, 1964).

The injection of 1 rat unit (R.U.) of FSH (purified sheep pituitary FSH, containing one part in ten of LH) each day for four days and 8 R.U. at the end of day four will produce ovulation; by injection of lactogenic hormone the corpora lutea can be maintained, and, if mating has occurred, pregnancy can be maintained to term in hypophysectomized rats (Carter et al., 1958).

If mating occurs, a release of a luteotropic hormone, probably prolactin, causes maintenance of the corpus luteum. Electrical stimulation of the cervix or stimulation of the cervical canal with a glass rod also will cause maintenance of the corpus luteum (CL). Meyer et al. (1929) showed that in high percentages of cases, anesthesia prevented the maintenance of the CL after stimulation of the cervical canal, indicating that a neural pathway is involved in this response. After sterile mating or after stimulation of the cervix, the corpora lutea are maintained for about 13 days, whereas the presence of deciduomata induced by trauma of the endometrium causes maintenance of the CL for about 20 days (see Table 6-18). After fertile mating, pregnancy lasts 22 days.

Functional Corpora Lutea and Long Cycles. The group of "spontaneously ovulating" mammals with long estrous cycles can be subdivided into two groups, Monoestrous (e.g. dog and skunk), and polyestrous animals (e.g. sheep, cattle, primates).

MONOESTROUS ANIMALS. Dogs, which come into heat in the fall and in the spring, have very small ovaries and follicles during the anestrous periods; follicles grow during a ten day period of proestrus; the estrous period lasts four to 13 days (Asdell, 1964) and ovulation occurs towards the end of estrus. Whether or not mating occurs, the corpus luteum is retained and remains functional for about two months. Pregnancy lasts 63 days.

The estrous cycle of spontaneous ovulators with long estrous cycles can be divided into a number of phases; the special case of the menstrual cycle will be discussed separately.

POLYESTROUS ANIMALS. In polyestrous animals the estrous cycle is followed by another cycle if no pregnancy or no pseudopregnancy occurs. The guinea pig will show pseudopregnancy after a sterile mating, but not all mammals of the spontaneous ovulators with long cycles, e.g. sheep, cow show this phenomenon.

DESCRIPTION OF THE ESTROUS CYCLE

Luteal Phase

If we consider the day of ovulation day 1 of the estrous cycle, we can make the following generalizations for the ovarian events. The corpus luteum increases in size for about one-half to two-thirds of the duration of the cycle (see Table 6-13 and Figure 9-2) and will then start to regress. In the guinea pig, for example, the corpus luteum increases from a diameter of about 1 mm. to a maximal diameter of 1.5 mm. at about day 12; after that time it regresses. This phase, from ovulation to the start of regression, is called the luteal phase. It is accompanied by a phase of glandular development of the endometrium as a result of the progesterone secreted by the corpus luteum.

Follicular Phase

During the luteal phase, groups of follicles have increased in diameter and part of these groups have become atretic at various intervals but a few follicles destined to be ovulated continue to grow so that the diameter of these follicles has increased from about 200 μ at day 1 of the cycle to about 800 μ at the end of the luteal phase. Some further atresia occurs and the other follicles continue to increase to about 1000 to 1200 μ in diameter at the time of ovulation. The large follicles secrete estrogen and the lowered level of progesterone (as a result of the regression of the corpus luteum) causes typical changes in the uterus, such as increased weight and mitotic activity in the epithelium, and also causes the development of estrous behavior close to the time of ovulation (see Table 9-2 for variations among species). The phase during which manifestations of estrogen secretion prevail is called the follicular phase. In most mammals, it lasts one-fourth to one-third the length of the cycle. In a number of species of bats, the Pipistrelle bat (*Pipistrellus pipistrellus*), the horseshoe bat (*Rhinolophus ferrumequinum*), the little brown bat (*Myotis lucifugus*), the gray bat (*M. grisescens*), the big brown bat (*Eptesicus fuscus*), and the lump-nosed bat (*Corynorhinus rafinesquii*), the follicular phase lasts several months. A follicle of 250 to 500 μ in diameter is present in the fall and secretes androgen. It matures and ovulates in the spring. After ovulation, the luteal phase starts if fertilization fails to occur.

The end of one estrous cycle and the beginning of the next cycle are the result of a decrease in progesterone secretion by the corpora lutea and an increase in the estrogen secretion of the new follicles. The decrease in the activity of the corpus luteum can be explained on the one hand by a decrease in the secretion of the luteotropic hormone (be it LH or prolactin) and on the other hand by an increased luteolytic activity. A consequence of a lack of stimulation may be that the corpus luteum loses its ability to secrete progesterone.

Armstrong and Black (1966) have

Table 9-2. The Estrous Cycle of Various Mammalian Species

SPECIES	LENGTH OF CYCLE (DAYS)	DURATION OF ESTRUS	OVULATION TYPE	OVULATION TIME
Cow (*Bos taurus*)	21	13–14 hours	Spontaneous	12–16 hours after end of estrus
Goat (*Capra hircus*)	20–21	1–3 days	Spontaneous	30–36 hours after onset of estrus
Sheep (*Ovis aries*)	16	20–48 hours	Spontaneous	12–24 hours before end of estrus
Pig (*Sus scrofa*)	21	2–3 days	Spontaneous	36 hours after onset of estrus
Horse (*Equus caballus*)	19–23	4–7 days	Spontaneous	1–2 days before end of estrus
Dog (*Canis familiaris*)	60	7–9 days	Spontaneous	1–3 days after start of estrus
Cat (*Felis catus*)	—	4 days with male 9–10 days without male	Induced	20–30 hours after mating
Ferret (*Mustela furo*)	—	Continuous	Induced	30 hours after mating
Mink (*Mustela vison*)	8–9	2 days	Induced	40–50 hours after mating
Fox (*Vulpes vulpes*)	90	1–5 days	Spontaneous	1–2 days after onset of estrus
Ground squirrel, (*Citellus tridecemlineatus*)	16	6–11 hours	Induced	8–12 hours after mating
Guinea pig (*Cavia porcellus*)	16	6–11 hours	Spontaneous	10 hours after start of estrus
Golden hamster (*Mesocricetus auratus*)	4	20 hours	Spontaneous	8–12 hours after start of estrus
Mouse (*Mus musculus*)	4	10 hours	Spontaneous	2–3 hours after start of estrus
Rat (*Rattus norvegicus*)	4–5	13–15 hours	Spontaneous	8–10 hours after start of estrus
Rabbit (*Oryctolagus cuniculus*)	No cycle	Continuous	Induced	10 hours after mating
Rhesus monkey (*Macaca mulatta*)	28*	None	Spontaneous	14 days prior to onset of menstrual bleeding
Man (*Homo sapiens*)	28*	None	Spontaneous	14 days prior to onset of menstrual bleeding

* Menstrual cycle.
References: Altman & Dittmer, 1962; Zarrow el al., 1964.

shown that the ability of the cow's corpus luteum to secrete progesterone in vitro decreases until the eighteenth day, after which secretion is undetectable. Addition of LH to the medium increased progesterone synthesis until day 18 of the cycle, but failed to do so after day 19. The inability to secrete progesterone could be restored by the addition of NADP plus glucose-6-phosphate. Further investigations showed that the corpora lutea obtained at the end of the cycle were unable to form pregnenolone, for if this precursor was added progesterone was formed. The inability to synthesize progesterone may, of course, be the result of inadequate hormonal stimulation or the result of a luteolytic factor.

THE MENSTRUAL CYCLE

The sequence of events in the ovaries of primates does not differ in its essentials from the sequence found in the mammals. However, the uterine reactions to the hormones differ. The experimental analysis of these events has yielded the following facts (see Hisaw and Hisaw, 1961, for details). In castrated monkeys and humans, uterine bleeding occurs if administration of estrogen is abruptly discontinued. If estrogen therapy is gradually withdrawn by decreasing the dose in small decrements over a longer period, no bleeding ensues. This would suggest that withdrawal of estrogen results in uterine bleeding. However, with progesterone administration and withdrawal the same effect can be obtained, although the endometrium in this case is a progestational one. It is even more interesting in relating the experimental analysis to the events occurring in the intact animal that if progesterone is withdrawn during an estrogen plus progesterone therapy, bleeding follows although the estrogen, if it had been given alone, would have prevented uterine bleeding. The sequence of events in this experiment was: treatment of ovariecto-

mized animals with estrogen for a few weeks, treatment with estrogen plus progesterone for about one week, treatment with estrogen. After the progesterone, which could be given in very small doses (0.5 to 1.0 mg.), was withdrawn, bleeding followed. Menstruation starts at the time that the corpus luteum starts to regress, and thus progesterone concentrations are decreasing although estrogen may start to increase. The reason for the prevention of menstrual bleeding in case of pregnancy is the secretion of progesterone by the corpus luteum.

The changes which occur in the uterus and cause menstrual bleeding are not entirely known. Markee (1940), in a beautiful study, transplanted pieces of endometrium to the anterior eye chamber so that it could be observed directly under a variety of endocrine conditions. He found a coiling of spiral arteries one to three days prior to bleeding and he postulated a theory that local anoxemia leads to necrosis of tissue and bleeding. However, this theory does not explain menstruation in some species of monkeys which lack such spiral arteries (Hisaw and Hisaw, 1961). Also, experimental ischemia or destruction of coiled vessels does not lead to menstruation. According to Hisaw and Hisaw (1961) it may involve mainly the stroma, but the exact events are not known. Nalbandov (1964) has presented evidence that animals which do not have menstrual cycles, such as sheep, show an extensive sloughing off of the endometrium. A cast of the uterine horn was obtained by flushing the horn. This sloughing off occurs midway between ovulations, at the time when the corpus luteum starts to regress. This time sequence is thus about the same as that for menstruation in primates.

With respect to ovarian events, the difference between the menstrual and estrous cycle is not a fundamental one but an arbitrary one, in that the start of the cycle is shifted. In the menstrual cycle, day 1 (the first day of bleeding) is related to the waning of the corpus luteum, whereas day 1 of the estrous cycle (the first day of heat) is related to the maximal size of the follicle and closely associated with ovulation in many mammals (the horse is an exception).

The lack of synchronization of estrus and ovulation has instigated a search for methods which can predict or indicate the time of ovulation. A number of methods will be listed:

1. In some women, ovulation is indicated by pain in the side somewhat similar to pain associated with appendicitis; the pain associated with ovulation is called "Mittelschmerz."

2. The basal body temperature (BBT), taken in the morning before arising, fluctuates around the normal body temperature, has a nadir on the day of ovulation, and subsequently rises to stay slightly above the preovulatory temperatures until the next menstrual period. If the cycles are regular, one can try to predict the time of ovulation on the basis of the indicated time of ovulation observed in prior cycles. This rise and the sustained higher body temperature are the consequence of progesterone secretion by the corpus luteum.

3. At the time just before and after ovulation, the cervical mucus is thin and clear, and can easily be stretched without breaking. As is the case with BBT, this test can be used to predict the approximate day of ovulation and at the same time to indicate whether ovulation is occurring or has just occurred.

4. The cervical mucus upon drying will form a fernlike pattern during the immediate preovulatory, ovulatory, and immediate postovulatory periods.

More complicated tests, which are not as easily adapted for routine use, are detection of the peak of LH secretion (see Table 9-5) by determining the gonadotropin content of 24 hour collections of urine, or of the first urine voided in the morning, or by measuring the increase in excretion of pregnanediol (the

major excretory product of progesterone) in the urine. In the case of the latter two methods, the major use is to predict the time of ovulation for the subsequent cycle.

The loss of the estrous period, which assures synchronization of insemination and ovulation, may have been important in pair-bond formation. The loss of estrus by itself, however, does not explain the occurrence of menstruation. The evolutionary significance of the menstrual cycle remains a mystery to the author.

It should be emphasized (Nalbandov, 1964) that the bleeding which occurs during the estrous cycle of dogs and which is limited to the estrous period is different from the menstrual bleeding in several respects:

1. The timing with respect to ovulation.

2. Endocrinologically, in that bleeding in bitches is caused by high estrogen titers and is discontinued when estrogen levels drop.

3. There is no sloughing off of the endometrium; rather, red blood cells pass through the tissue into the lumen of the genital tract.

In cattle, bleeding may occur from the vulva a day after ovulation; the endocrinological causes and physiological significance of this bleeding are not established. It is, apparently, not related to conception (Asdell, 1964; Nalbandov, 1964).

Hormonal Interrelationships During the Estrous and Menstrual Cycles. The advances made in the accurate chemical determination of estrogens and progestins in blood plasma and the high sensitivity of some of the newer bioassay methods for FSH and LH have enhanced the understanding of pituitary-ovary relationships.

Estrogens can be detected in the range of 0.05 μg. and in some cases in even smaller amounts (Preedy, 1962); progesterone can be detected by physical-chemical methods in the range of 0.5 to 2.0 μg. (Zander, 1962) and by bioassay methods in the range of 0.2×10^{-3} μg. (Hooker and Forbes, 1947), whereas FSH can be detected at levels of 50 μg. (Steelman and Pohley, 1953), LH at levels of 0.2 μg. (Sakiz and Guillemin, 1963) to 0.06 × 10^{-9} μg. (Bell et al., 1964) and prolactin at levels of 0.72 μg. (Grosvenor and Turner, 1958).

Unfortunately, only a few species have been investigated with respect to the circulating hormone concentrations during the cycle. In a number of animals, hormone concentrations have been determined after experimental treatments such as ovariectomy followed by hormone injections.

In the rabbit, an induced ovulator, estrogen levels are probably relatively high because the animals are in continuous heat. The variation in this level is probably minor. After mating the LH content of the anterior pituitary drops (Hill, 1934), the LH concentration of the blood increases and reaches a maximum in three to four hours and then decreases to nondetectable levels at eight hours (Hilliard et al., 1964). The progesterone production by the ovary increases from trace amounts to about 30 μg./ovary/hr. and that of 20-α-hydroxy-pregn-4 en-3-one increases about ten-fold (Hilliard et al., 1963). The 20-α-hydroxy-pregn-4 en-3 one may perform the function of a positive feedback and thus sustain the LH secretion (Hilliard et al., 1966). About six or seven hours after mating the amount of estrogen increases (Sawyer, Markee, and Hollinshead, 1947). At ten hours post coitum ovulation occurs. As inspection of Table 6-14 shows, the corpus luteum function is dependent upon the pituitary, although exogenous estrogen can cause maintenance of this structure. The uterus has, as we have seen, an effect on the maintenance of the corpus luteum of pseudopregnancy; removal of the uterus causes maintenance for about the same length of time as occurs in the case of pregnancy (see Table 6-17). During pregnancy the LH concentration of peripheral plasma is higher than during the cycle (see Table 9-3).

The high LH-like activity in the plasma is correlated with the maintenance of the corpora lutea. As we saw in Table 6-14, LH administration will cause functional maintenance of the corpora lutea after hypophysectomy. The drop in LH-like activity on day four or five was explained by Davies et al. (1965), as the result of a possible depletion of LH stores and a lack of adequate production of LH at this time.

The hormonal relationships in the rat are illustrated in Figure 9-4. Data on estrogen secretion by the rat's ovary are not plotted because only indirect estimates have been made. According to Schwartz (1964) the estrogen secretion is at its peak on the last day of diestrus (the day before proestrus). When the preovulatory LH release starts during proestrus the estrogen decreases.

The release of LH can be blocked by anti-adrenergic blocking agents (such as Dibenamine), anti-cholinergic blocking agents (such as atropine), and by barbiturates (such as Nembutal) and a number

Table 9-3.   Ovarian Ascorbic Acid Depletion Activity (OAAD) (LH?) in Pregnant Rabbit Blood

DAY	% OAAD
Estrus	2.57 ± 1.99
Day 1–3 pregnancy	24.36 ± 4.78
Day 4–5 pregnancy	4.10 ± 5.02
Day 6–17 pregnancy	23.19 ± 7.71
Day 18–23 pregnancy	21.50 ± 5.77
Day 24–30 pregnancy	7.83 ± 5.27

Reference: Davies et al., 1965.

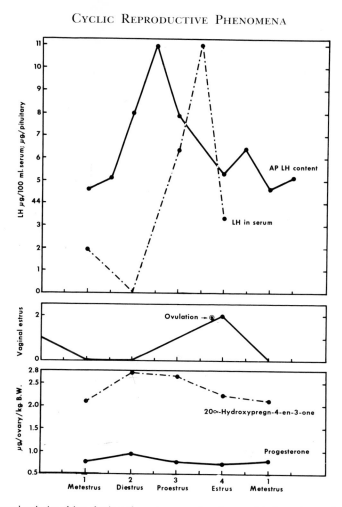

Figure 9-4. Hormonal relationships during the estrous cycle of rats with four-day cycles. For vaginal estrus in the middle graph, "2" represents full estrus. (Data for progesterone and 20-α-hydroxypregn-4-en-3-one from Telegdy and Endröczi, 1963; data for vaginal estrus from Everett, 1961; data for LH content of the anterior pituitary [AP] from Schwartz and Bartosik, 1962; LH concentration data for serum are taken from Ramirez and McCann, 1964.)

of other pharmacological agents (ether, morphine, reserpine, chlorpromazine, 2,4 dinitrophenol) (Everett, 1961). These agents are effective during a critical time of the day only; for rats kept under 14 hours of light (5 a.m. to 7 p.m.) the critical period is between 2 p.m. and 4 p.m. If Nembutal is given on the day of proestrus, ovulation is blocked; if no further treatment is imposed, ovulation takes place 24 hours later than it would have taken place had no Nembutal been given. If the rat is instead injected again at 2 p.m., she fails to ovulate and ovulation is shifted by another 24 hours. If injections are repeated every day between 2 p.m. and

4 p.m., ovulations fail to occur and eventually the follicles become atretic. The blocking of ovulation causes a concomitant prolonged vaginal estrus until the follicles become atretic. Schwartz (1964) has shown that Nembutal injections during this critical time during the day of proestrus prevent the decrease of pituitary LH content, and the increase in plasma LH is also prevented (Schwartz and Caldarelli, 1965).

Schwartz and Bartosik (1962) have suggested that the neurogenic mechanism which causes LH release operates daily between 2 p.m. and 4 p.m., and is set by an internal, biological clock (which in itself may be regulated by the environment) and that a steroid feedback from the ovary may lower the threshold for the stimulus to become effective. These workers explain the delay of exactly 24 hours in ovulation in rats which "spontaneously" have five day cycles by assuming that estrogen and/or progesterone secretion is slightly out of phase, preventing the surge in LH release, which now cannot occur until 24 hours later since this is "set" by the biological clock.

The dog, an example of a monoestrous species with a long cycle, has not received the same amount of attention with respect to the hormonal changes during its cycle as the rabbit, rat, and some farm animals.

Metzler et al. (1966) have presented data on the estrogen levels in the blood of dogs during various phases of the estrous period. These data given in Table 9-4 show the highest concentrations during early estrus and a subsequent gradual decrease. The levels of progesterone and of gonadotropic hormones in dogs during the various phases of the cycle seem not to have been determined.

I have selected sheep as an example of hormonal levels encountered in polyestrous mammals because information about the progesterone concentrations in the blood and the amounts of gonadotropins in the pituitaries during different days of the estrous cycle is available.

Apparently there is little information available on estrogen concentrations in sheep blood during the cycle. This may be the result of low concentrations, as is the case for cattle. According to Mellin and Erb (1965), "No endogenous estrogen

has been unequivocally identified in peripheral blood [of cattle]. However, low levels of biological estrogenic activity have been detected in bovine peripheral blood."

The progesterone concentrations during the estrous cycle have been determined by Short (1964) (see Figure 6-3).

Figure 9-5 summarizes some of the data reported on the gonadotropin content of the pituitary during the ewe's estrous cycle.

1. There is a decrease in LH content between four and 36 hours after the onset of estrus, according to Santolucito et al. (1960), and Robertson and Hutchinson (1962); however, Marincowitz (1964), did not find such a decrease.

2. There is a rather steady increase in FSH, LH, and total GTH between the end of estrus and day 15 according to Kammlade et al. (1952); Robertson and Hutchinson (1962); and Marincowitz (1964). The sharp decrease reported by Santolucito et al. (1960), at day 5 was not found by the other workers.

3. The "total gonadotropin" and LH content of the pituitary is higher during anestrus than during the breeding season (Kammlade et al., 1952; Robertson and Hutchinson, 1962). McDonald and Clegg (1966) also found a higher LH concentration in the serum of sheep during late anestrus than during early estrus or estrus.

It thus appears that between days 3 and 15 gonadotropin is stored in the pituitary to be released sometime between four and 36 hours after the start of estrus.

Dierschke and Clegg (1965) have obtained blood samples from the cavernous sinus, which drains the blood from the

Table 9-4. Free Estrogen Levels in Plasma of Dogs

PHASE OF ESTRUS	ESTRONE	ESTRADIOL-17-α	ESTRADIOL-17-β	ESTRIOL	16-EPIESTRIOL
			μg./100 ml.		
Early estrus	40	22	50	25	6
Middle estrus	30	8	8	15	8
Late estrus	10	5	5	12	6

Reference: Metzler et al., 1966.

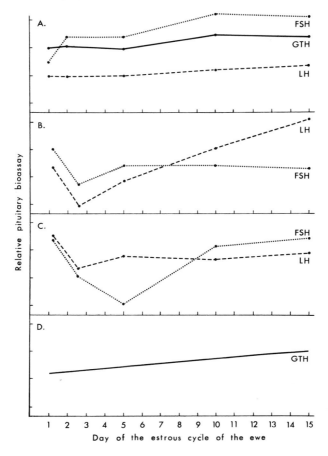

Figure 9-5. Relative pituitary bioassay value for gonadotropin content of the anterior pituitary during the estrous cycle of sheep. In *A*, the FSH data are expressed as the increase in testicular weight compared to initial testicular weight of rats injected with HCG and anterior pituitary (AP) preparation to be assayed (average of four experiments). The LH data are expressed as average seminal vesicle weights in rats injected with AP preparation (average of two experiments). The GTH data are expressed as average testicular weights in rats injected with AP preparation. In *B*, FSH and LH are expressed as percentage of standard FSH and LH preparations. In *C*, FSH data are expressed as percent increase in ovarian weight compared to HCG injected controls after injection of two pituitaries. LH data are expressed as percent increase in ventral prostate weight compared to uninjected controls. In *D*, the data are expressed as testicular weights of baby chicks injected with 15 mg. of AP powder. (*A* — Data from Marincowitz, 1964; *B* — data from Robertson and Hutchinson, 1962; *C* — data from Santolucito et al., 1960; *D* — data from Kammlade et al., 1952.)

pituitary, and assayed it for FSH and LH content. They found a preovulatory depletion of anterior pituitary LH while at the same time there was an increase in the serum LH from the cavernous sinus blood. This increase in serum LH probably represents the amount of LH required for ovulation.

Anderson and McShan (1966) observed that an increase in plasma LH concentration occurred 12 hours prior to ovulation in swine, six to 17 hours prior to ovulation in cattle, and six to 12 hours before ovulation in rats. The observations for the rat are in good agreement with those of Ramirez and McCann (1964), as shown in Figure 9-4. In all species investigated there is thus a good correlation between the time of LH concentration increases and time of ovulation.

Table 9-5 gives values concerning the circulating concentrations of LH, prolactin, and progesterone in the blood of women during the menstrual cycle. The

Table 9-5.   Hormonal Relationships During the Human Menstrual Cycle

DAY	PHASE	LH SERUM μG./100 ML.	LH PLASMA μG./100 ML.	PROLACTIN BLOOD I.U./100 ML.	PROGESTERONE PLASMA μG./100 ML.	PROGESTERONE OVARIAN VEIN BLOOD μG./100 ML.
1	M; EF				1.1	
2	M; EF					
3	M; EF	35		50	1.4	
4	M; EF					
5	EF					
6	EF	50			1.0	
7	EF		27 ± 3			
8	EF	50				
9	EF					
10	LF	80			1.1	
11	LF					
12	LF	110				
13	LF	130			0.9	
14	Ovulation	120	100			
15	EL					
16	EL				1.5	
17	EL					
18	EL	40				110
19	EL					
20	LL					
21	LL	35	15 ± 2		3.3	
22	LL					
23	LL			50		
24	LL	40			2.9	48
25	LL					29
26	LL					
27	LL	35				

M = menstruation; EF = early follicular phase; EL = early luteal phase; LF = late follicular phase; LL = late luteal phase.

Data for LH in serum estimated from Yokota et al., 1965; for LH in plasma from Ross et al., 1967; for prolactin from Simkin and Arce, 1963; for progesterone in peripheral blood from Short and Levett, 1961; and for progesterone in ovarian vein blood from Mikhail et al., 1963.

preovulatory rise in the concentration of LH is very similar to that found during the estrous cycle discussed above. The increase in the progesterone concentrations after ovulation are in accord with the concept that the corpus luteum secretes progesterone and that menstruation is the result of the decrease in progesterone concentration. The endocrinological sequence of events during the estrous and menstrual cycle are thus in essence the same. The response of the nervous system as reflected in the manifestation of estrus in lower mammals is not found in humans. On the other hand, the response of the uterus in humans is in its gross manifestations different from that found in the mammals below the primates.

THE OVARY DURING PREGNANCY

In most mammalian species investigated, the corpus luteum which forms after ovulation is maintained longer than the corpus luteum of the cycle or the corpus luteum of pseudopregnancy (e.g. in sheep and rabbits, respectively). According to Perry and Rowlands (1962) the life span of the corpus luteum of marsupials is not prolonged and the normal periodicity of estrus and ovulation is not disturbed. Table 9-6 shows the difference in the life span of the corpus luteum of the cycle and of pregnancy for a number of species.

In the species listed, except for the horse, the corpus luteum persists until the end of pregnancy or even after parturition. In the horse, the African elephant (*Loxodonta africana*), the black rhinoceros (*Diceros bicornis*), and in two African bats (*Nycteris luteola* and *Triaenops afer*), the corpora lutea disappear early in pregnancy (Amoroso and Finn, 1962). In the horse new corpora lutea (the accessory corpora lutea) are formed either from ruptured follicles or from luteinized follicles. These accessory corpora lutea secrete progesterone but disappear after about the one-hundred fiftieth day of pregnancy. The placenta probably secretes enough progesterone at this time to support pregnancy. In the African elephant, on the other hand, some of the accessory corpora lutea may persist until term (Amoroso and Finn, 1962). In the Canadian porcupine (*Erethizon dorsatum*) accessory corpora lutea are formed by luteinization of atretic follicles at estrus (Mossman and Judas, 1949). These corpora lutea persist only in an ovary that has the normal corpus luteum of pregnancy.

Accessory corpora lutea occur regularly in the mountain viscacha (*Lagidium peruanum*), the peccary (*Tayassu angulatus*), the nilgai (*Boselaphus tragocamelus*), and the fin whale (*Balaenoptera physalus*). These accessory corpora lutea arise during pregnancy, probably through luteinization of follicles (Amoroso and Finn, 1962). Occasionally, accessory corpora lutea are found in the rat (*Rattus norvegicus*), the Rhesus monkey (*Macaca mulatta*), the cat (*Felis catus*), the sow, and the bank vole (*Clethrionomys glareolus*); in most cases these accessory corpora lutea are formed during pregnancy.

During pregnancy, ovulation is usually abolished except in the mare (as noted above) but follicular growth may occur. In the rat, cycles of follicular growth with the same period as the estrous cycles have been noted (Perry and Rowlands, 1962). In sheep, on the other hand, there is an increase in number and size of follicles during early pregnancy, with a regression in size during the latter part of pregnancy

with the occurrence of estrus in 22 percent of a population of western ewes (Williams et al., 1956). However, no vesicular follicles are present during pregnancy in the vampire bat (*Desmodus rotundus*) (Wimsatt and Trapido, 1952).

The regulation of ovarian activity during pregnancy is under the control of hypophyseal gonadotropins and possibly of the uterus (either through a humoral or a neural mechanism or maybe through both) in a large number of species. Exception to this are species in which the uterus or the chorion secretes gonadotropins. The horse, the donkey (*Equus asinus*), the zebra (*Equus burchellii* ?), and possibly the giraffe (*Giraffa camelopardalis*), the nilgai, the African elephant, the Rhesus monkey, the chimpanzee (*Pan satyrus*), and man are examples. Of these, the horse and human have been studied in most detail. In the horse and the other perrissodactyla, a gonadotropic hormone (e.g. pregnant mare's serum gonadotropin, PMSG) is secreted by the endometrial cups. The PMSG concentration in the blood starts to increase at about the fiftieth day of pregnancy, it then rises sharply and remains at a high level to about the thirtieth to one-hundred fortieth day, after which it decreases sharply to zero. It is during the increase in concentration in the blood that the accessory corpora lutea are formed and during the decrease of gonadotropin concentration that they regress. The gonadotropin, which is high in FSH-like activity, also stimulates the fetal gonads (Nalbandov, 1964). A number of factors affect the secretion of PMSG, e.g. breed of horse (PMSG is higher in ponies than in larger breeds); parity (PMSG decreases during subsequent pregnancies); number of foals carried (there is a higher concentration with twins than with single pregnancies); nature of offspring (if the fetus is sired by a donkey, the concentration is about one-sixth of that found if the sire is a horse) (Rowlands, 1964).

The hormone present in the blood of pregnant women is high in LH-like activity and is secreted by the chorion; it is named human chorionic gonadotropin (HCG); it is excreted in the urine whereas PMSG is not. In the pregnant woman, HCG can be detected as early as the twenty-fourth day (day 1 is the first day of menstruation) and rises to a peak (100 to 120 I.U./ml. serum) at about the fiftieth day, remains at this concentration for about 14 days, and then falls to 5 to 35 I.U./ml. serum and remains at this concentration throughout the remainder of pregnancy (Rowlands, 1964). The Rhesus monkey secretes gonadotropin only between approximately the eighteenth and the twenty-fifth day, and the chimpanzee only between the twenty-fifth and the one-hundred thirtieth day of pregnancy; the amounts secreted are smaller than those secreted by humans. The presence of this hormone in urine of pregnant women is the basis for a number of pregnancy tests (e.g. ovulation in the rabbit).

There is evidence that the rat placenta may secrete prolactin, which acts as a luteotropic hormone (Amoroso and Finn, 1964, for details). For instance, rat placenta extracts can maintain pregnancy in the hypophysectomized rat; such extracts can also stimulate the pigeon crop gland (see Appendix). Yashinaga and Adams (1966) estimate that luteotropic activity is associated with the conceptus from day 7 of pregnancy until termination of pregnancy.

Ovarian activity during pregnancy in species which do not secrete endometrial or placental gonadotropins is regulated by the pituitary gonadotropic hormones and by the uterus. In a number of species, in which the uterine integrity is dependent upon ovarian steroids and not upon placental steroids, hypophysectomy at any time during pregnancy leads to termination of pregnancy (see Table 9-6). On the other hand, in the rat, mouse, guinea pig, Rhesus monkey, and human, hypophysectomy during the latter part of pregnancy does not result in termination of pregnancy. An explanation for this may be the production of placental gonadotropins, which stimulate the ovary and/or the placenta to produce estrogen and progesterone in sufficient quantities to maintain pregnancy. The data of Table 9-6 reveal that for the rat and mouse the ovary is essential for maintenance of pregnancy, indicating that the placental luteotropin may stimulate the ovaries. In the guinea pig, Rhesus monkey, and human, ovariectomy during the latter part of pregnancy does not terminate pregnancy, indicating that the placenta may secrete the required steroids; however, this does not exclude the possibility of ovarian stimulation by placental gonadotropins.

In rabbits, in which the pituitary is required for maintenance of pregnancy, the LH concentration in the blood is higher during gestation than at estrus (Table 9-3). The experimental evidence indicates that LH is required for maintenance of luteal function in this species, and the high LH levels thus may explain the sustained function of the corpus luteum through pregnancy.

For a few species, gonadotropin content of the anterior pituitary has been determined by modern assay methods. The data summarized in Table 9-7 show that in the guinea pig the amounts of FSH present during pregnancy were not different from those found during the cycle. In pigs, except for the low amounts of FSH found at 80 days of pregnancy there are relatively small fluctuations in FSH and LH content. The rat, which has been studied in more detail, shows a marked increase in FSH and LH content at day 4 of pregnancy with a sharp drop in FSH content at delivery but a higher LH content at delivery than at the first day of pregnancy.

The data concerning gonadotropin content of the pituitary are difficult to interpret in the absence of data on the concentrations found in the blood. The high content of a hormone may mean high secretion rate in the absence of release or with simultaneous release. The amounts found may represent storage or secretion,

Table 9-6. The Life Spans of the Corpus Luteum (CL) of the Cycle and of Pregnancy and the Effect of Ovariectomy in a Number of Mammalian Species

| SPECIES | CL OF CYCLE | | CL OF PREGNANCY | | EFFECT OF OVARIECTOMY |
	MAXIMAL DEVELOPMENT DAY	RETROGRESSIVE CHANGES DAY	MAXIMAL DEVELOPMENT DAY	RETROGRESSIVE CHANGES DAY	
American opossum (*Didelphis virginiana*)	3	7–8	3	12–13	Death of all embryos
European hedgehog (*Erinaceus europaeus*)	No luteinized granulosa	Shrinks after ovulation		During lactation	
Guinea pig (*Cavia porcellus*)	9–10	11	20	After parturition	Before day 14–27 termination of pregnancy. After 40 days occasionally pregnancy maintained
Golden hamster (*Mesocricetus auratus*)	2	3	2–3	After parturition	Before day 3 prevents implantation; day 11–13 results in abortion
Mouse (*Mus musculus*)	2	3	9–11	Slow regression, but functional at parturition	Abortion or resorption embryos
Rat (*Rattus rattus*)	2–3	After 3	9–11	After parturition	Abortion
Rabbit (*Oryctolagus cuniculus*)	–	–	8	After parturition	Abortion
European badger (*Meles meles*)	Ovulates during 10 month delay of implantation			After parturition	No effect (?)
Horse (*Equus caballus*)	12–14	14	14	35–40; followed by accessory CL which disappear after 150 days	Between 170 and 270 days no effect
Cow (*Bos taurus*)	9-10	14–16	90	150	Abortion if between day 92–236
Goat (*Capra hircus*)	9	12	30	After 60 days	Abortion
Sheep (*Ovis aries*)	6–8	14	14	120–140	Before day 55 abortion; later better chance for maintenance of pregnancy
Pig (*Sus scrofa*)	6–9	13–16	75	110	Abortion
Rhesus monkey (*Macaca mulatta*)	8	13	12	25	At day 25 or later pregnancy maintained
Man (*Homo sapiens*)	6	10	7–10th week	7–12th week	At day 40 or later pregnancy maintained

References: Altman and Dittmer, 1962; Amoroso and Finn, 1962.

depending on other conditions, and therefore it is difficult to draw any general conclusions.

The question "How does the corpus luteum know that the animal is pregnant?" may have a different answer for different species.

As was mentioned, the endometrium or the chorion may secrete the gonadotropins required for maintenance of the corpus luteum (Nalbandov, 1964), an interpretation which Short (1964) has questioned. However, in the absence of evidence against the operation of this mechanism it should be considered as a possible mechanism.

In species in which the endometrium and/or placenta do not secrete gonadotropic hormones other mechanisms are involved. Two main hypotheses have been proposed:

1. There is a neural mechanism that, via the hypothalamus, causes the appropriate changes in secretion by the anterior pituitary for maintenance of the corpus luteum.

2. There is a humoral mechanism that operates either via the pituitary or which acts directly on the ovary.

Experiments by Nalbandov et al. (1955) (see Table 6-18) have provided evidence in ewes in favor of the first hypothesis. Beads implanted into the uterus at different days of the cycle affected the length of the cycle. If implanted on day 3, the cycle was shorter than normal but an 8 mm. bead implanted on day 8 caused a lengthening of the cycle. Denervation of

Table 9-7. Pituitary Content of Gonadotropic Hormones During Pregnancy in Some Mammalian Species

SPECIES	STAGE OF CYCLE OR PREGNANCY	ANTERIOR PITUITARY CONTENT			REFERENCE
		FSH	LH	LTH	
Pig	Day 25 pregnancy	+	NC	+	Day et al., 1959
	Day 85 pregnancy	+	NC	+	
		(µg./mg. AP)	(µg./mg. AP)		
		MEAN 95% LIMITS	MEAN 95% LIMITS		
	Day 13 pregnancy	27.4 19-36	3.6 2.8-4.7		Melampy et al., 1966
	Day 18 pregnancy	31.0 20-42	4.7 3.7-6.0		
	Day 40 pregnancy	30.2 23-38	3.6 2.6-4.8		
	Day 80 pregnancy	14.7 11-19	3.1 2.1-4.5		
	Day 110 pregnancy	38.0 26-50	2.1 1.4-3.2		
Guinea pig	Day 22 pregnancy	Same as during	−	−	Labhsetwar and Dia- mond, 1965
	Day 44 pregnancy	Luteal phase	−	−	
	Day 66 pregnancy	of cycle	−	−	
Hamster			(I.U./AP)		
	Day 5 pregnancy		.026		Qazi and Kent, 1962
	Day 10 pregnancy		.045		
	Day 15 pregnancy		.041		
	Estrus		.0135		
		µg./AP mean ± S.E.			
Rat	Day 1 pregnancy	26.3 ± 4.46	4.6 ± 0.73		Greenwald, 1966
	Day 4 pregnancy	40.5 (no ±)	10.8 ± 1.10		
	Day 8 pregnancy	38.7 ± 4.34	15.6 ± 2.50		
	Day 12 pregnancy	60.2 ± 7.94	14.6 ± 2.37		
	Day 16 pregnancy	129.5 ± 9.92	16.9 ± 2.11		
	Day 20 pregnancy	138.5 ± 7.75	14.4 ± 2.63		
	Day 21 pregnancy	130.6 ± 11.23	12.7 ± 1.69		
	Day 22 pregnancy	137.1 ± 11.20	9.7 ± 0.70		
	Delivery	35.6 ± 4.01	10.4 ± 1.26		

+ = Above level during cycle; NC = No change from level during cycle.

the uterus eliminated the effect of beads on the length of the cycle.

Nalbandov and St. Clair (1958) (see Table 6-18) showed that denervation of the uterus prevented conception, presumably because the pituitary did not secrete the required hormones (as we saw, the pituitary hormone required for maintenance of the sheep corpus luteum is not known).

Bland and Donovan (1965) (see Table 6-18) repeated the experiments of Moore and Nalbandov with guinea pigs and found that if one bead was implanted in one horn only, the corpus luteum on the ipsilateral side regressed, which suggests a local effect of the distended uterus or the corpus luteum, presumably via a uterine luteolytic factor. Niswender and Dziuk (1966) inves-

tigated the possibility of a local effect of an eight-celled embryo on the uterus on the corpus luteum in sheep and did not find conclusive evidence for such a unilateral effect in this species. The difference between the results obtained for guinea pigs and sheep may well be the result of fundamental differences, e.g. a local humoral effect in the guinea pig and a neural effect in sheep.

In the cow, distention of the uterus also causes changes in the length of the cycle and, as the data of Table 6-18 show, the effect depends on the time during the cycle at which the distention is caused. In swine, on the other hand, uterine distention does not affect cycle length (Table 6-18). However, removal of the embryos causes regression of the corpora lutea, suggesting that some embryonic factor may be important in maintenance of the corpus luteum of this species.

There also exists a body of evidence that extracts from the endometrium can cause regression of corpora lutea in hysterectomized rats and rabbits (see Amoroso and Finn, 1962), and that transplants of uteri of estrous animals cause regression of the corpora lutea. It has been shown that uterine tissue metabolizes estrogen. Estrogens are capable of maintaining the corpora lutea of hypophysectomized rats and rabbits. The life span of the corpus luteum of hysterectomized rats and rabbits approaches the length of the life span of the corpus luteum of pregnancy. If the mechanisms for maintenance of the corpus luteum are indeed the same in the case of hysterectomy and of pregnancy, then one would have to assume that in the pregnant rat and rabbit less estrogen is metabolized by the pregnant than by the nonpregnant uterus or that the placenta produce sufficient estrogen to cause maintenance of the corpus luteum.

During pregnancy, estrogen and progesterone concentrations in the blood have been measured in a number of species. In some of these species the placenta secrete estrogens, progestins, or both. It is therefore difficult to evaluate the ovarian hormone secretion from peripheral blood concentrations unless it has been ascertained whether the placenta secreted these hormones also. Measurements of the concentrations of steroids in ovarian vein blood give a better measure of ovarian steroid hormone production (Figure 6-3). One could also measure peripheral blood concentrations of the hormones before and after ovariectomy and obtain an estimate of ovarian hormone production. Estrogens in the pregnant cow are apparently mainly of placental origin.

Progesterone concentrations (measured chemically) in the ovarian vein blood of the ewe, as reported by Edgar and Ronaldson (1958), show an increase from about 0 μg./ml. blood during the first week of pregnancy to about 2 μg./ml. during the fifth week, after which there is a steady decline to about 1 μg./ml. at 16 weeks and a sharper decline to about 0 μg./ml. at 20 weeks. Neher and Zarrow (1954) reported a steady increase of the concentration of blood gestagens (measured by bioassay) in the ewe. Between 20 and 140 days, the concentration rose from about 4 μg./ml. to about 10 μg./ml. Ovariectomy at 114 days had no effect on blood gestagens, showing that they were not of ovarian origin.

Thus one may expect that the secretion of progestins and estrogens by the ovary will vary considerably among species. Probably the secretion rates by the ovary are small when the secretions by the placenta are substantial enough to maintain pregnancy. In any event, peripheral blood concentrations are not a good measure of ovarian steroid secretions (see also Chapter 11).

During pregnancy the peripheral blood concentrations of relaxin increase in the rabbit, guinea pig, cow, and human (Zarrow, 1961). The concentration reaches a plateau at about two-thirds of the duration of pregnancy and drops sharply at parturition. Both the ovary and the placenta may be the source of relaxin. In ovariectomized rabbits, for instance, progesterone levels continue to rise provided pregnancy is maintained with progesterone injections. The exact contribution of the ovary to total relaxin secretion is not established, however, for most species.

REFERENCES

Altman, P. L., and Dittmer, D. S. 1962. Growth Including Reproduction and Morphological Development. Federation of American Societies for Experimental Biology, Washington, D.C.

Allen, E. 1922. The oestrous cycle in the mouse. Amer. J. Anat. *30*:297-371.

Amoroso, E. C., and Finn, C. A. 1962. Ovarian activity during gestation, ovum transport and implantation. *In* S. Zuckerman (ed.): The Ovary. Academic Press Inc., New York, Vol. 1, pp. 451-537.

Anderson, R. R., and McShan, W. H. 1966. Luteinizing hormone levels in pig, cow and rat blood plasma during the estrous cycle. Endocrinology 78:976-981.

Armstrong, D. T., and Black, D. L. 1966. Influence of luteinizing hormone on corpus luteum metabolism and progesterone biosynthesis throughout the bovine estrous cycle. Endocrinology 78:937-949.

Aron, C., Asch, G., Asch, L., Roos, J., and Luxembourger, M. M. 1965. Données nouvelles sur les facteurs neuro-hormonaux de la lutéinisation chez la ratte mise en evidence de l'action ovulatoire du coït au cours du cycle oestral. Pathol. Biol. 13:603-614.

Asdell, S. A. 1964. Patterns of Mammalian Reproduction. Ed. 2. Cornell University Press, Ithaca.

Asdell, S. A. 1966. Evolutionary trends in physiology of reproduction. *In* I. W. Rowlands (ed.): Comparative Biology of Reproduction in Mammals. Academic Press Inc., New York, pp. 1-13.

Bastian, J. W., and Zarrow, M. X. 1955. A new hypothesis for the asynchronous ovulatory cycle of the domestic hen *Gallus domesticus*. Poultry Sci. 34:776-788.

Bell, E. T., Mukerji, S., and Loraine, J. A. 1964. A new bioassay method for LH depending on the depletion of rat ovarian cholesterol. J. Endocrinol. 28:321-328.

Carter, F., Simpson, M. E., and Evans, H. M. 1958. Conditions necessary for the induction of ovulation in hypophysectomized rats. Anat. Rec. 130:283 (abstract).

Conaway, C. H. 1959. The reproductive cycle of the eastern mole. J. Mammal. 40:180-194.

Davies, J., Larsen, J. F., Davenport, G. B., and Schmelling, B. 1965. Plasma levels of ovarian ascorbic acid depleting activity (luteinizing hormone ?) in pregnant rabbits. Proc. Soc. Exp. Biol. Med. 119:925-930.

Day, B. N., Anderson, L. L. Hazel, L. N., and Melampy, R. M. 1959. Gonadotrophic and lactogenic hormone potencies of gilt pituitaries during the estrous cycle and pregnancy. J. Anim. Sci. 18:675-682.

Dempsey, E. W., and Searles, H. F. 1943. Environmental modification of certain endocrine phenomena. Endocrinology 32:119-128.

Dierschke, D. J., and Clegg, M. T. 1965. Gonadotrophins in anterior pituitary tissue and cavernous sinus serum of cycling ewes. Fed. Proc. 24:321 (abstract).

Eckstein, P. 1962. Ovarian physiology in the non-pregnant female. *In* S. Zuckerman (ed.): The Ovary. Academic Press Inc., New York, Vol. 1, pp. 311-359.

Eckstein, P., and Zuckerman, S. 1956. The oestrous cycle in the mammalia. *In* A. S. Parkes (ed.): Marshall's Physiology of Reproduction. Longmans Green & Co. Ltd., London, 1 (Pt. 1), pp. 226-396.

Edgar, D. G., and Ronaldson, J. W. 1958. Blood levels of progesterone in the ewe. J. Endocrinol. 16:378-384.

Enders, R. K., and Enders, A. C. 1963. Morphology of the female reproductive tract during delayed implantation in the mink. *In* A. C. Enders (ed.): Delayed Implantation. University of Chicago Press, Chicago, pp. 129-137.

Everett, J. W. 1952. Presumptive hypothalamic control of spontaneous ovulation. Ciba Found. Coll. Endocrinol. 4:166-177.

Everett, J. W. 1961. The mammalian female reproductive cycle and its controlling mechanisms. *In* W. C. Young (ed.): Sex and Internal Secretions. Williams & Wilkins Co., Baltimore, Vol. 1, pp. 496-555.

Fraps, R. M. 1955. Egg production and fertility in poultry. *In* J. Hammond (ed.): Progress in the Physiology of Farm Animals. Butterworth & Co. Ltd., London, Vol. 2, pp. 661-740.

Fraps, R. M. 1961. Ovulation in the domestic fowl. *In* C. A. Villee (ed.) Control of Ovulation. Pergamon Press, London, pp. 133-162.

Gorbman, A., and Bern, H. A. 1962. A Textbook of Comparative Endocrinology. John Wiley & Sons Inc., New York.

Greenwald, G. S. 1966. Ovarian follicular development and pituitary FSH and LH content in the pregnant rat. Endocrinology 79:572-578.

Grosvenor, C. E., and Turner, C. W. 1958. Assay of lactogenic hormone. Endocrinology 63:530-534.

Hansson, A. 1947. The physiology of reproduction in mink (Mustela vison, Schreb.) with special reference to delayed implantation. Acta Zool. 28:1-136.

Hill, R. T. 1934. Variation in the activity of the rabbit hypophysis during the reproductive cycle. J. Physiol. 83:129-136.

Hilliard, J., Archibald, D., and Sawyer, C. H. 1963. Gonadotropic activation of preovulatory synthesis and release of progestin in the rabbit. Endocrinology 72:59-66.

Hilliard, J., Hayward, J. N., and Sawyer, C. H. 1964. Postcoital patterns of secretion of pituitary gonadotropin and ovarian progestin in the rabbit. Endocrinology 75:957-963.

Hilliard, J., Rennie, P., and Sawyer, C. H. 1966. Role of the ovary in maintaining LH discharge in rabbits. Anat. Rec. 154:358 (abstract).

Hisaw, F. L., and Hisaw, F. L., Jr. 1961. Action of estrogen and progesterone on the reproductive tract of lower primates. *In* W. C. Young (ed.): Sex and Internal Secretions. Williams & Wilkins Co., Baltimore, Vol. 1, pp. 556-589.

Hooker, C. W., and Forbes, T. R., 1947. A bio-assay for minute amounts of progesterone. Endocrinology 41:158-169.

Kammlade, W. G., Jr., Welch, J. A., Nalbandov, A. V., and Norton, H. W. 1952. Pituitary activity of sheep in relation to the breeding season. J. Anim. Sci. 11:646-655.

Labhsetwar, A. P., and Diamond, M. 1965. Pituitary FSH levels and ovarian follicular growth in the pregnant guinea pig. Amer. Zool. 5:726-727 (abstract).

Libby, E. L., and Gilbert, P. W. 1960. Reproduction

in the clear-nosed skate *Raja eglanteria*. Anat. Rec. *138*:365 (abstract).

McDonald, P. G., and Clegg, M. T. 1966. Some factors affecting gonadotropin levels in sheep. Proc. Soc. Exp. Biol. Med. *121*:482-485.

Marincowitz, G. 1964. Follikel-stimulerende hormoon en interstisieelsel-stimulerende hormoon in die hipofisevoorlob van die ooi en die voorkoms van oestrus en ovulasie. Ph.D. thesis, University of Wageningen.

Markee, J. E. 1940. Menstruation in intraocular endometrial transplants in the rhesus monkey. Cont. Embryol. Carnegie Inst. Washington *28*:219-308.

Matthews, L. H., and Marshall, F. H. A. 1956. Cyclical changes in the reproductive organs of the lower vertebrates, *In* A. S. Parkes (ed.): Marshall's Physiology of Reproduction. Longmans Green & Co. Ltd., London, Vol. 1 (Pt. 1), pp. 156-225.

Melampy, R. M., Henricks, D. M., Anderson, L. L., Chen, C. L., and Schultz, J. R. 1966. Pituitary follicle-stimulating hormone and luteinizing hormone concentrations in pregnant and lactating pigs. Endocrinology *78*:801-804.

Mellin, T. N., and Erb, R. E. 1965. Estrogens in the bovine, a review. J. Dairy Sci. *48*:687-700.

Metzler, F., Jr., Eleftheriou, B. E., and Fox, M. 1966. Free estrogens in dog plasma during the estrous cycle and pregnancy. Proc. Soc. Exp. Biol. Med. *121*:374-377.

Meyer, R. K., Leonard, S. L., and Hisaw, F. L. 1929. Effect of anesthesia on artificial production of pseudopregnancy in the rat. Proc. Soc. Exp. Biol. Med. *27*:340-342.

Mikhail, G., Zander, J., and Allen, W. M. 1963. Steroids in human ovarian vein blood. J. Clin. Endocrinol. Metab. *23*:1267-1270.

Mossman, H. W., and Judas, I. 1949. Accessory corpora lutea, lutein cell origin, and the ovarian cycle in the Canadian porcupine. Amer. J. Anat. *85*:1-39.

Nalbandov, A. V. 1959. Neuroendocrine reflex mechanisms: bird ovulation, *In* A. Gorbman (ed.): Comparative Endocrinology. John Wiley & Sons Inc., New York, pp. 161-173.

Nalbandov, A. V. 1964. Reproductive Physiology, Ed. 2. W. H. Freeman and Company, San Francisco.

Nalbandov, A. V., and St. Clair, L. E. 1958. Relation of the nervous system to implantation. *In* F. X. Gassner (ed.): Reproduction and Infertility. Pergamon Press, New York, pp. 83-87.

Nalbandov, A. V., Moore, W. W., and Norton, H. W. 1955. Further studies on the neurogenic control of the estrous cycle by uterine distension. Endocrinology *56*:225-231.

Neher, G. M., and Zarrow, M. X. 1954. Concentration of progestin in the serum of the nonpregnant, pregnant and post-partum ewe. J. Endocrinol. *11*:323-330.

Nelson, D. M., Norton, H. W., and Nalbandov, À. V. 1965. Changes in hypophysial and plasma LH levels during the laying cycle of the hen. Endocrinology *77*:889-896.

Niswender, G. D., and Dziuk, P. J. 1966. A study of the unilateral relationship between the embryo and the corpus luteum by egg transfer in the ewe. Anat. Rec. *154*:394-395 (abstract).

Opel, H. 1966. The timing of oviposition and ovulation in the quail *(Coturnix coturnix japonica)*. Brit. Poultry Sci. 7:29-38.

Perry, J. S., and Rowlands, I. W., 1962. The ovarian cycle in vertebrates. *In* S. Zuckerman (ed.): The Ovary. Academic Press Inc., New York. Vol. 1, pp. 275-309.

Phillips, C. L. 1887. Egg-laying extraordinary in Colaptes auratus. Auk *4*:346.

Preedy, J. R. K. 1962. Estrogens. *In* R. I. Dorfman (ed.): Methods in Hormone Research. Academic Press Inc., New York, Vol. 1, pp. 1-50.

Qazi, M. H., and Kent, G. C. 1962. Pituitary prolactin levels in pregnancy pseudopregnancy and lactation: hamster. Amer. Zool. *2*:549 (abstract).

Ramirez, V. D., and McCann, S. M. 1964. Fluctuations in plasma luteinizing hormone concentrations during the estrous cycle of the rat. Endocrinology *74*:814-816.

Robertson, H. A., and Hutchinson, J. S. M. 1962. The levels of FSH and LH in the pituitary of the ewe in relation to follicular growth and ovulation. J. Endocrinol. *24*:143-151.

Ross, G. T., Odell, W. D., and Rayford, P. L. 1967. Luteinizing hormone activity in plásma during the menstrual cycle. Science *155*:1679-1680.

Rowlands, I. W. 1964. Levels of gonadotropins in tissues and fluids, with emphasis on domestic animals, *In* H. H. Cole (ed.): Gonadotropins. W. H. Freeman and Company, San Francisco, pp. 74-107.

Sakiz, E., and Guillemin, R. 1963. On the method of ovarian ascorbic acid depletion as a test for luteinizing hormone (LH). Endocrinology *72*;804-812.

Santolucito, J. A., Clegg, M. T., and Cole, H. H. 1960. Pituitary gonadotrophins in the ewe at different stages of the estrous cycle. Endocrinology *66*: 273-279.

Sawyer, C. H., Markee, J. E., and Hollinshead, W. H. 1947. Inhibition of ovulation in the rabbit by the adrenergic-blocking agent Dibenamine. Endocrinology *41*:395-402.

Schwartz, N. B. 1964. Acute effects of ovariectomy on pituitary LH, uterine weight, and vaginal cornification. Amer. J. Physiol. *207*:1251-1259.

Schwartz, N. B., and Bartosik, D. 1962. Changes in pituitary LH content during the rat estrous cycle. Endocrinology *71*:756-762.

Schwartz, N. B., and Caldarelli, D. 1965. Plasma LH in cyclic female rats. Proc. Soc. Exp. Biol. Med. *119*:16-20.

Short, R. V. 1964. Ovarian steroid synthesis and secretion *in vivo*. Recent Progr. Hormone Res. *20*: 339-340. (Discussion)

Short, R. V., and Levett, I. 1961. The fluorimetric determination of progesterone in human plasma during pregnancy and the menstrual cycle. J. Endocrinol. *25*:239-244.

Simkin, B., and Arce, R. 1963. Prolactin activity in blood during the normal human menstrual cycle. Proc. Soc. Exp. Biol. Med. *113*:485-488.

Smith, N. G. 1966. Adaptations to cliff-nesting in some arctic gulls *(Larus)*. Ibis *108*:68-83.

Steelman, S. L., and Pohley, F. M. 1953. Assay of follicle stimulating hormone based on the augmentation with human chorionic gonadotrophin.
Endocrinology 53:604-616.

Taleisnik, S., Caligaris, L., and Astrada, J. J. 1966. Effects of copulation on the release of pituitary
gonadotropins in male and female rats. Endocrinology 79:49-54.

Telegdy, G., and Endröczi, E. 1963. The ovarian secretion of progesterone and 20 α hydroxy-
pregn 4 en-3-one in rats during the estrous
cycle. Steroids 2:119-123.

van Tienhoven, A. 1961. Endocrinology of reproduction of birds. In W. C. Young (ed.): Sex and Internal Secretions. Williams & Wilkins Co., Baltimore, Vol. 2, pp. 1088-1169.

van Tienhoven, A., Nalbandov, A. V., and Norton,
H. W. 1954. Effect of Dibenamine on progesterone-induced and "spontaneous" ovulation in
the hen. Endocrinology 54:605-611.

Velardo, J. T. 1960. Induction of ovulation in immature hypophysectomized rats. Science 131:357-
359.

Williams, S. M., Carrigus, U. S., Norton, H. W., and
Nalbandov, A. V. 1956. The occurrence of es-

trus in pregnant ewes. J. Anim. Sci. 15:978-983.

Wimsatt, W. A., and Trapido, H. 1952. Reproduction
and the female reproductive cycle in the tropical American vampire bat Desmodus murinus.
Amer. J. Anat. 91:415-445.

Yokota, N., Igarashi, M., and Matsumoto, S. 1965.
Human serum luteinizing hormone (LH) levels
during the normal menstrual cycle and after
ovariectomy. Endocrinol. Jap. 12:92-101.

Young, W. C. 1961. The mammalian ovary. In W. C.
Young (ed.): Sex and Internal Secretions. Williams & Wilkins Co., Baltimore, Vol. 1, pp. 449-
496.

Yoshinaga, K., and Adams, C. E. 1966. Luteotrophic
activity of the early conceptus in the rat. Anat.
Rec. 154:445 (abstract).

Zander, J. 1962. Progesterone. In R. I. Dorfman
(ed.): Methods in Hormone Research. Academic Press Inc., New York, Vol. 1, pp. 91-138.

Zarrow, M. X. 1961. Gestation. In W. C. Young (ed.):
Sex and Internal Secretions. Williams & Wilkins
Co., Baltimore, Vol. 2, pp. 958-1031.

Zarrow, M. X., Yochim, J. M., and McCarthy, J. L.
1964. Experimental Endocrinology. Academic
Press Inc., New York.

Chapter 10

Insemination and Fertilization

COPULATION AND INSEMINATION

The manner in which a union of the male and female gametes is accomplished varies widely among species. In its most primitive form, sperm and ova are shed in a general area in the water; the union of the two gametes is very much endangered by wide dispersion, currents, etc., and at the same time the sperm and ova are exposed to a medium which is quite different from the body fluids which previously bathed the gametes, and which is generally damaging to the sperm, especially in fresh water fishes.

In cases of external fertilization, there are several ways in which the danger of wide dispersal of the gametes is reduced, and therefore the chances of gametes meeting are increased. Breder and Rosen (1966), in their excellent book, give a number of interesting examples of the mechanisms by which this is accomplished. For instance, in the Petromyzontidae the male loops his tail over that of the female near the vent and down against the opposite side of her body so the genital papilla of the male is near the cloaca of the female. In some bony fishes, e.g. the Clupeoidei, school spawning occurs and great masses of sperm and eggs are present in relatively high concentration, making the water appear milky.

Another mechanism to obtain a high concentration of gametes is used by the Gasterostoidei. The male builds a nest and causes the female to spawn in this nest, after which he spawns. Thus the eggs and sperm are located in a rather circumscribed area.

The European bitterling (Rhodeus amarus) lays its eggs, via a long ovipositor, in the excurrent siphon of a fresh water mussel. Sperm deposited outside the mussel are drawn into the mussel and fertilization takes place in the gill chamber of the mussel (Breder and Rosen, 1966). The eggs hatch in the gill chamber and the young fish remain there until they can swim.

In frogs (except *Ascaphus truei*) and toads, fertilization is external but the eggs are deposited on the back of the female during the complicated oviposition behavior in which the male keeps the female embraced. Eggs are laid when the female is in a horizontal and upside down position, and are caught by the male's belly and the temporary transverse skin folds. During the subsequent righting, the eggs fall on the back of the female where they are incubated (Rabb and Rabb, 1960).

Internal fertilization avoids the dispersion of the gametes and protects them against an inhospitable environment. Among the Cichlidae there are some interesting examples of a form of "internal fertilization" outside the genital tract. In *Haplochromis wingatii*, eggs are spawned, but are snapped up by the female prior to fertilization and kept in her mouth. The male has structures on the anal fin which resemble eggs; the female in trying to grasp these eggs takes in the semen spawned by the male (Wickler, 1962). In *Tilapia macrochir*, the female lays the eggs

297

in a spawning pit and, in trying to grasp the male's genital tassels, takes up the sperm, after which fertilization takes place in her mouth. The female may also snap up threads of semen deposited by the male near the spawning pit (Wickler, 1965).

Fertilization within the genital tract has evolved independently a number of times and is more efficient. It is found in the elasmobranchs, in some but not all teleost fishes, in some amphibia, and in reptiles, birds, and mammals.

A requirement for successful internal fertilization is that one of the following conditions be met: the ova or the sperm should retain their capability for a long time to become fertilized or to fertilize there must be a rather accurate synchronization between copulation and ovulation, or copulations must occur frequently throughout the breeding season to ensure the presence of viable sperm at the time of ovulation.

Examples of species in which sperm

Table 10-1.   Retention of Fertilizing Ability of Sperm for Extended Time Periods in the Genital System of the Female in Different Species

GENUS OR SPECIES	TIME FERTILIZING CAPACITY RETAINED	REFERENCE
Teleosts:		
Cymatogaster sp.	Several months	Turner, 1947
Heterandria formosa	10 months	Turner, 1947
Poecilia reticulata	4 months	Parkes, 1960
Reptiles:		
Malaclemmys centrata	4 years	Parkes, 1960
Terrapene carolina	4 years	Parkes, 1960
Microsaura punila punila	6 months	Parkes, 1960
Uta stansburiana	81 days	Cuellar, 1966
Vipera aspis	Over winter	Parkes, 1960
Causus rhombeatus	5 months	Parkes, 1960
Ancistrodon contortrix	11 days	Parkes, 1960
Crotalus viridis viridis	Over winter	Parkes, 1960
Tropidoclonion lineatum	Over winter	Parkes, 1960
Coronella austriaca	Over winter	Parkes, 1960
Thamnophis sirtalis	3 months	Parkes, 1960
Natrix natrix	Over winter	Parkes, 1960
Natrix vittata	1½ years	Parkes, 1960
Natrix subminiata	5 months	Parkes, 1960
Storeria dekayi	4 months	Parkes, 1960
Drymarchon corais couperi	4½ years	Parkes, 1960
Xenodon merremi	1 year	Parkes, 1960
Leptodeira annulata polysticta	6 years	Parkes, 1960
Leptodeira albofusca	1 year	Parkes, 1960
Boiga multimaculata	1 year	Parkes, 1960
Birds:		
Goose	9.7 days	Johnson, 1954
Chicken	10–14 days	Nalbandov and Card, 1943
Turkey	45.5 days	van Tienhoven and Steel, 1957
Ringdove	8 days	Riddle and Behre, 1921
Mallard duck	7–10 days	Elder and Weller, 1954
Ring-necked pheasant	22 days	Schick, 1947
Bobwhite quail	8.3 days	Kulenkamp et al., 1965
Mammals:		
Myotis l. lucifugus	138 days	Wimsatt, 1942
Eptesicus f. fuscus	156 days	Wimsatt, 1942
Horse	4–6 days	Parkes, 1960

In teleosts the sperm are stored in the ovary, whereas in reptiles, birds, and mammals the sperm are stored in parts of the oviduct or the vagina.

retain their fertilizing capacity for an extended period are given in Table 10-1. Recently Doak et al. (1967) reported that the motility of dog sperm was maintained for as long as 268 hours, but no data on the fertilizing capacity were given.

Accurate synchronization between ovulation and insemination is achieved in most mammals either by the fact that copulation induces ovulation or by the fact that the female accepts the male only during estrus which, in turn, is synchronized with ovulation. In some primates, e.g. humans, estrus does not manifest itself and insemination must occur frequently to ensure the presence of viable sperm at the time of ovulation (unless the time of ovulation can be predicted, as by methods discussed in Chapter 9).

Copulation normally requires the erection of the copulatory organs. The erectile tissues usually become engorged with blood (for details see Walton, 1960). After introduction of the copulatory organ into the female's genital tract ejaculation usually occurs, or may be caused by a back and forth movement of the penis. The ejaculate is not a homogeneous mixture at the time of ejaculation but consists of different portions, each portion with its own characteristics. An extensive review about the chemical composition of these different portions can be found in Mann's book (1964).

Walton (1960) has distinguished different types of insemination:

1. Uterine insemination of a large volume of semen with distention of the cervix (e.g. horse).
2. Uterine insemination of a large volume of semen and retention of the penis during ovulation (e.g. dog and pig).
3. Uterine insemination with a vaginal plug and spasmodic contractions of the vagina (e.g. rat and mouse).
4. Vaginal insemination with incipient plug or slight coagulation of semen (e.g. rabbit, human).
5. Vaginal insemination of a small volume of semen with a high sperm concentration (e.g. ewe, cow).

SPERM TRANSPORT

In elasmobranchs fishes, reptiles, birds, and in most laboratory and domestic mammals, fertilization occurs in the upper part of the Müllerian duct system. By special techniques, fertilization of the eggs can be obtained in the follicle in chickens, as was discussed in Chapter 6. In a few mammalian species, fertilization occurs in the ovary. In the short-tailed shrew (*Blarina brevicauda*), Pearson (1944) found eggs that were penetrated by sperm while still in the follicle. However, most of the eggs were fertilized in the upper part of the oviduct. In the Tenrecidae, fertilization normally takes place in the follicle prior to ovulation (see Chapter 6).

Fertilization of eggs in the ovary occurs in a number of species of bony fishes, as will be discussed in Chapter 11.

The site of fertilization is reached by some of the sperm in less than 15 minutes in chickens and turkeys (Allen and Grigg, 1957) and in sheep, rats, mice, cattle, and dogs (Austin and Bishop, 1957), or one to four hours in rabbits (see Austin and Bishop, 1957). In cattle, this time is two to four minutes (VanDemark and Moeller, 1951). However, in birds, sperm are stored in the oviduct and, if the contention of Bobr et al. (1964) that sperm are stored in the lower part of the oviduct is correct, a majority of the sperm may not reach this fertilization site until much later.

The transport of sperm to the site of fertilization may be aided by contractions of the female genital tract. Sperm have been found at the upper parts of the genital system at shorter intervals than could be accounted for by the swimming movements of the sperm; also, dead sperm are transported to the oviduct in the cow (VanDemark and Moeller, 1951) and the rat (Howe and Black, 1963).

Different mechanisms may cause these contractions. Good synchronization between insemination and uterine contractions could be obtained by introduction, with the semen, of agents which cause uterine contractions, or by stimulation of a reflex mechanism which causes uterine contractions by the act of copulation.

Mann and Prosser (1963) have presented evidence that the very high concentration of serotonin in the secretions of the clasper of the spiny dogfish *(Squalus acanthias)* may play a role in semen transport in this species. In vitro, the addition of either serotonin or of 0.1 to 0.2 cc. of claspersiphon sac fluid, added to the median, causes powerful brief contractions of the uterine muscle followed by smaller periodically occurring movements which can persist for several hours. These data suggest that upon insemination, enough serotonin is introduced to cause uterine contractions which may aid in the transport of the sperm.

The semen of rams and humans contain a group of very potent pharmacological agents, the prostaglandins. These agents are not produced by the prostate, as was originally thought, but rather by the seminal vesicles (von Euler, 1966). The structure of some of the prostaglandins is given in Figure 10-1. The effects of these compounds on the genital system of different species may be summarized as follows:

1. PGE_1 causes contractions of guinea pig and rat uteri in vitro (Pickles et al., 1966) but has an inhibitory effect on human myometrium in vitro (Bygdeman et al., 1966) as do PGE_2 and PGE_3.

2. PGE_1 potentiates (short term increase) the effect of electric stimulation or of vasopressin on the rat and guinea pig uterus and it also causes a prolonged increase in the response ("enhancement") to electrical and vasopressin stimulation (Pickles et al., 1966).

3. PGE_1 and $PGF_{2\alpha}$ initially potentiate the inhibitory effects of epinephrine and norepinephrine on in vitro uterine contractions of the rat, but after this initial effect the response to epinephrine and norepinephrine declines (Clegg, 1966).

4. PGE_1, PGE_2, and PGE_3 generally inhibit human uterine motility in vitro. Eliasson (1966), investigating the effects of partially purified extracts of human semen

(HSF-PG), found that small amounts caused stimulation of uterine strips in vitro, whereas larger doses caused inhibition. This reactivity pattern is observed mostly at midcycle. HSF-PG, placed in the vagina in amounts found in normal human ejaculates, caused increased motility of the body of the uterus in vivo around the estimated time of ovulation. At other times during the cycle the effects of HSF-PG were inconsistent, but this agent increased the tone of the uterotubal functions.

Eliasson (1966) proposed that prostaglandins may facilitate the transport of sperm from the vagina to the uterine cavity. Horton et al. (1965) found that effects on the genital system of ewes could be obtained only with doses in excess of amounts found in ram ejaculates, and thus the conclusion was drawn that it was unlikely that seminal prostaglandins acted as hormones on the oviduct.

Uterine contractions may also be induced by the release of posterior pituitary hormones as a result of behavior associated with mating and of coitus. The evidence concerning the possible importance of the release of these hormones in sperm transport has been reviewed in Chapter 8.

There are protective mechanisms against the entry of sperm into the uterus of pregnant cows. The contractions induced by mating only occur in uteri under the influence of estrogen, and not in uteri under the influence of progesterone. Secondly, a cervical seal is present that prevents entry of the sperm. As we discussed before, the resistance of the uterus to infection is low in pregnant cattle and entry of sperm could easily be accompanied by the entry of harmful bacteria. The protective mechanisms are important for the health of the pregnant animal.

Sperm may be transported to the site of fertilization by sperm motility, uterine contractions, ciliary actions in the female's genital system, or by a combination of these factors. Uterine contractions, in turn, may be the result of components of the semen and/or endogenous hormones

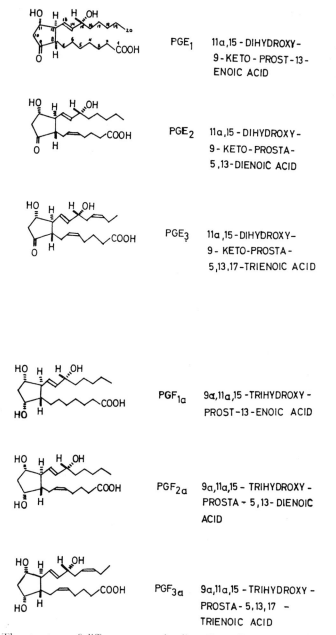

PGE$_1$	11a,15 - DIHYDROXY - 9 - KETO - PROST - 13 - ENOIC ACID
PGE$_2$	11a,15 - DIHYDROXY - 9 - KETO - PROSTA - 5,13 - DIENOIC ACID
PGE$_3$	11a,15 - DIHYDROXY - 9 - KETO - PROSTA - 5,13,17 - TRIENOIC ACID
PGF$_{1a}$	9a,11a,15 - TRIHYDROXY - PROST - 13 - ENOIC ACID
PGF$_{2a}$	9a,11a,15 - TRIHYDROXY - PROSTA - 5,13 - DIENOIC ACID
PGF$_{3a}$	9a,11a,15 - TRIHYDROXY - PROSTA - 5,13,17 - TRIENOIC ACID

Figure 10-1. The structure of different prostaglandins. (From Bergström and Samuelsson, 1965.)

released by the female. The importance of each of these mechanisms for different species needs to be determined.

It is generally assumed that the genes carried by the sperm do not affect their fertilizing capacity. The Mendelian laws of genetics are based on this assumption. An interesting exception to this assumption has been found for the alleles which deter-

mine tail length of the house mouse *(Mus musculus)*. Female mice, which are heterozygotic for this gene, transmit the two alleles in a 50:50 ratio to their offspring, but for males, significant deviations from the 50:50 ratio were found. The deviations can be in either direction, depending on the alleles involved. The alleles t[w6] of a male of genotype t[w6]/T may be transmitted to 99.1

percent of the offspring and only 0.9 percent of the T allele is transmitted (Yanagisawa et al., 1961). The physiological basis for this phenomenon has been investigated by different methods. Braden (1958) found that late mating of females by heterozygotic males (T/t¹, T/t⁰, T/t¹²) caused the ratio of transmission of the two alleles to approach the 50:50 ratio. The differences between the transmission ratios in semen for normal and late matings were significant ($P < 0.05$) in eight experiments. This suggests that there is a difference in the survival of the two types of sperm.

Yanagisawa et al. (1961) reinvestigated this question, using genotypes in which the transmission of the T allele was very low, 0.9 to 6.0 percent, and others in which this figure was 19 and 23 percent. It was found that late mating caused a shift towards a 50 percent transmission for those genotypes in which the transmission was 19 or 23 percent, but for the other genotypes no significant change was obtained. These data suggest that two different mechanisms might be operative for the two types of transmission.

Yanagisawa (1965a) investigated the survival of spermatozoa obtained from the ductus deferens of homozygous and heterozygous mice. For sperm from T/t¹ mice the survival declined gradually, then showed a sharp 5 to 15 percent decrease, and after this declined again gradually. Yanagisawa (1965a) suggested that the sharp decrease might represent differential survival values for the two types of sperm.

Ageing of sperm in the ligated epididymis did not affect the transmission ratio of the alleles (Yanagisawa, 1965b).

Electron microscopic examination of spermatozoa of T/t¹ showed abnormal configuration of the fibrils in 35/280 sperm cells, whereas only 1/103 of such abnormalities were found in T/+, and none of 109 sperm cells were abnormal for +/+ males (Yanagisawa, 1965c). These studies suggest that the alleles for tail length may affect some process between spermatogenesis and fertilization.

SPERMATOZOA NUMBERS AT THE SITE OF FERTILIZATION

The number of spermatozoa which reach the site of fertilization is very small in comparison with the huge numbers that are inseminated. Austin and Bishop (1957) cite figures for different species which range from 12 to 43 for the rat to 500 to 1000 for the rabbit. This loss of spermatocytes is probably partly the result of a failure of a large number of sperm to pass either the cervix or the uterotubal junction (which, as was pointed out in Chapter 3, can have villi or folds, or have a sigmoid flexure which may restrict sperm penetration).

CAPACITATION

Fresh sperm cells, if placed near the site of fertilization shortly before ovulation, are not capable of fertilizing the eggs unless they have undergone some important changes. This process is called capacitation and seems to be related to changes in the acrosome. The release of the enzyme hyaluronidase by the sperm cells occurs only after capacitation has taken place (Austin, 1965). Capacitation may take several hours and is apparently dependent upon the state of the reproductive cycle; e.g., complete capacitation occurs within six hours in the uterus of an estrous doe but is incomplete after incubation in the uterus of a pseudopregnant doe (Noyes, 1960).

Soupart and Orgebin-Crist (1966) showed that double ligation of the uterine horn of a rabbit and subsequent incubation of rabbit sperm in such a horn delays capacitation without, however, affecting the fertilizing capacity of the sperm. Soupart (1966) has investigated the effect of different doses of HCG injected into rabbits in which epididymal sperm were deposited in the uterine lumen. Ten hours after insemination, the uteri were removed and the sperm recovered and inseminated into another set of does. HCG did not affect the incidence of fertile eggs recovered from the "capacitating does" but the incidence of fertile eggs from the second set of rabbits was 15.4, 27.9, 43.6, 74.5, 14.1, 5.75, and 1.16 percent after HCG doses of 0, 25, 50, 75, 100, 200, and 400 I.U. respectively. Thus 75 I.U. HCG causes an apparently optimal environment, but at higher doses some inhibitory effect is triggered.

Although the conditions in the uterus may be of importance in capacitating the sperm, it is experimentally possible to capacitate sperm outside the genital tract. For instance, capacitation occurs after incubation in "surgically created diverticula of the bladder and colon of male and female donor animals" (Noyes, 1960), or in the anterior eye chamber or seminal vesicle. Kirton and Hafs (1965) have found that incubation with beta amylase in vitro capacitates rabbit sperm.

The process of capacitation is reversible by incubating the "capacitated" rabbit sperm with rabbit seminal plasma. Experiments to purify this decapacitation factor (DF) have yielded some information about its properties. The molecular weight is in the range of 300,000, but with subunits of smaller molecular weight. The DF is not destroyed by incubation with Pronase but destruction is obtained by beta amylase; fractionation of the Pronase digest gives separate carbohydrate and protein peaks, with most activity in the carbohydrate peak (Pinsker et al., 1966; Dukelow et al., 1966). Sperm, capacitated and then decapacitated, can be recapacitated by incubation in utero.

The changes which are invoked by capacitation are not entirely understood. Kirton and Hafs (1965) proposed that beta amylase or a similar enzyme changes a factor in seminal plasma which coats the sperm and makes them infertile. However, Dukelow et al. (1966) were not able to decapacitate rabbit sperm in vitro by incubation with beta amylase.

During the sojourn in the uterus the sperm cells lose their acrosomes (baglike structures at the tip of the sperm heads [Austin, 1965]), which results in the exposure of the perforatorium. This process has been linked with capacitation. However, the fact that decapacitation and recapacitation can take place seems to make it unlikely that acrosome removal and capacitation are identical, although under normal conditions both may occur simultaneously.

PENETRATION OF THE EGG MEMBRANES

The sperm may be brought into contact with the ovum by chemotaxis, but that this mechanism is operative has not been firmly established for vertebrates (Austin, 1965; Monroy, 1965; Rothschild, 1956).

Shaver (1966) and Shaver and Barch (1966) have analyzed in detail the interaction between the jelly coat of frog eggs and the spermatozoa. The jelly coat is secreted around the egg in the oviduct. Treatment of frog (*Rana pipiens*) eggs with antisera against jelly coat material prior to insemination decreased the incidence of fertilization. The jelly coat antigens are a mixture of components which are shared between species and of components unique for each species. On the basis of extensive analyses, Shaver (1966) proposed that there may be a series of interactions between the sperm and different surface components of the egg as the sperm traverse the jelly layers. According to his hypothesis, the first series of reactions would consist of complexing of combining sites of the sperm with the jelly coat molecules. If the sperm are of the same species as the egg, the species specific molecules of the jelly coat would react with complementary sites on the sperm and "capacitate" the sperm. These reactions would take place in the outer and middle jelly layers, because the species specific antigens are located there. As the sperm penetrate further, they would encounter jelly layer antigens common to several species and would react with these. The penetration of the egg surface proper would depend on reactions between complementary sites on egg and sperm. Sperm from a species different from that from which the egg is obtained would not be capacitated or would be capacitated incompletely by lack of combining sites between sperm surface molecules and the species specific jelly coat molecules.

Antibodies against frog tissue antigens may reach the surface of the egg rather rapidly and prevent fertilization by interaction with complementary binding sites, and thus prevent sperm from penetrating the egg surface, although the jelly coat may have been traversed successfully (Shaver and Barch, 1966).

A full discussion of the immunological aspects of reproduction falls outside the scope of this book; however, we want to enumerate the following findings:

1. Injection of testicular tissue or sperm, in such a manner that antibodies are obtained (for instance, by injection of antigens plus Freund's adjuvant) may lead to spermatogenesis, as has been found in the Japanese quail (Wentworth and Mellen, 1964) and guinea pigs (Katsh, 1960).

2. Antibodies against spermatozoa have been obtained after injection of sperm. In some strains of mice, guinea pigs, and rabbits fertility was reduced, while in others complete sterility was obtained (W.H.O., 1966).

3. Sensitization to foreign proteins can occur through the female reproductive tract.

The question has been raised by Menzoian and Ketchel (1966) why females do not become sensitized to proteins contained in seminal plasma after repeated inseminations. Investigation of this problem revealed that the same proteins present in the seminal plasma were also present in the female's reproductive tract. The possibility exists that these proteins may have been secreted by the accessory glands of the female which are homologous to protein secreting glands of the male.

The possible reason that females do not become sterile after repeated inseminations during which millions of sperm (and therefore antigens) enter the genital system is the rather weak antigenecity of the sperm. Katsh (1960) has pointed out that in the guinea pig it is necessary to inject sperm three or four times on alternate weeks to obtain immunity of about a year's duration. In addition, it is necessary that the females mate so that immunization can be maintained by continued coitus. It is, however, possible that in some cases infertility may be the result of sensitization of the female to sperm antigens.

The penetration of the ova by the sperm can occur in a number of different ways:

1. A micropylar canal is present in the egg membrane of fishes, but not of lampreys (Austin, 1965), and sperm can penetrate via these canals. The lamprey egg is surrounded by a membrane, which at one pole bears a jellylike tuft. It is at this end that sperm penetrate the egg, but how the membrane is penetrated is not established (Austin, 1965).

2. The spermatozoon has to penetrate the cumulus oophorus which surrounds mammalian eggs. The cumulus oophorus cells are coated by a mucopolysaccharide high in hyaluronic acid. The sperm fraction of the semen is high in hyaluronidase, and it is therefore possible that the sperm aid in the dispersion of the cumulus oophorus by action of this enzyme (Monroy, 1965). After penetration of the cumulus oophorus or dispersal of these cells by other means, the sperm penetrate the zona pellucida, which may consist of three concentric layers (e.g. in the pig) (Dickmann and Dziuk, 1964). The penetration of the zona probably is the result of the formation of a thin filament that is ejected by the spermatozoon. This ejection is accompanied by a change in the acrosome; these changes have been called the "acrosome reaction." During penetration of the zona, the spermatocyte loses its cell membrane and becomes denuded of its head cap (Hadek, 1963). This may liberate an enzyme or enzymes which may have

aided in the penetration of the outer egg membranes. Although more than one sperm cell can enter the zona pellucida, not all traverse it. In the pig, for instance, only one sperm penetrates into the inner zona of the zona pellucida. The others cannot penetrate deeper, because, apparently, a change has taken place in the zona pellucida; this is called the "zona reaction." The efficiency of this reaction is dependent upon the species; it is, for instance, highly effective in the dog, moderately so in the mouse and rat, but is lacking in the rabbit (see Monroy, 1965).

The sperm cells which have penetrated the zona pellucida but have not traversed it remain in the perivitelline space; they are called "supplementary," "supernumerary," or "accessory" spermatozoa. They have been found in the eggs of the rat, the mouse, the guinea pig, the cat, the mole, the bat, the pika, the rabbit, and the pig (Blandau, 1961). The strain of mice from which the sperm are obtained plays a role in the incidence of eggs with supplementary sperm cells (Blandau, 1961).

Penetration of the vitelline membrane by the sperm cell occurs after the fertilizing spermatozoon attaches itself to this membrane. The supplementary spermatocytes do not attach to the vitelline membrane (Austin and Walton, 1960). The exact mechanism by which the sperm penetrate this membrane is a matter of controversy. Austin and Walton (1960) compare the process to a kind of "phagocytosis" by the egg, whereas Blandau and Odor (1952) state that the sperm progress forward as a result of movements of the tail. The attachment of the sperm to the vitelline membrane is, according to Austin (1964), a prerequisite for preventing the penetration of sperm through the zona pellucida.

POLYSPERMY

Penetration of the vitelline membrane by more than one spermatocyte gives rise to polyspermy. The phenomenon is found regularly in elasmobranchs, urodeles, rep-

tiles, and birds (Rothschild, 1956; Pikó, 1961; Blandau, 1961). Only one sperm nucleus fuses with the nucleus of the ovum and the non-fertilizing sperm are destroyed, by a mechanism that has not been elucidated. A number of Russian workers (see Rothschild, 1956; Austin and Walton, 1960) have stated that polyspermy in birds and mammals has beneficial effects on the offspring, especially if the non-fertilizing and fertilizing sperm, which enter the egg or the perivitelline space, are from different sires; they also claim that the offspring in the case of chickens have characters of both "sires." In a rather careful experiment, Alterkirch et al. (1955) could not confirm this. Kushner (Rothschild, 1956) also obtained better fertility with mixtures of semen from different sires than with the semen from each sire by itself. Beatty (1960), in a well designed investigation in which the number of sperm contributed to the mixture by each male was made equal and in which sires with genetic markers were used, found that:

1. the fertilizing capacity of sperm by two or three donors may differ significantly among donors, although the sperm from each donor, when inseminated alone, may show normal fertility;

2. the conception rate may increase as the number of males contributing to the inseminate increases;

3. in one experiment, semen from one particular male yielded no offspring when inseminated alone, but when this semen was mixed with that of other males, young were born sired by this male. These data support Kushner's conclusions of a contribution by sperm from another male.

ACTIVATION AND FERTILIZATION OF THE EGG

The eggs of most species of fish, when exposed to fresh water, in many cases undergo abortive parthenogenetic activation and become unfertilizable. At parthenogenetic activation or after fertilization the following changes occur (Rothschild, 1958):

1. The cortical alveoli of the egg disintegrate.

2. The egg volume is reduced.

3. A perivitelline space appears as the result of the elevation of the chorion from the egg surface.

4. The second polar body is expelled.

5. Bipolar differentiation commences.

The features which fish and mammalian eggs have in common upon fertilization are, according to Rothschild (1958):

1. The fertilizing sperm initiates the propagation of an impulse around the egg surface. This impulse catalyzes disintegration of the cortical alveoli and makes the egg unreceptive to further sperm penetrations.

2. The mucopolysaccharides expelled from the cortical granules or alveoli cause the formation of a fluid-filled perivitelline space between the egg surface and the surrounding membrane.

3. The head of the sperm enters and the nucleus fuses with the nucleus of the ovum.

These changes have been beautifully illustrated for mammalian eggs in Austin and Walton's (1960) and Blandau's (1961) papers. The reader, interested in more detail, is referred to these excellent reviews.

Polyspermy in mammalian eggs occurs with much less frequency than in the groups mentioned above, but it has been observed in the rat, hamster, pig, vole, cat, ferret, and rabbit (Pikó, 1961, and Blandau, 1961). The incidence in rats is about 1.2 and in rabbits about 1.4 percent. Some of the dispermic eggs of rats show abnormal development, but others are normal at 12 days of gestation (Pikó, 1961).

The incidence of polyspermy can be increased experimentally by ageing the eggs (insemination after ovulation) or by subjecting female rats to hyperthermia (Blandau, 1961; Pikó, 1961).

After the spermatozoon contacts the vitelline membrane, changes occur in the structure and metabolism of the egg; these changes are called activation. Some of these changes consist of contraction of the vitellus (which caused a loss of as high as 25 percent in cytoplasmic volume in the goldfish eggs [Rothschild, 1956]), completion of meiosis, and extrusion of the second polar body. Such activation of eggs can also be induced by a number of experimental but nonspecific conditions, e.g. cold shock and ether treatment, while the activation can be prevented by "hot shock" or colchicine treatment (Blandau, 1961).

Morrill and Watson (1966), using frog (Rana pipiens) eggs, established that the membrane potential with respect to Ringer's solution was -63 ± 1 mV for the ovarian oocyte, $+41 \pm 1$ mV for the ovulated unfertilized egg, $+40 \pm 1$ mV for the fertilized uncleaved egg, and -58 ± 2 mV for the egg in the two cell stage. The corresponding figures for the potential difference between the deep cytoplasm and the medium were -37 ± 2 mV, $+26 \pm 2$ mV, and $+28 \pm 2$ mV, with the potential difference for the egg in the two cell stage not established. At the time of activation a slow monophasic change in the cortical membrane occurred but the potential returned to that of the ovulated egg in about ten minutes. Such a change may be associated with a transient increase in chloride ion permeability (Maéno, 1959).

After entrance of the sperm into the ooplasm, the sperm head undergoes a series of changes which result in detachment of the perforatorium, an increase in the size of the head, appearance of nucleoli within the sperm head; the number of nucleoli, in what is now called the male pronucleus, may reach 30 (Blandau, 1961).

The male pronucleus and the female pronucleus, which originates from the egg nucleus, approach each other, the nucleoli disappear, the nuclear membrane disappears, and the prophase chromosomes aggregate (Blandau, 1961).

DNA synthesis occurs in the male and the female pronucleus 3 to 6 hours after fertilization has taken place. This period of DNA synthesis is short, and is followed by a long postsynthetic period in rabbit eggs (Szollosi, 1966).

Ferrier (1967) has reported a case of experimentally induced gynogenesis (non-participation of the male pronucleus after fertilization) for eggs of *Pleurodeles waltlii* fertilized by sperm of *Salamandra salamandra*. A number of viable individuals with variable degrees of polyploidy developed. In this case the activation by the sperm penetration was apparently sufficient to induce embryonic development.

FERTILIZABLE LIFE OF THE EGG AND THE EFFECT OF AGEING OF EGGS

The time span during which an egg can be fertilized once it is ovulated is limited, and fertilization later than normal often leads to abnormalities in development.

We mentioned in a previous chapter how ageing of frog eggs before fertilization results in abnormal sex ratios (an excess of males). In a number of cases such ageing resulted in abnormal development.

Blandau (1961) lists the time span during which eggs can be successfully fertilized in a number of mammalian species. Generally, the life span is not over 30 hours (e.g. the ferret) and in some instances only five hours (e.g. the hamster).

Ageing of eggs before they are fertilized causes an increase in the incidence of embryonic mortality, of stillbirth, of abortions in guinea pigs and cattle (Nalbandov, 1964), and a failure of implantation in rabbits (Austin, 1967). By delaying the time of insemination of rabbits ovulated by gonadotropin injections, Austin (1967) established that as little as seven hours after ovulation pycnosis had occurred in 38 out of 67 eggs, whereas 34 eggs recovered three hours after ovulation were normal. The delayed insemination (three to seven hours after ovulation) caused the death of embryos during cleavage. The chromosomal abnormalities probably increased preimplantation losses. In postimplantation embryos no abnormal chromosome conditions other than tri-

ploidy were noted. The latter condition was probably the result of increased polyspermy associated with ageing of the eggs.

Hunter (1967) found that ageing pig eggs beyond eight hours after ovulation increased the incidence of unfertilized eggs, but that abnormal development of fertilized eggs did not increase until the egg was older than 12 hours at the time of fertilization. Polyspermy was 1.3 percent in eggs four hours old and 15.4 percent in those which were 16 hours old; in the 20-hour-old group polyspermy was 11.1 percent.

Ageing of spermatozoa also can affect embryonic mortality. Nalbandov and Card (1943) found that after removal of the male, fertility of chickens' eggs decreased and there was also an increase in the embryonic mortality of fertile eggs. Dharmarajan's (1950) investigations showed that the majority of abnormalities in embryos resulting from aged sperm were in the vascular and nervous system. Hale (1955) confirmed Nalbandov and Card's (1943) observations for turkeys. Salisbury (1965) has reviewed the evidence concerning the effect of ageing in the male and female reproductive tract. There is no clear cut evidence that ageing in the isolated scrotal epididymis (below body temperature) has a different effect than ageing in the female genital tract because several other variables are involved. It is suggested that in the female tract the sperm lose their fertilizing ability, but sperm which retain this ability do not cause subsequent abnormalities in embryonic development, whereas sperm aged in the isolated scrotal epididymis may undergo such changes that, if they are capable of fertilization, a certain incidence of abnormal embryonic development ensues. The decrease in embryonic viability is steeper than the decrease in fertilizing capacity of sperm after the sperm are aged in vitro at 4 to 5° C. or at −79° C.

A curious phenomenon concerning the preservation of the fertilizing capacity of rabbit sperm has been reported by Bedford (1967). The fertilizing capacity of rabbit sperm incubated in vivo in rabbit uteri started to decline sharply after about 20 hours, whereas the fertilizing ability of rabbit sperm incubated in vivo in uteri of estrous rats did not decline until after about 50 hours. Bedford (1967) has speculated that this longer survival of the sperm incubated in rat uteri may be related to the incomplete capacitation which occurs in these sperm.

The development of the fertilizing ability of sperm in the epididymis of the rabbit has been investigated by Bedford (1966). It was found that sperm obtained from the proximal to the middle of the body of the epididymis and from the head of the epididymis failed to make contact with the zona pellucida and that, consequently, no eggs were fertilized. Sperm from the lower part of the epididymis gave maximal fertility. However, polyploidy was observed in eggs fertilized by these sperm, whereas no polyploidy was observed after insemination with ejaculated sperm.

FATE OF NONFERTILIZED OVA AND UNUSED SPERM

Unfertilized ova, which have a rather short life, disintegrate. Rats eliminate such fragmented eggs via the vagina (Blandau, 1961). The fate of such unfertilized eggs in other mammals is not known.

The sperm which did not penetrate the zona pellucida or which did not reach the site of fertilization in mice are eliminated in two different ways. One is evacuation of uterine sperm via the vagina, the other is phagocytosis by polymorphonuclear neutrophil leukocytes and monocytes (Reid, 1965).

PARTHENOGENESIS

Parthenogenesis (birth from a virgin) occurs rarely in vertebrates, although it can be induced experimentally in fish *(Salmo salar, Salmo trutta)*, amphibia *(Rana nigromaculata, Triturus alpestris)*, and mammals (rabbit) (see Beatty, 1957, for documentation). However, in turkeys (Olsen, 1960) and in certain strains of chickens (Olsen, 1966a) parthenogenesis happens spontaneously and gives rise to diploid males only (Poole and Olsen, 1957). These males may not be completely homozygous, as indicated by homograft responses (Poole et al., 1963; Poole, 1965). These data suggest that probably meiosis II is suppressed or that the second polar body combines with the nucleus of the ootid.

The incidence of parthenogenetic development may be increased after vaccination of the hens with fowlpox vaccine or after an outbreak of lymphomatosis. The predisposition of parthenogenesis may be transmitted to the progeny (Olsen, 1956, 1966b).

The age of the hen laying the eggs is, apparently, also a factor in determining the incidence of parthenogenesis and the survival of the resulting embryos. Eggs from the same turkey hens show a higher incidence of parthenogenesis and better embryo survival during the first year of egg production than during the second year (Olsen, 1967).

REFERENCES

Allen, T. E., and Grigg, G. W. 1957. Sperm transport in the fowl. Austral. J. Agric. Res. 8:788-799.

Alterkirch, Hoffman, and Schaaf. 1955. Doppelpaarungen in der Geflügelzucht. Arch. Geflügelz. Kleintierk. 4:185-189.

Austin, C. R. 1964. Behaviour of spermatozoa in the female genital tract and fertilization. Fifth Int. Congr. Anim. Reprod. Art. Ins. 2:7-22.

Austin, C. R. 1965. Fertilization. Prentice-Hall Inc., New York.

Austin, C. R. 1967. Chromosome deterioration in ageing eggs of the rabbit. Nature 213:1018-1019.

Austin, C. R., and Bishop, M. W. H. 1957. Preliminaries to fertilization in mammals. In A. Tyler, R. C. von Borstel, and C. B. Metz (eds.): The Beginning of Embryonic Development. Amer. Ass. Adv. Sci., Washington, D. C. pp. 71-107.

Austin, C. R., and Walton, A. 1960. Fertilization.

In A. S. Parkes (ed.): Marshall's Physiology of Reproduction. Longmans Green & Co., Ltd., London, 1 (pt. 2), pp. 310-416.

Beatty, R. A. 1957. Parthenogenesis and Polyploidy in Mammalian Development. Cambridge University Press.

Beatty, R. A. 1960. Fertility of mixed semen from different rabbits. J. Reprod. Fertil. *1*:52-60.

Bedford, J. M. 1966. Development of the fertilizing ability of spermatozoa in the epididymis of the rabbit. J. Exp. Zool. *163*:319-330.

Bedford, J. M. 1967. Fertile life of rabbit spermatozoa in rat uterus. Nature *213*:1097-1099.

Bergström, S., and Samuelsson, B. 1965. Prostaglandins. Ann. Rev. Biochem. *34*:101-108.

Blandau, R. J. 1961. Biology of eggs and implantation. *In* W. C. Young (ed.): Sex and Internal Secretions. Williams & Wilkins Co., Baltimore. Vol. 2, pp. 797-882.

Blandau, R. J., and Odor, D. L. 1952. Observations on sperm penetration into the oöplasm and changes in the cytoplasmic components of the fertilizing spermatozoon in rat ova. Fertil. and Steril. *3*:13-26.

Bobr, L. W., Lorenz, F. W., and Ogasawara, F. X. 1964. Distribution of spermatozoa in the oviduct and fertility in domestic birds. J. Reprod. Fertil. *8*:39-47.

Braden, A. W. H. 1958. Influence of time of mating on the segregation ratio of alleles at the T locus in the house mouse. Nature *181*:786-787.

Breder, C. M., Jr., and Rosen, D. E. 1966. Modes of reproduction in fishes. The Natural History Press, Garden City, N. Y.

Bygdeman, M., Hamburg, M., and Samuelsson, B. 1966. The content of different prostaglandins in human seminal fluid and their threshold doses on the human myometrium. Mem. Soc. Endocrinol. *14*:49-63.

Chernoff, H. N., Pinsker, M. C., Dukelow, W. R., and Williams, W. L. 1966. Purification of sperm antifertility factor. Fed. Proc. *25*:284.

Clegg, P. C. 1966. The effect of prostaglandins on the response of isolated smooth-muscle preparations to sympathomimetic substances. Mem. Soc. Endocrinol. *14*:119-135.

Cuellar, O. 1966. Delayed fertilization in the lizard *Uta stansburiana*. Copeia *3*:549-552.

Dharmarajan, M. 1950. Effect on the embryo of staleness of the sperm at the time of fertilization in the domestic hen. Nature *165*:398.

Dickmann, Z., and Dziuk, P. J. 1964. Sperm penetration of the zona pellucida of the pig egg. J. Exp. Biol. *41*:603-608.

Doak, R. L., Hall, A., and Dale, H. E. 1967. Longevity of spermatozoa in the reproductive tract of the bitch. J. Reprod. Fertil. *13*:51-58.

Dukelow, W. R., Chernoff, H. N., Brackett, B. G., Williams, W. L., and Petersen, W. E. 1966. Properties of sperm antifertility factor. Fed. Proc. *25*:314 (abstract).

Elder, W. H., and Weller, M. W. 1954. Duration of fertility in the domestic mallard hen after isolation from the drake. J. Wildl. Mgmt. *18*:495-502.

Eliasson, R. 1966. The effect of different prosta-

glandins on the motility of the human myometrium. Mem. Soc. Endocrinol. *14*:77-87.

Ferrier, V. 1967. Gynogenèse diploïde et polyploïde réalisée expérimentallement chez le triton *Pleurodeles waltlii*. C. R. Soc. Biol. *160*:1526-1531.

Hadek, R. 1963. Submicroscopic changes in the penetrating spermatozoon of the rabbit. J. Ultra Structure Res. *8*:161-169.

Hale, E. B. 1955. Duration of fertility and hatchability following natural matings in turkeys. Poultry Sci. *34*:228-233.

Horton, E. W., Main, I. H. M., and Thompson, C. J. 1965. Effects of prostaglandins on the oviduct, studies in rabbits and ewes. J. Physiol. *180*:514-528.

Howe, G. R., and Black, D. L. 1963. Migration of rat and foreign spermatozoa through the uterotubal junction of the oestrous rat. J. Reprod. Fertil. *5*:95.

Hunter, R. H. F. 1967. The effects of delayed insemination on fertilization and early cleavage in the pig. J. Reprod. Fertil. *13*:133-148.

Johnson, A. S. 1954. Artificial insemination and duration of fertility of geese. Poultry Sci. *33*:638-640.

Katsh, S. 1960. Antigen-antibody reactions in relation to reproduction. J. Dairy Sci. Suppl. *43*:84-100.

Kirton, K. T., and Hafs, H. D. 1965. Sperm capacitation by uterine fluid or beta-amylase in vitro. Science *150*:618-619.

Kulenkamp, A. W., Coleman, T. H., and Ernst, R. A. 1965. Artificial insemination of bobwhite quail. Poultry Sci. *44*:1392.

Maéno, T. 1959. Electrical characteristics and activation potential of *Bufo* eggs. J. Gen. Physiol. *43*:139-157.

Mann, T. 1964. Biochemistry of Semen and of the Male Reproductive Tract. Methuen & Co., London.

Mann, T., and Prosser, L. C. 1963. Uterine response to 5-hydroxytryptamine in the clasper-siphon secretion of the spiny dogfish *Squalus acanthias*. Biol. Bull. *125*:384-385.

Menzoian, J. O., and Ketchel, M. M. 1966. Immunological tolerance of the female to homologous seminal plasma protein. Nature *211*:133-135.

Monroy, A. 1965. Chemistry and Physiology of Fertilization. Holt, Rinehart, and Winston Inc., New York.

Morrill, G. A., and Watson, D. E. 1966. Transmembrane electropotential changes in amphibian eggs at ovulation, activation and first cleavage. J. Cell. Comp. Physiol. *67*:85-92.

Nalbandov, A. V. 1964. Reproductive Physiology. W. H. Freeman and Co., San Francisco.

Nalbandov, A. V. and Card, L. E. 1943. Effects of stale sperm on fertility and hatchability of chicken eggs. Poultry Sci. *22*:218-226.

Noyes, R. W. 1960. The capacitation of spermatozoa. J. Dairy Sci. Suppl. *43*:68-80.

Olsen, M. W. 1956. Fowl pox vaccine associated with parthenogenesis in chicken and turkey eggs. Science *124*:1078-1079.

Olsen, M. W. 1960. Nine year summary of parthenogenesis in turkeys. Proc. Soc. Exp. Biol. Med. *105*:279-281.

Olsen, M. W. 1966a. Frequency of parthenogenesis in chicken eggs. J. Hered. *57*:23-25.

Olsen, M. W. 1966b. Parthenogenesis in eggs of White Leghorn chickens following an outbreak of visceral lymphomatosis. Proc. Soc. Exp. Biol. Med. *122*:977-980.

Olsen, M. W. 1967. Age as a factor influencing the level of parthenogenesis in eggs of turkeys. Proc. Soc. Exp. Biol. Med. *124*:617-619.

Parkes, A. S. 1960. The biology of spermatozoa and artificial insemination. *In* A. S. Parkes (ed.): Marshall's physiology of reproduction. Longmans Green & Co. Ltd., London, 1 (Pt. 2), pp. 161-263.

Pearson, P. O. 1944. Reproduction in the shrew (Blarina brevicauda Say). Amer. J. Anat. *75*: 39-93.

Pickles, V. R., Hall, W. J., Clegg, P. C., and Sullivan, T. J. 1966. Some experiments on the mechanism of action of prostaglandins on the guinea-pig and rat myometrium. Mem. Soc. Endocrinol. *14*:89-102.

Pikó, L. 1961. La polyspermie chez les animaux. Ann. Biol. Anim. Bioch. Biophys. *1*:323-383.

Poole, H. K. 1965. Further evidence of heterozygosity in parthenogenetic turkeys. Nature *206*:324.

Poole, H. K., and Olsen, M. W. 1957. The sex of parthenogenetic turkey embryos. J. Hered. *48*: 217-218.

Poole, H. K., Healey, M. V., Russell, P. S., and Olsen, M. W. 1963. Evidence of heterozygosity in parthenogenetic turkeys from homograft responses. Proc. Soc. Exp. Biol. Med. *113*:503-505.

Rabb, G. B., and Rabb, M. S. 1960. On the mating and egg-laying behavior of the Surinam toad, *Pipa pipa*. Copeia *4*:271-276.

Reid, B. L. 1965. The fate of uterine spermatozoa in the mouse *post coitum*. Austr. J. Zool. *13*: 189-199.

Riddle, O., and Behre, E. H. 1921. Studies on the physiology of reproduction in birds. IX. On the relation of stale sperm to fertility and sex in ring doves. Amer. J. Physiol. *57*:228-249.

Rothschild, Lord. 1956. Fertilization. Methuen & Co., Ltd., London.

Rothschild, Lord. 1958. Fertilization in fish and lampreys. Biol. Revs. *33*:372-392.

Salisbury, G. W. 1965. Ageing phenomena in gametes. J. Gerontol. *20*:281-288.

Shaver, J. R. 1966. Immunobiological studies of the jelly-coats of anuran eggs. Amer. Zool. *6*:75-87.

Shaver, J. R., and Barch, S. H. 1966. Time relationships of effects of antiserum treatment of frog eggs. Exp. Cell. Res. *43*:245-247.

Shick, C. 1947. Sex ratio—egg fertility relationships in the ring-necked pheasant. J. Wildl. Mgmt. *11*:302-306.

Soupart, P. 1966. Effect of human chorionic gonadotrophin on capacitation of rabbit spermatozoa. Nature *212*:408-410.

Soupart, P., and Orgebin-Crist, M. C. 1966. Capacitation of rabbit spermatozoa delayed *in vivo* by double ligation of uterine horn. J. Exp. Zool. *163*:311-318.

Szollosi, D. 1966. Time and duration of DNA synthesis in rabbit eggs after sperm penetration. Anat. Rec. *154*:209-212.

Turner, C. L. 1947. Viviparity in teleost fishes. Sci. Monthly *65*:508-518.

VanDemark, N. L., and Moeller, A. N. 1951. Speed of spermatozoan transport in reproductive tract of estrous cow. Amer. J. Physiol. *165*: 674-679.

van Tienhoven, A., and Steel, R. G. D. 1957. The effect of different diluents and dilution rates on fertilizing capacity of turkey semen. Poultry Sci. *36*:473-479.

von Euler, U. S. 1966. Introductory survey: Prostaglandins. Mem. Soc. Endocrinol. *14*:3-17.

Walton, A. 1960. Copulation and natural insemination. *In* A. S. Parkes (ed.): Marshall's Physiology of Reproduction. Longmans Green & Co. Ltd., London, 1 (Pt. 2), pp. 130-160.

Wentworth, B. C., and Mellen, W. J. 1964. Active immunity induced and spermatogenesis suppressed by testicular antigen in the male Japanese quail *(Coturnix coturnix japonica)*. J. Reprod. Fertil. *8*:215-223.

Wickler, W. 1962. 'Egg-dummies' as natural releasers in mouth-breeding Cichlids. Nature *194*:1092-1093.

Wickler, W. 1965. Signal value of the genital tassel in the male *Tilapia macrochir* Blgr (Pisces: Cichlidae). Nature *208*:595-596.

Wimsatt, W. A. 1942. Survival of spermatozoa in the female reproductive tract of the bat. Anat. Rec. *83*:299-307.

Wimsatt, W. A. 1944. Further studies on the survival of spermatozoa in the female reproductive tract of the bat. Anat. Rec. *88*:193-204.

World Health Organization. 1966. Immunological aspects of human reproduction. W.H.O. Tech. Rep. Serv. 34.

Yanagisawa, K. 1965a. Studies on the mechanism of abnormal transmission ratios at the T-locus in the house mouse. II Test for physiological differences between t- and T-bearing sperm manifested *in vitro*. Jap. J. Gen. *40*:87-92.

Yanagisawa, K. 1965b. Studies on the mechanism of abnormal transmission ratios at the T-locus in the house mouse. III Test for physiological differences between t¹- and T-sperm manifested during storage period in the *epididymis* and *vas deferens*. Jap. J. Gen. *40*:93-96.

Yanagisawa, K. 1965c. Studies on the mechanism of abnormal transmission ratios at the T-locus in the house mouse. IV Some morphological studies on the mature sperm in males heterozygous for t-alleles. Jap. J. Gen. *40*:97-104.

Yanagisawa, K., Dunn, L. C., and Bennett, D. 1961. On the mechanism of abnormal transmission ratios at the T-locus in the house mouse. Genetics *46*:1635-1644.

Chapter 11

Viviparity

OVIPARITY, OVOVIVIPARITY, AND VIVIPARITY

Internal fertilization prevents dispersal of sperm and improves the chances of survival as well as the duration of survival, although as we saw, in many mammals relatively few sperm reach the site of fertilization and the time of survival in the genital system of the female is usually one or two days only.

Eggs and parents may be exposed to the dangers of predation if the eggs require incubation by the parents. Various forms of parental care of the eggs and of the young will be discussed in a later chapter. Development of the embryos inside the mother's body generally will afford more protection of the embryos and of the mother. One of the consequences of such an arrangement may be a reduction in the number of offspring which are born during the reproductive life of the animal.

As far as the development of the embryos is concerned, a distinction can be made between oviparous, ovoviviparous, and viviparous forms. In oviparous forms the young emerge outside the mother's body from eggs; in ovoviviparous species the mother gives birth to live young which emerge from eggs containing enough yolk to nourish the embryo during its development but in which no nutritive connections between mother and young exist. In viviparous animals young are born after a term of intimate nutritive connections between embryo and mother (Amoroso, 1952).

Cyclostomes

As all cyclostomes have external fertilization, no consideration to ovoviviparity or viviparity needs to be given.

Elasmobranchs

Among the elasmobranchs, in which internal fertilization is the general rule, oviparous (some skates and rays), ovoviviparous, and viviparous species exist.

The embryos in ovoviviparous species are nourished by:

a. The yolk from the egg from which the embryo will develop.

b. Yolk as mentioned above, followed by yolk from immature ova taken up by the oviduct and eaten by the developing young, e.g. in *Lamna cornubica* (Amoroso, 1952).

c. Uterine milk secreted by the uterine wall, as in *Mustelus vulgaris* and *Torpedo ocellata*.

d. Uterine secretions via long villi, from the uterine wall, which enter the spiracle of the embryo extending to the esophagus; this arrangement is found in *Pteroplatea* (Amoroso, 1952).

Viviparity is frequent among the elasmobranchs. In all cases the connection between mother and embryo is made via a yolk placenta. In most of these placentae there is an intimate interdigitation of fetal and maternal tissue. The exchange between maternal and fetal blood systems occurs through the maternal endothelium, reduced maternal epithelium, egg case

311

membrane, reduced fetal epithelium, and fetal endothelium (Schlernitzauer and Gilbert, 1966). An exception to this arrangement is found in the silky shark *(Carcharhinus falciformis)* in which there is no interdigitation of fetal and maternal tissue. The layers which intervene between the two vascular systems are: the maternal endothelium, the maternal epithelium (essentially not reduced), under some conditions the egg case, the fetal epithelium (much reduced), and the fetal endothelium (Gilbert and Schlernitzauer, 1966).

In most species of *Scoliodon* two features of the yolk sac placenta make it resemble the mammalian placenta in the sense that the connection between mother and young is purely vascular (Amoroso, 1952). These modifications are (1) a network of cellular strands saturated with circulating blood in the cavity of the yolk sac, which is thus not filled with yolk as in other viviparous elasmobranchs; (2) obliteration of the yolk stalk so that a placental cord is formed.

Teleost Fishes

The viviparity among fishes has been investigated and discussed fascinatingly by C. L. Turner. The following account is largely taken from a paper by this author (1947), in which he has pointed out the differences between the reproductive processes of teleost fishes and the higher vertebrates. In the higher vertebrates the egg is ovulated and then transported through the oviduct, where fertilization occurs in species with internal fertilization. In viviparous vertebrates the embryo develops in the uterus and is nourished via a placenta.

The placenta, which makes the metabolic exchanges between mother and embryo possible, consists of the uterine wall, and on the part of the embryo, a chorion, the yolk sac, and the allantois. In fishes, however, no true (Müllerian) oviducts are present and this internal

fertilization, if it is to occur, must take place in either the gonaduct (extension of the wall of the ovary; see Chapter 3) or in the ovary, where gestation also must take place. Teleosts lack an allantois and an umbilical circulatory system. The heart of the teleost embryo lies upon the yolk sac. Blood which has circulated through the body passes through a portal system, which covers the yolk sac and the wall of the pericardial cavity, before entering the heart. Turner (1947) has emphasized that this circulation is not the same as the vitelline circulation of other vertebrates. The expansion of the pericardial cavity and the somato-pleural layer partially or entirely envelops the anterior part of the body by forming double folds. The external layer of these folds is structurally the equivalent of the chorion, whereas the inner layer is homologous to the amnion of higher vertebrates. An amniotic cavity is lacking because the amnion is in contact with the body of the embryo.

The order in which fertilization and ovulation occurs differs in various forms.

In *Zoarces,* ovulation probably occurs prior to fertilization and the embryo is retained in the ovarian cavity (Turner, 1947). This order of events seems to be rare, however.

Fertilization of the egg may take place within the follicle before ovulation; embryonic development is initiated and the embryo is released by rupture of the follicular wall. The follicle cells are changed after fertilization to take care of respiration, elimination of wastes, and nutrition (although enough yolk may be present to nourish the embryo). The portal circulation and the expanded pericardial sac, which may be drawn over the head, enables the exchange of oxygen, carbondioxide, and waste products between mother and young in cases where the amount of yolk is sufficient to supply the embryo with nutrients.

In species in which the amount of yolk in the follicle is small, nutrients must be transported to the embryo. This may be accomplished via large expanded pericardial and peritoneal sacs of the embryo and thin, very vascular, follicular walls (e.g. *Heterandria formosa*). In other species the pericardial and peritoneal sacs expand and the portal system covering these sacs has large protrusions increasing the vascular surface. Different parts of the intestines may become elongated. On the part of the follicle, highly vascular villi make loose contacts with the pericardial and peritoneal sacs (e.g. *Anableps*).

Superfetation, which was discussed in the previous chapter, occurs in forms exhibiting follicular gestation.

Gestation may also take place in the ovarian cavity of the follicle, which ruptures after fertilization has occurred, or, as discussed above, in cases in which ovulation preceded fertilization.

The embryos are contained in the ovarian cavity and are bathed by fluids secreted by the ovarian epithelium. Embryonic mortality is high, and surviving embryos may ingest the remains of dead embryos. During the sojourn of the embryos in the ovarian cavity, flat, leaf-shaped processes from the walls of the ovary grow into the opercular openings of the embryos and eventually fill the gill and mouth cavities. This condition is found in the Jenynsiidae. In the Goodeidae extensions grow out of the anal lips of the embryos, whereas in *Parabrotula* sp. ribbon-shaped structures grow out of the anal region and the urogenital pore; in the Embioticidae there are extensions between the ends of the rays of the vertical fins. These structures are probably involved in respiration rather than in nutritional transfers. The gut of the embryos in the ovarian cavity is enlarged in the Embioticidae and in *Zoarces*. The intestines frequently contain partly digested materials, indicating that nutrition probably occurs by ingestion of nutrients rather than by an exchange via extensions from the anal, urogenital, or fin ray areas.

Amphibia

Among amphibia there are no examples of true viviparity. Larvae of the salamander *(Salamandra atra)*, although ovoviviparous, not only utilize the yolk from their own egg but also eat other embryos and blood present in the uterus as a result of hemorrhages of the uterine wall. Of a total of 40 to 60 fertilized ova only one to four embryos may be born (Amoroso, 1952).

The Surinam toad (*Pipa pipa* [*Pipa dorsigera* ?]) and the marsupial toad *(Gastrotheca marsupiata,* or *Notrema marsupiatum)* incubate their eggs on the back, as was mentioned earlier (see Figure 3-12). The cavity in which the eggs of the Surinam toad are located consists of an invaginated epidermal pouch with vascular partitions between the eggs (Amoroso, 1952). The larvae have a large, highly vascular tail that, according to Amoroso (1952), acts as a placenta. In *Gastrotheca marsupiata,* the larval gills have very vascular bell-like extensions which spread out under the blood vessels of the maternal pouch (Amoroso, 1952, 1959). These placenta-like structures serve for respiratory and nutritional exchange (Amoroso, 1959). The ovaries of such pregnant females contain luteal structures, but whether the ovaries are required for maintenance of the functional connections between mother and larvae apparently has not been determined.

A curious phenomenon has been found in the Chilean toad *(Rhinoderma darwinii):* the male swallows the eggs and incubates them in two vocal pouches located lateral to the esophagus. The small frogs leap out when they are sufficiently developed (Noble, 1954).

The genus *Nectophrynoides* is ovoviviparous (it is not known how insemination occurs). The embryos, present in large numbers (over a hundred) in the uterus, have long slim tails which "apparently function as so many pipe lines bringing oxygen to the larvae kept away from the uterine wall by the bodies of their brothers and sisters" (Noble, 1954).

Reptiles

The Crocodilia and Chelonia are oviparous. Many species of snakes and lizards are ovoviviparous or viviparous (Matthews, 1955). Among the viviparous species different types of placentae are encountered. These types, as described by Amoroso (1952), are:

1. A yolk-sac placenta found in some Australian lizards and the Italian lizard *(Chalcides tridactylus)*. In this type of placenta there is no invasion of maternal tissue by fetal tissue, although the omphalochorionic membrane and the uterine epithelium may show interlocking folds.

2. Chorionic allantoic placentae which can be subdivided into three types:

Type A. The maternal and fetal blood streams are very close to each other, as the result of a reduction in uterine and chorionic epithelial tissues. (This placenta is found in e.g. *Chalcides ocellatus, Hoplodactylus maculatus, Demisonia superba, D. suta.*)

Type B. The intact maternal capillaries bulge at the surface of uterine folds, with grooves lined with a glandular epithelium between the folds. The enlarged chorionic epithelial cells interlock with the maternal grooves. Cytoplasmic processes may penetrate between the uterine epithelial cells. This type is encountered in some species of the genus *Lygosoma*.

Type C. The folded maternal tissues overlie the main longitudinal uterine blood vessels. The uterine folds indent the fetal placental face. The uterine epithelial cells are enlarged and cuboidal, as are the ectodermal chorion cells. This type is found in *Chalcides tridactylus*.

Birds

All birds are oviparous and will not be discussed here.

Mammals

Except for the duck-billed platypus and spiny anteater, all mammals are viviparous. There are some distinct differences between marsupials and eutherians, and therefore these groups will be discussed separately.

MARSUPIALS

Two main patterns for the sequence of estrus, ovulation, pregnancy, and lactation for the pouch young can be distinguished (Sharman, 1965). In the genera *Didelphis, Dasyurus,* and *Trichosurus,* pregnancy is shorter or has the same duration as the luteal phase in the nonpregnant animals. If the young are retained in the pouch, lactation will last for several months and upon weaning or removal of the young, estrus will manifest itself after several days (e.g. in *Trichosurus vulpecula*). Removal of the young results in estrus on the same day, as if no pregnancy had occurred.

The pattern found in the genera *Setonix* and *Megaleia* is as follows: Pregnancy lasts beyond the postluteal phase and the young are born at the end of the proestrous phase; the next estrus after pregnancy is a postpartum estrus which occurs whether the young are removed or not. The ovulation may, after mating, lead to another pregnancy, but as long as lactation occurs the embryo is not implanted. This matter of delayed implantation will be discussed later in this chapter. The removal of the pouch young results in implantation of the quiescent blastocyst and eventually to its birth and a subsequent post estrus. If the young are retained in the pouch, lactation will prevent implantation of the blastocyst, but as the young become older and are ready to leave the pouch, blastocyst implantation takes place. If no blastocyst was present, estrus occurs at approximately the same time as the postpartum estrus of fertile animals.

As was discussed briefly in Chapter 6, the arrival of the fertilized ovum and the physiological status of the uterus must be rather closely synchronized for implantation to occur in eutheria. This aspect will be discussed in more detail later in this chapter.

The relationship between blastocyst development and uterine status has been investigated for the marsupial quokka *(Setonix brachyurus)* by Tyndale-Biscoe (1963b). Quokkas, from which the pouch young were removed, were used because in this species removal of the young leads to implantation of the quiescent blastocysts. The day of pouch young removal (RPY) was taken as day 0. Some of the recipients were not pregnant, other recipients received the blastocyst in the horn contralateral to the side in which the corpus luteum was found. Synchronous transfers on day 0, 2, 4, and 6 were successful in 11 out of 22 cases. The transfers to non-pregnant females were also effective, thus demonstrating the equivalence of pregnant and non-pregnant uteri.

Asynchronous transfers were successful only if the blastocyst was retarded in relation to the recipient (as we shall see, the opposite is true in rats and mice); the discrepancy which could exist and still allow successful development was six days. This indicates that the ovarian secretions stimulate resumption of embryonic development and that subsequent development requires synchronization between the time of embryonic development and the status of the uterine endometrium.

Six-day blastocysts transferred to lactating quokkas grew slightly (indicating stimulation of the blastocyst by the donor's ovaries) but developed abnormally (in-dicating lack of synchronization between blastocyst and uterine endometrium).

The reason for the failure of transfers of day 0 blastocysts to day 8 recipients may be the result of lack of exposure of the blastocyst to the donor's ovarian hormones or to a detrimental effect of the older uterus.

Tyndale-Biscoe (1963a) has shown that the corpus luteum is essential for the resumption of embryonic development of the quiescent blastocyst of lactating quokkas and for induction of the secretory phase of the endometrium, required for implantation. The corpus luteum is required for stimulation of the blastocyst until day 4, but for pregnancy to progress normally it is required until day 7. This lack of normal progress if the corpus luteum is removed is probably due to its effect on the embryo, since even after removal of the corpus luteum on day 4, the uterus shows a normal luteal condition, which progresses for the same duration as in the intact animal. Progesterone substitution in ovariectomized quokkas will stimulate blastocyst development. Parturition fails to occur in ovariectomized animals whether given estrogen or oxytocin, but relaxin administration induces successful parturition. The corpus luteum, after day 2, also inhibits premature follicular development and ovulation in unilaterally ovariectomized quokkas, so ovulation does not occur before the postpartum estrus. Progesterone injections can prevent the follicular development but not ovulation, according to Tyndale-Biscoe (1963b), probably because of ovarian secretions from the remaining ovary.

Different types of placentae are found among the marsupials. Amoroso (1952) has emphasized the large yolk sac of the marsupials and the relatively small allantois, which only in the genera *Perameles, Phascolarctos,* and *Phascolomis* vascularizes a placenta; in all other marsupials the yolk sac placenta transfers nutrients from mother to embryo. Details of the anatomy of the marsupial placentae can be found in the excellent, illustrated paper by Amoroso (1952). The phylogenetic significance of the different forms found has been discussed by Sharman (1965).

EUTHERIA

Transportation of the fertilized egg may occur at different speeds in different species, and the egg arrives when the uterus is in the condition appropriate for further development of the egg. As we shall see, ovarian hormones play an important role in regulating the transport of the ova. Such a regulation assures that ova transport and the uterine condition are synchronized, as the development of the endometrium is under ovarian hormone control.

Ovum Transport. Hafez (1962) found that two injections of either 6 or 18 μg. estrone, or 2 or 6 μg. estradiol benzoate (EB) do not affect the ability of the fimbria of the rabbit oviduct to recover eggs transferred to the *bursa ovarii*, but that two injections of either 4 or 10 μg. progesterone increase the incidence of ovum pick up, and also that combinations of progesterone and estradiol benzoate (2 μg. EB at mating plus either 2 or 10 μg. progesterone at ovum transfer) are more effective. Estrogen treatment causes retention of

ova in the oviduct, an effect which is prevented if progesterone is also given.

Greenwald (1967), in a recent paper, reviewed the literature concerning the effects of estrogen on egg transport in different species and found that the evidence obtained for these species was not consistent because of differences among the experimental procedures used. He therefore compared the effects of estradiol cyclopentyl propionate (ECP) on ovum transport in the guinea pig, hamster, mouse, rat, and rabbit. The results of these experiments are given in Table 11-1. The data obtained with the mouse require some further explanation. At a dose of 0.1 μg. ECP, five out of ten mice had eggs in the oviduct on day 4 (in controls three out of three mice had eggs in the uterus), but in four out of ten mice, no eggs could be found (presumably because they were expelled), and in one out of ten mice the ova were in the uterus. The retained eggs were located mainly near the ampullary-isthmo junction of the oviduct, a result which is in agreement with those obtained by Chang and Harper (1966) after ethinyl estradiol injections into rabbits.

Greenwald (1967) suggested that the interruption of pregnancy was independent of the effect of ECP on ova transport, as the threshold for the former was con-

Table 11-1.   Effect of Estradiolcyclopentylpropionate on Ovum Transport in Different Laboratory Animals

SPECIES	DOSE REQUIRED FOR:			
	ACCELERATED TRANSPORT (μg.)	RETENTION IN OVIDUCT (μg.)	INTERRUPTION OF PREGNANCY IN 80% OF ANIMALS (μg.)	TIME EGGS ENTER UTERI OF CONTROLS (Day p.c.*)
Guinea pig	50–100	250	10	4
Hamster	100	250	25	3 (afternoon)
Rat	10	No dose	10	5
Mouse	1	1	1	4
Rabbit	25	100	50	3†

* p.c.=post coitum.
† From literature.
Reference: Greenwald, 1967.

siderably lower for guinea pigs and hamsters than the threshold for accelerated ovum transport. For the rabbit a higher dose was required to interrupt pregnancy. Chang and Harper (1966) found no difference, after transplantation studies, in the development of the fertilized egg when the egg or the endometrium had been exposed to estrogen treatment. Such a conclusion is compatible with the observations, by Greenwald (1967), that a higher dose is required for interruption of pregnancy, in 80 percent of the animals, than for acceleration of egg transport.

In rabbits, Harper (1966) has studied the effect of estrogen and progesterone in ovariectomized does and of progesterone in estrous does. The transport time through the ampulla in ovariectomized does was 16.8 ± 2 to 4 min; in similar does given progesterone (2 mg./day) the time was 29.8 ± 4.6 min., whereas in does given $4 \mu g.$ estradiol benzoate per day this figure was 8.7 ± 0.8 min. Additional progesterone injection to ovariectomized, estradiol benzoate-treated does did not affect the transport time significantly. The data show that estrogen can stimulate ovum transport and progesterone can depress it, and that the rate of transport in an intact animal is probably dependent upon the relative levels of the two hormones. Both hormones act on the ampullar musculature, and in this way affect the speed of travel of the ova.

Alden (1942a) has, however, shown that ovariectomy 7 to 20 hours after the vaginal plug is first seen did not affect either ovum transport or development of the egg, as determined by autopsy 62 to 120 hours after the vaginal plug's appearance.

Ovariectomy of guinea pigs two days after mating does not affect the transport of the eggs (Deanesly, 1963).

The rate of transport of the eggs through the oviduct is not uniform, as was shown by Harper et al. (1960) in experiments in which small, radioactively labeled resin spheres were used to simulate eggs. During the first eight hours after ovulation the spheres had been transported 49 percent of the length of the fallopian tube; at 48 hours after ovulation 79 percent of the length of the tube had been traversed. At 56 hours postovulation 55 percent and at 64 hours 90 percent of the spheres had passed into the uterus.

Changes of the Ovum in the Oviduct. During its sojourn in the oviduct, the egg may undergo a number of changes in addition to the cell divisions that started after fertilization. At the time of ovulation, mammalian eggs are often surrounded by the cumulus oophorus cell layers. These layers are few or absent in cattle, roe deer, pigs, horses, and opossums, but several cell layers are present around the eggs of rats, mice, hamsters, mink, rabbits, monkeys, and man (Blandau, 1961). The sperm penetration of these layers probably involves the release of hyaluronidase by the sperm and subsequent lysis of hyaluronic acid-protein matrix of the cumulus oophorus (Austin, 1965). The corona radiata cells, which are attached to the outer surface of the zona pellucida, can be removed by a tubal factor, and also by action of the sperm (Blandau, 1961).

Corona radiata cells are present around the eggs of rabbits, rats, mice, guinea pigs, dogs, cats, ferrets, Rhesus monkeys, and humans, but are absent from the eggs of horses, pigs, sheep, goats, and cattle (Altman and Dittmer, 1962).

The eggs of rabbits are free of cumulus and corona cells four to six hours after the ovulation following a fertile mating; however, after a sterile mating these cells can still be found seven to eight hours after ovulation. The rabbit egg loses cumulus and corona radiata cells in the oviduct, but acquires a coat of albumin. This coat may be one of the reasons for the limited time span during which fertilization can occur (Blandau, 1961). Monotreme eggs, as was mentioned, also are covered by a protein layer and, in addition, a thin shell membrane is deposited in the oviduct (Boyd and Hamilton, 1952).

Distribution of Blastocysts in the Uterus. The fertile eggs in many species have now become blastocysts. The blastocyst stage is defined as the stage at the end of cleavage and prior to gastrulation. After the arrival of the fertile egg in the uterus there arises the problem of distribution at the implantation sites.

Boyd and Hamilton (1952) list species of mammals in which transuterine migration of eggs from one horn to the other has been observed or experimentally induced. This phenomenon is found among ungulates, carnivores, chiroptera, insectivores and in one of the primates: *Lemur rufipes.* In some bats *(Miniopterus natalensis, Myotis lucifugus, M. myotis, Pipistrellus pipistrellus, Molossus m. crassicaudatus)* (Boyd and Hamilton, 1952; Asdell, 1964) and in some African bovidae: the Uganda kob *(Adenota kob),* the impala *(Aepyceros melampus),* the lechwe *(Kobus lechee)* and the common duiker *(Sylvicapra grimmia),* ovulation is either bilateral or sinistral, but implantation is always in the right horn, demonstrating that transuterine migration is normal in these species.

Dziuk et al. (1964) established by the use of genetic markers that eggs deposited in the oviduct or the uterus of one side become mixed with those placed in the opposite side. The distribution of the blastocysts is not completely random, since more eggs generally are implanted at the side at which they were deposited.

Beautiful quantitative studies of the spacing of rabbit blastocysts have shown that they become evenly spaced in spite of variations in the number of blastocysts per uterine horn (thus causing variations in the amount of space available and consequently introducing variation in the distance between implantation sites) (Böving, 1954, 1956). Such an evenly spaced distribution, regardless of the numbers of blastocysts involved, means that pre-

formed implantation sites cannot be the major factor in determining this distribution.

Böving (1956) established that at 73.5 hours post coitum, all eggs had entered the uterus and were located near the tubal end of the horn in a random fashion. At day 4 the blastocysts had been transported about 17 percent of the distance from the utero-tubal junction to the internal cervical os and the distribution was still random. At five days, 39 percent of the above mentioned distance had been traversed and distribution was random. Between day 5 and 6 a trend toward even spacing rather than random spacing was discernible. At day 7 the blastocysts were more evenly distributed (the even distribution was not perfect but was significantly different from random and closer to even).

This distribution of blastocysts is probably the result of uterine stimulation by the blastocysts, causing propulsion by the uterine muscle repelling adjacent blastocysts. Progesterone probably is involved in blastocyst transport by increasing the irritability of the myometrium and by reducing the spread of the response to stimuli (Böving, 1956).

Injection of estradiol 5 µg./day for three days disturbs the orderly spacing, and eggs are at the extreme ends of the horn with few or none in the middle portion (Greenwald, 1957).

The spacing of the implantation sites may also be a function of the lack of receptivity of areas close to an attached blastocyst. This is suggested by the experiments of Fawcett et al. (1947) in which mouse blastocysts were transplanted to the anterior eye chamber. In these experiments, implantation failed to occur until the most "precious" egg had started to implant. After this took place there was a rapid degeneration of the other blastocysts.

Hafez (1964a) studied the effect of large numbers of fertile eggs (40 to 50 hours post coitum) on implantation capacity and size and spacing of implantations by egg transfer in control and in superovulated (150 to 200 I.U. of PMSG plus 50 I.U. of HCG) rabbits. After the transfer of 20 to 40 embryos to control does, the number of implantation sites was increased four-fold (to 35.4 implantations per doe) in comparison with control does not receiving additional eggs (8.4 implantations per doe). Superovulated females to which eggs were transferred had 28.1 implantation sites per doe. Neither ovariectomy nor hysterectomy affected the incidence of implants per horn. The overcrowding by the embryos caused a fusing of some embryos and reduction in the diameter of the implants, as well as increased mortality. The maximum number of viable fetuses per litter was 15, with most of the embryonic deaths occurring between ten and 13 days post coitum. The overcrowding thus resulted in a breakdown of the spacing mechanism and subsequently in abnormalities of the developing embryo-uterine relationships.

A study of overcrowding in cattle by use of superovulation and subsequent insemination, conducted by Hafez (1964b), led to the following conclusions:

1. Transuterine migration was limited to one or two embryos.

2. The percentage of such migrations was 12.8 percent in ovariectomized and 6.38 percent in intact cows.

3. A single uterine horn could sustain one or two embryos only.

4. The embryo occupied the middle or upper two-thirds of one horn if only one embryo was present.

5. An increase in the number of embyros resulted in uneven spacing and overcrowding, with subsequent high embryonic mortality.

In cattle, the spacing mechanism present in rabbits does not appear to exist, which may not be too surprising in view of the fact that cows normally carry only one calf.

The implantation of embryos in ruminants occurs in special areas of the uterus, in contrast to the situation in rabbits. These areas are called caruncles or cotyledons, and consist of special regions of the mucosa characterized by many capillaries and the absence of glands.

Besides the spacing of the blastocysts from a longitudinal point of view, there is a spacing with respect to the sides of the horn where implantation occurs. Eggs may be implanted in the mesometrial (e.g. in Pteropodidae and Tarsiidae), in the antimesometrial part (e.g. most rodents, many insectivores), or in the orthomesometrial position [e.g. Tenrecs or Centetes and Hemicentetes (Blandau, 1961)]. The mechanisms which cause this orientation have not been elucidated. Reversal of the uterine mesometrial-antimesometrial axis does not change the orientation of the implanting blastocyst with respect to the uterus, indicating that gravity is not the factor which determines this type of orientation (Blandau, 1961).

Böving (1954) has explained the antimesometrial implantation of the rabbit's blastocyst by citing the local loss of uterine tone, and the formation of a dome by the ballooning out of the uterine wall. The formation of each dome is caused by mechanical stimulation by the blastocyst. The subsequent attachment between blastocyst and endometrium starts with an adhesion between the uterine epithelium and the outer layer of the egg, which consists of a gloiolemma (a noncellular adhesive layer) secreted by the uterus. This layer is deposited around the albuminous coat secreted in the oviduct (Böving, 1959). Near the time of membrane adhesion these noncellular membranes are perforated near knobs that become attached to the antimesometrial uterine epithelium. The knobs are aggregates of trophoblastic syncythium.

Implantation. Enders and Schlafke (1967), in a beautifully illustrated anatomical study of implantation of rat blastocysts, report that on the late afternoon of day 5 post coitum most of the eggs have lost their zonae pellucidae but are not yet implanted. The blastocysts at this time are located in shallow depressions that form the antimesometrial part of the lumen. By the evening of day 5 the uterus has become edematous (possibly as a result of estrogen secretion); and clasps the blastocyst, which still can easily be flushed out of the uterus. The trophoblast cells are in apposition to the uterine lumen, and one can occasionally see the tip of a uterine microvillus project into a caveloa of the trophoblast (Enders and Schalfke, 1967). The mechanical stimulation by the blastocyst probably starts a local decidual reaction, which results in a tubular pit surrounding the blastocyst, the antimesometrial extreme of the uterine lumen and extending beyond these structures. Glycogen appears in the decidual cells which originate from large-bodied fibroblasts, surrounding the uterine lumen. The transformation of these cells to decidual cells with epitheloid character results in a modification of the connective tissue space intervening between luminal epithelium and its vascular bed.

Shelesnyak (1965), on the basis of a long series of experiments, has proposed that the decidual reaction in the rat uterus in response to either a blastocyst or to trauma is the result of a histamine release, which occurs in response to an estrogen surge on day 3 post coitum. This estrogen surge will be discussed later in this chapter, but the evidence cited by Shelesnyak (1965) in favor of the mediation of histamine in eliciting the decidual response will be given here:

1. Application of antihistamines to the endometrium prevents decidualization.

2. Serial injections of histamine releasers (to deplete histamine stores) prevent or inhibit development of deciduomata. Deciduomata (the plural of deciduoma) are localized, tumorlike endometrial responses, generally obtained after traumatization of the endometrium. Coppola et al. (1966) have reported that

in 12 out of 70 rats, the uterus was not traumatized. These "spontaneous" deciduomata were in all respects similar to those obtained after traumatization.

3. Administration of histamine systemically or injection of histamine releasers in pseudopregnant rats causes decidualization.

4. Estrogen injection causes a decrease in mast cells that is correlated with histamine release (Shelesnyak and Kraicer, 1963).

5. Estrogen has a histamine-releasing action on the uterus (Shelesnyak and Kraicer, 1963; Szego, 1965).

Some difficulties have arisen with respect to the specificity of histamine in inducing the decidual reaction. Banik and Ketchel (1964), and Finn and Keen (1962) were unable to obtain decidual reactions after histamine injections into pseudopregnant rats, while Orsini (1963) was unable to produce deciduomata in rats and hamsters by injection of pyrathiazine (a histamine releaser which caused deciduomata in rats in Shelesnyak's experiments). The difference among the results obtained by different workers may be explained on the basis of genetic differences among the strains of rats used (Orsini, 1963; Shelesnyak and Kraicer, 1963).

Psychoyos (1965a) has expressed the opinion that the effect of histamine or other tissue metabolites may be mediated via an increase in capillary permeability.

In guinea pigs, there is an increase in the size and number of abembryonic pole cells (which make the first contact with the antimesometrial endometrial epithelium). These abembryonic pole cells send out cytoplasmic extensions through the zona pellucida. These cytoplasmic extensions increase in size and may extend as expansions beyond the zona pellucida; it is in this region that the zona disappears. The abembryonic cells increase in number and form the implantation cone (Blandau, 1961). Such cones have also been found in rabbits, squirrels, and chipmunks. Blandau (1961) has asked whether some substance might be secreted via the cytoplasmic extensions that would initiate the decidual response and cause the removal of the underlying endometrial tissue. Böving (1959, 1962), from his extensive studies on the interrelationship between blastocyst and uterus in rabbits, has proposed that the invasion of the uterine epithelium occurs near blood vessels. The increase in carbonic anhydrase by progesterone and the implantation-promoting effect of progesterone suggest that this enzyme would cause increased release of CO_2 and transfer of this gas to the maternal blood. This transfer, in turn, would facilitate transfer of CO_2 from the blastocyst to the maternal circulation. This exchange of CO_2 would result in a higher pH, thus making the blastocyst adhesive. However, the epithelial cells lose cohesion. The chemical transfer becomes restricted to areas with a capillary at their base. By day 8 the chemical transfer has become diffuse, and abembryonic attachment becomes general by overall adhesion of the thin trophoblast between knobs.

Eaton and Green (1963) reported on the implantation of the blastocyst of normal and homozygous yellow mice. The yellow gene in the homozygous condition is lethal and expresses itself in embryonic mortality before six days post coitum. In normal blastocysts, giant cells form filamentous pseudopodia, which penetrate between the cells of the uterine epithelium. The completion of this penetration is followed by extension of the pseudopodia between epithelium and basement membrane. Uterine epithelial cells are sloughed off and are phagocytosed by the giant cells, making attachment possible. The giant cells of homozygous yellow blastocysts either are retarded in their rate of development and fail to attach, apparently because the uterine sensitivity is past at the time the giant cells reach their normal size (the blastocyst and uterus are not

synchronized), or the giant cells fail to develop. Exogenous progesterone increases the incidence of implanting embryos either by stimulating the rate of development of the giant cells or by increasing the receptivity of the uterus.

Wilson (1963) has reported the presence of eosinophilic cells with a hyaline cytoplasm and rounded, dense homogeneous nuclei in the inner cell mass of the mouse blastocyst. At about 100 hours post coitum these cells, which have migrated, can be found between the trophoblast cells protruding from its surface and penetrating the uterine epithelium. The cells apparently fragment as they pass through the epithelium. The decidual reaction starts after the cells begin penetrating the epithelium. These cells are different from primary giant trophoblast cells of the rat and the attachment cone cells of the guinea pig, according to Wilson (1963).

It should be mentioned that the blastocyst of ungulates elongates and enlarges due to an accumulation of fluid in the blastocyst cavity. At this stage, the trophoblast is not implanted yet, but it fills part of the uterine cavity (Nalbandov, 1964). In pigs, the expansion of the trophoblast outstrips the fluid accumulation, so the walls of the blastocyst become folded. The expansion of the trophoblast brings it in contact with the uterine epithelium.

The manner in which the blastocyst is implanted differs considerably among species. The main forms of implantation, according to Boyd and Hamilton (1952), are:

1. Central implantation, in which the blastocyst remains in the uterine cavity and eventually fills the lumen. This arrangement is found, e.g. in ungulates, carnivores, and some vespertilionid bats.

2. Eccentric implantation, in which the small blastocyst occupies a small diverticulum or cleft of the lumen. When the placenta develops, the original lumen is obliterated. This type is found in many rodents.

3. Interstitial implantation, in which the blastocyst passes through the epithelium and becomes cut off from the uterine lumen. It is found, e.g. in guinea pigs, the European hedgehog, chimpanzees, and man.

Details about the morphological changes in the uterus and the implanting blastocyst can be found for a number of species, not mentioned here, in the publications by Boyd and Hamilton (1952).

Blastocysts do not require the uterus for implantation to occur. Experimentally it has been shown that mouse eggs have a greater tendency to implant in non-uterine tissue than rat eggs (Kirby, 1962a) and consequently most of the experimental evidence has been obtained with mouse eggs.

Mouse blastocysts transferred to the anterior eye chamber (Runner, 1947; Fawcett et al., 1947), to the surface of the kidney (Fawcett, 1950; Kirby, 1960, 1962a,b, 1965), to the spleen (Kirby, 1963a,b), or to the testis (Kirby, 1963b, 1965) will implant in these organs. The age, sex, or physiological state of the host plays no role in the success or failure of implants to occur (Fawcett, 1950). Mouse eggs will implant in rat kidneys, although the success is about one-third of that observed with mouse blastocysts transplanted to mouse kidneys (Kirby, 1962a). For blastocysts transplanted to scrotal testes, the incidence of implantation is higher than for transfers to cryptorchid testes. However, if implantation occurs, the growth of the trophoblast is greater in cryptorchid than in scrotal gonads. The difference is, apparently, mainly the result of the difference in temperature between the two locations (Kirby, 1963b).

The incidence of implantations of mouse eggs transferred to the peritoneal cavity is low (Fawcett et al, 1947; McLaren and Tarkowski, 1963). In one series of experiments, eggs were injected into the reproductive tract, and, apparently, some eggs escaped and implanted on the ovarian capsule, the mesosalpinx, and the outside of the uterine horn (McLaren and Tarkowski, 1963).

For embryonic development of the implanted blastocysts to occur it is necessary that the eggs be obtained from the uterus. Eggs obtained before this stage is reached will show development of trophoblast and extraembryonic membranes only (Kirby, 1962b, 1965). If ova are retained experimentally in the oviduct and transplanted (at the time they would normally have reached the uterus), development will be similar to that of normal tubal eggs. However, oviducal eggs, transferred first to the uterus and then to the extrauterine environments, will show normal embryonic development, indicating that a "uterine factor" is required for normal development (Kirby, 1962b, 1965).

The age of the egg at the time of transplantation affects the developmental stages which may be reached. Transplanted before the blastocyst stage, eggs will not show development of the embryonic shield (Kirby, 1960).

Rat blastocysts transferred to peritoneal cavity will implant, although the incidence is low (Jollie, 1961; Nicholas, 1934). Jollie (1961) increased the success of implantations from one percent to seven percent by injecting histamine. The incidence of successful rat blastocyst transfers to rat kidneys is about 18 percent and to mouse kidneys about 13 percent, which should be compared with a figure of 28 percent for mouse ova to rat kidney and an incidence of 78 percent for mouse ova transferred to mouse kidney (Kirby, 1962a). The sex of the host has no effect on the success of implants for rat egg transfers to rat kidneys (Nicholas, 1942). Eggs, transferred to intestinal mucosa fail to implant because of the sloughing of this mucosa (Nicholas, 1950).

Nine-day-old rat embryos transferred to a pocket upon the cecum developed to normal fetuses, showing that the uterine environment is not essential for development from nine days to term.

Guinea pig blastocysts transplanted

into kidney and abdominal muscle implanted, although ligature of the uterotubal junction failed to cause implantation of fertile eggs in the oviduct. The reason for this phenomenon is not clear. Postimplantation conceptuses transferred to the spleen, anterior eye chamber, or testes showed growth and differentiation (Bland and Donovan, 1965).

In view of the results obtained with mouse and rat eggs transplanted to rat and mouse kidneys, respectively, it is not surprising to find that eggs from one species placed in the uterus or oviduct of another species sometimes will implant and continue development.

The following transfers in which development continued in the uterus of the other species have been carried out: goat to sheep; sheep to goat; sheep ova to rabbit fallopian tube, with subsequent transfer to sheep uterus (Deanesly, 1966). Ova from mouse uterus and tube to rat ovarian capsule; mouse ova from tube to rabbit tube; rabbit ova from uterus to mouse tube; mouse ova from uterus to guinea pig uterus; rabbit ova from tube to rat ovarian capsule; ova from rabbit tube and uterus to rat uterus (Briones and Beatty, 1954). Snowshoe hare eggs *(Lepus americanus)* transferred to fallopian tubes of rabbits *(Oryctolagus cuniculus)* developed (Chang, 1965a), as did ferret eggs placed in rabbit fallopian tubes—if placed in the uterus these eggs did not develop and

neither did rabbit eggs transferred to ferret tubes or uteri. No decidual reaction was obtained in the rabbit uteri after transfer of either the snowshoe hare or the ferret eggs (Chang, 1965a, 1966).

No development has been obtained in transfer of rat ova to the mouse or rabbit, or in the transfer of guinea pig eggs to the mouse (Briones and Beatty, 1954) or in the transfer of roe deer eggs *(Capreolus capreolus)* to sheep (Short and Hay, 1965).

The time at which implantation occurs varies considerably among species, as can be ascertained from Table 11-2. The cases of delayed implantation will be discussed separately elsewhere in this chapter.

During the period of nonattachment, the blastocyst receives nutrients from the uterine milk secreted by the endometrium.

The Placenta. The attachment of the blastocyst to the uterine wall and the invasion of the latter by the former lead to the formation of the placenta, which enables an exchange of nutrients and gases between embryo and mother. The nutritive materials absorbed by the placenta or fetal membranes directly from the circulating blood are called the *hemotrophe*. The *histotrophe* refers to secretions and degradation products of the endometrium and also extravasated maternal blood which is absorbed.

On the basis of the relationships between fetal membranes and endometrium,

Table 11-2. Time of Implantation after Arrival in the Uterus in Different Species

SPECIES	DAYS	REFERENCE
Mouse	4½	Kirby, 1965
Mole	3–3½	Blandau, 1961
Shrew	3–3½	Blandau, 1961
Rat	½–1*	Greenwald, 1967; Enders and Schlafke, 1967
Guinea pig	3–3½	Blandau, 1961
Rabbit	4–4½	Böving, 1956, 1959
Cat	8–9	Blandau, 1961
Dog	9–10	Blandau, 1961
Rhesus monkey	4–6	Blandau, 1961
Man	4–6?	Blandau, 1961

* Calculated from data on ova transport by Greenwald and from implantation data by Enders and Schlafke.

one can distinguish three main types of placenta:

1. The chorionic placenta, in which the chorion adheres to the uterine mucosa. This type is a transitional type in some species.

2. The yolk sac placenta, which includes the nonvascular bilaminar omphalopleure (parietal surface of yolk sac plus chorion). If this bilaminar structure is invaded by mesoderm and area vasculosa, it becomes a trilaminar omphalopleure and forms the choriovitelline placenta. This arrangement is found as a permanent structure in certain marsupials, e.g. the American opossum, but it is also encountered as a temporary structure which exists concurrently with the chorioallantoic placenta, e.g. in the horse.

The inverted yolk sac placenta is formed by vascular splanchnopleure which is everted against the endometrium. This inverted yolk sac placenta is incomplete if the bilaminar omphalopleure separates the endoderm from the endometrium, as is the case in shrews, moles, and bats, or it is complete when the bilaminar omphalopleure has disappeared, e.g. in rabbits, guinea pigs, rats, mice (Amoroso, 1952). These inverted yolk sacs coexist with the chorioallantoic placenta until term, e.g. in rats. The yolk sac placenta is the sole mediator of antibody transfer from mother to fetus in rodents and lagomorphs (see Wislocki and Padykula, 1961).

3. The chorioallantoic placenta. The main types are listed in Table 11-3 together with the main zoological groups in which they occur and with the tissues which are present in each type. Björkman (1965) has pointed out for the sheep placenta that the various layers may be present, but that some can be bypassed by the presence of intraepithelial capillaries or by direct contact between maternal capillaries and cryptal syncytium.

The physiological exchange between mother and fetus via the placenta occurs by active transport, for which morphological evidence has been found in the form of pinocytotic vesicles in the syncytium and trophoblast, and in the capillary endothelium (Björkman, 1965).

Beautiful, detailed illustrations and scholarly discussions concerning the physiology, structure, histochemistry, and evolution of the placenta can be found in the papers by Amoroso (1952), Huggett (1959), Huggett and Hammond (1952), and Wislocki and Padykula (1961).

In addition to the placenta there are central and paraplacental hematomes found among carnivores, in the Madagascar hedgehog (*Setifer setosus* — also called *Ericulus setosus)*, and in some bats. "They consist of a mass of extravasated blood lying between the vascular chorioallantoic membrane lined by phagocytic cytotrophoblast and a glandular area of endometrium" (Sinha and Mossman, 1966). This hematome in the sea otter (*Enhydris lutris)* arises during the limb bud stage at the center of the antimesometrial portion of the placenta, as small pouches of vascular chorioallantoic membrane fill with blood from the mother. The lining of each pouch phagocytoses erythrocytes and probably products from the endometrial glands at its base. The hematome eventually consists of a large sac with a stalk, which may have smaller sacs at its base. Villous folds subdivide the stalk and the sac. The outer covering is formed by the endoderm of the allantoic sac as the result of invagination of this structure by the hematome.

Creed and Biggers (1964) suggested the name "hemophagous organ" instead of the name "hematome," because it indicates the function of the organ and lacks the pathological connotation of the word hematome. They described this organ for the raccoon (*Procyon lotor lotor)*, the olingo (*Bassaricyon gabbii orinomus)*, the Canadian river otter (*Lutra canadensis)*, the striped skunk (*Mephitis mephitis)*, the hooded skunk (*Mephitis macroura)*, and the spotted skunk (*Spilogale putorius)*. In each case, the hemophagous organ consists of a large fetal epithelium with large columnar cells which phagocytose maternal blood cells.

Table 11-3. Classification of Chorioallantoic Placentae According to Grosser

TYPE	MATERNAL TISSUE	FETAL TISSUE	SHAPE	FAMILIAR EXAMPLES	MAIN ZOOLOGIC GROUPS
Epitheliochorial	Endothelium Connective tissue Epithelium	Trophoblast Connective tissue Endothelium	Diffuse	Pig Horse Donkey	Prosimii (except Tupaiidae and Tarsiidae) Artiodactyla Perissodactyla Cetacea Polidota Insectivora
Syndesmochorial*	Endothelium Connective tissue	Trophoblast Connective tissue Endothelium	Cotyledonary	Sheep Goat Cow	
Endotheliochorial	Endothelium	Trophoblast Connective tissue Endothelium	Zonary or Discoid	Cat Dog Ferret	Elephantidae Tubilidenta Carnivora *Castor* *Pedetes* Bradypodidae Most of the Chiroptera Tupaiidae (?)
Hemochorial†		Trophoblast Connective tissue Endothelium	Zonary, Discoid, or Double discoid	Man Monkey	Anthropoidea Tarsiidae Sirenia Hyracoidea Most of the Rodentia Most of the Insectivora
Hemoendothelial‡		Endothelium	Discoid, Cup-shaped, or Spheroidal	Guinea pig Rat Rabbit	Caviidae Muroidea Geomyidea Lagomorpha

* According to Björkman and Bloom (1957) and Björkman (1965), this placenta does not exist in cattle and sheep because a syncytium is present between trophoblast and maternal connective tissue. The placenta is an epitheliochorial placenta.

† Enders (1965) has proposed a subdivision into *hemotrichorial* (found in rats, mice, hamsters, and deer mice), *hemodichorial* (found in rabbits), and *hemomonochorial* (found in the guinea pigs) placentae on the basis of the number of layers of trophoblast covering the fetal endothelium.

‡ Hemoendothelial placentae may not exist, as trophoblastic layers have been detected by electron microscopy in the guinea pig, rat, and rabbit (see above).

References: Altman and Dittmer, 1962; Amoroso, 1952.

The functions of the placenta are many; it provides physical protection for the embryo, attaches the fetus to the mother, mediates the exchange of nutrients from mother to fetus and the exchange of waste products from fetus to mother, converts substances absorbed from the maternal blood into other substances needed by the fetus or into materials which can be stored, and synthesizes steroid and gonadotropic hormones.

The gas exchange across the placenta has been discussed by Metcalfe et al. (1964). In such transfer, a number of factors should be taken into account:

1. The placenta contains two separate bloodstreams, which are separated by a number of layers (see Table 11-3).

2. The partial pressure of oxygen is higher on the maternal than on the fetal side of the membrane.

3. The main or probably the only process involved in oxygen transfer is diffusion.

4. The driving force for the oxygen diffusion is the difference in the oxygen tension between maternal and fetal blood. The affinity for oxygen is higher in fetal than in maternal blood. Therefore, at the same hemoglobin concentration and oxygen concentration, maternal blood has a higher oxygen tension, thus increasing the driving force.

As the fetal blood gives up CO_2 it becomes more alkaline, increasing its affinity for oxygen, while as the maternal blood takes up the CO_2 it becomes less alkaline, decreasing its affinity for oxygen; this effect increases the oxygen gradient.

In addition to these factors there exists a greater hemoglobin concentration in the fetal than in the maternal blood. This would increase the difference in oxygen tension and hence further increase the diffusion rate.

5. In some species, e.g. the rabbit and the cat, the maternal and fetal blood flow in different directions, thus creating a counter current exchange for transfer of substances from maternal to fetal circulation. This counter current arrangement has the greatest advantage when the diffusing capacity is high and the perfusion rate of the blood is low (as is the case in the rabbit). However, with a high rate of perfusion and a low oxygen diffusion rate (in sheep and human) such an arrangement is not as advantageous. Thus, in a system in which there is no active transport across membranes, many different factors enter into determination of the efficiency of the transfer.

The transfer of nutrients probably takes place largely by active transport, and, at least with respect to transfer of carbohydrates, is quite similar to that of many cell membranes (Dancis, 1964).

In addition to the transfer functions of the placenta, there is evidence of active metabolism of a number of nutrients. Glucose can be oxidized to lactic acid; the placenta can synthesize glycogen and can convert pyruvate and other intermediates of the tricarboxylic acid cycle to carbon dioxide and water (Hagerman, 1964). Enzymes involved in the urea cycle are absent in the human placenta, but some of the amino acid metabolizing enzymes, such as glutamic dehydrogenase, some transaminases and amino-oxidases can be found. Evidence is available that amino acids can be incorporated into placental proteins.

Neutral lipids and phospholipids are synthesized in the placenta (Hagerman, 1964). These lipids may later be used for fetal nutrition.

The synthesis of steroid hormones by the placenta will be discussed later in this chapter. The study of the physiology of placental transfers by different types of placentae must be extended before conclusions can be drawn about the significance of the anatomy with respect to the efficiency of such transfers.

Endocrine Control of the Fate of the Egg After Ovulation. The fate of the egg, assuming that sperm capable of fertilization are present, is determined by a number of endocrine events that must occur. The effect of estrogen on ovum pickup in the rabbit, on ovum transport in a number of species (Table 11-1), and on spacing of the blastocysts in rabbits has been discussed previously in this chapter.

The fertilized rat egg normally loses its zona pellucida (z.p.) about ten hours after it reaches the uterus, which is six hours prior to implantation. If rats are ovariectomized before noon of the fourth day of pregnancy, the z.p. is lost but the blastocyst does not implant. Ovariectomy on day 2 with subsequent progesterone administration does not cause implantation, although on day 8 the z.p. ruptures, but it remains in the uterine cavity. The z.p. is dissolved after injection of 17-β-estradiol at doses which are less than those required for implantation (Psychoyos, 1966). The removal of the z.p. from the egg does not, however, require a uterine environment, at least for mouse eggs (Fawcett et al., 1947; Runner, 1947). Dickmann and De Feo (1967) propose that the shedding of the z.p. is dependent upon the maturation of the trophoblast, which is inhibited by the "dormant" uterus (of pseudopregnant, ovariectomized rats treated with progesterone). However, once the trophoblast maturation has started, dormant uteri do not inhibit the process of the shedding of the z.p.

Psychoyos (1965a), in a review of the endocrine control of implantation of the rat's blastocyst, has pointed out that for success of implantation, the uterus must be receptive for implantation and the egg must be capable of inducing a response from the uterus.

As the work by a number of workers (Noyes et al., 1963) has shown, the development of the egg and of the uterus must be synchronized. Transfer of rat ova which were one day older than the uterus to which they were transplanted (age is determined with respect to time of ovulation) showed the same survival rate as eggs of the same age transferred to uteri of the same age as the eggs. Eggs which were one day younger than the uteri to which they were transferred showed a much lower incidence of survival, and transfers of eggs two days younger than the recipient were entirely unsuccessful. For mice, qualitatively similar results were obtained.

Chang (1950), in a study of synchronization of ova and uteri of rabbits, found that one-day-old ova transferred to tubes of rabbits ovulated the same day, one day before, or one day after the donors, develop normally. Such eggs transferred to hosts in estrus or in any stage of the luteal phase degenerate. The eggs in estrous rabbits were not transported.

Two-day-old ova obtained from the fallopian tubes showed a low incidence of development upon transfer to uteri days 2 or 3 of pseudopregnancy.

Four-day-old blastocysts developed in uteri of day 2 through 5 of pseudopregnancy but degenerated in the uteri of day 1; upon transfer to uteri of day 6, decidual tissue was formed but implantation failed to take place.

Six-day-old blastocysts developed normally upon transfer to uteri of days 5, 6, or 7, but showed a high incidence of degeneration if placed in uteri of days 3, 4, 8, 9, or 10.

For sheep, embryonic mortality is high when the egg and recipient uterus are more than two days out of phase in either direction. This was established for eggs collected on day 7 and day 9 (onset of estrus is day 0). For eggs of day 5 transferred to uteri of hosts, which were in heat two days before the donors, the incidence of pregnancies was as high as for synchronized transfers; however, if the hosts were in heat two days later than the donors the incidence of pregnancies was low. The time at which embryonic mortality occurred in these sheep was not recorded (Rowson and Moor, 1966).

Microscopic study of rat eggs, which were one day younger than the uteri to which they were transferred, showed that eggs which were either two days old and recovered after 48 hours in a day 3 uterus or which were three days old and stayed 24 hours in a day 4 uterus, were essentially normal. However, the sojourn of day 4 eggs in a day 5 uterus for as little as nine hours caused abnormalities. It thus appears that the uterine environment on day 3 and 4 was hospitable to younger ova, but that on day 5, just prior to normal implantation, the environment became deleterious to eggs too young for the uteri in which they were present. Mouse ova studied in a similar manner showed that the uterine environment was unsuitable for underdeveloped eggs on days 3, 4, and

5. The studies of eggs that were one day older than their hosts' uteri suggest that in the rat and the mouse the ova continue to develop while waiting for the uterus to develop to the stage of development suitable for implantation to start.

The question arises how one can separate the effect of hormones on the ovum from those exerted on the uterus. An experimental technique that can be used to evaluate the effect of hormones on the egg consists of making use of the delayed implantation that occurs in rats and mice under certain natural and experimental conditions.

Rats and mice will ovulate and show estrus the first or second night after delivery of the young ("postpartum heat"). If such rats and mice are mated and the eggs are fertilized, no implantation takes place if the female is nursing the pups. Parturition occurs 14 days after implantation in mice and 16 days after implantation in rats. The period during which the blastocyst does not implant (the delay period) is related to the number of young being suckled. For four young or less, the delay period is 2.18 ± 0.92 days for rats and none for mice, for five to eight young these figures are 3.68 ± 0.39 and 2.00 ± 0.43 days, for nine to 12 young, 4.22 ± 0.23 and 4.09 ± 0.18 days and for more than thirteen young, 4.76 ± 0.27 and $4.39 \pm$ to 0.20, respectively (Mantalenakis and Ketchel, 1966).

Experimentally, one can prevent implantation in the pregnant rat by ovariectomy and then study the effect of various hormones on the blastocyst, on the uterus, and on the incidence of implantation. The ovariectomy has to be performed before the afternoon of day 4 in order to prevent implantation. The blastocyst of such spayed animals can survive in the uterine lumen for several days in the absence of exogenous hormone treatments; this is also true in adrenalectomized-ovariectomized rats, and suggests that no steroid hormones are required for blastocyst survival (Mayer, 1963).

If progesterone is injected in such spayed rats, the blastocyst may survive for several weeks without implanting. A small dose of estrogen subsequent to progesterone treatment leads to implantation. Normal development will occur provided progesterone treatment is continued. Ageing of the blastocyst thus has no apparent effect, which is in marked contrast to the results obtained with ageing of ova prior to fertilization (see Chapter 10).

Estrogen in the absence of progesterone is detrimental to the blastocyst (Mayer, 1963).

The effect of estrogens and progesterone on fertilized eggs has also been studied in vitro. Fertile rabbit ova, obtained from the fallopian ducts, can be cultured in vitro and will show normal cleavage.

Addition of estradiol-17-β in concentrations of 5, 10, or 25 μg./ml. showed that 10 and 25 μg./ml. doses were detrimental to the egg and inhibited cleavage or caused fragmentation of the eggs; the 10 μg./ml. dose gave the highest incidence of fragmented eggs and the 25 μg./ml. dose the highest percentage of inhibited cleavage. Ten micrograms of estradiol-17-β per ml. plus 12.5 μg. progesterone per ml. resulted in 16 out of 22 fragmented and 2 out of 22 eggs in which cleavage was inhibited (McGaughey and Daniel, 1966). The fragmentation after progesterone plus estrogen treatment was less marked than after estrogen treatment alone. The controls used in this study were cultured in a steroid-free medium. It needs to be determined whether steroids without hormonal activity (e.g. cholesterol) may have similar effects.

In other experiments it was shown that progesterone alone inhibits cleavage of fertile rabbit ova. This effect can be reversed by removing the progesterone from the medium. Evidence was presented that progesterone may have prevented the entry of proteins and amino acids into the ovum, thus limiting the synthesis of proteins by the ovum (Daniel and Levy, 1964).

Unfortunately, rat ova do not seem to be very suitable for in vitro culture, thus the effect of hormones in vitro cannot be studied in this species, for which there is a considerable amount of information concerning the endocrine requirements for implantation. Of course, the findings made on rabbit eggs in vitro will not necessarily be applicable to rat ova.

Transfer of "dormant blastocyst" obtained from spayed, progesterone-treated rats, to "sensitive" uteri (of pseudopregnant rats on day 5) implanted and gave rise to normal fetuses; the same was true for "active" blastocysts (obtained from pregnant, intact rats on day 5) transferred to "dormant uteri" (of pseudopregnant rats ovariectomized on day 2 and given progesterone on day 7) (Dickmann and De Feo, 1967). The lack of difference between "dormant" and "active" blastocysts with respect to implantation exists in spite of morphological differences between these blastocysts. The experiments also show that the asynchrony, which plays such an important role in transfer of day 4 eggs to day 5 uteri, is not important in the case of blastocysts transferred to either "sensitive" or "dormant" uteri (Dickmann and De Feo, 1967).

The effect of ovarian and pituitary hormones on implantation can be conducted with pregnant rats hypophysectomized or ovariectomized at different days of pregnancy and treated with exogenous hormones.

The results of such studies with rats have led to the following conclusions:
1. The formation of the blastocyst, after fertilization of the egg, requires neither the uterus nor the ovary. Eggs retained in the oviduct by ligation in intact and ovariectomized rats developed into apparently normal blastocysts (Alden, 1942b).

2. Ovariectomy before the afternoon of day 4 results in failure of implantation (Mayer, 1963; Nutting and Meyer, 1963; Psychoyos, 1965a,b).

3. Progesterone treatment in doses between 3900 and 4000 μg. per day for ten days did not cause implantations in rats ovariectomized on day 3. The administration of this hormone was, however, required for implantation to take place when progesterone and estrogen were given subsequently (Nutting and Meyer, 1963). The number of implantation sites was linearly related to the dose of progesterone given between day 3 and 13, within the range of 125 to 8000 μg.

4. Injection of as little as 0.02 to 0.05 μg. estradiol together with progesterone will induce implantation within 24 hours in ovariectomized rats that have been treated with progesterone. If the estradiol is applied locally on the uterus, only 0.002-0.004 μg. estradiol is required (Psychoyos, 1965a,b). Nutting and Meyer (1963), using estrone, found that a minimal daily dose of 0.3 to 1.0 μg. was required for implantation but that 10 μg. estrone per day prevented implantation.

If estrogen and progesterone are given daily, the endometrial response to trauma is maximal at three days of treatment and then decreases. It has also been shown that the treatment of the ovariectomized recipients determines the success of implantation of transferred eggs (see Table 11-4).

On the basis of these experiments, Psychoyos (1965a) has proposed the concept of receptivity of the uterus, a period which is relatively short, followed by a period of nonreceptivity, which, under normal conditions in the mated rat, is the period of pregnancy.

Harper (1967), in analysis of the deciduomal response of pseudopregnant, intact, and ovariectomized rats, found that

Table 11-4. Effect of Progesterone (5 mg.) and Estradiol (0.1 μg.) Treatment of Ovariectomized Rats Prior to Transfer of Eggs on Implantation

4	3	2	1	0	PERCENT IMPLANTS
–	–	P	P	PE	44
–	–	PE	P	PE	63
P	P	P	P	PE	71
P	P	P	PE	P	66
P	P	PE	P	P	0
P	P	P	PE	PE	71
P	P	PE	P	PE	0

(column group header: DAYS PRIOR TO TRANSFER over columns 4, 3, 2, 1, 0)

P = Progesterone treatment.
PE = Progesterone plus estradiol treatment.
Reference: Psychoyos, 1965a.

spayed rats required estrogen plus progesterone to reach the same uterine response as intact controls. These results are in agreement with results obtained with egg implantation studies.

A biochemical analysis (Duncan et al., 1966) of the effects of estradiol (0.05 μg./day), progesterone (1.5 mg./day), and estradiol plus progesterone on deciduomata of ovariectomized rats showed that estradiol alone had no significant effect on any of the following parameters: fresh weight, percent dry weight, protein concentration, protein content, glycogen concentration, glycogen content, RNA concentration per unit of wet tissue, RNA concentration per unit of protein, RNA content, DNA concentrations (per unit of wet tissue or per unit of protein), DNA content, and RNA/DNA ratio of the ovariectomized uterus. Progesterone alone significantly increased: fresh weight, protein content, glycogen content, RNA content, DNA content, and RNA/DNA ratio. These responses were increased by the simultaneous injection of estradiol; in addition, the combination caused a significant increase in RNA concentration per unit of protein and in DNA concentration per unit of weight and per unit of protein. Analysis of this kind of uteri of ovariectomized rats, given progesterone and estrogen in different sequences (see Table 11-4) may reveal the biochemical

basis for the "receptive" condition of the uterus.

The evidence given so far strongly favors the hypothesis that estrogen causes implantation of the blastocyst by an action of the uterus. However, this does not exclude the possibility that progesterone and estrogen may also affect the fertile egg. Yasukawa and Meyer (1966) investigated this possibility by making a microscopic study of ova obtained from pregnant rats and from mated rats ovariectomized on day 3 and given progesterone (4 mg./day) from day 3 through 9. At day 9, one group was given progesterone alone to continue delayed implantation, another group received progesterone plus 1 μg. estrone (to induce implantation). Ova were obtained at 96, 102, 108, 114, 120, and 126 hours of pregnancy and at 6, 12, 18, 24, 30, and 36 hours after the steroid treatments on days 9 and 10.

Alterations in shape, axis lengths, and area of eggs from intact rats appeared during the afternoon of day 5. The zona pellucida was lost 18 hours prior to implantation or six hours after preimplantation changes in the blastocyst were first seen. In the ovariectomized rats, similar changes occurred 12 hours after the injection of estrone. Ova from rats receiving only progesterone did not show these changes in area shape and axis length, although the eggs were larger than the nondelayed ova except when the latter reached their full size at 126 hours of pregnancy.

5. Ovariectomy after the afternoon of day 4, followed by progesterone administration on day 6, results in implantation. This phenomenon can be explained on the basis of the experiments mentioned above. It is assumed that on day 4, release of estrogen ("estrogen surge") by the ovary takes place and causes implantation (Mayer, 1963; Nutting and Meyer, 1963; Psychoyos, 1965a; Shelesnyak and Kraicer, 1963).

6. Delayed implantation will occur in rats hypophysectomized on or after day 4, provided they are given either progesterone (Mayer, 1965) or prolactin (Zeilmaker, 1963), or that the pituitary is autotransplanted under the kidney (Mayer, 1963). If these procedures are used before day 4, implantation does not take place unless estrogen is given, a situation quite similar to the one discussed for ovariectomized rats.

In rats hypophysectomized before day 4 and given progesterone, one can analyze the effect of different gonadotropins on implantation. The occurrence of implantation would indicate that estrogen release from the ovary has been induced.

Implantation and maintenance of pregnancy has been obtained regularly in such hypophysectomized, progesterone-treated rats after daily administration of either LH (50 μg. in sesame oil plus five percent beeswax) (MacDonald et al., 1967), or 0.5 I.U. HCG, or 2 I.U. PMSG, or rat pituitary homogenates. Injection of either 1000 μg. FSH or 400 μg. LH occasionally results in ovo-implantation (Slough et al., 1965).

7. Drugs which interfere with gonadotropin secretion and/or release may be expected to prevent implantation in a manner similar to hypophysectomy. This is indeed the case with reserpine, prochlorpemazine, perphenazine, and 10-chlorodeserpidine. The effect can be overcome by estrogen injections (Mayer, 1965). One may expect that LH administration would have a similar effect.

8. For undetermined reasons, parabiosis of rats on day 1 of pregnancy with either similar rats, nonpregnant females, or male rats results in delayed implantation, provided the parabiosis involves the joining of skin and muscles between the partners. Estradiol given on day 4 prevents the parabiotic effect (Ketchel et al., 1966). These results suggest that parabiosis inhibits the release of estrogen from the ovary of the pregnant rat. Ketchel et al. (1966) showed that neither surgery nor the restricted movement is responsible for the effect.

The hormonal requirements for implantations in other species have been determined and will be mentioned here. Delayed implantation can be induced in mice by ovariectomy plus progesterone treatment. The highest incidence is obtained by spaying on day 3, with some implantations occurring when the operation is performed on days 1, 2, 4, or 5. The delayed blastocysts could be induced to implant by estrogen treatment (Yoshinaga and Adams, 1966). The mouse thus seems to be rather similar to the rat.

For the hamster, it appears that ovariectomy on day 1 or 4 causes failure of implantation, but it can be induced by the injection of progesterone (1-2 mg.) alone, although the same dose of progesterone plus 1 μg. estrone increases the number of implantations (Harper et al., 1966; Prassad et al., 1960).

The rabbit requires estrogen and progesterone (Elton, 1966; Deanesly, 1963) for deciduoma formation, but implantation requires only progesterone, suggesting, as Deanesly (1963) pointed out, that the blastocyst may carry a hormone or enzyme which contributes to the decidual reaction.

The guinea pig, which does not show delayed implantation (Deanesly, 1960), does not require estrogen even after long standing ovariectomy. Ovariectomy on day 3 does not prevent implantation, but

spaying on day 2 prevents this process unless progesterone is injected at either days
2, 3, or 4 (Deanesly, 1963). Continuous administration of this hormone (10 mg.) results in essentially normal embryonic
development, at least until day 21. Incidentally, injections of 1 μg. estradiol
and 5 mg. progesterone do not affect the
incidence of implantation but decrease
the incidence of live embryos on day 21
(Deanesly, 1963).

These examples illustrate the differences among species with respect to
the occurrence of delayed implantation
and to the requirements of normal and
delayed blastocysts, and thus emphasize
the importance of experiments carried
out with animals other than the rat.

Delayed implantation occurs in a
number of marsupials, implantation being
lactation controlled, as was discussed in
the beginning of this chapter. The species
which show this pattern are: *Setonix
brachyurus, Bettongia lesueuri, Pretemnodon
eugenii, P. irma, P. rufogrisea, Megaleia
ruffa, Potorous tridactylus, Thylogale thetis,
Macropus robustus, Lagostrophus fasciatus,*
and *Wallabia bicolor* (Sharman, 1963;
Sharman et al., 1965). A list of eutheria
in which delayed implantation has been
observed is given in Table 11-5.

The endocrinological requirements
for implantation of the delayed blastocysts
in the animals listed in Table 11-5 are
poorly understood, although morphological studies of the ovary and uterus before
and after implantation have been used to
obtain some leads, e.g. the reduced luteal
function of the corpora lutea (Canivenc,
1965).

Probably one of the most detailed
studies of the phenomenon of delayed
implantation and of the hormonal and
environmental requirements for implantation of the blastocyst has been made on
the European badger by Canivenc and his
associates. They first demonstrated that
there is a fertile postpartum coitus in
February, and that the fertilized eggs remain in a quiescent blastocyst stage until

December, when implantation takes place
(Canivenc and Bonnin-Laffargue, 1963).

In the roe deer (Short and Hay, 1966)
and the European badger (Canivenc and
Bonnin-Laffargue, 1963) ovulations may
occur at the time that implantation normally commences, and in the case of fertile
matings, implantation may take place
without delay, so that the young are born
at about the same time as those resulting
from the earlier matings of other females.

Enders (1966) found that many nulliparous nine-banded armadillos do not
ovulate until November, in contrast with
multiparous females which ovulate, generally, between July and August. Implantation takes place near the end of November
and in December in both groups; thus
the duration of the quiescent periods is
considerably shorter in the nulliparous
females.

The rationale and the results of several
types of experiments carried out to induce
earlier than normal blastocyst implantation will be discussed for various species.

1. Hansson (1947), in his study of
delayed implantation in mink, mentioned
that the estrous condition of the uterus
might be one of the causes for the failure
of the blastocyst to implant. One animal,
ovariectomized and treated with progesterone and estrogen, showed evidence of implantation.

In the nine-banded armadillo, bilateral
ovariectomy early in the quiescent period
causes implantation in 18 to 20 days according to Enders (1966) and in 30 to
34 days according to Buchanan et al.
(1956). Enders (1966) found similar results for animals ovariectomized later in
the quiescent period and he also established that spaying at the time of implantation did not interfere with this process.
Ovariectomy after the uterus shows evidence of implantation results in a loss of
embryos. Buchanan et al. (1956) showed
that the ovary, bearing the corpus luteum,
is apparently essential for maintenance of
pregnancy during the first one-third of
the postimplantation gestation period.

Table 11-5. Species in Which Delayed Ova Implantation Has Been Noted and Estimate of Duration of Dormant Period of Blastocyst

SPECIES	DORMANT PERIOD	REFERENCE
Nine-banded armadillo (*Dasypus novemcinctus*)	4 months	Canivenc, 1960
Mulita armadillo (*D. hybridus*)	4 months	Canivenc, 1960
Three-banded armadillo (*Tolypeutes tricinctus*)	4 months	Canivenc, 1960
Sloth (*Bradypus griseus*)	(?)	Canivenc, 1960
American badger (*Taxidea taxus*)	2 months	Wright, 1963
European badger (*Meles meles*)	10 months*	Canivenc and Bonnin-Laffargue, 1963
Short-tailed weasel (*Mustela erminea*)	(?)	Deanesly, 1966
	6 weeks	Canivenc, 1960
Long-tailed weasel (*M. frenata*)	27 days	Canivenc, 1960
Short-tailed weasel (*M. cicognanii*)	27 days	Canivenc, 1960
Mink (*M. vison*)	12–25 days†	Canivenc, 1960
Wolverine (*Gulo gulo*)	4 months	Wright, 1963
Marten (*Martes martes*)	(?)	Canivenc, 1960
American marten (*M. americana*)	7 months	Canivenc, 1960
Fisher (*M. pennanti, M. zibellina*)	9 months	Canivenc, 1960
	8 months	Canivenc, 1960
River otter (*Lutra canadensis*)	(?)	Wright, 1963
Black bear (*Ursus americanus*)	5 months	Wimsatt, 1963
Alaskan brown bear (*U. arctos*)	5–6 months	Canivenc, 1960
Polar bear (*Thalarctos maritimus*)	(?)	Asdell, 1964
South American sea lion (*Otaria byroni*)	3 months	Canivenc, 1960
Cape fur seal (*Arctocephalus pusillus*)	3–4 months	Canivenc, 1960
North Pacific fur seal (*Callorhinus ursinus*)	3½–4 months	Canivenc, 1960
South Atlantic elephant seal (*Mirounga leonina*)	4 months	Canivenc, 1960
Harbor seal (*Phoca vitulina*)	3–3½ months	Harrison, 1963
Gray seal (*Halichoerus grypus*)	3 months	Harrison, 1963
Weddell seal (*Leptonychotes weddellii*)	(?)	Harrison et al., 1952
Crab-eater seal (*Lobodon carcinophagus*)	(?)	Harrison et al., 1952
Hooded seal (*Cystophora cristata*)	(?)	Harrison et al., 1952
Harp seal (*Pagophilus groenlandicus*), (*Phoca groenlandica*)	(?)	Harrison et al., 1952
Fruit bat (*Eidolon helvum*)	4–6 months	Mutere, 1965
Roe deer (*Capreolus capreolus*)	4–5 months*	Canivenc, 1960

* Implantation occasionally is not delayed and the gestation period is 20 weeks instead of about 40 weeks (Asdell, 1964; Canivenc, 1966; Deanesly, 1966).
† See text for relationship between date of mating and length of gestation period.

Removal of the ovary containing the corpus luteum (nine-banded armadillos are monovular but give birth to four identical young) did not result in implantation but it did cause a decrease in fertility. This decrease could be prevented by daily injections of 10 to 25 mg. of progesterone (Enders, 1966).

Bilateral ovariectomy of the European badger during the quiescent period does not affect the blastocyst but fails to cause implantation (Canivenc, 1965; Canivenc and Bonnin-Laffargue, 1963).

2. Histological observations of the corpus luteum and the uterus revealed a lack of secretory function of the corpus luteum during the quiescent period and a change to secretory activity prior to implantation of the blastocyst in the European badger (Canivenc and Bonnin-Laffargue, 1963; Canivenc et al. 1966) and in the American badger (Wright, 1966). Wimsatt (1963) reported that the differences between the corpora lutea of delay and those of pregnancy consist of a dramatic increase in volume, as a result of hypertrophy of the luteal cells, an apparent increase in vascularity, and loss of the vacuolation.

In contrast to this, the corpora lutea

of the roe deer (Short and Hay, 1966) and of the nine-banded armadillo (Enders, 1966) show no difference between pre- and post-implantation periods.

In mink, the corpora lutea luteinize but do not hypertrophy until implantation. Changes in uterine histology and histochemistry also occur during the implantation period.

The histological appearance and the progesterone content of the corpora lutea were correlated in the European badger (Canivenc et al. 1966) and the roe deer (Short and Hay, 1966).

The observations and results given above provide a rationale for administration of ovarian hormones in an effort to induce implantation.

In the European badger, administration of either estrogen or estrogen plus progesterone fails to cause blastocyst implantation (Canivenc, 1960, 1965). Similar results were found in mink (M. vison) by Cochrane and Shackelford (1962), Hammond (1951), and Hansson (1947), although the last named author reported one case of an ovariectomized mink treated with estrogen and progesterone in which implantation had occurred.

Canivenc et al. (1967) were able to obtain progestational changes in the uterus of the European badger by local application of progesterone. In spite of these changes and in spite of the presence of blastocyst in the affected uterine areas, there was no evidence of implantation nor were there changes in diameter or appearance of the blastocysts.

3. Cytological examination of the anterior pituitary of the European badger reveals many lactation cells from February until July and a regression of LH cells during the phase of delayed implantation; these cells are large and show signs of secretory activity from October on, when the corpora lutea become active and implantation is initiated. It seemed logical, therefore, to attempt the injection of gonadotropic hormones for induction of implantation. FSH injections caused follicular stimulation, LH administration had no observable effect on the ovary but FSH plus LH caused formation of new corpora lutea. The cells of these new corpora lutea showed the same signs of inactivity which one finds in the corpora lutea of the delayed implantation phase (Canivenc, 1966). Prolactin injections failed to affect either the corpora lutea of the quiescent phase or those induced by FSH plus LH treatment (Canivenc and Bonnin-Laffargue, 1963).

The investigations by Canivenc (1966) showed that no new corpora lutea are formed and therefore that old corpora lutea, found during the postpartum period, become activated in the fall.

Hansson (1947) injected groups of mink during the first four days after ovulation with PMSG, pregnancy urine (PU), and a combination of these gonadotropins and obtained a prolonged gestation (6.8 days) in the PMSG treated mink. Only one animal in this group of eight became pregnant, so no great significance can be placed on this observation. In the two other groups the duration of gestation was prolonged 0.6 and 2.7 days.

4. The regularity with which implantation occurs with respect to the season in nonequatorial species suggests that some environmental factors may be involved in the initiation of implantation. Such a factor or factors might have their effect via the hypothalamus. Canivenc and Bonnin-Laffargue (1963) used intrasplenic grafts of the ovary in order to avoid a possible feedback of ovarian steroid on the hypothalamo-hypophyseal axis. In no case was evidence of the formation of active corpora lutea found.

5. Short and Hay (1965, 1966) attempted to obtain implantation of a quiescent blastocyst of the roe deer by transferring it to sheep in the early luteal phase of the cycle. No cases of implantation were encountered.

In a somewhat different approach, Chang (1965b) inseminated ferrets with mink sperm and found that the fertilized eggs showed no delay in reaching the expanded blastocyst stage; presumably such blastocysts would have implanted. Not too many conclusions can be drawn from this experiment because a number of factors may play a role in the expansion of the blastocyst, e.g. the contributions made by the ovum, the uterine environment, and the interactions between these two. Reciprocal crosses, which may eventually have to be supplemented by blastocyst transfer, may contribute to the solution of this problem. The experimental techniques are known, but whether they can be worked out for the mink remains to be investigated.

The possibility that nongonadotropic or nongonadal hormones have an effect on the time at which implantation occurs has not been excluded. It is entirely within the framework of endocrinological control of reproductive processes to assume that such hormones may have an effect, either directly or by interaction with the gonadotropic and gonadal hormones. It may be necessary to study delayed implantation by methods similar to those employed in the control of lactation, that is, by the use of hypophysectomized, adrenalectomized, ovariectomized, thyroidectomized animals. Such experiments obviously will be difficult and expensive to carry out, especially as some of the animals that have delayed implantation will show deviations from their normal reproductive pattern if kept in captivity.

In summary, it appears that the induction of implantation in nonlaboratory animals with delayed implantation has not been accomplished successfully by experimentally changing the endocrine status of the animal. An exception to this is found in the work on the nine-banded armadillo in which ovariectomy induced implantation.

After implantation has occurred, hormones may be needed in order to maintain the pregnancy and to terminate it at the normal time. Tables giving the length of the gestation period for a large number of mammals can be found in the publications of Altman and Dittmer, 1962 (Table 41); Kenneth, 1947; and Zarrow, 1961. It is difficult to determine the precise quantitative endocrine requirements for the maintenance of postimplantation gestation in some species because the placenta may secrete gonadotropic and/or steroid hormones (see Chapters 6 and 7). Quantitative requirements can thus be made only in species which do not have placentae with a significant endocrine function. For the sake of convenience, the discussion on the hormonal requirements for maintenance of postimplantation gestation will be discussed from the point of view of ablation and subsequent replacement therapy.

1. Hypophysectomy has different effects, which depend on the species used and the time during gestation that the operation is performed. Table 11-6 gives a brief summary of results obtained with this operation.

Data obtained after hypophysectomy of the goat, ferret, and cat were not included because the results were inconclusive (Amoroso and Porter, 1966).

The maintenance of pregnancy in the rat and the mouse after hypophysectomy can be explained on the basis of prolactin secretion by the placenta, which maintains the corpus luteum and therefore the gonadal hormones required for maintenance of the gestation. That hypophysectomy does not interrupt pregnancy in sheep, guinea pigs, monkeys, and women is the result of steroid hormone production by the placenta (see Tables 6-4, 6-12, and 9-6).

These data indicate that the steroid hormones are the ones principally involved in sustaining gestation and that the loss of adrenal and thyroid function, which would be expected after hypophysectomy, play relatively minor roles.

The "discrepancy" between the earliest time at which hypophysectomy does not interfere with pregnancy in women and the earliest date for ovariectomy is the

Table 11-6. Comparison of the Effects of Hypophysectomy (♂) and of Ovariectomy (♀) in Different Mammalian Species

SPECIES	EFFECT*		EARLIEST DATE†	
	♂	♀	♂	♀
Rabbit	Aborted	Aborted	Near term	Near term
Dog	Aborted	Continued	Near term	Day 30 (?)
Guinea pig	Continued	Continued	Day 40–41	Day 20
Mouse	Continued	Absorbed, aborted	Day 10	—
Rat	Continued	Absorbed, aborted	Day 11	—
Sheep	Continued	Continued	Day 50	Day 54
Rhesus monkey	Continued	Continued	Day 27	Day 25
Man	Continued	Continued	Week 12	Day 30

* Effect of hypophysectomy or ovariectomy is indicated as either *aborted* or *absorbed* if the operation caused these effects at any time during pregnancy except close to term, or as *continued* if pregnancy was not interrupted after the operation at some time during pregnancy.

† Earliest date at which the operation was compatible with maintenance of pregnancy.

References: Amoroso and Porter, 1966; Deanesly, 1966.

result of a lack of experimental data with respect to hypophysectomy. For guinea pigs, there is a more important difference between the ovariectomy and hypophysectomy data. Ovariectomy can be performed at 27 days and not interrupt gestation, whereas hypophysectomy performed on days 34 to 36 causes resorption of the fetuses (Pencharz and Lyons, 1934). This difference of four to six days may be the result of the more severe trauma associated with hypophysectomy as compared with ovariectomy, or it may be the result of a critical need for the other hypophyseal hormones during these four days.

Rats hypophysectomized at day 2 and treated with 60 to 120 I.U. prolactin daily and estrone (1 µg.) every other day show a fairly high incidence of live fetuses (but also, in many cases, resorption of some fetuses) near term (Lyons et al., 1943). This means that the prolactin causes sufficient progesterone production, that together with estrone, implantation is induced, and that the combination is also sufficient to maintain pregnancy, although the incidence of resorption is high.

The effectiveness of the placenta was demonstrated by implanting placentae into rats hypophysectomized at day 6 (when implantation has occurred). In such rats implantation of 1 to 4 whole placentae

each day resulted in maintenance of pregnancy till day 12 (when rats were killed but presumably the rat's own placenta would have secreted sufficient prolactin to maintain the pregnancy longer). The placentae of donors in their twelfth day of pregnancy were more effective than those of rats pregnant for 15 days (Averill et al., 1950).

After hypophysectomy and oophorectomy on day 7 to 8 pregnancy could be maintained by a combination of 3 or 4 mg. progesterone plus 1 µg. estrone (Lyons, 1943). In more recent experiments Macdonald and Greep (1966) reported that four days of LH treatment (50 µg. in sesame oil and beeswax) induced implantation in either prolactin-treated rats or in rats with pituitary transplants. Such pregnancies could then be maintained by progesterone treatment, with fetal death occurring late in pregnancy.

In virtually all the experiments mentioned above, the incidence of normal deliveries was small and in many cases fetuses died near term if the mothers were hypophysectomized (either early in pregnancy with maintenance of pregnancy by exogenous hormones, or after day 11 without exogenous hormones). Selye et al. (1933) reported, however, that after hypophysectomy on days 10 and 11 pregnancy was prolonged but delivery occurred normally. The reason for the difference among the results of these different experiments is not obvious, although it is possible that in some cases, pieces of posterior pituitary were left in place and that in other cases they were removed.

The abortions which occur after hypophysectomy of pregnant rabbits can be prevented by the injection of progesterone or estrogen (Deanesly, 1966). Progesterone administration replaces the hormones which are lacking as a result of the regression of the corpus luteum. Estrogen has its effect by maintaining the corpus luteum (see Chapter 6).

2. The effects of ovariectomy on established pregnancy in different species can be ascertained from Table 9-6; to this list needs to be added the ferret and ground squirrel in which ovariectomy even late in pregnancy causes termination of pregnancy (Deanesly, 1966) and the nine-banded armadillo which was discussed earlier in this chapter. In the rat, mouse, rabbit, guinea pig, and sheep, progesterone administration can prevent the interruption of pregnancy induced by ovariectomy (see Deanesly, 1966, and Zarrow, 1961 for documentation). The dose of progesterone in rats, mice, and rabbits can be reduced if estrogen is administered in conjunction with progesterone.

In general, the hormones required for maintenance of established pregnancy are progesterone alone or in combination with estrogen. These hormones can be secreted by either the ovary or the placenta.

The evidence indicates that in guinea pigs, cats, sheep, cattle, horses, Rhesus monkeys, and humans progestins are produced by the placenta in sufficient quantities to maintain pregnancy at least for the latter part of the gestation period. The relative duration of the period during which the placentae produce progestins with respect to the length of the gestation period is variable among species, e.g. in humans with a gestation period of nine months the placenta apparently produces progesterone after the first months, whereas in cows, with a similar gestation period, the ovaries are required until 207 days (Deanesly, 1966).

The different factors affecting the life span and secretory activity of the corpus luteum have been discussed in Chapters 6 and 9.

It is outside the scope of this book to give the concentration of progesterone and other gestagens in different species. Distinctions should be made between concentrations found by the Hooker-Forbes bioassay method and chemical determinations. Generally, the concentrations found by the bioassay method are considerably higher than the values found by chemical means. The discrepancy can be explained by the fact that the 17-α-hydroxyprogesterone, which has no progestational activity in other biological tests, is 60 times as active as progesterone in the Hooker-Forbes test (Short, 1960). We shall therefore not report values obtained with this method.

In comparing progesterone concentrations at different periods of pregnancy, it should be kept in mind that such concentrations in ovarian venous blood do not always reflect progesterone production. In the dog ovary the rate of blood flow also determines the rate of progesterone production (Romanoff et al., 1962).

It should also be considered that the lymph may transport a certain amount of progesterone from the ovary. Lindner et al. (1964) estimated that this amount would be less than ten percent of the total progesterone output in conscious ewes.

In all comparisons among species, care should be taken that only data reporting concentrations for either ovarian vein blood or for peripheral blood are compared. The progesterone concentration in the peripheral blood of rats gradually decreases from a concentration of 300 ng./ml. on day 10 to a concentration of 10 ng./ml. at parturition (Grota and Eik-Nes, 1967).

In pregnant rabbits the progesterone

concentrations in the ovarian blood reached their maximum between ten and 21 days (with a low value at 12 days) and then decreased to low but, in some cases, still detectable concentrations near parturition, whereas in non-pregnant controls, progesterone could not be detected (Okano et al., 1966). Data on 20-α-ol concentrations were incomplete and therefore insufficient to show a trend. Hafez et al. (1966) have reported values for progesterone and 20-α-ol concentrations which are about twice as high as those found by Okano et al. (1966). Hafez et al. (1966) found very low concentrations of progesterone and 20-α-ol on day 4, but there were no correlations between the day of pregnancy and the values for progesterone and 20-α-ol between days 4 and 20. There was also no correlation between these concentrations and either the number of corpora lutea or the number of viable young. The concentrations found in the ovaries and in the blood were, however, highly correlated.

The concentrations of progesterone in the peripheral blood of the guinea pig rise from about 64 ng./ml. between days 11 and 17 to a maximal level of about 265 ng./ml. between days 30 and 35; after this time the values drop to about 140 ng./ml. between day 60 and 65 (Heap and Deanesly, 1966).

In ovariectomized, pregnant animals, the concentrations at comparable times were about 100 ng./ml. lower than in the intact controls. This indicates that the ovary still contributes significantly to the progesterone production, although the placenta produces sufficient amounts to maintain pregnancy.

Progesterone concentration in ovarian blood of pregnant sheep remains close to the average found during the late luteal phase and decreases toward parturition (Edgar and Ronaldson, 1958). Short and Moore (1959) found little variation in the progesterone and 20-α-ol concentration of peripheral blood during pregnancy; there was no significant decrease prior to parturition (measured until two hours before parturition), but a decrease occurred after parturition.

Lindner et al. (1964) found a similar trend for the amount of progesterone put out via the lymph system.

Peripheral blood concentrations, which may reflect ovarian and placental progesterone productions, do not rise during pregnancy and, contrary to the ovarian blood levels, do not decrease at parturition. The 20-α-ol concentrations show a pattern similar to that of progesterone.

In cattle and sheep there is a rather constant level of progesterone during pregnancy that declines about ten days prior to parturition in cattle but not in sheep.

The production of progesterone by the ovaries of pregnant goats is estimated to be about 9 to 10.5 mg. of progesterone per day; the concentrations in the ovarian venous blood reach levels of 620 to 1600 ng./ml. (Heap and Linzell, 1966). The concentration of progesterone in peripheral blood was above 10 ng./ml. throughout pregnancy but decreased to 5.2 ng./ml. at parturition. The authors found that spinal anesthesia raised peripheral progesterone concentrations with further increase caused by laparotomy. It was also shown that the udder takes up about 20 percent of the progesterone produced during pregnancy.

In the mare, blood progesterone concentrations are high during the first four months (when the ovary is required for maintenance of pregnancy). After this time, when the placenta produces sufficient progesterone to maintain gestation in the absence of the ovaries, progesterone can no longer be detected (Short, 1960). At this time the ovary does not contain active corpora lutea. Progesterone seems to be absent from the peripheral blood, probably because of the epithiochorial structure of the placenta (Short, 1960). According to Short, the progesterone liberated by the chorion cells is metabolized before it can enter the maternal blood vessels.

The peripheral blood levels of progesterone in Rhesus monkeys are very low in comparison with those found in women (Short and Eckstein, 1961). The concentration found one to three weeks prior to Cesarean section was less than 10 ng./ml. (which is about one-thirtieth the concentration found in women at the comparable stage of gestation).

Uterine vein blood, at the time of Cesarean section, contained 24 ng./ml. and the umbilical cord blood contained 10.6 ng./ml. These low amounts of progesterone are probably the reflection of the low production rate of the placenta. The monkey placenta contained between 35 and 88 μg. progesterone/kg., in comparison with the concentration of 2220 μg./kg. in human placentae (Short and Eckstein, 1961).

In women, the progesterone that reaches the maternal blood per 24 hours is estimated to be 29 mg. during week 11 and to rise to 41 mg. during week 18, but during the last month of pregnancy to reach the level of 190 to 280 mg./day (Carey, 1963). This trend agrees fairly well with the pattern found by Short and Levett (1962) for progesterone concentrations in peripheral blood. During labor, the concentrations of progesterone were lower than at 37 or 39 weeks of pregnancy.

The possible role of progesterone in the initiation of parturition will be discussed later in this chapter.

Hormones, other than the gonadotropins and gonadal steroids, that may play a role in the maintenance of pregnancy are relaxin, adrenal cortical hormones, thyroid hormones, nongonadotropic hypophyseal and placental protein hormones, and pancreatic hormones. The effects of these hormones on reproduction have been discussed in Chapters 6 and 7. However, the effects of relaxin on maintenance of pregnancy require mention here. It is difficult to obtain an estimate of the requirement of relaxin for maintenance of pregnancy because the hormone is produced by the ovary, the placenta, and the uterus. In spayed rabbits, for instance, estrogen plus progesterone treatment results in release of relaxin, a release not found in spayed hysterectomized rabbits (Zarrow, 1961). The requirement for maintenance of pregnancy cannot be ascertained because the uterus is generally required for pregnancy (except in ectopic pregnancies). It has, however, been established that relaxin injections in ovariectomized mice synergize with estradiol and progesterone in maintaining pregnancy.

The concentration of relaxin in the blood of pregnant animals may give a possible indication of its significance. Zarrow (1961) has reviewed the evidence on this aspect of pregnancy hormones. In rabbits, cattle, and humans the relaxin concentration rises throughout gestation and drops shortly before or at parturition. In guinea pigs, a drop in relaxin concentration occurs at day 63 (gestation period 67 to 68 days) and drops to undetectable levels within 48 hours of parturition.

The endocrine function of the human placenta has been reviewed by Diczfalusy (1964), Diczfalusy and Troen (1961), and Diczfalusy et al. (1965).

The HCG is probably secreted by only the cytotrophoblast, but the specific cell type which produces the hormone has not been established. Diczfalusy and Troen (1961), after a critical review, concluded that the evidence designating the Langhans cells as the source of the HCG was insufficient.

The factors regulating HCG production by the placenta remain unknown.

The source of the prolactin-growth hormone complex secreted by the placenta seems not to have been established.

On the basis of perfusion studies of the placenta, it has been shown in different laboratories that the placenta does not carry out the total synthesis of certain steroid hormones, but that it requires extraplacental steroid precursors. In this sense Diczfalusy et al. (1965) do not consider the placenta a "true" endocrine organ but rather an "incomplete" one.

Diczfalusy et al. (1965) have proposed

the following series of events as a hypothesis for the production of the steroidal hormones produced by the placenta:

1. Pregnenolone sulfate from the maternal and the fetal compartments is partly hydrolyzed in the placenta.

2. The placenta converts the pregnenolone to progesterone (after injection of radioactive pregnenolone, 80 percent is converted to progesterone).

3. The progesterone is secreted to the maternal and fetal compartments.

4. Progesterone reaching the fetal adrenals is converted to various corticosteroids.

5. Pregnenolone sulfate is probably metabolized by the fetal adrenals into dehydro-epiandrosterone sulfate (DHEAS) via 17-α-hydroxypregnenolone sulfate; the same conversion may also take place in the maternal compartment.

6. Some of the 17-α-pregnenolone sulfate is hydrolyzed in the placenta to 17-α-hydroxyprogesterone, which is then secreted to the maternal and fetal compartments.

7. DHEAS is hydrolyzed by the placenta and converted into androstenedione, and then further converted into estrone and 17-β-estradiol, which are then secreted into the fetal and maternal blood. A minor part of the androstenedione secreted also reaches both.

8. Estrone and estradiol are sulphurylated in the fetal compartment; upon return to the placenta, a portion is desulphurylated.

9. Estrone sulfate, DHEA, androstenedione, and testosterone are exposed to 16-α-hydroxylation. The 16-α-hydroxylated steroids are converted into phenolic D-ketols and/or estriol in the placenta. The estriol is secreted in both directions. Most of the estriol which reaches the fetus is transferred into estriol sulfate and transported to the placenta where it is hydrolyzed.

Diczfalusy et al. (1965) have emphasized that the findings reported above apply to the human fetal-placental unit at midterm but that modifications may occur during pregnancy so that at term the situation may be quite different.

These investigations show the complicated nature of steroid secretion by the placenta, with different intermediates moving back and forth between fetal and maternal compartments. The role which fetal endocrine organs play in supplying the placenta with the intermediates for further metabolism of the steroid hormones is also demonstrated.

The fetus may have developed to term, which, in viviparous mammals, involves fertilization of the egg, transport to a receptive uterus, implantation, respiratory, and nutritive exchange via the placenta, and correct functioning of the endocrine system. It has yet to be born! The initiation of parturition is still poorly understood, There are a number of factors which have been studied, but the interactions between these factors have not been elucidated.

In only a few non-mammalian viviparous species has the endocrinology of parturition been studied. Ball (1962) found that in the teleost fish *Poecilia latipinna, (Mollienesia latipinna)* hypophysectomy did not prevent expulsion of the matured young from the ovary and oviduct by muscular contractions, although the completeness of the operation was attested by the lack of vitellogenesis. An occasional ovum which had not been fertilized was ovulated at the time the brood was expelled. This type of ovulation thus does not seem to require pituitary gonadotropins. The factors which cause the expulsion of the young remain unknown.

The "birth" of the tadpoles in the marsupial frog has been described by Amoroso (1959). The female immerses the opening of the pouch in pools of water by assuming a praying position. She then opens the lips of the pouch with her hind foot and the tadpoles can emerge. How the female "knows" that the tadpoles are ready to venture out on their own is not established.

Ovariectomy and hypophysectomy, which do not interfere with the maintenance of pregnancy in the snakes *Natrix* sp. and *Thamnophis* sp., do interfere with parturition (Forbes, 1961).

Most of the studies concerning parturition have been carried out with mammals, especially with domestic and laboratory animals and women.

Successful parturition involves dilation of the cervix, adaptation of the pelvis, contraction of the myometrium, and synchronization of the breaking of the union between mother and fetus, and the subsequent first breathing of the newborn.

As was discussed in Chapter 6, relaxin plays an important role in causing dilation of the cervix of the rat, cow, and pig. Progesterone and estrogen are required for a maximal effect in the rat (Zarrow, 1961).

The pelvis of many mammals, especially those which live in burrows, usually is too narrow for normal delivery. The problem of accommodating the young has been solved in different ways in various species. In the American mole *(Scalopus aquaticus)* the pubic arch is cartilaginous and is resorbed in males and females. This process is not endocrine dependent. The pelvis of the pocket gopher *(Geomys bursarius)* is rigid with ossified pubic cartilages when the animal is maturing, but in the female estrogen causes resorption of the pubic bones, and at the first estrus the pelvis becomes open ventrally.

In the mouse and guinea pig the ligaments of the pelvis and of the sacroiliac joint relax under the influence of relaxin, whereas in the ewe elongation of the sacroiliac ligament and relaxation of the sacroiliac joint can be induced by stilbestrol but not by relaxin (Zarrow, 1961).

The expulsion of the fetus requires not only that it pass through the pelvis and the dilated cervix, but also that the uterus contract. There is considerable evidence that such contractions are influenced by hormones, but the exact interactions and the control of hormonal levels for the initiation of parturition are poorly understood.

A few of the in vivo and in vitro experiments that have been carried out in trying to elucidate the control of the myometrium will be mentioned.

1. Uterine strips from castrated or immature rabbits show little motility in vitro and do not develop tension after electric stimulation; neither do they respond to oxytocin administration (Fuchs, 1966).

2. Strips similar to those mentioned under point 1 obtained from estrogen-treated rabbits show spontaneous motility; tension develops to maximal values after electrical stimulation and a strong response to oxytocin is obtained.

3. Treatment of the castrated rabbits with progesterone and estrogen abolishes the spontaneous activity and the response to oxytocin, but the uterine muscle responds to electrical stimulation.

In vivo the same type of relationships exists. The response to oxytocin consists of slowly declining rhythmic contractions which can be distinguished from contractions induced by either histamine, serotonin, acetylcholine, norepinephrine, epinephrine or vasopressin in vivo (Bisset et al., 1966; Fuchs, 1966) and in vitro (Bisset et al., 1966).

Analyses of the physiology of uterine muscle have shown that progesterone decreases the spontaneous contractions of the uteri of rats (Marshall, 1962). This lack of contractions is correlated with an asynchrony between the discharge of trains of action potentials and the mechanical activity of individual muscle fibers. In estrogen-dominated rabbit and rat uteri these discharges and mechanical activity are synchronized (Kuriyama and Csapo, 1961). Progesterone causes a conduction block and an associated increase in membrane potential. The membrane potential of ovariectomized rats was 35.2 mV. After treatment with estradiolbenzoate (6 μg. for five days) the membrane potential rose to 57.6 mV., and after estradiolbenzoate (6 μg. for three days) followed by 1.6 μg. EB plus 12 mg. progesterone for five days the membrane potential increased to 63.8 mV. (Marshall, 1959). Progesterone reduces contractions for mouse uterine (Kuriyama, 1961) and human uterine muscle (Bygdeman and Eliasson, 1964), and affects the electrical discharges of mouse uterine strips similar to the way it does in rats (Kuriyama, 1961).

The effects of estrogen and progesterone described for rabbit uteri in vitro and in vivo also apply to the responses obtained after stimulation of the hypogastric nerves in a uterine muscle hypogastric nerve preparation (Miller and Marshall, 1965).

Saldivar and Melton (1966) found that either estrogen or progesterone inhibited the electrical and the mechanical activity of uterine strips of spayed rats when the hormones were added in vitro. They found, however, no effect upon injection of progesterone (intramuscular, intraluminal and intraperitoneal injections were used). Neither in vitro nor in vivo administration of the hormones affected impulse velocity or minimal shock duration required for obtaining a response. These experiments are at variance with other experiments with respect to the effect of in vivo administered hormones on uterine activity. The reason for the difference is not apparent.

The question arises whether changes in progesterone concentrations in the blood might be causative factors in initiating parturition. As was mentioned previously, blood progesterone concentrations decrease before parturition in the rat and the rabbit. In the rabbit there is the additional evidence that either progesterone (Fuchs and Fuchs, 1958; Short, 1960; see also Amoroso, 1959, pp. 29 to 30) or HCG administration (Snyder, 1938),

which induce new functional corpora lutea, delay parturition. It seems that HCG and progesterone affect survival of the fetuses differently. Snyder (1938) noted that the fetuses, which had been delivered at 35 days, had hair and were alive, and Fuchs and Fuchs (1958) noted a high mortality of the fetuses which had not been delivered. The phenomenon of delayed parturition can be induced by progesterone also in rats (Fitzpatrick, 1966). It should be noted, as others have stated (Short, 1960), that this delayed parturition has been most consistently induced in rabbits and rats, both species in which ovariectomy interrupts pregnancy.

Other species, in which ovariectomy can be carried out without interruption of pregnancy at least at some stage during gestation, do not show delayed parturition after progesterone administration, e.g. cow, sheep, guinea pig, horse, Rhesus monkey, and man (Short, 1960; Fitzpatrick, 1966). Bengtsson and Schofield (1963) reported delay of parturition and high fetal mortality in sheep given 80 to 160 mg. progesterone. Such doses should be considered unphysiological, an interpretation which is supported by the persistent inactivity of the uteri. Short (1960) concluded that progesterone concentration is probably not the important factor in initiating labor in many species.

Csapo (1961) has proposed that placental progesterone may have a local effect on the myometrium so that during parturition contractions are strongest at locations a distance removed from the placenta; these contractions presumably detach the placenta during the final stages of labor (Schofield, 1963) and the entire uterus can contract to expel its contents. Measurements of myometrial activity in rabbits showed indeed that the placental sites differ from intraplacental sites with respect to membrane potential (Goto and Csapo, 1959) and the correlation between tension and frequency of stimulation (staircase effect) (Schofield, 1963). The concept of Csapo will be discussed later in connection with the effect of uterine volume on initiation of labor.

On the basis of indirect evidence, Biggers et al. (1963) suggested that the estrogen secretion increase at the end of pregnancy in mice may initiate parturition by increasing the sensitivity of the myometrium to oxytocin. This hypothesis is supported by the fact that estrogen injections cause abortions in the rat, mouse, rabbit, and cat (Deanesly, 1966); however, in order to be effective the estrogens have to be given early in the gestation period. It has also been noted that estrogen fails to induce abortion in guinea pigs, Rhesus monkeys, and women (Deanesly, 1966).

A third hormone, which has received considerable attention because of its stimulatory effect on the uterine musculature, is oxytocin. If one considers isolated observations in the different classes of animals, one can discern a reasonably consistent pattern that oxytocin or, at least neurohypophyseal hormones, may be involved in the ejection of ova or young. Fitzpatrick (1966) has reviewed much of the evidence, and cases mentioned here have been taken from his review.

In teleost fishes there is evidence which suggests that, in the Japanese rice fish *(Oryzias latipes),* neurohypophyseal extract may, under special experimental conditions, induce oviposition (Egami, 1959).

Hypophysectomy is associated with abnormal parturition in the viviparous snakes *Natrix sipedon* and *Thamnophis sirtalis,* and the lizard *Zootoca vivipara.* This evidence for involvement of hypophyseal hormones in reptiles is strengthened by the evidence that injection of mammalian posterior pituitary extracts can induce parturition in *Natrix* sp., *Storeria* sp., *Thamnophis* sp., and *Zootoca vivipara.*

Oviposition in birds is associated with a decrease in vasotocin content of the posterior pituitary (Fitzpatrick, 1966) and an increase in vasotocin concentration

in the blood (Douglas and Sturkie, 1964; Sturkie and Lin, 1966).

Injections of oxytocin cause premature oviposition (see Fitzpatrick, 1966 and van Tienhoven, 1961). The only weak point in the hypothesis that oviposition is caused by oxytocin lies in the fact that removal of the posterior pituitary does not interfere with oviposition (Shirley and Nalbandov, 1956; Opel, 1965). However, the neurohypophyseal hormones are secreted in the hypothalamus, thus removal of the posterior pituitary would not necessarily interfere with the release of oxytocin, although the release of antidiuretic hormone is inhibited, as is evident from the diuresis found in such chickens (Shirley and Nalbandov, 1956).

In a number of mammals, oxytocin causes uterine contractions provided the uterus is not under the influence of progesterone. The induction of labor by oxytocin has been observed in rabbits (Fitzpatrick, 1966) and guinea pigs (Schofield, 1960), but the effectiveness is smaller as the time interval to the normally expected time of parturition increases (Fuchs, 1964; Fuchs and Fuchs, 1958; Schofield, 1960). In mice, premature expulsion of fetuses has been obtained by combined administration of estrin and oxytocin (Newton, 1935), and in guinea pigs, at midterm, by injection of 5 I.U. of oxytocin (near term 1 I.U. is sufficient).

In women, oxytocin-induced labor is indistinguishable from natural labor in all respects investigated (see Fitzpatrick, 1966). Evidence that oxytocin is released during parturition is found in the milk ejection from lactating women during labor.

Observations have been made on rabbits showing that there is a sudden spurt of increased uterine activity (Fuchs, 1964) and that there is a milk letdown at the time of delivery of the young (Cross, 1958). Similarly, there have been findings of increased oxytocin concentration in the blood of sheep, goats, cattle, and horses during labor (Fitzpatrick, 1966; Folley and Knaggs, 1965; van Dongen and Hays, 1966b). The last named authors used an in vitro assay in which the end point was milk ejection; this assay can detect 1×10^{-12} to 1×10^{-10} I.U./ml. (van Dongen and Hays, 1966a) which is in the range where unextracted blood can be used. In none of the species investigated have there been significant increases in oxytocin concentrations in the blood prior to parturition; the large increases have been found during parturition. It thus seems that oxytocin aids in the expulsion of the young but that it does not initiate it.

The removal of the posterior pituitary from lactating rats interferes with the milk ejection and the dams can nurse the young only if oxytocin is administered. However, if such rats become pregnant later, parturition is normal and the young can subsequently nurse their pups (Benson and Cowie, 1956). The neural stalk shows hypertrophy. These data suggest that under these conditions the neural stalk can reorganize and release oxytocin, although it, apparently, cannot release vasopressin, for the rats show symptoms of diabetes insipidus.

The combination of data in ruminants, horses, and women show that there is neither a decrease in progesterone nor an increase in oxytocin concentration of the blood to account for the initiation of labor.

The question whether hormones initiate labor remains unresolved. Other factors of a nonendocrine nature may play a role in the initiation of labor. A series of classic experiments was carried out in the 1930's to investigate to what extent the placenta and the fetus were required for delivery. It was demonstrated that removal of the young (but leaving the placenta in situ) did not interfere with the delivery of such placenta at the time comparable to when young were delivered in controls. The same was true for ovariectomized rats treated in a similar manner. Paraffin pellets put into the emptied uteri of ovariectomized pregnant rats were expelled within 48 hours, but if they were implanted in one emptied horn and the other horn was left intact, pellets and young were born at the same, normal time (Kirsch, 1938). Thus, in the rat, the fetus is not required for normal parturition to take place, but the placenta is essential. The reason for the initiation of labor was not investigated, except for finding that removal of the placenta caused expulsion of the paraffin pellets.

Similar experiments, in which fetuses were removed but the placenta left intact, were carried out with mice, rabbits, guinea pigs, hamsters, cats, and Rhesus monkeys. Mice and hamsters will retain the placentae after removal of the fetus only if the ovary is present. Guinea pigs retain the placentae not more than five days after removal of the fetuses (see Holm, Zool. Soc. London Symp. 15, 1966, pp. 403–418).

Although the fetus may not be required for initiation of labor, it is conceivable that the number or size of fetuses could affect the time of delivery. There are different kinds of evidence which indicate that such factors may play a role in species other than the rat and that the genotype of the fetus also may be important.

As in most other cases, there are considerable variations among species, and factors which seem important in one species do not seem to be of importance in others.

Biggers et al. (1963), McLaren and Michie (1963), and McLaren (1967) studied the problem of litter size and of the mass of the conceptus on length of gestation in mice. It was first established that there was a negative regression of length of gestation on litter size (Biggers et al., 1963). This effect existed in intact and unilaterally ovariectomized mice (unilateral ovariectomy was performed to confine the embryos to one uterine horn) and the regressions between the two groups were not different (Biggers et al., 1963). These data indicate that crowding and the total number of conceptuses influence the length of gestation, and also that the total number of conceptuses in one horn is not a main factor. In another experiment the fallopian tube was tied off, restricting pregnancy to one horn, but at the same time increasing the number of corpora lutea per fetus. This operation also did not affect the regression of gestation length on number of fetuses. In other experiments with mice, fetal mass was varied without affecting fetal number (by using crosses in which hybrid fetuses were heavier than inbred ones, or by transplanting three and one-half-day-old embryos to uteri of mice pregnant for two and one-half days, thus accelerating development). The heavier young had shorter gestation periods, suggesting that the mass of placenta plus fetus influences the gestation period (McLaren and Michie, 1963). Crosses were made between strains of mice in such a manner that fetal weight was affected but not placental weight. In these crosses the length of gestation was inversely related to the mass of conceptuses (McLaren, 1967). The effect of the male on litter size, noted by Finn (1964) for mice, may have been mediated by an effect on the weight of the fetuses. Unfortunately, no data were reported on the effect of the sire on fetal and placental mass.

Biggers et al. (1963) critically reviewed the evidence on the phenomenon of a negative regression of gestation length on litter size and calculated such regressions from data available in the literature. On the basis of the evidence, it seems that such a regression exists in rabbits, guinea pigs (Deanesly, 1966), cattle, goats, sheep, and women; it also exists in mink (Dukelow, 1966), but is absent in pigs (Biggers et al., 1963; Cox, 1964a). This evidence suggests that the uterine volume, by stretching the uterus, may initiate parturition. This hypothesis has been tested by Csapo and his co-workers in experiments to be discussed:

1. It was first established that ovariectomy of pregnant rabbits resulted in premature delivery in about 48 hours, but that pregnancy could be maintained by progesterone, given in doses which became smaller every day; e.g. the following sequence maintained pregnancy: 2.0, 1.5, 1.25, 1.0, 0.75, and 0.5 mg./day (Csapo and Lloyd-Jacob, 1962, 1963).

2. At the low dose of progesterone, premature parturition occurred when the uterine volume was large, as was evident from:

a. Transfer of fetuses from one horn to the other in ovariectomized rabbits with dislocated placentae (to prevent localized progesterone secretion) maintained on progesterone resulted in delivery of the young of the crowded horn, but those in the uncrowded horn were not expelled. The same phenomenon occurred in rabbits in which one horn happened to contain more embryos than the other, provided that ovariectomized rabbits with dislocated placentae were used (Csapo and Lloyd-Jacob, 1963).

b. A comparison, in spayed rabbits, of horns with and without intact placenta, the horn with the placenta could support a larger volume than the horn without the placenta, at the same dose of exogenous progesterone (Csapo and Lloyd-Jacob, 1963).

c. Removal of all fetuses and placentae and subsequent replacement by paraffin dummy fetuses in such a manner that one horn contained 150 ml. and the other 15 ml. resulted in earlier delivery from the horn with the 150 ml. volume in ovariectomized rabbits on the progesterone treatment outlined above (Csapo and Lloyd-Jacob, 1963).

3. Insertion of a balloon into the uterus of parturient rabbits allowed regulation of the increases in volume of the uterine contents. It was established that an increase in volume to the optimal volume resulted in a greater frequency of spike discharges, a reduction in the delay of mechanical and electrical activity, a slight increase in the resting pressure, and an improvement in active pressure. As the optimal volume was surpassed,

train discharges became very frequent, the resting pressure increased sharply, and the active pressure dropped (Csapo et al., 1963a).

4. Recording of mechanical and electrical activity in pregnant and parturient rabbits (Csapo and Takeda, 1965) showed that:

a. progesterone suppressed electrical and mechanical activity.

b. as the amount of progesterone was decreased, asynchronous activity was generated at different portions of the myometrium, and mechanical activity improved.

c. after progesterone withdrawal action potentials were generated at the pace maker area in the form of regular trains of discharges which were propagated to distant portions. The electrical activity was synchronic and the resulting pressure cycles were of large amplitude and simple shape.

d. cyclic administration of progesterone induced cyclic evolution and suppression of activity.

These experiments support the hypothesis of Csapo (1961) that uterine activity is a function of the ratio $V : P_m$ in which V is the uterine volume and P_m stands for the myometrial progesterone content. This hypothesis was tested on pregnant women (Csapo et al., 1963b). Reduction of the volume by fluid withdrawal via amniocentesis did not induce labor until 13 to 58 hours later, whereas amniotomy resulted in labor four hours later.

In women in labor, withdrawal of amniotic fluid caused irregular uterine activity, and a decrease in the frequency and magnitude of cyclic active pressure. An increase in volume by injection of a glucose solution into the amnion induced labor in women, who were on the verge of being in labor or 1 to 3 days prior to the onset of labor (Csapo et al., 1963b).

Administration of oxytocin at very high doses (62 mU./min.) did not increase active amniotic pressure (21 mm. Hg) in women who were 16 to 24 weeks pregnant. The suppression of placental progesterone by replacing 100 to 200 ml. amniotic fluid by 100 to 200 ml. hypertonic saline resulted, 16 to 22 hours later, in an increase in active amniotic pressure to a level characteristic of first stage labor (30 mm. Hg). Oxytocin (3 mU./min.) increased the pressure to 48 mm. Hg. That the hypertonic saline reduced progesterone production was indicated by a drop in the progesterone concentration of the peripheral blood. The effects of the hypertonic saline could also be prevented in one case by administration of the progestin Provera (Csapo, 1961).

These experiments, in which each component of the ratio $V : P_m$ was experimentally modified, suggest that the hypothesis is substantially correct for rabbits and women. Fitzpatrick (1966) has raised questions about the correctness of the hypothesis that progesterone has a local effect, especially in view of the different types of placentae in which large areas of the uterus are involved. Only experimentation with other species can show the validity of Csapo's hypothesis.

The genotype of the fetus can affect the length of the gestation period, as is evident from the following findings:

1. Male calves are carried 1.97 days longer than heifer calves (Jafar et al., 1950), although they are heavier at birth so that one might have expected earlier birth, assuming that the theory that uterine volume determines the time of parturition was correct. Male foals are also carried longer than the female ones (Rossdale and Short, 1967). However, in sheep the sex of the fetus does not affect the duration of pregnancy (Terrill and Hazel, 1947).

2. Investigations of breeding records of dairy cattle have shown that heritability of the duration of the gestation considered as a fetal characteristic was 0.420, whereas considered as a characteristic of fetus plus dam this value was 0.474, showing that the genotype of the fetus

was a major factor for determining the length of the gestation period (DeFries et al., 1959). The estimate of heritability of the duration of gestation is 0.36 for horses (Rollins and Howell, 1951), 0.30 for swine (Cox, 1964b), between 0.40 and 0.50 for sheep (Terrill and Hazel, 1947), although no effort was made to separate the effect exerted by the fetus from that inherent in the ewe.

3. In Friesian cattle, an autosomal recessive gene present in the fetus prevents normal delivery of the calf. The cow carrying the calf does not show relaxation of the pelvic ligaments, edema of the vulva, softening of the cervix, enlargement of the udder, or a decrease in blood progesterone concentration about ten days prior to parturition (as found in normal cattle) at the time of expected delivery. The fetus is presented to the pelvic inlet but drops back into the abdomen and is not presented again. In order to obtain live fetuses, Cesarean section has to be performed. If the fetus dies in the uterus it is expelled. The affected calves have continued to grow in the uterus, but usually die after delivery as the result of adrenocortical insufficiency (Holm, 1966; Holm and Short, 1962).

In Guernsey cattle a similar lack of parturition at the normal time occurs when the calf is homozygously recessive for a gene which causes cessation of growth at about the seventh month of pregnancy; the affected animals lack a pituitary. The uteri of the dams carrying either the affected Friesian or Guernsey calves are unresponsive to exogenous oxytocin (Holm, 1966).

In sheep the feeding of skunk cabbage (*Veratrum californicum*) between days 1 and 15 of gestation causes abnormalities of the fetus which involve a cyclops-like malformation and absence of the pituitary. Such fetuses are carried longer than normal and may need to be delivered by Cesarean section. If twins are carried and one lamb is normal, length of gestation and parturition are also normal (Binns et al., 1959, 1963).

Liggins et al. (1966) removed the pituitaries of fetal lambs between the ninety-third and one hundred forty-third days of pregnancy (from one lamb when fetuses were twins, and from all but one in cases of multiple births). Ewes carrying hypophysectomized lambs only had prolonged gestations, and the lambs were delivered by Cesarean section, whereas ewes carrying at least one non-hypophysectomized lamb had normal gestation periods, as did sham-operated controls. Infusion of ACTH into one member of the hypophysectomized fetal twins led to parturition on the sixth day. ACTH did not cause parturition if the fetus was hypophysectomized and adrenalectomized. These data offer experimental evidence that the fetal pituitary affects parturition and that the pituitary-adrenal axis is probably the principal factor by which the effect is exerted.

The work by Diczfalusy, which was mentioned earlier, shows that the fetal adrenal is involved in human pregnancy, as it plays a role in the biosynthesis of placental steroids. The exact role of the fetal adrenal of sheep in steroid metabolism is not established, neither is the role it may play at different times during pregnancy; these steps need to be investigated.

As we have seen, the fetal adrenal is not required in all species for normal delivery, as in rats and rabbits paraffin pellets are delivered at the expected end of normal pregnancy, provided the placenta is present.

The season during which insemination occurs has an effect on the length of gestation, but this effect is not observed in all species. Sheep, which have a rather limited breeding season, will have a longer gestation if bred early in the season and a shorter gestation if bred late (Terrill and Hazel, 1947). Cattle, which can be bred throughout the year, do not show an effect of season on length of pregnancy (Jafar et al., 1950). However, in horses a definite effect of season was noted, with a gestation of 328.0 days observed for mares bred in September, October, and November, and a period of 342.2 days for mares bred in March, April, and May. The differences, are highly significant (Howell and Rollins, 1951). This effect is not the result of better nutrition during one season than during another one. In a comparison between mares fed a maintenance ration and well fed mares (and with the effect of season held constant) it was found that the gestation period was four days longer for the mares fed the maintenance ration (Howell and Rollins, 1951).

The hour of the day when parturition occurs is not distributed randomly throughout the 24 hour period. Rossdale and Short (1967) observed that 86 percent of the births of foals took place between 7 p.m. and 7 a.m., with the maximum between 10 and 11 p.m. They point out that animal husbandry practices may, however, have an effect and that close attendance to the mares may shift the foaling to daytime hours. These workers cite literature that such distributions, although not as pronounced, also occur in women, pigs, mice, and Chinese hamsters, and that in sheep and golden hamsters births take place most frequently during daytime hours; for cattle the distribution of parturitions is about evenly distributed over the 24 hour period. The mechanisms that regulate the onset of parturition during certain hours of the day have not been elucidated.

In view of the available evidence on an admittedly small number of species, mostly the rabbit, the rat, and the human), it seems that successful labor under natural conditions is caused by an interaction of the following factors, sometimes working simultaneously and other times in sequence:

1. Dilation of the cervix, so that the fetus can pass into the vagina; this dilation is not a requirement for contractions of the uterus and thus not required for the initiation of labor in the strict sense of the word; for normal childbirth it is, however, a necessity. This dilation seems to be largely under the control of estrogen, progesterone, and relaxin. The reasons for the changes in concentrations of these hormones before, during, and after labor are incompletely understood.

2. An increase in the volume of the uterine contents and a decrease in progesterone secretion either by the ovary, or the placenta, or both combined to change the ratio $V : P_m$ so that uterine contractions are initiated. The evidence for this has been discussed. The reasons for the decrease in progesterone concentration by the placenta, which would be most effective because of the local effect, are not obvious, however. Once contractions have started and the placenta becomes dislodged, further decrease can be explained by the reduction in progesterone-producing centers.

3. The uterus is not under the influence of progesterone and may become an estrogen-dominated uterus. In the estrogen-treated, spayed rabbit, stretching the uterus induces increased rhythmic activity of the uterus. Rapid distension is followed by an early stretch response and subsequently an increased rhythmic activity; a slowly increasing distension causes an increase in the frequency of contractions. The response is myogenic in origin (Setekleiv, 1964). It is conceivable that such contractions once started may cause a release of oxytocin, which then, in turn, would increase the contractions by the uterus.

4. Passage of the fetus through the cervix does not seem to affect uterine contractions. In postpartum rabbits, distension of one horn does not cause contractions in the other horn (Fuchs et al., 1965).

5. Distension of the vagina by the fetus causes uterine contractions which, in rabbits, are similar to epinephrine-induced contractions (Fuchs et al., 1965). In cattle, Debackere and Peeters (1960) could record oxytocin release after distension of the vagina of cows. This dis-

tension may be partly responsible for the increase in oxytocin concentrations of the blood observed during labor. Oxytocin release, if it occurs, increases the uterine contractions and aids in expelling the fetus.

The manner in which other factors, such as the genotype of the fetus, exert their effect is speculative, but may involve the endocrine organs of the fetus. Obviously, species differences are very important, for in rats and rabbits paraffin dummies can replace the fetuses without having an effect on the date of parturition, whereas in sheep and cattle the absence of the pituitary causes prolonged parturition.

REFERENCES

Alden, R. H. 1942a. Aspects of the egg-ovary-oviduct relationship in the albino rat. I. Egg passage and development following ovariectomy. J. Exp. Zool. 90:159-169.

Alden, R. H. 1942b. Aspects of the egg-ovary-oviduct relationship in the albino rat. II. Egg development within the oviduct. J. Exp. Zool. 90:171-181.

Altman, P. L., and Dittmer, D. S. 1962. Growth. Fed. Amer. Soc. Exp. Biol. Washington, D. C.

Amoroso, E. C. 1952. Placentation. In A. S. Parkes (ed.): Marshall's Physiology of Reproduction. Longmans Green & Co. Ltd., London, Vol. 2, pp. 127-311.

Amoroso, E. C. 1959. The biology of the placenta. Fifth conference on gestation. In C. A. Villee (ed.): Gestation. Josiah Macy Jr. Foundation, New York.

Amoroso, E. C., and Porter, D. G. 1966. Anterior pituitary function in pregnancy. In G. W. Harris and B. T. Donovan (eds.): The Pituitary Gland. University of California Press, Berkeley, Vol. 2, pp. 364-411.

Asdell, S. A. 1964. Patterns of Mammalian Reproduction. Ed. 2, Cornell University Press, Ithaca.

Austin, C. R. 1965. Fertilization. Prentice-Hall Inc., New York.

Averill, S. C., Ray, E.W., and Lyons, W. R. 1950. Maintenance of pregnancy in hypophysectomized rats with placental implants. Proc. Soc. Exp. Biol. Med. 75:3-6.

Ball, J. N. 1962. Brood-production after hypophysectomy in the viviparous teleost, *Mollienesia latipinna* Le Sueur. Nature 194:787.

Banik, U. K., and Ketchel, M. M. 1964. Inability of histamine to induce deciduomata in pregnant and pseudopregnant rats. J. Reprod. Fertil. 7:259-261.

Bengtsson, L. P., and Schofield, B. M. 1963. Progesterone and the accomplishment of parturition in the sheep. J. Reprod. Fertil. 5:423-431.

Benson, G. K., and Cowie, A. T. 1956. Lactation in the rat after hypophysial posterior lobectomy. J. Endocrinol. 14:54-65.

Biggers, J. D., Curnow, R. N., Finn, C. A., and McLaren, A. 1963. Regulation of the gestation period in mice. J. Reprod. Fertil. 6:125-138.

Binns, W., James, L. F., Shupe, J. L., and Everett, G. 1963. A congenital cyclopian-type malformation in lambs induced by maternal ingestion of a range plant *Veratrum californicum*. Amer. J. Vet. Res. 24:1164-1175.

Binns, W., Thacker, E. J., James, L. F., and Huffman, W. T. 1959. A congenital cyclopian-type malformation in lambs. J. Amer. Vet. Med. Ass. 134:180-183.

Bisset, G. W., Haldar, J., and Lewin, J. E. 1966. Actions of oxytocin and other biologically active peptides on the rat uterus. Mem. Soc. Endocrinol. 14:185-197.

Björkman, N. 1965. Fine structure of the ovine placentome. J. Anat. 99:283-297.

Björkman, N., and Bloom, G. 1957. On the fine structure of the foetal-maternal junction in the bovine placentome. Z. Zellforsch. 45:649-659.

Bland, K. P., and Donovan, B. T. 1965. Experimental ectopic implantation of eggs and early embryos in guinea-pigs. J. Reprod. Fertil. 10:189-196.

Blandau, R. J. 1961. Biology of eggs and implantation. In W. C. Young (ed.): Sex and Internal Secretions. Williams & Wilkins Co., Baltimore, Vol. 2, pp. 797-882.

Böving, B. G. 1954. Blastocyst-uterine relationships. Cold Spring Harbor Symp. Quant. Biol. 19: 9-25.

Böving, B. G. 1956. Rabbit blastocyst distribution. Amer. J. Anat. 98:403-434.

Böving, B. G. 1959. Endocrine influences on implantation. In C. W. Lloyd (ed.): Recent Progress in the Endocrinology of Reproduction. Academic Press Inc., New York, pp. 205-224.

Böving, B. G. 1962. Anatomical analysis of rabbit trophoblast invasion. Contribution to Embryol. Carnegie Inst. of Washington 38:254.

Boyd, J. D., and Hamilton, W. J. 1952. Cleavage, early development and implantation of the egg. In A. S. Parkes (ed.): Marshall's Physiology of Reproduction. Longmans Green & Co. Ltd., London, Vol. 2, pp. 1-126.

Briones, H., and Beatty, R. A. 1954. Interspecific transfer of rodent eggs. J. Exp. Zool. 125:99.

Buchanan, G. D., Enders, A. C., and Talmage, R. V. 1956. Implantation in armadillos ovariectomized during the period of delayed implantation. J. Endocrinol. 14:121-129.

Bygdeman, M., and Eliasson, R. 1964. Effect of progesterone and oestrone on the motility and reactivity of the pregnant human myometrium *in vitro*. J. Reprod. Fertil. 7:47-52.

Canivenc, R. 1960. L'ovo implantation différée des animaux sauvages. Les fonctions de nidation utérine et leurs troubles. Masson et Cie, Paris, pp. 33-86.

Canivenc, R. 1965. La fonction lutéale des mammifères sauvages à nidation différée. Arch.

Anat. Microscop. Morphol. Exp. *54*:105-118.

Canivenc, R. 1966. A study of progestation in the European badger *(Meles meles* L.*).* Symp. Zool. Soc. London *15*:15-26.

Canivenc, R., and Bonnin-Laffargue, M. 1963. Inventory of problems raised by the delayed ovo-implantation in the European badger *(Meles meles* L.*). In* A. C. Enders (ed.): Delayed Implantation. University of Chicago Press, Chicago, pp. 115-125.

Canivenc, R., Bonnin-Laffargue, M., and Lajus, M. 1967. Action locale de la progestérone sur l'utérus de blaireau pendant la phase diapause blastocytaire. C. R. Acad. Sci. *264*:1308-1310.

Canivenc, R., Short, R. V., and Bonnin-Laffargue, M. 1966. Étude histologique et biochimique du corps jaune du Blaireau européen *(Meles meles* L.*).* Ann. Endocrinol. *27*:401-413.

Carey, H. M. 1963. Progesterone. *In* H. M. Carey (ed.): Modern Trends in Human Reproductive Physiology. Butterworth and Co. Ltd., London, pp. 92-112.

Chang, M. C. 1950. Development and fate of transferred rabbit ova or blastocyst in relation to the ovulation time of recipients. J. Exp. Zool. *114*:197-225.

Chang, M. C. 1965a. Artificial insemination of snowshoe hares *(Lepus americanus)* and the transfer of their fertilized eggs to the rabbit *(Oryctolagus cuniculus).* J. Reprod. Fertil. *10*:447-449.

Chang, M. C. 1965b. Implantation of ferret ova fertilized by mink sperm. J. Exp. Zool. *160*:67-80.

Chang, M. C. 1966. Reciprocal transplantation of eggs between rabbit and ferret. J. Exp. Zool. *161*:297-305.

Chang, M. C., and Harper, M. J. K. 1966. Effects of ethinyl estradiol on egg transport and development in the rabbit. Endocrinology *78*: 860-872.

Child, G., and Mossman, A. S. 1965. Right horn implantation in the common duiker. Science *149*:1265-1266.

Cochrane, R. L., and Shackelford, R. M. 1962. Effects of exogenous estrogen alone and in combination with progesterone on pregnancy in the intact mink. J. Endocrinol. *25*:101-106.

Coppola, J. A., Ball, J. L., and Brown, H. W. 1966. The incidence of spontaneous deciduomata in pseudopropregnant *(sic)* rats. J. Reprod. Fertil. *12*:389-390.

Cox, D. F. 1964a. Relation of litter size and other factors to the duration of gestation in the pig. J. Reprod. Fertil. *7*:405-407.

Cox, D. F. 1964b. Genetic variation in the gestation period of swine. J. Anim. Sci. *23*:746-751.

Creed, R. F. S., and Biggers, J. D. 1964. Placental haemophagous organs in the procyonidae and mustelidae. J. Reprod. Fertil. *8*:133-137.

Cross, B. A. 1958. On the mechanism of labour in the rabbit. J. Endocrinol. *16*:261-271.

Csapo, A. 1961. Defence mechanism of pregnancy. CIBA Found. Study Group No. *9*:3-27. Little, Brown, & Co. Inc., Boston.

Csapo, A. I., and Lloyd-Jacob, M. A. 1962. Placenta, uterine volume and the control of the pregnant uterus in rabbits. Amer. J. Obstet. Gynec. *83*:1073-1082.

Csapo, A. I., and Lloyd-Jacob, M. A. 1963. Effect of uterine volume on parturition. Amer. J. Obstet. Gynec. *85*:806-812.

Csapo, A. I., and Takeda, H. 1965. Effect of progesterone on the electric activity and intrauterine pressure of pregnant and parturient rabbits. Amer. J. Obstet. Gynec. *91*:221-231.

Csapo, A. I., Takeda, H., and Wood, C. 1963a. Volume and activity of the parturient rabbit uterus. Amer. J. Obstet. Gynec. *85*:813-818.

Csapo, A. I., Jaffin, H., Kerenyi, T., Lipman, J. I., and Wood, C. 1963b. Volume and activity of the pregnant human uterus. Amer. J. Obstet. Gynec. *85*:819-835.

Dancis, J. 1964. The perfusion of guinea pig placenta in situ. Fed. Proc. *23*:781-784.

Daniel, J. C., and Levy, J. D. 1964. Action of progesterone as a cleavage inhibitor of rabbit ova *in vitro.* J. Reprod. Fertil. *7*:323-329.

Deanesly, R. 1960. Implantation and early pregnancy in ovariectomized guinea pigs. J. Reprod. Fertil. *1*:242-248.

Deanesly, R. 1963. The corpus luteum hormone during and after ovo-implantation: An experimental study of its mode of action in the guinea pig. *In* A. C. Enders (ed.): Delayed Implantation. University of Chicago Press, Chicago, pp. 253-261.

Deanesly, R. 1966. The endocrinology of pregnancy and foetal life. *In* A. S. Parkes (ed.): Marshall's Physiology of Reproduction. Longmans, Green and Co., London, Vol. 3, pp. 891-1063.

Debackere, M., and Peeters, G. 1960. The influence of vaginal distension on milk ejection and diuresis in the lactating cow. Arch. Int. Pharmacodyn. *123*:462-471.

DeFries, J. C., Touchberry, R. W., and Hays, R. L. 1959. Heritability of the length of the gestation period in dairy cattle. J. Dairy Sci. *42*:598-608.

Dickmann, Z., and De Feo, V. J. 1967. The rat blastocyst during normal pregnancy and during delayed implantation including an observation on the shedding of the zona pellucida. J. Reprod. Fertil. *13*:3-9.

Diczfalusy, E. 1964. Endocrine function of the human fetoplacental unit. Fed. Proc. *23*:791-798.

Diczfalusy, E., and Troen, P. 1961. Endocrine functions of the human placenta. Vitamins and Hormones *19*:229-311.

Diczfalusy, E., Pion, R., and Schwers, J. 1965. Steroid biogenesis and metabolism in the human foetoplacental unit at midpregnancy. Arch. Anat. Microscop. Morphol. Exp. *54*:67-84.

Douglas, D. S., and Sturkie, P. D. 1964. Plasma levels of antidiuretic hormone during oviposition. Fed. Proc. *23*:150 (abstract).

Dukelow, W. R. 1966. Variations in gestation length of mink *(Mustela vison).* Nature *211*:211.

Duncan, G. W., Cornette, J. C., Lyster, S. C., Northam, J. I., and Wyngarden, L. 1966. Biochemical aspects of rat deciduomata as affected by oxazolidinethione. Amer. J. Physiol. *211*:184-192.

Dziuk, P. J., Polge, C., and Rowson, L. E. 1964.

Intra-uterine migration and mixing of embryos in swine following egg transfer. J. Anim. Sci. *23*:37-42.

Eaton, G. J., and Green, M. M. 1963. Giant cell differentiation and lethality of homozygous *yellow* mouse embryos. Genetica *34*:155-161.

Edgar, D. G., and Ronaldson, J. W. 1958. Blood levels of progesterone in the ewe. J. Endocrinol. *16*:378-384.

Egami, N. 1959. Preliminary note on the injection of the spawning reflex and oviposition in *Oryzias latipes* by the administration of neurohypophyseal substances. Annot. Zool. Jap. *32*:13-17.

Elton, R. L. 1966. Induction of deciduoma in rabbits: The effect of dose of progesterone, time of trauma, nature of trauma and role played by oestrogens. Acta Endocrinol. *51*:551-556.

Enders, A. C. 1965. A comparative study of the fine structure of the trophoblast in several hemochorial placentas. Amer. J. Anat. *116*:29-67.

Enders, A. C. 1966. The reproductive cycle of the nine-banded armadillo *(Dasypus novemcinctus)*. Symp. Zool. Soc. London *15*:295-310.

Enders, A. C., and Schlafke, S. 1967. A morphological analysis of the early implantation stages in the rat. Amer. J. Anat. *120*:185-226.

Fawcett, D. W. 1950. The development of mouse ova under the capsule of the kidney. Anat. Rec. *108*:71-91.

Fawcett, D. W., Wislocki, G. B., and Waldo, C. M. 1947. The development of mouse ova in the anterior chamber of the eye and in the abdominal cavity. Amer. J. Anat. *81*:413-443.

Finn, C. A. 1964. Influence of the male on litter size in mice. J. Reprod. Fertil. *7*:107-111.

Finn, C. A., and Keen, P. M. 1962. Failure of histamine to induce deciduomata in the rat. Nature *194*:602.

Fitzpatrick, R. J. 1966. The posterior pituitary gland and the female reproductive tract. *In* G. W. Harris and B. T. Donovan (eds.): The Pituitary Gland. University of California Press, Berkeley, Vol. 3, pp. 453-504.

Folley, S. J., and Knaggs, G. S. 1965. Levels of oxytocin in the jugular vein blood of goats during parturition. J. Endocrinol. *33*:301-315.

Forbes, T. R. 1961. Endocrinology of reproduction in cold-blooded vertebrates. *In* W. C. Young (ed.): Sex and Internal Secretions. Williams & Wilkins Co., Baltimore, Vol. 2, pp. 1035-1087.

Fuchs, A. R. 1964. Oxytocin and the onset of labour in rabbits. J. Endocrinol. *30*:217-224.

Fuchs, A. R. 1966. The physiological role of oxytocin in the regulation of myometrial activity in the rabbit. Mem. Soc. Endocrinol. *14*:229-245.

Fuchs, A. R., Olsen, P., and Petersen, K. 1965. Effect of distension of uterus and vagina on uterine motility and oxytocin release in puerperal rabbits. Acta Endocrinol. *50*:239-248.

Fuchs, F., and Fuchs, A. R. 1958. Induction and inhibition of labour in the rabbit. Acta Endocrinol. *29*:615-624.

Gilbert, P. W., and Schlernitzauer, D. A. 1966. The placid and gravid uterus of *Carcharhinus falciformis*. Copeia *3*:451-457.

Goto, M., and Csapo, A. 1959. The effect of ovarian steroids on the membrane potential of uterine muscle. J. Gen. Physiol. *43*:455-466.

Greenwald, G. S. 1957. Interruption of pregnancy in the rabbit by estrogen. J. Exp. Zool. *135*: 461-481.

Greenwald, G. S. 1967. Species differences in egg transport in response to exogenous estrogen. Anat. Rec. *157*:163-172.

Grota, L. J., and Eik-Nes, K. B. 1967. Plasma progesterone concentrations during pregnancy and lactation in the rat. J. Reprod. Fertil. *13*:83-91.

Hafez, E. S. E. 1962. Endocrine control of reception, transport, development and loss of rabbit ova. J. Reprod. Fertil. *3*:14-25.

Hafez, E. S. E. 1964a. Effects of over-crowding *in utero* on implantation and fetal development in the rabbit. J. Exp. Zool. *156*:269-288.

Hafez, E. S. E. 1964b. Transuterine migration and spacing of bovine embryos during gonadotrophin-induced multiple pregnancy. Anat. Rec. *148*:203-208.

Hafez, E. S. E., Tsutsumi, Y., and Khan, M. A. 1965. Progestin levels in the ovaries and ovarian effluent blood in pregnant rabbits. Proc. Soc. Exp. Biol. Med. *120*:75-78.

Hagerman, D. D. 1964. Enzymatic capabilities of the placenta. Fed. Proc. *23*:785-790.

Hammond, J., Jr. 1951. Failure of progesterone treatment to affect delayed implantation in the mink. J. Endocrinol. *7*:330-334.

Hansson, A. 1947. The physiology of reproduction in mink (Mustela vison, Scheb) with special reference to delayed implantation. Acta Zool. *28*:1-136.

Harper, M. J. K. 1966. Hormonal control of transport of eggs in cumulus through the ampulla of the rabbit oviduct. Endocrinol. *78*:568-574.

Harper, M. J. K. 1967. Deciduomal response in ovariectomized pseudopregnant rats given oestrone and progesterone. Acta Endrocrinol. *54*:241-248.

Harper, M. J. K., Prostkoff, B., and Reeve, R. J. 1966. Implantation and embryonic development in the ovariectomized hamster. Acta Endocrinol. *52*:465-470.

Harper, M. J. K., Bennett, J. P., Boursnell, J. C., and Rowson, L. E. A. 1960. An autoradiographic method for the study of egg transport in the rabbit fallopian tube. J. Reprod. Fertil. *1*:249-267.

Harrison, R. J. 1963. A comparison of factors involved in delayed implantation in badgers and seals in Great Britain. *In* A. C. Enders (ed.): Delayed Implantation. University of Chicago Press, pp. 99-114.

Harrison, R. J., Matthews, L. H., and Roberts, J. M. 1952. Reproduction in some Pinnipedia. Trans. Zool. Soc. London *27*:437-540.

Heap, R. B., and Deanesly, R. 1966. Progesterone in systemic blood and placentae of intact and ovariectomized pregnant guinea pigs. J. Endocrinol. *34*:417-424.

Heap, R. B., and Linzell, J. L. 1966. Arterial concentration, ovarian secretion and mammary uptake of progesterone in goats during the reproductive cycle. J. Endocrinol. *36*:389-399.

Holm, L. W. 1966. The gestation period of mammals. Zool. Soc. London Symp. *15*:403-418.

Holm, L. W., and Short, R. V. 1962. Progesterone in the peripheral blood of Guernsey and Friesian cows during prolonged gestation. J. Reprod. Fertil. *4*:137-141.

Howell, C. E., and Rollins, W. C. 1951. Environmental sources of variation in the gestation length of the horse. J. Anim. Sci. *10*:789-796.

Huggett, A. S. G. 1959. Aspects of placental function. Ann. N. Y. Acad. Sci. *75*:873-888.

Huggett, A. S. G., and Hammond, J. 1952. Physiology of the placenta. *In* A. S. Parkes (ed.): Marshall's Physiology of Reproduction. Longmans Green & Co. Ltd., London, Vol. 2, pp. 312-441.

Jafar, S. M., Chapman, A. B., and Casida, L. E. 1950. Causes of variation in length of gestation of dairy cattle. J. Anim. Sci. *9*:593-601.

Jollie, W. P. 1961. The incidence of experimentally produced abdominal implantations in the rat. Anat. Rec. *141*:159-167.

Kenneth, J. H. 1947. Gestation periods. Techn. Communication No. 5. Imperial Bureau of Animal Breeding and Genetics, Edinburgh.

Ketchel, M. M., Banik, U. K., and Mantalenakis, S. J. 1966. A study of delayed implantation caused by parabiosis in pregnant rats. J. Reprod. Fertil. *11*:213-219.

Kirby, D. R. S. 1960. Development of mouse eggs beneath the kidney capsule. Nature *187*: 707-708.

Kirby, D. R. S. 1962a. Reciprocal transplantation of blastocysts between rats and mice. Nature *194*:785-786.

Kirby, D. R. S. 1962b. The influence of uterine environment on the development of mouse eggs. J. Embryol. Exp. Morphol. *10*:496-506.

Kirby, D. R. S. 1963a. Development of the mouse blastocyst transplanted to the spleen. J. Reprod. Fertil. *5*:1-12.

Kirby, D. R. S. 1963b. Development of mouse blastocysts transplanted to the scrotal and cryptorchid testis. J. Anat. *97*:119-130.

Kirby, D. R. S. 1965. The role of the uterus in the early stages of mouse development. *In* G. E. W. Wolstenholme and M. O'Connor (eds.): Preimplantation Stages of Pregnancy. Little, Brown, and Company, Boston, pp. 325-339.

Kirsch, R. E. 1938. A study of the control of length of gestation in the rat with notes on maintenance and termination of gestation. Amer. J. Physiol. *122*:86-93.

Kuriyama, H. 1961. The effect of progesterone and oxytocin on the mouse myometrium. J. Physiol. *159*:26-39.

Kuriyama, H., and Csapo, A. 1961. A study of the parturient uterus with the micro electrode technique. Endocrinol. *68*:1010-1025.

Liggins, G. C., Holm, L. W., and Kennedy, P. C. 1966. Prolonged pregnancy following surgical lesions of foetal lamb pituitary. J. Reprod. Fertil. *12*:419 (abstract).

Lindner, H. R., Sass, M. B., and Morris, B. 1964.

Steroids in the ovarian lymph and blood of conscious ewes. J. Endocrinol. *30*:361-376.

Lyons, W. R. 1943. Pregnancy maintained in hypophysectomized oophorectomized rats injected with oestrone and progesterone. Proc. Soc. Exp. Biol. Med. *54*:65-68.

Lyons, W. R., Simpson, M. E., and Evans, H. M. 1943. Hormonal requirements for pregnancy and mammary development in hypophysectomized rats. Proc. Soc. Exp. Biol. Med. *52*:134-136.

Macdonald, G. J., and Greep, R. O. 1966. Role of LH in blastocyst implantation. Fed. Proc. *25*:316 (abstract).

MacDonald, G. J., Armstrong, D. T., and Greep, R. O. 1967. Initiation of blastocyst implantation by luteinizing hormone. Endocrinol. *80*:172-176.

McGaughey, R. W., and Daniel, J. C., Jr. 1966. Effect of oestradiol-17-β on fertilized rabbit eggs in vitro. J. Reprod. Fertil. *11*:325-331.

McLaren, A. 1967. Effect of foetal mass on gestation period in mice. J. Reprod. Fertil. *13*:349-351.

McLaren, A., and Michie, D. 1963. Nature of systemic effect of litter size on gestation period in mice. J. Reprod. Fertil. *6*:139-141.

McLaren, A., and Tarkowski, A. K. 1963. Implantation of mouse eggs in the peritoneal cavity. J. Reprod. Fertil. *6*:385-392.

Mantalenakis, S. J., and Ketchel, M. M. 1966. Frequency and extent of delayed implantation in lactating rats and mice. J. Reprod. Fertil. *12*:391-394.

Marshall, J. M. 1959. Effects of estrogen and progesterone on single uterine muscle fibers in the rat. Amer. J. Physiol. *197*:935-942.

Marshall, J. M. 1962. Regulation of activity in uterine smooth muscle. Physiol. Revs. *42*:213-227.

Matthews, L. H. 1955. The evolution of viviparity in vertebrates. Mem. Soc. Endocrinol. *4*:129-144.

Mayer, G. 1963. Delayed nidation in rats: a method of exploring the mechanisms of ovo-implantation. *In* A. C. Enders (ed.): Delayed Implantation. University of Chicago Press, pp. 213-228.

Mayer, G. 1965. Tranquilizers and nidation. *In* C. R. Austin and J. W. Perry (eds.): Agents Affecting Fertility. J. and A. Churchill, Ltd., London, pp. 290-306.

Metcalfe, J., Moll, W. and Bartels, H. 1964. Gas exchange across the placenta. Fed. Proc. *23*: 774-780.

Miller, M. D., and Marshall, J. M. 1965. Uterine response to nerve stimulation in relation to hormonal status and catecholamines. Amer. J. Physiol. *209*:859-865.

Mutere, F. A. 1965. Delayed implantation in an equatorial fruit bat. Nature *207*:780.

Nalbandov, A. V. 1964. Reproductive Physiology. Ed. 2, W. H. Freeman and Co., San Francisco.

Newton, W. H. 1935. "Pseudo-parturition" in the mouse and the relation of the placenta to postpartum oestrus. J. Physiol. *84*:196-207.

Nicholas, J. S. 1934. Experiments on developing rats. I Limits to foetal regeneration, behavior of embryonic material in abnormal environments. Anat. Rec. *58*:387-413.

Nicholas, J. S. 1942. Experiments on developing rats. IV The growth and differentiation of eggs and egg cylinders when transplanted under the kidney capsule. J. Exp. Zool. *41*:71.

Nicholas, J. S. 1950. Experiments on developing rats. VII Transplantations to intestinal mucosa. J. Exp. Zool. *113*:741-759.

Noble, G. K. 1954. The Biology of the Amphibia. Dover Publications, New York.

Noyes, R. W., Dickmann, Z., Doyle, L. L., and Gates, A. H. 1963. Ovum transfers, synchronous and asynchronous, in the study of implantation. *In* A. C. Enders (ed.): Delayed Implantation. University of Chicago Press, pp. 197-209.

Nutting, E. F., and Meyer, R. K. 1963. Implantation delay, nidation and embryonal survival in rats treated with ovarian hormones. *In* A. C. Enders (ed.): Delayed Implantation. University of Chicago Press, Chicago, pp. 233-251.

Okano, K., Matsumoto, K., Kotoh, K., and Endo, H. 1966. Progestins in the ovarian vein blood of nonpregnant and pregnant rabbits before and after gonadotropic stimulation. Endocrinol. Jap. *13*:438-447.

Opel, H. 1965. Oviposition in chickens after removal of the posterior lobe of the pituitary by an improved method. Endocrinology *76*:673-677.

Orsini, M. W. 1963. Attempted decidualization in the hamster and the rat with pyrathiazine. J. Reprod. Fertil. *5*:323-330.

Pencharz, R. I., and Lyons, W. R. 1934. Hypophysectomy in the pregnant guinea pig. Proc. Soc. Exp. Biol. Med. *31*:1131-1132.

Prassad, M. R. N., Orsini, M. W., and Meyer, R. K. 1960. Nidation of progesterone-treated, estrogen-deficient hamsters. *Mesocricetus auratus* (Waterhouse). Proc. Soc. Exp. Biol. Med. *104*:48-51.

Psychoyos, A. 1965a. Contrôle de la nidation chez les mammifères. Arch. Anat. Microscop. Morphol. Exp. *54*:85-102.

Psychoyos, A. 1965b. Neurohormonal aspects of implantation. Proc. Second Int. Congr. Endocrinol. *1*:508-512.

Psychoyos, A. 1966. Influence of oestrogen on the loss of the zona pellucida in the rat. Nature *211*:864.

Rollins, W. C., and Howell, C. E. 1951. Genetic sources of variation in the gestation length of the horse. J. Anim. Sci. *10*:797-805.

Romanoff, E. B., Deshpande, N., and Pincus, G. 1962. Rate of ovarian progesterone secretion in the dog. Endocrinology *70*:532-539.

Rossdale, P. D., and Short, R. V. 1967. The time of foaling of thoroughbred mares. J. Reprod. Fertil. *13*:341-343.

Rowson, L. E. A., and Moor, R. M. 1966. Embryo transfer in the sheep: The significance of synchronizing oestrus in the donor and recipient animal. J. Reprod. Fertil. *11*:207-212.

Runner, M. N. 1947. Development of mouse eggs in the anterior chamber of the eye. Anat. Rec. *98*:1-17.

Saldivar, J. T., Jr., and Melton, C. E., Jr. 1966. Effects in vivo and in vitro of sex steroids on the myometrium. Amer. J. Physiol. *211*:835-843.

Schlernitzauer, D. A., and Gilbert, P. W. 1966. Placentation and associated aspects of gestation in the bonnethead shark, *Sphyrna tiburo*. J. Morphol. *120*:219-232.

Schofield, B. M. 1960. Myometrial activity in the pregnant guinea pig. J. Endocrinol. *30*:347-354.

Schofield, B. M. 1963. The local effect of the placenta on myometrial activity in the rabbit. J. Physiol. *166*:191-196.

Selye, H., Collip, J. B., and Thompson, D. L. 1933. Effect of hypophysectomy upon pregnancy and lactation. Proc. Soc. Exp. Biol. Med. *30*:589-590.

Setekleiv, J. 1964. Uterine motility of estrogenized rabbit. II Response to distension. Acta Physiol. Scand. *62*:79-93.

Sharman, G. B. 1963. Delayed implantation in marsupials. *In* A. C. Enders (ed.): Delayed Implantation. University of Chicago Press, pp. 3-14.

Sharman, G. B. 1965. Marsupials and the evolution of viviparity. *In* J. D. Carthy and C. L. Duddington (eds.): Viewpoints in Biology. Butterworth & Co., London, Vol. 4, pp. 1-28.

Sharman, G. B., Callaby, J. H., and Poole, W. E. 1965. Patterns of reproduction in female diprodont marsupials. J. Reprod. Fertil. *9*:375-376.

Shelesnyak, M. C. 1965. Inhibition of decidualization. *In* C. R. Austin and J. S. Perry (eds.): Agents Affecting Fertility. J. & A. Churchill Ltd., London, pp. 275-289.

Shelesnyak, M. C., and Kraicer, P. F. 1963. The role of estrogen in nidation. *In* A. C. Enders (ed.): Delayed Implantation. University of Chicago Press, pp. 265-274.

Shirley, H. V., and Nalbandov, A. V. 1956. Effects of neurohypophysectomy in domestic chickens. Endocrinology *58*:477-483.

Short, R. V. 1960. Blood progesterone levels in relation to parturition. J. Reprod. Fertil. *1*:61-70.

Short, R. V., and Eckstein, P. 1961. Oestrogen and progesterone levels in pregnant Rhesus monkeys. J. Endocrinol. *12*:15-22.

Short, R. V., and Hay, M. F. 1965. Delayed implantation in the roe deer, *Capreolus capreolus*. J. Reprod. Fertil. *9*:372-374.

Short, R. V., and Hay, M. F. 1966. Delayed implantation in the roe deer, *Capreolus capreolus*. Symp. Zool. Soc. London, *15*:173-194.

Short, R. V., and Levett, I. 1962. The fluorimetric determination of progesterone in human plasma during pregnancy and the menstrual cycle. J. Endocrinol. *25*:239-244.

Short, R. V., and Moore, N. W. 1959. Progesterone in blood. V. Progesterone and 20α-hydroxypregn-4-en-3-one in the placenta and blood of ewes. J. Endocrinol. *19*:288-293.

Sinha, A. A., and Mossman, H. W. 1966. Placentation of the sea otter. Amer. J. Anat. *119*:521-554.

Slough, J. S., Schuetz, A. W., and Meyer, R. K. 1965. Induction of implantation in the hypophysectomized rat with gonadotrophins. Proc. Soc. Exp. Biol. Med. *120*:458-463.

Snyder, F. F. 1938. Factors concerned in the duration of pregnancy. Physiol. Rev. *18*:578-596.

Sturkie, P. D., and Lin, Y. C. 1966. Release of vasotocin and oviposition in the hen. J. Endocrinol. *35*:325-326.

Szego, C. M. 1965. Role of histamine in mediation of hormone action. Fed. Proc. *24*:1343-1352.

Terrill, C. E., and Hazel, L. N. 1947. Length of gestation in range sheep. Amer. J. Vet. Res. *8*:66-71.

Turner, C. L. 1947. Viviparity in teleost fishes. Sci. Monthly *65*:508-518.

Tyndale-Biscoe, C. H. 1963a. Effects of ovariectomy in the marsupial *Setonix brachyurus*. J. Reprod. Fertil. *6*:25-40.

Tyndale-Biscoe, C. H. 1963b. Blastocyst transfer in the marsupial *Setonix brachyurus,* J. Reprod. Fertil. *6*:41-48.

van Dongen, C. G., and Hays, R. L. 1966a. A sensitive *in vitro* assay for oxytocin. Endocrinology *78*:1-6.

van Dongen, C. G., and Hays, R. L. 1966b. Oxytocic activity in unextracted blood plasma during calving. J. Reprod. Fertil. *11*:317-323.

van Tienhoven, A. 1961. Endocrinology of reproduction in birds. *In* W. C. Young (ed.): Sex and Internal Secretions. Williams & Wilkins Co., Baltimore, Vol. 2, pp. 1088-1169.

Wilson, I. B. 1963. A new factor associated with the implantation of the mouse egg. J. Reprod. Fertil. *5*:281-282.

Wimsatt, W. A. 1963. Delayed implantation in the ursidae, with particular reference to the black bear (*Ursus americanus* Pallus). *In* A. C. Enders (ed.): Delayed Implantation. University of Chicago Press, pp. 49-74.

Wislocki, G. B., and Padykula, H. 1961. Histochemistry and electron microscopy of the placenta. *In* W. C. Young (ed.): Sex and Internal Secretions. Williams & Wilkins Co., Baltimore, Vol. 2, pp. 883-957.

Wright, P. L. 1963. Variations in reproductive cycles in North American mustelids. *In* A. C. Enders (ed.): Delayed Implantation. University of Chicago Press, pp. 77-95.

Wright, P. L. 1966. Observations on the reproductive cycle of the American badger (*Taxidea taxus*). Symp. Zool. Soc. London *15*:27-45.

Yasukawa, J. J., and Meyer, R. K. 1966. Effect of progesterone and oestrone on the pre-implantation and implantation stages of embryo development in the rat. J. Reprod. Fertil. *11*: 245-255.

Yoshinaga, K., and Adams, C. E. 1966. Delayed implantation in the spayed, progesterone treated adult mouse. J. Reprod. Fertil. *12*: 593-595.

Zarrow, M. X. 1961. Gestation. *In* W. C. Young (ed.): Sex and Internal Secretions. Williams & Wilkins Co., Baltimore, Vol. 2, pp. 958-1031.

Zeilmaker, G. H. 1963. Experimental studies on the effects of ovariectomy and hypophysectomy on blastocyst implantation in the rat. Acta Endocrinol. *44*:355-366.

Effects of Nutrition on Reproduction

The discussion of the interrelationships between nutrition and reproduction will be restricted to the effects of specific nutrients and of energy on reproductive performance, and it will exclude the effects of drugs and of hormones which may be present in natural feedstuffs such as alfalfa and other legumes.

The study of the effect of specific nutrients on different systems has some inherent difficulties that have to be avoided. A short discussion of experimental methods used to avoid these difficulties and the shortcomings of these methods will be given first.

In the case of some mineral, vitamin, and amino acid deficiencies, the animal will eat less, and therefore it will consume less of the nutrient under study, and will also consume less of the other nutrients in the diet than a control animal fed the adequate diet ad libitum. Thus, in reality, one cannot distinguish between the indirect effect of the vitamin (indirect because food intake is diminished) and a direct effect on the organ or system under study. There are several methods to avoid this difficulty.

The pair-feeding method is often used. Under these conditions, each day the pair-fed control animals receive the same amount of food as has been eaten the previous day by the experimental animals. This method, although better than ad libitum feeding, still has a few disadvantages: (a) often the pair-fed animals may gain more weight because they are more efficient in converting the food. (b) the animals are usually fed only once a day, which changes their rhythm of activity from that of animals fed ad libitum (Reinberg and Ghatta, 1964). (The effect of deficient ration on this rhythm has not been studied specifically, but it is assumed here that it may be more similar to that of animals fed an adequate ration ad libitum than to that of pair-fed animals fed once a day). This change of rhythm may well affect other functions, and it is entirely conceivable (although, as far as I know, not specifically tested) that hypothalamic centers regulating endocrine output by the anterior pituitary will be affected by this change in rhythm. It is, of course, possible to feed the pair-fed animals many times a day and alleviate the effect on the animals' rhythm. (c) the pair-fed animals are presumably hungry a large part of the time and this in itself may be a stress reflected in abnormal functioning of the neuroendocrine system.

One can regulate the diet of the controls and experimental animals in such a manner that their intake of calories, proteins, vitamins, and minerals is quite similar for the two groups. One can increase the percentage of fat (at the expense of, e.g., sucrose or starch), proteins, vitamins, and minerals such that even at the reduced feed intake, the diet supplies the same amount of each nutrient as is eaten by the controls fed ad libitum. This, of course, can be done only within certain limits, because not all animals can eat high fat diets.

It also assumes that the nutrient under study is not involved in fat metabolism. If a vitamin is involved in fat metabolism the method should probably be avoided. As an alternative, one can add enough cellulose or other inert material and determine how much animals will eat of the food containing the cellulose. One can then compose the diet in such a manner that control animals eat the same amount of calories, proteins, vitamins, and minerals as the animals fed the deficient diet. The use of this method assumes that the cellulose does not have any effect other than reducing caloric intake.

In the majority of the experiments to be discussed, either ad libitum fed controls or pair-feeding has been used. In only a few cases was use made of the second method. An effort has been made to indicate whether pair-fed or changed diets were used to determine the effect of the nutrient under consideration on reproduction.

The major part of experimental work in which diets of known composition have been fed has been carried out with laboratory and domestic farm animals. The work reviewed in this chapter deals almost exclusively with birds and mammals for this reason.

ENERGY INTAKE

STARVATION

Total starvation of drakes for 17 days during the spring resulted in a lack of testicular weight increase, in failure of spermatogenesis to proceed beyond secondary spermatocytes, and in Leydig cells which remained in the resting stage. These phenomena were correlated with regression of the FSH cells in the pituitary and a failure of neurosecretory material mobilization from the median eminence. The testicular changes were quite similar to those observed after hypophysectomy (Assenmacher et al., 1965). In the fall, similar starvation and subsequent exposure to continuous light resulted in a considerable increase in testicular weight (from 5.43 ± 1.28 g. of full-fed controls on natural light to 48.1 ± 6.1 g.; full-fed controls on continuous light had testes of 78.9 ± 17.33 g.), spermatogenesis which was completed, and active Leydig cells, but FSH, LH, and prolactin cells in the pituitary were less active than those of full-fed controls on continuous light. The testes and pituitaries of drakes fed 50 percent of the food intake of birds fed ad libitum were not different from these controls. The authors explain the results by assuming that an intensive stimulation of the hypothalamus can overcome the nutritional inhibition of gonadotropic function of the pituitary. It is unfortunate that the same light conditions were not used during both seasons so that the effect of season as a contributing factor in the difference in response could have been eliminated.

The increase in neurosecretory material in the median eminence as a result of starvation has also been observed in the toad (Bufo arenarum) by Rodriguez (1964).

The concept that starvation has its effect on the gonads via an effect on the pituitary is supported by experiments on laying chickens. Withdrawal of feed results in atresia of the large follicles; however, injection of FSH, PMSG, or avian pituitary extracts prevents such atresia and the follicles can be ovulated (Hosoda et al., 1955, 1956; Morris and Nalbandov, 1961).

Leathem (1961) reviewed the experimental evidence concerning the effect of inanition on mammals and came to the conclusion that variations in experimental design made it difficult to compare results among experiments carried out in different laboratories, and conclusions concerning the effect of starvation on gonadotropin secretion cannot be generalized. It is, of course, important when the restriction of energy intake is imposed and when the effects are measured.

Short time fasting of male mice has no effect on mating behavior and fertility if it is limited to a 30 hour period. If the starvation period is extended to 36 or 48 hours the proportion of mated females decreases; this effect lasts for about 48 hours after starvation is ended (McClure, 1966). Fasting for as long as 48 hours does not affect fertility, which is not surprising because of the long duration of spermatogenesis and the time that it takes for sperm to be transported from the testes to the ductus deferens (see Chapter 5).

Similar experiments were carried out in which males and females were fasted for different time periods. Such an experiment, in the absence of groups in which females alone are fasted, precludes a separation of the effects on the females per se and possible interactions between fasted males and fasted females. With this provision made, it appears that starvation for 18 to 30 hours reduces fertility but has no effect on estrous behavior. Starvation for 36 hours inhibits estrous behavior (McClure, 1966). The main component which seemed to be missing when mice were starved seemed to be energy, not proteins, vitamins, or minerals, because a "fasted" group given 75 percent glucose solution did not differ from normally fed controls with respect to the incidence of mated females which had litters (McClure, 1966).

Food withdrawal from mated female rats, starting on the day sperm were found in the vagina, for one, two, or three 48 hour periods; one, two or three 72 hour periods; or one or three 96 hour periods, separated by 48 hour periods of feeding ad libitum, resulted in a sharp decrease in the incidence of pregnancies (McClure, 1961) with the lowest percentage found for rats starved 2×72, 3×72, or 3×96 hours.

Mice fasted for 48 hours from the end of the third day p.c. showed a high incidence of degenerating embryos on days 6 and 7, and a high incidence of failures to conceive. Treatment with either 0.5 mg. or 1.5 mg. progesterone from either days 3 to 5 or 3 to 10 decreased the incidence of degenerating embryos but did not permit pregnancies to be carried until term. Five I.U. HCG per day had effects similar to those of progesterone. With these two hormone treatments, most of the failures

of normal pregnancy occurred at about day 12. Neither adrenalectomy nor desoxycorticosterone acetate seemed to prevent the effects of starvation. The prevention of these effects by exogenous gonadotropins suggest that food withdrawal causes a reduction in gonadotropin secretion similar to that observed in chickens.

Starvation has its most pronounced effect if it occurs at or close to the time of implantation in rats and mice. The first sign of the lesion consists of intercellular hemorrhage close to the periphery of the unattached parts of the deciduomata. Subsequently, the deciduomata and embryos become necrotic, the tissue is invaded by leukocytes, the deciduomata liquefy, and debris is absorbed, but sometimes blood and debris are discharged through the cervix (McClure, 1959, 1961, 1962).

The claim by Teitelbaum and Gantt, (1956) that starvation of dogs for ten days may increase sperm counts has been shown to be based on inadequate evidence (Chang and Sheaffer, 1956).

Starvation of swine for 24, 48, or 72 hours after mating affected neither fertility nor embryonic survival during spring experiments in South Dakota, but improved embryonic survival during an experiment conducted in the winter. However, the starved animals were kept indoors and the controls outdoors so that the effect cannot be ascribed to starvation alone (Ray and McCarty, 1965).

EXCESSIVE FOOD INTAKE

Ingle (1950) has stated in a discussion that obesity induced in animals by overfeeding and restricted exercise causes some atrophy of the testes, but whether the tubules or interstitial cells were affected was not further clarified.

A hereditary defect in mice, in which the animals become obese, has allowed the study of the problem of excessive food intake (Ingalls et al., 1950). In the hereditary obese mice, sperm are present in the ductus deferens (Lane and Dickie, 1954) but the males are sterile if fed ad libitum. Restriction of the food intake reveals that at least some males with this genotype can be fertile (Lane and Dickie, 1954). The endocrine function of mice with this syndrome is also impaired, as indicated by the small seminal vesicles and the histology of the testis. Food restriction does not cause improvement of the hormonal production of the testes, indicating that overeating per se is not the cause of the impairment (Lidell and Hellman, 1966).

Obesity induced by gold-thioglucose injections (which causes overeating) does not affect the testicular interstitium (Lidell and Hellman, 1966) substantiating the evidence obtained with hereditary obese mice kept on a restricted food intake.

Obese female mice are also sterile, but ovulation can be induced by gonadotropin treatment. Either unfertilized or fertilized eggs can then be transferred to nonobese foster mothers, and either fertilization and gestation or gestation only will occur in the foster mother (Runner and Gates, 1954). These investigations suggest that one probable reason for the sterility of obese mice is a lack of gonadotropin secretion.

Electrolytic lesions of the ventromedial nucleus induce hyperphagia and obesity in rats and also cause an initial nonspecific pseudopregnancy. Subsequently these rats show normal estrous cycles; however, mating behavior did not occur even in animals which showed vaginal estrus. Food restriction of lesioned rats or of control rats resulted in constant vaginal cornification; after refeeding, cycles became normal again (Kennedy and Mitra, 1963a,c). These data indicate that underfeeding as such causes abnormal estrous cycles whether the animal is normal or obese, so the amount of energy which the animal has stored does not seem to be an important factor in determining the response.

RESTRICTED FOOD INTAKE

The effects of restricted food intake are different depending on when during

the development of the animal the treatment is imposed and on the length of time the food intake is restricted.

It is most convenient to discuss the aspects of this treatment with respect to the onset of sexual maturity, which is defined as either the production of sperm or the first ovulation or appearance of estrus.

Before Sexual Maturity. The economics of raising large numbers of chicks for about four months before the pullets start to lay eggs have initiated a number of studies on the effects of feed restriction on age at which the first egg is laid, on egg production, egg size, and mortality during a subsequent 500 day laying test. The experiments restricting the food intake during the growing period to 70 percent of the amount eaten by the birds fed ad libitum resulted in:

1. A 12-day delay in sexual maturity.

2. The total number of eggs laid during the test period was the same for full-fed and restricted-fed birds, but the rate of egg production was higher for the restricted-fed birds. (They started 12 days later but laid the same number of eggs as the controls.)

3. The restricted-fed pullets laid fewer small eggs than the full-fed birds.

4. The mortality was 14.7 percent for the full-fed and 11.4 percent for the restricted-fed birds when the average for the six farms was taken. On five of the six farms the mortality was lower for the restricted-fed pullets.

In a subsequent experiment these results, except for the beneficial effect of restricted feeding on egg size, were confirmed. Actually, in this experiment more eggs were laid by the birds which had received a restricted amount of feed and the total egg mass produced by these birds was higher than for full-fed controls. Also, in this experiment the hens were force-moulted at the end of their first year of production and then brought back into production. During the second year the restricted-fed birds again laid at a higher rate and produced a greater egg mass than the controls. During the period of restricted feeding mortality was higher but after housing it was lower for birds which had received less food during the rearing period than the mortality of controls. The results obtained by Gowe et al. (1960) and Hollands and Gowe (1961) agree with most of the results reported.

Food restriction (85 percent of ad libitum intake) of growing turkeys during weeks 12 to 24, 24 to 40, or 12 to 40 resulted in later appearance of sperm when compared to full-fed toms (197.4 versus 205.1 days of age) according to Anderson et al. (1963). The number of eggs laid by hens treated in a similar manner was not affected, but fertility was higher for eggs laid by hens restricted-fed from 12 to 24 weeks of age and from 12 to 40 weeks than for eggs from hens fed either ad libitum or receiving a restricted diet from 24 to 40 weeks of age. The mechanism whereby feed restriction improves the hatchability of the eggs laid is not clear.

Other experiments with turkeys, in which food intake was restricted between 20 and 34 weeks of age, showed no effect on egg production, mortality, fertility, or hatchability of fertile eggs (Mitchell et al., 1962).

Kennedy and Mitra (1963b) have pointed out that food restriction can be imposed for a limited time during various stages of development and can have entirely different effects. Retardation was induced by having one rat nurse three pups and another rat 15 to 17 pups. At weaning, the average weight of the young was about 40 g. for the first group and 15 to 25 g. for the second one; after weaning the young were fed ad libitum. In other experiments restriction of food was imposed after weaning. These experiments showed:

1. In the most optimally grown control rats, vaginal opening, first estrus, and mating occurred on the same day.

2. For rats retarded during the preweaning period, vaginal opening preceded first estrus by about three days and first mating took place during the second, third, or fourth cycle. The running activity that normally accompanies estrus also failed to appear at the first estrus, but became apparent during subsequent ones.

3. Vaginal opening occurred at a higher body weight in optimally grown rats than in retarded rats. Widowson et al. (1964) found that 18 out of 31 rats on a restricted diet after weaning had open vaginas at 41 to 67 days at weight of 41 to 72 g., control rats had open vaginas at 31 to 50 days and 61 to 112 g. respectively. The 13 remaining restricted-fed rats had closed vaginas at 77 days.

4. First estrus and first mating were noted at approximately the same body weight in fast growing and retarded rats (Kennedy and Mitra, 1963b). The follicles of undernourished rats were normal in the experiments conducted by Widowson et al. (1964) but no corpora lutea were seen by the eleventh week, with controls showing corpora lutea at seven weeks. Kennedy and Mitra (1963b) also found no estrous cycles if food restriction was started after weaning and continued. Estrous cycles started within a week after refeeding was instigated (Kennedy and Mitra, 1963b; Widowson et al., 1963).

5. Chronic underfeeding led to development of vaginal cornification and follicular cysts (Kennedy and Mitra, 1963b).

6. Food intake and skeletal maturation bore a rather constant relation to body weight in rats retarded during either the pre- or the postweaning period (Kennedy and Mitra, 1963b).

7. Underfeeding started after weaning resulted in regressed interstitial cells in the testes and increased testicular weight expressed as a percentage of body weight. No effect was noted on the development of the seminiferous tubules (Widowson et al., 1964). Upon refeeding, the testes remained larger than those of well fed controls.

8. After postweaning undernourishment and upon the start of refeeding protrusion of the penis was observed in 6 out

of 10 rats for the first five days but by the fourth day it had disappeared (Widowson et al., 1964).

Hahn and Koldovský (1966) have reported that male rats weaned early showed repercussions at one year of age, although at six months no differences could be noted. The early weaning resulted in a high incidence of animals with impaired spermatogenesis and a smaller diameter of the seminiferous tubules. Premature weaning results in a reduced food intake, for during the first two days no food is eaten. The prematurely weaned rats consume more calories than normal once they start to eat; this greater food intake continues to about 40 days of age. It appears from these data that body size and food intake determine, to a large extent, the onset of puberty in the rat, and that these factors are greater when undernutrition starts earlier.

Ball et al. (1947) reduced the incidence of pregnancies in mice by caloric restriction after weaning. Full feeding, started at eight months of age, resulted in a high incidence of pregnancies between eight and 12 months of age; however, the incidence was low at this age in mice kept either on the restricted or on the full feeding treatment after weaning.

Puberty can be advanced in guinea pigs by increasing energy intake above normal and it can be delayed by reducing feed intake (see Rombauts et al., 1961).

Reid (1960) and Rombauts et al. (1961) have reviewed the literature on the effect of energy intake in farm animals. The most extensive experiments have been carried out with cattle. Comparisons between calves fed from birth to about 18 months of age 65, 100, and 140 percent of recommended feed intake showed:

1. The age at which puberty (first motile sperm in ejaculate or first estrus) was attained was dependent on the amount of energy consumed during the growing period. The weight of the bulls at the time of puberty was about the same for the three levels of nutrition; the same was

true for the heifers. The age at which puberty was first noted differed widely, with the animals on the high level of energy reaching puberty at younger age (Sorenson et al., 1959; Bratton et al., 1959, 1961; Reid et al., 1964). With identical twins the differences were in a similar direction but less pronounced (see Rombauts et al., 1961).

2. After puberty was reached, no effect of the rearing treatment on the fertility of the cows or on embryonic survival was detected (Reid et al., 1964).

Reid (1960), from a review of the literature, concluded that the relationship between energy intake (between weaning and puberty) and onset of puberty of gilts was to a certain extent an inverse relationship. Hafez (1960) reported that gilts fed 70 percent of full feed intake reached puberty at 186 days, whereas those that were full fed reached this stage of development at 195 days. In this experiment, these treatments had been used for ten generations.

O'Bannon et al. (1966) manipulated the diet to restrict energy intake and found a slight delay in the age at which puberty was reached by gilts on a restricted caloric intake, but rather large differences in body weight at puberty (91 to 92 versus 102 kg.). It thus seems that in these experiments energy restriction did not delay puberty as it did in cattle, and that age is probably more important in determining onset of puberty than the plane of nutrition. The restriction of energy intake before puberty reduced the rate of ovulation in gilts when compared to full-fed controls (O'Bannon et al., 1966; Reid, 1960), but did not affect the concentration of sperm, percentage motility, percentage of abnormal sperm, or libido; the restricted feeding of boars reduced the volume of semen produced. Embryonic survival seems to be favorably influenced by feed restriction beginning between weaning time and 120 days of age (Reid, 1960).

Caloric intake restriction seemed to have only a relatively minor effect on the age at which puberty is reached by boars. Full-fed controls weighed 223 lbs. and were 203 days old at puberty, whereas restriction to 70 and 50 percent of the caloric intake of controls resulted in a weight at puberty of 171 lbs. and an age of 212 days, and of 135 lbs. and 219 days respectively. Libido, motility, number of sperm, percent abnormal sperm, and fertility did not seem to be affected by food restriction prior to puberty; however, the volume of semen was reduced progressively as the energy intake was decreased (Dutt and Barnhart, 1959).

Dickerson et al. (1964) restricted feed intake after weaning to the extent that pigs weighed only 5 to 6 kg. when they were a year old. Histological and gross examination of the reproductive system showed: (1) Development of the tubules of the testes. (2) Regressed Leydig cells. (3) An enlarged and edematous glans penis. (4) Ovaries with primary and cystic follicles but without corpora lutea. (5) Enlarged uteri and vulvae.

Rapid rehabilitation resulted in larger testes and vulvae with respect to body size than in the controls, disappearance of the edema of the penis, ovulations, spermatogenesis, and delayed appearance of the interstitial cells.

Experiments carried out with sheep suggest that energy intake may play a somewhat more important role in determining the onset of puberty than it does in swine, but that it is not as important as in cattle (Allen, 1961).

Ewe lambs, fed concentrates to increase their energy intake, reached puberty sooner and at a higher body weight than ewes kept on bare pasture. There was no difference between these two groups with respect to the response to an 800 I.U. dose of PMSG, suggesting that the delayed puberty and smaller ovarian weights were not the result of hypofunction of the anterior pituitary. Average fertility and amount of luteal tissue after puberty was not affected by energy intake.

Hafez (1952) and Allen (1961) have proposed that the lambs have to reach a certain weight (which is different for each breed) before puberty can be reached, regardless of the animal's age. In this respect the ewe would take a position between cattle and swine.

After Puberty. The energy requirement of male birds for reproduction has not been investigated in great detail. Parker and Arscott (1964) fed diets containing either 2553 kCal. metabolizable energy (ME)/kg. or 2068 kCal./kg. or 1584 kCal./kg. to seven-month-old roosters. The diets were composed in such a manner that the intake of all other nutrients was the same for each bird. Each rooster received 90 g. of food per day. At the lowest energy intake, the testes decreased to 1.86 ± 1.25 g. in birds with an average body weight of about 1.7 kg. The amount of semen collected decreased rapidly from the time the diet was fed and fertilizing capacity decreased after the birds had been treated for six weeks. On the intermediate level of energy the decrease in volume of semen and in fertility was slow, and at the end of the 13-week experimental period the testis weighed 9.44 ± 6.31 g. in birds with a body weight of about 2.2 kg. The high energy level maintained semen volume and fertilizing capacity at pre-experimental values; the testis weighed 18.45 ± 2.88 g. in roosters with an average body weight of approximately 2.5 kg. (Parker and Arscott, 1964). Energy intake thus is an extremely important factor in maintaining the reproductive performance of sexually mature roosters.

Card and Nesheim (1966) have pointed out that the amount of feed consumed is primarily determined by the energy level of the ration in laying hens, provided other nutrients are present in adequate amounts. To ensure maximum rate of production the amount of energy should not be less than 2640 kCal. per kg. of feed. The statement implies that restriction of energy intake will reduce egg production. The situation is somewhat different for the so-called heavy breeds. Singsen et al. (1961) were able to reduce energy intake of White Plymouth Rock hens without affecting egg production (which was between 55 and 58 percent as compared to 75 to 80 percent egg production for White Leghorns in full production). The energy intake was reduced by feeding a measured amount of food each day, calculated on the basis of the formula found at the bottom of this page.

This system of feeding reduced the increase in body weight, reduced mortality, and decreased the amount of feed needed per dozen eggs. It appears that heavy breeds may overeat if fed ad libitum and will store the excess energy as fat, whereas in the laying breeds the energy is deposited into the egg.

It seems preferable to discuss the effects of feed restriction after puberty by species investigated rather than by the effect on different phases of reproductive performance. In the rat, the restriction of food intake to either 25 to 50 or 75 percent of that of controls (this reduces not only energy intake but also that of all other nutrients) between days 0 and 20 of pregnancy increased the incidence of resorption of fetuses. For each rat the effect was an all or none effect; either all implants were resorbed or none were. Transitory unrestricted feeding reduced the incidence of resorptions with feeding started on day 8 having the most effect and feeding started on day 10 having no effect (Berg, 1965). Whether these resorptions were the result of general inanition or the lack of one or more specific nutrients was not established. The data indicate, however, that the period between days 8 and 11 of pregnancy are crucial with respect to the onset of resorptions.

Hammond (1965), using an inbred strain of rabbits with a high incidence of fetal atrophy, found that restriction of food intake (which restricted not only energy but also other nutrients) so that animals did not put on weight depressed conception rate but increased litter size. Ovulation rates on the two treatments were similar, but the number of fetuses in the uteri was 3.8 for the animals on the high plane of nutrition and 6.0 on the low plane.

In the nutritional management of sheep it has been common knowledge that increasing the plane of nutrition and thus increasing the gain in body weight of ewes, prior to mating, results in higher ovulation rates and in more lambs per ewe (Reid, 1960). This management practice is called "flushing." The flushing can be started with the greatest economic advantage about three to five weeks prior to mating. Allen and Lamming (1961) found that flushing did not increase the ovulation rate above that of ewes kept in fat condition.

Ewes kept on submaintenance or on maintenance diets had lower ovulation rates than the flushed ewes. According to Allen and Lamming (1961) gonadotropin release for ewes on the submaintenance rations may be incomplete. PMSG injections increased ovulation rates, particularly in ewes on submaintenance diets, showing that the ovary can give a normal response to exogenous gonadotropins.

In a detailed analysis on the effect of nutrition on reproduction of ewes it was found that:

1. Feeding of a high energy diet for seven months prior to mating increased the number of ova shed by yearling ewes above that found in ewes kept on a low energy diet (El Sheikh et al., 1955).

2. Flushing of the ewes which had

Daily food allowance (lbs.) =

$$\frac{25 + 8 \times \text{Body weight (lbs.)} + \dfrac{\text{Number of 2 ounce eggs per year}}{7}}{365} \times 85\%$$

been on the low level of nutrition increased the incidence of multiple ovulations in one of three years and the incidence was lower than that obtained with ewes kept on a high plane of nutrition for seven months. Full feeding resulted in higher embryonic mortality in one of the three years during which the investigations were conducted (Foote el al., 1959).

3. Use of regression calculations revealed that the way the animal grew out had a greater effect on the number of ova shed than the nutritive state at the time of breeding (Foote et al., 1959).

4. The effect of flushing on ovulation rate was noted in the Columbia ewes but not in Hampshires (Bellows et al., 1963).

5. A high level of nutrition was associated with higher plasma glucose concentrations, lower concentration of free fatty acids, higher pituitary and adrenal weights, higher ovulation rates, more numerous large follicles, more follicular fluid and probably higher LH concentrations in the pituitary (Howland et al., 1966a). The higher LH concentration (ascorbic acid depletion test, see appendix) in the pituitary was interpreted as a higher rate of production, whereas Allen and Lamming (1961), finding a higher content of gonadotropins (chick testes weight assay, see appendix) in the ewes on a low level of nutrition, considered this evidence of lack of release of gonadotropins. The pituitary-gonadotropin content is not a valid criterion for either production or release unless one also has values for the plasma concentrations of the hormone.

6. Drenching with glucose twice daily during the estrous cycle increased blood glucose concentrations but depressed follicular development (Howland et al., 1966b).

These data all indicate that energy restriction prior to mating reduced the number of ovulations and that the body weight of the ewe is of importance in affecting the rate of ovulation.

Undernutrition during early gestation increased embryonic mortality. Feed restriction between days 0 and 7 post coitum

(p.c.) resulted in 40.9 percent embryonic mortality between days 0 and 7, 48.8 percent mortality between days 6 and 13, and 51.2 percent mortality between days 13 and 20 but in controls the mortality was between 27.9 and 34.1 percent (Edey, 1965).

Reduction of energy intake of 14-month-old rams to 25 percent of the recommended requirements did not affect libido, fertility, semen motility, or total number of sperm collected, although the body weight decreased from an initial value of 120 lbs. to a final value of 85 lbs. at the end of the experiment (Tilton et al., 1964).

Testosterone output of adult rams, underfed so that they lost between 0.6 to 1.2 kg./week for three months, was 0.4 ± 0.2 mg./ram per day, whereas full-fed rams produced 3.5 ± 0.7 mg./ram per day. This level of undernutrition also reduced the diameter of the seminiferous tubules, the sperm content of the epididymis, and the weight and fructose content of the seminal vesicles, but it increased the extent of tubular damage in the testes. However, spermatogenesis was found in all of the rams (Setchell et al., 1965).

These data, when considered together, seem to indicate that reproductive performance need not be affected, although there exists a suboptimal function of the testes.

The effects of energy restriction in pigs depend on the stage of development at which the restriction is started. Reid (1960) pointed out that one might expect optimal reproductive performance by a sequence of limited feeding prepubertally (to attain earlier puberty and save feed at the same time), a high level of energy intake for a brief period prior to breeding (flushing), and a low energy intake during pregnancy. The effects of feeding before puberty have been discussed previously.

Restriction of feed intake prior to mating reduces the ovulation rate of gilts (Reid, 1960); similarly, energy restriction imposed during the first estrous cycle reduces the number of ovulations at the second heat.

Flushing at the time of puberty increases the incidence of ovulations beyond the increase found between first and second heat in controls (Reid, 1960). Flushing started at day 16, 12, or eight of the first heat increased the number of ova shed more than the continuous feeding of the restricted energy diet. The inclusion of more glucose or lard in the diet fed two weeks prior to ovulation increased the number of ovulations (Zimmerman et al., 1960).

Feeding of either glucose or corn oil, in addition to the basal diet, starting about 14 days prior to ovulation during the second estrous cycle of gilts, increased the ovulation rate in three breeds of pigs (Chester White, Poland China and Hampshires). The Chester Whites had the highest ovulation rate (Kirkpatrick et al., 1967a).

Further analysis of the effect of additional glucose feeding for about 14 days prior to slaughter on days 3, 7, 11, 15, or 19 of the cycle showed that the ovulation rate increases if the glucose is fed either eight or 12 days prior to ovulation, and corpus luteum weights and higher progesterone concentrations in the corpora lutea of gilts killed on days 15 or 19 increase. Bioassays of the pituitaries for FSH and LH activity revealed no effect of feed on the assay values nor of a feed-day interaction. Partitioning of the interaction showed significant quadratic regressions of FSH and LH activity on the day of the cycle, suggesting differences in the pattern of gonadotropin release or production as a result of the treatment (Kirkpatrick et al., 1967b).

Bellows et al. (1966) fed mature rats in such a manner that the energy intake was reduced in one group to 60 percent of that of controls but the intake of other nutrients was similar in the full-fed and restricted-fed group. All rats were first fed the restricted diet for ten days and half of the rats were continued on this diet; the other half were full-fed from the first day of estrus after the ten day conditioning period. On the second proestrus

rats were autopsied. The diet had no effect on ovarian weight, anterior pituitary weight, total pituitary FSH, or LH content. The ovarian response to exogenous PMSG also was not different for the two groups of rats. The higher energy intake did result in greater weight gains.

The effects of energy intake after mating have been studied rather extensively. In general, these studies have shown that embryonic survival in gilts is improved by lowered energy intake (Clawson et al., 1963; Goode et al., 1965; Reid, 1960). Heap et al. (1967) found no effect of feeding either 3, 6, or 9 lbs. of meal (containing similar amounts of energy, protein, ether extract, crude fiber, calcium and phosphorus per pound but so adjusted that mineral and vitamin intakes for all groups of sows would be adequate) on embryo survival in *sows*, when adjustments were made for differences in body weight at the time of mating. It needs to be established whether the differences between these results and those cited above are the result of differences between sows and gilts or whether they are the result of differences in experimental techniques.

The mechanisms whereby overfeeding of gilts increase embryonic mortality have not been elucidated and investigations into the mechanisms causing these effects should be fruitful.

The review of the effect of energy intake on reproductive phenomena shows that there are important differences between species and that any phase of the reproductive cycle of females may be influenced by energy intake in one species or another. It also shows that by careful manipulation of the diet during different reproductive phases it may be possible to improve reproductive efficiency. Too little information is available to even speculate whether in nondomesticated mammals energy intake plays as important a role (as long as minimal requirements are met) and whether there are feedback mechanisms which ensure attainment of maximal reproductive efficiency. In domestic hens there seems to be such a mechanism. When the pullet approaches sexual maturity the ovary starts to secrete estrogen, which not only stimulates the oviduct and mobilizes precursors, but also stimulates appetite so that she takes in the energy required for the deposition of the large amount of calories in the yolk.

Pregnancy causes an increase in food consumption of rats to the extent that a female may gain 50 grams during the first 15 days, although the fetuses and membranes are small. The maternal gain in energy is reflected in increased fat and a positive nitrogen balance. These reserves are probably used during the latter part of pregnancy when food intake declines and the conceptuses increase in size (Leathem, 1961). As was discussed in Chapter 6, progesterone may increase food intake as a secondary response to increased energy expenditure; progesterone also increases nitrogen retention. It remains to be investigated whether mechanisms exist to make energy intake optimal for each particular phase of reproduction in animals which have different optima at different stages.

PROTEIN INTAKE

The interrelationships between protein intake and reproduction, especially in mammals, have been reviewed by Blaxter (1964), Leathem (1961, 1964, 1966), Mason (1959), and Moustgaard (1959). The major part of this discussion will be based on these reviews.

The effects of the quality and quantity of protein on reproduction of birds have been evaluated mostly for female chickens, turkeys, and pheasants. The criteria for establishing the protein requirements in terms of percent protein and of amounts of amino acids have been egg production, and fertility and hatchability of the eggs. The different aspects of these requirements have been discussed by Mitchell (1962).

In general, the protein requirements

for reproduction of male birds have not received much attention. Wilson et al. (1965) fed rations with 16.0, 9.0, 6.75, and 4.5 percent protein to roosters from nine to 23 weeks of age and then fed them a ration with 17 percent protein. As expected, growth was decreased by feeding of the rations containing less than 16 percent protein with virtually no increase in weight obtained on the 4.5 percent protein ration. Subsequent to the feeding of the 17 percent protein diet there was a sharp increase in the growth of the roosters fed the deficient diets, and at 33 weeks of age differences in body weight were reduced to about ten to 15 percent. Sperm production before 24 weeks of age was obtained only in the cocks fed the 16 percent and the nine percent protein diets, but on the latter diet sperm production was considerably below that found on the former diet. After the feeding of the 17 percent protein diet started there was a sharp increase in sperm production, and by 30 weeks of age the groups produced similar amounts of sperm. Fertility increased rapidly after the birds had been placed on the protein-sufficient diet, and by 29 weeks it was at least as good as in the birds fed the 16 percent protein diet; as a matter of fact, the birds receiving the 9.0 and 6.75 percent protein rations had higher fertility by 26 to 27 weeks of age. Testicular weights at 40 weeks, expressed as percent of body weight, were 0.29, 0.68, 0.62, and 0.77 for the 16.0, 9.0, 6.75, and 4.5 percent protein diets fed between nine and 23 weeks of age, respectively. These results thus show that the protein requirement for early and optimal sperm production and fertility is 16 percent and that no permanent damage was done to reproductive performance by feeding diets lower in protein content between nine and 23 weeks of age. For these experiments the energy intake was not given, thus the effects noted could be the result of a diminished energy and protein intake.

For laying hens the amino acid requirements for egg production have been determined (Johnson and Fisher, 1956). These authors noted that leaving out one of the essential amino acids (arginine, lysine, methionine, tryptophan, glycine, histidine, leucine, isoleucine, phenylalanine, or phenylalanine and tyrosine, threonine, and valine) resulted in an immediate decrease of food intake. Forced feeding of such a ration did not support normal egg production, however, indicating that the interruption of egg production was not the result of the decreased energy intake. The suggestion by Morris and Nalbandov (1961) that the amino acid deficiency may exert its effect by reducing gonadotropin secretion and/or release, as it does during total starvation, needs to be investigated. For quantitative requirements of the different amino acids, see Card and Nesheim (1966).

The aspects of protein deficiency in relation to reproduction have been studied most extensively in rats.

Feeding of protein-free diets to male rats and mice prevents sexual maturation of testes and secondary sex organs and causes an increase in lipid content of the testes (Leathem, 1961). The damage to the testis is not permanent, for subsequent feeding of an adequate ration causes a rapid onset of spermatogenesis. A diet deficient in one of the essential amino acids causes changes similar to those described above; by pair-feeding or forcefeeding the deficient diet it was possible to show that the observed effects are probably not the result of inanition (Ershoff, 1952).

Adult rats fed a protein-deficient diet lose their libido before sperm disappear from the tubules and epididymis; this loss of libido can be correlated with the observation that seminal vesicle weights decrease before the testes (see Leathem, 1961, for documentation).

The observed effects may be the result of a diminished gonadotropin secretion (exogenous PMSG stimulates spermatogenesis and seminal vesicle weights of immature rats on a protein deficient diet

and protein deficiency tends to decrease the gonadotropin content of the pituitary [Leathem, 1958; Srebnik and Nelson, 1962]) and a diminished responsiveness to exogenous gonadotropins and gonadal hormones. Testosterone does not maintain spermatogenesis and testicular weight as well in rats fed a protein deficient diet as in rats fed an adequate diet (Leathem, 1961).

Female rats on a protein-free or protein-deficient diet exhibit the same general symptoms as the male on such treatments, i.e. delayed sexual maturity, and if the treatment is started in adults, atrophy of the ovaries, abnormal estrous cycles. Refeeding of an adequate diet causes rapid changes in the ovary, vesicular follicles can be seen, estrogen is released (Leathem, 1961). Similar results are obtained if one or more of the essential amino acids are omitted from the diet. As such omission usually results in decreased food intake, the relationship becomes confounded by insufficient intake of other nutrients.

The gonads of rats fed protein-deficient diets respond to exogenous gonadotropic hormones, although the response is qualitatively different (the follicles are stimulated but do not become luteinized after PMSG in protein-deficient rats but they luteinize in rats on an 18 percent casein diet) and quantitatively diminished. They are, however, more sensitive to PMSG when they are on protein-deficient diets. In hypophysectomized rats, protein-deficient diets cause an increased sensitivity to LH, HCG, and PMSG, but not to FSH (see Leathem, 1961).

Bioassays of the pituitaries and plasma of intact and spayed rats on protein-deficient and on adequate diets revealed a slight increase in FSH content of the pituitary (the statistical significance of this increase was not analyzed and from the data given it could not be analyzed by me) as a result of feeding the deficient diet, but no differences were apparent for the gonadotropin concentration in the plasma. Ovariectomy resulted in an increase in pituitary FSH and LH content and in circulating FSH in both groups of rats (Srebnik et al., 1961). These observations were interpreted as a lack of FSH release, which would account for the atrophy of the ovaries observed after feeding protein-deficient diets (Srebnik et al., 1958). The findings for the female rat differ from those for the male rat, in which protein-deficient diets cause decreased gonadal and secondary accessory gland weights and decreased gonadotropin content of the pituitary, as pointed out by Srebnik and Nelson (1962).

One of the most interesting facets of nutritional-reproductive interrelationships is the elucidation of the mechanism whereby protein deficiency causes diminished reproductive performance.

Removal of protein from the diet of the rat at the time of mating did not prevent implantation (Leathem, 1961), an effect different from that observed after total starvation at about the same time. The repercussions of protein deficiency become evident in the smaller number of fetuses born as a result of resorptions (Nelson and Evans, 1953). At first thought, this effect is not surprising because one might expect a lack of protein for synthesis of fetal tissue and extra embryonic membranes if a diet does not supply enough protein. However, this "explanation" is incorrect, for pregnancy can be maintained by the injection of estrone and/or progesterone, as has been found by Nelson and Evans (1954) and confirmed by many others (Fisher and Leathem, 1965; Hays and Kendall, 1961; Hays et al., 1965; Hazelwood and Nelson, 1965; Kendall and Hays, 1960; Kinzey and Srebnik, 1963; Nelson and Evans, 1955). The question on how the mother manages to deliver normal, albeit small (1.8 versus 3.6 grams for the controls), fetuses in spite of the absence of protein from the diet has been studied by chemical analyses of the uterus, of the uterine contents, and of the maternal tissues.

Hazelwood and Nelson (1965) concluded, on the basis of such analyses, that proteins were mobilized from skeletal muscles and that such mobilization could account for the proteins deposited in the conceptuses. Fisher and Leathem (1965) concluded that the principal action of the injected steroid hormones was to sustain placental function, and that the presence of viable fetuses and placentas, regardless of diet or of hormone treatment, resulted in higher RNA : DNA ratios and higher total protein content of the uterus and liver than found in similar rats with resorbed fetuses. The two explanations are not mutually exclusive and both effects can be exerted by steroid hormone treatment.

Another set of data may be useful for consideration of this question. Kinzey and Srebnik (1963) injected protein-deprived pregnant rats with 1 μg. estrone and 4 mg. progesterone for different intervals of the gestation period (days 1 to 5; days 3 to 7; days 3 to 8; days 6 to 10 and days 5 to 9). Injections from days 5 to 9 maintained pregnancy in 100 percent of the 28 cases; injections from days 3 to 8 and 6 to 10 were quite effective in maintaining pregnancy (in 80 and 89 percent of the cases), but injections from days 3 to 7 were not effective, as only 30 percent of the pregnancies were maintained. This indicates that the period around day 8 is extremely important, but that once the pregnancy is firmly "established" no further steroid hormone support is needed. This can be interpreted as sustaining placental and/or pituitary function. The fact that in hypophysectomized rats on a complete diet the steroid hormone injections between days 5 and 11 could maintain 100 percent of the pregnancies indicates that the hypophyseal secretions are not required. The placenta, once well established, might, by its secretion of prolactin and of a growth hormone-like substance (Ray et al., 1955), cause adequate mobilization of proteins from the muscles. This interpretation is supported by the evidence obtained by Fisher and Leathem (1965) that RNA : DNA ratios are higher in the presence of viable than in the presence of resorbed fetuses. The determination of prolactin in the blood of pregnant rats under varying conditions may shed light on this question. The injection of prolactin in ovariectomized rats treated with estrogen and progesterone could determine whether prolactin can mobilize proteins for the synthesis of fetal tissues. Evidence for the mobilization of proteins by prolactin has been provided by Lyons (1966) in experiments with lactating rats on protein-free diets.

Alternative explanations for the effects of estrogen and progesterone on maintenance of pregnancy would be a series of reactions set in motion by estrogen and progesterone per se which mobilize or make proteins available even after the injections have been discontinued.

Hays et al. (1965) found little difference in the number of young born from estrogen-progesterone-treated ovariectomized rats fed either a complete diet or a sucrose diet. Intact, steroid-hormone-treated rats, fed a complete diet, gave birth to 10.1 young, but those on a sucrose diet had only 5.2 pups; intact controls, fed a complete diet, had 11.6 young, whereas similar rats, fed a sucrose diet, had only 0.2 young. These data suggest that the sucrose diet had an effect on embryonic survival similar to that of ovariectomy on control rats. It seems reasonable to assume that feeding only sucrose impairs steroidogenesis by the ovary. Ovarian steroid hormone secretion is under the control of the pituitary and it is, therefore, pertinent to evaluate to what extent pituitary function is affected by protein-deficient diets.

Two types of evidence suggest that protein-free diets cause insufficient prolactin secretion by the pituitary. Injection of prolactin causes maintenance of pregnancy in rats fed sucrose only (Hays and Kendall, 1961). This apparent prolactin insufficiency might, however, be the result of inadequate placental or pituitary hormone secretion. Reserpine, at levels of 10 mg./100 g. body weight, increased the percentage of rats (on a protein-free diet) 64 percent, while there was a ten percent increase in the controls (Kalivas and Nelson, 1966). There is evidence from different sources that reserpine causes prolactin release from the pituitary (Everett, 1966).

Unfortunately, no data seem to be available on the prolactin content in the pituitary on the circulating levels of this hormone in protein-deprived rats. A new radio-immunoassay (Kwa and Verhofstad, 1967a), which can detect prolactin in the blood of mice (Kwa and Verhofstad, 1967b) may elucidate this problem.

Protein-deficient diets fed to female rabbits do not affect the increase in pituitary gonadotropin content which follows the coitus-induced depletion of gonadotropic hormones. Does, on these rations, not only received little protein, but, because appetite was affected, also fewer calories per day than control does (Friedman and Friedman, 1940).

Studies with pigs have shown that as little as five percent protein (either provided by sesame meal, or gelatin, or corn plus soybean meal) was sufficient to obtain litter size, number of live pigs farrowed, weight of live pigs, and survival of piglets similar to figures obtained with a 16 percent protein diet (Rippel et al., 1965a). Nitrogen balance studies revealed that for pregnant gilts an intake of three percent protein at a food intake of 1.82 kg./day was slightly in excess of maintenance requirement (Rippel et al., 1965b).

LIPID INTAKE

The effects of lipids on reproductive performance will be discussed mainly from the point of view of requirements of essential fatty acids.

In chickens, linoleic acid is required for optimal egg production, egg weight, fertility, and hatchability (Menge et al., 1965a,b). In the case of linoleic acid deficiency there is an increase in the concentration of eicosatrionic acid in the tissues, yolk, and plasma. The concentration of this fatty acid is negatively correlated with the expression of the above mentioned reproductive characteristics (Menge et al., 1965b). Some of the menhaden oil poly-unsaturated fatty acids, which are not linoleic acids, seem to depress the formation of eicosatrionic acid and in this manner improve reproductive performance. Calvert (1967), on analysis of the mortality of embryos, found:

a. Major peaks of mortality between zero and four days of incubation.

b. Seventy-five percent of the surviving embryos had the head over the wing instead of the normal (head under the wing) position. Two thirds of the dead embryos were in abnormal positions in the egg, but no specific lesions could be found in the embryos.

c. The linoleic acid and arachidonic acid content of the eggs from hens on the linoleic acid-deficient diet contained only trace amounts of arachidonic and linoleic acid, whereas these fatty acids made up 1.26 and 21.28 percent of the total fatty acids in the yolks from hens fed three percent linoleic acid in the diet.

d. The percentages of yolk, dry matter, and lipid were lower in eggs from hens on the linoleic acid-deficient diet than from hens on the three percent linoleic acid diet.

These results thus show a definite requirement for linoleic acid for reproduction of chickens.

Feeding of excessive amounts of unsaturated fatty acids, among them linoleic acid, will cause vitamin E deficiency because of the destruction of the vitamin; addition of antioxidants will prevent such destruction.

Linoleic acid deficiency in the diet of rats causes degeneration of the testicular tubules, irregular ovulation, and atrophic changes of the uterine mucosa (Leathem, 1961). The addition of hydrogenated arachis oil (14 percent) to the diet caused testicular degeneration in the males, decreased the conception rate in females, and increased embryonic mortality to 100 percent (Aaes-Jørgensen et al., 1956).

The feeding of as little as 25 mg. of *Sterculia foetida* oil, which is high in sterculic acid and malvelonic acid (both cycloprenoid fatty acids), to laying hens caused 80 percent embryonic mortality; the reasons for the mortality were not determined (Schneider et al., 1961).

The addition of certain fatty acids to the diet causes impairment of reproduction. Noble and Carroll (1961) found that addition of ten percent erucic acid (cis, 13-docosenoic acid 22:1) to the diet of male rats caused a decrease in testicular weights, degeneration of the tubules, and complete infertility, whereas five percent erucic acid caused infertility in three out of six rats without affecting testicular weights. After atrophy of the testis has progressed recovery to normal is poor, even when the animals are placed on a normal diet. The observation that erucic acid does not have these effects when added to a semisynthetic diet has not been explained.

Females fed ten percent erucic acid had regular estrous cycles, mated normally, but were often sterile. During the early part of the experimental period such mated rats would become pseudopregnant, but later the mating would not induce pseudopregnancy.

Pups from females that had been on the erucic acid diet for four months and had conceived died because of involution of the mammary glands after parturition. Recovery of treated females after they were placed on a normal diet was generally poor. The effect of erucic acid on lactation could be prevented by adding vitamin E to the diet; however, this vitamin did not prevent the damage to the testes induced by erucic acid.

The mechanism whereby erucic acid diminishes reproductive performance has not been determined.

Feeding of *Sterculia foetida* oil to mammals has no apparent effect on the reproductive organs or performance of the males. In the females, the following observations were made: a high incidence of atresia was present, many of the atretic vesicular follicles had turned into lobules of interstitial tissue with central cavities formed by the zonae pellucidae, the granulosa of medium-sized follicles seemed to undergo luteinization, and the uteri had underdeveloped myometria and endometria.

When the diet contained 3 percent foetida oil, embryonic mortality was 100 percent (Rascop et al., 1966).

The mechanism whereby these changes are mediated has not been determined, nor is it known why males respond differently than females to this oil.

VITAMINS

The specific effects of vitamin deficiencies on reproduction need to be assessed by paired-feeding trials if the deficiency of the vitamin causes a decrease in food intake, for, as was discussed previously, energy and also protein intake have an influence on reproductive performance.

As Lutwak-Mann (1958) has pointed out, not many experiments carried out with male birds have met this requirement. In the present discussion much of the earlier work, which has been reviewed extensively by Leathem (1961), Lutwak-Mann (1958), Mason (1959), and Moustgaard (1959) will not be considered in detail and only where new developments have occurred will specific mention be made of the original papers.

FAT SOLUBLE VITAMINS

Vitamin A. One of the most recent interesting discoveries in the study of the function of vitamin A, especially with respect to reproduction, has been the interrelationship among three forms of vitamin A. These relationships are (Thompson et al., 1965a):

Chickens, rats, guinea pigs, and probably most other mammals show none of the following symptoms of classical vitamin A deficiency if they are fed vitamin A acid: defective epithelia, susceptibility to infections, and inanition. However, chickens, rats, and guinea pigs grow totally blind, because vitamin A aldehyde is required for the formation of the visual pigments. With respect to reproduction, there are differences between different classes of animals.

Roosters fed a vitamin A deficient diet but containing vitamin A acid appear to be normal with respect to testicular histology and fertility (Thompson et al., 1965a,b). Male rats and guinea pigs, however, show degeneration of the germinal epithelium (Howell et al., 1963, 1967; Thompson et al., 1964, 1965a), but some spermatocytes and spermatogonia remain present, so that on refeeding the epithelium can regenerate (Thompson et al., 1965a). Neither FSH nor testosterone injections could prevent the degeneration of the seminiferous epithelium (Coward et al., 1966). The castration cells in the pituitary (Thompson et al., 1965a) seem to be secondary to the degeneration of the germinal epithelium.

Palludan (1966) injected vitamin A into the testes of vitamin A-deficient boars and observed a local effect on the histology of the germinal epithelium. These experiments suggest a direct effect of vitamin A on the seminiferous tubules. Scott and Scott (1964) found that gonadotropin injections can reverse the effects of vitamin A deficiency in cats, which suggests that the deficiency affected pituitary gonadotropin secretion.

Female chickens fed a diet deficient in vitamin A alcohol or aldehyde, but supplied with vitamin A acid lay normally; the eggs are fertile, but upon incubation the embryos die within two days. Injection

reversible   irreversible

Vitamin A alcohol $\rightleftharpoons$ Vitamin A aldehyde ——— Vitamin A acid of vitamin A alcohol prevents this mortality and healthy chicks hatch (Thompson et al., 1965a). Apparently, vitamin A acid either does not reach the egg or else the embryo cannot utilize vitamin A acid.

Female rats fed a diet lacking vitamin A alcohol, but containing vitamin A acid have normal estrous cycles, conceive normally, but resorb the fetuses during the last one third of gestation. At day 15 or 16, necrosis can be observed at the edge of the placental labyrinth (Thompson et al., 1964, 1965a); if vitamin A alcohol is given in sufficient quantities pregnancy continues normally. Similar effects have been noted in guinea pigs.

The beauty of these experiments is that the researchers were able to induce a vitamin A deficiency which affected the reproductive organs but in which no complications of inanition, infection, etc., occurred. In this system one can now study the effects of vitamin A hormonal interactions for specific effects. In chickens it had not been possible to study the effect of vitamin A deficiency satisfactorily, for the requirements for laying hens are higher than the requirements for the embryo.

Thompson et al. (1965a) cite evidence that progesterone did not prevent resorption of fetuses of rats on a vitamin A-deficient diet but given vitamin A acid. The exact reason for the discrepancy between these results and those reported by Hays and Kendall (1956), in which progesterone maintained pregnancy in vitamin A-deficient rats, is not known. It is possible that on the totally vitamin A-deficient diet, the rats resorbed fetuses while there were still some vitamin A stores and that progesterone mobilized this stored vitamin A thus relieving the symptoms. The fact that Hays and Kendall (1956) found no increase in plasma vitamin A concentrations after progesterone treatment does not argue against this, for the increased number of embryos kept alive could have metabolized the vitamin A that was mobilized. An alternate explanation would be that resorption is the result of defects that can be prevented by

vitamin A acid and that progesterone cures these effects, rather than that effects are, specifically, the result of vitamin A alcohol deficiency.

This new evidence that vitamin A acid can prevent many of the lesions associated with vitamin A deficiency but allows development of lesions of the reproductive system requires a reassessment of the effect of vitamin A deficiency on reproductive performance. This is especially true for species in which vitamin A deficiency has been reported to have a deleterious effect. The experiments showing that in roosters vitamin A deficiency in the presence of vitamin A acid does not cause testicular degeneration but does so in the rat, hamster and guinea pig, emphasize this.

An interesting relationship exists between vitamin A and estrogen with respect to the uterine epithelium and the vaginal mucosa.

Intact female vitamin A-deficient rats show metaplastic changes in the uterine epithelium but in ovariectomized rats such changes fail to occur. Castrated vitamin A-deficient rats treated with estrogen show metaplasia, but, if vitamin A is given also, no adverse effects can be noted (Leathem, 1961). Vitamin A alcohol is effective but vitamin A acid is not, in preventing these morphological changes (Bo and Smith, 1966).

For the vagina the situation is different; vitamin A deficiency causes cornification of the epithelium in intact and spayed rats. Such a vagina is histologically indistinguishable from that of a rat in estrus. Vitamin A will not only prevent the vitamin A deficiency-induced cornification but it also will prevent the effect of simultaneous local application of estrogen on the vagina of spayed rats (Kahn, 1964). The relationship between vitamin A and α estradiol was quantified by applying 0.6 I.U. of α estradiol (to obtain a 100 percent response) and applying different doses of vitamin A. The relationship proved to be a log dose response curve. Kahn (1954) interpreted the results to indicate that vitamin A inhibited keratinization through an effect on protein anabolism. In vitro experiments have shown that vitamin A deficiency can cause keratinization of epithelia (Fell, 1964).

The vaginal epithelium of vitamin A deficient rats fails to undergo mucification in response to progesterone, which suggests an exaggerated albuminoid production by the vitamin A deficient vaginal epithelium (Mason, 1959).

An excess of vitamin A can have deleterious effects on a number of functions, e.g., bone lesions can be induced, in conjunction with estrogen the effects on bone resorption become more severe, but methyltestosterone counteracts the effect of hypervitaminosis A (Selye, 1957).

Hypervitaminosis A in immature male rats causes complete degeneration of the germinal epithelium (Lutwak-Mann, 1958) and a decrease in the weight per 100 g. body weight of seminal vesicles and prostate (Biswas and Deb, 1966), but in adult males these effects are either absent or small (Lutwak-Mann, 1958).

Excessive intake of vitamin A by pregnant rats causes exencephaly, cleft palates, and inner ear abnormalities of the fetuses (Baba and Araki, 1959; Baba and Yukioka, 1959; and Baba and Nakamura, 1959).

Whether the effects of hypervitaminosis A on reproduction are primary or the consequence of other disturbances has not been established.

Vitamin D. The effect of vitamin D deficiency on reproductive performance of mammals seems to be small or absent (Mason, 1959; Moustgaard, 1959).

Excessive vitamin D_2 impedes fertilization, changes the estrous cycle, alters the implantation process, and causes resorption of implanted embryos if administered to rats before mating or during the first five days of gestation. Gestation is normal when administration of the vitamin is started after day 5 of pregnancy (Nebel and Ornstein, 1966).

Vitamin D deficiency in laying hens results in reduced egg production, smaller eggs, decreased shell thickness, and increased incidence of blood spots in the eggs, although the ovaries are normal and the hens seem to be in good health (Turk and McGinnis, 1964). In roosters, vitamin D deficiency causes small testes and combs (Buckner et al., 1951).

Vitamin D deficiency can only be obtained by feeding a vitamin D deficient diet and by preventing ultraviolet irradiation from reaching the skin; otherwise steroid precursors can be converted into vitamin D. Deficiency of this vitamin in the dam is reflected by poor hatchability, probably because the embryo is unable to utilize calcium and phosphorus (Cravens, 1949; Landauer, 1961).

The effect of vitamin D deficiency in roosters was studied by Buckner et al. (1951), who found a depression of testicular weights and of secondary sex characteristics. However, the vitamin D deficient roosters also weighed less, which may reflect a lower food intake, and thus the effects of vitamin D deficiency per se and of lowered energy and protein intake cannot be separated.

Vitamin E. The induction of vitamin E deficiency in birds requires that either the hens, from which the chicks are to be obtained, be placed on a vitamin E deficient diet or that vitamin E present in the animal be destroyed. Such in vivo destruction can be accomplished by feeding of unsaturated fatty acids, such as linoleic acid, cod liver oil, and other polyunsaturated fatty acids. However, some symptoms of vitamin E deficiency (e.g. encephalomalacia in chicks) can be induced by certain unsaturated fatty acids: linoleic acid and arachidonic acid are effective, but linolenic acid is not (Dam, 1962).

If the chicken has vitamin E stored, it is extremely difficult to deplete it without the use of unsaturated fatty acid administration. It took Adamstone and Card (1934) about two years to obtain effects in roosters fed a vitamin E deficient diet. The testes of some of the roosters were atrophic, but the incidence was not 100 percent. By feeding of a diet containing

7.3 percent linoleic acid Arscott et al. (1965) were able to induce a decrease in fertility in about five weeks, and near the end of the experiment fertility had dropped to zero. There was also a significant decrease in sperm concentration noticeable during the 25 week experimental period. On a low linoleic acid diet these effects were not observed; the effects of the high linoleic acid intake could be prevented by feeding of the antioxidant ethoxyquin or of vitamin E.

Vitamin E deficiency in male rats causes irreversible damage to the germinal epithelium (histologically vitamin A and vitamin E deficiency damage to the testes is quite similar, but the effects of lack of vitamin A are reversible). Mason (1959) has, however, obtained regeneration of damaged testes in hamsters after vitamin E supplementation. The reversibility of vitamin E deficiency-induced testicular damage in guinea pigs, roosters, and guppies (*Poecilia reticulata*) has not been established (Mason, 1933, 1959).

Blaxter (1962) has stated that simple dietary vitamin E deficiency does not affect reproduction in sheep and cattle.

The first observations leading to the discovery of vitamin E were made by Evans and Bishop, who observed absorption of fetuses caused by rancid diets. The scientific name for vitamin E, tocopherol, is derived from tocos (childbirth) and phero (to bring or confer); the ending "ol" indicates that the compound is an alcohol (Evans, 1962). Female rats on a vitamin E deficient diet have normal estrous cycles, mate normally, the blastocysts implant, but at about day 3 of pregnancy, resorption starts. Administration of 2 mg. vitamin E on day 10 of pregnancy permitted some fetal development, but the incidence of abnormalities among the young born was high (37 to 40 percent) in experiments carried out by Cheng et al. (1960). Either progesterone or estrone, or estrone plus progesterone administration from the third day of gestation to such vitamin E-deficient rats, given 2 mg. vitamin E on day 10, increased the incidence of resorptions from 77 percent

in the nonhormone-treated to 89 to 100 percent in the hormone-treated rats. The hormone treatment reduced the incidence of abnormalities to zero (Cheng, 1959). Gortner and Ekwurtzel (1965), however, could not confirm that vitamin E administration at day 10 of pregnancy causes a high incidence of fetal abnormalities; only 4 to 5 percent were obtained.

Kenney and Roderuck (1963) gave 2 mg. vitamin E on day 8 or 9 of gestation, which permitted some fetal development, but only 1 out of the 15 young born was alive and eight out of the 15 died at parturition (no mention was made of the incidence of abnormalities). As the dose of vitamin E was increased, the incidence of mortality decreased, which was also the case for the dams. These workers found a 53 percent mortality of the mothers at or after parturition if 2 mg. of vitamin E was given on day 8 or 9; these rats showed dyspnea, vaginal bleeding, hemorrhagic large kidneys, enlarged adrenals, accumulation of pleural fluid, and high nonprotein nitrogen concentration in the plasma. Other workers have not reported these phenomena when vitamin E was given on day 10. The reasons for some of these differences are not obvious from differences among experimental methods.

The deficiency of vitamin E in the diet of turkey hens had no effect on egg production or fertility, but decreased hatchability. Embryos from such eggs were smaller than normal and had lens defects (Atkinson et al., 1955). Feeding of a diet high in linoleic acid and without antioxidants causes a decrease in egg production, low fertility, and 100 percent embryonic mortality; either ethoxyquin or vitamin E can prevent these disturbances of reproduction, as can feeding of a diet low in linoleic acid (Machlin et al., 1962). Chick embryos in vitamin E-deficient eggs show hemorrhages and disturbances of the circulatory system (Landauer, 1961).

From the evidence given above, it appears that vitamin E acts as a biological antioxidant rather than as a vitamin, for other antioxidants have the same effect as vitamin E.

Vitamin K. There seems to be little evidence that vitamin K is required for reproduction per se, although vitamin K deficiency does cause hemorrhages, and may also cause placental hemorrhages, thus causing fetal and early postnatal death in chicks.

WATER SOLUBLE VITAMINS

Much of the evidence concerning the effects of water soluble vitamins has been summarized by Lutwak-Mann (1958) and has also been reviewed by Leathem (1961).

For normal development of the embryo it is necessary to feed the dams higher amounts of the water soluble vitamins than are required for optimal egg production.

Some of the relationships among the water soluble vitamins and the oviducal response to estrogen administration have been reviewed (van Tienhoven, 1961), and the highlights will be mentioned.

Folic acid deficiency, independent of inanition, diminishes the response to estrogen, probably because the deficiency prevents adequate nucleic acid synthesis. Brown (1953) has shown that the oviducal response to estrogen and progesterone in folic acid deficient rats can be obtained after administration of DNA.

The increased response of the oviduct to estrogen in cases of nicotinic acid and thiamine deficiency have been discussed. This increased response is probably the result of a decreased inactivation of estrogen by the liver, causing the amount of circulating estrogen to be higher than in control birds (van Tienhoven, 1961).

Deficiency of either of the following vitamins results in reduced food intake and in reduced egg production in chickens: thiamine, riboflavin, pantothenic acid, nicotinic acid, pyridoxine, and folic acid. To what extent the deficiency of each of these vitamins is a specific one or a secondary one has not been established because the deficiency reduces feed intake.

For optimal embryonic viability and minimal malformations the following vitamins must be present in the egg: thiamine, riboflavin, pantothenic acid, nicotinic acid, pyridoxine, biotin, folic acid, and vitamin B_{12}.

The lack of any of these vitamins, either because of its absence in the egg or because an antimetabolite has been injected into the egg, thus creating a deficiency, causes embryonic mortality.

A short account will be given here of the various deficiency symptoms for each vitamin, as observed in chick embryos:

(a) Thiamine — After injections of thiamine analogs into eggs the embryonic mortality increases. The affected chicks show hemorrhages, edema, and abdominal hernia (Naber et al., 1954).

(b) Riboflavin — Embryos from eggs deficient in riboflavin (either because riboflavin is present in insufficient quantities or because the hen can not transfer the vitamin into the egg [Maw, 1954]) results in high mortality. Embryos from such eggs show edema, degeneration of the Wolffian bodies, "clubbed" down, and dwarfism (Cravens, 1949; Landauer, 1961).

(c) Biotin — Deficiency of this vitamin causes high embryonic mortality, mainly on the third day and toward the end of the incubation period. The embryos have crooked tibia, twisted tarsometatarsi, and parrot beaks.

(d) Pantothenic acid — The lack of this vitamin results in high embryonic mortality at 12 to 14 days of incubation. The embryos show subcutaneous hemorrhages and severe edema (Beer et al., 1963).

(e) B_{12} — The presence of this vitamin in insufficient amounts decreases the cephalin and sphingomyelin in the embryo. Embryonic mortality is so early that it may seem that the eggs had not been fertilized (Landauer, 1961).

(f) Niacin — Induction of niacin deficiency usually requires that a low tryptophan diet be fed, because niacin can be formed from tryptophan. Injection of a niacin antagonist, such as 3-acetyl pyridine, into the egg also creates a lack of available niacin for the embryo. Mortality is 100 percent. The embryos show hypoplasia of the musculature, sometimes shortened upper beaks, and generalized edema. 6-amino nicotinamide (also a niacin antagonist) injected at 24 hours of incubation, caused a high incidence of rumplessness, whereas injection at 96 hours caused micromelia and parrot beaks (Landauer, 1961). The symptoms induced either by 3-acteyl pyridine or by 6-amino nicotinamide could be prevented by niacin injection.

(g) Pyridoxine — Deficiency of this vitamin affects egg production more severely than hatchability. Injection of desoxypyridoxine or methoxypyridoxine to induce pyridoxine deficiency inhibits early embryonic development (Landauer, 1961).

(h) Folic acid — This vitamin seems to be required in very small amounts. Lack of the vitamin causes mortality of embryos exhibiting bends in the tibio tarsus, syndactylism, and beak defects (Landauer, 1961).

Little information seems to be available on the relationship between the deficiency of the water soluble vitamins and the testicular development of the rooster. It is has been established that folic acid is not required for the response of the comb to testosterone (see van Tienhoven, 1961), but the testicular tubules are diminished in diameter. Vitamin B_{12} deficiency causes smaller than normal testes (Terroine and Delost, 1961).

The effect of vitamin deficiencies on reproductive organs has been thoroughly reviewed by Terroine and Delost (1961), and on gestation by Bourdel et al. (1961). These authors stressed the necessity of using normal and pair-fed controls to distinguish between the specific effect of the vitamin and undernutrition. Here some of the major effects will be mentioned.

Thiamine deficiency in rats causes smaller than normal testes, small diameters of the seminiferous tubules, abnormal spermatogenesis, underdeveloped Leydig cells, small seminal vesicles, but there is still some androgen secretion, as indicated by the normal ventral lobes of the prostate and the ductus deferens. Comparisons were made with pair-fed controls. The addition of ascorbic acid to the diet prevented these effects to a large extent (Terroine and Delost, 1961).

The effect of thiamine deficiency on the female rat does not seem to have been studied in great detail. The estrous cycle is abnormal; if the female becomes pregnant resorptions occur, gestation is prolonged, many of the young born are not viable (Bourdel et al., 1961). The abortions and effects on the fetus can be prevented by estrone plus progesterone treatment (Srebnik and Nelson, 1962).

Biotin deficiency affects the male reproductive system in a way similar to thiamine deficiency, but the effects on the germinal epithelium can be distinguished histologically. In thiamine deficiency the primary spermatocytes do not undergo chromatin reduction, whereas in the case of biotin deficiency there is condensation of multinucleated giant cells, a phenomenon which also occurs during either vitamin E, riboflavin, or pantothenic acid deficiency. Lesions of the paraprostatic ganglion are found in the case of biotin deficiency and also in the case of vitamin E deficiency (Terroine and Delost, 1961). In these experiments pair-fed controls were used.

The effects of biotin deficiency on the female's genital tract have not been studied sufficiently. Atresia of follicles has been observed in rats and mice, but in the rat the estrous cycle seems to remain normal (Terroine and Delost, 1961). Although the evidence is incomplete, it appears that biotin deficiency does not affect gestation adversely (Bourdel et al., 1961).

Riboflavin deficiency in rats causes small testes, damage to the germinal epithelium (the damage being more severe than in the case of thiamine or biotin deficiencies), and atrophy of the Leydig cells, the seminal vesicles, and prostates. Comparisons made with pair-fed controls, by Terroine and Delost (1961), show that the ovaries of riboflavin-deficient rats are atrophied and lack corpora lutea, the rats are in anestrus, and the uterus is also atrophied. Pregnancies can be obtained after instituting a riboflavin-deficient diet a few days prior to mating so that the effect of the deficiency can be studied with respect to pregnancy. Resorptions are found in riboflavin deficient rats.

Another method of inducing short-term riboflavin deficiencies consists of injecting of galactoflavin, which is a riboflavin antimetabolite. After the injections are stopped, one administers riboflavin to restore the riboflavin adequate condition. With this method one can study the days of gestation during which the deficiency is most effective. Administration of galactoflavin causes abnormal fetal development in rats and mice, although there are genetic differences among strains of mice with respect to the incidence of malformations in response to galactoflavin administration (Bourdel et al., 1961).

Pantothenic acid is required for normal testicular function; deficiency causes the appearance of multinuclear giant cells in the seminiferous tubules. Seminal vesicles of rats and mice are diminished in size as the result of pantothenic acid deficiency.

Deficiency of this vitamin causes delayed puberty. In sexually mature rats, the deficiency results in small ovaries that lack mature follicles, atrophy of the uteri, and permanent anestrus. Uterine weight can be increased and estrus can be induced by estrogen injections. In pigs, atretic follicles and smaller than normal corpora lutea are noted under pantothenic acid deficiency conditions (Terroine and Delost, 1961). If the deficiency is instituted during pregnancy it leads to abortions and malformations. The incidence can be decreased by the addition of ascorbic acid to the diet (Bourdel et al., 1961). Injections of estrogen and progesterone do not maintain pregnancy (Nelson and Evans, 1956), although such injections maintain pregnancy in the case of thiamine, pyridoxine, protein or potassium deficiency (Srebnik and Nelson, 1962).

An insufficient vitamin B_{12} supply causes degeneration of the germinal epithelium, reduction of testicular size, and a decrease in the number of Leydig cells of rats and reduces testicular size in cockerels (Terroine and Delost, 1961).

Vitamin B_{12}-deficient female rats have atrophic ovaries and uteri. In pregnant rats the deficiency results in hydroencephaly and malformation of the eye of the fetuses (Bourdel et al., 1961).

Folic acid deficiency causes a decrease in tubule diameter of the testis of cockerels but little effect has been noted on the testes of guinea pigs, although the seminal vesicles and prostates are smaller than normal. The response to PMSG of the testes is diminished but the response of the prostates and seminal vesicles to androgen is normal (Terroine and Delost, 1961).

The effect of the deficiency of folic acid on the oviduct of the chicken has been discussed previously. The effect on the rat is similar; that is, there is no response of the uterus to estrogen. The involvement of folic acid in nucleic acid is well documented and the lack of a response of the oviduct to estrogen has been "explained." However, the reason for a response by the seminal vesicles and prostate in spite of folic acid deficiency is not clear. It is possible that there are metabolic preferences so that one organ can still respond to hormonal stimulation but others cannot (Terroine and Delost, 1961).

Folic acid deficiency can be caused by the feeding of a folic acid-deficient diet and also by the administration of the folic acid antimetabolite aminopterin. By the administration of aminopterin for a selected number of days and subsequent administration of folic acid, one can pinpoint the deficiency to a certain number of days and one can determine during which stage of development the deficiency has the most severe effects. It was found that as short a period as 48 hours of folic acid deficiency, between days 7 and 12 of pregnancy, results in 70 to 100 percent abnormalities (Nelson et al., 1955) which consisted of edema, cleft palate, and abnormalities of the paw and lung (Nelson et al., 1952). Estrogen and progesterone do not prevent folic acid deficiency-induced abnormalities and resorptions (Srebnik and Nelson, 1962).

Aminopterin administration prevents the uterine response to progesterone in the Hooker-Forbes bioassay (Velardo and Hisaw, 1952) and of the crop gland to prolactin (Cowie and Folley, 1955); both responses involve synthesis of nucleic acids (Cowie and Folley, 1955).

The deficiency of pyridoxine causes lesions in the seminiferous tubules and Leydig cells of rats and reduced testicular weight to 50 percent of that of pair-fed controls (Delost and Terroine, 1961). The secondary sex organs are small, indicating low androgen secretion. In the female rat, normal mature follicles are present but atretic follicles are found, while the interstitial cells are atrophic, the cycles are irregular. As Terroine and Delost (1961) pointed out, no pair-fed controls were used.

In mice, lack of pyridoxine results in atrophy of the ovaries, small follicles, atretic follicles, and contracted interstitial cells. However, in these experiments the same effects were found in pair-fed controls. It thus seems that pyridoxine is not required for normal gonadal function except in the sense that the deficiency reduces food intake.

During gestation the imposition of pyridoxine deficiency by administering a pyridoxine antimetabolite causes resorption of the fetuses. A 100 percent incidence can be accomplished by administration of the antimetabolite 22 days prior to mating (Terroine and Delost, 1961). Resorptions can be prevented by injecting estrogen and progesterone (Srebnik and Nelson, 1962).

The response of the pigeon crop gland to prolactin is not affected by pyridoxine deficiency (Hsu, 1963).

Niacin deficiency is difficult to impose because of its metabolic interrelationship with tryptophan, and there is insufficient information to draw satisfactory conclusions. The response of the pigeon crop gland to prolactin injections is inhibited by niacin deficiency (Masahito, 1959).

Ascorbic acid deficiency is, of course, of importance only in the relatively few species for which this acid has to be supplied in the diet (guinea pigs, monkeys, man). Deficiency of this vitamin causes degeneration of the germinal epithelium starting near the center of the seminiferous tubule and progressing toward the periphery. The Leydig cells are not affected. No pair-fed controls seem to have been used, however (Terroine and Delost, 1961). The effect of ascorbic acid deficiency consists of atresia and degeneration of follicles, regression of the corpora lutea, and hyperplasia of the endometrium (Terroine and Delost, 1961). If the deficiency occurs during early pregnancy, abortions and resorptions may occur; during late pregnancy the effect consists mainly of premature delivery (Bourdel et al., 1961).

MINERALS

The mineral requirements for laying and breeding hens have been listed as the same by Card and Nesheim (1966), but the requirements for good hatchability are probably more critical than for laying (Nesheim, personal communication). The requirements are: Ca 3 percent, P 0.6 percent, Na 0.15 percent, K 0.16 percent, Mn 33 mg./kg. feed, I 0.30 mg./kg., Zn 35 mg./kg. The requirements for magnesium, iron, and copper have not been determined.

Calcium deficiency, if it is marginal, may express itself first in the thin shells of eggs and, as the deficiency becomes more severe, egg production is unfavorably affected. Hatchability, as is the case with vitamin D deficiency, is also affected unfavorably.

The lesions induced by deficiencies of any of these minerals are not readily distinguishable except for magnesium, iodine, and zinc deficiencies.

Lack of magnesium results in chondrodystrophy of the embryos, characterized by short wings and legs, a parrot beak, bulging heads, and straight tibia (Cravens, 1949).

Iodine deficiency is expressed by delayed hatching, enlarged thyroids, and abnormal thyroid histology (Rogler et al., 1961).

Lack of zinc, in an isolated soy protein diet high in calcium (to aggravate zinc deficiency) causes micromelia, dorsal curvature of the spine, abnormally shortened and fused thoracic and lumbar vertebrae, and edematous swelling of the neck muscles (Kienholz et al., 1961). Survival of apparently normal chicks from hens on zinc-deficient diets was low; the chicks were weak, unable to stand, eat, or drink, and had a high respiratory rate and labored breathing.

In their review on the effects of nutrition on mammalian reproduction Bourdel et al. (1961) discuss only the following minerals with respect to reproduction: calcium, phosphorus, iodine, sodium, potassium, copper, and iron.

Lack of calcium apparently does not affect gestation of either the rat or the pig. However, if such a ration is fed to rats for several generations a decrease in fertility and an increase in embryonic mortality is found (Bourdel et al., 1961; Rombauts et al., 1961). A probable reason for a lack of an effect of calcium deficiency in the first generation is the mobilization of calcium from the skeleton of the dam.

Phosphorus deficiency causes decreased fertility in cattle but apparently has little effect in pigs (Rombauts et al., 1961).

Iodine is required for normal development of the thyroid of the embryo; if present in insufficient amounts, myxedemous young are born.

Sodium deficiency causes irregular cycles and reduces fertility. Lack of potassium results in resorptions and abortions, which can be prevented by estrogen and progesterone treatment (Srebnik and Nelson, 1962).

Manganese does not seem to be required for normal estrous cycles and ovu-

lations, but young born are abnormal and show ataxia (Hurley et al., 1958).

Iron deficiency may result in anemia of mother and young.

Copper is apparently involved in the myelinization of the fetus, for lambs and calves born from copper-deficient dams show degeneration of the brain and motor nerves (Bourdel et al., 1961).

Zinc deficiency caused testicular degeneration, whereas pair-fed controls receiving 100 μg. Zn/g. of food had normal testes. Germinal vesicles and prostates of the deficient rats were small (Millar et al., 1960).

Zinc administration was ineffective in restoring normal testes and epididymides once the degeneration had occurred (Millar et al., 1958).

Testosterone or gonadotropin injections to rats on a low zinc diet (0.5 μg./g.) caused a marked growth of the accessory reproductive glands, although the dorsolateral prostate was low in zinc content. Testosterone did not affect the atrophic testes. Gonadotropin injected into immature zinc-deficient rats caused an increased rate of growth. Degeneration of the germinal epithelium, as a result of feeding a zinc-deficient diet to sexually mature rats, could not be prevented by gonadotropin injections (Millar et al., 1960). It thus appears that there are two sites at which zinc is important for reproduction in the male rat. During the development of the testes, zinc deficiency seems to affect mainly the gonadotropin secretion, whereas once sexual maturity is reached, zinc seems to be required by the testes for normal spermatogenesis (Millar et al., 1960). No significant effects of zinc deficiency were observed on the reproductive performance of bulls (Pitts et al., 1966).

Feeding a zinc-deficient diet to pregnant rats results in a high incidence (152 out of 280) resorptions and a high incidence (125 out of 128) of abnormalities in the fetuses which survive. Forty-nine percent of the fetuses have abnormalities of the urogenital system, 80 percent of the digits of the feet, 85 percent of the tail, and many other abnormalities which occurred with somewhat smaller frequency (Hurley and Swenerton, 1966).

A low zinc (35 p.p.m.) + high calcium (1.4 percent) diet fed after weaning to gilts decreased their weight gains below that of gilts fed this diet with zinc at 85 p.p.m., but reproductive performance was not affected (Pond and Jones, 1964).

Sodium deficiency delays spermatogenesis in rats so that at 99 days only a few primary spermatocytes are evident, whereas in pair-fed controls spermatogenesis is complete. The deficient rats also had smaller secondary sex organs than pair-fed controls.

The reproductive system of the female on a sodium-deficient diet is characterized by normal ovarian weight, with a few corpora lutea and fewer large follicles, probably accounting for the weight difference. The vaginal epithelium is multilayered and the lumen is filled with keratinized cells and leukocytes; the uteri have columnar epithelial cells which show secretory activity (Follis et al., 1942).

Potassium-low diets (0.01 percent K) caused abnormal spermatozoa to be prevalent, lowered sperm motility, and resulted in sterility, although matings occurred. The females on this treatment reached puberty later than normal, the estrous cycle was abnormal, and ovulations were irregular (Orent-Keiles and McCollum, 1941).

Some minerals found in feed may be toxic and cause reproductive disturbances. An example is selenium, which can be present in toxic amounts in grains grown on selenium-rich soils.

Hens fed such grains will deposit selenium in the egg, where it may cause damage to the embryo. Mortality is high during the last few days of the incubation period, and the chicks cannot hatch, although they are alive. Heads, wings and legs are abnormal. Injection of selenium into the normal hatching eggs causes the same symptoms (Landauer, 1961).

This mineral can cause infertility in rats and swine, but the presence of this element in the ration of pregnant rats did not cause congenital malformations. Selenium intake by a pregnant horse and by pregnant ewes has been reported to result in congenital malformations. The lambs had abnormal eyes (microphthalmia, microcornea), rudimentary development, and colobomas of various organs (Rosenfeld and Beath, 1964).

A specific and a rather curious series of effects has been observed after *injection* of cadmium salts.

Pařízek and Záhoř (1965) were the first to report that injections of cadmium salts caused severe testicular damage in rats. Zinc at 80 to 100 times the dose of cadmium protected against this effect. A large number of papers reporting on the investigation of this phenomenon have been published. The most salient findings are:

1. The testicular damage by cadmium injections either subcutaneously or intravenously occurs in rats (Pařízek, 1957, 1960; Gunn et al., 1965a), mice (Chiquone, 1964), rabbits (Pařízek, 1960; Cameron and Foster, 1963), hamsters (Pařízek, 1960), guinea pigs (Pařízek, 1960), and monkeys *(Macacus irus)* (Girod and Chauvineau, 1965), but not in opossums (Chiquone, 1964), and ferrets (Chiquone and Suntzeff, 1965), although in the latter two species intratesticular cadmium salt injection will cause damage to the epithelium (Chiquone and Suntzeff, 1965). No damage to the testes occurred in roosters upon subcutaneous injection (Erickson and Pincus, 1964) although the animals were affected by the cadmium, as was evident from their lethargy. The subcutaneous administration of $CdCl_2$ caused a retardation of the photoperiodic response of the testes of wood pigeons *(Columba palumbus)*. In animals with postnuptial regression of the testes there was no effect. The testes of feral pigeons *(C. livia)* in full breeding condition showed no necrosis but showed disturbance of the radial coordination of the cells of the germinal epithelium after

CdCl₂ injections. Intratesticular injections caused local necrotic damage, but spermatogenesis occurred in other tubules (Lofts and Murton, 1967).

2. At low doses of cadmium the seminiferous tubules may show degeneration without necrosis, and the Leydig cells apparently remain unaffected (Mason et al., 1964).

3. The cadmium injections are effective only after the testis has reached a certain state of maturity (at about 15 days of age) (Pařízek, 1960).

4. Cadmium-induced necrosis of the germinal epithelium is irreversible, but after partial damage surviving germ cells can proliferate and normal spermatogenesis can be attained (Kar and Das, 1961).

5. The primary effect of cadmium seems to be on the blood flow to the testis. Twelve hours after injection, the amount of blood reaching the rat's testis is about 2 to 9 percent of normal (Waites and Setchell, 1965). A reduction in blood flow to the accessory reproductive organs also occurs (Waites and Setchell, 1965). Citric acid and fructose content of the seminal vesicles decreases to levels found in castrates (Favino et al., 1966).

6. Cadmium salt injections cause injury to the vasculature of the rat's testis, the internal spermatic artery, and the pampiniform plexus, but do not affect the vessels accompanying the ductus deferens (Gunn et al., 1965b). Niemi and Kormano (1965) found a dramatic disappearance of blood vessels from the testicular surface. Four weeks after injection, new blood vessels started to reappear.

7. Testosterone synthesis decreases after cadmium injections, but recovery occurs about 100 days after injection (Favino et al., 1966). Gunn et al. (1965b) found that interstitial cell tumors occurred after cadmium salt injections but they also were found after ligation of the testicular blood vessels. Androgenic activity was higher in rats treated with cadmium or that had only the spermatic vessels ligated than in rats with spermatic and ductus deferens vessels ligated. Zinc prevents the cadmium-induced tumors but not those induced by ligation of the blood vessels, suggesting that other factors than "chemical ligation" are involved in the cadmium-induced tumor development (Gunn et al., 1965b).

8. There are genetic differences within species with respect to the sensitivity of the testes to cadmium salts (Chiquone and Suntzeff, 1965; Gunn et al., 1965a).

9. Protection against the effects of cadmium salt injection on the testes is afforded by zinc (Pařízek, 1957, Pařízek and Záhoř, 1957), selenium (Kar and Das, 1963), thiol compounds (Gunn et al., 1966) and the following steroids: testosterone propionate, dehydroepiandrosterone, progesterone, 17-β-hydroxy estran-3-one (Maekawa and Hosoyama, 1965).

The effect of cadmium salt injections into female rats depends on the stage of development and the reproductive phase during which the material is injected. Injected to estrous females, it does not prevent fertilization and birth (Pařízek, 1960). Injection of these salts during days 17 to 21 of pregnancy results in damage to the fetal part of the placenta, and pregnancy is terminated. However, there is also damage independent of the fetus, for after its removal, cadmium salt administration also results in placental damage (Pařízek, 1964).

Chiquone (1965) injected (0.02 mM./kg.) CdCl₂ at different times during pregnancy in mice and found no effect if injections occurred before day 5 (day of implantation); administration on day 5, 14, 15, 16, or 17 caused placental necrosis and termination of pregnancy. Injections of zinc (2 mM./kg.) either 12 or seven hours prior to the CdCl₂ prevented the interruption of pregnancy.

The damaging effects of cadmium salts on the testes seem to be rather specific in two ways:

1. Salts of metals and rare earth other than cadmium do not cause similar damage to the testes. Sometimes one injection

may have a temporary effect, but recovery is rapid and virtually complete (Hoey, 1966; Kamboj and Kar, 1964).

2. The effect of cadmium salts is rather selectively deleterious to the testes, although changes in spleen, liver and kidney are found (Cameron and Foster, 1963). The animals, after a temporary cessation of growth, recover and seem normal (Pařízek, 1960).

The mode of action of cadmium salts has not been elucidated. It may be involved with the sulfhydryl groups of different enzymes, and the evidence that thiol compounds can prevent cadmium-induced damage supports this. However, such an explanation does not account for the selectivity of the location of the damage.

SUMMARY

It appears from the data and experiments reviewed that energy restriction has a relatively minor effect on reproductive performance. The effect is often unfavorable, but in pigs it may be beneficial. It should be kept in mind that in swine breeding there has been much emphasis on the selection of fast growing animals that have, in general, a higher feed consumption. This selection may have been somewhat detrimental to reproductive performance. The breeders, of course, have not neglected reproductive ability in their selection programs. It would be of interest to compare the effects of different energy intakes on reproductive performance in beef and dairy cattle.

Inadequate supplies of amino acids (resulting from a diet deficient in either protein or amino acids) have severe repercussions on reproduction. Sperm production and ovulation are inhibited, and no young can be produced. (Teleologically, this would be an advantage for the preservation of the individuals.) Protein deficiency imposed on a pregnant animal results in abortion, which can, in the rat, be prevented by progesterone and estrogen treatment. The evidence that the amino acid deficiency acts on the same system, i.e., the anterior pituitary, during puberty and pregnancy is indirect (response to exogenous gonadotropins, lowered gonadotropin content of the pituitary) but reasonably convincing.

As one might expect, the effect of amino acid deficiency is not selective; other parts of the endocrine system are affected, e.g. the thyroid and adrenals (see Aschkenasy, 1961), but the fact that gonadotropic and gonadal hormones can maintain pregnancy suggests that the main effect on reproduction is via the pituitary-gonadal axis. Why the animal can mobilize amino acids for synthesis of the proteins for the embryo but not for gonadotropin synthesis is not known. However, the mechanism, again, tends to preserve the individual at the cost of reproduction of the species.

It is not surprising, in view of the role which vitamins and minerals play in enzymatically catalyzed reactions, that deficiencies of these nutrients have severe consequences on reproductive performance. Often the deficiency is accompanied by a decrease in intake of all nutrients.

To what extent this has influenced the outcome of experiments is not always discernible, and since many of the requirements are determined per unit of feed rather than per individual, these effects may not be important. The exact mechanism of action of these nutrient deficiencies has not been determined.

The experiments in which pregnancy was maintained during nutrient deficiency conditions (potassium, protein, thiamine, pyridoxine) by estrogen and progesterone suggest that these nutrients affect mainly the hormone production by the dam. The malformations induced by, e.g., folic acid and pantothenic acid indicate damage primarily to the embryo, although it is possible, of course, that damage to the placenta causes embryonic abnormalities because of lack of nutrient and oxygen supply during crucial phases of development.

Nutrition is thus an important factor in obtaining optimal reproductive performance and the specificity of some lesions may provide a clue that indicates which nutrient is missing from the diet or is not available to the animal or the fetus for some reason.

REFERENCES

Aaes-Jørgensen, E., Funch, J. P., and Dam, H. 1956. The role of fat in the diet. 10. Influence on reproduction of hydrogenated arachis oil as the sole dietary fat. Brit. J. Nutrit. 10:317-324.

Adamstone, F. B., and Card, L. E. 1934. The effects of vitamin E deficiency on the testis of the male fowl (Gallus domesticus). J. Morphol. 56:339-352.

Allen, D. M. 1961. Some effects of malnutrition on the growth and sexual development of ewe lambs. J. Agr. Sci. 57:87-95.

Allen, D. M., and Lamming, G. E. 1961. Nutrition and reproduction in the ewe. J. Agr. Sci. 56:69-79.

Anderson, D. L., Smyth, J. R., Jr., and Gleason, R. E. 1963. Effect of restricted feeding during the growing period on reproductive performance of large type white turkeys. Poultry Sci. 42:8-15.

Arscott, G. H., Parker, J. E. and Dickinson, E. M. 1965. Effect of dietary linoleic acid, vitamin E and ethoxyquin on fertility of male chickens. J. Nutrit. 87:63-68.

Aschkenasy, A. 1961. Le retentissement de la carence alimentaire en protéines sur la thyroïde et les surrénales. La part revenant à un dysfonctionnement de ces deux glandes dans la genèse de diverses manifestations de la carence. Ann. Nutrit Alim. 15:B165-202.

Assenmacher, I., Tixier-Vidal, A., and Astier, H. 1965. Effets de la sous-alimentation et du jeûne sur la gonadostimulation du canard. Ann. Endocrinol. 26:1-26.

Atkinson, R. L., Ferguson, T. M., Quisenberry, J. H., and Couch, J. R. 1955. Vitamin E and reproduction in turkeys. J. Nutrit. 55:387-397.

Baba, T., and Araki, E. 1959. Morphogenesis of malformation due to excessive vitamin A. I. Morphogenesis of exencephaly. Biol. Abstr. 36, ref. 24479, 1961.

Baba, T., and Nakamura, S. 1959. Changes in the rat fetus inner ear due to an excessive vitamin A. Biol. Abstr. 36, ref. 24481, 1961.

Baba, T., and Yukioka, K. 1959. Morphogenesis of malformation due to excessive vitamin A. II. Morphogenesis of cleft palate and its critical phase. Biol. Abstr. 36, ref. 24480, 1961.

Ball, Z. B., Barnes, R. H., and Visscher, M. B. 1947. The effects of dietary caloric restriction on maturity and senescence with particular reference to fertility and longevity. Amer. J. Physiol. 150:511-519.

Beer, A. E., Scott, M. L., and Nesheim, M. C. 1963. The effects of graded levels of pantothenic acid on the breeding performance of White Leghorn pullets. Brit. Poultry Sci. 4:243-253.

Bellows, R. A., Meyer, R. K., Hoekstra, W. G., and Casida, L. E. 1966. Pituitary potency and ovarian activity in rats on two levels of dietary energy. J. Anim. Sci. 25:381-385.

Bellows, R. A., Pope, A. L., Chapman, A. B., and Casida, L. E. 1963. Effect of level and sequence of feeding and breed on ovulation rate, embryo survival, and fetal growth in the mature ewe. J. Anim. Sci. 22:101-108.

Berg, B. N. 1965. Dietary restriction and reproduction in the rat. J. Nutrit. 87:344-348.

Biswas, M. M., and Deb, C. 1966. Testicular degeneration in rats during hypervitaminosis A. Endokrinologie 49:64-69.

Blaxter, K. L. 1962. Vitamin E in health and disease of cattle and sheep. Vitamins and Hormones 20:633-643.

Blaxter, K. L. 1964. Protein metabolism and requirements in pregnancy and lactation. In H. N. Munro and J. B. Allison (eds.): Mammalian Protein Metabolism. Academic Press Inc., New York, Vol. 2, pp. 173-221.

Bo, W. J., and Smith, M. S. 1966. The effect of retinol and retinoic acid on the morphology of the rat uterus. Anat. Rec. 156:5-10.

Bourdel, G., Jacquot, R., Klein, M., and Mayer, G. 1961. Nutrition and gestation. Ann. Nutrit. Alim. 15B:337-380.

Bratton, R. W., Musgrave, S. D., Dunn, H. O., and Foote, R. H. 1959. Causes and prevention of reproductive failures in dairy cattle. II. Influence of underfeeding and overfeeding from birth to 80 weeks of age on growth, sexual development, and semen production of Holstein bulls. Cornell Agr. Exp. Sta. Bull. 940.

Bratton, R. W., Musgrave, S. D., Dunn, H. O., and Foote, R. H. 1961. Causes and prevention of reproductive failures in dairy cattle. III. Influence of underfeeding and overfeeding from birth through 80 weeks of age on growth, sexual development, semen production, and fertility of Holstein bulls. Cornell Agr. Exp. Sta. Bull. 964.

Brown, W. O. 1953. The effect of deoxypentosenucleic acid on the impaired oviduct response to oestrogen in the folic acid-deficient chick. Biochim. Biophys. Acta 11:162-163.

Buckner, S. O., Insko, W. M., Henry, A. H., and Wachs, E. F. 1951. Influence of vitamin D on the growth of New Hampshire cockerels, their combs, wattles, gonads and uropygeal glands. Poultry Sci. 30:267-268.

Calvert, C. C. 1967. Studies on hatchability of fertile eggs from hens receiving a linoleic acid deficient diet. Poultry Sci. 46:967-973.

Cameron, E., and Foster, C. L. 1963. Observations on the histological effects of sub-lethal doses of cadmium chloride in the rabbit. J. Anat. 97:269-280.

Card, L. E., and Nesheim, M. C. 1966. Poultry Production, Ed. 10. Lea & Febiger, Philadelphia.

Chang, M. C., and Sheaffer, D. 1956. Does starvation increase sperm count? Science 124:1203.

Cheng, D. W. 1959. Effect of progesterone and estrone on the incidence of congenital malformations due to maternal vitamin E deficiency. Endocrinology 64:270-275.

Cheng, D. W., Bairnson, T. A., Ras, A. N., and Subbammal, S. J. 1960. Effect of variations of rations on the incidence of teratogeny in vitamin E-deficient rats. J. Nutrit. 71:54-60.

Chiquone, A. D. 1964. Observations on the early events of cadmium necrosis in the testis. Anat. Rec. 149:23-36.

Chiquone, A. D. 1965. Effect of cadmium chloride on the pregnant albino mouse. J. Reprod. Fertil. 10:263-265.

Chiquone, A. D., and Suntzeff, V. 1965. Sensitivity of mammals to cadmium necrosis of the testis. J. Reprod. Fertil. 10:455-457.

Clawson, A. J., Richards, H. L., Matrone, G., and Barrick, E. R. 1963. Influence of level of total nutrient and protein intake on reproductive performance in swine. J. Anim. Sci. 22:662-669.

Coward, W. A., Howell, J. McC., Pitt, G. A. J., and Thompson, J. N. 1966. Effects of hormones on reproduction in rats fed a diet deficient in retinol (vitamin A alcohol) but containing methyl retinoate (vitamin A acid methyl ester). J. Reprod. Fertil. 12:309-317.

Cowie, A. T., and Folley, S. J. 1955. Physiology of the gonadotropins and the lactogenic hormone. In G. Pincus and K. V. Thimann (eds.): The Hormones. Academic Press Inc., New York, Vol. 3, pp. 309-388.

Cravens, W. W. 1949. The nutrition of the breeding flock. In L. W. Taylor (ed.): Fertility and Hatchability of Chicken and Turkey Eggs. John Wiley & Sons Inc., New York, pp. 1-51.

Dam, H. 1962. Interrelations between vitamin E and polyunsaturated fatty acids in animals. Vitamins and Hormones 20:527-540.

Delost, P., and Terroine, T. 1961. Lésions du tube séminifère et de la glande interstitielle chez le rat carencé en pyridoxine. C. R. Soc. Biol. 155:1513-1516.

Dickerson, J. W. T., Gresham, G. A., and McCance, R. A. 1964. The effect of undernutrition and rehabilitation on the development of the reproductive organs: pigs. J. Endocrinol. 29:111-118.

Dutt, R. H., and Barnhart, C. E. 1959. Effect of plane of nutrition upon reproduction and maintenance of boars. J. Anim. Sci. 18:3-13.

Edey, T. N. 1965. Undernutrition in early embryonic mortality in merino ewes. Nature 208:1232.

El Sheihk, A. S., Hulet, C. V., Pope, A. L., and Casida, L. E. 1955. The effect of level of feeding on the reproductive capacity of the ewe. J. Anim. Sci. 14:919-929.

Erickson, A. E., and Pincus, G. 1964. Insensitivity of fowl testes to cadmium. J. Reprod. Fertil. 7:379-382.

Ershoff, B. H. 1952. Nutrition and the anterior pituitary with special reference to the general adaptation syndrome. Vitamins and Hormones 10:79-140.

Evans, H. M. 1962. The pioneer history of vitamin E. Vitamins and Hormones 20:379-387.

Everett, J. W. 1966. The control of the secretion of prolactin. In G. W. Harris and B. T. Donovan (eds.): The Pituitary Gland. University of California Press, Berkeley, Vol. 2, pp. 166-194.

Favino, A., Baillie, A. H., and Griffiths, K. 1966. Androgen synthesis by the testes and adrenal glands of rats poisoned with cadmium chloride. J. Endocrinol. 35:185-192.

Fell, H. B. 1964. The role of organ cultures in the study of vitamins and hormones. Vitamins and Hormones 22:81-127.

Fisher, C. J., and Leathem, J. H. 1965. Effect of a protein-free diet on protein metabolism in the pregnant rat. Endocrinology 76:454-462.

Follis, R. H., Jr., Orent-Keiles, E., and McCollum, E. V. 1942. Histological studies of the tissues of rats fed a diet extremely low in sodium. Arch. Pathol. 33:504-512.

Foote, W. C., Pope, A. L., Chapman, A. B., and Casida, L. E. 1959. Reproduction in the yearling ewe as affected by breed and sequence of feeding level. I Effects on ovulation rate and embryo survival. J. Anim. Sci. 18:453-462.

Friedman, M. H., and Friedman, G. S. 1940. The relation of diet to the restitution of the gonadotropic hormone content of the discharged rabbit pituitary. Amer. J. Physiol. 128:493-499.

Girod, C., and Chauvineau, A. 1965. Nouvelles observations concernant l'influence du chlorure de cadmium sur le testicule du singe Macacus irus F. Cuv. C. R. Soc. Biol. 158:2113-2115.

Goode, L., Warnick, A. C., and Wallace, H. D. 1965. Effect of dietary energy levels upon reproduction and the relation of endometrial phosphatase activity to embryo survival in gilts. J. Anim. Sci. 24:959-963.

Gortner, R. A., and Ekwurtzel, J. B. 1965. Incidence of teratogeny induced by vitamin E deficiency in the rat. Proc. Soc. Exp. Biol. Med. 119:1069-1071.

Gowe, R. S., Johnson, A. S., Crawford, R. D., Downs, J. H., Hill, A. T., Mountain, W. F., Pelletier, J. R., and Strain, J. H. 1960. Restricted versus full-feeding during the growing period for egg production. Brit. Poultry Sci. 1:37-56.

Gunn, S. A., and Gould, T. C. 1958. Role of zinc in fertility and fecundity in the rat. Amer. J. Physiol. 193:505-508.

Gunn, S. A., Gould, T. C., and Anderson, W. A. D. 1965a. Strain differences in susceptibility of mice and rats to cadmium-induced testicular damage. J. Reprod. Fertil. 10:273-275.

Gunn, S. A., Gould, T. C., and Anderson, W. A. D. 1965b. Comparative study of interstitial cell tumors of rat testis induced by cadmium injection and vascular ligation. J. Nat. Cancer Inst. 35:329-337.

Gunn, S. A., Gould, T. C., and Anderson, W. A. D. 1966. Protective effect of thiol compounds against cadmium-induced vascular damage to testis. Proc. Soc. Exp. Biol. Med. *122*:1036-1039.

Hafez, E. S. E. 1952. Studies on the breeding season and reproduction of the ewe. J. Agr. Sci. *42*:189-231.

Hafez, E. S. E. 1960. Nutrition in relation to reproduction in sows. J. Agr. Sci. *54*:170-178.

Hahn, P., and Koldovský, O. 1966. Utilization of Nutrients During Postnatal Development. Pergamon Press, New York.

Hammond, J. 1965. The effects of high and low planes of nutrition on reproduction in rabbits. New Zeal. J. Agr. Res. *8*:708-717.

Hays, R. L., and Kendall, K. A. 1956. The beneficial effect of progesterone on pregnancy in the vitamin A-deficient rabbit. J. Nutrit. *59*:337-341.

Hays, R. L., and Kendall, K. A. 1961. Maintenance of pregnancy with prolactin or progesterone in rats on a sucrose diet. Endocrinology *68*:177-178.

Hays, R. L., Hahn, E. W., and Kendall, K. A. 1965. Evidence for decreased steroidogenesis in pregnant rats fed a sucrose diet. Endocrinology *76*:771-772.

Hazelwood, R. L., and Nelson, M. M. 1965. Steroid maintenance of pregnancy in rats in the absence of dietary protein. Endocrinology *77*:999-1013.

Heap, F. C., Lodge, G. A., and Lamming, G. E. 1967. The influence of plane of nutrition in early pregnancy on the survival and development of embryos in the sow. J. Reprod. Fertil. *13*:269-280.

Hoey, M. J. 1966. The effects of metallic salts on the histology and functioning of the rat testis. J. Reprod. Fertil. *12*:461-471.

Hollands, K. G., and Gowe, R. S. 1961. The effect of restricted and full-feeding during confinement rearing on first and second year laying house performance. Poultry Sci. *40*:574-583.

Hosoda, T., Kaneko, T., Mogi, K., and Abe, T. 1955. Effect of gonadotrophic hormone on ovarian follicles and serum vitellin of fasting hens. Proc. Soc. Exp. Biol. Med. *88*:502-504.

Hosoda, T., Kaneko, T., Mogi, K., and Abe, T. 1956. Forced ovulation in gonadotrophin-treated fasting hens. Proc. Soc. Exp. Biol. Med. *92*:360-362.

Howell, J. McC., Thompson, J. N., and Pitt, G. A. J. 1963. Histology of the lesions produced in the reproductive tract of animals fed a diet deficient in vitamin A alcohol but containing vitamin A acid. I. The male rat. J. Reprod. Fertil. *5*:159-167.

Howell, J. McC., Thompson, J. N., and Pitt, G. A. J. 1967. Changes in the tissues of guinea-pigs fed on a diet free from vitamin A but containing methyl retinoate. Brit. J. Nutrit. *21*:37-44.

Howland, B. E., Bellows, R. A., Pope, A. L., and Casida, L. E. 1966b. Ovarian activity in ewes treated with glucose and triiodothyronine. J. Anim. Sci. *25*:836-838.

Howland, B. E., Kirkpatrick, R. L., Pope, A. L., and Casida, L. E. 1966a. Pituitary and ovarian function in ewes fed on two nutritional levels. J. Anim. Sci. *25*:716-721.

Hsu, J. M. 1963. Interrelations between vitamin B$_6$ and hormones. Vitamins and Hormones *21*:113-134.

Hurley, L. S., and Swenerton, H. 1966. Congenital malformations resulting from zinc deficiency in rats. Proc. Soc. Exp. Biol. Med. *123*:692-696.

Hurley, L. S., Everson, G. J., and Geiger, J. F. 1958. Manganese deficiency in rats: Congenital nature of ataxia. J. Nutrit. *66*:309-319.

Ingalls, A. M., Dickie, M. M., and Snell, G. D. 1950. Obese, a new mutation in the mouse. J. Hered. *41*:317-318.

Ingle, D. J. 1950. In "Discussion" of "The virilizing syndrome in man." Recent Progr. Hormone Res. *5*:436.

Johnson, D., Jr., and Fisher, H. 1956. The amino acid requirement of the laying hen. II Classification of essential amino acids required for egg production. J. Nutrit. *60*:275-282.

Kahn, R. H. 1954. Effect of locally applied vitamin A and estrogen on the rat vagina. Amer. J. Anat. *95*:309-336.

Kalivas, D. T., and Nelson, M. M. 1966. Maintenance of pregnancy by reserpine in the absence of dietary protein. Endocrinology *79*:460-462.

Kamboj, V. P., and Kar, A. B. 1964. Antitesticular effect of metallic and rare earth salts. J. Reprod. Fertil. *7*:21-28.

Kar, A. B., and Das, R. P. 1963. The nature of protective action of selenium on cadmium-induced degeneration of the rat testis. Biol. Abstr. 46, ref. 93279, 1965.

Kar, A. B., Dasgupta, P. R., and Das, R. P. 1961. Effect of low dose of cadmium chloride on the genital organs and fertility of male rats. Biol. Abstr. 39, ref. 1952, 1962.

Kendall, K. A., and Hays, R. L. 1960. Maintained pregnancy in the rat as associated with progesterone administration and multiple-nutrient deficiency. J. Nutrit. *70*:10-12.

Kennedy, G. C., and Mitra, J. 1963a. Hypothalamic control of energy balance and the reproductive cycle in the rat. J. Physiol. *166*:395-407.

Kennedy, G. C., and Mitra, J. 1963b. Body weight and food intake as initiating factors for puberty in the rat. J. Physiol. *166*:408-418.

Kennedy, G. C., and Mitra, J. 1963c. Spontaneous pseudopregnancy and obesity in the rat. J. Physiol. *166*:419-424.

Kenney, M. A., and Roderuck, C. E. 1963. Fatal syndrome associated with Vitamin E status of pregnant rats. Proc. Soc. Exp. Biol. Med. *114*:257-261.

Kienholz, E. W., Turk, D. E., Sunde, M. L., and Hoekstra, W. G. 1961. Effect of zinc deficiency in the diets of hens. J. Nutrit. *75*:211-221.

Kinzey, W. G., and Srebnik, H. H. 1963. Maintenance of pregnancy in protein-deficient rats with short term injections of ovarian hormones. Proc. Soc. Exp. Biol. Med. *114*:158-160.

Kirkpatrick, R. L., Howland, B. E., First, N. L., and Casida, L. E. 1967a. Some characteristics associated with feed and breed differences in ovulation rate in the gilt. J. Anim. Sci. *26*:188-192.

Kirkpatrick, R. L., Howland, B. E., First, N. L., and Casida, L. E. 1967b. Ovarian and pituitary gland changes in gilts on two nutrient energy levels. J. Anim. Sci. 26:358-364.

Kwa, H. G., and Verhofstad, F. 1967a. Radio immuno assay of rat prolactin. Biochim. Biophys. Acta 133:186-188.

Kwa, H. G., and Verhofstad, F. 1967b. Prolactin levels in the plasma of female (C57BL × CBA) F1 mice. J. Endocrinol. 38:81-82.

Landauer, W. 1961. The hatchability of chicken eggs as influenced by environment and heredity. Monograph I, Univ. Conn. Agr. Exp. Sta.

Lane, P. W., and Dickie, M. M. 1954. Fertile obese male mouse. J. Hered. 45:56-58.

Leathem, J. H. 1958. Hormones and protein nutrition. Recent Progr. Hormone Res. 14:141-182.

Leathem, J. H. 1961. Nutritional effects on endocrine secretions. In W. C. Young (ed.): Sex and Internal Secretions. Williams & Wilkins Co., Baltimore, Vol. 1, pp. 666-704.

Leathem, J. H. 1964. Some aspects of hormone and protein metabolic interrelationships. In H. N. Munro and J. B. Allison (eds.): Mammalian Protein Metabolism. Academic Press Inc., New York, Vol. 1, pp. 343-380.

Leathem, J. H. 1966. Nutritional effects on hormone production. J. Anim. Sci. 25:68-78. (suppl.)

Lidell, C., and Hellman, B. 1966. The influence of overeating on the endocrine testis function. Metabolism 15:444-448.

Lofts, B., and Murton, R. K. 1967. The effects of cadmium on the avian testis. J. Reprod. Fertil. 13:155-164.

Lutwak-Mann, C. 1958. Dependence of gonadal function upon vitamins and other nutritional factors. Vitamins and Hormones 16:35-75.

Lyons, W. R. 1966. Hormonal treatment of lactating rats on a protein-free diet. Endocrinology 78:575-580.

McClure, T. J. 1959. Temporary nutritional stress and infertility in female mice. J. Physiol. 147:221-225.

McClure, T. J. 1961. Uterine pathology of temporarily-fasted pregnant mice. J. Comp. Pathol. 71:16-19.

McClure, T. J. 1962. Infertility in female rodents caused by temporary inanition at or about the time of implantation. J. Reprod. Fertil. 4:241.

McClure, T. J. 1966. Infertility in mice caused by fasting at about the time of mating. I Mating behaviour and littering rates. J. Reprod. Fertil. 12:243-248.

Machlin, L. J., Gordon, R. S., Marr, J. E., and Pope, C. W. 1962. Effects of antioxidants and unsaturated fatty acids on reproduction in the hen. J. Nutrit. 76:284-290.

Maekawa, K., and Hosoyama, Y. 1965. Protective effects of steroidal hormones on rat testis against injurious actions of cadmium. Zool. Mag. 74:17-23 (Japanese with English abstr.).

Masahito. 1959. The effect of nicotinamide on prolactin-induced mitosis of crop sac epithelium in the pigeon. J. Fac. Sci., Univ. Tokyo, Sec. IV:411-417.

Mason, K. E. 1933. Differences in testis injury and repair after vitamin A deficiency, vitamin E deficiency and inanition. Amer. J. Anat. 52:153-240.

Mason, K. E. 1959. Nutrition and reproduction. Survey Biol. Progr. 1:89-114.

Mason, K. E., Brown, J. A., Young, J. O., and Nesbit, R. R. 1964. Cadmium-induced injury of the rat testis. Anat. Rec. 149:135-148.

Maw, A. J. R. 1954. Inherited riboflavin deficiency in chicken eggs. Poultry Sci. 33:216-217.

Menge, H., Calvert, C. C., and Denton, C. A. 1965a. Further studies on the effect of linoleic acid on reproduction in the hen. J. Nutrit. 86:115-119.

Menge, H., Calvert, C. C., and Denton, C. A. 1965b. Influence of dietary oils on reproduction in the hen. J. Nutrit. 87:365-370.

Millar, M. J., Elcoate, P. V., Fischer, M. I., and Mawson, C. A. 1960. Effect of testosterone and gonadotrophin injections on the sex organ development of zinc-deficient male rats. Can. J. Biochem. Physiol. 38:1457-1466.

Millar, M. J., Fischer, M. I., Elcoate, P. V., and Mawson, C. A. 1958. The effects of dietary zinc deficiency on the reproductive system of the male rat. Can. J. Biochem. Physiol. 36:557-569.

Mitchell, H. H. 1962. Comparative Nutrition of Man and Domestic Animals. Academic Press Inc., New York. Two volumes.

Mitchell, R. H., Creger, C. R., Davies, R. E., Atkinson, R. L., Ferguson, T. M., and Couch, J. R. 1962. The effect of restricted feeding of Broad Breasted Bronze turkeys during the holding period on subsequent reproductive performance. Poultry Sci. 41:91-98.

Moore, T. 1965. Nutritional factors affecting fertility: vitamin E and other nutrients. In C. R. Austin and J. S. Perry (eds.): Agents Affecting Fertility. J. and A. Churchill, Ltd., London, pp. 18-33.

Morris, T. R., and Nalbandov, A. V. 1961. The induction of ovulation in starving pullets using mammalian and avian gonadotropins. Endocrinology 68:687-697.

Moustgaard, J. 1959. Nutrition and reproduction in domestic animals. In H. H. Cole and P. T. Cupps (eds.): Reproduction in Domestic Animals. Academic Press Inc., New York, Vol. 2, pp. 170-223.

Naber, E. C., Cravens, W. W., Baumann, C. A., and Bird, H. R. 1954. The effect of thiamine analogs on embryonic development and growth of the chick. J. Nutrit. 54:579-591.

Nebel, L., and Ornstein, A. 1966. Effect of hypervitaminosis D2 on fertility and pregnancy in rats. Biol. Abstr. 48, ref. 1030, 1967.

Nelson, M. M., and Evans, H. M. 1953. Relation of dietary protein levels to reproduction in the rat. J. Nutrit. 51:71-84.

Nelson, M. M., and Evans, H. M., 1954. Maintenance of pregnancy in the absence of dietary protein with estrone and progesterone. Endocrinology 55:543-549.

Nelson, M. M., and Evans, H. M. 1955. Maintenance of pregnancy in absence of dietary protein with progesterone. Proc. Soc. Exp. Biol. Med. 88:444-446.

Nelson, M. M., and Evans, H. M. 1956. Failure of ovarian hormones to maintain pregnancy in rats deficient in pantothenic or pteroylglutamic acid. Proc. Soc. Exp. Biol. Med. 91:614-617.

Nelson, M. M., Asling, C. W., and Evans, H. M. 1952.

Production of multiple congenital abnormalities in young by maternal pteroylglutamic acid deficiency during gestation. J. Nutrit. *48*:61-74.

Nelson, M. M., Wright, H. V., Asling, C. W., and Evans, H. M. 1955. Multiple congenital abnormalities resulting from transitory deficiency of pteroylglutamic acid during gestation in the rat. J. Nutrit. *56*:349-363.

Niemi, M., and Kormano, M. 1965. Angiographic study of cadmium-induced vascular lesions in the testis and epididymis of the rat. Acta Path. Microbiol. Scand. *63*:513-521.

Noble, R. L., and Carroll, K. K. 1961. Erucic acid and reproduction. Recent Progr. Hormone Res. *17*: 97-118.

O'Bannon, R. H., Wallace, H. D., Warnick, A. C., and Combs, G. E. 1966. Influence of energy intake on reproductive performance of gilts. J. Anim. Sci. *25*:706-710.

Orent-Keiles, E., and McCollum, E. V. 1941. Potassium in animal nutrition. J. Biol. Chem. *140*: 337-352.

Palludan, B. 1966. Direct effect of vitamin A on boar testis. Nature *211*:639-640.

Pařízek, J. 1957. The destructive effect of cadmium ion on testicular tissue and its prevention by zinc. J. Endocrinol. *15*:56-63.

Pařízek, J. 1960. Sterilization of the male by cadmium salts. J. Reprod. Fertil. *1*:294-309.

Pařízek, J. 1964. Vascular changes at sites of oestrogen biosynthesis produced by parenteral injection of cadmium salts: The destruction of placenta by cadmium salts. J. Reprod. Fertil. *7*:263-265.

Pařízek, J., and Záhoř, Z. 1956. Effect of cadmium salts on testicular tissue. Nature *177*:1036-1037.

Parker, J. E., and Arscott, G. H. 1964. Energy intake and fertility of male chickens. J. Nutrit. *82*:183-187.

Pitts, W. J., Miller, W. J., Fosgate, O. T., Morton, J. D., and Clifton, C. M. 1966. Effect of zinc deficiency and restricted feeding from two to five months of age on reproduction in Holstein bulls. J. Dairy Sci. *49*:995-1000.

Pond, W. G., and Jones, J. R. 1964. Effect of level of zinc in high calcium diets on pigs from weaning through one reproductive cycle and on subsequent growth of their offspring. J. Anim. Sci. *23*:1057-1060.

Rascop, A. M., Sheenan, E. T., and Vavich, M. G. 1966. Histomorphological changes in reproductive organs of rats fed cycloprenoid fatty acids. Proc. Soc. Exp. Biol. Med. *122*:142-145.

Ray, D. E., and McCarty, J. W. 1965. Effect of temporary fasting on reproduction in gilts. J. Anim. Sci. *24*:660-663.

Ray, E. W., Averill, S. C., Lyons, W. R., and Johnson, R. E. 1955. Rat placental hormonal activities corresponding to those of pituitary mammotrophin. Endocrinology *56*:359-373.

Reid, J. T. 1960. Effect of energy intake upon reproduction in farm animals. J. Dairy Sci. *43 suppl.*: 103-120.

Reid, J. T., Loosli, J. K., Trimberger, G. W., Turk, K. L., Asdell, S. A., and Smith, S. E. 1964. Causes and prevention of reproductive failures in dairy cattle. IV Effect of plane of nutrition during early life on growth, production, health and longevity of Holstein cows. Cornell Agr. Exp. Sta. Bull. 987.

Reinberg, A., and Ghatta, J. 1964. Biological Rhythms. Walker & Co., New York.

Rippel, R. H., Harmon, B. G., Jensen, A. H., Norton, H. W., and Becker, D. E. 1965b. Response of the gravid gilt to levels of protein as determined by nitrogen balance. J. Anim. Sci. *24*:209-215.

Rippel, R. H., Rasmussen, O. G., Jensen, A. H., Norton, H. W., and Becker, D. E. 1965a. Effect of level and source of protein on reproductive performance of swine. J. Anim. Sci. *24*:203-208.

Rodriguez, E. M. 1964. Neurosecretory system of the toad *Bufo arenarum* Hensel and its changes during inanition. Gen. Comp. Endocrinol. *4*:684-695.

Rogler, J. C., Parker, H. E., Andrews, F. N., and Carrick, C. W. 1961. The iodine requirement of the breeding hen. 2. Hens reared on diet deficient in iodine. Poultry Sci. *40*:1554-1562.

Rombauts, P., Courot, M., Levasseur, M. C., and Thibault, C. 1961. Nutrition et puberté. Ann. Nutrit. Alim. *15B*:263-284.

Rosenfeld, I., and Beath, O. A. 1964. Selenium, Geobotany, Biochemistry, Toxicity, and Nutrition. Academic Press, New York.

Runner, M. N., and Gates, A. 1954. Sterile, obese mothers. J. Hered. *45*:51-55.

Schneider, D. L., Vavich, M. G., Kurnick, A. A., and Kemmerer, A. R. 1961. Effects of *Sterculia foetida* oil on mortality of the chick embryo. Poultry Sci. *40*:1644-1647.

Scott, P. P., and Scott, M. G. 1964. Vitamin A and reproduction in the cat. J. Reprod. Fertil. *8*:270-271.

Selye, H. 1957. Effect of sex hormones upon hypervitaminosis-A. Rev. Suisse Zool. *64*:757-761.

Setchell, B. P., Waites, G. M. H., and Lindner, H. R. 1965. Effect of undernutrition on testicular blood flow and metabolism and the output of testosterone in the ram. J. Reprod. Fertil. *9*:149-162.

Singsen, E. P., Matterson, L. D., Tlustohowicz, J., and Potter, L. M. 1961. The effect of controlled feeding, energy intake, and type of diet on the performance of heavy-type laying hens. Storrs Agr. Exp. Sta. Bull. 346.

Sorensen, A. M., Hansel, W., Hough, W. H., Armstrong, D. T., McEnter, K., and Bratton, R. W. 1959. Causes and prevention of reproductive failures in dairy cattle. I. Influence of underfeeding and overfeeding on growth and development of Holstein heifers. Cornell Agr. Exp. Sta. Bull. 936.

Srebnik, H. H., and Nelson, M. M. 1962. Anterior pituitary function in male rats deprived of dietary protein. Endocrinology *70*:723-730.

Srebnik, H. H., Nelson, M. M., and Simpson, M. E. 1958. Response to exogenous gonadotrophins in absence of dietary protein. Proc. Soc. Exp. Biol. Med. *99*:57-61.

Srebnik, H. H., Nelson, M. M., and Simpson, M. E. 1961. Follicle-stimulating hormone (FSH) and interstitial-cell-stimulating hormone (ICSH) in pituitary and plasma of intact and ovariectomized protein-deficient rats. Endocrinology 68: 317-326.

Teitelbaum, H. A., and Gantt, W. H. 1956. Effect of starvation on sperm count and sexual reflexes. Science 124:363-364.

Terroine, T., and Delost, P. 1961. Influence des carances vitaminiques sur le développement des organes sexuels. Ann. Nutrit. Alim. 15B:291-329.

Thompson, J. N., Howell, J. McC., and Pitt, G. A. J. 1964. Vitamin A and reproduction in rats. Proc. Roy. Soc. (London) B 159:510-535.

Thompson, J. N., Howell, J. McC., and Pitt, G. A. J. 1965a. Nutritional factors affecting fertility. In C. R. Austin and J. S. Perry (eds.): Agents Affecting Fertility. J. & A. Churchill Ltd., London, pp. 34-45.

Thompson, J. N., Howell, J. McC., Pitt, G. A. J., and Houghton, C. I. 1965b. Biological activity of retinoic ester in the domestic fowl. Production of vitamin A deficiency in the early chick embryo. Nature 205:1006-1007.

Tilton, W. A., Warnick, A. C., Cunha, T. J., Loggins, P. E., and Shirley, R. L. 1964. Effect of low energy and protein intake on growth and reproductive performance of young rams. J. Anim. Sci. 23:645-650.

Turk, J. L., and McGinnis, J. 1964. Influence of vitamin D on various aspects of the reproductive processes in mature hens. Poultry Sci. 43:539-546.

van Tienhoven, A. 1961. Endocrinology of reproduction in birds. In W. C. Young (ed.): Sex and Internal Secretions. Williams & Wilkins Co., Baltimore, Vol. 2, pp. 1088-1169.

Velardo, J. T., and Hisaw, F. L. 1952. Inhibition of the Hooker-Forbes response by aminopterin. Proc. Soc. Exp. Biol. Med. 81:653-654.

Waites, G. M. H., and Setchell, B. P. 1965. Changes in blood flow and vascular permeability of the testis, epididymis, and accessory reproductive organs of the rat after administration of cadmium chloride. J. Endocrinol. 34:329-342.

Widowson, E. M., Mavor, W. O., and McCance, R. A. 1964. The effect of undernutrition and rehabilitation on the development of the reproductive organs: rats. J. Endocrinol. 29:119-126.

Wilson, H. R., Waldroup, P. W., Jones, J. E., Duerre, D. J., and Harms, R. H. 1965. Protein level in growing diets and reproductive performance of cockerels. J. Nutrit. 85:29-37.

Zimmerman, D. R., Spies, H. G., Self, H. L., and Casida, L. E. 1960. Ovulation rate in swine as affected by increased energy intake just prior to ovulation. J. Anim. Sci. 19:295-301.

Environment and Reproduction

The performance of animals and plants is dependent upon the interaction between the inherited characteristics (and mutations) and the environment. In the previous chapter we have seen that nutrition may play an important role in obtaining optimal reproductive performance. Most of the literature concerning adequately controlled experiments pertained to the common laboratory and domestic animals. The chapter on nutrition was purposely not included under environment because it was one of the most easily manipulated factors influencing reproduction and because the effect of different nutrients was considered rather than the availability of food.

In this chapter we will first discuss the role of environment in determination of the breeding season and subsequently the effect of various environmental factors on reproductive performance and expression of sexuality.

Natural selection has favored the retention of control systems which use the most reliable information and which cause reproduction to occur at the time which is optimal for the survival of the young (Farner and Follett, 1966). Two sets of causes have been proposed by Baker (1938 a, b), i.e. (1) ultimate causes, which exert selection pressure so that *populations* survive that reproduce at the optimal season, and (2) proximate causes, which provide *individuals* with the appropriate information so that reproductive processes are initiated and continued at

such a time that the young are born at the optimal time for survival.

Consideration will be given to the question whether the rhythms of reproduction are induced by environmental factors only or whether there are also endogenous rhythms, with which environmental factors interact.

ENDOGENOUS RHYTHMS

A voluminous amount of literature has been published on this subject, and for the purpose of this presentation, reviews have been consulted to a large extent.

Halberg and Reinberg (1967) have divided biological rhythms into the following categories:

1. High frequency rhythms, with a period of less than 0.5 hours. Examples are electrical activity of the brain (such as alpha waves), heart beat, respiration rate.

2. Medium frequency rhythms subdivided into: (a) Ultradian rhythms, with a period of more than 0.5 but less than 20 hours. (b) Circadian rhythms, with a period of more than 20 but less than 28 hours. (c) Infradian rhythms, with a period of more than 28 hours but less than 2.5 days.

3. Low frequency rhythms, with a period of more than 2.5 days. These rhythms can be subdivided into: (a) Circaseptidian rhythms, with a period of approximately seven days. (b) Cir-

cavignitidian rhythms, with a period of about 20 days. (c) Circatrigintian rhythms, with a period of about 30 days (e.g. menstrual cycle). (d) Circennian or circaannual rhythms, with a period of about a year.

All these rhythms may be present simultaneously in one individual and in one organ.

In the discussion to follow we will be most concerned with circadian and circennian rhythms. The circadian rhythms have been studied most extensively and a number of concepts have been developed on the basis of these studies. For a consideration of the seasonal reproductive cycles, obviously the circennian rhythms are of prime importance. We will, however, discuss the circadian rhythms first, in terms of the concepts developed and the evidence that supports these concepts.

A great number of physiological phenomena in the animal and plant kingdom show "circadian" rhythmicity: some species of flowers open at the same time each day, bees can be trained to fly to a foraging place at the same time each day, and some people can train themselves to wake up at the same hour each day (Bünning, 1964). These phenomena, one may argue, are timed by the light of the sun. However, the plants and animals placed under constant conditions of either constant light or constant darkness will continue to show these phenomena at the expected time. One remarkable thing also happens—the occurrence of the phenomena slowly shifts to another chronological time. One can measure the interval between the successive occurrences and find the period. This period is seldom if ever 24 hours.

The rhythms with a period between 20 and 28 hours have been called "circadian," but confusion exists about the terminology (Baker, 1964; Clark, 1964; Palmer, 1964; Wurtman, 1967). The term *circadian rhythm* will be used here for rhythms which exist in the absence of rhythmic environmental changes (light,

temperature, etc.), the so-called free running rhythms with periods between 20 and 28 hours. Cycles existing in the presence of external rhythmic changes (called synchronizers, signals, "Zeitgeber," and entraining agents) will be called *diurnal* if there is a rhythm of 24 hours.

A number of difficulties in proving the existence of a circadian rhythm prevail. One of these is that it is difficult to make an environment that is constant in every sense, e.g. barometric pressure changes occur, the magnetic field to which the system under study is exposed changes, etc. (Brown, 1960, 1965). In some experiments these factors have been compensated for by transporting the organisms east or west and observing the time at which the studied phenomena occurred. Such experiments have shown that organisms have indeed an "endogenous" rhythm of about 24 hours (Bünning, 1964; Marler and Hamilton, 1966). The fact that such rhythms are found in plants as well as animals proves that a nervous system is not required. The occurrence of circadian rhythms in cells, organs, and organisms indicates its universality (Halberg and Reinberg, 1967).

The considerations outlined above indicate the existence of an internal biological clock in cells and organisms. This clock, as Bünning (1964) has pointed out, not only indicates the time but is also used by the organism to time events. The opening of flowers before sunrise is an illustration of such timing.

Discussion of the methodology and analysis involved in the establishment of various parameters of the rhythms (period, phase angle, and amplitude) and the determination of their statistical validity falls outside the scope of this book. A valuable discussion can be found in the extensive paper by Halberg and Reinberg (1967).

For the purpose of discussion it appears useful to consider the biological clock as an oscillator. This oscillator, in the absence of external synchronizers, has a period of 20 to 28 hours. However, the internal clock can become coupled with and synchronized by an external oscillator. This synchronization can be either unilateral, which means that one system completely determines the characteristics of the other, or it can be mutual, in which there is a feedback from the driven system to the driving system and the period of the oscillator is intermediate between the periods of the two oscillators under consideration (Pittendrigh and Bruce, 1959). From the point of view of energetics, the period of the driving system is most easily imposed on the second oscillator if the frequencies are approximately the same. The biological clock's endogenous (free running) circadian rhythm can, for instance, be changed by external signals to a new rhythm only within certain limits. The activity of mice with a circadian rhythm of 22.5 hours could be changed to activities between 19 and 26 hours by photoperiod cycles with such rhythms. However, on longer or shorter photocycles the mice retained their 22.5 hour rhythm (Tribukait, 1956).

Properties of the internal oscillator which need to be mentioned are:

1. The circadian rhythm is relatively independent of temperature, that is, the frequency is not increased or decreased by high or low temperatures (Sollberger, 1965), although the clock can be stopped by very low temperatures (0 to 5° C.) (Bünning, 1964).

2. Circadian rhythms are inherited, not imprinted (Bünning, 1964; Marler and Hamilton, 1966).

3. In all probability Aschoff's rule applies to animals. This rule states that under conditions of continuous light the period of circadian rhythm is longer than under conditions of continuous darkness for nocturnal animals and shorter for diurnal animals (Sollberger, 1965).

4. The free running cycle can be reset by external stimuli (to be discussed later). The time at which the external stimulus occurs with respect to the phase of the cycle

is important. Assuming that the stimuli are out of phase with the organism's endogenous cycle, what events will occur? Eventually the synchronizing cycle and the organism's cycle become in phase; this can be accomplished by a series of phase shifts until synchrony between the two oscillators is reached. These shifts may consist of either delays or advances. In the case of organisms sensitive to the onset of light, presentation of a light stimulus close to the onset of activity may cause the greatest delay; this delay decreases as the stimulus is presented later in the activity cycle and eventually it may cause an advance instead of a delay (Marler and Hamilton, 1966).

It is also possible that under constant conditions a resetting of the cycle occurs; this would take place if the response to light at the onset of activity differed from that at the end of the cycle. In this manner one could explain some of the deviation of the circadian cycle from an exact 24 hour cycle (Marler and Hamilton, 1966).

5. The period of the cycle can be affected by light treatments prior to exposure to the constant environment (Marler and Hamilton, 1966).

The considerations given so far to the endogenous cycle have shown that apparently the cycle is almost universal (it occurs in plants and animals, in organs and organisms). This universality suggests that the circadian rhythm may be a fundamental property of the cell (Harker, 1964). This does not mean that all cells or functions are regulated by the same clock but that they are regulated by similar clocks. Where the clock is located in the organism has been experimentally investigated by Harker (1964). In the cockroach (*Periplaneta* sp.), she found a correlation between the activity of the neurosecretory cells of the subesophageal ganglion and the activity of the animal. Transplantation of these cells from one cockroach to a decapitated cockroach caused activity in the host at about the time of day at which the donor was expected to show activity.

This experimental technique allowed the investigation of the effects of light (used as a synchronizer) during different times of the day. Such investigations revealed:

1. There is a "possible" secretion stage during which the system will respond to a light-off stimulus.

2. A stage during which no secretion will occur, an "impossible" secretion stage.

3. A stage during which secretion occurs regardless of the occurrence of light stimulation.

If the neurosecretory system is left in situ (not transplanted), the animal's activity differs from that of an animal to which a similar system has been transplanted, suggesting resetting of the clock by the animal with the system left in situ.

Further investigations showed that chilling the neurosecretory system in situ without cooling the animal stops secretion by the neurosecretory cells, as is evidenced by implantation tests. The delay in the secretory cycle corresponded to the length of time the system is chilled. However, if the neurosecretory cells were not transplanted the delay was not always apparent, suggesting that there is another clock in the animal that keeps time and resets the neurosecretory "clock."

The question remains why the clock is reset when left in situ but not when transplanted. The hosts receiving the neurosecretory cells are decapitated and either the resetting mechanism or a relay in this mechanism is probably located in the head. In any event, the experiments demonstrate that a clock mechanism can be located in this cockroach, but it also shows that there may be other clocks or, at least, feedback mechanisms that affect the neurosecretory clock.

In a recent paper Ehret and Trucco (1967) have proposed a molecular model for the circadian clock. In this model the cell is regarded as a clock whose circadian escapement consists of a sequential transcription component and a recycling component. The essential part of the model is the *chronon*, defined as a very long poly-cistron complex with a transcription rate which is limited by cell functions which are rather independent of temperature. Transcription is unidirectional, and starts at the initiator cistron and ends at the terminator cistron. The recycling component consists of:

1. a posttranscriptional interval, during which protein synthesis and polymer assembly occur.

2. a pretranscriptional preinitiator interval, during which substances, such as amino acids, diffuse into the inner region of the nucleus so that an initiator substance can accumulate. This initiator, upon arrival at the proper cistron sets the sequential transcription cycle in motion again.

The authors also derive from this model and the experimental evidence that the phase shift induced by light is mediated via the recycling component of the circadian escapement.

Not all rhythms which show diurnal variation are, however, circadian rhythms. In the rat's pineal gland the activity of hydroxyindole-O-methyltransferase (HIOMT) shows a diurnal rhythm as long as the animal is on a light-dark schedule. The rhythm is abolished when the rats are placed either in continuous darkness or in continuous light (Axelrod et al, 1965). The content of the serotonin of the pineal gland varies diurnally (Fiske, 1964; Quay, 1963; Snyder et al., 1965) with a nocturnal minimum and a midday maximum. Under constant darkness the rhythm persists for at least two weeks, but under continuous light the serotonin content remains high. In blinded animals the rhythm persists and continuous light does not abolish the rhythm in such blinded rats (Snyder et al., 1965). Superior cervical ganglionectomy abolishes the rhythm by preventing the nocturnal decrease in serotonin content. Light given at the time that the lights are normally turned off prevents the nocturnal decrease, but if the lights are turned off earlier than normal, the decrease occurs at the same time as in the controls. The darkness can induce the earlier decrease if given within a few hours of the start of darkness on previous days (Quay, 1963). Thus, within the same organ there exists an endogenous rhythm (serotonin content) and a purely exogenously-induced rhythm (HIOMT activity), which also demonstrates that rhythms can be created by variation in the environment.

The existence of circadian rhythms for many physiological phenomena should be taken into account in experiments in which the time of sampling for the determination of the parameter may play a role. For instance, in an experiment with many treatments, animals of each treatment group need to be sampled as near the same time as possible, rather than first sampling animals from one treatment and then from another one. In bioassays the time of optimal sensitivity should be determined. Halberg and Reinberg (1967) cite experiments in which the corticosterone production of mouse adrenals in vitro in response to a standard dose of ACTH was measured at two hour intervals. The adrenals of the mice, which received light from 7 a.m. to 7 p.m., showed a response of 40 percent of the mean if taken at 4 p.m. and of 180 percent if taken at 4 a.m. Thus the sensitivity of the assay can be increased 4.5 times by taking the adrenals at 4 a.m. rather than at 4 p.m.

Halberg and Reinberg (1967) also present data on the concentration of corticosterone in the serum, of ACTH in the pituitary, and ACTH-RF in the hypothalamus of mice kept under the conditions given above. These data, which show a peak in ACTH content of the pituitary about four hours prior to the peak of corticosterone concentration in the blood and a peak of adrenal sensitivity, coincide with the lowest serum corticosterone concentration. The ACTH-RF is more or less in phase with the serum corticosterone secretion.

These authors state "let us emphasize that this experimental demonstration con-

cerning a coherent circadian* system describes in time some of the variations which contribute to the circadian* variations of plasma corticosterone. *For these observations the idea of a feed-back can not exist* [italics mine]. This, in effect, does not normally give precise information relative to the duration (and period) of the observed phenomena and because of this does not give entirely satisfactory explanation in the absence of temporal information."

It appears to me that the statement in italics is not justified because the organs assayed all had been subject to possible feedback mechanisms. The sensitivity of the adrenal may well have been partly determined by the endogenous ACTH concentrations to which it had been exposed. The diurnal rhythm of the pituitary should have been determined in adrenalectomized mice and the rhythm of the adrenal sensitivity in hypophysectomized mice. In addition to these considerations, it should be emphasized that pituitary contents of hormones only indicate what is present, not what is released. ACTH concentrations in the blood are required in addition to pituitary contents for an evaluation of synthesis and release.

It is highly probable that there are diurnal rhythms of the adrenal, pituitary, and hypothalamus with respect to secretion of hormones in the absence of target organs, and thus in the absence of feedbacks from these organs. A direct feedback of ACTH or the pituitary would nevertheless still be possible; as was discussed in Chapter 8, such direct feedbacks of pituitary hormones on the pituitary do exist. It is my opinion that the concentration of corticosterone is regulated by an interaction between the diurnal rhythm of the hypothalamus, pituitary, and adrenal on the one hand and the feedback systems of the hypothalamus-pituitary-adrenal axis on the other hand. In the absence of data on

---

*Diurnal, in the terminology used in the present discussion.

diurnal rhythms in adrenalectomized and in hypophysectomized mice this relationship cannot be determined.

SYNCHRONIZING STIMULI

The external factors that can synchronize the circadian rhythm so that the new frequency corresponds to the external agent are light and temperature. Although factors such as meteotropic agents, gravitational force, and magnetic fields cannot be excluded, they are in all probability either weak synchronizers or they interact with other agents (Sollberger, 1965).

INITIATION OF THE BREEDING SEASON

Light. The evidence that light is one of the principal synchronizing agents for many species in determining the diurnal rhythms has been reviewed and documented extensively in recent publications (Bünning, 1964; Cloudsley-Thompson, 1961; Halberg et al., 1959; Marler and Hamilton, 1966; Pittendrigh and Bruce, 1959; Pittendrigh and Minis, 1964; Rawson, 1959; Sollberger, 1965).

It was mentioned earlier that the period of the circadian rhythm is relatively temperature independent; this statement refers to the period at constant temperatures. Cyclic temperature changes can act as synchronizers not only for poikilotherms but also for homoiotherms (Bünning, 1964; Sollberger, 1965).

Other synchronizing agents, usually imposed by the experimenter but which may or may not be important for animals under natural conditions, are:

1. Cycles at which food is made available (Fraps, Neher, and Rothchild, 1947; McNally, 1947; Sollberger, 1965).

2. Sound, e.g. bird songs, presented in cycles synchronized the locomotor rhythm of house sparrows (*Passer domesticus*) (Menaker and Eskin, 1966). Noise which is generated by the care of animals, refrigerator units, experimenters buzzing about, can also act as synchronizing factors (Sollberger, 1965).

3. The social environment, herd instinct, may in some cases be important in synchronizing the diurnal rhythm (Sollberger, 1965).

The fact that these agents can be important in establishing diurnal rhythms emphasizes the need for very careful control of any factor which may be cyclic in nature, if one wishes to determine the existence of circadian rhythms.

It is pertinent to compare the seasonal rhythms and circadian and diurnal rhythms with respect to some of their basic properties.

Two important questions are whether the seasonal reproductive rhythms are endogenous (as the circadian rhythms are) and whether the synchronizers can determine the period only within a rather limited range (as is the case for diurnal rhythms). It appears that the answers to these questions depend on the animal species to which they apply. The experimental basis for an endogenous seasonal (circennian) rhythm is not as solid as for the circadian rhythm, which seems to be almost universal.

Evidence of an endogenous rhythm for reproductive phenomena in animals kept under constant conditions for an extended time has been obtained for ducks (kept in either total darkness or continuous light) (Benoit et al., 1956, 1959). Under these conditions the size of the testes showed cyclic changes. The amplitude of the changes was smaller than observed during the seasonal changes and the periods were shorter. The authors state that the periods are irregular, but no detailed analysis as, e.g. was used by Halberg and Reinberg (1967) for the analysis of circadian rhythms, was carried out. It has been shown that exposure of sheep to continuous light for three years results in breeding seasons at the normal time of the year (Thibault et al., 1966). Indirect evidence for an endogenous reproductive rhythm has been derived from the cycle of the short-tailed shearwater *(Puffinus tenuirostris)*. The birds breed near South Australia between mid-November and the first week of December. They leave for the Aleutians via Japan and return along the coast of the American continent to their breeding grounds in the last week of September; the return is very regular. This migratory and breeding cycle could well be under the control of the photoperiod. However, exposure of captive birds to different light regimens did not alter the gonadal cycles substantially (Marshall, 1960).

Other indirect evidence for the endogenous rhythm can be found in the 9.6 month breeding cycle of the sooty tern *(Sterna fusca)* (Chapin, 1951), the eight month cycle of the booby *(Sula leucogaster)* (Dorward, 1962), and the approximately eight month cycle of the black noddy *(Anous tenuirostris)* (Ashmole, 1962). All three species breed on Ascension Island. In one year of the three year study the interval was one year for the black noddy, but Ashmole (1962) considers this the result of food shortage.

In the population of the sooty tern breeding on Christmas Island, birds successful in rearing a young breed at six month intervals, whereas those unsuccessful in rearing a young breed at an interval of 12 months. Most populations of this species breed at annual intervals, and where sea surface temperatures are 23° C. or above for only part of the year, breeding occurs during that particular period (Ashmole, 1963).

The molting of the sooty terns of the Christmas Island population is continuous during the nonbreeding season. Birds unable to rear their chick often do not complete their molt by the time they start to breed again. However, all birds of the Ascension Island population complete a molt in the nine month interval between breeding periods, and the annual breeders molt after breeding. Ashmole (1965)

proposes "that continuous breeding among sea birds in seasonless environments is prevented by selection favoring a regime in which breeding activity alternates continuously with minimal feather replacement rather than by any fundamental physiological need for a quiescent period in the pituitary gonad cycle."

The breeding cycle of the Ascension Island population of sooty terns appears to be controlled by an endogenous rhythm. However, the flexibility of the breeding cycle of this species in other areas, as mentioned above, argues against a rigid clock explanation. Ashmole (1963, 1965) has proposed that the 9.6 month interval is an adaptation which has led to the greatest frequency of cycles while allowing molting to occur. However, this cycle can be expected only in environments where seasons do not prevent successful rearing of chicks during any month. Ashmole (1963) has speculated that the synchrony of the breeding population at Ascension Island may be an adaptation which reduces the impact of predators (in this case cats).

The breeding cycle of the sooty tern population of Christmas Island seems to be regulated by some seasonal changes which keep the breeding in phase. However, the nature of these seasonal changes is unknown (Ashmole, 1965).

The insectivorous tropical bat *(Miniopterus australis)* may be another species with an endogenous circennian rhythm. This bat, in spite of a constant climate (the animals stay all day in a dark cave with a constant temperature) has a definite breeding season; the females become pregnant in September (Baker, 1938a). The cycle cannot be free running because one would expect it to become out of phase over a number of years, but the signals used to keep the cycle in phase are not known. It is most probable that the cycle is endogenous and that some subtle synchronizer keeps it in phase.

That populations of tropical sea birds do not always breed in synchrony is evident from the fact that eggs of the red-billed boatswain bird *(Phaethon aethereus aethereus)* and the yellow-billed boatswain bird *(P. lepturus ascensionis)* are laid during every month of the year on Ascension Island (Stonehouse, 1962). Individual birds of the yellow-billed boatswain bird breed at five to ten month intervals and those of the red-billed boatswain bird at nine to 12 month intervals. The data are not sufficient to allow one to determine an exact period, nor is it certain that interactions with the environment (nesting places, etc.) do not determine the frequency of breeding so that no conclusion can be drawn with respect to an internal rhythm.

Two species of *Sula* showed different breeding intervals on Ascension Island. The white booby *(S. dactylatra)* has an annual cycle in which 55 percent of the clutches are laid in July and 19 percent in June. The brown booby *(S. leucogaster)* has an eight and one-third month cycle. In spite of the lack of identifiable seasonal variations (temperature, day length), individual animals that had become out of phase with the population were in phase again the next breeding period (Dorward, 1962). It is, of course, entirely possible that flock behavior is the synchronizing factor that brings the individuals in phase.

The "breaking-through" of the internal rhythm that was found in Australian silver gulls in captivity in the Washington Zoo, may also be considered as indirect evidence of an internal rhythm. For two seasons these birds nested in November (Australian spring), then adapted to nesting in the Northern spring and summer, and later reverted to nesting in November (Davis, 1945).

There is, however, substantial evidence that in other avian species the internal rhythm either does not exist or plays a minor role. It is, for instance, possible to induce as many as five cyclic variations in testicular size and spermatogenesis in slate-colored Juncos *(Junco hyemalis)* and white-throated sparrows *(Zonotrichia albicollis)* by manipulation of the photoperiod (the circadian rhythm period can only be changed within rather narrow limits). For many other species the existence of a circennian endogenous rhythm has not been determined, but in many respects the response of the animals to light suggests that photoperiod is the cause of the onset or termination of breeding (see Farner, 1965). We will consider the environmental factors which have been shown to affect the onset of the breeding season in different vertebrates.

The most consistent variable from year to year in middle and high latitudes is the day length; it is not surprising that photoperiod has been used by organisms to time their breeding season (Farner, 1965).

As can be seen from Table 13-1, the effect of light on gonadal activity has been observed in representatives of the bony fishes, amphibia, reptiles, and mammals. The number of avian species, in which photoperiod affects the gonads is too long to be given here (see Benoit and Assenmacher, 1955; Farner, 1959). It should not be surprising that in the poikilothermic fishes and reptiles (amphibia not having been investigated in enough detail to make generalizations) the effect of photoperiod is influenced by the temperature at which the experiments are conducted. Harrington (1957, 1959a) found that in *Phoxinus phoxinus* kept under short day conditions, high temperature arrests egg development, a phenomenon also observed in the European bitterling, the banded sunfish, the four-spined stickleback, and during certain phases of development in the three-spined stickleback (see Harrington, 1959a). In the Eastern brook trout, temperature (8.5° C. versus 16° C.) has no effect on maturation of the ova. Exposure to short days and 8.5° C. temperatures results in earlier gonadal development than obtained at 16° C. temperatures. The growth rate of the ova is retarded at 8.5° C. but normal at 16° C., however, the ova continued to grow for a longer than usual period, resulting in larger ova. Under long

Table 13-1.   Species of Fish, Amphibia, Reptiles, and Mammals in which Photoperiod Has Been Shown to Affect the Gonads

SPECIES	REFERENCE
Fishes:	
Salmonidae	
Salvelinus fontinalis, eastern brook trout	Henderson, 1963a,b
Cyprinidae	
Couesius plumbeus, lake chub	Ahsan, 1966
Notropis bifrenatus, bridled shiner	Harrington, 1959a
Phoxinus phoxinus, minnow	Bullough, 1959, 1940
Rhodeus amarus, European bitterling	Harrington, 1959a
Carassius auratus, goldfish	Hoar and Robertson, 1959
Oryzias latipes, Japanese rice fish	Yoshioka, 1962
Gasterosteidae	
Gasterosteus aculeatus, three-spined stickleback	Baggerman, 1959
Apeltes quadracus, four-spined stickleback	Merriman and Schedl, 1941
Cyprinodontidae	
Fundulus confluentus, marsh killifish	Harrington, 1959b
Centrarchidae	
Enneacanthus obesus, banded sunfish	Harrington, 1956
Amphibia:	
Rana esculenta, edible frog	Farner, 1965
Rana temporaria, European common frog	Bullough, 1959
Reptiles:	
Phrynosoma m'calli, MacCall's horned lizard	Mayhew, 1964
P. cornutum, texas horned lizard	Mayhew, 1964
Xantusia vigilis, desert night lizard	Bartholomew, 1959
Anolis carolinensis, american chameleon	Bartholomew, 1959
Lacerta sicula, wall lizard	Bartholomew, 1959
Uma notata, fringe-toed lizard	Mayhew, 1964
U. inornata, fringe-toed lizard	Mayhew, 1964
U. scoparia, fringe-toed lizard	Mayhew, 1964
Pseudemys elegans (Pseudemys scripta elegans), red-eared pond turtle	Bartholomew, 1959
Mammals:	
Erinaceus europaeus, euorpean hedgehog	Allanson and Deanesly, 1934
Lepus timidus,* hare	Farner, 1961
Oryctolagus cuniculus, rabbit	Thibault et al., 1966
Glaucomys volans, flying squirrel	Muul, 1966
Mesocricetus auratus, golden hamster	Hoffman et al., 1965;
	Gaston and Menaka, 1966
Microtus montanus, vole	Pinter, 1964
Microtus arvalis, field vole	Thibault et al., 1966
Mus musculus, mouse	Bloch, 1964
Rattus norvegicus, laboratory rat	Everett, 1961
Vulpes fulva, silver fox	Farner, 1961
Felis catus, cat	Scott and Lloyd-Jacob, 1959
Procyon lotor, raccoon	Bissonnette and Csech, 1937
Mustela putorius, ferret	Donovan, 1966
Mustela vison, mink	Hammond, 1953
Martes zibellina,* sable	Farner, 1961
Equus caballus horse	Yeates, 1954
Capra hircus, goat	Bissonnette, 1941
Ovis aries, sheep	Yeates, 1954

* A response is probable in these species.

photoperiods the growth rate of maturing ova was retarded at 16° C. Resorption of these ova took place, and ova of the succeeding year underwent precocious development. At 8.5° C. the growth rate of the maturing ova was retarded and the fish became functionally mature in midwinter (Henderson, 1963a). Neither the mechanisms involved nor the significance of these phenomena for the animal have been elucidated. In contrast to the significant effect of photoperiod on the ovary, no effect of photoperiod on early spermatogenesis was found. Spermiation could be delayed by continuous long photoperiods at 8.5 and 16° C., by continuous short photoperiods at 8.5° C., or short photoperiods followed by long photoperiods at 8.5° C. A different response of males and females to photo stimulation is found in *Phoxinus phoxinus*, in which short photoperiods delay the growth of the ova, but spermatogenesis, although it will be somewhat delayed, can be completed in total darkness (Bullough, 1940).

In the banded sunfish there is a postspawning refractory period during which no testicular response is obtained after exposure to long photoperiods (Harrington, 1959a). In contrast to many bird species, this fish will respond at the end of the refractory period in spite of continued exposure to long photoperiods. The refractory period ends without having required exposure of the animals to short photoperiods. The refractoriness of the response in the banded sunfish is probably the result of an inability of the testes to respond at this time to gonadotropins (Harrington, 1957), whereas in birds the refractory period is probably the result of a failure of the hypothalamo-hypophyseal system to respond (Farner and Follett, 1966; Wolfson, 1966). The refractory period of the banded sunfish lasts from mid-July to mid-November (Harrington, 1959a).

Licht (1966), using the American chameleon *(Anolis carolinesis)*, observed that at low temperatures light was not effective in stimulating the increase in testicular size. The temperature must be about 32° C. at least during part of the light period to induce a response. However, in the desert night lizard the response to light is not affected by low temperatures (8°, 19° C.) (Bartholomew, 1953). These interspecific differences with respect to the temperature dependence of the photoperiodic response may be related to the different ecologies of the different species. It does not explain the physiological differences.

The photoperiodic control of reproductive activity in birds probably has been investigated more thoroughly than that of the other classes of vertebrates. It is impossible to review, within the scope of this chapter, the original contributions of the various workers, and therefore I refer the interested reader to the excellent recent reviews by Farner and Follett (1966), and Wolfson (1965, 1966).

Most of the experiments concerning the effect of photoperiod on the gonadal cycle have been carried out with males; the testicular size, molting, and fat deposition have been measured. Females have not been used mainly because it is so difficult to obtain full ovarian development in the majority of species caught in the wild. It appears that captivity puts more restraint on stimulation of the female gonad than on that of the male.

Many of the avian species that breed at middle or high altitudes show a photoperiodic testicular response. As Farner and Follett (1966) point out, photoperiod is the most consistent cue for indicating the time of the year when breeding may be most advantageous. Other factors, such as rainfall, availability of nesting sites, nesting material, etc., may be required to bring the gonads to full development. These factors will be discussed separately. Farner and Follett (1966) have recognized three main patterns in photoperiodic importance to various avian species, i.e.: (a) Species which are obligately dependent upon long days; examples are the white-crowned sparrow (Zonotrichia leucophrys gambelii), the white-throated sparrow (Z. albicollis), and the brambling (Fringilla montifringilla). (b) Species in which an endogenous circa-annual rhythm of testicular size exists, but in which the precise annual testicular cycle is dependent on long days; an example is the domestic drake (Anas platy-rhynchos). (c) Species in which testicular development can occur on short days as well as on long days, e.g. the house sparrow (Passer domesticus).

The adaptive and multiple origin of the photoperiodic mechanism can explain why many different patterns of response are to be found among birds (Farner and Follett, 1966).

The testicular response (increase in size, stimulation of spermatogenesis) cannot be obtained all the time in birds with small testes. In the house sparrow, the red start (Phoenicurus phoenicurus), the starling (Sturnus vulgaris), the slate colored junco, and the white-crowned sparrow, exposure to long days immediately after the testis has regressed not only does not invoke a response but also prevents the testicular response from occurring as long as the birds are exposed to long days. This refractoriness can be removed by exposure of the birds to short days (Wolfson, 1966). Wolfson exposed white-throated sparrows, within a period of 369 days, to five periods of long days (16 hours of light, eight hours of darkness = 16L-8D) alternated by four periods of short days (8L-16D) and obtained five periods of gonadal activity, five periods of fat deposition, and two molts, showing that this bird's gonadal and fat deposition cycle can be regulated entirely by day length.

The refractory period is not present in some species, e.g. the bobwhite quail (Colinus virginianus), and the Baya weaver (Ploceus phillipinus), whereas the domestic drake does not show a testicular response to long days after testicular regression, but the refractory period does not need to be eliminated by exposure of the birds to short days. The red-billed dioch (Quelea quelea), an equatorial bird whose breeding cycle probably is not regulated by day length, shows a photoperiodic response when exposed to long days. However, the length of the refractory period after testicular regression is independent of day length (Farner and Follett, 1966).

It should be recalled that in the starling and the spotted munia, thyroidectomy prevents testicular regression, which normally occurs at the end of the breeding season; in effect then, in these species refractoriness is prevented by thyroidectomy (see Chapter 7).

In some species, e.g. Zonotrichia leucophrys, Z. albicollis, and Z. atricapilla, there is a postjuvenile photorefractory period, but in the equatorial Andean sparrow (Z. capensis) such a refractory period is lacking, as it is in the Japanese quail (Coturnix coturnix japonica) (Farner and Follett, 1966). However, in the latter species males start to produce semen at five to six weeks of age—thus any refractory period would be expected to be very short.

There have been numerous investigations of the effect of different day length on testicular growth of avian testes and of the effect of the same duration of light in different dosages [e.g. (1L-2D repeated seven times) + 1L + 16D)]. Only a brief summary of the most important aspects of these investigations will be given.

The rate of the testicular response, which can be expressed as:

$$k = \frac{\log w_t - \log w_o}{t}$$

in which k = rate constant; w_t = testicular weight at time t; w_o = testicular weight at time zero, and t = the t day of the experiment, is dependent on:

1. The length of the photoperiod (given in one dose). The relationship is essentially a linear one between nine and 18 hours of light for white-crowned

sparrows, bramblings, chaffinches *(Fringilla coelebs)*, green finches *(Carduelis chloris)*, and house sparrows (Farner, 1965).

2. Temperature. The rate constant of the testicular growth is only slightly affected by temperature in white-crowned sparrows, juncos, and starlings (Farner and Wilson, 1957).

3. Light intensity. This seems to play a minor role in obtaining the gonadal response as long as the threshold intensity is reached. The testicular response of starlings tended to increase with increasing intensity up to about 180 lux, but the number of birds used was small and no statistical analysis was carried out (Bissonnette, 1931). Similar results, also with small numbers of birds, were obtained by Bartholomew (1949) who used English sparrows and intensities between 0.4 and 2600 lux. The response of the testis of bobwhite quail was not affected by intensities above 0.4 lux; in the female, intensities of 1.0, 10, and 100 had no apparent effect on the age at which the first egg was laid, but at 3200 lux eggs were laid at an earlier age (Kirkpatrick, 1955). The rate constant of testicular growth of testes of white-crowned sparrows increased between 11 and 31 lux, but no further increase was obtained at 375 lux (Farner, 1959). Egg production of chickens is not affected by light intensities between 0.6 and 405 lux (see van Tienhoven, 1961). Wilson et al. (1956) found that at low intensities (0 to 74 lux) sexual maturity of pullets receiving restricted exposure to light was delayed as compared to pullets receiving 5 to 340 lux. Rollo and Domm (1943) found a graded response of the nuptial plumage (which is dependent upon LH) in *Euplectes pyromelana* exposed to intensities between 40 and 225 lux.

It thus appears that only at low intensities is there a relationship between the light intensity and gonadal response. There is the possibility that a relationship between intensity and response exists over a wider range of intensities under special conditions, such as restricted lighting.

It should be pointed out that the period of circadian activity rhythms of wall lizards *(Lacerta sicula)*, starlings and finches (Fringilidae) decreases with increasing intensity of illumination (ranges tested were between 1 and 800 lux under conditions of continuous illumination (Hastings, 1964).

4. Wave length. The ingenious, classic studies of Benoit and his co-workers, reviewed by Benoit (1964) and Benoit and Assenmacher (1959), have shown that in intact drakes the stimulation of the gonads could be obtained with orange and red lights (6640 to 7400 Å) and not with shorter wave lengths. Similar findings have been reported for starlings, sparrows, and turkeys (Farner, 1959).

In drakes with cut optic nerves, the response to light is still obtained, although it is smaller. The same wave lengths that are effective in the intact birds are effective in the blinded ones. If the light is directed on the hypothalamus via a quartz rod, it is found that blue light, which is normally not stimulatory, has the same effect as red light at the same energy level. The failure of blue light to stimulate the testis in the intact and blinded birds is the result of its failure to penetrate to the hypothalamus and of the apparent lack of a response by the optic-hypothalamic system to blue light. Light has been shown to penetrate to the hypothalamus in intact drakes, and in rats, rabbits, sheep, and dogs (Ganong et al., 1963; Van Brunt et al., 1964). The possible significance of this phenomenon will be discussed later in this chapter.

The time between testicular stimulation and regression is dependent, to a certain extent, on the rate of response (Wolfson, 1966). There was no regression, however, of the white-throated sparrow testis when exposed to 12L-12D.

When light is given either in non-24-hour cycles, e.g. 18L-8D or in divided dosages within 24 hour or in non-24-hour cycles, it appears that there is a circadian rhythm of photoresponsitivity. Hamner (1963), using the house finch (Carpodacus mexicanus), first discovered that cycles of 6L-18D, 6L-42D, 6L-66D, did not stimulate the testicular size, but cycles of 6L-6D, 6L-30D, 6L-54D stimulated the testes.

Subsequently, by interrupting the dark period in these different cycles at different times it was established that the the same dose of light has a greater stimulatory effect at different intervals after the onset of darkness (Hamner, 1964). Farner and Follett (1966) have confirmed these findings for white-crowned sparrows on a 6L-18D period, in which the dark period was interrupted by a two hour light period at different intervals. No response or a minimal one is obtained when the two hour light period comes up to four hours after the onset of the dark period, or just prior to the six hour light period; the maximal response is obtained when the two hour light period comes between ten and 14 hours after the onset of darkness.

Hamner and Enright (1967) investigated the hypothesis: "whether there is within an organism a single physiological time-measuring system responsible for all manifestations of daily rhythmicity" (one master clock whose hands can be read by examining any endogenous rhythm of the organism under investigation). The hypothesis was tested by measuring the testicular size and the daily locomotor activity of house finches:

1. on different light-dark cycles (6L-30D, 6L-54D versus 6L-18D, 6L-42D, 6L-66D);

2. on cycles of 6L-20D and 3L-23D versus 6L-16D and 3L-19D. The rationale for the use of these light cycles was derived from a locomotor activity experiment that indicated that on a 22 hour LD cycle with a short main light period, activity should be completely synchronized to the light phase of the cycle, i.e., all activity should occur during the light period, whereas birds on the 26 hour LD cycle with a short light period should be synchronized, but activity should be anticipated as much as ten hours before the onset of lights. If the locomotor activity and photoresponsitivity, with respect to testicular size, are regulated by the same clock, birds on the 22 hour cycle should always receive the light stimulus early in the "day" and at a time of low photoresponsitivity, whereas birds on the 26 hour cycle should always receive the light during the time of high photoresponsitivity.

3. in experiments in which the birds were allowed to establish their free running circadian activity rhythm for four days, and in which they received a non-synchronizing six hour light period either early (within 90 minutes after onset of activity) or later (12 hours after onset of activity) with respect to the "day" that the birds had established under the free running condition. The early light treatment should not cause testicular growth, but the late light treatment should.

In all three experimental conditions, there were strong correlations between testicular growth and onset of activity, if only groups of birds were considered. However, in some of the groups there were exceptions; a few birds showed testicular responses against expectations. Hamner and Enright (1967), therefore, consider the hypothesis of "single master clock" inadequate, and suggest as alternatives two independent circadian rhythms for locomotor activity and photoresponsitivity, or a single "master clock" for which the two manifestations investigated were not phase locked.

Wolfson (1966) exposed birds (either slate colored juncos or white-throated sparrows—the species is not indicated) to 16L-8D for eight days to induce a long day activity pattern, and then exposed the birds to continuous darkness. Controls were placed on a 9L-15D cycle instead of under continuous darkness. The testes of the experimental group weighed 117.9

mg. (N = 4), whereas the control testes weighed 7.9 mg. (N = 7). In another experiment Wolfson (1966) found that highly photosensitive white-throated sparrows (they had been for four months on 9L-15D) did not show a testicular response when placed in continuous darkness. These experiments thus show that long days are necessary for a testicular response, and also that once the new period of the biological clock is set, the clock retains this period provided no new synchronizing rhythm is imposed. An implication of these experiments is that the hypothalamo-hypophyseal system, once having acquired the new rhythm, can keep releasing the gonadotropins required for testicular stimulation (see also discussion of diurnal rhythms in rats later in this chapter).

Equatorial species can respond to long photoperiods by an acceleration of the testicular growth (Marshall, 1960), but this does not necessarily mean that the breeding cycle of such species is regulated by photoperiod. Marshall (1960) points out that rainfall seems to be an important factor for the red-billed dioch *(Quelea quelea)*. The fact that in its breeding area this species experiences differences in photoperiod of only a few minutes seems to argue against the idea that the photoperiod is the principal factor in regulating the breeding season of these species.

Among mammals, long photoperiods or extra light given during the night increases gonadal activity of rabbits, voles *(Microtus montanus* and *M. arvalis)*, hamsters, cats, raccoons, ferrets, mink, horses, and hedgehogs. The exposure of flying squirrels to long photoperiods causes a delay in sexual maturity and the absence of litters in females. In some breeds of sheep and in goats (Bissonnette, 1941) there is evidence that decreasing day lengths (either natural or artificial) cause gonadal stimulation. By exposing sheep to long days during the winter and short days during the summer a reversal of breeding seasons is obtained (Yeates,

1954). The breeds of sheep most susceptible to changes of the light schedule were "high latitude" sheep, whereas sheep from tropical areas were less susceptible. The tropical sheep can breed any time of the year (Hafez, 1964). It should be remembered that Thibault et al. (1966) have obtained data indicating an endogenous rhythm of sheep under constant light. These investigators have also been able, by experimental six month cycles of photoperiodic variation, to induce a breeding period every six months during the quarterly increasing light photoperiods. The breeding period usually lasted into the longer photoperiod.

The different responses of various breeds of sheep to long photoperiods are the result of the selective advantage of breeding seasons at high latitudes (Yeates, 1954).

Exposure of immature rats to long photoperiods results in earlier than normal estrus (Everett, 1961). The persistent estrus induced by continuous illumination in mature rats will be discussed later in this chapter.

In sheep and voles the gonads regress while remaining under the same light regime that initially stimulates the gonads, indicating a refractory period (Thibault et al., 1966). There is no evidence that a dark period is required to abolish this refractory period in these species. In ferrets there is, however, evidence that under certain conditions refractoriness to light exists, and that this is abolished by exposure to short days (females transferred to long days in July did not respond to long days in two out of five cases) (Donovan, 1967). Thorpe (1967), however, obtained repeated estrous periods at irregular intervals over a period of two years in females kept under continuous light.

Investigations with ferrets of different ages showed that both young and old ones, under normal daylight conditions, come into estrus in the spring, and, under continuous light, may come into heat at any time of the year. Adult ferrets become anestrous with an imposed short photo-period, which causes early estrus in young ferrets; a long photoperiod each day causes estrus in adults, but causes a delay in immature ferrets (Thorpe, 1967).

The fact that estrus can occur under continuous illumination at any time of the year indicates the absence of an endogenous circennian rhythm. The puzzling fact remains, however, that blinded ferrets did not respond to long photoperiods (whereas controls did) but in the spring these animals came into estrus.

The pathways by which light affects gonadal function in birds have been the subject of extensive investigations, es-pecially by Benoit and his associates. These investigations have been ably and ex-tensively reviewed by Benoit (1964), Benoit and Assenmacher (1955, 1959) and Farner and Follett (1966) for birds, and by Critchlow (1963) for mammals. The following findings are most important:

1. The gonadal response to the photoperiod requires the presence of the anterior pituitary.

2. Neither the eyes nor the optic nerves are required for the response in drakes, although the rate of response is reduced by removal of the eyes or section-ing of the optic nerve. These structures are essential for obtaining persistent estrus in rats (Critchlow, 1963), or out of season estrus in ferrets (Thorpe, 1967).

3. Light directed via a quartz rod to the hypothalamus or to the rhinencephalon of drakes induces a testicular response. The response is induced by the entire spectrum of visible light, whereas the re-sponse in intact drakes is obtained only in the red and orange part of the spectrum (Benoit, 1964).

Implantation of fine glass rods (optic fibers) into the brain of rats allows light to be directed to selected areas of the brain. Lisk and Kannwischer (1964), by the use of this technique, found that light directed on the suprachiasmatic region of blinded rats caused constant estrus. Exposure of the arcuate region caused an increase in ovarian and pituitary weights and the presence of many corpora lutea. These experiments thus indicate a direct effect of light on the neurons of the hypo-thalamus. However, it is not possible to state what the receptors are, as no pigment has been found in these areas. There is a possibility that light causes a local increase in temperature which is responsible for the response rather than light per se. This point has not yet been investigated.

4. In a comparison of intact and blinded drakes, operated so that light could fall directly on the hypothalamus (see Benoit, 1964), it was found that the operated drakes responded to lower amounts of energy from white light than intact ones; thus the sensitivity via the retinal pathway is lower than via the hypothalamic pathway. (It should be kept in mind that in intact drakes light can penetrate to the hypothalamus, but that much of the energy is absorbed by inter-vening tissues, so intact drakes would be more sensitive than blinded ones in which the hypothalamus was not exposed).

5. Lesions of the suprachiasmatic regions prevent the induction of con-stant estrus in rats under continuous light, but damage to the optic tracts does not cause this effect.

6. Evidence that there is a retinal-hypothalamic pathway is controversial (see Critchlow, 1963).

7. Evoked potentials recorded from the hypothalamus in response to light stimulation suggest the existence of optic connections to the hypothalamus (Feld-man, 1964; Massopust and Daigle, 1961; van Tienhoven [unpublished data], but Critchlow (1963) points out that such find-ings need to be confirmed in animals with bilaterally transected optic tracts.

8. The presence of the pineal eye in a lizard, showing a gonadal response to long photoperiods, has made it possible to investigate the role of this photoreceptor organ in the photosexual response. Clausen and Poris (1937) found that re-

moval of the pineal body caused an increase in testicular size of the American chameleon held under natural light conditions, but does not affect the response of the testis to long photoperiods. This suggests that the pineal body, either via its photoreceptor action or by a possible endocrine activity (see Chapter 7), inhibits testicular development in animals under natural daylight conditions. This finding is quite similar to that observed in mammals in which the pineal body has no photoreceptor cells.

Exposure of intact and pinealectomized Japanese quail to long and short photoperiods showed that the removal of the pineal body does not affect testicular or ovarian weight and increases oviduct weights under 14L-10D (Homma et al., 1967).

Pinealectomized rats kept in continuous darkness have larger ovaries than the controls; under continuous light the ovarian weights of controls and pinealectomized rats were not different. The uterine weight of rats in constant darkness was the same in sham-operated and operated rats; the same was true for rats in continuous light. Light did increase ovarian and uterine weights in the sham-operated rats (Wurtman et al., 1961). It thus appears that the effect of light on the ovary involves the pineal gland with constant darkness causing the secretion of a pineal substance which inhibits the gonads; the substance is in all probability melatonin (see Chapter 7). The mechanism by which light affects gonadal activity in birds and mammals may thus be different.

Cervical ganglionectomy, which affects pineal function (see Chapter 7), prevents the estrous response of the ferret to long photoperiods (Donovan and van der Werff ten Bosch, 1956; Marshall, 1962). This effect is not mediated via the thyroid (Donovan and van der Werff ten Bosch, 1956), nor is it the result of the drooping eyelids associated with the ganglionectomy (Marshall, 1962). Bilateral superior cervical ganglionectomy of rats prevents the

increase in size of ovaries and uteri and the increase in the incidence of estrous smears in rats exposed to continuous illumination. This operation also prevents the decrease in pineal weight and in HIOMT activity induced by continuous light in sham-operated rats (Wurtman et al., 1964). Blinding has the same effect as ganglionectomy. This evidence suggests that the photosexual response of the rat is mediated via the pineal gland. The possibility exists that the same mechanism operates in the ferret.

The relationship of the hypothalamus to the pituitary's gonadotropin function has been discussed in Chapter 8. On the basis of the available evidence, it appears that the pathway for the photosexual response of drakes differs from that of rats and ferrets in that the mammals require intact optic nerves and that the effect of the short photoperiod in pinealectomized animals differs.

The difficulties in the interpretation of the direct effect of light on the hypothalamus have not been resolved. The direct effect of light on neurons in the absence of pigment would be unusual. The possibility that light has its effect by raising the temperature has not been excluded.

The question whether an animal can reach sexual maturity without exposure to any light does not seem to have been answered experimentally. Jöchle (1964) states, in reference to laying hens, that "All animals reared in permanent light and in daylight change started normal egg laying, the former somewhat later than the latter. But hens hatched in permanent light produced more and heavier eggs compared with controls. Only one-third of the hens hatched in darkness started egg-laying (Figure 13)." The legend for Figure 13 states: "Egg laying performance (average daily production of g-egg) of groups of hens hatched and kept in different environments between the sixth and fourteenth month of life." It is not clear from these two statements whether the animals were kept in constant darkness from hatching to 14 months of age or whether they were raised under light until six months and then placed in constant darkness. It is unfortunate that the ambiguous statements make it impossible to draw a conclusion from these experiments, because it would be one of the few experiments, of which the author is aware, in which animals normally exposed to light become sexually mature without exposure to any light.

Temperature. The effectiveness of temperature as a synchronizer of the endogenous rhythm has not been investigated with respect to reproductive functions as extensively as has light. As a signal for the timing of the breeding season, one might expect that temperature would be of particular value to fishes, because water temperatures, especially of the ocean, are relatively constant from year to year, and may be correlated with the availability of food at the time the young hatch.

Harrington (1959a) reviewed much of the evidence concerning the effect of temperature and the interaction between temperature and photoperiod on fish reproduction. In the minnow (*Phoxinus phoxinus*) and in the bridled shiner, a combination of high temperature and long photoperiod are required to obtain maturity of males and females. With short photoperiods, high temperature inhibits development of the eggs.

Inhibition of egg development by high temperature under short day conditions has also been found in the European bitterling (*Rhodeus amarus*) and in the three-spined stickleback. In the lake chub (*Couesius plumbeus*) temperature is the major environmental factor controlling spermatogenesis. High temperatures (16 to 21° C.) stimulate proliferation of the spermatogonia and spermiation; low temperatures (5 to 12° C.) are required for increase in gonadal size and for the formation of primary spermatocytes.

Short photoperiods seemed to enhance the effects of low temperature on primary spermatocyte formation and

spermiogenesis, but neither 18L-6D nor 6L-18D did overcome the effects of temperature (Ahsan, 1966). During fall and winter, experimental variations of light and temperature were ineffective in stimulating testicular maturation. This may be considered evidence for an endogenous rhythm synchronized by temperature, but evidence of variation in the gonads in the absence of either temperature or light variations is not available.

The testis of the killifish (*Fundulus heteroclitus*) does not seem to be affected by photoperiod, but temperatures of 10° C. initiate spermatogenesis, and at higher temperatures spermatogenesis can be completed (Burger, 1939). Temperatures of 5.5° C. inhibit spermatogenesis (S. A. Matthews, 1939), but whether temperature acts as a synchronizer is not known. Whether an endogenous circennian cycle exists under constant conditions has not been established.

The possibility that temperature variations time the breeding season of amphibia has been investigated for different species. van Oordt (1960) has reviewed much of the evidence critically. Temperatures equivalent to summer temperatures in the breeding regions (about 20° C.) induce spermatogenesis in frogs (*R. esculenta, R. graeca,* and *Leptoductylus ocellatus*) in newts (*Triturus cristatus carnifex* and *T. viridescens*) and in *Geotriton fuscus*; lower temperatures inhibit spermatogenesis. In these species the cycle is regulated by environmental factors and there seems to be no yearly endogenous rhythm (van Oordt, 1960).

Interesting experiments have been carried out with the common European frog (*R. temporaria*) in which there are races which differ in the timing of the spermatogenetic cycle. The early race found in the lower parts of Western Europe has a spermatogenetic cycle which takes place from May until September with breeding occurring in March. In the late race, found in the Alps and Northern Europe, spermatogenesis begins in April and ends in August, with breeding occurring in May. Transfer of males of the late race to breeding regions of the early race did not affect the spermatogenetic cycle, suggesting an endogenous rhythm. Further investigations showed that the initiation of spermatogenesis can be induced by high temperatures, but that the beginning of the resting period is genetically determined and has an endogenous rhythm (van Oordt, 1960). In *R. arvalis* the initiation of spermatogenesis seems to be endogenous, as high temperatures do not initiate spermatogenesis. In *R. dalmatina* spermatogenesis was induced only by high temperature towards the end of the resting period.

A number of species show continuous spermatogenesis, e.g. *R. erytrea, R. grahami, R. tigrina, Bufo melanostictus, B. arenarum, B. paracnemis, B. granulosus d'orbignyi, Leptodactylus ocellatus reticulata, L. ocellatus bonaerensis,* all tropical or subtropical species, but also *Telmatobius schreiteri* and *Hyla raddiana andina,* which live in areas with low winter temperatures. In these species, spermatogenesis is probably independent of temperature. *Leptodactylus ocellatus typica* has a cycle which shows a resting period during the winter and one during the hot summer (van Oordt, 1960).

Low temperature can inhibit spermatogenesis in species that, in subtropical climates, have a continuous spermatogenetic cycle, thus making the cycle discontinuous, e.g. *R. esculenta ridibunda* and *Discoglossus pictus* (see van Oordt, 1960).

Reproduction of the lizard *(Uta stansburiana)* seems to be affected by temperature and not by photoperiod. There is, however, a refractory period during which the ovaries cannot be stimulated (Tinkle and Irwin, 1965), although in one year (out of three), after exposure to 27° C., 4 out of 16 females bore young in October through December.

There is no direct evidence that temperature regulates the timing of the breeding season of birds, although there is evidence that in unusually cold springs the start of the breeding season is delayed and that in unusually mild falls the birds may renest and lay eggs "out of season." Spermatogenesis and androgen secretion of the males may be stimulated (Riley, 1937; Marshall, 1961).

Among mammals the sexual cycle of the ground squirrel *(Citellus tridecimlineatus)* seems to be partly regulated by temperature variations. The breeding season normally starts in the spring. During the summer the reproductive system of males and females regresses. This regression can be prevented by exposing the animals to a constant temperature of 4° C., whereas photoperiod has no effect (Wells, 1959). It thus appears that the end of the breeding season is initiated by high temperatures. Whether these animals have an endogenous circennian rhythm and whether temperature can act as a synchronizer apparently have not been determined. Hoffman et al. (1965), using the golden hamster, which normally is a seasonal breeder (spring to fall), found that short photoperiod (two hours) and low temperature (6° C.) had additive effects in causing weight loss and testicular atrophy, and that high temperature (20° C.) and long photoperiod could induce continuous breeding. Temperature as such does not seem to regulate the breeding cycle of the European hamster *(Cricetus cricetus)*. Animals kept at 20° C. to prevent hibernation show seasonal regression of the gonads (Kayser, 1961).

In most, if not all, species there are a number of environmental factors which interact to initiate and end the breeding season. The optimal combination of such factors is often unknown, and differences exist between sexes in the same species. For example, male white-crowned sparrows will reach full breeding condition in captivity if given the proper photoperiod and food, but under the same conditions the females fail to show complete development of the ovary and ovulations fail to occur (Farner and Follett, 1966). The factors causing incomplete ovarian development are unknown.

In the following discussion some of

the factors that have been isolated will be discussed. These factors, unlike those discussed above, are not synchronizers of a circennial rhythm, although they may be synchronizers of an endogenous circadian rhythm. The author is aware that an attempt to isolate these factors on the basis of their sensory input is somewhat artificial, but it provides a basis for classification which seems useful.

DURING THE BREEDING SEASON

Light.   Ovulation in the Japanese rice fish, under natural light conditions, occurs from 1 to 5 a.m. This process is affected by light period (see Hoar, 1965). Harrington (1963) has made the interesting observation that in the self-fertilizing *Rivulus marmorata*, fertilization is largely confined to the dark period with few fertilizations occurring during the hours of light. Ovipositions occurred around noon in August but shifted to about 9 a.m. in November. No experiments were reported in which these events were made to occur at different times by changing the timing of the photoperiod.

The oviposition and ovulation cycle of the domestic chicken and the Japanese quail have been studied under a variety of photoperiods. The cycles of these two species have been discussed in Chapter 9.

Laying chickens placed under continuous light after they had been under a regime of 14L-10D, have been reported to distribute ovipositions evenly over the 24 hour period (Warren and Scott, 1936) and to retain their established oviposition cycle (Fraps et al., 1947). The reasons for the difference between these two sets of results is not obvious from the methods used by the two groups of workers. The data of Warren and Scott (1936) suggest that either the oviposition rhythm is entirely regulated exogenously or that the period of the endogenous circadian rhythm differs significantly from 24 hours, so that the endogenous rhythm becomes out of phase

and oviposition times of the population become distributed equally over 24 hour periods. The data of Fraps et al. (1947), however, indicate an endogenous rhythm with a period close to 24 hours, so the oviposition times remain in phase.

The timing of ovipositions of laying hens in continuous darkness seems to become synchronized by the visits of the caretaker (gathering of eggs, feeding; light was excluded) (Wilson, 1964). Egg production of laying hens drops sharply when they are placed in continuous darkness (Wilson and Woodard, 1958).

The oviposition cycle of the Japanese quail as discussed in Chapter 9 differs from that of the chicken in that the largest percentage of eggs is laid during the last six or seven hours of the light period (Arrington et al., 1962; Opel, 1966). Exposure of Japanese quail to continuous light, after their laying pattern has been established under 14L-10D, results in a rapid (three to five days) change into an even distribution over the 24 hour period (Arrington et al., 1962) as was observed for laying chickens by Warren and Scott (1936).

Light is a synchronizer for timing of oviposition, as has been demonstrated for chickens and Japanese quail by reversal of light treatments (Arrington et al., 1962; Fraps et al., 1947; Warren and Scott, 1936; Wilson, 1964; Wilson et al., 1964), or shifting the time of onset of light, or of light flashes (Arrington et al., 1962; Wilson et al., 1964), or by the use of unnatural days with equal length of darkness and light (21 to 42 hour days) (Biellier and Ostmann, 1960).

On the basis of the available evidence, Wilson et al. (1964) concluded that the release of LH in the chicken occurs about five hours after the onset of darkness, that LH release is followed eight hours later by ovulation, and that oviposition follows ovulation by an interval of 24 to 25 hours so that the total interval between stimulus and oviposition is 37 to 38 hours.

The ovulation cycle and the effects of

photoperiods have been critically reviewed by Fraps (1955, 1961). The data are consistent with the concept of a 24 hour periodicity of gonadotropin release, which can be synchronized by external factors such as light (Fraps, 1965).

Photoperiod also can affect egg production, which is not surprising as the photoperiod affects the length of the sequence; the fewer the intervals between successive eggs, the higher the egg production can be, provided the birds start and end the reproductive season at the same time.

Exposure of pullets that have started to lay to continuous light increases early egg production but not yearly production, probably because of a refractoriness also observed in other animals. It appears from the data obtained by Biellier and Ostmann (1960) that on a 29 hour cycle (14.5L-14.5D) egg production was highest, when eggs, incidentally, were mostly laid during the dark period. Byerly and Moore (1941) obtained about a 20 percent increase in egg production by exposing hens to 16L-10D instead of 14L-10D. The experiments by Biellier and Ostmann (1960) and Byerly and Moore (1941) were of short duration and apparently it has not been investigated whether such unnatural day length periods increase yearly egg production.

Riley (1937) found that spermatogenesis of sparrows showed a diurnal rhythm in which there was a correlation between low body temperature and the incidence of mitotic figures. Whether such a rhythm persists under continuous light or darkness has apparently not been investigated. Riley caused a lowering of the body temperature of the birds by clipping the feathers and found mitoses during the hours of light whereas such figures were absent in controls. The data presented by Riley show little effect of increased body temperature (caused by forced activity) on the incidence of mitosis between 4.05 and 5.40 a.m. when mitotic activity is highest in control sparrows.

The effects of season and of light on reproduction of domestic mammals have been reviewed by Ortavant et al. (1964) and the following account is based on the data assembled from the literature and from their own experiments:

Artificial illumination, apparently, increased fertility of cattle in Alaska, but spermatogenesis of bulls in the Netherlands was not affected by long (16L) or short photoperiods (8L).

The ovarian weight, number of follicles, number of corpora lutea of swine were larger on 18L-6D than either on 7L-4D-5L-8D or on 3L-8D-3L-10D. As Ortavant et al. (1964) point out it is unfortunate that no short photoperiods with uninterrupted dark periods were used.

Photoperiods have a pronounced effect on seasonally reproducing sheep. Long photoperiods have an unfavorable effect on spermatogenesis; e.g. a spermatogonium A which normally produces 64 spermatids produces about 40 under long photoperiods. The FSH and LH content of the sheep pituitary are decreased by long photoperiods. Information on other species is rather incomplete and no conclusions seem to be warranted.

In some of the species that show delayed implantation, long photoperiods can cause earlier implantation than natural daylight. This is the case for the mink (*Mustela vison*), the marten (*Martes americana*) (Pearson and Enders, 1944) and the sable (*Martes zibellina*) (Farner, 1961).

The exposure of rats to continuous light results in constant estrus (Critchlow, 1963; Everett, 1961). This constant estrus is associated with lower than normal LH concentrations in the pituitary (Bradshaw and Critchlow, 1966). The mechanism whereby continuous light prevents the secretion and release of LH is not known. It is, however, apparent that continuous light prevents the periodic release of LH. It was discussed in Chapter 8 that LH release was dependent upon stimulation during a two hour "critical period" that occurs, under conditions of 14L-10D, between 2 and 4 p.m. on the day of proestrus. The occurrence of this critical period can be shifted by changing the light regime. An abrupt three hour advance of the time at which the light turns on causes a readjustment of the time at which the "critical period" occurs over a two to three week period. Full reversal of the light-dark schedule also causes a shift of the "critical period." This shift requires about two to three weeks for completion (Everett, 1961).

In immature rats injected with PMSG there is also a "critical period" between 2 and 4 p.m. required for ovulation. The time of this critical period can be shifted by shifting the light-dark periods (Strauss and Meyer, 1962).

Temperature. Aronson (1965) lists the following spring-breeding species of teleosts in which increasing temperatures induce gonadal maturation: *Fundulus, Gambusia*, the European bitterling, the carp, the pike, *(Esox lucius)*, darters and sticklebacks, and the following fall-breeding species in which decreasing temperatures cause gonadal maturation: the char *(Salmo alpinus)*, the lake trout *(Salvelinus* sp.), the whitefish *(Coregonus lavaretus)*, and the Caspian sturgeon.

In the three-spined stickleback and the green sunfish *(Lepomis cyanellus)* spawning behavior is related to the water temperature, and in the green sunfish nesting behavior also seems to be regulated by water temperature (Aronson, 1965).

The oviposition time of the Japanese rice fish is delayed by low temperature, the length of the delay is a function of the length of the cooling period, and of the length of the cooling period falling between 2 and 5 a.m. (Egami, 1959).

Harrington (1967), in an interesting set of experiments, showed that exposure of embryos, after the onset of blood circulation, to low temperatures (19.5 ± 0.5° C.) induced the appearance of 72 percent males in *Rivulus marmoratus* in which normally not more than five percent males occur, the remainder being hermaphrodites. In this species females have not been found either in the wild or in the laboratory experiments.

Among amphibia, van Oordt and Lofts (1963) found that high temperatures (20 to 24° C.) impeded the secretion of LH, as reflected in the regression of the interstitial testicular cells, reduced androgen secretion, and cytologic appearance of the pituitary of the common European frog *(Rana temporaria)*. The secretion of FSH is stimulated by the high temperatures, resulting in new spermatogenetic activity. A similar relationship between temperature and gonadal activity seems to occur in the edible frog *(R. esculenta)* (de Kort and van Oordt, 1965).

In salamanders *(Pleurodeles waltlii)* exposure to cold and subsequent transfer to warmer water causes spawning, indicating that oviposition is stimulated by this sequence of temperature changes (Noble, 1931).

Among birds the effect of temperature on the time of oviposition has been investigated in chickens and Japanese quail. Payne et al. (1965) found that, under continuous light, cycles of either nine hours of 18.3° C. and 15 hours of 29.5° C. or nine hours of 29.5° C. and 15 hours of 18.3° C. caused ovipositions to be predominant during the warm hours, whereas under continuous temperature of either 18.3° C. or 29.5° C. ovipositions were distributed evenly over the 24 hour periods. Arrington et al. (1962) did not affect the distribution of ovipositions of Japanese quail by cycles of additional heat.

Spermatogenesis in roosters is relatively resistent to high environmental temperatures. After heat stress (37 to 39° C.), Boone and Huston (1963) found no significant differences in spermatogenesis and fertility of roosters.

High temperatures (about 25 to 30° C.) will adversely affect egg production, size, and shell thickness, which, in turn, may decrease hatchability (Glick et al., 1959; Hutchinson, 1954).

The egg production of turkey hens starts earlier if the birds are protected from low temperatures, but exposure of the animals to constant temperatures throughout the year results in lower egg production than exposure to changing temperatures. This effect is mainly the result of the higher incidence of broodiness of hens in the constant temperature environment (see van Tienhoven, 1961, for review).

The fertility of turkey toms was improved during the cold winter months (Minimum temperature is −29° C.) in Pullman, Washington, by keeping the birds in warm pens (18.3° C.) and in the hot summers (with 37.7° C. temperatures) the fertility was improved by keeping the birds in cool pens (18.3° C.) (see Hafez, 1964, and van Tienhoven, 1961, for reviews).

The effects of high temperatures on spermatogenesis in mammals have been discussed in Chapter 5. Among domestic animals, the fertility of rams seems to be particularly affected by high temperatures. Exposure for 24 hours to a temperature of about 38° C. causes a decrease in semen quality (motility, sperm concentration, incidence of abnormal spermatozoa) (Simpson, 1966). Air conditioning (even free choice by the rams of air conditioned or conventional barns), or shearing of the rams may improve semen quality (see Hafez, 1964).

Beef calves of the Brahma and Shorthorn breeds reach puberty about 157 and 137 days later, respectively, when they are raised at 32.2° C. than when raised at 10° C. For the Santa Gertrudis breed there was no such difference (Dale et al., 1959).

Exposure of either *Bos indicus* or *Bos taurus* bulls to 40° C. for 12 hours had a detrimental effect on spermatogenesis; the effect is most severe in *Bos taurus* (Skinner and Louw, 1966).

The length of the estrous cycle of sheep is not affected by temperature, but the ova of sheep exposed before, at, or after breeding to 32° C. are frequently abnormal (Dutt, 1964), as indicated by shrunken cytoplasm, vacuoles in the cytoplasm, ruptured vitelline membranes, and ruptured zonae pellucidae. It is not surprising that fertility is adversely affected by high environmental temperature (Hafez, 1964).

Ulberg (1966) has discussed the effects of exposure to 40° C. of sheep on different steps of the reproductive process. Environmental temperature of 40° C. during the time that capacitation occurs results in death of the blastocysts before implantation. Postimplantation mortality is increased after exposure of the sheep to 40° C. when the egg is undergoing its first cell division, but if this condition is applied during the second cell division this effect is not found.

Woody and Ulberg (1964) showed, by transfer of ova between two groups of sheep held at either 21.1 or 32.2° C., that the uteri of the sheep kept at 32.2° C. provided an unfavorable environment for embryonic development.

Exposure of pregnant sheep to high temperatures (40.6° C.) during the last two-thirds of the gestation period frequently results in dwarfed lambs. The pituitaries of the dwarfs have cells smaller than those in the controls and with intensely chromophilic nuclei; the adrenal cortices are also smaller (Ryle and Morris, 1961). The dwarfism is not the result of reduced feed intake (Hafez, 1964).

Ryle (1961) found that thyroxine administration reduced embryonic mortality in sheep exposed to high temperature which it also did in control ewes, so that it seems that the effect of high temperature on embryonic mortality is not mediated via the thyroid.

There are seasonal variations in the duration of gestation in sheep: lambs born early in the spring are carried longer, but experimental exposure to high temperatures does not affect the length of gestation (Hafez, 1964).

Swine apparently are not affected by high temperatures as far as reproduction is concerned.

Rats exposed to temperatures of 35° C. between days 6 and 12 of gestation show fetal resorption, which can be reduced by progesterone administration (MacFarlane et al., 1959; Pennycuik, 1964). By acclimatizing the animals for 14 to 79 days prior to breeding, embryonic losses can be reduced. A system of breeding and selection created strains of rats which are resistant to high temperatures (MacFarlane et al., 1959).

Low temperatures generally are less detrimental to nonhibernating mammals than high temperatures.

Barnett and Manly (1954) have demonstrated that mice can breed at −3° C. for several generations. There are strain differences with respect to the reproductive performance of mice transferred from 21° C. to −3° C. Generally, the number of litters per pair of mice decreased, as did the number of young weaned per pair, but the mean number of young per litter was reduced in one out of three strains (Barnett and Manly, 1956). Barnett and Little (1965) showed that the loss of young was lower for mice which had been bred at −3° C. for 17 to 19 generations than for mice whose parents and grandparents had been transferred as young adults to the −3° C. environment, but the differences were not statistically significant.

It is obvious that animals receive a multitude of stimuli which affect their behavior and their reproductive performance. Often it is difficult to neatly separate these effects into categories, and in many cases the optimal combination may not have been established.

For the sake of convenience, the effects of various categories of stimuli will be discussed separately and examples will be used to illustrate whether such stimuli have been effective in stimulating the genital system.

Visual Stimuli.   Visual stimuli are important, not only for eliciting a response from the other sex, inducing courtship behavior, but also for the development of the gonads.

In the three-spined stickleback (*Gasterosteus aculeatus*) it has been demonstrated that visual signals (by the use of models) are important in eliciting courtship behavior in the male, with a swollen silver underside being the most important charac-

teristic, and the head up position being most effective (Marler and Hamilton, 1966).

Tilapia macrocephala females in isolation spawn, on the average, about three times per year. If the females are allowed to see another *T. macrocephala,* male or female, intact or gonadectomized, she spawns seven to eight times per year, showing that visual stimuli increase the incidence of spawning (Aronson, 1957).

The classical experiment in which a visual stimulus was shown to affect gonadal activity of birds is the experiment by L. H. Matthews (1939) in which pigeons *(Columba livia)* were either isolated, or isolated but with a mirror, or isolated but so that they could hear and see a male, or together with a male. The female with the mirror laid later than the females which could hear and see males, and the female housed with the male laid first. The isolated female did not lay until a male was introduced; she ovulated 11 days after the introduction of the male. Subsequent experimental results by Lott and Brody (1966) showed that two out of ten ring doves (*Streptopelia risoria*) laid when they were in a sound reducing chamber with a mirror. Although the authors dispute Matthews' conclusion that visual stimuli rather than auditory stimuli stimulated ovulation, their own design did not include a group of birds in a sound reducing chamber without a mirror. Their experiments do show rather clearly that introducing sound from the breeding room interacted with the visual stimulus from the mirror and caused nine out of 12 to lay eggs.

Erickson and Lehrman (1964) placed male and female ring doves in cages so that the pair was separated by a glass plate. Males were either intact or had been castrated for five weeks. After seven days the females paired with intact males had oviducts about 1.8 times as heavy as those of females paired with castrated males; in other experiments females tested without males had oviducts which weighed about

47 percent of what those of the females paired with castrated males in the experiments above. Castration may have reduced the effect of males on the female's estrogen secretion by difference in either auditory, visual, or auditory and visual stimuli.

In a beautifully conceived and executed series of experiments carried out in the Arctic, Smith (1963) investigated the stimulus value of different morphological characteristics in four species of gulls, i.e. the glaucus gull *(Larus hyperboreus)*, the herring gull *(Larus argentatus)*, Thayer's gull *(L. thayeri)*, and Kumlien's gull *(L. glaucoides kumlieni)*; these gulls are sympatric in various combinations in the Eastern Canadian Arctic. The main features used by the gulls for "recognition" of their own species were the yellow eye ring and yellow iris in the glaucus gull, the orange eye ring and yellow iris in the herring gull, the reddish-purple eye ring and dark iris in Thayer's gull, and the reddish-purple eye ring and irises varying between very light and dark in Kumlien's gull. By capturing these gulls and painting their eye rings, Smith (1963) established that the contrasts between eye ring and head feather color acts as an isolating mechanism. These experiments revealed that:

1. The female selects the male and chooses only males with an eye-head contrast like her own.

2. In mated pairs the female's eye-head contrast serves as a release for the male to mount.

3. Changing the eye-head contrast pattern of the female of mated pairs to the eye-head contrast of another species resulted in regression of the testes, whereas in control pairs testes increased in size. The regression of testicular size on time after change of contrast was linear. The difference between the regression coefficients of control males and for males with a changed partner was statistically significant.

4. By changing the eye-head contrast of males of different species to that of the female and by changing the eye-head con-

trast of the female after pairing had occurred, Smith was able to obtain hybrids between different species of arctic gulls.

These experiments clearly indicate the effect of a visual stimulus on the testes of these gulls.

In animals other than birds, visual stimuli have not been clearly separated from acoustic, olfactory, and tactile stimuli, but this does not imply that visual stimuli are not important.

Hale (1966) has presented evidence that visual stimuli are important for sexual behavior in bulls. The absence of visual stimuli reduced the probability that a bull will identify the sexual situation and try to start a response. Blind bulls were deficient in only one response, i.e. to a new stimulus animal. Blind bulls show no defects of spermatogenetic function and sperm output (Hafs, 1966). Estrous cows used as "teasers" for obtaining semen with an artificial vagina were more effective than nonestrous cows, as measured by the time between presentation of the cow and the attempt of the bull to mount and by sperm output by the bull. The sensory pathways whereby this effect was mediated were not determined.

Beach (1951) cites work by Enders that indicates that visual isolation of female mink retards their ovarian development, suggesting that visual stimuli enhance the development of the ovary, but not proving that visual stimuli would be effective in the absence of olfactory and auditory stimuli.

Auditory Stimuli. The male gobiid fish *(Bathygobius soporator)* makes grunting sounds to which gravid females respond by quick darting movements. The response of the female to these sounds in the absence of a visual stimulus is unoriented, but in the presence of another goby the movements are oriented.

Brockway (1960), using pairs of budgerigars as an experimental unit, investigated the effects of visual and auditory stimuli in a factorial experiment and found that either visual or auditory stimuli caused gonadal development and the effects seemed to be additive. In another series of experiments, pairs of budgerigars were placed in isolation and tapes of vocalizations were played either in three sessions of two hours or in one session of three hours. The soft warble, which is closely associated with visible male precopulatory behavior, stimulates egg laying; other vocalization or no vocalizations did not result in egg laying (Brockway, 1965). Six hours of stimulation were more effective than three hours. It needs to be emphasized that reference is made to pairs of budgerigars. The reaction of single males and females has not been tested, as far as I am aware. In isolated pairs, the male does not seem to vocalize without auditory stimulation from other males (Brockway, 1960).

The sound made by the boar increases the incidence of estrous posture among sows and gilts by about 25 percent (Signoret et al., 1960). The odors of the boar act synergistically with these vocalizations in inducing this behavior (Signoret and du Mesnil du Buisson, 1961).

Cow vocalizations will increase the amount of semen and will reduce the time it takes a bull to ejaculate into the artificial vagina (de Vuyst et al., 1964).

Experiments with mammals have shown that "unphysiological" stimuli, such as the ringing of electric bells, can affect reproduction.

Stimulation consisting of the ringing of an electric bell (3 to 12kHz* and peaks of 100 decibels (db.) at 4kHz and 95 db. at 10kHz) at ten minute intervals for one minute day and night (Zondek and Tamari, 1967) resulted in:

1. Permanent estrus in rats, with heavier ovaries, more corpora lutea, and heavier uteri than in controls. Male rats were not affected, as determined by spermatogenesis.

2. Ovulations, large ovaries, and sometimes milk secretion in rabbits.

3. Decreased ability of the male rats to

---

* 1Hz = 1 cycle/sec.

fertilize, and of the females to be fertilized, when stimulation occurred during the premating period.

4. Reduced incidence of pregnancies and reduced number of fetuses if stimulated during a four day mating period.

5. Interruption of pregnancy if stimulation occurred during the first 48 hours p.c.

Deaf rats did not show these effects after exposure to the ringing of the bell.

Árvay (1967), using complex neural stimuli which included continuous illumination (at 1.900 to 2.000 Lux), ringing bells (five minutes every hour), and electrical stimuli (70 to 80 V. at 30 to 45 mA.), increased the incidence of abnormal fetuses by application before mating during pregnancy and reduced fertility by application either before or after mating. Onset of puberty was hastened by exposing the rats to these stimuli shortly before the expected onset of puberty, but a delayed onset occurred if the rats were exposed well in advance of expected puberty. In these experiments enlarged ovaries and enlarged corpora lutea were found in the experimental groups, suggesting an increase of gonadotropin secretion, which can also account for the earlier onset of puberty. However, the delayed puberty after long exposure and the high incidence of fetal abnormalities may be the result of damage to the germ cells (stimulation prior to mating being effective) and/or increased corticosteroid and epinephrine concentrations. (The concentration of these hormones was not determined.)

The significance of these findings in the normal reproductive cycle of rats and rabbits cannot be determined from these experiments. However, the experiments do indicate that such effects exist in mammals and may be of importance in human reproduction. Árvay (1967) cites the increased incidence of abnormal babies in the period following the war during which a particular area had been a battlefield. Of course, nutritional and other factors may also have contributed to such abnormalities, but the evidence suggests the possible effect of psychotraumatic experience on human reproduction.

Olfactory Stimuli. Olfactory stimuli play an important part in the communication between animals, and a special terminology has been used for the substances which function in this manner. "Pheromones" are defined as "substances or mixtures of substances, which are produced to the exterior by one animal and may be received by a second individual of the same species, in which they produce one or more specific reactions" (Whitten, 1966).

The effects of pheromones and the importance of olfactory stimuli in mammalian reproduction have been reviewed extensively (Bruce, 1966, 1967; Whitten, 1966) and for vertebrates and invertebrates by Wilson and Bossert (1963).

The gobiid fish *(Bathygobius soporator)* normally attacks males or nongravid females intruding into his territory, but gravid females are courted; the color of the courting male becomes different from that of a noncourting one. Tavolga (1955) discovered that water in which gravid females had been present induced courtship behavior in five to ten seconds after introduction of the water. Males with either plugged nostrils or cauterized nostrils did not respond (Tavolga, 1955, 1956). The fluid from the ovaries of gravid females was the only fluid which caused this response. Ovarian fluid from nongravid females gave a short incomplete response. A similar effect has been reported for the shad *(Alosa alosa)* (Aronson, 1957).

Visual stimuli interacted with the olfactory stimuli, especially in the orientation of the behavior. In the absence of visual stimuli the behavior was more or less random all through the aquarium. In the presence of a visual stimulus (which may be either a gravid or nongravid female, a male, dead or alive, and even a male showing combat behavior) the aggressive behavior was oriented. Thus the visual stimuli not only oriented the behavior, but also enhanced it to the extent that objects not normally courted were now courted, but only if the olfactory stimulus was given.

Visual stimuli in the absence of olfactory stimuli (e.g. males placed in an Erlenmeyer flask that was lowered into the tank of the resident male) elicited courtship response, but the response showed great variation from animal to animal. Males, that courted on the first test (in response to a gravid female), also courted nongravid females or males in subsequent tests. These courted animals, had they been in the tank, would probably have been chased rather than courted (Tavolga, 1956).

Noble (1931) has discussed the significance of the hedonic glands in a number of salamanders with respect to the courtship behavior. No experiments were, however, carried out to demonstrate the relative effectiveness of olfactory stimuli.

Sex and species recognition among garter snakes *(Thamnophis sirtalis)* was shown to be at least partly on the basis of odors, as indicated by the following of trails made on a glass plate by females; the trail was not followed by males if it was made by a male or by a male or female of another species (Noble, 1937).

Among mammals, the importance of olfactory stimuli in reproduction has been shown in the mouse *(Mus musculus)*, the deer mouse *(Peromyscus sp.)*, the vole, the cat, the sheep, the pig, and the goat. The mouse and the deer mouse have probably been investigated most intensively in this respect. In the mouse, three effects have been noted:

1. The van der Lee-Boot effect. Female mice housed in groups of four or more show a higher incidence of pseudopregnancies and maintenance of corpora lutea in the absence of matings than controls kept in smaller groups. Removal of the olfactory bulbs prevents this effect (Whitten, 1966). In the presence of a male, intact mice will show regular cycles. If female mice are housed in groups of thirty or more the incidence of anestrus increases. These anestrous mice have a high incidence of atrophic uteri, the ovaries lack

luteal tissue or have atrophic corpora lutea, and the ovarian weight is reduced (Whitten, 1959). Placing a male with the females causes regular cycles, an effect also obtained after exposing the females to urine of males from the same strain (Marsden and Bronson, 1965a).

These experiments show, as Whitten (1966) has pointed out, that female mice secrete pheromones which affect the estrous cycle. With groups of four mice this pheromone or these pheromones cause pseudopregnancy; in groups of 30 mice they (it) cause(s) anestrus. It is not determined whether one or two pheromones are involved (see Whitten, 1966).

With male urine, four effects can be obtained: earlier estrus, suppression of pseudopregnancy (induced by female pheromones), synchronization of estrous cycles, and blocking of pregnancy or pseudopregnancy (induced by mating).

2. The Whitten effect. If one takes into account that the estrous cycle of the mouse is four or five days, one would expect that 20 or 25 percent of the nonpregnant and nonpseudopregnant females would be in estrus on any one day. After a male is introduced, one would expect 20 or 25 percent of the population to mate each day. However, after the male is placed with the females the incidence of matings on days 1 and 4 is less than 25 percent, but 46 to 50 percent of the mice mate on day 3 (Whitten, 1956a). The male must be introduced at the start of metestrus in order to affect the current cycle (Bruce, 1967). The presence of the males or of the male's urine (Marsden and Bronson, 1964) suppresses anestrus among grouped females.

As Nalbandov (1964) has pointed out, the endocrinology of this rapid response is not well understood.

Matings reach the highest frequency one day after release of a male that had been placed in a wire basket in a box with females for two days; this peak thus occurs on the third day after exposure of the females to male odors (Whitten, 1966). Castration of the male prevents the synchronization of the estrous cycles (Bruce, 1966, 1967; Whitten, 1966).

The Whitten effect also has been observed in rats (Hughes, 1964), and in the deer mouse (Bronson and Marsden, 1964).

The introduction of a ram accelerates the occurrence of estrus in sheep and synchronizes the cycles of ewes which were not yet cyclic. However, if the ram is continuously with the flock, neither the acceleration of estrus, nor the synchronization of the cycles are observed, nor does the ram cause synchronization among sheep which already had estrous cycles (Bruce, 1966; Hulet, 1966).

A male goat placed in a herd of Angora does stimulated the initiation of estrus and ovulation and also synchronized the cycles so that the greatest frequences of births was between the eighth and twelfth day of the kidding season (Shelton, 1960).

3. The Bruce effect. If newly mated mice are removed from the stud male and are exposed to males of either the same or of another strain, pregnancy and pseudopregnancy are blocked. The female returns to heat three to seven days after coitus (p.c.) with the stud male. The blockade of pregnancy is more effective if the exposure to strange males (or male urine, as will be discussed) occurs during the first four days p.c. and becomes gradually less effective as the time interval between coitus and exposure to the strange male increases.

This block to pregnancy, the Bruce effect can be prevented by either the injection of prolactin or the grafting of an ectopic pituitary (Dominic, 1966c), suggesting that the olfactory stimuli (to be discussed) decrease prolactin secretion or release. This effect is probably mediated via the hypothalamus. Evidence in support of this concept is found in the fact that reserpine, which inhibits the hypothalamic center controlling prolactin release, also prevents the pregnancy blockade by strange males or urine of those males (Dominic 1966 a,c). The Bruce effect, unlike the Whitten effect, has not been observed in rats (Davis and de Groot, 1964;

Whitten, 1966), but has been found in the deer mouse (Bronson and Eleftheriou 1963).

Several quantitative aspects of the blockade of pregnancy have been investigated. The findings are summarized here:

1. The farther the new male is removed from the stud male, genetically, the higher the incidence of blocked pregnancies (Bruce, 1966). It should be emphasized that it is the genetic relationship between the males which determines the effectiveness of the blockade and not the relationship between either of the two males and the female. Thus a female mated with a male from a different strain will have her pregnancy blocked by exposure to a male of her own strain.

2. The incidence of blocked pregnancies is higher when six males are used than when one or three males are used (Chipman and Fox, 1966).

3. Older females are less susceptible than younger females (Chipman and Fox, 1966).

4. There are no significant differences between parous and nonparous females.

5. A 15 minute exposure to a wild male mouse was as effective as a continuous exposure (Chipman et al., 1966).

6. Castrated males do not block implantation (Bruce, 1965).

7. Pregnancy is not blocked by the presence of strange males when the females are made anosmic, showing that the effect is mediated via the olfactory system (Bruce, 1966).

8. The material causing the pregnancy block is present in the urine of intact males (Dominic, 1966b) but not in the urine of castrated males (Bruce, 1966, 1967). Androgen induces the occurrence of the active factors upon injection to spayed females (Dominic, 1965).

9. Removal of the preputial glands, which produce a sex attractant (Bronson, 1966), does not affect the response of the females (see Bruce, 1966).

10. Strange males and also strange females can block pregnancy in deer mice. Bronson et al. (1964) exposed inseminated deer mice (Peromyscus maniculatus bairdii) to either strange males or females of the mouse (Mus musculus), strain C57BL/10J, or of the bairdii, or of the gracilis subspecies. Males of bairdii, gracilis, and the mouse were effective in blocking implantation, but females of P. maniculatus bairdii and of the mouse were not. These experiments indicate, but do not prove (no anosomic females were used), that females may also secrete substances interfering with pregnancy of females of another subspecies.

11. The blockade of implantation can be repeated several times by mating the female to the stud male and again exposing her to a strange male. The females so treated show an increased incidence of pseudopregnancies, following the pregnancy block rather than the return to normal 4 day estrous cycles; fertility is, however, not affected (Bruce, 1962).

12. Marsden and Bronson (1965b) found among strains of inbred mice that neither strange males of the same strain nor males from a different strain blocked pregnancy. Strains used were C57BL/6J, CBA/J, CBA/ca, SWR/J, 129/J. The 129/J females were tested with CBA/J and C57BL/6J males, and the C57BL/6J females were tested with CBA/J males. The reasons for this failure to show the Bruce effect in these inbred strains are not known.

Removal of the olfactory bulbs causes regression of the ovary and uterus in rabbits (Franck, 1966), in mice (Whitten, 1956b), and in swine (Signoret and Mauleon, 1962). In swine this operation resulted in an increased FSH content of the pituitary, suggesting a failure of FSH release (Signoret, 1965).

In the guinea pig ablation of the olfactory bulbs had little effect on the estrous cycle, but it did seen to inhibit estrous behavior (Donovan and Kopriva, 1965).

Young stallions that did not attempt to mount a dummy did so in 37 percent of the cases when the dummy was sprinkled with the urine of a pregnant mare (Wierz-bowski and Hafez, 1961), suggesting that olfactory cues stimulated the mating behavior; strangely enough this same procedure inhibited the mounting by adult stallions. The adult stallions attempted to mate the dummy in 79 percent of the cases, but after sprinkling with urine they did so in only 38 percent.

Olfactory cues play an important role in the discrimination by the male between estrous and nonestrous rats (Bruce, 1966, 1967); castrated males do not lose this ability to discriminate (Carr and Caul, 1962).

Anosmic rams approach estrous and nonestrous ewes alike, whereas intact rams preferentially approach estrous ewes. Anosmic rams are able to mate, but the amount and type of foreplay is different from that of intact rams (Lindsay, 1965).

Exposure of anestrous cats to valeric acid causes the development of ovarian follicles, which ovulate upon vaginal stimulation; valeric acid and vaginal secretions cause mating behavior in anestrous cats, as will be discussed in Chapter 14 (Lissák, 1962).

Miscellaneous Factors.   Marshall (1960, 1961) has repeatedly emphasized that factors other than light and temperature can stimulate or inhibit the maturation or development of the gonads. Some of such factors will be mentioned here:

RAINFALL. The spawning of the Indian carp is correlated with rainfall. It is difficult to determine whether the rainfall per se is the stimulus or whether the rainfall changes the amount of food available, the pH, the oxygen content, the water temperature, or the concentration of dissolved chemicals. Experimentally, spawning can be induced in a few days by oxygenation of the aquarium water in *Barbus stigma* and *Amblyopharyngodon mola* (Aronson, 1965). The nest building and fanning of the eggs by three-spined sticklebacks are affected by the concentrations of oxygen and carbon dioxide in the water.

Ovulation in some species of frogs and toads is stimulated by rain, and as the female usually only is receptive after ovulation, sexual receptivity is also affected by rain (Aronson, 1965).

The equatorial species of lizard, *Agama agama lionotus*, shows distinct breeding seasons in spite of the lack of any substantial variation in photoperiod and temperature. The breeding occurs after the period of the so-called long rains, which apparently makes protein food available and thus allow gonadal development to occur (Marshall and Hook, 1960).

The time of breeding of the fringe-toed lizard *(Uma notata)*, the zebra finch *(Taeniopygia castanotis-Poephila castanotis)* and the budgerigar, follows the falling of rain (Marshall, 1960, 1961; Mayhew, 1966); whether the maturation of the gonads is the result of the increased amount of the proper food is not certain, but it seems probable.

Serventy and Marshall (1957) made field studies of the effects of heavy rains in 1953 and of a summer deluge in 1955 in Western Australia on a large number of avian species. There were 39 species that showed evidence of unseasonal reproductive activity, presumably as a result of the heavy rains or factors associated with these rains. A gradient of response was observed; individuals in areas where rainfall is normally lower showed a greater response to the heavy rains than individuals in areas which normally have a greater yearly precipitation.

Low temperatures seemed to inhibit reproduction in these species, and Serventy and Marshall (1957) proposed that rainfall and temperature may regulate the occurrence of breeding in these species.

In Australian ducks, the pink-eared duck *(Malacorhynchos membranaceus)* and the gray teal *(Anas gibberifrons),* rain stimulates reproduction by causing a rise in water levels. The gray teal breeds shortly after the rise of the water level starts, the pink-eared duck when the water level recedes. Breeding can occur at any time of the year, and water level seems to be the signal for the onset of the breeding activity (Marshall, 1960).

For the red-billed dioch, the presence of green grass after rainfall affects nest building activity, but rainfall itself also stimulates this activity (Marshall, 1961).

NEST SITES. Marshall and Roberts (1959) found that the equatorial cormorants *(Phalocrocorax carbo* and *P. africanus)* reproduce from late May to December, but only segments of the population reproduce at any one time, so no pair breeds without a pause long enough for another pair to breed at the nest site abandoned by the first pair. Nesting sites seem to determine how large a segment of the population will breed. Experimentally, the removal of suitable nest sites has delayed egg laying in canaries (Hinde and Warren, 1959).

LUNAR EFFECTS. The grunion *(Leuresthes tenuis)* is a fish with a breeding season which extends from March to September, with the greatest frequency of breeding in late spring and summer. The fish spawn in the wet sand and fertilization occurs there. The animals come ashore on one wave and return to the sea with the next wave. Eggs develop for about two weeks in wet sand before they hatch; the high tide assures a sufficient amount of water. The spawning is predictable on the basis of the occurrence of high tides. The New Zealand white bait shows similar behavior. The stimuli that cause the timing of the maturation of the gametes and of the spawning, are not known (Cloudsley-Thompson, 1961; Marler and Hamilton, 1966).

The effects of lunar rhythms on reproduction of terrestial animals seem to be limited to a few species.

The nightjar *(Carprimulgus europaeus)* lays its two eggs during the last quarter of the lunar cycle. When eggs are removed, three weeks must pass before she can lay again (Cloudsley-Thompson, 1961).

The incidence of conceptions among the nocturnal Malayan forest rats *(Rattus mulleri, R. sabanus, R. whiteheadi, R. r. jalorensis, R. rajah)* is highest in the period before the full moon (Harrison, 1952; van den Bijl and Harrison, 1954); the house rat *(R. r. diardii)* shows a less pronounced but similar trend. In the diurnal forest squirrels *(Callosciurus notatus, C. nigrovittatus* and *C. caniceps)* this phenomenon did not occur (Harrison, 1952), and it also was absent in the diurnal tree shrews *(Tupaia glis* and *T. minor)* which eat similar food as the rats (van den Bijl and Harris, 1954).

The relationship between lunar cycles and reproductive activity of invertebrates has been reviewed by Cloudsley-Thompson (1961).

CAPTIVITY. Hediger (1965) has given a fascinating account of the various factors which influence the success or failure of animals to breed in captivity. Some of these involve the behavior of the animals, some the environment, and some both. In summary, the following points seem to be important:

1. Social learning; some animals, brought to the zoo while young, did not "know" how to copulate, and others had to learn how to take care of their young.

2. Aggressiveness, which leads to fighting and prevents copulation from taking place.

3. Synchronization of male and female behavior.

4. Fear of men or of other animals that under natural conditions, may be their enemies.

5. Parasites that cause deterioration of the animal's health.

6. Imprinting on the wrong animal, e.g. man.

7. Space (crowding).

8. Territory which can be explored by the male and female separately before they encounter each other.

9. Special requirements for spawning (nesting material, depth of water) (Aronson, 1965).

10. Temperatures, humidity, light.

11. Endogenous circennian rhythm; e.g. the emu and the Australian black swan

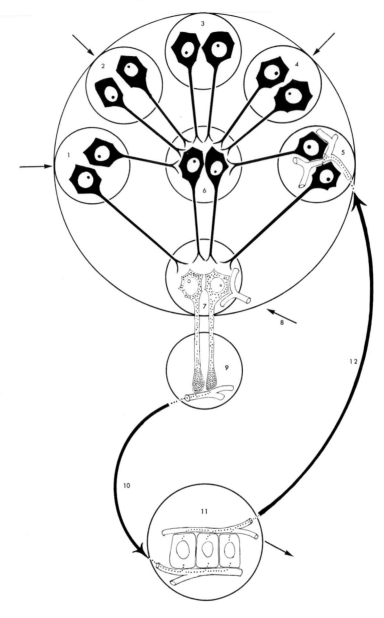

Figure 13-1. Diagram illustrating the principle of neuroendocrine integration. Nervous pathways from organs of special senses *(1)* receiving photic, chemical and acoustic stimuli reach neurosecretory cells either directly or via mesencephalic reticular formation, limbic system, and hypothalamus *(6)* in the vertebrates or via analogous neurocircuits in the invertebrates. In higher animals, cortical centers *(2)*, through their connections with related stations *(6)*, may affect neuroendocrine functions. Another cell group *(3)*, of unidentified location, represents sites in which intrinsic rhythms originate. Afferent spinal pathways *(4)* carrying a large variety of sensory stimuli, e.g., pain and touch, have access to hypothalamic centers via the thalamus. Hormone-sensitive cells *(5)* are located in different parts of the central nervous system. They may be supposed to pass on stimuli thus received by hypothalamic centers *(6)* which may themselves directly respond to circulating hormones *(8)*. The vessels may also carry other blood-borne stimuli, e.g., changes in osmolarity and temperature that directly affect neurosecretory cells. The axons of the latter terminate in a neurohemal organ *(9)* from which neurohormones *(10)* are released. These may stimulate an endocrine organ *(11)* to release its hormones which reach all tissues and organs including the central nervous system *(5)*. In this way a feedback mechanism *(12)* is established which contributes its information to that derived from neural stimuli. The neurosecretory cells *(7)* represent the final common path for the sum total of the different kinds of input. (From Scharrer, 1966.)

(Cygnus attratus) continue to lay eggs in Europe during the winter with difficulties of the eggs freezing, etc.

12. Nutrition.

13. Freedom of movement.

The optimal combination of factors for a certain species often has to be determined by trial and error.

An example of the importance of rather subtle differences in the environment, which determine whether an animal will breed or not, can be found in experiments by Brockway (1962) with budgerigars. When the vertical distance between the roosting perch and the hole in the nest box (above the roosting perch) was less than 10 cm. (four inches) the birds did not visit the nest box nor did the gonads develop.

Experiments involving the escape behavior of wild mallard ducks *(Anas platyrhynchos)* by Phillips (1964) showed that development of the ovary could be enhanced by either destroying connections between archistriatum and hypothalamus (see Chapter 8) or by imprinting the ducklings on the experimenter. These experimental ducks showed a reduced escape behavior, which was correlated with larger ovaries.

Most of the factors listed by Hediger (1965) as of importance for successful breeding in captivity are, of course, of importance in nature also. Several of them have been discussed in Chapter 12, and the effect of crowding has been considered in Chapter 7.

The question of the pathways involved in the transfer of the environmental input to the anterior pituitary has been explored only to a small extent. In a beautiful analysis of the principles of neuroendocrine integration, Scharrer (1966) has discussed the interrelations between the nervous system and the endocrine system. The diagram in Figure 13-1 illustrates the pathways which may be involved once the stimuli reach the hypothalamic-hypophysial system. The diagram and the legend should be consulted.

There is less controversy about the pathways for the olfactory stimuli (Nauta, 1963) than about the pathways by which photic stimuli reach the hypothalamus (which has been discussed in this chapter). As far as we are aware, the pathways involved in the sexual stimulation by auditory stimuli have not been explored experimentally.

For successful reproduction, a rather accurate timing of the gonadal activities and synchronization of these activities in the male and the female are not sufficient by themselves because the appropriate behavior must be obtained in order to bring the gametes into enough proximity. As will be discussed in the next chapter, this requires an interaction between the hormones (gonadal and hypophyseal) and the nervous system.

REFERENCES

Ahsan, S. N. 1966. Effects of temperature and light on the cyclical changes in the spermatogenetic activity of the lake chub Couesius plumbeus (Agassiz). Can. J. Zool. *44*:161-171.

Allanson, M., and Deanesly, R. 1934. Reaction of anoestrus hedge hogs to experimental conditions. Proc. Roy. Soc. (London) *116 B*:170-185.

Amoroso, E. C., and Marshall, F. H. A. 1960. External factors in sexual periodicity. *In* A. S. Parkes (ed.): Marshall's Physiology of Reproduction. Longmans Green & Co. Ltd., London, 1 pt. 2, pp. 707-831.

Aronson, L. R. 1957. Reproductive and parental behavior. *In* M. E. Brown (ed.): The Physiology of Fishes. Academic Press Inc., New York, Vol. 2, pp. 271-304.

Aronson, L. R. 1965. Environmental stimuli altering the physiological condition of the individual among lower vertebrates. *In* F. A. Beach (ed.): Sex and Behavior. John Wiley & Sons Inc., New York, pp. 290-318.

Arrington, L. C., Abplanalp, H., and Wilson, W. O. 1962. Experimental modification of the laying pattern in Japanese quail. Brit. Poultry Sci. *3*:105-113.

Árvay, A. 1967. Effects of exteroceptive stimuli on fertility and their role in the genesis of malformations. Ciba Found. Study Group *26*:20-28.

Ashmole, N. P. 1962. The black noddy *Anous tenuirostris* on Ascension Island. Ibis *103 b*:235-273.

Ashmole, N. P. 1963. The biology of the wideawake or sooty tern *Sterna fuscata* on Ascension Island. Ibis *103 b*:297-364.

Ashmole, N. P. 1965. Adaptive variation in the

breeding regime of a tropical sea bird. Proc. Nat. Acad. Sci. *53*:311-318.

Axelrod, J., Wurtman, R. J., and Snyder, S. H. 1965. Control of hydroxindole-O-methyltransferase activity in the rat pineal gland by environmental lighting. J. Biol. Chem. *240*:949-954.

Baggerman, B. 1959. The role of external factors and hormones in migration of sticklebacks and juvenile salmon. *In* A. Gorbman (ed.): Comparative Endocrinology. John Wiley & Sons Inc., New York, pp. 24-37.

Baker, B. L. 1964. Circadian. Science *145*:296.

Baker, J. R. 1938a. The evolution of breeding seasons. *In* G. R. de Beer (ed.): Evolution: Essays on Aspects of Evolutionary Biology. Clarendon Press, Oxford, pp. 161-177.

Baker, J. R. 1938b. The relation between latitude and breeding season in birds. Proc. Zool. Soc. London *108 A*:557-582.

Barnett, S. A., and Little, M. J. 1965. Maternal performance in mice at −3° C: food consumption and fertility. Proc. Roy. Soc. London. *162 B*: 492-501.

Barnett, S. A., and Manly, B. M. 1954. Breeding of mice at −3° C. Nature *173*:355.

Barnett, S. A., and Manly, B. M. 1956. Reproduction and growth of mice of three strains, after transfer to −3° C. J. Exp. Biol. *33*:325-329.

Bartholomew, G. A. 1949. The effect of light intensity and day length on reproduction in the English sparrow. Bull. Mus. Comp. Zool. Harvard Coll. *101*:433-476.

Bartholomew, G. A. 1959. Photoperiodism in reptiles. *In* R. B. Withrow (ed.): Photoperiodism and Related Phenomena in Plants and Animals. American Association for the Advancement of Science, Washington, D. C., pp. 669-676.

Bartholomew, G. A., Jr. 1953. The modification by temperature of the photoperiodic control of gonadal development in the lizard *Xantusia vigilis*. Copeia:45-50.

Beach, F. A. 1951. Instinctive behavior. Reproductive activities. *In* S. S. Stevens (ed.): Handbook of Experimental Psychology. John Wiley & Sons Inc., New York, pp. 387-434.

Benoit, J. 1964. The role of the eye and of the hypothalamus in the photostimulation of gonads of the duck. Ann. N. Y. Acad. Sci. *(117:1)*:204-215.

Benoit, J., and Assenmacher, I. 1955. Le contrôle hypothalamique de l'activité préhypophysaire gonadotrope. J. de Physiol. *47*:427-567.

Benoit, J., and Assenmacher, I. 1959. The control by visible radiations of gonadotrophic activity of the duck hypophysis. Recent Progr. Hormone Res. *15*:143-164.

Benoit, J., Assenmacher, I., and Brard, E. 1956. Apparition et maintien de cycles sexuels non saisonniers chez le canard domestique placé pendant plus de trois ans à l'obscurité totale. J. de Physiol. *48*:388-391.

Benoit, J., Assenmacher, I., and Brard, E. 1959. Action d'un éclairement permanent prolongé sur l'évolution testiculaire du canard Pékin. Arch. Anat. Microscop. Morphol. Exp. *48*(bis): 5-11.

Biellier, H. V., and Ostmann, O. W. 1960. Effect of varying day-length on time of oviposition in domestic fowl. Univ. Missouri Agr. Sta. Res. Bull. 747.

Bissonnette, T. H. 1931. Studies on the sexual cycle in birds. V Effect of light of different intensities upon the testis activity of the European starling *(Sturnus vulgaris)*. Physiol. Zool. *4*:542-574.

Bissonnette, T. H. 1941. Experimental modification of the breeding cycles in goats. Physiol. Zool. *14*:379-383.

Bissonnette, T. H., and Csech, A. G. 1937. Modification of mammalian sexual cycles. VII Fertile matings of raccoons in December instead of February induced by increasing daily periods of light. Proc. Roy. Soc. (London) *212 B*:246-254.

Bloch, S. 1964. Experiments on the influence of illumination and darkness on the genital function of the mouse. Biol. Abstr. 47, ref. 111542, 1966.

Boone, M. A., and Huston, T. M. 1963. Effects of high temperatures on semen production and fertility in the domestic fowl. Poultry Sci. *42*: 670-676.

Bradshaw, M., and Critchlow, V. 1966. Pituitary concentration of luteinizing hormone (LH) in three types of "constant estrous" rats. Endocrinology. *78*:1007-1014.

Brockway, B. F. 1960. The effects of visual and vocal stimuli upon the reproductive ethology and physiology of paired budgerigars *Melopsittacus undulatus*. Amer. Zool. *1*:346-347.

Brockway, B. F. 1962. The effects of nest-entrance positions and male vocalizations on reproduction in budgerigars. The living bird. First Annual Cornell Lab. Ornithol.:93-101.

Brockway, B. F. 1965. Stimulation of ovarian development and egg laying by male courtship vocalization in budgerigars *(Melopsittacus undulatus)*. Anim. Behav. *13*:575-578.

Bronson, F. H. 1966. A sex attractant function for mouse preputial glands. Amer. Zool. *6*:535 (abstract).

Bronson, F. H., and Eleftheriou, B. E. 1963. Influence of strange males on implantation in the deer mouse. Gen. Comp. Endocrinol. *3*:515-518.

Bronson, F. H., and Marsden, H. M. 1964. Male-induced synchrony of estrus in deer mice. Gen. Comp. Endocrinol. *4*:634-637.

Bronson, F. H., Eleftheriou, B. E., and Garick, E. I. 1964. Effects of intra- and interspecific social stimulation on implantation in deer mice. J. Reprod. Fert:. *8*:23-27.

Brown, F. A., Jr. 1960. Response to pervasive geophysical factors and the biological clock problem. Cold Spring Harbor Symp. Quant. Biol. *25*:57-70.

Brown, F. A., Jr. 1965. A unified theory for biological rhythms. *In* J. Aschoff (ed.): Circadian Clocks. North Holland Publishing Co., Amsterdam, pp. 231-261.

Bruce, H. M. 1962. Continued suppression of pituitary luteotrophic activity and fertility in the mouse. J. Reprod. Fertil. *4*:313-318.

Bruce, H. M. 1965. Effect of castration on the reproductive pheromones of male mice. J. Reprod. Fertil. *10*:141-143.

Bruce, H. M. 1966. Smell as an exteroceptive factor. J. Anim. Sci. *25* (supplement):83-87.

Bruce, H. M. 1967. Effects of olfactory stimuli on reproduction in mammals. Ciba Found. Study Group *26*:29-38.

Bünning, E. 1964. The Physiological Clock. Academic Press Inc., New York.

Bullough, W. S. 1939. A study of the reproductive cycle of the minnow in relation to environment. Proc. Zool. Soc. London *109*:79-102.

Bullough, W. S. 1940. The effect of the reduction of light in spring on the breeding season of the minnow *(Phoxinus laevis)*. Proc. Zool. Soc. London *110*:149-157.

Burger, J. W. 1939. Some experiments on the relation of the external environment to the spermatogenetic cycle of Fundulus heteroclitus (L.). Biol. Bull. *77*:96-103.

Byerly, T. C., and Moore, O. K. 1941. Clutch length in relation to period of illumination in the domestic fowl. Poultry Sci. *20*:387-390.

Carr, W. J., and Caul, W. F. 1962. The effect of castration in the rat upon the discrimination of sex odours. Anim. Behav. *10*:20-27.

Chapin, J. P. 1951. The calendar of the Wideawake Fair. Auk *71*:1-15.

Chipman, R. K., and Fox, K. A. 1966. Factors in pregnancy blocking: age and reproductive background of females: number of strange males. J. Reprod. Fertil. *12*:399-403.

Chipman, R. K., Holt, J. A., and Fox, K. A. 1966. Pregnancy failure in laboratory mice after multiple short-term exposure to strange males. Nature *210*:653.

Clark, R. H. 1964. Circadian. Science *145*:296.

Clausen, H. J., and Poris, E. G. 1937. The effect of light upon sexual activity in the lizard Anolis carolinensis, with special reference to the pineal body. Anat. Rec. *69*:39-53.

Cloudsley-Thompson, J. L. 1961. Rhythmic activity in animal physiology and behaviour. Academic Press Inc., New York.

Critchlow, V. 1963. The role of light in the neuroendocrine system. *In* A. V. Nalbandov (ed.): Advances in Neuroendocrinology. Univ. of Illinois Press, Urbana, pp. 377-402.

Dale, H. E., Ragsdale, A. C., and Cheng, C. S. 1959. Effect of constant environmental temperatures, 50° and 80° F, on appearance of puberty in beef calves. J. Anim. Sci. *18*:1363-1366.

Davis, D. L., and de Groot, J. 1964. Failure to demonstrate olfactory inhibition of pregnancy ("Bruce effect") in the rat. Anat. Rec. *148*:366. (abstract).

Davis, M. 1945. A change of breeding season by Australian gulls. Auk *62*:137.

de Kort, E. J. M., and van Oordt, P. G. W. J. 1965. The effects of high temperature upon the testes and thumb pads in the green frog *Rana esculenta*. Gen. Comp. Endocrinol. *5*:692-693 (abstract).

De Vuyst, A., Thinès, G., Henriet, L., and Soffié, M. 1964. Influence de stimulations auditives sur le comportement sexuel du taureau. Experientia *20*:648-650.

Dominic, C. J. 1965. The origin of the pheromones causing pregnancy block in mice. J. Reprod. Fertil. *10*:469-472.

Dominic, C. J. 1966a. Reserpine: inhibition of olfactory blockage of pregnancy in mice. Science *152*:1764-1765.

Dominic, C. J. 1966b. Observations on the reproductive pheromones of mice. I Source. J. Reprod. Fertil. *11*:407-414.

Dominic, C. J. 1966c. Observations on the reproductive pheromones of mice. II Neuro-endocrine mechanisms involved in the olfactory block to pregnancy. J. Reprod. Fertil. *11*:415-421.

Donovan, B. T. 1966. The regulation of the secretion of follicle-stimulating hormone. *In* G. W. Harris and B. T. Donovan (eds.): The Pituitary Gland. Univ. of California Press, Berkeley, Vol. 2, pp. 49-98.

Donovan, B. T. 1967. The effect of light upon reproductive mechanisms, as illustrated by the ferret. Ciba Found. Study Group *26*:43-52.

Donovan, B. T., and Kopriva, P. C. 1965. Effect of removal or stimulation of the olfactory bulbs on the estrous cycle of the guinea pig. Endocrinol. *77*:213-217.

Donovan, B. T., and van der Werff ten Bosch, J. J. 1956. The cervical sympathetic system and light-induced oestrus in the ferret. J. Physiol. *132*:123-129.

Dorward, D. F. 1962. Comparative biology of the white booby and the brown booby Sula spp. at Ascension. Ibis *103 b*:174-220.

Dutt, R. H. 1964. Detrimental effects of high ambient temperature on fertility and early embryo survival in sheep. Int. J. Biometeor. *8*:47-56.

Egami, N. 1959. Effect of exposure to low temperature on the time of oviposition and the growth of the oocytes in the fish *Oryzias latipes*. J. Fac. Sci. Univ. Tokyo Sec. IV *8*:539-548.

Ehret, C. F., and Trucco, E. 1967. Molecular models for the circadian clock. J. Theoret. Biol. *15*:240-262.

Erickson, C. J., and Lehrman, D. S. 1964. Effect of castration on male ring doves upon ovarian activity of females. J. Comp. Physiol. Psychol. *58*:164-166.

Everett, J. W. 1961. The mammalian female reproductive cycle and its controlling mechanisms. *In* W. C. Young (ed.): Sex and Internal Secretions. Williams & Wilkins Co., Baltimore, Vol. 1, pp. 497-556.

Farner, D. S. 1959. Photoperiodic control of annual gonadal cycles in birds. *In* R. B. Withrow (ed.): Photoperiodism and Related Phenomena in Plants and Animals. American Association for the Advancement of Science, Washington, D. C., pp. 717-750.

Farner, D. S. 1961. Comparative physiology: photoperiodicity. Ann. Rev. Physiol. *23*:71-96.

Farner, D. S. 1965. Circadian systems in the photoperiodic responses of vertebrates. *In* J. Aschoff (ed.): Circadian Clocks. North Holland Publishing Co., Amsterdam, pp. 356-369.

Farner, D. S., and Follett, B. K. 1966. Light and other environmental factors affecting avian reproduction. J. Anim. Sci. *25* (suppl.):90-115.

Farner, D. S., and Wilson, A. C. 1957. A quantitative

examination of testicular growth in the white-crowned sparrow. Biol. Bull. *113*:254-267.

Feldman, S. 1964. Visual projections to the hypothalamus and preoptic area. Ann. N. Y. Acad. Sci. *(117:1)*:53-68.

Fiske, V. M. 1964. Serotonin rhythm in the pineal organ: control by the sympathetic nervous system. Science *146*:253-254.

Franck, H. 1966. Effets de l'ablation des bulbes olfactifs sur la physiologie génitale chez la lapine adulte. C. R. Soc. Biol. *160*:863-865.

Fraps, R. M. 1955. Egg production and fertility in poultry. *In* J. Hammond (ed.): Progress in the Physiology of Farm Animals. Butterworth & Co. Ltd., London, Vol. 2, pp. 661-740.

Fraps, R. M. 1961. Ovulation in the domestic fowl. *In* C. A. Villee (ed.): Control of Ovulation. Pergamon Press Ltd., Oxford, pp. 133-162.

Fraps, R. M. 1965. Twenty-four hour periodicity in the mechanism of pituitary gonadotrophin release for follicular maturation and ovulation in the chicken. Endocrinology 77:5-18.

Fraps, R. M., Neher, B. H., and Rothchild, I. 1947. The imposition of diurnal ovulatory and temperature rhythms by periodic feeding of hens maintained under continuous light. Proc. Soc. Exp. Biol. Med. 50:313-317.

Ganong, W. F., Shepherd, M. D., Wall, J. R., Van Brunt, E. E., and Clegg, M. T. 1963. Penetration of light into the brain of mammals. Endocrinology 72:962-963.

Gaston, S., and Menaker, M. 1966. Photoperiodic response of hamster testes. Amer. Zool. 6:508-509 (abstract).

Glick, B., Griffin, J., and van Tienhoven, A. 1959. The effect of environment on reproductive characters and endocrine organs of New Hampshire chickens. Poultry Sci. *38*:1078-1087.

Hafez, E. S. E. 1964. Environment and reproduction in domesticated species. Inter. Rev. Gen. Exp. Zool. *1*:113-164.

Hafs, H. D. 1966. Introduction to discussion. J. Anim. Sci. 25 (suppl.):44-47.

Halberg, F., and Reinberg, A., 1967. Rythmes circadiens et rythmes de basses fréquences en physiologie humaine. J. de Physiol. *59* (1 bis): 117-200.

Halberg, F., Halberg, E., Barnum, C. P., and Bittner, J. J. 1959. Physiologic 24-hour periodicity in human beings and mice, the lighting regimen and daily routine. *In* R. B. Withrow (ed.): Photoperiodism and Related Phenomena in Plants and Animals. American Association for the Advancement of Science, Washington, D. C., pp. 803-878.

Hale, E. B. 1966. Visual stimuli in reproductive behavior in bulls. J. Anim. Sci. 25 (suppl.):36-44.

Hammond, J., Jr. 1953. Effects of Artificial Lighting on the Reproductive and Pelt Cycles of Mink. W. Heffer & Sons Ltd., Cambridge.

Hamner, W. M. 1963. Diurnal rhythm and photoperiodism in testicular recrudescence of the house finch. Science *142*:1294-1295.

Hamner, W. M. 1964. Circadian control of photoperiodism in the house finch demonstrated by interrupted-night experiments. Nature *203*: 1400-1401.

Hamner, W. M., and Enright, J. T. 1967. Relationships between photoperiodism and circadian rhythms of activity of the house finch. J. Exp. Biol. *46*:43-61.

Harker, J. E. 1964. Diurnal rhythms and homeostatic mechanisms. Symp. Soc. Exp. Biol. *18*: 283-300.

Harrington, R. W., Jr. 1956. An experiment on the effects of contrasting daily photoperiods on gametogenesis and reproduction in the centrarchid fish Ennecanthus obesus (Girard). J. Exp. Zool. *131*:203-223.

Harrington, R. W., Jr. 1957. Sexual photoperiodicity of the cyprinid fish *Notropis bifrenatus* (Cope) in relation to the phases of its annual reproductive cycle. J. Exp. Zool. *135*:529-556.

Harrington, R. W., Jr. 1959a. Photoperiodism in fishes in relation to the annual sexual cycle. *In* R. B. Withrow (ed.): Photoperiodism and Related Phenomena in Plants and Animals. American Association for the Advancement of Science, Washington, D. C., pp. 651-667.

Harrington, R. W., Jr. 1959b. Effect of four combinations of temperature and daylength on the oogenetic cycle of a low-latitude fish *Fundulus confluentus* (Goode and Bean). Zoologica *44*: 149-165.

Harrington, R. W., Jr. 1963. Twenty-four-hour rhythms of internal self-fertilization and oviposition by hermaphrodites of Rivulus marmoratus. Physiol. Zool. *36*:325-341.

Harrington, R. W., Jr. 1967. Environmentally controlled induction of primary male gonochorists from eggs of the self-fertilizing hermaphroditic fish Rivulus marmoratus Poey. Biol. Bull. *132*: 174-199.

Harrison, J. L. 1952. Moonlight and the pregnancy of Malayan forest rats. Nature *170*:73-74.

Hastings, J. W. 1964. The role of light in persistent daily rhythms. *In* A. C. Giese (ed.): Photophysiology. Academic Press Inc., New York, Vol. 1, pp. 333-361.

Hediger, H. 1965. Environmental factors influencing the reproduction of zoo animals. *In* F. A. Beach (ed.): Sex and Behavior. John Wiley & Sons Inc., New York, pp. 319-354.

Henderson, N. E. 1963a. Influence of light and temperature on the reproductive cycle of the Eastern brook trout Salvelinus fontinalis (Mitchill). J. Fisheries Res. Bd. Can. *20*:859-897.

Henderson, N. E. 1963b. Extent of atresia in maturing ovaries of the Eastern brook trout Salvelinus fontinalis (Mitchill). J. Fisheries Res. Bd. Can. *20*:899-908.

Hinde, R. A., and Warren, R. P. 1959. The effect of nest building on later reproductive behaviour in domesticated canaries. Anim. Behav. 7:35-41.

Hoar, W. S. 1965. Comparative physiology: Hormones and reproduction in fishes. Ann. Rev. Physiol. 27:51-70.

Hoar, W. S., and Robertson, G. B. 1959. Temperature resistance of goldfish maintained under controlled photoperiods. Can. J. Zool. *37*:419-428.

Hoffman, R. A., Hester, R. J., and Towns, C. 1965.

Effect of light and temperature on the endocrine system of the golden hamster *(Mesocricetus auratus* Waterhouse). Comp. Biochem. Physiol. *15*:525-533.

Homma, K., McFarland, L. Z., and Wilson, W. O. 1967. Response of the reproductive organs of the Japanese quail to pinealectomy and melatonin injections. Poultry Sci. *46*:314-319.

Hughes, R. L. 1964. Effect of changing cages, introduction of the male and other procedures on the oestrous cycle of the rat. C. S. I. R. O. Wildlife Res. *9*:115-122.

Hulet, C. V. 1966. Behavioral, social, and psychological factors affecting mating time and breeding efficiency in sheep. J. Anim. Sci. *25*(suppl.): 5-16.

Hutchinson, J. C. D. 1954. Heat regulation in birds. *In* J. Hammond (ed.): Progress in the Physiology of Farm Animals. Butterworth & Co. Ltd., London, Vol. 1, pp. 299-362.

Jöchle, W. 1964. Trends in photophysiological concepts. Ann. N. Y. Acad. Sci. *(117:1)*:88-104.

Kayser, C. 1961. The Physiology of Natural Hibernation. Pergamon Press Ltd., Oxford.

Kirkpatrick, C. M. 1955. Factors in photoperiodism of bobwhite quail. Physiol. Zool. *28*:255-264.

Licht, P. 1966. Reproduction in lizards: Influence of temperature on photoperiodism in testicular recrudescence. Science *154*:1668-1670.

Lindsay, D. R. 1965. The importance of olfactory stimuli in the mating behaviour of the ram. Anim. Behav. *13*:75-78.

Lisk, R. D., and Kannwischer, L. R. 1964. Light: Evidence for its direct effect on hypothalamic neurons. Science *146*:272-273.

Lissák, K. 1962. Olfactory-induced sexual behaviour in female cats. Proc. 22nd Int. Congr. Physiol. Sci., Leiden *1(pt. 2)*:653-656.

Lott, D. F., and Brody, P. N. 1966. Support of ovulation in the ring dove by auditory and visual stimuli. J. Comp. Physiol. Psychol. *62*:311-313.

MacFarlane, W. V., Pennycuik, R. R., Yeates, N. T. M., and Thrift, E. 1959. Reproduction in hot environment. *In* C. W. Lloyd (ed.): Recent Progress in Endocrinology of Reproduction. Academic Press Inc., New York, pp. 81-95.

McNally, E. H. 1947. Some factors that affect oviposition in domestic fowl. Poultry Sci. *26*:396-399.

Marler, P., and Hamilton, W. J., III. 1966. Mechanisms of Animal Behavior. John Wiley & Sons Inc., New York.

Marsden, H. M., and Bronson, F. H. 1964. Estrous synchrony in mice. Alteration by exposure to male urine. Science *144*:1469.

Marsden, H. M., and Bronson, F. H. 1965a. The synchrony of oestrus in mice: relative roles of the male and female environments. J. Endocrinol. *32*:313-319.

Marsden, H. M., and Bronson, F. H. 1965b. Strange male block to pregnancy: Its absence in inbred mouse strains. Nature *207*:878.

Marshall, A. J. 1960. Annual periodicity in the migration and reproduction of birds. Cold Spring Harbor Symp. Quant. Biol. *25*:499-505.

Marshall, A. J. 1961. Breeding seasons and migration. *In* A. J. Marshall (ed.): Biology and Comparative Physiology of Birds. Academic Press Inc., New York, Vol. 2, pp. 307-339.

Marshall, A. J., and Hook, R. 1960. The breeding biology of equatorial vertebrates: reproduction of the lizard *Agama agama liononotus* Boulenger at latitude 0° 01′ N. Proc. Zool. Soc. London *134*:197-205.

Marshall, A. J., and Roberts, J. D. 1959. The breeding biology of equatorial vertebrates: reproduction of cormorants (Phalacrocoracidae) at latitude 0° 20′ N. Proc. Zool. Soc. London *132*:617-625.

Marshall, W. A. 1962. The effect of altering the size of the palpebral fissure on the induction of oestrus by light in normal ferrets after removal of both superior cervical sympathetic ganglia. J. Physiol. *165*:27-28P.

Massopust, L. C., Jr., and H. J. Daigle. 1961. Hypothalamic and antero ventral mesencephalic photic responses in the cat. Exp. Neurol. *3*:476-486.

Matthews, L. H. 1939. Visual stimulation and ovulation in pigeons. Proc. Roy. Soc. London *126 B*: 557-560.

Matthews, S. A. 1939. The effects of light and temperature on the male sexual cycle in Fundulus. Biol. Bull. *77*:92-95.

Mayhew, W. W. 1964. Photoperiodic responses in three species of the lizard genus *Uma*. Herpetologica *20*:95-113.

Mayhew, W. W. 1966. Reproduction in the arenicolous lizard *Uma notata*. Ecology *47*:9-18.

Menaker, M., and Eskin, A. 1966. Entrainment of circadian rhythms by sound in Passer domesticus. Science *154*:1579-1580.

Merriman, D., and Schedl, H. P. 1941. The effects of light and temperature on gametogenesis in the four-spined stickleback Apeltes quadracus (Mitchill). J. Exp. Zool. *88*:413-449.

Muul, I. 1966. Photoperiodic influence on seasonal breeding cycles of *Glaucomys volans*. Amer. Zoologist *6*:583 (abstract).

Nalbandov, A. V. 1964. Reproductive Physiology. Ed. 2. W. H. Freemen and Co., San Francisco.

Nauta, W. J. H. 1963. Central nervous organization and the endocrine motor system. *In* A. V. Nalbandov (ed.): Advances in Neuroendocrinology. Univ. of Illinois Press, Urbana, pp. 5-27.

Noble, G. K. 1931. The Biology of Amphibia. McGraw-Hill Book Company, New York.

Noble, G. K. 1937. The sense organs involved in the courtship of *Storeria, Thamnophis* and other snakes. Bull. Amer. Mus. Nat. Hist. *73*:673-725.

Opel, H. 1966. The timing of oviposition and ovulation in the quail *Coturnix coturnix japonica*. Brit. Poultry Sci. *7*:29-38.

Ortavant, R., Mauleon, P., and Thibault, C. 1964. Photoperiodic control of gonadal and hypophyseal activity in domestic mammals. Ann. N. Y. Acad. Sci. *(117:1)*:157-193.

Palmer, J. D. 1964. Circadian. Science *145*:296.

Payne, C. G., Lincoln, D. W., and Charles, D. R. 1965. The influence of constant and fluctuating environmental temperatures on time of oviposition under continuous lighting. Brit. Poultry Sci. *6*:93-95.

Pearson, O. P., and Enders, R. K. 1944. Duration of

pregnancy in certain mustelids. J. Exp. Zool. 95:21-35.

Pennycuik, P. R. 1964. The effects in rats of chronic exposure to 34° C. Austr. J. Med. Biol. Sci. 17: 245-260.

Phillips, R. E. 1964. "Wildness" in the mallard duck: Effects of brain lesions and stimulation on "escape behavior" and reproduction. J. Comp. Neurol. 122:139-155.

Pinter, A. J. 1964. Effects of nutrition and photoperiod on reproductive physiology, growth, and maturation in Microtus montanus. Diss. Abstr. 25:710.

Pittendrigh, C. S., and Bruce, V. C. 1959. Daily rhythms as coupled oscillator systems and their relation to thermoperiodism and photoperiodism. In R. B. Withrow (ed.): Photoperiodism and Related Phenomena in Plants and Animals. American Association for the Advancement of Science, Washington, D. C., pp. 475-505.

Pittendrigh, C. S., and Minis, D. H. 1964. The entrainment of circadian oscillations by light and their role as photo periodic clocks. Amer. Natural. 98:261-294.

Quay, W. B. 1963. Circadian rhythm in rat pineal serotonin and its modifications by estrous cycle and photoperiod. Gen. Comp. Endocrinol. 3: 473-479.

Rawson, K. S. 1959. Experimental modification of mammalian endogenous activity rhythms. In R. B. Withrow (ed.): Photoperiodism and Related Phenomena in Plants and Animals. American Association for the Advancement of Science, Washington, D. C., pp. 791-800.

Riley, G. M. 1937. Experimental studies on spermatogenesis in the house sparrow, Passer domesticus (Linnaeus). Anat. Rec. 67:327-351.

Rollo, M., and Domm, L. V. 1943. Light requirement of the weaver finch. I Light period and intensity. Auk 60:357-367.

Ryle, M. 1961. Early reproductive failures in hot environment. I Ovulation rate and embryonic mortality. J. Agr. Sci. 57:1-9.

Ryle, M., and Morris, L. R. 1961. Some quantitative studies on tissues of lambs dwarfed by high temperature during gestation. Austr. J. Exp. Biol. Med. Sci. 39:79-92.

Scharrer, E. 1966. Principles of neuroendocrine integration. Res. Publ. Ass. Res. Nerv. Ment. Dis. 43:1-33.

Scott, P. P., and Lloyd-Jacob, L. 1959. Reduction in the anoestrus period of laboratory cats by increased illumination. Nature 184:2022.

Serventy, D. L., and Marshall, A. J. 1957. Breeding periodicity in Western Australian birds. Emu 57:99-126.

Shelton, M. 1960. Influence of the presence of a male goat on the initiation of estrous cycling and ovulation of Angora does. J. Anim. Sci. 19:368-375.

Signoret, J. P. 1965. Action de l'ablation des bulbes olfactifs sur les mécanismes de la reproduction. Proc. Second Int. Congr. Reprod. 1:198-202.

Signoret, J. P., and DU Mesnil DU Buisson, F. 1961. Étude du comportement de la truie en oestrus. Fourth Int. Congr. Anim. Reprod. 2:171-175.

Signoret, J. P., and Mauléon, P. 1962. Action de l'ablation des bulbes olfactifs sur les mécanismes de la reproduction chez la truie. Ann. Biol. Anim. Biochem. Biophys. 2:167-174.

Signoret, J. P., DU Mesnil DU Buisson, F., and Busnel, R. G. 1960. Rôle d'un signal acoustique de verrat dans le comportement réactionnel de la truie en oestrus. C. R. Acad. Sci. 250:1355-1357.

Simpson, E. C. 1966. Semen production and fertility of rams following exposure to controlled ambient temperatures. Diss. Abstr. 26:4143-4144.

Skinner, J. D., and Louw, G. N. 1966. Heat stress and spermatogenesis in Bos indicus and Bos taurus cattle. J. Appl. Physiol. 21:1784-1790.

Smith, N. G. 1963. Evolution of Some Arctic Gulls (Larus): A Study of Isolating Mechanisms. Ph.D. Thesis, Cornell University.

Snyder, S. H., Zweig, M., Axelrod, J., and Fischer, J. E. 1965. Control of the circadian rhythm in serotonin content of the rat pineal gland. Proc. Nat. Acad. Sci. 53:301-305.

Sollberger, A. 1965. Biological Rhythm Research. Elsevier Publishing Co., Amsterdam.

Stonehouse, B. 1962. The tropic birds (Genus Phaethon) of Ascension Island. Ibis 103 b:124-161.

Strauss, W. F., and Meyer, R. K. 1962. Neural timing of ovulation in immature rats treated with gonadotrophin. Science 137:860-861.

Tavolga, W. N. 1955. Ovarian fluids as stimuli to courtship behavior in the gobiid fish Bathygobius soporator (C and V). Anat. Rec. 122: 425 (abstract).

Tavolga, W. N. 1956. Visual, chemical and sound stimuli as cues in the sex discriminatory behavior of the gobiid fish, Bathygobius soporator. Zoologica 41 pt. (2:7):49-64.

Thibault, C., Courot, M., Martinet, L., Mauléon, P., DU Mesnil DU Buisson, F., Ortavant, R., Pelletier, J., and Signoret, J. P. 1966. Regulation of breeding season and estrous cycles by light and external stimuli in some mammals. J. Anim. Sci. 25 (suppl.):119-139.

Thorpe, D. H. 1967. Basic parameters in the reaction of ferrets to light. Ciba Found. Study Group 26:53-66.

Tinkle, D. W., and Irwin, L. N. 1965. Lizard reproduction: Refractory period and response to warmth in Uta stansburiana females. Science 148:1613-1614.

Tribukait, B. 1956. Die Aktivitätsperiodik der weissen Maus im Kunsttag von 16-29 Stunden Länge. Z. Vergl. Physiol. 38:479-490.

Ulberg, L. C. 1966. Introduction to discussion. J. Anim. Sci. 26(suppl.):16-18.

Van Brunt, E. E., Shepherd, M. D., Wall, J. R., Ganong, W. F., and Clegg, M. T. 1964. Penetration of light into the brain of mammals. Ann. N. Y. Acad. Sci. (117:1):217-224.

van den Bijl, W., and Harrison, J. L. 1954. Moonlight and the pregnancy of Malayan forest rats. Nature 173:1002.

van Oordt, P. G. W. J. 1960. The influence of internal and external factors in the regulation of the spermatogenetic cycle in amphibia. Symp. Zool. Soc. London 2:29-52.

van Oordt, P. G. W. J., and Lofts, B. 1963. The

effects of high temperature on gonadotrophin secretion in the male common frog *(Rana temporaria)* during autumn. J. Endocrinol. *27:* 137-146.

van Tienhoven, A. 1961. Endocrinology of reproduction in birds. *In* W. C. Young (ed.): Sex and Internal Secretions. Williams & Wilkins Co., Baltimore, Vol. 2, pp. 1088-1169.

Warren, D. C., and Scott, H. M. 1936. Influence of light on ovulation in the fowl. J. Exp. Zool. *74:*137-156.

Wells, L. J. 1959. Experiments on light and temperature in a wild mammal with an annual breeding season. *In* R. B. Withrow (ed.): Photoperiodism and Related Phenomena in Plants and Animals. American Association for the Advancement of Science, Washington, D. C., pp. 801-802.

Whitten, W. K. 1956a. Modification of the oestrous cycle of the mouse by external stimuli associated with the male. J. Endocrinol. *13:*399-404.

Whitten, W. K. 1956b. The effect of removal of the olfactory bulb on the gonads of mice. J. Endocrinol. *14:*160-163.

Whitten, W. K. 1959. Occurrence of anoestrus in mice caged in groups. J. Endocrinol. *18:*102-107.

Whitten, W. K. 1966. Pheromones and mammalian reproduction. Adv. Reprod. Physiol. *1:*155-177.

Wierzbowski, S., and Hafez, E. S. E. 1961. Analysis of copulatory reflexes in the stallion. Fourth Int. Congr. Anim. Reprod. *2:*176-179.

Wilson, O. E., and Bossert, W. H. 1963. Chemical communication among animals. Recent Progr. Hormone Res. *19:*673-716.

Wilson, W. O. 1964. Photocontrol of oviposition in gallinaceous birds. Ann. N. Y. Acad. Sci. *(117:1):*194-202.

Wilson, W. O., and Woodard, A. E. 1958. Egg production of chickens kept in darkness. Poultry Sci. *37:*1054-1057.

Wilson, W. O., Woodard, A. E., and Abplanalp, H.

1956. The effect and after-effect of varied exposure to light on chicken development. Biol. Bull. *111:*415-422.

Wilson, W. O., Woodard, A. E., and Abplanalp, H. 1964. Exogenous regulation of oviposition in chicken. Poultry Sci. *43:*1187-1192.

Wolfson, A. 1965. Circadian rhythm and the photoperiodic regulation of the annual reproductive cycle in birds. *In* J. Aschoff (ed.): Circadian Clocks. North Holland Publishing Co., Amsterdam, pp. 370-378.

Wolfson, A. 1966. Environmental and neuroendocrine regulation of annual gonadal cycles and migratory behavior in birds. Recent Progr. Hormone Res. *22:*177-239.

Woody, C. O., and Ulberg, L. C. 1964. Viability of one-cell sheep ova as affected by high environmental temperature. J. Reprod. Fertil. *7:*275-280.

Wurtman, R. J. 1967. Ambiguities in the use of the term circadian. Science *156:*104.

Wurtman, R. J., Axelrod, J., Chu, E. W., and Fischer, J. E. 1964. Mediation of some effects of illumination on the rat estrous cycle by the sympathetic nervous system. Endocrinol. *75:*266-272.

Wurtman, R. J., Roth, W., Altschule, M. D., and Wurtman, J. J. 1961. Interactions of the pineal and exposure to continuous light on organ weights of female rats. Acta Endocrinol. *36:*617-624.

Yeates, N. T. M. 1954. Daylight changes. *In* J. Hammond (ed.): Progress in the Physiology of Farm Animals. Butterworth and Co., Ltd., London, Vol. 1, pp. 363-392.

Yoshioka, H. 1962. On the effects of environmental factors upon the reproduction of fishes. I The effects of day-length on the reproduction of the Japanese killifish *Oryzias latipes*. Bull. Fac. Fish. Hokkaido Univ. *13:*123-136.

Zondek, B., and Tamari, I. 1967. Effects of auditory stimuli on reproduction. Ciba Found. Study Group *26:*4-16.

Chapter 14

Hormonally Induced Reproductive Behavior

The discussion of reproductive behavior will include some aspects of behavior which are required to bring males and females together in the breeding territory, e.g. migration, sexual behavior per se (to be defined), and parental behavior. Some of the concepts and experimental evidence discussed in previous chapters will be mentioned and the reader should refer to these chapters for specific references.

Little or no information seems to be available concerning the role of specific parts of the nervous system in the initiation of migration. We will, therefore, consider the effect of external stimuli and of the activity of the endocrine system on migration.

MIGRATORY BEHAVIOR

In a laboratory experiment in which aquaria were divided into two compartments, one with salt and one with fresh water, but in such a manner that the animals could swim from one compartment to the other, Baggerman (1957) demonstrated that for the three-spined stickleback *(Gasterosteus aculeatus)*:

1. Adult specimens captured during the early months of the year preferred fresh water, and at the end of the breeding season preferred salt water.

2. Young fish, hatched in April and May preferred salt water, but in the early months of the next year preferred fresh water.

These two patterns agreed with those found in nature, demonstrating the suitability of the laboratory method for testing the preference of the animals.

In the captured animals there existed a strong correlation between the size of the testes and the preference for fresh water. It was demonstrated experimentally that gonadectomy did not result in an immediate change in preference from fresh to salt water; eventually this change occurred, but later than in control males, thus showing that the observed correlation was not one of cause and effect.

Thyroxine administration caused a preference for fresh water in fish that initially preferred salt water; the change occurred in about five days. Hypothyroidism, induced by thiourea, caused a preference for salt water in fish that initially preferred fresh water. Gonadectomy had no effect on this response.

These experiments suggest that seasonal changes in water temperature may act via the thyroid to induce preference for fresh water, causing the animals to go to the rivers and ditches where they breed. The correlation between gonadal activity and the preference for fresh water that exists in these fish is not a cause and effect relationship, but rather one in which the two activities are correlated because other factors affect both testes and thyroids.

Experiments by Baggerman (1959)

with Pacific salmon *(Oncorhynchus keta, O. gorbuscha, O. kisutch,* and *O. nerka),* given thyroxine or thiourea, yielded inconsistent results. Exposure to short photoperiods (8L-16D) postponed the change in preference of *O. kisutch,* and long photoperiods (16L-8D) caused an earlier preference change from fresh to salt water. The hormones involved in this change have not been determined.

Extensive studies have been made concerning the migration of birds which breed in the Northern temperate and arctic zones. As Farner and Follett (1966) pointed out, "migration may be regarded as an adaptation to permit the use of a seasonally favorable region for reproduction. Therefore, in principle, the mechanisms that control migration are similar to and coordinated with those that control reproductive cycles." One of the phenomena that accompanies migration is the deposition of fat, correlated with hyperphagia, of birds prior to migration (King and Farner, 1965). In the white-crowned sparrow *(Z. leucophrys gambelii)* such fat despositions may account for 20 percent of the total body weight; the increase in body weight is completed in about eight days in the spring. In the late summer the total increase in body weight and fat deposition is less than in the spring. The difference between spring and late summer fattening is probably correlated with the more favorable weather and with the fact that the southward migration requires less energy expenditure than the northward migration (King and Farner, 1965).

In feral populations and also in laboratory experiments, there seemed to be a correlation between the vernal (spring) fattening, increased testicular size, and migration in some species (white-crowned sparrows, white-throated sparrows [*Z. albicollis*], golden-crowned sparrows [*Z. atricapilla*], slate-colored juncos [*Junco hyemalis*], and others). Systematic investigations have shown that all three of these con-

ditions (migratory activity, fattening, and testicular size increase) can be induced by long photoperiods, but they are not dependent upon each other. The following experiments illustrate this:

1. After castration, migratory restlessness *(Zugunruhe)* occurs after exposure to long photoperiod in the brambling *(Fringilla montifringilla)* (Lofts and Marshall, 1960). The authors pointed out that some birds were incompletely castrated and that these birds might have induced migratory restlessness in the castrated ones. Morton and Mewaldt (1962), using the golden-crowned sparrow, found that *Zugunruhe* occurred in castrated as well as in intact birds, although it occurred about one week later in the castrates than in controls. King and Farner (1963) confirmed these observations for the white-crowned sparrow.

2. Castration does not prevent fat deposition in response to long photoperiods; however, in the golden-crowned sparrow (Morton and Mewaldt, 1962) and in the white-crowned sparrow (King and Farner, 1963) the amounts of fat deposited are larger in controls than in castrates.

3. Restriction of food intake prevents fat deposition but does not affect the onset of *Zugunruhe* under long photoperiods in white-crowned sparrows (King and Farner, 1963), white-throated sparrows, slate-colored juncos, and bramblings (Lofts et al., 1963).

The increased food intake of white-crowned sparrows kept under long photoperiods is not the result of the longer time the animals have available for eating. Exposing the animals to nine hours of light per day plus one minute of light every 20 minutes yielded results similar to long photoperiods, whereas controls receiving nine hours and 27 minutes of light in a continuous dose showed no fat deposition (King, 1961).

The fat deposition shows a refractoriness similar to that discussed for the testicular response to light in Chapter 13. The metabolic refractory period lasts longer than the gonadotropic one (King and Farner, 1965).

The occurrence of the late summer fat deposition cannot be explained on the basis of photoperiod, but this fattening, as well as the spring fat deposition, may be the result of endogenous* cycles that are timed by photoperiodic changes (King, 1967).

Wolfson (1966), by alternating periods of long days to induce a response and periods of short days to shorten the refractory period, was able to obtain five periods of gonadal activity, five of fat deposition, and two molts in 369 days.

The endocrine control of molting is a complex subject, and falls outside the scope of this book. I mention briefly that the thyroid, prolactin, and gonadotropic hormones have been implicated at various times in different species.

Prolactin injection into either photosensitive or photorefractory white-crowned sparrows causes increased food intake and fat deposition; gonadotropins (FSH and LH) act synergistically with prolactin, but by themselves are not effective (Meier and Farner, 1964). In subsequent experiments, Meier and Davis (1967) found that the same is true for the white-throated sparrow and that a diurnal rhythm exists with respect to the effectiveness of prolactin. Injections of 21 I.U. five and ten hours after the beginning of a 16 hour photoperiod were effective, and at zero and five hours suppressed body weight and deposition of fat.

The same hormone was also shown to be effective in inducing migratory restlessness in white-crowned sparrows. Adrenocortical hormones, which by themselves had no effect, acted synergistically with prolactin in inducing nocturnal migratory restlessness (Meier et al., 1965).

The antigonadotropic effect which prolactin possesses in nonmigratory birds

seems to be absent in migratory species (Meier et al., 1966). As a matter of fact, data by Meier and Farner (1964) show that prolactin acts synergistically with gonadotropins in increasing testicular and ovarian size of photorefractory white-crowned sparrows; neither prolactin nor gonadotropins alone produced any appreciable effect. The prolactin content of the pituitaries of white-crowned sparrows was higher during premigratory periods than at others (Meier et al., 1965).

From the available evidence it appears that there may be circennian rhythms of prolactin secretion and release in white-crowned sparrows and that photoperiod may act as a synchronizer. Prolactin may cause fat deposition either by having a direct effect on feeding centers of the hypothalamus, causing hyperphagia and subsequently fat deposition, or by affecting metabolic pathways, causing fat deposition with hyperphagia as a compensating mechanism. The effect of prolactin on migratory behavior suggests at least that there may be a direct effect of this hormone on the central nervous system. Which of the above alternatives will prove to be the correct one can only be determined by experimentation.

It is consistent with other observations made on the white-crowned sparrow to propose that photoperiod causes an increase in prolactin and gonadotropin secretion that results in testicular size increase and fat deposition, and also in an increase in adrenocortical hormones (the adrenal cortex appears histologically active in photosensitive birds [Lorenzen and Farner, 1964]).

After migration and use of some of the fat deposits, the birds become refractory: the fat deposits decrease further and testes and ovaries regress. Prolactin probably plays a role in the formation of the incubation patch, which in the white-crowned sparrow is present in the female only. In the late summer, after the molt, the "spontaneous" (or endogenous ?) release of prolactin again can cause fattening

---

* King prefers to call the rhythm spontaneous because the data were available for one year only.

(to a lesser extent, probably as the result of a lack of gonadotropins) and migratory behavior. The difficulties of accounting for the late summer migratory behavior and fat deposition have not been solved, but the experiments carried out so far very strongly suggest that prolactin plays a role at this time also. It has not been shown whether prolactin plays an identical or similar role in species other than the white-crowned and golden-crowned sparrow.

Fattening may be the result of different hormonal factors in different species, as can be ascertained from a comparison between chickens and pigeons. Hypophysectomized pigeons lose weight and the amount of body fat decreases, presumably because they eat less than intact birds. Prolactin injection causes an increase in food intake and an increase in liver, pancreas, intestinal, kidney, and crop sac weights (Bates et al., 1962); no data on fat deposition were reported. Thyroxine, prednisone, and growth hormone acted synergistically with prolactin, with the combination of all four hormones giving the highest stimulation of fat deposition and organ weight increase.

Hypophysectomized chickens, in spite of a decrease in food intake of about 50 percent, become so obese that 50 percent of the dry matter consists of lipids (Gibson and Nalbandov, 1966a,b). This obesity is reminiscent of the genetic obesity observed in chickens in which the thyroid is either absent or functions at a lower than normal level (van Tienhoven and Cole, 1962). It thus appears that the reduction of thyroid activity in the chicken is the major reason for fat deposition, and other hormones play minor roles. In the pigeon, however, the adrenals seem to be of primary importance in fat deposition, as prednisone is the most effective single hormone in causing fat deposition (Bates et al., 1962). This fat deposition is dependent upon increased food intake, whereas the response in hypophysectomized roosters occurs in spite of a low food intake. It remains to be determined whether prolactin

or any of the other hormones that promote food intake in the hypophysectomized pigeon have a similar effect on the hypophysectomized chicken and to what extent these hormones increase the deposition of fat above that of hypophysectomized controls. Not enough data are available to make a valid comparison between chickens and pigeons with respect to the hormonal causes for the apparent differences.

It is of interest to note that prolactin injections enhance food intake of the American chameleon (*Anolis carolinensis*), but that contrary to the effect observed in white-crowned sparrows, gonadotropins reduce the effect of prolactin. The principal effect of the prolactin injections is an increase in growth, rather than an increase in fat deposition. The storage of lipids by this lizard in the late summer and early fall seems to occur while prolactin levels probably are low (Licht, 1967).

AGGRESSIVE BEHAVIOR

Under the term aggressive behavior will be included territorial behavior and dominance relationships. These types of behavior are interwoven with sexual behavior, and the separation into aggressive and sexual behavior is somewhat arbitrary in certain situations.

Excellent reviews on the relationship among the endocrine system, the nervous system, and behavior have been published (Benoit, 1956; Guhl, 1961; Marler and Hamilton, 1966). It is obviously arbitrary to divide the effects of hormones and the effects of changes in the central nervous system into separate groups, but for the purpose of discussion such a grouping is rather useful.

Effect of Hormones

The methods used to test the effect of either ablation of endocrine glands or the administration of hormones can determine, to some extent, the results that will be obtained. For the purpose of illustration, some experiments carried out with chickens will be used to emphasize this point (Guhl, 1961).

Androgen administration to certain hens in a flock did not cause a rise in social rank, probably because the social habits withstood the effects that androgen may have had on aggressive behavior of the individual hens. When hens were tested in pairs to establish the aggressiveness for the individual of each pair, androgen administration caused a rise in rank (Guhl, 1961).

The importance of the territory in which the test is made has been demonstrated by experiments of Buchholz, as cited by Guhl (1961). The lowest ranking male of a group of seven roosters was placed in an unoccupied pen for one week. A hen was introduced and was easily dominated. After her removal two days later a former penmate, which had been ranked sixth, was introduced and the "resident" male dominated him. Successively introduced males from the former group of seven were introduced in the reverse of the former peck order and were dominated by the male which originally ranked lowest.

The stability of a social hierarchy also plays an important role in the extent of the response one may obtain. For many of the animals investigated, the stability of these hierarchies has not been investigated, as far as I am aware, and contradictory results between experiments may be the result of such stability differences.

The relationships between hormones and aggressive behavior have been reviewed by Aronson (1957, 1958, 1965), Johnson et al. (1962), Guhl (1961), and Marler and Hamilton (1966). My own review has relied on these reviews to a large extent.

Vivien (1941) found that 30 percent of male rock gobies (*Gobius paganellus*) still spawned after hypophysectomy and retained their aggressive behavior. The fact that this occurred only in a minority of the cases suggests the possibility of incomplete hypophysectomy. Vivien (1941) made histological investigations of remnants of pituitaries in hypophysectomized females that laid eggs two weeks after hypophysectomy. It is not specifically stated that serial sections were made in the males which spawned after the operation. It seems reasonable to assume that this was done, however. In any event, the experiments suggest a relationship between testicular activity and aggressive behavior. Survival of rock gobies after gonadectomy was poor and no conclusions concerning behavior can be made.

Ablation of the pituitary of the frill-finned goby *(Bathygobius soporator)* resulted in a loss of aggressiveness and in regression of the gonads (Tavolga, 1955). Gonadectomy had the same effect on aggressive behavior (Tavolga, 1955) as hypophysectomy and it seems therefore most probable that the effect of pituitary ablation was mediated by a decreased gonadal hormone secretion.

Baggerman (1966) established that aggressive behavior of three-spined stickleback males was correlated with the gonadal cycle. After gonadectomy, shortly before the onset of the breeding season, there was no decrease in agonistic behavior; as a matter of fact, it increased. However, gonadectomy during the breeding season caused a sharp decrease in agonistic behavior. Baggerman (1966) proposed that in the period prior to breeding the increasing level of gonadotropins regulates aggressive behavior and that the mechanism underlying this behavior becomes less sensitive to gonadotropins and more sensitive to gonadal hormones. Experiments by Hoar (1962a) yielded results consistent with Baggerman's hypothesis. Methyltestosterone administered to castrated three-spined sticklebacks kept under 8L–16D did not increase their aggressive behavior as much as it did in fish kept under 16L–8D, suggesting that pituitary hormone secretion, stimulated by the long photoperiod, may have interacted with the methyltestosterone effects.

Hoar (1962b) has also presented evidence indicating that LH injections increased the level of aggressive behavior of three-spined sticklebacks (TSH and prolactin had no effect and FSH gave inconsistent results). These experiments indicate that LH and/or androgens play an important role in regulating the aggressive behavior of the three-spined stickleback.

Luteinizing hormone injections into the Cichlid fish *Symphysodon aequifasciata axelrodi* caused a marked increase in fighting tendency (snaps and pushes), whereas FSH was not effective (Blüm and Fiedler, 1965). This effect may be a direct one, but the LH also may have stimulated androgen secretion, an interpretation which is supported by the fact that LH caused protrusion of the genital papilla.

Androgen administration caused an advancement in rank of treated female and spayed female swordtails *(Xiphophorus helleri)* (see Guhl, 1961).

In the American chameleon *(Anolis carolinensis)*, castration does not eliminate fighting, but androgen administration causes an increased amount of fighting. Females rarely fight unless they have been ovariectomized (Guhl, 1961).

Treatment of the lizard *(Sceloporus grammicus)* with androgen caused an advancement in rank of subordinate males.

In a preliminary note, Evans (1956) has stated that testosterone and LH caused previously subordinate newts *(Triturus viridescens)* to become dominant; the LH, of course, may have had its effect via the stimulation of androgen secretion.

Davis (1957, 1963, 1964) and Vandenbergh (1964) have stated that the aggressiveness of starlings *(Sturnus vulgaris)* is under the control of gonadotropic hormones, specifically LH, rather than under the control of gonadal hormones. Critical evaluation of the evidence does not seem to support this contention. In the first series of experiments castrated birds kept singing, and testosterone injections did not affect aggressiveness. Out of 11 birds, those ranked 1, 3, and 8 had testicular remnants. The dose of testosterone injected is not

given in the paper and therefore it is difficult to interpret the results, especially because two high ranking birds had testicular remnants (Davis, 1957).

In a second series of experiments, five castrated starlings were allowed to establish their hierarchy for two weeks and then received a 20 mg. testosterone pellet. The starlings that ranked fourth and fifth prior to implantation reversed rank during a two-week postimplantation period (Davis, 1963).

The effect of luteinizing hormone (LH) was evaluated by injecting 200 μg. LH into starlings ranked third and fifth among a group of five birds (Davis, 1963). This treatment increased the rank of number 5 to number 4 but did not affect the place of number 3 in the hierarchy. The starlings were subsequently castrated and allowed to establish a new hierarchy. The castration changed the ranks as follows: number 1 did not change in the social hierarchy, number 2 became number 4, number 3 became number 5, number 4 became number 3, and number 5 became number 2. The birds that ranked second and fifth after castration received 200 μg. LH. The rank of number 2 was not affected and number 5 tied for fourth place with the starling that, prior to the injection period, had been number 3 in the rank order. These experiments do not show any significant effect of LH on either rank or on the number of fights engaged in or on the number of fights won.

Other experiments, in which castrated birds were paired with intact ones and in which the domination for each pair was established, showed that in five out of six pairs the castrates dominated. This is not significantly different from the 3:3 ratio expected on the basis of chance.

Subordinate intact birds given large doses of LH (250 and 3000 μg.) gained the dominant position in one out of two cases tested; testosterone had no effect on dominance reversal in one out of one case (Davis, 1963).

Other experiments of a similar nature

either lack sufficient data to warrant a statistically validated conclusion or doses of
hormones injected are entirely outside the
physiological range. The same is true for
the experiments by Mathewson (1961).

Vandenbergh (1964) compared the
dominance of starlings kept under 15
hours of light with others kept under eight
hours of light per day. The number of encounters won (58 out of 85) by birds under
eight hours of light was significantly higher
than would be expected by chance. The investigator interpreted these data in support of the concept that "gonadotropins or
other pituitary hormones may influence
aggressive behavior."

Long day length increased testicular
volume, and thus, obviously, caused an increased gonadotropin secretion; nevertheless, these birds *lost* most of the encounters.
It seems to me that this evidence hardly
supports the contention that gonadotropins increase aggressive behavior (if win-
ning an encounter is accepted as a measure
of aggressiveness).

These data by Davis (1957, 1963),
Mathewson (1961), and Vandenbergh
(1964) provide indirect negative evidence
that gonadal hormones of the male do not
dominate the control of aggressive behavior but they do not provide positive evidence that gonadotropins regulate this
type of behavior. It is, of course, possible
that hormones do not affect aggressive behavior of starlings.

Davis (1957, 1963) noted that castration did not affect the singing by the starlings. We may recall that in canaries, singing is induced by androgen (see Chapter 5).

The evidence that androgens may not
be required for aggressive behavior in starlings is in agreement with data obtained
with castrated pigeons which continued to
fight after castration (Guhl, 1961). Androgen increased aggressiveness in male and
female ring doves *(Streptopelia risoria)*, immature male herring gulls *(Larus argentatus)*, unilaterally ovariectomized chickens,
young chicks, castrated mallard drakes
(Anas plathyrynchos), and valley quail *(Lo-*

phortyx californica vallicola), whereas castration diminished fighting in capons, turkey
toms *(Meleagris gallopavo)*, and mallards
(Beach, 1948; Guhl, 1961; Etienne and
Fischer, 1964).

In a detailed study of the behavior of
ring doves, Vowles and Harwood (1966)
found that aggressive behavior towards
other doves is high for males just prior to
laying of the eggs and during incubation,
whereas for females it is high during incubation and decreases during brooding.
Seven daily injections of estrogen cause a
minor increase in aggressive behavior of
males, while progesterone is more effective
in this respect. The combination of estrogen plus progesterone has the effect that
would be expected on the basis of additive
effects of the two hormones. Prolactin has
about the same effect as estrogen. In hens,
defense behavior towards other ring doves
is increased by progesterone, by estrogen
plus progesterone, and by prolactin.

The latency between intramuscular injection and response was in the range of
one-half to two hours for estrogen and
prolactin, but for progesterone it was 12 to
18 hours, suggesting an indirect effect on
the central nervous system.

Testosterone had no effect in either
the male or female when given in seven
daily injections, but single injections increased defensive behavior towards females but did not increase aggressive behavior towards other doves.

The differences between males and females could be the result of differences in
the animals' own hormonal levels. The experiments, having been carried out in intact animals, do not allow for an evaluation
of this possibility.

Aggressiveness is inherited and, by selection, lines of high and low aggressiveness have been obtained in chickens. The
heritability estimates were 0.22 when based
on the percentage of contests won, and
0.18 when based on the percentage of individuals dominated (Guhl et al., 1960).
Experimental evidence indicates that androgen increases aggressiveness in chick-

ens; for instance, after the injection of testosterone propionate into six-week-old cockerels their aggressiveness increased (Wood-Gush, 1957). As we shall see later, androgens also induce sexual behavior, and it was, therefore, of interest to determine to what extent aggressiveness and sexual behavior were correlated. Wood-Gush (1957) and Guhl et al. (1945) found that the levels of aggressiveness and of sexual behavior of cockerels are not correlated, and Wood-Gush (1957) observed that after testosterone injections these characteristics remain uncorrelated. McDaniel and Craig (1959), on the other hand, found a correlation between aggressiveness and completed matings in roosters. Aggressiveness is also correlated with age at sexual maturity, with sperm concentration, and with the number of crouches received from females. Selection for sexual effectiveness may thus lead to more aggressive roosters in the lines of White Leghorns used by McDaniel and Craig (1959). The reason for the differences between the experiments by Guhl et al. (1945) and Wood-Gush (1957), and those of McDaniel and Craig (1959) is not easy to determine since different breeds were used, and testing situations may have been sufficiently different to introduce variables affecting one type of behavior more than another.

The agonistic behavior of rats and mice, the stimuli that elicit aggression, the effects of lactation, the genetic differences among strains and between sexes, and the effects of early experience, fighting, and defeat have been reviewed recently by Scott (1966).

Castration reduces the aggressiveness of rats and mice (Beach, 1948; Johnson et al., 1962). Injection of androgens restores fighting in mice, but not in females, suggesting differences in the responsiveness of the nervous system of males and females (Scott, 1966). In two species of rodents, the short-tailed shrew (Blarina brevicauda) and the hamster, the females are aggressive towards the males of their own species except during estrus. Ovariectomy reduces

this agonistic behavior, which is restored by estrogen replacement therapy. Estrogen and progesterone are required to reduce the aggressive tendencies towards the level found in female short-tailed shrews in estrus (Beach, 1948; Johnson et al., 1962). The female marten (Martes americana) fights with the males during estrus (Beach, 1948), indicating that estrogen or estrogen and progesterone may induce this behavior.

The variety of the aggressive responses in different species indicates that no single rule can be made with respect to the effect of hormones on aggressive behavior.

The evolution of the animals made it more advantageous in one species to "capture" one hormone, whereas, for another species, another hormone or combination of hormones was of greater advantage. The aggressive behavior may not have come under the controlling influence of hormones because the lack of such hormonal control offers certain advantages.

Effect of Brain Lesions and of Electrical Stimulation

The effect of brain lesions on aggressive behavior has been explored in only relatively few species.

Hale (1956), in an extensive series of experiments, investigated the effect of lesions of the fish brain of the green sunfish (Lepomis cyanellus) under a number of different conditions. On the basis of these experiments, he concluded that the forebrain functions mainly to provide facilitation of aggressive behavior patterns organized at lower brain levels. Visual and tactile stimuli seemed to be the main stimuli eliciting aggressive behavior. After the aggressive behavior was elicited it was normal in all respects. Hale (1956) has pointed out that it is difficult to compare his results with those obtained by Noble and Borne (1941) with swordtails (Xiphophorus helleri), the Siamese fighting fish (Betta splendens), and the jewel fish *(Hemichromis bimaculatus)* since no details were provided in their preliminary notes. Brain lesions in these fish did not seem to affect aggressive behavior markedly.

Segaar and Nieuwenhuys (1963), using the three-spined stickleback, found that either frontal or bilateral lesions in the telencephalon lowered aggressive tendencies, but that after bimediocaudal lesions aggressiveness was increased. Bimediocentral and bimediocaudal lesions did not affect aggressive behavior.

Electric stimulation (0.05 to 1.0 mA; 50 Hz, 3 msec.) of the preoptic area, the area ventralis, or the border area of septum and paleostriatum of pigeons causes aggressive behavior either in empty space, towards another pigeon, or towards threatening objects. The attack behavior is only carried out when the other pigeon comes close. Defense and escape responses are obtained from an area extending from the hypothalamus and the diencephalic paraventricular gray via the area ventralis anterior and the posterior parts of the cerebral peduncles up into the paleostriatum and archistriatum (Åkerman, 1966b).

Stimulation (0.05 to 0.35 mA; 50 Hz, 2 msec.) of the medial archistriatum, including the nucleus taenia, the telencephalic part of the tractus occipito-mesencephalicus, the area septalis, or near the nucleus paraventricularis magnocellularis of the chicken elicits attacks on other chickens (including attacks on roosters by hens) and threat displays. These displays are often, but not always, accompanied by attacks (Putkonen, 1967). These observations concerning the area of the brain apparently most involved in aggressive behavior agree rather well with experiments by Barfield (1965b), in which testosterone propionate implants in the area extending from paleostriatum to the lateral diencephalon caused aggressive behavior in capons.

Delgado, in a review (1966), discussed the possible interpretations of the results obtained by electrical stimulation of different brain areas of Rhesus monkeys *(Macacus mulatta)* with respect to aggressive behavior. Aggressive behavior could be elicited against other members of the colony. For some of the electrode sites it is not possible to exclude the possibility that pain pathways were stimulated, which in turn caused aggression. Stimuli in the midline thalamus caused attacks and threatening, and, apparently, no pain stimuli were involved. However, it is not possible, on the basis of present knowledge, to state what the anatomical and neurophysiological relationships involved in aggressive behavior are.

Lesion studies suggest that the hypothalamus is an important site for the excitation and integration of autonomic and hormonal effects involved in aggressive behavior. Inhibition of this behavior involves the septum (Heimer and Larsson, 1967b), whereas the amygdala appears to have an excitatory function. Lesions of the amygdala have given different results in different laboratories. Green et al. (1957) noted that cats with amygdalar lesions, which caused seizures, were also more aggressive towards the investigator and other animals. Wood (1958) found that after bilateral lesions, in either the basal nucleus or the central nucleus of the amygdala, five out of ten and four out of ten cats, respectively, became more aggressive towards other cats. The operated animals would go across the room to attack the other cats. Schreiner and Kling (1953), on the other hand, found that amygdalar lesions caused greater docility of cats towards other species (dog, monkeys, agoutis). They also found an increased threshold for eliciting anger in these animals. After amygdalectomy, lynx *(Lynx rufus)*, agoutis *(Dasyprocta agouti),* and monkeys *(Macacus mulatta)* showed a noticeable decrease in aggressiveness towards the investigator and toward other species. Lynx and agoutis, which normally are ferocious, could actually be petted after the operation (Schreiner and Kling, 1956). The aggressiveness towards individuals of their own species apparently was not tested.

Kling (1962) found that amygdalectomy of cats younger than 13 weeks old did not affect their behavior. The hypopituitarism and lack of appetite observed in adults after this operation were absent in kittens after the same operation. Summers and Kaebler (1962) tested the aggressiveness towards man and the behavior after presentation of mice to amygdalectomized cats and found that nine out of 13 cats were indifferent towards the mice and were nonaggressive towards man. The differences among the results of different investigators may be due to slight differences in the location and extent of the lesions and differences in the testing situation. Green et al. (1957) noted that one cat would behave savagely in its own cage but would not do so outside its own territory. Thus the territory where the test occurred was apparently of major importance in eliciting aggressive behavior.

SEXUAL BEHAVIOR

For the purpose of the present discussion, sexual behavior will be defined as the behavior of males and females that promotes bringing the male and female gametes into the closest possible proximity. In general, mating and the release of gametes are the climax of a sometimes very intricate pattern of male and female behavior, which is rather specific for each species. Behavioral differences can act as isolating mechanisms in sympathetic species and thus prevent hybridization.

Phoenix et al. (1967)* have pointed out that "the pattern of sexual behavior is a somewhat idealized concept of the sexual behavior characteristic of a species." These same authors have also emphasized the

---

* A recent review by Bastock (1967) became available too late to be considered in this discussion.

variability in the occurrence of the sequence of behavior and that not all the behavioral sequences have the same probability of occurring.

Uniformity of terminology used for the description of behavior for the rat and guinea pig has been achieved (Phoenix et al., 1967), but there is still a certain amount of ambiguity. Estrus, e.g., means to some workers that the rat, mouse, cat, or other animal, which shows variability in the vaginal smear correlated with gonadal events, shows the typical smear expected at estrus (prior to ovulation), i.e., the smear contains nucleated and cornified epithelium (Chapters 6 and 9). For other animals, e.g. cow, sheep, and horse, the term estrus is frequently used to mean that the animal will stand still and accept the male when he tries to copulate. In cattle, the cow in estrus may attempt to mount other cows and, in turn, other cows may try to mount the estrous cow.

As Beach (1967) has pointed out, the term estrual or estrous behavior implicitly assumes that the particular behavior is dependent upon the presence of estrogen. Beach (1967) and Phoenix et al. (1967) have stressed the importance of defining behavior in descriptive terms. An attempt will be made here to do so, but, in some of the papers to which we will refer, the behavior is not described in these terms; nevertheless, the implications of the work are important and should be mentioned.

Aronson (1957), from a survey of the modes of reproduction of many species of fish, concluded that there are considerable similarities in courtship behavior even among widely separated groups. The existence of a positive feedback is suggested by the fact that courtship behavior may induce color changes which, in turn, may increase courtship activity.

Effects of Hormones

Gonadal maturation is associated with changes in color in many species of fish. As was mentioned, such colorations may be important in inducing courtship behavior in other members of the species. Such behavior then may affect the particular animal under consideration and induce courtship and other sexual behavior in it. We shall consider here the effects of hypophysectomy, gonadectomy, and hormone administration on the hypophysectomized animal only.

In the gobiid fish *(Bathygobius soporator)* hypophysectomy causes the loss of sexual behavior and the regression of the gonads. The effects of the operation on behavior, therefore, may have been the result of pituitary and/or gonadal, interenal, or thyroidal hormones. Castration of the males does not affect courtship behavior towards gravid females. The intact male courted nongravid females for a shorter time than gravid ones, but the castrated males courted gravid and nongravid females for about the same length of time (Tavolga, 1955). These experiments indicate that there may be an effect of pituitary hormones per se, or that gonadal hormones interact with pituitary hormones, or that adrenal and thyroid hormones play a role in this behavior.

In a detailed study, Baggerman (1966) showed that castration of male three-spined sticklebacks, whether it occurred before or during the breeding season, reduced the frequency of zigzagging (one of the components of sexual behavior) and also reduced the frequency of leading if castration occurred after the onset of the breeding season (the frequency is too low before the breeding season to show a substantial decrease). Nest building activity, especially boring, is decreased by castration after the onset of the breeding season (Baggerman, 1966; Hoar, 1962a,b).

The effectiveness of androgen (methyltestosterone) replacement therapy in restoring nest building behavior depends on the photoperiod. Under long photoperiods (16L–8D) the incidence of responses is higher and the interval between hormone treatment and response is shorter than under short photoperiods (8L–16D) (Hoar, 1962b).

Castration of male jewel fish *(Hemichromis bimaculatus)* and of Siamese fighting fish *(Betta splendens)* did not affect their courtship behavior. Castrated male *Tilapia macrocephala*, separated from females by a transparent partition, were as active in nest building as intact males (Aronson, 1957).

Gonadectomy of the blue acara *(Aquidens latifrons)* affected mainly nest building activity, but had little effect on mating patterns except for causing an increase in the rubbing of the genital papilla over the nest (Aronson, 1958). In the viviparous platyfish *(Xiphophorus maculatus)* castration reduced the frequency of copulations, thrusts, and swings (undirected forward and lateral movement of the gonopodium), but other parts of the behavior were not affected (Aronson, 1958).

Spaying of jewel fish and Siamese fighting fish resulted in a lack of sexual behavior and, in *Tilapia macrocephala*, a lack of nest building (Aronson, 1957). However, in the guppy *(Poecilia reticulata)*, gonadectomy did not affect female sexual behavior (Liley, 1965). In the hermaphrodite fish *Serranus subligarius*, two courting fishes, in which one has assumed the "male" role and the other the "female" role, may within a minute reverse their behavior completely (Clark, 1959). In this species one might expect that hormones play a minor role, if any, in controlling or modifying the sexual behavior, and it appears that sensory stimuli or the relative abundance of sperm or ova in an individual determine its behavior.

These data suggest that in the male the gonads (androgens ?) are generally not required for sexual behavior, but that the ovaries (estrogens ?) in some species are required for the genetic female. There is, however, the puzzling observation that after incomplete ovariectomy of the Siamese fighting fish the regenerating gonad is testicular and causes male behavior (Aronson, 1957).

The administration of androgens to

adult, intact, or spayed swordtails induces elements of male behavior, but in castrated male adult salmon, testosterone causes following of the females, but no other element of spawning behavior.

The evidence that androgens cause male sexual behavior in immature fish seems to be limited to swordtails and guppies *(Poecilia reticulata)*. In *Platypoecilus variatus* only the preliminary courtship pattern occurs after treatment of adult females with methyltestosterone, as is the case with adult females (Aronson, 1957). The evidence that estrogens cause female sexual behavior seems inadequate.

In intact, castrated, or hypophysectomized killifish *(Fundulus heteroclitus)*, in male and female Japanese rice fish, in the Japanese bitterling *(Rhodeus* sp.*)*, and in *Gambusia* sp., injection of oxytocin or vasopressin causes "S" shaped spawning movements (Wilhelmi et al., 1955). The spawning reflex may be the result of stimulation of the oviduct and body musculature (Aronson, 1965) and, therefore, the behavioral response to the posterior pituitary hormones may be a secondary one.

The hypothesis has been posed that in the evolution of the teleosts some elements of reproductive behavior have been released from the functional control of the gonadal hormones (Aronson, 1957).

According to the review by Aronson (1958), in the following species the clasp reflex is abolished by castration: the leopard frog *(Rana pipiens)*, the toad *(Bufo arenarum)*, the American chameleon, and the lizard *(Eumeces fasciatus)*. Treatment of immature animals with gonadal hormones causes the clasp reflex to occur in the American chameleon and the toad *(Bufo fowleri)*. In *Bufo vulgaris* and *Bufo arenarum* testosterone and gonadotropins are required to induce the clasp reflex in either castrated or intact males. In *Xenopus laevis* pregnancy urine causes the appearance of the mating clasp (Beach, 1967).

Beach (1967) has discussed the evidence concerning the neural control of this reflex. In males of *Rana fusca, R. escu-*

lenta, R. temporaria, R. pipiens, and *Xenopus laevis*, transection of the brain in the anterior medulla causes the clasping reflex to occur outside the breeding season (this reflex does not occur in most females or in immature males, but female *Xenopus laevis* will exhibit this behavior after transection of the brain at the indicated level).

The behavior obtained after brain transection may not be normal in the sense that the males of *R. pipiens* and *Xenopus laevis* are unable to reorient themselves to the correct position if they are clasping in the wrong position, and that they are unable to terminate the clasping spell once it has started (Beach, 1967).

Transection at other levels or destruction of other brain areas either leads to uncoordinated behavior or fails to induce the clasp reflex.

Stimulation of the midbrain of an intact *R. temporaria* or *B. vulgaris* during clasping results in release of the clasp, suggesting the presence of an inhibitory center in the midbrain.

All the evidence indicates the presence of such a center in the species mentioned above, and the hypothesis has been presented that gonadal hormones and/or gonadotropic hormones act on this center to depress this inhibitory effect (Beach, 1967).

Courtship behavior, which involves a series of advances with the male, body spasms, and fanning oriented towards the male, was induced in European newts *(Triturus cristatus, T. vulgaris, and T. helveticus)* by prolactin. This behavior seemed to be independent of the gonads, which continued to regress (Grant, 1966).

Considerable research has been carried out on the sexual behavior of birds, although much of this work has been concentrated on chickens and turkeys. Excellent reviews of the sequence of events in the mating behavior of these two species can be found in the papers by Guhl (1962), and Hale and Schein (1962).

Castration or bilateral ovariectomy results in diminished sexual behavior of chickens. The male behavior can be restored in capons. In bilaterally ovariectomized hens waltzing behavior can be induced but copulation attempts are not made. In ovariectomized hens estrogen replacement therapy caused crouching for a normal rooster; the same treatment in capons caused waltzing and copulation but did not induce crowing. Estrogen treatment of males may increase the frequency of sexual behavior, including attempts to copulate. Generally, androgens are more effective in inducing male behavior than estrogens, and male chicks respond more easily to androgens than do females (Guhl, 1962).

As was discussed earlier, sinistral ovariectomy of chickens results in the development of the right (rudimentary) gonad into an ovotestis or testis. Such sinistrally ovariectomized hens will take on a male appearance and will show male sexual behavior, but will not tread females (Domm, 1939).

It appears from these investigations that it is difficult to induce female behavior by estrogen in males, but that male-like behavior can be induced in genetic males and females by either androgen or estrogen.

The correlation between mating frequency and semen quality (volume, sperm concentration, and sperm morphology) was nonsignificant in experiments conducted by Wood-Gush and Osborne (1956), and McDaniel and Craig (1959). There was a significant negative correlation between comb size and mating frequency (Wood-Gush and Osborne, 1956). Comb size as such was not cause for lesser mating frequency because dubbing (removal of the comb) did not affect mating frequency.

It is possible, by mass selection, to increase or decrease the mating ability in a population of chickens. Siegel (1965) selected for high and low mating ability (measured as the cumulative number of matings within a ten minute observation period) and found that the phenotypic expression of this trait changed little in the first few generations, but then changed in the direction for which selection was made.

The heritability was 0.18 ± 0.05 in the line selected for increased mating ability and 0.31 ± 0.11 for the line selected for decreased mating ability. The phenotypic correlations between the selected trait and courting, mounting, and treading were 0.60, 0.94, and 0.96, respectively. The phenotypic correlation between the selected trait and aggressiveness, sperm concentration, and semen volume was small; however, the genetic correlation between mating ability and sperm concentration was -0.67 and between mating ability and semen volume was -0.38. Thus, by selection for mating ability one might select against sperm production.

Crawford and Smyth (1965) investigated the effect of comb type, Rose (RR or Rr) or single (rr), on mating behavior of a strain of chickens selected for meat production. Females of RR genotype were courted more often than either Rr or rr females; this courting, in turn, appeared to be the result of greater aggressiveness of these females. Single comb males were not different from the other males with respect to sexual displays but copulated more frequently. Heterozygote males copulated more often than RR males, but the difference was small.

After mating to RR males, fertility was lower and duration of fertility was shorter than after mating to other males (Crawford and Smyth, 1964a,b). This result may be partly explained by the behavioral deficiency.

In turkeys, precocious sexual behavior (strutting, gobbling, copulatory attempts) can be induced in poults by injections of androgens. The head of the female turkey provides the primary stimulus eliciting complete mating patterns, while the body is not required for obtaining the sexual response. In chickens, both head and body are required for inducing the complete response (Hale and Schein, 1962).

The turkey hen, after complete eversion of the oviduct has been achieved during mating (which may or may not include copulation), becomes refractory for an average of about five days. The incidence of matings has a high heritability and probably is not affected extensively by environmental factors. The observations that the incidence of matings during the prebreeding season is slightly correlated with that during the breeding season is of practical importance, because it allows a certain amount of selection to be exercized prior to making up the breeding pens. Unfortunately, there is also a correlation, but this one negative, between mating frequency and egg production. Turkeys differ from chickens in that the mating frequency of chickens can be modified by changing the frequency at which females are dominated; in turkeys this procedure has no effect on mating frequency (Hale and Schein, 1962). Schein and Hart (1962) obtained male sexual behavior in female turkeys by electrical stimulation of the brain, but the locus of the electrode was not given.

In mallard ducks, gonadectomy reduced sexual behavior in males and females (Collias, 1962; Etienne and Fischer, 1964; Phillips and McKinney, 1962). Replacement therapy induced aggressive behavior, sexual displays, and sexual behavior in that sequence. Two of three ovariectomized females responded to testosterone by showing intense female sexual behavior and male warning cries; the other female showed masculine sexual behavior after testosterone treatment (Etienne and Fischer, 1964). In young ducks (up to 23 days old) (*Anas acuta, Anas platyrhynchos,* and *Aythyas americana*), testosterone induced male courtship displays in both sexes (Phillips and McKinney, 1962).

In the ducks investigated there seems to be good evidence that testosterone induces male sexual behavior and increases aggressiveness and that androgens are required to maintain these types of behavior.

After castration all sexual activity disappeared from male Japanese quail (*Coturnix coturnix japonica*) and returned to normal after testosterone propionate treatment (Beach and Inman, 1965).

Other examples of male sexual behavior induced by testosterone have been found in the black-crowned night heron (*Nycticorax n. hoactli*) male and females (Noble and Wurm, 1940).

Höhn and Cheng (1967) compared the testosterone content of the testes and ovaries of chickens, mallard ducks, and red-winged blackbirds (*Agelaius phoeniceus*) (species in which the male initiates sexual behavior, has the bright plumage, and is more aggressive than the female), with that of pigeons (the male and female are about equal with respect to the behavioral characteristics mentioned), and with Wilson's phalarope (*Steganopus tricolor*), in which the female is bright and the male dull colored and in which the female is more aggressive and initiates pair formation. The testosterone content of the testis and ovary of the killdeer (*Charadrius vociferus*), in which the relative dominance position of the male and female is not well established, was also determined.

The testis of the mallard, chicken, and red-winged blackbird contains more testosterone than the ovary, whereas in the phalarope, pigeon, and killdeer, the ovary contains more testosterone than the testis. These data need to be interpreted cautiously because the hormone content of an endocrine organ may not be related to hormonal content in the blood. Nevertheless, there seems to be a good correlation, with the few species investigated, between ovarian and testicular testosterone content and the behavior of females and males.

Castration of pigeons did not abolish copulatory behavior in all animals (the completeness of castration was verified histologically) (Carpenter, 1933). This type of variability was also noted by Beach (1952) after unilateral and bilateral decerebration of male pigeons on which preoperative copulation behavior was determined. None out of four unilaterally decerebrated males showed copulatory behavior, but after testosterone propionate treatment, this behavior was restored in two males; other aspects of male behavior, such as billing, cooing, and strutting, were eliminated by the operation in all males, but were restored in all by testosterone. Bilateral decerebration had no effect on copulatory behavior in eight out of 12, but eliminated it in four out of 12 animals. Testosterone reestablished copulation in one of these four males. Beach (1952) interpreted this as the maintenance of a high level of responsiveness of male sex performance by forebrain centers.

Nest building activity behavior can be induced by testosterone administration to black-crowned night herons (Noble and Wurm, 1940).

Female ring doves will engage in nest building after estrogen injections (Lehrman, 1958). The effect of androgen on this behavior, apparently has not been investigated.

In many species of wild birds, nest building is associated with gonadal development (Eisner, 1960). One might suppose that this behavior is induced by gonadal or hypophyseal hormones, but which hormones are involved and to what extent exogenous hormones can induce this behavior apparently has been determined in only a few species. Orcutt (1965) induced cutting of paper strips (nesting material) by ten-week-old peach-faced lovebirds (*Agapornis roseicollis*) by estrogen treatment; this behavior does not normally occur until the birds are about four months old, when they become sexually mature.

Visiting of the so-called trap nest by chickens in floor pens occurs regularly prior to laying of the egg. The presence of the oviduct is not required for this behavior (Wood-Gush, 1963). Removal or ligation of the most recently ruptured follicle (surgery which causes delay of the laying of the egg present in the oviduct) caused 15 out of 34 hens to lay without nest visits, one out of 34 to lay at the normal time without going to the nest, three

out of 34 to lay prematurely without nest visits, two out of 34 to nest more than once within 24 hours, one out of 34 to nest for a prolonged period, and in two out of 34 nesting and oviposition were divorced. In sham operated hens, or in birds in which other follicles were removed, only two out of 62 nested twice within 24 hours, two out of 62 failed to nest with oviposition delayed, and in one out of 62 nesting and oviposition were divorced (Wood-Gush and Gilbert, 1964). In subsequent experiments, Gilbert and Wood-Gush (1965) injected cocaine into the walls and stalk of the latest postovulatory follicle and observed ten out of 24 birds with abnormal nesting behavior versus two out of 24 for the controls. On this basis they proposed that a neural component from the ovary plays a role in the nesting behavior, but the possibility that endocrine mechanisms also play a role was not excluded.

The effects of gonadal hormones on sexual behavior and the probable mechanisms of actions in mammals have been extensively reviewed (Beach, 1948, 1967; Benoit, 1956; Clegg and Doyle, 1966; Guhl, 1961; Lehrman, 1961; Lisk, 1966; Phoenix et al., 1967; Marler and Hamilton, 1966; Mason et al., 1966; Sawyer et al., 1966; Soulairac, 1963; Young, 1961, 1964 [see also the books edited by Beach, 1965; Etkin, 1964, and Hafez, 1962]).

It should be recalled that gonadal hormones affect the organization of the behavioral substrate during embryonic or early postnatal development. Much of this evidence has been reviewed in Chapter 5 (see also Barraclough, 1967; Goy, 1966, for extensive critical reviews), but some new evidence has become available which requires mention here:

1. Genetic males and females, gonadectomized neonatally and implanted as adults with estrogen and progesterone, do not behave the same way. Genetic females and males both gave the lordosis response, but males also showed male sexual behavior (Lisk and Suydam, 1967). Thus

genotypic males seem to possess the potential for male and female sexual response patterns, and androgen acting at birth prevents the development of the female response pattern. It should be noted that intact control females or females ovariectomized after four days of age and implanted with estrogen and progesterone sometimes attempt to mount other females and show pelvic thrusts, but that this does not occur if ovariectomy occurs before day 4 of age (Lisk and Suydam, 1967).

2. The effect of testosterone propionate administration to neonatal rats on the incidence of lordosis to mount ratio is dependent upon:

a. The dose of testosterone propionate; with a greater lordosis mount ratio obtained after 5 to 10 μg. testosterone propionate and a much smaller ratio when 500 to 1000 μg. testosterone propionate is administered.

b. The age of the rat; there is a slow decrease in the lordosis to mount ratio between day 1 and day 4. The testosterone propionate-treated female showed maintenance of lordosis for longer than normal periods and was very passive and inactive (Levine and Mullins, 1966).

3. Male rats castrated neonatally mounted females after administration of testosterone, but after this experience the administration of estrogen plus progesterone to these castrated males caused them to exhibit lordosis. Administration of estrogen plus progesterone to another group of neonatally castrated male rats caused the lordosis response to occur after mounting by a male; rats, having shown this lordosis response, would mount females after testosterone administration. Neonatally castrated rats, which had been treated with either testosterone or estrogen plus progesterone but had not been allowed sexual experience, showed the appropriate response when they were injected with estrogen plus progesterone and testosterone, respectively.

The behavioral response to the hormone remained appropriate to the hormone administered whether the rats had had sexual experience or whether they had received other gonadal hormone treatment (Whalen and Edwards, 1966). This shows that in the adult, neonatally castrated, rats the gonadal hormones did not change the qualitative responsiveness to testosterone and estrogen plus progesterone, whereas in the neonatal rat testosterone and estrogen have profound effects in determining the future behavioral responsiveness of the animal.

4. Goy et al. (1967) found that androgen treatment of pregnant guinea pigs so that the female young were pseudohermaphrodites did not affect the lordosis response on day of birth (control males also showed the response). The lordosis response at this time probably is involved in elimination of urine and feces (Beach, 1967).

The sensitivity of male and female guinea pigs to androgens and estrogens increases steadily between birth and 90 days of age; pseudohermaphrodites respond to estrogens at a later age than control females and the incidence of lordosis responses is infrequent and abbreviated (Goy et al., 1967).

5. Genetic female pseudohermaphroditic Rhesus monkeys (obtained as the result of androgen treatment of the pregnant mother) exhibited mounting of females, whereas control females did not. The number of mounts by the pseudohermaphrodites was lower than the number found in either males castrated at three months of age or in intact males. The pseudohermaphrodites showed an aspect of female behavior ("presents") that was about the same as that seen in males castrated at three months of age; however, this number was considerably lower than the number seen in normal females and higher than that seen in normal males. The pseudohermaphrodites were

also intermediate in social threat, play inanition, and rough-and-tumble play frequencies between males and females (Goy, 1966).

For the mammalian species investigated, there is thus considerable evidence that androgen affects the differentiation of the behavioral substrate, but the work by Lisk and Suydam (1967) indicates that the substrates of neonatally gonadectomized genetic males and females are not identical.

The behavior of the male rat and guinea pig during mating has been described by Young (1961). Upon introduction of a female rat into the cage of a male, the male may examine her anogenital region and he may nibble at the head or body. The copulatory behavior can be classified in different categories according to Young (1961):

1. *Clasp without palpation,* which is characterized by the male mounting the female from the rear and clasping her about the laterolumbar region.

2. *Palpation with pelvic thrusts,* which consists of clasping of the female by the male, palpation of the female's sides by rapid movements of the front legs, and rapid pistonlike thrusts of the male's pelvis. If he fails to achieve intromission, the male slips off the female rather weakly. This behavior indicates incomplete copulation.

3. *Complete copulation,* which consists of palpation with pelvic thrusts, but, instead of slipping off the female's back, the male gives a final forceful thrust and in many instances throws himself back several inches. This behavior is indicative of intromission.

4. *Ejaculation,* which consists of behavior similar to that observed under complete copulation; however instead of the backward lunge the male remains pressed against the female, and subsequently releases his clasp, slowly raises his forelegs, emits the ejaculate, and withdraws his penis.

After ejaculation there is a refractory period during which the male is not affected by sexual stimuli. This period has been found to be between 324 and 818 seconds.

The male guinea pig's behavior consists of sniffing, nibbling, nuzzling, abortive mounting, mounting, intromission, and ejaculation.

Castration causes a gradual decrease in mating behavior in rats, guinea pigs, rabbits, hamsters, cats, dogs, sheep, pigs, and horses, but some elements, including copulation, may be retained (Banks, 1962; Davidson, 1966; Young, 1961). In the rat all components may be retained for a relatively long time (in one animal an ejaculatory pattern was noted 147 days after operation). Of the sexual behavior patterns, mounting was retained longer than intromission; ejaculation was usually present when intromission occurred. In the castrated guinea pig, ejaculation disappeared first, followed by intromission and mounting (Young, 1961).

The effect of age at castration on development of sexual behavior after administration of androgens has been investigated for cats, rats, guinea pigs and Rhesus monkeys. These investigations have shown that some of the male sexual behavior patterns can develop in these species after prepubertal castration (Beach, 1948, 1958; Phoenix et al., 1967; Rosenblatt, 1965). However, sexual experience, social factors (e.g. rearing in isolation) have qualitative and quantitative effects on the sexual behavior of the animals (for review see Rosenblatt, 1965). Some of the effects of age at castration on sexual behavior after androgen treatment have been indicated in Table 5-5.

The tendency of the rat and hamster to mate after castration varies with the level of these activities at the time of castration. For the guinea pig the percentage change after castration was the same for high, low and medium scoring males (Young, 1961).

Androgen administration can restore male mating behavior, usually to precastration levels and no higher, in guinea pigs, but in rats the mating levels can be raised above precastration levels by exogenous testosterone. In intact rats and rabbits testosterone propionate can increase the mating frequency (Young, 1961).

Pregnant guinea pigs will show some clitoral hypertrophy after androgen administration but will not show male-like mounting, whereas nonpregnant guinea pigs will mount other females and have hypertrophied clitorides. Progesterone injections inhibited the male-like androgen-induced mounting, but had no effect on androgen-induced clitoral hypertrophy (Diamond, 1967; Diamond and Young, 1963).

The administration of progesterone to male guinea pigs caused a decrease in the sex behavior score to a level intermediate between that of controls and castrated guinea pigs (Diamond, 1967). The histologic study showed that the testes of these males were normal; this does not mean, however, that androgen concentrations in the blood may not have been affected. The fact that progesterone inhibits the male-like mounting in female guinea pigs injected with androgen indicates that progesterone probably has its effect on the nervous system. The effect of progesterone on the electrical activity, on thresholds for EEG arousal, and on the EEG after reaction have been discussed in Chapter 8.

Occasionally, male rabbits, hamsters and rats will show feminine behavior. Castration eliminated this behavior in one such rat and testosterone propionate treatment restored it. Large doses of estrogen (about 86 times higher than required for females) may induce female behavior (lordosis) in intact and castrated male guinea pigs and rats (Young, 1961).

Among mice there exist definite strain differences in mating ability (number of ejaculations, number of days between ejaculations) e.g. C75BL/65 males showed only two ejaculations, whereas DBA/2J mice showed 15 in the same observation period. After castration the ejaculatory reflex was more rapidly lost in the more homozygous mice than in the more heterozygous ones. In the latter the reflex was still seen as long as 60 days after the operation (McGill and Tucker, 1964).

In an experienced ram, castration caused a decrease in sexual behavior in an orderly sequence of disappearance of the components of sexual behavior, e.g. copulation, nudging, and nosing frequency. Androgen administration restored the frequency of nosing, nudging, and mounting above the frequency observed before castration. Intromission was seen but ejaculation was not recorded.

One ram, castrated at 139 days of age, completed a copulatory response when 396 days old, although intromission was not achieved, probably as a result of the small size of the penis. Another ram, castrated at 118 days of age, never displayed sexual behavior over a one-and-a-half year period but after administration of testosterone nosing, nudging and mounting increased; however, the precision of movement with which a normal ram courts the ewe was not present (Banks, 1962).

The sexual behavior of the tom cat shows some peculiarities not encountered in the other species discussed so far. As is the case with rats and guinea pigs castration causes a loss of sexual drive, and after about ten days intromissions seem to be impossible (Green et al., 1957). This loss is somewhat faster than in rats and guinea pigs but this is a quantitative rather than a qualitative difference. Aronson (1958) divided the reactions of cats to castration into three categories:

1. Animals in which the capacity for intromissions lasted for months or even years and for mounting lasted almost indefinitely.

2. Cats in which the capacity for intromissions lasted for about two months, but in which mounts without intromissions increased in frequency and in which mounting continued for a year or more.

3. Cats in which the capacity for intro-

missions dropped rapidly and mounting was weak, sporadic, and disappeared rapidly.

It is not clear why the cats used by Green et al. (1957) all apparently belonged to this third group.

The same three basic groups of responses were found after testosterone withdrawal from prepubertally castrated rats treated with testosterone. Aronson (1958) interprets the behavioral changes after castration or after testosterone withdrawal to changes in the sensory receptive mechanisms of the male. These changes will be discussed later in this chapter.

Castration of cats at the age when the sensitive spines on the glans penis develop (three to four months of age) resulted in mounting in only one out of 13 cats and a failure of intromissions. These experiments indicate that androgen is required for the develpment of the complete sexual behavior pattern.

Green et al. (1957) restored sexual behavior in castrated cats with testosterone propionate and also with estradiol (60,000 R. U.) or 1 to 5 mg. of stilbestrol pellet implants. However, restoration with any of these hormones is effective only in recently castrated tom cats (Green et al., 1957). In one apparently exceptional cat, 75 mg. of testosterone propionate, given one year after gonadectomy, caused violent sexual behavior that included an attempt to copulate with a teddy bear.

The lack of specificity of the gonadal hormones required for induction of sexual behavior in the cat also applies to the female. Testosterone propionate can induce female sexual behavior in spayed females. The uteri of these cats were atrophic, indicating that the androgen had not been converted to estrogen. Thus androgen seemed to have induced female sexual behavior probably by a direct effect on the nervous system. In young males, estrogens can induce some aspects of female sexual behavior, although these males were never receptive (Green et al., 1957).

Palen and Goddard (1966) compared the behavior of a cat in heat and a cat exposed to catnip *(Nepata cataria)*. The unique rolling pattern found in estrous cats was also observed after exposure to catnip; there was also an increase in the attention paid to a stuffed object, an attention similar to that observed in estrous cats with respect to a male. Sexual mounting was not seen. The reaction to catnip was shown by males as well as by females. The possible connection between catnip and estrous behavior is not clear, however.

Effects of Brain Lesions

Much research has been done to determine in what manner sexual behavior is initiated, to what extent hormones play a role in the initiation of sexual behavior and in the execution of copulation and ejaculation, and at which sites the hormones act to have their effects. Two excellent critical reviews (Beach, 1967; Lisk, 1967) have been published recently that connect many of the concepts with detailed information.

Beach (1967) has evaluated the evidence:

1. Whether there are species specific copulatory patterns that partly consist of reflexes mediated by spinal and myelencephalic mechanisms that are capable of functioning after separation from the more rostral parts of the central nervous system.

2. Whether there are "lower centers" under varying degrees of control by more anteriorly placed neural tissue and whether such control is inhibitory.

3. Whether gonadal hormones have any direct effects on the centers located in the spinal cord and the myelencephalon.

4. Whether gonadal hormones affect the occurrence of copulatory behavior by modifying cerebral control of the lower, reflexive mechanisms.

With respect to the first question there is evidence mentioned previously in this chapter that in amphibia the clasp reflex of the male produces a *species specific* copulatory response; for instance, the *Xenopus laevis* male displays an extremely posterior clasp, whereas *Rana esculanta* and *R. temporaria* use a postaxillary clasp. Spinal toads and frogs display the pattern which normally occurs in the male of the particular species.

Spinal rats will show a series of erections, two or three quick dorsal flips and one to three extended long dorsal flips of the glans, when the animal is restrained on its back and the preputial sheath is held behind the glans penis. The pattern of response resembles the pattern and duration of the ejaculatory response of the intact rat (Hart, 1967). In these tests, sexually naive rats, castrated between 120 and 131 days of age, to which testosterone was administered, were used. Withdrawal of androgen reduced the number of erections and quick and long flips. The prewithdrawal level could be reestablished by testosterone administration. These data suggest that the androgen affected spinal neurons. Hart (1967) considered the possibility that testosterone may have affected the sensitivity of the sensory receptors, but cites several arguments against this explanation.

Spinal dogs (transection between thoracic vertebrae 7 and 10) display reflexes characteristic of the copulatory behavior, i.e., shallow pelvic thrusts, leg movements associated with initial penetration, and protracted erection, after manipulation of the penis (Beach, 1967). Hart and Kitchell (1966) also obtained erection and detumescence reflexes in spinal dogs upon manipulation of the penis. Different reflexes were obtained depending upon the site of manipulation. Beach (1967) compared the behavior of castrated dogs that had received testosterone with that of untreated castrated dogs, and concluded that androgens were not required for the maintenance of these reflexes, but that androgen can probably influence the reflexes; for example, in

some castrated dogs the time that male and female were tied together during coitus was shorter than in intact dogs.

Spinal cats show marked priapism; dorsiflexion of the tail by the experimenter induced augmentation of the penile erection, quick twitching of the anal and perineal musculature, and increased flexion of the hind legs. All of these reactions are also seen in male cats during copulation.

Sleeping rats and cats may show phenomena that resemble ejaculation; presumably, they may occur as a result of the diminished inhibition by higher brain centers during sleep.

Beach (1967) cites several examples of men who, although paraplegic, could have intercourse or showed other evidence of a coital reflex.

The evidence seems to support the hypothesis that certain aspects of copulation can be preserved in male spinal animals. There are not sufficient experiments to determine to what extent androgens modify these reflexes which do not require androgen for their maintenance.

Beach (1967) discusses in detail the ontogeny of the lordosis reflex, which, in sexually receptive rats and guinea pigs, is an essential part of the feminine copulatory patterns. In neonatal guinea pigs the lordosis response can be obtained by human stimulation of the rump of the animal. In guinea pigs nursed by their dams, this reflex disappears within a few hours, whereas in similar but bottle-fed animals, the reflex may be retained for several days (Beach, 1966). In young guinea pigs, which do not exhibit lordosis upon human stimulation, lordosis is obtained upon licking by the dam. According to Beach (1966) this reflex at this age may be involved in voiding of urine and feces. The lordosis reflex is obtained at a time when gonadal hormone secretion is still low.

Decerebrate rigidity in a female cat can be inhibited by vaginal stimulation; this reaction can be obtained in cats that are in heat or in anestrus. Beach (1967) has emphasized the importance of this reaction and of the failure to observe it in decerebrate bitches. The female cat during coitus flexes its legs, whereas the bitch's legs are rigid. This evidence, therefore, favors the interpretation of species-specific reflexes.

Spinal cats will, upon gentle tapping of the perineal region, show flexion of the hind legs, a greater flexion of the front legs so that the rear end is elevated, and lateral deviation of the tail and alternate stepping movements of the hind legs. All these reflexes are parts of the normal copulatory behavior of female cats. The reflex responses can be obtained in spayed cats and cats in heat. This suggests that, as in the male, the reflexes do not require gonadal hormones.

The available evidence for mammals shows that reflexes associated or, at least, similar to coital reactions can be obtained in spinal cats. Whether gonadal hormones influence different aspects of the reflex (duration and latency) has not been sufficiently investigated to warrant definite conclusions.

The second point evaluated by Beach (1967), "whether the lower centers are under inhibitory control of more anterior centers," has been the subject of many investigations, which have also been reviewed by Lisk (1967). The evidence will be reviewed according to the category of the effect of the lesion and the effect of stimulation.

Removal of substanital parts of cerebral cortex, dorsolateral cortex, median surface, frontal lobes, or posterior lobes of male rats did not consistently interfere with sexual activity and sexual behavior. Some elements of the behavior were affected. After removal of the dorsolateral cortex, four out of 20 rats showed complete suppression of activity, but the remaining 16 showed slower mounting and had fewer ejaculations per unit of time. Removal of the median surface resulted in a failure to ejaculate in two out of 20 rats, but recovery occurred in one rat

after testosterone treatment; both rats mounted and had intromissions (Larsson, 1962).

Removal of the frontal lobes led to suppression of mating in eight out of 20 rats, but in the unaffected rats the behavior was normal, although in one of the three experiments the ejaculatory latency was slightly longer. After posterior lobectomy, intromission latency was longer, as were the ejaculatory latency and the postejaculatory interval. There was also an increased proportion of mounts which did not culminate in intromission. The investigator thought that these effects were secondary to visual deficits (Larsson, 1964). Testosterone propionate administration did not restore sexual activity in the inactive rats.

Cortical lesions in the rat, cat, and rabbit do not seem to affect the male sexual behavior unless the motor-sensory area and the overlapping sensory-motor area are damaged (Lisk, 1967).

Ablation of the neocortex of male rabbits does not seem to affect their sexual interest in the female. However, if lesions in the somatesthetic, auditory, and visual areas are made in combination with lesions of the olfactory bulb, sexual behavior of the male disappears, although lesions of the olfactory bulb alone do not have this effect (Lisk, 1967).

Removal of the cingulate and the retrosplenial cortex of the male hamster reduced intromission frequency but had no effect on the sequence of behavior. Lesions of the lateral cortex did not seem to influence sexual activity of this animal (Bunnell et al., 1966).

Removal of the neocortex of rats, guinea pigs, and rabbits may result in an exaggerated lordosis reflex, and the animals sometimes maintain the lordosis posture after the male has dismounted (Beach, 1967).

The application of potassium chloride solution to the surface of the cerebral hemispheres causes depression of its activity. This treatment leads to temporary inhibition of the female's sexual behavior, i.e., lordosis and acceptance of the male, and eliminates the hopping responses and the pursuit of the male (Lisk, 1967). Clemens et al. (1967), however, found that potassium chloride applied to the surface of the cerebrum increased the incidence and frequency of lordosis in estrogen-treated spayed rats. Potassium chloride, in the absence of estradiol benzoate, had no effect on lordosis in spayed rats. Treatment with estrogen plus progesterone was more effective than estrogen plus KC1 application.

These data indicate that in the male, sexual behavior culminating in ejaculation is possible in rats with lesions in the dorsolateral median or posterior lobes, but that the frontal lobes are required. No evidence for an inhibitory center was found in these studies. The experiments with the females suggest inhibitory centers in view of the exaggerated lordosis after removal of the cortex and in view of the induction of lordosis by estrogen when the cortical activity is depressed.

Anestrous cats exposed to valeric acid and either treated with estrogen (Endröczi et al., 1958) or not treated with estrogen (Lissák, 1962) will, upon vaginal stimulation, show mating behavior and the after-reaction. The estrogen treatment of anestrous cats is, apparently, not necessary because the valeric acid causes stimulation of the pituitary-gonad axis, as is evident from the many enlarged follicles. Upon vaginal stimulation, ovulation occurred in five out of seven of these cats (Lissák, 1962). Application of the vaginal smear obtained from estrous cats to the nose of anestrous cats caused a violent orienting reaction, and, after vaginal stimulation, mating behavior and the after-reaction. After spaying, these phenomena do not occur, but treatment with estrogen will restore this behavior (Endröczi et al., 1958). Testosterone injections in anestrous cats will not prevent the lordosis response after valeric acid exposure, but they will inhibit the copulatory behavior and after-

reaction that follow vaginal stimulation in control or in estrogen-treated cats (Endröczi et al., 1958). Removal of the fronto-orbital area of the cortex facilitates the sexual behavior to the extent that it may occur upon exposure to valeric acid, but without mechanical stimulation. The duration of the behavior, which normally is less than half an hour, may be several hours after the lesions have been made. Similar effects were obtained after lesions in the preoptic areas, in the paraventricular areas, and in the septum (Endröczi et al., 1958).

Lesions of the olfactory bulbs of male rats cause a prolonged latency in the response to estrous females, reduce the number of ejaculations, and increase the tendency to remain unresponsive to sexual stimulation (Heimer and Larsson, 1967a). The removal of the olfactory bulbs may cause a decrease in androgen secretion for, as we saw in Chapter 8, transection of the olfactory stalk resulted in decreased body and testicular weight in rats.

Lesions in the rhinencephalon have given somewhat controversial results. On the one hand, Green et al. (1957), Schreiner and Kling (1953, 1956), and Wood (1958) observed "hypersexuality" in rats with amygdalar lesions. The "hypersexuality" was expressed in homosexual mounts, mounting of animals of other species (e.g. dogs, chickens), tandem mounting, and mounting of inanimate objects (e.g. teddy bears). On the other hand, Shealy and Peele (1957) found no such effects in cats, and Kling (1962) did not obtain hypersexuality in young kittens with lesions in the amygdala. With respect to the kittens it should be recalled that in other behavioral aspects (grooming, eating, aggressiveness) they differed from adult cats. The reasons for the difference between the results obtained by Shealy and Peele (1957) and the other workers are not clear.

During sexual activity changes in electrical activity were observed in recordings from the amygdala, but not in the recordings from the suprasylvian cortex, the anterior, and the posterior hypothalamus (Schwartz and Whalen, 1965). This evidence also suggests that the amygdala is involved in the sexual behavior of the male cat.

Female cats with amygdalar lesions showed neither hypersexuality nor permanent estrus, according to Green et al. (1957). In experiments by Wood (1958) females with such lesions showed no precopulatory activity, did not court, and would spit at hypersexual males. When the male succeeded in obtaining the neck grasp the female assumed the mating crouch, would exhibit treading activity, and exhibit postcopulatory activity similar to that of a normal estrous cat.

In male rats, amygdalar lesions resulted in inactive animals which avoided the female and which, during mating tests, exhibited a high frequency of biting the female; however, the sexual behavior was not disrupted, although it was modified (Michal, 1966).

Bilateral lesions, made by heat coagulation, in the basolateral amygdaloid nucleus of adult female deer mice (*Peromyscus maniculatus bairdii*) had no apparent effect on vaginal smears and on mating behavior in 70 percent of the animals, but caused mating during diestrus as well as during estrus. In the medial amygdaloid nucleus, bilateral lesions did not affect the vaginal smears, but none of the females mated (Eleftheriou and Zolovick, 1966). These results indicate that inhibitory centers may be present in the basolateral amygdaloid nucleus and that excitatory centers are present in the medial amygdaloid nucleus.

Ablation of olfactory bulbs and section of the fornix of rabbits caused mounting by females and acceptance of the male at times when their vaginal orifices appeared pale, and the animals seemed to be in anestrus endocrinologically. In one of these rabbits the ovary was atrophic, but in four others the ovaries were normal (Sawyer, 1959).

These experiments thus indicate that there may be inhibitory centers in the amygdalar region, but that the inhibitory effect may play a greater role in the male than in the female cat. In the rabbit, the combined effect of olfactory bulb and amygdalar lesions suggests that two centers may be involved in the sexual behavior of this species.

Kim (1960) reported that hippocampal lesions in male rats caused an increase in the number of matings with either estrous rats or rats taken at random from a population. Michal (1966) found increased exploring activity in rats with such lesions, but the incidence of mounting decreased.

Lesions of the septum resulted in persistent pursuit of the female, but a partial blockage occurred in the behavioral sequence between display of courtship behavior and mounting (Michal, 1966).

Some of the results to be discussed seem to be contradictory with respect to the effects obtained after lesions in the hypothalamus. It is important to remember that the use of stainless steel or nickel electrodes may cause deposition of irritative deposits and that, therefore, results obtained after use of such electrodes may differ from those obtained after lesions made with platinum electrodes (see Chapter 8).

Lesions of the basal preoptic area of testosterone propionate-treated roosters abolished copulatory behavior, but inhibited waltzing temporarily (Barfield, 1965a).

Brookhart and Dey (1941) were, apparently, the first workers to observe that lesions between the optic chiasma and the pituitary stalk of male guinea pigs resulted in a loss of sexual activity, with only a few mountings taking place after the lesion. The testes and secondary sex organs appeared normal, indicating that androgen secretion was probably normal.

Soulairac (1963), carried out an extensive series of experiments over a number of years, but does not give the composition of the electrodes he used when he made bilateral lesions in the medial preoptic area, in the mamillary bodies, and in the median eminence. Lesions in any of these three areas resulted in loss of sexual activity. After lesions in the mamillary bodies or in the median eminence the testes were atrophied. Neither androgen treatment nor HCG injections caused restoration of mating behavior after lesions of the mamillary bodies. Apparently these treatments were not tried in rats with median eminence lesions. The testis and ductus deferens were normal in rats with lesions in the anterior hypothalamus. Larsson and Heimer (1964), after making lesions with nickel-plated electrodes in the medial preoptic area, found that two out of 16 rats showed normal sexual behavior, six out of 16 showed depression in this behavior, and eight out of 16 showed no sexual behavior. No data were given concerning the weight or activity of the gonads. The effect on behavior may, therefore, have been secondary to gonadal hypofunction. Lott (1966), using stainless steel electrodes to make lesions, found no effect of the lesions in either the lateral or the medial preoptic area on sexual behavior.

Heimer and Larsson (1967b) made lesions in the medial preoptic anterior hypothalamus and found, when the lesions were small, that sexual behavior was never completely abolished, although temporary impairment occurred. After extensive lesions, all sexual behavior was eliminated and then could not be restored by androgen treatment. According to Heimer and Larsson (1967b) the preoptic anterior hypothalamus is, in effect, an interstitial nucleus of the medial forebrain bundle. The fiber tract is the major reciprocal link between the mediobasal telencephalon and the midbrain tegmentum. It seems probable that the medial preoptic region receives impulses from visceral and somatic sensory structures of the lower brain stem, the hippocampal formation, the cingulate gyrus, the septal area, the amygdaloid complex, and, in macrosomal animals, also from olfactory structures.

Lisk (1966, 1967) used platinum electrodes to make lesions and measured the number of copulation plugs under the cage after housing of the male with an estrous female rat. Lesions involving the suprachiasmatic nucleus, the area dorsal to the arcuate nucleus, or the habenula caused a decline in the number of copulation plugs, whereas a marked increase occurred after lesions were placed in the mamillary region. There were no changes in either testicular, pituitary, or accessory sex gland structures after lesions in either the habenula, the arcuate nucleus region, or the mamillary region (Lisk, 1966, 1967). The most striking difference is that between the results of Soulairac (1963) and Lisk (1966) with respect to lesions in the mamillary region. There is the probability that Soulairac did not use platinum electrodes, in view of the fact that the deposition of iron during lesioning with stainless steel electrodes and its effect on the hypothalamus had not been discovered (see Chapter 8). If such stainless steel electrodes were used, it is possible that the difference between the two sets of results is due to deposition of irritative deposits in Soulairac's experiments.

Law and Meagher (1958) made lesions in the anterior, central, or posterior hypothalamus of intact female rats, and spayed rats treated with estrogen plus progesterone (the composition of the electrodes was not given). In the nonspayed females, lesions either in the anterior or in the posterior hypothalamus increased the incidence of lordosis and the incidence of mating during vaginal diestrus, whereas lesions in the central hypothalamus eliminated mating during vaginal diestrus and estrus, but increased the incidence of lordosis during diestrus. In spayed rats, anterior, central, and posterior hypothalamic lesions increased the frequency of lordosis during diestrus, with the sharpest increase occurring in rats with posterior hypothalamic lesions. During vaginal estrus, central hypothalamic lesions eliminated the lordosis response, whereas lesions in the anterior hypothalamus caused a marked increase in this behavior.

It should be recalled that "behavioral centers" may be in different regions for different species (see Figure 8-7).

In female cats, lesions of the anterior hypothalamic region rostral to the ventromedial nucleus and medial to or within the area of the medial forebrain bundle, caused a loss of sexual interest which could not be restored by gonadal hormone administration. Lesions in the area of the ventromedial nucleus, the premamillary region, or the mamillary body caused loss of sexual behavior, which could be restored by gonadal hormone administration; the loss of the behavior was the result of the gonadal atrophy which occurred after the lesion (Lisk, 1967).

Anestrous estrogen-treated cats exposted to valeric acid will exhibit normal sexual behavior after vaginal stimulation when they have lesions in either the area of the mamillary body, the dorsomedial nucleus, the premamillary nuclei, or the nucleus arcuatus. Lesions between the preoptic and paraventricular region, on the other hand, facilitated the sexual behavior of such cats in a manner similar to that observed after fronto-orbital lesions (Endröczi et al., 1958).

The mamillary bodies, which do not seem to be essential for sexual behavior in the cat, are essential for this behavior in the female rabbit. Does with lesions of the mamillary bodies have normal ovaries, but lack the female sexual behavioral responses to a male rabbit; estrogen injections in such does do not restore normal sexual behavior (Sawyer and Kawakami, 1961).

In the spayed guinea pig, treated with estrogen and progesterone, lesions of the mamillary and premamillary region with stainless steel electrodes did not cause changes in sexual behavior, whereas lesions in the midventral hypothalamus resulted in a complete loss of sexual behavior (no lordosis) in nine out of 21 females and in an incomplete loss in ten out of 21 females; in two females sexual behavior

was seen in the absence of exogenous hormones and while the reproductive tract was atrophic. The lesions in these two animals may have been slightly more anterior and medial than in the ones that caused loss of sexual behavior (Goy and Phoenix, 1963).

Clegg et al. (1958) found that lesions of the ventral hypothalamus just above the anterior third of the median eminence abolished estrous behavior in nine ewes. Seven of the nine ewes had normal ovaries and had uteri which indicated cyclic patterns (Clegg et al., 1958). Further experiments showed that lesions of the pituitary stalk and adjacent ventral hypothalamus abolished ovarian cycles and sexual behavior (not receptive to male), whereas destruction of the anterior median eminence did not result in a disturbance of normal cyclic changes in the ovary, but inhibited estrous behavior (Clegg and Ganong, 1960).

The data obtained with females of different species are consistent with the hypothesis of dual inhibitory-excitatory system in the brain regulating sexual behavior. Lesions of one area may abolish the sexual behavior, whereas lesions elsewhere may cause an increased interest ("hypersexuality"), or may cause mating behavior in the absence of gonadal hormones.

Effects of Electrical Stimulation

There is also evidence from stimulation studies that has a bearing on the problem of the regulation of sexual behavior in the central nervous system.

Some parts of the courting behavior, e.g. bowing, displacement preening, pecking, and nest demonstration, have been induced in male and female pigeons by electrical stimulation (0.05 to 1.0 mA, 50 Hz, 3 msec.) in an area extending medially from the anterior diencephalic paraventricular and preoptic nuclei up into the paleo-, neo-, and hyperstriatum (Åkerman, 1966a).

Electrical stimulation of the anterior dorsolateral hypothalamus of male rats in the presence of estrous females caused the complete repertoire of sexual behavior: mounting, intromissions, and ejaculations. This behavior occurred within seconds after the stimulation was given and stopped when stimulation was discontinued (Vaughan and Fisher, 1962). In the presence of an ovariectomized female one male rat only achieved mounts without intromissions, whereas the same animal under the same electrical stimulation conditions achieved 19 ejaculations in the same time period in the presence of an estrous female. This indicates that stimuli from the female may lower the threshold for inducing certain parts of the behavioral repertoire, or that these stimuli are required for obtaining a coordinated and complete response.

Postintromission grooming was absent in some animals; the grooming behavior seemed to be related to the stimulation current. Grooming occurred at 4 and 6 mA, but not at 8 mA.

In these experiments no reference is made to the effect of the presence or absence of gonadal hormones on the behavior of the stimulated male; only intact males seem to have been used.

Rats, cats, monkeys, and other mammals can be trained to deliver electric stimuli to themselves via permanently implanted electrodes. At certain sites the electrical stimulus seems to act as a primary reward, and the animals, once taught, will self-stimulate, sometimes at very high rates, 5000 stimulations per hour for an extended length of time. Fasted rats given a choice between food and self-stimulation may choose self-stimulation (see Olds, 1962, for an extensive discussion concerning self-stimulation and the possible interpretations). The "rewarding sites" are located largely in the hypothalamus and the rhinencephalon and involve areas which, in other experiments, have resulted in different aspects of reproductive behavior after electrical stim-

ulation. Constant stimulation (controlled by the experimenter) via platinum electrodes of the medial forebrain bundle near the lateral fornix at the level of the premamillary nuclei resulted in copulation with estrous females. These copulations soon became "stimulus-bound," that is, they occurred during stimulation and rarely without it. Such stimulated rats would open a door to obtain access to the females, even shortly after ejaculation had taken place, and would exhibit sexual behavior. Upon self-stimulation of this same area, ejaculation without erection or other sexual behavior would occur in the absence of a female (the authors do not state that either erection or other aspects of male sexual behavior occur in the presence of a female, although the statement that "Penile erection was usually absent during self-stimulation, and neither pelvic thrusts nor the customary postejaculatory posture ever occurred in the absence of a female" may imply that these reactions were seen in the presence of estrous females). Androgen treatment (50 μg. testosterone propionate per day) increased the rate of self-stimulation 17 and 37 percent in two males (Caggiula and Hoebel, 1966). The region in which stimulation resulted in sexual behavior agrees with the region in which Miller (1957) obtained ejaculation in male rats.

Caggiula and Hoebel (1966) concluded that posterior hypothalamic stimulation resembled normal sexual stimulation in that it is rewarding, that the reward varies with the amount of sex hormone, and that it elicits motivated copulation.

Male cats and rats show some parts of courtship behavior (grooming, penile erection) after chemical excitation of the dorsal hippocampus, or following electrical simulation (see Lisk, 1967). MacLean (1963, 1966), using the squirrel monkey *(Saimiri sciureus)*, obtained penile erection after stimulation of:

1. Areas that have known hippo-

campal connection with septum, anterior thalamus, and hypothalamus.

2. Areas that are parts of the so-called Papez circuit (mamillary bodies, mamillothalamic tract, parts of the anterior thalamic nucleus and the anterior cingulate gyrus).

3. Parts of the medial orbital gyrus and along its connections with the medial part of the medial dorsal nucleus.

4. The anterior medial hypothalamus, the rostral and caudal tuberal regions, dorsomedial and lateral hypothalamic areas, and the mamillary region.

The medial septopreoptic region and the medial part of the medial dorsal nucleus seem to be nodal points for erection.

On the basis of this evidence MacLean (1966) concluded that afferents involved in genital sensation follow the spinothalamic tract to the caudal intralaminar region of the thalamus, which, probably, articulates with the part of the medial dorsal nucleus that is nodal with respect to erection.

The descending pathway, the major autonomic pathway for erection, comes into association with neocortical, extrapyramidal, and cerebellar systems. The pathway descends along the medial forebrain bundle, runs through the dorsal aspect of the substantia nigra into the lateral field of this nucleus, and then descends through the lateral triangular region of the pons bounded by peduncular fibers and the brachium pontis; from here the pathway descends past the ventrolateral aspects of the superior olive and continues medially to a point lateral to the pyramids (MacLean, 1966).

Ejaculations have been obtained after the discontinuance of stimulation along the spinothalamic pathway which connects the medial dorsal thalamic and the intralaminar nuclei. In many cases genital scratching occurred during the stimulation. Seminal discharge occurred without or before erection after stimulation of the ventromedial part of the medial dorsal nucleus and the mid-dorsal portion of the parafascicular centromedian complex (MacLean, 1966).

Electrical after-discharges in the hippocampus were often associated with maximal erections obtained by stimulation of the septum and the rostral diencephalon, suggesting that the hippocampus may modify the excitability of the effective neurons involved in erection (MacLean, 1963).

Erection and ejaculation, often accompanied by pelvic thrusting, took place after stimulation of the preoptic area of one Rhesus monkey *(Macaca mulatta)*. The monkey self-stimulated at a very low rate, although, when electrodes at other sites were used, it self-stimulated at rates of over 500 times per five minutes (Robinson and Mishkin, 1966).

The evidence discussed so far indicates that certain aspects of male and female sexual behavior can occur in spinal animals. There is also evidence for inhibitory and excitatory systems in the hypothalamic and higher brain centers. Electrical stimulation can cause completely normal sexual behavior. For the squirrel monkey the ascending and descending pathways have been partly outlined. Testosterone increases self-stimulation of centers which, upon stimulation, cause normal male sexual behavior.

Hormone Implants in the Brain

The centers, or regions at which the gonadal hormones have their effect, have been investigated with different experimental techniques, i.e. the effect on behavior of gonadal hormones implanted in different regions of the brain, and the concentration of gonadal hormones in different brain areas after injection. The results with these techniques have been largely obtained with mammals, although some experiments with birds have been carried out.

Barfield (1964) induced copulatory

behavior without courting behavior by bilateral and unilateral implants of testosterone propionate in the basal medial preoptic region; the occurrence of the copulatory behavior was not correlated with comb growth, indicating that the hormone acted in the area described rather than systemically. Capons could be induced to court and copulate after an initial implant of testosterone propionate in the aggression area (described previously) and a subsequent implant in the preoptic area. The area in which these implants were effective in inducing sexual behavior corresponds to the one in which lesions abolished copulatory behavior (Barfield, 1965a,b).

Progesterone injections into ring-doves *(Streptopelia risoria)* induce incubation behavior and inhibit courtship behavior. Implants of progesterone in the preoptic nuclei, the supraoptic decussation, and the paleostriatum elicited incubation behavior, whereas courtship behavior was suppressed after progesterone was implanted in the preoptic nuclei, the occipitomesencephalic tract and the archistriatum. The two systems, which are sensitive to progesterone and are responsible for the two types of behavior, overlap to a certain extent (Komisaruk, 1965). The effects of lesions in these areas on behavior do not seem to have been studied and, therefore, no statement concerning the agreement between the two methods of localizing the important areas involved in sexual behavior can be made.

Stilbestrol implanted via hypodermic needle tubing into the brain of spayed cats (which retained anestrous genital tracts and vaginal smears after the implant) between the posterior mamillary region and the anterior preoptic region induced mating behavior. The estrogen sensitive system is diffuse in the mid-hypothalamic region and is restricted and localized to the basal medial area at the level of the optic chiasma. The estrogen in these experiments did not spread beyond 600 to 800 μ from the implantation

site (Michael, 1966a). Sawyer's results (1963), obtained with ovariectomized cats indicated that implants of estradiol benzoate in the posterior hypothalamus were not effective, but in the lateral anterior hypothalamus area, including the medial forebrain bundle, implants caused sexual behavior. The sites found to be sensitive to estrogen in inducing behavior in Sawyer's experiments agree with the sites found to be required for sexual behavior in the ablation experiments mentioned earlier.

Estrous behavior could be induced in ovariectomized rabbits after implants of estradiol benzoate, diluted with cholesterol, bilaterally or unilaterally in the ventromedial-premamillary region about 1 mm. lateral to the midline; the latency between implant and behavioral changes was one to two days. The diffusion of the implanted estrogen was estimated to be about 2 mm. The uteri of these rabbits were atrophic. When undiluted estradiol benzoate was implanted all rabbits showed an effect on the uterus, but only those with implants in the hypothalamus showed estrous behavior, indicating that the threshold for uterine stimulation is lower than for sexual behavior in the rabbit (Palka and Sawyer, 1966). The estrogen sensitive ventromedial-premamillary region lies anterior to the mamillary area which, in ablation studies, was shown to be required for normal sexual behavior, suggesting that the mamillary area is not the "steroid receptor" center but part of the pathway necessary for the expression of the behavior (Palka and Sawyer, 1966). Progesterone injections or progesterone implants in the ventromedial-premamillary area of rabbits, bearing estradiol benzoate implants in the ventromedial-premamillary area and showing estrous behavior, did not block estrous behavior. In ovariectomized rabbits injected with estradiol benzoate, or in intact rabbits in heat, estrous behavior is blocked by progesterone. Palka and Sawyer (1966) suggest that the high local concentrations of estradiol benzoate may either saturate the "steroid receptors" or that the estrogen prevents the progesterone from acting elsewhere in the central nervous system.

Lisk (1967) concluded, on the basis of the rather extensive evidence obtained with either intact or spayed rats, that the "mating center" is in the preoptic-anterior hypothalamic area. Estradiol, which, upon injection, does not cause sexual behavior unless progesterone is also administered, induces the lordosis response if placed in the anterior hypothalamic region. Progesterone implants together with estrogen implants increased the incidence and shortened the latency (period between implant and response) of the lordosis response in prepubertally ovariectomized rats. Neither progesterone nor testosterone alone induced the lordosis response when implanted in the brain (Lisk, 1967).

The agreement between the location of the "mating center" by lesion techniques and by implantation techniques is, as Lisk (1967) has pointed out, unusually good for the female rat.

The location of the mating centers in rats has been investigated by Davidson (1966a) and Lisk and Suydam (1967). Davidson (1966a), using castrated rats that had failed to ejaculate in three successive tests after the operation, implanted small pellets of testosterone propionate, or 20 gauge needle tubing containing testosterone propionate into different brain areas and found restoration of the complete pattern of male sexual behavior in the absence of stimulation of the secondary accessory organs. The frequency of positive responses was highest after implantation into the medial preoptic and the anterior hypothalamic areas. A relatively large area had to be exposed and the author concluded that there are probably no discrete centers. Lisk and Suydam (1967) found that either testosterone or androstenedione implanted in the preoptic region or in the hypothalamus was ineffective in eliciting male copulatory behavior in prepubertally castrated male

rats; however, implants of estrogen and progesterone in the preoptic anterior hypothalamic area induced male behavior (mounting, pelvic thrusts) in rats castrated when three to five days old. This behavior occurred 34 to 60 days after the implants were made. The same animals had shown a lordosis response as soon as three to 12 days after the implants and showed lordosis even when they also showed the male behavior. In males castrated after puberty, rather large testosterone implants were capable of restoring male behavior only if the males had been proven to be sexually responsive prior to castration and had been trained to copulate in the box for testing (Lisk and Suydam, 1967). The fact that rather large implants were needed, indicates that the steroid sensitive area is rather diffuse.

The experiments by Fisher (1956, 1964), in which female sexual behavior was induced in male rats after injections of androgens, have been discussed in Chapters 5 and 8.

Selective Concentration of Gonadal Hormones by Brain Areas

Biochemical and autoradiographic techniques have been used to determine whether certain tissues and certain parts of the central nervous system selectively concentrate injected radioactive hormones.

Resko et al. (1967), using biochemical techniques, found that after testosterone injections free testosterone was present in higher concentrations in the hypothalamus, cerebellum, and the pituitary than in the plasma, but the concentration of testosterone was not significantly higher than plasma in the prostate and seminal vesicles. The hypothalamus, cerebellum, and pituitary also contained higher concentrations of androstenedione and etiocholanolone than plasma, but the seminal vesicles and prostate contained about twice as much of these hormones as the neural tissues and pituitary.

Hamburg (1966) studied the effect of time on the distribution of radioactive progesterone in different parts of the brain of ovariectomized estrogen-treated rats. The principal findings showed:

1. There is a rapid uptake of progesterone by the brain, and uptake that is about ten times as high as the uptake by the uterus, five minutes after injection.

2. Radioactivity disappears more rapidly from other parts of the brain than from the hypothalamus. The concentration 22 hours after injection was 60 percent of the concentration at five minutes postinjection, whereas for other parts of the brain the corresponding figure was 2.5 percent. Other experiments by Balman and Clayton, cited by Hamburg (1966), confirm this retention of progesterone by the hypothalamus.

The anterior pituitary, uterus, vagina, adrenal, hypothalamus, preoptic area, cerebellum, and cerebrum retain radioactive estradiol. There may be some nonspecific absorption of the estradiol by neural tissue; Eisenfeld and Axelrod (1965, 1966) have subtracted the radioactivity found per mg. cerebral or cerebellar tissue from the radioactivity per mg. hypothalamic tissue to obtain values which express the specific binding in the hypothalamus and septum. It was found that norethynodrel (17-α-ethynyl-est-5(10)-en-17-β-ol-3-one), an oral contraceptive, administered before the tritiated estradiol, reduced the accumulation in the anterior pituitary, vagina, hypothalamus, and preoptic area, but administration after the tritiated estradiol caused a reduced uptake in the uterus and vagina only.

Nonradioactive estradiol, injected prior to radioactive estradiol, reduced the concentration of the labeled estrogen in the anterior pituitary, uterus, vagina, and hypothalamus, which suggests that saturable sites for steriod binding are present in these tissues. The uptake of tritiated estradiol by the preoptic region and other tissues was not affected by administration of nonlabeled estradiol (Eisenfeld and Axelrod, 1965). Subsequent experiments showed that the concentration of tritiated estradiol was similar for male and female, for ovariectomized, and for intact rats. Ovariectomized rats, treated either with estrone or with estriol, showed a decreased concentration of radioactive estradiol in the pituitary, hypothalamus, uterus, and vagina; high doses of either progesterone, testosterone, or hydrocortisone did not have this effect. This evidence suggests a high specificity for attachment to the estradiol binding sites (Eisenfeld and Axelrod, 1966).

Autoradiographic studies have shown that the specific binding sites in the hypothalamus, median eminence, and anterior pituitary take up and retain the radioactive 17-β-estradiol (Kato and Villee, 1967a,b). The specificity of the binding sites was demonstrated in experiments in which pretreatment with 17-β-estradiol decreased the uptake of the labeled hormone by the anterior hypothalamus and anterior pituitary, but it did not affect the uptake by the cerebral cortex and by the cerebellum. It was also shown that 17-α-estradiol injections did not affect the concentration of 17-β-estradiol by these tissues (Kato and Villee, 1967b).

The neonatal rat concentrates injected tritiated hexestrol in the nucleus arcuatus and the basal part of the ventromedial nucleus (Michael, 1966b).

Experiments by Attramadal (1964) showed that the labeled estrogen is mainly found in the cell nuclei of the hypothalamic nuclei, but that in the pituitary cells it is found only in the cytoplasma.

The ovariectomized cat, injected with tritiated hexestrol, concentrates the labeled material in the uterus, vagina, anterior pituitary, septum, and hypothalamus (Glascock and Michael, 1962; Michael, 1966a).

These experiments show that progesterone, estrogen, and testosterone are taken up selectively by certain brain areas, but it does not give information by itself concerning the location of the sexual behavior centers or areas; however, in conjunction with the lesion and implantation studies these findings have provided additional evidence concerning the localization of these centers or areas.

Mention should be made of reports by Glascock and Michael (1962) and Michael (1962) that after a single injection of 1.20 μg./kg. of hexestrol the material was present in the brain within five hours and had disappeared 24 hours after injection, while mating occurred 48 hours after injection, when the radioactive hexestrol was not present in either the hypothalamus or the preoptic area in concentrations higher than those found in blood or muscle. The manner in which the hormone might have affected a threshold after it had been absent from the tissue for 24 hours is not at all clear.

A new technique that can be used to provide answers to the questions concerning the location of mating centers is microelectrophoresis, by which hormones can be introduced in minute quantities in very small areas of the brain, and which allows simultaneous monitoring of the electrical activity of the neurons where the hormone is introduced (Ruf and Steiner, 1967).

After coitus, male and female rabbits will show elements of the so-called olfactory-bucco-alimentary-anal-genital syndrome (OBAGS), consisting of licking, sniffing, licking of the perineal area, pulling of the skin in this area, and coprophagia (Faure, 1964). The behavior is preceded by sleep with a hyperactivity recorded from the hippocampus and limbic cortex, and a desynchronized activity from the frontal cortex; this has been called the EEG after reaction and is equivalent with paradoxic or activated sleep (Faure, 1964; Faure et al., 1966; Sawyer et al., 1966).

Microinjections of either vasopressin-oxytocin or of luteotropic hormone into the nucleus of Gudden caused the appearance of the OBAGS and of paradoxic and normal sleep after a short latency (0 to 40 seconds). After longer latencies

(one to seven minutes), microinjections of HCG, PMSG, vasopressin, oxytocin, luteotropin, or estrogen plus progesterone, in either the nucleus reticularis pontis caudalis or in the nucleus of Gudden, resulted in the appearance of the OBAGS. Implants of estrogen into the tuberobasal hypothalamus resulted 24 hours later in the OBAGS and the EEG after reaction, with estrous behavior towards the male. Three days after implantation the OBAGS was expressed weakly and the female refused the male. Injection of estrogen 17 to 18 days after the implant induced the appearance of the OBAGS, and of the EEG after reaction, and of mating behavior (acceptance of the male). Faure (1964) interprets these experiments as evidence for the effect of hormones on thresholds in different parts of the nervous system. The techniques used by Faure (1964) and Faure et al. (1966) are somewhat different than those used by Sawyer et al. (1966), but both groups of workers arrived at similar conclusions. Interactions between hypophyseal hormones, gonadal hormones, and the reticular hypothalamic and the limbic hypothalamic systems are mainly responsible for the coordination of behavior, hormone release, and eventually the termination of certain hormone secretions, so that all events occur in the orderly sequence required for optimal reproductive activity of the animal.

Faure et al. (1966) have proposed that serotonin may also be involved in the appearance of paradoxic sleep. The evidence seems to be insufficient to support this contention. In one group of rabbits the controls showed paradoxic sleep and mated ("realized a complete program"), but animals with estrogen implants in the habenula showed little luteinization, did not conceive, and showed an excessive occurrence of the OBAGS, whereas in a second group the controls failed to ovulate, showed few symptoms of the OBAGS, and little paradoxic sleep. However, the animals with habenular estrogen implants conceived, showed the normal OBAGS and exhibited paradoxic sleep before copulation. It is not clear from the publication to what extent the two control groups could be distinguished *prior* to the experiment. In view of this, it seems that the variability among control rabbits was sufficient to account for the variability found among the experimental animals. The hypothesis that estrogen implants caused serotonin secretion was based on experiments by others, in which such estrogen implants caused regression of the pineal gland. It appears that the hypothesis of Faure et al. (1966) requires further experimental verification before it can be accepted.

Electrical Activity of the Brain Correlated with Sexual Behavior

The manner in which hormones affect the central nervous system so that it appears to be correlated with the animal's behavior has been studied by Sawyer and his co-workers. These studies have been reviewed by Sawyer et al. (1966); part of the evidence has been discussed also in Chapter 8.

The EEG arousal threshold is affected by progesterone in the estrogen-treated spayed rabbit. As should be recalled, progesterone has a biphasic effect on mating behavior, first facilitating and later inhibiting this behavior. The EEG arousal threshold decreases sharply during the first few hours after progesterone injection and then increases sharply. The mating behavior is inhibited at the same time interval that the EEG arousal threshold increases. Norethindrone, given orally, blocks copulation-induced ovulation but does not inhibit sexual behavior and does not affect the EEG arousal threshold. These experiments suggest that the EEG arousal threshold is related to the estrous behavior of the rabbit. Some of the other effects of hormones on electrical activity of the brain were discussed in Chapter 8.

Sensory Feedback During Copulation

During copulation there may exist sensory feedback, which is required for the completion of the copulatory act. Whether such a feedback exists and is required has been investigated by different techniques.

Adler and Bermant (1966) placed lidocaine, a local anesthetic, on the rat's penis and found that the animal could not achieve intromission although it mounted at relatively high frequencies. Aronson and Cooper (1966) performed surgical desensitization of the glans penis of cats, which resulted in disoriented mounting and failure of intromission. The cat's penis is equipped with spines that are under the control of androgen; the increase in size of the spines is correlated with increased mating behavior (which is not too surprising, as both seem to be controlled by androgen secretion). After castration, some cats, with reduced spines, still attempted to copulate, but others stopped attempting to copulate before the spines had regressed (Aronson and Cooper, 1967).

Rosenblatt (1965) has pointed out that as the sexual behavior progesses, various components of this behavior are elicited in succession; this succession is dependent on the interplay of the behavior of the male and female. These stimuli, male-female and vice versa, and the effect of new or fresh females on the latency for a subsequent mating, have been reviewed by Schein and Hale (1965) and will not be discussed here.

PARENTAL BEHAVIOR

Extensive reviews concerning parental behavior in vertebrates have been published in recent years (Eisner, 1960; Lehrman, 1961, 1965; Richards, 1967), and, in the author's opinion, no purpose would be served by reviewing the same data again. One aspect, however, namely the role that prolactin plays in different classes, is of sufficient interest to mention here.

Pickford and Atz (1957) considered the evidence whether prolactin induces parental care by jewel fish toward young introduced in the aquarium, and found that the response was not hormone-specific. However, the evidence showed that fish that had not spawned could not be induced to take care of the young, and fish that had spawned but had no brooding experience were induced to take care of the young in a smaller percentage of cases than fish that had had experience in brooding young.

In recent years experiments have shown that prolactin can induce the secretion of mucus on the body surface of the Cichlid fish (*Symphysodon aquifasciata axelrodi*) and in *Aequidens latifrons* (Blüm and Fiedler, 1964, 1965). In addition to this effect prolactin caused fanning (a form of parental care of the eggs and young), and decreased fighting activity in *Pterophyllum scalare* and the two species mentioned above. Fiedler (1962) had observed earlier that prolactin injections caused fanning in *Crenilabris ocellatus*. However, in the three-spined stickleback prolactin failed to induce either parental fanning or so-called displacement fanning (Smith and Hoar, 1967). In this species, methyl testosterone injections restored the fanning behavior, which had disappeared after castration. Thus, apparently the same behavior is under the influence of two entirely different hormones in Cichlid fishes and the three-spined stickleback.

Little, if anything, is known about the effects of prolactin in amphibia and reptiles, except for the water drive in the red eft, which is discussed in the Appendix.

In birds, prolactin may affect a number of physiological phenomena, which are involved in incubation and care of the young:

1. The formation of the brood patch or incubation patch, which was discussed in Chapter 7.

2. Maintenance of incubation of the eggs by ring doves after this behavior is initiated by progesterone (Lehrman, 1965).

3. The brooding of the young by domestic hens, turkeys, and pheasants after prolactin injection (Lehrman, 1961). The fact that the prolactin content of the pituitaries of broody domestic hens and pheasants is higher than in nonbroody hens supports the contention that prolactin may control this type of behavior. Injection of prolactin in roosters may also induce care of the young, a phenomenon not normally seen in roosters (Lehrman, 1961). The effects of the prolactin injections may have been the result of the depression of gonadal activity. Capons will become broody when exposed to chicks (see Lehrman, 1961).

This response to prolactin, although it is probably physiological, should be considered in the light of recent experiments by Kovach (1967), which showed that 9 ml./kg. of 33 percent ethanol given orally induced maternal behavior in roosters. It is possible that prolactin and alcohol have in common, albeit probably by different mechanisms, that they reduce aggressiveness of roosters; once this aggressive tendency is removed roosters may respond to the chicks by sheltering them.

4. Formation of pigeon milk by the crop gland (see Chapter 7 and Appendix).

5. Feeding of the young by pigeons, which regurgitate feed from the crop (Lehrman, 1965).

In mammals, nest building does not appear to require prolactin; as a matter of fact, hypophysectomy increases nest building activity (Lehrman, 1961) and reduces the latency (Rosenblatt, 1967).

Retrieving of pups, crouching over the young, and licking them all occur in hypophysectomized rats, so there seems to be no requirement for pituitary hormones for this behavior (Rosenblatt, 1967), although hormones may play a role in timing the occurrence of this behavior.

A definite role of prolactin in care of the young has been demonstrated in the stimulation and initiation of milk secretion (Cowie, 1966).

Riddle (1963), in a rather polemic review of the role of prolactin in vertebrate function and organization, emphasized the important role of prolactin, and, although some of the arguments, especially with respect to the function of prolactin in initiation of incubation behavior, do not seem well founded, there is no doubt about the interesting role that prolactin plays in behavior, which involves care of the young in different classes of vertebrates; however, this does not mean that prolactin plays such a role in every species.

The view expressed by Medawar (1953) that "Endocrine evolution is not an evolution of hormones but an evolution of the uses to which they are part; an evolution not, to put it crudely, of chemical formulae but of reactivities, reaction patterns and tissue competences" should be kept in mind in any discussion of the effects of endocrines on behavior. The timing of behavioral reactions is probably even more important than the timing of such processes as spermatogenesis and ovulation, because the male and female are in constant interaction with each other and even small deviations in the behavior may prevent successful mating and raising of young. The hormones, which may have been present at high levels for other purposes, may have been used for other functions as they became required during the evolution of a species. It is remarkable that the nervous system has this "plasticity" to use different hormones as compared to the somewhat more "standardized" responses of organs such as the gonads and secondary sex organs to hypophyseal and gonadal hormones.

Throughout this book the author has tried to emphasize the control of the events that lead to the successful sexual reproduction of vertebrates. It is obvious that the interaction between the body's two coordinating systems, the nervous system and the endocrine system, is required, and that the interactions occur in both directions.

Starting with the mammalian embryo and neonatal young, there is convincing evidence that steroid hormones affect the differentiation of the nervous system with respect to its future physiology and role in the release of pituitary hormones, and with respect to the future behavior reactions of the animal. In the maturing and mature animal its reaction, with respect to reproduction, to the environment is mediated via the nervous system (often by unknown pathways to the hypothalamus) and the hypophyseal portal system to the pituitary. Feedback mechanisms between pituitary and end organ involve the nervous system. Hormones, acting on the nervous system, may change the animal's behavior so that it migrates, advertises its presence by song or scent, defends its territory, and, eventually, mates successfully. Hormones may then again affect the nervous system to induce parental behavior, but, on the other hand, the presence of young may, via the nervous system, induce new endocrine secretions that are important for taking care of the young.

The synopsis given above shows the many interactions that occur, but, as we hope has been clear from the text, this is an oversimplification that only attempts to illustrate the general principles and does not indicate the many delicate balances.

REFERENCES

Adler, N., and Bermant, G. 1966. Sexual behavior of male rats: effects of reduced sensory feedback. J. Comp. Physiol. Psycho. *61*:240-243.

Åkerman, B. 1966a. Behavioural effects of electrical stimulation in the forebrain of the pigeon. I. Reproductive behaviour. Behaviour *26*:323-338.

Åkerman, B. 1966b. Behavioural effects of electrical stimulation in the forebrain of the pigeon. II. Protective behaviour. Behaviour *26*:339-350.

Aronson, L. R. 1957. Reproductive and parental behavior. *In* M. E. Brown (ed.): The Physiology of Fishes. Academic Press Inc., New York, Vol. 2, pp. 271-304.

Aronson, L. R. 1958. Hormones and reproductive behavior. Some phylogenetic considerations. *In* A. Gorbman (ed.): Comparative Endocrinology. John Wiley & Sons Inc., New York, pp. 98-120.

Aronson, L. R. 1965. Environmental stimuli altering the physiological condition of the individual among lower vertebrates. *In* F. A. Beach (ed.): Sex and Behavior. John Wiley & Sons Inc., New York, pp. 290-318.

Aronson, L. R., and Cooper, M. L. 1966. Seasonal variation in mating behavior in cats after desensitization of glans penis. Science *152*:226-230.

Aronson, L. R., and Cooper, M. L. 1967. Penile spines of the domestic cat, their endocrine-behavior relations. Anat. Rec. *157*:71-78.

Attramadal, A. 1964. The uptake and intracellular localization of oestradiol-17β.6.7-H^3 in the anterior pituitary and the hypothalamus of the rat. Acta Pathol. Microbiol. Scand. *61*:151-152 (abstract).

Baggerman, B. 1957. An experimental study on the timing of breeding and migration of the three-spined stickleback. Arch. Neerl. Zool. *12*:105-317.

Baggerman, B. 1959. The role of external factors and hormones in migration of sticklebacks and juvenile salmon. *In* A. Gorbman (ed.): Comparative Endocrinology. John Wiley & Sons Inc., New York, pp. 26-37.

Baggerman, B. 1966. On the endocrine control of reproductive behaviour in the male three-spined stickleback *(Gasterosteus aculeatus* L.). Symp. Soc. Exp. Biol. *20*:427-456.

Banks, E. M. 1962. Some aspects of sexual behavior in domestic sheep, *Ovis aries*. Behaviour *23*:249-279.

Barfield, R. J. 1964. Induction of copulatory behavior by intracranial placement of androgens in capons. Amer. Zool. *4*:301 (abstract).

Barfield, R. J. 1965a. Effects of preoptic lesions on the sexual behavior of male domestic fowl. Amer. Zool. *5*:686-687 (abstract).

Barfield, R. J. 1965b. Induction of aggressive and courtship behavior by intracerebral implants of androgen in capons. Amer. Zool. *5*:202 (abstract).

Barraclough, C. A. 1967. Modifications in reproductive function after exposure to hormones during the prenatal and early postnatal period. *In* L. Martini and W. F. Ganong (eds.): Neuroendocrinology. Academic Press Inc., New York, Vol. 2, pp. 61-99.

Bastock, M. 1967. The physiology of courtship and mating behaviour. Adv. Reprod. Physiol. *2*:9-51.

Bates, R. W., Miller, R. A., and Garrison, M. M. 1962. Evidence in the hypophysectomized pigeon of a synergism among prolactin, growth hormone, thyroxine and prednisone upon weight of the body, digestive tract, kidney and fat stores. Endocrinology *71*:345-360.

Beach, F. A. 1948. Hormones and Behavior. P. B. Hoeber, Inc., New York.

Beach, F. A. 1952. Effects of forebrain injury upon mating behavior in male pigeons. Behaviour *4*:36-59.

Beach, F. A. 1958. Evolutionary aspects of psychoendocrinology. *In* A. Roe and G. G. Simpson (eds.): Behavior and Evolution. Yale University Press, New Haven, pp. 81-103.

Beach, F. A. (ed): 1965. Sex and Behavior. John Wiley & Sons Inc., New York.

Beach, F. A. 1966. Ontogeny of "coitus-related" reflexes in the female guinea pig. Proc. Nat. Acad. Sci. *56*:526-532.

Beach, F. A. 1967. Cerebral and hormonal control of reflexive mechanisms involved in copulatory behavior. Physiol. Revs. *47*:289-316.

Beach, F. A., and Inman, N. G. 1965. Effects of castration and androgen replacement on mating in male quail. Proc. Natl. Acad. Sci. *54*:1426-1431.

Benoit, J. 1956. Etats physiologiques et instinct de reproduction chez les oiseaux. *In* P. P. Grassé (ed.): L'Instinct dans le Comportement des Animaux et de l'Homme. Masson et Cie., Paris. pp. 177-260.

Blüm, V., and Fiedler, K. 1964. Der Einfluss von Prolactin auf das Brutpflegeverhalten von Symphysodon aquifasciata axelrodi L. P. Schultz (Cichlidae, Teleostei). Naturwissensch. *51*:149-150.

Blüm, V., and Fiedler, K. 1965. Hormonal control of reproductive behavior in some cichlid fish. Gen. Comp. Endocrinol. *5*:185-196.

Brookhart, J. M., and Dey, F. L. 1941. Reduction of sexual behavior in male guinea pigs by hypothalamic lesions. Amer. J. Physiol. *133*:551-554.

Bunnell, B. N., Friel, J., and Flesher, C. K. 1966. Effects of median cortical lesions on the sexual behavior of the male hamster. J. Comp. Physiol. Psychol. *61*:492-495.

Caggiula, A. R., and Hoebel, B. G. 1966. "Copulation-reward site" in the posterior hypothalamus. Science *153*:1284-1285.

Carpenter, C. R. 1933. Psychological studies of social behavior in *Aves*. I. The effect of complete and incomplete gonadectomy on the primary sexual activity of the male pigeon. J. Comp. Psychol. *16*:25-57.

Clark, E. 1959. Functional hermaphroditism and self-fertilization in serranid fish. Science *129*:215-216.

Clegg, M. T., and Doyle, L. L. 1966. Role in reproductive physiology of afferent impulses from the genital and other regions. *In* L. Martini and W. F. Ganong (eds.): Neuroendocrinology. Academic Press Inc., New York, Vol. 2, pp. 1-17.

Clegg, M. T., and Ganong, W. F. 1960. The effect of hypothalamic lesions on ovarian function in the ewe. Endocrinology *67*:179-186.

Clegg, M. T., Santolucito, J. A., Smith, J. D., and Ganong, W. F. 1958. The effect of hypothalamic lesions on sexual behavior and estrous cycles in the ewe. Endocrinology. *62*:790-797.

Clemens, L. G., Wallen, K., and Gorski, R. A. 1967. Mating behavior: Facilitation in the female rat after cortical application of potassium chloride. Science *157*:1208-1209.

Collias, N. E. 1962. The behaviour of ducks. *In* E. S. E. Hafez (ed.): The Sexual Behaviour of Domestic Animals. Williams & Wilkins Co., Baltimore, pp. 565-585.

Cowie, A. T. 1966. Anterior pituitary function in lactation. *In* G. W. Harris and B. T. Donovan (eds.): The Pituitary Gland. University of California Press, Berkeley, Vol. 2, pp. 412-443.

Crawford, R. D., and Smyth, J. R., Jr. 1964a. Studies of the relationship between fertility and the gene for rose comb in the domestic fowl. 1. The relationship between comb genotype and fertility. Poultry Sci. *43*:1009-1017.

Crawford, R. D., and Smyth, J. R., Jr. 1964b. Studies of the relationship between fertility and the gene for rose comb in the domestic fowl. 2. The relationship between comb genotype and duration of fertility. Poultry Sci. *43*:1193-1199.

Crawford, R. D., and Smyth, J. R., Jr. 1965. The influence of comb genotype on mating behavior in the domestic fowl. Poultry Sci. *44*:115-122.

Davidson, J. M. 1966. Characteristics of sex behaviour in male rats following castration. Anim. Behav. *14*:266-272.

Davidson, J. M. 1966a. Activation of the male rat's sexual behavior by intracerebral implantation of androgen. Endocrinology *79*:783-794.

Davis, D. E. 1957. Aggressive behavior in castrated starlings. Science *126*:253.

Davis, D. E. 1963. The hormonal control of aggressive behavior. Proc. XIII Int. Ornithol. Congr. 994-1003.

Davis, D. E. 1964. The physiological analysis of aggressive behavior. *In* W. Etkin (ed.): Social Behavior and Organization Among Vertebrates. University of Chicago Press, Chicago, pp. 53-74.

Delgado, J. M. R. 1966. Aggressive behavior evoked by radio stimulation in monkey colonies. Amer. Zool. *6*:669-682.

Diamond, M. 1967. Androgen-induced masculinization in the ovariectomized and hysterectomized guinea pig. Anat. Rec. *157*:47-52.

Diamond, M., and Young, W. C. 1963. Differential responsiveness of pregnant and non-pregnant guinea pigs to the masculinizing action of testosterone propionate. Endocrinology *74*: 429-438.

Domm, L. V. 1939. Modifications in sex and secondary sexual characters in birds. Ed. 2. *In* E. Allen, C. H. Danforth, and E. A. Doisy (eds.): Sex and Internal Secretions. Williams & Wilkin Co., Baltimore, pp. 227-327.

Eisenfeld, A. J., and Axelrod, J. 1965. Selectivity of estrogen distribution in tissues. J. Pharmacol. Exp. Therap. *150*:469-475.

Eisenfeld, A. J., and Axelrod, J. 1966. Effect of steroid hormones, ovariectomy, estrogen pretreatment, sex and immaturity on the distribution of ^{3}H-estradiol. Endocrinology *79*:38-42.

Eisner, E. 1960. The relationship of hormones to the reproductive behaviour of birds, referring especially to parental behaviour: A review. Anim. Behav. *8*:155-179.

Eleftheriou, B. E., and Zolovick, A. J. 1966. Effect of amygdaloid lesions on oestrous behaviour in the deer mouse. J. Reprod. Fertil. *11*:451-453.

Endröczi, E., Lissák, K., Bata, G., Illey, J., and Tolnay, T. 1958. Beobachtungen über die endokrine and neurale Organisation des Sexualverhaltens an weiblichen Katzen. Endokrinologie *36*:13-23.

Etienne, A., and Fischer, H. 1964. Untersuchung über das Verhalten kastrierter Stockenten (Anas platyrhynchos L.) und dessen Beeinflussung durch Testosteron. Z. Tierpsychol. *21*:348-358.

Etkin, W. (ed.): 1964. Social Behavior and Organization Among Vertebrates. University of Chicago Press, Chicago.

Evans, L. T. 1956. Endocrine effects upon urodele hierarchies. Anat. Rec. *124*:400 (abstract).

Farner, D. S., and Follett, B. K. 1966. Light and other environmental factors affecting avian reproduction. J. Anim. Sci. *26* (suppl.):90-115.

Faure, J. M. A. 1964. Hormones in relation to sleep-wakefulness mechanisms. Proc. Soc. Int. Congr. Endocrinol. 606-611.

Faure, J., Vincent, J. D., and Bensch, C. 1966. "Sommeil paradoxal' et équilibre hormonal; interdépendances entre "sommeil paradoxal" et fonctions sexuelles. Rev. Neurol. *115*: 443-454.

Fiedler, K. 1962. Die Wirkung von Prolactin auf das Verhalten des Lippfisches *Crenilabrus ocellatus* (Forskål). Zool. Jb. (Allg. Zool.) *69*:609-620.

Fisher, A. E. 1956. Maternal and sexual behavior induced by intracranial chemical stimulation. Science *124*:228-229.

Fisher, A. E. 1964. Chemical stimulation of the brain. Sci. Amer. *210(6)*:60-68.

Gibson, W. R., and Nalbandov, A. V. 1966a. Lipid mobilization in obese hypophysectomized cockerels. Amer. J. Physiol. *211*:1345-1351.

Gibson, W. R., and Nalbandov, A. V. 1966b. Lipolysis and lipogenesis in liver and adipose tissue of hypophysectomized cockerels. Amer. J. Physiol. *211*:1352-1356.

Gilbert, A. B., and Wood-Gush, D. G. M. 1965. The control of the nesting behaviour of the domestic hen. III The effect of cocaine in the post-ovulatory follicle. Anim. Behav. *13*:284-285.

Glascock, R. F., and Michael, R. P. 1962. The localization of oestrogen in a neurological system in the brain of the female cat. J. Physiol. *163*: 38P-39P.

Goy, R. W. 1966. Role of androgens in the establishment and regulation of behavioral sex differences in mammals. J. Anim. Sci. *25* (suppl.): 21-31.

Goy, R. W., and Phoenix, C. H. 1963. Hypothalamic regulation of female sexual behaviour: establishment of behavioural oestrus in spayed guinea-pigs following hypothalamic lesion. J. Reprod. Fertil. *5*:23-40.

Goy, R. W., Phoenix, C. H., and Meidinger, R. 1967. Postnatal development of sensitivity to estrogen and androgen in male, female and pseudo-hermaphroditic guinea pigs. Anat. Rec. *157*: 87-96.

Grant, W. C., Jr. 1966. Endocrine induced courtship in three species of European newts. Amer. Zool. *6*:585 (abstract).

Green, J. D., Clemente, C. D., and de Groot, J. 1957. Rhinencephalic lesions and behavior in cats: An analysis of the Klüver-Bucy syndrome with particular reference to normal and abnormal sexual behavior. J. Comp. Neurol. *108*:505-536.

Guhl, A. M. 1961. Gonadal hormones and social behavior in infra human vertebrates. *In* W. C. Young (ed.): Sex and Internal Secretions. Williams & Wilkins Co., Baltimore, Vol. 2, 1240-1267.

Guhl, A. M. 1962. The behaviour of chickens. *In* E. S. E. Hafez (ed.): The Behaviour of Domestic Animals. Williams & Wilkins Co., Baltimore, pp. 491-530.

Guhl, A. M., Collias, N. E., and Allee, W. C. 1945. Mating behavior and the social hierarchy in small flocks of White Leghorn. Physiol. Zool. *18*:365-390.

Guhl, A. M., Craig, J. V., and Mueller, C. D. 1960. Selective breeding for aggressiveness in chickens. Poultry Sci. *39*:970-980.

Hafez, E. S. E. (ed.): 1962. The Behaviour of Domestic Animals. Williams & Wilkins Co., Baltimore.

Hale, E. B. 1956. Effects of forebrain lesions on the aggressive behavior of green sunfish Lepomis cyanellus. Physiol. Zool. *29*:107-125.

Hale, E. B., and Schein, M. W. 1962. The behaviour of turkeys. *In* E. S. E. Hafez (ed.): The Behaviour of Domestic Animals. Williams & Wilkins Co., Baltimore, pp. 531-564.

Hamburg, D. A. 1966. Effects of progestrone on behavior. Res. Publ. Ass. Nerv. Ment. Dis. *43*:251-263.

Hart, B. L. 1967. Testosterone regulation of sexual reflexes in spinal male rats. Science *155*:1283-1284.

Hart, B. L., and Kitchell, R. L. 1966. Penile erection and contraction of penile muscles in the spinal and intact dog. Amer. J. Physiol. *210*:257-262.

Heimer, L., and Larsson, K. 1967a. Mating behavior of male rats after olfactory bulb lesions. Physiol. Behav. *2*:207-209.

Heimer, L., and Larsson, K. 1967b. Impairment of mating behavior in male rats following lesions in the preoptic anterior hypothalamic continuum. Brain Res. *3*:248-263.

Hoar, W. S. 1962a. Hormones and the reproductive behaviour of the three-spined stickleback, *Gasterosteus aculeatus*. Anim. Behav. *10*:247-266.

Hoar, W. S. 1962b. Reproductive behavior of fish. Gen. Comp. Endocrinol. Suppl. *1*:206-216.

Höhn, E. O., and Cheng, S. C. 1967. Gonadal hormones in Wilson's phalarope *(Steganopus tricolor)* and other birds in relation to plumage and sex behavior. Gen. Comp. Endocrinol. *8*:1-11.

Johnson, J. I., Goy, R. W., and Michels, K. M. 1962. Physiological mechanisms and behaviour patterns. *In* E. S. E. Hafez (ed.): The Behaviour of Domestic Animals. Williams & Wilkins Co., Baltimore, pp. 139-179.

Kato, J., and Villee, C. A. 1967a. Preferential uptake of estradiol by the anterior hypothalamus of the rat. Endocrinology. *80*:567-575.

Kato, J., and Villee, C. A. 1967b. Factors affecting uptake of estradiol-6-7-H³ by the hypophysis and hypothalamus. Endocrinology *80*:1133-1138.

Kim, C. 1960. Sexual activity of male rats following ablation of hippocampus. J. Comp. Physiol. Psychol. *53*:553-557.

King, J. R. 1961. On the regulation of vernal premigratory fattening in the white-crowned sparrow. Physiol. Zool. *34*:145-157.

King, J. R. 1967. Photoregulation of food intake and fat metabolism in relation to avian sexual cycles. Coll. Int. C.N.R.S. "La Photorégulation de la reproduction chez les oiseaux et les mammifères". In Press.

King, J. R., and Farner, D. S. 1963. The relationship of fat deposition to Zugunruhe and migration. Condor *65*:200-223.

King, J. R., and Farner, D. S. 1965. Studies of fat deposition in migratory birds. Ann. N. Y. Acad. Sci. *131*(1):422-440.

Kling, A. 1962. Amygdalectomy in the kitten. Science *137*:429-430.

Komisaruk, B. R. 1965. Localization in brain of reproductive behavior responses to progesterone in ring doves. Amer. Zool. *5*:687 (abstract).

Kovach, J. K. 1967. Maternal behavior in the domestic cock under the influence of alcohol. Science *156*:835-836.

Larsson, K. 1962. Mating behavior in male rats after cerebral cortex ablation. I Effects of lesions in the dorsolateral and the median cortex. J. Exp. Zool. *151*:167-176.

Larsson, K. 1964. Mating behavior in male rats after cerebral cortex ablation. II Effects of lesions in the frontal lobes compared to lesions in the posterior half of the hemispheres. J. Exp. Zool. *155*:203-214.

Larsson, K., and Heimer, L. 1964. Mating behaviour of male rats after lesions in the preoptic area. Nature *202*:413-414.

Law, T., and Meagher, W. 1958. Hypothalamic lesions and sexual behavior in the female rat. Science *128*:1626-1627.

Lehrman, D. S. 1958. Effect of female sex hormones on incubation behavior in the ring dove *(Streptopelia risoria)*. J. Comp. Physiol. Psychol. *51*:142-145.

Lehrman, D. S. 1961. Hormonal regulation of parental behavior in birds and infra human mammals. *In* W. C. Young (ed.): Sex and Internal Secretions. Williams & Wilkins Co., Baltimore, Vol. 2, pp. 1268-1382.

Lehrman, D. S. 1965. Interaction between internal and external environments in the regulation of the reproductive cycle of the ring dove. *In* F. A. Beach (ed.): Sex and Behavior. John Wiley & Sons Inc., New York, pp. 355-380.

Levine, S., and Mullins, R. F., Jr. 1966. Hormonal influences on brain organization in infant rats. Science *152*:1585-1592.

Licht, P. 1967. Interaction of prolactin and gonadotropins on appetite, growth, and tail regeneration in the lizard *Anolis carolinensis*. Gen. Comp. Endocrinol. *9*:49-63.

Liley, N. R. 1965. The role of the gonad in the control of sexual behavior in the female guppy, *Poecilia reticulata*. Amer. Zool. *5*:686 (abstract).

Lisk, R. D. 1966. Increased sexual behavior in male rat following lesions in the mamillary region. J. Exp. Zool. *161*:129-136.

Lisk, R. D. 1967. Sexual behavior: hormonal control. *In* L. Martini and W. F. Ganong (eds.): Neuroendocrinology. Academic Press Inc., New York, Vol. 2, pp. 197-239.

Lisk, R. D., and Suydam, A. J. 1967. Sexual behavior patterns in the prepubertally castrated rat. Anat. Rec. *157*:181-190.

Lissák, K. 1962. Olfactory-induced sexual behavior in female cats. Proc. 22nd Int. Physiol. Congr. Leiden *1(pt. 2)*:653-656.

Lofts, B., and Marshall, A. J. 1960. The experimental regulation of *Zugunruhe* and the sexual cycle in the brambling, *Fringilla montifringilla*. Ibis *102*:209-214.

Lofts, B., Marshall, A. J., and Wolfson, A. 1963. The experimental demonstration of premigratory activity in the absence of fat deposition in birds. Ibis *105*:99-105.

Lorenzen, L. C., and Farner, D. S. 1964. An annual cycle in the interrenal tissue of the adrenal gland of the white-crowned sparrow, *Zonotrichia leucophrys gambelii*. Gen. Comp. Endocrinol. *4*:253-263.

Lott, D. F. 1966. Effect of preoptic lesions on the sexual behavior of male rats. J. Comp. Physiol. Psychol. *61*:284-291.

McDaniel, G. R., and Craig, J. V. 1959. Behavior traits, semen measurements and fertility of White Leghorn males. Poultry Sci. *38*:1005-1014.

McGill, T. E., and Tucker, G. R. 1964. Genotype and sex drive in intact and in castrated male mice. Science *145*:514-515.

MacLean, P. D. 1963. Some neuroanatomic and neurophysiologic correlates of sexual functions. *In* A. V. Nalbandov (ed.): Advances in Neuroendocrinology. University of Illinois Press, Urbana, pp. 21-27.

MacLean, P. D. 1966. Studies on the cerebral representation of certain basic sexual functions. *In* R. A. Gorski and R. E. Whalen (eds.): Brain and Behavior. The Brain and Gonadal Function. U.C.L.A. Forum Med. Sci. Ill. University of California Press, Los Angeles, pp. 35-79.

Marler, P., and Hamilton, W. J., III. 1966. Mechanisms of Animal Behavior. John Wiley & Sons Inc., New York.

Mason, J. W., Brady, J. V., and Tolson, W. W. 1966. Behavioral adaptations and endocrine activity. Psychoendocrine differentiation of emotional states. Res. Publ. Ass. Nerv. Ment. Dis. *43*: 227-248.

Mathewson, S. F. 1961. Gonadotrophic hormones affect aggressive behavior in starlings. Science *134*:1522-1523.

Medawar, P. B. 1953. Some immunological and endocrinological problems raised by the evolution of viviparity in vertebrates. Symp. Soc. Exp. Biol. *7*:320-338.

Meier, A. H., and Davis, K. B. 1967. Diurnal variations of the fattening response to prolactin in the white throated sparrow, *Zonotrichia albicollis*. Gen. Comp. Endocrinol. *8*:110-114.

Meier, A. H., and Farner, D. S. 1964. A possible endocrine basis for premigratory fattening in the white-crowned sparrow, *Zonotrichia leucophrys gambelii* (nuttall). Gen Comp. Endocrinol. *4*: 584-595.

Meier, A. H., Davis, K. B., and Dusseau, J. 1966. P olactin and the antigonadal response in the migratory white-throated sparrow. Amer. Zool. *6*:312 (abstract).

Meier, A. H., Farner, D. S., and King, J. R. 1965. A possible endocrine basis for migratory behaviour in the white-crowned sparrow, *Zonotrichia leucophrys gambelii*. Anim. Behav. *13*:453-465.

Michael, R. P. 1962. The selective accumulation of estrogens in the neural and genital tissues of the cat. Proc. First Int. Congr. Horm. Steroids *2*: 469-481.

Michael, R. P. 1966a. Action of hormones on the cat brain. *In* R. A. Gorski and R. E. Whalen (eds.): Brain and Behavior. U.C.L.A. Forum Med. Sci. III. University of California Press, Los Angeles, Vol. 3, pp. 81-98.

Michael, R. P. 1966b. The affinity of the neonatal rat brain for gonadal hormone. Anim. Behav. *14*: 584 (abstract).

Michal, E. K. 1966. Effects of lesions in limbic system on courtship and mating behavior of male rats. Diss. Abstr. *26*:7464.

Miller, N. E. 1957. Experiments on motivation. Science *126*:1271-1278.

Morton, M. L., and Mewaldt, L. R. 1962. Some effects of castration on a migratory sparrow (*Zonotrichia atricapilla*). Physiol. Zool. *35*:237-247.

Noble, G. K., and Borne, R. 1941. The effect of forebrain lesions on the sexual and fighting behavior of *Betta splendens* and other fishes. Anat. Rec. Suppl. *79*:49 (abstract).

Noble, G. K., and Wurm, M. 1940. The effect of testosterone propionate in the black crowned night heron. Endocrinology *26*:837-850.

Olds, J. 1962. Hypothalamic substrates of reward. Physiol. Revs. *42*:554-604.

Orcutt, F. S. 1965. Estrogen stimulation of nest material cutting in the immature peach-faced love bird (*Agapornis roseicollis*). Amer. Zool. *5*:197 (abstract).

Palen, G. F., and Goddard, G. V. 1966. Catnip and oestrous behaviour in the cat. Anim. Behav. *14*:372-377.

Palka, Y. S., and Sawyer, C. H. 1966. The effects of hypothalamic implants of ovarian steroids on oestrous behaviour in rabbits. J. Physiol. *185*: 251-269.

Phillips, R. E., and McKinney, F. 1962. The role of testosterone in the displays of some ducks. Anim. Behav. *10*:244-246.

Phoenix, C. H., Goy, R. W., and Young, W. C. 1967. Sexual behavior: general aspects. *In* L. Martini and W. F. Ganong (eds.): Neuroendocrinology. Academic Press Inc., New York, Vol. 2, pp. 163-196.

Pickford, G. E., and Atz, J. A. 1957. The Physiology of the Pituitary Gland of Fishes. New York Zool. Soc., New York.

Putkonen, P. T. S. 1967. Electrical stimulation of the avian brain. Ann Acad. Sci. Fennicae, Series A V Medica 130.

Resko, J. A., Goy, R. W., and Phoenix, C. H. 1967. Uptake and distribution of exogenous testosterone-1,2-³H in neural and genital tissues of the castrated guinea pig. Endocrinology 80:490-498.

Richards, M. P. M. 1967. Maternal behaviour in rodents and lagomorphs. Adv. Reprod. Physiol. 2:53-110.

Riddle, O. 1963. Prolactin in vertebrates function and organization. J. Nat. Cancer Inst. 31: 1039-1110.

Robinson, B. W., and Mishkin, M. 1966. Ejaculation evoked by stimulation of the preoptic area in the monkey. Physiol. Behav. 1:269-272.

Rosenblatt, J. S. 1965. Effects of experience on sexual behavior in male cats. In F. A. Beach (ed.): Sex and Behavior. John Wiley & Sons Inc., New York, pp. 416-439.

Rosenblatt, J. S. 1967. Nonhormonal basis of maternal behavior in the rat. Science 156:1512-1514.

Ruf, K., and Steiner, F. A. 1967. Steroid-sensitive single neurons in rat hypothalamus and midbrain: Identification by microelectrophoresis. Science 156:667-669.

Sawyer, C. H. 1959. Effect of brain lesions on estrous behavior and refexogenous ovulation in the rabbit. J. Exp. Zool. 142:227-246.

Sawyer, C. H. 1963. Induction of estrus in the ovariectomized cat by local hypothalamic treatment with estrogen. Anat. Rec. 145:280 (abstract).

Sawyer, C. H., and Kawakami, M. 1961. Interactions between the central nervous system and hormones influencing ovulation. In C. A. Villee (ed.): Control of Ovulation. Pergamon Press, New York, pp. 79-97.

Sawyer, C. H., Kawakami, M., and Kanematsu, S. 1966. Neuroendocrine aspects of reproduction. Res. Publ. Ass. Nerv. Ment. Dis. 43:59-84.

Schein, M. W., and Hale, E. B. 1965. Stimuli eliciting sexual behavior. In F. A. Beach (ed.): Sex and Behavior. John Wiley & Sons, New York, pp. 440-482.

Schein, M. W., and Hart, F. N. 1962. Male sexual behavior induced in female turkeys by brain stimulation. Amer. Zool. 2:555-556 (abstract).

Schreiner, L., and Kling, A. 1953. Behavioral changes following rhinencephalic injury in the cat. J. Neurophysiol. 16:643-659.

Schreiner, L., and Kling, A. 1956. Rhinencephalon and Behavior. Amer. J. Physiol. 184:486-490.

Schwartz, A. S., and Whalen, R. E. 1965. Amygdala activity during sexual behavior in the male cat. Life Sci. 4:1359-1366.

Scott, J. P. 1966. Agonistic behavior of mice and rats: a review. Amer. Zool. 6:683-701.

Segaar, J., and Nieuwenhuys, R. 1963. New ethophysiological experiments with male Gasterosteus aculeatus, with an anatomical comment. Anim. Behav. 11:331-344.

Shealy, C. N., and Peele, T. L. 1957. Studies on the amygdaloid nucleus of the cat. J. Neurophysiol. 20:125-139.

Siegel, P. B. 1965. Genetics of behavior: Selection for mating ability in chickens. Genetics 52:1269-1277.

Smith, R. J. F., and Hoar, W. S. 1967. The effects of prolactin and testosterone on the parental behaviour of the male stickleback Gasterosteus aculeatus. Anim. Behav. 15:342-352.

Souiairac, M. L. 1963. Etude expérimentale des régulations hormono-nerveuses du comportement sexuel du rat mâle. Ann. Endocrinol. 24 (suppl.):1-98.

Summers, T. B., and Kaebler, W. W. 1962. Amygdalectomy: effects in cats and a survey of its present status. Amer. J. Physiol. 203:1117-1119.

Tavolga, W. N. 1955. Effects of gonadectomy and hypophysectomy on prespawning behavior in males of the gobiid fish Bathygobius soporator. Physiol. Zool. 28:218-232.

Vandenbergh, J. G. 1964. The effects of photoperiod on testicular activity and aggressive behavior of starlings. J. Exp. Zool. 156:323-330.

van Tienhoven, A., and Cole, R. K. 1962. Endocrine disturbances in obese chickens. Anat. Rec. 142:111-122.

Vaughan, E., and Fisher, A. E. 1962. Male sexual behavior induced by intracranial electrical stimulation. Science 137:759-760.

Vivien, J. 1941. Contribution à l'étude de la physiologie hypophysaire dans ses relations avec l'appareil génital, la thyroïde et les corps suprarénaux chez les poissons sélaciens et téléostéens, Scylliorhinus canicula et Gobius paganellus. Bull. biol. France et Belg. 75: 257-309.

Vowles, D. M., and Harwood, D. 1966. The effect of exogenous hormones on aggressive and defensive behaviour in the ring dove (Streptopelia risoria). J. Endocrinol. 36:35-51.

Whalen, R. E., and Edwards, D. A. 1966. Sexual reversibility in neonatally castrated male rats. J. Comp. Physiol. Psychol. 62:307-310.

Wilhelmi, A., Pickford, G. E., and Sawyer, W. 1955. Initiation of the spawning reflex response in Fundulus by the administration of fish and mammalian neurohypophysial preparations and synthetic oxytocin. Endocrinology 57:243-252.

Wolfson, A. 1966. Environmental and neuroendocrine regulation of annual gonadal cycles and migratory behavior in birds. Recent Progr. Hormone Res. 22:177-239.

Wood, C. D. 1958. Behavioral changes following discrete lesions of temporal lobe structures. Neurology 8:215-220.

Wood-Gush, D. G. M. 1957. Aggression and sexual activity in the brown Leghorn cock. Brit. J. Anim. Behav. 5:1-6.

Wood-Gush, D. G. M. 1963. The control of the

nesting behaviour of the domestic hen. I. The role of the oviduct. Anim. Behav. *11*:293-299.

Wood-Gush, D. G. M., and Gilbert, A. B. 1964. The control of the nesting behaviour of the domestic hen. II. The role of the ovary. Anim. Behav. *12*:451-453.

Wood-Gush, D. G. M., and Osborne, R. 1956. A study of differences in the sex drive of cockerels. Brit. J. Anim. Behav. *4*:102-110.

Young, W. C. 1961. The hormones and mating behavior. *In* W. C. Young (ed.): Sex and Internal Secretions. Williams & Wilkins Co., Baltimore, Vol. 2, pp. 1173-1239.

Young, W. C. 1964. The hormones and behavior. *In* M. Florkin and H. S. Mason (eds.): Comparative Biochemistry. Academic Press Inc., New York, Vol. 7, pp. 203-251.

Appendix

The amounts of FSH, LH, and prolactin present in pituitaries and body fluids are determined by bioassay methods. A bioassay, to be of greatest value, should meet the following criteria:

a. It should be specific for the hormone under consideration and there should be a minimal interference by other hormones on the response.

b. It should have minimal variability in relation to the slope. The numerical value used to express this relationship is the index of precision. The smaller the index of precision, the more precise the assay and the fewer the animals required to carry it out, and thus the smaller the total amounts of tissue or fluid required for a satisfactory assay (Bliss, 1952).

Siegel and Siegel (1964a,b) demonstrated that the precision of bioassays for PMSG, FSH, or LH in which chicks were used could be increased considerably if the analyses were made on an intrasire basis. The differences among sire families were significant and of sufficient importance to take into account. Thus one could reduce the variability of the assays by selecting the sires on the basis of the response of their progeny in a sire test. It would be of interest to determine whether such selections in mammalian populations used for bioassays would have similar effects of reducing the index of precision. The specific bioassays used by Siegel and Siegel (1964a,b) will not be discussed

further because the responses were not specific for the hormones used.

c. The bioassay should have a fairly large range of doses over which the response is linear; there should be either a linear dose response or a linear log dose response relationship. Most of the bioassays in endocrinological experiments have a linear log dose response.

d. Preferably, the bioassay should be simple and subject to routine procedures.

e. The assay should be repeatable from laboratory to laboratory if carried out by competent personnel.

f. It is preferable that the assay involves the measurement of the response in a target organ (e.g. in the ovary in gonadotropin assays) rather than the response of a secondary organ (e.g. uterine weight in a gonadotropin assay). The response of the secondary organ often makes the response nonspecific; e.g. estrogen can also cause a response in the uterus, and thus, for example in a plasma bioassay one may need to remove the estrogens or other contaminants.

For FSH, the tests most frequently used are:

1. The Steelman-Pohley (1953) test in which immature female rats are pretreated with 20 I.U. HCG and FSH for three days and the ovarian weight is measured 72 hours after the first injection. The assay will detect 0.10 mg. FSH; the index of precision is between 0.100 and

467

0.136 if injections are made twice daily and between 0.102 and 0.201 if injections are made once daily. The higher index of precision is obtained with porcine FSH (Parlow and Reichert, 1963). The assay is not affected by additon of either TSH, LH, prolactin, ACTH or growth hormone (Steelman and Pohley, 1953). The dose range over which the assay is effective is small, 0.1 to 0.2 mg. FSH.

2. Gans and van Rees (1966) used immature hypophysectomized male rats, removed the right testis, and weighed it. After this, 20 I.U. HCG was injected and FSH was administered once a day for six days. The weight of the left testis was determined and the difference between the weight of left and right testis was used in the statistical analysis. With this method, a total dose of 45 μg. FSH per rat was detected; the index of precision varied between 0.145 and 0.251. The response was not altered by the presence of either LH, prolactin, TSH, growth hormone, or ACTH. The serum of hypophysectomized males and females gave a response in one of two experiments. The assay method needs further testing.

3. Igarashi and McCann (1964) injected the test material together with 0.25 or 0.1 I.U. HCG into intact immature mice for three days. On the fourth day the uterine weight without fluid was determined. A linear log dose response was found between 0.4 and 50.0 μg. FSH. The minimal effective dose of FSH (ovine) was 2.0 μg. As much as 6 μg. of LH did not affect the test, but 10 μg. sometimes reduced the response to FSH. LH (20 to 200 μg.), or ACTH (10 mU.), or TSH (200 mU.), or growth hormone (200 mU.), or prolactin (200 mU.) did not give a response. The index of precision was 0.337 if 0.25 I.U. of HCG, and 0.307 if 0.1 I.U. of HCG, was used.

This test, in the hands of other investigators (de Reviers and Mauléon, 1965), has given positive responses to LH (0.625 and 2.5 μg.), prolactin (25 to 400 mU.),

and growth hormone (2.5 to 80 μg.) in three different strains of mice tested, thus making the test nonspecific.

4. Lamond and Bindon (1966) have proposed that uterine weights be determined in immature mice injected five hours after hypophysectomy with 4.5 I.U. HCG and the substance under investigation. This test can detect about 3 μg. of FSH; the index of precision was 0.20 and LH addition to the FSH did not interfere with the assay. This test is new and needs further investigation to determine its usefulness. The hypophysectomy of large numbers of mice may make it too difficult for routine assay procedures. If PMSG is injected after hypophysectomy the mice can be used 24 hours later instead of five hours after the operation.

LH ASSAYS

1. The ovarian ascorbic acid depletion (OAAD) test, or the Parlow test, in which 29 to 30-day-old rats are treated with 50 I.U. PMSG followed 56 to 65 hours later by 25 I.U. HCG. Six to nine days later the rats are injected with LH and the ascorbic acid concentration in the ovary is determined. One can remove one ovary and use it as the control value for each rat or one can use a group of rats injected with saline to obtain the control value. Adjusting the ascorbic acid to the same ovarian weight by covariance analysis increases the precision (reduces the index of precision) of the experiment (Sakiz and Guillemin, 1963).

The strain or rats used determines both the precision and the sensitivity of the assay (Yokota et al. 1965). Holtzmann rats are more sensitive and yield a lower index of precision than Wistar rats, but by genetic selection the sensitivity and index of precision can be improved within the Wistar strain. Pelletier (1963), by the use of 23-day-old rats, 30 I.U. PMSG, and interval of 70 hours between PMSG and HCG injections, and by killing the rats three hours after the LH injection obtained an index of precision of 0.228 with one strain of Wistar rats and could detect a dose of 0.4 μg. of LH.

Novella et al. (1965) found that injection of 1 mg./day trifluoperazine (TFP) for three days prior to the assay increased the sensitivity of the assay so that with this treatment 0.2 μg. LH could be detected, whereas without the TFP (in the same experiment) 2.4 μg. LH did not give a significant response.

Guillemin and Sakiz (1963) established that hypophysectomized rats could also be used provided they received prolactin. Such rats are useful for making a distinction between LH and LHRF; the former should give a response in intact and in hypophysectomized rats, the latter should give a response only in intact rats.

The response has also been obtained with starch gel which has been subjected to electrophoresis (Gibson et al., 1965) demonstrating that care must be taken with interpreting results obtained with this method if tissue or body fluids are subjected to purification procedures.

2. The increase in ventral prostate weight of hypophysectomized male rats has been used to measure LH activity. This test is not as sensitive as the OAAD test when the comparison between the tests is made with ovine LH preparation, but there are no differences between the two tests if LH of the urine of men, postmenopausal women, or of castrated men is used (Rosemberg et al.,1964). FSH can interfere with this LH assay (Parlow and Reichert, 1963). The assay has a precision of 0.13 (Albert et al., 1965).

3. The rat hyperemia tests in which immature rats are injected with radioiodinated serum albumin to label the blood and two hours later with LH. The ovaries are removed 15 minutes later and the amount of I^{131} is determined. The method can detect between 0.5 and 1.0 μg. of LH, the log dose response is linear between 0.5 and 2.0 μg., and the index of

precision is 0.14. FSH, if present in large amounts, affects the slope of the log dose response line. Prolactin has no effect (Ellis, 1961). According to Parlow and Reichert (1963) the sensitivity of this assay is about 0.4 of that of the OAAD test and the index of precision is 0.29. Reichert (1966) found that the hyperemia test gave a value four to six times higher for human LH when compared with the ovine LH standard rather than the OAAD test. For bovine, porcine, and equine LH, the ratio of potencies determined by hyperemia and OAAD test were close to one. The higher value for human LH may be the result of the fact that human LH has a longer half life than the other luteinizing hormones (Reichert, 1966).

4. Bell et al. (1964) and Mukerji et al. (1965) have published an ovarian cholesterol depletion test which is very sensitive and can detect 0.06 to 0.3 picogram of LH; prolactin, ACTH, and TSH do not interfere with the response; the index of precision is above 0.35, generally. Other workers have not been able to use this test successfully (Heald and Furnival, 1966; Skosey and Goldstein, 1966) probably because of diurnal variations in cholesterol content of the ovaries. Clark and Zarrow (1966) used rats treated with either 0.5 or 1.25 mg. testosterone propionate at two days of age. The 0.5 mg. dose allowed detection of 0.03 μg. of LH but it did not eliminate the variability in cholesterol content; the dose of 1.25 mg. testosterone propionate lowered the sensitivity of the test so that the lowest detectable dose was 0.25 μg.; however, the index of precision was 0.17 and diurnal variation in cholesterol content was eliminated.

5. The test of repair of interstitial cells of the ovary of hypophysectomized immature female rats. This assay depends on an all or none response which usually requires a large number of animals for each dose of LH tested in order to make the assay statistically valid.

6. The African weaver finch test. In

this assay, abdominal and subtail feathers are plucked from sexually quiescent males or females which may be intact or castrated. The test material is injected in two doses, subcutaneously, five days after removal of the feathers. A positive test is indicated by the presence of a black bar on the new feathers. The response is obtained with LH, PMS, or HCG. Doses of 5 μg. LH/bird or 30 I.U. HCG/bird can be detected (Segal, 1957). FSH does not give a response nor does it affect the response to LH (Witschi 1955). According to Witschi (1955), finches from the genera *Euplectes, Steganura,* and *Quelea* can be used for this assay, whereas Ortman (1966) found *Steganura paradisea* unsatisfactory. The test has disadvantages for quantitative assays similar to the interstitial repair test.

7. Radiophosphate uptake by testes of baby chicks is enhanced by LH. The method can detect 0.5 to 1.0 μg. of LH if the material is injected intracardially (Florsheim et al., 1959) and 1.0 μg. if injected subcutaneously (Breneman et al., 1962). The index of precision according to Breneman is 0.20, but others have not been able to obtain this (van Tienhoven et al., 1965) although a good agreement among indices of precision were found when PMSG was used instead of LH. The response is not specific for LH because FSH also augments P^{32} uptake (Breneman et al., 1962; Florsheim et al., 1959; van Tienhoven et al., 1965) as does thyroxine (Florsheim et al., 1959; van Tienhoven et al., 1965).

PROLACTIN ASSAYS

The determination of prolactin activity needs to be defined in terms of the response and the classes of vertebrates used. Nicoll et al. (1966) have investigated this problem and their main conclusions can be summarized as follows:

1. The "eft water drive" response is marked by the migration of young salamanders to seek water, a behavior which normally occurs only in breeding salamanders. (Water is the only medium in which mating and egg laying occurs successfully [Gorbman and Bern, 1962]). The only mammalian hormone that causes this activity is prolactin. This hormonal activity is found in the pituitaries of all vertebrates except, possibly, cyclostomes, although the latter have not been investigated thoroughly.

2. Hypophysectomized euryhaline fishes (e.g. *Fundulus heteroclitus, Poecilia latipinna*) do not survive in fresh water unless they receive hormone injections. The only mammalian hormone which has the property to maintain these fish in fresh water is prolactin. The activity has been found also in some teleosts, and in Dipnoans, amphibia, reptiles, and birds.

3. Stimulation of the pigeon crop gland (see page 163) can be obtained with pituitaries from Dipnoans, amphibia, reptiles, birds, and mammals.

4. Stimulation of the mammary gland has been obtained with pituitaries from amphibia, reptiles, and birds.

5. Maintenance of the corpus luteum of rats and mice has been obtained with pituitaries from mammals, although avian pituitaries may also have this property.

For bioassay purposes, the pigeon crop gland stimulation, the mammary gland stimulation, and luteotropic activity have been used; in addition to these, an effect on a testicular enzyme of the rat has been employed.

The main procedures used and responses obtained are:

1. A sensitive specific method for prolactin bioassay is the one proposed by Grosvenor and Turner (1958). Pigeons *(Columba livia)* between 240 to 360 gm. are kept in a room maintained at 31 to 32° C. An intradermal injection of 0.1 ml. test solution is made four times, at 24 hour intervals, in the same area. The birds are killed 24 hours after the last injection and the crop sac is taken out; it is then stretched over a light and the size is estimated with

the aid of a series of discs which differ by 0.5 cm. in diameter. The crop gland on the two sides can be injected with different solutions so that each pigeon yields two observations. The test can detect 0.0144 I.U. of prolactin; the log dose response is linear between 0.0144 and 0.448 I.U.; the index of precision is 0.11.

2. In the systemic pigeon crop assay test (Bates et al., 1963) prolactin is injected once daily for four or seven days into adult pigeons and the crops are weighed the day after the last injection. By the use of adult birds, indices of precision of between 0.046 and 0.206 provided crop glands weigh less than ten grams. The total dose which can be detected by this method is between 2 to 4 I.U. per pigeon, and thus the sensitivity is considerably less than for the intradermal assay. With juvenile pigeons the index of precision is between 0.127 and 0.389, so the number of pigeons required is considerably higher than when adult pigeons are used.

3. Wolthuis (1963a,b) has proposed an assay based on a direct effect on the corpus luteum. Immature (three-week-old) female rats were hypophysectomized and received daily injections of 10 I.U. HCG and 10 I.U. PMSG daily for ten days. From the fifth through the eleventh day after hypophysectomy the rats received prolactin. The rats were killed, corpora lutea with a connective tissue center and a radial structure were selected, and the corpus luteum cell nuclei per unit of surface were counted. The higher dose of prolactin the smaller the number of corpus luteum cell nuclei per unit of surface. The addition of growth hormone, TSH, ACTH, FSH, or LH did not effect the response. Unfortunately, the author does not give the index of precision and does not state what the smallest detectable dose is. The data show that a total dose of 0.50 I.U. prolactin per rat can be detected.

4. Kovačić (1962) used the prolongation of diestrus in mature mice. The percentages of positive responses were transformed into probits for statistical analysis of the data. The response was linear over a range of 0.620 to 2.5 I.U. of prolactin. The index of precision was 0.2 to 0.25. The assay is not specific and can be used only for purified preparations.

5. Kovačić (1964, 1965) employed the decidual response of adult, female mice hypophysectomized on the first day of diestrus and injected with the hormone immediately after operation and each day thereafter for four days. On day 3 the right uterine horn was damaged and the animals were killed on day 6. The increase in weight of the damaged horn over that of the undamaged horn was used in the statistical assay. The ovaries of these mice were also examined histologically. A decidual response was obtained with ovine prolactin, human LH, HCG, and PMSG. Hypertrophy of luteal cells was observed after injections of ovine prolactin, human LH, human and bovine growth hormone, and bovine TSH. The assay is therefore not specific, but may be usable for purified preparations. For the deciduomata test the index of precision was between 0.09 and 0.22. The method can detect approximately 1.4 I.U. of prolactin.

6. Evans (1966) has published a sensitive method which is simple and because of its low variability requires few animals. One adult rat is sufficient! The testes of an adult rat are removed, homogenized in Krebs-Ringer-bicarbonate at pH = 6.9 – 7.3, and incubated for 30 minutes at 34° C. The homogenates is centrifuged at 4000 g. for five minutes, the residue is retained and resuspended in fresh buffer so that it contains 0.10 to 0.15 g./ml. The hormone is added, 0.1 ml. in 0.001 N HCl per 0.5 ml. homogenate. The medium plus homogenate is gassed with 95 percent O_2, 5 percent CO_2, and incubated at 34° C. for 2 to 3 hours. At the end of incubation 0.05 ml. 1 M ammonium acetate (pH = 4.3) is added, the homogenate centrifuged at 2000 g. for two minutes. The material is filtered 0.2 ml., filtrate is incubated with 1.0 ml.

phenolphthalein glucuronide (250 μg./ml.) in 0.1 M. ammonium acetate buffer (pH = 4.2 to 4.5) at 37° C. for 1.5 hours and 2 ml. glycine buffer is added to develop the color. Optical density is determined at 550 mμ. The index of precision is 0.03 to 0.05. The method can detect 0.320 I.U. of prolactin. Insulin causes a small inhibition of the effect of prolactin and large doses of LH and HCG give a positive response although the slopes of the log dose response lines are not as steep as those obtained with prolactin.

7. Nicoll et al. (1966) using mammary tissue of ten to 12 day pseudopregnant mice cultured in a medium containing insulin (5 μg./ml.) and either aldosterone (1 μg./ml.) or cortisol (5 μg./ml.) could detect histological changes in the tissue after addition of as little as 1 μg. of ovine prolactin per ml. of medium.

ASSAYS FOR HUMAN CHORIONIC GONADOTROPIN (HCG)

Many methods have been proposed and used. The various methods have advantages and disadvantages that sometimes depend on the circumstances under which a laboratory operates. In a recent review, Loraine (1966) does not refer to any bioassay method proposed after his extensive 1956 review. Some of the methods given in that review will be listed here together with their index of precision. Loraine (1956) divides the assay methods into two groups: those based on primary effects of the HCG on the test animal (e.g. ovarian weight), and those based on secondary effects (e.g. uterine weight).

The methods based on primary effects are:

1. Ovarian weight determination of the immature rat; this method is insensitive.

2. The determination of ovarian hyperemia in adult rats; the success depends on the strain of rats used. The method is not specific and the index of precision is 0.450, but the test is sensitive.

3. The induction of spermiation in amphibia. The sensitivity varies with the season. The index of precision is 0.120 to 0.176.

The methods based on secondary effects that have a good index of precision are:

1. The determination of the prostate weight of rats; the index of precision is 0.100.

2. The determination of the seminal vesicle weight of rats; the index of precision is 0.195.

3. The determination of uterine weights of immature rats. The index of precision varies from 0.149 to 0.329, but the response is affected by serum, so the method is not suitable for assays of untreated serum. In all the indirect methods one always needs to be sure that no androgen (in the case of prostate or seminal vesicle weight determinations) or estrogen is present.

Loraine (1966) also lists three immunological assays for HCG determination:

1. Hemagglutination-inhibition tests: this method depends on the inhibition by the test material of the agglutination of HCG-coated red cells and antiserum produced in rabbits by injection of HCG. The method is suitable for qualitative but not for quantitative use.

2. Complement-fixation tests: The method is qualitative rather than quantitative.

3. Radio immunological assays: Midgley (1966) has published a sensitive method in which radioiodinated HCG is precipitated by a specific HCG antiserum and the activity of the precipitate is counted. To 0.5 ml. diluted anti-HCG serum 0.5 ml. of the unknown or the standard preparation is added. After incubation at 37° C. for 30 minutes, 0.5 ml. radioiodinated HCG and 0.5 ml. antirab-

bit gamma globulin (to separate antibody bound HCG I^{131} from free HCG I^{131}) are added. The precipitate is centrifuged and the radioactivity is determined. This method has an excellent index of precision 0.068 to 0.085 and sensitivity. 5 to 10 m. I.U./ml. can be detected so that HCG in 0.1 ml. blood plasma and 0.1 ml. urine can be determined. Human LH can also be determined by this method.

Odell et al. (1966) have published a preliminary note on the use of a radio immunoassay for HCG and for human LH. In this method the following reactants are added:

a. Phosphate buffer (0.01 M.) containing 0.15 M. NaCl, 2.5 percent normal rabbit serum and 0.1 percent sodium azide to make a final volume of 1 ml.

b. 0.1 ml. of 0.1 M. EDTA.

c. 0.005 to 0.2 ml. of material to be assayed (serum or plasma).

d. 0.1 ml. of either human LH-I^{131} or HCG-I^{131} containing 0.1 mμg. of human LH-I^{131} or HCG-I^{131} with a specific activity of 100-500 μc./μg.

e. 0.1 ml. of antiserum to human LH or HCG (obtained by injection of either purified human LH or HCG together with Freund's adjuvant) suitably diluted so that 50 to 75 percent is antibody-bound in tubes containing no unlabeled human LH (or HCG).

The mixture is incubated for five days at 4° C. and an excess of sheep antirabbit globulin is added. After an additional 24 hours of incubation the tubes are centrifuged at 500 g. for 20 minutes. The radioactivity of the precipitate gives a measure of the amount of LH in the sample under investigation. Amounts of 0.39 to 1.6 mμg. were located in the useful part of the standard curve.

PREGNANT MARE'S SERUM GONADOTROPIN (PMSG)

This hormone, which has FSH and LH activity (but in which the activity can-

not be separated, in contrast with the pituitary gonadotropins), can be assayed as follows:

1. By determining the follicular growth in hypophysectomized immature rats (Catchpole, 1964); the interstitial cells also show repair, thus one can distinguish PMSG from FSH and LH.

2. By determining ovarian and uterine growth in immature intact rats (Catchpole, 1964); at doses < 10 I.U. the uterine response is detectable but no increase or only a small increase in ovarian weight is found, at dose of about 20 I.U. an increase in ovarian and in uterine weight is found (D'Amour and D'Amour, 1940).

3. The radiophosphorus uptake by chick testes is increased by 0.05 I.U. of PMSG (Florsheim et al., 1959); the response is not specific, but the assay can be used for standardization of PMSG preparations although the index of precision is rather poor (0.41).

For a recent review of various assay methods for pituitary hormones see also Bell (1966).

REFERENCES

Albert, A., Gentner, D., Rosemberg, E., and Ferrechio, G. 1965. Assay characteristics of tannate complexes of human pituitary gonadotropin. Endocrinology 77:226-230.

Anderson, R. R., and McShan, W. H. 1966. Luteinizing hormone levels in pig, cow and rat blood plasma during the estrous cycle. Endocrinology 78:976-982.

Bates, R. W., Garrison, M. M., and Cornfield, J. 1963. An improved bio-assay for prolactin using adult pigeons. Endocrinology 73:217-223.

Bell, E. T. 1966. Some observations on the assay of anterior pituitary hormones. Vitamins and Hormones 24:64-113.

Bell, E. T., Mukerji, S., and Loraine, J. A. 1964. A new bioassay method for LH depending on the depletion of rat ovarian cholesterol. J. Endocrinol. 28:321-328.

Bliss, L. C. 1952. The Statistics of Bioassay. Academic Press Inc., New York.

Breneman, W. R., Zeller, F. J., and Creek, R. O. 1962. Radioactive phosphorus uptake by chick testes as an end-point for gonadotropin assay. Endocrinology 71:790-798.

Catchpole, H. R. 1964. Physiology of the gonadotropic hormones. *In* H. H. Cole (ed.): Gonado-tropins. W. H. Freeman & Company, San Francisco, pp. 40-70.

Clark, J. H., and Zarrow, M. X. 1966. Ovarian cholesterol depletion assay for LH in the andro-gen-sterilized rat. Fed. Proc. *25*:315 (abstract).

D'Amour, F. E., and D'Amour, M. C. 1940. A comparison of the international gonadotropin standards. Endocrinology *27*:68-70.

de Reviers, M. M., and Mauléon, P. 1965. Étude critique du dosage de l'hormone folliculo-stimulante par la méthode d'Igarashi et McCann. C. R. Acad. Sci. *261*:540-543.

Ellis, S. 1961. Bioassay of luteinizing hormone. Endocrinology *68*:334-340.

Evans, A. J. 1966. Further investigations of an assay *in vitro* for prolactin. J. Endocrinol. *34*:319-328.

Florsheim, W. H., Velcoff, S. M., and Bodfish, R. E. 1959. Gonadotrophin assay based on augmentation of radiophosphate uptake by the chicken testis. Acta Endocrinol. *30*:175-182.

Gans, E., and van Rees, G. R. 1966. Studies on the testicular augmentation assay method for follicle stimulating hormone. Acta Endocrinol. *52*:573-582.

Gibson, W. R., Frankel, A. I., Graber, J. W., Nalbandov, A. V. 1965. An ovarian ascorbic acid depletion factor in starch gel preparations following electrophoresis. Proc. Soc. Exp. Biol. Med. *120*:143-146.

Gorbman, A., and Bern, H. A. 1962. A Textbook of Comparative Endocrinology. John Wiley & Sons Inc., New York.

Grosvenor, C. E., and Turner, C. W. 1958. Assay of lactogenic hormone. Endocrinology *63*:530-534.

Guillemin, R., and Sakiz, E. 1963. Quantitative study of the response to LH after hypophysectomy in the ovarian ascorbic acid depletion test: Effect of prolactin. Endocrinology *72*:813-816.

Heald, P. J., and Furnival, B. E. 1966. The ovarian cholesterol depletion assay for luteinizing hormone. J. Endocrinol. *34*:525-526.

Igarashi, M., and McCann, S. M. 1964. A new sensitive bio-assay for follicle-stimulating hormone (FSH). Endocrinology *74*:440-445.

Kovačić, N. 1962. Prolongation of dioestrus in the mouse as a quantitative assay of luteotrophic activity of prolactin. J. Endocrinol. *24*:227-231.

Kovačić, N. 1964. Biological characteristics of pituitary and placental hormones. J. Reprod. Fertil. *8*:165-186.

Kovačić, N. 1965. Prolactin assay by decidual reaction in the mouse. J. Endocrinol. *33*:295-299.

Lamond, D. R., and Bindon, B. M. 1966. The biological assay of follicle-stimulating hormone in hypophysectomized immature mice. J. Endocrinol. *34*:365-376.

Loraine, J. A. 1956. Bioassay of pituitary and placental gonadotropins in relation to clinical problems in man. Vitamins and Hormones *14*: 305-357.

Loraine, J. A. 1966. Assays of human chorionic gonadotrophin in relation to clinical practice. J. Reprod. Fertil. *12*:23-31.

Midgley, A. R., Jr. 1966. Radioimmuno assay: A method for human chorionic gonadotropin and human luteinizing hormone. Endocrinology *79*: 10-18.

Mukerji, S., Bell, E. T., and Loraine, J. A. 1965. The effect of pregnant mare serum gonadotrophin and human chorionic gonadotrophin on rat ovarian ascorbic acid and cholesterol. J. Endocrinol. *31*:197-205.

Nicoll, C. S., Bern, H. A., and Brown, D. 1966. Occurrence of mammotrophic activity (prolactin) in the vertebrate adenohypophysis. J. Endocrinol. *34*:343-354.

Novella, M. A., Acker, G., Alloiteau, J. J., and Aschheim, P. 1965. Intérêt d'un prétraitement par un tranquillisant (trifluopérazine) pour le dosage de l'hormone lutéinisante par la méthode de Parlow. C. R. Acad. Sci. *261*:1742-1745.

Odell, W. D., Ross, G. T., and Rayford, P. L. 1966. Radioimmunoassay for human luteinizing hormone. Metabolism *15*:287-289.

Ortman, R. 1966. The paradise whydah in the weaver finch test. Amer. Zool. *6*:518 (abstract).

Parlow, A. F., and Reichert, L. E., Jr. 1963. Species differences in follicle-stimulating hormone as revealed by the slope of the Steelman-Pohley assay. Endocrinology *73*:740-743.

Pelletier, J. 1963. Étude critique du dosage de ICSH par la méthode de l'acide ascorbique ovarien. Ann. Biol. Anim. Biochim. Biophys. *3*:307-323.

Reichert, L. E., Jr. 1966. Measurement of luteinizing hormone by the hyperemia and ovarian ascorbic acid depletion assays. Endocrinology *78*: 815-818.

Rosemberg, E., Solod, E. A., and Albert, A. 1964. Luteinizing hormone activity of human pituitary gonadotropin as determined by the ventral prostate weight and the ovarian ascorbic acid depletion methods of assay. J. Clinic. Endocrinol. *24*:714-728.

Sakiz, E., and Guillemin, R. 1963. On the method of ovarian ascorbic acid depletion as a test for luteinizing hormone (LH). Endocrinol. *72*: 804-812.

Segal, S. J. 1957. Response of weaver finch to chorionic gonadotrophin and hypophysial luteinizing hormone. Science *126*:1242-1243.

Siegel, H. S., and Siegel, P. B. 1964b. Genetic variation in chick bioassays for gonadotropins. II Histological and histochemical responses. Virginia J. Sci. *15*:204-217.

Siegel, P. B., and Siegel, H. S. 1964a. Genetic variation in chick bioassays for gonadotropins. I. Testes weight and response. Virginia J. Sci. *15*:187-203.

Skosey, J. L., and Goldstein, D. P. 1966. Observations on ovarian cholesterol depletion (OCD) as a test for luteinizing hormone activity. Endocrinology *78*:218-219.

Steelman, S. L., and Pohley, F. M. 1953. Assay of the follicle stimulating hormone based on the augmentation with human chorionic gonadotropin. Endocrinology *53*:604-616.

van Tienhoven, A., Simkin, D., Weske, J., and Barr, G. R. 1965. Effect of thyroxine on the gonadotrophin dose response line using the chick's testicular response. Endocrinology 76:194-197.

Witschi, E. 1955. Vertebrate gonadotrophins. Mem. Soc. Endocrinology 4:149-163.

Wolthuis, O. L. 1963a. An assay of prolactin based on a direct effect of this hormone on cells of the corpus luteum. Acta Endocrinol. 42:364-379.

Wolthuis, O. L. 1963b. A new prolactin assay method; some experiments which provide arguments for its specificity. Acta Endocrinol. 42:380-388.

Yokota, N., Igarashi, M., and Matsumoto, S. 1965. Studies on the ovarian ascorbic acid depletion test (OAAD) for luteinizing hormone (LH). Endocrinol. Jap. 12:83-91.

Index

Note: The Index is centered on major concepts, and animals are not listed by species name. To find out about *Rana pipiens*, for example, one would look under *Frog*, *Amphibian*, and the topic of discussion (say, *Testosterone*).

The following abbreviations are used:

ACTH—Adrenocorticotropic hormone
CL—Corpus luteum
DHEA—Dehydroepiandrosterone
FSH—Follicle-stimulating hormone
FSH-RF—FSH-releasing factor
HCG—Human chorionic gonadotropin
HIOMT—Hydroxyindole-O-methyltransferase
ICSH—Interstitial cell-stimulating hormone
LH—Luteinizing hormone
LH-RF—LH-releasing factor
LIHN—Laterodorsal interstitial hypothalamic nucleus

MSH—Melanophore-stimulating hormone
NSM—Neurosecretory material
OAAD test—Ovarian ascorbic acid depletion test
OBAGS—Olfactory-bucco-alimentary-anal-genital syndrome
20α-ol—20α-OH-Δ⁴-pregnene-3-one
20β-ol—20β-OH-Δ⁴-pregnene-3-one
PMSG—Pregnant mare's serum gonadotropin
TP—Testosterone propionate
TSH—Thyroid-stimulating hormone

Italic folios indicate pages with illustrations.
Folios followed by "t" indicate pages with tables.

Abembryonic pole cells, and implantation, 320
Abortion, diabetes and, 189, 190
Accessory sperm, 305
Acetylcholine, in median eminence, 212
Acrosome, and sperm capacitation, 302
Acrosome reaction, 304
ACTH, and adrenogenital syndrome, 186
  and hyperadrenal function, 188
  and pituitary, 213, 214, 216
  and population density control, 188
  and spermatogenesis, 97
  implants of, in median eminence, 233
  release of, and LH release, 251
    nonspecific stress agents and, 250
Actinomycin D, and ovulation, 150
Activation, of ovum, 305-307
Adrenal, 181-188
  and metabolism, 183
  and population density, 186, 187, 188
  fetal, and pregnancy, 347
Adrenal cortex, and gonads, 183
Adrenaline, 181, 182
  and spermiogenesis, 91
Adrenogenital syndrome, in man, 186
African weaver finch test, 469
"Aged" eggs, and sex differentiation, 19, 20
Aggressive behavior, 429-435
  and sexual behavior, 433
  androgens and, 431
    in birds, 84
  brain lesions and, 433-435
  heritability of, 432

  LH and, 431
  pituitary and, 430
Amino acids, and reproduction, 381
  requirements of, for chicken, 366
  sequence of, in neurohypophyseal hormones, 210t
Aminopterin, and folic acid, 376
  and uterine response to progesterone, 377
Amniotes, embryogenesis of genital system in, *21*
Amphibian, Bidder's organ of, 40
  androgen and sex differentiation in, 24
  breeding patterns of, 271-272, 404
  brood pouch of, *40*
  corpora lutea of, 39
  diencephalon of, destruction of, 222
  epinephrine in, 182
  estrogen secretion of, site of, 106
  fertilization in, 271, 297
  gonadectomy of, and differentiation of secondary sex organs, 22
  hermaphroditism in, 69
  hypophysectomy of, and spermatogenesis, 90
  hypothalamus of, electric stimulation of, 235
    histology of, 241
    lesions of, 222
  interstitial cells in, 38
  neurosecretory material in, 241
  ovary of, 39
  ovoviviparity of, 313
  pars distalis of, ectopic transplantation of, 215
  parturition of, endocrinology of, 340
  pineal body of, 191, 192

477

Amphibian *(Continued)*
  pituitary stalk section in, 219
  pituitary transplantation in, 213
  rainfall and reproduction in, 416
  reproductive system of, 38-40
  sexual behavior of, 437
  temperature and reproduction in, 408
  testis of, and androgen secretion, 74
  thyroid in, 176
Amygdala, and aggression, 434
Amygdalar lesions, and sexual behavior, 448
  in immature rats, 256
Androgens, 79-89. See also *Testosterone.*
  and aggressive behavior, 431
    in birds, 84
    in chameleon, 83
    in chicken, 430
    in frill-finned goby, 82
    in higher vertebrates, 84
    in rat, 433
  and behavior, 82
    in mammals, 88
  and corpora lutea, in rabbit, 145
  and epididymis, 81
  and external genitalia, 24
  and genital system, 79-81
  and gonadal development, 23, 24
  and gonadotropin secretion, 81
  and mating behavior, 83t
  and nest building activity, 436
  and neural tissue, differentiation of, 84-89
  and organization of hypothalamus, 86, 87t, 88t
  and pituitary gonadotropin secretion, 80
  and precocious sexual behavior in turkey, 438
  and restoration of mating behavior in castrated mammals, 442, 443
  and secondary sex characters, 81, 82t
  and secondary sex structures, 81
  and sex differentiation, 17t, 18, 84-89
  and sexual behavior, 436, 437
  and testis, 79, 80
  and thyroid, 181
  biochemistry of, 76, 78
  in castrated teleosts, 74, 74t
  metabolic effects of, 89
  ovarian, 144-145
  secretion of, by testis, 73-89
    source of, 74, 75
    control of, 77
    diabetes and, 189
    cryptorchidism and, 99
  with prolactin, and reproductive system, male, 165
Androstenedione, and adrenogenital syndrome, 186
  metabolism of, by placenta, 14
  secretion by mammalian testis, 77
Androstenedione implant, in rat brain, and sexual behavior, 454
Androsterone, pineal body and secretion of, 195
Anovular ovarian follicles, 53
Anterior pituitary, ablation of, in mammals, 162
  anterior, and corpora lutea, 135
  and male, reproductive system, 218
  and pregnancy, 290, 292t
  basophilic cells in, 217
  blood supply of, 209
  control of, 211, 212, 225

Anterior pituitary *(Continued)*
  environmental input and, 419
  gonadotropins of, control of, 212
    hypothalamus and, 249
  in birds, 161
  in vitro culture of, 218
  photoperiod and, 402
  replacement therapy and, in mammals, 162
  transplantation of, function of, 213-218
    in mammals, 216
    to different parts of hypothalamus, 217
Anti-androgen, and sex differentiation, 24
Antigens, and insemination, 303, 304
Antihistamine, and decidual reaction in uterus, 320
Antimesometrial implantation, 319
Anura, breeding patterns of, 272
  pineal body of, 191
  testis of, 38
Appetite, estrogens and, 122
  nutrition and, 355
  progestins and, 143
  reproduction and, 364, 365
Archistriatum, and reproductive system, in duck, 254
Arrhenogens, 13
Ascension Island, breeding cycles of birds on, 394
Ascorbic acid, and reproduction, 377
Atretic follicles, 52
Auditory stimuli, reproduction and, 411, 412

Bacteria, resistance of uterus to, progesterone and, 141, 142
Baculum, mammalian, 50
Badger, delayed implantation in, 332
Banded sunfish, photoperiod and reproduction in. 397
Barr body, 5, 6
Bartholin's glands, 54
Basking shark, female, reproductive system of, *33*
  male, reproductive system of, *30, 32*
Basophilic cells, in anterior pituitary, after transplantation to hypothalamus, 217
Bat, endogenous rhythm in, 394
  estrous cycle of, 281
Beak color, estrogen and, in birds, 116
Behavior, androgens and, 82
  in mammals, 88
  courtship, in inframammalian vertebrates, ovariectomy and, 123
  sexual. See *Sexual behavior.*
"Behavioral substrate," differentiation of, androgens and, 86
  estrogen and, 124
  in mammals, 442, 443
Bidder's organ, amphibian, 40
  in Bufonidae, 38
Bioassay methods, 467-475
Biological clock, 389
Biological rhythms, 388
Biotin, and reproduction, 375
  in chickens, 374
Bird, androgens and aggressive behavior in, 84, 430, 431
  anterior pituitary hormones of, 161
  breeding cycle in, temperature and, 405
  breeding patterns of, 272-274

Bird *(Continued)*
cortisone in, 184
determinate egg layers in, 272
electric stimulation of brain of, and aggressiveness, 434
endogenous rhythm in, 394
energy intake of, after puberty, and reproduction, 361
epinephrine in, 182
estrogens and ovary in, 109
hermaphroditism in, 69
hypophyseal portal vessels of, destruction of, 220
hypophysectomy and spermatogenesis in, 93
hypothalamo-hypophyseal system of, 207
hypothalamus of, electric stimulation of, 235
lesions of, 222
incubation and prolactin in, 458
indeterminate egg layers in, 272
Leydig cells of, and sexual activity, 75
LH of, 162
lunar effects on reproduction of, 417
migratory behavior of, 163, 205, 427, 428, 429
prolactin and, 163
nonphotoperiodic, 240
ovarian androgen in, 144
ovarian follicle of, 44
oviducts of, estrogens and, 115
oviposition of, oxytocin and, 343
oviposition and ovulation cycle of, photoperiod and, 406
oxytocin in, 170
pancreas in, 188
parental behavior of, prolactin and, 458
parthenogenesis in, 308
photoperiod in, 239, 395-402
pineal body of, 191
pituitary of, stalk section of, 220
transplantation of, 215
posterior pituitary hormones in, 173
prolactin in, 428
protein intake of, and reproduction, 365
rainfall and reproduction in, 416
refractory period in, 239, 398
thyroid and, 176
reproductive system of, 42-46
secondary sex characters of, estrogen and, 116
sex determination of, 4t
sexual behavior of, 437, 438, 439, 440
progestins and, 143
sexual maturity of, estrogen and, 117
sperm storage in, 299
spermatogenesis in, 93, 93t, 94, 95, 272
temperature and reproduction in, 405, 408
testis of, 42, 399
and androgen secretion, 75
testosterone in, 439
thyroid in, 176, 177
Blastocyst, definition of, 318
development of, uterus and, in eutheria, 315
estradiol-17-β and, 328
formation of, requirements of, 329
hormonal control of, 328
implantation of, spacing of, 318
in uterus, distribution of, 318, 319
transport of, steroid hormones and, 318
uterine stimulation by, 318

Bleeding, menstrual, cause of, 282
Blood, composition of, estrogen and, 117, 118t, 119, 119t
ovarian, progesterone in, 337, 338
Bloodstreams, placental, 325
Bone marrow chimera, 14
Bony fishes, reproductive system of, 34-37. See also Fish.
Brain, and control of pituitary functions, *228*
cortex of, and ovulation, in rabbit, 254
electric activity of, and gonadotropin release, 252-257
and sexual behavior, 457
frontal lobe of, extirpation of, effects of, 255
lesions of, and sexual behavior, 446, 447
gonadal hormone concentration in, 454
hormone implants in, and sexual behavior, 452
lesions of, and aggressive behavior, 433-435
and sexual behavior, 444-450
sex differentiation of, in rat, 86
Breeding cycle, events of, 269
in viviparous teleosts, 270
photoperiod and temperature in, 395
seasonal, 269
temperature and, 404, 405
wave length (of light) and, 399
Breeding patterns, 269-293
of amphibia, 271-272
of anura, 272
of birds, 272-274
of eutheria, 274
of marsupials, 274
of monotremes, 274
of reptiles, 272
of teleosts, 270-271
Breeding season, environment and, 389-425
photoperiod and. See *Photoperiod.*
synchronizing stimuli of, 393
temperature and, 404-406
Brood patch, hormones and, 163, 164, 458
Brood pouch, amphibian, *40*
Bruce effect, 255
in deer mouse, 415
in mouse and rat, 414
Budgerigars, auditory stimuli and reproduction in, 411
neurosecretory material of, continuous darkness and, 240
Bufonidae, Bidder's organ in, 38

Cadmium salts, injection of, and reproduction, 379, 380
Calcium, and reproduction, 378
in chicken, 121, 377
in chicken blood, and estrogen, 119, 119t
retention of, gonadal hormones and, in pullets, 120t
Calyx nutricus, 36
Capacitation, of sperm, 302
reversibility of, 303
Captivity, and reproduction, 417, 419
Carp, rainfall and spawning in, 416
Castration, and FSH-RF, in male rat, 248
and gonadotropin secretion, in neonatal rats, 85
and LH-RF concentration, in male rats, 246

Castration (*Continued*)
  and mating behavior, 83t
    in cat, 443, 444
  and sexual behavior, in fish, 436
  and TSH, thyroid activity and, 181
  scrotum after, 81
Castration cells, caused by cryptorchidism, 99
Cat, aggressiveness of, amygdala and, 434
  brain lesions of, and sexual behavior, 447, 448, 450
  cerebrum of, removal of, and sexual behavior, 445, 446
  cyclic patterns of, reproduction of, 276
  estrus of, estrogen implants and, 233
  hermaphroditism of, 70
  hormone implant in brain of, and sexual behavior, 453
  hypothalamus of, electric stimulation of, 235
    suprachiasmatic nucleus of, lesions of, 224
  mating behavior of, castration and, 443, 444
  spinal lesions of, and sexual behavior, 445, 446
  stria terminalis of, transection of, effect of, 256
Catfish, hypophyseal hormones in, 161
Cattle, auditory stimuli and reproduction in, 412
  blastocysts of, overcrowding of, 319
  corpora lutea of, oxytocin and, 172
  diestrus in, thyroid and, 180
  energy intake of, and puberty, 360
  estrous cycle in, 282
  freemartinism in, 12
  parturition of, and fetus genotype, 346, 347
  photoperiod and, 407
  pineal body in, 194
  sex differentiation in, 11
  sigmoid flexure of penis in, 49, *50*
  temperature and reproduction in, 409
  thyroid of, 179
    and estrus and diestrus, 180
  visual stimuli and reproduction in, 411
Caudate nucleus, lesions of, effects of, 256
Cell, and circadian rhythm, 390
Central nervous system, hypothalamic effects on anterior pituitary and, 254
Cerebellum, removal of, effect of, in sheep, 256
Cerebral hemispheres, and reproduction, 254, 446
Cerebrum, removal of, and sexual behavior, in female cats and dogs, 445, 446
Cervical ganglion, photoperiod and, in ferret, 403
Cervix, dilation of, and labor, 348
  progesterone and, 142
Chameleon, androgens and aggressiveness in, 83
  photoperiod and reproduction in, 397
Chemical stimulation, of hippocampus, and sexual behavior, 451
Chemotaxis, and penetration of ovum by sperm, 303
Chemotransmitters, hypophyseal portal system and, 257
  in hypothalamus, 243-250
  in mammals, 244
Chicken, aggressive behavior and androgens in, 430
  amino acid requirements of, 366
  calcium in, 121, 377
  egg formation in, gonadotropins and, 118
  egg laying cycle of, 273, *273*, 274
  eggs of, yolk composition of, 119t
  electric stimulation of brain of, and aggressiveness, 434
  embryo of, vitamins in, 374

Chicken (*Continued*)
  energy intake of, after puberty, and reproduction, 361
  epinephrine in, 182
  essential fatty acids for, 368-369
  estrogens in blood of, 118t
  fat deposition in, 429
  food intake of, and egg-laying, 358
  gonadectomy of, and differentiation of secondary sex organs, 23
  hyperadrenalism of, and population density, 187
  light intensity and reproduction in, 399
  LH in egg laying cycle of, 273, 274
  LH measurement in, ovulation and, 234
  male, reproductive system of, *43*
  mineral requirements of, and reproduction, 377, 378
  neurosecretory material and annual cycles of, 240
  ovarian follicle of, *44*
    fertilization of, 148
    rupture of, 150
  ovariectomy of, effects of, 124
  oviduct of, *45*, 45t
    epithelial cells of, *46*
  oviposition and ovulation cycle of, photoperiod and, 406
  pancreas of, 188
  pineal body of, 192
  pituitary transplantation in, 215
  posterior pituitary hormones in, 173
  protein intake of, and reproduction, 365, 366
  sexual behavior of, brain lesions and, 448
  sexual behavior of, hormones and, 438
  sperm nests in, 44
  temperature and reproduction in, 408
  thyroid of, estrogens and, 179
  thyroidectomy of, 176
  vitamin A in, 370
  vitamin D in, 372
  vitamin E in, and reproduction, 372
  water soluble vitamins in, 374
Chorioallantoic placenta, classification of, 325t
  definition of, 324
Chorionic placenta, definition of, 324
Chromosomes, and gonadal sex, in vertebrates, 5t
  and sex determination, 3
Chronon, 391
Circadian clock, molecular model of, 391
Circadian rhythm, 389
  and internal oscillator, 390
  light intensity and, 399
  universality of, 390
Circennian rhythm, 389
  of prolactin secretion, in birds, 428
  photoperiod and, 395
Clasp reflex, brain and, 437
Cloaca, and spermatophores, 38, 40
Coitus, and vasopressin, 175
Collagenase, and ovulation, 150
Congenital abnormalities, pancreas and, 190
Constant heat, of cattle, 123
Continuous estrus, sex steroids of, 232
Continuous light, and LH release, 407
Copper, and reproduction, 378
Copulation, 297-299
  and ovulation, in mammals, 276, 277
  sensory feedback during, 457

Copulatory behavior, of rat and guinea pig, 84, 442
Cormorant, reproduction of, nesting site and, 417
Corpora lutea, amphibian, 39
  and breeding cycle, in teleosts, 270
  and implantation, 334
  and progesterone, 108, 128, 129
  and progestin secretion, 126
  and relaxin secretion, 145
  and theca interna cells, 127t
  androgens and, in rabbits, 145
  anterior pituitary and, 135
  estrogen and, 110, 114
  estradiol and, 109, 129
  estrous cycle and, 280
  formation of, FSH and DES and, 109
  FSH and, 109, 130t, 131
  FSH plus LH and, 164
  formation of, genital tract stimulation and, 136
    HCG and, 109
  function of, regulation of, 126-136
  functional, and long cycles, in mammals, 280
  hormone administration and, 130t
  hypothalamus and, 129
  hypophyseal control of, 130t
  hysterectomy and, 128, 132, 132t, 134t, 135
  implantation and, 334
  in menstrual cycle, 282, 283
  in pregnancy, in mammals, 289, 291t
  in reptiles, 272
  maintenance of, as prolactin assay, 470
    control of, 127
    during pregnancy, 290, 291, 291t
    endometrium and, 292, 293
    estrogens and, 293
      in rabbit, 114
    in sheep, 128
  nonfunctional, and short cycles, in mammals, 278
  of estrus cycle, development and regression of, in
    mammals, 128t
  of pregnancy, mammalian, theca interna cells and,
    127t
  of rat, maintenance of, 163
  oxytocin and, 171
    in cattle, 172
    in mammals, 171, 172
  pituitary and, 131, 135, 216, 220
  progestins and, 130t, 131
  prolactin and, 129, 130t, 131
  uterus and, 129, 132, 135, 291, 292
Cortex, of genital ridge, after differentiation, *11*
Cortical lesions of brain, and sexual behavior, 446
Corticosteroids, 182-188
  biosynthetic pathways of, *183*
  in migratory fish, 185
Corticosterone, function of, in rats, 186
Cortisone. See also *Corticosteroids.*
  and estrus, in rats, 185
  and gonadotropin secretion, 185
  and ovary, in rats, 185
  in birds, 184
  in frog, 184
  in rats, 184, 185
Courtship behavior. See also *Sexual behavior.*
  electric stimulation and, 450
  in inframammalian vertebrates, ovariectomy and,
    123
  prolactin and, 437

Crop gland, of pigeon, prolactin and, 163, 470, 471
Cryptorchidism, 99
Cumulus oophorus, in egg penetration, in mammals,
  304
Cycle, breeding. See *Breeding cycle.*
  mammalian, 122t
Cyclic reproductive phenomena, 269-296. See also
    Breeding patterns and *Breeding cycles.*
  in elasmobranchs, 269-270
  in cyclostomes, 269
Cyclostomes, brain and pars distalis of, connections
    of, 208
  cyclic reproductive phenomena of, 269
  hypophysectomy of, and spermatogenesis, 89
  pineal organ of, 191
  reproductive system of, 29, 30
  sexual differentiation in, 9
  testes of, and androgen secretion, 73
  thyroid in, 175

Darkness, continuous, and neurosecretory material,
  240. See *Photoperiod.*
Day length. See *Photoperiod.*
Decidual response, as prolactin assay, 471
Deciduomata, serotonin injection and, in mice, 197
Deer mouse, sexual behavior of, brain lesions and,
  448
Dehydroepiandrosterone, 75-77
Desoxycorticosterone, and sex differentiation, 18
  physiologic effects of, in rats, 185
Determinate egg layers (birds), 272
DHEA, 75-77
Diabetes, and abortion, 189, 190
  and androgen secretion, 189
  in female rats, 189
  in man, and abortion rate, 190
  in rabbits, 189
Diencephalon, destruction of, in amphibians, 222
Diestrus, prolonged, as prolactin assay, 471
  thyroid and, in cattle, 180
Diethylstilbestrol, and sexual behavior, 123
  and corpora lutea formation, 109
Differentiation, of brain, sex differences in, 86
  of gonads, 8-20. See also *Sex differentiation.*
  of neural tissue, androgen and, 84
Dimorphism, sexual, androgen and, 81
Diurnal rhythm, and feedback mechanism, 392
  and photoperiod, 406-408
  and serotonin, melatonin, and noradrenaline, 195
  and spermatogenesis, 407
  definition of, 389
  glands with, 392
  noncircadian, 391
Dog, breeding patterns of, 280
  cerebrum of, removal of, 445, 446
  estrous cycle of, estrogen in, 286, 286t
  ovary of, and steroid synthesis, 78-79
  spinal lesions of, and sexual behavior, 445
  thyroid in, 179
Dominance relationships. See *Aggressive Behavior.*
"Drumsticks," in polymorphonuclear leukocytes, 6
Duck, captive, reproductive system in, 254
  freemartinism in, 14
  hypophyseal portal vessels of, destruction of, 220
  penis of, *43*
  photoperiod in, 239, 402

Duck *(Continued)*
  pituitary stalk section in, 220
  pituitary transplantation in, 215
  rainfall and reproduction in, 416
  reproductive system of archistriatum and, 254
  sex differentiation of, in vitro, 15, 15t
  sexual behavior of, 439
  spermatogenetic cycle of, 93t, 94, 95, *96*
  spermiogenesis stages in, 91
  starvation of, and reproduction, 356
  thyroidectomy of, effects of, 176

EEG after-reaction, 253
EEG arousal threshold, 456, 457
Eel, neurosecretory material in, 241
  sex differentiation of, in salt water, 19
Eft water drive, 162
  as prolactin assay, 470
Egg, activation of, 305-307
  ageing of, 19, 20, 307
  cell layers of, at ovulation, 317
  development of, after meiotic prophase, 149
    receptivity of uterus and, 327
  fate of, endocrine control of, 326
  fertilization of, 303, 305, 306, 307, 308
    site of, in teleosts, 312
  in oviduct, 317
  penetration of, by sperm cell, 303
    species specificity and, 303, 304
  transport of, estradiol cyclopentyl propionate and, 316
    in eutheria, 316
    ovariectomy and, 317
    progesterone and, 317
  unfertilized, life span of, 307
Egg laying, and energy intake, in chickens, 362
  paraventricular nucleus lesions and, 225
  photoperiod and, 407
Egg laying cycle, in birds, 272, 273, 274
Elasmobranchs, cyclic reproductive phenomena of, 269-270
  estrogen in, and sex differentiation, 14
  hermaphroditism in, 68
  hypophysectomy of, effects of, 89
  neurosecretory material of, transportation of, 208
  oogenesis in, 146
  ovoviviparous, embryo of, nourishment of, 311
  pars distalis of, blood supply of, 208
  reproductive systems of, 22t, 30
  testes of, and androgen secretion, 73
  viviparous, embryo of, nourishment of, 311
    reproductive system of, 32
Electrical activity of brain, and gonadotropin release, 252-257
  and sexual behavior, 457
Electrical stimulation, and sexual behavior, 450, 451, 452
  of brain, and aggressiveness, 434
Electrocoagulation, of hypothalamic nuclei, 221-228
Electrodes, permanent, advantages of, 235
Electrolytic lesions, of hypothalamic nuclei, 221
Embryo, and uterus, 322
  nutrition of, in teleosts, 313
Embryogenesis, of genital system, in amniotes, *21*
Embryology, 8-28
Embryonic development, CL and, in marsupials, 315

Embryonic mortality, ageing of gametes and, 307
  energy and, 362, 363, 364
  vitamin deficiency and, 371-377
Endocrine glands, nongonadal, 160-206
Endocrine hormones, and fate of ovum, 326
Endocrine organs, of fetus, and labor, 347, 349
Endogenous rhythms, 388-393
  and temperature, 404-406
  animals with, 394
  in frogs, 405
Endometrial hormones, secretion of, 290
Endometrium, and corpora lutea maintenance, 292, 293
  progesterone and 142
Energy intake, and reproduction, 356-365, 381
Environment, and reproduction, 334, 389-425
  and sex differentiation, 19
Environmental input, and anterior pituitary, 419
Epididymis, androgens and, 81
Epinephrine, 181, 182
Epiphysis cerebri, 190-197. See also *Pineal organ.*
Erection, medial dorsal nucleus and, 452
Erucic acid, and reproduction, 369
Erythrocinophilic cells, hypophysis transplantation and, in birds, 215
Essential fatty acids, 368-370
Estradiol, and blastocyst transport, 318
  and corpora lutea, 109, 129
  and estrogen concentration, 455
  and granulosa cell proliferation, 109
  and radioiodine uptake by thyroid, 180
  implants of, and LH-RF concentration, 246
  retention of, 455
  plus progesterone, and implantation, 329, 330, 330t
Estradiol-17-β, and blastocyst, 328
α-Estradiol, vitamin A and, 371
Estradiol benzoate, and LH-RF concentration, 246
  in rabbit brain, and sexual behavior, 453
Estradiol cyclopentyl propionate, ovum transport and, 316t
Estriol, and ovary, 108
Estrogens. See also *Estradiol, Estriol,* and *Estrone.*
  added to rat pituitary, and LTH secretion, 115
  administration of, to males, 114
  and appetite, 122
  and behavioral substrate differentiation, 124
  and blastocyst, 328
  and blood composition, 117, 118t, 119, 119t
  and corpora lutea, 110, 114
  and egg, formation of, 117
    transport of, 316
  and estrus, 122, 233, 280, 283, 284, 286t
  and external genitalia, 24
  and fallopian tube, 116
  and fat deposition, in chickens, 122
  and gonadal development, 23, 24
  and gonadotropins, release of, 109, 124
    synergistic effect of, 110
  and granulosa cells, in hypophysectomized rodents, 109
  and histamine, in decidual reaction in uterus, 320
  and hypothalamo-hypophyseal system, 229
  and hypothalamus, 86, 87t, 88t, 222, 223
  and implantation, 330, 331
  and incubation patch, 164
  and Leydig cells, 89, 110

Estrogens (*Continued*)
  and LH release, 111, 114
  and LH-RF concentration, 246
  and nest building, 440
  and neural tissue differentiation, 124
  and neurosecretory material, in median eminence, 242
  and oviduct, 115
  and ovulation, 108, 111
  and parturition, 343
  and pituitary, 110
    in nutrient deficiencies, 381
  and relaxin, 146
  and reproductive system, 108, 142
  and RNA, and uterine cell growth, 116
  and pregnancy, 367, 368
  and secondary sex characters, 116, 117
  and sex differentiation, 16t, 18
  and sexual behavior, in chickens, 438
    in mammals, 122
  and sperm transport, 300
  and uterine contractions, 342
  and uterus, during labor, 348
  and uterus, of primates, 282
  effects of, 108
    thresholds of, 111
  electric activity of brain and, 254
  in chicken blood, 188t
  in estrous and menstrual cycles, 283
  in estrous cycle, of dog, 286, 286t
  in endocrine organs, of female mammals, 107t
  in follicular phase of estrous cycle, 281
  in median eminence, 232
  in polyestrous mammals, 286
  plus progesterone, and reproductive system, 142
  pregnancy and, in mammals, 293
  source of, 107
  thyroid and, in chickens, 177, 179
  transport of, 114
  vitamin A and, 371
  water soluble vitamins and, 374
Estrogen secretion, by Leydig cell, 89
  by ovary, 104-124
  by Sertoli cell tumor, 89
  by testis, 89
  control of, 108
  in inframammalian vertebrates, 105, 105t, 106, 106t
  progesterone and, 137
Estrogen concentration, estradiol and, 455
Estrogen feedback mechanism, 242
Estrone, 336
Estrous cycle. See also *Estrus.*
  and corpora lutea, 280
  and LH-RF concentration, 246
  and radioiodine uptake by thyroid, 180
  corpora lutea of, development and regression of, in mammals, 128t
  cortisone and, in rats, 185
  duration of, in mammals, 128t
  estrogen and, 122, 233, 280, 283, 284, 286, 286t, 287
  hypophyseal gonadotropins in, in sheep, 287
  hypophysis and, stalk section of, in mammals, 220
  hysterectomy and, subtotal, 133t
  in rat, 278, 279t, 280, 285
  luteal phase of, and appetite, 143

Estrous cycle (*Continued*)
  oxytocin and, 171
  phases of, 280-282
  sex steroids of, 233
  TSH and, 180
  uterus and, 139t
Estrus, continuous, sex steroids of, 232
  definition of, 122, 435
  estrogen and, 122, 233, 280, 283, 284, 286t
  luteotropic effect of estrogen in, electric activity of brain and, 254
  progesterone and, 123, *129*, 281
  starvation and, in mice, 357
  thyroid and, in cattle, 180
European bitterling, ovarian follicle of, *36*
Eutheria, blastocyst of, development of, uterus and, 315
  breeding patterns of, 274
  egg transport in, 316
  puberty in, 275
External fertilization, 297
External genitalia, estrogen and, 24
  and estrogen and androgen, 24
  mammalian, female, 54
Fallopian tube, estrogen administration and, 116
Farm animals, energy intake of, and reproduction, 360
Fat deposition, and migration of birds, 427, 429
  estrogens and, in chickens, 122
  hypophysectomy and, 429
  in chickens, causes of, 429
Fat intake, and reproduction, 368-370
Fat soluble vitamins, and reproduction, 370-374
Fatty acids, essential, 368-370
Feedback mechanism, and diurnal rhythm, 392
Ferret, photoperiod in, 401
  cervical ganglion and, 403
Fertility, polyspermy and, 305
  prolactin and, 165
Fertilization, 297-310
  external, 297
  in mammals, 299
  internal, 269, 297, 298, 299
  site of, numbers of sperm at, 302
Fetus, adrenal of, and pregnancy, 347
  development of, in mammals, 340
  endocrine organs of, and labor, 347, 349
  expulsion of, requirements of, 341
  genotype of, duration of pregnancy and, 346, 347
  in uterine horn, crowding of, and parturition, 345
  mass of, and initiation of parturition, 345
  pituitary of, and parturition, 347
  protein deficiency and, 367
  sex of, duration of pregnancy and, 346, 347
Fish(es). See also *Elasmobranchs* and *Teleosts.*
  aggressive behavior of, brain lesions and, 433, 434
    LH in, 431
  auditory stimuli and reproduction in, 411
  bony, reproductive system of, 34-37
  breeding cycle of, temperature and, 404
  fertilization in, 297, 306
  lunar effects on reproduction of, 417
  migratory behavior of, 426
    corticosteroids in, 185
  oxytocin in, 173
  parental behavior of, prolactin and, 458

Fish(es) *(Continued)*
  parthenogenesis in, experimental induction of, 308
  parturition of, endocrinology of, 340
  photoperiodic, 241. See also *Photoperiod.*
  pineal body of, 191
  pinealectomy of, 192
  prolactin and gonads of, 163
  rainfall and reproduction in, 416
  sexual behavior of, 435, 436, 437
  temperature and maturation of gonads in, 408
  thyroid in, 175
  viviparity of, 311-313
Foetida oil, and embryonic mortality, 369
Folic acid, and reproduction, 374, 375, 376
Follicle. See *Ovarian follicle.*
Follicular phase, of estrous cycle, 281
Follicular fluid, depolymerization theory of, 151
Food, availability of, and circadian rhythms, 393
  intake of, and reproduction, 356-365. See also
    Energy intake.
Forebrain, and aggression, in green sunfish, 433
Fornix, lesions of, effects of, 256
Freemartins, 12, 13, 14
Fresh water, survival of fish in, as prolactin assay, 470
Frill-finned goby, aggressive behavior in, androgens
    and, 82
    pituitary and, 430
  auditory stimuli and reproduction in, 411
  hypophysectomy and sexual behavior of, 436
  olfactory stimuli and reproduction in, 413
Frog, breeding cycle of, temperature and, 404
  cortisone in, 184
  eggs of, ageing of, effects of, 307
    penetration by sperm cells, 303
  endogenous rhythm in, 405
  fertilization in, 297
  rainfall and ovulation in, 416
  thyroid in, 176
Frontal lobe of brain, extirpation of, 255
  lesions of, and sexual behavior, 446, 447
FSH. See also *Gonadotropins.*
  and corpora lutea, 109, 130t, 131, 164
  and implantation, 334
  and ovulation, in birds, 162
  and spermatogenesis, 91, 97
  assays of, 467, 468
  definition of, 110
  hypothalamic lesions and, 223, 227
  implants of, in median eminence, 233
  in pregnancy, in mammals, 290, 292t
  oxytocin and, 171, 172
  pituitary transplantation and, in amphibians, 214
  plus LH, in female hypophysectomized rats, 164
  secretion of, pituitary transplantation and, in mam-
    mals, 216
    testosterone and, 81
FSH-RF, 247
  and castration, in male rat, 248
  and LH-RF, similarities of, 248
  in extracts of median eminence, 247
  in hypothalamus, measurement of, 244

Gametes, ageing of, effects of, 307, 308
  unused, fate of, 308
Garter snake, olfactory stimuli and reproduction in,
  413

Gas exchange, placenta and, 325
Gene-effector interactions, and Müllerian duct system
  control, 115
Genes, and sperm fertilizing capacity, 301
  regulation of, hypothesis for, 115
Genital duct system, oxytocin and, in mammals, 174
Genital ridge, 8
  after differentiation, *11*
  in female, development of, 146
Genital system, anatomy of, 29-67
  androgens and, 79-81
  embryogenesis of, in amniotes, *21*
  progesterone and, 144
  female, and sperm transport, 299
  stimulation of, ovulation and, 136
Genotype, and sperm fertilizing capacity, 301, 302
Germ cells, primordial, 8, 9
  and derivation of oogonia, 147
Germinal epithelium, heat and, 98, 99
  LH and, 97
Gestagens. See hormone name.
Gestation, hormonal requirements of, 335
  hypophysis and, 335, 336t
  length of, and litter size, 345, 347
    and season of insemination, 347
  ovary and, 336t
  postimplantation, hormonal requirements of, 335,
    336
  prolonged, PMSG and, 334
GH, and spermatogenesis, 97
  pituitary and, 213, 216
  species differences in, 162
Giant baby syndrome, 190
Glands, reproductive. See *Reproductive glands.*
Glaucus gull, visual stimuli and reproduction in, 411
Glucagon, 188-190
Glucuronidase activity, prolactin and, 165
Goats, pseudohermaphroditism of, 70
Gobiid fish, auditory stimuli and reproduction in, 411
  olfactory stimuli and reproduction in, 413
  sexual behavior of, hypophysectomy and, 436
Goldthioglucose, and ventromedial nucleus of hypothalamus, 221
Gonadal development, and nest building, in birds, 440
  androgens and, 23, 24
  estrogen and, 23, 24
Gonadal hormones, and calcium retention, in pullets,
  120t
  and organization of the hypothalamus, 86, 87t
  and sexual behavior of mammals, 440
  and thyroid, 179
Gonadal hormone concentration, in brain areas, and
  sexual behavior, 454
Gonadectomy, of embryo, and differentiation of
  secondary sex organs, 22, 23t
Gonadotropic cells, differentiation of, pituitary transplants and, 213
  stalk section of, hypophysis and, 219
Gonadotropins. See also hormone name.
  and aggressive behavior, 431
  and egg formation, 118
  and ovarian follicle maturation, 276
  and oocyte growth, 151
  and sex differentiation, 19
  and testosterone, 79
  avian, 162

Gonadotropins *(Continued)*
  definition of, 110
  effects of, 168
  endogenous, site of release of, 225, *225*
  estrogens and, 110
  hypothalamus and, 245
  implantation into hypothalamo-hypophyseal system, 233
  in hypothalamus, areas of localization of, *228*, 229
  in urine, 167
  pituitary, 80t, 212, 257
  ovariectomy and, in rat, 110
  placental. See *Placenta.*
  release of, electric activity of brain and, 252-257
    estrogens and, 109, 124
    hypothalamus and, 238
Gonadotropin administration, effects of, 77t, 78t
Gonadotropin complex, dualistic, hypothesis of, 166
  single, hypothesis of, 166
Gonadotropin secretion, cortisone and, 185
  in castrated neonatal rats, 85
  pineal organ and, 192
  pituitary, androgen and, 80
  stalk section of pituitary and, 220
Gonadotropin secretion regulating centers, androgen and, 84
  estrogen and 124
Gonads, activity of, and photoperiod, 395, 396t, 401
  and adrenal cortex, 183
  and protein intake, 365, 366
  differentiation of, 8-20
  functions of, 29
    pituitary and, 160-175
  morphology of, 8
  primordial germ cells and development of, 9
  transplantation of, and sex differentiation, 12, 13t
  undifferentiated, *9*
Gonaducts, progesterone and, 138
Gonopodium, 35
Grafting, and sex differentiation, 12, 13t
Granulosa cell proliferation, estrogens and, 109
Green sunfish, aggressiveness of, brain lesions and, 433
Ground squirrel, breeding cycle of, regulation of, 405
Growth hormone, pituitary and, 213, 216
  species differences in, 162
Grunion, reproduction of, lunar effects and, 417
Guinea pig, copulatory behavior of, 442
  energy intake of, and puberty, 360
  hypophysis transplantation in and male reproductive system, 215
  LIHN in, 242
  olfactory stimuli and, in reproduction, 415
  sexual behavior of, and androgen, 443
  gonadal hormones and, 441
  thyroid in, 178
Gulls, breeding patterns of, 272
Guppy, pinealectomy of, 192
  sex determination of, 3
Gynogenesis, in fish, 307

Haldané's rule, 3
Hamster, breeding cycle of, regulation of, 405
  pinealectomy of, 196
HCG, and thyroid, 180

HCG *(Continued)*
  and corpora lutea, 130t, 131
  and LH, relation of, 167
  and ovary, in hypophysectomized mice, 167
  and ovulation, 150
  and prolactin, 165
  and spermatogenesis, 90
  in urine, 167
  plus prolactin, 165
  secretion of, 290, 339
HCG assays, 472, 473
Heat. See *Estrus* or *Temperature.*
Hedonic glands, in salamander, 413
Hematomes, and placenta, 324
Hermaphroditism, definition of, 68
  in amphibians, 69
  in birds, 69
  in elasmobranchs, 68
  in mammals, 70, 71
  in reptiles, 69
  in teleosts, 68
  rudimentary, in mammals, 70
Herring gull, visual stimuli and reproduction in, 411
Heterogametic sex, 3
Heterozygous sex, 3
Hexestrol, retention of, 455, 456
Hibernating gland, of bats, 75
HIOMT, activity of, estrous cycle and, 196
  and diurnal rhythm, 391, 392
Hippocampus, chemical stimulation of, and sexual behavior, 451
  lesions of, 256, 448
Histamine, and decidual reaction in uterus, 320
  and implantation, 322
Homogametic sex, 3
Hormones, and aggressive behavior, 84, 429, 431. See also name of hormone.
  and androgen secretion, 77
  and gonadal development, 23, 24
  and implantation, 141
  and reproductive behavior, induction of, 427
  and sexual behavior, 435
  hypophyseal, 161
  implants of, in brain, 452
  of anterior pituitary, 161
  steroid, and sex differentiation, 15. See also name of hormone.
Horse, olfactory stimuli and, in reproduction, 415, 416
  placenta of, gonadotropin secretion of, 167
3β-HSD, in ovary, 105-107
  inhibition of, effects of, 186
Hyaluronic acid, in egg penetration, 304
Hydrocortisone, in female rats, 185
21-Hydroxylase, deficiency of, 186
Hydroxyindole-O-methyltransferase. See *HIOMT.*
Hyperadrenalism, and population density, 187, 188
Hyperadrenocorticism, 185, 186
Hyperphagia, and migration of birds, 427, 429
Hyperthyroidism, mild, and reproduction, 179
Hypervitaminosis A, in rats, 372
Hypervitaminosis D, and reproduction, 372
Hypoglycemia, and congenital abnormalities, in mice, 190
  and reproductive system, in rats, 189
Hypophyseal homografts, *218*

Hypophyseal hormones, 160-175
Hypophyseal portal system, 209
  chemotransmitters and, 257
  transection of, 219
Hypophyseal portal vessels, function of, 217
Hypophysectomy, 77t, 78t, 160-175
  and corpora lutea, 130t
  and fat deposition, 429
  and oocyte growth, 151
  and ovulation, 128, 162
  and pregnancy, 220, 336, 337
  and Sertoli cells, 90
  and sex differentiation, 18
  and sexual behavior, in gobiid fish, 436
  and spermatogenesis, 89, 90, 91, 93, 94
  with replacement therapy, 160-175
    and gestation, 335, 336, 337
Hypophysiotropic area, hypophysis transplantation
  to, 217
Hypophysis cerebri, 160-175. See *Pituitary gland* and
  Hypophysectomy.
Hypothalamic nuclei, electrocoagulation of, 221
  electrolytic lesions of, 221
Hypothalamo-hypophyseal (neurosecretory) system,
  207, 213-229
  annual cycle of chickens and, 240
  electric stimulation of, 233-238
  estrogen, 229
  gonadotropin implantation into, 233
  sex steroid administration to, 229-233
    and reproductive organs, 230, 232t
Hypothalamus, 207-268
  anatomy of, 207-213
  and aggressive behavior, 434
  and anterior pituitary control, 212
  and gonadotropin release, 85, 238
  and gonadotropins, 245, 257
  and implantation, 334
  and oxytocin, 242
  and uterus, 222, 223
  anterior, and estrogen, 223
    castration cells in, cryptorchidism and, 99
    lesions of, in mammals, 222
  central nervous system and, 254
  chemotransmitters in, 234-250
  corpora lutea function and, 129
  electric stimulation of, 235
  estrogens and, 86, 87t, 88t, 222, 223
  extracts of, and pituitary LH release, in rat, 219
  FSH-RF in, measurement of, 244
  functions of, 207
  gonadotropic and sex behavioral areas in, localiza-
    tion of, *228*, 229
  gonadotropin release and, 238
  histologic, histochemical, and biochemical correla-
    tions of, 238-243
  histology of, 241
  hormone synthesis of, hypothalamic lesions and,
    221, 223
  hormones of, and anterior pituitary function, 249
  hormones of, vs. LH-RF, 249, 250
  hypophyseal hormones in, *243*
  in pregnancy, 242, 243
  lesions of, 221-229
    and precocious sexual maturity, 227
    and reproduction, 226
    and sexual behavior, 449, 450

Hypothalamus *(Continued)*
  lesions of, electrolytic, in rats, 222
    experimental production of, 221
    FSH and, 227, 233
    in amphibians, 221
    in birds, 222
    in mammals, 222
  medial basal, interruption of connections to, and
    gonadotropic function of anterior pituitary, 226t
  nuclei of, destruction of, effects of, 221
    electrocoagulation of, 221
  electrolytic lesions of, effects of, 221-229
  organization of, gonadal hormones and, 86, 87t
  oxytocin and, 174
  pharmacologic agents and, 250-252
  photoperiod and, 402
  preoptic, lesions of, and oviposition, 173
  progesterone and, 85
  progesterone retention of, 455
  releasing factors in, 243-250. See also *Chemotrans-
    mitters.*
  rhinencephalic and reticular formation of nerve
    pathways of, *255*
  structure of, in rat, 233
  supraoptic lesions of, 174
  testosterone and, 86, 87, 88t
  tissue of, and pituitary, 248
Hysterectomy. See also *Uterus.*
  and corpora lutea, 128, 132, 132t, 134t, 135
  estrous cycle, 139t
  progestins and, 134t, 135
  subtotal, and estrous cycle, 133t

ICSH, definition of, 110
Immunology, and reproduction, 304
Implantation, 319
  abembryonic pole cells and, 320
  antimesometrial, 319
  corpora lutea and, 334
  delayed, 331, 332-335
  early, 332
  environment and, 334
  estrogen and, 330, 331
  FSH and, 334
  hormonal and uterine requirements for, 141
  hormonal requirements of, 326-335
  hypothalamus and, 334
  in mice, 321
  LH and, 334
  non-uterine, 322
  nursing and, in rats and mice, 328
  ovary and, 326
  prolactin and, 331
  site of, 318
  starvation and, in mice, 357
  time of, in mammals, 323t
  types of, 321
  uterus and, 141, 322
Incubation, by amphibia, 39
  by birds, 82
Incubation patch, hormones and formation of, 163,
  164, 428
Indeterminate egg layers (birds), 272
Indian carp, rainfall and spawning in, 416
Induced ovulators, cyclic patterns of reproduction
  in, 276

Infundibulum, lesions of, in toad, 222
Inhibitors, thyroid, and sex differentiation, 19
Insemination, 297-310
  antigens and, 303, 304
  season of, and gestation length, 347
  types of, 299
Insulin, 188-190
Internal fertilization, 269, 297, 298, 299
Internal oscillator, and circadian rhythm, 390
Internal rhythm. See *Endogenous rhythm.*
Intersexes, 68-71
  in mammals, 70
  in man, 71t
Interstitial cell repair test, 469
Interstitial cells, and sexual activity of birds, 75
  in amphibia, 38
Intromittent organ, of amphibia, 38
  of elasmobranchs, 31
  of fishes, 34-36
  of reptiles, 41, *41*
Iron, and reproduction, 378

Japanese rice fish, breeding patterns of, 270
  photoperiod and ovulation in, 406
  sex determination of, 3, 4t
Japanese quail, photoperiod and oviposition and ovulation cycle in, 406
Jewel fish, parental behavior of, and prolactin, 458

Klinefelter syndrome, 71

Labia majora, 54
Labia minora, 54
Labor. See also *Parturition.*
  initiation of, hormones and, 344
  oxytocin and, 174
  successful, factors in, 348
Lactation, erucic acid and, 369
  pituitary stalk section and, 220
Lamprey, hypophyseal hormones in, 160
  urogenital system of, *30*
L-D. See *Photoperiod.*
Lepomis cyanellis, aggressiveness of, brain lesions and, 433
Leukocytes, progesterone and, 142
Leydig cells, androgen secretion and, 74, 75
  estrogens and, 89, 110
  in reptiles, 40
  in teleosts, 34
  pituitary transplantation in mammals and, 216
LH. See also *Gonadotropins.*
  ACTH release and, 251
  activity of, half-life of, 170
  and aggressive behavior, 431
  and corpora lutea, 129, 130t, 131
  and estrogens, effects of, thresholds of, 111
  and germinal epithelium, 97
  and HCG, relation of, 167
  and implantation, 334
  and induction of ovulation, 149
  and 20-α-ol synthesis, 168
  and ovulation, in birds, 162
    in sheep, 286
    in swine, 287
  and release of spermatozoa, 91
  and rupture of follicle, 150

LH *(Continued)*
  and spermatogenesis, 91
    in hypophysectomized rats, 97
  assays of, 468-470
  avian, 162
  blockage of, agents of, 284
  definition of, 110
  electric stimulation of hypothalamus and, in amphibians, 235
  estrogen implants in median eminence and, 232
  hypophysis transplantation and, in amphibians, 214
  hypothalamus lesions and, 223, 227
  implants of, in median eminence, 233
  in egg laying cycle of chicken, 273, 274
  in hypophysis, estrogen implant and in rabbit, *232*
  ovariectomy, 112t, 113t
  mammalian, 162
  negative feedback of, LH-RF secretion and, 247
  oxytocin and, 171, 172
  photoperiod and, 406, 407
  secretion and release of, estrogens and, 111
  serotonin and, 197
  specificity of, 93, 170
  thyroid and, 180
LH release, continuous light and, 407
  and egg laying cycle of chickens, 273, 274
LH secretion, and ovulation, in primates, 283
  electric stimulation of hypothalamus and, 235, 236, 237
  estrogens and, 111, 114
  from pituitary, hypothalamus and, in rat, 219
  measurement of, 233, 234
  mechanism of; 285
  pituitary transplantation and, in mammals, 216
  site of, 225, *225*
  temperature and, 408
  vasopressin and, 175
LH-RF, 246, 247, 248
  concentration of, 246, 247, 248
  identification of, 245
  in hypothalamus, measurement of, 244
  in median eminence, 246
  purification of, 245
  secretion of, and negative LH feedback, 247
  vs. hypothalamic hormones, 249, 250
  vs. PIF, 249
Light. See also *Photoperiod.*
  and circadian rhythm, 393-404
  and diurnal variations in pineal body, 195
  and testis, in birds, 239
  transplanted pituitary, 213
  pathways of response to, in birds, 402
  wave length of, and breeding cycle, 399
Light intensity, and circadian rhythm, 399
Light-dark cycles. See *Photoperiod.*
LIHN, in mammals, 242
Linoleic acid, 368, 369
Lipid intake, and reproduction, 368-370
Lizard, breeding cycle of, 405
  pineal eye of, photoperiod and, 402
  rainfall and reproduction in, 416
Lordosis reflex, in rodents, 445
LTH, 110. See *Prolactin.*
Lunar effects, and reproduction, 417
Luteal phase, of estrous cycle, 280
Luteinized ovarian follicles, 53
Luteinizing hormone. See *LH.*

Luteotropic hormone, 110. See also *Prolactin*.
  and olfactory-bucco-alimentary-anal-genital syndrome, 456
  secretion of, pituitary stalk section and, 220
Lymph, and progesterone transport, 337

Magnesium, and reproduction, in chicken, 377
Mammal, aggressive behavior of, androgen and, 433
  anterior pituitary hormones of, 162
  castration of, and mating behavior, 442, 443
  chemotransmitters and, 244
  corpora lutea of, in pregnancy, theca interna cells and, 127t
  cyclic activity of, 122t
  cyclic reproductive phenomena of, 274-293
  egg laying, breeding patterns of, 274
  epinephrine in, 182
  estrogens in, 107, 107t, 109, 117, 122
  fertilization in, 299, 306
  fetal development in, 340
  hermaphroditism in, rudimentary, 70
  hypothalamo-hypophyseal system of, *207*
  hypothalamus of, chemotransmitters in, 244
    electric stimulation of, 235, 451, 452
    histology of, 241
    lesions of, 222
  intersexuality in, 70
  LIHN in, 242
  neurosecretory material in, 241
  norepinephrine in, 182
  olfactory stimuli and reproduction in, 413
  oogenesis in, 148
  os penis of, 50
  ovary of, 50, *51*
    in pregnancy, 288
  oviducts of, 53
    estrogen and, 115
  oxytocin in, 170, 171, 174, 175, 343
  pancreas in, 188, 189, 190
  parental behavior of, prolactin and, 458
  parturition of, oxytocin and initiation of, 343. See also *Parturition*.
  pineal organ of, 192, 194, 195
  pituitary of, pinealectomy and, 193t
  pituitary stalk section of, 220
  pituitary transplantation in, 215
  polyestrous, estrogen in, 286
  polyspermy in, 306
  pregnancy and ovulation in, 289
  pregnancy in, FSH and, 290, 292t
    corpora lutea and, 291t
    ovary and, 291
    relaxin secretion in, 293
  progesterone in pregnancy of, 293, 338, 339
  progesterone secretion of, site of, 126
  prolactin in, 163, 165
  relaxin in, 145, 146
  reproductive system of, 46-54
    pinealectomy and, 193t
    progestins and, 136-142
  secondary sex characters of, estrogen and, 117
  secondary sex glands of, 49, 49t
  seminiferous epithelium cycle of, duration of, 97t
  sexual behavior of, gonadal hormones and, 440
    progestins and, 143
  spermatogenetic cycle of, 94, 97t
  temperature and reproduction in, 405, 409

Mammal *(Continued)*
  testis of, 46, 46t, 47, *47*
    and androgen secretion, 75
    androstenedione secretion of, 77
    temperature regulation by scrotum, 47
    thyroid in, 176
    visual stimuli and reproduction in, 411
    viviparity of, 314
Mammary glands, estrogen and, 117
  progesterone and, 143
  prolactin and, 165
  stimulation of, as prolactin assay, 470
Mammillary bodies, lesions of, and sexual behavior, 449
Mammillary peduncle, and ovulation, 256
Man, diabetes in, abortion and, 190
  intersexuality in, 71t
  menstrual cycle of, hormonal relationships of, 288, 288t
  ovarian androgen in, 145
  placenta of, gonadotropin secretion of, 168
Manganese, and reproduction, 378
Marmoset, bone marrow chimera in, 14
Marsupials, breeding patterns of, 274
  embryos of, development of, 314
  oviduct of, 53
  puberty in, 275
Maternal behavior, and prolactin, 458
Mating, and milk ejection, 174
  and oxytocin release, 171
  and protein intake, in rat, 367
  energy intake and, 364
  fertile, and ovum, cell layers of, 317
  in salamanders, 271
Mating ability, heritability of, 438, 443
Mating behavior, See also *Behavior, sexual*.
  androgen and, 83t, 442, 443
  castration and, 83t, 442, 443
  of rat, 84
Mating center, in rat, 454
Medial dorsal nucleus, and erection, 452
Medial habenula, damage of, effect of, 256
Median eminence, acetylcholine in, 212
  ACTH implants in, 233
  and anterior pituitary control, 212
  destruction of, in amphibians, 220
  estrogen implants in, 232
  extracts of, and vaginal opening, 248
    FSH-RF in, 247
  FSH implants in, 233
  granules of, function of, 212
  lesions of, 227, 449
  LH-RF in, 246
  vesicles in, 212
Median lobe of brain, lesions of, and sexual behavior, 447
Medulla, of genital ridge, after differentiation, *11*
Medulla oblongata, lesions of, in rats, 256
Medullary bone, and egg calcification, in chickens, 121t
Medullary hormones, of adrenal, 181, 182. See also *Epinephrine and Norepenephrine*.
Meiosis, and oogenesis, 146
Melatonin, and serotonin, 195
  biogenesis of, pathway of, *196*
  synthesis of, pineal organ and, in mammals, 194, 195

Menstrual cycle, 282-288
Metabolism, adrenal and, 183
  androgens and, 89
Microelectrophoresis, and mating centers, determination of, 456
Micropylar canal, 304
Migratory behavior, 426-429
  prolactin and, 163, 428
Milk ejection, and mating, 174
Minerals, and reproduction, 377-381
Miniopterus australis, endogenous rhythm in, 394
Mink, cyclic patterns of, reproduction in, 276, 277
  photoperiod and, 407
  thyroid in, 179
Mole, LIHN in, 242
Monoestrous animals, 280
Monotremes, breeding patterns of, 274
Mouse, brain lesions of, and sexual behavior, 448
  dwarf, prevention of sterility, by ovine prolactin, 165
  gonadectomy of, and differentiation of secondary sex organs, 23
  hypoglycemia in, 190
  hypophysis of, gonadotropin secretion of, 216
    transplantation of, and reproductive system, 218
  hyperadrenalism of, and population density, 187
  implantation in, 321, 322
  obesity and reproduction in, 357, 358
  olfactory stimuli and reproduction in, 255, 413
  pheromones of, 414
  protein intake of, and reproduction, 366
  serotonin administration in, 197
  starvation and reproduction in, 356, 357
  temperature and reproduction in, 410
  thyroidectomy of, results of, 178
  van der Lee-Boot effect in, 413
MSH, and reproductive system, male, 170
Müllerian duct system, anatomy of, progesterone and, 142
  and fertilization, 299
  development of, hormone administration and, 23, 24, 25
  estrogens and, 115
  gene-effector interactions and, 115
  mammalian, separation of, 53
  progesterone and, 142
Myometrium, epinephrine and, 182

Nagrase, and ovulation, 150
Nervous system, hormones and, 253
Nest building, and gonadal development, in birds, 440
  androgens and, 436
  castration and, 436
  estrogen and, 440
  prolactin and, in mammals, 458, 459
Nest site, and reproduction, in cormorant, 417
Neural tissue, differentiation of, 84, 124, 144
Neuroendocrine integration, *418*
Neurohumeral control, of hypothalamus, 225, 257
Neurohumeral mechanism, for gonadotropin activity of pituitary, 257
Neurohypophyseal hormones, *210*, 210t
Neurosecretion, of hypothalamo-hypophyseal system, in mammals, 242
  starvation and, 356

Neurosecretory area, and neurohypophysis, relationship of, 208
Neurosecretory cells, 209, 238
Neurosecretory material, amphibian, 241
  and hypophysis, in teleosts, 241
  estrogens and, in median eminence, 242
  identification of, 238
  in chickens, 240
  in eels, 241
  in mammals, 241
  in rat, 241
  of median eminence, and portal capillaries, 238
  photoperiod and, 240, 241
  production of, 209
  transportation of, 209
    hypothalamic lesions and, 221
    in fish, 208, 241
Neurosecretory system, and circadian rhythm, 390, 391
Neurotransmitters, and ovulation, 251
Niacin, and reproduction, 374, 377
Nongonadal endocrine glands, 160-206. See also *Endocrine glands, nongonadal.*
Nonuterine implantation, 322
Noradrenaline, 181, 182
Norepinephrine, 181, 182
Norethindrone, and EEG arousal threshold, 457
Northern phalarope, incubation patch of, 164
Nucleus tuberalis, lesions of, 226
Nursing, and implantation, in rats and mice, 328
  and oxytocin, 344
Nutrients, transfer of, placenta and, 326
Nutrition, and reproduction, 355-387
  appetite and, 355
Nymphomania, of cattle, 123

OAAD test, 468
OBAGS, 456
Obesity, and reproduction, 357-358
20-α-ol, concentration of, 338
  synthesis of, LH and, 168
Olfactory-bucco-alimentary-anal-genital syndrome, 456
Olfactory bulb, and behavior, 255, 256, 415, 447, 448
Olfactory stalk, lesions of, effects of, in rats, 256
Olfactory stimuli, and visual stimuli, in reproduction, 413
Oncorhynchus nerka, breeding patterns of, 270
  corticosteroids in, 185
Oocyte, derivation of, 147, 148
  gonadotropins and, 151
  maturation of, in mammals, 148
Oocytogenesis, in rabbit, 148
Oogenesis, 146-151
  enzymatic control of, 150, 151
  hypophyseal control of, 151
  time of occurrence, 147, 147t, 148
Oogonia, development of, *10*, 10, 147, 148
Optic nerve, and circadian rhythms, 399
Os penis, mammalian, 50
Ovarian ascorbic acid depletion test, 468
Ovarian blood, progesterone in, 337, 338
Ovarian cavity, breeding in, without superfetation, in teleosts, 271
Ovarian cholesterol depletion test, 469
Ovarian follicle, avian, 44

Ovarian follicle (Continued)
  cystic, luteinized, and progestin secretion, 126
  chicken, 44, 148, 150
  hypothalamic lesions and, in mammals, 222
  in European bitterling, fate of, 36
  in rat, fertilization of, 149
  in teleosts, 37
  LH and, 149
  maturation of, gonadotropins and, 276
  pituitary and, 214, 220
  pituitary transplantation and, in rats, 216
  PMSG and, 167
  rupture of, 149, 150
  types of, 52, 53
Ovariectomy, 110
  and egg transport, 317
  and FSH-RF concentration, 248
  and gonadotropins, in rat, 110
  and LH levels, 112t, 113t
  and LH-RF concentration, 246
  and sexual behavior, in chicken, 438
  of chicken, 124
  with replacement therapy, and gestation, 335, 336, 337
Ovary, 104-159
  and gestation, 336t
  and implantation, 326, 329
  and oogenesis, 146
  and ovum, after ovulation, 326
    transport, 317
  and pituitary, relationships of, 283
  and testis, 104-104t
  and thyroid, in rabbits, 180
  and zona pellucida, 326
  androgen secretion of, 144-145
  anterior hypothalamus and, 223
  ascorbic acid depletion of, in pregnant rabbit blood, 284t
  cortisone and, in rats, 185
  cyclic activity of, 275, 276
  development of, 11
  estrogen secretion of, 104-124
  FSH plus LH and, 164
  hormones of, and ovum transport, 316
  hypophysectomy and, 160, 161t, 290
  in menstrual cycle, 282
  in pregnancy, 288, 289, 290, 291, 337
    estrogen and, 109
  of amphibia, 39, 62
  of birds, 42, 43, 63, 64
  of bony fishes, 35, 36, 36, 61
  of cyclostomes, 29, 30, 59, 60
  of elasmobranchs, 31, 32, 60, 61
  of mammals, 50, 51, 51, 64
  of reptiles, 41, 62
  of teleosts, 35
  PMSG and, 167
  progesterone production of, LH and, 168
  progestin secretion of, 124-144
  relaxin secretion of, 145-146
  removal of, and hypophyseal FSH potency, 166
  stalk section of, hypophysis and, 219, 220
  testosterone and, 86
  uterine distention and, 135
Oviduct, avian, 44, 115
  chicken, 45, 45t, 76

Oviduct (Continued)
  estrogens and, 115
  increased weight of, estrogen-induced, and progesterone, 140t
  mammalian, 53, 115
    progestins and, 138
  ovum in, 317
  reptilian, 41
  right, regression of, in birds, 24, 25
  water soluble vitamins and, and estrogen, 374
Oviparity, definition of, 311
Ovipositor, 36
Oviposition, and photoperiod, 406
  posterior pituitary hormones and, 173
  temperature and, in fish, 408
Ovoviviparity, definition of, 311
  of amphibia, 313
  progesterone and, 126
Ovulation, actinomycin D and, 150
  and insemination, synchronization of, in mammals, 299
  and measurement of LH release, 233
  and oviposition, time sequence of, in Coturnix c. japonica, 274
  and radioiodine uptake by thyroid, 180
  blockage of, agents of, 251, 252
  copulation and, in mammals, 276, 277
  corticosteroids and, 184
  electrical stimulation and, 234, 235
  energy intake, and, 363
  estrogens and, 108, 111
  FSH and, in birds, 162
  genital tract stimulation and, 136
  hypophysectomy and, 128, 160, 162
  hypothalamic stimulation and, 224, 224, 235
  hypothalamus lesions and, in birds, 222
  induction of, LH and, 149
  infundibulum lesions and, in toad, 222
  LH and, in birds, 162
    in sheep, 286
    in swine, 287
  mechanism of, 237
  neurotransmitters and, 251
  oxytocin and, in rabbits, 171
  pharmacologic agents and, 250
  pituitary transplantation and, in amphibians, 214
  PMSG and, 150, 162, 167
  pregnancy and, in mammals, 289
  prediction of, time of, in primates, 283
  progesterone and, 137
  pronase and, 150
  puromycin and, 150
  thyroid and, 178
  vasopressin and, 175
  verification of, 234
Ovum, 305-309. See also Egg.
Oxygen, placental transfer of, 326
Oxygenation, of water, and reproduction, in fish, 416
Oxytocin, action of, pathways of, 171
  and expulsion of young, 174
  and gonadotropins, 170, 171, 172
  and estrous cycle, 171
  and prolactin release, 172, 173
  and uterine contractions, 343
  hypothalamus and, 242

Oxytocin (*Continued*)
  in fishes, 173
  in mammals, 170, 171, 174, 175, 343
  in nursing, 344
  in parturition, 343
  progesterone and uterine sensitivity to, 141
  release of, causes of, 171
  specificity of, in mammals, 171
  vs. LH-RF, 249, 250

Pair-feeding, 355
Pancreas, 188-190
Pantothenic acid, and reproduction, 374, 376
Paradoxic sleep, serotonin and, 456
Parathyroids, 181
Paraventricular nucleus, and neurosecretory material production, 209
  lesions of, 225, 226
Parental behavior, 457-459
Parlow test, 468
Pars distalis, and brain, connection of, 208
  and hypothalamus, connection of, 211
  blood supply of, 208
  cells of, hormone production of, 166
  ectopic transplantation of, in *Ambystoma mexicanum*, 215
Pars tuberalis, extracts of, and vaginal opening, 248
Parthenogenesis, 308
Parturition, and endocrine organs of fetus, 347, 349
  endocrinology of, 340, 341
  estrogens in, 343
  factors in 341, 348
  fetus and, 345, 347
  hour of, 348
  initiation of, 342, 343, 344, 345
  progesterone and, in rabbit, 141
  uterus and, 345, 346
Penis, 49, *50*
Perikaryon, and neurosecretory material production, 209
Perissodactylae, placental gonadotropins of, 167
Peritoneal cavity, implantation in, 322
Pheromones, 413, 414
Phosphorus, and fertility, 82, 83, 378
Photoperiod, and aggressiveness, 432
  and cervical ganglion, in ferret, 403
  and hypothalamus, 402
  and LH release 406, 407
  and migratory behavior in birds, 427
  and neurosecretory material, in chickens, 240
    in rat, 241
  and oviposition, 406
  and ovulation, in Japanese rice fish, 406
  and pineal organ, 403
  and refractory period, 398
  and spermatogenesis, 397, 407
  and temperature, in breeding cycle, 404, 405
  and testis, avian, 397, 398, 399, 400
  anterior pituitary and, 402
  effectiveness of, 240
  gonadal activity and, 395, 396t, 401
  in American chameleon, 397
  in banded sunfish, 397
  in birds, 239, 395-402
  in domestic animals, 407

Photoperiod (*Continued*)
  in mammals, 401
  long, 401
Photosensory cells, of pineal organ, 191
Photosexual response. See *Photoperiod*.
PIF, 248, 249
Pig, auditory stimuli and reproduction in, 412
  energy intake of, and reproduction, 360, 361, 363
  hermaphroditism in, 70
  olfactory bulb of, removal of, 255
  ovulation in, LH and, 286
  photoperiod in, 407
  protein requirement of, 368
  temperature and reproduction in, 409
  vitamin A requirements of, 370
  zinc and reproduction in, 379
Pigeon, electric stimulation of brain of, and aggressiveness, 434
  and sexual behavior, 450
  hypophysectomy of, and progesterone, 93
    and spermatogenesis in, 93
  median eminence of, granules of, 212
  milk formation in, prolactin and, 163, 458
  parental behavior of, prolactin and, 458
  pituitary transplantation in, and prolactin, 215
  sexual behavior of, gonadectomy and, 439
  visual stimuli and reproduction in, 410
Pigeon crop gland stimulation, as prolactin assay, 470, 471
Pineal extract, preparations of, 194
Pineal eye, photoperiod and, 402. See also *Pineal organ*.
Pineal body, 190-197
  absence of, in vertebrates, 191
  and diurnal variations, 195
  and gonadotropin secretion, 192
  as endocrine organ, 195
  bovine, 194
  development of, 191
  inhibitory effect of, 194
  photoperiod and, 403
Pinealectomy, age of experimental animal and, 192
  and thyroid, in rat, 195
Pipid toads, *39*
Pituitary gland, 160-175
  ablation of, and replacement therapy, 161
  and aggressiveness, 430
  and androgen secretion, 77, 78t
  and corpora lutea, 216, 220, 131, 135
  and FSH secretion, 166
  and gestation, 335, 336t
  and hypothalamus, anatomy of, 207
    tissue, 248
  and LH secretion, 166
  and neurosecretory material in fish, 241
  and oogenesis, 151
  and ovary, 283
  and photostimulation, in birds, 239
  and progesterone secretion control, 127
  and spermatogenesis, 89, 90, 93
  anterior. See *Anterior pituitary*.
  control of, in brain, areas of, *228*
  estrogens and, 110
  fetal, and parturition, 347
  FSH secretion of, testosterone and, 81
  growth hormone and, 213, 216

Pituitary gland (*Continued*)
 hormones of, and sex differentiation, 18
  in hypothalamus, *243*
 LH and prolactin in, estrogen implant and, in rabbit, *232*
 neurohumoral control of, 257
 photostimulation and, in birds, 239
 pinealectomy and, in mammals, 193t, 199
 portal system of, transection of, 219
 posterior. See *Posterior pituitary.*
 protein intake and, in rats, 366
 stalk section of, 219, 220
 transplantation of, and gonadotropin secretion of, 216
  and sex differentiation, 19
  in amphibia, 213
  in birds, 215
  in mammals, 215
  in teleosts, 213
  in vivo, 213
   to hypophysiotropic area, and gonadotropin secretion, 217
 ventral lobe of, ablation of, 160
Pituitary gonadotropins, 80, 80t, 212, 257
 and ovarian activity in pregnancy, 289
 androgen and, 80
 in estrous cycle of sheep, *287*
 in pregnancy, 292t
 testosterone propionate and, 80t
Pituitary homografts, *218*
Placenta, 323
 and nutrient transfer, 326
 chorioallantoic, 324, 325t
 formation of, 323
 functions of, 325
 gonadotropin secretions of, 167, 168, 289, 290, 335, 336, 337, 340. See also hormone names.
 hormones of, and maintenance of pregnancy, 337
 in reptiles, 314
 in teleosts, 312
 types of, 324
Platinum electrodes, advantages of, 234, 235
Plumage, and hormones, 81, 82, 116, 117
PMSG, and ovulation, 150, 162, 167
 and spermatogenesis, 90
 and thyroid, 180
 assays of, 473
 half-life of, 170
 properties of, 167
 secretion of, 289
Polar bodies, formation of, 148
Polyestrous animals, 280
Polyestrous mammals, estrogen in, 286
Polyspermy, 305, 306
Population, control of, by adrenal, 186, 187, 188
Portal vessels, hypophyseal, function of, 210, 217
Posterior lobe of brain, lesions of, and sexual behavior, 447
Posterior pituitary, hormones of, 170
  and sperm transport, 300
  in birds, 173
  in reptiles, 173
Postimplantation gestation, hormonal requirements of, 335
Potassium, and reproduction, 378, 379
Pregnancy, and fetal adrenal, 347

Pregnancy (*Continued*)
 and progesterone, 293, 338, 339
 and relaxin, 145, 146, 293, 339, 341
 anterior pituitary and, in mammals, 290, 292t
 appetite and, 365
 blockage of, Bruce effect and, 415
 corpora lutea in, in mammals, 289
 duration of, and fetus genotype, 346, 347
 estrogens in, in mammals, 293
 fetal adrenal and, 347
 hypothalamus in, 242, 243
 maintenance of, estrogens and, in nutrient deficiency, 381
  hormonal requirements of, 337-341
 ovary and, 289, 290, 291
 ovulation in, in mammals, 289
 pituitary and, 220, 292t, 336, 337
 pituitary and ovary in, in mammals, 289
 protein deficiency and, 367, 368
 starvation and, in mice, 257
Preoptic nucleus, destruction of, in amphibians, 222
Preoptic hypothalamus, lesions of, and oviposition, 173
 and sexual behavior, 448, 449
Primates, ovulation in, prediction of, time of, 283
 uterus of, reaction to hormones, 282
Primordial germ cells, 8, 9, 147
Progesterone, aminopterin and, 377
 and blastocyst, 328
  transport of, 318
 and cervix, 142
 and corpora lutea, 108, 128, 129
 and egg transport, 317
 and electroencephalogram arousal threshold, 457
 and endometrium, 142
 and estrogen secretion by ovarian follicle, 137
 and estrogen-induced increase in oviduct weight, 140t
 and estrus, 123, 281
  in sheep, *129*
 and follicular growth, in mammals, 137
 and gestation, 336
 and gonaducts, 138
 and hypothalamus, 85, 455
 and implantation, 141, 329, 330, 331
 and leukocytes, 142
 and LH-RF concentration, 246
 and life span of ovum, 141
 and maintenance of pregnancy, in nutrient deficiencies, 381
  protein deficiency and, 367, 368
 and mechanical activity in uterus, 346
 and Müllerian duct system, 142
 and neural tissue differentiation, 144
 and ovulation, 137
 and ovum transport, 317
 and parturition, delay of, 342
  in rabbit, 141
 and radioiodine uptake by thyroid, 180
 and sensitivity of uterus to posterior pituitary hormones, 141
 and sex differentiation, 18
 and sperm transport, 300
 and uterus, contraction of, 341
  resistance to bacteria of, in rabbit, 141
 concentration of, and initiation of parturition, 342

Progesterone (*Continued*)
  effect of, 245
  in brain areas, 455
  in hypophysectomized pigeons, 93
  in ovarian blood, 337, 338
  in pregnancy of mammals, 293, 338, 339
  ovoviviparity and, 126
  pituitary transplantation and, in mammals, 216
  plus estradiol, and implantation, 329, 330, 330t
  plus estrogen, synergistic effects of on reproductive system, 142
  production of, in pregnancy, 338, 339
    LH and, 168
  synthesis of, site of, 108
  viviparity and, 126
Progesterone implants in brain, and sexual behavior, 453
Progestins, 124-144
  and appetite, 143
  and gonaducts, 138
  and hysterectomy, 134t, 135
  and mammalian reproductive system, 136-142
  and neural tissue differentiation, 144
  and secondary sex characters, 142
  and sex differentiation, 18
  and sexual behavior, 143
  occurrence of, 125t, 126
  placental, and maintenance of pregnancy, 337
  secretion of, control of, 126
Progestogens, 124-144. See also *Progestins.*
Prolactin, 162
  and brood patch, 148, 163
  and corpora lutea, 129, 130t, 131
  and courtship behavior, 437
  and fertility, 165
  and gestation, 336
  and glucuronidase activity, 165
  and implantation, 331
  and male reproductive system, 165
  and migratory behavior in birds, 163, 215, 428
  and parental behavior, 458
  and pigeon crop gland, 163
  and protein, 368
  androgen with, and reproductive system, 165
  assays of, 162, 163, 470-472
  definition of, 110
  estrogen addition to rat pituitary and, 115
  estrogen implants in median eminence and, 232
  extragonadal effects of, 163
  in circennian rhythms, in bird, 428
  in pituitary estrogen implant and, in rabbit, *232*
  in rat, 163
  in vitro, production of, 219
  mammalian, effects of, 165
  pituitary transplantation and, in amphibians, 214
    in birds, 215
  placental, 335
  plus HCG, 165
  release of, 219, 249
    electric stimulation of hypothalamus and, 237
    oxytocin and, 172, 173
  secretion of, by rat placenta, 290
    determination of, 237
    inhibition of, 248
  spermatogenesis and, 97
Prolactin-inhibiting factor, 248, 249

Pronase, and ovulation, 150
Prostaglandins, and sperm transport, 300
  structures of, *301*
Prostate gland, in female mammals, 54
Protandrous hermaphroditism, definition of, 68
Proteases, and ovulation, 150
Protein intake, and reproduction, 365-370
Protogynous hermaphroditism, definition of, 68
Pseudohermaphroditism, 68, 70
Puberty, and energy intake, 360, 361
  in marsupials and eutheria, 275
Pubic bones, resorption of, and parturition, 341
Puffinus tenuirostris, breeding cycle of, 394
Puromycin, and ovulation, 150
Pyridoxine, and reproduction, 375, 377

Quail, Japanese, ovulation and oviposition of, time sequence of, 274
Quelea quelea, photoperiod and, 401

Rabbit, blastocysts of, implantation of, spacing of, 318, 319
  brain lesions, and sexual behavior, 448, 450
  cyclic patterns of reproduction in, 276
  diabetes in, 189
  electric activity of brain, and gonadotropin release, 253
  energy intake of, after puberty, and reproduction, 362
  estrous cycle of, estrogens in, 284
  hormone implant in brain of, and sexual behavior, 453
  hypothalamus of, electric stimulation of, 235
  olfactory stimuli and, in reproduction, 415
  ovarian androgen in, 145
  ovum of, transport of, 317
  oxytocin, in, 171
  pancreas in, 189
  pregnancy of, hypophysis and, 290
    progesterone and, 141
  serotonin administration in, 197
  sex steroids of, functions of, 232
  thyroid in, 177, 179, 180
  uterine contractions of, 341
Radioiodine uptake by thyroid, ovulation and, 180
Rainbow trout, migratory, corticosteroids in, 185
Rainfall, and reproduction, 416
Rat, amygdalar lesions of, 256
  androgens and aggressiveness in, 433
  anterior hypothalamus of, 233
  auditory stimuli and reproduction in, 412
  behavioral substrate in, 124
  blastocyst of, implantation of, 319
  continuous light and, 407
  copulatory behavior of, 84, 442
  cortisone in, 184, 185, 186
  desoxycorticosterone in, 185
  diabetes in, 189
  energy intake of, after puberty, and reproduction, 362, 364
  essential amino acids for, 369
  estrous cycle of, *278*, 279t, 280, 285
  fertilization in, 149
  FSH-RF and castration in, 248
  heat to testis of, and spermatogenesis, 98

Rat *(Continued)*
  hypervitaminosis A in, 372
  hypoglycemia in, 189
  hypophysectomized, FSH plus LH and, 164
    requirements for spermatogenesis in, 97
  hypophysectomized, spermatogenesis in, 94
  hypothalamic lesions in, and sexual behavior, 227, 449
  hypothalamic nuclei of, electrocoagulation of, 221
  hypothalamus of, chemotransmitters in, 244
    electric stimulation of, and ovulation, 224, *224*, 236
    lesions of, 222, 223, 235
  LH-RF of, concentration of, 246, 247
  lunar effects and reproduction in, 417
  male, early weaning of, and reproduction, 360
  mating behavior of, 84, 442
  "mating center" of, 454
  median eminence of, vesicles in, 212
  neurosecretory material in, 241
  ovarian androgen in, 145
  ovariectomy of, and gonadotropins, 110
  pancreas in, 188, 189
  photoperiod and, 401, 407
  pineal body of, photoperiod and, 403
  pinealectomy of, 195
  pituitary transplantation in, 215, 216
  placenta of, gonadotropin secretion of, 168, 290
  prolactin in, 163, 290
  protein intake of, and reproduction, 366, 367
  serotonin administration in, 197
  sex steroids of, functions of, 233
  sexual behavior of, brain lesions and, 446, 447, 448, 449
    castration and, 444
    electric stimulation and, 451
    gonadal hormones and, 440, 441, 453
  sodium and reproduction in, 379
    spinal lesions and, 445
  spermatogonia of, development of, *96*
  thiamine in, 375
  thyroid in, 177, 178
  undernourished, reproduction of, 359
  unphysiologic stimuli and reproduction in, 412
  uterus of, decidual reaction in, 320
  vitamin A in, and reproduction, 371, 372
  vitamin E in, 373
  zinc in, and reproduction, 378
Rat hyperemia test, 469
Red-billed dioch, photoperiod and, 401
  rainfall and reproduction in, 417
Refractory period, photoperiod and, 239, 398, 401
  thyroid and, in birds, 176
Relaxin, 145-146
  and parturition, 341
  and pregnancy, 293, 339
  production of, sites of, 339
Reproduction, auditory stimuli and, 411-413
  captivity and, 417, 419
  cyclic phenomena of, 269-293
  energy intake and, 356-365
  environment and, 389-425
  hypothalamic lesions and, 226
  immunology and, 304
  minerals and, 377-381
  nongonadal endocrine glands and, 160-197

Reproduction *(Continued)*
  nutrition and, 355-387
  obesity and, 357-358
  olfactory stimuli and, 413
  population density and, 186-188
  restricted food intake and, 358-365
  starvation and, 356
  temperature and, 408-410
  visual stimuli and, 410-411
Reproductive behavior, hormonally induced, 426-465
Reproductive glands, accessory, in bony fishes, 34
Reproductive organs, and vitamin deficiency, 375
Reproductive rhythms, 388. See *Breeding season.*
Reproductive system, estrogens and, 108, 142. See also specific organs.
  hypothalamus and, 222, 223
  oxytocin and, 175
  pancreas and, in rats, 189
  pituitary stalk section and, 220
  thyroid and, 177
  male, anterior pituitary and, 218
    corticosteroids and, in rats, 184
    cortisone and, in birds, 184
    pancreas and, in rabbits, 189
    pinealectomy and, in birds, 192
    pituitary transplantation and, in mammals, 215
    oxytocin and, 175
    starvation and, in ducks, 356
    thyroid and, 176, 177
  of amphibia, 38-40
  of basking shark, female, *33*
  of bony fishes, 34-37
  of cyclostomes, 29, 30
  of elasmobranchs, 30-34
  of gymnophiona, 38
  of mammals, 46-54
  of teleosts, 34
  of vertebrates, anatomy of, 29-67
  pinealectomy and, in mammals, 193t, 194
  progestins and, 136
  sex steroid administration, into hypothalamo-hypophyseal system and, 230-232t
  stalk section of hypophysis and, 219, 220
Reptiles, aggressive behavior and androgens in, 431
  anatomy of reproductive system of, 40-42
  breeding patterns of, 272
  estrogen secretion of, site of, 107
  hermaphroditism in, 69
  hypophysectomy and replacement therapy in, 161
  hypophysectomy of, and spermatocytes, 91
  oviduct of, 41
  parturition of, endocrinology of, 341
  pineal body of, 191
  placenta of, 314
  posterior pituitary hormones in, 173
  sexual behavior of, 437
  testis of, 40
    and androgen secretion, 75
  thyroid in, 176
  viviparity of, 314
Retina, of eye, and pineal body, 196
Rhesus monkey, sexual behavior of, gonadal hormones and, 441
  thyroid in, 179
Rhinencephalon, lesions of, and sexual behavior, 447

Rhinencephalon (*Continued*)
    photoperiod and, 402
Rhythms, biological, 388
Riboflavin, and reproduction, 374, 375
Ribonucleic acid and uterine cell growth, 116
Ring doves, aggressive behavior in, 432
    visual stimuli and reproduction in, 410
Ringer's solution, and sex differentiation, 19
Rudimentary hermaphroditism, 68, 70

Salamanders, hedonic glands in, 413
    mating of, 271
    pineal organ of, 191
    reproductive system of, 38
    spermatogenesis in, 271
    temperature and spawning in, 408
Salmon, breeding patterns of, 270
    corticosteroids in, 185
    migration of, thyroxine administration and, 427
Salt water, and sex differentiation, 19
    hypophyseal hormones in, 160
Scrotum, castration and, 81
    in mammals, and temperature regulation of testis, 47
    in sheep, temperature readings of, *48*
Secondary sex characters, androgens and, 81, 82t
    estrogens and, 116, 117
    maintenance of in nonbreeding season, 75
    progestins and, 142
Secondary sex glands, mammalian, 49, 49t
Secondary sex organs, differentiation of, 20-26
Selenium, and reproduction, 379
Semen, and sperm transport, 299, 300
Semen volume, 81
Seminal plasma, and sperm capacitation, 303
Seminiferous epithelium, and spermiogenesis, 91
Seminiferous epithelium cycle, in mammals, duration of, 97t
Septum, lesions of, and sexual behavior, 448
    effects of, in rabbits, 256
Serotonin, and deciduomata, in mice, 197
    and LH, 197
    and melatonin, 195
    and paradoxic sleep, 456
    and sperm transport, 300
Serotonin administration, in rats, 197
Sertoli cell tumors, and estrogen secretion, 89
Sertoli cells, and hypophysectomy, 90
Sex, heterogametic, 3
    heterozygous, 3
    homogametic, 3
    notation of, 3
Sex chromatin, 6
Sex chromosome, 3
    inactive, 5, 6
    mode of action of, 5
Sex determination, 3-7
Sex differentiation, "aged" eggs and, 19
    analysis of, 12
    androgen and, 17t, 18
    desoxycorticosterone and, 18
    environment and, 19
    in cyclostomes and teleosts, 9
    in vitro, of ducks and chicken gonads, 15, 15t
    of secondary sex organs, 20-26

Sex differentiation (*Continued*)
    progesterone and, 18
    Ringer's solution and, 19
    steroid hormones and, 15, 16t, 17t
    temperature and, 19
Sex glands, secondary. See *Secondary sex glands.*
Sex inversion, definition of, 68
Sex organs, secondary. See *Secondary sex organs.*
Sex reversal, androgen-induced, 17t
    definition of, 68
    estrogen and, 16t, 124
Sex steroids, administration into hypothalamo-hypophyseal system, and reproductive organs, 230-232
    of estrous cycle, 233
Sexual behavior, 435-457
    aggressiveness and, 433
    brain lesions and, 444-450
    chemical stimulation of hippocampus and, 451
    description of, 84
    estrogens and, 122, 438
    hormones and, 435-437
    progestins and, 143
    spinal lesions and, 445, 446
Sexual dimorphism. See *Secondary sex characters.*
Sexual skin, progestins and, in monkeys, 142
Sexual maturity, precocious, and hypothalamic lesions, 227
Sharks, cyclic reproductive phenomena of, 269
    relaxin in, 145
    reproductive system of, 31
Sheep, brain lesions of, and sexual behavior, 450
    cerebellum of, removal of, 256
    corpora lutea of, estradiol and, 129
        maintenance of, 128
    energy intake of, and reproduction, 361, 362
    estrous cycle of, estrogen implants and, 233
        estrogen in, 286
        hypophyseal gonadotropins in, *287*
    LH and corpora lutea in, 129
    mating behavior of, androgen and, 443
    olfactory stimuli and, 416
    ovulation in, LH and, 286
    photoperiod and, 401, 407
    pituitary stalk section of, 220
    progesterone of, in pregnancy, 293
    scrotum of, temperature readings of, *48*
    temperature and reproduction in, 409
Short-tailed shearwater, breeding cycle of, 394
Sigmoid flexure, of penis, in cattle, 49, *50*
Silent heat, 275
Skate, breeding pattern of, 270
Skunk, hypothalamo-hypophyseal system of, neurosecretory activity of, 242
Social environment, and circadian rhythm, 393
Sodium, and reproduction, 378, 379
Sooty tern, breeding cycle of, 394
Sparrow, light intensity and sexual maturity in, 399
    photoperiod and, 239, 427
    prolactin secretion and, 428
Spawning behavior, temperature and, in fish, 408
Sperm, antigenicity of, 304
    capacitation of, 302, 303
    duration of fertility of, in female genital tract, 298, 298t, 299
    egg penetration by, 303

Sperm *(Continued)*
  fertilizing capacity of, genes and, 301, 302
  in ooplasm, changes in, 306
  motility of, 300
  numbers of, at site of fertilization, 302
  protein and, in chicken, 365
  storage of, in birds, 299
  supplementary, 305
  transport of, 174, 299-302
  unused, fate of, 308
Sperm nests, in chickens, 44
Spermatogenesis, 89-99
  androgens and, 79
  corticosteroids and, in rats, 184
  diurnal rhythm and, 407
  FSH and, 91, 97
  in birds, 93, 93t, 94, 95, 272
  in mammals, 94, 97t
  in salamanders, 271
  periods of, 91
  photoperiod and, 397, 407
  pituitary and, 89, 90, 93
    transplantation of, in amphibians, 214
  PMSG and, 90
  quantitative analysis of, advantages of, 94
  starvation and, 356, 357
  temperature and, 98, 404, 405, 407
  testosterone and, 79, 80, 80t
  thyroid and, 176, 177
Spermatogonia, development of, *10*, 10
Spermatophore, of elasmobranchs, 31
  of salamanders, 38
Spermatozoa, ageing of, 307
  numbers of, at site of fertilization, 302
  release of, LH and, 91
Spermiation, LH and, 91
Spermiogenesis, hypophysectomy and, 160
  stages of, 91, *92*, 94
Spine, lesions of, and sexual behavior, 445, 446
Spontaneous ovulators, 276, 277
Starling, aggressive behavior in, 431
Starvation, and reproduction, 356, 357
Steelman-Pohley test, 468
Steganopus tricolor, incubation patch of, 164
Sterculia foetida oil, and embryonic mortality, 369
Sterility, prevention of in mouse, by ovine prolactin, 165
Sterna fusca, breeding cycle of, 394
Sternus vulgaris, aggressive behavior and androgens in, 431
Steroid hormones. See also name of hormone.
  and maintenance of pregnancy, in protein-deficient mother, 367, 368
  and sex differentiation, 15
  biosynthetic pathways of, 76t
  intracerebral administration of, effects of, 257
  nervous system effects of, measurement of, 253
  secretion of, mechanism of, *237*
Stilbestrol implants, in cat brain, and sexual behavior, 453
Stratum basale, in pigeon, prolactin and, 163
Superfecundation, in mink, 277
Superfetation, in teleosts, 270, 313
Stress, nonspecific agents of, and ACTH release, 250
Stria terminalis, transection of, effect of, in immature cat, 256
Supernumerary sperm, 305

Suprachiasmatic nucleus, lesions of, and sexual behavior, 449
  in cats, 224
Suprachiasmatic regions, photoperiod and, 402
Supraoptic-hypophyseal connection, 225
Supraoptic hypothalamus, lesions of, 174
Supraoptic nucleus, and neurosecretory material production, 209
  lesions of, 225
Synchronizing stimuli, of circadian rhythm, 393
Synchronous hermaphroditism, definition of, 68

Target organs, anterior pituitary hormones and, 170
Telencephalon, and aggressiveness, 434
  and mammary gland, in rabbit, 254
Teleosts, breeding patterns of, 270-271
  castration and androgen administration and, 74, 74t
  hermaphroditism in, 68
  hypophysectomized, survival of, and replacement therapy, 163
    in fresh and brackish water, 162
  Leydig cells in, 34
  ovarian follicle of, *37*
  oviparous, breeding patterns of, 270
  oxytocin in, 173
  pars distalis of, and brain, connection of, 208
  pineal organ of, 191
  pituitary of, and NSM, 241
  pituitary transplantation in, 213
  reproductive system of, 34
  sexual differentiation in, 9
  superfetation in, 270, 313
  testes of, and androgen secretion, 73
  thyroid in, 175
  viviparity of, 312
  viviparous, breeding patterns of, 270, 271
Temperature, and breeding cycle, 404, 405
  and circadian rhythm, 390
Temperature, and endogenous rhythm, 404-406
  and germinal epithelium, 98, 99
  and gonadal maturation, in fish, 408
  and LH secretion, 408
  and photoperiod, in breeding cycle, 395, 404, 405
  and reproduction, 408-410
  and sex differentiation, 19
  and spermatogenesis, 98, 404, 405, 407
Territorial behavior. See *Aggressive behavior.*
Testicular gland, 34
Testis, 73-101
  and heat, in spermatogenesis of rat, 98
  and pineal eye, in lizards, 403
  and scrotum, 81
  androgen and, 73-89
  descent of, 46, *47*
  development of, 110
  hypophysectomy and, 160, 160t
  in anura, 38
  in birds, 42, 75, 399
  in mammals, 46, 46t, 47, *47*, 75, 77
  in reptiles, 40, 75
  in salamanders, 38
  light and, in birds, 239, 399
  photoperiod and, in birds, 397, 398, 399
  retained in body cavity, and spermatogenesis, 98

Testis *(Continued)*
pituitary transplantation and, 217
secretion of by mammalian testes, 77
sexual behavior and, in birds, 639
stalk section of pituitary, and, 219, 220
temperature and, in birds, 399
in mammals, 47
testosterone propionate and, 80, 80t
vs. ovary, 104, 104t
Testosterone. See also *Androgens.*
aggressive behavior and, 432
and behavior, in mammals, 88
and external genitalia, 24
and FSH secretion, 81
and gonadal development, 24
and gonadotropins, 79
and LH-RF concentration, 247
and organization of the hypothalamus, 86, 87t, 88t
and ovary, 86
and spermatogenesis, 79, 80, 80t
concentration of, in brain areas, 454
in peripheral blood, 77
effects of, 80, 80t
in basal medial preoptic region of brain, and sexual behavior, 453
in rat, 80t
in testis of birds, 439
inhibitory effect of, 79
Testosterone implant, in rat brain, and sexual behavior, 454
local, in dogs, 81
Tetrapods, oogenesis in, 146
Thalamus, lesions of, effects of, 256
Thayer's gull, visual stimuli and reproduction in, 411
Theca interna cells, function of, 127t
of birds, 42, 44
of fish, 29, 31, 36
Thiamine, and reproduction, 374, 375
Three-spined stickleback, aggressive behavior of, brain lesions and, 434
breeding patterns of, 270
gonadal cycle of, aggressive behavior and, 430
migratory behavior of, 426
sexual behavior of, castration and, 436
visual stimuli and reproduction in, 410
Thyrocalcitonin, and reproduction, 181
Thymus, and differentiation of brain, 124
Thyroid, 175-179
and fat deposition, 429
and estrus, in cattle, 180
and female reproductive system, 177
and LH, 180
and male reproductive system, 176, 177
and migration, in three-spined stickleback, 426
androgen and, 181
castration and, 181
gonadal hormones and, 177, 179
PMSG and, 180
pinealectomy and, in rats, 195
Thyroid inhibitors, and sex differentiation, 19
Thyroid-stimulating hormone. See *TSH.*
Thyroidectomy, 176, 178
Thyroxine. See *Thyroid.*
Toad, fertilization in, 297
lesions of infundibulum in, 222
TP. See *Testosterone.*
Trypsin, and ovulation, 150

TSH, and estrous cycle, 180
and spermatogenesis, 97
castration and, 181
hypophysis and, in teleosts, 213
Turkey, androgen and precocious sexual behavior in, 438
food intake of, and reproduction, 359
vitamin E in, 373
Turner's syndrome, 71t

Urodeles, reproductive system of, 38. See *Salamander.*
Uterus. See also *Hysterectomy.*
anatomy of, 53
and blastocyst, 315, 318, 319
and corpora lutea, 129, 132, 135, 291, 292
and embryo, normal development of, 322
and estrogen, 282, 341, 342, 348
and estrous cycle, 139t
and fetus, expulsion of, 341
and implantation, 141, 322
and sperm capacitation, 302, 303
and parturition, 345, 346
contractions of, 341
and sperm transport, 174, 299, 300
decidual reaction in, in rat, 320
distention of, and corpora lutea, 135, 292
and estrous cycle, 135, 139
and ovary, 135
hypothalamus and, 222, 223
implantation in, site of, 318
mechanical activity of, progesterone and, 346
reaction to hormones, in primates, 282
receptivity of, 327, 329
relaxin and, 146
resistance to bacteria of, progesterone and, in rabbit, 141
volume of, and labor, 348

Vagina, distention of, and labor, 348
hypothalamic lesions and, in mammals, 222
progesterone and, 142
Valeric acid, and sexual behavior, in cat, 450
Van der Lee-Boot effect, 255, 413
Vasopressin, 175
vs. LH-RF, 249, 250
Vasopressin-oxytocin, and olfactory-bucco-alimentary-anal-genital syndrome, 456
Vertebrates, inframammalian. See also name of animal or class of animals.
and behavioral substrate, 124
courtship behavior of, ovariectomy and, 123
estrogen secretion of, 105t, 106t
ovarian androgen in, 144
ovary of, progestins and, 136
pineal organ in, 191
sexual behavior of, progestins and, 143
Visual stimuli, and olfactory stimuli, in reproduction, 413
and reproduction, 410
in gulls, 411
Vitamin A, and reproduction, 370-372
Vitamin B₁₂, and reproduction, 374, 376
Vitamin D, and reproduction, 372
Vitamin E, and reproduction, 372, 373

Vitamin K, and reproduction, 374
Vitamins, and reproduction, 370-377, 381
Vitelline membrane, 42, 44
Viviparity, 311-354
Vole, photoperiod and, 401

Water balance, control of, 207
Water soluble vitamins, and reproduction, 374-377
Wave length (of light), and breeding cycles, 399
Weaning, and reproduction, in male rats, 360
Whitten effect, in mice, 414
Wilson's phalarope, incubation patch of, 164
Wolffian ducts, development of, hormone administration and, 23, 24

Yolk, composition of, in chicken eggs, 119t
Yolk deposition, and second polar body, extrusion of, 149
  gonadotropins and, 118, 119
  rupture of follicle and, 149
Yolk sac placenta, definition of, 324

Zinc, and reproduction, in chickens, 378
Zona pellucida, formation of, 149
  in ovum penetration, 305
  ovary and, 326
Zugunruhe, 427, 428, 429